MW00448633

THE OXFORD HANDBOOK OF

LATIN PALAEOGRAPHY

THE OXFORD HANDBOOK OF

LATIN

PALAEOGRAPHY

Edited by

FRANK T. COULSON

and

ROBERT G. BABCOCK

OXFORD

UNIVERSITY PRESS

OXFORD
UNIVERSITY PRESS

Oxford University Press is a department of the University of Oxford. It furthers
the University's objective of excellence in research, scholarship, and education
by publishing worldwide. Oxford is a registered trade mark of Oxford University
Press in the UK and certain other countries.

Published in the United States of America by Oxford University Press
198 Madison Avenue, New York, NY 10016, United States of America.

© Oxford University Press 2020

All rights reserved. No part of this publication may be reproduced, stored in
a retrieval system, or transmitted, in any form or by any means, without the
prior permission in writing of Oxford University Press, or as expressly permitted
by law, by license, or under terms agreed with the appropriate reproduction
rights organization. Inquiries concerning reproduction outside the scope of the
above should be sent to the Rights Department, Oxford University Press, at the
address above.

You must not circulate this work in any other form
and you must impose this same condition on any acquirer.

ISBN 978-0-19-533694-8

Library of Congress Control Number: 2020944631

3 5 7 9 8 6 4 2

Printed by Sheridan Books, Inc., United States of America

PREFACE AND ACKNOWLEDGMENTS

In organizing the *Oxford Handbook of Latin Palaeography*, we have been guided by the dictates of Leonard Boyle, who first coined the term "integral palaeography," whereby he encouraged the study of palaeography not as an isolated discipline but as one bound up with other aspects of the manuscript book. To quote from the preface of his collected essays:

> On y retrouve sa préoccupation constante d'étudier le codex comme un ensemble et de l'analyser sous divers angles permettant de mieux reconstituer l'histoire du livre médiéval. Il utilise toutes les ressources de la paléographie, de la codicologie, de l'histoire du livre et de sa décoration pour retrouver les traces du milieu d'origine.
> (*Integral Palaeography*, Preface vii)

The present handbook consists of five parts devoted to Script, Material Embodiment and Techniques, Cultural Setting, Selected Scriptoria and Libraries, and Varieties of Book Usage. The emphasis throughout is on Latin palaeography. We deemed it impossible to include a section on decoration and illumination for reasons of length and cost. Part I, devoted to script, of necessity, looms large and details the evolution of Latin book hands from late antiquity to the Renaissance. The coverage given to these varied scripts is both traditional and innovative. Each contributor was asked to provide a detailed history of the script, its nomenclature, its particular letterforms (including abbreviations and ligatures) and to include some discussion of the cultural relevancy of the script (when appropriate). In contrast with earlier overviews, we have given rather full coverage to the scripts of late antiquity, particularly Old Roman Cursive and New Roman Cursive. In one instance, namely the section dealing with Visigothic script, the author has been granted some latitude, since we felt that Visigothic script in general had received short shrift in earlier handbooks and therefore merited a more extensive treatment (particularly under the magisterial guidance of Jesús Alturo i Perucho). The discussion of the evolution of Gothic script in Europe may also call for some words of explanation. The section opens with an expertly presented overview by Albert Derolez of the problems involved in the nomenclature of Gothic script. Subsequent articles deal with the evolution of Gothic script in various regions, including the traditional division of Northern (France, Germany, and England) and Southern Gothic (Italy), but also covering less well-mapped areas such as Hungary, the Czech Republic, and Slovakia. We have also attempted throughout to provide readers with copious plates and illustrations to guide their assimilation of the specifics of individual scripts. This practice contrasts somewhat with earlier treatments where illustrative material had been kept to a minimum.

We are very grateful to our editors at Oxford University Press for their generous indulgence.

Part II, devoted to the material embodiment of the codex, contains the standard articles on the stages of manuscript production, the *mise-en-page* of the manuscript book, and the format of the manuscript book. In addition, we have commissioned two articles which deal more exclusively with newly established disciplines in the field of codicology, namely quantitative and comparative codicology.

Part III of the handbook discusses cultural aspects of manuscripts with chapters by Alison Beach on "Who were the Scribes", Paul Saenger on "Orality and Visible Language", and Guglielmo Cavallo and Kouky Fianu on the book trade in antiquity and the Middle Ages. Part IV provides an overview of medieval libraries: Donatella Nebbiai of the Institut de recherche et d'histoire des textes opens with an overview of the organization of the medieval library, followed by discrete articles on a selection of the most important libraries and centers of book production of the Middle Ages and Renaissance, including Lindisfarne, north Italy in the seventh and eighth centuries, St. Gall, Monte Cassino, Paris, Florence, and Salisbury Cathedral. The final part of the handbook, Part V: Varieties of Book Usage, guides the graduate student and incipient palaeographer through selected genres of the manuscript book that may pose specific problems for the researcher. Herein, the reader will find overviews of such topics as legal manuscripts at Bologna, Books of Hours, glossed manuscripts and glossaries, the manuscript miscellany, florilegia, and theological texts. The emphasis in this final part is placed squarely on specifics of page layout, decoration, and other vagaries of the genre, though authors have been encouraged, where appropriate, to include some discussion of the cultural and intellectual importance of the genre. The editors of the volume also commissioned a lengthy article on manuscript cataloguing from Consuelo Dutschke, cataloguer of Western Manuscripts at Columbia University, which we hope will serve as a practical guide to the cataloguing of Latin manuscripts.

The handbook, it is hoped, will be accessible to the broadest audience. To this end, all articles are published in English (though many were originally written in Italian, German, Spanish, and French). We have benefited throughout the editing of the handbook from the tireless work of many scholars who labored to render the original contributions into easily accessible English. In particular, we are extremely grateful to Consuelo Dutschke and Anna A. Grotans, who labored long and tirelessly on many of the translations from Italian and German.

The handbook could not have been produced without the generosity of the individual contributors who shared so freely of their knowledge and expertise. We are extremely indebted to each for his or her patience, indulgence, and goodwill. We would also like to thank the many people behind the scenes who gave of their time and energies during what can only be described as an elephantine gestation prior to publication. Michael Jean, Quinn Griffin, and William Little helped to format bibliography and notes and provided expert help on technical matters. We are also most grateful to Harald Anderson for putting together so expertly the two indices, and to John Beeby who provided the abstracts for each article. Wendy Watkins, Curator of the Center for Epigraphical and Palaeographical Studies at the Ohio State University, readily answered our many queries regarding bibliography. Our thanks also to Ornella Rossi and to John Beeby for editorial assistance. We are indebted to the College of Humanities and the Arts of The Ohio State University and the Department of Classics at The Ohio State University and its Chair, Benjamin Acosta-Hughes, for much appreciated support. We are also grateful to Stefan Vranka, acquisitions editor at Oxford University Press, who first broached the idea of a new handbook with Prof. Coulson and who has expertly shepherded the project to conclusion.

Contents

I.6 HUMANIST

PART II. MATERIAL EMBODIMENT
AND TECHNIQUES

PART III. CULTURAL SETTING

List of Contributors

Jesús Alturo i Perucho, Universitat Autònoma di Barcelona

Robert G. Babcock, University of North Carolina at Chapel Hill

Alison I. Beach, Professor of Mediaeval History, University of St Andrews

Malachi Beit-Arié, Professor Emeritus of Codicology and Palaeography, Hebrew University of Jerusalem

Walter Berschin, Professor Emeritus, Universität Heidelberg

Michelle P. Brown, FSA, Professor Emerita, SAS, University of London

Charles Burnett, Professor of the History of Islamic Influences on Europe, Warburg Institute

Guglielmo Cavallo, Accademia Nazionale dei Lincei, Roma

Paolo Cherubini, Professore ordinario, Università degli Studi di Milano-Bicocca

Frank T. Coulson, Department of Classics, The Ohio State University

Teresa De Robertis, Dipartimento di Storia, Archeologia, Geografia, Arte, Spettacolo—Università di Firenze

Albert Derolez, Emeritus Professor at the Free Universities of Brussels

Greti Dinkova-Bruun, Pontifical Institute of Mediaeval Studies, Toronto

Consuelo W. Dutschke, Columbia University

Mirella Ferrari, Università Cattolica del S. Cuore, Milano

Kouky Fianu, Université d'Ottawa/University of Ottawa

Richard Gameson, Durham University

David Ganz, Visiting Professor of Palaeography, the Medieval Institute, University of Notre Dame

Simona Gavinelli, Università Cattolica del S. Cuore, Milano

Anna A. Grotans, Department of Germanic Languages and Literatures, The Ohio State University

†**J. P. Gumbert**, Professor Emeritus, Leiden University

Olivier Guyotjeannin, Directeur d'études à l'École nationale des chartes, Paris

Jacqueline Hamesse, Professor Emerita, L'Université catholique de Louvain

Gregory Hays, Department of Classics, University of Virginia

Patrizia Lendinara, Professor Emeritus, Dipartimento Culture e Società, Università di Palermo

Susan L'Engle, Center for Medieval and Renaissance Studies, Saint Louis University

Donatella Nebbiai, Institut de recherche et d'histoire des textes, Paris

Paul Needham, Scheide Librarian, Princeton University

Francis Newton, Professor Emeritus of Classical Studies, Duke University

Ezio Ornato, CNRS, Paris

Marianne Pade, Department of Classical Studies, Aarhus University

Hana Pátková, Charles University, Prague

Karl-Georg Pfändtner, Director, Staats- und Stadtbibliothek, Augsburg

Olaf Pluta, Institut für Philosophie, Ruhr-Universität Bochum

Lucien Reynhout, Curator at the Department of Manuscripts, Royal Library of Belgium, Brussels, Belgium

†**George Rigg**, Professor Emeritus, University of Toronto

Pamela Robinson, University of London

Richard and Mary Rouse, University of California, Los Angeles

Paul Saenger, Newberry Library, Chicago

Juraj Šedivý, Comenius-University in Bratislava/Faculty of Arts

Lesley Smith, Professor of Medieval Intellectual History, University of Oxford, Fellow in Politics and Senior Tutor, Harris Manchester College

Peter A. Stokes, King's College, University of London

Alison Stones, Professor Emerita, University of Pittsburgh

Marie-Hélène Tesnière, Conservateur général au département des manuscrits de la Bibliothèque nationale de France

Xavier van Binnebeke, Katholieke Universiteit Leuven, Seminarium Philologiae Humanisticae

Rowan Watson, Senior Curator, National Art Library, Word & Image Department, Victoria and Albert Museum

Teresa Webber, Trinity College, Cambridge

†**David Wright**, Professor Emeritus, University of California at Berkeley

Stefano Zamponi, Università di Firenze

INTRODUCTION[1]

FRANK T. COULSON

ORIGINS

THE discipline of palaeography arose from a religious controversy that erupted in the seventeenth century between the Jesuit and Benedictine orders. A Jesuit named Daniel van Papenbroeck (1628–1714) claimed in a short pamphlet of 56 pages entitled "Propylaeum antiquarium circa veri ac falsi discrimen in vetustis membranis" (1675) that a charter purportedly issued by the Merovingian king Dagobert in 646 guaranteeing certain privileges to the Benedictine order was a forgery. Jean Mabillon (1637–1707), a member of the Benedictine order, took up the challenge and over several years studied medieval manuscripts with a view to establishing criteria to prove a work genuine or a forgery. Published in 1681, *De re diplomatica* focused, in particular, on ancient legal and administrative documents (it is to the title that we owe the term diplomatics), though chapter 11 of Book One dealt more extensively with questions related to palaeography. Mabillon was chiefly concerned with pre-Caroline scripts, which he classified into five broad categories: "antiqua romana," "gothica," "longobardica," "saxonica," and "franco-gallica," and it is to this Maurist scholar that we owe the term "national hands." Mabillon, however, refrained from discussing any possible relationship between the scripts.

Scipione Maffei (1675–1755), a Veronese aristocrat and antiquarian, had a particular interest in the fate of ancient Latin manuscripts once in the possession of the Chapter House Library in Verona. In 1712, the librarian found them, apparently stored on the top of a cupboard, where they had been placed in the previous century. Maffei immediately began to study these texts, and the resulting work, *Istoria diplomatica* (1727), represented a major theoretical advance on the earlier study of Mabillon. Maffei

---

[1] The essays in the *Handbook* aim at enduring introductions to the subject matter, not up-to-the minute bibliographic surveys. But it should be noted that most contributors completed their essays for this volume by 2014, and publications which appeared after that date have only rarely been mentioned.

advocated a study of all types of writing, attacked Mabillon's notion of "national hands," and stressed the continuity of handwriting, dividing script into three broad types: majuscule, minuscule, and cursive.

DEVELOPMENTS IN THE NINETEENTH AND TWENTIETH CENTURIES

The establishment of the École des Chartes by royal decree of Louis XVIII in 1821 gave added impetus to the study of medieval manuscripts and charters. It soon became an important institution in the field of manuscript studies, and its students, recruited by competitive examination, receive the designation of palaeographer-archivist after the completion of a thesis. Other important figures who dominated the field of palaeography in France during the nineteenth century include Léopold Delisle (1826–1910) and Émile Chatelain (1851–1933). Delisle, by virtue of his position as Director of the Bibliothèque nationale from 1874, had daily contact with the manuscripts housed therein, and he is particularly remembered for his publications dealing with the manuscripts in the library and on the script at Tours. Chatelain, who was affiliated with the École pratique des hautes études, continued the work inaugurated by Champollion on the study of the palaeography of the Latin classics.

In Germany, Ludwig Traube (1861–1907) demonstrated that manuscripts were important not only as our primary sources for classical and medieval texts, but also as documents that illuminate medieval culture. While a manuscript that is a direct copy of another may hold no interest as a textual witness, it may serve to illuminate the intellectual and cultural milieu in which it was produced. Traube also made a lasting contribution as the director of the Monumenta Germaniae Historica (MGH) from 1897–1904 and as a teacher whose pupils at Munich included E. A. Lowe, arguably one of the towering figures in the discipline during the twentieth century.

Paul Lehmann (1884–1964), Traube's successor at the University of Munich, held the professorship in medieval philology there from 1914. Best known for his two works on parody and pseudo-antique literature in the Middle Ages, from 1953 until his death in 1964 he served on the central committee of the MGH, which since 1949 had been housed in Munich. Bernhard Bischoff (1906–91), Lehmann's pupil and successor in the chair of Medieval Latin Philology at Munich, was arguably the most influential German palaeographer of the twentieth century. He was an expert in localizing and dating medieval manuscripts, particularly those written in Caroline minuscule, and his textbook on palaeography, originally published in German and now translated into English and French, is fundamental to the discipline.

E.A. Lowe (1879–1969) published in 1914 his monumental study of the Beneventan script, the minuscule which dominated the Duchy of Benevento in the Middle Ages. Subsequently, he delved into the pre-Caroline scripts of Western Europe in his *Codices*

Latini Antiquiores, wherein scholars may survey the vast panorama of manuscripts written before 800. His pioneering work on the Beneventan script has been greatly expanded upon by Virginia Brown (1940–2009), who as a senior Fellow at the Pontifical Institute of Mediaeval Studies (1970–2009) trained several generations of manuscript scholars, and by Roger E. Reynolds (1936–2014), who as director of the *Monumenta Liturgica Beneventana* project did so much to refine our knowledge of Beneventan liturgical manuscripts.

The establishment of research centers and institutes dedicated to the preservation and reproduction of medieval and humanistic manuscripts was a further significant development in the study of palaeography. Most noteworthy among these various centers is, of course, the Institut de recherche et d'histoire des textes (IRHT) in Paris, founded in 1937 by Félix Grat (1898–1940) under the auspices of the CNRS. The IRHT contains an important library and an extensive collection of reproductions of manuscripts in photograph or microfilm. In addition, its holdings of unpublished "fichiers" (file-card catalogues) on medieval manuscripts is an unrivalled resource. Equally important are its collection of medieval incipits, now online as the In Principio database, and the seminal palaeographical journals (*Revue d'histoire des textes* and *Scriptorium*) published under its aegis.

Two other centers worthy of the attention of the manuscript researcher are the Vatican Film Library in St. Louis, Missouri, and the Hill Monastic Manuscript Library in Collegeville, Minnesota. The Vatican Film Library, established with generous funding of the Knights of Columbus Foundation and housed in the Pius XII Memorial Library of St. Louis University, has a unique collection of nearly 37,000 microfilmed manuscripts from the Biblioteca Apostolica Vaticana. The Hill Monastic Manuscript library contains an impressive microfilmed collection of manuscripts housed primarily in Austrian monasteries.

In the twenty-first century, the advent of new technology has revolutionized the study of manuscripts. Many entire collections may now be consulted online, and the digital scan, most often in color, has enormously facilitated the study of scripts. It is impossible within the confines of the present handbook to list all significant digitization projects, but the following may merit particular note: Manuscriptlink, E-codices-Virtual Library of Switzerland, Gallica (BnF), Biblioteca Palatina-digital, and Europeana Regia.

BIBLIOGRAPHY

Bischoff, B. 1990. *Latin Palaeography: Antiquity and the Middle Ages*, trans. D. Ó Cróínin and David Ganz. Cambridge: Cambridge University Press.

Boyle, L. 1984. *Medieval Latin Palaeography. A Bibliographical Introduction*. Toronto: University of Toronto Press.

Boyle, L. 2001. *Integral Palaeography*. Turnhout: Brepols.

Clemens, R. and T. Graham. 2007. *Manuscript Studies*. Ithaca, NY: Cornell University Press.

Lehmann, P. 1922. *Die Parodie im Mitelalter*. Munich: Drei Masken Verlag.

Lehmann, P. 1927. *Pseudo-antike Literatur des Mittelalters*. Berlin: Teubner.

Lowe, E. A. 1972. *Codices latini antiquiores; A Palaeographical Guide to Latin Manuscripts Prior to the Ninth Century*. Oxford: Clarendon.

Mabillon, J. 1681. *De re diplomatica*. Paris: Ludovici Billaine.

Maffei, S. 1727. *Istoria diplomatica*. Mantua: Alberto Tumermani.

Stiennon, J. 1973. *La Paléographie du Moyen Âge*. Paris: Armand Colin.

Ullman, L. B. 1932. *Ancient Writing and its Influence*. New York: Longmans, Green and Co.

van Papenbroeck, D. 1675. "Propylæum antiquarium, circa veri falsique discrimen in vetustis monumentis, præsertim diplomatis" in *Acta sanctorvm quotquot toto orbe coluntur, vel à catholicis scriptoribus celebrantur, / Aprilis / Godefridus Henschenius. Tomvs II, Quo medii XI dies continentur. Præponitur illis Propylæum antiquarium, circa veri falsique discrimen in vetustis monumentis, præsertim diplomatis, obseruandum subiunguntur Acta Græca ad eosdem dies pertinentia*, ed. Godefroid Henschen and Daniel van Papenbroeck. Antwerp: Michael Cnobarus.

PART I

SCRIPT

I . 1

ORGANIZING SCRIPT

CHAPTER 1

....

PUNCTUATION

....

FRANK T. COULSON

THROUGHOUT the early and high Middle Ages, punctuation in manuscripts often remained erratic. It was subject to much variation from period to period, from region to region, and even within an individual manuscript. Indeed, the reader of medieval manuscripts would be well advised to heed the warning of Malcolm Parkes, who in the introduction to his study of punctuation in medieval manuscripts opined: "The fundamental principle for interpreting punctuation is that the value and function of each symbol must be assessed in relation to the symbols in the same immediate context, rather than in relation to a supposed absolute value and function for that symbol when considered in isolation" (Parkes 1993, 2). The systems of abbreviation outlined below (*distinctiones* and *positurae*) are therefore to be interpreted not as absolute guidelines but rather as general guidance (as noted by Clemens and Graham 2007, 82).

In the early Roman imperial period, Latin texts were generally written without the aid of punctuation marks and were laid out *per cola et commata*, which meant that each sense unit was written on a new line. The terms *cola* and *commata* refer not to marks of punctuation but to divisions within a periodic sentence. Thus, the *colon* represented a major division where the sense was complete but the meaning was not, while the *comma* referred to a lesser division where, for example, the speaker might need to pause for breath. St. Jerome used such a layout in his text of the Bible, though it was not carried over into other types of text.

In late antiquity, scribes employed *scriptura* (or *scriptio*) *continua* in writing texts. The text was laid out continuously on a line without word division. Punctuation was often inserted later by individual readers in an effort to facilitate the reading aloud of the text. One method (called *distinctio*) involved placing a point (*punctus*) after the word at varying heights to denote pauses of differing value. A *punctus* placed low, at the level of the line of writing, indicated a brief pause (*subdistinctio*); a *punctus* placed at mid-level indicated a pause of medium value (*media distinctio*); and a *punctus* placed high carried the greatest value and marked the end of a sentence (*distinctio*). Donatus refers specifically to this system in his *Ars grammatica* (1.26), as does Isidore of Seville in his *Etymologiae* (1.20).

Irish and Anglo-Saxon scribes, for whom Latin was not a native language, introduced word separation to facilitate reading and comprehension. Insular scribes often added additional punctuation marks to earlier manuscripts that had been written in *scriptura continua*, and they adapted the system of *distinctiones* outlined by Donatus and Isidore, employing new symbols.

A second system of punctuation (*positurae*), in which the type of pause was indicated by different symbols rather than by the placement of a single *punctus*, developed in the Carolingian period. Originally employed in liturgical manuscripts to indicate when a voice should rise and fall, the marks gradually became universally used. There are four basic symbols in the *positurae* system:

The *punctus* . indicates a minor pause.
The *punctus elevatus* ⸵ indicates a major medial pause.
The *punctus versus* ⸵ indicates the end of a sentence.
The *punctus interrogativus* ⸮ indicates a question.

By the twelfth century, the *punctus versus* had fallen into disfavor and was replaced by a simple *punctus*, followed by a *littera notabilior* (capital letter).

Humanist scholars introduced several new punctuation signs:

Virgulae convexae (. . .) (labeled *lanulae* by Erasmus) were used to indicate parentheses. An example of the use of *virgulae convexae* can be found in Parkes 1993, Plate 31, lines 18–19)

The *punctus exclamativus* or *admirativus* ! (exclamation mark) first appeared in the second half of the fourteenth century (Iacopo Alpoleio da Urbisaglia lays claim to its invention, Parkes 1993, 49). In 1399, Coluccio Salutati used the mark in his manuscript of the *De nobilitate legum et medicinae,* Paris, BnF, lat. 8687 (see Parkes 1993, Plate 30, line 2).

The semicolon ; first appeared in the circle of humanists surrounding Aldus Manutius the Elder. It can be found in the edition of Pietro Bembo's *De Aetna* printed by Aldus at Venice in 1494 (Parkes 1993, Plate 31, lines 3, 11, and 12) and also in Bembo's edition of Petrarch printed by Aldus at Venice in 1501 (Parkes 1993, 49). Aldus Manutius the Younger in his *Interpugendi ratio* (Venice, 1566) views the semicolon as a figure of compromise between the two punctuation marks of the comma and colon, taking the semicircle from the comma and high point from the colon (Parkes 1993, 49).

Scribes indicated syllabic division at the end of a line with a single stroke (beginning in the eleventh century) and with a double stroke from the fourteenth century onward. Italian scribes, particularly during the thirteenth to fifteenth centuries, "justified" the right-hand margins of the manuscript by filling up empty spaces with an expuncted or crossed stroke. The vocative case is generally denoted by a small "o" with an accent stroke to the right placed over the word in the vocative case.

Certain punctuation signs were also to be found in specific types of texts. For example, the paragraph sign (essentially a "C" with a stroke through it) was used to indicate the beginning of a paragraph, proposition, or section and was particularly useful in manuscripts of *quaestiones* to enable the reader to identify quickly the principal stages of an argument. The *signe de renvoi* (return sign) could designate any sign used by a scribe to link the text to matter added in the margin.

Scribes used several methods to correct a text. *Cancellation* entailed crossing out the offending letters. *Expunction* entailed placing a small dot or series of dots beneath the offending letters. Another method used the Latin word *uacat*—usually separated into its two component parts, *ua* and *cat*—placed at the beginning and end of an offending passage.

Certain scripts also had punctuation marks peculiar to that script. In Beneventan script, the punctuation is notable: the mark for a full stop consists of a comma surmounted by two dots. Most striking is the suprascript "2 sign" (𝟤) to indicate an interrogation sign. It stands over the interrogative word or first word in a question or exclamation. Alongside it is the "assertion sign" (⊢), which cancels an earlier 2 sign or negates the implication that the word above which it stands can be interrogative. Related to this is the heavy grave bar, used in some Beneventan centers, especially Benevento itself, for exclamation. Beneventan punctuation was subtle in a manner far beyond that applied in most medieval scripts (adapted from Newton, Chapter 10 of this volume, p. 122).

Punctuation in medieval manuscripts, therefore, could vary from period to period, region to region, and script to script. The system used in *scriptura continua* during late antiquity was supplemented in the Carolingian age by a system called *positurae*. Certain scripts, particularly Beneventan, contained punctuation symbols unique to that script. Parkes 1993 is the fullest and best treatment of punctuation in medieval manuscripts and early printed texts; see also Clemens and Graham 2007, 82–9 with plates.

BIBLIOGRAPHY

Bischoff, B. 1990. *Latin Palaeography: Antiquity and the Middle Ages.* Translated by Dáibhí Ó Cróinín and David Ganz. Cambridge and New York: Cambridge University Press.

Clemens, R. and T. Graham. 2007. *Introduction to Manuscript Studies.* Ithaca, NY, and London: Cornell University Press.

Donatus, Aelius. 1864. *Grammatici latini*: IV: *Probi, Donati, Servii qui feruntur de arte grammatica libri*, ed. H. Keil. Leipzig: B. G. Teubner.

Gilles, Anne-Véronique. 1987. "La Ponctuation dans les manuscrits liturgiques au Moyen Âge." In *Grafia e interpunzione del latino nel medioevo. Seminario internazionale, Roma, 27–29 settembre 1984*, ed. Alfonso Maierù, 113–33. Rome: Edizioni dell'Ateneo.

Grotans, A. A. 1997. "'Sih dir selbo lector': Cues for Reading in Tenth- and Eleventh-Century St. Gall." *Scriptorium* 51: 251–302.

Hubert, M. 1970. "Corpus stigmatologicum minus." *Archivum latinitatis medii aevi* 37: 5–171.

Hubert, M. 1971–2. "Le Vocabulaire de la 'ponctuation' aux temps médiévaux: Un Cas d'incertitude lexicale."*Archivum latinitatis medii aevi* 38: 57–167.

Isidore of Seville. 1911. *Isidori Hispalensis episcopi Etymologiarum sive Originum libri XX,* 2 vols., ed. W. M. Lindsay. Oxford: Oxford University Press.

Moreau-Maréchal, J. 1968. "Recherches sur la ponctuation." *Scriptorium* 22: 56–66.

Müller, R. W. 1964. "Rhetorische und syntaktische Interpunktion. Untersuchungen zur Pausenbezeichnung im antiken Latein." Ph.D. diss., Tübingen: Eberhard-Karl-Universität.

Parkes, M. B. 1993. *Pause and Effect: An Introduction to the History of Punctuation in the West.* Berkeley, CA: University of California Press.

Saenger, P. 1997. *Space between Words: The Origins of Silent Reading.* Stanford, CA: Stanford University Press.

Treitler, L. 1981. "Oral, Written, and Literate Process in the Transmission of Medieval Music." *Speculum* 56: 471–91.

Treitler, L. 1984. "Reading and Singing: On the Genesis of Occidental Music-Writing." *Early Music History* 4: 135–208.

CHAPTER 2

ABBREVIATIONS

OLAF PLUTA

THE Middle Ages (or medieval period) is present in our daily lives in many ways.[1] The same is also true of medieval abbreviations. For instance, the @ symbol (at sign) in our email addresses can be traced back to a letter written by Francesco Lapi, an Italian merchant, dated May 4, 1536, and sent from Seville to Rome.[2] In this letter, the @ denotes 'anfora' (amphora), then a common unit of measurement.[3] Later, the @ symbol acquired the general commercial meanings 'at the price of' or per-unit cost.

The & symbol (and sign, or ampersand) as it is written today—originally a ligature of 'et', which is still discernible in the italic ampersand *&*—can frequently be found in medieval Latin manuscripts from the eighth century onward in abbreviations such as 'hab&', 'ten&', 'ſcilic&', 'app&it', 'uari&aſ', 'l&itia', '&iam' (Fig. 2.1), '&ſi', and '&c&era', or used separately as '&' denoting 'et'.[4]

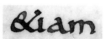

FIG. 2.1 Lyons, Bibliothèque municipale, MS 324, fol. 3r (Date: 825–50).[5]

The ∅ symbol (zero sign)—today used to signify the empty set, which has zero members—can be found in manuscripts of the fourteenth and fifteenth centuries. In those cases, the ∅ symbol denotes 'instans' (instant), a moment in time, the duration of which is zero.[6] It can also be found in combinations such as $\emptyset^{ns}$ (instans), $\emptyset^{tis}$ (instantis), $\emptyset^{ti}$ (instanti) (Fig. 2.2), or in derivatives like $\emptyset^{ea}$ (instantanea).[7]

FIG. 2.2 Fribourg, Bibliothèque des Cordeliers, MS 51, fol. 30v (Date: 1364).[8]

Apart from these special abbreviation marks, which can stand for themselves—there are other, less obvious ones, such as ≈ (esse) or ÷ (est)—the Middle Ages developed a wealth of abbreviation marks that can only be used in combination with letters.[9] To start with, there is a three-shaped mark (ȝ) used for *et* and for 'm' (vertical m), in combination with 'b' for 'bus' or with 'q' for the enclitic 'que'. A raised nine-shaped mark (ꝰ) is frequently used for 'us'. A zigzag-shaped mark above a letter (č) is used for 'er' or 're'. A wavelike mark above a letter (c̃), actually an open 'flat' a—the open form being the standard in some medieval scripts such as the Carolingian 'ɑ'—often replaces 'ar' or 'ra' but, generally speaking, it may replace any syllable that contains an 'a'. A two-shaped mark on top of letters (t²), actually a round r, stands for 'ur' or 'tur'. And the same two-shaped mark on the baseline, combined with a downward stroke, may stand for 'ris' as in aȥ^les (Aristoteles), though it is more often used at the end for 'rum'. A dot on or above the baseline after a letter usually signifies a suspension. A horizontal stroke (or two horizontal strokes) above a letter signifies a contraction, which can also be denoted by superscript letters or abbreviation marks.

What we have learned so far allows us to decipher the following abbreviations, all of which are combinations of the letters 'ca' with various abbreviation marks: c̃a (cura), ca² (capitur), caꝰ (casus), cā (causa), cāȝ (causam), c̄ā (causam), cāȥ (causarum), caȥ (carum), c̃a (cera), c̆ā (charta), č̆ā (creatura), č̆a² (creatur), and ca· (capitulum, capitulo). On its own, 'ca' may also denote a name like Cassiodorus.[10]

Abbreviations can be very short, sometimes consisting of a single letter combined with an abbreviation mark. If you know how a particular abbreviation has evolved over time, its various forms are easy to recognize: aꝥparȝ, aꝥpaȝ, aꝥpȝ, apȝ, and, ultimately, aȝ have all been used to denote 'apparet'.[11] There are, however, no rules that proscribe reading aȝ as 'absolvet', 'accidet', 'adesset', or any other word that begins with 'a-' and ends with '-et'. Since the three-shaped mark (ȝ) has, as mentioned earlier, various other meanings as well, the word could have a different ending. To make things even more complicated, abbreviations were not only used to represent words but also sometimes replaced whole phrases, which resulted in a reading that could be even more farfetched. For example, in medieval disputations, which are often highly logical, aȝ is sometimes used to denote 'maior patet'.[12]

Copying books by hand was a time-consuming task. When Jacobus van Enkhuysen, librarian of the Brethren of the Common Life in Zwolle, produced a copy of the entire Bible in six parchment volumes in folio, it took him 12 years to complete his work.[13] Understandably, the scribes sought to ease their gargantuan task by using scribal abbreviations. At the same time, the dignity of the manuscript dictated the extent to which an abbreviation could be used. In precious and ostentatious manuscripts such as the Zwolle Bible, abbreviations tend to be rare or are even entirely absent, with the exception of *nomina sacra*.[14] In academic manuscripts, however, abbreviations tend to be frequent. Even though university lectures were sometimes read "ad pennam"—slowly and accentuated to allow the students to write down the lecture carefully—lecture notes are often hastily written and full of strong abbreviations. This also extends to other texts that were copied and compiled for study purposes.

When a text contained a strong abbreviation for a particular word, even medieval scribes were sometimes at a loss when trying to figure out the correct word. For example, in the very first sentence of a treatise on the soul from the fourteenth century, the copyists came across a strong abbreviation that they successively read as 'discernere', 'discutere', and 'disserere'—all of which make sense in the given context.[15]

With ambiguities like these, the textual tradition branched out into a multitude of readings. When scribes had access to two or more copies of a particular text, they sometimes added variant readings in the margin or above the line if they were unsure about the correct reading. In a case comparable to the preceding example, the scribe of a commentary on Aristotle's *Physics* read 'distinguere' (diſtī^{re}) in the main manuscript ("quia est difficile distinguere") but added 'discernere' (diſčně) (Plate 2.1) as a variant reading from another manuscript in the margin.[16]

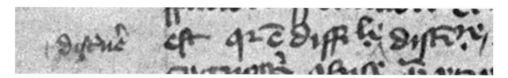

PLATE 2.1 København, Kongelige Bibliotek, MS Ny kgl. Saml. 108 fol., fol. 12ra.

While 'distinguere' and 'discernere' are largely synonymous, there are other cases where the variant readings change the meaning of the text. For example, it does make a difference whether Aristotle puts forward something as a mere question (quaestio) or as a demonstrative conclusion (conclusio).[17] Apparently, at some point in the textual tradition, a scribe misread the nine-shaped abbreviation mark on the baseline for prefixes standing for con-/com- (9) as the letter 'q', the original abbreviation being something like '9^{o³}' or '9̣ně' (conclusionem), which he interpreted as 'q^{o³}' or 'q̣ně' (quaestionem). The scribe of our commentary read 'quaestionem' (queſtionē) (Plate 2.2) in the main manuscript and added 'conclusionem' (9cluſionē) as a variant reading from another manuscript above the line.

PLATE 2.2 København, Kongelige Bibliotek, MS Ny kgl. Saml. 108 fol., fol. 3va.

In the following example, the original abbreviation may have been something like '9^{ib}' or '9īt', which one could read as 'contingit' or 'convenit', among other possibilities.[18] The scribe of our commentary read 'contingit' (9tīg^t) in the main manuscript, but added 'concipit' (ſeu 9cipit) as a variant reading in the margin (Plate 2.3).

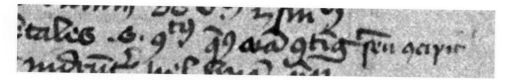

PLATE 2.3 København, Kongelige Bibliotek, MS Ny kgl. Saml. 108 fol., fol. 9vb.

In fact, an abbreviation such as '9ᵗ ᵇ' or '9īt' can have many more readings. Depending on the context, it may also be read as 'consistit', 'constituit', 'contigit', 'concludit', 'convertit', 'contulit', 'consuevit', or 'congruit', to name but a few options.

It is worthwhile briefly to remind ourselves of how many different readings are possible with a strong abbreviation. Take, for example, the common abbreviation "añs". Looking at this abbreviation through the eyes of a novice reader, "añs" may signify any word that starts with the letter *a*, ends with the letter *s*, and has the letter *n* somewhere in between. Searching the *Thesaurus Formarum Totius Latinitatis*,[19] a database of Latin word forms, for instances of "a*n*s" (with the asterisk denoting any string of characters, or no character at all), we get a total of 7,820 results.[20] Even when we apply some heuristic rules to narrow down the number of results, the figure is still considerable. For example, we may say that the first two letters ("añ") frequently stand for the preposition *ante*. When searching for "ante*s" we get 178 results.[21] Likewise, we may say that the last two letters ("ñs") are frequently used for the ending *ens*. When searching for "a*ens", we get 322 results.[22]

Experience shows that in nine out of ten cases, the abbreviation "añs" stands for "antecedens".[23] This, however, cannot be deduced *a priori* by applying scribal or heuristic rules; it can only be known *a posteriori* by collating as many instances as possible. In general, one may say that frequently used words or phrases are abbreviated the most. Ultimately, however, only experience can tell what words or phrases are frequent in a given context and which abbreviations were actually used.[24]

For this reason, collections of abbreviations have been compiled from the earliest days.[25] In the late Middle Ages, more and more lists of abbreviations were put together.[26] This is unsurprising, since both the sheer volume of texts and the number of abbreviations used increased significantly during the thirteenth, fourteenth, and fifteenth centuries. In the age of printing, the anonymous *Modus legendi abbreviaturas in utroque iure* was reissued many times over.[27] The first edition of this book was probably printed in Cologne around 1475, and subsequent editions were published in Basle, Strasbourg, Nuremberg, Louvain, Paris, and elsewhere.[28] It was reprinted continuously until 1623.[29] In the sixteenth century, we have the *Nuova regoletta nella quale troverai ogni sorta de abbreviatura usuale*,[30] which contains around 900 abbreviations, and Manutius' *De veterum notarum explanatione quae in antiquis monumentis occurrunt*.[31]

In the eighteenth century, the first attempts were made to devise a comprehensive collection of abbreviations. Daniel Eberhard Baring published his *Clavis diplomatica* in 1737,[32] followed by Johann Ludolf Walther's *Lexicon Diplomaticum* in two volumes in 1747.[33] In the late nineteenth century, two major dictionaries of Latin abbreviations were compiled. The first was Alphonse Chassant's *Dictionnaire des abréviations latines et françaises* in 1846, which was corrected and augmented several times;[34] the second was Ramón Álvarez de la Braña's *Siglas y abreviaturas latinas* in 1884.[35]

Still in use today is Adriano Cappelli's *Lexicon abbreviaturarum*. It first appeared in 1899 as part of the series "Manuali Hoepli."[36] It has since been revised four times, twice in Italian for the same series (1912, 1929) and twice in German for "Webers illustrierte Handbücher" (Leipzig 1901, 1928).[37] A longer version of the Latin title was used in 1899—*Lexicon abbreviaturarum quae in lapidibus, codicibus et chartis praesertim medii-aevi occurrunt*—but all subsequent editions have reduced the title to two words, following the example of the German translator: *Lexicon abbreviaturarum: Wörterbuch lateinischer und italienischer Abkürzungen*. The first Italian edition contained 10,000 entries, and although a further 3,000 entries were added in the German translation of 1901, the next Italian edition in 1912 was enlarged by only a thousand entries; its present size stands at approximately 14,000 entries. Since 1929 no changes have been introduced into the Italian text, which continues to be reprinted under the title *Lexicon abbreviaturarum: Dizionario di abbreviature latine ed italiane usate nelle carte e codici specialmente del medio-evo riprodotte con oltre 14000 segni incisi con l'aggiunta di uno studio sulla brachigrafia medioevale, un prontuario di Sigle Epigrafiche, l'antica numerazione romana ed arabica ed i segni indicanti monete, pesi, misure, etc.*[38]

The *Lexicon* was never available in an English edition, as it was in German, but Cappelli's prefatory treatise on the elements of Latin abbreviation has been published in an English translation under the title *The elements of abbreviation in medieval Latin paleography by Adriano Cappelli*, Lawrence, Kansas 1982.[39]

Auguste Pelzer's *Abréviations latines médiévales: Supplément au Dizionario di abbreviature latine ed italiane de Adriano Cappelli* presents a valuable supplement based on Vatican manuscripts.[40] It contains approximately 1,500 entries that cannot be found in Cappelli.

According to Adriano Cappelli's *Lexicon abbreviaturarum*, all medieval abbreviations can be divided into six categories (some of these abbreviation techniques are still in use today).

1. *Truncation*. A word is abbreviated by *truncation* when only the first part of the word is actually written out, while an abbreviation mark replaces the missing final letters. Examples are: b. (beatus), a.t. (alia translatio), fi· (fide), and oſ (omnis). Today, only the dot on the baseline has survived in abbreviations of titles, such as Prof. (Professor), and in commercial abbreviations as part of firm names such as Co. (Company), Corp. (Corporation), and Inc. (Incorporated).

2. *Contraction*. A word is abbreviated by contraction when one or more of the middle letters are missing. Such an omission is indicated by one of the general signs of abbreviation: ſp̄ſ (spiritus), grā (gratia), rō (ratio), and añs (antecedens). Today, we frequently use contractions, but usually without any sign of abbreviation, in abbreviations such as Mme (Madame) and Mlle (Mademoiselle) in social titles, or in the last part of street names such as Blvd (boulevard), Pkwy (parkway), and Rd (road).

3. *Abbreviation marks significant in themselves.* These signs indicate which elements of the abbreviated word are missing, no matter what letter the symbol is placed above or joined with as a ligature. Examples are: ꝓ (pro), ꝓbō (probatio), ꝓba^le (probabile), and ꝓlog⁹ (prologus).

4. *Abbreviation marks significant in context.* In this category are signs that indicate which elements are missing in an abbreviated word whose meaning is not set and constant but varies relative to the letter for which the sign stands. Examples are: p̄ (per), pfcō (perfectio), pcial' (partialis), and pcio (portio).

5. *Superscript letters.* With a few exceptions, a word is abbreviated with superscript letters at the end of a word where a superscript letter, whether a vowel or a consonant, simply indicates the ending of the word. Examples are: a^d (aliud), a^a (maior nota), g̊ci (Graeci), and ꝓ̇e^te (proprietate). Today, we use abbreviations such as n° (numero/number) as well as in ordinal numerals such as 1st, 2nd, 3rd, and 4th.

6. *Conventional signs.* This category includes all signs that stand for a frequently used word or phrase; in most cases these are not recognizable as letters and they are almost always isolated. Examples are: ≈ (esse), ≈n^r (essentialiter), ∅ (instans), and ∅^ti (instanti). Today, our currency symbols €, £, $, and ¥ fall into this category as do ® (registered trademark) and © (copyright), as well as many conventional signs in the sciences that are not recognizable as letters such as ×, ÷, =, ≠, ≈, ∅, ⊕, ⊗, ∞, and so on.

It should be noted that not all medieval abbreviations start with the initial letters of the words they represent. Examples include l' (vel), ·n· (enim), g° (ergo), and g^i (igitur). As our examples illustrate, it should be noted that the six categories discussed here are not mutually exclusive.

There were no restrictions on which techniques could be used to abbreviate a particular word. For example, the word 'consequentia', a frequent word in logical argumentations, has been abbreviated variously as: ꝯ̈, 9^a, 9n̈, 9n^a, 9n̄a, 9n̄a, 9ncia, 9ſeq^a, 9ſequētia, coña, and concia.

It remains a matter of debate whence exactly these different abbreviation techniques originated. Contraction, for example, which is clearly the most frequently used abbreviation technique in late-medieval manuscripts, can be traced back to the abbreviation of *nomina sacra*, which in turn can already be found in early Greek Christian manuscripts.[41] The most common of these abbreviations are: ΘΣ = θεός, ΚΣ = κύριος, ΙΣ or ΙΗΣ = Ἰησοῦς, ΧΣ or ΧΡΣ = Χριστός, and ΠΝΑ = πνεῦμα. Following the Greek example, these abbreviations were written in Latin texts as D̄S = Deus; D̄N̄S or D̄M̄S = Dominus; IH̄S = Iesus; XP̄S = Christus; and SP̄S = Spiritus. These Latin abbreviations sometimes imitated the Greek letters by using visually similar letters from the Latin alphabet.[42] The origin of the usage of contracting the *nomina sacra*, however, remains unclear to this day. The Christian scribes may have received their inspiration from the Jewish tradition of writing the inexpressible tetragram in the Greek versions of the Old Testament, or, alternatively, from a similar usage of writing the names of emperors in Greek cursive script.[43]

It can be useful to be aware of the fact that some abbreviations originated in the British Isles, while others were invented (and frequently used) in Spain or on the Italian

Peninsula. In Italy, for example, 'qui' was represented by a distinctive abbreviation, written with a horizontal stroke through the descender of the letter *q*.[44] This abbreviation was also used in combinations, such as 'qa' (quia), 'qdē' (quidem), or 'aliqd' (aliquid). Thomas Aquinas used this abbreviation in his own handwriting, the famous "littera inintelligibilis" as it was dubbed by contemporaries,[45] which, however, is only 'illegible' as far as Thomas's script is concerned, while the abbreviations used are not exceptionally difficult to decipher.[46]

Notably, however, scholars traveled, and so did their books and their abbreviations. A scribe who, like Thomas Aquinas, was trained in Naples, Italy did not immediately change his abbreviation techniques when he traveled to Paris and started to copy manuscripts there. Hence, we should be careful not to use abbreviations as the sole instrument in dating or locating a particular manuscript, even though they are undoubtedly useful as additional evidence.

Little is known about scribal training in the use of abbreviations. It should thus be all the more worthwhile briefly to look at one of the rare examples of a medieval tutorial for novice scribes. Our example is special in that it is an attempt to reform scribal practice, which apparently had got somewhat out of hand. The multitude of abbreviations in use during the Late Middle Ages had become a danger when it came to the transmission of religious texts. If a text is considered to be *holy*, as in the case of the *Holy Scripture*, it is naturally of the utmost importance that every single word is transmitted correctly. There must not be the slightest doubt as to what word the scribe has copied. It is certainly no coincidence that the Congregation of Windesheim, where this tutorial was compiled in the late fourteenth or early fifteenth century, prepared, at around the same time, a critical revision of the Latin Bible (Vulgate).

The title of the treatise as given in the *Incipit* reads as follows: "*Quaedam regulae de modo titulandi seu apificandi pro novellis scriptoribus copulatae.*"[47] This title introduces us to some technical terms related to the art of abbreviating. The term '*titulare*' literally means 'to add a *titulus* to a letter'. The term '*apificare*' is used as a synonym and literally means 'to add an *apex* to a letter'.

At the beginning of the text, the terms '*titulus*' or '*titellus*'—the text does not use the term '*apex*'—refers to the abbreviation strokes placed on top of letters to indicate contraction. Later on in the treatise, however, the term is also used to refer to other abbreviation marks. We may thus readily say that '*titulus*' or '*titellus*' refers to any sign that is used to indicate an omission.

Since the text is aimed at novice scribes, the abbreviation rules are fairly simple. Usually, only individual syllables are abbreviated. Hence, the term '*syllabicare*' is used in an alternative title of the treatise given in the initial table of contents: "*Quaedam regulae scribendi et syllabicandi bonos libros*".

As this second title makes clear, the collection of scribal rules should be used to copy 'good books', which the text of our treatise identifies further as 'precious books, that is to say, Bibles and the like' (*iste modus titulandi servari potest in libris pretiosis, scilicet in bibliis et huiusmodi*). However, the scribe may, if he so wishes, also apply these rules to the writing of missals, sermons, or homilies (*nisi scriptori autem placuerit, scilicet in messalibus, sermonibus, homilariis et sic de aliis*).

The scribal rules of the treatise are straightforward: special rules refer to syllables at the beginning of words (rules 1–3), at any position within a word (rules 4–5), or at the end of a word (rules 6–9 and 12). A special case refers to polysyllabic words (rule 13) where every single syllable is "*titellabilis*", i.e., where every syllable can be abbreviated with a "*titulus*"; in such cases, one needs to determine which syllables should be abbreviated. Two general rules (rules 14–15) determine when and where the '*titulus*' has to be placed in order to avoid doubt in the reader. Finally, three rules (rules 10, 11, and 16) refer to when and where to use special letterforms: the round *u*, the round *r*, and the long *s*.

As an example, let us look at two general rules that aim at avoiding ambiguity in abbreviation.

Rule 14. Every "*titellus*" must always be placed exactly where it replaces a number of characters; otherwise, it raises doubt in the reader and also often changes the meaning of the word, as is evident in the following example: If in "rapia" the "*titellus*" is put directly over the *a* (rapiā), this signifies a verb and is read as "rapiam". If, however, the "*titellus*" is put directly over the *i* (rapīa), this signifies a noun and is read as "rapina". For this reason, the "titellus" must be put in the exact place where it replaces a number of letters (*suppletio*) or where it modifies the meaning of a letter (*combinatio*). For example, when using a "*titellus*" in writing "gratia" or "littera", the "*titellus*" must not be placed over the last letter, but instead over the middle letter (grā, līa). Likewise, in 'frēs' (*fratres*) and 'pɔēs' (*patres*), the "*titellus*" must be put over the *r* as in 'frē' (*fratre*) and 'pɔē' (*patre*).`

Rule 15. If a "*titellus*" allows us to read a word in various ways, then it must not be written with a "*titellus*", as in the examples provided, for these can be read in two ways: 'cōfŏɔre' ("*confortare*" or "*conformare*"), 'tpare' ("*temperare*" or "*temporare*"), 'gēitus' ("*genitus*" or "*gemitus*"), and so forth. This general rule drastically reduces the number of abbreviations. Here, as well as in other places, the treatise emphasizes that an abbreviation must not generate any doubt in the reader; if there is the slightest possibility of doubt concerning the "*significatum dictionis*" (i.e., the meaning of a given abbreviation), the word must not be abbreviated. Strong contractions are only allowed for well-known and frequently used abbreviations signifying words such as *dominus, Deus, gratia, littera, ecclesia, fratres, patres,* and so forth. Ambiguity in abbreviations must be avoided at any cost in order to make sure that the texts of precious books, that is to say, Bibles and the like, are transmitted correctly.

Despite such late-medieval attempts to reform scribal practice, the reader of a medieval Latin manuscript usually has to solve a three-dimensional puzzle: one has to read a text in a foreign language (medieval Latin), which is written in an unfamiliar script, and, on top of that and more often than not, which is heavily abbreviated. The three dimensions are tightly interconnected: if you cannot recognize a letter in a particular script, you may have a hard time deciphering the abbreviation used; likewise, if you do not know the many technical terms of medieval Latin, you may have no idea what a particular abbreviation stands for. If you are an expert in Latin palaeography, and widely read in a particular field, you will probably have a good idea of what a given abbreviation stands for; this intuitive knowledge can, however, sometimes be misleading. Solving the compound puzzle presented by medieval Latin manuscripts is both an art and a science. Fortunately, Latin palaeography is becoming more of a science today.

The humanities have become more and more computational in recent years, and Latin palaeography is no exception. The first database of medieval Latin abbreviations, aptly named "Abbreviationes™," was developed by Olaf Pluta at Ruhr-Universität Bochum, Germany.[48] Originally written for the Apple Macintosh family of computers, the database is now published exclusively on the Internet, following the long-term trend away from native applications to web-based applications ("cloud computing").[49] Today, you can access Abbreviationes™ from anywhere with an Internet connection and a web browser, even from your smartphone (Plate 2.4). A medieval scribe would certainly be amazed at the ease and speed with which a current reader can today search for abbreviations on a small handheld device, tapping on a mirror-like surface where letters and abbreviation marks appear as if by magic.

PLATE 2.4 Abbreviationes™ on the Apple iPhone 3G.[50]

And th@'s th@!

NOTES

1. For a list of medieval inventions such as books and bookcases, the printing press, and eyeglasses, see Frugoni (2003).

2. The Italian newspaper *La Repubblica* reported on its website on July 28, 2000 (and in print on July 29, 2000) that Giorgio Stabile, then professor of the History of Science at Sapienza University of Rome, had come across this letter while carrying out research for a visual history of the twentieth century: https://ricerca.repubblica.it/repubblica/archivio/repubblica/2000/07/29/la-madre-di-tutte-le-chiocciole.html, accessed January 17, 2020. Medieval financial institutions—the bourse, a market for trading commercial paper, is another medieval invention—may have earlier examples in their documents. Stabile's finding does not, however, completely rule out a Latin or Middle English origin of the @. The @ may, in fact, have several independent roots.

   For a printed facsimile edition of the letter, see Melis (1972, no. 44, 214–17). Note that Francesco Lapi begins his letter with the date written as "@ddì 4 di maggio 1536"; the @ is used for purely decorative purposes here.

3. The Spanish word for amphora was 'arroba', and in modern Spanish the @ is still called 'arroba'; likewise in modern French, the @ is called 'arobase' or 'arrobe'.

4. These examples are taken from the following manuscripts: München (Munich), Bayerische Staatsbibliothek, MS lat. 14500 (ninth century); and Paris, Bibliothèque nationale de France, MS lat. 13956 (ninth century). Sometimes, the & symbol spans two words, such as in 'd&erra' (de terra) or 'qua&amen' (quae tamen). Occasionally, the & is also used for 'ec' as in 'm&um' (mecum), 'n&' (nec), 'fp&ulū' (speculum), 'intell&tum' (intellectum), or 'gr&e' (Graece). Furthermore, it could also be used for 'ed' as in 'f&' (sed).

5. https://florus.bm-lyon.fr/visualisation.php?cote=MS0324&vue=11. You will find the abbreviation in question in line 15.

6. See Meersseman (1955, 87–9). See also Steffan (1980, 155–7). On the adaptation of the medieval zero sign in contemporary modal logic, see Weidemann (1981, 8–9).

7. The examples are taken from the following manuscripts: Fribourg (Switzerland), Bibliothèque des Cordeliers, MS 51 (1364); Wien (Vienna), Dominikanerkloster, MS 138/108 (fourteenth century); Wien (Vienna), Dominikanerkloster, MS 107/73 (fifteenth century). In logical contexts, however, the ∅ is used for 'instantia' (counterinstance) as in '∅^{ie}' (instantiae) or '∅^{as}' (instantias).

8. https://www.e-codices.unifr.ch/en/fcc/0051/30v/0/Sequence-775. You will find the abbreviation in question in line 20: "motus non possit fieri in instanti, sed in tempore". On this manuscript, see Putallaz (1998, 304–11).

9. The medieval abbreviation system goes back to the ancient Roman system of *sigla*. In part at least, it also derives from the system of Tironian notes, a Roman shorthand. A third line of influence is the *nomina sacra*, which were abbreviated in the Christian tradition. While some elements of these precursors survived through the Middle Ages, the medieval abbreviation system is highly original in its use of many different abbreviation techniques.

10. The examples are taken from the following manuscripts: Città del Vaticano, Biblioteca Apostolica, MS Vat. lat. 694 (thirteenth century), MS Vat. lat. 781 (thirteenth century), MS Urb. Lat. 198 (fourteenth century), MS Ottob. lat. 21 (fourteenth century); Fribourg (Switzerland), Bibliothèque des Cordeliers, MS 51 (1364); Köln (Cologne), Historisches Archiv, MS W 258 a (thirteenth century); København, Kongelige Bibliotek, MS Ny

kgl. Saml. 1801 fol. (fourteenth century); Kraków, Biblioteka Jagiellońska, MS 659 (fourteenth century), MS 1771 (fourteenth century); Paris, Bibliothèque Mazarine, MS 934 (fourteenth century); Wien (Vienna), Österreichische Nationalbibliothek, MS 5437 (fourteenth century); Wolfenbüttel, Herzog August Bibliothek, MS 40 Weissenb. (fifteenth century).

11. There are, of course, further abbreviations such as 'appar&' or 'aṗpaět'. Apart from a₃, frequent abbreviations of this type include d₃ (debet), e₃ (esset), h₃ (habet), l₃ (licet), o₃ (oportet), p₃ (patet), f₃ (scilicet), t₃ (tenet), and v₃ (valet, videlicet).

12. In logical texts, 'a' is frequently used for the major premise and 'b' is for the minor premise of a conclusion. This results in abbreviations such as a^a (maior nota) and b^2 (minor probatur).

13. This Bible (now Utrecht, Universiteitsbibliotheek, MS 31) was commissioned by Herman Droem, dean of the chapter of St. Mary in Utrecht, and produced after the invention of printing in the years 1464–76. For a description of the manuscript, see Horst (1984, 138–40), (1989, No. 76).

14. See Bischoff (1990, 154). For the *nomina sacra* as an origin of the use of abbreviations, see Traube (1907).

15. Peter of Ailly (1987, xxxi). Further (singular) readings are 'dicere', 'asserere', and 'recitare', but here the scribes obviously deviate from the original text. The original sentence reads as follows: "Quidditatem animae umbratice somniantes philosophi de ea diversa et adversa senserunt, quae omnia disserere longum esset."

16. The variant readings in this manuscript are often accompanied by terms like "alias …", "aliter …", "aut …", "seu …", or "vel …".

17. The passage in question reads: "quia in secundo *Posteriorum* ponit Aristoteles unam conclusionem demonstrative scibilem."

18. The passage in question reads: "termini mentales, scilicet conceptus, quibus anima concipit plures res simul indifferenter."

19. Tombeur (1998).

20. The asterisk, which is used as a wildcard character, takes the place of any series of characters. Searching for "*ualere", for example, delivers the following results: *aequiualere, beneualere, conualere, equiualere, inualere, praeualere, preualere, squalere,* and *ualere* itself. The database allows a maximum of two asterisks (*) per search.

21. From *anteactas* to *anteus*. The results include frequent word forms such as *antecedens, antecedentes, antecedentibus, antecedentis, antecessores, antecessoribus, antedictis, anteponens, anteriores, anterioribus, anterioris,* and *anterius*, with the most frequent word form being *antecedens*.

22. From *abdens* to *auriens*. The results include frequent word forms such as *absens, accedens, accidens, accipiens, addens, adhaerens, adolescens, adueniens, adulescens, agens, agnoscens, aliquotiens, amens, antecedens, aperiens, apparens, appetens, ardens, arguens, ascendens, aspiciens, asserens, assumens, attendens, audiens,* and *auferens*, with the most frequent word forms being *accidens, agens,* and *audiens*.

23. The abbreviation "añs" is also used in abbreviations of common phrases such as "añs₃" (antecedens patet) and "añs²" (antecedens probatur).

24. When searching for instances of "a*n*s", the ten most frequent word forms are *Augustinus, angelus, annos, annis, accidens, angelis, animus, animas, agens,* and *angelos*. Evidently, frequency is not the reason for choosing the abbreviation "añs" for "antecedens", which is not even among the top 50 most frequent word forms.

25. On the oldest lists of abbreviations, see Traube (1909, 129–56).

26. These inventories were collected and published by Lehmann (1929).

27. See Sawicki (1973, 109–34). The question of authorship is still not decisively resolved (see ibid., 111–13).

28. For the incunable editions, see Feenstra (1998, 221–48). Feenstra lists (p. 248) 36 printed editions from 1475 to 1500.

29. *Modvs legendi abbreviatvras* (1623).

30. *Nuova regoletta* (1534): see Omont (1902, 5–9).

31. Manutius (1566).

32. Baring (1737).

33. Walther (1745–7).

34. Chassant, (1846). Chassant was the first to try and categorize the huge volume of abbreviations; for this purpose, he introduced the terms "contraction" and "suspension."

35. Álvarez de la Braña (1884).

36. Cappelli (1899).

37. Cappelli (1901), (1928).

38. Cappelli (2011).

39. Cappelli (1982).

40. Pelzer (1966).

41. See Traube (1907). Similarly, Bischoff views the "ubiquitous model of the nomina sacra" as the origin of the abbreviation technique of contraction (Bischoff 1990, 153). This view contradicts Schiaparelli's opinion, which regards the contractions of legal terms as the model for the development of the medieval system. See Schiaparelli (1914, 241–75), (1915, 275–322). These two articles were reprinted in Schiaparelli (1969, 94–186). Schiaparelli denies a major role of the *nomina sacra*: "I nomi sacri formarono un gruppo di vocaboli scritti o abbreviati in tal maniera pressoché chiuso, pur avendo esercitato qualche influenza" (Schiaparelli,1928, 86).

42. See Christianus Stabulensis, *Expositio in evangelium Matthaei*, col. 1278, linea 43: "Scribitur autem Iesus iota et eta et sigma et apice desuper apud nos. Nam in Grecorum libris solummodo per iota et sigma et apice desuper invenitur scriptum, et sicut alia nomina dei comprehensive [i.e. abbreviated] debent scribi, quia nomen dei non potest litteris explicari. Quando purum hominem significat, per omnes litteras scribitur" (Migne 1864, 106, col.1278CD).

43. For a summary of the discussion, see Paap (1959).

44. See Derolez (2003, 68).

45. According to Dondaine and Shooner (1967, 7) 'inintelligibilis' is a misreading of 'illegibilis', but it has held the field for a long time. See Boyle (2005, 294).

46. In the autograph manuscript Città del Vaticano, Biblioteca Apostolica Vaticana, MS Vat. lat. 9850, we find, for example: q (qui) (fol. 105ra), qa (quia) (fol. 105ra), qb; (quibus) (fol. 105rb), qđ (quidem) (fol. 48ra), qdā (quidam) (fol. 48ra), eqtatē (aequitatem) (fol. 105ra), eqtatiſ (aequitatis) (fol. 105rb), eqnoſ (equinos) (fol. 105rb), ppīq (propinqui) (fol. 105ra), reqeſcēt (requiescent) (fol. 105rb), reqrite (requirite) (fol. 105rb); and in the autograph manuscript MS Vat. lat. 9851, we find, for example: loqm² (loquimur) (fol. 12va), ſeqt² (sequitur) (fol. 12va), qa (quia) (fol. 13rb).

47. See Pluta (2010).

48. See Pluta (2004).

49. The Abbreviationes™ Online Web site is available at https://abbreviationes.net/, accessed January 19, 2020.
50. You can use your smartphone (or laptop or netbook) anywhere in the world to access Abbreviationes™ through your university's VPN or proxy server.

BIBLIOGRAPHY

Álvarez de la Braña, R. 1884. *Siglas y abreviaturas latinas con su significado por órden alfabético, seguidas del calendario romano y de un catálogo de las abreviaturas que de usan en los documentos pontificos*. León: Garzo [repr. Hildesheim and New York: Olms, 1978].

Baring, Daniel Eberhard. 1737. *Clavis diplomatica, specimina veterum scripturarum tradens, alphabeta nimirum varia, medii aevi compendia scribendi, notariorum veterum signa perplura et singula tabulis aeneis expressa. Praemissa est bibliotheca scriptorum rei diplomaticae. Iterata hac editione sic ab auctore recognita, emendata ac locupletata, ut novum opus videri possit*. Hanover: Förster.

Bischoff, B. 1990. *Latin Palaeography: Antiquity and the Middle Ages*, trans. Dáibhí Ó Cróinín and David Ganz. Cambridge: Cambridge University Press.

Boyle, L. E. 2005. "St. Thomas Aquinas and the Third Millennium." In *Omnia disce— Medieval Studies in Memory of Leonard Boyle, O.P.* (Church, Faith and Culture in the Medieval West), ed. Anne J. Duggan, Joan Greatrex, and Brenda Bolton, 294. Aldershot: Ashgate.

Cappelli, A. 1899. *Lexicon abbreviaturarum quae in lapidibus, codicibus et chartis praesertim medii-aevi occurrunt: Dizionario di abbreviature latine ed italiane: usate nelle carte e codici specialmente del medio-evo riprodotte con oltre 13000 segni incisi; aggiuntovi uno studio sulla brachigrafia medioevale, un prontuario di Sigle Epigrafiche, l'antica numerazione romana ed arabica, i monogrammi, ed i segni indicanti monete, pesi, misure*. Milan: Hoepli.

Cappelli, A. 1901. *Lexicon abbreviaturarum: Wörterbuch lateinischer und italienischer Abkürzungen, wie sie in Urkunden und Handschriften besonders des Mittelalters gebräuchlich sind, dargestellt in über 16000 Zeichen, nebst einer Abhandlung über die mittelalterliche Kurzschrift, einer Zusammenstellung epigraphischer Sigel, der alten römischen und arabischen Zählung und der Zeichen für Münzen, Masse und Gewichte* (Webers illustrierte Handbücher 3). Leipzig: Weber.

Cappelli, A. 1928. *Lexicon abbreviaturarum: Wörterbuch lateinischer und italienischer Abkürzungen, wie sie in Urkunden und Handschriften besonders des Mittelalters gebräuchlich sind, dargestellt in über 14000 Holzschnittzeichen* (Webers illustrierte Handbücher 3), 2nd ed. Leipzig: Weber.

Cappelli, A. 1982. *The Elements of Abbreviation in Medieval Latin Paleography*, trans. David Heimann and Richard Kay (University of Kansas Publications, Library Series 47). Lawrence, KS: University of Kansas Libraries.

Cappelli, A. 2011. *Lexicon abbreviaturarum: Dizionario di abbreviature latine ed italiane usate nelle carte e codici specialmente del medio-evo riprodotte con oltre 14000 segni incisi con l'aggiunta di uno studio sulla brachigrafia medioevale, un prontuario di Sigle Epigrafiche, l'antica numerazione romana ed arabica ed i segni indicanti monete, pesi, misure, etc.*, 6th ed. with 9 plates. Milan: Ulrico Hoepli.

Chassant, A. A. L. 1846. *Dictionnaire des abréviations latines et françaises usitées dans les inscriptions lapidaires et métalliques, les manuscrits et les chartes du Moyen Age*. Évreux: Cornemillot [2nd ed. Paris: Aubry, 1862; 3rd ed. Paris: Aubry, 1866; 4th ed. Paris: Aubrey, 1876; 5th ed. Paris: Martin, 1884; repr. of 5th ed. Paris 1884: Hildesheim and New York: Olms, 1965].

Derolez, A. 2003. *The Palaeography of Gothic Manuscript Books: From the Twelfth to the Early Sixteenth Century*. Cambridge: Cambridge University Press.

Dondaine, H. F. and H. V. Shooner. 1967. *Codices manuscripti operum Thomae de Aquino*, vol. 1. Rome: Commissio Leonina.

Feenstra, R. 1998. "La Genèse du 'Modus legendi abbreviaturas in utroque iure.' Éditions incunables et manuscripts." In *Life, Law and Letters: Historical Studies in Honour of Antonio García y García*, vol. 1 (Studia Gratiana 28), ed. Peter Linehan, 221–48. Rome: Libreria Ateneo Salesiano.

Frugoni, C. 2003. *Books, Banks, Buttons, and Other Inventions from the Middle Ages*, trans. William McCuaig. New York: Columbia University Press.

Horst, K. van der. 1984. *Handschriften en Oude Drukken van de Utrechtse Universiteitsbibliotheek: Samengesteld bij jet 400-jarig bestaan van de bibliotheek der Rijksuniversiteit, 1584–1984*, 2nd ed. Utrecht: Universiteitsbibliotheek.

Horst, K. van der. 1989. *Illuminated and Decorated Medieval Manuscripts in the University Library, Utrecht: An Illustrated Catalogue*. Maarssen's-Gravenhage: Gary Schwartz.

Lehmann, P. 1929. *Sammlungen und Erörterungen lateinischer Abkürzungen in Altertum und Mittelalter* (Abhandlungen der Bayerischen Akademie der Wissenschaften. Philosophisch-historische Abteilung. Neue Folge, 3). Munich: Verlag der Bayerischen Akademie der Wissenschaften.

Manutius, A. 1566. *De veterum notarum explanatione quae in antiquis monumentis occurrunt*. Venice [repr. Milan: La Goliardica, 1971].

Meersseman, G. G. 1955. "Einige Siglen der mittelalterlichen Logik." *Freiburger Zeitschrift für Philosophie und Theologie* 2: 87–9.

Melis, F. 1972. *Documenti per la storia economica dei secoli XIII–XVI, Con una nota di Paleografia Commerciale a cura di Elena Cecchi* (Istituto internazionale di storia economica "F. Datini", Prato—Pubblicazioni Serie I: Documenti, vol. 1). Florence: Olschki.

Migne, J. P. 1864. *Patrologiae cursus completus... Series Latina*, vol. 106. Paris: Garnier and J. P. Migne.

Modvs legendi abbreviatvras passim in ivre tam civili, qvam pontificio occvrrrentes. 1623. Rome: Facciotti. [repr. Bononia: Forni, 1989, http://works.bepress.com/david_freidenreich/28, accessed January 18, 2020].

Nuova regoletta nella quale troverai ogni sorta de abbreviatura usuale. 1534. Brescia: Damiano e Jacobo Philippo fratelli.

Omont, H. 1902. "Dictionnaire d'abréviations latines publié à Brescia en 1534." *Bibliothèque de l'École des Chartes* 63: 5–9.

Paap, A. H. R. E. 1959. *Nomina Sacra in the Greek Papyri of the First Five Centuries A.D.: The Sources and Some Deductions* (Papyrologica Lugduno-Batava 8). Leiden: Brill.

Pelzer, A. 1966. *Abréviations latines médiévales. Supplément au Dizionario di abbreviature latine ed italiane de Adriano Cappelli* (Centre de Wulf-Mansion, Recherches de philosophie ancienne et médiévale), 2nd ed. Louvain: Publications Universitaires and Paris: Béatrice-Nauwelaerts.

Peter of Ailly. 1987. "Tractatus de anima (ed. Pluta)." In Olaf Pluta, *Die philosophische Psychologie des Peter von Ailly: Ein Beitrag zur Geschichte der Philosophie des späten Mittelalters* (Bochumer Studien zur Philosophie 6, Part II (Edition)). Amsterdam: Grüner.

Pluta, O. 2004. "Abbreviationes™: A Database of Medieval Latin Abbreviations." In *Mediaevistik und Neue Medien*, ed. Klaus van Eickels, Ruth Weichselbaumer, and Ingrid Bennewitz, 183–9. Stuttgart: Jan Thorbecke.

Pluta, O. 2010. "*Quaedam regulae de modo titulandi seu apificandi pro novellis scriptoribus copulatae*: A Late Medieval Tutorial for Novice Scribes." In *Teaching Writing, Learning to Write*: (Proceedings of the XVIth Colloquium of the Comité International de Paléographie Latine, Held at the Institute of English Studies, University of London, 2–5 September 2008) (King's College London Medieval Studies, XXII), ed. Pamela R. Robinson, 241–71. London: King's College London, Centre for Late Antique & Medieval Studies.

Putallaz, F.-X. 1998. "Cherchez l'auteur! Un curieux manuscrit du XIVe siècle." In *Was ist Philosophie im Mittelalter? Qu'est-ce que la philosophie au Moyen Âge?* (What Is Philosophy in the Middle Ages?) (Akten des X. Internationalen Kongresses für mittelalterliche Philosophie der Société Internationale pour l'Étude de la Philosophie Médiévale, 25 bis 30 August 1997 in Erfurt, Miscellanea Mediaevalia 26), ed. Jan A. Aertsen and Andreas Speer, 304–11. Berlin and New York: Walter de Gruyter.

Sawicki, J. T. 1973. "Der 'Modus legendi abbreviaturas in utroque iure' in der Breslauer Handschrift I Q 69: Ein Denkmal der populären Rechtsliteratur und der juristischen Paläographie in Polen aus dem XV. Jahrhundert." *Bulletin of Medieval Canon Law*, n.s. 3: 109–34.

Schiaparelli, L. 1914. "Note paleografiche: Segni tachigrafici nelle *Notae iuris*." *Archivio storico italiano* 72/1: 241–75.

Schiaparelli, L. 1915. "Le *Notae iuris* e il sistema delle abbreviature medievali." *Archivio storico italiano* 73/1: 275–322.

Schiaparelli, L. 1928. "Tachigrafia sillabica latina in Italia." *Bollettino della Accademia di Stenografia* 4: 11–18, 80–90, 157–68.

Schiaparelli, L. 1969. *Note paleografiche (1910–1932)*, ed. Giorgio Cencetti. Turin: Bottega d'Erasmo.

Steffan, H., ed. 1980. "Magistri Theodorici Ordinis Fratrum Praedicatorum Tractatus de cognitione entium separatorum et maxime animarum separatarum, Einleitung, III. Paläographischer Exkurs zu einem Sigel in D." In Dietrich von Freiberg, *Schriften zur Metaphysik und Theologie*, with an Introduction by Kurt Flasch [=Dietrich von Freiberg, *Opera Omnia*, II], 155–7. Hamburg: Meiner.

Tombeur, P., ed. 1998. *Thesaurus Formarum Totius Latinitatis, Cetedoc Index of Latin Forms: Database for the Study of the Vocabulary of the Entire Latin World/Base de données pour l'étude du vocabulaire de toute la latinité*. Brepols: Catholic University of Leuven.

Traube, L. 1907. *Nomina sacra: Versuch einer Geschichte der christlichen Kürzung* (Quellen und Untersuchungen zur lateinischen Philologie des Mittelalters, 2). Munich: Beck [repr. Darmstadt: Wissenschaftliche Buchgesellschaft, 1967].

Traube, L. 1909. "Lehre und Geschichte der Abkürzungen (Vorgetragen in der historischen Klasse der K. B. Akademie der Wissenschaften zu München am 4. Februar 1899)." In L. Traube, *Zur Paläographie und Handschriftenkunde*, ed. P. Lehmann, 129–56. Munich: Beck [repr. =Ludwig Traube, *Vorlesungen und Abhandlungen*. ed. Franz Boll, 1. Munich: Beck, 1965].

Walther, J. L. 1745–7. *Lexicon Diplomaticum, abbreviationes syllabarum et vocum in diplomatibus et codicibus a saeculo viii. ad xvi. usque occurrentes exponens, iunctis alphabetis et scripturae speciminibus integris.* Göttingen: Schmid [repr. Ulm: Gaum, 1756; New York: Franklin, 1966 (Burt Franklin bibliography and reference series, 101); Hildesheim and New York: Olms, 1973].

Weidemann, H. 1981. "Zur Semantik der Modalbegriffe bei Peter Abaelard." *Medioevo* 7: 1–40.

CHAPTER 3

··

THE PALAEOGRAPHY
OF NUMERALS

··

CHARLES BURNETT

NUMERALS are symbols that are independent of language. The same symbol in the Middle Ages "iii" could be read as "tres, trois, tre, three...," just as the modern equivalent "3" can be pronounced in any language of the world. This chapter investigates how numbers were represented in manuscripts, documents, and in epigraphy in the context of Latin and the European vernacular writings from classical times to the early modern period. It takes a taxonomical rather than a historical approach, since several numerical systems were often used simultaneously. There is no attempt to explain how calculations were made in premodern times, but a basic distinction should be established first: "number" is the value, either cardinal or ordinal, which can be expressed in words (*tres*, *triginta*, etc.), or in numerals (Roman numerals, Hindu-Arabic numerals, etc.); "numerals," called "caracteres" or "figurae" in Latin, are the written expressions of numbers.

THE FORMS OF NUMERALS

··

1 Numbers may be expressed in words: unus, duo, tres... for the cardinal numbers; primus, secundus, tertius... for the ordinal numbers. To write numbers in full was regarded as the safest way to make sure that the correct amounts were recorded, and to avoid fraud. Hence, in legal documents it is especially common to find numbers written in full. Note the contorted example in a charter written by Miró Bonfill

> Exarata est igitur haec adclamationis scedula elapsis Dominice Humanationis annis ter senis quinquagenis ($3 \times 6 \times 50 = 900$) ebdeque denis ($7 \times 10 = 70$) ter binisque ($3 \times 2 = 6$) indicione tetra ($= 4$), die bisterna ($2 \times 3 = 6$) kalendarum martiarum, anno tetrapendo dipondio ($4 \times 5 + 2 = 22$) Leuthario Francorum rege oblinente regno.

2 But it is very cumbersome to write numbers in full. The most transparent abbreviation of numbers was simply to retain the ending of the written form of the numeral and to express the numerical value in the current numeral system. This again "fixes" the significance of the number and marks it as cardinal, ordinal, or iterative (most commonly, ordinal numbers, because they decline). This mixed form is particularly common in dates, where the appropriate ending of the thousands, hundreds, tens, and units is added to the numeral: anno .m.° ccc.° xx.° ii.° (1322).

3 Numbers could also be expressed by images of the calculation instruments that engender them. Calculation on the fingers was commonly employed by merchants and other members of society. Bede started his book on the calculation of the church calendar, the *De ratione temporum*, with a chapter on finger reckoning, showing the positions of the units, tens, and hundreds, extending to the use of the whole body to represent the ten thousands (Bede 1999, 10–11; Murdoch 1984, 79). The hand positions of figures in medieval illustrations may sometimes represent these numbers symbolically (a possible example in Paris, BnF, lat. 6734 (d'Alverny 1993 VI).

4 The other instrument commonly used in calculation was the abacus, which was a board marked out in columns, sometimes for units, tens, hundreds, and further powers of ten, at other times, for currency: *denarii, solidi, librae.* The relevant number of counters was placed in each column (sometimes with a counter representing "5" of the item). For a brief period from the late tenth century to the mid-twelfth century, a special kind of abacus was used (the "Gerbertian" abacus, or "abacus with "apices"") which employed a different counter for each digit; the digits, from 0 to 9 were inscribed on the counters: (Burnett 2010a, I). Numerical values could be recorded in manuscripts by depicting the arrangement of the counters on the abacus (Plate 3.1). In the case of the "Gerbertian" abacus, in which the counters could, and were, differentiated by Greek alphabetical numeration or by Hindu-Arabic numerals, a group of manuscripts illustrates the stages of calculation on such an abacus (Plate 3.2).

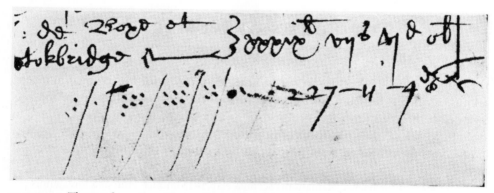

PLATE 3.1 The configuration of counters on the abacus drawn to show a numerical value.
Kew, National Archives, Exchequer Augmentation Office. Misc. Books. 1600. Temp. Elizabeth.

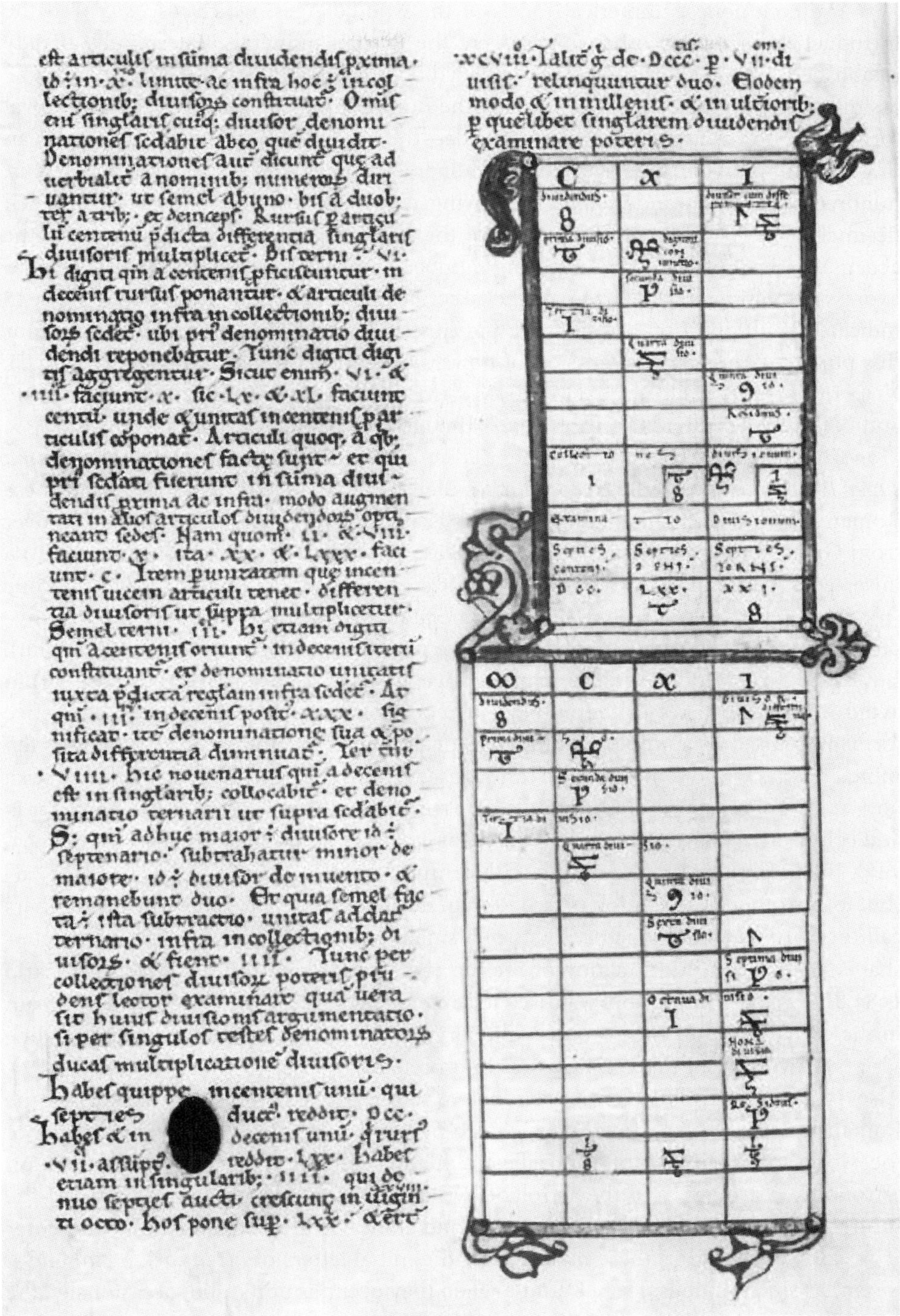

PLATE 3.2 Arabic numerals on the counters of an abacus, with Roman numerals in the text.
Oxford, Bodleian Library, Auct. F.1.9 (AD 1120–1140), fol. 56v.

5 The commonest numerical forms of the Middle Ages, which also survived the introduction of several other forms, were the Roman numerals. These were already established in Antiquity, when certain symbols (originally Etruscan) had become assimilated to their closest equivalents in the Roman alphabet. Only the early medieval form of "1000" (a figure of eight on its side—the present-day infinity sign) retains an original non-alphabetical form. Roman numerals differentiate between the units, tens, hundreds, and thousands, while employing a distinct symbol for the "5" in each decimal place (perhaps as a reflection of the use of a separate counter for 5 on the abacus). Instead of using an increasing number of forward-facing and reverse "Cs" to express increasing powers of ten, medieval scribes and mathematicians used the tilde to indicate a multiplication by one thousand (just as the Greeks had used the comma for this purpose): thus the progression of powers of ten took the form: I, X, C, $\bar{\text{M}}$ (or $\bar{\text{I}}$), $\bar{\text{X}}, \bar{\text{C}}, \bar{\text{I}}\bar{\text{M}}$(or$\bar{\text{M}}\bar{\text{I}}$), $\text{X}\bar{\text{I}}\bar{\text{M}}$($\bar{\text{X}}\bar{\text{I}}\bar{\text{M}}$), $\text{C}\bar{\text{I}}\bar{\text{M}}$($\bar{\text{C}}\bar{\text{I}}\bar{\text{M}}$), $\bar{\text{I}}\bar{\text{M}}\bar{\text{I}}$ (or $\bar{\text{M}}\bar{\text{I}}\bar{\text{M}}$ or $\bar{\text{M}}\bar{\text{M}}\bar{\text{M}}$). Note that "M" and "$\bar{\text{I}}$" are used interchangeably, even though "M" should strictly mean "1000" × "1000" (Burnett 2010a, I). This system is set out in detail in Petrus Helias's *Summa super Priscianum* from the 1140s (Petrus Helias, 1993, 147–8). An addition to these Roman numerals in mathematical contexts is a symbol for zero, which was taken over from Greek, and which varies in appearance from a circle with tilde on top of it, to a lower-case "t" (Plate 3.3). Roman numerals were originally "additive": 2 is one plus one (ii), 3 is one plus one plus one (iii), 4 is one plus one plus one plus one (iiii), 6 is five plus one (vi), 7 is five plus two (vii), 8 is five plus three (viii), 9 is five plus four (viiii). But in the early Middle Ages, as an alternative, in order to save space and (perhaps) to avoid making mistakes in the number of repetitions of the single stroke, subtractive forms were used for numbers ending in -4 or -9: four is five minus one (iv), nine is ten minus one (ix). The same strategy can be used at each decimal level (40 = 50 – 10: xl; 90 = 100 – 10: xc; 400 = 500 – 100: cd). The subtractive form is given as the norm for iv and ix by Petrus Helias, who retains lxxxx for 90 and dcccc for 900 (Petrus Helias, 1993, 147). In Visigothic script, from the sixth century onwards, a ligature was used for "xl" (but for no other combination of two Roman numerals), which Spanish palaeographers call the *x-aspada*, and which consists of a small "L" (often reduced to a hook or cup-shape) written as a continuation of the top right-hand arm of the "x" (Millares Carlo 1983, II, 273–4). This symbol was used in some mathematical works translated in Spain in the early to mid-twelfth century and survives in copies of these works in Caroline script; but very often the *x-aspada* was interpreted as a simple "x" (Burnett 2010a IV). Also in the mid-twelfth century further experiments were made to abbreviate the Roman numerals—experiments which are particularly prominent in manuscripts of the works of Raymond of Marseilles, a highly cultured Latin writer of texts on astronomy, astrology, and the astrolabe, writing in Marseilles in 1141. Instead of the subtractive forms of the Roman numerals, and alongside the *x-aspada* for 40 and (after "l" = 50) 90, we find in these manuscripts the initial letters of *q(uatuor)*, *o(cto)* and *n (ovem)* as small capitals, for 4, 8, and 9 when they occur as units, and, occasionally, the initial letter of *t(riginta)*, in lower case, for the first numeral in numbers between 31 and 39 (Raymond of Marseilles 2009, 10). Roman numerals remained the most familiar

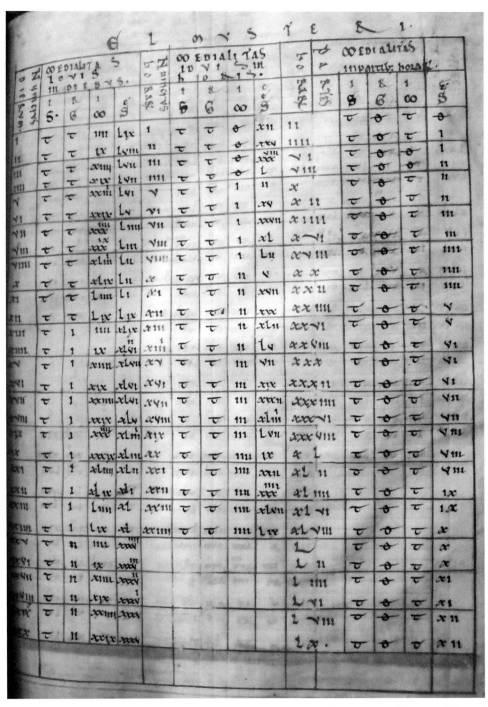

PLATE 3.3 An astronomical table, showing different forms of the symbol for zero ("t" and crossed-out "o").

Oxford, Bodleian Library, Auct. F.1.9 (AD 1120–1140), fol. 106r.

form of numeration for the whole of the Middle Ages and into the early modern period. They are occasionally used in texts where Hindu-Arabic numerals are used in examples; or for final totals when Hindu-Arabic numerals are used for the calculation. They are frequently used in year values for the thousands and hundreds, where Hindu-Arabic numerals are used for the tens and units (e.g., MS Avignon, Bibliothèque municipale, 1086, fol. 68r: M°CCCC43°; see Crossley (2013).

6 From classical times the numerical values of Greek letters appear in Latin contexts. These Greek letters (plus three extra symbols which were obsolete letters), as numerals, were used in the early church computus literature (e.g., Bede 1999, 12). Latin letters are sometimes used to transliterate alphanumeric letters in Arabic (as in the markings on the late tenth-century "Carolingian" astrolabe (Stevens 1998) and Hebrew (in onomantic contexts: Juste 2007, 675; Cambridge, Library of the Fitzwilliam Museum, McClean 165, fol. 47v and London, Wellcome Institute for the History of Science, MS 21, fol. 4r).

7 A truly Latin alphanumeric notation, where the units, tens, and hundreds follow the order of the Latin alphabet, apparently was not used in the early Middle Ages. It occurs in an onomantic context, amongst a large number of other Latin alphabetical-numerical equivalents in Burgo de Osma, Archivo y Biblioteca de la Catedral, 7, fol. 104v (Juste 2007, 681), but was used systematically for the first time, it appears, in Latin translations and original texts in the second quarter of the twelfth century associated with "Stephen the Philosopher" and Antioch and Pisa (Burnett 2009, IV). One work that may have arisen in the same context (a translation from Arabic of Ptolemy's *Almagest* by a certain "'Abd al-Masih of Winchester," uses a more complicated (and apparently unparallelled) form of this alphanumeric notation, in which the initial Latin letters of the alphabet, as in other texts, are used for the units, and the letters towards the end of the alphabet are used for the hundreds, but the tens have been represented by means of dots and tildes and a small apostrophe, respectively, attached to the unit (discovered by Grupe, see Grupe 2013, 83–88). Latin alphanumeric notation reappears sporadically, usually in connection with onomancy, in later periods (e.g., Agrippa 1992, 307).

8 The major alternatives to Roman numerals were Arabic numerals—or, to be more precise, in recognition of their ultimate origin—Hindu-Arabic numerals. These first appear, as an illustration of "the nine digits of the Indians," in two manuscripts of Isidore's *Etymologies* written in northern Spain in the late ninth century, and as the "caracteres" written on the abacus counters in the "Gerbertian" abacus, from *c.*1000 onward (as mentioned in 4 above). In the early twelfth century they were introduced into the Latin world as symbols to be written on parchment or paper, together with texts on the principles of "calculation the Indian way." Unlike any of the forms of numeration mentioned so far, the value of Hindu-Arabic numerals is determined by their "place" (a "two" in the place of the units is "2," in the place of the tens "20," in the place of the hundreds "200," etc.); the zero has to "hold" the place when there is no other digit present. The "algorisms" (named after the ninth-century Arabic mathematician, al-Khwarizmi), which described how to calculate with numerals which had place value, generally include a table which shows how the same numerical symbol can be used to represent numbers in the units, tens, hundreds, thousands, etc. (Plate 3.4). Although these numerals had a common origin in seventh-century northwest India (Ifrah 1998, 356–591), they developed different shapes in al-Andalus and the Maghreb (the Western forms) from those in the Central Islamic realm (the Eastern forms). While the "abacus" numerals and the Latin texts arising from Toledo reflect the Western forms, certain Latin manuscripts of the twelfth century, especially those associated with Italy and the Crusader States, preserve the Eastern forms. By the early thirteenth century (e.g., in the manuscripts of the works of Fibonacci) the Western forms have prevailed. A certain simplification can be observed in respect to the shapes of the numerals in Arabic manuscripts and the "abacus" numerals (especially in regard to the numeral "4"), but from the early thirteenth century onward the Western forms remain remarkably constant in their appearance, and it is only at the turn of the fifteenth to the sixteenth century that the 4 and 5 change their medieval shape into that which is familiar nowadays (Hill 1915 documents this change).

9 Certain other numerical systems were devised on the model of the Hindu-Arabic numerals with their place value. At first this may have been to avoid the introduction of unrecognizable and difficult-to-remember symbols. Thus, Abraham Ibn Ezra in the

PLATE 3.4 A table showing how the same numerical symbol can be used to represent a number in any decimal place.

Paris, Bibliothèque nationale de France, lat. 15461, fol. 13r.

1140s used the first nine letters of the Hebrew alphabet as the nine digits with place value. At about the same time a pupil of Adelard of Bath used the first nine Roman numerals as digits with place value, and "t" for zero, in a text on the algorism which survives in two manuscripts (thus iii iii = 33, i ii t t = 1,200; (Burnett 2010, III)). In Flanders in the late thirteenth century, the first nine letters of the Roman alphabet were similarly used (Gilisson 1976).

10 Beside numeral systems which can be and were used in calculation, there are numerals used in cryptographs or codes. In one such system, which had a long history, from the mid-twelfth century until the early modern period, every number was represented by a single grapheme; see Bischoff 1966 and King 2001.

THE SYNTAX OF NUMERALS

Numerals, whatever their form, occupy an ambiguous position in medieval and Renaissance manuscripts. It is usual for numerals to have *puncta* on each side of them, as if to emphasize that they are not part of the text. The earliest algorism manuscripts sometimes put the numerals in boxes within the script. The algorisms also enjoin the reader to write Hindu-Arabic numerals from right to left (John of Sacrobosco, 1983–4, 177; Alexander of Villa Dei, 1841, 74), examples of which we

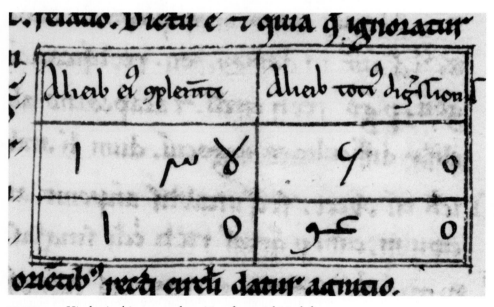

PLATE 3.5 Hindu-Arabic numerals written from right to left.

Oxford, Bodleian Library, MS Arch. Seld. B.34, fol. 33r.

occasionally find in manuscripts: see Burnett 2010b, and Plate 3.5. Sometimes Hindu-Arabic numerals were reversed, with the lower values on the left (Burnett 2010a VII). Hindu-Arabic numerals were regarded as being particularly useful for writing large numbers; where a mixture of numeral forms is found, Latin alphanumeric notation is used for the two-digit numbers and Hindu-Arabic for higher numerals: (Burnett 2009, IV). Sometimes superscript dots are used to mark each group of three digits in a large number (Abu Ma'shar, *Great Conjunctions*, Vienna, ÖNB, 5478, fol. 105r); Fibonacci advocates the use of "arches" ("arcus") to bracket every three digits: (Burnett 2010a, IX, 95). For fractions, the symbols for the twelve-part division of the Roman weight, the *as*, remain in use throughout the Middle Ages. Divisions of the astronomical degree are expressed in terms of the sexagesimal parts: minutes, seconds, thirds, etc. Other mathematical symbols are gradually added: "x" for the unknown quantity appears in works on algebra from the mid-twelfth century, and a vertical line separating the numerator from the denominator in fractions appears in thirteenth-century copies of a mathematical work translated from Arabic by Gerard of Cremona (d. 1187) (Benoit *et al.* 1992, Moyon 2017). But for most of the Middle Ages mathematical formulae were expressed rhetorically— with words rather than symbols, and it is only in the seventeenth century that the decimal point was introduced for decimal fractions, together with signs for plus, minus, division, and equality.

BIBLIOGRAPHICAL SURVEY

Numerals are referred to only briefly in manuals of palaeography. A short, but accurate account can be found in Bischoff 1989, 176–7, and certain Hispanic idiosyncracies are mentioned in Millares Carlo 1983, II, 273–4. The writing of numerals was the subject of a classical Latin work (Priscian), and an introduction to Hindu-Arabic numerals (*Liber Alchorismi*; see Burnett 2010a, V, 240) discusses the different written forms of the numerals. Lists of the forms and meanings of Roman numerals are given in Petrus Helias, 1993, 147–8, from which they have been extracted and joined by Hindu-Arabic in MS Dublin, Trinity College, 667, p. 59. Modern scholarship, however, has tended to concentrate on the syntax and semantics of numerals rather than on their shapes (Ifrah 1998; Chrisomalis 2010). Cappelli 1929, 419–28, provides a selection of Roman and Hindu-Arabic numerals without giving their provenance, while Abbreviationes[TM]Online (updated April 24, 2020) does not include variants in numeral forms at all. The only substantial collection of numeral forms is that of Hindu-Arabic numerals compiled by Hill (1915); other studies reproduce numerals only in specific manuscripts: Folkerts 1970; Becker 1995; Bartoli Langeli 2000. Crossley (2013) establishes the framework for a study of numerals from 1200–1500. The work remains to be done.

Table of the Different Forms of Numerals Used in the Middle Ages

1	2	3	4	5	6	7	8	9
i	ii	iii	iv/iiii	v	vi	vii	viii	ix/viiii
			q				o	N
A	B	Γ	Δ	E	F	Z	H	Θ
a	b	c	d	e	f	g	h	I

10	20	30	40	50	60	70	80	90
x	xx	xxx	xl/xxxx	l	lx	lxx	lxxx	xc/lxxxx
		t						
I	K	Λ	M	N	Ξ	O	Π	Ϙ
k	l	m	n	o	p	q	r	s

100	200	300	400	500	600	700	800	900
c	cc	ccc	cccc	d	dc	dcc	dccc	dcccc
P	Σ	T	Y	Φ	X	Ψ	Ω	Ϡ
t	u	x	y	z	θ	φ		

1000	10,000	100,000	1,000,000	etc.				0
m	xm	cm	mm	etc.				
∞/ī	xī	cī	mī/īm	etc.				t
A′	B′	Γ′	Δ′	etc.				Θ

Note the contents of the rows are as follows:

(1) our present-day numerals;

(2) Roman numerals with their additive or subtractive variants;

(3) variants in the Roman numeral system (e.g., in the works of Raymond of Marseilles);

(4) Greek alphanumeric notation (using capital letters);

(5) Latin alphanumeric notation;

(6) abacus numerals;
(7) Western forms of the Hebrew-Arabic numerals;
(8) variants of the Western forms;
(9) Eastern forms of the Hebrew-Arabic numerals;
(10) variants of the Eastern forms.

BIBLIOGRAPHY

Agrippa, H. C. 1992. *De occulta philosophia*, ed. V. Perrone Compagni. Leiden: Brill.

Alexander of Villa Dei, 1841. "Carmen de Algorismo." In *Rara Mathematica: A Collection of Treatises on Mathematics*, ed. J. O. Halliwell, 73–83. London: John William Parker.

Alverny, M.T. d'. 1993. *Études sur le symbolisme de la sagesse et sur l'iconographie*, Variorum Collected Studies Series (cited by article number). Aldershot: Variorum.

Bartoli Langeli, A. 2000. "I notai e i numeri (con un caso perugino, 1184–1206)." In *Scienze matematiche e insegnamento in epoca medioevale: Atti del convegno internazionale di studio. Chieti, 2–4 maggio 1996*, ed. P. Freguglia, L. Pellegrini, and R. Pacciocco, 225–54. Naples: Edizioni scientifiche italiane.

Becker, W. 1995. *Frühformen indisch-arabischer Ziffern in einer Handschrift des Soester Stadtarchivs*. Soest: Universität Paderborn/Abteilung Soest.

Bede. 1999. *The Reckoning of Time*, trans. and comm. F. Wallis. Liverpool: Liverpool University Press.

Benoit, P., K. Chemla, and J. Ritter. 1992. *Histoire de fractions, fractions d'histoire*, Basel: Birkhäuser.

Bischoff, B. 1989. *Latin Palaeography: Antiquity and the Middle Ages (Paläographie des römischen Altertums und des abendländlischen Mittelalters)*, trans. David Ganz and Daíbhí Ó Cróinín. Cambridge: Cambridge University Press.

Bischoff, B. 1996. "Die sogenannten "griechischen" und "chaldäischen" Zahlzeichen des abendländischen Mittelalters." In *Mittelalterliche Studien: Ausgewählte Aufsätze zur Schriftkunde und Literaturgeschichte*, vol. I, 67–73. Stuttgart: Hiersemann.

Burnett, C. 2009. *Arabic into Latin in the Middle Ages*, Variorum Collected Studies Series (cited by article number). Farnham: Variorum.

Burnett, C. 2010a. *Numerals and Arithmetic in the Middle Ages*, Variorum Collected Studies Series (cited by article number). Farnham: Variorum.

Burnett, C. 2010b. "Learning to Write Numerals in the Middle Ages." In *Teaching Writing, Learning to Write: Proceedings of the XVI Colloquium of the Comité internationale de paléographie latine*, ed. P. Robinson, 233–40. London: Kings College.

Chrisomalis, S. 2010. *Numerical Notation: A Comparative History*. Cambridge: Cambridge University Press.

Crossley, J. N. 2013. "Old-fashioned versus Newfangled: Reading and Writing Numbers, 1200–1500" *Studies in Medieval and Renaissance History*, 3rd ser., 10: 79–109.

Folkerts, M. 1970. *Boethius' Geometrie II, ein mathematisches Lehrbuch des Mittelalters*. Wiesbaden: Franz Steiner Verlag.

Gerbert d'Aurillac. 1899. *De abaco*. In *Gerberti postea Silvestri II papae Opera Mathematica*, ed. N. Bubnov. Berlin: R. Friedländer und Sohn [repr. Hildesheim 1963].

Gilissen, L. 1976. "Curieux foliotage d'un manuscrit de droit civil: la somma d'Azzon (Bruxelles 9251 et 9252)" *Studia Gratiana* 19: 303–11.

Grupe, D. 2013. *The Latin Reception of Arabic Astronomy and Cosmology in Mid-Twelfth-Century Antioch: The Liber Mamonis and the Dresden Almagest.* PhD dissertation, University of London.

Hill, G. F. 1915. *The Development of Arabic Numerals in Europe, Exhibited in Sixty-Four Tables.* Oxford: Clarendon Press.

Ifrah, G. 1998. *The Universal History of Numbers,* trans. D. Bellos *et al.* London: Wiley.

John of Sacrobosco. 1983–4. In *Algorismus vulgaris,* ed. F. S. Pedersen in Petrus Philomena de Dacia et Petrus de S. Audomaro, *Opera quadrivialia,* 2. vols, I, 174–201 [An annotated partial English translation by Edward Grant (1974) in *A Source Book in Medieval Science,* ed. E. Grant, Leipzig. Cambridge, MA: Harvard University Press].

Juste, D. 2007. *Les Alchandreana primitifs: Étude sur les plus anciens traités astrologiques latins d'origine arabe (Xe siècle).* Leiden: Brill.

King, D. 2001. *The Ciphers of the Monks. A Forgotten Number-Notation of the Middle Ages,* Stuttgart: Franz Steiner Verlag.

Kunitzsch, P. 2003. "The Transmission of Hindu-Arabic Numerals Reconsidered." In *The Scientific Enterprise in Islam,* ed. J. P. Hogendijk and A. I. Sabra, 3–21. Cambridge, MA: MIT Press.

Lemay, R. 1977. "The Hispanic Origin of Our Present Numeral Forms, *Viator* 8: 435–62.

Menninger, K. 1958. *Zahlwort und Ziffer. Eine Kulturgeschichte der Zahl,* 2nd revised ed, 2 vols. Göttingen: Vandenhoeck & Ruprecht [English translation: 1969. *Number Words and Number Symbols,* Cambridge, MA: M.I.T. Press)].

Millares Carlo, A. 1983. *Tratado de paleografía española,* 3rd ed., 2 vols. Madrid: Espasa-Calpe.

Moyon, M. 2017. *La géométrie de la mesure dans les traductions arabo-latines médiévales,* Turnhout: Brepols.

Muhammad ibn Musa al-Khwarizmi. 1992. *Le Calcul indien (Algorismus),* edited by A. Allard. Paris: A. Blanchard and Namur: Société des études classiques.

Muhammad ibn Musa al-Khwarizmi. 1997. *Die älteste lateinische Schrift über das indische Rechnen nach al-Hwārizmī,* ed., trans., and comm. Menso Folkerts, with the collaboration of Paul Kunitzsch. Munich: Verlag der Bayerischen Akademie der Wissenschaften [= *Dixit Algorizmi*].

Murdoch, J. 1984. *Album of Science: Antiquity and the Middle Ages,* New York: MacMillan.

Petrus Helias. 1993. *Summa super Priscianum,* ed. L. Reilly, CSB, 2 vols, Toronto: Pontifical Institute of Mediaeval Studies.

Priscian. 1855–80. *De figuris numerorum. Grammatici Latini,* ed. H. Kiels, 8 vols, III: 406–17. Leipzig: Teubner [repr: Hildesheim, 1961].

Raymond of Marseilles. 2009. *Opera omnia,* vol. 1, ed. M.-T. d'Alverny, C. Burnett, and E. Poulle. Paris: CNRS.

Stevens, W., G. Beaujouan and A. J. Turner, eds. 1998. *The Oldest Latin Astrolabe,* 2nd ed. Florence: Olschki.

I . 2

GRECO-ROMAN HERITAGE

CHAPTER 4

OLD ROMAN CURSIVE

TERESA DE ROBERTIS
(Translated by Consuelo Dutschke)

WE begin with a definition of cursive that is valid for the cursive scripts of the Roman era, but also for medieval and modern cursives. When we speak of cursive, we mean a script in which the strokes that constitute a letter[1] (all or only some of the strokes), or two strokes that belong to adjacent letters, are produced in a single movement of the pen or other writing implement (which is to say, all at one time) without raising the pen from the writing surface (i.e. *currenti calamo scribere*, from which we derive *littera* or *scriptura cursiva*) (see Figs. 4.1 and 4.2).

FIG. 4.1 In the second and third variants of m, all four strokes are written without raising the pen, in one movement; in the first variant of m, only strokes 2, 3, and 4 are united; in the fourth, each stroke is written separately.

FIG. 4.2 In the sequence *–ritate esse* strokes of adjacent letters are written at one time, without lifting the calamus from the papyrus (for example, the second stroke of *t* with the first stroke of *a*, or the second stroke of *a* with the first stroke of *t*, and so forth). PLond.229 (*ChLA* III.200).

By ligature we mean the linking together of two or more strokes. We speak of internal ligatures (within a letter) if the tie occurs between the structural strokes of a single letter; we speak of external ligatures when the tie is between the last stroke of one letter and the first stroke of the next. A cursive is, therefore, a script that contains internal and/or external ligatures. A writing instrument that allows ascending and circular strokes (such as a calamus or a quill pen with a narrow and relatively hard point, but also a metal pen) is necessary to produce such ligatures. Internal and/or external ligatures allow production of rapid, synthetic, and terse writing, which is particularly useful in all forms of documentation and pro memoria connected with the practical aspects of life, so much so that the term *documentary script* is often used instead of *cursive script.*

From the standpoint of graphic technique and speed in production, the opposite of a cursive script is one that is executed in a segmented manner, stroke by stroke, a set or analytical script. If we employ a musical metaphor, cursive script is equivalent to playing musical notes "legato," while a script produced with individual strokes is "staccato." While it is not always easy to identify each stroke of a letter in a cursive script (which is to say, to understand where one stroke ends and the next stroke begins), in a set script the number of elements necessary for building the shape of a letter is always very clear, and it coincides with pauses in the rhythm of writing, with the lifting of the writing instrument. A stroke-by-stroke or set script, composed of rectilinear and curvilinear *articuli*, mainly in descending direction, certainly takes longer to write and lends itself to execution by instruments with a wide point, bringing about an alternation between thick and thin strokes. Because of this, set and "posed" scripts find prevalent but not exclusive use in book production.

In the definitions proposed for a cursive script and for a constructed script, we have referred implicitly to a fundamental concept in analyses of scripts: the *ductus* (literally, the act of writing, the tracing of the letters) as it was first formulated by Jean Mallon.[2] For Mallon, *ductus* is the relationship between the number, direction, and succession of the strokes that make up the shape, the form of a letter. In other words, we recognize in the *ductus* the dynamic moment of the writing, the process itself; in the morphology of a letter, on the other hand, we recognize the result of this process. But if a separation between *ductus* and morphology is possible as a theory (and useful while analyzing a script), in practice *ductus* and morphology represent two aspects of the same reality (*ductus* does not exist independently of the form of the letter, and vice versa).

Even if some variants of cursive letters, and occasionally even elementary ligatures between the letters occur in incised scripts produced by scratching, and especially in wax tablets and *tabellae defixionum*,[3] it is only with papyrus and with the use of ink and writing instruments of thin and somewhat rigid points that, during the Roman period, one may begin to speak of an actual cursive script, sometimes of extremely rapid execution.

Therefore, it is not entirely wrong to assert that the discovery of the cursive Latin script of the Roman era is one of the most important results, albeit an indirect result, of the Napoleonic expedition to Egypt (1798) and of the very real mania for its ancient civilization provoked by the publication of the *Description de l'Égypte* (1809 and 1812). It was in fact from that point that papyri (especially Egyptian but also Greek) began to enter Europe along with other antiquities as souvenirs of diplomats and travelers or as objects of not always legal trafficking. Later, around 1877, large numbers of papyri appeared on the antiquarian market of Cairo, most from Fayum, among which there were also some papyri in the Latin alphabet; this material was acquired by the consuls of Austria, Germany, France, and Britain, acting in the names of their respective governments, with the intention of placing the papyri in public collections. Towards the end of the nineteenth century, with the advent of large-scale excavations carried out in a systematic and scientific manner by European and American scholars, publication of texts and early photographs began to bring radical change to what was known about the ways Romans wrote.

Some papyri were already known to erudite scholars of the sixteenth to the eighteenth centuries,[4] but the cursive scripts found in these papyri seemed so unusual and exotic that they were sometimes taken for Turkish or Chinese; or else, even when the script was recognized as Latin, it was labeled "longobardica" or "Gotica," which is to say, barbarian.[5] Until the discovery of the Latin papyri of Egypt, in fact, the only script certainly assignable to the Roman era was *capitalis*, visible on the ruins of sacred and civil buildings, on commemorative or funerary inscriptions, and on coins or seals. And even if already by the time of the Italian humanists, some scholars had the vague notion that other manners of writing had existed in ancient Rome, it was only with the Latin papyri originating in Egypt that one arrived at a first concrete knowledge of cursive script during Roman times. This knowledge was considerably expanded by archeological discoveries in other areas, such as Syria (some one hundred military documents from Dura Europos, datable to the span between AD 200 and 250), Palestine (military documents from Masada and papyri from Murabba'at of the first century AD), or Algeria (bills of sale of real estate written on wooden tablets, from the end of the fifth century),[6] characterized by similar climatic conditions as those that preserved the Egyptian papyri.[7] From 1973, the number of extant examples increased with the wooden tablets discovered in England (at Bardon Mill, in Northumberland, near Hadrian's Wall) in a completely different climate from that of Egypt: several hundred military documents and letters addressed to soldiers and civilians who lived in the fort of Vindolanda, datable to the span AD 95–115.

In total, the picture of written records of a practical nature (excluding, that is, books), copied with ink, is as follows: for the first through the sixth centuries, the *Chartae Latinae antiquiores* (*ChLA*) publish 558 documents on papyrus, often reduced to tiny fragments; there are also, as has been noted, the 736 tablets from Vindolanda[8] and the 34 Algerian tablets, and somewhat fewer than 400 wax tablets with traces of writing and ink on the wooden side of the object.[9] Therefore, in sum, we have at our disposal approximately 1,700 examples, mainly concentrated between the first and the third centuries (we count 396 papyri from the first to the third centuries, but only 162 from the fourth to the sixth centuries).[10] There is, however, a significant lacuna in the documentation for the second half of the third century, and therein lies the origin of divergent interpretations of the evolution of Roman cursive.

If we consider only the numbers, the picture may appear disheartening, and all the more so when compared to the amount of Greek material that has come down to us (Greek papyri exist in the thousands, of which *c.*30,000 have been published to date);[11] equally disheartening are the numbers of surviving Latin documents when we compare them to what we know of the Roman world, with its very high level of literacy and the intense and diffuse graphic practices in every corner of the empire, as the documentary finds themselves bear witness.[12] If, on the other hand, we take into consideration the places where materials with Latin writing were found, we see that there is not one far-flung district of the empire that has not handed something down to us. From such documentation, numerically small, but of diverse and distant geographic provenance, we draw an important lesson: that the Latin graphic system is essentially uniform, and that, when chronology matches (i.e. simultaneously), the phenomena of morphological evolution and even of stylistic elaboration are more or less the same throughout the empire, in spite of the diversity of the writing surfaces and of the writing techniques.

The surviving material allows us to recognize that, during the course of the third century AD, there was a profound transformation of Latin cursive, which has been interpreted in various ways (as an out-and-out fracture, by Jean Mallon, who speaks of a "fossé" and of a "solution de continuité"; as a graphic change and division into two branches, by Casamassima and Staraz). This metamorphosis is usually defined as the passage from the Old Roman cursive (or classical common writing)[13] to the New Roman cursive (or new common writing). Especially in the case of ancient cursive it is more appropriate to speak of a system of scripts, rather than of a single script, because for more than two centuries we find ourselves facing not one cursive, but a rich and varied complex of scripts, within which one specialized script becomes recognizable (without the disappearance of the other cursives), although it will disappear shortly after the middle of the third century. Instead, for the new Roman cursive, witnessed in coherent forms from the early years of the fourth century, we may employ both terms (system and script) equally; more problematic is to define the limits of its life.

As has been noticed, cursive script is the script par excellence in practical life. During the first three centuries of the Christian era we find it used (in conjunction with occasional examples of *capitalis*)[14] in military documents (far and away the most numerous group of examples that have come down to us), and in the interactions of Roman citizens with bureaucracies: contracts, wills, marriages, manumissions, receipts, and letters.[15]

The range of these documents leaves us with the impression of a highly varied graphic reality that is not easily classifiable. This impression is due to a number of factors: certainly, to the fact that there are relatively few documents and yet they are very diverse in origin, in content, and in what they tell us of the graphic capabilities of the writers and their intentions (we have scribes who are barely literate next to bureaucrats of the highest level; simple writing next to true exercises in calligraphy);[16] in the second place, our impression is due to the fact that the documents present differing degrees of haste in writing (and this is a constant with cursive scripts, no matter which period they belong to); and finally, it is due to the fact that the system of ancient cursives permits notable morphological diversification: it is, in other words, possible that one letter could be written (even within the same document) in forms that are so different that they seem to have nothing in common. Such strong morphological diversification is an exception in the history of the Latin alphabet.

It has been mentioned that *capitalis* can also occur in documents. A comparison between the coherent series of letters of this alphabet (we can speak of an alphabet because, in this case, no variant forms are permitted) and the cursive letterforms can help us understand the successive steps in the process of simplification that lead to a cursive script.

In Fig. 4.3 the morphology of *capitalis* is reproduced faithfully, even in the alternation of thick and thin strokes or in the use of flourishes or "grazie" at the terminal points of vertical strokes (the script is not different from that used in books or in inscriptions). In Fig. 4.4 the overall design of the letters is respected, but the *ductus* is sometimes simplified, thanks to the fusion of certain strokes (*b* and *r*). In Fig. 4.5 some letters present significant alterations in the development of the strokes (some are shorter, some longer) or in their relative positions, but above all certain letters occur in notably simplified forms or even in different variants: the most macroscopic difference is the one that affects the letter *b* with three variants. In Fig. 4.6 almost all the letters occur in extremely synthetic and economical forms, in which two or more strokes seem to have merged into one, or their dimensions are modified (some strokes are reduced, others emphasized), or the strokes are traced in a different direction and succession; in the same document, we also see a great number of external ligatures, tying one letter to another.

FIG. 4.3 PSI XI 1183 (*ChLA* XXV 785), AD 45–54, Oxyrhynchos, declaration of Roman citizenship for fiscal purposes.

FIG. 4.4 PBerol. Inv. 6870+14907 (*ChLA* X 411), AD 156, Fayum, Pridianum of the cohors I Augusta Praetoria Lusitanorum equitata.

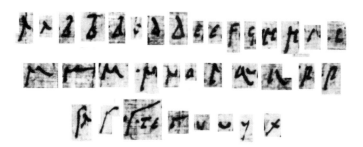

FIG. 4.5 POxy. 3208, of the Augustan era, letter of Syneros.

The difference between capital and cursive letters becomes clear if we observe in particular *b* and *d* (but lesser degrees of differentiation are visible in all the letters): the cursive variants have forms with no apparent relationship to those of the capital letters. Nevertheless, in papyri and in the Vindolanda tablets the entire sequence of minor and minimal variants is visible, and this allows us to establish relationships between the variants.

In Fig. 4.7 we can see how the simplification of the *ductus* began with a series of small and subtle variations toward more economical writing: first of all, by connecting, in one continuous movement without lifting the calamus from the writing surface, the strokes that end and begin more or less at the same point (strokes 1 and 2 of *b* and *d*; strokes 3 and 4 of *b*); secondly, by transforming angles into curves (it is easier and more rapid to trace a curve than an angle, since the latter implies a halt in the motion of the calamus); and finally, by reducing the swell of the curves (shorter strokes are more economical to write than longer ones). It is at this point in the evolution of the letter, while some part of the more set and posed form of the letter is still recognizable, that the most severe change takes place: in *b*, stroke 4 changes direction; in *d* both the order and the direction of the *articuli* change (stroke 3 is written first in its "normal" direction, starting at the top; then, strokes 2 and 1 are written in reversed direction).

The process of simplification involves other letters as well (Plate 4.1): the more complex the structure of a letter is, the larger the amount of simplification that can occur in that letter; the simpler the structure of the letter is, the smaller will be the differences. We should also note that not all letters evolve in the same way and that,

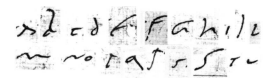

FIG. 4. 6 PBerol. Inv. 8507 (*ChLA* X 418), after AD 41–54, copy of an oration of the Emperor Claudius about justice.

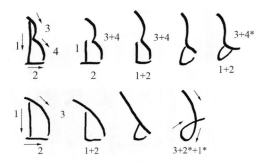

FIG. 4.7 Variant forms of letters and the process of change in the *ductus*.

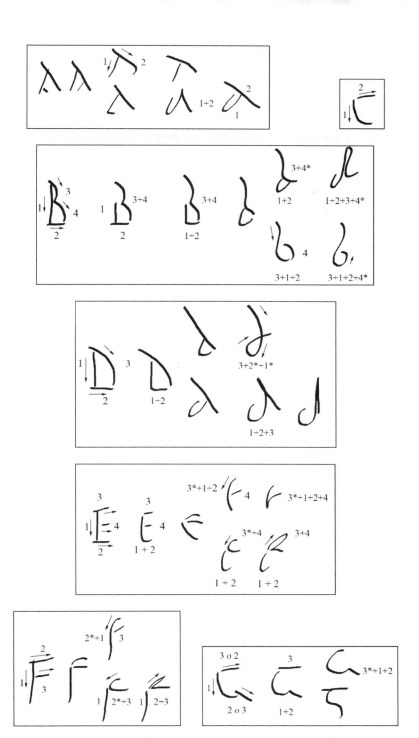

PLATE 4.1 (a) Variants of letters in Latin cursive of the first to the fourth centuries.

Numbers indicate the succession of strokes, the arrows their direction; the asterisk indicates that the stroke has changed direction relative to the previous form; strokes made without lifting the pen from the writing surface are indicated with the sign +.

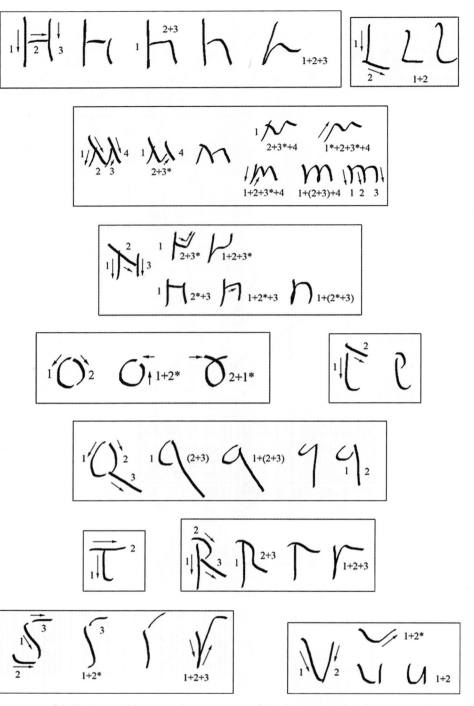

PLATE 4.1(b) Variants of letters in Latin cursive of the first to the fourth centuries (letters h–u/v).

from a given stage, the process of alteration of certain letters (*a, b, d, e, f, g, m, n*) continues forward in bifurcated directions. It is important to remember that, up until a certain moment, the system of cursive script retains all the forms that have gradually come into being. It happens, therefore, that both complex and simplified forms, i.e., the cursive forms, may coexist even within a single document: sometimes the different forms have different functions; very often there is no difference in usage between them, even within a single word. In PSI XI 1183 (*ChLA* XXV 785) *capitalis* is employed in the *scriptio exterior*, i.e., in the open section of the document, for requirements of solemnity and communication,[17] while in the *scriptio interior*, i.e. in the closed parts of the document (reserved for a specialized reading),[18] the same scribe uses a more cursive script. On the other hand, in PSI VI 729 (*ChLA* XXV 782; Plate 4.2) cursive variants are mixed with the complex or set variants (Fig. 4.8): notice in particular the three different forms of *e*, two forms of *n*, two forms of *s*, and two forms of *u*; for the scribe these letterforms are evidently equivalent and interchangeable.

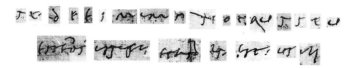

FIG. 4.8 PSI VI 729 (*ChLA* XXV 782), AD 77, bill for the purchase of a horse. In line 2: *esse bi-, -us Rufu-, et hab-, -la, est, -us, -uli-*.

Almost contemporaneously with the process of simplification of the letters, we witness the beginning of a system of ligatures that will endure, without substantial changes, until the thirteenth century. A ligature (i.e., the tie between the final stroke of one letter and the first stroke of the following letter, realized without lifting the pen from the writing surface) comes about during Roman times according to a simple yet rigorous pattern: with a movement that is first horizontal and then descending (i.e., angular, starting from the top, clockwise). The system is founded on the *ductus*, on the structure of the letters, with no use of added strokes ("sine virgula superius," according to the definition given in the medieval *Modus scribendi* of Kremsmünster).[19] Ligatures are possible when the first letter ends with a horizontal stroke and when the following letter begins with a descending vertical stroke.

Not all letters (or rather, not all variants of letters) possess characteristics that allow for ligatures (for example, the letter *i*, consisting only of one vertical stroke, hampers the pen in a natural movement to the next letter). In a number of cases it is clear that certain modifications of the *ductus* are not only useful for producing ligatures, but actually seem to have been devised for this purpose.[20] Such may be the situation of the *b* "panse à gauche" (i.e. with its bowl to the left) which with this function will survive for several decades even into the new cursive. In the examples of Fig. 4.9, one can also observe that the writing is conceived of as a rhythmical succession of descending and inclined strokes (and almost all of the same height) and more or less horizontal strokes,

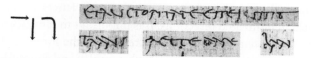

FIG. 4.9 Pattern of ligatures in Roman era and groups of ligatured letters from PLond. 229 (*ChLA* III 200), AD 166, Seleucia Pieria, act of purchase of a slave: (line 1) *et auctoritate esse iussit*; (line 2) *trans-*, *recte dare*, *-ban*.

in which at times it is difficult to recognize the single letters, since they have been assimilated to one another so thoroughly. All this is not by chance, but is the result of a stylistic process that will have important outcomes during the course of the third century; this process is born as the sum of two patterns: the pattern that brings about ligatures, discussed above, and the pattern that arranges the single strokes of each letter, even in view of potential ligatures (in PLond. 299 [Plate 4.3], the letters *a*, *c*, *p* with an open bowl, *r*, *s*, and *t* are formed by an initial descending and inclined stroke, and by a second stroke that is more or less horizontal). In Roman times (and in every other period in the history of the Latin alphabet), ligatures are an important factor in ordering the sequence of writing.

In the Latin papyri of the first and second centuries, but also in the Vindolanda tablets, Latin cursive script is in a phase of expansion and enrichment in which various forms of the same letter are to be found sometimes even within a single document; these multiple forms are perceived by the scribes as equivalent, as simple gradations tied to the speed of execution, as functional adaptations toward the making of ligatures: the sum of all these variant letters, attested to in the documents, delimits the system of cursive script and constitutes the complete repertory available to the community of scribes.

The situation appears profoundly changed at the beginning of the third century, at least in one part of the documentation. In the papyri produced in high-level civil and military *officia*, that alternation of variants which had been so characteristic of the earlier period is no longer present. On the contrary, we now see clearly how certain variants begin to form a coherent series, or even an alphabet: the scribes working in the *officia* concentrate their choices on the most rapid variants, on those most essential to the structure and most readily allowing for ligatures (Fig. 4.10); at the same time they eliminate the variants of opposite value (the variants that are more complex and posed, less economical, in many cases not functional to ligaturing). The result is that, as Cencetti has already noticed,[21] a specialized script, an "official" or "scribal" cursive, comes into being in the documents produced by the Roman bureaucracy (which constitute the greatest number of survivals from the second half of the second century through the third century).

The process has already taken shape around the middle of the second century, as is seen, for example, in PGen. lat. 8 + PLond. 730 (*ChLA* I 12 + III 204; AD 167, receipt of goods) in which the only contradiction is the *p* with an open bowl coexisting with the *p* with a closed bowl. During the first years of the following century, the phase of elaboration of the new official style concluded: alternation of opposing variants is by

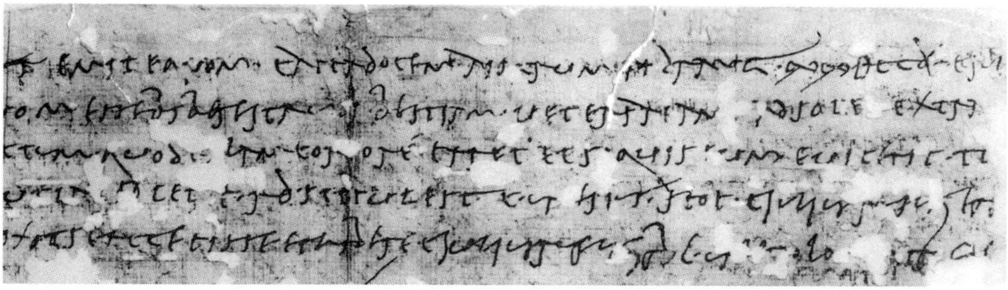

PLATE 4.2 PSI VI 729 (*ChLA* XXV 782), AD 77, bill for the sale of a horse.

A]pr(iana) emit equom Cappadocem nigrum M dr(achnis) Aug(ustis) MMDCC de C. Iul[io
equ]om esse bibere ita uti bestiam veterinam adsolet extra[
destri]ctum quod palam corpore esset et si quis eum evicerit tu[nc
uti a[d]solet p(robam) r(ecte) d(ari) stipul(atus) est C. Va[l]erius spop(ondit) C. Ilius Rufus
(centurio) ea[s
d]ixit se accepisse et habere C. Iulius Rufus ab C. Valerio Lo[ngo em]tore

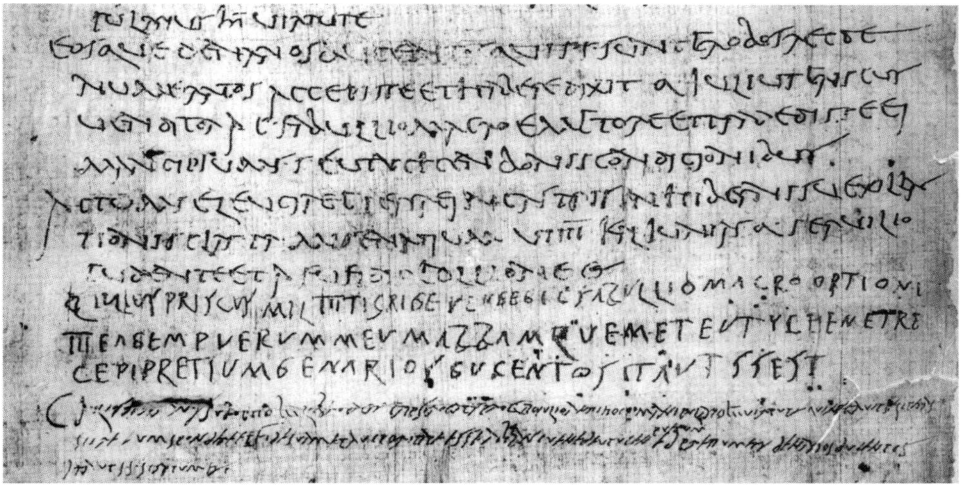

PLATE 4.3 PLond. 229 (*ChLA* III 200), AD 166, Seleucia Pieria, bill for the purchase of a slave.

(First hand) -pularius (triere) Virtute.
Eosque denarios ducentos qui s(upra) s(scripti) sunt probos recte
numeratos accepisse et habere dixit Q. Iulius Priscus
venditor a C. Fabullio Macro emptore et tradedisse ei
manicipium s(upra) s(criptum) Eutychen bonis condicionibus.
Actum Seleuciae Pieriae in castris in hibernis vexilla-
tionis clas(sis) pr(aetoriae) Misenatium viiii kal. iunias Q. Servilio
Pudente et A. Fufidio Pollione cos.
(Second hand) *Q. Iulius Priscus mil(es) (triere) Tigride vendedi C. Fabullio Macro optioni (triere)*
eadem puerum meum Abbam quem et Eutychenm et recepi pretium denarios ducentos ita ut
s(upra) s(criptum) est.
(Third hand) *C. Iulius Titianus suboptio (triere) Libero Patre et ipse rogatus pro Gaio Iulio*
Antihoco manipulario (triere) Virtute qui negavit se literas
scire eum spondere et fide suam et auctoritate esse Abban cuen et Eutucen puerum ed pretium eius
denarios ducentos
ita ut s(upra) s(criptum) scritum est.

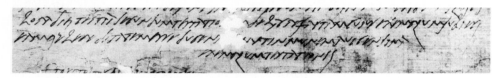

FIG. 4.10 Forms of letters standardized for use in bureaucratic writing.

now a rare event; the variants deriving from the more rapid *ductus* constitute a completely coherent series, and writing comes about according to a precise stylistic plan. Most letters, leaning decidedly to the right, are formed in two sections: the first section is an oblique stroke, descending from right to left, while the characteristic strokes of the letter give rise to the second section, which is shifted to the right and upward (Fig. 4.11); normally, the oblique and descending strokes are all of the same length, contributing to the impression of a script that mainly arranges itself within a two-line pattern (letters such as *l* do not follow the pattern, with a second stroke developed downward; nor do letters such as *b*, *d*, *h* and sometimes *i* and *s* fit the pattern, since they are more developed in their upper part). The result is an extremely economical, assimilated and stylistically recognizable script that is open to the highest level of calligraphy, as can be seen in the letters from the office of the governor of Syria (for example, PDura 56 = *ChLA* VI 311, AD 208 [Plate 4.4] and PDura 59 = *ChLA* VI 314, AD 241) and four fragments now in Vienna (PVindob. L 15 = *ChLA* XLIII 1254, third century, possibly writing exercises).

FIG. 4.11 PLond. 2059 = POxy. 1114 (*ChLA* III 216), AD 237, process for inheritance *ab intestato*: (line 1) *hora diei tertia secundum testatio[ne]m de hac re factam cuius exemplum subieci*; (line 2) *eamque hereditatem esse ducena[aria]m et inmunem a vicensima*; (line 3) *exemplum testationis*.

However, the official documentation (although numerically significant) is only one part of the material, and the special script does not represent all cursives. Thus, in an exiguous group of papyri we can still observe at the beginning of the third century the simultaneous presence of variants with opposing signs: as, for example, in PDura 60 (*ChLA* VI 315, *c*. AD 208, Dura Europos, circular letter announcing the arrival of the ambassador of the Parthians) in which we find both forms of *a*, *e*, *n* and *p* (Fig. 4.12 and Plate 4.5).

But this situation is not destined to last. Through a long and uncertain course which goes on for almost a century, a stable series of variants begins to establish itself even in

PLATE 4.4 PDura 56 fragm. A (*ChLA* VI 311), *c.* AD 280, letter of Marius Maximus, governor of Syria, regarding a horse of the twentieth cohort of the Palmyreni.

(Second hand in a smaller script) *Acc(epta) septimum decimum [kal(endas) apriles d(omino) n(ostro) imp(eratore) A]ntonino Aug[usto*
(First hand) *Ecum quadrimum rus(seum) person[a]tum*
s(ine) n(ota) probatum a me Iulio Basso eq(uiti) coh(ortis) XX Pal(myrenorum)
c(ui) p(rees) (denariis) centum viginti [q]uin[que i]n a[cta ut
mos refer et [. . .] nota ex die [qu]ar[to.

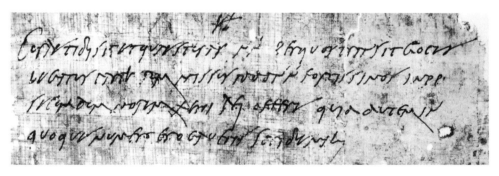

PLATE 4.5 PDura 60 (*ChLA* VI 315), *c.* AD 208, Dura Europos, letter announcing the arrival of the ambassador of the Parthians.

ex(emplum)
Curae tibi sit ut quaesturas n(umerorum) per quos transit Goces
legatus Parthorum missus ad d(ominos) n(umerorum) fortissimos imp(eratores)
secundum morem xenia ei offere quid autem in
quoque numero erogaveris scribe mihi.

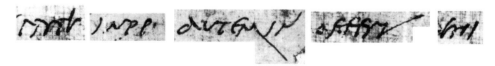

FIG. 4.12 PDura 60 (*ChLA* VI 315), *c.* AD 208: *parth-, impp., autem in, offere, -eni-.*

the field of "common"-use script, gradually eliminating the variants by now typical of the bureaucratic script; the "common"-use script is defined, therefore, as difference, as subtraction, as opposition. The result is a script in which the less rapid variants and, often, those ill-equipped for ligaturing (Fig. 4.13; see also Plate 4.6) remain in place.

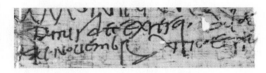

FIG. 4.13 PMich. 164 (*ChLA* V 281), AD 242–4, list of decurions and centurions (detail); (line 1) *factus dec(curio) ex sesq(uiplicario) alae*; (line 2) *kal(endas) novembr(es) Attico et pr-*.

The official, bureaucratic script seems to sink into invisibility during the second half of the third century (the last examples of dated documents are from the 270s and the 280s).[22] With the disappearance of this script, all its characteristic letterforms are also lost; they leave the system of the Latin alphabet forever (with two brief exceptions, because of their usefulness for ligature: the *b* "panse à gauche" and the *n* written in one or two moments with the final stroke moving from the bottom upward). And yet, during the entire second half of the third century, we have only five or six examples of the other cursive, the one that from the fourth century onward will be the only script used for practical purposes, even by high-ranking civil servants. This situation, accentuated by a dearth of documentation (for the entire second half of the third century we have only some twenty examples), lies at the heart of what we may call an optical illusion: that the bureaucratic script and the other cursive might represent in some fashion two successive graphic systems.

Ever since early studies on Latin writing of the Roman era, the problem of these two cursives, of what seemed to be a transformation of the first cursive into the second, represented a fundamental problem for palaeographers, who produced various explanations for it. Against the traditional opinions of scholars such as Van Hoesen and Schiaparelli (founded, it must be remembered, on the tiniest number of examples),[23] who spoke in a general manner of a natural evolution from one form to the other, stands Mallon (1952), who, instead, asserted the impossibility of such an evolution.

By concentrating his attention on the morphology of certain letters that are particularly representative of the two scripts (*a, b, e, n, p*; Fig. 4.14), Mallon affirmed that what can explain the passage from one script to the other is not the mechanics of *ductus*, but rather a matter of a technical nature. According to Mallon, the typical forms of the new cursive and with them the profound metamorphosis of cursive script are the reflection of a radical change that took place elsewhere, that is, in the book scripts of the late second century, following a change in the angle of writing (from about 45° to 90°).[24]

The work of Mallon on Roman writing left its mark on an era of scholarship and placed palaeographic studies on a new methodological and conceptual plane for matters well beyond those regarding Roman times. Nevertheless, his theory on the "solution de continuité" was later criticized for its premises and for its results (Casamassima and Staraz, 1977). Among the variants examined by Mallon there is,

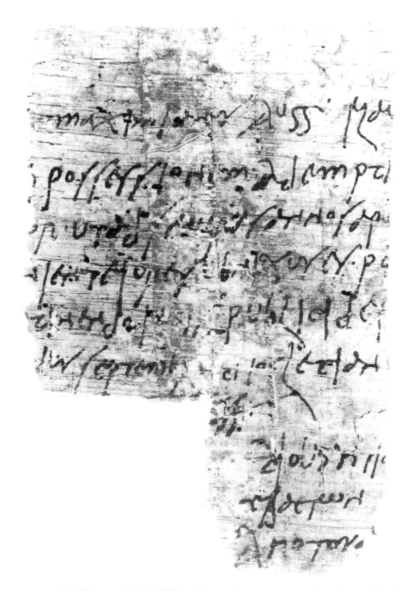

PLATE 4.6 PSI I 111 (*ChLA* XXV 780) AD 287–304, copy of an Imperial edict.

]*et Maximianus aug(usti) Flav*[
]*possesionem ad empt*[
]*ur ut adseveras annos ap*[
]*niente iure subnixus es po*[
]*tinendo iuris publici dep*[
]*dus septembr*[*es*] *Diocletiano et*[
]*cos.*
(3 lines in Greek).

FIG. 4.14 The letters used in Mallon's demonstration (on the left, the series considered representative of the ancient cursive; on the right the series of the new cursive).

in fact, not only opposition but actual impossibility of derivation; nevertheless, those variants are not characteristic of two systems, the one following the other chronologically, but of two coeval scripts that represent the two branches into which the cursive script of the classical period had divided itself. Mallon's error was to describe the entire cursive writing of the classical period by means of the variants that belong to only one of the two branches, that of special and bureaucratic writing. By ignoring the many letter variants that, as has been said, are produced by the very nature of cursive writing, and that are present in abundance in papyri of the first and second centuries, Mallon refused to look within the cursive scripts themselves for the reasons for their transformation, and instead he found the reasons for change within book hands, attributing the dissolution of an entire system to a simple shift in the angle of writing. According to Casamassima and Staraz what happened during the course of the third century internally to cursive writing was a conscious effort to select and reorganize the graphic matter (variants and ligatures) that was already present in the system; they proposed that this effort took place initially within the bureaucracies, and later within the remaining script areas. Profoundly new, on the other hand, is the stylistic structure of the two scripts.

A source of later date than that of the events described suggests that an external and conscious action with the intent of controlling script, did in effect take place. In a rescript of the emperors Valentinian and Valens dated AD 367, a highly placed functionary of the empire, the proconsul of Africa, was reminded to respect the habit that reserved the *litterae caelestes* for the imperial chancery alone; on that occasion the prohibition against the use of the script was invoked, requiring all functionaries instead

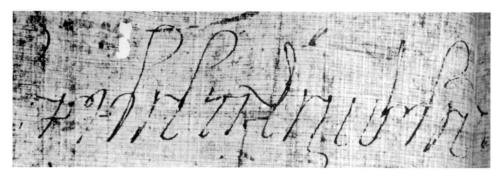

FIG. 4.15 PLouvre 2404 + PLeiden 421 (*ChLA* XVII 657), fifth century, fragment of an imperial rescript; *non secuta legibus ra-*.

to use the *litterae communes*.[25] By the manner in which the text is formulated, we understand not only that the imperial chancery had enjoyed its own special script already for a notable period of time, but also that the exclusive use of this script was known to all functionaries in the periphery. What appearance the script referred to by Valentinian and Valens had we can see in a fragment of a fifth-century imperial rescript (Fig. 4.15): the *litterae caelestes* are an extremely mannered and artificial variety of that bureaucratic script of which we had lost track in the second half of the third century, but which survived only in the imperial chancery, courtesy of a precept or habit to which the rescript implicitly refers. How, then, to explain the disappearance of the bureaucratic script during the 270s and 280s? We cannot exclude the possibility that the special script was abandoned by the outlying chanceries in favor of the new Roman script (the *litterae communes*), and that this abandonment might have taken place concurrently with a turnover in the bureaucracies, when a new class of scribes, with a different training, replaced the older generation that had been tied to the bureaucratic script tradition of the early parts of the century. The dates of the last examples of bureaucratic script, if the synchronicity is not pure chance, point to a moment of general upheaval and restructuring in the political and administrative organizations of the empire, culminating in the reforms of Diocletian.

SUGGESTED READING

Fundamental works are: Jean Mallon, *Paléographie romaine*. Madrid: Consejo Superior de Investigaciones Científicas, Instituto Antonio de Nebrija de Filologia 1952, and Emanuele Casamassima and Elena Staraz, "Varianti e cambio grafico nella scrittura dei papiri latini. Note paleografiche," *Scrittura e civiltà* 1 (1977): 9–110. For bibliography after 1952: Teresa De Robertis, "La scrittura romana," in *Tagung des Comité International de Paléographie Latine*, ed. Walter Koch and Theo Kölzer (Enghien-les-Bains, 19–20 September 2003) = *Archiv für Diplomatik* 50 (2004): 221–46. Photographic documentation and editions of all documentary papyri of the Roman era in Albert Bruckner and Robert Marichal, eds., *Chartae Latinae antiquiores. Facsimile-edition of the Latin charters prior to the ninth century*, vols. I–XIL,

Olten-Lausanne, later Dietikon Zurich: Urs Graf Verlag 1954–98; an ample selection of documents is to be found in Richard Seider, *Paläographie der lateinischen Papyri*, I, Stuttgart: Hiersemann, 1972. In Guglielmo Cavallo, *La scrittura greca e latina dei papiri. Una introduzione*, Pisa and Rome: Fabrizio Serra, 2008, 143–67 there is a palaeographic overview of the most important documents of the first to the third centuries. On the scripts of the Vindolanda tablets, see Alan K. Bowman and John David Thomas, *Vindolanda: The Latin Writing Tablets*, London: Society for the Promotion of Roman Studies 1983, 53–67 and *The Vindolanda Writing Tablets (Tabulae Vindolandenses II)* London: British Museum Press, 1994, 40–6; on incised writing, see Guglielmo Bartoletti, "La scrittura romana nelle *tabellae defixionum* (secc. I a.C.–IV d.C.). Note paleografiche," *Scrittura e civiltà* 14 (1990): 7–47.

Notes

1. In ancient sources, these are termed *articuli, baculi, virgulae*.
2. Mallon (1952: 22).
3. Bartoletti (1990).
4. Sixteen papyri from the year 445 until the eighth century were published and annotated by Maffei (1727). There are 146 papyri in the edition by Marini (1805), which also includes papal documents (until the eleventh century) and Merovingian charters.
5. At least on chronological grounds, the assessment is not too far from the truth. In fact, the largest number of the papyri that were copied in the West and came to us via direct transmission are dated to the period that runs from the second half of the fifth century until the end of the seventh. For the complete list, see Tjäder (1982: I, 35–133).
6. Courtois, Leschi, Perrat, and Saumagne (1952).
7. Egyptian papyri do not survive from the delta of the Nile, which is too humid, but from areas south of Cairo (in the valley of the Nile but out of reach of the annual flooding of the river) or on the edges of the desert. The dry climate and the sand aid in the preservation of organic materials such as papyrus.
8. Such is the complete number to date of the tablets, not counting, however, the dozens of small fragments that contain only a few letters. The tablets are now held in the British Museum. Edition and photographic documentation of the tablets as published in the first two volumes of the series *Tab. Vindol.* may be seen at http://vindolanda.csad.ox.ac.uk/.
9. Information about the wax tablets is derived from the census by Bartoletti and Pescini (1994, 63–100).
10. Chart with the numeric distribution in De Robertis (2004, 228–30).
11. We should not forget, however, that during Roman domination in Egypt, the number of Latin-speaking residents was relatively low (functionaries in high positions, soldiers, bankers, an occasional merchant or businessman) and that the administrative language remained Greek, as was the case in all Hellenized countries; only the army spoke Latin. This social and linguistic situation preselected the occasions for writing in Latin and determined from the start an uneven numeric balance in favor of Greek: Latin is, in fact, used only in military documents and in those drawn up for Roman citizens and according to Roman law.
12. For example, in PLond. 229 (*ChLA* III 200, AD 166, Seleucia Pieria), a sales contract for a slave boy between two sailors of the Roman navy, there are, as well as the hand of the *tabellio*, another six Latin hands, all of soldiers of rather low rank.

13. Inappropriately, the script of this period is also called majuscule cursive or *capitalis* cursive.

14. See Wright, Chapter of 6 this volume, pp. 79–97.

15. The most ancient Latin papyri are letters: POxy. 3208 (*ChLA* XLVII 1420, Augustan age: a certain Syneros warns a friend); PBerol. 13956 (*ChLA* X 428, second half of the first century BC: the slave Phileros writes to his fellow slaves); and PVindob. Lat. 1 (*ChLA* XLIII 1241, 26-2 BC.: four or perhaps five letters sent to a certain Macedo, glued together to form a *volumen*).

16. The scribes of the letters sent to Macedo (cf. n. 15), coming from environments that were culturally and geographically not distant from one another and although employing essentially the same script (form and *ductus* are, in fact, the same), produce stylistically very different results: compare the extreme sobriety of *ChLA* XLIII 1241, Fragment B, with the mannered execution of *ChLA* XLIII 1241, Fragment C.

17. With this same function, also in PDura 54 (*ChLA* VI 309), AD 225–35, *Feriale Duranum*.

18. In documents drawn up in two copies (on wax tablet, papyrus, and even bronze), the *scriptio interior* could be opened in case of controversy in the presence of a judge or an arbiter charged with verification that the terms of the contract were the same in both parts. Even in some wax tablets we find, as in PSI 1183, differences in graphic style between the *scriptio interior* and the *scriptio exterior*.

19. Gasparri (1979, 265).

20. De Robertis (2007).

21. Cencetti (1993).

22. The last two dated documents are POxy. 2951 (*ChLA* XVII 1415: 267, sale of a female slave) and PPrinc. Garrett Dep. 7734 (*ChLA* IX 404: 276–82, Greco-Latin register of accounts).

23. Van Hoesen (1915); Schiaparelli (1976).

24. His demonstration is founded on a comparison of the script in the fragment of the *De bellis Macedonicis* (PLond. 745 = *CLA* II 207) of the end of the first century with the script of the *Epitome Livii* (PLond. 1532 = *CLA* II 208) of the second–third century. In this case, too, Mallon considers the forms of the letters in the two fragments as representatives of two chronologically sequential scripts (Mallon (1952, 77–104)).

25.

> Impp. Valentinianus et Valens AA. ad Festum proconsulem Africae. Serenitas nostra prospexit inde caelestium litterarum coepisse imitationem, quod his apicibus tuae gravitatis officium consultationes relationesque complectitur, quibus scrinia nostrae perennitatis utuntur. Quam ob rem istius sanctionis auctoritate praecipimus ut posthac magistra falsorum consuetudo tollatur et communibus litteris universa mandentur, quae vel de provincia fuerint scribenda vel a iudice, ut nemo stili huius exemplum aut privatim sumat aut publice. Dat. v id. iun. Treviris Lupicino et Iovino conss.

English translation by Clyde Pharr, et al.:

> Emperors Valentinian and Valens Augustuses to Festus, Proconsul of Africa. Our Serenity has observed that the practice of imitating Our celestial imperial letters has arisen from the fact that the office of Your Gravity, in composing references of cases to the Emperor and reports to Him, uses the same kind of script as that which the bureaus of Our Eternity use. Wherefore, by the authority of this sanction, We command that hereafter this custom, a teacher of forgery, shall be abolished and that everything which must be written

either from a province or by a judge shall be entrusted to commonly used letters, so that no person shall have the right to appropriate a copy of this style, either privately or publicly. Given on the fifth day before the Ides of June at Trier in the year of the consulship of Lupicinus and Jovinus [Ju 9, 367].   Pharr (1952, 241): 19.19.3

Since this rescript is included in the Codex Theodosianus (9.19.3), it still retained the force of law in the fifth century.

BIBLIOGRAPHY

Bartoletti, G. and I. Pescini. 1994. *Fonti documentarie in scrittura latina. Repertorio (sec. VII a. C.-VII d.C.)* Florence: Olschki.

Bowman, A. and D. Thomas. 1983. *Vindolanda: The Latin Writing Tablets.* London: Society for the Promotion of Roman Studies.

Bowman, A. and D. Thomas. 1994–2003. *The Vindolanda Writing Tablets (Tabulae Vindolandenses II-III).* London: British Museum Press.

Bruckner, A. and R. Marichal, eds. 1954-1998. *Chartae Latinae antiquiores (ChLA). Facsimile-edition of the latin charters prior to the ninth century,* voll. I-XIL. Zurich: Urs Graf Verlag.

Casamassima, E. and E. Staraz, 1977. "Varianti e cambio grafico nella scrittura dei papiri latini. Note paleografiche." *Scrittura e civiltà* 1: 9–110.

Cavallo, G. 2008. *La scrittura greca e latina dei papiri. Una introduzione.* Pisa and Rome: Fabrizio Serra.

Cencetti, Giorgio. 1950. "Note paleografiche sulla scrittura dei papiri latini dal I al III secolo d. C." *Memorie dell'Accademia delle scienze dell'Istituto di Bologna. Classe di scienze morali* serie V 1: 3–54 (now in *Scritti di paleografia*, ed. Giovanna Nicolaj. Dietikon Zurich: Urs Graf Verlag, 1993: 47–107).

De Robertis, T. 2004. "La scrittura romana". In *Tagung des Comité International de Paléographie Latine,* ed. Walter Koch and Theo Kölzer. *Archiv für Diplomatik* 50: 221–46.

De Robertis, T. 2007. "Quelques remarques sur les conditions et les principes de la ligature dans l'écriture romaine." *Bibliothèque de l'École des chartes* 165: 29–45.

Gasparri, F. 1979. "L'Enseignement de l'écriture à la fin du Moyen Âge: à propos du 'Tractatus in omne modum scribendi', ms. 76 de l'abbaye de Kremsmünster". *Scrittura e civiltà* 3: 243–65.

Maffei, S. 1727. *Istoria diplomatica che serve d'introduzione all'arte critica in tal materia, Con raccolta de'documenti non ancor divulgati, che rimangono in papiro egizio.* Mantua: Alberto Tumermani [republished Rome: Bibliopola 1964].

Mallon, Jean. 1952. *Paléographie romaine.* Madrid: Consejo superior de Investigaciones Cientificas. Instituto Antonio de Nebrija de Filologia.

Marini, G. 1805. *I papiri diplomatici raccolti e illustrati dall'abate G. M.* Rome: Stamperia della Sacra Congregazione de Propaganda Fide.

Pharr, C., T. S. Davidson and M. B. Pharr. 1952. *The Theodosian Code and Novels and the Sirmondian Constitutions: A Translation with Commentary, Glossary and Bibliography.* Princeton, NJ: Princeton University Press.

Schiaparelli, L. 1921. *La scrittura latina nell'età romana (Note Paleografiche).* Como: Tipografia Ostinelli [republished Turin: Bottega d'Erasmo, 1976].

Tablettes Albertini. Actes privés de l'époque vandale (fin du Ve siècle), ed. C. Courtois, L. Leschi, C. Perrat, and C. Saumagne. Paris : Arts et metiers, 1952.

Tjäder, J-O. 1982. *Die nichtliterarischen lateinischen Papyri Italiens aus der Zeit 445–700*, voll. I–II. Lund 1955 –Stockholm 1982.

Van Hoesen, H. B. 1915. *Roman Cursive Writing*. Princeton, NJ: Princeton University Press.

CHAPTER 5

NEW ROMAN CURSIVE
(IVth–VIIth centuries)

TERESA DE ROBERTIS
(Translated by Consuelo Dutschke)

In Chapter 4 of this volume we examined the slow and uncertain process whereby the script commonly called "New Roman cursive" developed (Mallon speaks of a "*nouvelle écriture commune*"; "*corsiva nuova*" is the term used most frequently in the Italian tradition). Nevertheless, certain crucial events, already adumbrated by the end of the third century, came more clearly into focus by the beginning of the fourth.

I. The paradigm of the letterforms of the new cursive has become essentially stable; an occasional rare "ancient" variant resists (the *b* "panse à gauche" produced in a single movement, because it allows for the presence of ligatures; the *n* formed as a capital letter, produced in two movements and, more rarely, in one), but generally speaking, in this alphabet, which combines the earliest of letter variants from the schematic and rapid variants of the bureaucratic script of the third century, we are able to recognize the archetype from which all the forms of letters of the so-called "national" cursives of the high Middle Ages will derive, whether in documents or in books (the scripts called Merovingian, Visigothic, Beneventan, and so forth).

II. The arrangement of these letterforms (both in isolation and in ligature) in the graphic chain, or rather their disposition within the written space, is controlled by a different and new principle that will never be abandoned from now on, and that becomes instead a constituent force in all cursive scripts (and not just of these) to the present day: if the ancient cursive could be defined as an essentially majuscule script (all the vertical strokes retained essentially the same height, and the script, or at least the major part of it, was inscribed within a bilinear system), the new Roman cursive is called a minuscule script, whereby the majority of the letters are inscribed within a four-line system.

III. The new Roman cursive was a private and personal script, but it was also employed in the outlying offices of the empire. In its character as a bureaucratic script, already before the rescript of the emperors Valentinian and Valens of the year 367[1], but even more so as a consequence of it, it presents all the typical characteristics that define an official script and that are at the same time a guarantee of the provenance of a document and, at least in part, a guarantee of its authenticity: strokes that are somewhat artificial (cursive but neither economic nor quick), a high level of execution, and an expressive and decorative use of graphic elements.

The papyri of the first half of the fourth century clearly demonstrate this situation, among which may be singled out the subscription added in 310 by Ulpius Alexander, *censitor* (public official) of the Heptanomia (also called Middle Egypt), to a declaration of citizenship (PStrasb. gr. 1592, *ChLA* XIX 685; Fig. 5.1); the very famous letter of credentials written in the years 317–24 dictated by Vitalis to one of his secretaries, which miraculously survives in two copies, one complete and one fragmentary (PStrasb. lat. 1, *ChLA* XIX 687, letter to Achillius, governor of Phoenicia; PRyl. IV 623, *ChLA* IV 253, letter to Delphinius); the scratch copy of the petition sent in 342–4 by the *praefectus alae* Flavius Abinneus to the emperors (PLond. II 447, *ChLA* III 202). In particular, we call attention to the fact that both in PStrasb. lat. 1 (Plate 5.1) and in PLond. II 447 (Plate 5.2) two hands are present: in PStrab. lat. 1, in addition to the hand of the secretary who writes the greater part of the text, there is also the hand of Vitalis, added at the end, in the formulaic greeting; in PRyl. IV 623 Flavius Abinneus corrects and modifies in his own hand several parts of the petition copied by a professional scribe of notable ability.

In these papyri we can see various levels of execution: the hands of the two secretaries are professional, elegant, stylized; those of Vitalis and Flavius Abinneus are certainly expert but less mannered. But the behavior is the same in the choice of variants, in the manner of realizing the ligatures, and in the general arrangement of the script. In particular, in the letter of Vitalis to Achillius (Fig. 5.2), we see the use of "old" and "new" variants for the letters *d* and *n*, and the tenacious resistance of the *b* "panse à gauche," in one or two movements (this last is the only form attested to here, and it occurs only in ligature);[2] the same variant of *b* is present in Fig. 5.1.

In the forms of the other letters—executed more or less rapidly, in isolation and in ligature (and, in this last case, sometimes deformed)—we recognize variants already attested to in the third century (see Plate 4.1 of Chapter 4 of this volume) in a more advanced stage of evolution; these variants will, at the same time, form the graphic patrimony of the following centuries (Fig. 5.3). Among the most significant letters and variants, we note *a*, *b*, *d*, *e*, *g*, *m*, *n*, *p*, *q*, and *u*.

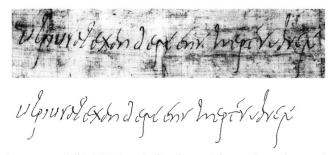

FIG. 5.1 PStrasb. gr. 1592 (*ChLA* XIX 685), dated 310: *Ulpius Alexander cens(itor)Hept(anomiae) subscr(ipsi)*.

(a)

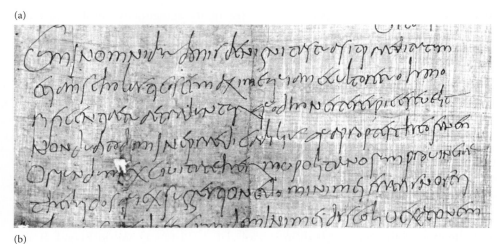

(b)

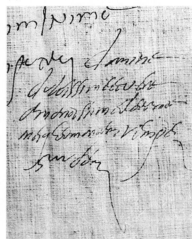

PLATE 5.1 PStrasb. lat. 1 (*ChLA* XIX 687), AD 317–24, letter of Vitalis to Achilles governor of Pheonicia: (a) hand of the secretary, (b) autograph greeting of Vitalis.

(a) *Cum in omnibus bonis benignitas tua sit praedita tum*
etiam scholasticos et maxime qui a me cultore tuo hono-
rificentiae tuae traduntur quod honeste respicere velit
non dubito domine praedicabilis quapropter Theofanen
oriundum ex civitate Hermupolitanorum provinciae
Thebaidos qui ex suggestione domini mei fratris nostri

(b) *Domine*
dulcissime et vere
amantissime beatum te
meique amantem semper
gaudear

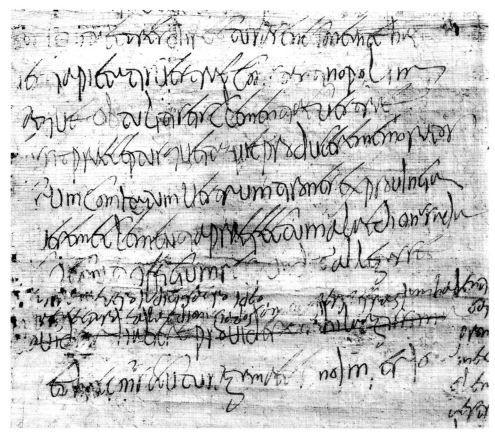

PLATE 5.2 PLond. II 447 (*ChLA* III 202), AD 342–4, petition of the *praefatus alae* Flavius Abinneus.

(first hand)

]*triginta et tres directus a Senecione ante hac*

]*estia pietatis vestrae Constantinopolim*

atque obtulitis eis clementiae vestrae

iu]*ssit praeceptusque itaque producere memoratos*

sac]*rum comitatum vestrum tirones ex provincia*

vere me clementia praefectum alae Dionysada

]*cio comiti officium respondit allegasse*

]*o videor habere provides et mihi largissima*

]*et hoc consecutus agam aeterno imperio*

(second hand)

] . . . *e uero iudicio sacro ideo*

pr]*aefectura alae Dionysiados am . . . per suffragium haben-*

Between the fourth and the fifth centuries, the system for ligatures remains essentially the same as that described for the preceding period: the ligatures are still realized by means of a movement that is initially horizontal, toward the right, and then descending (i.e. at an angle, clockwise). Obviously, the condition whereby a letter may connect with the following letter remains the same: to have a final stroke that is more or less horizontal. The letters whose structures favor this are, in this phase, *e*, *f*, *g*, *r*, and *t*, and very much less so the letters *c* and *s*, for stylistic reasons, as we will see.

There are, however, two important innovations. The first consists of the fact that *a* and *l*, with increasing frequency, tie to the following letter with a movement that begins at the bottom (Fig. 5.4), in which we recognize in embryo (but here on the foundation of a structural element) the anticlockwise principle (i.e. a ligature that begins at the bottom) that will constitute the most important innovation of medieval cursive scripts. One also detects an analogous behavior enacted in the letter *c* (in an anomalous but very frequent ligature between its first stroke and the following letter).

The second innovation consists in the fact that *a* and *l* form a ligature with *c*, *e*, and *t* also by means of an imposition of similar elements: the first *articulus* of *c*, *e*, and *t* is, in fact, identical in structure and in movement to the last section of *a* and *l* (Fig. 5.5). We find ourselves facing, so to speak, a cursive nexus, a type of ligature *per compositionem*.[3]

FIG. 5.2 PStrasb. lat. 1 (*ChLA* XIX 687), dated 317–24: *-fanem, non dubito dom-, ben-* (first hand); *d, -eb-* (second hand).

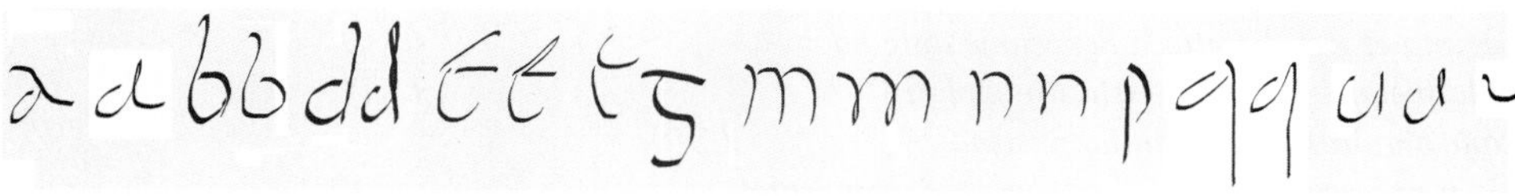

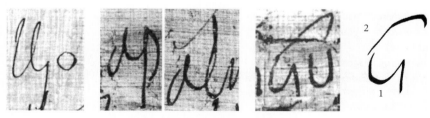

FIG. 5.3 Main letterforms of the new Roman cursive.

FIG. 5.4 Ligatures moving from the bottom upwards in PStrasb. lat. 1 (*llio*) and in PLond. II 447 (*ap, al, ci*).

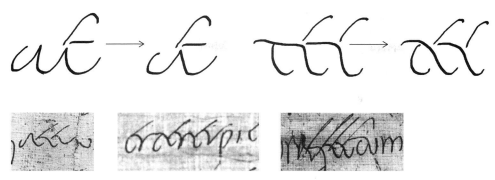

FIG. 5.5 -aeeun-, -esterespic- (P. Strasb. lat. 1); -raefectu- (P. Lond. II 447).

Also e, g, r, and t, in ligature with c and t (and sometimes with a and u) behave similarly thanks to a partial modification of the final stroke, which from the horizontal becomes oblique and descending.

In the new Roman cursive, the letters that do not allow for ligature (because they do not have a final horizontal stroke, or one that can be modified in such a manner) are far more numerous than was the case during the first three centuries: because of their morphology from b, d, m, n, p, and u in old Roman cursive one cannot make a ligature after these letters (the letters no longer have an active function; a passive function is always possible); q did not tie to the right even in the old system; h occasionally ties to the following letter by means of a graphic prothesis (Plate 5.1.(a), r. 4 Theofanen); i, which earlier (even though very rarely) tied to the right by means of a prothesis, from now on is instead the letter that breaks the rhythm of the script. This is already sufficient to show that the system of ligatures of the new cursive includes a smaller number of alphabetical combinations compared to the previous period. The matter is confirmed by the table reproduced as Fig. 5.6 (constructed on the basis of a corpus of 251 documents datable between the third and the fifth centuries), from which we realize that approximately one-third of the combinations of letters attested to in the third century disappears in the two following centuries and that this drastic disappearance is not compensated, except in a minimal way, by new combinations (some of which are attested to only in a single document, and may be classified as marginal).[4] In the face of this situation, it is important to note how the sequences of letters in ligature tend to become very complex (including, that is, a high number of letters). In Fig. 5.7, the scribe interrupts the chain of letters in ligature at the presence of the letters b, i, n, o, s (in two cases out of three) and u, that is, when he encounters letters whose morphology makes it impossible to proceed past them.

But the characteristic and, in fact, new aspect of the late antique Roman cursive is not due only to its predictable letters, or to its system of ligatures, which (with the exception of the decrease in alphabetical combinations and of the two novelties indicated above) remains substantially those of the previous period. Far more impor-tant is the general organization of this new cursive, which develops from two factors: the tendency to realize in an identical manner and according to a new style the segments of letters that are perceived of as similar, and the positioning of letters in

Lettera anteriore	Lettera posteriore																						
	A	B	C	D	E	F	G	H	I	K	L	M	N	O	P	Q	R	S	T	U	X	Y	Z
A	•	•	•	•	•	•	•	*1	•		•	•	•	*1	•	•	•	•	•	•	•		[•]
B	•	[•]	*1	[•]	•		[•]		•		[•]			•			[•]	[•]	•	•		*1	
C	•				•		•	•		•	•		•				•		•	•	*1		
D	[•]		[•]	[•]	[•]			[•]	•		[•]	[•]	[•]	[•]	[•]		[•]	[•]		[•]		[•]	
E	•	•	•	•	•	•	•	•	*		•	•	•	•	•	•	•	•	•	•	•		
F	•				•	•			•		•		*	•	*		•		*	•			
G	•	[•]	[•]	*1	•		•	*1	•		[•]		•	•	[•]		•	[•]		•		[•]	
H	•	[•]			•				•				•	[•]						[•]			
I	•		[•]	*1	[•]	*1		*1	[•]	[•]		[•]	•	•			[•]	•	•	[•]			
K	•																						
L	•			•	*		•		*		*	*	*	*					*	*			
M	•	[•]	[•]		•		•		[•]	[•]	[•]	[•]	[•]		[•]					[•]	[•]		
N	•			•	•	[•]	*1	[•]	•			[•]	•				[•]	•	•				
O	•	[•]	•	•	•	•	[•]	[•]	[•]		•	•	•				•	•	•	•	*	*	
P	[•]			[•]	[•]			[•]			[•]	[•]		[•]			[•]	[•]	[•]	[•]			
Q																							
R	•	•	•	•	•	•	[•]	•			*	•	•	•	•	[•]	•	•	•	•		[•]	
S	•		[•]	[•]	•	[•]	*		•		•	[•]	•				[•]	[•]	•	•	•	[•]	
T	•		•	*	•	*1	*	•	•		•	•	•	[•]	•		•	•	•	•			
U	•	[•]	•	[•]	•	[•]	•		•		•	•	•	•			•	•	•				
X	[•]		[•]				•						•	[•]	[•]						*		
Y												*	[•]				[•]						
Z	[•]																						

FIG. 5.6 Combination of letters in ligature: third–fifth century (corpus of 251 documents).

• Combinations attested for the third century
[•] Combinations no longer attested for the fourth–fifth century
* New combinations attested for the fourth–fifth century. The numeral 1 indicates that the combination is found in a single document.
Total combinations for the third–fifth century: 273
Combinations attested for the third century: 246
Combinations attested for the fourth–fifth century: 186
Combinations attested for the third century not present in the fourth–fifth century: 87
Combinations attested only for the period fourth–fifth century: 27 (11 of which are attested a single time.

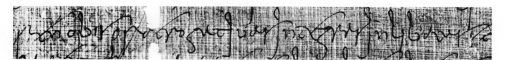

FIG. 5.7 PLips. I 44 (*ChLA* XII 526), after the years 293–5: *ren|o|b|i|s|p|raero|gati|u|as|i|n| tegrasi|n|li|b|atas.*

one in relation to the other (in ligature or outside of it) and of the *articuli* internal to the letter on differing planes or levels. The most visible phenomenon consists in the rounding and lengthening towards the right of the vertical strokes: this occurs for the first stroke of the *t* (which thus assumes the same movement as the first stroke of the *c*); it occurs for what is now the first stroke of the *e*, as well as for the second strokes of *l* and of *a*. With the same movement toward the right, we now see the internal ligature between the first and the second strokes of *a, d, g, q,* and *u* (note that the principal morphological difference between *a* and *u* consists from this point forward in the fact that the second stroke of *u* retains a rigorously vertical direction, thus rendering impossible a ligature towards the right). The combination of terminal roundings and internal and external ligatures reaching upward from the bottom identifies visually the line that the script rests on, above which is situated another important zone for articulation of script: the area that contains the point of attachment of the various short strokes, and in which, as we have seen, ligatures formed from on high and at an angle occur (Fig. 5.8). Above this area are the attachment points of *b*, *h*, *i* (in its tall variant), and *l*, and the area in which one can develop (in this case with ascending and oblique movement) the second stroke of *c*, *e*, and *s*; below this we see the prolonged vertical strokes of *f*, *p*, and *q*, the so-called tail of *g*, and in a less systematic manner (at least in this phase) the letters *i*, *r*, *s*, and *x*.

Dynamic relationships (i.e., ligatures between letters) take place preferably in the central zone of the written ribbon. An indirect proof of this is in the notable reduction, with respect to the period of first to the third century, of the ligatures that follow *c* and *s*, which can be explained by the fact that the second stroke, prolonged upward, distances itself from the point of attachment of the short strokes; only if the second stroke remains near the stream of letters do *c* and *s* form a ligature with the following letter; for a "high" *c* we have numerous attestations of a ligature that leaves off from the first stroke (cf. Fig. 5.4), with the second stroke of the letter then written at the end of the sequence.

The upper zone is instead the area in which we see formations of stylistic nature. This is where, for example, various types of loops (simple, double, triple) are developed at the end of the fifth century (Fig. 5.9), loops that are only rarely useful or utilized for ligatures, but which remain deeply important for the definition of various chancery styles, even beyond the period when this new cursive was in use (it will be enough to consider the long elaborated ascenders in diplomatic minuscule script from the German imperial chancery or from the papal chancery during the eleventh and twelfth centuries, or the hooks of the multiple European cursives during the so-called Gothic period).

FIG. 5.8 Significant aspects in the ordering of script.

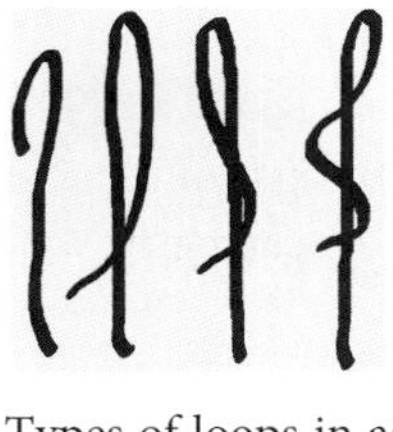

FIG. 5.9 Types of loops in ascenders.

The ample success of ligatures effected by superimposition of shared elements between two letters seems to be connected to questions of ordering, to preferences, in one part of the documentation, for a *ductus* in which the point of attachment of the short vertical lines (line 2 in Fig. 5.8) comes very close to the line on which the script rests (line 3 in Fig. 5.8): the letters reach out, the short strokes become almost horizontal, and in the ligature they dissolve to such a point that it becomes almost impossible to establish where the break between two marks occurs (Fig. 5.10); in the word, the ligatures and the connections between the various *articuli* that form the letters seem to all take place in a single zone of writing.

This cursive with an inclined axis, which will have great success especially in areas of Italy during the course of the sixth and seventh centuries (and indeed beyond), is flanked by a cursive that answers to the opposite principle, as is evident in PVindob. L.31 (*ChLA* XLIV 1264 + XLVIII 1264*, a copy of an imperial rescript of 386 recopied towards the beginning of the fifth century; Fig. 5.11 and Plate 5.3). The expert main hand handles the vertical strokes with a greater extension than what he uses for the horizontal strokes, (Fig. 5.11), or, in other words, he takes as his spatial reference a schema in which the lines indicated as 2 and 3 in Fig. 5.8 are a good distance apart. The contrast between these two concepts of graphic space remains very clear thanks to the presence of a second hand, which adds an occasional word in a script that is not far from what we described as the first style.

These are, in synthetic manner, the characteristics of the new cursive of the fourth and fifth centuries, such as they can be deduced from a corpus formed of some one hundred documentary papyri, in the largest part still of African or Eastern origin, to which, from the middle of the fifth century, we begin to add Italian papyri. An important group of some forty wooden tablets, made of cedar and dating from the end of the fifth century, attests to this same new Roman cursive; the tablets contain acts of sales of land in the area of Tebessa (Algeria); their script, produced by a writing

FIG. 5.10 Pomersfeld lat. 14 (*ChLA* XII 547), end of the fifth century (after 433): *ate, raefati, ot.*

FIG. 5.11 PVindob. L.31 (*ChLA* XLIV 1264+XLVIII 1264*), fifth century (after 386): *-aec que con-, -egaretur, -sam vil-* (first hand); *provinciae arcadi-* (second hand).

PLATE 5.3 PVindob. L.31 (*ChLA* XLIV 1264 + XLVIII 1264*), beginning of fifth century, copy of an imperial rescript from 386 (first hand).

]anus II Fl(avius) Vincentius Fl[
]dem ipsam vilissimam[
]negaretur exact[io
]ntentionibus[
]co secundum sa[
]raeteritorum te[
]aec que continu[
]o procurando[
(second hand)
praesidi provinciae Arcadiae.

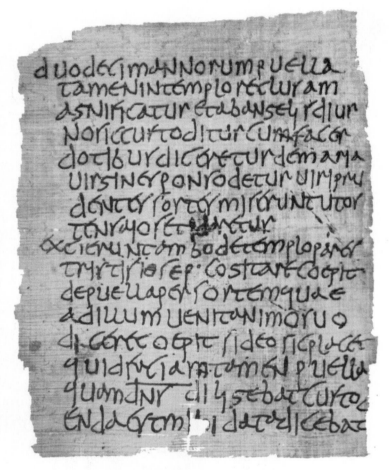

PLATE 5.4 PBarc. 149*b*-153 (*CLA* XII 178), fourth century, *Psalmus responsorius*.

Duodecim annorum puella
tamen in templo reclusa m-
agnificatur et ab angelis diur-
no sic custoditur cum sacer-
dotibus diceretur de Maria
virgine sponso detur viri pru-
dentes sortes miserunt ut os-
tensa Ioseti dareur
Excierunt ambo de templo pares
tristis Iosep cogitare coepit
de puella per sortem quae
ad illum venit animo suo
dicere coepit si Deo sic placet
quid faciam tamen puella
quam d(omi)n(u)s diligebat custod[i]-
enda est mihi data dicebat.

instrument with a wide point that significantly limits the ascenders (it might have been a small stick with a softened point so as to function like a paint brush), has many points of contact with what we find in books, classified according to necessity as a minuscule or a primitive half-uncial, or as a cursive half-uncial, or as a quarter-uncial.

The new cursive, in fact, made its first precocious entry into the world of books in a natural manner as script of glosses,[5] and with some adaptation as the script of the text.[6] The reproduction in Plate 5.4 is of a page of a small codex of the fourth century that contains, together with materials in Greek, a responsorial psalm dedicated to the Virgin (PBarc. 149b-153, *CLA* XII 1782) and fragments of the First Catilinarian of Cicero (PBarc. 149a+PRobinson inv. 201, *CLA* XI 1650):[7] as far as variants, ligatures, and order are concerned, the script is not far from PStrab. lat. 1 or PLond. II 447, even though their execution is obviously more formal. Jean Mallon noted examples of the epigraphic use of the new cursive in Spanish territories: in the epitaph of Rogata (fourth or fifth century) and in an inscription on raw clay (fourth century),[8] both also important as being the oldest examples of cursive script from the Visigothic period.

There are no significant morphological changes during the sixth and seventh centuries: the forms of the letters remain substantially the same, even if for *e* and *t* we register the appearance of variants made in one movement[9] that will find favor especially in the eighth century and beyond (see Fig. 5.12); other letters, on the other hand, can be written more formally, reconstructing their *ductus* in a different manner (this is what happens to the letter *a*, which is built in two moments, pulling together two strokes of similar structure, or to *d* and *q*, which present an occasional horizontal stroke to close the upper part of the body of the letter, as in Fig. 5.12); the two-stroke variant or uncial form of the letter *a* disappears; the letter *d* done as a variant in one movement from a higher point is now attested to only in ligature; the capital variant of *n* is very rare, and it remains associated with a distinctive function. Far more significant is the mutation that occurs in the second stroke of the *t* and the *g* (see Fig. 5.12), which ever more frequently begins with the ornament of an ample opening flourish; to write this second stroke, the writing instrument performs an ascending movement starting from the baseline, or else it inserts itself into the attack stroke of the first vertical stroke. At this point we are looking only at a stylistic shift, but it is easy to recognize in it the first link in an evolution that for the letter *g* will bring us to the formation of the upper so-called bowl, and for the letter *t* will signal the beginning of the (improperly called) double-hook *t* attested to in Visigothic script, in Beneventan, and in various other pre-Caroline scripts (as well as documentary scripts, for a very long time).

During the course of the sixth and seventh centuries, we note the growing persistence and even the widening of the bifurcation between the two stylistic lines that were

FIG. 5.12 Variants made in one movement (*e* and *t*); reconstructed *ductus* (*a*, *d*, *q*, *t*, and *g*).

already recognizable in papyri of African or eastern origin in the preceding two centuries. In the sixth century, the most calligraphic example of the vertical style (at two levels of execution) is without doubt represented by the so-called Butini Papyrus, copied in Italy and deriving from the chancery of a "comes Sacri Stabuli," who may be Bloody John, the *magister militum* of the Emperor Justinian (PTjäder 55, *ChLA* I 5): in the protocol we see one of the first attestations of the use of *litterae elongatae*, which was realized through exaggeration, almost to the limits of legibility, of the vertical strokes, reducing to almost ignorable appendices the horizontal strokes, as well as the upper portions of the letters, and moving to the top, with a reduction in size, the vowels *o* and *a*.[10] In the rest of the document, even if in forms that are less exaggerated, the phenomena remain the same: what we have called the middle zone of the four-line system is well individualized, the downward strokes are rigorously vertical, their point of attachment is rigorously distanced from the baseline of the script, and the ligatures are almost all formed from the top downward (with the exception of the *l*).

Phenomena analogous to those described for the Butini Papyrus are found in the cursive script used in the records of the chancery of the Merovingian kings, whose first examples go back to the end of the sixth century. If we examine the two precepts of Theodoric III dispatched on 12 and 15 September 677 (these are the most ancient Latin documents on parchment, *ChLA* XIII 566 and 565), we note that the letters constructed only of vertical strokes (*a*, *m*, *n*, and *u*) appear compressed; that the vertical strokes of *b*, *d*, *h*, and *l* are emphatically elongated so as to render it impossible to form a natural ligature with the preceding letter by reaching for the attaching point; and that while the letters have a cursive "design," they have been written in more than one stroke and the actual ligatures are, in fact, not so numerous, and pertain to short sequences (usually not more than two or three letters). In examples such as these, we have the impression that the tendency to verticality is in contradiction to an effective cursivity.

Examples of considerable elegance of the vertical style and the other cursive style—with inclined axis, with the letters and ligatures a good distance apart—can live together within a writing context and even within a single document with differing functions (Plate 5.5). This is what we see in the important series of Italian papyri, largely from Ravenna or at least connected to that city's environment. These papyri are written for the most part by hands that exhibit a very high technical competency that is mirrored in the articulated formulary of its rhetorical and juridical world; and the fact does not surprise us, if we consider that the lay and ecclesiastical bureaucracy of Ravenna is that of a capital city, initially imperial (from 402), then of the kingdom of the Goths (from 476) and, after the reconquest under Justinian (539), of the Prefecture and then the Exarchate of Italy. Of the more daily or private level all we have are an occasional photogram: some autograph subscriptions,[11] an inventory of papers of various type from the archive of the *praefectus praetorio per Italiam* in Ravenna,[12] a list of relics perhaps copied in Rome and now in the treasury of the cathedral of Monza.[13] And examples of books in cursive scripts are rare for the sixth and seventh centuries. A codex of the *Antiquitates Iudaicae* of Flavius Josephus in the Latin version of Rufinus was copied in Italy (in Milan? in Ravenna?), in the sixth century (Milan,

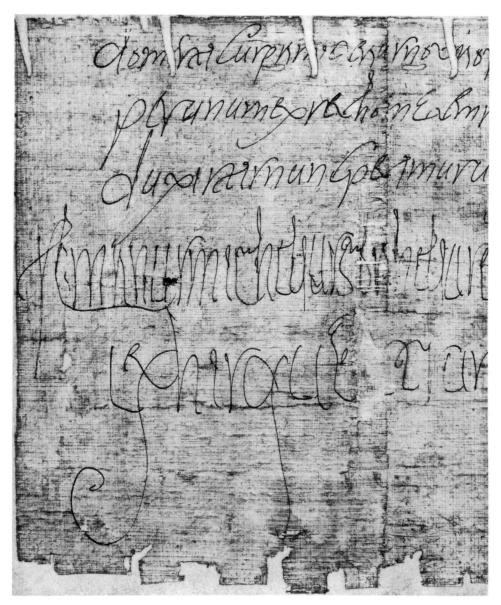

PLATE 5.5 PTjäder 4–5B, col. VIII (*ChLA* XVII 653), AD 552–75, registration of the *Gesta* of the Prefecture of Ravenna of five wills connected with the property of the Church of Ravenna.

domesticus primicerius notario[rum . . .
per unum ex se Thomatem s[ecundocirium . . .
duxistis nunc petimus u[t . . .
Fl(avius) Marianus Micahelius Gabrihelius P[etrus . . .
ex his quae quae acta sun[i . . .

PLATE 5.6 Paris, BnF, lat. 8913, sixth century (after 515), Avitus episcopus Viennensis, *Homiliae et Epistolae*: c. 7r, part. (end of *Hom.* XXIV, beginning of *Hom.* XXV, with partial interlinear transcription in a hand of the sixteenth century).

pra]estolatio nostra concepit porrigitur hic praeludens per coniecturam prae-
sen]tium contemplatio subsequentum iuste \aestimatur/ tantum
in n]obis quantum per te potior eris in summa. Certe sicut te rationem
illi]c operum perpendemus hic donorum non quidem solus in praesentibu[s
as]pecis quod delectet sed solus in futuris poteris proferre quod superet. Fin[it
Dic]ta in basilica s(an)c(t)orum Acaunensium in innovatione monasterii
ip]sius vel passione martyrum
P]raeconium felicis exercitus in cuius congregatione beatissima nem[o]
per]it dum nullus evasit cum iniustam s(an)c(t)orum martyr(u)m mortem quas.
sor]tis iustitia iudecarit qua bis super aciem dispersa mansuetam, cen-
tuple]x decimatis fructus adcriscerit, et hodio in prosperum suffragante
eatenus eliger]entur singoli donec simul collegerentur elicti ex consu[etu-

Biblioteca Ambrosiana, Cimelio MS 1, *CLA* III 304): of this book, 92 leaves survive, copied by several hands in an elegant cursive of the inclined style. From France is Paris, BnF, lat. 8913+8914 (*CLA* V 573),[14] which contains the *Homiliae et epistolae* of St. Avitus, bishop of Vienne from 494 to c.525; from the text of one homily we know that it was delivered after September 22, 515 and this offers a sure *terminus post quem* for the dating of the codex (Plate 5.6). The French origin of the book is established (other than by its history) by the characteristics of the script, which seems to announce the stylization that we will see in actual practice from the first years of the seventh century in Merovingian diplomas. The copyist is to be traced to a secretary of the holy bishop; proof of this is the shared presence of scripts of varying size that take on precise functions: the larger size is reserved for the *inscriptio* of the letters and the *actum* of the sermons, i.e. the indication of the place and occasion for the sermon. We are within a book context, but the habits (as well as the script) are documentary. To the Ambrosian codex of the *Antiquitates Iudaicae* and to the St. Avitus of Paris, we may also add the *scriptio inferior* of the manuscript, Milan, Biblioteca Ambrosiana, C.105.inf. (*Carmen de septem fratribus Machabeis* and medical recipes, *CLA* III 324, assigned by Lowe to the sixth century, but more likely of the late seventh century) and the Greek-Latin glossary, PLouvre 2329 (*CLA* V 696, of the sixth century), of Egyptian provenance.

The Italian papyri are the oldest documents that have come down to us in an uninterrupted tradition, and they constitute a unique corpus: knowledge of them goes back to Italian humanism, when the main nucleus was still preserved in Ravenna in the chancery of the bishopric (today they are dispersed throughout the major collections of Europe, but with a large group in the Archivio Vaticano). Their existence was known to Ambrogio Traversari, who refers to them in a letter to Cosimo de' Medici dated 1433, even though the first person to describe them, with an exaggeratedly early date, was Ponticus Virunius in the early years of the sixteenth century in his *De inventione litterarum*.[15] From that point onward, and up until the archeological discoveries in Egypt, it is upon these documents that we found our knowledge of papyrus as a support for writing and the cursive scripts of the Roman tradition.[16]

For the seventh century we still have an occasional rare example of Latin script originating in North Africa, but by now all the examples are western European. One important contribution to the story of the final period of cursive scripts of late antique tradition, before the period called "graphic particularism," comes not just from the papyri of Ravenna and from the Merovingian charters, but also from the 153 documents copied by means of scratching on slate found in Spain, in the area of Avila and Salamanca, and datable to the end of the sixth and through the eighth century. With the exception of an occasional and obvious deformation or limitation (for example, in the frequency and complexity of the ligatures) due to the material and to the writing instrument, the graphic stage attested to in these *pizarras* is perfectly coherent with what we see in contemporary Italian or French *chartae*. We recognize, in substance, the fundamental graphic unity that still resists the general political and institutional collapse of the western Roman empire and its fragmentation.

SUGGESTED READING

Jean Mallon, *Paléographie romaine*. Madrid: Consejo Superior de Investigaciones Cientificas, Instituto Antonio de Nebrija de Filologia, 1952, 114–22 ("L'Écriture diplomatique de l'empire et des royaumes barbares") and 123–52 ("La Nouvelle Écriture romaine"); Giorgio Cencetti, "Dall'unità al particolarismo grafico. Le scritture cancelleresche romane e quelle dell'alto medioevo", in *Il passaggio dall'antichità al medioevo in Occidente*, Spoleto: CISAM, 1962, 237–64 (now in *Scritti di paleografia*, ed. Giovanna Nicolaj, Dietikon-Zurich: Urs Graf Verlag, 1993, 227–71); Emanuele Casamassima and Elena Staraz, "Varianti e cambio grafico nella scrittura dei papiri latini. Note paleografiche," *Scrittura e civiltà* 1 (1977): 9–110 (esp. 83–95).

Photographic documentation and editions of all documentary papyri and earlier charters are to be found in Albert Bruckner and Robert Marichal, eds., *Chartae Latinae antiquiores. Facsimile-Edition of the Latin Charters Prior to the Ninth Century*, vols. I–XIL, Olten-Lausanne, later Dietikon-Zurich: Urs Graf Verlag, 1954–98. For all Latin books, see E. A. Lowe, *Codices Latini Antiquiores: A Palaeographical Guide to Latin Manuscripts Prior to the Ninth Century*, vols. I–XII, Oxford: Clarendon Press, 1954–71. For an ample selection of documents and books, see Richard Seider, *Paläographie der lateinischen Papyri*, I, II/1–2, Stuttgart: Hiersemann, 1972–81, with transcriptions and commentary of the facsimiles. In Guglielmo Cavallo, *La scrittura greca e latina dei papiri. Una introduzione*, Pisa and Rome: Fabrizio Serra, 2008, 167–90 there is a palaeographic overview of the most important papyri (documents and books) of the fourth–sixth centuries. On the scripts of the Algerian tablets, see Christian Courtois, Louis Leschi, Charles Perrat, and Charles Saumagne, *Tablettes Albertini, actes privés de l'époque vandale (fin du Vᵉ siècle)*, Paris: Arts et métiers graphiques, 1952, I, 15–62; on the scripts of Italian papyri, see Jan-Olof Tjäder, *Die nichtliterarischen lateinischen Papyri Italiens aus der Zeit 445–700*, vol. I, Lund: C. W. K. Gleerup 1955, 86–156; on incised writing of the Visigothic *pizarras*, see Isabel Velásquez Soriano, *Documentos de época visigoda escritos en pizarra (siglos VI–VIII)*, vols. I–II, Turnhout: Brepols, 2000, II, 24–68. On the evolution of the new cursive in Italy from the eighth century, other than Cencetti, "Dall'unità al particolarismo grafico," see Emanuele Casamassima, *Tradizione corsiva e tradizione libraria nella scrittura latina del Medioevo*, 2nd ed., Rome: Vecchiarelli 1998 (in particular 31–69); a detailed outline of the diffusion of this script from the era of the Lombards until the eleventh century (in urban locations such as Milan, Bergamo, Lucca, Pisa, Rome, and Salerno) is to be found in Armando Petrucci and Carlo Romeo, *Scriptores in urbibus. Alfabetismo e cultura scritta nell'Italia Altomedievale*, Bologna: Il Mulino, 1992; see also Francesca Santoni, "Palazzi vecchi e nuovi: il fenomeno grafico tra Ravenna, Pavia e Milano (sec. VII–IX)," *Ravenna Studi e Ricerche*, vol. 9 (2002): 115–36.

Notes

1. Cf. Chapter 4 of this volume, pp. 57–8 n. 25.
2. Among the ancient variants, *b* "panse á gauche" is the only one that we find until the middle of the sixth century: see PTjäder 10–11 (*ChLA* XX 703 + XLV 1331), AD 489, donation of Odoacre; PTjäder 12 (*ChLA* XXV 791), AD 491; PTjäder 29 (*ChLA* XLV 1332), AD 504; PTjäder 34 (*ChLA* XX 704), AD 551, in the subscription of Deusdedit; PTjäder 13 (*ChLA* XIX 880), AD 553; PTjäder 4–5 (*ChLA* XIX 878 + XVII 653), AD 552–75. Its resistance is surely due to the fact that it allows for ligature, but we cannot exclude that this variant is used also for its characteristic appearance, both archaic and special.
3. The definition comes from the *Tractatus* published by Gasparri (1979): "'compositionem' voco quando taliter connectuntur quod una [littera] alteram ingreditur, et ejusdem substancie cum ea efficitur sic quod unus baculus interdum erit duarum litterarum substancia" (p. 264).

4. In Casamassima (1998, 82–3), there is a table with all the morphological combinations of ligatures for the fourth and fifth centuries (every letter in all its attested variants, with all the letters with which there is a ligature at least once).

5. The oldest and most extended set of annotations in new cursive are those in the margins of the Bembo Terence (Vatican City, BAV, Vat. lat. 3226, *CLA* I 12, fourth–fifth century); but see also (all of the fifth century) Bologna, Biblioteca Universitaria, 701, Lactantius (*CLA* III 280); Vatican City, BAV, Urb. lat. 1154, Probus (*CLA* I 117); PRyl. 477, Cicero (*CLA* II 226); Cambridge, University Library, Nn.II.41, *Codex Bezae* (*CLA* II 140); Paris, BnF, lat. 8907, Hilary of Poitiers, Ambrosius and others (*CLA* V 572).

6. Adaptations, of variable intensity, consist essentially in a fragmentary execution of the letter and in a lessening of the frequency and complexity of the ligatures; see the grammatical treatises copied during the course of the fifth century in Italy, contained in occasional leaves Naples, Biblioteca Nazionale, lat. 2, formerly Vindob. 16 (*CLA* III 397*a* and 398), and in Turin, Biblioteca Nazionale, G.V.4+Varia 186*bis* (*CLA* IV 462). In various ways tied to the world of schools, see also the Greek-Latin glossary PChester Beatty *s.n.* (*CLA* XII 1683), the paraphrase of the *Aeneid* contained in PSI 142 (*CLA* III 289) and probably also PSI 21, Vergil (*CLA* III 287) and PSI 110, Sallust (*CLA* III 288), not to mention the very interesting series of fragments of a codex with the speeches of Cicero, PLond. 2057 (*CLA* II 210); the examples listed here are all of the fifth century and from Egypt.

7. The portion that contains the psalm is reproduced in its entirety in Roca-Puig (1965); for the American fragments of the *Catilinaria*, see Willis (1963).

8. Mallon (1952, plate XXIII 1 and 2).

9. For *T* produced in a single stroke (used especially in ligature), see PTjäder 30, hand of Deutherius (*ChLA* XX 706, AD 539), PTjäder 31 (*ChLA* XX 707, AD 540), PTjäder 34, hand of Petrus (*ChLA* XX 704, AD 551), PTjäder 4–5 (*ChLA* XVII 653 + XIX 878, AD 552–75), PTjäder 44 (*ChLA* XXII 721, AD 648–61). For *e* (more rare in this phase), see PRyl. Gk. IV 609 (*ChLA* IV 246, AD 505) and PTjäder 27 (*ChLA* IX 406, middle of the sixth century). There are also two attestations of this in the fifth century (POxy. XVI 1879, *ChLA* XLVII 1409 and PPommersfeld lat. 14, *ChLA* XII 547).

10. It is to this script that we may apply the definition offered by the glossary published by Bischoff (1966, 5): "Longarie, que grece syrmata dicuntur. Syrma enim grece, latine dicuntur longa scriptura vel manus, quibus cartule et edicta scribuntur et precepta" ("Longarie" are the letters that in Greek are called "syrmata." That which in Greek is "syrma" in Latin is a script or a longhand, with which charters, edicts, and precepts are written).

11. See, for example, the subscriptions of PTjäder 25 (*ChLA* XXVIII 843, *c.* AD 600).

12. PTjäder 47–8 AB (*ChLA* XXV 792 and XXIX, 870, first half of the sixth century, after 510).

13. PTjäder 50 (*ChLA* XXVIII 863, AD 590–604).

14. For a complete reproduction of the fragments contained in the two manuscripts, see http://gallica.bnf.fr/ark:/12148/btv1b10303684w, accessed December 23, 2019, and http://gallica.bnf.fr/ark:/12148/btv1b10303685b, accessed December 23, 2019.

15. "[Extant] similiter et Ravennae et alibi tabulas publicas sub Hadriano Augusto ex papyro herba palustri longas quinque passus, brachii latitudine, sed inter lineas quattuor digitorum quasi schiza descriptas, non intelligibiles mille e trecentorum annorum" (There remain also in Ravenna and elsewhere certain public documents made of papyrus,

written during the time of Hadrian, five feet long, and as wide as one arm, with lines separated by a space of four fingers, incomprehensible for one thousand and three hundred years); in *Erotemata Guarini cum multis additamentis et cum commentariis Latinis*, Ferrariae 1509, fol. 13r.

16. Mabillon (1709, 344–5, 460 and 457*–460*); Maffei (1727).

BIBLIOGRAPHY

Bischoff, B. 1966. "Die alten Namen der lateinischen Schriftarten." In Bernhard Bischoff, *Mittelalterliche Studien: Ausgewählte Aufsätze zur Schriftkunde und Literaturgeschichte*, vol. I, 1–5. Stuttgart: Hiersemann.

Casamassima, E. 1998. *Tradizione corsiva e tradizione libraria nella scrittura latina del Medioevo*, 2nd ed. Rome: Vecchiarelli.

Gasparri, F. 1979. "L'Enseignement de l'écriture à la fin du Moyen Âge: à propos du 'Tractatus in omne modum scribendi', ms. 76 de l'abbaye de Kremsmünster." *Scrittura e civiltà* 3: 243–65.

Mabillon, J. 1709. *De re diplomatica libri VI, editio secunda ab ipso Auctore recognita, emendata et aucta*, Luteciae Parisiorum, sumptibus Caroli Robustel.

Maffei, S. 1727. *Istoria diplomatica che serve d'introduzione all'arte critica in tal materia, Con raccolta de' documenti non ancor divulgati, che rimangono in papiro egizio*. Mantua: Alberto Tumermani [repr. Rome: Bibliopola, 1964].

Mallon, J. 1952. *Paléographie romaine*. Madrid: Consejo Superior de Investigaciones Cientificas, Instituto Antonio de Nebrija de Filologia.

Roca-Puig, R. 1965. *Himne a la Verge Maria. "Psalmus responsorius." Papir llatí del segle IV*, Barcelona: Asociación de Bibliófilos.

Willis, W. H. 1963. "A Papyrus Fragment of Cicero." *Transactions and Proceedings of the American Philological Association* 94: 321–7.

CHAPTER 6

CAPITAL SCRIPTS

†DAVID WRIGHT

THE letterforms[1] we think of as capitals were stabilized for Roman inscriptions in the second century BC.[2] In the Middle Ages, especially around the thirteenth and four-teenth centuries, they were frequently deformed, or hidden in ornament, but they were revived in pure form in the Italian Renaissance. During the Augustan era two distinct styles of rendering the basic letters developed: the very formal "Square Capitals," where round shapes are as nearly as possible circular and the overall shape is as close to square as possible (standard for Imperial inscriptions on marble) and the informal "Rustic Capitals," where the shapes are more slender, more compressed, and refinements suggest the use of pen or brush.

Square Capitals, always stressing the geometry underlying the letterforms, were perfected for inscriptions on stone, where in the best imperial examples serifs and careful distinctions between broad and narrow strokes were carved with great preci-sion, as in the dedication of the Column of Trajan (AD 113) (Fig. 6.1), a masterpiece of the stone carver's art, (*CIL* 6.960). This style of lettering is also known from the main headings of advertisements painted on walls in Pompeii, or later in books for titles or colophons, or for section initials, but not normally for the main text.

FIG. 6.1 Column of Trajan, Rome (AD 113), detail of letters 11 cm high.

The basic capital letterforms (without refinements) continued in use for more routine inscriptions, such as military diplomas (Figs. 6.2 and 6.3), or the bronze tablets posted on the Capitol (which they record).

FIG. 6.2 Detail of diploma dated AD 79 (British Museum 1923,0116.1 = *CIL* XVI, 24).

FIG. 6.3 Detail of diploma dated AD 122 (British Museum 1930,0419.1 = *CIL* XVI, 69).

These were all official documents made in Rome, ordered by a veteran finishing his military duty, wanting a certificate of citizenship and his right to marry. A horizontal stroke was made with one sharp blow of a hammer on a pointed chisel going from right to left, leaving a very small lump of excess bronze at the end of the stroke, and a vertical stroke was made in the same way from bottom to top. Curved strokes were more difficult, and had to be made carefully, with small repeated taps of the hammer on a chisel constantly moved to make the curve. Occasionally the chisel was also struck across the end of a long stroke (as at both ends of the letter I and at the bottom of T) to give a small serif comparable to those in Rustic capitals.

As the demand for these diplomas increased, the workmanship deteriorated and letterforms were simplified somewhat, minimizing the curvature of round shapes. In this way the letter O may even appear as ( ) to reduce the constant repositioning of the chisel, but the basic letterforms remain those used at the end of the Republic.

Essentially the same letterforms, casually written with reed pen on papyrus, were used for important military documents written in the provinces, as in the semi-annual roster of a cohort stationed in Upper Egypt in 156 shown in Fig. 6.4. Although C, N, O, and T retain their square proportions, other letters approach the Rustic form, as in the A with a dwarfed left stroke and no cross bar; furthermore downward diagonal strokes tend to curve slightly with the natural motion of the hand, so that V approaches uncial U. This happened gradually in the evolution of common capital script.

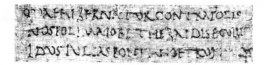

FIG. 6.4 Detail of cohort roster dated AD 156 (P. Berol. 6870).

MATURE RUSTIC CAPITALS

··

The term "Rustic" for the capital script with relatively slender proportions, regular serifs, and less rounded forms is arbitrary, but was established by the *Nouveau traité de diplomatique... par deux religieux Bénédictins de la Congrégation de S. Maur* (6 vols. published in Paris, 1750–65) and remains in common use today.

This script is frequent on the walls of Pompeii, where Square Capitals were also used for the most important announcements. It was painted with a square-headed brush by a very skilled worker, using, in Fig. 6.5, compressed letterforms appropriate for a rather long line of advertisement. Many details conform to the natural motions of the painter's hand, such as the slight curve of a downward diagonal stroke to the right and the shape of the serifs at the top and bottom of vertical strokes. Note also at the top edge of the photograph in Fig. 6.5 the details of very large Square Capital serifs at the bottom of the main heading of this announcement of entertainment sponsored by a citizen of Pompeii and his son.

FIG. 6.5 Detail from Pompeii, house III.2.1, advertisement with letters 11 cm high, for an entertainment in the reign of Nero (54–68), *CIL* 4 suppl. 3 (1952) p. 844.

The same combination of a very large initial line in Square Capitals followed by a long text in small Rustic Capitals is common in imperial inscriptions, as in an inscription on marble in honor of Hadrian in Athens dated 112.[3]

Surviving papyrus fragments with literary texts, rather than a documentary purpose, also show the development of Rustic capitals, but they are generally in poor condition and few can be dated accurately. Ten fragments of a roll from Herculaneum (i.e. before AD 79) have an unidentified oratorical text written with a broad pen in bold capitals about 5 mm high (P. Herc. 1475; *CLA* 3.387); the letters follow essentially the same canon of forms as the wall inscription of Fig. 6.5, with the same tendency to draw a strong horizontal serif at the top of a thin vertical stroke, but the proportions are very different; letters are generally so much broader that N fills a square, while O remains an oval clearly showing the 60 degree orientation of the pen. It is worth noting that the new fragment of a papyrus roll with elegiacs by Gallus generally resembles this script; it was probably written shortly before 25 BC, and found in Qasr Ibrim (between the first and second cataracts in Egypt) in 1978.[4]

Reliably datable codices of literary texts written in capital script do not survive before about AD 400, when the Vatican Vergil (Fig. 6.6) can be dated on the basis of the figure

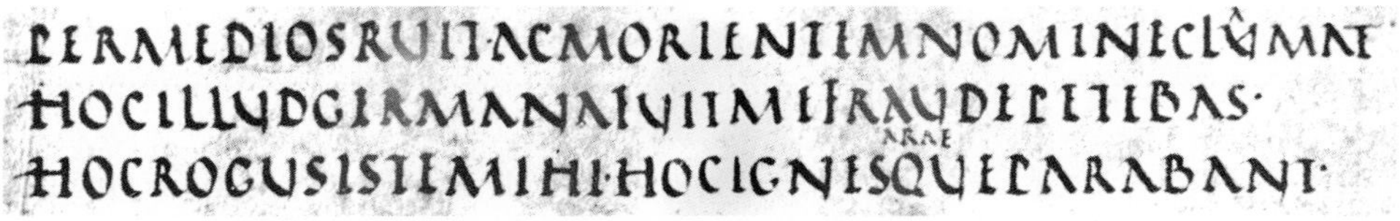

ΕΕRΑΜΕDΙΟSRVΠΑCΜΟRΙΕΝΠΙΜΝΟΜΙΝΕCΙ̂ΜΑΤ
ΗΟCΙLLVDGΙRΜΑΝΑΙVΙΤΜΙΙRΑVDΙΕΕΠΙBΑS·
ΗΟCRΟGVSΙSΠΑΙΗΙΗΟCΙGΝΙSQVΕΕΑRΑBΑΝΤ·

FIG. 6.6 Detail from the Vatican Vergil, (Vatican City, BAV, Vat. lat. 3225, *CLA* 1.11) fol. 41r.

style and spatial composition of its best paintings, as compared with dated wall paintings and ivory carvings.[5] By this time the parchment codex had become the normal form for books of literary character, for they were much easier to handle than a papyrus roll that must always be rewound after reading, and a codex could contain (for example) the complete works of Vergil in one volume, with gatherings consisting of four or five sheets of parchment folded and arranged with flesh and hair sides facing each other for uniform appearance, and then sewn along the fold for binding between stiff covers. The Vatican Vergil was a fully illustrated luxury edition, with originally some 280 framed paintings occupying part of the page, placed just before the episode illustrated; it had some 435 folios about 24 by 21 cm, but only 75 scattered folios survive, ranging from *Georg.* 3.1 to *Aen.* 11.895. The book is clearly the work of one expert scribe writing mature Rustic capitals with a wide pen oriented at about 60 degrees, yielding strongly differentiated thick and thin strokes. It should be noted that by this time *scriptura continua* no longer allows word separation by a space or a medial dot (as on the Column of Trajan), and that there are no abbreviations except suspensions for *-bus* and *-que* and a raised horizontal stroke where M or N is omitted at the end of a line.

Now the letterforms are less compressed than in the Rustic used in carved inscriptions or painted on walls, but they have developed further from the Rustic known from early scraps of literary rolls, for N is essentially square, H nearly so, and M extends horizontally beyond a square, because the two outer strokes slope outward. The first stroke of V is so rounded at the bottom that it approaches the form of an uncial u. Broad rounded strokes clearly reveal the 60 degree orientation of the pen, but for some vertical strokes the hand was turned to about 30 degrees to draw a thinner line, as in the descender at the left of M. Simple vertical strokes, as in E, I, L, and T, are normally slightly narrower than the bold diagonal of M or N, but in drawing the narrow left stroke of N or the stroke at the right of V the scribe usually turns his pen to an angle even lower than in the left stroke of M. While this writing gives the impression of being a natural script, particularly in the easy curves of D, S, or V, or the tilde-shaped top of T, there is significant artifice in some of the adjustments to the width of strokes.[6]

There is also one unusual letterform here: this scribe uses two forms of G interchangeably, the normal capital form with a small curving stroke of closure at the right, and an uncial form with a very thin short descender at the right.

A truly monumental copy of Lucan's *Bellum civile* (Fig.6.7) had the same letterforms (except the uncial G) written between two ruled lines with extraordinary regularity and refinement of shading and serifs. Only fifteen scattered folios survive, palimpsested in the eighth century by an Irish scribe at Bobbio, but we have enough to establish the

FIG. 6.7 Detail of Lucan, Naples, Biblioteca Nazionale, lat. 2, fols. 31v–33v (*CLA* 3.392).

character of the original, which must have measured about 38 × 36 cm, and had letters 7 mm high on lines 12.5 mm apart—fully twice the size of the Vatican Vergil. It is also noteworthy for enlarging the first letter on a page almost three times, when the norm for enlarging a letter in that position was less than two times in this period. In character this book was analogous to the substantially later Square capital "Augusteus" of Vergil discussed below.

Another famous Vergil, which reached the Medici collection (Fig. 6.8), is a much more intimate book, small enough to be held comfortably in the hand (originally 230 folios, about 21.5 × 15 cm). It has essentially the same letterforms only half as big as those in the Vatican Vergil, with 29 lines to a page instead of 21, and no illustrations.[7] This smaller script is very close to that of the Vatican Vergil, but the page appears lighter because the letters are spaced further apart and the contrast between thick and thin strokes is less marked. It may seem slightly later because this scribe regularly starts the horizontal stroke of H just to the left of the first vertical, while that is true in the Vatican Vergil only if the H comes at the start of a line. The modestly decorated colophons point toward a development prominent in the sixth century, so it seems reasonable to place the Medici Vergil in the middle of the fifth.

QUISEURORISTENOUUSQUONUNCQUOTENDITISINQUII
HEUMISERAECIUES·NONHOSTEMINIMICAQ·CASTRA
ARGUUMYESTRASSPESURITIS·ENEGOUESTER
ASCANIUSGALEAMANTEPIDESPROIECITINANEM·

FIG. 6.8 Detail of Medici Vergil, Florence, BML, 39.1, fol. 110v (*CLA* 3.296).

These three books may be taken as exemplifying the classic phase of Rustic capitals as a book hand. There are a few fragments of other fine books of this character, mostly palimpsested, that seem to belong to this phase. Half of a thoroughly erased folio of Terence in St. Gall, Stiftsbibliothek, 912 (*CLA* 7.974) seems to have the same letterforms at the same size and *ductus* as the Vatican Vergil, while a palimpsested fragment of Livy (in Vatican City, BAV, Pal. lat. 24, *CLA* 1.75) matches the Medici Vergil very closely in size and spacing as well as in letterforms, and a miserably palimpsested fragment of Fronto (*CLA* 1.72, also in Vatican City, BAV, Pal. lat. 24) has similar very small letters spaced much more closely together.

A palimpsested Cicero in Turin (*CLA* 4.442, destroyed in the 1904 fire but known from surviving photographs) had the same letterforms as the Vatican Vergil, slightly smaller, written with a slightly narrower pen and spaced slightly further apart; it must have been an elegant book, in character halfway between the Medici and Vatican Vergils. A scrap of a different Cicero manuscript that met the same fate in Turin (*CLA* 4.445) had a less skillful version of the same script. A corner of one parchment folio of Vergil found at Antinoopolis (Pap. Ant. 30, *CLA* Suppl.1709) has a slightly more elaborate and larger version of that writing, with N no longer square in shape and V now clearly an uncial u (suggesting a slightly later date). It must have been written in Italy, and if we assume no illustrations, it required some 260 folios with 24 lines to a page—an imposing volume.

A palimpsested Cicero in Vatican City, BAV, Reg. lat. 2077 (*CLA* 1.115) is similar in letterforms but has a more distinctly rounded uncial U and boldly shaded letters a full millimeter higher than in the Vatican Vergil, with slightly larger letters placed in the margin to mark new sections. It is also interesting for giving the titles of the evidence cited by Cicero in slightly smaller uncials. A palimpsested Aulus Gellius in Vatican City, BAV, Pal. lat. 24 (*CLA* 1.74) has letters another millimeter larger and more boldly formed, but seems still to belong to the classic phase of Rustic capitals.

As usual in any art, this classic phase seems to have been followed by mannered exaggerations and variations. A palimpsested bifolium in the Vatican from a copy of the satires of Juvenal and Persius (Fig. 6.9), Vatican City, BAV, Vat. lat. 5750 (*CLA* 1.30), follows the basic letterforms of the Vatican Vergil, including an uncial G, this time with a long tail, and takes care in drawing delicate serifs, but allows some very exaggerated letters, particularly Y, which rises well above the tops of other letters, and on the first line of a page blossoms out in sweeping curves, while the downward diagonals of U and X may start higher than normal, reaching almost to the line above them. But this seems to have been an eccentric scribe trying out his elaborations, and we have no trace of close followers, no evidence for a specific date.

FIG. 6.9 Detail of Vatican Juvenal–Persius fragment, Vatican City, BAV, Vat. lat. 5750, p. 78.

One such exaggeration, however, does become a criterion for dating: the strange development of the K-shaped H. The letter H is a symmetrical rectangle in the classic phase, with identical broad vertical strokes, and a somewhat narrower horizontal stroke that may start just to the left of the first vertical.

A first hint of a new development is seen in two fragments of a bifolium of Sallust from Oxyrhynchus (Fig. 6.10), now in Berlin (*CLA* 8.1054). The letterforms are generally good examples of the classic phase, including a proper capital G, but the H is no longer symmetrical. The cross stroke of H begins slightly to the left, as we have seen occasionally, but the first vertical stroke of H is now narrow (like the letter I, or the verticals of P and T), while the second vertical stroke is much wider than other vertical strokes and has a hint of curvature to the right at the top; also, the serif at the bottom of that stroke can be read as another slight curve to the right. This is not one of the special forms that soon develop, but it seems to suggest some experimentation with the shape of the letter H, a letter that is relatively rare in Latin.

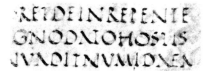

FIG. 6.10 Detail of Berlin, Staatsbibliothek zu Berlin-Preussischer Kulturbesitz, Lat. Qu. 914, Sallust fragments from Oxyrhynchus.

The severely palimpsested Vergil in Verona (Verona, Biblioteca Capitolare, XL (38), *CLA* 4.498) (Fig. 6.11) was originally produced on a grand scale, with 13 verses of Vergil boldly written by a very good scribe in a ruled area 130 × 175 mm, with letters about 6 mm high, in the middle of pages roughly 29 × 23 cm, leaving the vast upper and lower margins for scholia. The letterforms follow the types used in the Vatican Vergil with one exception, the letter H. As before, the first stroke is a wide vertical with a serif at the bottom, and the cross stroke is a narrow horizontal line starting near the left edge of the first vertical, drawn to the right to reach the right half of H, but that half is now a normal capital C, drawn in two strokes as usual, but with its curved shape slightly compressed to make this I–C combination approximately square. It is hard to imagine why this form was developed, but it seems to be uniform in what can still be read in this book, and it seems to be the source of the evolving K-shaped H.

FIG 6.11 Three details with the letter H in the Verona Vergil, (Verona, Biblioteca Capitolare, XL (38), fols. 223r, 222v, 219r (*CLA* 4.498).

This development can be followed in the Palatine Vergil (Vatican City, BAV, Pal lat. 1631, *CLA* 1.99) (Fig. 6.12), the work of a very skillful scribe whose letters are taller, more compressed laterally, and drawn with a pen broader than in the Vatican Vergil. This led to stronger shading and more vigorous curving strokes, which this scribe

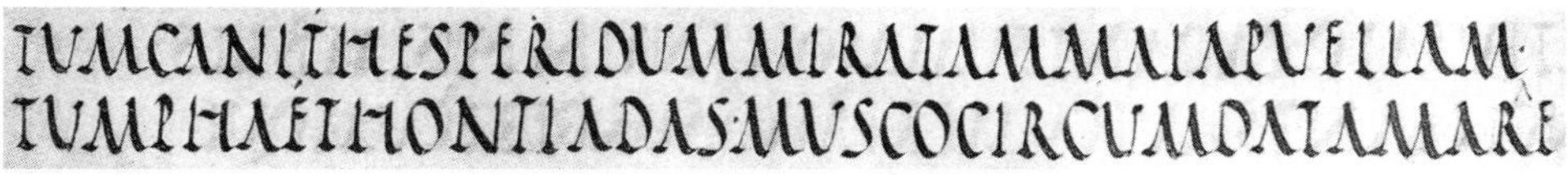

TUMCANITHESPERIDUMMIRATAMMAIAPUELLAM·
TUMPHAETHONTIADASMUSCOCIRCUMDATAMARE

FIG. 6.12 Detail of Palatine Vergil, Vatican City, BAV, Pal. lat. 1631, fol. 20v.

seems sometimes to have enjoyed exaggerating decoratively, especially at the top or bottom of a page. The letter H in an early part of his book has a form comparable to that in the Berlin-Oxyrhynchus Sallust, but the cross stroke is now a tilde, starting inside the first narrow vertical stroke and curving up, where a pen lift was needed before making the broad second vertical stroke, which at the bottom curves up in a small hook (not really a serif), almost like the broad stroke of A or the first stroke of V.

But this skillful and disciplined scribe used this transitional form for only about a dozen folios, and only after he had used his mature and more decorative form on the first five folios. Then he resumed the more decorative form on folio 22r and used it for the rest of the book (Fig. 6.13). In this mature form the cross stroke is a bolder tilde, starting to the left of the narrow first vertical stroke and swinging up almost to the top of the broad second vertical, which was made after a pen lift (though sometimes it looks as if there were only a pause to reverse the motion of the hand) and curved slightly outward at the bottom. That second vertical starts lower than the first narrow vertical and is crowned by a separate stroke, an outward-curving *virgula* (twig), which does not produce a normal C like the right half of the H in the Verona Vergil. This feature and the projecting tilde may be exaggerated for decorative effect, as at the top of a page (fol. 145r) or the beginning of a line (fol. 111r).

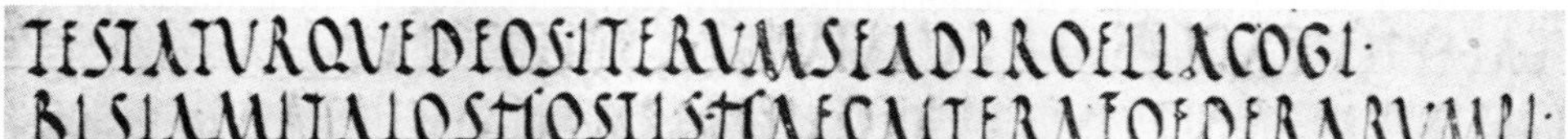

TESTATVRQVEDEOSITERVMSEADPROELIACOGI·
BISIAMITALOSHOSTISHAECALTERAFOEDERARVMII·

FIG. 6.13 Detail of Palatine Vergil, Vatican City, BAV, Pal. lat. 1631, fol. 248v.

The next step in this strange development is clear in the Vergilius Romanus (Vatican City, BAV, Vat. lat. 3867, *CLA* 1.13) (Fig. 6.14), where the broad downward stroke at the right of H is gently curved near the bottom and has a separate cap at the top curving to the right. This is not actually a K-shaped H: it is, rather, a very compressed version of the combination I–C in the Verona Vergil, but it has the proportions of a compressed H. This book is much larger and more pretentious than any other ancient illustrated manuscript, originally 410 folios about 35 × 33.5 cm, with a small illustration before each of the *Eclogues* and a pair of frontispiece illustrations before each book of the *Georgics* and of the *Aeneid* (instead of small narrative illustrations placed just before the passage they illustrate, as in the *Vaticanus*). The flattened figure style of these illustrations, the spatial suppression, and the clumsy execution—a dramatic contrast with the superb control and skill of the scribe—point to a date around 480, by comparison with dated consular diptychs in ivory.[8] It should also be noted that

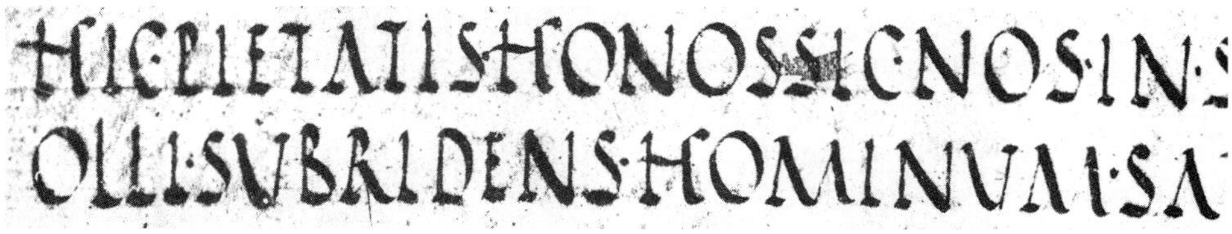

FIG. 6.14 Detail of Vergilius Romanus, Vatican city, BAV, Vat. lat. 3867, fol. 85r.

this innovative book has much more elaborate colophon ornament than the Medici Vergil, and also for the first time has a framed preface before each book, setting a precedent for later sumptuous manuscripts of Vergil. The bulk of the volume made it impractical to handle: it must have been displayed open on a stand, for admiration, especially to display the pairs of facing illustrations at the start of each book, separated from the text. But the very large letters (M measures 9 × 10 mm) made it possible to read this manuscript when on display.

A splendid manuscript of the poems of Prudentius in Paris (Paris, BnF, lat. 8084, *CLA* 5.571a) (Fig. 6.15) shows the true K-shaped H. Now it is clear that the first stroke is a narrow vertical with horizontal serifs at top and bottom (just like the I), and the second stroke is a broad curving diagonal starting from the middle of the I, curving down and turning slightly up at the bottom, resembling the letter h; the third stroke is a hairline diagonal starting from the bend in the second stroke and going up to the right before being pulled down to make a small hook-serif. This letterform would be better designated "h-plus-*virgula*"; it makes sense as a rapid simplification of the form of H in the Palatine Vergil, omitting the pen lift, and must come after the sequence of changes to H just described. The Prudentius script has a number of other mannered features, such as the letters F and L that rise far above the line and the cross bar of E, shaped like a tilde and placed crossing the middle of the vertical stroke. The former assumption that the very small sloping uncial entry on fol. 45r "+ . . . ttius Agorius Basilius" referred to Mavortius, Consul in 527, has been disproven by Alan Cameron.[9]

FIG. 6.15 Detail of Paris Prudentius (Paris, BnF, lat. 8084, *CLA* 5.571a), folio 29v.

It is significant that in this survey of capital scripts, which has included many copies of Vergil, some of Cicero, Livy, Sallust, Terence, etc., this is the only example of a Christian text, which we would normally expect to be in uncial script, as are early copies of biblical texts. There is, however, a miserable parchment fragment of St. John found in Egypt, now in Aberdeen (Aberdeen, University Library, Papyrus 21, *CLA*

2.118), with only a few legible words in small Rustic capitals, just 2.5 mm high, and there is a much better parchment fragment from Egypt of Latin-Greek Pauline Epistles in Florence (Florence, BML, P. S. I. 1306, *CLA Suppl.*1695) with four lines of classic Rustic capitals. Clearly producers of fine books in Late Antiquity normally reserved Rustic capitals for classical authors.

One other famous manuscript has this K-shaped H boldly and consistently, the Terence proudly owned by the humanist Bernardo Bembo (Fig. 6.16), who wrote on a flyleaf "codex mihi carior auro." It has been dated as early as around 400 (Vatican City, BAV, Vat. lat. 3226, *CLA* 1.12), but the writing has a character quite different from the classic Rustic capitals of the Vatican Vergil, and it must now be dated early in the sixth century. The broad strokes are wider in relation to the size of the whole letter, and they lack the easy curving rhythm of the Vergil; the letter S appears to be a zigzag because there is not enough room to exploit the curves of its intrinsic form in a line that is so compressed; the relatively long tail of Q is bold but usually straight (giving the line of script a jagged appearance), the F descends well below the line, and G always has the uncial form with a small descender. The *ductus* is uneven, for this is not a scribe with the highest skill, but he would seem to have enjoyed making the exaggerated *virgula* for the letter H, sometimes extending it decoratively. There are, on the other hand, some interesting features here taken from an early exemplar: the use of Greek letters in red to identify the speakers, placed by each name in the cast list at the start of each scene and then repeated at the start of each speech (instead of giving abbreviated names), and also the adjustment of line length according to the meter, indenting the left margin for passages with short lines.

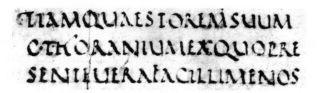

FIG. 6.16 Detail of Bembine Terence, (Vatican City, BAV, Vat. lat. 3226, fol. 58r).

Three folios in the Vatican (Vatican City, BAV, Reg. lat. 1283B) from a Sallust that was broken up in Fleury in the seventh or eighth century and mostly palimpsested display a skillful rounded version of Rustic capitals from this phase (*CLA* 1, p. 34 and 6.809) (Fig. 6.17), including a boldly rising *virgula* on the K-shaped H, and use the

FIG. 6.17 Detail of Vatican City, BAV, Reg. lat. 1283B Sallust, fol. 92r.

uncial G with a short tail and an F rising above the line (though an L that does not rise) but otherwise generally following classic Rustic forms.

There are a few other manuscripts with the developed K-shaped H, which must be put in this chronological group. The palimpsest Plautus in Milan (Milan, Biblioteca Ambrosiana, G 82 sup., *CLA* 3.345) is famously difficult to read, but the K-shaped H is reported, and it uses the uncial G with a rather long tail, and has F and L rising slightly above the line. Five folios of Seneca (Medea, Oedipus) in the same palimpsest collection in Milan (Milan, Biblioteca Ambrosiana, G 82 sup., *CLA* 3.346) also have the K-shaped H and the uncial G, but here F descends below the line. Another Bobbio palimpsest in Milan (Milan, Biblioteca Ambrosiana, R 57 sup., *CLA* 3.363, containing Cicero) has the K-shaped H, uncial G, and V that approaches the uncial form. A palimpsested fragment of Lucan in the Vatican (Vatican City, BAV, Pal. lat. 24, *CLA* 1.70) has the K-shaped H, the uncial G and V, and the descending F, but the character of the rather small script seems otherwise close to the classic phase.

It is not possible to establish a tight chronology for these books, but the K-shaped H in this late form is so distinctive, and so clearly the result of an evolution beginning with the Verona Vergil (Verona, Biblioteca Capitolare 40.51), passing through the strange form in the datable Romanus of Vergil (Vatican City, BAV, Vat. lat. 3867), leading to the flourishing form in the Paris Prudentius (Paris, BnF, lat. 8084), that the K-shaped H must be accepted as pointing to the first part of the sixth century.

By the middle of the sixth century, on the other hand, it seems that the production of grand volumes of classical authors in Rustic capitals ceased, and it is hard to imagine such production continuing in the Italy ravaged by the Longobard invasion of 568, although the use of Rustic capitals survived for special purposes such as titles or colophons.

MANUSCRIPTS IN SQUARE CAPITALS

Grand imperial inscriptions in the tradition of the Column of Trajan continued well into the fourth century, and a recognizable, if inelegant version of that lettering was still in use in Rome as late as 441–5.[10] But the refinements of Square Capitals are difficult to form with a pen and therefore were very rarely used for continuous text in a book. We have fragments of only three literary books written entirely in this script.

The best are the remnants of an enormous and elegantly simple copy of Vergil (Fig. 6.18) that was partly palimpsested late in the twelfth century, and finally cut up to repair bindings in the library of St. Gall (St. Gall, Stiftsbibliothek, 1394, *CLA* 7.977) in 1461—at a time when a full generation of Italian humanists had already been searching the libraries of German monasteries for unrecognized classical texts. Only eleven substantial fragments and one small scrap survive, but the sumptuous design of the book is evident from the first of the palimpsested folios, which has two lines of colophon on the recto for the end of the *Eclogues* and the beginning of the *Georgics*, but was left empty on the verso. If we allow for similar features elsewhere (but not for illustrations), it seems the book must have contained about 350 folios. It has 19 lines of text written between pairs of ruled lines, in an area 223 × 275 mm. In the wide top margin of each page was an abbreviated running title in Square capitals half the size of the text script. If we allow for some loss to the top margin and assume a broader bottom margin, it seems the book measured something around 36 × 35 cm. It is also characteristic of the monumental character of this book that its only abbreviation is the suspension for *-que*.

The letterforms are essentially the same as on the Column of Trajan, except that G here has a curved inward hook at the lower right, and F and L rise slightly above the line, while the custom of extending the long vowel I (as on the Column) has been abandoned. The first scribe (shown in Fig. 6.18) was clearly the most skillful, but the refinements of serifs and shading in the manner of the Column cannot be perfect when writing with a broad pen, making letters six mm high, and copying the whole of Vergil. Some triangular serifs are drawn accurately (as at the top of C, G, and S), and wide vertical lines can have a small hairline terminal at the bottom (and also at the top of I) made by sliding the pen slightly to each side without lifting it, while a similar terminal at the right of the narrow horizontals of E may become a shapeless little blob. The small serif at the bottom of the narrow stroke of A is usually more successful (and also on the corresponding narrow stroke of M), though it is not always regular. Such details that are simple to carve in marble required extraordinary skill and discipline when drawn with pen and ink at this size. The broad sloping stroke of V sometimes curves very slightly at the bottom, as is natural in Rustic capitals, and it does so more frequently in work by the less skilled second and third hands.

FIG. 6.18 Detail of the St. Gall Vergil (St. Gall, Stiftsbibliothek, 1394, *CLA* 7.977).

A scrap of one folio of parchment found in Oxyrhynchus contains parts of *Aen.*2.16–23 and 39–46 (Fig. 6.19) written in expert Square capitals between 3 and 4

FIG. 6.19 Detail of Oxyrhynchus 1098, Vergil fragment (*CLA* 10.1569).

mm high on ruled lines not quite 8 mm apart, with a preserved outer margin of 56 mm. For a copy of Vergil written in such a formal script it is a safe assumption that each book began at the top of a page; therefore, this book must have been ruled for 23 lines (the same as the Palatine Vergil, slightly more than the 21 lines of the Vatican Vergil) and required about 290 folios (or more if there were elaborate colophons or accessories). With a ruled area about 170 mm wide (to judge by the text lost at the left on the recto), the broad surviving outer margin, and if we allow about 25 mm for the inner margin, we can reconstruct a page width at around 25 cm. The ruled area was about 180 mm high, and if we allow a top margin wider than the outer margin and a bottom margin substantially larger than that, we can imagine a page size around 30 × 25 cm. The letters are the normal Square capital forms, including G, except that A has no cross bar and E no serifs (presumably because they would be too small to draw reliably). They are carefully shaded and rather generously spaced. Some are stretched slightly to make them wider than square, so that M with sloping verticals measures roughly 3 × 6 mm, N 3 × 5, D and O 3 × 4. Though hardly the equal of the St. Gall Vergil, this was a very showy book.

The other major example of Square capitals used for a literary manuscript was much more ambitious but departs significantly from the canon of the Column of Trajan. The script of the Augusteus (Vatican City, BAV, Vat. lat. 3256) (Fig. 6.20) is actually hybrid capitals, for although most letters have the Square form (conspicuously D, H, O, and V), A has no cross bar, R has a narrow vertical stroke, E, F, and L have very short thin horizontal strokes without any terminal to suggest a serif, and F and T generally have a curving top stroke shaped like a tilde, also without any hint of a serif.

FIG. 6.20 Detail of the Augustan Vergil, Vatican City, BAV, Vat, lat. 3256, fol. 1r (*CLA* 1.13, and 8, p. 9).

This book was in St. Denis in the Middle Ages, but apparently was broken up in the sixteenth century; two bifolia survive in the Vatican and three separate folios bought at auction in 1862 by the Berlin librarian (Berlin, Staatsbibliothek zu Berlin-Preussischer Kulturbesitz, Lat. fol. 416), who thought them so splendid they should have belonged to Augustus, the patron of Vergil. Combining the Vatican and Berlin holdings, we have what seems to be two-thirds of a ternion with *Georg.* 1.41–280 (but more likely it was originally a quaternion, or perhaps a quinion with a title page on the first recto and further text on the last folios) and a single leaf with *Georg.* 3.181–220. There is also an engraving published in 1709 recording a page with part of Book IV of the *Aeneid*;

extrapolating from this, we expect 330 folios for the complete book, or a little more if there were textual accessories or elaborate colophons. The best-preserved leaves establish a size of about 43 × 36 cm, the largest known ancient literary manuscript, much taller than even the palimpsested Lucan in Naples (about 38 × 36 cm), the St. Gall Vergil (about 36 × 35 cm), or the Romanus of Vergil (about 35 × 33.5 cm).

But the most conspicuously grandiose quality of this book is the large initial at the start of every page (even when there is no pause in the meaning). They are typically 4 cm high, drawn with compass and rule and decorated with color. To begin a page with a slightly enlarged letter was a normal habit early in the evolution of the codex—in the Vatican and Medici Vergils the first letter is often 30 to 50% taller, but the Naples Lucan seems unique in beginning a page with a letter slightly more than twice the normal size, carefully drawn but not decorated. The Augusteus places its initials at the beginning of the top line but makes them about eight times the normal size; they are shaped as Square capitals except that A has a v-shaped cross stroke. They have washes of color (verdigris for green, an unidentified mineral red, and a very light yellow) and simple pen-drawn decoration (including circles and triangles within the broad strokes and strange little curls extending from the ends of some narrow strokes). The irregularities in script suggest that this scribe was not accustomed to writing continuous text in Square capitals, and the decoration seems improvised from page to page, showing no logical development.

There is no specific evidence for dating these three books. The St Gall manuscript, as elsewhere, has clearly mature Square capital script and is extraordinarily sumptuous; it is tempting, therefore, with historical intuition, to put it in the first half of the fifth century. The Oxyrhynchus fragment seems to be a modest version of that production and thus of about the same date. The improvisational quality of the Augusteus decoration shows no symptoms of the widespread development of decorated initials in the middle of the sixth century, and therefore must be earlier than that; the effect of boastful display in size and decoration is similar to the Romanus of Vergil, and therefore the late fifth century seems the most likely date.[11]

It should also be mentioned that large expertly formed Square capitals were frequently used for colophons and section initials in fine Italian sixth-century books, as in the uncial Gospel Books in Cividale del Friuli, Museo Archeologico Nazionale. Archivi e Biblioteca (*CLA* 3.285), London, BL, Harley 1775 (*CLA* 2.197), and Milan, Biblioteca Ambrosiana, C 39 inf. (*CLA* 3.313).

RUSTIC CAPITALS IN ENGLAND

The Codex Amiatinus in Florence, BML, Amiatino 1 (*CLA* 3.299), a complete Bible written in expert uncials, finished at Wearmouth-Jarrow early in 716, usually has colophons and titles in Rustic capitals, sometimes admitting an uncial form, sometimes written rather awkwardly, rarely using a K-shaped H (e.g. fol. 86v).

The scribe who wrote the label for the image of Esdras (part of the first gathering, which was probably a last-minute addition) (Fig. 6.21) wrote this script more confidently, and it remained in current use in Wearmouth-Jarrow at least through 746, when the St. Petersburg Bede (Saint Petersburg, National Library of Russia, lat. Q. v. I.18) used it for titles.

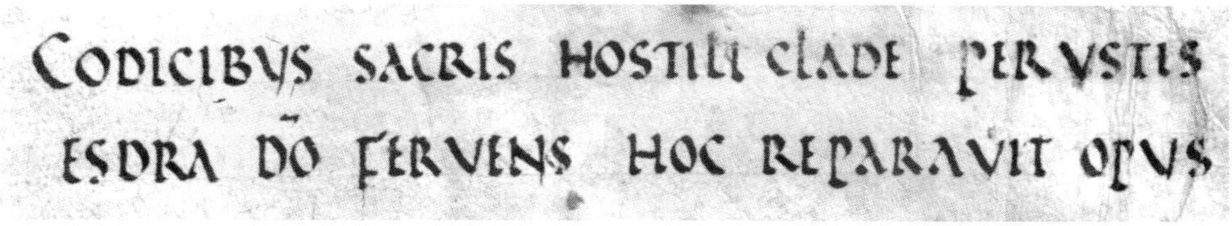

FIG. 6.21 Detail of label to Esdras, Codex Amiatinus (Florence BML, Amiatino 1), fol. 4r.

In Canterbury, around the second quarter of the eighth century, the main scribe of the Vespasian Psalter (Fig. 6.22) wrote text in excellent artificial uncials, with triangular serifs, but wrote titles in red in confident normative Rustic capitals; he also developed a smaller version of Rustic capitals with squarer proportions and more curving finials, which he used for the text of prefaces (as in Fig. 6.22). None of the correctors in this book used Rustic, but a slightly later scribe added three more prefaces and a prayer by Cassiodorus (fols. 2–3, 109 and 141v), writing an awkward version of normative Rustic capitals. A generation later in Canterbury the Codex Aureus now in Stockholm, Kungliga Biblioteket, A 35, was written in relatively clumsy uncials, without any Rustic capitals.

FIG. 6.22 Detail of Vespasian Psalter preface (London, BL, Cotton Vespasian A.1, fol. 4r; *CLA* 2.193).

A large and pretentious Gospel Book now in Paris, BnF, lat. 281 (Fig. 6.23) produced probably in southern England late in the eighth century, has elegant strongly shaded uncials for the Gospel text, but bold and rather awkward Rustic for prefaces and chapter lists. This scribe seems to have taught himself Rustic by copying a sixth-century Italian model with the K-shaped H. The decorated incipits show elements of

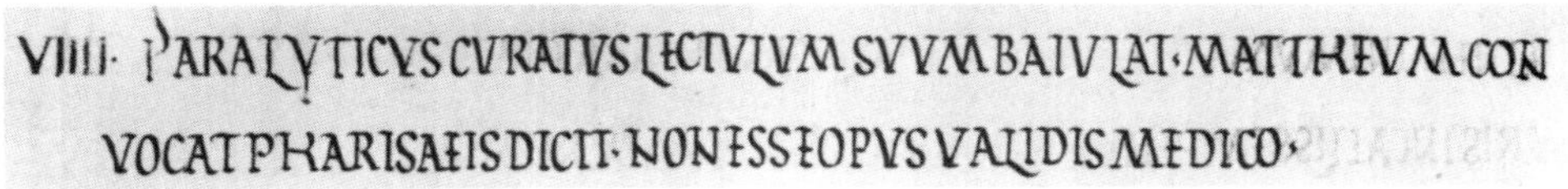

FIG. 6.23 Detail of preface in Bigotianus Gospels, Paris, BnF, lat. 281, fol. 6r (*CLA* 5.526).

the Northumbrian tradition and also some of the Canterbury tradition but there is no evidence for a specific localization.

CAROLINGIAN CAPITAL SCRIPTS

During the Merovingian period capital scripts were not normally written in *Francia*, and in display pages capital letterforms were usually submerged in ornament and often distorted, but a double Psalter (Gallicanum and *Iuxta Hebraeos*, Vatican City, BAV, Reg. lat. 11, [*CLA* 1.101]) was produced around the middle of the eighth century, probably in northern France, with the *Hebreos* written in uncials, and on facing pages the Gallican written in curiously mannered Square capitals. Serifs are exaggerated, G has both a tail curving inward, as expected, and a descending tail with a heavy serif at the end, Q has a similar tail, and H has a clumsy K shape imitating the form used in Italy early in the sixth century. While Merovingian decoration took many features from the classical tradition, and elaborated them, Merovingian writing normally ignored that source.

After Charlemagne's conquest of Lombardy and his visit to Pope Hadrian in Rome (774) his interest and knowledge of the classical tradition in art increased dramatically and turned his patronage in that direction. Perhaps the most dramatic example of this is the black marble tomb slab for Hadrian (who died at the end of 795) with verses composed in the name of Charlemagne, carved in excellent Square capitals, about 3.3 cm. high, originally gilded, and framed with an elegant classical vine scroll (Fig. 6.24). The refinements of shape and spacing of letters are not as careful as in Trajan's time, but nothing as expert as this could have been produced in Rome around 795.

FIG. 6.24 Detail of Pope Hadrian's tombstone carved for Charlemagne in Aachen.

The earliest manuscripts made specifically for Charlemagne use uncials for their main text but use canonical capital scripts for titles, colophons, and other special purposes. The Gospel lectionary made by Godescalc between 781 and 783 (Paris, BnF, Nouv. acq. lat. 1203, *CLA* 5.681) (Fig. 6.25) has precisely drawn monumental

FIG. 6.25 Detail of a heading in Godescalc's Gospel lectionary, Paris, Bnf, Nouv. acq. lat. 1203, fol. 45r.

Square capitals on illuminated pages and in the text expert Square capitals (which may use an uncial E) for special headings.

All the Gospel prefaces and chapter lists in Charlemagne's magnificent purple Schatzkammer Gospels (Vienna, Hofburg, S.N., *CLA* 10.1469, supposedly found in his tomb and subsequently used in the coronation of the Holy Roman Emperor) were written in gold in confident Rustic Capitals early in the 790s. Decorated incipits in this book have large Square capitals, but the main text is in gold uncials with prominent serifs. All four manuscripts in this group associated with Charlemagne personally use both types of capital script for special purposes, and when the court circle broke up after the emperor's death, Ebo was made archbishop of Reims in 816 and took these artistic traditions with him, displacing the mixed Insular elements previously used in Reims. So, around 820 the Ebo Gospels (Épernay, Bibliothèque municipale, 1) has excellent capital scripts, used as they had been in Charlemagne's best books. Also in Reims at that time the famous Utrecht Psalter follows ancient tradition in writing the text in three narrow columns of Rustic capitals in a text block that is nearly square (yet the psalm titles are in red uncials, reversing the hierarchy we might expect).

When Alcuin was sent by Charlemagne to take charge in Tours in 796, he complained of the "rusticity" of the scribes there, but by his death in 804 the standards had improved markedly, and under his successor Fridugisus (807–34) the mature Tours hierarchy of scripts became well established, and led to the production of a remarkable series of complete bibles, and also Gospel books and secular manuscripts. Major decorated pages were normally written in monumental Square capitals; smaller incipits (as in a two-column format) begin with smaller but no less elegant Square capitals and sometimes continue in uncials with precise shading and serifs, for in effect uncial was treated as a capital script. Rustic capitals were always available (as for an explicit, a less prominent title, or labels in illustrations), and sometimes a few lines of half uncials mark a transition to the normal minuscule script. These books set the standard for three centuries.

NOTES

1. All reproductions here are at actual size except those of monumental inscriptions, for which the height of letters is given.
2. See examples discussed and illustrated by Gordon (1983, 82–95).
3. Gordon (1983, 137–8).
4. See Nisbet (1979).
5. See illustrations and analysis in Wright (1993, 84–91); the original areas of the apse mosaic of S. Pudenziana in Rome (*c*.410) should also be compared for their close resemblance in figure style and coloristic modeling to the work of the first painter in this book, who developed original illustrations for the *Georgics*. A detailed reconstruction of the book, including information gained from surviving offsets, is given in my commentary volume to the facsimile: Wright (1984).

6. For a well-illustrated further discussion, see Wright (1993, 76–9). Students of palaeography are well advised to study also the comments of modern calligraphers, such as Knight (2003), which includes excellent enlarged details of the manuscripts. Drogin (1980) gives large drawings showing how he would form the letters, but some ancient practice was different, as revealed by close examination with magnification. Thus, the broad stroke of the letter A could be made first, and the pen then turned to make the narrow stroke at the left, which sometimes blotted slightly with the ink at the top of the still wet broad stroke (and similarly in forming the M).

7. The added entry naming Asterius, Consul in 494, long assumed to date the codex, has been convincingly rejected as a later copy rather than an authentic owner's work: Cameron (1998). Furthermore, this entry is very clumsily written in uncials between the lines of the colophon at the start of the *Georgics*, hardly what one would expect from a Consul proud of his elegant copy of Vergil.

8. Conveniently illustrated in Wright (2001). The clumsy stuccoes in the cathedral baptistery at Ravenna, dedicated 458, may also be cited as evidence for the date. What became the Justinianic style, with figures better coordinated and more spatially involved, began to appear around 500 in the mosaics made for Theoderic in Ravenna (the second phase of the dome of the Arian baptistery and the side walls of S. Apollinare Nuovo) In judging the style of these paintings it is important to realize that the illustration to the first *Eclogue* is strangely clumsy in execution because this painter was not yet accustomed to painting in a book, but that in this case he copies accurately an older model in "papyrus style," while the other surviving illustrations for the *Eclogues* and *Georgics* are clumsily improvised from stock decorative motifs and do not properly illustrate their texts. The *Aeneid* illustrations, on the contrary, are based on authentic iconography, except for the final battle scene, which is again a very clumsy compilation of standard elements that contradict the text in many ways. For further details of this manuscript, including correctors and dots added for word division, see Wright (1992).

9. See n. 8. The inscription is illustrated in Delisle (1881, plate 2.16). It should also be noted that the illustration given in *CLA* shows a section title awkwardly written in red, in pseudo-Square capitals, by a corrector, not by the main scribe. But this book must still be placed early in the sixth century.

10. Gordon (1983, No. 97, 182–3).

11. My long friendship and deep admiration for Carl Nordenfalk does not prevent me from rejecting his case for an earlier date; see his introduction to Nordenfalk (1976).

BIBLIOGRAPHY

Cameron, A. 1998. "Basilius, Mavortius, Asterius." In *Aetos: Studies in Honour of Cyril Mango*, ed. Ihor Sevcenko and Irmgard Hutter, 28–39. Stuttgart: Walter de Gruyter.

Delisle, L. 1881. *Cabinet des Manuscrits de la Biliothèque impériale*. Paris: Paris Imprimerie impériale.

Drogin, M. 1980. *Medieval Calligraphy, its History and Technique*, Montclair, NJ: Dover.

Gordon, A. E. 1983. *Illustrated Introduction to Latin Epigraphy*. Berkeley, CA: University of California Press.

Knight, S. 2003. *Historical Scripts from Classical Times to the Renaissance*. New Castle, DE: Oak Knoll Press.

Nisbet, R. G. M. 1979. "Elegiacs by Gallus from Qasr Ibrîm." *JRS* 69: 125–55.

Nordenfalk, C. 1976. "Introduction." In *Vergilius Augusteus: Vollständige Faksimile-Ausgabe.* Graz: Staatsbibliothek Preussischer Kulturbesitz.

Wright, D. H. 1984. *Vergilius Vaticanus: vollständige Faksimile-Ausgabe im Originalformat des Codex Vaticanus Latinus 3225 der Biblioteca Apostolica Vaticana.* Graz: Akademische Druck- und Verlagsanstalt.

Wright, D. H. 1992. *Codicological Notes on the Vergilius Romanus.* Studi e testi 345. Vatican City: Biblioteca apostolica vaticana.

Wright, D. H. 1993. *The Vatican Vergil.* Berkeley, CA: University of California Press.

Wright, D. H. 2001. *The Roman Vergil and the Origins of Medieval Book Design.* London: British Library.

CHAPTER 7

···

UNCIAL SCRIPT

···

ROBERT G. BABCOCK

UNCIAL is the name used today by Latin palaeographers to designate a type of bilinear, rounded, majuscule book script that is especially distinguished from other ancient majuscule scripts (e.g., Rustic Capital) by the forms of the letters *A* ( ), *D* ( ), *E* ( ), and *M* ( ).[1] A classic example of Uncial script is the *Basilicanus* of Hilary (Plate 7.1; Vatican, Arch. Cap. S. Pietro, D. 182, fol. 298; *CLA* 1.1b). Uncial script is not, in the strictest sense, entirely bilinear (that is, written between two lines); but in the early examples very few letters (e.g., *d*, *h*, *l*, *p*, and *q*) have ascenders or descenders, and these are typically rather short, so the script has a predominantly bilinear appearance. Later examples of the script can exhibit much longer ascenders and descenders, and more letters have them (including *b*, *f*, *g*, and *r*), giving the script a more quadrilinear aspect. Early Uncial script—that is, the script of the fourth or fifth centuries—is distinguished by a writing angle of 45–50°. Beginning in the sixth century, an angle of writing of 90° becomes common for the Uncial hand. Whatever the angle, the heavy shading of the script remains a constant feature; in other words, there is a marked difference between the thick and thin strokes within a letter. More than four hundred books or fragments written in Uncial script survive, dating from the fourth to the ninth centuries; and Uncial continued to be used in later periods as a display script (and for colophons, running heads, titles, etc.) after it had ceased to be used as a text script. The use of Uncial as a display script has been relatively neglected and warrants a more extensive study.

The Uncial script is sometimes said to have been particularly favored for Christian texts.[2] It is certainly the case that the surviving manuscripts in Uncial script predominantly contain Christian works, and those in Rustic Capital script, pagan. To what extent the surviving evidence reflects an intentional choice of script on the part of Late Antique scribes or patrons is less clear. The monumental study by Chatelain, in spite of needing updating in many respects, is the starting place for any investigation of Uncial.[3] The various volumes of Lowe's *CLA* (along with the supplements to the series)

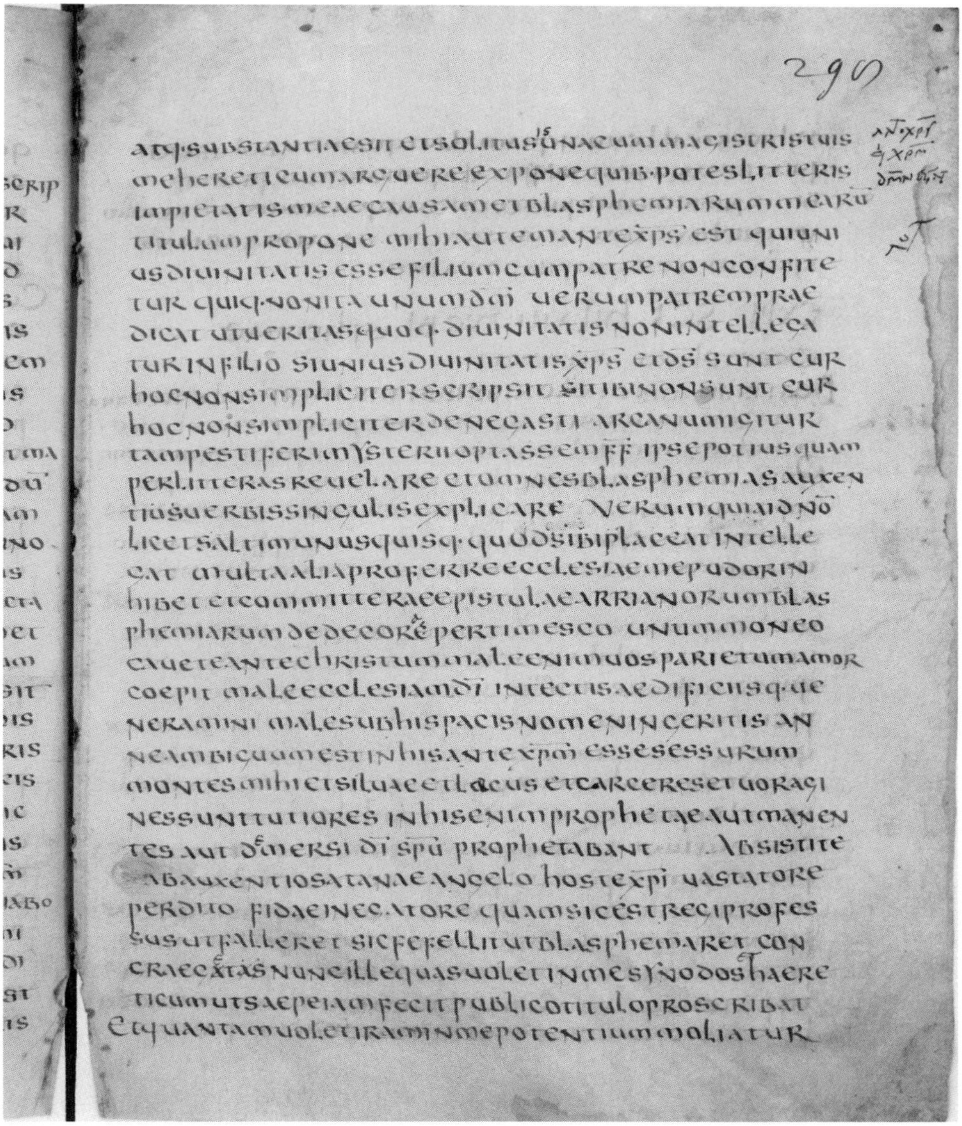

PLATE 7.1 Vatican, Arch. Cap. S. Pietro, D. 182, fol. 298r; *CLA* 1.1b (Hilary): probably Cagliari, Sardinia, saec. VI^in (post 509–10) © 2015 Biblioteca Apostolica Vaticana.

provide a comprehensive listing of the surviving specimens and succinct descriptions of them.[4]

The Latin adjective *uncialis* means "of one ounce" or "of one inch." The term Uncial was introduced to modern scholarship by Jean Mabillon, although he uses it in a broader sense for a variety of types of majuscule script.[5] The source of the name is a passage in Jerome: "Those who want them can have their old books, or those inscribed on purple skins with gold and silver, or executed in what are commonly called 'Uncial letters'—burdens more than codices."[6] Since Jerome is describing, albeit hyperbolically, luxury books of his day that were written in large (or weighty) letters, some readers have assumed that he is talking about a specific type of majuscule script known in his day by the name "Uncial." It is unclear whether Jerome is referring to the size of the letters or the weight of gold or silver used to produce them (or both), although by labeling the books "burdens" he may intend to emphasize the weight of the letters as well as of the volumes. Precisely what type of script Jerome has in mind is not clear from the passage, and it is debatable whether he is even referring to a specific type of script, rather than to the enlarged letters that appear at the beginning of each page in books like the *Vergilius Augusteus*.[7] But the name Uncial has stuck, and since its use by modern palaeographers to describe one particular script type is relatively consistent and specific, there seems little reason to abandon it.

The origins of the script are unclear because of the paucity of surviving Latin manuscripts before the fourth century that are written in book scripts; but Uncial may be described as a descendant of Roman capital script, under cursive influence. The latter contributed to the roundness of the script as well as to specific letterforms (e.g., *a*, *e*, *d*, and *m*).[8] By the fourth century, Uncial is a well-developed script, apparently the product of many generations of evolution and refinement. Earlier specimens of Latin book scripts, for example the fragment of "*De bellis Macedonicis*,"[9] illustrate this developmental stage with their mixture of letters in Rustic Capital, Uncial, Half-uncial, and cursive forms. Such mixed scripts must have been common, and the occasional mingling of elements from other scripts is still found in some of the earliest Uncial manuscripts, as also in some of the later regional types of Uncial (e.g., the b-d Uncial mentioned below).

Dated examples of Uncial writing are extremely rare; but a sufficient body of material from the period between the fourth and the eighth centuries has been preserved to allow, in conjunction with the evidence from the few dated or datable examples, a rough dating of the surviving specimens.[10] The major guideposts for dating Uncial, in chronological order, are the *Codex Vercellensis* of the Gospels, *c.*371 (Plate 7.2; Vercelli, Biblioteca Capitolare, s.n., fol. 267; *CLA* 4.467), the Bodleian manuscript of Jerome's *Chronicle*, after 435 or 442 (Plate 7.3; Oxford, Bodleian Library, Auct. T. II. 26, fol. 121; *CLA* 2.233a), the Berlin Easter Tables, 447, (Berlin, Staatsbibliothek zu Berlin, Lat. qu. 298; *CLA* 8.1053;), the *Basilicanus* of Hilary, after 509/510 (Plate 7.1; *CLA* 1.1b), the *Codex Pisanus* of Justinian, after 533 (Plate 7.4; Florence, BML, s.n., vol. 1, fol. 325r; *CLA* 3.295), the *Codex Fuldensis* of the Gospels, before 546/547 (Fulda, Landesbibliothek, Bonifatianus 1; *CLA* 8.1196), the Toulouse *Canons*, 666/667 (Toulouse, Bibliothèque municipale, 364 + Paris, BnF, Lat. 8901; *CLA* 6.836), the Morgan Augustine from Luxeuil, 669 (New York, Pierpont Morgan Library, M. 334; *CLA* 11.1659), the Bern manuscript of Jerome's *Chronicle*, 699/700 (Bern, Burgerbibliothek, 219; *CLA* 7.860), the Brussels collection of *Varia Patristica* from Soissons, 695–711 (Brussels, Bibliothèque Royale, 9850–2; *CLA* 10.1547a), the *Codex Amiatinus* of the Bible, 681–716 (Plate 7.5; Florence, BML, Amiatino 1, fol. 1006v; *CLA* 3.299), the

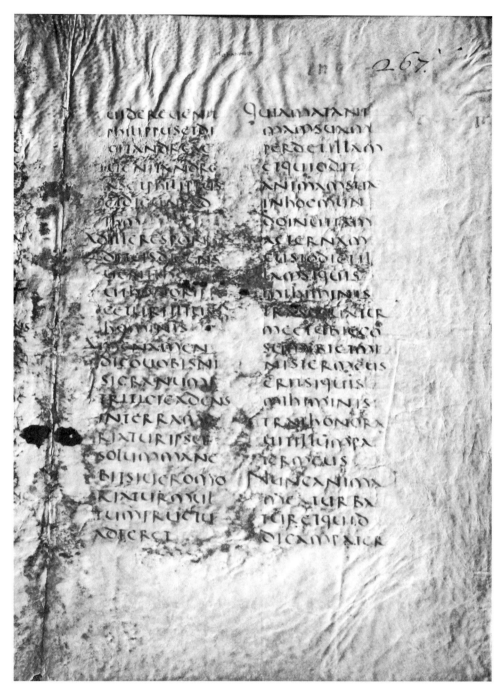

PLATE 7.2 Vercelli, Biblioteca Capitolare, s.n., fol. 267r; *CLA* 4.467 (*Codex Vercellensis* of Gospels): Italy, saec. IV² (*c.*371).

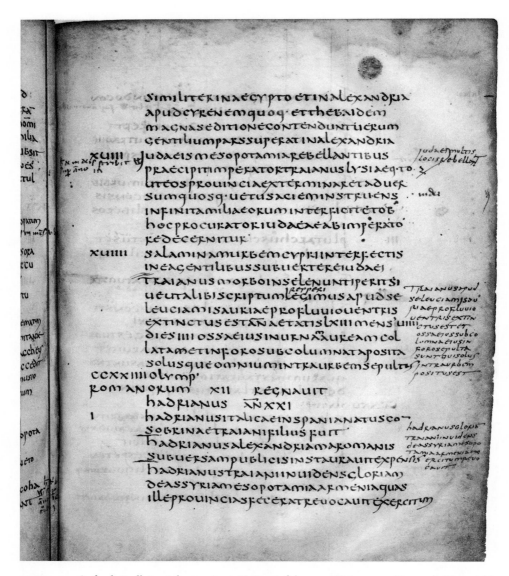

PLATE 7.3 Oxford, Bodleian Library, Auct. T. II. 26, fol. 121r; *CLA* 2.233a (Jerome's *Chronicle*): Italy, saec. V^med (post AD 435 vel 442).

Trier Quodvultdeus, 719 (Trier, Stadtbibliothek, 36; *CLA* 9.1367), the Milan manuscript of Gregory's *Moralia*, around 750 (Plate 7.6; Milan, Biblioteca Ambrosiana, B. 159 sup., fol. 14v; *CLA* 3.309), the Autun Gospels, 754 (Autun, Bibliothèque municipale, 3 (S. 2); *CLA* 6.716), the *Codex Beneventanus* of the Gospels, 736–60 (London, BL, Add. MS 5463; *CLA* 2.162), and the collection of texts in Lucca 490, after 787 (Plate 7.7; Lucca, Biblioteca Capitolare, 490, fol. 322v; *CLA* 3.303e).[11]

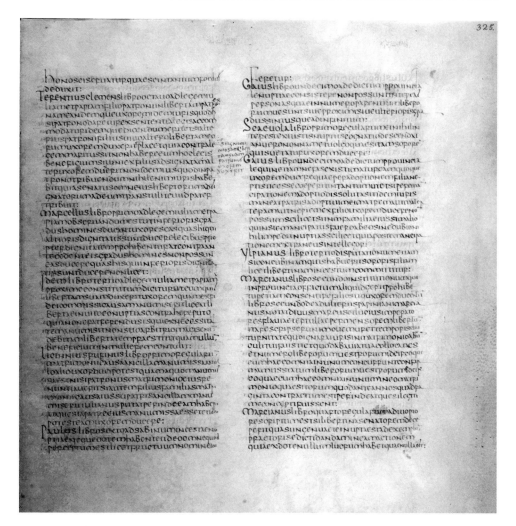

325.

PLATE 7.4 Florence, BML, ms. Pandette s.n., cassetta 1, fol. 325r; *CLA* 3.295 (*Codex Pisanus*, Justinian): Byzantium, saec. VI (soon after 533).

Scholars have identified and described regional variations of the Uncial script that were used in Italy,[12] North Africa,[13] England,[14] France,[15] and the Eastern Empire (Byzantium?).[16] Only from Italy is there surviving material from all periods of the writing of Uncial script; elsewhere, the extant evidence comes from comparatively short periods of production (so, e.g., the North African examples are predominantly from the fourth and fifth centuries, the French from the seventh and eighth). Consequently, the localization and the dating of Uncial manuscripts are intimately connected.

Lowe's naming of the varieties of Uncial script, which can serve to isolate distinct regional and chronological groupings, is primarily based on the *Basilicanus* of Hilary

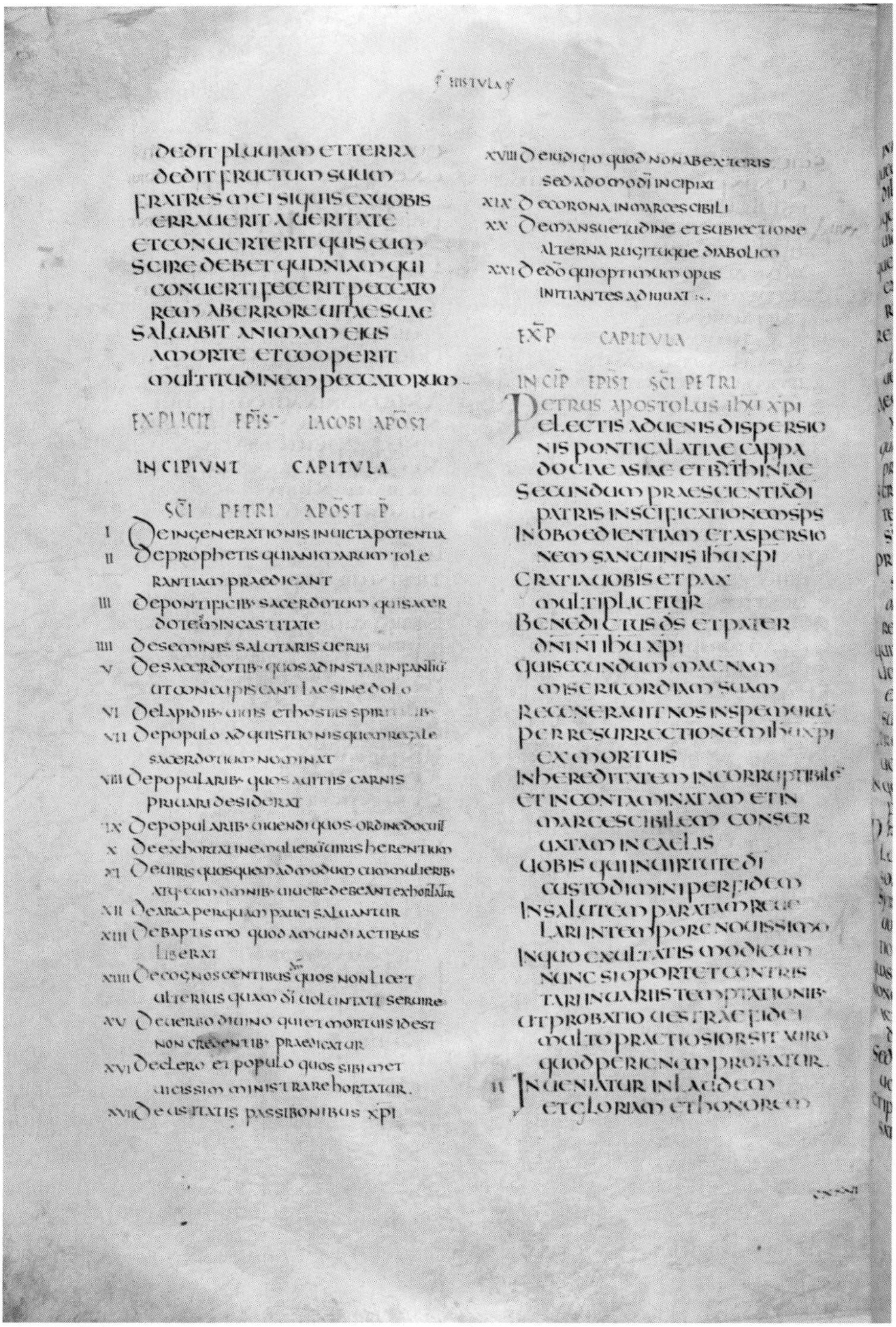

ꝼ EPISTVLA ꝼ

DEDIT PLUUIAM ET TERRA
DEDIT FRUCTUM SUUM
FRATRES MEI SIQUIS EXUOBIS
ERRAUERIT A UERITATE
ET CONUERTERIT QUIS EUM
SCIRE DEBET QUONIAM QUI
CONUERTI FECERIT PECCATO
REM AB ERRORE UITAE SUAE
SALUABIT ANIMAM EIUS
AMORTE ET COOPERIT
MULTITUDINEM PECCATORUM

EXPLICIT EPIS IACOBI APOST

INCIPIUNT   CAPITULA

      SCI PETRI APOST P
I   DE INGENERATIONIS INUICTA POTENTIA
II DE PROPHETIS QUIANIMARUM TOLE
    RANTIAM PRAEDICANT
III DE PONTIFICIBUS SACERDOTUM QUISACER
    DOTES IN CASTITATE
IIII DE SEMINIS SALUTARIS UERBI
V   DE SACERDOTIB QUOS ADINSTAR INFANTIU
    UT OMNI CAPISCANT LAC SINE DOLO
VI DE LAPIDIBUS UIUIS ET HOSTIIS SPIR IB
VII DE POPULO AD QUISITIONIS QUEM REGALE
    SACERDOTIUM NOMINAT
VIII DE POPULARIB QUOS AUT HIS CARNIS
    PRIUARI DESIDERAT
IX DE POPULARIB UIUENDI QUOS ORDINE DOCUIT
X   DE EXHORTATIONE MULIERU TAMIS HERENTIUM
XI DE UIRIS QUOSQUEM ADMODUM CUM MULIERIB
    ATQ CUM OMNIB UIUERE DEBEANT EXHORTATUR
XII DE ARCA PERQUAM PAUCI SALUANTUR
XIII DE BAPTISMO QUOD AMUNDI ACTIBUS
    LIBERAT
XIIII DE COGNOSCENTIBUS QUOS NON LICET
    ALTERIUS QUAM DI UOLUNTATI SERUIRE
XV DE UERBO DIUINO QUIET MORTUIS IDEST
    NON CREDENTIB PRAEDICATUR
XVI DE CLERO ET POPULO QUOS SIBI INET
    UICISSIM MINISTRARE HORTATUR
XVII DE AESTATIS PASSIONIBUS XPI

XVIII DE ERUDICIO QUOD NON ABEXTERIS
    SED ADOMODI INCIPIAT
XIX DE CORONA INMARCESCIBILI
XX DE MANSUETUDINE ET SUBIECTIONE
    ALTERNA RUGITUQUE DIABOLICO
XXI DE EO QUIOPTIMUM OPUS
    INITIANTES ADIUUAT

EXP   CAPITULA

INCIP EPIST SCI PETRI
PETRUS APOSTOLUS IHU XPI
ELECTIS ADUENIS DISPERSIO
NIS PONTI GALATIAE CAPPA
DOCIAE ASIAE ET BITHINIAE
SECUNDUM PRAESCIENTIA DI
PATRIS INSCIFICATIONE MSPS
INOBOEDIENTIAM ET ASPERSIO
NEM SANGUINIS IHU XPI
GRATIA UOBIS ET PAX
MULTIPLICETUR
BENEDICTUS DS ET PATER
DNI NRI IHU XPI
QUISECUNDUM MAGNAM
MISERICORDIAM SUAM
REGENERAUIT NOS INSPEM UIUA
PER RESURRECTIONEM IHU XPI
EX MORTUIS
INHEREDITATEM INCORRUPTIBILE
ET INCONTAMINATAM ET IN
MARCESCIBILEM CONSER
UATAM IN CAELIS
UOBIS QUI IN UIRTUTE DI
CUSTODIMINI PER FIDEM
INSALUTEM PARATAM REUE
LARI INTEMPORE NOUISSIMO
INQUO EXULTATIS MODICUM
NUNC SIOPORTET CONTRIS
TARI IN UARIIS TEMPTATIONIB
ET PROBATIO UESTRAE FIDEI
MULTO PRAETIOSIOR SIT AURO
QUOD PER IGNEM PROBATUR
INUENIATUR IN LAUDEM
ET GLORIAM ET HONOREM

PLATE 7.5 Florence, BML, Amiatino 1, fol. 1006v; *CLA* 3.299 (*Codex Amiatinus* of Bible): Wearmouth or Jarrow, saec. VII–VIII (ante AD 716).

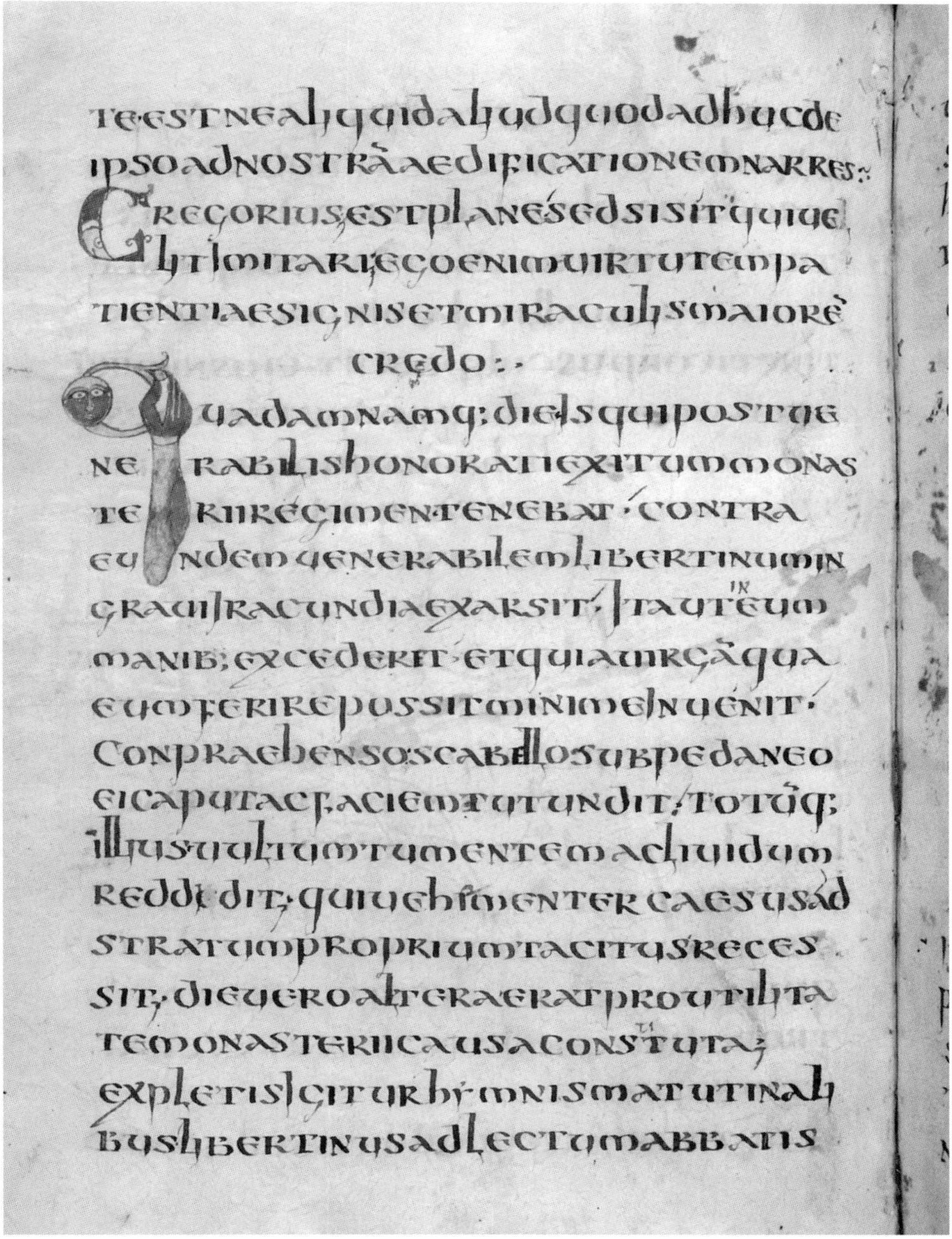

PLATE 7.6 Milan, Biblioteca Ambrosiana, B. 159 sup., fol. 14v; *CLA* 3.309 (Gregory, *Moralia*): Bobbio, saec. VIII[med] (*c*.749).

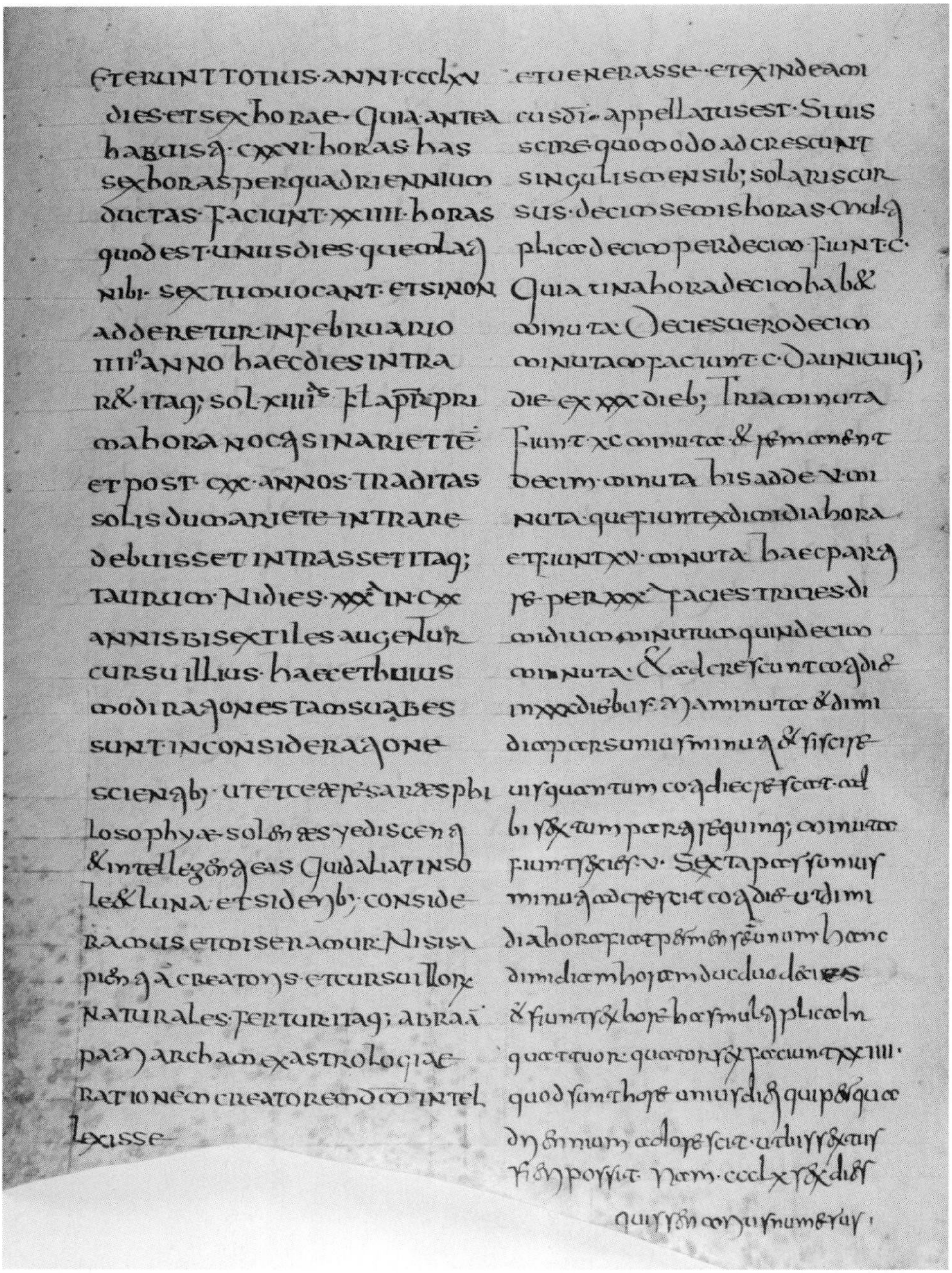

PLATE 7.7 Lucca, Biblioteca Capitolare, 490, fol. 322v; *CLA* 3.303e (Bede): Lucca, saec. VIII–IX (post 787).

(*CLA* 1.1b; Plate 7.1). The forms of the letters in that manuscript are taken by him to be canonical for Uncial script, and variant types are described in terms of their deviations from it.[17] So, for example, "b-uncial" has generally the letterforms found in the *Basilicanus*, with the exception of the *b*, which has the minuscule (or Half-uncial) form; "b-d Uncial" has the *Basilicanus* forms except for its use of minuscule (Half-uncial) *b* and *d*. More work needs to be done in defining stylistic groupings among the surviving manuscripts.

Notes

1. Calligraphers apply the term more broadly to a variety of different modern script types and fonts, most of them characterized, to some extent, by rounded letterforms. Based on similarities of some of their letters and letterforms to the Latin Uncial, some Greek and Coptic scripts are also called Uncial by some scholars.
2. E.g., by Ullman (1932, 66–8).
3. Chatelain (1901–2).
4. Lowe (1934–71); further supplements by Bernhard Bischoff, Virginia Brown, and James John, in *Mediaeval Studies* 47 (1985, 317–66); 54 (1992, 286–307); 58 (1996, 291–303).
5. Mabillon (1709, 47). The restriction of the term to its current palaeographical meaning dates from the publication of Toustain and Tassin (1750–65).
6. "Habeant qui uolunt ueteres libros uel in membranis purpureis auro argentoque descriptos, uel uncialibus, ut uulgo aiunt, litteris onera magis exarata quam codices." Jerome (1975, 1:732).
7. *CLA* 1.13.
8. Cf. Tjäder (1974, 9–40). The third- and fourth-century Greek book script may also have influenced the formation of the Latin Uncial: see, e.g., Cavallo (1967); Cavallo and Maehler (1987).
9. London, BL, Papyrus 745; *CLA* 2.207, a mixed script that is close to Uncial. The dating of this fragment is debated, but it is generally agreed to be before the fourth century.
10. Useful discussions of dating are found in Lowe and Rand (1922); Battelli (1949, 73–80); and Bischoff (1990, 66–72). But the safest guide to the dating of Uncial script comes from E. A. Lowe's discussions in the introductions to the various volumes of *CLA*, and especially from his descriptions in the individual entries in those volumes.
11. This list based on Lowe and Rand (1922) and *CLA*.
12. The fundamental study is that of Petrucci (1971, 75–132).
13. Cf. E. A. Lowe, *CLA*, Suppl., pp. vii–x.
14. Lowe (1960), and Parkes (1982).
15. Cf. Lowe (1924).
16. For Eastern Uncial, see, e.g., *CLA* 10.1535. The descriptions of the peculiar characteristics of these regional variations given in works cited in the Bibliography seem to me to justify calling them distinct types of Uncial script. Battelli (1949, 77) did not consider them regional types, but he wrote before many of the studies cited here were published.
17. Lowe did not, of course, consider the *Basilicanus* to be a standard for judging the quality of Uncial script, just a well-known example of the script, whose letterforms could be compared and contrasted with other examples in order to pinpoint the distinctions. So the *Basilicanus* is canonical only in so far as naming some of the variants of Uncial script.

BIBLIOGRAPHY

Battelli, G. 1949. *Lezioni di paleografia*. Vatican City: Libreria Editrice Vaticana.

Bischoff, B. 1990. *Latin Paleography*. Cambridge: Cambridge University Press.

Cavallo, G. 1967. *Ricerche sulla maiuscola biblica*. Florence: Le Monnier.

Cavallo, G. and H. Maehler. 1987. *Greek Bookhands of the Early Byzantine Period, A. D. 300–800*. London: University of London, Institute of Classical Studies.

Chatelain, É. 1901–1902. *Uncialis scriptura*. 2 vols. Paris: Welter.

Jerome. 1975. *Prologus in libro Iob de hebraeo translato*. In R. Weber, *Biblia sacra iuxta Vulgatam versionem*, 2 vols. Stuttgart: Württembergische Bibelanstalt, 1:732.

Lowe, E. A. 1924. *Codices Lugdunenses antiquissimi. Le scriptorium de Lyon, la plus ancienne école calligraphique de France*. Lyons: : Société des amis de la bibliothèque.

Lowe, E. A. 1934–71. *Codices Latini Antiquiores*. 11 vols. + Supplement. Oxford: Clarendon Press.

Lowe, E. A. 1960. *English Uncial*. Oxford: Clarendon Press.

Lowe, E. A. and E. K. Rand. 1922. *A Sixth-Century Fragment of the Letters of Pliny the Younger*. Washington D.C.: Carnegie Institution.

Mabillon, J. 1709. *De re diplomatica*, 2nd ed. Paris: Robustel.

Parkes, M. B. 1982. *The Scriptorium of Wearmouth-Jarrow*. Jarrow Lecture. Jarrow: St. Paul's Church.

Petrucci, A. 1971. "L'onciale romana. Origini, sviluppo e diffusione di una stilizzazione grafica altomedievale (sec. vi–ix)," *Studi Medievali*, ser. 3, 12: 75–132.

Tjäder, J.-O. 1974. "Der Ursprung der Unzialschrift," *Basler Zeitschrift für Geschichte und Altertumskunde* 74: 9–40.

Toustain, C.-F. and R.-P. Tassin. 1750–65. *Nouveau traité de diplomatique*. 6 vols. Paris: G. Desprez.

Ullman, B. L. 1932. *Ancient Writing and its Influence*. New York: Longmans.

CHAPTER 8

···

HALF-UNCIAL

···

ROBERT G. BABCOCK

HALF-UNCIAL, also called Semi-uncial, is a minuscule script, that is to say, the letters are written between four lines: the shafts of *b, d, f, h, l*, and tall *s* normally ascend above the height of the minims, and the tails of *g, p*, and *q* (and occasionally of other letters) normally descend below the baseline. The Half-uncial script was used as a book hand from the fourth century through the eighth; after that it served as a display or ornamental script for another century or more, most notably in Tours bibles. The canonical form of Half-uncial has the modern miniscule (lower-case Roman) forms of *b, d, e, m*, and *r*. The letter *a* has a short, straight shaft, and the bowl of the letter is large and round; *g* has a flat top at the height of the minims and does not form a bowl at the top; it has an elongated, sinuous tail, descending below the baseline (similar in appearance to the Arabic numeral 3).[1] The *s* has a tall, straight shaft and resembles the minuscule *r* (which itself often resembles the miniscule *n*). The *s* is distinguished from the *r* by having a continuous arch for a shoulder, whereas the shoulder of the *r* breaks downward and then rises again. The *n* has the capital form (*N*). The script is written with the pen at a 90° angle to the baseline, so the tall vertical strokes are straight and upright, not rounded as in the Uncial hand.

A comprehensive account of the script was written for the first time in 2018 by Tino Licht; much of the surviving material is illustrated by Émile Chatelain;[2] and the individual items are all described and illustrated in *CLA* and its supplements by E. A. Lowe and his successors.[3] Dated examples of the script are especially scarce; the earliest surviving ones are from the sixth century: the *Basilicanus* of Hilary, ante 509/510 (Plate 8.1; Vatican, Arch. Cap. S. Pietro, D. 182, fol. 159v; *CLA* 1.1a),[4] the Sulpicius Severus in Verona, signed by the scribe Ursicinus, from 517 (Verona, Biblioteca Capitolare, XXXVIII (36); *CLA* 4.494), and the Monte Cassino Ambrosiaster, 570/571 (Plate 8.2; Monte Cassino, Biblioteca dell'Abbazia, MS 150, p. 270; *CLA* 3.374a).

Though widely used for books in the early Middle Ages, Half-uncial script seems not to have been as popular as Uncial, of which approximately four times as many examples survive.[5] It is, however, possible that the surviving evidence, which is probably skewed towards the greater survival of more luxurious volumes, provides

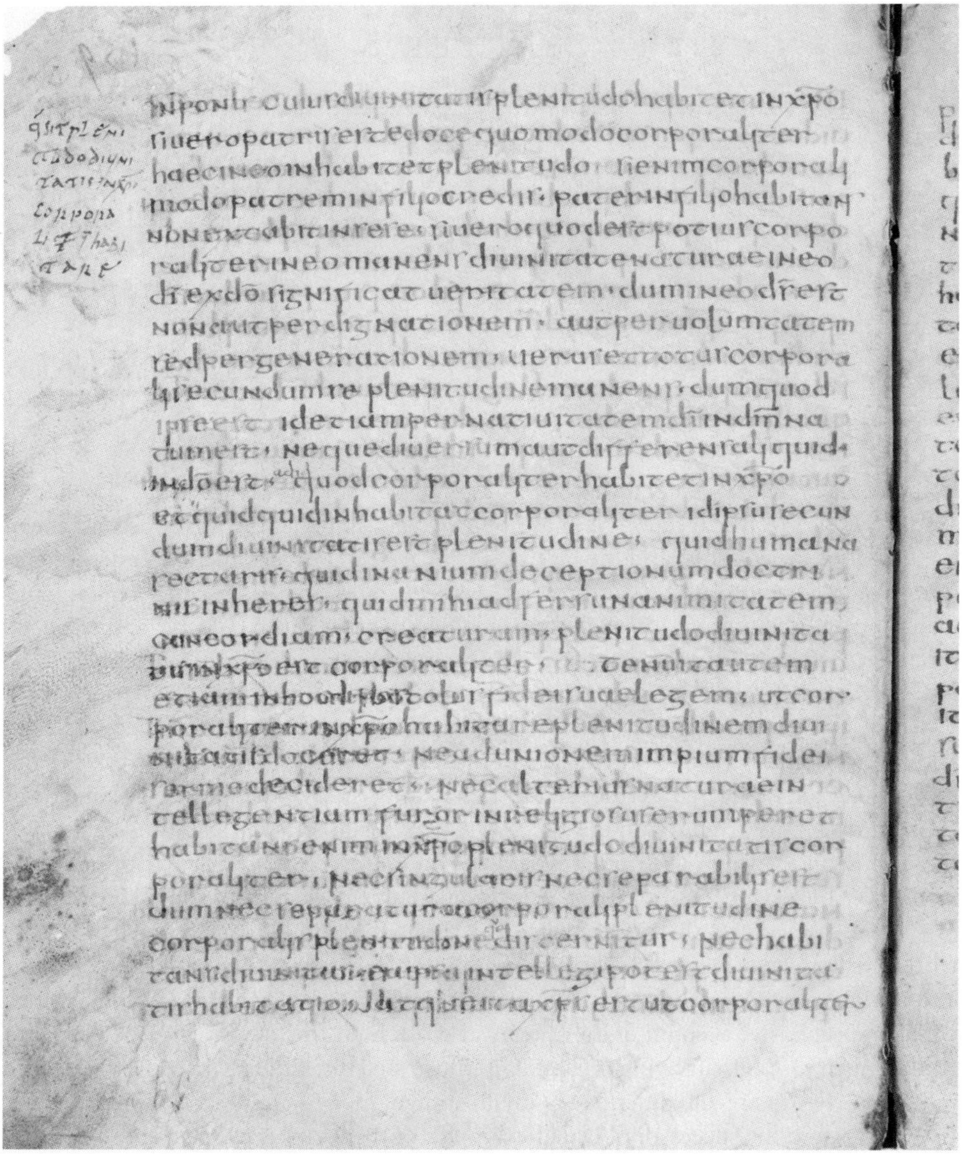

PLATE 8.1 Vatican, Arch. Cap. S. Pietro, D. 182, fol. 159v; *CLA* 1.1a (Hilary): probably Cagliari, Sardinia, sec. V–VI (ante AD 509–10).

an inaccurate picture of the relative popularity of Uncial and Half-uncial as book hands during the periods when both were in widespread use. In the hierarchy of scripts in medieval manuscripts, Half-uncial sometimes appears in a subordinate role to Uncial, and it is used for less formal parts of the text. The continuing use of Half-uncial in the ninth century, for instance in Tours bibles, reflects its position as a script that is less

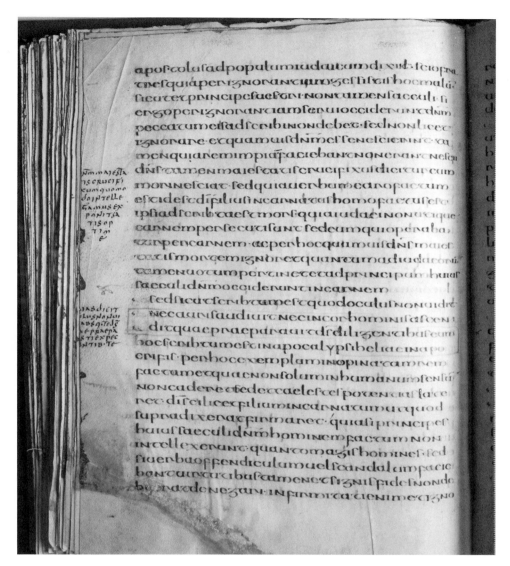

PLATE 8.2 Monte Cassino, Archivio dell'Abbazia, cod. 150, p. 270; *CLA* 3.374a (Ambrosiaster): South Italy, saec. VI² (ante AD 570).

formal than Uncial, but more formal than Carolingian minuscule. In addition to its survival in the ninth century at Tours, Half-Uncial was also used as an ornamental script in that period at Corbie and Reims (see Plate 8.3; New Haven, Beinecke Library, MS 413, fol. 7v).[6] The most enduring legacy of the script is its influence (direct or indirect) on the formation of Insular minuscule, to which it contributed a number of letterforms still in use in modern Gaelic fonts, most notably the form of *g*.

The script must have been developed in the first centuries of the Common Era, but evidence for the earliest phases of the script is sparse. The name Half-Uncial was

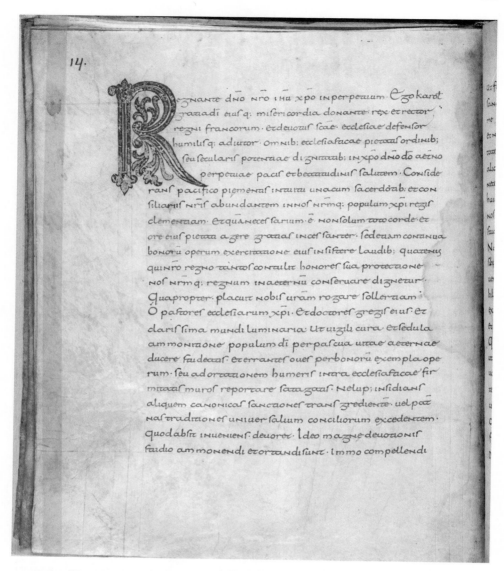

PLATE 8.3 New Haven, Beinecke Library, MS 413, fol. 7v (Capitularies): "a court scriptorium for Charles the Bald, 873 or later."

applied to the script by modern scholars, who considered it a reduced version of Uncial, with letterforms roughly half the size of those of the Uncial script.[7] But the name is misleading, for Half-uncial is not derived from Uncial. It developed principally from ancient cursive script ("Ancient Common Writing"), of which it is a calligraphic elaboration, employed as a book hand. There are a few surviving examples from the first centuries of the Common Era of hybrid scripts combining some elements of capital, Uncial, and/or cursive scripts with some that are typical of the later fully formed Half-uncial. The celebrated fragment of a papyrus roll known as the "*Epitome Livii*" (London, BL, Papyrus 1532; *CLA* 2.208), perhaps dating from the late third or early fourth century, is one such early example of a miniscule script with many of the characteristics of Half-uncial (it has the Half-uncial forms of *b*, *d*, *m*, and *r*; but not of *a*, *e*, *g*, or *s*).[8]

Half-uncial is the most calligraphic of a group of similar—and perhaps related—miniscule scripts used in the Late Antique and early medieval periods, many of them markedly more cursive than canonical Half-uncial.[9] Some of these are differentiated by scholars as distinct scripts, and labeled "quarter-uncial," "cursive Half-uncial" *vel sim*. Too few examples survive to allow a coherent account of the development and use of these scripts types, or subtypes. But since they are, in general, more cursive than Half-uncial, it is likely that they were generally used for less formal writing. If they served their practitioners as casual, everyday hands, it is likely that they were influential not only in the development of the various miniscule scripts (Carolingian, Insular, Visigothic, etc.), but also in the development of and the changes to the Uncial and Half-uncial scripts over the centuries.

NOTES

1. To be more precise, it resembles the shape of 3 in the Harrington font.
2. Licht (2018); Chatelain (1901–2, plates 61–100).
3. Lowe (1934–71); further supplements by Bernhard Bischoff, Virginia Brown, and James John, in *Medieval Studies* 47 (1985, 317–66); 54 (1992, 286–307); 58 (1996, 291–303).
4. The same volume has portions in Uncial and in Half-uncial, and it is equally important for the study of both scripts. On this manuscript, see Boyle (2001, 105–17).
5. Cf. Boyle (1984, 76).
6. According to Bischoff (2004: 2, 311), the volume was written in a "Hofskriptorium für Karl den Kahlen, 873 oder später."
7. It seems that the first scholars to describe the script in its modern sense, distinguishing it from Uncial, on the one hand, and from other types of miniscule script, on the other, were Tassin and Toustain (1750–65: 3, 204–6, who refer to it as "demi-onciale." Although they identify the script by its characteristic letters, they take the name to refer entirely to the size of the script.
8. Lowe (*CLA* 2.208, 1st ed., 1935) dates the script "sec. III–IV"; in the second edition of *CLA* vol. 2 (1972), Lowe dates the fragment earlier, "III¹"; Mallon (1952, 80–9 and 180–1 dates the fragment to the second or third century; Cavallo (2008, 170) opts for Lowe's first dating. A careful examination is provided by Ammirati (2008–9, 58–60).
9. Examples in Seider (1972).

BIBLIOGRAPHY

Ammirati, S. 2008–9. "Bibliologia e codicologia del libro latino antico." Dottorato di ricerca, Università degli Studi Roma Tre.

Bischoff, B. 2004. *Katalog der festländischen Handschriften des neunten Jahrhunderts: (mit Ausnahme der wisigotischen)*, vol. 2. Wiesbaden: Harrasowitz.

Boyle, L. 1984. *Medieval Latin Palaeography: A Bibliographical Introduction.* Toronto: University of Toronto Press.

Boyle, L. 2001. "The 'Basilicanus' of Hilary Revisited." In *Integral Palaeography,* ed. Leonard Boyle, 105–17. Turnhout: Brepols.

Cavallo, G. 2008. "La scrittura greca e latina dei papiri. Una introduzione." *Studia erudita* 8: 170.

Chatelain, É. 1901–2. *Uncialis Scriptura.* 2 vols. Paris: Welter.

Licht, T. 2018. *Halbunziale.* Stuttgart: Hiersemann.

Lowe, E. A. 1934–71. *Codices Latini Antiquiores.* 11 vols. with Supplement. Oxford: Clarendon Press.

Mallon, J. 1952. *Paléographie romaine.* Madrid: Consejo Superior de Investigaciones Científicas, Instituto Antonio de Nebrija, de Filología.

Seider, R. 1972. *Paläographie der lateinischen Papyri.* Stuttgart: A. Hiersemann.

Tassin, R.-P. and C.-F. Toustain. 1750–65. *Nouveau traité de diplomatique.* 6 vols. Paris: G. Desprez.

CHAPTER 9

GREEK SCRIPT IN LATIN MANUSCRIPTS

WALTER BERSCHIN
(Translated by Robert G. Babcock)

THE Greek alphabet is found in a considerable number of Latin manuscripts of the late antique and medieval periods, for it is imbedded in the text of such widely circulated works as Isidore of Seville's *Etymologiae* (I, 3, 6–9), Bede's *De temporum ratione* (ch. 1), Rabanus Maurus' *De computo* (ch. 7), and Hugh of St. Victor's *De grammatica* (ch. 1). Frequently the numerical value of the Greek letters is also provided in such works. An alphabet table, entitled *Formae litterarum secundum Grecos*, survives from the school of Alcuin. It includes variant forms of some of the Greek letters, phonetic transcriptions of the names of the letters, Roman equivalents, and numerical values of the letters up to 900.[1] The most remarkable, yet also typical Western variant that is found in this alphabet table is the "M-siglum,")–(for M. Also characteristic of Western practice is the interchange of H and E, Y and I, Θ and T, ω and O; or, to put it more precisely, the preference in the West for employing the "Greek-looking" letters H, Y, Θ, and ω, instead of E, I, T, and O. This preference accounts for the widespread practice in the High Middle Ages of cloaking the *nomen sacrum* 'Christus' in hyper-Greek forms like XPYCΘI (*Christi*). The signs for the numbers 6, 90, and 900 appear in widely diverging forms in Western manuscripts. The sign Ꝡ for 900 is frequently misunderstood (as in the *Formae litterarum secundum Grecos,* where it has the form ↑); likewise often confused is the sign ⊢ for the rough-breathing mark (*spiritus asper*), which was known from Isidore (*Etym.* I, 19, 10). The Greek letters used in the West during the Middle Ages were consistently majuscule in form; they were written in Uncial script. The new minuscule Greek alphabet appears in only a few precious examples from the ninth and tenth centuries, and even in the High Middle Ages it is found only sporadically. In his *Grammatica*, Roger Bacon (died 1292) taught both the majuscule and minuscule alphabets.[2]

In the monastic scriptoria of the Latin West, the Greek alphabet was used for encryption or for giving ornamental emphasis to proper names,[3] subscriptions (e.g., A)–(HN), quire signatures, etc. The *Epistola formata*, a letter of recommendation for traveling clerics, employed Greek for a practical purpose; certain characters were encoded as Greek numbers in order to protect the document from being forged.[4] Additionally, alphabet tables provided Latin scribes with the ability to reproduce correctly the Greek words found so abundantly in the works of Late Latin writers like Lactantius, Jerome, Macrobius, Servius, and Priscian. Many scribes attempted to do this; and even when the surrounding Latin characters were written in minuscule script, the majuscule script was maintained for writing the Greek characters. The medieval efforts at rendering these Greek words were rarely flawless, and the proper restoration of these texts was left to the humanists.

Greek-Latin glossaries were, on occasion, copied in the early Middle Ages. One example is the "Cyrillus-Glossary" preserved in a manuscript of the eighth century that formerly belonged to the library of Nicholas of Cusa, and is today in London.[5] Closely related to this glossary is the one found in Laon, Bibliothèque municipale, MS 444; it was produced by Irishmen in Laon in the second half of the ninth century. There are no surviving manuscripts from the High or Late Middle Ages preserving any of the substantial ancient glossaries of Greek.

Greek texts of any substantial length copied by Western scribes are rare before the humanist period. Bilingual Greek-Latin manuscripts of books of the Bible constitute the largest group of such texts. A representative example is the Acts of the Apostles preserved in Oxford, Bodleian Library, Laud gr. 35, which was written in Greek and Latin uncials around the year 600. There are also surviving bilinguals of the Pauline Epistles,[6] of the Gospels, and especially of the Psalter. These bilinguals do not all employ Greek script. The oldest extant bilingual of the Psalter, Verona, Biblioteca Capitolare I(1), is written entirely in Latin characters, and so also is the *Psalterium quadrupartitum* of Salomo III of Constance, the most frequently copied bilingual of the medieval period.[7] Among the works of the High Middle Ages, the bilingual liturgical and polemical treatises of Abbot Nicholas-Nectarius of Otranto (1220–35) deserve special notice.[8] The Dominican preacher Buonaccorsi of Bologna (died *c*.1275) continued in the same tradition with his bilingual Latin-Greek *Thesaurus veritatis fidei*.

The Greek theologian who attracted the most attention in the medieval West was Dionysius the Areopagite. Considerable effort was expended in trying to interpret his works, and there were multiple attempts at translation.[9] Robert Grosseteste, bishop of Lincoln (1235–53), produced a *Corpus Dionysiacum* in Greek minuscule script, combining works by Dionysius with scholia, introductions, biographies, etc. "In the meticulous care with which [the Greek script of the manuscript] is made to hang from the ruled line instead of standing on it as Latin would, it rivals the most Greek of Greek manuscripts."[10]

A new period for Greek studies in the West began with the arrival of Greek teachers from Constantinople. Manuel Chrysoloras, who began teaching Greek in Florence in 1397, composed a Greek grammar, the *Erōtēmata tēs ellinikēs glōssēs*, which, after it was translated into Latin by Guarino of Verona, made it possible for anyone who so desired to attain proficiency in Greek. All the same, the typical medieval teaching tools continued to be widely used: in 1516 in Basel, Johannes Froben printed for his son an *Alphabetum graecum*; and many more such volumes followed in the course of the sixteenth century.[11]

NOTES

1. The best witness to this table is in Vienna, Österreichische Nationalbibliothek, 795, fol. 19r. It is illustrated in Berschin (1988, 2).
2. Nolan and Hirsch (1902, 7).
3. E.g., HEPI)-(ANNUS = Herimannus. Manitius (1911, 609–10) refers to this eleventh-century author as "Hepidannus."
4. The text of the *Regula formatarum* can be found in Berschin (1988, 71–2).
5. London, BL, Harley 5792, Goetz and Gundermann (1888, 215–483 [*glossae graeco-latina*] and 487–506 [*idiomata*]).
6. Frede (1964); Berschin (2007).
7. Cf. Berschin (2005).
8. Hoeck and Loenertz, (1965, 79–82 and 88–105).
9. Chevallier (1937–50).
10. Barbour (1957–61).
11. *Alphabetum Graecum* (1516).

BIBLIOGRAPHY

Alphabetum Graecum, Oratio dominica, Angelica Salutatio, Symbolum Apostolorum . . . Graece et latine, In usum iuventutis Graecarum adyta literarum subingressurae. 1516. Basle: Johannes Froben. Universitätsbibliothek, Basel, *Bc VI 9:1* VD16 A 1945 ; Hieronymus/Griechischer Geist, Nr. 19.

Barbour, R. 1957–61. "A Manuscript of Ps.-Dionysius Areopagita Copied for Robert Grosseteste," *The Bodleian Library Record* 6: 401–16.

Berschin, W. 1988. *Greek Letters and the Latin Middle Ages*, tr. Jerold C. Frakes. Washington, D.C.: Catholic University of America Press.

Berschin, W. 2005. "Neun *Psalteria quadrupartita* Solomons III. von Konstanz (Abt von St. Gallen 890-920)." In *Mittellateinische Studien*, 1: 203–13. Heidelberg: Mattes.

Berschin, W. 2007. "Die griechisch-lateinische Paulus-Handschrift der Reichenau 'Codex Paulinus Augiensis' (Cambridge, Trinity College, B.17.1)." *Zeitschrift für die Geschichte des Oberrheins* 155: 1–17.

Chevallier, P. ed. 1937–50. *Dionysiaca*, vols. 1–2. Paris and Bruges: Desclée, de Brouwer & Cie.

Frede, H. 1964. *Altlateinische Paulus-Handschriften.* Freiburg im Breisgau: Herder.

Goetz, G. and G. Gundermann, et al., eds. 1888. *Corpus Glossariorum Latinorum*, vol. 2. Leipzig: B. G. Teubner.

Hoeck, J. and R. J. Loenertz. 1965. *Nikolaos-Nektarios von Otranto Abt von Casole*. Ettal: Buch-Kunstverlag.

Manitius, M. 1911. *Geschichte der lateinischen Literatur des Mittelalters*, vol. 1. Munich: C. H. Beck.

Nolan, E. and S. A. Hirsch, eds. 1902. *The Greek Grammar of Roger Bacon.* Cambridge: Cambridge University Press.

I . 3

EARLY MEDIEVAL HANDS

CHAPTER 10

··

BENEVENTAN (SOUTH ITALIAN/LANGOBARDIC) SCRIPT

··

FRANCIS NEWTON

THE high *auctoritas* of E. A. Lowe has singled out the name "Beneventan" (not from the city name, but from the medieval duchy, "ducatus Beneventanus") for the dominant script of Southern Italy in the Middle Ages. The same scholar provided, in his masterpiece of 1914, what Bernhard Bischoff has called a "biography" of the script. The book is a model for "study in regional palaeography," as Lowe put it, rich in detail and thoroughly researched. In one aspect, however, recent scholarship has suggested the limitations of its nature as "biography": the biological, evolutionary paradigm serves as a straitjacket that does not allow scope for describing the polymorphic richness of the script. Beneventan, it seems, did not trace a single, unitary, undeviating development; instead, it achieved a number of canonical types (the term "canonical" is borrowed from Cavallo 1970, 134), each characterized by its own individual and independent calligraphic ideal.

The Beneventan book script is first attested, as far as is now known, in Monte Cassino, Archivio e Biblioteca dell'Abbazia, 753, a manuscript of Isidore of the second half of the eighth century. The descent of this script type from a variety of Roman cursive is evident in the letters *a* like two *c*'s and *t* with loop to left, and in the ligatures. The non-*t* ligatures are as follows: *ae, ct, ei, et, fi, gi, li, nt, rum, ri, rp, sp, st, sti, xp*. The ligatures of *t* plus vowel are particularly interesting; Beneventan had a complete set of these available for *ta, te, ti* (hard), *ti* (soft or assibilated), *to*, and *tu*. In its developed form, Beneventan script reflected speech patterns closely: the *ti*, when hard, was written with the former ligature; when soft, with the latter. So the word "iustitia" would illustrate both types: the first *ti* the hard ligature, the second, the soft.

Of the ligatures, only the *ei, fi, gi, li, ri,* and the two *ti*'s were obligatory. *I*-longa (▎), the tall form of the letter *i,* is obligatory at the beginning of a word, unless the next letter has an ascender (under the principle of dissimilation of forms), and always when it is the consonantal *i.* The most characteristic Beneventan abbreviations are, especially, *au* with macron above for "autem," and the *ei* ligature with stroke through the tail for "eius" (ℭ). The punctuation is notable; the mark for a full stop consists of comma surmounted by two dots. But most striking is the suprascript "2 sign" (✓) for raised pitch or raised volume (a better term than "interrogation sign"). It stands over the interrogative word or first word in a question or exclamation, as (the 2 sign stands over the part in italics) in Venice, Biblioteca Nazionale Marciana, Marc. Z. L. 497 when the mother frog in Horace's fable asks: "Num *tanto*" ("Was it *this much* bigger?"), and in Monte Cassino, Archivio e Biblioteca dell'Abbazia, 75, when Gregory quotes Luke's Gospel: "V*e* vobis divitibus" ("*Woe* unto you that are rich!"). Alongside it is the "assertion-sign" (⊢), which cancels an earlier 2 sign or negates the implication that the word it stands above can be interrogative. Related to this is the heavy grave bar, used in some Beneventan centers, especially Benevento itself, for exclamation. Beneventan punctuation was subtle, far beyond that of most medieval scripts.

Recent research has shown that the productivity and duration of Beneventan script was greater than had been thought. Lowe in his survey listed about 600 manuscripts or fragments in Beneventan. The investigations of the late Virginia Brown (2012) have expanded this to more than 2000 items. The same heroic scholar has discovered that, far from dying out at the end of the thirteenth century, as had been supposed, the script was in use in the sixteenth century.

THE EARLY STAGE

The earliest dated (and placed) manuscripts in this hand fall at the end of the eighth century and were produced at Monte Cassino or, possibly, also Benevento (Plate 10.1). These early examples, crabbed and charming, do not approach calligraphy. Spacing seems arbitrary. Word separation has hardly been begun. Some hands show lateral spacing that echoes the amplitude and breadth of uncial script; these tend to possess more contrast between thick and thin strokes. Other hands emphasize the contrast between tall ascenders and the short, cramped space between head line and baseline; here the strokes are more uniform throughout. In either type, the abundant ligatures (especially those with *e,* such as *en, er, te*) create knots of letters that militate strongly against regularity. Occasionally in this early period a ligature may have two forms, as *fi* with *i* depending from the top of the *f* (the form that endures), or from its cross bar. The letter *m* may be abbreviated by a macron above the head line or else by a quite

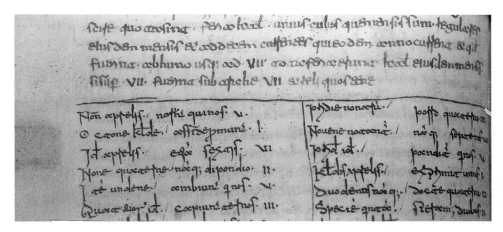

PLATE 10.1 Cava 3 (a. 779–97), Isidore; *Kalendarium*, etc., fol. 67v. A single page shows the two main early Beneventan types. Both types show the characteristic Beneventan *a* and *t* with loop closed. Above, the low, broad, stately look with uncial proportions and rather few abbreviations, aside from the most basic calendarial ones. The *ri* and *ra* ligatures are notable; *rr* forms a narrow knot. Below, a dashing, laterally compressed type of early Beneventan, with tall ascenders (including tall *d* often), tall *s* having a swaying shaft; many abbreviations. This hand is rich in ligatures, including *tu* in "Quattuor." The suprascript stroke for final *m* is like a fine *s*; that for *ur* is 3-shaped and upright.

strictly vertical 3-shaped sign. The *c* may have two forms, the usual one, or the broken one (**c**, **c**), the latter a standard feature of the later Bari type. The parts that may achieve regularity are (where present) the headings in late uncial—well formed and well spaced.

There is a strong similarity between the Beneventan script of Monte Cassino in an early stage and the contemporary (early ninth century) script of the famous house of Nonantola, near Modena, so strong a similarity that the unwary novice might confuse them. Cencetti saw the Nonantola type as the model for the Monte Cassino one; Palma (1979 and 1983) has refuted this thesis and sees the influence as running from Monte Cassino northward. By the middle of the ninth century the Nonantola type had disappeared under the domination of Caroline over all of Northern Italy and much of Central Italy, but in its period of efflorescence Nonantola achieved a regular and splendid calligraphic penmanship.[1]

By the latter half of the ninth century, Beneventan itself had, at times, developed a new regularity and clarity in many specimens (Plate 10.2). Word separation is strikingly improved. In this period, the broader style survives, with its uncialesque look and with contrast between thick and thin strokes, alongside the quite different laterally compressed form with no breaking or contrast in the minims and with relatively tall verticals for the ascenders. The tight knots of *e*-ligatures have opened up laterally so as no longer to impede the flow of script to so great an extent.

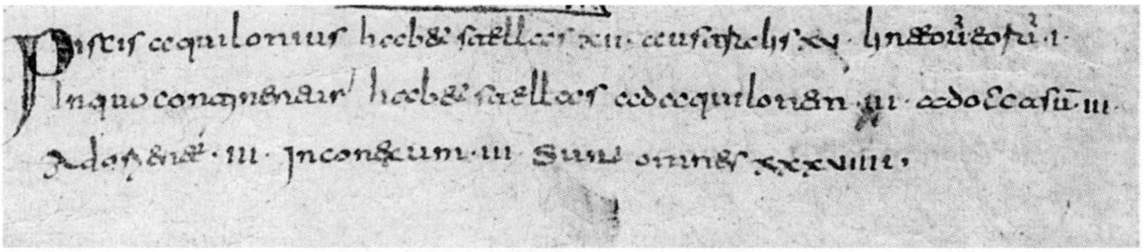

PLATE 10.2 MC 3 (a. 874–92), Alcuin; *astronomica*; *computi*, etc., p. 184. In this broad type the *a* is open; double *c* has both common and broken forms, for *variatio*. The ligatures are relatively well spaced (e.g., early *tu* in "continentur"). The only abbreviation in these three lines is the macron or 3-shaped stroke for final *m*.

THE TENTH CENTURY

After the disaster of the sack of their monastery by the Saracens in 883, the Cassinese community took refuge, first in Teano, and then in Capua. It was a period of exile, until Abbot Aligern reestablished the monks in their own mountain-top home above ancient Casinum in 950. But from a cultural and specifically palaeographical point of view, the period of exile was not a matter of marking time. The manuscript Monte Cassino, Archivio e Biblioteca dell'Abbazia, 175, *Regula S. Benedicti* and other texts (Plate 10.3), is in fact a great repository of the community's traditions. As such, it is written in a style that shows a conscious striving towards a script of greater dignity and clarity. Both vertically, with an evenly observed baseline, and laterally with careful spacing of letters and words, the writing reveals a new measured and deliberately handsome concern for showing honor to this fundamental text. As the angels flanking the central mandorla bow in homage to Christ as Light (LUX), the surrounding display capitals for incipit and opening word—no longer uncial—and the chastened, ordered Beneventan for the text below combine to mark a new level of respect for the words of the saint, a level not seen before (so far as is now known) in Cassinese history.

It may be that Naples possessed the first truly calligraphic form of our script. Lowe (1929) compared the description of the reign of Duke John of that city (928–68) preserved in a Bamberg codex, with the surviving manuscripts from the era. His brilliant discovery enabled him to identify the tattered, stained Livy leaves now in Prague (Universitní knihovna, VII A 16/9) and the Josephus, the first part of a MS (Monte Cassino 123) in the same style of Beneventan writing, with the Chronicler's reference to "ioseppum . . . et Titum Livium," written for Duke John. These two in turn permitted the identification of other books in the same style as Neapolitan products, such as Naples, Biblioteca Nazionale,. ex-Vindob. lat 6, which contains a Virgil, and Vatican City, BAV, Vat. lat. 3317, which contains Servius (Plate 10.4). The layout has an ordered disposition of strokes between head line and baseline, with ascenders rising relatively high above that upper line; straight-backed *d* is often preferred to the uncial

PLATE 10.3 MC 175 (915–34), Paulus Diaconus, *Commentarius in Regulam S. Benedicti*, p. 3. This refined version of the laterally compressed Beneventan (tall ascenders, as in *i*-longa (in "inclina"), and descenders) shows delicately curving *ri* and *et* ligatures and shoulder of the final *r*. The three-part final punctuation (after "recesseras") is evenly balanced; indeed, the entire effect is one of balance and control. The 3-shaped *m*-abbreviation stroke now inclines, in careful relationship to the right side of the vowel it stands over.

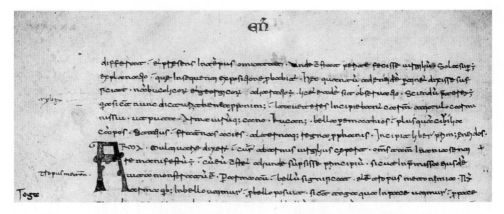

PLATE 10.4 Vat. lat. 3317 (saec. x^2), Servius, fol. 86v. This beautiful script foreshadows the later Fine Script; there is little contrast in thickness of the strokes, an effect as of writing by stylus. The lowercase letters are strongly confined within head line and baseline, except for the rogue letter c; the continuous head line is clear in such words as "ueteres" (l. 4) and "teste" (last line). Relatively new is the abbreviation for "-tur" by t with comma above. "Est" is abbreviated both by e with macron above and by the "division sign." The 2-shaped sign for a question (over "cur" in l. 7) is here, unusually, employed for an indirect question. The lemma "ARMA" in majuscules shows that those letter forms were less carefully worked out than was the minuscule. The running head at top (for *Aeneid*) is a later Gothic addition.

form, and this adds to the vertical emphasis. Word separation is perspicuous. The minims are bent, more uniformly than in earlier Beneventan. The 3-shaped m-stroke is now inclined, upper left to lower right. The older ligatures with e have been unknotted or loosened, to make a smooth line of script. The effect is one of enormous finesse and spidery grace.

Two famous rolls, Rome, Biblioteca Casanatense, 724 (B I 13) 1, Pontificale, and 724 (B I 13) 2, Benedictionale, have a Benevento provenance and are tied by inscriptions to its Bishop Landulf (granted the use of the pallium by papal decree in 969), the first an owner's mark from within his lifetime, and the second verses singing his praises after his death (a third roll, the Exultet in Vatican City, BAV, Vat. lat. 9820, also belongs close to this tenth-century group of Benevento provenance.) The script of the Pontificale (Plate 10.5) is rounded, the rightmost minims of m and n delicately bent as in the *i*. Proportions are excellent; the most distinctive characteristic is the breadth of the letters, with lateral spacing for each carefully observed. Ligatures, especially those with *e*, had often constituted a disfiguring knot in early Beneventan, but in the hands of these rolls ligatures are harmonious, and those with p (the sp of "spiritus", the rp of "corpore") have a graceful balloon effect that adds to the overall impression of roundness about the head line. Landulf's rolls represent a high point in South Italian script, as in its painting. Astoundingly, considering its *luxe*, the Pontificale has near-contemporary rubrics added in Caroline in fine black ink (see Section 10.3 on Caroline in the Beneventan zone).

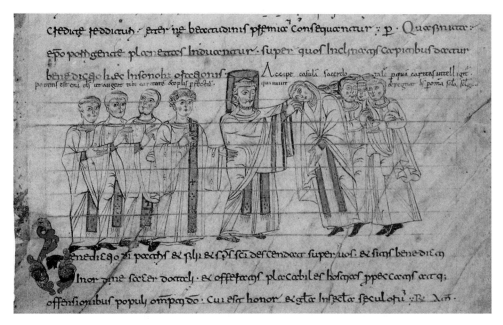

PLATE 10.5 Rome, Biblioteca Casanatense 724, 1 (saec. X, time of Bp. Landulf of Benevento), Pontificale: showing vesting of priests with chasuble. The letters are broad and set apart without lateral crowding, while ascenders and descenders are relatively short; the descent of this type from the rounded type of early Beneventan with uncial-like proportions is clear. The script type emphasizes respect for the baseline; the *s* does not descend below it, nor does final *r*. Abbreviations are rare, except for the usual *nomina sacra*. The finely-written 11th-century Caroline, in which the letters are crowded laterally, contrasts with the Beneventan text type.

THE ELEVENTH CENTURY

In the late tenth century the monks of Monte Cassino, settled once more on St. Benedict's mountain, were producing a few works of the major Fathers, the first that were deemed by their successors to be well enough written to be preserved and hence ones that have come down to us. But the eleventh century was Monte Cassino's golden age. That age opened with the abbacy of Theobald (1022–*c*.1030 effectively). The lists of books copied under this abbot give evidence of his zeal in the creation of a library worthy of Monte Cassino's great traditions. The look, characteristic of Monte Cassino with its emphasis upon contrast between thick and thin strokes, was established in the house, but still with considerable freedom in the play of the pen; see Plate 10. 6, the famous encyclopedia of Rabanus Maurus (Monte Cassino, 132).

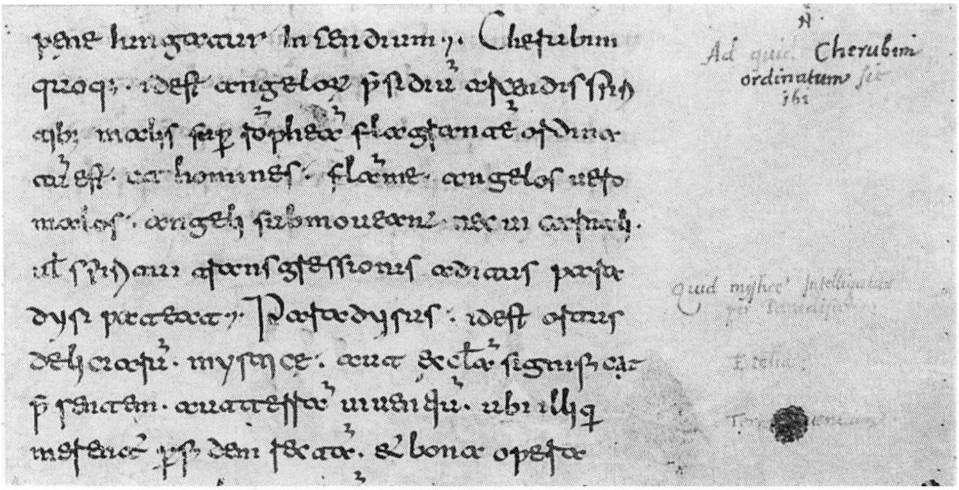

PLATE 10.6 MC 132 (Theobaldan (1022–*c*.1030)), Rabanus Maurus, *De Origine Rerum*, p. 299. The script gives a low-slung impression, because letters are wide, spaces between letters are generous, and ascenders are short (though descenders are long). The soft effect is only occasionally (l. 1, *t* in "iungatur") broken by diamond points of usually rounded letters at the baseline. The lemma "Paradysus" is in slightly larger module. The *ri* ligature is the acid test of gracefulness in Beneventan; here it is bold rather than graceful. In the last line, the word "merentur" has the comma abbreviation for *ur* (hardly found after the first third of the eleventh century).

No book production is attested for the politically difficult interval of struggle with the Capuan princes (from *c*.1030) that followed. The arrival of Desiderius as abbot in 1058 marks a renewal of the Theobaldan ideal; the new abbot's first new building project was that of a library, and, to fill it, book copying began again in earnest. The leader of the scriptorium may have been the master scribe Grimoald; at any rate, his superb homiliaries, Monte Cassino, 104 and 109 (the latter containing his portrait) (Plate 10.7), once misdated as Theobaldan, are now firmly placed in the early Desiderian period by the identification of his hand as scribe/artist of the handsome Exultet roll in Vatican City, BAV, Vat. lat. 3784, which has always been ascribed to Desiderius' era by palaeographers and art historians. The scriptorium of Desiderius embarked on "the most dramatic single event in the history of Latin scholarship in the eleventh century," namely, the "abbey's phenomenal revival" (Reynolds and Wilson 2013, 110). In parallel to Desiderius' campaign to renew all the monastic buildings, the abbey entered upon a *renovatio* of learning and the campaign to acquire, by copying, a collection of patristic works, e.g., the magnificent series of works of Augustine, some of them of the highest textual significance. It is clear that among the texts uncovered and copied was a group of most rare African texts, perhaps preserved in the Campanian area since late antiquity. Even more remarkable is the list of rare and even unique classical texts that were copied. (See Newton, Chapter 50 of this volume.)

PLATE 10.7A MC 109 (Desiderian (1058–87), Homiliarium, early), p. 264. Both MC 104 and 109 are, script and decoration, the work of the master scribe Grimoald, deacon and monk. It has remarkable finesse. Four varieties of script are seen here: the small majuscules beside the figure of Gregory the Great and for the *ex* of "Textum"; and three types of Beneventan: Fine Script for the quotation from the lesson; the slightly larger script type for the heading; the handsome text hand.

Many of the manuscripts from near the opening of Desiderius' rule show an exploitation of thick, inky masses, in what may be called a "clotted effect." This rich and striking stage (Plate 10.8) betrays the scribes' preoccupation with the potential inherent in the play of contrasting shapes. But the major shift in this era is a change in the angle of the script (Plates 10.9a and 10.9b), from the traditional Old Angle, with

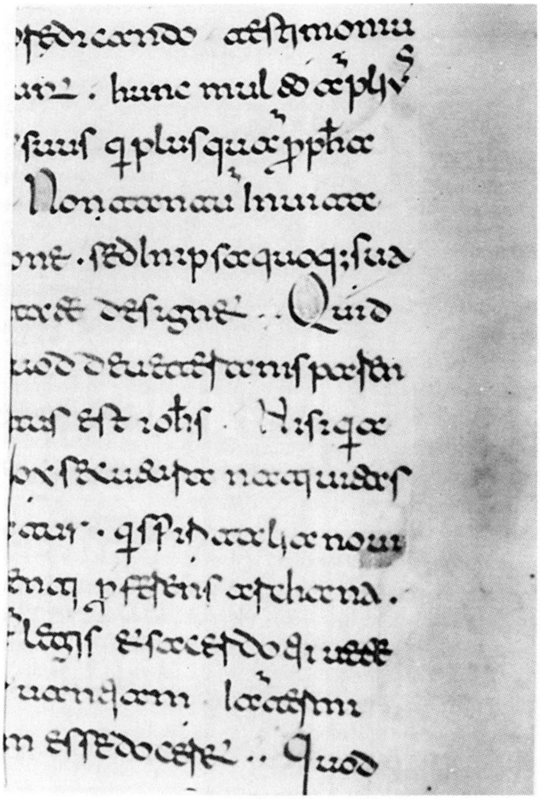

PLATE 10.7B MC 109, Homiliarium, p. 21. To justify the right margin, Grimoald employed the now old-fashioned ligatures *to* (l. 2, "multo"); *tu* (l. 9, "secutura"); *ta* (l. 9, "nativitas"); and *te* (l. 12 "vete—").

heavy curving strokes at the base of round letters such as *b*, *d* and *o* (the last being ο). Within a decade of Desiderius' accession, in the work of the more advanced scribes, this has given way to the New Angle, in which the same round letters present an increasingly sharp point at the bottom, on the baseline (*o* is now ο, shaped like a diamond). This is the most salient feature of the developed or canonical style at Monte Cassino; the resulting emphasis upon a broken quality lends a striking geometric quality to the new script form. Also contributing to the mathematical regularity of the new form was a great new clarity in the marshaling of strokes so that the fundamental elements of the script received the same treatment throughout; the parts of letters that lie between baseline and head line are carefully aligned at those points; ascenders and descenders stand at the same angle; and the rational spacing of letters in the line of script and the perspicuous separation of words produce a new order never seen before in the Cassinese atelier. So powerful was the example of this type that it ultimately influenced not only the writing of the immediate region, which can be studied, e.g., in the manuscripts preserved at the Archivio di Stato in Frosinone

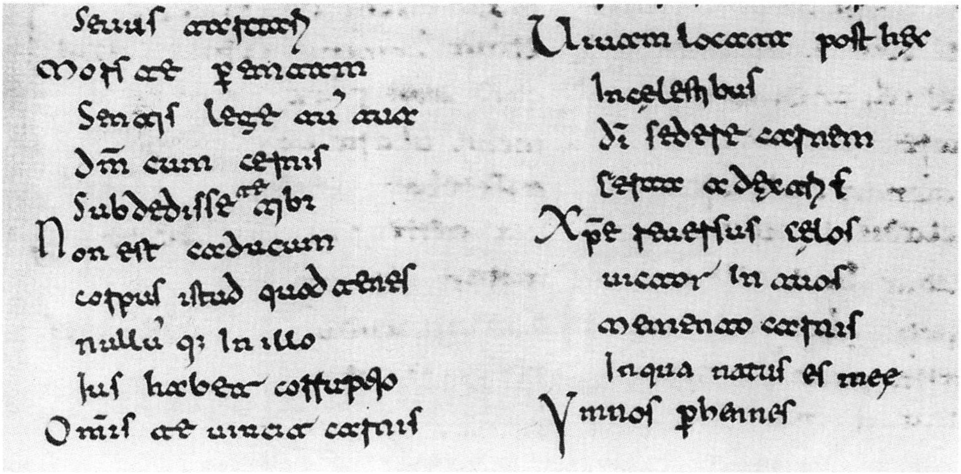

PLATE 10.8 Arezzo 405 (Desiderian (1058–87), early), Hilarius, *Hymni*, p. 29. The MS is listed in the *Chronicle* of MC as one copied under Desiderius. The frequently dense clusters of letters with rich, thick strokes (as third line from bottom, "memento carnis") give an inky, "clotted" appearance to the page of script. This fascination with the heaviness of many pen strokes foreshadows the development of strong contrast between thick and thin strokes in the developed Desiderian hand. The last two lines of text are in Caroline, a feature—lurking, generally unnoticed—of a number of Beneventan manuscripts.

today, but eventually over virtually all the script region. Alongside this type, the Monte Cassino brothers perfected a second, smaller type, which still maintained the Old Angle (Plate 10.10), for marginalia and, sometimes, for entire manuscripts, that has been denominated "Fine Script." The splendid array of volumes, patristic and classical, continued unabated under Abbot Oderisius (1087–1105). Also characteristic of his era are a series of service books of small dimensions but great refinement.

The Desiderian and Oderisian periods saw a revolution in decoration as well as in script. The Gospel Book of Henry II (Vatican City, BAV, Ottob. lat. 74), copied at St. Emmeram of Regensburg, was presented to Monte Cassino in the year 1023. But, from the standpoint of decoration, it was almost fifty years later, as H. Bloch (1986, 19–30 and 71–82) demonstrated, that Cassinese artists began to imitate aspects of its initials and thus transformed the appearance of their codices and rolls (Plate 10.11).

It is useful to consider, immediately alongside the Monte Cassino type, another superb form of Beneventan that reached its apogee in the eleventh century. It is the "Bari Type," to use Lowe's (1980, 150–2) name (Plate 10.12). This beautiful form stands at the opposite extreme from the canonical Monte Cassino type of the script. A developed example like the Benedictional Roll still preserved in the Archivio del Capitolo Metropolitano at Bari shows the rounded letters (*b, d, o* etc.) marked by fine strokes everywhere and thus a greatly reduced contrast between thick and thin strokes. Rather than breaking, as in the classic developed Monte Cassino type, the Bari type

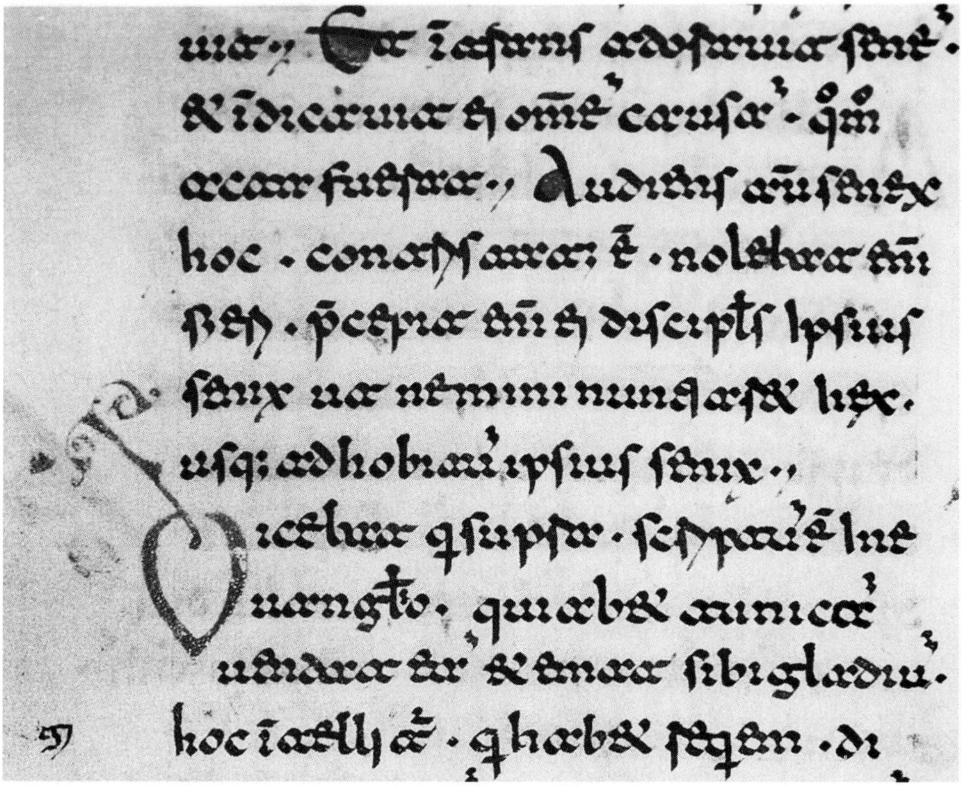

PLATE 10.9A MC 143 (Desiderian (1058–87), early), *Vitae PP. Anachoretarum*, etc., p. 252. Old Angle. Most of the letters whose bottom rests on the baseline have at that point a gently rounded pad. This early Desiderian scribe either was poorly educated or was copying blindly a barbarous text; note "ad hobitum ipsius senix" for "ad obitum ipsius senis," among other errors.

flows evenly, smoothly, and without drama. It goes without saying that it retains the Old Angle traditional in Beneventan script for centuries. If the look of Monte Cassino script became sharply and monumentally geometrical, the look of Bari type insisted upon a rounded grace. The curving aspects are emphasized by the descenders of the *i*-ligatures, which curve back gracefully to the left; above the head line the balloon effect of such ligatures as *ct, rp, sp* and *xp* provides especially striking curves. The curving broken *c*, a virtually obligatory form in this script type, enhances the rounded effect on the page. The only place where the double-loop form is not allowed is after the letter *e*, on the principle of dissimilation of forms; thus, in the Canon of the Mass, in the words of institution, "Hoc est enim corpus meum . . . hic est enim calix sanguinis mei" ("This is my body . . . this is the cup of my blood"), the final letter of "Hoc" and "hic" would have had the broken-*c* form, but in the next sentence, "Haec quotienscumque feceritis . . ." ("These, as oft as ye shall do them . . ."), the *c* in the word "Haec," since it followed *e*, would not have been permitted to have that form. The baseline is emphasized by the

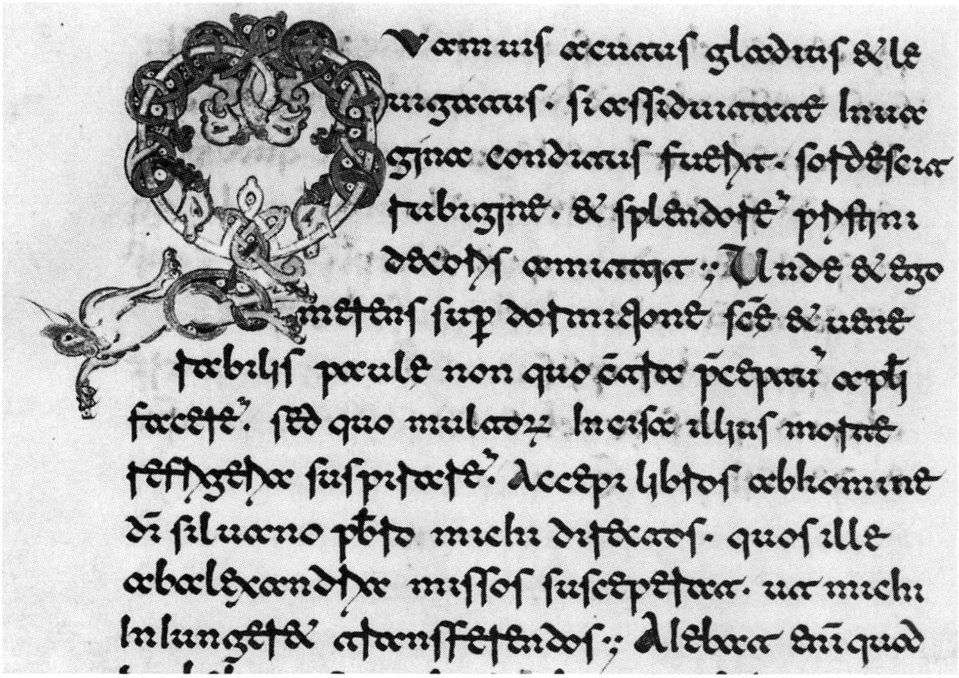

PLATE 10.9B MC 444 (1075–90, late Desiderian or early Oderisian), *Kalendarium et Regula S. Benedicti*, p. 228. New Angle. In this, the fully developed Desiderian canonical script, the letters that rest on the baseline are pointed at the bottom, so that the letter forms a diamond, or nearly so. Minims are uniformly broken and therefore consist of two diamonds, or quasi-diamonds. The result is a more sharply geometrical pattern of thicks and thins. Overall organization at head line and baseline is tighter. One result is the continuous head line, seen briefly in the bottom line, "fere" in "transferendos."

fact that the shaft of *f* and *s* rests on it, as do small capitals. In further distinction from the eleventh-century Cassinese type, *de* and other adjacent rounded letters regularly show fusion of strokes. In decorated initials the shafts in the developed type are like the elements of the letters in being markedly slender and of uniform thickness. The curving influence is seen in the tondos with saints' portraits in the borders. The interlace in small initials may often end in human heads in profile; pearls are also frequent decorative elements in initials. The "Bari type" is seen in a wide range of manuscripts, and not only in service books but also in such classical manuscripts as the Naples Ovid, *Metamorphoses* (Naples, Biblioteca Nazionale, IV F 3), and the Oxford Vergil (Oxford, Bodleian Library, Canon. Class. lat. 50). When the Ovid, the oldest illustrated *Metamorphoses* in existence, came as a gift to Monte Cassino by the twelfth century, it would have struck the brothers there as different from their own hand, a particularly graceful Apulian importation (Cavallo, Fedeli, and Papponetti 1998).

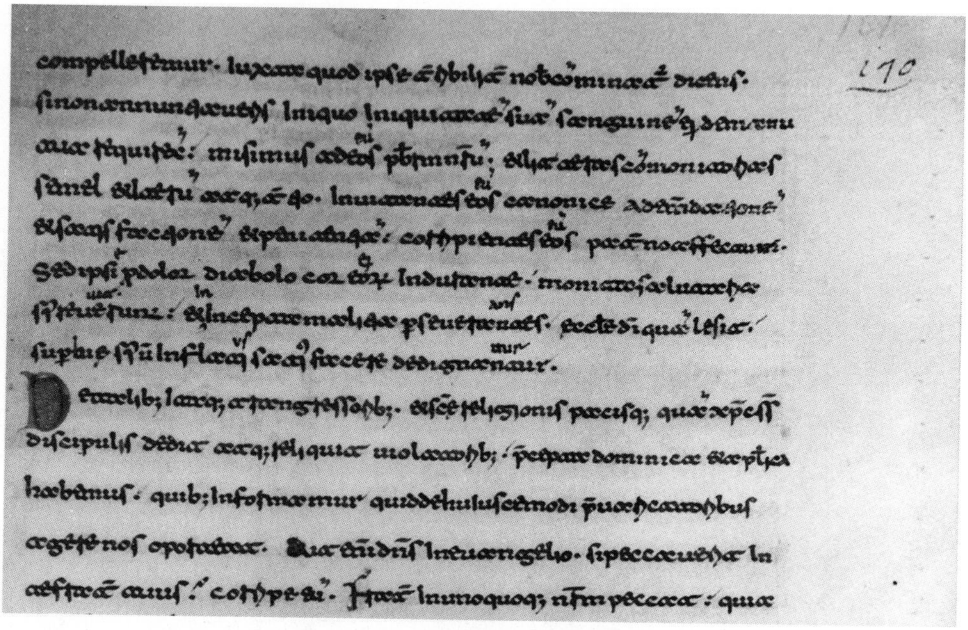

PLATE 10.10 MC 451 (Desiderian), *Ordo Romanus*, p. 161. Fine Script continues to be written at the Old Angle, and with less obvious breaking of minims. The older final *r* standing on the baseline is retained. Caroline *a* is frequent (l. 4, "ad emendationem"). This page shows the editorial work of a reviser, also writing Fine Script.

In the larger view, from the old Beneventan stock came a number of calligraphic sister types, but at the end of the eleventh century none more strongly contrasting than the handsomely angular, broken Cassinese and the gracefully rounded Bari types. The history of Beneventan is not the story of a single undeviating line of development.

That old Beneventan stock, with its cursive-derived letterforms and archaic ligatures, was not, for outsiders, readily legible and, furthermore, in its production did not possess the economy of strokes that Lowe (1953, xii) ascribed to the comely Caroline, with its "economy, grace, and legibility." But Beneventan had its compensating virtues. Because of such user-friendly aspects as its hard/soft *ti* distinction and its fascinatingly subtle array of punctuation signs, it could be asserted that the old script type probably provided more help (*adiutorium*) and support to the lector than any other script of medieval Europe. Perhaps that contributed to its striking longevity.

The Caroline that had overwhelmed the fair local Nonantola style in the north by the middle of the ninth century was an ever-present neighbor and rival to Beneventan, throughout its history, in the south. It is now clear that in the Beneventan zone there were scribes who were "digraphic" or could write both scripts. It is only recently that the evidence for Caroline there—much of it lurking inconspicuously in margins, or in corrections between the lines of Beneventan, or in blank spaces in prefatory material of

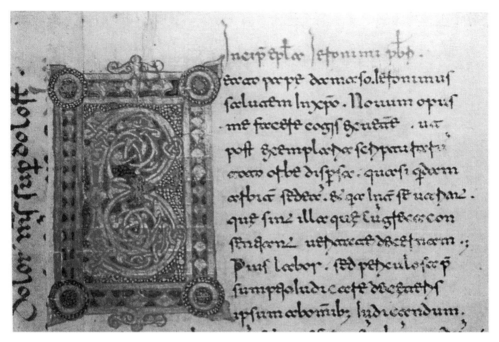

PLATE 10.11 MC 211 (Oderisian), Gospels, p. 13. The small but distinguished initial *B* of "Beato" (the opening of Jerome's address to Pope Damasus) is understated, like the rest of the book production of Abbot Oderisius. The frame is gold, but shows a blue ground with white stippling, as does the inner space. This is part of the Cassinese adaptation, beginning around 1066, of the decoration of the Gospel Book of Henry II (now Vat. Ottob. lat 74). The foliage also is gold, outlined in red. To the left, a fragment taken from a dismembered Monte Cassino MS used for binding the book.

a codex—has begun to be seriously examined. Palma and Supino Martini (1987) have published (Plate 10.13) a draft document of Abbot Desiderius of Monte Cassino for the venerable Peter Damian, and the draft of the letter is written in Caroline. The draft signature of the abbot, however (not a genuine signature of his), is in the honored Beneventan. And some Caroline entries are not so inconspicuous. The master Grimoald supplied textual omissions in his homiliaries and elsewhere prominently in the margins in his stately Caroline (Plate 10.14). Or the text itself, similarly, could be in Caroline. What may be called "codices nobiliores"—liturgical books, especially, and the finer copies of the Fathers or historians—were always in Beneventan. But at the opposite end of the scale, in "libri plebeii" such as technical works ("Fachliteratur") or schoolbooks, where the quality control was relaxed or nonexistent, the copy could be made in Caroline, or even partly in Beneventan and partly in Caroline. The schoolbook Monte Cassino, 580 of the Desiderian era, first studied by Willard (1929), shows such a disorderly mixture, all by the same hand. And, recently, the fair copy of a technical treatise of Desiderian date and dedicated to the abbot, Constantinus Africanus'

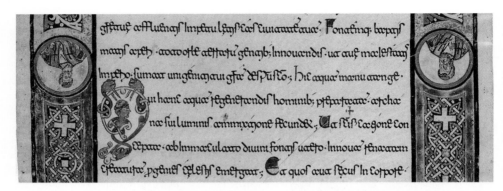

PLATE 10.12 Bari, Archivio del Cap. Metropol., Benedictional. The style of Bari is characterized by a slender-limbed grace. The outline of every letter is traced in a thin stroke that hardly varies in thickness, like finely-wrought wire or filigree. Even the decorated initials show a uniformly slender frame. Broken *c* is the rule. The ligature *sp* has the double-arch form. A special exception to the soft *ti* rule specifies that, when following *s* or *x* (as in "ammixtione" here), *ti* was pronounced hard and written with the hard ligature. Unlike contemporary Monte Cassino script, the Bari type makes use of fusion; where rounded letters abut, they share a single stroke (as in l. 1, the *pe* in "impetus" and the *pt* in "baptismatis.")

Pantegni, has come to light (The Hague, Koninklijke Bibliothek, 73 J 6); it is entirely in Caroline, though the hand regularly uses the *ri* ligature familiar from Beneventan and other Italian scripts.

Yet it should not be supposed that Beneventan, with the comely, economical rival within its gates, was weak or on the defensive. The scholarship of recent decades has shown that the script was practiced vigorously in houses in the Abruzzi and the Marche, and it has long been known that it spread to Dalmatia, where beautiful and most valuable manuscripts in the local form of Beneventan—akin to the Bari type— were produced. Practitioners of Beneventan and their products were *scribes (ou— également—livres) sans frontières*. There are pages written by a Beneventan scribe in a manuscript produced in Normandy, now in Rouen. The only copy of the translation of Nemesius' *Peri physeos anthropou* that records the name of the translator— Desiderius' friend, Alfanus of Salerno—is one from Mont St. Michel, and the Paris manuscript (BnF, lat. 15078) of this text—also in France in the Middle Ages—preserves a suprascript 2-shaped sign of interrogation in one passage, showing its descent from a Beneventan manuscript (another manuscript, very rich in this and other Beneventan features, shows that it was copied directly from a South Italian exemplar; it is Lawrence of Amalfi's handbook of the Liberal Arts, Venice, Biblioteca Nazionale Marciana, Zan. Lat. 497). England had a particularly close relationship with southern Italy and its medical resources; an important medical manuscript in Beneventan reached Bury St. Edmunds by the late twelfth or early thirteenth century. At the frontiers to the east, Mount Athos had a handsome Bible (or parts of one) in Beneventan in the Middle

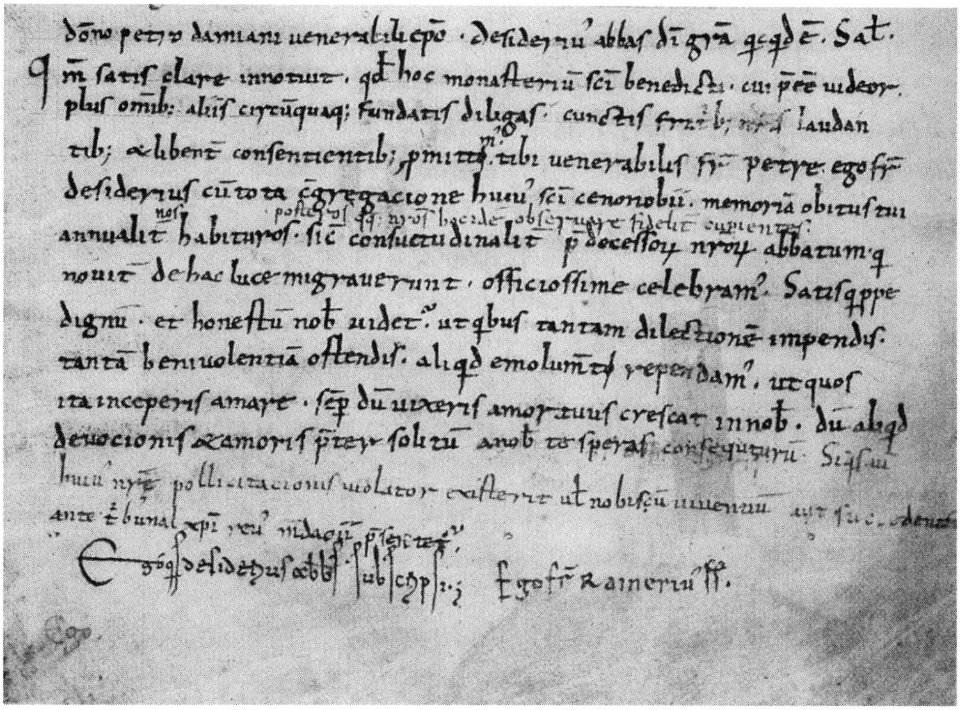

PLATE 10.13 MC 3 (entry 1058–71), Alcuin, *De Trinitate*, etc., p. 17. Inserted in a blank space in the ninth-century MS, a draft document from Abbot Desiderius to Peter Damian (so no later than beginning of 1072, the year of Damian's death), assures the latter of the abbot's intention to observe every year the anniversary of his death with commemorative prayer as for those who had served as abbots of the community. The salutation line and the text that follows are in rough Caroline with occasional errors ("officiossime" by haplography) and a very occasional Beneventan touch (as "amor tuus" with Beneventan *t*). The abbot's signature, however, is written, with the same pen, in Beneventan: "Ego qui supra Desiderius abbas subscripsi." The other signature, of "Frater Rainerius," is in the same Caroline as the main text. Caroline was a working script, even within the abbey.

Ages; partly palimpsested, the fragments today lie at the monastery of Koutloumousiou and in Paris (where the latter were brought, from Mt. Athos, in the nineteenth century). There is in Paris a Greek manuscript (BnF gr. 1053, see Brown 2012, 31) with interesting marginal notes in Beneventan. A Vatican manuscript of Solinus in Beneventan (Vat. Lat. 3342) has *probationes* in the form of an Arabic version of a verse from the Psalms. The Naples Ovid (IV f 3) contains, among many delightful illustrations *in margine*, pseudo-Kufic designs beside some passages; it has been shown that these Islamic decorative elements mark episodes in the poem connected with the Near East and reveal the scribe/artist's awareness of geography and culture.[2]

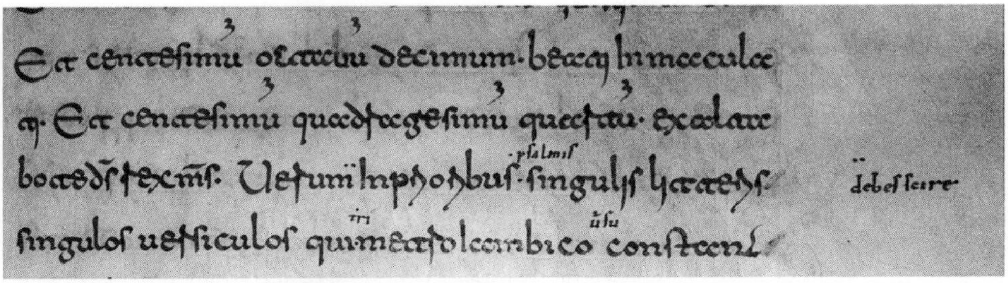

PLATE 10.14 MC 434 (Desiderian (1058–87), early), *Psalterium cum expositionibus*, p. 23. Grimoald corrects the text (in his own beautiful Beneventan hand), and the corrections are in Caroline. Where the correction stands in the margin, it is linked to its proper place in the text by *signes de renvoi*. One of the master scribes of the early Desiderian scriptorium was "digraphic," or skilled in both scripts. It has been demonstrated that scribes of common MSS fell from Beneventan into their native Caroline script through clumsiness, inattention, or drowsiness, but in this case of a handsome book Grimoald deliberately chose to write his textual suppletions in a contrasting hand.

THE LATER PERIOD

Late Beneventan in the Monte Cassino style (Plate 10.15, Monte Cassino, 440) shows a script that is ever more angular and even, at times, disarticulated. This last aspect can give it, at times, the look of old, somewhat tattered lace. Some of the script rules cease to be observed, and Gothic elements begin to appear, but the monumentality remains.

It was in the twelfth century that the balance began to shift decisively towards the ordinary minuscule, and even more so in the following one. But the prestige of books in Beneventan was so great that in the thirteenth century a Monte Cassino brother or brothers laboriously retraced the faded, flaking Beneventan writing of liturgical books, the Fathers, and classics alike—thousands of pages—so that the volumes in that script might continue in use. In fact, the honored hand retained its *auctoritas* in some quarters even in the age of the Humanists; as late as the sixteenth century, as Brown (2005) has demonstrated, nuns in Naples revived the Beneventana in their own fascinatingly idiosyncratic form ("Nuns' Beneventan"), to produce the liturgical books they used in their services. And, as Ullman (1973, 401–28) has observed, a very famous humanist, Giovanni Pontano (d.1503), chancellor of the same city, paid tribute to the medieval script of southern Italy when he copied out the elegies of Tibullus (the MS is today Wolfenbüttel, Herzog. August Bibliothek, Cod. Guelf. Aug. 82.6) and introduced in his elegant humanist hand the Beneventan *e* and the Beneventan *r*. Like the scribe of Ovid's *Metamorphoses* just cited, Pontano had a sense of poetic color. In the Ovid that regional atmosphere is conveyed by the evocative Islamic decoration in the margins; the humanist has incorporated the haunting allusions to southern Italy in the very script of his text.

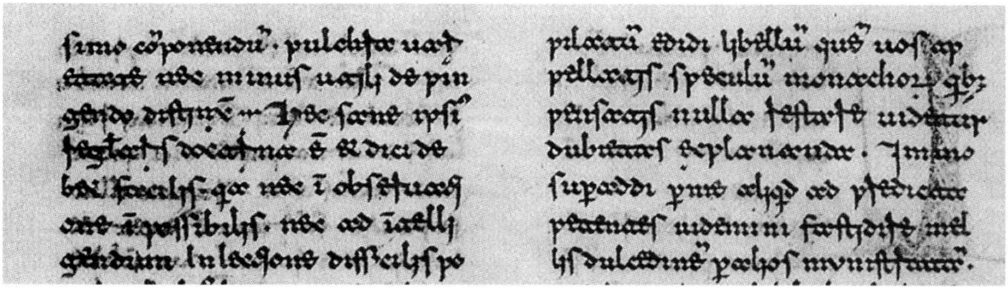

PLATE 10.15 MC 440 (saec. XIII ex.), Bernardus Ayglerius, *Commentarius in Regulam S. Benedicti*, p. 6. The broken quality of classic Cassinese Beneventan has become quite brittle. In earliest Beneventan the 3-shaped *m*-stroke is vertical; here it is sharply pointed and almost horizontal. The Beneventan period (comma surmounted by two points) has become a particularly jagged horizontal. The small initial *H* in "Hec" (l. 3) has a Gothic-style form; here and everywhere *ae* has given way to *e*. Fusion may occur (col. 2, l. 4 *da* in "explananda"). Unorthodox spellings (e.g., col. 2, l. 7, "mynistratam") creep in.

NOTES

1. This handsome script-type is described in Bischoff (1983, 99–124); in Cencetti (1957, 187–219); in Belloni (1984, 1–16); and in Feo and Modesti (2009, 5-12). On the relationship to South Italian script, see especially Palma (1983, 141–49 and 1979, 77–88).
2. See Newton (2011, 25–69, esp. 34–5).

BIBLIOGRAPHY

The classic study is Elias Avery Lowe [Loew], *The Beneventan Script. A History of the South Italian Minuscule* (Oxford: Oxford University Press, 1914; second edition prepared and enlarged by Virginia Brown, Rome: Edizioni di Storia e Letteratura, 1980, 2 vols.). The list of MSS in the second volume and of MSS subsequently discovered is now available in Virginia Brown, *Beneventan Discoveries: Collected Manuscript Catalogues, 1978–2008* (Toronto: Pontifical Institute of Mediaeval Studies, 2011). The invaluable annual bibliography on Beneventan script and MSS is BMB: *Bibliografia dei manoscritti in scrittura beneventana 1–* (Università degli studi di Cassino, Dipartimento di Filologia e Storia; Scuola di specializzazione per conservatori di beni archivistici e librari della civiltà monastica), (Rome: Viella, 1993–).

Alfanus. 1974. *I carmi di Alfano I, Arcivescovo di Salerno*, ed. Anselmo Lentini and Faustino Avagliano, Miscellanea Cassinese 38. Montecassino.
Anderson, D. W. 2002. "Medieval Teaching Texts on Syllable Quantities and the Innovations from the School of Alberic of Monte Cassino." In *Latin Grammar and Rhetoric. From Classical Theory to Medieval Practice*, ed. Carol Dana Lanham, 180–211. London and New York: Continuum.

Avagliano, F., and P. Oronzo, eds. 1992. *L'età dell'abate Desiderio. Miscellanea Cassinese 67.* Montecassino: Pubblicazioni Cassinesi.

Belloni, A. 1984. "La 'Translatio Benedicti' a Fleury e gli antichi monasteri dell'Italia settentrionale." *Italia medioevale e umanistica* 27: 1–16.

Bibliotheca Casinensis, vols. 1–5. 1873–94. Monte Cassino: Typographia Casinensis.

Bloch, H. 1986. *Monte Cassino in the Middle Ages,* 3 vols. Cambridge, MA: Harvard University Press.

Bischoff, B. 1983. "Manoscritti Nonantolani dispersi dell'epoca Carolingia." *La Bibliofilia* 85: 99–124.

BMB. 1993–. *Bibliografia dei manoscritti in scrittura beneventana.* Rome: Viella.

Brenk, B., ed. 1981. *Lektionar zu den Festen der heiligen Benedikt, Maurus und Scholastica: Vat. lat. 1202 (Codices e Vaticanis selecti quam simillime expressi 50),* Zurich: Belser.

Brown, V. 2005. *Terra Sancti Benedicti. Studies in the Palaeography, History and Liturgy of Medieval Southern Italy.* Rome: Edizioni di storia e letteratura.

Brown, V. 2012. *Beneventan Discoveries: Collected Manuscript Catalogues, 1978–2008.* Toronto: Pontifical Institute of Mediaeval Studies.

Campana, Augusto. 1958. "Per il 'Textus Evangelii' donato da Enrico II a Montecassino (Vat. Ottob. lat. 74)." *La Bibliofilia* 60: 34–47.

Cavallo, G. 1970. "Struttura e articolazione della minuscola beneventana libraria tra i secoli X–XII." *Studi medioevali* 3rd ser., 11/1: 343–68.

Cavallo, G., P. Fedeli, and G. Papponetti (eds.). 1998. *L'Ovidio napoletano.* Sulmona: Centro Ovidiano di Studi e Ricerche.

Cavallo, G., G. Orofino, and O. Pecere, eds. 1994. *Exultet: Rotoli liturgici del medioevo meridionale.* Rome: Istituto Poligrafico e Zecca dello Stato.

Cencetti, Giorgio. 1957. "Scriptoria e scritture nel monachesimo benedettino." In *Settimane di studio del Centro italiano di studi sull'alto Medioevo 4: Il monachesimo nell'alto Medioevo e la formazione della civiltà occidentale* 187–219. Spoleto: CISAM.

Coulson, F. T. and A. A. Grotans, eds. 2008. *Classica et Beneventana. Essays Presented to Virginia Brown on the Occasion of her 65th Birthday,* Fédération Internationale des Instituts d'Études Médiévales, Textes et Études du Moyen Âge, 36. Turnhout: Brepols.

Dell'Omo, M. 1992. "Cultura liturgica e preghiera a Montecassino negli anni dell'abate Desiderio (1058–1087) (con una giunta sulla raccolta di preghiere del cod. Casin. 442)." In *L'età dell'abate Desiderio. Miscellanea Cassinese 67,* ed. Faustino Avagliano and Oronzo Pecere, 279–361. Montecassino: Pubblicazioni Cassinesi.

Dell'Omo, M., ed. 1996. *Virgilio e il chiostro. Manoscritti di autori classici e civiltà monastica,* Rome: Palombi.

Dell'Omo, M., ed. 1998. *I Fiori e' Frutti santi. S. Benedetto, la Regola, la santità nelle testimonianze dei manoscritti cassinesi,* Milan: Ministero per i beni culturali e ambientali.

Dell'Omo, M. 1999. *Montecassino. Un'abbazia nella storia* (Biblioteca della Miscellanea Cassinese 6), Monte Cassino: Pubblicazioni cassinesi.

Dell'Omo, M. 2008 *Montecassino medievale. Genesi di un simbolo, storia di una realtà,* Monte Cassino: Pubblicazioni cassinesi.

Feo, G. and M. Modesti, eds. 2009. *Chartae Latinae Antiquiores,* vol. 89, Italy vol. 61. Dietikon: Urs Graf.

Hoffmann, H. 1973. "Studien zur Chronik von Montecassino," *Deutsches Archiv* 29: 59–162.

Hoffmann, H., ed. 1980. *Chronica monasterii Casinensis, M.G. SS. 34.* Hanover: Hahn.

Kelly, T. 1989. *The Beneventan Chant*, Cambridge: Cambridge University Press.

Kelly, T. 1996. *The Exultet in Southern Italy*, Oxford: Oxford University Press.

Leccisotti, T. (and, for vols. IX–XI, Avagliano, Faustino). 1964–77. *Abbazia di Montecassino. I Regesti dell'Archivio, vols. I, II, VI-XI (Ministero dell'Interno, Pubblicazioni dell'Archivio di Stato*, vols. LIV, LVI, LXXIV, LXXVIII, LXXIX, LXXXI, LXXXVI, XCV), Rome: Ministero per i beni culturali e ambientali.

Lohrmann, D. 1968. *Das Register Papst Johannes' VIII. (872-882). Neue Studien zur Abschrift Reg. Vat. I, zum verlorenen Originalregister und zum Diktat der Briefe (Bibliothek des Deutschen Historischen Instituts in Rom 30)*, Tübingen: Niemeyer.

Lo Monaco, F. 1984. "Note su codici cassinesi tra Quattro e Cinquecento." *Miscellanea Cassinese* 48: 229–57 [= *Miscellanea Cassinese* 66 (1992), 329–64].

Lowe [Loew], E. A. 1910. *Studia Palaeographica: A Contribution to the History of Early Latin Minuscule and to the Dating of Visigothic Manuscripts*, Munich: G. Franz [= *Pal. Pap. I*, 2–65].

Lowe, E. A. 1920. "The Unique Manuscript of Apuleius' *Metamorphoses* (Laurentian. 68.2) and its Oldest Transcript (Laurentian. 29.2)." *Classical Quarterly* 14: 150–5 [= *Pal. Pap. I*, 92–8].

Lowe, E. A. 1929a. *Scriptura Beneventana*, 2 vols. Oxford: Clarendon.

Lowe, E. A. 1929b. "The Unique Manuscript of Tacitus' Histories (Florence, Laur. 68. 2)." In *Casinensia I*, 257–72. Monte Cassino: Typographia Casinensis [= *Pal. Pap. I*, 289–302].

Lowe, E. A. 1932. "Virgil in South Italy: Facsimiles of Eight Manuscripts of Virgil in Beneventan Script," *Studi medievali*, new ser. 5: 43–51 [= *Pal. Pap. I*, 326–34].

Lowe, E. A. 1953. *Codices Latini Antiquiores*, vol. 6. Oxford: Clarendon.

Lowe, E. A. 1972. *Palaeographical Papers 1907-1965*, ed. Ludwig Bieler, 2 vols. Oxford: Clarendon.

Lowe, E. A. 1980. *The Beneventan Script: A History of the South Italian Minuscule*. 2nd ed. prepared by Virginia Brown. 2 vols. Rome: Edizioni di Storia e Letteratura [original edition Oxford: Oxford University Press, 1914].

Meyvaert, P., ed. 1982. *The Codex Benedictus: An Eleventh-Century Lectionary from Monte Cassino (Vat. lat. 1202: Codices e Vaticanis selecti quam simillime expressi 50)*. New York: Johnson Reprint Corporation.

Newton, F. 1973. "Beneventan Scribes and Subscriptions, With a List of Those Known at the Present Time," *The Book Mark* (Friends of the University of North Carolina Library) 43: 1–35.

Newton, F. 1991. "One Scriptorium, Two Scripts: Beneventan, Caroline, and the Problem of Marston 112." In *Beinecke Studies in Early Manuscripts (Yale University Library Gazette*, Supplement 66), ed. R. G. Babcock, 118–33. New Haven, CT: Yale University Library.

Newton, F. 1999. *The Scriptorium and Library at Monte Cassino, 1058-1105* (Cambridge Studies in Palaeography and Codicology 7). Cambridge: Cambridge University Press.

Newton, F. 2003. "'Expolitio' per l'umanesimo: la formazione classica dei monaci cassinesi nel XI secolo." In Pecere, 169–79, 224–35.

Newton, F. 2004. "Fifty Years of Beneventan Studies." *Archiv für Diplomatik* 50: 327–45.

Newton, F. 2011. "Arabic Medicine and Other Arabic Cultural Influences in Southern Italy in the Time of Constantinus Africanus (Saec. XI²)." In *Between Text and Patient. The Medical Enterprise in Medieval and Early Modern Europe*, Micrologus Library 39, ed. Florence Eliza Glaze and Brian Nance, 25–69. Florence: SISMEL.

Orofino, G. 1983. "Considerazioni sulla produzione miniaturistica altomedievale a Monte-cassino attraverso alcuni manoscritti conservati nell'Archivio della Badia." *Miscellanea Cassinese* 47: 131–85.

Orofino, G. 1989. "La prima fase della miniatura desideriana (1058–1071)." In *L'età dell'abate Desiderio. 2. La decorazione libraria. Miscellanea Cassinese* 60, 47–63. Monte Cassino: Pubblicazioni Cassinesi.

Orofino, G. 1994–2006. *I codici decorati dell'Archivio di Montecassino* 1–3, Rome: Istituto Poligrafico e Zecca dello Stato.

Palma, M. 1979. "Nonantola e il Sud. Contributo alla storia della scrittura libraria nell'Italia dell'ottavo secolo." *Scrittura e Civiltà* 3: 77–88.

Palma, M. 1983. "Alle origini del 'tipo di Nonantola': nuove testimonianze meridionali." *Scrittura e Civiltà* 7: 141–9.

Palma, M., and P. Supino Martini. 1987. "Desiderio e S. Pier Damiani: Osservazioni su di una testimonianza scritta." *Nuovi Annali della Scuola Speciale per Archivisti e Bibliotecari* 1: 225–9.

Pecere, O., ed. 2003. *Il monaco il libro la biblioteca. Atti del Convegno Cassino–Montecassino 5-8 settembre 2000*, Cassino: Edizioni dell'Università degli studi di Cassino.

Reynolds, L. D. 1968. "The Medieval Tradition of Seneca's *Dialogues*." *Classical Quarterly*, N. S., 18: 355–72.

Reynolds, L. D. and N. G. Wilson. 2013. *Scribes and Scholars. A Guide to the Transmission of Greek and Latin Literature*, 4th ed. Oxford: Oxford University Press.

Reynolds, R. E. 2009. *Studies on Medieval Liturgical and Legal Manuscripts from Spain and Southern Italy*, Burlington, VT: Ashgate.

Toubert. H. 1990. *Un Art dirigé: Réforme grégorienne et iconographie*, Paris: Éditions du Cerf.

Tristano, C. 1979. "Scrittura beneventana e scrittura carolina in manoscritti dell'Italia meridionale." *Scrittura e Civiltà* 3: 89–150.

Ullman, B. L. 1973. *Studies in the Italian Renaissance*, 2nd ed. Rome: Edizioni di Storia e Letteratura.

Willard, H. M. 1929. "Codex Casinensis 580T, Lexicon Prosodiacum saec. XI." In *Casinensia I*, 297–304. Monte Cassino: Typographia Casinensis.

CHAPTER 11

THE VISIGOTHIC SCRIPT

JESÚS ALTURO I PERUCHO
(Translated by Pablo Molina and Robert G. Babcock)

DEFINITION

THE script generally known today as 'Visigothic' refers to the most common graphic form that the Latin alphabet acquired in the Iberian Peninsula and Septimania in the High Middle Ages. There are, however, chronological differences in each of the territories that adopted the script. Witnesses to this type of script appear at the beginning of the eighth century and continue until the end of thirteenth. The fact that witnesses earlier than the eighth century have not survived, however, does not necessarily imply that the script did not exist before then.

The Visigothic script was not the only type of script that was widely known and practiced in this period and geographical region. To a greater or lesser extent, other scripts coexisted with it: square capital,[1] uncial, and half-uncial;[2] and, in its last stage, as attested particularly in Galicia and in the liturgical books of the suburban Mozarabic parishes of Toledo, Visigothic script was also practiced alongside Caroline, Proto-gothic, and even Gothic script itself.[3] And we must not forget the contemporaneous presence of the *escritura prolongada*[4] (also known as *littera longaria* or *elongata*) derived from the cursive script used in the provincial Roman chanceries[5] which continued to be used in the chanceries of the barbarian kings, including that of the Visigoths.[6]

NAMES

Before the coining of the term Visigothic, this type of script was known by a variety of different names, including *toletana, gallega, moçaraua,* and *gotica.* The last-named designation, *Gothic,* had a long lifespan, continuing into the modern period.[7] One could say that the terms *littera toletana, littera gallega* and *littera moçaraua* are based on (real or supposed) geographical origins.[8] The equation of *littera gothica* and *littera toletana* seems to stem from the belief that the script was introduced to Spain by the Goths when they built their capital in Toledo[9].

Another term, *ulfiliana*, was given by scholars who believed the script derived from the alphabet invented by the Arian bishop Ulfilas[10], or, later, *ataúlfica*, so called by F. Pérez Bayer[11] because he believed it originated in the period of the Gothic king Ataulfo. J. Mabillon chose the term *gotica*,[12] Ángel de Módena was the first to call it *hispana*,[13] and it was also referred to as *española*.[14] C. M. Vigil considered the terms *gótica* and *isidoriana* synonymous.[15] W. Weinberger opted for a technical term "*escritura g-t*."[16] M. Gómez Moreno used the terms *mozárabe* and *toledana*;[17] and Tomás Marín believed that the most reasonable position was to call it *visigótico-mozárabe*.[18] The first scholar to give precedence to the name "Visigoda" (though he also sometimes used the term "Visigothic") was Jesús Muñoz y Rivero, who notably titled his book *Paleografía visigoda*.[19] But it is D. Agustín Millares who established the modern preference for the term Visigothic by the frequent use that he makes of this term in his influential works (although purely for *variatio sermonis*, he does at times also use the term Gothic).[20]

None of the proposed terms is entirely accurate for our script. Some scholars date its origin later than the period of the Visigoths; and even if its origin is from that period, it certainly continued in use well beyond that period. We cannot correctly call it *Spanish* script because it was also used in Portugal and in Septimania; and for this reason the term *Hispanic* is also incorrect, as also the designation *Iberian*. Although it continued to be used in the Mozarabic territory after the Saracen invasion, its most abundant and best witnesses are found in the centers of Christian territories.[21]

In conclusion, although the term *Visigothic* is not precise, it seems best to adopt it in the sense given it by Muñoz ("the Roman script used in Spain in the first centuries of the Middle Ages"),[22] if only for the simple merit of its having become deeply rooted in modern scholarship.

TYPES OF VISIGOTHIC SCRIPT

Like other scripts, Visigothic manifests itself in diverse forms. A greater or lesser degree of perfection results from a variety of influences: the competence, experience, and care of the scribes (producing different levels of script—calligraphic, semi-calligraphic, rudimentary, semi-rudimentary);[23] the greater or lesser deliberateness or rapidity of the strokes (book-hand, cursive, semi-cursive); the stage of the evolution of the script (incipient, formed, decadent); the degree of canonicity of the alphabet and system of abbreviations; or the influence of other scripts (genuine, mixed).

In my opinion, we should not equate cursive writing with coarseness.[24] Indeed, I would argue that these terms are radically opposed to each other, since rapidity of execution always presupposes familiarity with the script and even mastery of the act of writing. In contrast, it is to be expected of a rudimentary or elementary hand that the execution be slow and struggling. In cursive writing, an uncalligraphic result can be due to the speed of the writing or to the mediocre professional level of the scribe; in rudimentary writing, it is always due to a lack of talent or practice. Furthermore, there is a calligraphic form of cursive, an aesthetically pleasing style which is called cursive only because of the graphic forms that it uses. The difficulty and care that its execution demands make it a slowly written script and one restricted to seasoned and expert hands. Its extensive use for documents justifies naming it *visigótica cancilleresca*.[25]

In conclusion, Visigothic calligraphy must be understood as writing performed by professionals who produced an elegant and refined script. And we will find this type of script in the aforementioned chancery script (*cancilleresca*) and also in the round script (*redonda*).

The round script (*redonda*), typical of books but also used in documents,[26] is the more regular and clear type of script. Muñoz defines it very well. For him it is a script written with regularity, preserving the proper separation of the characters, maintaining a distinction between thick and thin strokes, and observing a consistent inclination, which is normally vertical.[27] The term 'book-hand' (*sentada*), since it always refers to a calligraphic script, will be applied both to the round and to the chancery (*cancilleresca*) script;[28] and the terms cursive and semi-cursive, implying no roughness but only swiftness, will also be attributed exclusively to professional variants.[29]

In addition to the scripts produced by professional or highly trained scribes, which vary from the spectacularly beautiful to the simply satisfactory, we find others of rough execution, characteristic of scribes with less training or of those who wrote only sporadically. This type is called rudimentary, and it is an elementary version of the round script (it may appear in a slightly more refined version in the semi-rudimentary variant).

It is principally within the round (*redonda*) category that it is possible to distinguish between majuscule and minuscule. The majuscule letterforms may derive from the square capital and uncial alphabets, sometimes reinterpreted capriciously, or they may simply appear as enlarged Visigothic minuscule letters. In majuscule writing, it is common to incorporate some letters inside of others.

A mixed script is a type that exhibits so many influences and importations of letters from another script that it has lost its original identity (unlike the pure or genuine script which, once formed, lacks foreign elements).[30] For present purposes, the mixed script refers to a transitional script that is moving from Visigothic to Caroline, Protogothic, or even Gothic. It thus includes letterforms and elements of the abbreviation systems typical of these scripts, mixed to various degrees with those of the standard Visigothic script, resulting in a hybrid product. So, from a morphological perspective, there are only two distinct forms: the round (*redonda*) and the cursive. The remainder derive from these two.[31]

GENETIC ORIGIN OF THE ROUND
AND CURSIVE SCRIPTS

The Visigothic cursive obviously arises from a local evolution of the Roman cursive minuscule, in particular, from the cursive used in the provincial chanceries. The only difficulty lies in determining the precise time of its appearance as a distinctive type.

The more complex question is determining the genetic origin of the round script (*redonda*). On this question there are many opinions. A notable group of palaeographers trace its origin to the half-uncial script under cursive influence. According to J. Armengol Rovira, "the Visigothic book script...developed through a process of reduction of the module of the half-uncial script...accompanied by the adoption of some cursive elements."[32] E. A. Lowe also traced the origins of Visigothic round script to half-uncial (in a Spanish version which used the uncial *g*) under cursive influence.[33] P. Lehman thought it derived from a rough half-uncial with cursive tendencies, which, when mixed with a late Roman cursive, developed again into a calligraphic script in the eighth century.[34]

A. M. Mundó differs in that he downplays the influence of cursive, instead deriving round Visigothic directly from the type of "half-uncial which in [BAV] Reginensis latinus 1024 admits the Uncial *g* and the horizontal stroke of the *t* with a slight curve on the left side; a style of writing which in the second part of Autun [Bibliothèque municipale] 27 [fols. 63–76] turns into minuscule writing with decidedly Visigothic characteristics."[35] In his opinion, this derivation is evident from the half-uncial script of the earlier portion of Autun 27 (fols. 16–62). Mundó thus agrees to some extent with T. Marin, who derives Visigothic round script simply from a "slightly evolved form of Roman minuscule."[36]

L. Schiaparelli, however, reversed the order of influence of the scripts that generated Visigothic round script. While recognizing the importance of half-uncial (and even of uncial), he thought that *redonda* derived from a calligraphic development of a previously formed Visigothic cursive.[37] This theory, though later rejected by Millares himself,[38] is still widely accepted.[39] G. Cencetti suggested a new hypothesis, which, in my opinion, is the most plausible. He proposed a parallel development of Visigothic cursive and *redonda* "within the framework of the uninterrupted development of Roman writing in the Iberian peninsula."[40]

Cencetti, moreover, noted that in the Iberian Peninsula in the sixth century, cursive minuscule script was used for everyday purposes, alongside the formal uncial and the less formal half-uncial. But at the same time the semi-cursive script was used not only for scholia and marginal notes, but also for whole codices. Thus:

> it does not seem impossible that the development of the cursive script in its use for everyday purposes and for chancery writing produced the Leonese and Mozarabic cursive, while the other scripts (uncial, half-uncial, and semi-cursive), which were familiar to scholars and other readers, formed the basis for the creation of the [round] minuscule.[41]

I agree with Cencetti. His hypothesis obviates the need to postulate influences from other scripts in order to explain the distinctive use of uncial *g* in Visigothic minuscule, for this same *g* is also present in semi-cursive minuscule.[42]

In sum, it is my opinion that Visigothic round script (*redonda*) arose from a calligraphic development of the semi-cursive minuscule used in the copying of books. I would argue that not only the origin but also the evolution of the cursive and round scripts are independent, without denying specific mutual influences, for example the semi-cursive form.[43]

CHRONOLOGICAL ORIGIN

An equally difficult issue is determining the period at which one can speak of Visigothic script as a completely differentiated type. When can we say that our script presents some formal peculiarities that set it apart from other scripts, in particular from the one that generated it? When do its features make it distinctive? The earliest scholars place its birth in the fifth century, e.g., Francisco Javier de Santiago Palomares,[44] A. M. Burriel and E. de Terreros y Pando,[45] Andrés Merino,[46] and Jesús Muñoz y Rivero,[47] the last two not unequivocally. But this view was overturned by A. Millares, who postulated different chronologies for Visigothic cursive and *redonda*. Initially, he thought that the Visigothic cursive had arisen between the sixth and seventh centuries. Indeed, he stated in 1941 that the Roman cursive minuscule script:

> which was of primary importance as the fundamental original source of the so-called national hands of the Continent, and among them of the Visigothic hand, is the result of a natural development from the majuscule cursive, a development which we may consider as having been completed in the course of the fourth century.[48]

He continued, "the existence in Spain of a cursive diplomatic script, which at least from the sixth century, and then certainly in the seventh, already incorporated the characteristics which after the Arab invasion are seen in the most ancient documents, is beyond question;" and further, "After the careful and in-depth study of Prof. Robinson ... it is impossible to doubt that the writing [of Autun 27] represents the most ancient witness that has been identified of the cursive Visigothic script, one attributable to the middle of the seventh century."[49] He concluded, "by the middle of the seventh century there already existed a Spanish cursive with characters that distinguish it from the common type."[50]

He had, however, a different opinion about the time of the emergence of the round Visigothic script. Since he agreed with Schiaparelli that the Visigothic *redonda* derived from the Visigothic cursive, he naturally assigned to it a later date, "In the domain of book scripts this cursive—which was only exceptionally employed at that time and later—became more calligraphic, absorbing influences from uncial and half-uncial, and gradually acquiring the peculiar characteristics of the round script. We can already see this process in the eighth century;" he concluded, "I am inclined to affirm that before the eighth century, the Spanish scribes had only uncial and half-uncial scripts for their fundamental book hands, and that there was no calligraphic minuscule available other than half-uncial."[51]

Millares dealt with this topic again in 1973,[52] analyzing not only the well-known codicological examples of Autun (MS 27) and of El Escorial (*CLA* 11.1628b), but also epigraphical specimens, particularly the Visigothic slate tablets published by M. Gómez Moreno,[53] and, especially, the diplomas discovered and studied by A. M. Mundó.[54] This examination led him to alter his opinion about the date of the Visigothic cursive. He concluded that the script of these documents was essentially that of the common Roman cursive, "even if in this script, just as in the script of the slate tablets and in that of the few pages of codices that have survived . . . it is possible to glimpse some of the characteristics that would become established in the following period."[55] He emphasized that the seventh-century date generally assigned to the earliest Spanish examples of cursive used as a book script, in Autun 27 and *CLA* 11.1628b, appeared to him acceptable (and the similarity of their writing to that of the slate tablets and documents provided a further justification for attributing the codices to Spain). But he believed that calling this script Visigothic cursive, as though it already had the peculiar features of the script from the beginning of the eighth century that is generally called by that name, was unjustified.[56] His change of heart was influenced by Schiaparelli, who had denied the existence of any Visigothic cursive characteristics in *CLA* 11.1628b.[57] So, Millares redated the origin of the Visigothic cursive to the same century in which the origin of the *redonda* took place, namely the eighth. His opinion is still considered correct by the majority of scholars.[58]

Nonetheless, I believe that some reservations are appropriate. Although a distinctive Visigothic cursive, according to Millares' analysis, does not appear before the eighth century,[59] some form of cursive script is known in many earlier Spanish witnesses. Since cursive was being widely used before the eighth century, and many examples survive from this period, it is reasonable to think that some examples of Visigothic cursive from this period would survive if they had existed. Consequently, we can conclude that Visigothic cursive originated in this century, not earlier. But the round Visigothic script poses a different problem, given that it originated genetically, as I have stated before, in the context of book production. Although the most ancient books known in round Visigothic are also from the eighth century and the previous extant codices are copied in rustic capital, uncial or half-uncial, I do not believe that this observation necessarily implies that other previous witnesses written in Visigothic *redonda* did not exist (even though they have not reached us). Rather I believe the opposite.

There are many reasons that lead me to this view. Firstly, the existence of the *Oracional* of Verona.[60] Its Visigothic *redonda* presents a fully formed and perfected writing system which can hardly have developed overnight.[61] Since all indications are that the *Oracional* was made around AD 700, we must assume that the type of script employed in it was developed at least a generation earlier. But there is more. The sporadic incorporation of some letters of the *redonda* alphabet in the writings of the

Visigothic slates, as well as the frequent use in these tablets of peculiar Visigothic orthography, presupposes the existence of the round script in a finished form at least by the end of the sixth century or the beginning of the seventh.[62]

On the other hand, the aforementioned codices in uncial and half-uncial script that are commonly dated to the middle of the seventh century and assigned an Hispanic origin (on account of their letterforms, abbreviation systems, and orthography), presuppose and indirectly demonstrate, in my view, the existence and contemporaneous use of a Visigothic book script—even more so if we accept the previously proposed genetic origin. In my opinion, the similarities are due to the influence of coexisting writing systems rather than to the evolution of one toward the other.

There is yet another issue, namely the problems raised by the existence of the Visigothic script north of the Pyrenees. Even aside from the examples of codices copied beyond the Pyrenees by copyists who were exiled or removed from their own cultural environment (studied or mentioned by S. Tafel,[63] A. M. Mundó,[64] J. Vezin,[65] and L. Schiaparelli,[66] among others), the recognition of exemplars in Visigothic script copied by local scribes in active scriptoria of Aquitaine would lead us, of necessity, to conclude that the Visigothic script originated in the Visigothic kingdom of Toulouse by the end of the fifth century. How otherwise could we explain the use of that script in Aquitaine after the Visigoths were expelled from it by Clovis' Franks after the defeat at Vouillé, near Poitiers, in the year 507?

But even in the absence of certainty,[67] we cannot forget that Septimania was a territory where the Visigothic script was undoubtedly used. It remained under Gothic control only until its conquest by the Arabs in the year 720. When it was later recovered by the Christians, this was done by the Frankish king Pepin in 759, not by the Goths. It seems to me that there is a new argument here in favor of the formation of the Visigothic *redonda* long before the eighth century. Its origin in that century would hardly account for its continuous use in the Septimania region until, at least, the first quarter of the ninth century;[68] and it would fail to explain its use in the Mozarabic area occupied by the Muslims from the year 711, after the defeat at Guadalete.

Hence, I believe that it is not entirely mistaken to propose again an ancient chronology—between the end of the fifth century and the beginning of the sixth—for the origin of our script. We must also take into account that certain isolated, yet very characteristic elements of the Visigothic script (such as the "X aspada," the ligature of XL for the Roman numeral 40) are already found in inscriptions, for example that of the bishop Vincolmalos (AD 509), today at the Museum of Huelva.[69] It seems logical to think that, in spite of the common Roman basis of its alphabet, the Latin script being used throughout the empire by the indigenous peoples of various regions would evolve slowly but surely, in a natural and constant manner, toward a peculiar local type. Afterwards, with the fall of the empire and its cultural consequences, this process of scribal differentiation ought to accelerate and the script develop national characteristics under the first few generations of scribes trained after the year 476.[70] On the other hand, despite the lack of witnesses, it seems more logical that this change manifested itself earlier in the book script than in the documentary. The latter is more frequently used than the former, and public documents possess an official character; so the documentary script ought to maintain longer its original graphic form.

In conclusion, I would situate the birth of the round Visigothic script (*redonda*) at the beginning of the sixth century; and I would assign a date in the eighth century to the origin of cursive Visigothic.[71]

GEOGRAPHICAL ORIGIN

Intimately related to the question of dating the origins of Visigothic script is the question of its geographical origin. This too is a thorny issue for which various solutions have been proposed. Millares was the first to address it. He is reported to have stated in 1978—in light of the likely Catalan origin of the most ancient Visigothic codices and documents known— that the script had its origin "in the area of the Pyrenees, from the coastal part of the province of Tarragona through the province of Gallia Narbonensis."[72]

Mundó also raised the problem of the geographical origin of our script. He rejected Millares' hypothesis because it did not explain how a script that originated in Catalonia could have expanded to the rest of the peninsula in the period after the Saracen invasion, a period in which the different territories became isolated and removed from the nucleus of the Pyrenees. (This difficulty certainly disappears if we accept the sixth century origin for the script that I have proposed in Section 11.5 above.) Mundó postulated, as did Merino,[73] a Toledan origin for the script because of "the cultural leadership Toledo exercised...during the seventh century" and because of Toledo's "rôle in the dissemination of culture throughout the realm." Hence he believed that it was "more logical to think that it was there, in the center, that the graphic synthesis which produced the national hand called Visigothic was forged."[74]

Seville has also been proposed as the center of the origin and dissemination of the script. This argument is based on the cultural importance of the most eminent Hispanic bishops in the seventh century. Various scholars, including Díaz y Díaz and Ch. Higounet have subscribed to this theory.[75] Bischoff postulated North Africa as the place of birth and diffusion of Visigothic script, basing his suggestion on the possible northwestern African origin of the Latin codices of Saint Catherine's on Mount Sinai.[76]

In sum, an origin for the script is assigned to one place or another based on: (a) the origin of the oldest known codices and diplomas written in Visigothic script; (b) the most important centers of production by virtue of their political leadership or cultural primacy; or (c) the supposed origin of graphic monuments unknown until relatively recently. But if we assign the beginning of the Visigothic *redonda* to the early sixth century, Narbonne or Barcelona, the successive capitals of the Visigothic kingdom from the second quarter of the sixth century, are not unworthy candidates, especially Narbonne, a metropolitan capital.[77] This hypothesis is even more plausible since in other nearby areas we already find clear examples of "national scripts," for example, the Merovingian cursive used in copying the homilies of Avitus, apparently in the sixth century.[78] It should also be remembered that among the pre-Carolingian scripts, there is a great similarity between the Merovingian script and Visigothic.[79] This could have arisen from the proximity of their respective geographical origins. In sum, the assignment of a geographical origin for the Visigothic script depends on the chronology that we attribute to the birth of round Visigothic. For my part, on the basis of my proposed date of origin for the script, I would locate the birthplace of the *redonda* in the Narbonese region, or, more specifically, in Narbonne.[80]

FIXATION OF TYPES AND HEYDAY
OF THE SCRIPT

In the absence of more ancient witnesses, it is necessary to place the crystallization of the basic features of round Visigothic no earlier than 700. But its calligraphic highpoint certainly occurred in the middle of the tenth century,[81] the period of the scribes Florencio de Valeránica[82] and Vigila de Albelda, two of the greatest masters of Visigothic calligraphy. This efflorescence continued, to some extent, into the eleventh century but saw its decline at the end of that century.[83]

Hence, the codices and diplomas written in territories such as Septimania and Catalonia were excluded from this culmination of the Visigothic graphic process, for they had already abandoned the script. Also excluded were areas in which the use of Visigothic script belonged only to a limited community, subject to a power with a different language and script, namely the Mozarabic zone. In these areas the script followed another kind of evolution, characterized by the maintenance of archaic features.[84] The splendor, therefore, only occurred in the northwestern part of the Iberian Peninsula, particularly in Castile and León, including la Rioja. Another question that remains unsolved is the precise identification of the principal center where this new graphic synthesis of high calligraphic quality flourished for the first time. San Pedro de Cardeña has been tentatively proposed as that center.[85]

In any case, the round Visigothic script continued in its pure state until the third quarter of the eleventh century, at which time a process of contamination begins under the influence of the newly introduced continental Caroline minuscule. A conscious and deliberate opposition to this influence arose. This resistance came from liturgical traditions maintained by papal privilege and kept in books that not only contained texts of the old Hispanic liturgy, but continued to be transmitted in the old Visigothic script. This occurred, for example, in Toledo as late as the thirteenth century, and perhaps even the fourteenth.[86] Further sources of opposition were the mechanical and involuntarily conservative attitudes typical of remote areas far from the major cultural centers. A document in decadent Visigothic of the year 1234 reflects this conservatism in Galicia.[87]

Regarding the cursive variant, if the originality of the diploma of King Silo is ruled out, there is an excellent example of cursive Visigothic in a Catalan diploma of the year

PLATE 11.1 La Seu d'Urgell, Arxiu de la Catedral d'Urgell, fons Codinet, perg. 1, AD 815, Visigothic cursive, Catalan variant.

815, which demonstrates that, at least by the beginning of the ninth century, this script had reached its maturity (Plate 11.1). There are also magnificent examples from Asturias and León dating to the tenth century. Millares established a formal distinction for the regional varieties that he studied: the Asturias-León variant and the Mozarabic.[88] There are very few witnesses to the latter, though they suffice, in my opinion, to allow us to compare it to the Visigothic Catalan cursive, even though each has its own peculiarities.[89]

LETTERFORMS AND ABBREVIATIONS IN VISIGOTHIC SCRIPT AT ITS PEAK

The Visigothic round script

Letterforms

The *a* is open. It is distinguished from the *u* by the second stroke, which is curved in the *a* and straight in the *u*. The *a* is one of the most distinctive letters.

The *b* can have a bowl that is either closed or slightly open. The top of the shaft, as with other tall letters (*d, l, l*), has an introductory stroke that is large and rounded in the most ancient manuscripts and in the archaizing Mozarabic witnesses. In the examples from the Castile-León region, broadly speaking, it is straight, and bevel-cut.

The *c*, like the *o*, the *p*, and the *q*, is basically the same as the modern letter.

The *d* can have a straight shaft (the half-uncial form) or a rounded shaft (the uncial form).

The most characteristic form of *e* resembles the Greek epsilon, but it can also be similar to the modern letter. The *e-caudata* is also used.

The *f* is almost always open, that is to say, the upper loop does not rejoin the shaft. The shaft generally descends visibly below the baseline.

The *g* is uncial and is one of the most distinctive characteristics of the Visigothic script.

The *h*, just as the *m* and *n*, has its last stroke perpendicular to the line of writing or with a slight turn to the left or the right, the latter being the most common (though not exclusive) form from the eleventh century onward.

The *i* is like the modern letter, but also occurs in a tall form, like the majuscule (*I*), and in a descending form, like a *j*. It acquires the latter form in the *tj* ligature when the *t* has a sibilant sound 𝖺.[90] On the other hand, the *i* is tall or long (*i-longa*) at the beginning of a word (unless the following letter also extends above the baseline) or when it functions as a semi-consonant. This form can also be used in the interior of compound words since the inner element is perceived to be the beginning of a new word, as in *deInde*.

The final stroke of the *k* is horizontal and joins to the following letter.

The *l* resembles the *i-longa*, but it has a small curved stroke at the baseline, which usually connects to the next letter.

The *r* and *s* are quite similar in shape, but the former has a more elongated and, at times, more pointed shoulder, while in the *s*, it is shorter and more rounded.

The *t* is one of the most typical letters of the Visigothic script. It occurs in three forms. (i) The most frequent is the one with the horizontal stroke lengthened to the left, descending and curving back until it joins the vertical shaft at the baseline to form a closed semicircle. (ii) The upper stroke can also lengthen to the left, but in an upward direction and then curl to the right until it reaches the shaft near its base; the result is a letter that resembles a backwards Greek *beta* (β). This form usually appears when the following letter is *e, i, r,* or *s*. (iii) Occasionally, in the Visigothic round script, the cursive *t*—similar to a *c*—is also used. This form can appear at the end of words or syllables that are separated from the following word (or syllable).

The *u*, as mentioned above, differs from the *a* in having its second stroke almost always straight and descending below the baseline. A form similar to a *v* is used when it is written superscript (this is not an abbreviation), for example, -*t*ᵛ*r* and -*t*ᵛ*s*.

The *x* can have either the form of the letter in current use or a form similar to a *c* with a slightly concave vertical stroke on the left side, which extends further below the baseline than it ascends above the headline.

The *y* can be elevated, with the base of its shaft resting on the baseline, or it can descend below the baseline, as in the letter in current use.

The *z* can have an upper curl that is relatively large and a lower curl that descends to varying degrees below the baseline.

But, as Mabillon wrote, *rectius docent specimina quam verba*. Consequently, I give as an example of the Visigothic round script the alphabet of Vigila (Fig. 11.1), one of the best scribes of Visigothic.[91] This example comes from the *Codex Albeldensis*, a manuscript also known as the *Codex Vigilanus* from its main copyist. Vigila produced this codex in collaboration with Sarracino in the monastery of San Martín de Albelda between the years 974 and 976.[92]

Joinings and ligatures

The terms 'joinings' and 'ligatures' are often used without sufficient distinction. By 'joining' I understand the scribe's purposeful union of two or more consecutive letters presenting, at a minimum, one common stroke. By 'ligature' (or linkage) I understand the natural union of strokes in consecutive letters resulting from the cursive nature of the writing or from the rapidity with which it is executed. The joinings, initially only used at the end of a line, arose intentionally from the need to fit an entire word in the same line of writing—an absolute necessity in the case of verses—while the ligatures have a more spontaneous origin.

I believe that it is desirable to distinguish between two types of ligatures: primary and secondary. Indeed, in addition to the original ligatures created in a free and unplanned manner, there are others that are used intentionally rather than sporadically since they have become part of the tradition of the script. This is the case for most of the ligatures that are habitually found in the round Visigothic script. In the round script there are more secondary joinings and secondary ligatures than primary ligatures. The opposite phenomenon is found in the cursive script.

Some characteristic joinings are those formed by the syllable *iT* or *it*, and by *or* or *os*. In the uppercase alphabet they are somewhat more abundant; for example, the joinings

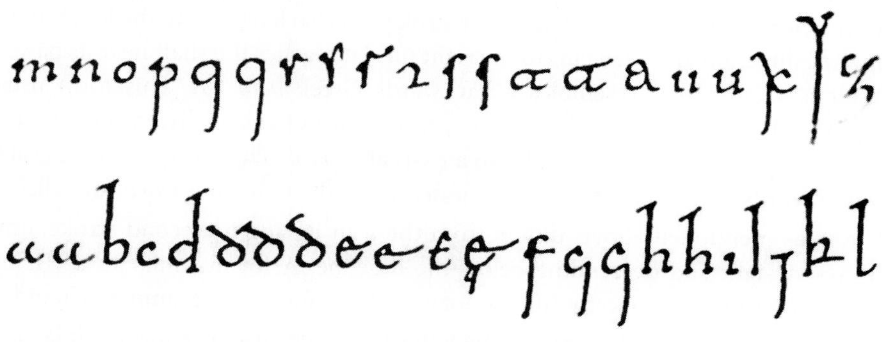

FIG. 11.1 The letterforms used by Vigila in the *Codex Albeldensis* (Madrid, Escorial, MS D.I.2).

FR, ND, NE, and *TE.* As previously mentioned, in the uppercase alphabet, scribes sometimes include miniature letters in the interior spaces of larger letters.[93]

The round Visigothic could naturally be written with increased or decreased rapidity and permit, at least sporadically, some primary ligatures. Moreover, we constantly find secondary ligatures formed from a letter that finishes with a horizontal stroke toward the right, which serves to join it to the following letter. This is the case, for example, of the letters *a, e, f, k, l, r, t,* and sometimes *n.* And these ligatures were formed with as many letters as possible that could be subsumed into the horizontal line to the right. This can extend through an entire word, as in the case of *terra.*

The ligature *XL* for forty is very typical, having a cross-shaped *X* with an *L* of smaller dimension in the shape of a comma hanging from the tip of the second stroke of the *X*.

The Visigothic cursive script

Letterforms

The *a* is open and has a long tail. It is written above the line, with only its final stroke touching the line (see Fig. 11.2).

The *b* generally has a long shaft, and the bowl is normally closed.

The *c* can have either a simple form, like the modern letter, or a fine stroke of cursive origin on the left side of its base, a vestige of the elongation of the preceding letter which, in the cursive script, had joined the *c* to the previous letter **ſ**. This stroke eventually became naturalized as a regular part of the new form of the letter in isolation. In some cases, this same fine stroke has folded back toward the main body of the letter; and as it closes, it gives the letter an *s*-shape. On other occasions this adventitious stroke, after extending and closing at the top, has become a reduplication of the initial semicircle of *c*, which ends up having a double concentric stroke **ℂ**.

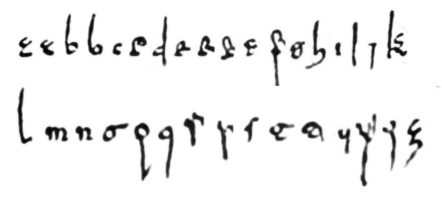

FIG. 11.2 Cursive Visigothic letterforms in a document of June 12, 918 written by the priest Sisvieno (ACLugo, Libro X de pergaminos, leg. 2, n°. 3).

The *d* looks like a *c* joined to an *i-longa* with its stem dropping below the baseline; but it can also have the same adventitious stroke found in the letter *c*, with an identical formal result: (1) the curling of the stroke until it acquires the shape of a *c*, so that the *d* looks like *cd* ȡ; or (2) reduplication of the curved stroke until it forms a concentric stroke ɖ.

The *e*, like the *c*, can have the aforementioned stroke. Since it is a letter that has an initial convex stroke, it can end up either resembling the syllable *ce* or reduplicating the curved stroke until it forms the same concentric semicircle found in the *c* and the *d*. Another characteristic form of *e* resembles an inverted numeral 3. In final position, the horizontal stroke is elongated to the right.

The cursive *f* either is like the *f* of the round script or turns the vertex of its shaft clockwise until it closes on itself reaching the transversal stroke. Thus, it looks like the top half of an *e* with a long descending tail.

The *g* is generally closed in the cursive script of the Astur-Leonese region and normally open in the Mozarabic and Catalan varieties. It often resembles the numeral 8. In the Catalan variant, its base may rest on the baseline.

The *h* can have a straight or a rightward-leaning shaft.

The *i* of the cursive script, that of the round script, can sit on the baseline and rise to the height of the other minims; or it can ascend or descend.

The cursive forms of the letters *k*, *l*, *m* and *n* are similar to the corresponding letters in the round script.

The *o* either is like the modern letter or can have an adventitious stroke at the top, of cursive origin, a vestige of the stroke that unites it to the next letter. This can also be present when the letter appears in isolation.

The *p* can be like the modern letter, or it can have a *q*-shaped form. Alternatively, it can be open on the left, so that it resembles an inverted Uncial *g*. Sometimes the descender terminates in a hook-like stroke.

The *q* can be like the modern letter, or it may resemble the numeral 9.

The *r* and the *s* are very similar to their counterparts in the round script. But the *r* in ligatures has an extended shoulder which forms a point (similar to an inverted *v*), and the shaft descends below the baseline. The *t* can be closed as in the round script, but executed in a single stroke. Alternatively, it can have the form of an inverted beta, or resemble a *c*.

The cursive *u* is like the *u* of the round script, but with the second stroke more elongated downwards. In a more cursive form, it acquires a shape similar to an inverted numeral 3 but with the top portion being triple the size of the lower portion. This can be explained as resulting from a single stroke for the whole body of the *u*, with the lower part representing only that portion of the second stroke of the *u* that extends below the baseline. This form is standard in the *-ue* following a *q* in the enclitic *-que*.

The *x* can resemble the same letter in the round script, or it may be similar to Greek ψ or, in its more cursive variant, φ.

The *y* is usually written in a single stroke.

The *z* may or may not have a crest; and, according to Millares, from the eleventh century onwards the crest normally rests on the baseline, acquiring the appearance of a *c* with a standard *z* attached to its base.[94]

Joinings and ligatures

Among genuine joinings we find *om*, *or*, *tr*, and *ts*. Naturally, ligatures are more abundant, since they constitute an essential element of the cursive script. Letters that never or almost never bind with the following letter in the round Visigothic may do so in the cursive script, including *c*, *g*, short *i*, *n*, *o*, *s*, *x*, and *y*.

To conclude this section we may say in accord with Millares that the characteristic traits of Mozarabic cursive are its slightly leftward inclination[95] and the following details: *g* with an open lower bowl; the form of *t* when followed by *e* and exceptionally, by *r*, and that of the ligatures *e-t* and *i-t*; it does not use the high *u* and, on the other hand, it does employ to a greater or lesser degree the hooked *u*, a form unknown to the script of the Asturias-León region;[96] the assibilated *ti* appears either as a joining of the cursive *t* and *i*, or as the combination resembling an inverted beta.[97] Millares further declared that the ligatures *a-g*, *a-m*, *a-s*, and *a-t* are regular, in the final case preserving the alteration of the form of *t* if it is followed by *e* or *i*; the abbreviation of *per* consists of a small line through the descender of the *p*; *us* is only abbreviated by means of the semicolon or the raised *s* when it follows *b*, *i-longa*, *m*, *n*, and *p*; the cursive sign (the treble clef) abbreviates *um* in the syllables *num*, *rum*, and *tum*.[98]

ABBREVIATIONS

Aside from the system of superimposed letters in the pure Visigothic script—found only in the hybrid transitional script— abbreviations are indicated by a straight or somewhat wavy horizontal stroke placed above the abbreviated word. In general, this line is surmounted by a point (*punctus*) which, under cursive influence, can become a line (though a shorter one than the line below it). Cursive influence is also the source of an abbreviation stroke that is reminiscent of the numeral 2; and this may, in turn, develop a shape similar to a *v* with the second stroke more elongated. The superimposed point is normally not used when the abbreviation stroke passes through the shaft of any tall letter. In the cursive script the abbreviation stroke may have the shape of a loop or a spiral.

When the abbreviation stroke indicates the omission of *m*, it is generally surmounted by a point. This is not normally the case when it is used for an *n*. But this is a scribal tendency rather than a rule. The superimposed point does not appear in abbreviations in the cursive Visigothic script.

To abbreviate the letters -*ue* in the enclitic –*que* or -*us* after any other consonant, either the semicolon or a sign similar to an *s* is used. Millares thought that both signs had coexisted since antiquity and that they had independent origins. He agreed, therefore, with E. M. Thompson,[99] and disagreed with Lowe, since he believed that the sign similar to an *s* derived from a cursive superscript *u*.[100] For Millares this sign was older because it is attested in more ancient Visigothic manuscripts, such as the *Oracional de Verona* (Verona, Biblioteca Capitolare, LXXXIX), Madrid, Escorial, MS R. II.18, and Paris, BN lat. 4667. In reality, the semicolon appears in earlier non-Visigothic manuscripts; and even if there are no surviving witnesses in Visigothic, this does not necessarily mean it is younger. I believe that the *s*-shaped sign simply evolved from the cursive semicolon, as the scribe quickly traced the point and the comma without lifting the pen. It should also be noted that the *s*-shaped sign additionally appears in the ending –*is* of *nobis* and *uobis*, and sometimes in -*lis*, -*nis* and -*tis*, (that is, at the end of words that have no *u*).[101]

In the cursive Visigothic script, final -*us* is abbreviated with a stroke that starts on the left side of the shafts of tall letters, rotates on itself toward the right, and passes through the shaft. But in this script, a sign reminiscent of a treble clef is even more common.

The endings in -*um* can be indicated by a vertical or slightly inclined line that bisects the final stroke of the preceding letter (usually *c*, *g*, *l*, *m*, *n*, *r*, or *t*). In the cursive script this stroke acquires a characteristic shape similar to a treble clef.

The abbreviation for *per* was, in the oldest exemplars, a straight or slightly wavy stroke that horizontally bisected the descender. Under cursive influence, this stroke was joined to the end of the stroke that produced the bowl of the *p*, which explains the oblique stroke so characteristic of standard Visigothic script.

The pronoun or syllable *qui* is abbreviated with an oblique or straight stroke that bisects the descender of the *q*.

The possessives are abbreviated with a medial *s* instead of with the medial *r* that is characteristic of the other Latin scripts. Thus we find *nsm* or *usm,* instead of *nrm* or *urm* (for *nostrum* or *uestrum,* respectively).

Other characteristic abbreviations of Visigothic script include: *apstls* (*apostolus*), *aum* (*autem*), *epscps* (*episcopus*), *famls* (*famulus*), *prsbtr* (*presbiter*), *qnm* (*quoniam*), *Srl* (*Israel*).

It is useful to emphasize that the alleged influence of Semitic practices in the Visigothic abbreviation system, in which vowels are deleted and only the consonants of the abbreviated word remain, was already noted by Antonio Nasarre in the prologue to Cristóval Rodríguez' *Bibliotheca universal de la polygraphia española*.[102] But given that this practice is already attested in Hispano-Visigothic inscriptions prior to the Muslim invasion, it seems unlikely that it derives from Arabic script.[103]

ORTHOGRAPHY

When dealing with the Visigothic script, we cannot omit reference to the peculiar spelling of its texts. E. Flórez gathered information on its general features, adding that this spelling "was a vice, or a matter of taste, in certain periods,"[104] and that, occasionally, some orthographic detail may serve, if only indirectly, for making chronological distinctions.[105]

The following are some of the characteristics of Visigothic spelling: the addition of *i* at the beginning of a word that starts with an *s* followed by another consonant (*iscriptura*), or its suppression by hypercorrection (*sta* for *ista*). The reduction of consecutive double consonants (*eclesia*). The apparently random use of the *h*, often incorporated when it is not necessary from an etymological point of view and omitted otherwise (*homnes, anc*). The use of *g* instead of *j* (that is, semiconsonantal *i*) (*magor*) or *i* instead of *g* (*ienitor*). Confusion of *u* and *b* (*haueo* for *habeo*) or vice versa (*pabor* for *pauor*). The use of *b* instead of *p* (*abtum*) or *p* for *b* (*puplicum*), *g* for *c* (*eglesia*) or the reverse (*intecritate*), *k* for *c* (*kaput*), *t* for *d* (*aput*) or *d* for *t* (*sustinead*). Confusion between *m* and *n* (*conpetet, uolumtas*) or between *s* and *x* (*testum, dextruxi*). The preference of *qu* for *c* (*quur*), but also the use of *c* for *qu* (*corum*).

The occasional inclusion of punctuation marks that indicate a pause within a word is surely a consequence of reading under the breath, and also, frequently, of syllabic reading (*clari.ficare, uas.culum, proprie.tate*).

NUMERALS

As regards the graphic representation of the numerals, in addition to the distinctiveness of the numeral XL (mentioned in Section 11.5 above), it should be noted that the first use of Arabic numerals in a Latin text is in a miscellaneous codex in Visigothic script, currently preserved in the Arxiu Capitular of La Seu d'Urgell (*Codex miscellaneus*, AD 938), but surely copied in Cordoba in 938, as attested by its colophon. The chart in Figure 11.3 shows the single digits (1–10), the tens (from 10–90), and 100, with

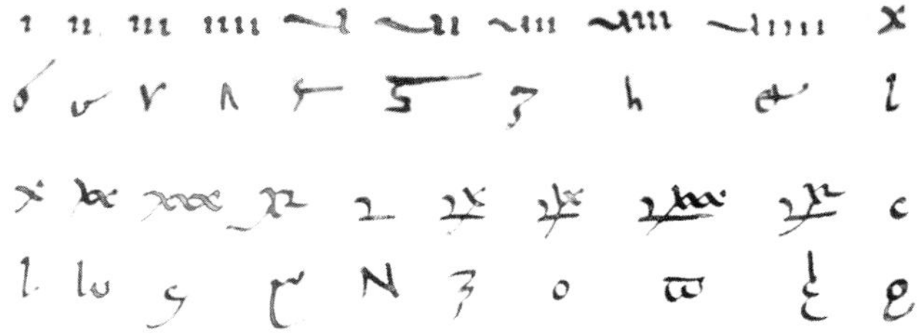

FIG. 11.3 Arabic and Latin numerals in Visigothic script (from La Seu d'Urgell, Arxiu Capitular, *Codex miscellaneus*, AD 938).

the Roman characters above the Arabic equivalents. Note that zero does not yet appear in this document.

REGIONAL VARIATIONS

The Visigothic script changed over time during the period in which it was used, and there were also variations within the different geographical regions where it was employed.

It is not always easy to assign a particular codex to a specific region; indeed, the contrary is true.[106] Nonetheless, regional variations do, in fact, exist.[107] The following regional variants may be distinguished, though each has a greater or lesser degree of individual differentiation:[108] Septimanian (Plate 11.2), Catalan, Aragonese (Plate 11.3), Navarran, Riojan (Plate 11.4), Asturian, Leonese, Castilian, Galician, Portuguese, and Mozarabic.[109]

The identification of regional types was made in a gradual way over a long period of time.[110] Merino was responsible for important progress in this field, as he distinguished two regional variants of round Visigothic. He wrote:

> I believe that if one traces a line from Cartagena, passing through Toledo and ending in Santiago de Galicia . . . we have a division between two zones of writing. [The Visigothic Bible conserved in the Bibliotheca de la Santa Iglesia of Toledo] pertains to the region south of this line . . . ; every Visigothic manuscript that has this type of letters belongs to the southern regions . . . The Visigothic script of Old Castile is much more regular, more clear, and almost always written with a fine pen.[111]

Muñoz also approached the study of Visigothic script on the basis of the ancient kingdoms. After endorsing Merino's account of the Mozarabic variant, he described its main features and even established specific differences between the Andalusian (Plate 11.5) and Toledan variants of the Mozarabic type:

> The Mozarabic script has different proportions than that used in the Christian realms . . . It is shorter and its width more pronounced. The letter strokes are fatter, perhaps because the Mozarabic scribes adopted the Muslim use of reed pens for writing. The writing has an archaic aspect . . . especially in the manuscripts of Andalusía . . . which was most separated from [northern] influence.

He saw this distinction disappearing as the Christians advanced further and further to the south, bringing with them more up-to-date script types that began to influence the southern scribes, so that, to cite one example, the script of Toledo in the eleventh century began to take on the appearance of the Northern script. It became better proportioned, less fat, and conformed more to the style of León and Castile: airy with a curved outline, and admitting few abbreviations (though a greater number than in earlier periods).[112]

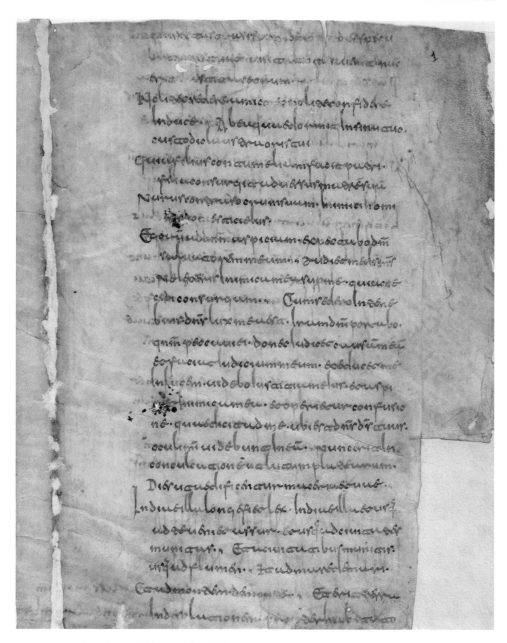

PLATE 11.2 Barcelona, Biblioteca de Catalunya, MS. 2541/1, *c.*800, Visigothic script of probable Septimanian origin.

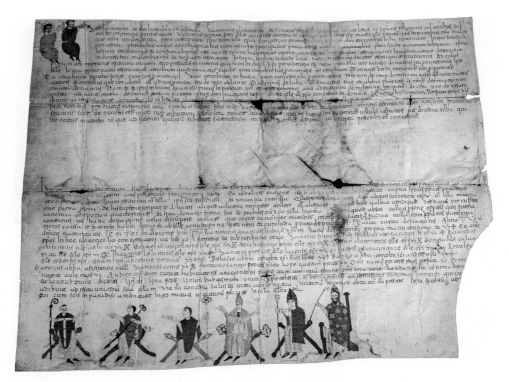

PLATE 11.3 Huesca, Archivo de la Catedral de Huesca, *Actas del Concilio de Jaca*, end of the eleventh century, round Visigothic script of the Aragonese variety.

In fact, the characteristics that Muñoz assigned to the Mozarabic variant of the Visigothic script are, in essence, those currently accepted as such.[113] These characteristics, along with those outlined by Merino for the Castilian-Leonese variant at its peak, allow for a better generic differentiation of the two most important regional varieties of Visigothic script.[114] It must be acknowledged that, in the absence of detailed studies, the regional differences are not sufficiently understood;[115] and that, because the attention of palaeographers has primarily focused on establishing the moment at which the old Visigothic script was abandoned for the new Caroline script, only scant attention has been given to the morphological characteristics and systems of abbreviation of the mixed transitional script.

THE DECLINE OF THE VISIGOTHIC SCRIPT

The decline of the Visigothic script occurred at different times in different regions, but it always occurred through a transition process characterized by the combination of

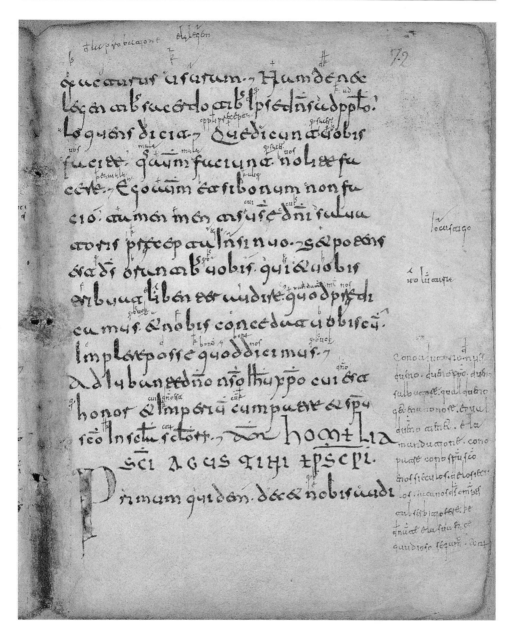

PLATE 11.4 Madrid, Real Academia de la Historia, cód. 60, f. 72r, end of the ninth century, provenance: Monastery of San Millán de la Cogolla.

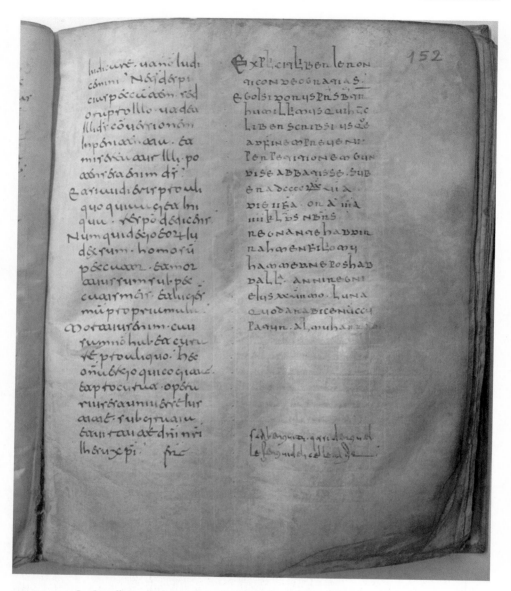

PLATE 11.5 La Seu d'Urgell, Arxiu de la Catedral d'Urgell, *Codex miscellaneus*, AD 938, f. 152r, round and cursive Visigothic script of the Andalusian type, probably from Cordoba.

older elements with newer ones. E. Terreros first called attention to a type of script that was transitioning from Visigothic to Caroline, and he stated that:

> the abrogation of the Visigothic script could not compel all Spaniards to give it up until many years later. The number of teachers of the new French script could not have been so great, nor the opposition to their teaching of it so minimal, that it instantly became universal throughout the entire nation. But from this point onwards, a French script flavored with Visigothic began to be written.[116]

Terreros described the Caroline script as an introduction after the year 1100, resulting from a decree of King Alfonso el Conquistador, or from other reasons that are unknown to us.[117]

According to Merino:

> whether as a result of the Council of Leon or of the decree to introduce French script, after the year 1100 there is an innovation in the style of script. And even if Visigothic script is still used, it has a foreign flavor. I would say that the participation of so many Frenchmen, especially from Gascony, in the conquest of Toledo and their settling in the regions of this city (as shown by various grants and privileges) caused the style of writing there to change a great deal. And so we find that the writing style of Toledo took on the French flavor much earlier than did that of Castile and Leon.[118]

Muñoz offered an overview of the chronology of the survival of the Visigothic script in the kingdoms of Galicia, Asturias, León, and Castile. He rejected the idea that this script disappeared during the reign of Alfonso VI (1065–1109), or that Alfonso was involved in trying to outlaw it.[119] He summarized his conclusions in five points: (1) the French script appears during the reign of Alfonso VI, but the documents emanating from his chancery were normally copied in Visigothic script; (2) Doña Urraca used both scripts but gave preference to Visigothic in Galician documents and to the French script in Castilian and Leonese documents; (3) during the reign of Alfonso VII (1126–57), the French script predominated, but the Visigothic script still survived; (4) in private charters, the French script became frequent only after 1115; (5) in Galicia, it is not uncommon to find documents in Visigothic script as late as the end of the twelfth century.[120]

This assessment appears to be confirmed by recent studies. According to data provided by Ruiz Asencio,[121] the Visigothic script lingers in León and Castile until 1120 (and sporadically until 1130–5), and the Caroline script begins to be used normally after 1110–20.[122] Therefore, the key date for this change should be located at the end of the first quarter of the twelfth century.

Asturias was also a region in which the Visigothic script persisted longer. M. Calleja found the Caroline script in use there already in 1116, but notes the use of Visigothic until 1166.[123] The use of Visigothic is documented by Rosa Maria Blasco in the Monastery of Belmonte until 1157 and in the Monastery of San Vicente of Oviedo until 1166.[124] And we should not forget the *Liber testamentorum ecclesiae Ouetensis*, copied during the first part of the pontificate of Bishop Pelayo (1098–1130 and 1142–3).[125]

In Cantabria, as well, Blasco found also that the use of Visigothic continued for the better part of the twelfth century. She cites examples from the Monastery of Santa Juliana in Santillana del Mar until 1136 and from Santa María del Puerto, in Santoña, until 1120.[126]

At the beginning of the nineteenth century, the Portuguese palaeographer J. P. Ribeiro, called attention to the individuality of the Portuguese style of Visigothic.[127] More recently, M. J. Azevedo Santos documented the use of Visigothic script in Portugal until 1123, after a period of transition that had already begun in 1054. Fully Caroline examples are found as early as 1108.[128]

It appears then that the developments in Portugal, in general terms, run parallel to those in Castile, León, Asturias, and Cantabria, and that Portugal does not exhibit archaizing tendencies like those found in Galicia,[129] where there are more, but isolated examples of Visigothic survival for a longer period. For Galicia, according to M. Lucas Alvarez:[130]

> In San Martín of Santiago, there are only two documents [in Visigothic script] after 1150; Carboeiro has four that are later than this date, one of them from 1199; Sobrado preserves six that are later, one from 1194; Lugo only two, from 1152 and 1156; Samos one from 1191; Penamayor one from 1164; Melón three from 1152, 1159, and 1165; Meira four between 1150 and 1163; in the Cathedral of Orense there is one from 1176; in Oseira, eight, dated between 1150 and 1189. In all, there are forty documents in Visigothic later than the year 1150, and in comparison, many hundreds of the same period written in Caroline minuscule.[131]

It appears then that in Cantabria and Asturias (and even in Galicia and Portugal), just as in León and Castile, we can locate the crucial date of the change from Visigothic to Caroline around the year 1120. This does not mean that some archaizing tendencies did not persist in these areas, especially in Galicia. Be that as it may, from the third quarter of the eleventh century there is evidence in the Western territories of the gradual introduction of Caroline influence in the Visigothic script. Generally, the new continental script solidifies its preeminence between the years 1110 and 1120.

The reasons for its introduction are known: (a) the relations of the sovereigns of Asturias with Cluny and Rome, beginning with Ferdinand, but especially under Alfonso VI; (b) the French orientation of Alfonso VI's successive marriages; (c) the Gregorian reform and the subsequent presence of papal legates in Castile and León; (d) the holding of councils, particularly that of Burgos in 1080 to change the liturgy and that of León (less securely known) for the replacement of the old script; and (e) the exchanges facilitated by the pilgrimage route to Santiago de Compostela.[132]

As regards the Visigothic script of the eastern territories, A. Canellas attributed the beginning of the influence of the Caroline script in Aragón to the reign of Alfonso I (1104–34).[133] However, he confirms the maintenance of the Visigothic script until the reign of Alfonso II (1162–96). M. Usón described the Aragonese territory as one that aligned itself with the archaizing regions and was "the last Spanish territory to use Visigothic script in its chancery. It persisted here approximately thirty years longer than in Castile, where it disappeared already in 1134 during the reign of Alfonso VII."[134] Canellas finds Visigothic witnesses in Aragón even in the year 1162.[135] On the other hand, he notes the preferential use of the round form both for chancery and for private documents.

In Septimania, Visigothic script was used for a briefer period than in any other territory. I myself have tried to describe a precise chronology for its use there as well as for its later replacement by Caroline minuscule. I have also addressed some of the characteristic features and abbreviation system of Septimanian Visigothic. The influence of the Caroline script on the Septimanian Visigothic is already observable at the beginning of the ninth century. A change in scribal training occurs generation by generation. Already by the end of the first decade of the ninth century the younger copyists who write in Visigothic in Septimania (a) do not use, or rarely use, the abbreviation stroke with a point over a horizontal stroke; (b) replace, entirely or partially, the sign similar to *s* (in the endings *–bus* and *–que*) with the semicolon; (c) begin using the Caroline abbreviations of the possessive pronouns (which use medial *r*) instead of the Visigothic-style abbreviation of these words; (d) prefer *au* to *aum* for *autem* and begin to favor *qm* over *qnm* for *quoniam* and *propr* over *ppr* for *propter*; (f) employ the common continental abbreviation for *per*.

As for the alphabet, in the Septimanian variety of Visigothic script the Caroline *a* is the first letter that gets incorporated into the Visigothic system. This introduction was certainly favored by the fact that the uncial *a* was already regularly appearing in *tituli* and epigraphs. After the *a*, the Caroline *t* appears and then the closed *g*. Finally, by about the year 825, the Caroline script triumphs in the most important centers of production and for executing significant documents.[136]

As for Catalonia,[137] a quite precise periodization of the gradual substitution of Caroline for the Visigothic script (by way of the mixed transitional script) is possible (Plate 11.6). The change took place in the course of the ninth century. The change to

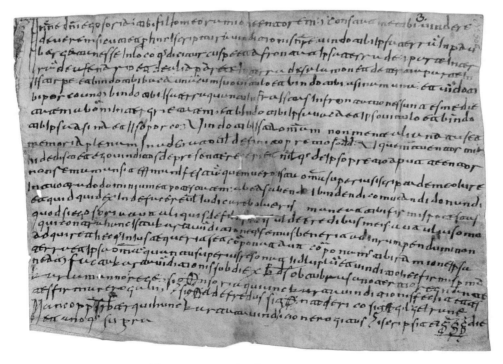

PLATE 11.6 Vic, Arxiu i Biblioteca Episcopal, cal. 9, episc. I, perg. 3, AD 881, mixed, transitional script, between Visigothic and Caroline minuscule.

the new international script was swifter in the eastern Catalan counties and dioceses than in the western ones during the first half of this century, but afterward there was a more equal evolution in both areas. This gave way to a mixed type of script that is especially common in the decade from 870 to 880. From this time onward one finds witnesses in perfected Caroline script.[138]

The change of script in Catalonia was favored by the influence of imported codices copied in the new continental script, transmitters of the Franco-Roman liturgy imposed on the Catalan dioceses dependent on Narbonne. An additional influence on the scribes was the arrival of French documents (not infrequently copied in Caroline script) in the Catalan counties dependent on that kingdom.[139]

In Mozarabic territory, as Muñoz observed, a chronologically unequal evolution took place, as the Andalusian Visigothic was initially less permeable to the Caroline innovations than was the Toledan variety. It may be added that a document written in Denia around 1056, undoubtedly by a Mozarabic copyist of this kingdom, demonstrates that no later than the middle of the eleventh century, in the eastern part of the peninsula, the Mozarabic community had already been influenced by the new continental script, since a mixed transitional alphabet (Visigothic to Caroline) was in use.

The script of the Latin manuscripts of St. Catherine's on Mount Sinai exhibits some graphical features that resemble the transitional Visigothic script of the Mozarabic region. In light of the new twelfth-century date for the Mount Sinai codices proposed by J. Vezin, (whose arguments, in my view, are conclusive), we may ask if that type of script is not also a Visigothic Mozarabic transitional script. If so, the domain of our "national" script must be expanded, directly or indirectly, since this African Mozarabic Visigothic would also be the one used by the Christian communities of North Africa, at least in the aforementioned century. They were certainly in contact with the Mozarabs of the south of the peninsula, since on several occasions the peninsular Mozarabs had to go into exile in the Maghreb.[140] For this reason the Northern African area would also be influenced by the new Caroline script, which was destined to end this peculiar early medieval graphical system.

NOTES

1. e.g., folios 23v–24r of the Codex Ouetensis (Madrid, Escorial R.II.18); cf. Díaz y Díaz (1983, 115–53) and (1995, 64–9). There are also epigraphic texts in square capitals (including numismatic texts); cf. Vives (1962) and García Lobo and Martín (1995).
2. Cf. *CLA*, vol. 11, Oxford 1966, pp. 13–18; Millares Carlo (1983, 25–31). For cursive and semi-cursive scripts, cf. Velázquez (2000), (2012).
3. In addition to Latin scripts, there were also in this period Ulfilan, Greek, Arabic, and Hebrew scripts used in Spain.
4. Cf. Muñoz y Rivero (1881, 33).
5. e.g., Vienna, ÖNB, papyrus Rainer 523 (fifth cent.); Geneva, Bibliothèque Publique et Universitaire MS. lat. 75 (sixth cent.); Paris, Archives Nationales, K.2 n. 12 (Diploma of Theodoric III, AD 677). Cf. Mundó (1970), soon to be published in his *Obres Completes*.

6. Cf. Mundó (1970) on Madrid, Archivo Histórico Nacional, cód. 1452B, no. 15. The use of the *escritura prolongada* is widely attested in the royal documentation of Asturias-León, e.g., León, Archivo de la Catedral, no. 978. This script is also attested in the first line of documents, in the complete text of diplomas, and in some parts of codices. It was used by calligraphers such as Florencio de Valeránica (Covarrubias, Archivo de la Canónica, leg. I, núm. 4) and Vigila de Albelda (Logroño, Archivo de la Catedral, perg. 1ter; and the catchwords in Madrid, El Escorial, MS. D. I. 2). On these scribes, cf. Fernández Flórez and Herrero (2003). Further examples in Ruiz Asencio (2007, 265–312) and Floriano (1949–51, vol. 1, *Liber testamentorum ecclesiae Ouetensis*, plate 3; vol. 2, doc. 174 and 181). Cf. also Compte and Recasens (1967).

7. It was used, on occasion, by Millares Carlo.

8. On the other hand, Millares Carlo (1983, 77–8) thinks that the term *toletana* arises from the importance of one of the principal centers of production of writings in this script, an opinion shared by Cencetti (1997, 132). Clearly the same criterion could be applied to references to the *gallega* and Mozarabic scripts, though less credibly. Cf. also Merino (1780, 53); Merino saw in the Visigothic Bible of Toledo the origin of the Visigothic script.

9. This equation was already made in the thirteenth century by Alfonso X, el Sabio (1977, vol. 2, 547), following Rodrigo Jiménez de Rada (1987, lib. 6, cap. 28, p. 213–14). The idea persisted; cf., e.g., Garibay (1571, 244) and Alderete (1606, 249).

10. Jiménez de Rada and Alfonso X, el Sabio; see n. 9 above.

11. Pérez Bayer (1872).

12. Mabillon (1681, 432).

13. Marín (2001, 479) makes this assertion. Ljublinskaja (1969, 78–9) also prefers the term *hispana* or *hispánica.*

14. Lehmann (1927, 57).

15. Vigil (1887, 47).

16. Quoted by Cencetti (1997, 130).

17. Gómez Moreno (1919, 130).

18. Marín (2001, 480).

19. Muñoz (1881). Muñoz is following in the steps of Ribeiro (1819, 83–4), who sometimes refers to our script as *wisigothica.*

20. Collected in Millares Carlo (1983).

21. In spite of this, Floriano (1946, 330–1) thinks that "if one gives this word a broader sense, as signifying a period in which the Mozarabic culture flourished (the ninth to the eleventh centuries), exercising its influence not only among the subjugated Christians, but also in the independent zone, the term may be employed quite properly."

22. Muñoz (1881, 9).

23. It seems to me convenient to maintain a distinction between semi-calligraphic and semi-rudimentary based on whether the predominant characteristic of the product is elegant or elementary, since it is evident that even among notaries it is possible to distinguish different levels. Certainly, in addition to calligraphers such as Florencio de Valeránica, we encounter others who are rather novices, but in no way mediocre. So the writing of a professional of the second rank, like Cidi for example, cannot be called calligraphic, but also not semi-rudimentary. The term semi-calligraphic appears to define his style rather adequately. On Cidi, cf. Herrero and Fernández Flórez (2004).

24. Llió (2000, 411–12) gives a good definition of cursivity.

25. Muñoz (1881, 20), and defined (ibid. 75). The *cancilleresca* script, in less polished final products, also has a *semicancilleresca* variant.

26. See Mundó (1983, 184). Mundó, in agreement with Millares, attributes the gradual substitution of the cursive handwriting by semi-cursive or round in the diplomatic production to the influence of the copyists of codices. While acknowledging this possible influence, I believe that this change was mainly due to the greater number of charters produced by documentary scribes lacking the training required for the execution of the elegant *cancilleresca* cursive. In this environment it began to be abandoned as demand for documents increased, given that it must have been faster to write in semi-cursive or even round script rather than in *cancilleresca*. This change occurred later in Castile and León; cf. Ruiz Asencio (2007, 272).

27. And he adds: "It has more abbreviations than the cursive script, because the scribes want to compensate for the greater slowness which the writing of the round letterforms requires by the time-saving device of using abbreviations" (Muñoz 1881, 27–8).

28. If one uses the term *sentada* to mean a script executed slowly (in opposition to cursive), then the name could also be applied to the *rudimentaria*. But the word *sentada* is a concept that applies only to scripts written calligraphically.

29. It is only in this sense that I can accept Millares Carlo's definition (1983, 28) of the semi-cursive as being characterized by the mingling of the forms of certain letters and of some of the abbreviations proper to the cursive and round varieties.

30. The mixed and transitional Visigothic-Caroline script was identified to a certain extent by de Terreros (1758, 106–7) and more clearly by Merino (1870, 40 and 135). Muñoz also talks about a transitional script (1881, 29). Millares Carlo (1961, 338) locates this transitional period at the end of the eleventh century and the beginning of the twelfth.

31. There is also cryptographic script; cf. Galende (1995) and (2009). Mention should also be made of Visigothic musical notation; cf., e.g., Zapke (2007).

32. Armengol Rovira (1950, 17). Cf. del Camino (1990), (1992), (1987).

33. Lowe (1969, 23).

34. Lehmann (1927, 57).

35. Mundó (1983, 180).

36. Marin (2001, 481).

37. Schiaparelli (1929, 199).

38. Millares (1932, 47); later, in the third edition of his treatise, he rejects this hypothesis criticizing its weak points.

39. e.g., by Floriano (1946, 329); Foerster (1949, 120); Battelli (1999, 138). Earlier, Merino (1780, 26) and Bretholz (1926, 75) had stated that it derived directly from the Roman cursive minuscule. García Villada (1974, vol. 1, 87) derived it from Roman cursive and Roman minuscule (half-uncial).

40. Cencetti (1997, 133).

41. Millares Carlo (1983, 79) seems to accept the thesis of Cencetti.

42. Cf., e.g., Alturo (2000, 32).

43. On the various genetic, chronological, and geographical origins of the Visigothic script, I have already laid out my hypothesis in Alturo (2004).

44. *Polygraphia góthico-española. Origen de los caracteres o letras de los godos en España,* manuscript dated 1764, [Madrid, Real Academia de la Historia, sign. 12-23-1*a*; A. núm. 2] of which a study and edition is being prepared by M. Torras Cortina.

45. de Terreros (1758, 123).

46. Merino (1780, prologue and 53).
47. Muñoz (1881, 9 and 43).
48. Millares Carlo (1941, 10–11). His observations draw to some extent on Robinson (1939).
49. Millares Carlo (1941, 21–2).
50. Ibid. (22).
51. Ibid. (23).
52. Millares Carlo (1973).
53. Gómez Moreno (1954) and (1966).
54. Mundó (1970); cf. also Canellas (1979).
55. Millares Carlo (1973, 19).
56. Ibid. (20).
57. Schiaparelli (1924).
58. Ruiz Asencio (1991, 199). Likewise Pratesi and Cherubini (2010, 227).
59. Or perhaps later, if we consider that the celebrated document of King Silo, although probably authentic, does not appear to be original, but rather a copy of the tenth century. Cf. Díaz y Díaz (2001, 29, n. 38); Pacheco (2001); García Leal (2007, 61). This diploma was presented as original by Millares Carlo (1971). If the document of King Silo is not original, the most ancient Spanish document becomes one dated 803, on which, cf. Sanz Fuentes (2006).
60. Cf. Díaz y Díaz (1997); Petrucci and Romeo (1998); and Vivancos (2006).
61. Cf. Merino (1780, 30).
62. e.g., slate tablet nº. 53, on which, cf. I. Velázquez (2000, 72) (with has closed-*t,* in various forms, and tall-*i*). Cf. Díaz y Díaz (1975, 26). Battelli (1999, 139) believes that the new script form dates from the middle of the seventh century, and that by the end of this century its characters are, in part, already established.
63. Tafel (1923–5, esp. 1925, 64).
64. Mundó (1952), (1988).
65. Vezin (1988), (1992). Cf. also Riché (1992).
66. Schiaparelli (1927, 3–15). See also Petrucci (1973).
67. Cf. Díaz y Díaz (2002, 52) on the possible Aquitanian origin of that manuscript.
68. This was demonstrated in Alturo (1994b).
69. For further inscriptions with this detail, cf. Fernández Flórez and Herrero (2012). Mallon (1952, 129–36) observed the presence of this unusual ligature from the fifth century onward. De Santiago Fernández (2009), referring to the epitaph of Pierius, remarks on the elision *er* in the word *era,* with minuscule *r* and *e* (which appears to me rather Protovisigothic than Uncial, since it does not have a perfectly curved arch, but one slightly drawn in at the middle), and he also indicates the presence of *t* with a curl to the left at least since the seventh century, e.g., in the inscription of the votive crown of Abbot Teodosio. He also states that he can confirm the presence of the *u* with the second stroke upright and extended below the baseline in numerous epigraphic texts of the same century (p. 301), a characteristic, in my view, of Visigothic script. Furthermore, in accord with the studies of Mundó and Velázquez, the most ancient cursive texts appear to presage since the sixth or seventh century some, if not all, of the characteristics that will be typical of Visigothic cursive, especially since, as Millares Carlo observed, Visigothic cursive presents few formal changes in the broad period of time in which it was used, a circumstance that creates a serious difficulty for dating the undated or undatable examples. Mundó (1983, 179), after an account of the witnesses to cursive from the

sixth and seventh centuries and an analysis of the characteristics of the script, concludes that "this cursive cannot yet be called typical Visigothic because it lacks certain specific features," but, "it has other features that permit granting it its own name, from the historical period in which it appears, of '*cursiva visigoda*.'"

70. The Iberian Peninsula was already independent of the Roman Empire before its fall. Eurico (466–84) annexed Tarragona in 472, later occupying as well the southern part of the peninsula along with part of Lusitania, and held under his dominion the southern portion of Gaul, which since 462 had passed under the control of the Visigoths under Teodorico II (453–66).

71. The greater longevity of the Roman cursive is clear in other regions as well. For example, the Ravenna papyri demonstrate this continuity until the year 700; cf. Bischoff (1985, 113).

72. Millares Carlo's opinion is reported by Mundó (1978).

73. Merino (1780, 53).

74. Mundó (1983, 181).

75. Seville is mentioned in Marín, Ruiz Asencio, *et al.* (1982, 114); Battelli (1999, 139); Stiennon (1973, 81). Prof. Díaz y Díaz, during a meeting in San Millán de la Cogolla, told me that he believes in "the possibility" of a Sevillian origin for the Visigothic script. This possibility also seems to be suggested by Higounet (1982, 83).

76. Bischoff (1985, 110). On the St. Catherine's manuscripts, cf. Lowe (1955), (1964), (1965); Fischer (1964); Tarracó (1992); Gros (2002–3); Vezin (2002–3; 2010, 17–45). The fragility of Bischoff's thesis of a possible North African origin for Visigothic script was addressed by del Camino (1990, 30, n. 8).

77. The most important ecclesiastics of the sixth century were bishops in the northeast, e.g., Caesarius of Arles and the brothers Justinianus, Justus, Nebridius, and Elpidius (bishops, respectively, of Valencia, Urgel, Égara, and Huesca.) Later, hegemony passed to Seville with the brothers Leander and Isidore.

78. Bischoff (1985, 117). Some scholars date this papyrus codex to the beginning of the seventh century; cf. Vezin (2004, 266).

79. Cf. Schiaparelli (1929, 178, 180); and Ruiz Asencio (2007, 272).

80. It became part of the Visigothic realm in 462. On the other hand, Liuva I (567–72), before becoming king of the Visigoths in Toledo, had been duke of Narbonne.

81. Cf. Muñoz (1881, 29); Millares Carlo (1983, 58); Merino (1780, 74); Fernández Flórez (2000).

82. He is called the "prince of our calligraphy" by Gómez Moreno (1919, 361); and "the perpetual enemy of idleness" by de Argáiz (1675, 289).

83. Muñoz, *Paleografía visigoda* (1881, 29). Lowe (1910) followed Muñoz, but introduced a twist in distinguishing four stages of development: (1) the eighth to the ninth century; (2) the end of the ninth century until the beginning of the tenth; (3) the tenth and eleventh centuries; (4) the period of decadence and of the influence of the new Caroline script. Millares Carlo (1925, 255) summarized the position of Lowe as follows:

[For the first period] he references the surprising compactness of the characters, the breadth of the letters, which lack slenderness, the inward curve of the final minims of *m*, *n*, and *h*, the use of the semicolon above *b* and *q* to abbreviate the endings –*bus* and –*que*, and the imperfect separation of words. In contrast, the codices made in the tenth century offer letter types whose bodies are taller and narrow. The final stroke of the three aforementioned letters normally turns outwards. The ascenders terminate at the top in a hook or hammer-head, and the semicolon of the first period has changed to the conventional sign *s* with the meanings -*us* and -*ue*.

But Millares Carlo added the qualification that Lowe's "affirmations err on the side of too much certainty," and he gave various examples from the tenth century that do not comply with Lowe's rule about the final strokes of *m*, *n*, and *h*.

84. To prove the superiority of the calligraphy of the codices of the northern part of the peninsula over those of the Mozarabic ones of the south, it suffices to compare the Bible of Seville (Madrid, Biblioteca Nacional, MS Vitr.13.1) with that of León (León, Archivo de la Colegiata de San Isidoro, MS 2), both from the tenth century.

85. e.g., tentatively by Cencetti (1997, 140). Cf. also Pérez de Urbel (1975, 80); and Millares Carlo (1983, 137). This question is being studied by A. Serna. Fernández Flórez (2010, 66) has stressed the importance of the two monasteries of Cardeña and Silos.

86. The dating of the codices in Visigothic script remains a thorny issue. Cf. García Larragueta (1990). Quite a stir was created by the study of A. M. Mundó (1965). He redates Madrid, BN, 10.110 (formerly Toledo, Archivo de la Catedral 35.2) from the tenth or eleventh century to "no earlier than the second half of the thirteenth, or a little later"; Toledo, Archivo de la Catedral 35.4 from "IX–X sec." "to around 1200"; Toledo, Museo de Santa Cruz, 1325, previously dated between the ninth and eleventh centuries to "the middle of the thirteenth"; and others as well. He concluded (p. 21):

> Until recently it was asserted that the last books in peninsular Visigothic script were the *Becerro gótico de Sahagún* (1110) [Madrid, AHN 989B] and the "Libro de los testamentos de Oviedo" (1101–29) [Oviedo, Archivo de la Catedral, *Liber testamentorum,*sine num.]. In addition to a small group of Portuguese fragments in Visigothic script of the twelfth and thirteenth centuries, there are now an entire series of magnificent Toledan codices that continued a tradition of writing in the national script up to the threshold of the fourteenth century.

> Cf. also Mundó (1994). Mundó was preceded, to varying degrees, in dating the survival of Visigothic to a later period by Merino (1780, 126); Tassin and Toustain (1759, 324); A. Nasarre (1738, 24). Merino, with good judgement, dates the end of the period of the use of Visigothic script to "the year 1100; it being of little consequence that, after this date, there is one example or another of writing in the old style" (p. 136).

87. Martínez Salazar (1913). Rodríguez (2011, 93).

88. Millares Carlo (1973, 23).

89. Among its characteristics, observable in Seu d'Urgell, Arxiu Capitular, Codinet n°. 1 (AD 815) are the leftward slant of the writing; notable extension of the ascenders and descenders; the *b* with the bowl slightly open; the *g* in two forms, but both with the lower portion not closed (in the first case, with its base on the ruling; in the second dropping well below it); the *m* and the *n* extending the first stroke below the baseline and ending, at times, with a finial which gives the impression of being a point; the *o* may have a vestigial stroke at the upper right side, or may acquire a form similar to a closed *a*; the *f*, *r*, *s*, and *x* go a little below the ruling, as does the right stroke of the *u*, and this ends with a turn to the right; the ligature *et* is formed with a *t* with an upright stroke slightly inclined to the right at the top; generally, there is no distinction between *ti* and *tj*, the latter being used only in the word *uinditjonis*; the abbreviation for–*bus* is indicated by a sign similar to an *s* adhered to the shaft a little above the beginning of the semicircle, but when this same sign abbreviates –*ue* after *q*, it is placed above it; *per* is abbreviated with a horizontal stroke crossing the descender of the *p*; in *dni* for *Domini*, the *i* hangs from the horizontal abbreviation stroke, to which it is directly joined.

90. The distinction between the form *ti* or *tj*, depending on whether it represents a syllable with a hard or a sibilant sound, was considered a dating criterion by Lowe, who believed that this differentiation never occurred in manuscripts of the eighth century or the beginning of the ninth, and that it was consistent after the second half of the tenth. But one cannot speak of a "rule" but simply of a tendency with many exceptions. Cf. the recent study of Ruiz (2004).

91. I want to acknowledge Ainoa Castro, research scholar at the Seminari de Paleografia, Codicologia i Diplomàtica of the Universitat Autònoma de Barcelona, who was working under my direction on his doctoral thesis, "La escritura visigótica en Galicia. 1. Las diócesis lucense y mindoniense," for his generous assistance in producing these images from the originals.

92. Madrid, Escorial, MS D.I.2 (from San Lorenzo). Vigila and Sarracino, were extremely erudite and multifaceted scribes; cf. Díaz y Díaz (1980) and Fernández Flórez (2000).

93. On majuscule script, cf. García Lobo (2008), (2007), (1999); and García Lobo and Martín (1996).

94. I owe this alphabet also to the generosity of A. Castro, who extracted it from a document of June 12, 918 written by the priest Sisvieno (ACLugo, Libro X de pergaminos, leg. 2, nº. 3).

95. In a document from Lugo being studied by A. Castro (Lugo, Archivo de la Catedral, perg. 23), dated January 8, 1009 and lacking the name of the scribe, one observes a Visigothic cursive slanted slightly to the left. Could it be owing to a Mozarabic scribe? Or is it simply that the affirmation of Millares Carlo does not permit generalization?

96. This characteristic is not exclusive to Mozarabic script; A. Castro informs me that it appears frequently in the Visigothic cursive of Galicia.

97. Millares Carlo (1973, 29).

98. Ibid. Muñoz (1881, 31–2), in reference to the cursive of the ninth century, points out the regularity of its writing, its leftward inclination, its sparse use of abbreviations, its frequent ligatures with *e*, *a*, *t*, *r*, and *s*. But he says that in the tenth and eleventh centuries it presents even a greater sameness and regularity in its alphabet, although the ligatures and joinings increase and the abbreviation signs multiply; so the cedilla is used for terminations in *is;* the sign resembling an inverted *ce* to indicate *con;* and there are other signs not previously common.

99. Thompson (1906, 103, n.1).

100. Millares Carlo (1925, 256–7), (1983, 91). Muñoz (1881, 101) considered that this abbreviation sign came directly from an *s*.

101. Cf. Alturo (2003a, n. 26).

102. Rodriguez (1738, 3).

103. Yet this style of abbreviation could have been introduced by Christian copyists who were refugees in Spain after the conquest of the Magreb by the Muslims; cf. Vezin (2001, 97). It is used already in the celebrated *Basilicanus* of Hilary (*CLA* 1.1a) copied in half-uncial and revised in Cagliari in AD 509/510, where it may have come with one of the bishops from Byzantium exiled there; cf. Vezin (2005, 26–7). However, the use of this system in inscriptions from Merida and Andalusia from ancient times, as was observed by Rodríguez (2011, 88) makes it more difficult to see in it any Arabic influence.

104. Flórez (1770, vol. 2, 55).

105. E.g., Merino (1780, 112–13) argued that the spellings *mici* and *nicil* for *mihi* and *nihil* was an abuse that was introduced in the tenth century, and that this spelling was normal in the eleventh. But this practice can already be observed in the Visigothic slate tablets; cf. Vezin (2005, 25).

106. It is especially difficult to distinguish differences in script, whether in detail or in general terms, in the period of the flowering of the script when an effort is made at uniformity. For this period, there is a dearth of scholarly studies because the distinctions are imprecise and particularly difficult to define. Cf. note 83, above; Fernández Flórez (2000, 166); T. Marín (2001, 490, n. 36).

107. On this point I do not share the skepticism of Fernández Flórez (2000, 166) because, in addition to the insufficient attention this topic has received in palaeographical and codicological studies, there has been little effort devoted to the study of the documents (and inscriptions). An outline of codicological distinctions by regions is given by Ostos (2003).

108. Millares (1935, 18) established the importance for Visigothic palaeography of the study of geographical origin.

109. Within this general division, the Septimanian and Catalan types are more closely related; so are the Navarran and Aragonese; likewise the Leonese, Castilian and Riojan; and also the Galician and Portuguese. Additionally, subgroups can be distinguished within these, such as the Toledan and Andalusian variants of Mozarabic. Too little effort is made in much of the scholarship to distinguish these groups, to identify the important schools, or to define the basic characteristics of each.

110. There is a rapid review of this subject in Alturo (1994b). Mundó (1956) made particularly significant contributions to this field.

111. Merino (1780, 53–4).

112. Muñoz (1881, 50–1).

113. Díaz y Díaz (1995, 181–7) described the traits particularly characteristic of Andalusian script (especially in Cordoba):

> The ascenders have a great tendency to end in a wide club shape . . . ; on the contrary, the descenders vacillate between slimming at the end . . . or having a beveled finial that maintains its thickness . . . the general orientation of the script is leftwards . . . the use of the semicolon is preserved for a long time.   (Díaz y Díaz 1995, 183)

A summary of the Mozarabic variant is made by del Camino (2012, 131). She states that the *t* in the Mozarabic script:

> is distinguished by the addition of its final stroke not at the height of the beginning of the second stroke, but somewhat below this, in the most characteristic cases at half this height and with a markedly ascending oblique orientation. Furthermore, when the letter is isolated, this final stroke normally becomes very slender in comparison with the thickness of the remainder of the letter.

114. The geographic zones are defined more precisely by Millares Carlo (1983, 132). He adds that an important characteristic of Castilian script is, "the manner of terminating the ascenders with a small horizontal flourish. In contrast [the Mozarabic books] terminate these strokes in a greater thickening, which gives the letters a less attractive aspect" (pp. 59–60). Millares Carlo also noted that this difference was observed by Lowe, but that Lowe had wrongly seen it as a dating criterion, not a localizing one (p. 60). I will add that an essential component of the regional style of Mozarabic script is its archaic quality. This is a product of the isolation of the Christian communities in this region from those in the north and resulted in a style of writing that evolved little or not at all over time.

115. There are, however, some detailed studies, such as those gathered in Turza (2002).

116. Terreros (1758, 106–7); cf. also n. 30 above.

117. Terreros (1758, 106–7).

118. Merino (1780, 127).

119. Muñoz (1881, 36).

120. Ibid., 39–40.

121. Ruiz Asencio (2008). Cf. also, Ostolaza Elizondo (1990, 161); Herrero de la Fuente (2000); Mendo (2001); Vezin (2003); and Keller (1990).

122. More precise documentation is provided by Fernández Flórez (2002, 127). In analyzing the documentation for the monastery of Sahagún, he establishes that:

> during the years 1100-1109, of a total of 56 original documents, 52 are written in Visigothic and only 4 in Caroline (the earliest being from the year 1104); for the years 1110-1119, of a total of 18, there are 8 in Visigothic and 10 in Caroline; from 1120-1129, out of 30 documents, only 2 are Visigothic (from the years 1122 and 1123), and 28 are Caroline; and from 1130-1139, out of 23 documents, only 1 is Visigothic (from 1131).

123. Calleja (2008).

124. Blasco (1994–5, 217, n.19).

125. See n. 6 above.

126. Blasco (1994–5, 217). On the Visigothic script in Cantabria, cf. Blasco (1988, esp. 97–8).

127. Ribeiro (1819, 86).

128. M. J. Azevedo Santos (1994) and (2000–1, 105–6):

> the Monastery of S. Salvador de Moreira, a bastion of Visigothic, was among the last to accept the new script, in 1102. It took at least 118 years for the "notaries" of Portugal to completely abandon Visigothic script (1054–1172).... [the Abbey of Pendorada] used a transitional Visigothic from 1054 to 1152 (98 years); that of Pedroso from 1079 to 1172 (93 years); that of Lorvâo from 1086 to 1168 (82 years) as far as the Colegiada of Guimarâes and the Cathedral of Coimbra, they gave up Visigothic definitively in 1135 and 1137, respectively. In the early years of the twelfth century, many European script types were introduced: from Caroline in 1108 to Carolina-Gotica in 1111 to Gothic in 1123.

> For the Monastery of Santa Cruz de Coimbra, she affirms that the Visigothic script for documentary use ended in 1145 (p. 108).

129. All the more since one of the Portuguese codices considered the most archaizing with respect to the use of the Visigothic script, the *Livro dos Testamentos do Mosteiro de Lorvâo*, appears to have been put together around the year 1120. Cf. Nascimento and Fernández Catón (2008).

130. Lucas Alvarez (1991, 441) distinguishes three phases in the Galician form of Visigothic, focusing exclusively on the analysis of documents.

131. Ibid., 445. Alvarez does not specify the date of the introduction of the Caroline script in Galicia, nor does he provide statistical data on the ratio between Visigothic and Caroline documents once the latter script was introduced. A. Castro informs me that the first examples of Caroline script in Galicia, at least for the dioceses of Lugo and Mondoñedo, date from 1113.

132. Cf. del Camino (2008).

133. Canellas (1991). Cf. also, Muñoz (1881, 45). Information on Rioja and Navarra is lacking; but on Rioja, cf. Turza (2002) and Díaz y Díaz (1979); and on Navarra, Ubieto (1957).

134. Usón (1940, 21). Yet he recognizes (p. 23) that "it is true that since the reign of Sancho Ramírez [1063–94] one begins to see here and there some inroads of the Caroline script in the abbreviations and ligatures of *ct* and *st*."

135. Canellas (1991, 25 and plate 4).

136. Alturo (1994b); cf. also (1992a), (1992b), (1994a).

137. Mundó and Alturo (1990); on transitional and marginal scripts, cf. Mundó and Alturo (1998); Alturo (1991b), (1991a), (1999), (2003a), and (2003b, 69–74). On the transitional script and the early Catalan Caroline, cf. Alturo (1994–5) and (1997).

138. But an archaic mixed script does survive in some rural zones, such as in the parish of Sant Esteve de Vilanova, where the rector, the priest Miró, used a semi-rudimentary Caroline script for a sale contract (January 22, 1032), consistently employing Uncial *g* and the common Visigothic abbreviation for *qui*; cf. Alturo (1985, doc. 36). Cf. also the imitation of Visigothic in codices (e.g., Girona, Arxiu Capitular, ms. 3) and in documents (e.g., Barcelona, Arxiu Reial, ACA, Monacals, Amer, prg.5).

139. Alturo (2010).

140. Cf. Vezin (2005, 37) and Aillet (2010, 7 and 136).

BIBLIOGRAPHY

Aillet, C. 2010. *Les Mozarabes. Christianisme, islamisation et arabisation en Péninsule Ibérique (IXe–XIIe siècle)*. Madrid: Casa de Velázquez.

Alderete, B. 1606. *Del origen y principio de la lengua castellana o romance que oi se usa en España*. Rome: C. Vullietto.

Alfonso X, Rey de Castilla. 1977. *Primera crónica general de España*, ed. R. Menéndez Pidal. 2 vols. Madrid: Editorial Gredos.

Alturo, J. 1985. *L'Arxiu Antic de Santa Anna de Barcelona del 942 a 1200. Aproximació històrico-lingüística*, vol. 2. Barcelona: Fundació Noguera.

Alturo, J. 1991a. "Els manuscrits i documents llatins d'origen català del segle IX." In *Symposium Internacional sobre els orígens de Catalunya (Segles VIII–XI)*, vol. 1, 273–80. Barcelona: Real Academia de Buenas Letras.

Alturo, J. 1991b. "Escritura visigótica y escritura carolina en el contexto cultural de la Cataluña del siglo IX." *Memoria Ecclesiae* 2: 33–44, 298.

Alturo, J. 1992a. "El glossari llatí en escriptura visigòtica de la Burgerbibliothek de Berna, ms. A.92.3." *Fauentia* 14/1: 43–52.

Alturo, J. 1992b. "Los folios de guarda del manuscrito París, Bibl. Nat. lat. 6113, un *Commentarium in Lucam* de Beda del siglo IX." *Historia. Instituciones. Documentos* 19: 1–6.

Alturo, J. 1994a. "El glosario del ms. París, Bibl. Nat. lat. 609." *Euphrosyne* 22: 185–200.

Alturo, J. 1994b. "La escritura visigótica de origen transpirenaico. Una aproximación a sus particularidades." *Hispania Sacra* 46: 33–64.

Alturo, J. 1994–5. "El fragment de còdex 2541, IV de la Biblioteca de Catalunya amb algunes notes sobre característiques paleogràfiques de la primitiva minúscula carolina catalana." *Estudis Castellonencs* 6: 95–103.

Alturo, J. 1997. "Un *Liber de dono perseuerantiae* de san Austín copiado en Gerona entorno a 870–80." *Revue des Études Augustiniennes* 43/1: 105–10.

Alturo, J. 1999. "Tipus d'escriptura a la Catalunya dels segles VIII–X." In *Catalunya a l'època carolíngia. Art i cultura abans del romànic (segles IX i X)*, ed. J. Camps, 131–4, 485–7. Barcelona: Museu Nacional d'Art de Catalunya.

Alturo, J. 2000. *El llibre manuscrit a Catalunya. Orígens i esplendor.* Barcelona: Generalitat de Catalunya.

Alturo, J. 2003a. "El *Liber iudicum* manuscrito latino 4667 de la Biblioteca Nacional de Francia. Análisis paleográfico." *Historia. Instituciones. Documentos* 30: 9–54.

Alturo, J. 2003b. *Historia del llibre manuscrit a Catalunya.* Barcelona: Entitat Autònoma del Diari Oficial i de Publicacions.

Alturo, J. 2004. "La escritura visigótica. Estado de la cuestión." *Archiv für Diplomatik* 50: 347–86.

Alturo, J. 2010. "L'Enseignement et l'apprentissage de l'écriture en Catalogne au Moyen Âge." In *Teaching Writing, Learning to Write: Proceedings of the XVIth Colloquium of the Comité International de Paléographie Latine*, ed. P. R. Robinson, 193–204. London: Kings College London Medieval Studies.

Argáiz, G. de. 1675. *La soledad laureada.* Madrid: Bernardo de Herbada.

Armengol Rovira, J. 1950. "Sobre los orígenes de la redonda visigótica." *Cuadernos de Historia de España* 12: 5–18.

Azevedo Santos, M. J. 1994. *Da visigótica à carolina. A escrita em Portugal de 882 a 1172.* Lisbon: FCG-JNICT.

Azevedo Santos, M. J. 2000–1. "Os modos de escrever no século XII em Portugal. O caso do Mosteiro de Santa Cruz de Coimbra." *Bibliotheca Portucalensis*, 2nd series 15–16: 99–111.

Battelli, G. 1999. *Lezioni di paleografia*, 4th ed. Vatican City: Libreria Editrice Vaticana.

Bischoff, B. 1985. *Paléographie de l'Antiquité romaine et du Moyen Âge occidental.* Paris: Picard.

Bretholz, B. 1926. *Lateinische Paläographie*, 2nd ed. Leipzig and Berlin: B. G. Teubner.

Blasco, R. M. 1988. "Aproximación a la escritura visigótica en Cantabria. La documentación conservada en Santillana." *Altamira. Revista del Centro de Estudios Montañeses* 47: 75–128.

Blasco, R. M. 1994–5. "La escritura de la zona norte peninsular en los siglos XI y XII." *Estudis Castellonencs* 6: 213–23.

Calleja, M. 2008. "De la visigótica a la carolina en los documentos del Archivo de San Vicente de Oviedo: la escritura de Dominicus y Pelagius." In *Actas de las IV Jornadas de la Sociedad Española de Ciencias y Técnicas Historiográficas. Paleografía I: La escritura en España hasta 1250*, ed. J. A. Fernández Flórez and S. Serna Serna, 191–200. Burgos: Universidad de Burgos.

Camino, C. del. 1987. "La obra paleográfica de L. Schiaparelli: Orígenes de escrituras altomedievales." Ph.D. diss., Universidad de Sevilla.

Camino, C. del. 1990. "Los orígenes de la escritura visigótica. ¿Otras posibilidades para su estudio?" In *Actas del VIII Coloquio del Comité Internacional de Paleografía Latina*, 29–37. Madrid: Joyas Bibliográficas.

Camino, C. del. 1992. "Luigi Schiaparelli y los orígenes de la escritura visigótica." *Historia. Instituciones. Documentos* 19: 125–32.

Camino, C. del. 2008. "La escritura carolina en la Península Ibérica." In *Actas de las IV Jornadas de la Sociedad Española de Ciencias y Técnicas Historiográficas. Paleografía I: La escritura en España hasta 1250*, ed. J. A. Fernández Flórez and S. Serna Serna, 121–40. Burgos: Universidad de Burgos.

Camino, C. del. 2012. "La escritura visigótica de los centros mozárabes en su período primitivo." In *La escriura visigótica en la Península Ibérica: nuevas aportaciones*, ed. J. Alturo, M. Torras, and A. Castro, 115–44. Barcelona: Servei de Publicacions de la Universitat Autònoma de Barcelona.

Canellas, A. 1979. *Diplomática hispano-visigoda*. Zaragoza: Institución Fernando el Cathólico.

Canellas, A. 1991. "Paleografía aragonesa de la Alta Edad Media anterior al año 1137." *Anuario de Estudios Medievales* 21: 471–92.

Cencetti, G. 1997. *Lineamenti di storia della scrittura latina*, ed. G. Guerrini Ferri. Bologna: Patron.

Compte, E. and J. Recasens. 1967. "L'escriptura de les cancelleries franques en els documents de la Marca Hispànica." In *I Col·loqui d'història del monaquisme català*, vol. 2, 51–7. Santes Creus: Impr. del Monastir de Poblet.

Díaz y Díaz, M. C. 1975. "Consideraciones sobre las pizarras visigóticas." In *Actas de las I Jornadas de metodología aplicada de las ciencias históricas*, vol. V. *Paleografía y Archivística*, 23–30. Santiago de Compostela: Universidad de Santiago de Compostela.

Díaz y Díaz, M. C. 1979. *Libros y librerías en la Rioja altomedieval*. Logroño: Servicio de Cultura de la Diputación Provincial.

Díaz y Díaz, M. C. 1980. "Vigilán y Sarracino. Sobre composiciones figurativas en la Rioja del siglo X." In *Lateinische Dichtungen des X. und XI. Jahrhunderts. Festgabe für W. Bulst*, ed. W. Berschin and R. Düchting, 60–92. Heidelberg: Schneider.

Díaz y Díaz, M. C. 1983. "El códice ovetense del Escorial." In *Códices visigóticos en la monarquía leonesa*, ed. M. C. Díaz y Díaz, 115–53. León: Centro de Estudios e Investigación San Isidoro.

Díaz y Díaz, M. C. 1995. *Manuscritos visigóticos del Sur de la Península. Ensayo de distribución regional*. Seville: Universidad de Sevilla.

Díaz y Díaz, M. C. 1997. "Consideraciones sobre el Oracional visigótico de Verona." In *Petrarca, Verona e l'Europa*, ed. G. Billanovich and G. Frasso, 13–29. Padua: Antenore.

Díaz y Díaz, M. C. 2001. *Asturias en el siglo VIII. La cultura literaria*. Oviedo: Sueve.

Díaz y Díaz, M. C. 2002. "El códice latino 2855 de la Biblioteca Nacional de Francia en Paris." In *Los manuscriptos visigóticos: Estudio paleográfico y codicológico (I): Códices riojanos datados*, ed. Claudio Garcia Turza, 49–76. Logroño: Fundación San Millán de la Cogolla.

Fernández Flórez, J. A. 2000. "Un calígrafo-miniaturista del año mil: Vigila de Albelda." In *Los protagonistas del año mil. Codex Aquilarensis 16 (Actas del XIII Seminario sobre Historia del Monacato)*, ed. J. A. García de Cortázar, 153–80. Aguilar de Campoo: Fundación Santa María La Real.

Fernández Flórez, J. A. 2002. *La elaboración de los documentos en los reinos hispánicos occidentales (ss. VI–XIII)*. Burgos: Diputación Provincial de Burgos.

Fernández Flórez, J. A. 2010. "Documentos y códices en el Reino de León." In *XI Reino de León*, 60–6. Madrid: Consejo Superior de la Casa de León.

Fernández Flórez, J. A. and M. Herrero. 2003. "Copistas y colaboradores en el Monasterio de Albelda." In *Actes du XIIIe colloque international de paléographie latine*, ed. H. Spilling, 105–30. Paris: École nationale des chartes.

Fernández Flórez, J. A. and M. Herrero. 2012. "Sobre la escritura visigótica en León y Castilla durante su etapa primitiva (ss. VII–X): algunas reflexiones." In *La escriura visigótica en la Península Ibérica: nuevas aportaciones*, ed. J. Alturo, M. Torras, and A. Castro, 55–104. Barcelona: Servei de Publicacions de la Universitat Autònoma de Barcelona.

Fischer, B. 1964. "Zur Liturgie der lateinischen Handschriften von Sinai." *Revue Bénédictine* 74: 284–97.

Flórez, E. 1770. *España sagrada : theatro geographico-historico de la Iglesia de España: origen, divisiones, y limites de todas sus provincias; antiguedad, traslaciones, y estado antiguo, y presente de sus sillas, con varias dissertaciones criticas*. Madrid: Marin.

Floriano, A. C. 1946. *Curso general de paleografía y diplomática españolas.* Oviedo: Imprenta La Cruz.

Floriano, A. C. 1949–51. *Diplomática española del período astur. Estudio de las fuentes documentales del reino de Asturias (718–910),* 2 vols. Oviedo: Imprenta La Cruz.

Foerster, H. 1949. *Abriss der lateinischen Paläographie.* Bern: Paul Haupt.

Galende, J. C. 1995. *Criptografía. Historia de la escritura cifrada.* Madrid: Complutense.

Galende, J. C. 2009. "Elementos y sistemas criptográficos en la escritura visigótica." In *VIII Jornadas Científicas sobre Documentación de la Hispania altomedieval (siglos VI–X),* ed. N. Ávila Seoane, M. Salamanca López, and L. Zozaya Montes, 173–83. Madrid: Universidad Complutense de Madrid.

García Larragueta, S. 1990. "Consideraciones sobre la datación de códices en escritura visigótica." In *Actas del VIII Coloquio del Comité Internacional de Paleografía Latina,* ed. M. C. Díaz y Díaz, 51–8. Madrid: Joyas Bibliográficas.

García Leal, A. 2007. *El diploma del rey Silo,* La Coruña: Fundación Pedro Barrié de la Maza.

García Lobo, V. and E. Martín. 1995. *De epigrafía medieval. Introducción y album.* León: Universidad de León, Departamento de Patrimonio Histórico Artístico y de la Cultura Escrita.

García Lobo, V. and E. Martín. 1996. "La escritura publicitaria en la Edad Media. Su funcionalidad." *Estudios humanísticos. Geografía, historia, arte* 18: 125–45.

García Lobo, V. and E. Martín. 1999. "La escritura publicitaria en la Península Ibérica. Siglos X–XIII." In *Inschrift und Material. Inschrift und Buchschrift. Fachtagung für mittelalterliche und neuzeitliche Epigraphik Ingolstadt,* ed. W. Koch and C. Steininger, 151–90. Munich: Bayerischen Akademie der Wissenschaften.

García Lobo, V. and E. Martín. 2007. "La escritura publicitaria en los documentos." In *De litteris, manuscriptis, inscriptionibus... Festschrift zum 65. Geburtstag von Walter Koch,* ed. T. Kölzer, F. Bornschlegel, C. Friedl, and G. Vogeler, 229–55. Vienna: Bohlau.

García Lobo, V. and E. Martín. 2008. "La escritura visigótica publicitaria." In *Actas de las IV Jornadas de la Sociedad Española de Ciencias y Técnicas Historiográficas. Paleografía I: La escritura en España hasta 1250,* ed. J. A. Fernández Flórez and S. Serna Serna, 61–91. Burgos: Universidad de Burgos.

García Villada, Z. 1974. *Paleografía española,* 2 vols. Barcelona: El Albir.

Garibay, E. 1571. *Los quarenta libros del compendio historial de las chrónicas y universal historia de todos los reynos de España.* Amberes: C. Plantino.

Gómez Moreno, M. 1919. *Iglesias mozárabes: arte español de los siglos IX al XI.* Madrid: Centro de Estudios Históricos.

Gómez Moreno, M. 1954. "Documentación goda en pizarra." *Boletín de la Real Academia Española* 34: 25–58.

Gómez Moreno, M. 1966. *Documentación goda en pizarra. Estudio y transcripción.* Madrid: Real Academia de la Historia.

Gros, M. S. 2002–3. "Les Fragments de l'épistolier latin du Sinaï. Étude liturgique." *Ecclesia orans* 19: 391–404.

Herrero, M. and J. A. Fernández Flórez. 2004. "Cidi, *scriptor* de documentos altomedievales del fondo monástico de Otero de las Dueñas." In *Escritos dedicados a José María Fernández Catón,* ed. M. C. Díaz y Díaz, vol. 1, 651–88. León: Centro de Estudios e Investigación San Isidoro.

Herrero de la Fuente, M. 2000. "De Cluny a Sahagún: la escritura carolina en el monasterio de Sahagún (siglos XI–XII)." In *Le Statut du scripteur au Moyen Âge. Actes du XIIe Colloque Scientifique du Comité International de Paléographie Latine,* ed. M.-C. Hubert, E. Poulle, and M. Smith, 29–40. Paris: École de Chartes.

Higounet, Ch. 1982. *L'Écriture*, 6th ed. Paris: Presses Universitaires de France.

Jiménez de Rada, R. 1987. *Historia de rebus Hispanie siue Historia Gothica*, ed. J. Fernández Valverde. Turnhout: Brepols.

Keller, A. 1990. "Le Système espagnol de réglure dans les manuscrits wisigothiques." In *Actas del VIII Coloquio del Comité Internacional de Paleografía Latina*, ed. M. C. Díaz y Díaz, 107–14. Madrid: Joyas Bibliográficas.

Lehmann, P. 1927. "Lateinische Paläographie bis zum Siege der karolingischen Minuskel." In *Einleitung in die Altertumswissenschaft*, 3rd ed., vol. 1, ed. A. Gercke and E. Norden, 38–68. Leipzig: B. G. Teubner.

Ljublinskaja, A. D. 1969. *Latinskaja paleografija*. Moscow: Izd. Vysšaja Škola.

Llió, Marqués de. 2000. *Observaciones sobre los principios elementales de la historia*. Barcelona: Barcelona Associació de Bibliòfils de Barcelona [Originally published in 2 vols., 1756–1868].

Lowe, E. A. 1910. *Studia Palaeographica : A Contribution to the History of Early Latin Minuscule and the Dating of Visigothic Manuscripts*. Munich: Königlich Bayerische Akademie der Wissenschaften. (=*Paleographical Papers 1907–1965*, ed. L. Bieler, Oxford: Clarendon, 1972, vol. 1, pp. 2–65).

Lowe, E. A. 1955. "An Unknown Latin Psalter on Mount Sinai." *Scriptorium* 9: 177–99.

Lowe, E. A. 1964. "Two New Latin Liturgical Fragments on Mount Sinai." *Revue Bénédictine* 74: 252–83.

Lowe, E. A. 1965. "Two Other Unknown Latin Liturgical Fragments on Mount Sinai." *Scriptorium* 19: 3–29.

Lowe, E. A. 1969. *Handwriting. Our Medieval Legacy*. Rome: Edizioni di storia e letteratura.

Lucas Alvarez, M. 1991. "Paleografía gallega. Estado de la cuestión." *Anuario de Estudios Medievales* 21: 419–69.

Mabillon, J. 1681. *De re diplomatica libri sex*. Paris: L. Billaine.

Mallon, J. 1952. *Paléographie romaine*. Madrid: Consejo Superior de Investigaciones Científicas.

Marín, T. 2001. "La escritura de los Beatos." In *Studia paleographica, diplomatica et epigraphica D. Tomás Marín Martínez, magistri Universitatis Complutensis*, 471–510. Madrid: Consejería de Educación.

Marín, T., J. M. Ruiz Asencio, *et al.* 1982. *Paleografía y Diplomática*. Madrid: Universidad Nacional de Educación a Distancia.

Martínez Salazar, A. 1913. "Diplomática gallega. ¿El último representante de la escritura visigoda?" *Boletín de la Real Academia Gallega* 8: 49–56.

Merino, P. 1780. *Escuela paleográphica o de leer letras cursivas antiguas y modernas desde la entrada de los godos en España hasta nuestros tiempos*, Madrid: J. A. Lozano.

Mendo, C. 2001. "La escritura de los documentos leoneses en el siglo X." *Signo. Revista de Historia de la Cultura Escrita* 8: 179–210.

Millares Carlo, A. 1925. "De paleografía visigótica. A propósito del 'Codex Toletanus.'" *Revista de Filología Española* 12: 252–70.

Millares Carlo, A. 1935. *Los códices visigóticos de la catedral toledana. Cuestiones cronológicas y de procedencia*. Madrid: Ignacio de Noreña.

Millares Carlo, A. 1941. *Nuevos estudios de Paleografía Española*. Mexico City: La Casa de España en México.

Millares Carlo, A. 1961. "Manuscritos visigóticos. Notas bibliográficas." *Hispania Sacra* 14: 337–444.

Millares Carlo, A. 1971. *El diploma del rey Silo*. Madrid: Joyas Bibliográficas.

Millares Carlo, A. 1973. *Consideraciones sobre la escritura visigótica cursiva.* León: Centro de Estudios e Investigación San Isidoro.

Millares Carlo, A. 1983. *Tratado de paleografía española,* 3rd ed., 3 vols. Madrid: Espasa-Calpe [1st edition 1932].

Mundó, A. M. 1952. "El 'Cod. Parisinus Lat. 2036' y sus añadiduras hispánicas." *Hispania Sacra* 5: 67–78.

Mundó, A. M. 1956. "El commicus palimpsest Paris lat. 2269. Amb notes sobre litúrgia i manuscrits visigòtics a Septimània i Catalunya." In *Liturgica 1. Cardinali I. A. Schuster in memoriam,* 151–275. Montserrat: Abbatia Montisserrati.

Mundó, A. M. 1965. "La datación de los códices litúrgicos visigóticos toledanos." *Hispania sacra* 18: 1–25.

Mundó, A. M. 1970. "Los diplomas visigodos originales en pergamino. Transcripción y comentario con un regesto de documentos de época visigoda." Ph.D. diss., Universitat de Barcelona.

Mundó, A. M. 1978. "Problemas que suscita la escritura de los *Beatos.*" In *Actas del Simposio para el estudio de los códices del "Comentario al Apocalipsis" de Beato de Liébana,* vol. 1, 193–212. Madrid: Joyas Bibliográficas.

Mundó, A. M. 1983. "Notas para la historia de la escritura visigótica en su período primitivo." In *Bivium. Homenaje a Manuel Cecilio Díaz y Díaz,* 175–96. Madrid: Gredos.

Mundó, A. M. 1988. "Importación, exportación y expoliaciones de códices en Cataluña (siglos VIII al XIII)." In *Coloquio sobre circulación de códices y escritos entre Europa y la Península en los siglos VIII-XIII, 16–19 de septiembre 1982. Actas,* 87–134. Santiago de Compostela: Universidad de Santiago de Compostela.

Mundó, A. M. 1994. "Millares Carlo y las dataciones de códices visigóticos." *Boletín Millares Carlo* 13: 39–50.

Mundó, A. M. and J. Alturo. 1990. "La escritura de transición de la visigótica a la carolina en la Cataluña del siglo IX." In *Actas del VIII Coloquio del Comité Internacional de Paleografía Latina,* ed. M. C. Díaz y Díaz, 131–8. Madrid: Joyas Bibliográficas.

Mundó, A. M. and J. Alturo. 1998. "Problemàtica de les escriptures dels períodes de transició i de les marginals." *Cultura Neolatina* 58: 121–48.

Muñoz y Rivero, J. 1881. *Paleografía visigoda. Método teórico-práctico para aprender a leer los códices y documentos españoles de los siglos V al XII.* Madrid: Impr. y Lit. de la Guirnalda.

Nasarre, A. 1738. "Prólogo." In Cristóval Rodríguez, *Bibliotheca universal de la polygraphia española.* Madrid: A. Marin.

Nascimento, A. A. and J. M. Fernández Catón, eds. 2008. *Liber testamentorum coenobii Laurbanensis.* 2 vols. León: Centro de Estudios e Investigación San Isidoro.

Ostolaza Elizondo, M. I. 1990. "La transición de la escritura visigótica a la carolina en los monasterios del reino de León." In *Actas del VIII Coloquio del Comité Internacional de Paleografia Latina,* ed. M.C. Díaz y Díaz, 149–63. Madrid: Joyas Bibliográficas.

Ostos, P. 2003. "Producción libraria altomedieval y códices isidorianos. Aproximación codicológica." In *San Isidoro, doctor de las Españas,* ed. J. González Fernández, 271–307. Sevilla: Fundación El Monte.

Pacheco, R. 2001. "El diploma del rey Silo. Datos de semiótica para un estudio diplomático." *Signo. Revista de historia de cultura escrita* 8: 121–78.

Pérez Bayer, D. F. 1872. "Extracto del Catálogo de la Biblioteca del Escorial." *Revista de Archivos, Bibliotecas y Museos* 2: 218–22, 233–7.

Pérez de Urbel, J. 1975. "El monasterio de Valeránica y su escritorio." In *Homenaje a D. Agustín Millares Carlo*, vol. 2, 71–89. Las Palmas: Caja Insular de Ahorros.

Petrucci, A. 1973. "Il codice n. 490 della Biblioteca Capitolare di Lucca: un problema di storia della cultura medievale ancora da risolvere." *Actum Luce. Studi Lucchesi* 2: 159–75.

Petrucci, A. and C. Romeo. 1998. "L'Orazionale visigotico di Verona : aggiunte avventizie, indovinello grafico, tagli maffeiani." *Scrittura e Civiltà* 22: 13–30.

Pratesi, A. and P. Cherubini. 2010. *Paleografia latina: l'avventura grafica del mondo occidentale*. Vatican City: Scuola Vaticana di Paleografia, Diplomatica e Archivistica.

Ribeiro, J. P. 1819. *Dissertações chronologicas e criticas sobre a historia e jurisprudencia em Portugal*, 2nd ed., vol. 4. Lisbon: Academia das Sciencias de Lisboa.

Riché, P. 1992. "Les Réfugiés wisigoths dans le monde carolingien." In *L'Europe héritière de l'Espagne wisigothique*, ed. J. Fontaine and C. Pellistrandi, 177–83. Madrid: Casa de Velázquez.

Robinson, R. P. 1939. *Manuscripts 27 (S 29) and 107 (S 129) of the Municipal Library of Autun: A Study of Spanish Half-Uncial and Early Visigothic Minuscule and Cursive Scripts*. New York: American Academy in Rome.

Rodríguez, C. 1738. *Bibliotheca universal de la polygraphia española*. Madrid: A. Marin.

Rodríguez, E. 2011. "Los manuscritos mozárabes: una encrucijada de culturas." In *Die Mozaraber. Definitionen und Perspektiven der Forschung*, ed. M. Maser and K. Herbers, 75–103. Berlin: LIT Verlag.

Ruiz, I. 2004. "La distinción gráfica de '*ti/tj*' en los documentos visigóticos del Archivo de la Catedral de León." In *Orígenes de las lenguas romances en el Reino de León. Siglos IX–XII*, vol. 2, 439–56. León: Centro de Estudios e Investigación San Isidoro.

Ruiz Asencio, J. M. 1991. "La escritura y el libro." In *Historia de España Menéndez Pidal III, España visigoda II*, ed. J. M. Jover Zamora, 161–205. Madrid: Espasa-Calpe.

Ruiz Asencio, J. M. 2007. "Notas sobre la escritura y monogramas regios en la documentación real astur-leonesa." In *Monarquía y sociedad en el reino de León. De Alfonso III a Alfonso VII*, ed. J. M. Fernández Catón, 265–312. León: Centro de Estudios e Investigación San Isidoro.

Ruiz Asencio, J. M. 2008. "Cronología de la desaparición de la escritura visigótica en los documentos de León y Castilla." In *Actas de las IV Jornadas de la Sociedad Española de Ciencias y Técnicas Historiográficas. Paleografía I: La escritura en España hasta 1250*, ed. J. A. Fernández Flórez and S. Serna Serna, 93–117. Burgos: Universidad de Burgos.

Santiago Fernández, J. de. 2009. "El hábito epigráfico en la Hispania visigoda." In *VIII Jornada Científicas sobre Documentacion de la Hispania altomedieval (siglos VI-X)*, ed. N. Avila Seoane, M.J. Salamanca López, and L. Zozaya Montes, 291–344. Madrid: Universidad Complutense de Madrid.

Sanz Fuentes, J. 2006. "El documento de Fakilo (803): estudio y edición." In *Estudios en homenagem aô Professor Doutor José Marques*, 31–40. Porto: Universidade do Porto.

Schiaparelli, L. 1924. "Sulla data e provenienza del cod. LXXXIX della Biblioteca Capitolare di Verona." *Archivio Storico Italiano* 1: 106–17.

Schiaparelli, L. 1927. Influenze straniere nella scrittura italiana dei secoli VIII e IX. Note paleografiche. Rome: Biblioteca Apostolica Vaticana.

Schiaparelli, L. 1929. "Note paleografiche: Intorno all'origine della scrittura visigotica." *Archivo Storico Italiano* 7th ser. 12: 165–207.

Stiennon, J. 1973. *Paléographie du Moyen Âge*. Paris: A. Colin.

Tafel, S. 1923-5. "The Lyons Scriptorium." *Palaeographia Latina*, 2: 66–73 and 4: 40–70.

Tarracó, L. M. 1992. "Notas para la historia del monasterio de San Isidoro de Dueñas. III. ¿Procedería del monasterio de San Isidoro de (las) Dueñas el manuscrito latino nº 5 del fondo eslavo del Sinaí?" *Publicaciones de la Institución Tello Telles de Meneses* 63: 163–204.

Tassin, R. P. and C. Toustain. 1759. *Nouveau Traité de diplomatique*, vol. 3. Paris: G. Desprez.

Terreros, E. de. 1758. *Paleografía española, que contiene todos los modos conocidos que ha habido de escribir en España*. Madrid: J. Ibarra.

Thompson, E. M. 1906. *An Introduction to Greek and Latin Palaeography*. Oxford: Clarendon Press.

Turza, C. G., ed. 2002. *Los manuscriptos visigóticos: Estudio paleográfico y codicológico (I): Códices riojanos datados*. Logroño: Fundación San Millán de la Cogolla.

Ubieto, A. 1957. "¿Con qué tipo de letra se escribió en Navarra hace mil años?" *Revista de Archivos, Bibliotecas y Museos* 53: 409–22.

Usón, M. 1940. *Contribución al estudio de la cultura medieval aragonesa. La escritura en Aragón del siglo XI al XVI*. Zaragoza: Universidad de Zaragoza.

Velázquez, I. 2000. *Documentos de la época visigoda escritos en pizarra, siglos VI–VIII*. 2 vols. Turnhout: Brepols.

Velázquez, I. 2012. "La escritura visigótica cursiva en su período primitivo." In *La escritura visigótica en la Península Ibérica: nuevas aportaciones*, ed. J. Alturo, M. Torras, and A. Castro, 15–52. Bellaterra: Universitat Autònoma de Barcelona.

Vezin, J. 1988. "Manuscrits présentant des traces de l'activité en Gaule de Théodulphe d'Orléans, Claude de Turin, Agobard de Lyon et Prudence de Troyes." In *Coloquio sobre circulación de códices y escritos entre Europa y la Península en los siglos VIII–XIII, 16–19 de septiembre 1982. Actas*, 157–71. Santiago de Compostela: Universidad de Santiago de Compostela.

Vezin, J. 1992. "Le Commentaire sur la Genèse de Claude de Turin, un cas singulier de transmission des textes wisigothiques dans la Gaule carolingienne." In *L'Europe héritière de l'Espagne wisigothique*, ed. J. Fontaine and C. Pellistrandi, 223–9. Madrid: Casa de Velázquez.

Vezin, J. 2001. "Lire le latin dans le texte: la question des abréviations." In *Les Historiens et le latin médiéval*, ed. M. Goullet and M. Parisse. Paris: Publications de la Sorbonne.

Vezin, J. 2002–3. "À propos des manuscrits latins du Sinaï. Problèmes de localisation et de datation." *Antiquités africaines* 38–9: 313–20.

Vezin, J. 2003. "El códice British Library add. 30849 y la introducción de la carolina en España." *Studia Silensia* 26: 211–22.

Vezin, J. 2004. "Un Demi-siècle de recherches et de découvertes dans le domaine de l'écriture mérovingienne." *Archiv für Diplomatik* 50: 266.

Vezin, J. 2005. *À propos des manuscrits latins du Sinaï. Problèmes de localisation et de datation*. Paris: CNRS.

Vezin, J. 2010. "Les Manuscrits latins du Sinaï." In *Doctor honoris causa Jean Vezin*, 17–45. Bellaterra: Universitat Autònoma de Barcelona.

Vigil, C. M. 1887. *Asturias monumental, epigráfica y diplomática*. Oviedo: Imprenta del Hospicio Provincial.

Vivancos, M. C. 2006. "El oracional visigótico de Verona: notas codicológicas y paleográficas." *Cuadernos de Filología Clásica. Estudios Latinos*, 26: 121–44.

Vives, J. 1962. *Inscripciones cristianas de la España romana y visigoda*. Barcelona: Biblioteca Balmes.

Zapke, S., ed. 2007. *Hispana Vetus. Manuscritos litúrgico-musicales de los orígenes visigóticos a la transición francorromana (siglos IX–XII)*. Bilbao: Fundación BBVA.

CHAPTER 12

··

LUXEUIL

··

PAOLO CHERUBINI

Aᴛ the beginning of the Middle Ages, an authentic 'national' book script had not yet developed in the Frankish region comparable to the Insular scripts in Ireland and Great Britain, the Visigothic script in the Iberian Peninsula, or the Beneventan script in southern Italy. In fact, during the first centuries of the Middle Ages, there is evidence that Uncial and Half-uncial continued to be used for the copying of works of literature in several writing centers in Gaul including Lyons[1] and Autun.

It is likely that a national script began to be used for documents at the end of the sixth century or at the beginning of the seventh in a territory roughly corresponding to the Merovingian kingdom founded by Clovis in the northern part of Austrasia and Neustria. This script, the Merovingian, which originated from New Roman Cursive, was still used in chanceries at the time of the first Carolingian kings. Prefigured in a codex containing the *Homilies* of St Avitus of Vienne written in the region of Lyons in the sixth century (*CLA* V.573), the Merovingian script developed by pursuing the documentary tradition of the ancient *curia municipalia*, or perhaps thanks to the recovery by the chancery of the Merovingian kings of the *litterae officiales* of the late Roman Empire's provincial chanceries.

The most ancient chancery witnesses date to the first decades of the seventh century: two diplomas belonging to Chlothar II (*ChLA* XIII.550 and 552), some fragments of a private document from the early seventh century (*ChLA* XIII.549), a few collections containing the most ancient financial records of the Abbey of Saint Martin at Tours (overall about thirty sheets: *ChLA* XVIII.659), a very large number of relic labels from various churches and abbeys, mostly from the north—Chartres (*ChLA* XVIII.668), Saint Vivant at Vergy (*ChLA* XIX.691), Baume-les-Messieurs (*ChLA* XVIII.665 and 666), Saint Philibert at Tournus (*ChLA* XIX.690), Sainte Foy at Conques (*ChLA* XIX.677), Sens (*ChLA* XIX.682), Saint Maurice d'Agaune (*ChLA* I.14–39), Saint Pierre at Solignac (*ChLA* XIX.683), and especially Jouarre (*ChLA* XIX.678) and Chelles (*ChLA* XVIII.669)—as well as frequent notations in the margins of codices written in other scripts. During the central phase of its use it spread throughout the Frankish kingdom even beyond the boundaries of present-day France, as far as St Gall in northeastern Switzerland (*ChLA* I.49, 96; II.135).[2] Occasionally, it was used in northern Italy, for example, by the Frankish nobleman Abbo to edit the founding document of Novalesa abbey in 726 (*ChLA* XXVII.837).[3]

Merovingian script was used both for documentary and (less often and almost exclusively in the regions of Neustria, Austrasia, and northern Burgundy) for book use. In the latter use, it has a smaller size and less contrast between the bodies and stems of individual letters, as can be seen in the *Historia Francorum* by Gregory of Tours at the end of the seventh century (*CLA* V.671),[4] in the prayer added on a white sheet in the *Missale Gallicanum* not much later (*CLA*. I.106),[5] in the *De viris illustribus* by Saint Jerome and Gennadius, once the property of the Abbey of Corbie (*CLA* V. 664), in the *Sermones* by Augustine and St Caesarius copied in a codex of the monastery of Moutiers-Saint-Jean (*CLA* V.624), and in a few other manuscripts.[6] Since its earliest appearance, the presence of the letter *b*, with a small horizontal segment to the right of the stem at approximately one third of its height, is typical: it is without a doubt the most significant letter, which is never found outside the territories of Frankish domination.[7]

We must again look at the northern part of Gaul, corresponding by and large to the regions of Neustria, Austrasia, and part of Burgundy (the Vosges area), to follow the development of the first book minuscules in the Frankish region that may be called a distinct type. It is in this area, between the sixth and the seventh centuries, that new monastic foundations tied to insular preaching arose (beginning with those founded by St Columbanus), and, with them, new writing centers. Unfortunately, handwritten documentation from these centers has been unequally preserved: a clearer picture emerges from a more detailed examination of such as that found at Luxeuil, Corbie, Soissons, Saint-Amand, Fleury, Chelles, and Tours, though we know almost nothing, for instance, of the book production of Saint-Denis, for which no codices prior to the end of the eighth century survive, despite its great political importance.[8] From beginning of the Carolingian period, these areas began to develop their own cultural life, including, under the rule of Pepin III (714–68), a radical reform of the clergy and the introduction in Gaul of both Roman Liturgy and Gregorian chant. At this period, St. Denis begins to play a leading role, and it is not surprising that the transcription of the *Liber historiae Francorum* and the revision of the *lex salica* were undertaken there. Important late antique manuscripts (among these, the Virgilius Augusteus and Romanus) were kept in the library of the abbey on the outskirts of Paris at the time of the abbot Fulrad (750–84), and the pontiff Paul I (757–67) sent to the abbey codices in Greek, including the works of Dionysius the Areopagite.[9]

The creation of book minuscules in the Frankish territory followed two courses: on the one hand, the progressive calligraphy of the Merovingian script employed for editing documents, starting with those in the chanceries, on which, in different ways and at different times, the Insular scripts exercised their influence; on the other hand, the adaptation of Half-uncial to increasingly agile and economic forms. The first minuscule on a Merovingian base appeared at Luxeuil, the monastery founded *c.*590 by St. Columbanus at the foot of the Vosges, which shortly thereafter became a center not only for religious studies and asceticism, but also for the copying and export of manuscripts.[10] The guiding codex for the study of this minuscule, which was kept in the monastery's library until the French Revolution, is the famous *Luxeuil Lectionary*, now Paris, BnF, lat. 9427, *CLA* V.579),[11] dated with relative certainty to around 680; about thirty other related manuscripts in this script have been identified.[12]

The script, which Ludwig Traube first called *Luxoviensis*, appears fairly uniform on the whole; it is characterized by very thick vertical strokes that make the script compact and heavily shaded, by ascenders which are often almost semi-clubbed (Fig. 12.1a):

Fig. 12.1a *b, h, l, d.*

and by descenders equipped with distinctly visible wedges betraying the strong insular imprint (Fig. 12.1b):[13]

Fig. 12.1b *i, m, n, N, u.*

Ligatures are frequent, although the ductus is altogether quite formal; moreover, the letters extend in height rather than width, as in Merovingian cursive. The Merovingian base continuously surfaces in the morphology of single letters: *a* in the form of two *c*'s written together and with curves that tend to break (Fig. 12.1c):

Fig. 12.1c *a.*

c at times in two strokes with a small serif at the start of the lower stroke (Fig. 12.1d):

Fig. 12.1d *c.*

d with an open bowl when in ligature with the previous letter (Fig. 12.1e):

Fig. 12.1e *od.*

with a high and narrow bowl when linked to the next; the *ec* and *ex* ligature typical of documentary Merovingian is not rare (Fig. 12.1f):

$$\&\quad\&x$$

Fig. 12.1f *ec, ex.*

a drop-shaped *o* flattened at the top right, similar to that seen in royal diplomas (Fig. 12.1g):

$$\mathfrak{G}$$

Fig. 12.1g *o.*

the *o* also retains the Merovingian little horn, usually functional to the ligature (or the pseudo-ligature) with the following letter (Fig. 12.1h)

$$\text{ob}\quad\text{oc}\quad\text{ol}\quad\text{om}\quad\text{on}\quad\text{op}\quad\text{or}$$

Fig. 12.1h *ob, oc, ol, om, on, op, or.*

but which is sometimes present even when the letter is isolated or at the end of a word after an *r* or, less frequently, after another letter (Fig. 12.1i):

$$\text{ro}\quad\text{eo}$$

Fig. 12.1i *ro, eo.*

letters *p* and *q* also have a similar "drop-shaped" bowl, that of the *p* at times open toward the bottom and that of the *q* toward the top if the letter links to the previous (Fig. 12.1j):

$$p\quad\text{eoq}$$

Fig. 12.1j *p, eo q.*

Lastly, the upper stroke of the *t* is arched when in a ligature with *e, i, u* (rarely with *a*) as in all scripts originating from New Roman Cursive, though in a narrower form in line with common taste (Fig. 12.1k):

$$\text{te}\quad\text{ti}\quad\text{tu}$$

Fig. 12.1k *te, ti, tu.*

The New Roman Cursive origin can be recognized, furthermore, in the use of ligatures and particularly in the behavior of the *i*, which descends under the baseline almost every time it is in a ligature with the previous letter (besides *ti*, see Fig. 12.1l):

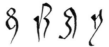

Fig. 12.1l *ei, fi, gi, ri.*

A few years after editing the *Lectionary* in 1944, the Benedictine Pierre Salmon carried out an accurate study of the handwriting used within it and of its decorative apparatus;[14] he provided an overview of the other manuscripts belonging to the *Luxoviensis* type and concluded that three periods could be distinguished in the evolution of the graphic type, which he believed reflected the activity of as many schools in different regional areas.[15] Meanwhile, other scholars had questioned the attribution of the *Lectionary* to Luxeuil, and, thereby, of its script. On the basis of liturgical and hagiographical arguments, it seemed indeed that the codex was to be assigned to a different geographical area: the preeminence given to saints Genevieve, Julian and Basilissa had induced the Benedictine Germain Morin (followed by Louis M. Olivier Duchesne and by François Masai), a few decades before Salmon, to assign it to the Church of Paris, or in any case to the Parisian region, where their cult was much more established than in the Vosges. In 1948 C. Charlier advocated an attribution to Lyons or Clermont. Salmon knew the *Lectionary* was not intended for the Columbanian abbey but for the Church of Langres; even so, he did not exclude the possibility that it had been produced at Luxeuil. The matter was made more complicated by the fact that two of the manuscripts of the group, both containing works of Gregory the Great, were associated with Italian scriptoria, one in Verona (*CLA* IV.497–501: *Moralia in Iob*, with parts written in Uncial and Half-uncial) and the other in Ivrea (*CLA* III.300: *Regula pastoralis*).[16] The area of diffusion of the *Luxoviensis* thus seemed to have spread as far as Italy.

Elias Avery Lowe made a decisive intervention on the matter in 1953 when he proposed an important comparison with another manuscript containing the *Homilies* of Augustine, written on papyrus and parchment in Uncial with a brief section in Half-uncial, most certainly copied in Luxeuil between September 1 and November 15, 669, as can be deduced from the note "Explecitum opus, favente Domino, apud coenubium Lussovium, anno duodecimo regis Chlothacarii, indictione tercia decima" referring to Clothar III king of Neustria in the years 657–73 (*CLA* XI.1659).[17] Alongside the Uncial used for the text, a decorative majuscule with a distinctive function and with a strong Insular reminiscence was used here; it is characterized by peculiar shapes (Fig. 12.2):

Fig. 12.2 *A, G, H, O, X.*

A with a central stroke split in two parts, where the left part is curved, 'spiral-shaped' *G*, *H* with a waved horizontal stroke, 'diamond-shaped' *O*, *X* with its second stroke split in two short and slightly curved elements, three dots placed vertically one on top of the other to highlight the separation between words.[18]

A decorative majuscule of the same type can be found in the *Lectionary* and in other manuscripts that can be traced to Luxeuil; the only difference is that, while in the *Homilies* codex, one of the abbey's most ancient, it is coupled with Uncial and Half-uncial, in those dating immediately afterwards the script used for the text is always the minuscule. Most though not all manuscripts written in *Luxoviensis* were transcribed at Luxeuil, and the Burgundian abbey was beyond doubt its main production center. Of the two Italian manuscripts mentioned above, the one from Verona is surely of the same school, if not of the same hand, as a papyrus manuscript containing works of Augustine (*CLA* V.614) with which it shares the abbreviation system and the omission marks (*hd/hs*); the same is found in the *Missale Gallicanum* (or *Gothicum*), one of the most ancient examples of Gallican liturgy, also belonging to the Burgundian area and whose decorative apparatus points precisely to Luxeuil.[19] The attribution of the *Regula pastoralis* to Ivrea is indicated by a dedication in capital letters on fol. 1*v*: "DESIDERIUS PAPA—VIVAT DIU" (Desiderius was the city's bishop from 679 to the turn of the century), but it is possible that the codex was written in Burgundy and brought to Ivrea as a gift, or that the manuscript was copied by a French monk visiting the city or by a French-educated Italian scribe.[20] Just as the *Regula* was produced for Ivrea and the *Lectionary* for a church in northeastern France, so another manuscript of varied content was produced for the nun Ragyndrudis (Ragentruth) of Fulda (*CLA* VIII.1197), while the *Missale Gallicanum* was intended for the Church of Langres. One can, therefore, imagine that an "export" handwriting production center was active for some time in Luxeuil; this would explain the presence of codices in *Luxoviensis* found at very advanced dates in Würzburg, Regensburg, Salzburg, Reichenau, and Weltenburg.[21] The role played in the evangelization of Rhenish Germany by Eustace and Waldebert, abbots of Luxeuil, favored the script's imitation in peripheral centers.[22]

NOTES

1. For Lyons, see Lowe (1924) and Tafel (1923–5). Perhaps the only case in Gaul at the time, a tradition of philological *notae*, later found in Corbie and Tours, was long maintained in the capital of the Burgundian kingdom: Ganz (1990, 70–1).
2. Steffens (1909, Tables 38 and 44a–b).
3. Federici (1964, Table XIV).
4. Steffens (1909, Table 49) and Mallon, Marichal, and Perrat (1939, No. 68).
5. Ehrle and Liebaert (1912, Table 18); cf. Vezin (1971); see also Tjäder (1973).
6. Vezin (2004, 267).
7. Vezin (2004, 254).
8. Vezin (1989, 307–9). The most ancient codex from Saint-Denis is a commentary of St. Jerome on *Jeremiah* commissioned by the abbot Fardulfus (793–806): *CLA*. V.668; for the abbey's codices see *CLA* VI.
9. Riché (1989, 299–300).

10. The extent of Luxeuil's spiritual and cultural influence was such that its lineage included Remiremont, Grandval, Rebais, Faremoutiers, etc., and the rule of Luxeuil became a model for the monasteries of Jouarre (founded in 629–36), Solignac (632), Rebais (636), Sens (660), Corbie (c.659), Chelles (660), Soissons (667), Montierender (692), Flavigny (721), and Murbach (728). For this reason it is correct to speak of the region of Luxeuil rather than of the single center.

11. Mallon, Marichal, and Perrat (1939, No. 66). Facsimiles of *Luxoviensis* script from Par. lat. 9377 (*CLA Supplement*, 1746) and from Ms. Wolfenbüttel, Herzog August Bibliothek, Weiss. 99 (*CLA*. IX, 1396), are found in Kirchner (1970, Table 31a–b).

12. A first list by Lowe in *CLA* VI, pp. XVI–XVII has been updated by Ganz (2002, 200–2).

13. Lowe had recognized the strong Irish imprint in the script of Luxeuil in other phenomena such as the classic *diminuendo* which accompanies the incipitary letter.

14. Salmon (1944) and Salmon (1953). Visigothic is one of the scripts that can be found in the marginalia to the *Lectionary*. The relation to the Iberian area has recently emerged through another manuscript in *Luxoviensis* containing the *Prophets* (*CLA* IX.1337), which completely follows the Iberian textual tradition (Ganz, 1991, 110).

15. He discerned the following production areas: Burgundy and Southern Austrasia (the Paris region), Rhenish Germany, and northern Italy.

16. The reproduction of a page of the latter may be found in Ehrle and Liebaert (1912, Table 19).

17. Lowe (1953), discussed and expanded in Ganz (2002, 188).

18. For the recovery of indigenous motives (from Burgundian inscriptions of the late fifth and sixth centuries) as well as the intrinsic Insular culture of this decorative majuscule, see Ganz (2002, 193).

19. Cf. Vezin (1971) (who favors a generic Burgundian writing center, perhaps Autun) and Ganz (2002, 193); for the attribution of the decoration to Luxeuil, see Mütherich (1989).

20. Putnam (1963) continues to consider the Ivrea codex Italian, but see Ferrari (1998, 511–17).

21. Ganz (2002, 195–6). For Weltenburg, see Ganz (1991, 110–12).

22. I hereby revise chapters 18 and 19 of Cherubini and Pratesi (2010).

BIBLIOGRAPHY

Atsma, H., ed. 1989. *La Neustrie. Les Pays au nord de la Loire de 650 à 850. Colloque historique international* (Beihefte der Francia, 16). Sigmaringen: Jan Thorbecke.

Cherubini, P. and A. Pratesi. 2004. *Paleografia latina. Tavole* (Littera Antiqua, 10). Vatican City: Scuola Vaticana di Paleografia, Diplomatica e Archivistica.

Cherubini, P. and A. Pratesi. 2010. *Paleografia latina. L'Avventura grafica del mondo occidentale* (Littera Antiqua, 15). Vatican City: Scuola Vaticana di Paleografia, Diplomatica e Archivistica.

Ehrle, F. and P. Liebaert. 1912. *Specimina codicum Latinorum Vaticanorum. Tabulae in usum scholarum*, ed. J. Lietzmann, 3, Berlin and Leipzig: W. De Gruyter et Socios [2nd ed., 1927; repr. Berlin, 1968].

Federici, V., ed. 1964. *La scrittura delle cancellerie Italiane dal secolo XII al XVII. Fac-simili per le Scuole di Paleografia degli Archivi di Stato raccolti ed illustrati a cura di V. Federici*. Rome: P. Sansaini [repr. Turin, 1964].

Ferrari, M. 1998. "Libri e testi prima del Mille." In *Storia della Chiesa di Ivrea. Dalle origini al XV secolo* (Chiese d'Italia, 1), ed G. Cracco, with A. Piazza, 511–33. Rome: Viella.

Ganz, D. 1990. *Corbie in the Carolingian Renaissance* (Beihefte der Francia, 20). Sigmaringen: Jan Thorbecke.

Ganz, D. 2002. "Texts and Scripts in Surviving Manuscripts in the Script of Luxeuil." In *Ireland and Europe in the Early Middle Ages: Texts and Transmission*, ed. P. Ní Chatáin and M. Richter, 186–204. Dublin and Portland, OR: Four Courts Press.

Ganz, D. 1991. "The Luxeuil Prophets and Merovingian Missionary Strategies." In *Beinecke Studies in Early Manuscripts* (Yale University Library Gazette. Supplement, 66), ed. R. Babcock, 105–17. New Haven, CT: Yale University Press.

Kirchner, J. 1970. *Scriptura latina libraria a saeculo primo usque ad finem medii aevi*, 2nd ed. Munich: R. Oldenbourg.

Lowe, E. A. 1924. *Codices Lugdunenses Antiquissimi. Le "scriptorium" de Lyon, la plus ancienne école calligraphique de France*. Lyons: Bibliothèque de la Ville.

Lowe, E. A. 1953. "The 'Script of Luxeuil.' A Title Vindicated." *Revue bénédictine* 63: 132–42 [=*Palaeographical Papers*, II, 389–98 and tables 74–9].

Mallon, J., R. Marichal, and C. Perrat. 1939. *L'Écriture latine de la capitale romaine à la minuscule: 54 planches reproduisant 85 documents originaux*. Paris: Arts et métiers graphiques.

Müterich, F. 1989. "Les Manuscrits enluminés en Neustrie." In *La Neustrie. Les Pays au nord de la Loire de 650 à 850. Colloque historique international* (Beihefte der Francia, 16), ed. H. Atsma, vol. 2, 319–38. Sigmaringen: Jan Thorbecke.

Ní Chatáin, P. and M. Richter, eds. 2002. *Ireland and Europe in the Early Middle Ages: Texts and Transmission*. Dublin and Portland, OR: Four Courts Press.

Putnam, M. C. 1963. "Evidence for the Origin of the 'Script of Luxeuil.'" *Speculum* 38: 256–66.

Riché, P. 1989. "Les Centres de culture en Neustrie de 650 à 850." In *La Neustrie. Les Pays au nord de la Loire de 650 à 850. Colloque historique international* (Beihefte der Francia, 16), ed. H. Atsma, vol. 2, 297–305. Sigmaringen: Jan Thorbecke.

Salmon, P. 1944. *Le Lectionnaire de Luxeuil (Paris, ms. lat. 9427). Édition et étude comparative. Contribution à l'histoire de la Vulgate et de la liturgie en France au temps des Mérovingiens* (Collectanea biblica Latina, VII). Rome and Vatican City: Abbey of St. Jerome and Vatican Publishing House.

Salmon, P. 1953. *Le Lectionnaire de Luxeuil (Paris, ms. lat. 9427). Édition paléographique et liturgique suivie d'un choix de planches* (Collectanea biblica Latina, IX). Rome and Vatican City: Abbey of St. Jerome and Vatican Publishing House.

Steffens, F. 1909. *Lateinische Paläographie*, 2nd ed. Trier: Schaar and Dathe [repr. Berlin, 1929, 1964; French ed: *Paléographie latine*, tr. R. Coulon. Trier: Schaar and Dathe and Paris: H. Champion, 1910; repr. Rome: Multigrafica, 1982)].

Tafel, S. 1923–5. "The Lyons Scriptorium." *Palaeographia Latina* 2: 66–73 and 4: 40–71.

Tjäder, J.-O. 1973. "L'origine della b merovingica," In *Miscellanea in memoria di Giorgio Cencetti* (Università degli studi di Roma. Scuola Speciale per archivisti e bibliotecari), ed. P. Supino Martini, 47–79. Turin: Bottega d'Erasmo.

Vezin, J. 1971. "Le B en ligature à droite dans les écritures du VIIe et du VIIIe siècles." *Journal des Savants* 4: 281–6.

Vezin, J. 1989. "Les Scriptoria de Neustrie, 650–850." In *La Neustrie. Les Pays au nord de la Loire de 650 à 850. Colloque historique international* (Beihefte der Francia, 16), ed. H. Atsma, vol. 2, 307–18. Sigmaringen: Jan Thorbecke.

Vezin, J. 2004. "Un Demi-siècle de recherches et de découvertes dans le domaine de l'écriture mérovingienne." *Archiv für Diplomatik* 50: 247–75.

CHAPTER 13

....

SCRIPTS OF
MEROVINGIAN GAUL

....

DAVID GANZ

DURING the eighth century distinctive minuscule scripts were developed in several Merovingian writing centers, as also in Italy. Many of these scripts were rich in cursive ligatures. The most celebrated examples are discussed below.

LAON *AZ* SCRIPT

....

A small group of manuscripts that can be linked to the libraries of Laon cathedral and of the abbey of Corbie are copied in an angular Merovingian minuscule script. This script was first discussed and was named "Laon az" script by W. M. Lindsay.[1] The distinctive letterforms are an open *a* formed of two angular strokes; curving *t*; the *ti* ligature; a deeply forked *r*; the *ri* ligature; *g* with a head stroke; the *ei* ligature; and a large *z*. Laon *az* script derives from the script of Luxeuil, and may be compared with the angular versions of Luxeuil script used at Corbie (for example, *CLA* 11.1617 containing Gregory the Great's *Homiliae in Ezechielem*) and at the unidentified center where the collection of homilies now in Wolfenbüttel (*CLA* 9.1396) was written. The surviving manuscripts in the *az* script are copies of substantial works which were copied by several collaborating scribes. They comprise Augustine, *De civitate Dei* (Basel, Universitätsbibilothek, N 1 4), Origen, *Homiliae* (Cambridge, CCC 334), Orosius, *Historiarum adversum paganos* (Laon, Bibliothèque municipale 137) and Isidore, *De natura rerum* (Laon, Bibliothèque municipale, 423) (Plate 13.1), Gregory, *Moralia in Job* (London, BL, Add. 31031), and Augustine, *Quaestiones in Hepateuchem* (Paris, BnF, lat. 12168). The script has been linked to the nunnery of St. John in Laon. The aforementioned manuscript of Isidore contains a colophon, not in *az* script, naming a certain Dulcia as its scribe: *Ego dulcia scripsi et susscripsi istum librum.*[2]

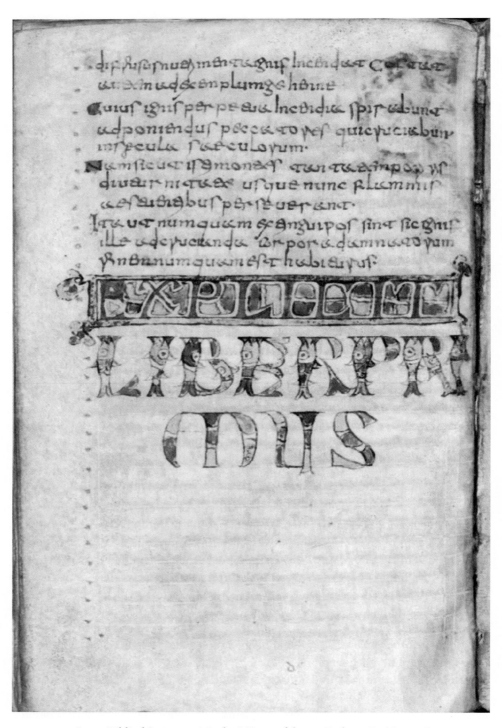

CORBIE

The abbey of Corbie was founded by the Merovingian queen Balthild between 657 and 661, receiving an episcopal privilege in 664.The first abbot, Theudefrid, had been a monk at Luxeuil, and Corbie owned a copy of Gregory the Great's *Homeliae in Ezechielem* in Luxeuil script (*CLA* 11.1617), as well as a copy of the abridged version of Gregory of Tours's *Historia Francorum.* which starts in Luxeuil script (*CLA* 5.671). Abbot Grimo of Corbie went to Rome from 739 to 741, and he is mentioned in a letter to Boniface. He may have brought back the Italian manuscripts which had entered the Corbie library by the early eighth century. The *Annales Petaviani* assert that Charles Martel confessed his sins to Martin, a monk of Corbie who died in 726, showing that the abbey had close links with the Merovingian court. Abbot Leodegar is mentioned in the prayer alliance of Attigny of 762, and he is known to have commissioned manuscripts.

eN Script

The eN script, first studied by Paul Liebaert, is found in six manuscripts from Corbie, where it was used in the eighth century. It preserves some of the ligatures and letterforms of Merovingian cursive script, such as are found in Merovingian charters, relic labels, and marginal notes. Distinctive letterforms are the high *e* in ligature with following *m*, or *r*; the Uncial *N*, and open *a*. The seven manuscripts in eN script are: Amiens, Bibliothèque municipale, 220 (Paterius, *Liber testimoniorum veteris testamenti*); St. Petersburg, National Library of Russia, O v I 4 (Cassian, *Collationes*); Paris, BnF, lat. 12239 (Cassiodorus, *Expositio Psalmorum*); BnF, lat. 13028 (Isidore, *Etymologiae*); BnF, lat. 13347 (Jerome, *Quaestiones hebraicae in Genesim* and *De situ et nominibus locorum hebraicorum*); BnF, lat. 13348 (Jerome, *Quaestiones hebraicae in Genesim*, Pseudo-Methodius, etc.) (Plate 13.2); and BnF, lat. 13349 (Jerome, *Commentarius in Ecclesiasten*). The eN script was also used to copy a single folio in an insular manuscript (*CLA* 11.1618: Isidore, *Differentiae*) and for a marginal entry in an Uncial manuscript (*CLA* 5.633: *Regula Magistri*). The eN script is combined with an informal minuscule in Paris, BnF, lat. 12239 and in Amiens, Bibliothèque municipale, 220. It was from such experiments that the Caroline minuscule of Corbie developed.

AB Script

The *ab* script, first discussed by Traube, Lindsay, and Liebaert, is found in 39 manuscripts, including a group of 11 manuscripts from the library of Corbie; but the script is

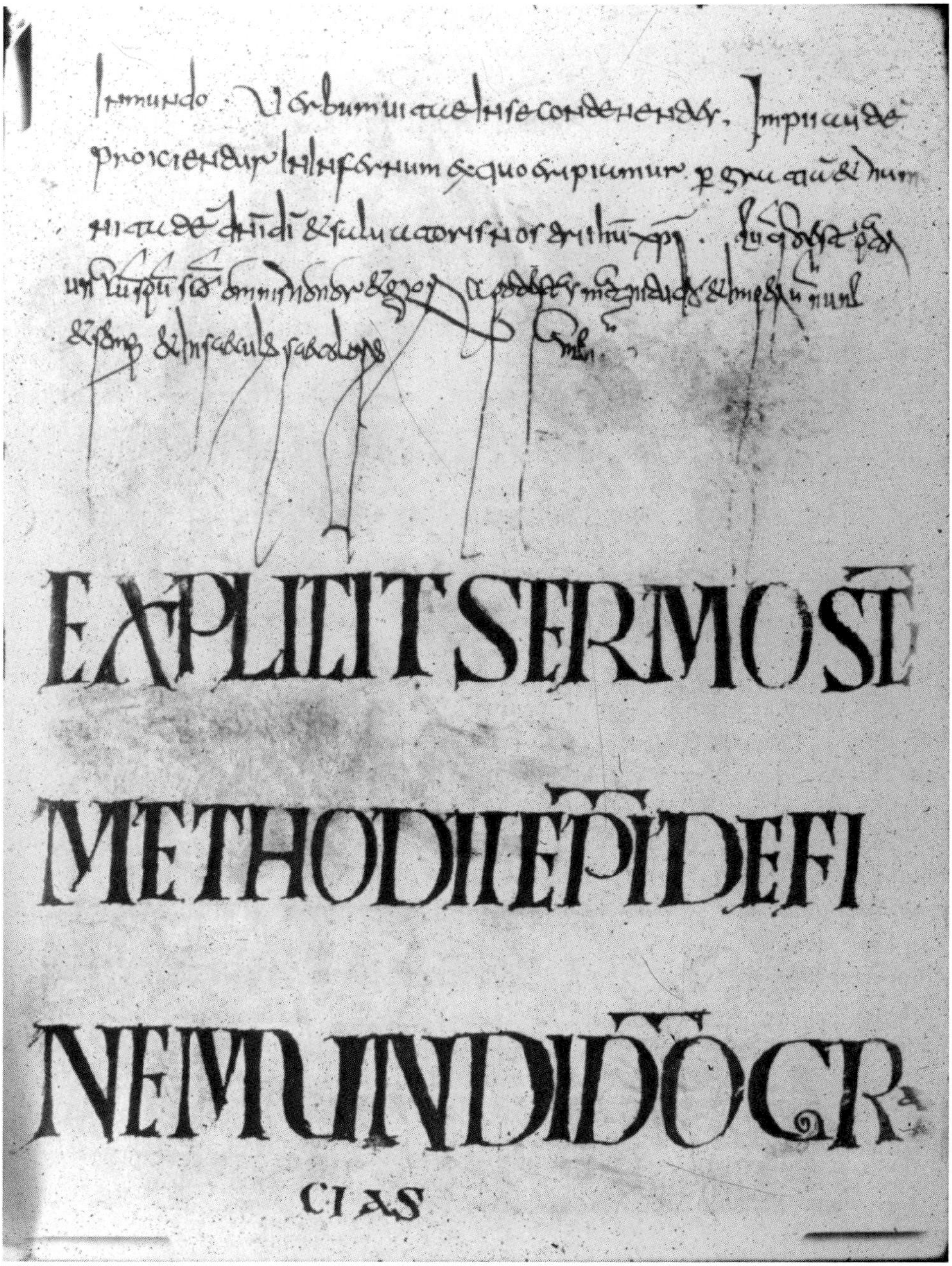

PLATE 13.2 Paris, BnF lat. 13348, Pseudo-Methodius in EN script (photo DG).

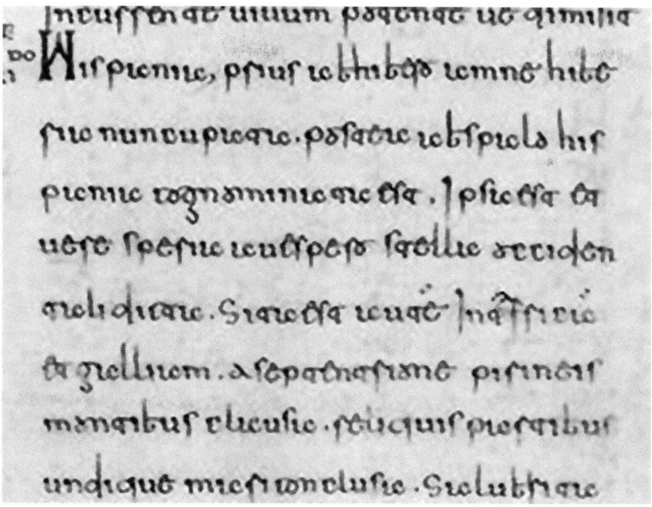

PLATE 13.3 Paris, BnF, lat. 11530, fol. 69r, showing the *a* and *b*.

also found in manuscripts which have no link with that abbey. The script is similar to the *b* minuscule (described below) and has a distinctive open form of the letter *a*, and a *b* with an open bowl and a crossbar on the shaft (see Plates 13.3 and 13.4).

Though the *ab* script is frequently dated to the last quarter of the eighth century, the earliest extant specimens can hardly be much earlier than the beginning of the ninth. T. A. M. Bishop identified 68 different *ab* scribes, one of whom he recognized in 12 distinct manuscripts. An unusual codicological feature of the *ab* manuscripts is that the quires are composed such that flesh side faces hair side in the openings (this contrasts with the more common Carolingian practice of making each opening consistent). The *ab* manuscripts from Corbie are found in *CLA*, volume 5, numbers 570, 611, 612, 615, 621, 622, 623, 636, 650, and *CLA*, volume 11, 1606, and 1620.

Works copied in *ab* script which appear to have been produced for houses other than Corbie include *CLA* 6.669, 10.1554, 8.1183, 2.201, 6.792, 5.574, and 5.662. There are two copies of the massive three-column encyclopedic glossary *Liber Glossarum* (*CLA* 5.611 and 6.743), so at least one of them must have been produced for export. Bishop believed that several surviving examples of the *ab* script were copied at Soissons: a copy of Ambrose, *Hexameron* (*CLA* 2.124); a manuscript of Orosius now in private hands; a collection of saints lives (*CLA* 4.446); and a canon law manuscript (*CLA* 5.554).

The date of the *ab* script must be inferred from existing specimens. Several of the *ab* manuscripts from Corbie have corrections or replacement leaves in the Maurdramnus script developed at the abbey from the 770s. A manuscript of Cassiodorus' *Historia Tripartita* (St. Petersburg, National Library of Russia, F. v. I. 11) has two eleventh-century inscriptions on the flyleaf recording that the manuscript was written at the

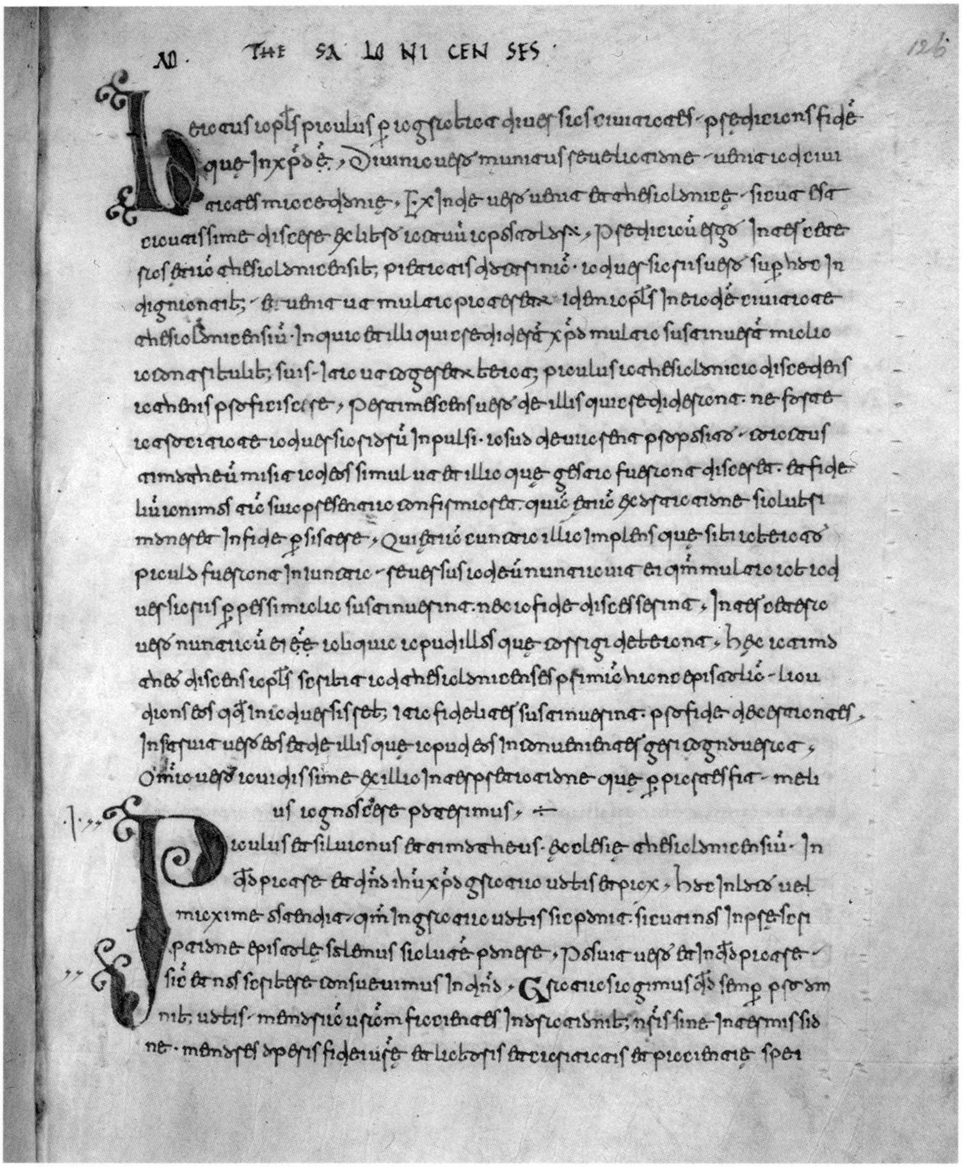

PLATE 13.4 London, BL, Harley 3063, Theodore of Mopsuestia, *In Epistulas Pauli.*

monastery of Noirmoutier, by command of Abbot Adalhard while he was in exile there (between 814 and 821). An *ab* manuscript of canon law in Berlin, Staatsbibliothek zu Berlin-Preussischer Kulturbesitz, Hamilton 132 contains a reference to the Emperor Charlemagne, and so dates after 800; a copy of Claudius of Turin's and Alcuin's commentaries on Genesis (*CLA* 8.1183) was copied after 811.

MAURDRAMNUS SCRIPT

The Maurdramnus script is named for Abbot Maurdramnus of Corbie, who is known from a colophon in one of the volumes of a multivolume Bible now in Amiens (Bibliothèque municipale, 6-9, 11): *Ego Maurdramnus abbas propter dei amorem et propter compendium legentium hoc volumen fieri iussi.* The Bible is written in a distinctive regular minuscule, with very few variant letterforms, generally recognized as the earliest form of Caroline minuscule. Ascenders are clubbed; the upper compartment of *g* is open; *s* has a pronounced knob on the shaft. Several of the scribes who copied the Bible also shared in the copying of a multivolume set containing Augustine, *Ennarationes in Psalmos*, now in Paris (BnF, lat. 12171–83). The Maudramnus script was used for copies of exegetical works of Augustine, Hilary, Jerome (Plate 13.5), and Bede, and for works of grammar and canon law. Over 60 volumes survive in this script. It was used at Corbie for some 50 years and was replaced by a smaller and rounder Caroline minuscule.

b MINUSCULE

This minuscule script is found in additions to manuscripts from Northern Francia copied in N-uncial, most notably in Vatican City, BAV, Reg. lat. 316 (the Gelasian Sacramentary), Oxford, Bodleian Library, Laud Misc. 126 (Augustine, *De Trinitate*) (Plate 13.6), and Paris, BnF, lat. 6413 (Isidore, *Sententiae* and *De Natura Rerum*). The distinctive letterforms are the *b* with a short horizontal tag to the right of the shaft and a long open bow; and the *a*, which is shaped like two **c**'s. The script is also found in Autun, Bibliothèque municipale, 20 (*CLA* 6.719: Gregory, *Dialogi* and Augustine, *Enchiridion*), Montpellier, Bibliothèque de la Faculté de Médecine, 3 (Gospels), and the single leaf now in Paris, BnF, lat. 4808, fol. 121 (Symphosius, *Aenigmata*).

Bernhard Bischoff suggested that *b* minuscule was written at Chelles during the abbacy of Charlemagne's sister Gisela. The script is also found on relic labels from Chelles (reproduced in *ChLA* XVIII.669, item LXVII). It is found in the following manuscripts: Cologne, Dombibliothek, MSS 63, 65, 67 (Augustine, *Enarrationes in Psalmos*) with quires signed by 9 female scribes; Oxford, Bodleian Library, Douce 176 (*CLA* 2.238: Evangelistarium); Paris, BnF, lat. 1564 (*Concilia*); BnF, lat. 12240 and 12241 (Cassiodorus, *Expositio psalmorum*); BnF, lat. 18282 (Rufinus's Latin translation of Eusebius's *Historia ecclesiastica*); St. Gall, Stiftsbibliothek, 435 (Smaragdus, *Expositio libri comitis*); Quedlinburg, Stifts- und Gymnasialbibliothek, 74 (Jerome, *Epistulae*); Berlin, Staatsbibliothek zu Berlin-Preussischer Kulturbesitz, Phillipps 1657 (Augustine, *Enarrationes in Psalmos*). The script of Chelles is a minuscule which retains the ligatures *nt*, *ra*, *re*, and *ri*.

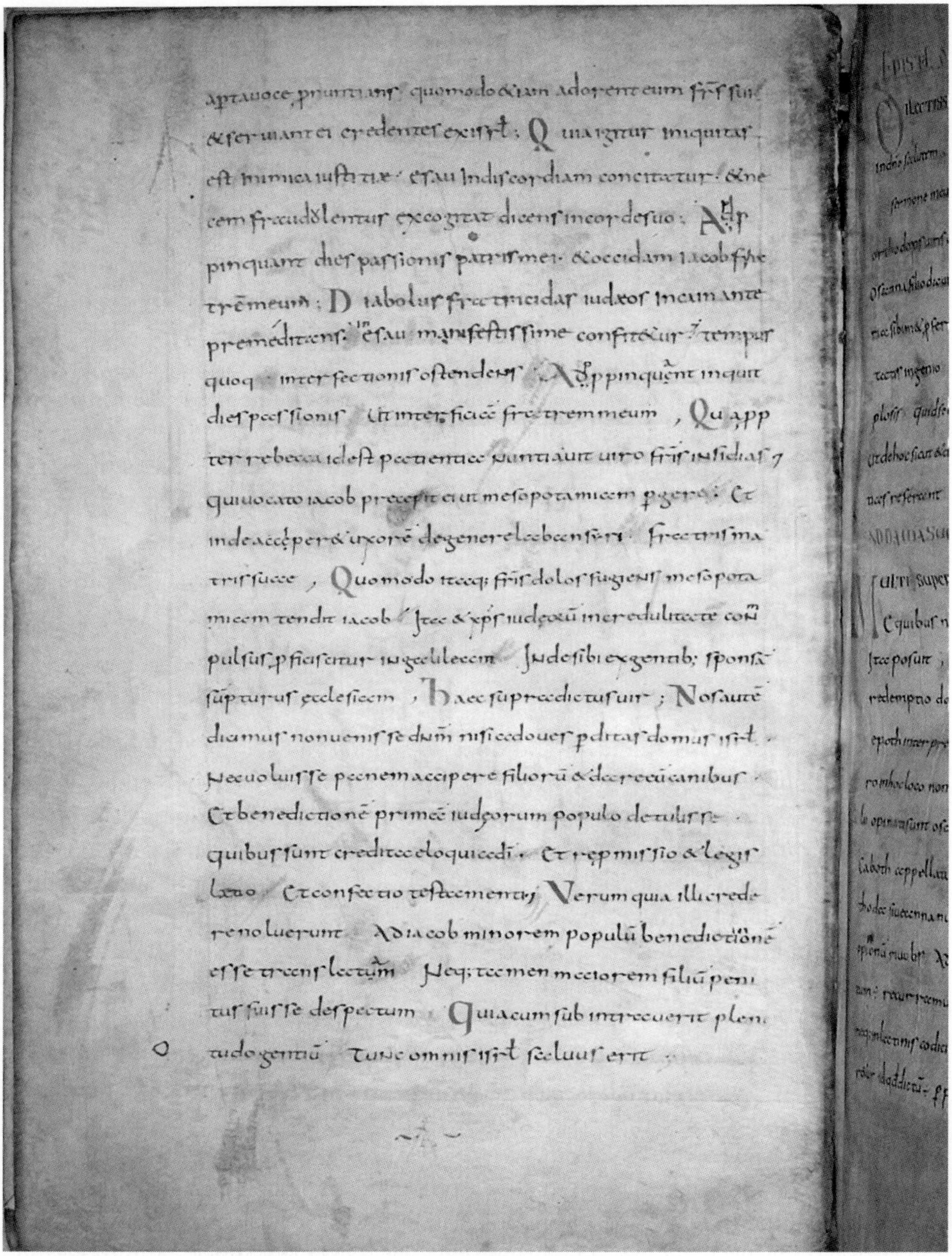

PLATE 13.5 Cologne, Dombibliothek, 60, fol. 8v, Jerome, *Epistolae*, Corbie, s. IX 1/3.

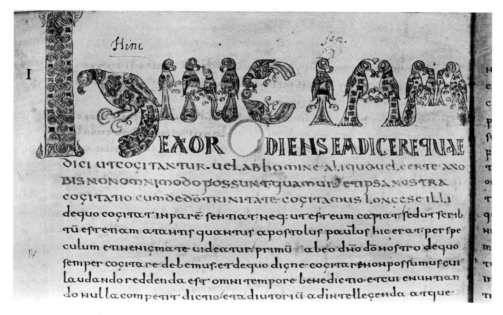

PLATE 13.6 Oxford, Bodleian Library, Ms Laud Misc. 126, fol. 87v, Augustine, *De Trinitate*, Chelles.

NOTES

1. Lindsay (1914, 15–27).
2. Plate in Dosière (1987, 40).

BIBLIOGRAPHY

Laon *az* Script

Dosière, René. 1987. *Laon citadelle royale carolingienne*. Laon: Association "Archives, Bibliothèque, Musée à Laon."
Lindsay, W. M. 1914. "The Laon az Type." *Revue des bibliothèques* 24: 15–27.

eN Script

Ganz, David. 1990. *Corbie in the Carolingian Renaissance*. Sigmaringen: Jan Thorbecke.
Liebaert, P. 1922. "Some Early Scripts of the Corbie Scriptorium." *Palaeographica latina* 1: 62–6.

ab Script

Bishop, T. A. M. 1978. "The Prototype of *Liber Glossarum.*" In *Medieval Scribes, Manuscripts and Libraries Essays presented to Neil Ker,* ed. M. B. Parkes and A. G. Watson, 69–86. London: Scolar.

Bishop, T. A. M. 1990. "The Scribes of the Corbie *a-b.*" In *Charlemagne's Heir: New Perspectives on the Reign of Louis the Pious (814–840),* ed. R. Collins and P. Godman, 523–53. Oxford: Oxford University Press.

Ganz, D. 1990. *Corbie in the Carolingian Renaissance.* Sigmaringen: Jan Thorbecke.

Gasparri, F. 1966. "Le Scriptorium de Corbie à la fin du VIIIe siècle et le problème de l'écriture *ab.*" *Scriptorium* 20: 265–72.

Goullet, M., S. Isetta, and I. Tessarolo. 2014. Le Légendier de Turin. Ms. D.V.3 de la Bibliothèque Nationale Universitaire. Avec DVD. Florence: SISMEL-Edizioni del Galluzzo.

Lindsay, W. M. 1912. "The Old Script of Corbie, its Abbreviation Symbols." *Revue des bibliothèques* 22: 405–29.

b Minuscule

Bischoff, B. 1966. "Die Kölner Nonnenhandschriften und das Skriptorium von Chelles." In *Mittelalterliche Studien* 1, 16–34. Stuttgart: Hiersemann.

Vezin, J. 2004. "Un Demi-siècle de recherches et de découvertes dans le domaine de l'écriture mérovingienne." *Archiv für Diplomatik* 50: 247–75.

Ziegler, U. 1976. "Das Sacramentarium Gelasianum bibl. Vat. Reg. Lat. 316 und die Schule von Chelles." *Archiv für Geschichte des Buchwesens* 16: 2–148.

CHAPTER 14

....

ST. GALL SCRIPTS

....

ANNA A. GROTANS

OF the 2,100 volumes on deposit in the St. Gall Abbey library, or *Stiftsbibliothek*, *c.*400 can be dated before AD 1000. Manuscripts originally produced at St. Gall are found strewn in libraries across Europe and North America. Some of these were produced at St. Gall for export; others were lent out and never found their way back. Four St. Gall library catalogues survive from the ninth century and together they list 580 titles; a later catalogue from the fifteenth century lists 480 works. Scholars estimate that in the mid-twelfth century the library housed 800–1,000 manuscripts. In addition, the neighboring abbey archive, or *Stiftsarchiv*, houses more than 800 original charters and other documents produced from the eighth to the tenth centuries. Of course, not all of the manuscripts preserved in the *Stiftsbibliothek* were produced there. Scarpatetti estimates that of the 450 early manuscripts, 232 were produced on location, 125 are of mixed or questionable provenance, and 101 were produced elsewhere (Scarpatetti 1999, 37–8). To the last group belong manuscripts written in Ireland, Anglo-Saxon England, Italy, and western and eastern Francia. Provenance can sometimes be difficult to determine because scripts closely related the St. Gall styles can be found elsewhere, e.g., on the Reichenau, in Rhaetia or Lombardy, later in Einsiedeln, Rheinau, and Bavarian centers such as Freising and Salzburg.

Contemporary sources about the scriptorium, the scribes, and library are found in the historical accounts by Ratpert and Ekkehard IV. On the ideal Carolingian architectural "Plan of St. Gall" dating from the first quarter of the ninth century, the scriptorium and library are situated next to the church on the north side in a two-storied building with the caption "below the seats of the scribes; above the library." Whether the scriptorium and chancery were located in the same space and how often chancery scribes also participated in book production are unclear. Bruckner in his monumental study of St. Gall manuscripts argued for numerous correspondences between the two and often attributed manuscripts to named charter scribes. Earlier scholars in general often stressed the role of individual scribes and their schools in tracing innovations and changes. Although some ascriptions are fairly certain, others are questionable and should be treated with healthy skepticism (cf. Scarpatetti 1995).

St. Gall Scripts

Functional style is an important consideration when evaluating and dating a script and scribal hand. At St. Gall, two to three levels of script are generally recognized. The highest level, the "book" script, was used for biblical and liturgical texts, as well as for saints' lives and some collections of canons. The "middle" or "documentary" style is used for texts such as charters, calendars, martyrologies, and patristic and contemporary works; it contains some cursive characteristics and uses frequent ligatures and abbreviations. The third level is the "school" style, which was used for teaching materials and in glosses. It is marked by *notae*, copious abbreviations, and ligatures, including superscript or suspended vowels. According to Daniel the distinction in styles was common at St. Gall already by the mid-ninth century (1973, 3–10). The levels were not always clearly distinguished, though, and the lines between them can be very fluid, especially from the mid-tenth century on (Scarpatetti 1999, 67).

The dating and provenance of St. Gall manuscripts as listed in Scherrer's nineteenth-century catalogue and Bruckner's *Scriptoria Medii Aevi Helvetica* are for the most part reliable, but can vary and should always be verified by additional sources if possible. The catalogue of datable Swiss manuscripts by Beat von Scarpatetti *et al.* (1991), as well as the new catalogue volumes edited by him (2003, 2007, and Scarpatetti, Lenz, and Ortelli 2014), von Euw's study of medieval book art (2008), and Hartmut Hoffmann's study of Ottonian manuscripts (1986) provide excellent additional resources. Scholars also now have at their disposal the superb resources found online at "e-codices. Virtual Manuscript Library of Switzerland," including manuscript facsimiles, descriptions, and bibliographies. As of March 2020, 675 of the *Stiftsbibliothek*'s manuscripts were available in the virtual electronic library. Facsimiles of all manuscripts discussed below can be found there.

The palaeography of medieval St. Gall can roughly be divided into three periods: Pre-Caroline, St. Gall Caroline, and late Caroline. An early high point was reached in the late ninth and early tenth centuries, at which time the St. Gall type of Caroline minuscule and other scribal practices associated with the abbey exerted major influence on many southern German scriptoria. This same script continued to be used well into the eleventh century with only minimal variation, and reached a refined maturity at the end of the tenth and early eleventh century. The description of any script is based on the impression given by several hands over time, and it is important to remember that individual characteristics will always be present. Some scribes will write modern forms, whereas others will reintroduce older forms from a previous generation or a foreign scriptorium. The summaries that follow are meant to give a general impression of the script used at St. Gall from the mid-eighth through the twelfth century.

Pre-Caroline Scripts: Rhaetian, Alemannic, and St. Gall Minuscule

The development of script at St. Gall in the eighth century is difficult to trace with any certainty. Although *c.*40 manuscripts from the eighth century survive at St. Gall, not all were copied there, and the provenance of some is unclear. In this early period, the abbey lay between the cultural and scribal influence of two important ecclesiastical centers, Chur and Constance. At the former the Rhaetian-Lombardic script flourished; the latter lay on the border of an area in which various Burgundian and Merovingian scripts were in use. The first generation of monks who populated the abbey after its founding in 719 were adults, and we can assume that the scribes among them introduced styles of writing from elsewhere; how much they eventually conformed to a "house style" and how quickly is unclear. The first abbot, Otmar (719–59), was trained at Chur, where the Rhaetian script flourished.

We have evidence that the scriptorium existed from 760 onwards. Early books and charters were written in either the Rhaetian or Alemannic minuscule, local script styles that developed independently of the roman cursive and Half-uncial scripts. According to Bruckner, the "Rhaetian" script was that used in the area of Grisons; "Alemannic" appears in the Alemannic and Alsatian regions at St. Gall, Reichenau, and perhaps Constance and contains some Merovingian traits. He admits that the individual styles of the Alemannic type can be difficult—if not impossible—to distinguish; the distance between St. Gall and Reichenau was minimal, and scribes probably moved back and forth (1936, 15–16). The Rhaetian script is also found in the very early period at St. Gall, but more often in charters and in only a few early manuscripts. CSang 229 (of questionable St. Gall provenance) is written in a Rhaetian-cast script, with typical Beneventan and Visigothic characteristics such as the cc-form of *a* and *t* with a loop on its back extending to the left of its top stroke, sometimes reaching to the baseline.

In its early form, the Alemannic minuscule is a composite script which absorbs some cursive elements. Its appearance can be primitive, written with a thick-cut quill: lineation is not always respected and some letterforms cross over the baselines and head lines, especially ligatures. Likewise ductus and pen control are not always uniform or stable, and letterforms can at times be erratic. The small *a* derived from Uncial appears already in the 760s, although the cc-form is far more common. The Half-uncial *e* is used; notched *e* is found only in ligatures (with *c*, *t*, *x*, and, less commonly, *m*, *n*, *r*, and *s*). *f* descends a bit below the line, *s* rests directly on the line; *g* is found in a Semi-uncial form with open bows, resembling the numeral *3*; the first shafts of *m* and *n* can bend slightly to the left, and the last shaft only rarely bends out to the right.

Ligatures are kept to a minimum; in addition to the common *&*, *rt*, and *st*, are found *nt*, *r-* ligatures (with *a*, *e*, *o*, *n*, *r*, *s*, *u*, and *t*) and the *e*-ligatures. A good example of early book hands is seen in CSang 194, which was written partially on a palimpsest sometime toward the middle of the century at a Swiss scriptorium, probably St. Gall. In it we find scribes writing both the Rhaetian and Alemannic minuscule types.

One group of early St. Gall manuscripts is associated with the scribe Winithar, who himself copied several codices, including CSang 2, 70, 238, 907, and parts of 11, 109, and perhaps 1399; he also wrote a charter in the year 763 (Wartmann 1863, I, 39). Winithar's script deviates from the Alemannic minuscule and is far from polished; Scarpatetti sees in it clear western and late Merovingian influence, with fewer ligatures and a more frequent use of simpler, more modern letterforms than those used in Rhaetian scripts of the time (1999, 46). Another figure associated with this early period is Waldo, who either wrote or signed some 17 charters between 770 and 779. Bruckner stressed Waldo's influence in the scriptorium and attributed to him numerous manuscripts as well; today, only CSang 125 can probably be attributed to him. He was, nonetheless, influential in the abbey and also served as deacon and abbot (782–4) and later assumed the same office at Reichenau, where he founded the library. The writing from Waldo's period is characterized by a more cursive and dense script, in which ligatures are common.

The Alemannic minuscule reached an early highpoint at St. Gall at the turn of the ninth century and into Gozbert's abbacy (816–37). The later, more refined form is characterized by broad, rounded, and plump strokes with a clear vertical aspect that can give it a static appearance. The weight of letters falls on the headline; ascenders and descenders are well proportioned to the elements of mid height. The curves of letters such as *m*, *n*, *s*, and *u* are wide and exhibit architectural balance; the final two shafts of the *m* bend in to the left, as does the final shaft of the *n*; the cross strokes of *f*, *r*, and *t* are given ample space. Spacing between letters and lines is in general very generous. Two older letterforms still used are an occasional cc-form of *a* and *g* with both a bowl and bow open to the left [3]. Common ligatures are *&*, *rt*, and *st*; *ri* is found only rarely. Small octave-format codices are often written with a finer quill and the spacing is less generous, which can at times give a stiff appearance. Bruckner attributes a group of *c*.30 manuscripts from this period to Wolfcoz, who wrote several charters from *c*.817–22, and to a group of scribes influenced by him. He describes the minuscule of this "Wolfcoz group" as having a perfected harmony evident in the carefully placed shafts and the proportion of the letterforms with their evenly broad and well-formed descenders and ascenders; *g* can be written with a closed upper bowl, although the form with two open bowls is more common; ligatures are kept to a minimum except for *&*, *nt*, and *st* (1936, 26–8). Several illuminated manuscripts are also associated with this group, e.g., the "Wolfcoz Psalter" in CSang 20, the "Wolfcoz Evangeliary" in CSang 367, which is the first St. Gall manuscript to use gold and silver lettering, and the "Zürich Psalter" in Zürich, Zentralbibliothek, C 12.

At the same time that scribes were writing this highly developed form of the Alemannic minuscule, they were also copying texts in the new Caroline minuscule.

The concurrence of both scripts can make it very difficult to date manuscripts at the turn of the ninth century. Bruckner points out that some scribes show uncertainty in their writing, which lends it an unsure, "unrestful," and unharmonious appearance (1936, 26). Scarpatetti and Bruckner estimate that *c.*20 manuscripts were written in the period from 800–25, bringing the total number of MSS for the early period to *c.*60.

CAROLINE SCRIPTS

Early and High St. Gall Caroline

The transition from the local Alemannic minuscule to a Caroline version occurred at St. Gall *c.*820–40. Exactly why is not known and, as pointed out in Section 14.2 above, both scripts were used by the same scribes. The Alemannic minuscule was not outdated, and the Caroline minuscule new and foreign. Yet, as Scarpatetti points out, the change was probably inevitable given the cultural and political strength of the new empire and the role that St. Gall's leaders wanted the abbey to play in it. Once the abbey gained in prestige at the beginning of the ninth century, we also have to assume that its monks came from far and wide, including scribes from areas where forms of the Caroline script were already in use. The early form at St. Gall was probably based on the Frankish variety used at Tours, such as that found in CSang 75, which contains the earliest complete copy of Alcuin's pandect Bible, although Löffler warns against placing too much importance on one particular manuscript as a model. It, along with other manuscripts, however, must have formed the basis for the St. Gall production of several biblical manuscripts *c.*850, e.g., CSang 77, 78, 79, 81, 82, and 83.

By the mid-ninth century, a Caroline minuscule specific to St. Gall had developed, and the scriptorium held to this style with very few changes well into the eleventh century. According to Scherrer's count, *c.*120 manuscripts were produced in the years 825–900. In the tenth century, its influence reached beyond the abbey walls, especially into southern Germany, where it can be found at Freising and Regensburg. Traces of influence have even been suggested in Italy. Because of the wide influence that the St. Gall script enjoyed, it can sometimes be difficult to distinguish the hand of an inexperienced St. Gall scribe from that of foreign scribes who wrote a very similar script. A leveling of scripts can also be seen in charters from the Alemannic area. Whereas in the eighth and early ninth centuries there is a clear distinction between the cursive scripts of local scribes and the book hands of the scriptorium, in the course of the ninth century the scripts become more uniform. McKitterick suggests that this may indicate that the number of St. Gall scribes redacting documents grew, whereas that of local scribes decreased (1991, 223–5).

Traditionally the development of the St. Gall type of the Caroline minuscule is divided into four periods: (1) early (*c.*820–50); (2) a "Golden Age," with its grand display MSS dating roughly from 850–920 and including the abbacies of Grimald

(842–72), Hartmut (872–83; with a sub-period called "Hartmut-minuscule"), and Salomo (890–920); (3) the "Silver Age" from the mid tenth century to the mid-eleventh century, during which the script itself reached a high point and large numbers of MSS were exported; and (4) finally a "late" period from the mid-eleventh century until the twelfth century.

In general, the St. Gall Caroline minuscule is characterized by a thinner and steeper, less rounded script than the Alemannic minuscule. The quill is cut with a broader tip, and scribes distinguish more between horizontal and full strokes. Letters rest firmly on the baseline, and attention is given to the careful grouping of shafts and bows. Focus falls on the head line, where the horizontal head strokes of letters such as *t*, *r*, *a*, *e*, and *g* and the initial hook of *i*, *u*, *m*, and *n* meld into a visible horizontal line. The general appearance of the script is round, soft, and even; in aspect it slants slightly toward the right. Short descenders give the script a compact appearance. Slight clubbing appears on the shafts of *m*, *n*, and, to some extent, *l* and *q*. Some hands adopt the technique of "turning the quill," which occasionally results in the breaking of letter bows (Daniel 1973, 13–14). Individual characteristic letterforms to look for are *a* with a fairly vertical right back stroke; *g* is written in various ways, with both open and closed bowls; sometimes *g* is found with a back stroke of the top bow that leans inward and a thick initial stroke of the lower bow that protrudes prominently to the right; Uncial *d* is common; the head of *e* is small and the base begins with a short horizontal stroke to the right; the shafts of *m*, *n*, and *h* are often short and reach the baseline only with the very left tip of the shaft, adding to the rounded impression of the script; the middle stroke of *m* is not written parallel to the first and third and tips up to the left; the final shafts of *m* and *n* have a final tick that rests horizontal on the baseline. Common ligatures found at this time are *ct*, *&*, *rt*, *st*, and *or*, with the *oR* abbreviation; occasionally *nt* is found.

The script develops more quickly in charters from the period, where one finds a more careless style than in the book script of the manuscripts, with more abbreviations and ligatures being used, including *ti*. An interesting mix of the charter and book styles can be found in copies of Augustine's *Commentary on the Psalms* in CSang 162–6 from *c.*850 and Cassiodorus' *Expositio Psalmorum* in CSang 200–2 from the third quarter of the ninth century. The scribes all use both the closed and open cc-form of *a*. The first shaft of *m* and *n* has a tendency to lean to the left, and the last shaft is written with a slight foot protruding the right. The only ligatures used are *ct*, *&*, *rt*, and *st*; the *rt* ligature begins to appear with a small horn in order to distinguish it from *st*. According to Bruckner, the "Hartmut-minuscule" from the last third of the ninth century displays characteristics of a pure Caroline minuscule: both *u* and *v* occur for both the vowel and semivowel; both Uncial and minuscule *d*; *m* and *n* with left shafts (and with *m* also the middle shaft) that tip up to the left; occasional use of suspended vowels, perhaps under Insular influence (1938, 40).

Examples of the extreme book-hand style can be found in several of the magnificent display codices produced at the end of the ninth and the beginning of the tenth century, e.g., the Folchert Psalter in CSang 23, the *Evangelium longum* in CSang 53, the Gundis Evangeliary in CSang 54, and the Epistolary of St. Gall in Geneva, Bibliothèque publique et universitaire, lat. 37a; the Golden Psalter in CSang 22 may also stem from St. Gall. Bruckner and Scherrer often disagree on the dating of c.40 MSS from the period 875–925: Scherrer lists the tenth century, whereas Bruckner dates earlier in the ninth. Scarpatetti suggests that one reason for the discrepancies might be Bruckner's preference for the ninth century, against which the tenth lay "in the shadows." In such cases Scherrer's dating should be given precedence unless more recent studies are available (Scarpatetti, 1999, 231, n. 9).

In the middle of the ninth century, St. Gall experienced a period of Irish influence with the monks Marcus and Moengal. Next to Bobbio, St. Gall preserves the largest number of Irish MSS on the Continent; most of these were not produced at St. Gall, but served as a further model in the development of script there (see Ó Corráin 2017). Examples are the Irish Evangeliary in CSang 51, the Greek-Latin Evangeliary written by Irish monks at Bobbio in CSang 48, Priscian's *Grammatica* in CSang 904, and fragments in CSang 1395 and 1299a. In the earliest library catalogue in CSang 728 these are listed under the title "Libri scottice scripti." Irish influence is evident in the "middle" documentary style, and particularly in the "school" style, where typical Hibernian abbreviations and suspensions can be found, many of them stemming from Insular school scripts. The use of accents to mark syllable stress and vowel length, found in several post-950 manuscripts may also hark back to an Irish tradition (Löffler 1929, 12–18).

Tenth and early eleventh centuries

Following the death of Salomo in 919, the abbey experienced several physical and economic setbacks: Hungarian invasions, a fire, and then, toward the middle of the century, internal political unrest. The second half of the century was calmer, and during it the scriptorium experienced a second blossoming, traditionally called its "Silver Age." It was during this time that numerous manuscripts, largely illuminated liturgical texts, were produced also for export. Preserved at St. Gall are 88 tenth- and 45 eleventh-century manuscripts. To these can be added the c.100 Ottonian and early Salic manuscripts to which Hoffmann ascribes a St. Gall provenance. The turn of the eleventh century saw the first sizeable production of Old High German texts with the works of Notker Labeo. Another important scribal figure at this time is Ekkehard IV, Notker's pupil. Ekkehard's unique hand, especially in his later years, is found in no fewer than 59 St. Gall codices, both in the text and in glosses, e.g., CSang 621. The copy of his *Liber Benedictionum* in CSang 393 is an autograph and contains many of his later glosses and corrections.

The conservative nature of the St. Gall minuscule and its strong influence on other scriptoria make it difficult to date some manuscripts from the second half of the tenth century. One possible source for comparing scripts is CSang 915, which contains the *Annales Sangallenses maiores* up to the year 1080, as well as the Abbey's necrology begun in the tenth and ending in the eleventh century. Charters are also helpful, although their production slows down greatly by the end of the tenth century; furthermore, the difference in writing style between them and book-hand MSS often makes comparison difficult.

In the last quarter of the tenth century, the script of the St. Gall minuscule is ample and has what Scarpatetti calls a "sugar-coated" character, which he associates with elements of Ottonian and Romanesque art (1999, 57; see his description on pp. 57–60). The script leans to the right, and the height of ascenders and descenders is controlled with a focus on the head line and the middle of the letterforms. The script achieves an angular effect that is more disciplined than in the previous century. It is no longer the arches of letters such as *s, f, d, b, p, q,* and *l* that dominate, but rather their vertical downward strokes. The middle stroke of *m* turns to the left, whereas the first and last strokes are vertical; the bowl of the *e* is extremely small; Uncial *d* is rare, although it is picked up again in the mid-eleventh century and used then quite frequently; the horizontal stroke of the *r*, which earlier was drawn out, is finished up with a short tip followed by a stroke joining it to the next letter. A tell-tale sign for the period is the *rt*-ligature, which is reintroduced and often appears with an elongated stroke that reaches up to the right, where the two letters are joined. As Scarpatetti points out: "Unity, regularity, discipline and a clearly paced writing tempo point to a high level of professionalism among some scribes. Here we no longer have the pious community of monks, which primarily wrote texts slowly in a large script, but rather a team of experienced specialists at work" (1999, 58). Because of the conservative style of some scribes, dating early eleventh-century manuscripts can be tricky, e.g., the case of CSang 269, which Bruckner placed at the beginning of the tenth century but Scherrer in the eleventh; the latter is most probably correct.

Late Caroline

The period from 1050–1150 marks the end of the Caroline minuscule at St. Gall and coincides with the abbey's "Iron Age," a dark period, replete with political strife and economic turmoil. Nonetheless, some 50 MSS were copied there in the twelfth century (as compared to only 46 in the eleventh century), among them lectionaries and homilaries, a gradual, antiphonaries, saints' lives, and hymnals; the Bible in CSang 76 contains a complete text of 850 pages. The development of the late St. Gall minuscule has received little scholarly treatment, having lain in the shadows of the glorious early Middle Ages.

The script becomes even more angular, vertical, and drawn out. In some cases scribes begin to employ ticks, tabs, and tines almost reminiscent of an early Gothic script, e.g., CSang 139, especially in the later portions of the text. The backstroke of the *a* is nearly vertical to the baseline; clubbing is evident in the initial strokes of *s, f,* and *l*. Rustic capitals appear squarer, and some illuminated initials demonstrate early stages of Romanesque book art (e.g., CSang 564). Ligatures are rare, and abbreviations can be more copious and at times reminiscent of the new "insular" types; examples of MSS produced during this period are CSang 76, 360, 375, 395, 399, 427, 565, and the copies of Ekkehard IV's *Casus Sancti Galli* and other abbey histories in CSang 615.

BIBLIOGRAPHY

Berschin, Walter. 1991. "The Medieval Culture of Penmanship in the Abbey of St. Gall." In *The Culture of the Abbey of St. Gall. An Overview*, ed. James C. King and Werner Volger, 69–80. Stuttgart: Belser.

Bischoff, B. 1994. "Manuscripts in the Age of Charlemagne." In *Manuscripts and Libraries in the Age of Charlemagne*, tra. Michael Gorman, 20–55. Cambridge: Cambridge University Press.

Bruckner, A. 1936–8. *Scriptoria Medii Aevi Helvetica. Denkmäler schweizerischer Schreibkunst des Mittelalters*. Vols. II, and III. Geneva: Roto-Sadag.

Bruckner, A. 1937. *Paläographische Studien zu den älteren St. Galler Urkunden*. Turin: Chiantore.

Daniel, N. 1973. *Handschiften des zehnten Jahrhunderts aus der Freisinger Dombibliothek. Studien über Schriftcharakter und Herkunft der nachkarolingischen und ottonischen Handschriften einer bayerischen Bibliothek*. Münchner Beiträge zur Mediävistik und Renaissance-Forschung, 11. Munich: Arbeo-Gesellschaft.

e-codices. Virtual Manuscript Library of Switzerland. http://www.e-codices.unifr.ch/en, accessed December 30, 2019.

Eisenhut, H. 2009. *Die Glossen Ekkeharts IV. von St. Gallen im Codex Sangallensis 621*. Monasterium Sancti Galli, 4. St. Gall: Verlag am Klosterhof.

Euw, A. von. 2008. *Die St. Galler Buchkunst vom 8. bis zum Ende des 11. Jahrhunderts*. 2 vols. St. Gall: Verlag am Klosterhof.

Ganz, D. and C. Dora. 2017. Tuotilo. *Archäologie eines frühmittelalterlichen Künstlers*. Monasterium Sancti Galli, 8. St. Gall: Verlag am Klosterhof.

Hoffmann, H. 1986. *Buchkunst und Königtum im ottonischen und frühsalischen Reich*. Textband. Schriften der Monumenta Germaniae Historica, 30.1. Stuttgart: Hiersemann.

Löffler, K. 1929. "Die Sankt Galler Schreibschule in der 2. Hälfte des 8. Jahrhunderts." *Palaeographia Latina* 6: 5–66.

Löffler, K. 1937. "Die Sankt Galler Schreibschule in der ersten Hälfte des 9. Jahrhunderts." *Neue Heidelberger Jahrbücher* (N.S.): 28–54.

Lowe, E. 1934–71. *Codices Latini Antiquiores. A Palaeographical Guide to Latin Manuscripts Prior to the Ninth Century*. Oxford: Oxford University Press.

Maag, N. 2014. *Alemannische Minuskel (744–846 n. Chr.). Frühe Schriftkultur im Bodenseeraum und Voralpenland* (Quellen und Untersuchungen zur lateinischen Philologie des Mittelalters, 18). Stuttgart: Hiersemann.

McKitterick, R. 1991. "Literacy in Alemannia and the Role of St. Gall." In *The Culture of the Abbey of St. Gall. An Overview*, ed. James C. King and Werner Vogler, 217–26. Stuttgart: Belser.

McKitterick, R. 1999. "Schriftlichkeit im Spiegel der frühen Urkunden St. Gallens." In *Das Kloster St. Gallen im Mittelalter. Die kulturelle Blüte vom 8. bis zum 12. Jahrhundert*, ed. Peter Ochsenbein, 69–82. Darmstadt: Wissenschaftliche Buchgesellschaft.

Ó Corráin, D. 2017. *Clavis litterarum Hibernensium: Medieval Irish Books and Texts (c. 400–1600).* 3 vols. Turnhout: Brepols.

Scarpatetti, B. von. 1995. "Schreiber-Zuweisungen in St Galler Handschriften des achten und neuenten Jahrhunderts." In *Codices Sangallenses. Festschrift für Johannes Duft zum 80. Geburtstag,* ed. Peter Ochsenbein and Ernst Ziegler, 25–56. Sigmaringen: Thorbecke.

Scarpatetti, B. von. 1999. "Das St. Galler Scriptorium." In *Das Kloster St. Gallen im Mittelalter. Die kulturelle Blüte vom 8. bis zum 12. Jahrhundert,* ed. Peter Ochsenbein, 31–67. Darmstadt: Wissenschaftliche Buchgesellschaft.

Scarpatetti, B. von. 2003. *Die Handschriften der Stiftsbibliothek St. Gallen.* Vol. 1, Abt. IV. *Codices 547–669: Hagiographica, Historica, Geographica, 8.–18 Jahrhundert.* Wiesbaden: Harrassowitz.

Scarpatetti, B. von. 2007. *Die Handschriften der Stiftsbibliothek St. Gallen.* Vol. 2, Abt. III/2. *Codices 450–546: Liturgica, Libri precum, deutsche Gebetbücher, Spiritualia, Musikhandschriften, 9.–16. Jahrhundert.* Wiesbaden: Harrassowitz.

Scarpatetti, B. von. 2015. "Ego Wolfoz scripsi? Fragen um Subskriptionen und Schriftvarianten im St. Gallen des 9./10. Jahrhunderts." In *Urkunden—Schriften—Lebensordnungen: neue Beiträge zur Mediävistik: Vorträge der Jahrestagung des Instituts für Österreichische Geschichtsforschung aus Anlass des 100. Geburtstags von Heinrich Fichtenau (1912–2012). Wien, 13.–15. Dezember 2012,* ed. Andreas Schwarcz and Katharina Kaska, 39–59. Vienna: Böhlau.

Scarpatetti, B. von, R. Gamper, and M. Stähli, eds. 1991. *Katalog der datierten Handschriften in der Schweiz in lateinischer Schrift vom Anfang des Mittelalters bis 1550.* Vol. III. *Die Handschriften der Bibliotheken St. Gallen–Zürich.* 2 vols. Zurich: Urs Graf.

Scarpatetti, B. von, P. Lenz, and S. Ortelli. 2014. *Die Handschriften der Stiftsbibliothek St. Gallen: beschreibendes Verzeichnis. 3, Abt. V. Codices 670–749: Iuridica, kanonisches, römisches und germanisches Recht.* Wiesbaden: Harrassowitz.

Scherrer, G. 1875. *Verzeichniss der Handschriften der Stiftsbibliothek von St. Gallen,* repr. 1975. Hildesheim: Olms.

Schmuki, K., P. Ochsenbein, and C. Dora, eds. 1998. *Cimelia Sangallensia. Hundert Kostbarkeiten aus der Stiftsbibliothek St. Gallen.* St. Gall: Verlag am Klosterhof.

Wartmann, H. 1863–82. *Urkundenbuch der Abtei Sanct Gallen.* 3 vols. Zurich: Höhr.

CHAPTER 15

....

INSULAR SCRIPT

....

PETER A. STOKES

INTRODUCTION/OVERVIEW

....

ONE distinctive feature of Insular script is its polymorphism: that is to say, scribes had a variety of scripts available to them and could select which script to use depending on the text being written and the degree of formality which was sought. By no means unique or unprecedented, this polymorphism was still relatively highly developed among Insular scribes compared to their contemporaries in the early Middle Ages. As a result, there is not a single Insular script, but rather a system of at least two and as many as five distinct grades.

The two broad grades of Insular script are majuscule and minuscule. The "pure" majuscule script is now often referred to as Insular Half-uncial (represented in Plate 15.1). It is distinguished by its very short ascenders and descenders and by its use of majuscule (capital) forms of *N*, *R*, and *S*, all three of which can be found even in the middle of words where a minuscule form would normally be expected. It also features a form of *a* shaped somewhat like an *o* or *c* joined to a following *c* (e.g., Plate 15.1 line 1:), and *d* with a vertical ascender (as opposed to the more typically Insular ð). This script was written with the pen held very flat, such that vertical strokes are the thickest and horizontal ones thinnest. In contrast, the minuscule forms of Insular script (e.g., Plates 15.2 and 15.3) were typically written without these majuscule letterforms, with the stem of **d** angled at approximately 45° (ð), and with a form of *a* lacking the hook on the upper right shoulder, and thus similar to our modern italic *a* but without the rightward slant (e.g., Plate 15.2, line 2:). Some forms of Insular minuscule also show a characteristically pointed, often slightly curved termination at the baseline on the minims and descenders; these curves have been likened to cat's claws (e.g., Plate 15.3 line 4:). This stands in contrast to the flat bottoms on the minims in the majuscule script (e.g., Plate 15.1 line 1:). It also contrasts with the serifs which are sometimes found on an intermediate script, one that typically exhibits some majuscule letters but is written without the use of the very flat pen. Julian Brown (1993, 201–2)

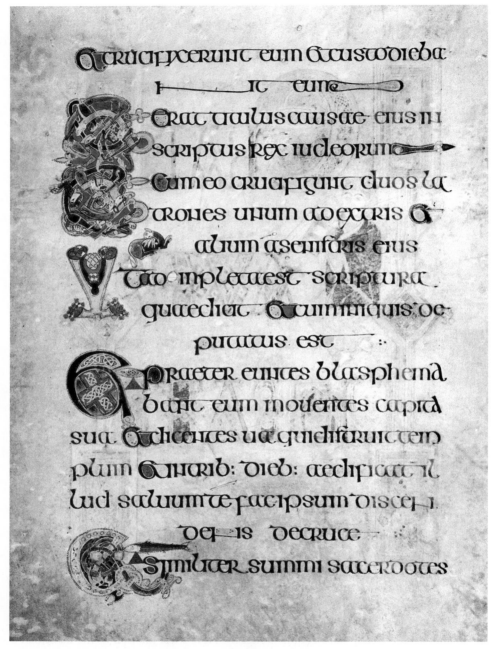

PLATE 15.1 *Insular Half-uncial*: Book of Kells. Dublin, Trinity College 58, 183v. Gospels. *saec.* ix[1].
(Trinity College Dublin: Reproduced by kind permission of the Board of Trinity College Dublin.)

1. Et crucifixerunt eum et custodieba
2. nt eum
3. Erat titulus causae eius in
4. scriptus rex iudeorum

5. Cum eo crucifigunt duos la
6. trones unum a dextris et
7. alium a senistris [*sic*] eius
8. Vt ad inpleta est scriptura
9. quae dicit Et cum iniquis de
10. putatus est :.
11. Et praetereuntes blasphema
12. bant eum mouentes capita
13. sua Et dicentes ua quid istruit tem
14. plum Et in tribus diebus aedificat il
15. lud saluum te fac ipsum discen
16. dens de cruce :.
17. Et similiter summi sacerdotes

Perhaps the archetypal example of Insular Half-uncial, this hand very clearly shows all the characteristics of that script. Insular wedges are consistently present on minims and ascenders, and the characteristic letterforms include *f* with tongue on the line (ꝼ). Slight diminuendo can be seen particularly after decorated initials (ll. 1, 8, 11, and 17). Ascenders and descenders are very short relative to the bodies of letters, giving the characteristic "shorn" (*tonsae*) and approximately two-line look. The flat pen is evident in horizontal strokes such as the top of *d*, *g*, and *t*, the tongue of *e* and *f*, and in the wedges on minims and ascenders and feet of minims and, to a lesser extent, descenders. In contrast, the pen angle is also evident in the thick vertical strokes of minims, ascenders, and descenders. Round "uncial" ꝺ and vertical-backed *d* are both found (compare *duos*, l. 5, with *ad*, l. 6), as well as majuscule N and R, and both majuscule and tall s (both forms found, for example in *senistris*, l. 7). Insular decoration is found throughout, particularly dotting, interlace, and zoomorphism. Abbreviations are almost absent (but note –*b*: twice in l. 14). Punctuation is primarily achieved by layout, including word separation, and enlarged or decorated letters, but groups of three dots are used (ll. 10 and 16). Monosyllabic words and long vowels are sometimes indicated with marks (*ásenistrís*, l. 7; *saluumtéfacipsum*, l. 15). The distinctive Insular form of *e+t* ligature is used throughout, particularly for *et* (ll. 1, 11, 13, 14, 17).

has termed this Insular Hybrid minuscule. Some of its characteristics survived in the descendants of Insular script which developed in England and Wales between the ninth century and the eleventh. Brown (1993, 201–2) also proposed three further grades of minuscule script—Set, Cursive and Current, in decreasing order of formality—which he distinguished primarily by the degree of pen lift and the number of abbreviations and ligatures. Brown's Cursive grade is perhaps the "classic" Insular minuscule script, with its distinctive pointed appearance, particularly in the wedged tops and pointed bottoms of minims, and it was certainly used for a number of important manuscripts. But it is by no means clear that it was necessarily the most frequently used, particularly in the earlier periods. It is represented in Plates 15.2 and 15.3.

DEVELOPMENT

The earliest stages of the distinctive Insular script have been the subject of some debate. Scholars generally agree that the early examples include the Springmount Bog tablets

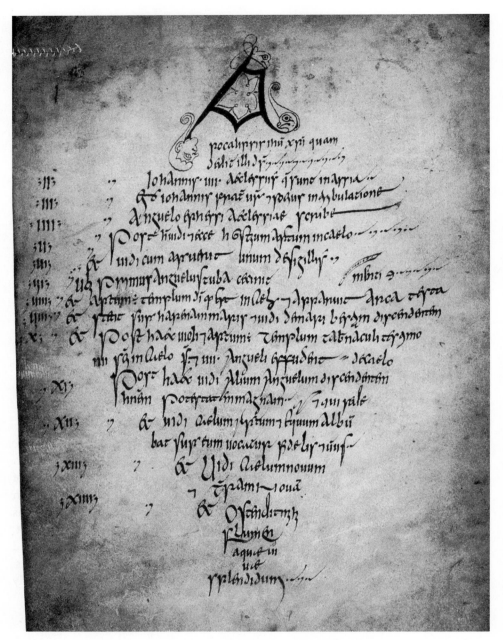

PLATE 15.2 *Insular Cursive minuscule*: Book of Armagh. Dublin, Trinity College MS 52, fol 159v. Extracts from the Book of Revelations. Armagh, Ireland, *c*.807. (Trinity College Dublin: Reproduced by kind permission of the Board of Trinity College Dublin.)

1.	.i.	A
2.		pocalipsis iesu Christi quam
3.		dedit illi deus
4.	.ii.	Iohannis .uii. aeclessiis quae sunt in assia
5.	.iii.	Ego iohannis frater uester et socius in tribulatione
6.	.iiii.	Anguelo ephessi aeclessiae scribe
7.	.u.	Post hoc uidi et ecce hostium apertum in caelo
8.	.ui.	Et uidi cum aperuerit unum de sigillis
9.	.uii.	Ubi primus anguelus tuba cecinit / menti eius
10.	.uiii.	Et apertum est templum dei quod est in caelo et apparuit arca testa
11.	.uiiii.	Et stetit super harenam maris et uidi de mari bestiam discendentem
12.	.x.	Et post haec uidi et apertum est templum tabernaculi testimo
13.		nii sancti in caelo sed et uii angueli effudent // de caelo
14.	.xi.	Post haec uidi alium anguelum discendentem
15.		hominem Potestatem magnam / et qui sede
16.	.xii.	Et uidi caelum apertum et equum album
17.		bat super eum uocatur fidelis et uersus.
18.	.xiii.	Et uidi caelum nouum
19.		et terram nouam
20.	.xiiii.	Et ostendit mihi
21.		flumen
22.		aquae in
23.		uae
24.		splendidum

This calligraphic example shows all the features of Insular Cursive minuscule, although showing some features more typical normally of higher-grade script but others normally only found in more current minuscule. Insular wedges are found throughout, as well as distinctive Insular forms of low *f*, *r*, and *s* (e.g., *frat'…socius*, l. 5). More typical of Hybrid minuscule or Half-uncial is the use of Uncial *a* as well as the more typical Insular single-compartment forms (both of which are found in *assia*, l. 3, but note also the more clearly Uncial *a* in *angueli*, *alium anguelum*, and *apertum*, ll. 13, 14, and 16), and both straight-backed and more typically Insular Cursive round ð (compare the two forms in *dedit*, l. 3). Open-topped *a* is also found, looking somewhat like *u*; this appears particularly but not exclusively in ligatures (e.g., *caelum*, l. 18, and regularly in the *–ae* ending such as *aquae…uae*, ll. 22–3, but also *uocatur*, l. 17). Abbreviations are frequent, including the 7-shaped Tironian nota for *et* (ll. 5, 7, 10, 11, etc.), the reversed open *e* for *eius* (l. 9), and *p* with a hook for *per* (ll. 7, 8, 10–12, etc.). Ligatures are used freely and imaginatively (note *hostium*, l. 7; *caelo*, l. 10). However, they are generally based on forms common to Insular cursive script, including underslung i (*hostium* just cited, but also *testimonii*, ll. 12–13, *fidelis*, l. 17, and *mihi*, l. 20), as well as *t+i+a* (*bestiam*, l. 11) and *t+r+i* (*tribulatione*, l. 5). Ligatures with *e* plus following letter are common, including the typically Insular *e+t* (ll. 8, 10, 11, 12, etc.), but also *e+g* (*ego*, l. 5), *e* plus minim (*templum*, l. 10) or descender (*bestiam*, l. 11), and the less common *e+c* (*aeclessiis*, l. 4, etc.). Reverse-*ductus e* is also found in *potestatem*, l. 15, a form normally reserved to Current minuscule, the lowest grade of Insular script.

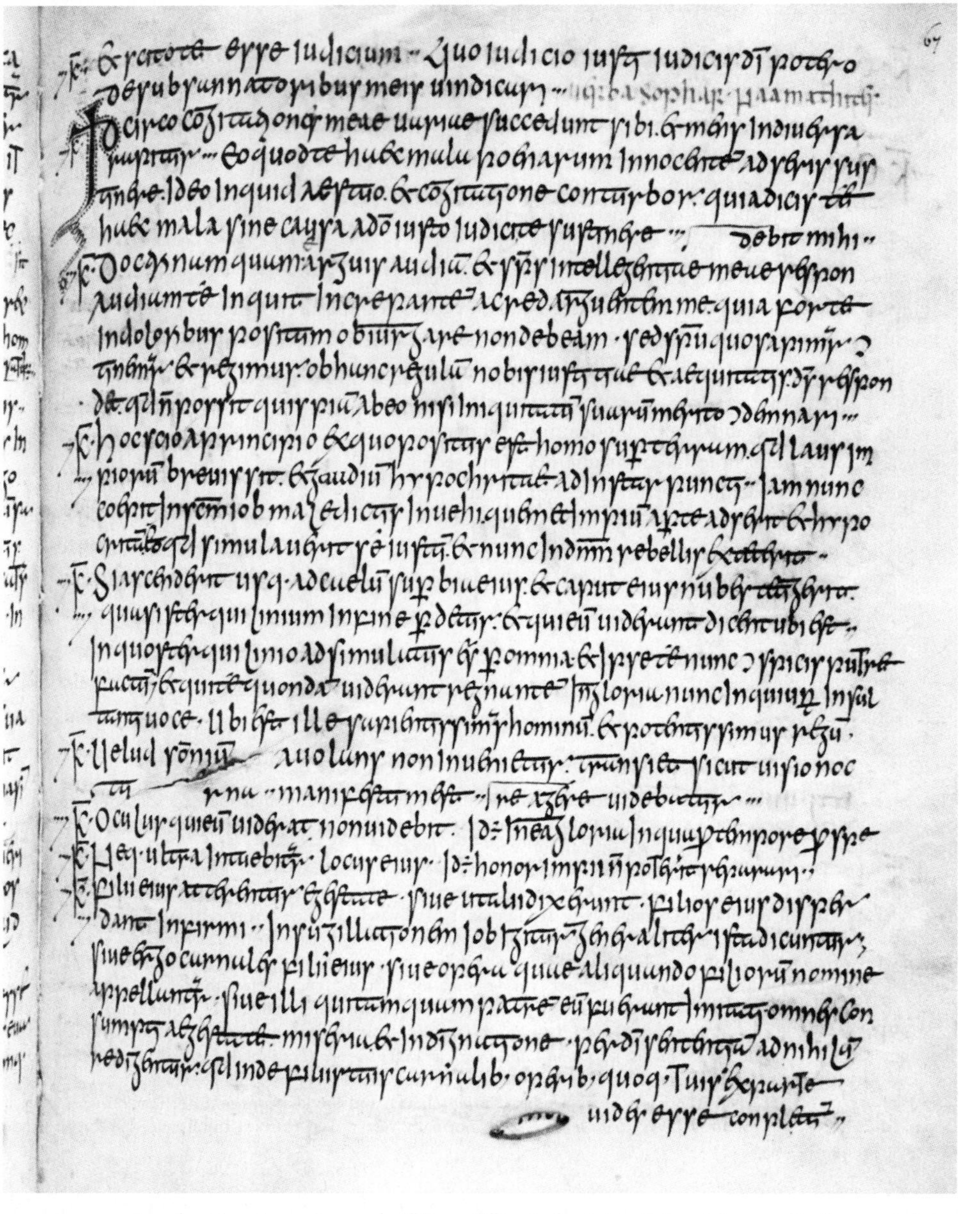

PLATE 15.3 *Insular Cursive minuscule* ("Type B"): Oxford, Bodleian Library, Bodley 426, fol. 67r. Philippus *Commentarii in Iob*. Wessex, England, *saec.* ix¹. (Bodleian: Reproduced by kind permission of The Bodleian Libraries, The University of Oxford.)

1. k. Et scitote esse iudicium . . . Quo iudicio iusti iudicis dei potero
2. de subsannatoribus meis uindicari . . . uerba sophar naamathites
3. k. Id circo cogitationes meae uariae succedunt sibi. Et mens in diuersa
4. rapitur . . . Eo quod te haec mala poenarum innocentem adseris sus

5. tinere. Ideo inquid aestuo. Et cogitatione conturbor. quia dicis te
6. haec mala sine causa a deo iusto iudicite sustinere...Γ debit mihi ..
7. k. Doctrinam qua m\e/ arguis audiam. Et spiritus intellegentiae meae respon
8. Audiam te inquit increpantem ac redarguentem me . quia forte
9. In doloribus positum obiurgare non debeam . sed spiritu quo sapimur con
10. tinemur et regimur. ob hanc regulam nobis iustitiae et aequitatis . deus respon
11. det . quod non possit quispiam ab eo nisi iniquitatum suarum merito condemnari ...
12. k. Hoc scio a principio ex quo positus est homo super terram. quod laus im
13. piorum breuis sit. et gaudium hypochritae ad instar puncti .. Iam nunc
14. coepit in sanctum iob maledictis inuehi . quem et impium aperte ad serit et hypo
15. critam et quod simulauerit se iustum. Et nunc in dominum rebellis exteterit ..
16. K. Si ascenderit usque ad caelum superbia eius . Et caput eius nubes tetigerit .
17. quasi sterquilinium in fine perdetur . Et qui eum uiderant dicent ubi est ..
18. In quo sterquilinio adsimulatus es per omnia . Et ipse te nunc conspicis putre
19. factum ; Et qui te quondam uiderant regnantem In gloria nunc inquiunt insul
20. tanti uoce . Ubi est ille sapientissimus hominum. Et potentissimus regum.
21. K. Uelud somnium auolans non inuienietur . transiet sicut uisio noc
22. turna .. manifestam est .. / re agere uidebatur ...
23. K. Oculus qui eum uiderat non uidebit. Id est in ea gloria in qua pro tempore pro spe
24. K. Neque ultra intuebitur locus eius . Id est honor impii non poterit separari ..
25. K. Filii eius atterentur egestate . siue ut alii dixerunt . filios eius disper
26. dant infirmi .. In sugillationem Iob igitur generaliter ista dicuntur ;
27. siue ergo carnales filii eius . siue opera quae aliquando filiorum nomine
28. appellantur . siue illi qui tamquam patrem eum fuerant imitati . omnes con
29. sumpti aegestate . miseria et indignatione. per dei sententiam ad nihilum
30. redigentur . quod inde filiis tuis carnalibus operibus quoque tuis ex parte
31. uides esse conpletam..

This example of Insular Cursive minuscule includes the characteristically long top strokes of *g* and *t* which seem to be distinctive of writing from Wessex (southern England). Insular forms include the consistent wedges on minims and ascenders, though ascenders can sometimes be more clubbed. Typical of Cursive minuscule is the angled pen, lack of pen lift within letters, and the curved minims with pointed bottoms and no feet. The usual Insular letterforms are found, including low *f*, *r*, and *s* (ꝼ, ꞃ, and ꞅ, e.g., *subsannatoribus*, l. 2), open-topped *a* (*subsannatoribus* again), though again a more Uncial or Caroline *a* is also found (*mala*, l. 6); round ꝺ (*dei*, l. 1) but also straight-backed *d* (*iudicium, iudicio*, l. 1). Ligatures are most commonly with *e* plus following letter, including the distinctive *e+t* (*et*, l. 1; cf. also *e+c* in *haec*, l. 4), as well as *t+i* and *t+r+i* (*cogitationes*, l. 3; *doctrinam*, l. 7) but also underslung *i* (*iusti*, l. 1; *cogitationes*, l. 3) and *t* (*inquiunt*, l. 19); although not in ligature, *l* sometimes also extends under the following letter (*sterquilinium*, l. 17). Abbreviations include a reversed *c* for *con* (e.g., end of l. 9), the "division sign" for *est* (e.g., ll. 23 and 24), and per, which is not the distinctively Insular form but rather the more widespread *p* with a stroke through the descender (e.g., the middle of ll. 16, 17, and 18). Majuscule *T* is sometimes found (*putrefactum*, ll. 18–19; *poterit*, l. 24; *tuis ex parte*, l. 30): this is not common but is found in some Mercian charters. The relatively late date is demonstrated by influence from Caroline script such as the form of *a* and the per abbreviations mentioned, as well as the relative lack of abbreviations, the turned-down toe of *t* which is distinctive of the long ninth century, here at word ends (e.g., *est*, ll. 20 and 22; *inquit*, l. 8). Punctuation is primarily the *punctus*, sometimes followed by a comma, and monosyllabic words are sometimes marked (*té*, ll. 5 and 8; *sé*, l. 15). Three words are written in Insular Hybrid minuscule (*uerba sophar* . *Naamathites*, l. 2): these show much more pen lift, majuscule *R* and *s*, and foot serifs, and they indicate the speaker of the biblical passage which follows (Job 20:2).

now preserved in the National Museum of Ireland; the Cathach of St. Columba, now Dublin, Royal Irish Academy MS 12.R.33; and a set of fragments now preserved at Durham Cathedral as MSS A.ii.10, C.iii.16 and C.iii.20. All of these manuscripts show the features recognized as distinctive of Insular script as outlined in Section 15.1 above. A difficulty arises, however, from the almost complete lack of evidence for dating them, and scholars differ widely in their assignments of dates, with consequential disagreements about when and how the script first developed. The problem is compounded by the relative lack of surviving evidence for writing in Roman Britain, including some disagreement about what scripts British and, subsequently, Irish and Anglo-Saxon scribes would have had available as models. Whether the scribes began with a higher-grade script such as Half-uncial or Uncial and developed "down," or started with Cursive Half-uncial (also known as Quarter-uncial) or even Cursive and worked "up," or some combination of the two, has been debated at length. What seems clear is that scribes in an early Insular context were familiar with some forms of writing practiced throughout the Roman Empire, and that some of these scribes, most probably Irish ones, developed distinctive features from this. The resulting script system with its distinctive characteristics seems to have emerged by the seventh century, although securely datable examples have not been found from before the eighth.

Some scholars, most notably Julian Brown (1993), have argued for chronological developments in the script, dividing the script used before 850 into two phases. The earlier phase has been seen as less regular and consistent, not so much in terms of variant letterforms but rather because of a lack of consistency in how the minims, descenders, and other strokes were produced. The result has been described as "agitated," as compared to the "restful" consistency perceived in writing of the later phase. Scribes writing "Phase II" also show greater attention to page layout, particularly to the justification of the right-hand margin. Additionally, their work is characterized by a reduction in the range of abbreviations and idiosyncratic ligatures. The date and the circumstances of this transition between phases have been debated, but it seems to have taken place during the first half of the eighth century. It may be due to new Roman influences being introduced to northern England at that time, in particular at the twin monastery of Wearmouth-Jarrow. Certainly this period saw the introduction of manuscripts written in Uncial script from Rome and elsewhere, and scribes at Wearmouth-Jarrow began writing this script themselves. They also adopted Rustic Capitals for headings and lists of chapters. The best-known examples of these new practices include the Codex Amiatinus (Florence, BML, Amiatino 1) and the St. Cuthbert Gospels (London, BL, Additional MS 89000). These "Roman" scripts were never part of the Insular script system as such, but were used alongside it. This is demonstrated most clearly by manuscripts of the mid-eighth century written principally in Insular Cursive minuscule but with headings or lemmata in a distinctive form of "Capitular" Uncial. All of the localizable examples of this were produced at Wearmouth-Jarrow.

The system of Insular scripts described here was practiced in Ireland and Anglo-Saxon England, in Wales by the ninth century and probably much earlier, and perhaps also in Scotland. It was also practiced by missionaries from Ireland and then Anglo-

Saxon England who founded houses on the Continent. These include Columbanus and his disciples at Luxeuil, Bobbio, and St. Gall; Willibrord at Echternach; and Boniface and his disciples at Würzburg, Fulda, and Mainz. It is striking how uniform practices seem to have been in the different regions, at least in the early stages. Attempts have been made to identify local variations: some details that seem to withstand scrutiny include a form of script apparently local to Wessex with very long top strokes of *g* and *t* (see Figure 15.3, e.g., line 5: *cognatione*); use of a long, majuscule *t* which seems to be specific to London and Mercia; a tendency at some Continental houses—particularly Anglo-Saxon foundations in Germany—to write with elongated proportions, reduced wedges, and "theta-shaped" *e* (*θ*); and some variation in abbreviations, particularly forms which seem to be distinctive of the Celtic regions such as *h* with various strokes for *haec* and *huius*, *mr* for *mater*, *g* with suprascript *o* (*g̊*) for *ergo*. However, this relative uniformity of scribal practice did not last indefinitely. The Continental houses adopted relatively quickly the local scripts for which they are known, such as Luxeuil minuscule at Luxeuil, *ab*-script at Corbie, etc. Ultimately, they all began using Caroline minuscule. In Britain, change began with the Viking incursions into England in the second half of the ninth century. As a result of this, Anglo-Saxon scribes seem to have lost their knowledge of the Insular script system, and they subsequently developed a distinctive new form known as Anglo-Saxon Square minuscule (represented in Figure 15.4). This was written throughout the tenth century before another dramatic change occurred: from the second half of the tenth century Anglo-Saxon scribes began to adopt Caroline minuscule for writing in Latin and retained Square minuscule only for Old English. They then transformed Square minuscule at the end of the tenth and start of the eleventh century, going first through another period of significant trans-formation with substantial regional variation. Finally, from about the middle of the eleventh century, they produced a very rounded English Vernacular minuscule. The key distinguishing letters were retained throughout the tenth and eleventh centuries, with the Caroline *a, d, f, g, r,* and *ſ* as well as *h* with rounded leg carefully distinguished from the old Insular ƀ, ꝼ, ȝ, ꞑ and ꞃ (or *s*) as well as *h* with straight leg and turned-out foot. In contrast, Irish and Welsh scribes continued to produce something very close to Insular script in the second half of the ninth century and throughout the tenth (see, for example, Figure 15.5), and some evidence survives for similar practice also in Scotland at this time, and perhaps also in Brittany, at least for the earlier part of this time period. The distinctive Insular letterforms were retained, as were the wedges and most of the abbreviations and ligatures. However, the clear distinction between different grades of script seems to have broken down, and scribes combined features from different grades which had previously been kept very much distinct. They also introduced some new abbreviations.

Evidence for the period *c.*950–*c.*1050 in Wales is very scarce, but a group of manuscripts produced at Llanbadarn Fawr and datable to the 1060s through 1080s was written in a distinctive script which is rounded in a way not entirely unlike contemporary production in England. It has, however, a marked propensity to empha-size horizontal strokes at minim height, sometimes giving almost a sense of a

nat · quietum expectatione futuræ beatitudinis
diem duxit adusq; psbium ; Cuietiam uigiliam qui
etiam insequibus continuauit &noctem ; itaubi con
suetum nocturnæ orationis tempus aderat · accep
tis armæ sacramentis peluiaenib; &tuum uiuiuu · quem
iam uenisse cognouit · dominici corporis &san
guinis comunione muniuit · atq; eleuatis ad
cælum oculis · &thesisq; maituu maenib; litteris
tæ supnis laudib; animæ adgaudia regni cæ
lestis emisit ;   XXXVIIII

Ergo fata gnefius numquam obitum eius fiuteni
bus · qui etipsi noctem uigilando atq; oriando
mans egitiant; & tunc forte subonore noct
ny laudis · dicebant psalmum quinquæ gesi
mu nonu ; Cuius inrqum ÷ ; dr refppulistinos &
dr truxistinos · miatus es & misitcus es nobis ;
ipse monia cunctis unus gei &eis · accendit duas
candelas · &utraeq; thesis manu · accendit simi
nstrqonetin locum · adofendisthou fiateqib; quin lui
dis ferunchsi monastehuo maenebant · quia pea
illa anima lamini gnaffes acdonim ; tale næq;
intehse signu scifisimi eius obitus condixeriant ;
Quodeuuiodhet fiatchi quin spetula lindif fai
nehris insule longe dteonena euitieus eius de
psuirgil expectauisiant honie · cucurint eteius
adetetam · ubi collêtus omnis fiim cotuif noc

PLATE 15.4 *Anglo-Saxon Square minuscule*: Cambridge, Corpus Christi College 183, fol. 49r. (Corpus Christi College Cambridge: Reproduced by kind permission of the Master and Fellows of Corpus Christi College.) Southern England, 930s.

1. rat . quietum expectatione futurę beatitudinis
2. diem duxit ad uesperam ; cui etiam per uigilem qui
3. etus in precibus continuauit et noctem ; at ubi con
4. suetum nocturnę orationis tempus aderat ./ accep
5. tis á me sacramentis salutaribus exitum suum . quem
6. iam uenisse cognouit . dominici corporis et san
7. guinis communione muniuit . atque eleuatis ad
8. cælum oculis . extensisque in altum manibus . Inten
9. tam supernis laudibus animam ad gaudia regni cæ
10. lestis emisit ; XXXVIIII
11. At ego statim egressus nuntiaui obitum eius fratri
12. bus . qui et ipsi noctem uigilando atque orando
13. transegerant ; Et túnc forte sub ordine noctur
14. nę laudis . dicebant psalmum quinquagesi
15. mum nonum ; Cuius initium est ; Deus reppulsisti nós et
16. destruxisti nós ./ iratus és et misertus és nobis ./
17. Néc mora currens unus ex eís . accendit duas
18. candelas ./ et utraque tenens manu . ascendit emi
19. nentiorem locum . ad ostendendum fratribus qui in lin
20. disfarnensi monasterio manebant . quia sancta
21. illa anima iam migrasset ad dominum ; tale namque
22. inter sé signum sanctissimi eiús obitus condixerant ;
23. Quod cum uideret frater qui in specula lindisfar
24. nensis insulę longe de contra euentus eiúsdem
25. per uigil expectauerat horam ./ cucurrit citius
26. ad ecclesiam . ubi collectus omnis fratrum coetus noc

This sample of Anglo-Saxon Square minuscule shows the characteristically square proportions which are particularly evident in *m*, *n*, *u*, and especially the flat top of *a*. Both round and low *s* are found throughout, as are square and "*oc*" forms of *a*, and a short descender on *r* such that it looks near majuscule. These letterforms, along with the high degree of pen lift and regular foot serifs on minims, reflect the script's origins in Insular Hybrid minuscule. The low *s* and *r* also descend directly from the Insular forms, as does the regular use of wedges, the low *f*, and continued use of "uncial" round-backed ð and flat-topped *g* (ᵹ). The vertical minim stroke of *h* with its horizontal foot also stands in contrast to the rounded Caroline form used throughout most of Europe by this date, and the tall *s* before *t* (ſt) probably reflects some Caroline influence (*destruxisti*, l. 16, etc.), as well as *e caudata* (*futurę*, l. 1; *nocturnę*, ll. 13–14; *insulę*, l. 24). Punctuation is also closer to Caroline, with use of *punctus*, *punctus uersus* (ll. 2, 3, 10, 13 etc.), and *punctus elevatus* (ll. 4, 16, 18, 25); abbreviations are infrequent but still retain some distinctive forms such as the hook on *t* for -*tur* (ll. 13–14). The turned-down toe of *t* is also found throughout in final position, despite the relatively late date. Monosyllabic words are indicated (*nós*, l. 16; *néc*, l. 17; *sé* and *eiús*, l. 22; but also *eiúsdem*, l. 24). Ligatures are infrequent and commonly *e* with following letter, including the Insular form of *e+t* (e.g., *quietum*, l. 1), but ligatures also include *s+s* (*migrasset*, l. 21); although not a true ligature, conjoined *t+i* is also distinctive of this phase of Square minuscule (*expectatione*, l. 1).

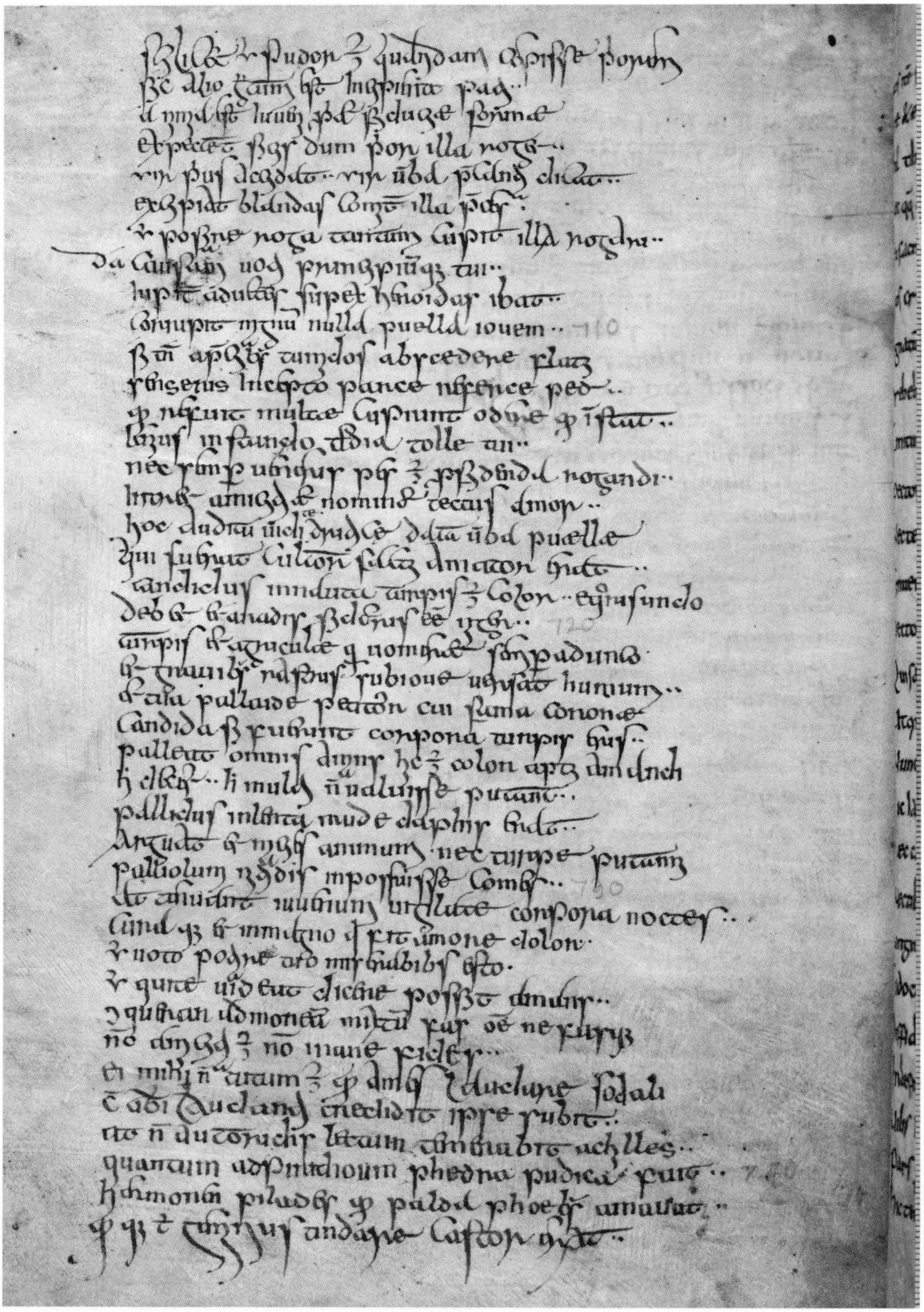

PLATE 15.5 *"Late Celtic" minuscule.* Oxford, Bodleian Library, Auct. F.4.32, fol. 46v. Wales, *saec.* ix/x. (Bodleian: Reproduced by kind permission of The Bodleian Libraries, The University of Oxford.)

1. scilicet ut pudor est quandam [*for* quaedam] cepisse priorem
2. sic alio gratum est incipiente pati [corrected from *priati*] ..
3. a nimia est iuueni propriæ fiduciæ [*sic*] formae
4. expectet sicis [*for* si quis] dum prior illa roget ..
5. uir prius accidat [*for* prior accedat].. uir uerba precantia dicat ..
6. excipiat [*for* excipiet] blandas comiter illa preces .

7. ut posiare [*recte* potiare] roga tantum cupit illa rogari ..

8. dá causam uoti principiumque tui ..

9. Iupiter ad ueteres sup[pl]ex heroidas ibat ..

10. corripit [*for* -rupit] magnum nulla puella iouem ..

11. si tamen a precibus tumidos abscedere flatum [*for* accedere fastus]

12. senseris incepto parce referce pedem ..

13. quod refu[g]it multæ cupiunt odere quod instat ..

14. lenius instando tedia tolle tui ..

15. nec semper ueneris [s]pes est profidenda rogandi [*for* profitenda roganti]..

16. Intret amicitiæ nomine tectus amor ..

17. Hoc aditu uidi \ te / tritice [*for* tetricæ] data uerba puællæ

18. qui fuerat cultor factus amator erat ..

19. candidus in nauta turpis est color .. equoris undo [*for* unda]

20. debet et a radi[i]s sideris esse niger ..

21. turpis et agriculæ qui uomeræ semper adunco

22. et grauibus rastris sub ioue uersat humum ..

23. et tua [tibi] pallaide [Palladiae] petitur [*corrected from* petitor] cui fama coronæ

24. candida si fuerint corpora turpis eris ..

25. palleat omnis amans hic est color aptus amandi [-ti]

26. hoc decet .. hoc multi [*for* stulti] non ualuisse putant ..

27. [Pallidus in side siluis errabat orion - *line missing*]

28. pallidus in lenta mude [*for* naide] daph[n]is erat ..

29. arguat et macies animum . nec turpe putamus [*recte* putaris]

30. palliolum nitidis inpossuisse comes [-is] ..

31. attenuant iuuenum uigilate corpora noctes ..

32. curaque et in magno qui fit amore dolor ..

33. ut uoto potiare tuo miserabilis esto .

34. ut qui te uideat dicere possit amans [amas] ..

35. conquerar admoneam [an moneam] mixtum fas omne nefasque

36. nomen amicitia est nomen inane fides ..

37. ei mihi non tutum est quod ames laudare sodali

38. cum tibi laudanti credidit ipse subit ..

39. at non autoridis [actorides] lectum temerabit [-uit] achilles ..

40. quantum ad pirithoum phedra pudica fuit ..

41. hermonen [Hermionem] pilades quod [quo] palda [Pallada] phoebus amauat [-bat]..

42. quodque tibi geminus tindare [Tyndari] castor erat ..

This very calligraphic and somewhat idiosyncratic example represents Late Celtic minuscule. The Insular wedges and letterforms are still in use, including Insular *r* (ꞃ) with a short descender and so looking very close to *n* (e.g., *senseris... parce*, l. 12), but also the typical low *f* and *s* (ꝼ and ꞅ), round-backed ꝺ (but note also the upright *d*, e.g., *instando*, l. 14), and a single-compartment *a*, as well as a more Caroline and sometimes even Uncial form (all three are found in *tantum cupit illa rogari*, l. 7). Underslung letters are found throughout; as with earlier Insular hands these particularly include *i* but also *a* (e.g., *posiare*, l. 7), and the familiar *e+t* and *t+i* ligatures are used throughout (*scilicet* and *roget*, ll. 1 and 4; *pati* and *-tritice*, ll. 2 and 17), as well as combinations of the above (*precantia*, l. 5; *potiare*, l. 33). Insular abbreviations are also used throughout, including some apparently more distinctive of Celtic scribes such as *oe* for *omne* and *no* for *nomen* (ll. 35–6). Abbreviations are also sometimes combined, such as *p* with both the hook for *pro* and also the suprascript *i* for *pri* (*propriae*, l. 3). Distinctive "Late Celtic" forms include the bird-silhouette *u* found throughout (e.g., *ut*, l. 1), the distinctive forms of abbreviation for *-tra-* and *-gra-* (*gratum*, l. 2;), the 2-shaped abbreviation for *est* (e.g., in line 1), and the suprascript *i* touching the *p* or *q* in *pri-* and *qui* respectively (*qui*, l. 32). Also indicative of date is the use of high-grade features such as such as straight-backed *d*, round *s*, flat feet or small serifs on the bottom of minims, and substantial pen lift, alongside low-grade features such as very frequent use of ligatures and abbreviations. Distinctive of this scribe are the many errors and spelling variants, many of which seem to reflect errors of similar sound; they range from b/v and t/d substitutions (*profidenda rogandi* for *profitenda roganti*, l. 15; *amauat* for *amabat*, l. 41) to errors of vowel (*accidat* for *accedat*, l. 5; *corripit* for *corrupit*, l. 10), substitution of similar-sounding words (*quondam* for *quaedam*, l. 1; *prius* for *prior*, l. 4; *pes* for *spes*, l. 15; *multi* for *stulti*, l. 26), or outright nonsense (*sicis* for *si quis*, l. 4; *posiare* for *potiare*, l. 7; *refuit* for *refugit*, l. 13). Also unusual is the b+s ligature with suprascript *u* for *-bus* (*precibus*, l. 11; *phoebus*, l. 41, etc.). Tall *e* is not uncommon in Insular script and its descendants, particularly in ligature, but an unusual form is often used here where the top hook is placed forward at the top of the following letter rather than the more normal position at the left of the letter (see, for example, both forms in *ueneris*, l. 15).

continuous horizontal head line (this is also found in a small number of samples of Square minuscule). There is also a similar horizontal emphasis to the wedges (Figure 15.6). Examples of this script also show greater retention of Insular forms and especially Insular abbreviations, including some of the "Late Celtic" forms discussed in Section 15.4 below which are first found in the ninth century and which were apparently not used by Anglo-Saxon scribes. In contrast, scribes in Ireland and Scotland developed a characteristically pointed script from around the start of the eleventh century, and this "Gaelic" minuscule survived largely unchanged for a further nine hundred years (see Figure 15.7).

CHARACTERISTICS AND LETTERFORMS

Probably the best-known and most distinctive aspect of Insular script is the wedge which appears at the top of all minims, ascenders, and descenders (𝖍), and which survived on all the regional descendants of the script. These pointed, triangular features are distinct from (but perhaps descended from) the rounded clubs or loops which are more typical of Continental Half-uncial (𝒍); they are also distinct from the tapering ascenders which are characteristic of Anglo-Caroline minuscule (𝖽). The distinctive letterforms of the Insular scripts can be divided into groups of characters that share common features. One such group is *f*, *r*, and *s*, all of which have a similar shape and are formed in similar ways. In Insular minuscule hands, these typically have descenders which drop clearly below the baseline, and the top parts of the letters normally remain at minim height (ꝼ, ꞃ, ꞅ). In contrast non-Insular forms, particularly from the Caroline period onward, normally stand on the baseline and reach above minim height (*f*, *r*, ſ). It should be noted, however, that this is true of minuscule scripts but not necessarily of Insular Half-uncial, where majuscule *N*, *S*, and *R* are found (as noted in Section 15.1 above: see, for example, Figure 15.1). Something similar to majuscule *R* is also found in some early examples of Insular minuscule, where the form can look deceptively like an *n*; it is essentially the normal form (ꞃ) without a descender. In contrast to "typical" Caroline minuscule, the Insular letterforms also include a flat-topped *g* (ᵹ) and a form of *h* in which the minim stroke is vertical and has a horizontal foot (𝖍) instead of the inward turning minim stroke normally found in (Anglo-)Caroline scripts (𝒽). Also distinctively Insular is the *cc* or *oc* form of *a* (e.g., Figure 15.1 line 1: ꭇ, referred to in Section 15.1 above), and the angled-back minuscule form of *d* (ð), although care must be taken here as a similar form is also found in Uncial script. The majuscule form of *N* is by no means unique to the Insular world, but the combination of *cc*-shaped *a*, vertical-backed *d* (as opposed to ð), and majuscule *N*, *R*, and *S* is very distinctive of the "pure" Insular Half-uncial and Hybrid scripts. In the more cursive and current forms of

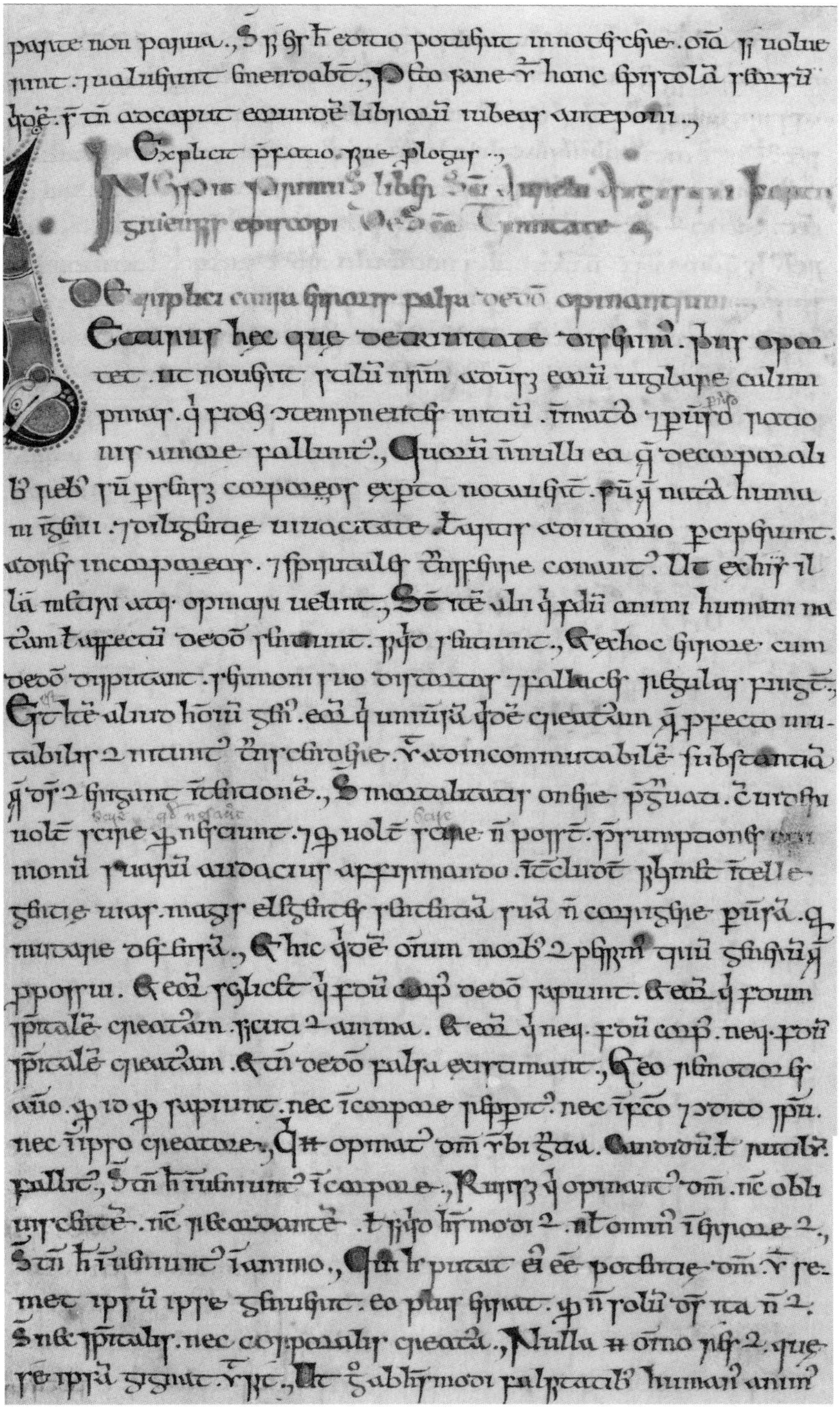

PLATE 15.6 *"Welsh National" minuscule*: Cambridge, Corpus Christi College 193, fol. 2r. Wales (Llanbadarn Fawr, Ceredigion?), 1085×1091. (Corpus Christi College Cambridge: Reproduced by kind permission of the Master and Fellows of Corpus Christi College.)

1. parte non parua ., Sed si eis haec editio potuerit innotescere . omnia si uolue
2. rint . et ualuerint emendabunt ., Peto sane ut hanc epistolam seorsum
3. quidem . sed tamen ad caput eorundem librorum iubeas anteponi .,

4. Explicit prefatio siue prologus ..,
5. Incipit primus liber Sancti Aurelii Augustini karta
6. ginensis episcopi De Sancta Trinitate,
7. De triplici causa erroris falsa de deo opinantium ...
8. Lecturus hęc quę de trinitate diserimus . prius opor
9. tet . ut nouerit stilum nostrum aduersus eorum uigilare calum
10. pnias . qui fidei contempnentes initium . inmaturo et peruerso ratio
11. nis amore falluntur., Quorum nonnulli ea quae de corporali
12. bus rebus siue per sensus corporeos experta notauerunt . siue quae natura huma
13. ni ingenii . et diligentię uiuacitate uel artis adiutorio perciperunt .
14. ad rés incorporeas . et spiritales transferre conantur. Ut ex hís il
15. la[s] metiri atque opinari uelint ., Sunt item alii qui secundum animi humani na
16. turam uel affectum de deo sentiunt . si quid sentiunt ., Et ex hoc errore cum
17. de deo disputant . sermoni suo distortas et fallaces regulas fingunt .,
18. Est item aliud hominum genus . eorum qui uniuersam quidem creaturam quae profecto
mu
19. tabilis est nituntur transcendere . ut ad incommutabilem substantiam
20. quae deus est erigant intentionem ., Sed mortalitatis onere pregrauati . cum uideri
21. uolunt scire quod nesciunt . et quod uolunt scire non possunt . presumptiones opi
22. nionum suarum audacius affirmando. intercludunt sibimet intelle
23. gentię uias . magis elegentes sententiam suam non corrigere peruersam. quam
24. mutare defensam ., Et hic quidem omnium morbus est pessimus trium generum quae
25. propossui [sic]. Et eorum scilicet qui secundum corpus de deo sapiunt . Et eorum qui
secundum
26. spiritalem creaturam . sicuti est anima . Et eorum qui neque secundum corpus . neque
secundum
27. spiritalem creaturam . Et tamen de deo falsa existimant ., Et eo remotiores
28. á uero . quod [sic] id quod sapiunt . nec in corpore repperitur . nec in facto et condito
spiritu .
29. nec in ipso creatore ., Qui enim opinatur deum uerbi gratia . Candidum uel rutilum .
30. fallitur ., Sed tamen haec inueniuntur in corpore ., Rursus qui opinantur deum . nunc obli
31. uiscentem . nunc recordantem . uel si quid huiusmodi est . nihilominus in errore est .,
32. Sed tamen haec inueniuntur in animo ., Qui autem putat eius esse potentię deum . ut se
33. met ipsum ipse genuerit . eo plus errat . quod non solum deus ita non est .
34. Sed nec spiritalis . nec corporalis creatura ., Nulla enim omnino rés est . quę
35. sé ipsam gignat . ut sít ., Ut ergo ab huiusmodi falsitatibus humanus animus

This sample shows the distinct form of script that survives from eleventh-century Wales. Most characteristic is the combination of very flat tops of letters, including *a* and the horizontal backs of *d*, but also the tops of wedges which are splayed and so very wide; these combine to give a very strong sense of head line, namely the line across minim height. It also tends to produce joined letters, which can lead to difficulties in reading, particularly in resolving minims (e.g., *animi humani*, l. 15). The Insular letterforms are still evident in contrast to the Caroline script now practiced even in England by this date; *a*, *d*, *f*, *g*, *h*, *r*, and *s* are all consistently distinguished, despite Caroline influence evident in the 2-shaped *r* following *o* (e.g., *eorundem*, l. 3). Insular ligatures remain, including underslung *i* even from *b* (*sibimet*, l. 22). The old Insular abbreviations are still found, including the н-shaped form of *enim* and *h* with hook for *autem* (ll. 29 and 32), as well as "Celtic" *haec, huius* (ll. 1 and 32), and others. The large curve on letters can function either as the "Insular" -*ur* or the "Caroline" -*us* (*cf.* *creaturam* and *corpus*, both l. 26) "Late Celtic" features are also still found throughout, including bird-silhouette *u* (e.g., *ut*, l. 2), 2-shaped *est* (ll. 20 and 21), the distinctive form of *gra* and *tra* (*transferre, pregrauati*, ll. 14 and 20), and the wedge-shaped suprascript *i* joining onto *p* and *q* (*quidem*, l. 3). *E caudata* (ę) is found throughout, even when the *e* is omitted due to abbreviation, in which case the *cauda* is attached to the nearest letter that remains (*quae*, first word of l. 20). As also with the Late Celtic script, the Insular principles of grade are no longer followed: the sample here shows much pen lift and regular foot serifs on minims, both suggesting Set or even Hybrid minuscule, alongside very frequent abbreviations and ligatures to a degree normally found no higher than Cursive minuscule.

the script an open *a*, which looks rather like a *u*, was often employed (e.g., Figure 15.3 line 4, *haec*: ![glyph]), and in the most rapid script a "reverse ductus" *e* is also found. To form the latter, the scribes began near the bottom of the letter, moved the pen down and to the right before curving back up and over, and then added the tongue with a downward stroke that ligatured to the following letter.

Some of the ligatures used by Insular scribes were not commonly used elsewhere. The most characteristic of these is *e+t*, a form which was used throughout all of the Insular world. In this ligature, the tongue of *e* is brought down to form the lower stroke of *t*, and the top of *t* is then extended horizontally from this at minim height (e.g., Figure 15.1 line 1: ![glyph]). Such a form is distinct from that produced in Continental scriptoria, where the top of the *t* begins low and is brought diagonally upward, almost looking like a majuscule form which has been rotated approximately 135° counter-clockwise ![glyph]). The Insular form survived in all areas until at least the eleventh century; the "Continental" one is still in use today as the modern ampersand, &. Insular scribes also employed other ligatures after *e* when writing more informal scripts; for example, *e +g*, where flat the top stroke of *g* (![glyph]) presented the same structure as that of *t* (written as ![glyph], e.g., Figure 15.3 line 7: ![glyph]). The practice of forming ligatures after **e** extended to the point that any descender or minim after *e* might be ligatured (Figure 15.3 line 4: ![glyph]); sometimes scribes even used it before curves such as *e+c* or *e+o*. This ligature was produced again in the late tenth century, for instance by the second scribe of the *Beowulf* manuscript (London, British Library, Cotton Vitellius A.xv, folios 94–209). Other ligatures include the subscript **i** (particularly after minims but also after other letters including *t*), and even a -*tio* or -*tia* ligature in which the cross bar of the *t* begins high on the left, is brought down diagonally to minim height as it crosses the downstroke, and then descends further as an (implied) *i* before being either looped below the baseline to produce the *o* or curved below the baseline to make the *a*; similar forms were used for other ligatures, such as *tri* (e.g., Figure 15.2: line 4, *tri* ![glyph], and Figure 15.3 line 7: ![glyph]).

As noted in Section 15.2 above, the clearest dating criterion for script produced after the mid-ninth century is confusion over the grades of script. Examples of this typically include majuscule letterforms in an otherwise rapid and cursive script, or a highly set script with foot serifs and few ligatures or abbreviations but no majuscule forms. Square minuscule is distinguished unsurprisingly by its square proportions but also by the distinctive form of *a*, which is typically written much like a *u*, but with a horizontal stroke across the top (![glyph]). Scribes also often wrote Square minuscule with foot serifs and occasional majuscule letters, particularly *s*. In contrast, the English Vernacular minuscule of the early eleventh century can be very tall and narrow in proportion. It is often written with a thin pen and sometimes with tall, bulging forms of *e* and *æ* when in ligature with a following letter (e.g., London, British Library, Royal 1. D.ix, fol. 44v: ![glyph], *pæron*). These proportions then changed until about the mid-eleventh century, by which time ligatures of any form were no longer in use when writing in the vernacular, bodies of letters were very round, ascenders were often written with deeply split tops, and descenders curved to the left (e.g., Oxford, Bodleian

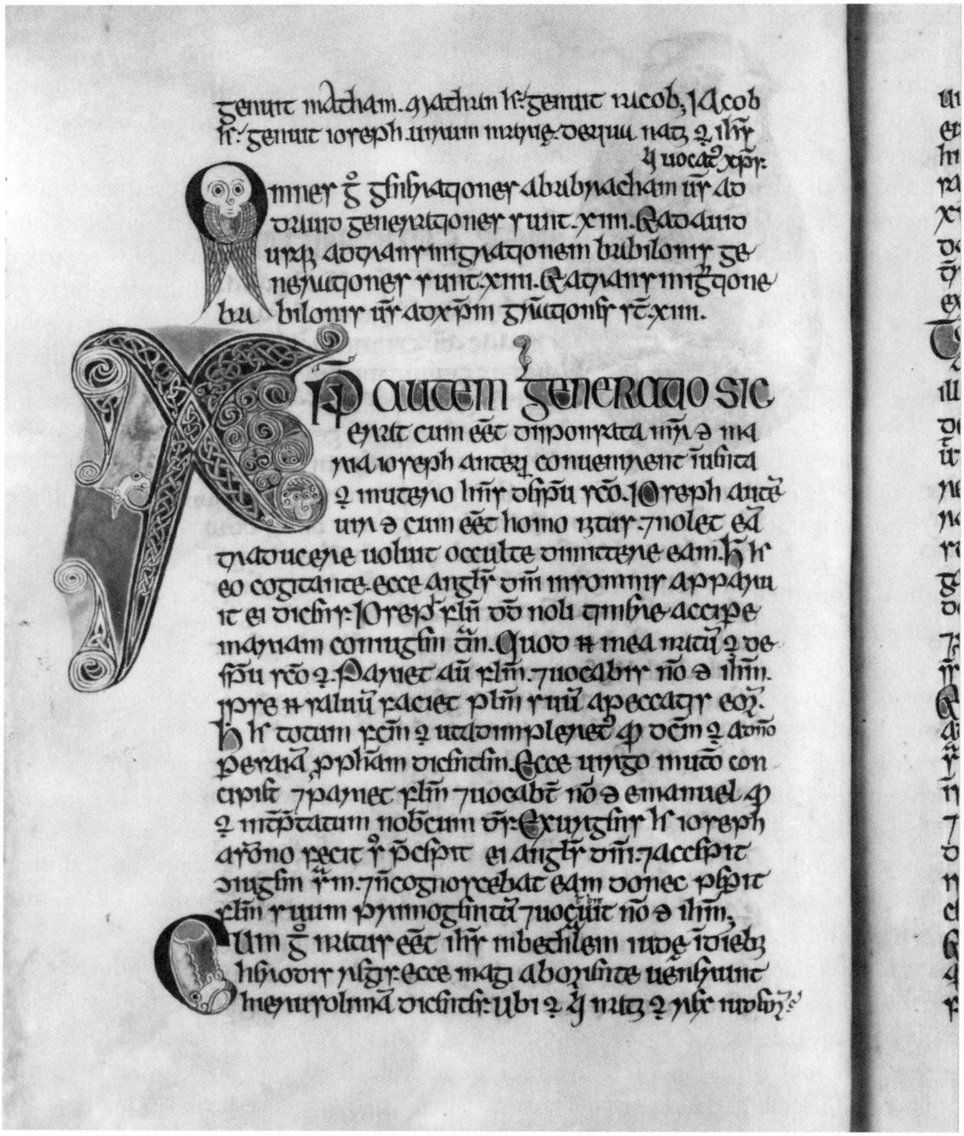

PLATE 15.7 *"Gaelic National" minuscule*: Oxford, Corpus Christi College 122, fol. 10v. Ireland (Armagh?), *saec.* xii *ex.* (Corpus Christi College Oxford: Reproduced by kind permission of Corpus Christi College, Oxford.)

1. genuit matham . matham <u>autem</u> ./ genuit iacobus ; iacob
2. <u>autem</u> ./ genuit ioseph . uirum marie . de qua <u>natus</u> <u>est</u> ihesus
3.   qui uocatur <u>christus</u>
4. Omnes <u>ergo</u> generationes ab abracham us<u>que</u> ad
5. dauid generationes sunt .xiiii. Et a dauid

6. usque ad transmigrationem babilonis ge
7. nerationes sunt .xiiii. Et a transmigratione
8. babilonis usque ad christum generationes sunt .xiiii.
9. Christi autem generatio sic
10. erat cum esset disponsata mater eius ma
11. ria ioseph antequam conuenirent inuenta
12. est in utero habens de spiritu sancto. Ioseph autem
13. uir eius cum esset homo iustus . et nolet eam
14. traducere uoluit occulte dimittere eam. Haec autem
15. eo cogitante . ecce angelus domini in somnis apparu
16. it ei dicens Iosep' filii dauid noli timere accipere
17. mariam coniugem tuam. Quod enim in ea natum est de
18. spiritu sancto est. Pariet autem filium. et uocabis nomen eius ihesum.
19. ipse enim saluum faciet populum suum a peccatis eorum .
20. Hoc autem totum factum est ut adimpleretur quod dictum est a domino
21. per esaiam prophetam dicentem . Ecce uirgo in utero con
22. cipiet et pariet filium et uocabunt nomen eius emanuel quod
23. est interpretatum nobiscum deus. Ex[s]urgens autem ioseph
24. a somno fecit sicut precepit ei andelus domini . et accepit
25. coniugem suam . et non cognoscebat eam donec peperit
26. filium suum primogenitum et uocauit \ uel -bit / nomen eius ihesum;
27. Cum ergo natus esset ihesus in bethlem iude in diebus
28. herodis regis . ecce magi ab oriente uenerunt
29. hierusolimam dicentes . ubi est qui natus est rex iudeorum?

This sample clearly shows the heavy, angular script distinctive of Gaelic writing from the eleventh century onward. Particularly distinctive is the three-stroke construction of *a* and *r*. The former shows a very pointed top and a slight but thin upper-left side with curved bottom stroke; the same construction is often used for the body of *q* (as here: *qui*, l.3). The descender of *r* is angled back toward the left, and the hook is produced in two distinct sections: a straight diagonally rising stroke which then turns sharply into a diagonally descending stroke down to the baseline. Alternative forms of *a* include Caroline (the first in *matham*, l. 1), an open-topped form similar to *cc* (*generationes*, ll. 6–7), and one similar to the "basic" three-stroke *a*, but where the top left stroke approaches from the left and curves almost to form a reversed *c* (*iacob*, l. 1); this last variant is also used for *q* (*qua*, l. 2). Other letterforms are also typically Insular, including low *f* and *s* (ꝼ and ꞃ), and ð here consistently with a horizontal back, as is common for this script type. Abbreviations still show distinctive Insular forms, most notably *h* with a hook for *autem* (e.g., ll. 1 and 2) but also the hook for -*ur* (*uocatur*, l. 3) and -3 for -*us* (*iustus*, l. 13), the "Greek" *xps* for *Christus* (l. 3, the spelling presumably in imitation of Greek Χριστός), ʜ-shaped *enim* (ll. 17 and 19), ꝫ for *eius* (l. 10) and ꝯ for *con* (*coniugem*, l. 25). Numerous "Celtic" abbreviations are also still found, including *g* with suprascript *o* (ᵍₒ) for *ergo*, mr for *mater*, hns for *habens*, flm for *filium*, no for *nomen*, and h' for *hoc*, (ll. 4, 10, 12, 18 twice, and 20 respectively). Also not unprecedented in Irish script is the use of an aspiration marker shaped like ⊦ which derives directly from that in Greek (*iosep[h]*, l. 16). "Late Celtic" abbreviations are also found throughout, including 2-shaped *est*, the distinctive *gra* (though here not *tra*), and pointed suprascript *i* pressing down on *q* for *qui* (ll. 2, 7, and 3 respectively); *tra* and *pri* here are spelled in full (see lines 6, 7, 14, and 26). Some Caroline influence is evident, particularly in the use of 2-shaped *r* after *o* (*oriente*, l. 28), and perhaps also in the relative lack of variety in abbreviations and ligatures when compared with earlier Insular samples. Indeed, ligatures are confined principally to tall *e* plus letters with minims or descenders, and the distinctive Insular *e+t* ligature is used for the word *et* rather than in words (compare *et*, ll. 5 and 7, with *esset*, *pariet*, etc., lines 10, 13, 18); the ligature was also used in *concipiet*, however (ll. 21–2), and Latin *et* was often written with the Tironian 7, as again is typical of Insular script (e.g., l. 22 again).

Library, Auct.D.2.16, fol. 1r:). In the Celtic context, some mixture of majuscule forms can be observed even in otherwise minuscule scripts from the tenth century, and distinctive forms of abbreviations were introduced (for which, see Section 15.4 below). Irish and Scottish scribes from the eleventh century write a very angular script (represented in Figure 15.7); distinctive forms include pointed *a* with a diagonal top stroke (Figure 15.7 line 1:), a form typically used also for the body of *q* (Figure 15.7 line 6: , *usque*), and an angular, forward-leaning *r* produced with three distinct strokes (Figure 15.7 line 2:). Scribes from across the Insular world also gradually introduced increasing numbers of letterforms, ligatures, and abbreviations from Caroline minuscule. This is most evident in the work of Anglo-Saxon scribes, many of whom by the late tenth century were proficient in both Caroline and Square minuscule. But a similar if more subtle influence can also be observed in the work of Irish and Welsh scribes, such as their use of the 2-shaped form of *r* after *o* (oꝛ), which is found in some tenth-century books.

Abbreviations and Ligatures

Insular scribes made heavy use of abbreviations, and this was continued particularly by Welsh scribes into the eleventh century and Irish ones far beyond that. Nevertheless, scribes seem to have reduced the use of abbreviations from about the ninth century onward, particularly in Anglo-Saxon England, where they perhaps made less use of them in the earlier period as well (or at least seem to have been less inventive in their use). Abbreviations used by Insular scribes are frequently not those more typically found elsewhere. Some seem to be highly distinctive, for example *h* with a curved hook coming off the shoulder for *autem* (Figure 15.6 line 33:), *p* with a similar hook for *per*, a form looking somewhat like a small majuscule *H* with extended horizontal stroke for *enim* (Figure 15.7 line 18:), a "backwards" *c* for *con* (ɔ), and a "backwards", open (small Uncial) *e* for *eius* (ɘ). Other abbreviations may look the same as those used elsewhere but with different expansions, such as *t* with a curved stroke (ꞇꝰ) for *-tur* rather than the more common *-tus*, or *q* with a curved loop through it for *quod*, rather than the more typical *qd* with a horizontal stroke through the ascender of the *d* (the latter form also used by Anglo-Saxon scribes). Dumville, in his summary reworking of Lindsay's *Notae Latinae*, listed 97 words or syllables which were commonly abbreviated by scribes writing Insular script before *c*.850, many of which appear with more than one possible abbreviation. Of these words, 85 have abbreviations which seem to have been used only by Celtic scribes, and 24 have abbreviations apparently distinctive to Anglo-Saxon practice. Also noteworthy are the so-called "Late Celtic" abbreviations or forms which characterize writing in the Celtic regions from about the mid-ninth century. These include *p* and *q* with suprascript *i* touching the letter and often triangular-shaped for *pri* and *qui* (Figure 15.5 line 5:); a "bird-silhouette" form of *u*, initially in abbreviations such as *ut* and *uero* but then more widely (Figure 15.5

line 1: 🜂); *g* and *t* with "commas" above them for *gra* and *tra* (Figure 15.5 line 2: 🜄); and a 2-shaped form, sometimes more like two commas separated by a horizontal line, for *est* (Figure 15.5 line 1: 🜃). Although designated "Late Celtic," these forms were used beyond the period of Late Celtic script. They are still found in eleventh-century examples from Wales, and even later in Irish script.

BIBLIOGRAPHY

Brown, M. P. 2004. "Fifty Years of Insular Palaeography, 1953–2003: An Outline of some Landmarks and Issues." *Archiv für Diplomatik, Schriftgeschichte, Siegel- und Wappenkunde* 50: 277– 325.

Brown, M. P. 2012. "Writing in the Insular World." In *Cambridge History of the Book in Britain*, vol. I, 121–66.

Brown, T. J. 1993. *A Palaeographer's View*, ed. J. M. Bately, M. P. Brown, and J. Roberts. London: Harvey Miller.

Crick, J. 2012. "English Vernacular Script." In *Cambridge History of the Book in Britain*, vol. I. 174–86.

Dumville, D. N. 1999. *A Palaeographer's Review: The Insular System of Scripts in the Early Middle Ages*. Osaka: Institute of Oriental and Occidental Studies, Kansai University.

Dumville, D. N. 2004. *Abbreviations Used in Insular Script before A.D. 850: Tabulation Based on the Work of W. M. Lindsay*. Cambridge: Department of Anglo-Saxon, Norse and Celtic.

Gameson, R., ed. 2012. *Cambridge History of the Book in Britain*, vol. I: *c.400–1100*.Cambridge: Cambridge University Press.

Ganz, D., R. Rushforth, and T. Webber, 2012. "Latin Script in England, c. 990– 1100." In *Cambridge History of the Book in Britain*, vol. I, 187–224.

Lindsay, W. M. 1915. *Notae Latinae: An Account of Abbreviations in Latin MSS. of the Early Minuscule Period (c. 700–850)*. Cambridge: Cambridge University Press.

McKee, H. 2012. "Script in Wales, Scotland and Cornwall." In *Cambridge History of the Book in Britain*, vol. I, 167–73.

O'Sullivan, W. 2005. "Manuscripts and Palaeography." In *A New History of Ireland*, vol. I: *Prehistoric and Early Ireland*, ed. D. Ó Crónín, 511–48. Oxford.

Descendents of the Insular Script System

Dumville, D. N. 1987. "English Square Minuscule: The Background and Earliest Phases." *Anglo-Saxon England* 16: 147–79.

Dumville, D. N. 1994. "English Square Minuscule: The Mid-Century Phases." *Anglo-Saxon England* 23: 133–64.

Duncan, E. 2010. "A History of Gaelic Script, AD 1000–1200." Diss., University of Aberdeen.

Stokes, P. A. 2014. *English Vernacular Minuscule*. Cambridge: D.S. Brewer.

I . 4

CAROLINGIAN
MINUSCULE

CHAPTER 16

EARLY CAROLINE

France and Germany

DAVID GANZ

THE development of Caroline minuscule can be traced at Tours, where the earliest books copied in the second quarter of the eighth century use Uncial, Half-uncial, and Cursive scripts. Creation of a uniform script was aided by the collaboration of scribes in the copying of a single manuscript. Caroline minuscule is a disciplined and formal book hand using well-proportioned letterforms which have been simplified by using fewer ligatures between letters, and often achieving a uniform alphabet in which each letter had a single shape. Distinctive features are the consistent heights of ascenders and descenders; a natural slanted pen angle; uncial *a*; and the minuscule forms of *g*, *r*, and *s* (see Plate 16.1). The script is called *coequaria*, modern script, in a late eighth-century source.[1] Carolingian legislation was concerned with the copying of books and sought to impose standards. The *Admonitio Generalis* of 789 stipulates that Gospel books, Psalters, and Missals were to be copied by mature scribes with all care. A decree of 805 ordered scribes not to write badly, and one of 816 insisted that the acts of imperial assemblies be copied clearly.[2]

The majority of ninth-century manuscripts can only be assigned to a general area, north or south of the Loire or the Alps, east or west of the Rhine. In some cases it is possible to localize the scriptoria where manuscripts in Carolingian scripts were copied, though few of these can be dated precisely.

WESTERN FRANCIA

The major writing centres of the Carolingian empire west of the Rhine were Saint-Denis, Paris, Fleury, Tours, Saint-Amand, Corbie, Reims, and the scriptoria at the imperial courts. In the south, Lyons, Flavigny, and Burgundy were important: the differences between manuscripts copied at Auxerre and at Orléans need further study.

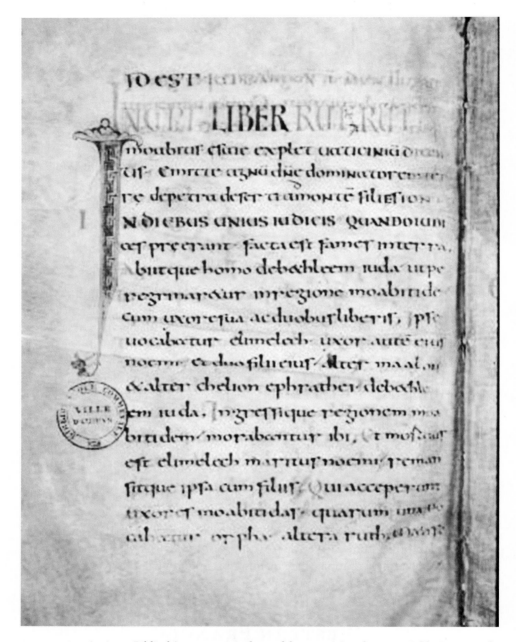

PLATE 16.1 Amiens, Bibliothèque municipale, 7, fol. 120v, Maurdramnus Bible Pentateuch, Corbie 773–81 (lines 3–5 are in Half-uncial, line 6 in Uncial).

The Court of Charlemagne

The manuscripts copied for Charlemagne by calligraphers who wrote verses describing their activity are Paris, BnF, nouv. acq. lat. 1203 (*CLA* 5.681) the Gospel lectionary copied by Godescalc (781–3), written in Uncial but with a final poem in Caroline minuscule (Plate 16.2); and the so-called Dagulf Psalter, now Vienna, ÖNB, 1861 (*CLA* 10.1504), copied in minuscule for Pope Hadrian (793–5). Both manuscripts are written in gold ink on purple dyed parchment, the purple probably derived from seaweed, but used to convey imperial pretensions. Further Gospel books copied at the court school are now in Abbeville, London, Paris, Rome, Trier, and Vienna.

Saint-Denis

The earliest manuscripts from Saint-Denis, now Paris, BnF, lat. 17371 (*CLA* 5.668: Jerome, *in Hieremiam*) and lat. 15304 (*CLA* 5.665: Cassiodorus, *Expositio Psalmorum*), were copied for abbot Fardulfus (797–807). Other Saint-Denis volumes are London, British Library, Harley 4831, *Epistulae* of Paulinus of Nola (Plate 16.3); Reims, Bibliothèque municipale, 435 (*CLA* 6.824: Defensor); Paris, BnF, lat. 528 (*Poetae*); the Bamberg copy of Amalarius (Bamberg, Staatsbibliothek, Lit. 131) with the colophon "*Haec a coenobio dionisii venit*" (Plate 16.4); two copies of the *Epistulae* of Alcuin and Dungal (Paris, BnF, nouv. acq. lat.1096 and London, BL, Harley 208); an Ambrosiaster in Paris (*CLA* 5.535: BnF, lat. 1759); and Aeneas of Paris' *Liber adversus Graecos* (Paris, BnF, lat. 2864).

Saint-Germain-des-Prés

The script used at the Parisian abbey of Saint-Germain-des-Prés was a Caroline minuscule with Half-uncial as well as minuscule forms of *a*, and *h* with a characteristic round bow. There are distinctive *ct*, *et*, *ex*, *or*, *re*, *rt*, *rs*, and *st* ligatures (see Plate 16.5). Two datable manuscripts are the *Polyptique* of Abbot Irminon (812–17) now in Paris, BnF, lat. 12832 (Plate 16.5), and the martyrology of Ususard copied around 865 and now in Paris, BnF, lat. 13745.[3] Other manuscripts from Saint-Germain-des-Prés are Bologna, Biblioteca Universitaria, 1702 (Constantius of Lyons, *Vita Germani*); Copenhagen, Kongelige Bibliotek, S. 28 Fol. (Jerome, *Epistulae*); Copenhagen, Kongelige Bibliotek, GkS. 157 Fol. (Josephus, *Antiquitates*); Leiden, Bibliotheek der Rijksuniversiteit, Voss. lat. F 82 (Isidore, *Etymologiae*); Berlin, Staatsbibliothek zu Berlin-Preussischer Kulturbesitz, Theol. Lat. Oct. 96 (Venantius Fortunatus, *Vita Germani*); Bern, Burgerbibliothek, 16 (*Liber Glossarum*); Paris, BnF, lat. 14144 (Venantius Fortunatus); BnF, lat. 11642 (Eugippius); BnF, lat.1695 (Hilary); BnF 12242-6 (Gregory

PLATE 16.2 Paris, BnF, nouv. acq. lat. 1203, fol. 126v, Godescalc Gospel lectionary, showing the poem by Godescalc.

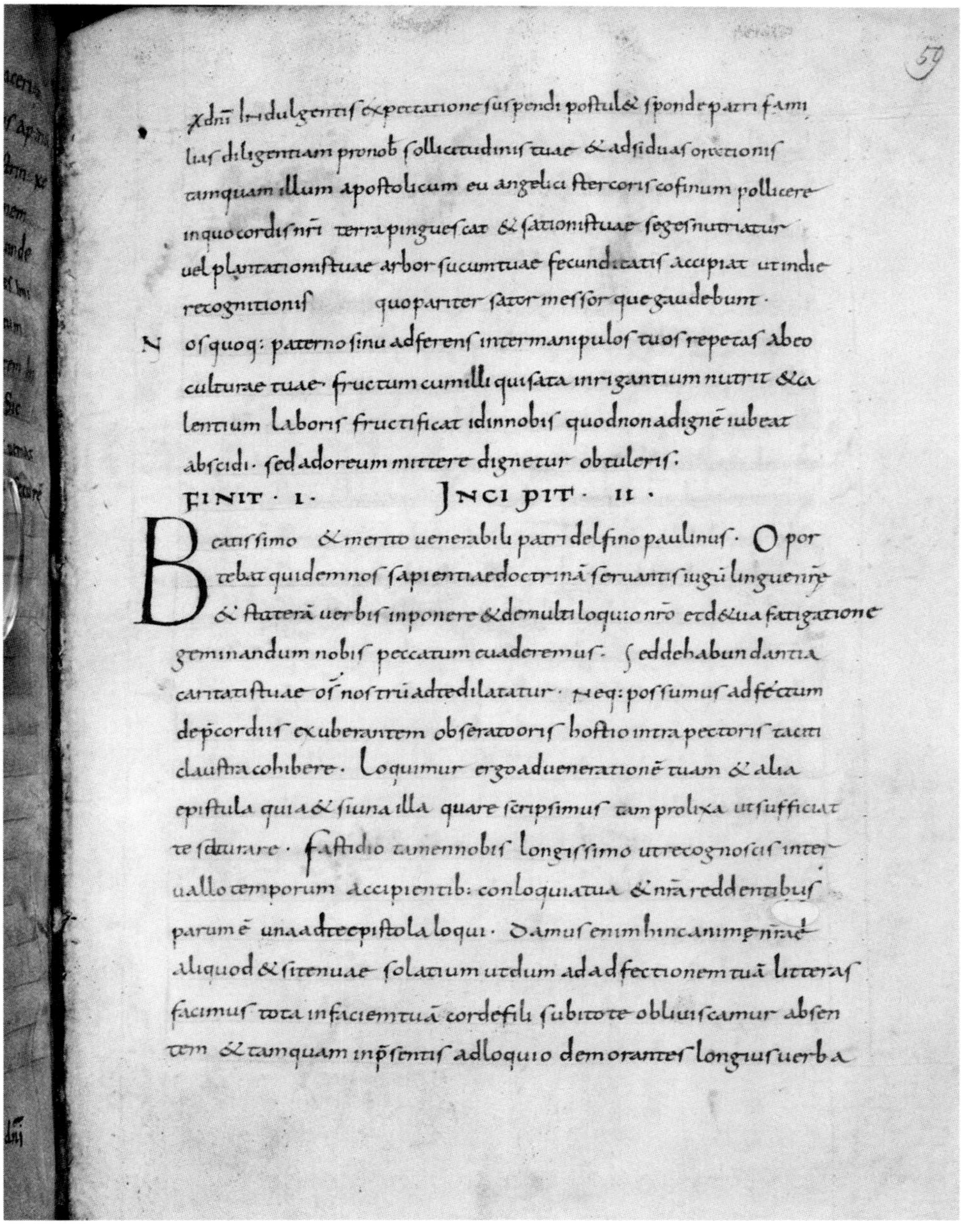

59

Xdnī lridulgentis expectatione suspendi postul& sponde patri fam
lias diligentiam pronob sollicitudinis tuae & adsiduas orationis
tamquam illum apostolicum eu angelica stercoris cofinum pollicere
inquo cordis nrī terra pinguescat & sationis tuae seges nutriatur
uel plantationis tuae arbor sucum tuae fecunditatis accipiat ut indie
recognitionis quo pariter sator messor que gaudebunt ·
N os quoq: paterno sinu adferens inter manipulos tuos repetas abeo
culturae tuae · fructum cum illi qui sata inrigantium nutrit & ca
lentium laboris fructificat id innobis quod non adignē iubeat
abscidi · sed adoreum mittere dignetur obtuleris ·
FINIT · I · INCIPIT · II ·
B eatissimo & merito uenerabili patri delfino paulinus · O por
tebat quidem nos sapientiae doctrinā seruantis iugū linguae nrē
& stateram uerbis inponere & de multiloquio nrō et de sua fatigatione
geminandum nobis peccatum euaderemus · sed de habundantia
caritatis tuae os nostrū adte dilatatur · neq: possumus ad fectum
de pcordiis exuberantem obseratoris hostio intra pectoris taciti
claustra cohibere · Loquimur ergo ad uenerationē tuam & alia
epistula quia & si una illa quare scripsimus tam prolixa ut sufficiat
te saturare · fastidio tamen nobis longissimo ut recognoscis inter
uallo temporum accipientib: conloquia tua & nra reddentibus
parum ē una adte epistola loqui · Damus enim hinc animę nrē
aliquod & si tenuae solatium ut dum ad adfectionem tuā litteras
facimus tota in faciem tuā corde fili subito te obliuiscamur absen
tem & tamquam inpsentis adloquio demorantes longius uerba

PLATE 16.3 London, British Library, Harley 4831, fol. 59r. Paulinus of Nola, *Epistulae*. St Denis *c.* 825–50.

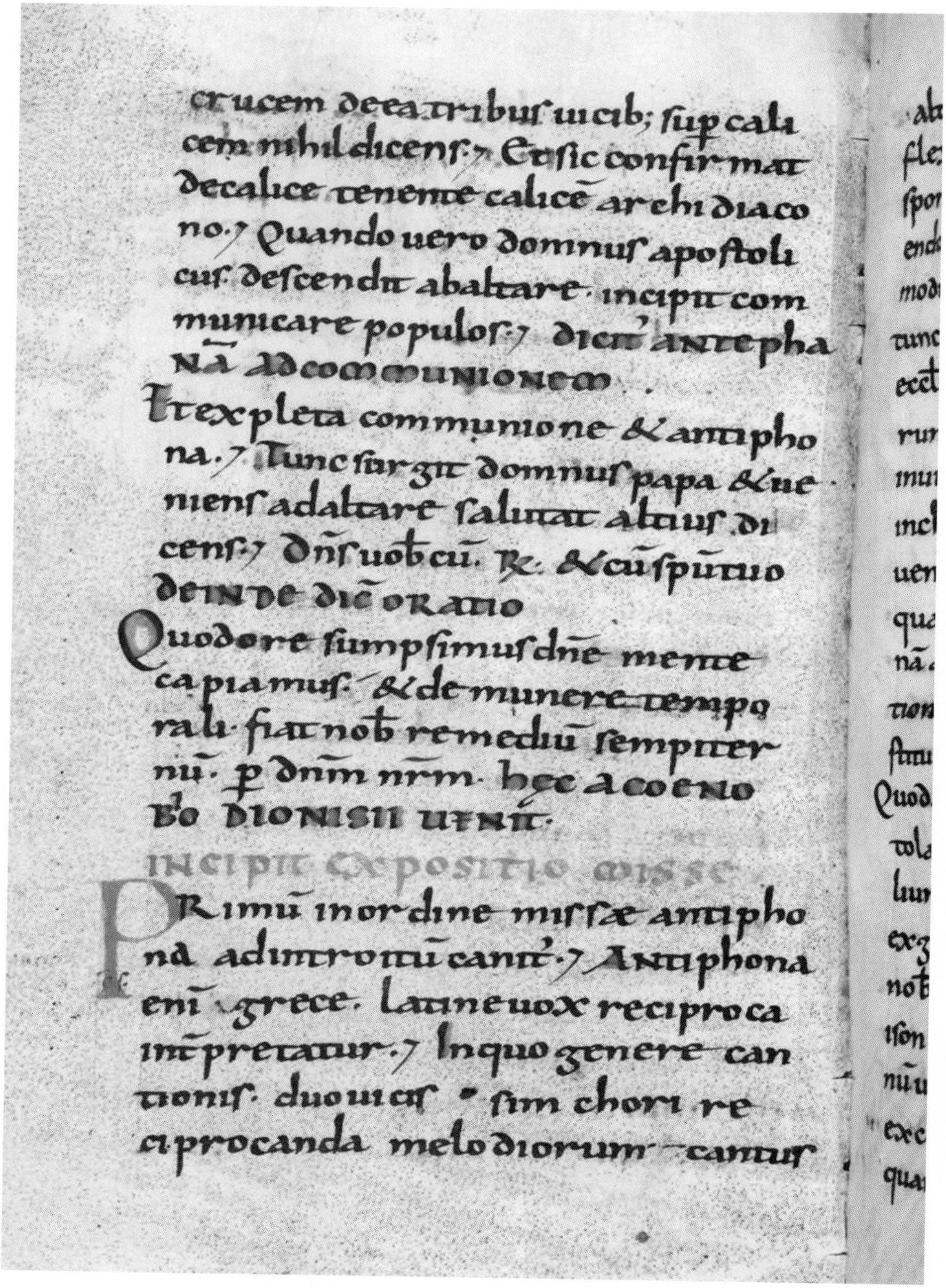

PLATE 16.4 Bamberg Amalarius. Bamberg, Staatsbibliothek, Lit. 131, 30v. St Denis.

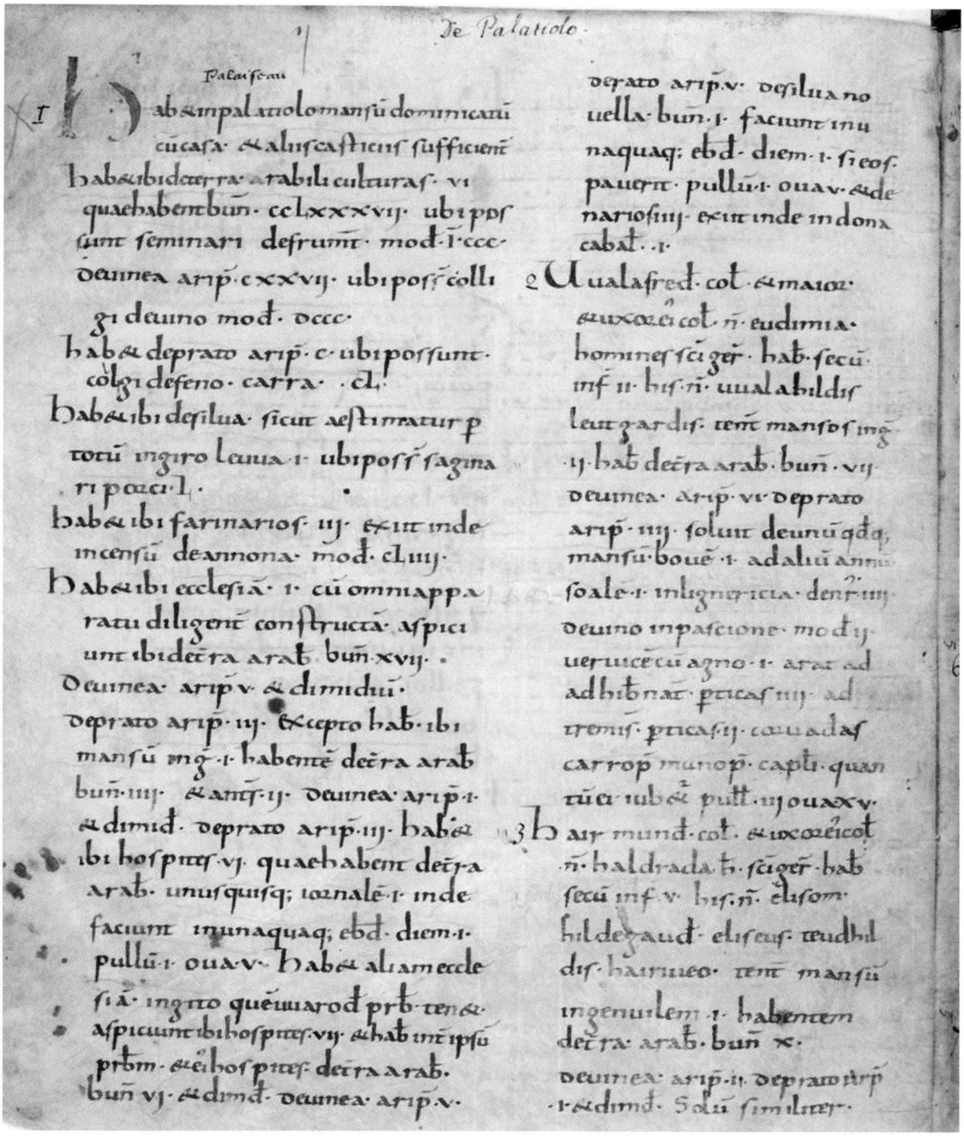

PLATE 16.5 Paris, BnF, lat. 12832, fol. 3v, *Polyptique* of Abbot Irminon (812–17). St Germain-des-Prés.

Moralia in Job); and Laon, Bibliothèque municipale, 439 (Boethius, *De consolatione philosophiae*). Half-uncial is used as a display script during the mid-ninth century in Vatican City, BAV, Reg. lat. 581, fols. 40–116 (*Vita s. Germani*), Vienna, ÖNB, 483 (*Vita s. Germani*), and Copenhagen, Kongelige Bibliotek, Saml. 163 Fol. (Rufinus's Latin translation of Eusebius's *Historia ecclesiastica*).

Paris

The following manuscripts are attributed to Paris by Bernhard Bischoff: Antwerp, Museum Plantin Moretus, 312 (Sedulius and Iuvencus); Bern, Burgerbibliothek, 109 (Priscian) and 180 (Hegesippus); Laon, Bibliothèque municipale, 131 (Augustine, *Opuscula*); London, BL, Harley 2666 (Frontinus); Harley 3033 (Gregory, *Moralia in Job*); and Milan, Biblioteca Ambrosiana, A 135 inf. (Origen, *in Epistulam ad Romanos*).

Tours

Tours had developed a distinctive Caroline minuscule by the 790s with a very elegant and distinctive *g*, the Uncial form of *a*, minuscule *n*, a tall *s* which curves over the following letter, and a distinctive *quoniam* abbreviation visible in the last line of BL Harley 2793 (Plate 16.6).

Manuscripts from the time of Alcuin (796–804) are Tours, Bibliothèque municipale, 10 (Octateuch); Vatican City, BAV, Reg. lat. 762 (Livy); Paris, BnF, lat. 5581 (Martinellus) and 13759 (Martinellus) (both the Martinellus manuscripts use an elegant Half-uncial close to sixth-century models); Leiden, Bibliotheek der Rijksuniversiteit, Voss. lat. F 73 (Nonius); London, BL, Harley 2793 (*Psalterium Hebraicum*); Monza, Biblioteca Capitolare, G.1 (Bible); Troyes, Bibliothèque municipale, 1742 (Alcuin, *De Virtutibus et vitiis*); Ghent, Universiteitsbibliotheek, MS 102 (Jerome, *in Esaiam*), and MS 240 (Bede, *in Regum librum, in apocalypsin*); Berlin, Staatsbibliothek zu Berlin-Preussischer Kulturbesitz, Lat. Qu. 404 (Cicero, *De Amicitia*). Manuscripts from the mid-century, which use the New Style of ruling, include Bamberg, Staatsbibliothek, Class. 5 (Boethius, *De Instituione Arithmetica*) copied for Charles the Bald (Plate 16.7); Bern, Burgerbibliothek, 167 (Virgil copied by Berno); Laon, Bibliothèque municipale, 220 (Amalarius); Paris, BnF, lat. 7774A (Cicero, *De inventione*); Vatican City, BAV, Reg. lat. 1484 (Tiberius Claudius Donatus) and Autun, Bibliothèque municipale, 19 (*Sacramentarium* dated to 846).

The main products of the Tours scriptoria were the twenty-five Gospel books, over fifty complete bibles, and at least eighteen copies of a collection of texts about St. Martin of Tours. The bibles were copied at the rate of two per year, by groups of scribes working together. Eight scribes are to be found in Paris, BnF, lat. 3 (the so-called Rorigo Bible); 12 in London, BL, Harley 2805; over a dozen in Zürich, Zentralbibliothek, Cod. Car. C. 1; 24 in London, BL, Add. 10546 (the so-called Moutier Grandval Bible); and at least six in Paris, BnF, lat. 1 (the so-called 'First Bible of Charles the Bald'). The main features of the script type are tall ascenders with heavily wedged serifs, the use of Half-uncial for Bible prologues and opening lines, and Uncial at the start of the text. The wide circulation of Tours bibles and Gospel books throughout the Carolingian empire provided a model which contributed to the standardization of Caroline minuscule.

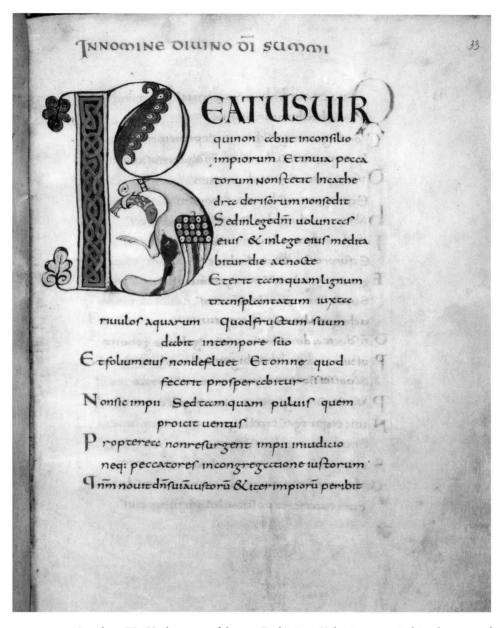

INNOMINE DIUINO DI SUMMI   33

BEATUSUIR
quinon cebut inconfilio
impiorum Etinuia pecca
torum Nonftetit Incathe
dree derifôrum nonfedit
Sedinlegedñi uoluntcef
eiuf & inlege eiuf medita
bitur die acnocte
Eterit tecm quam lignum
trcenfplecntatum iuxtee
riuulof aquarum   Quodfructum fuum
debit intempore fuo
Etfoliumeiuf nondefluet Etomne quod
fecerit profperebitur
Nonfic impii Sedtecm quam puluif quem
proicit uentuf
Proptereec nonrefurgent impii iniudicio
neq: peccatoref incongregectione iuftorum ·
Qñm nouit dñfuïãiuftorü & iterimpiorü peribit

PLATE 16.6 London, BL, Harley 2793, fol. 33r, *Psalterium Hebraicum*, copied in the time of Alcuin.

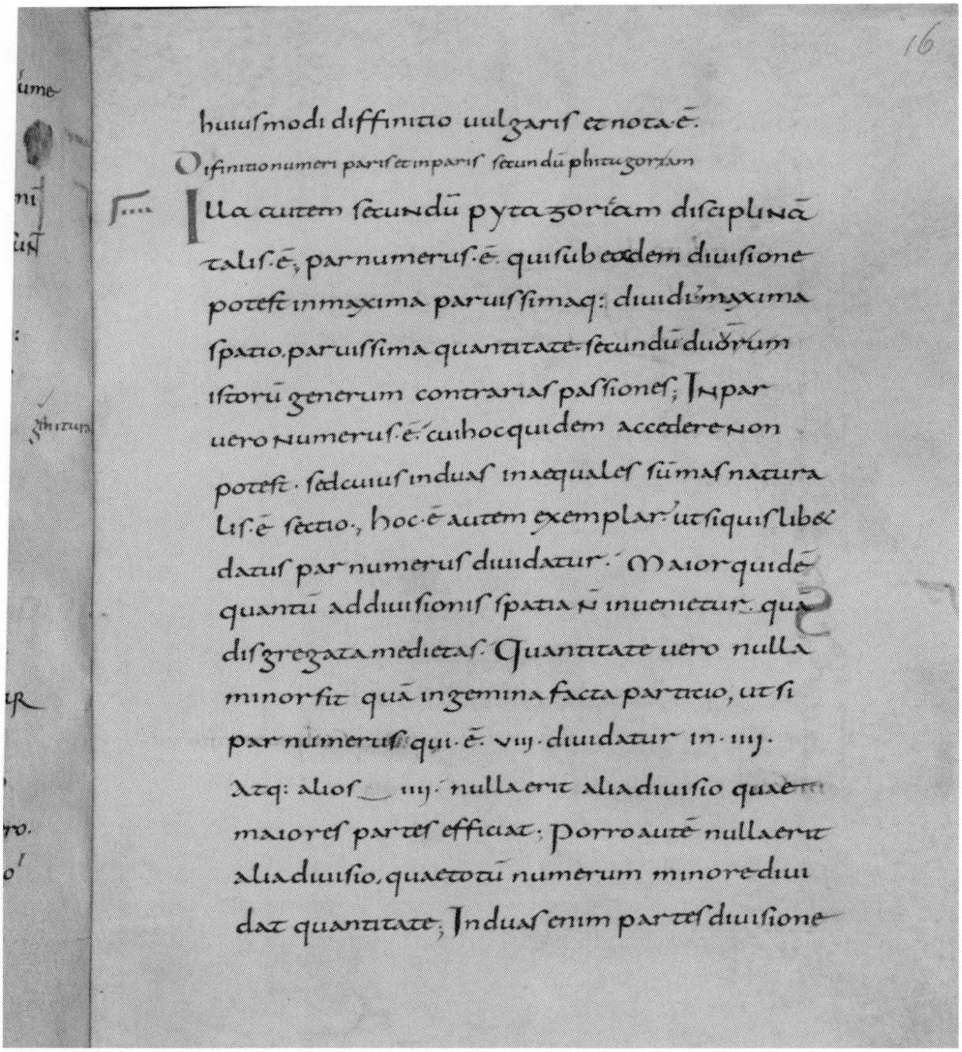

16

huiusmodi diffinitio uulgaris et nota est.

Diffinitio numeri paris et inparis secundum phitagoricam

Illa autem secundum pytagoricam disciplinam
talis est, par numerus est qui sub eadem diuisione
potest in maxima paruissimaque diuidi: maxima
spatio, paruissima quantitate, secundum duorum
istorum generum contrarias passiones; Inpar
uero numerus est cui hoc quidem accedere non
potest. sed eius in duas inaequales summas natura
lis est sectio., hoc est autem exemplar. ut si quislibet
datus par numerus diuidatur. Maior quidem
quantitate ad diuisionis spatia non inuenietur. quam
disgregata medietas. Quantitate uero nulla
minor fit quam ingemina facta partitio, ut si
par numerus qui est viii. diuidatur in iiii.
Atque alios iiii. nulla erit alia diuisio quae
maiores partes efficiat; porro autem nulla erit
alia diuisio, quae totum numerum minore diui
dat quantitate; In duas enim partes diuisione

PLATE 16.7 Bamberg, Staatsbibliothek, Class 5, fol. 16r, Boethius *De Institutione Arithmetica*. Tours, *c*.845.

Saint-Amand

Arno was abbot of Saint-Amand from 783; in 784 he was made bishop of Salzburg. Many manuscripts produced at Saint-Amand are now in the Bibliothèque municipale at Valenciennes, and some 40 more can be found in the Bibliothèque nationale de France in Paris. The earliest manuscripts include Valenciennes, Bibliothèque municipale, 51 (Augustine, *De trinitate*, et al.); 100 (a biblical glossary with a dedication inscription); MS 170 (Fulgentius); and 395 (Marius Victorinus, *Ars grammatica*, et al.). The scribe Lotharius copied four manuscripts with verse dedication inscriptions before his death in 828: Vatican City, BAV, Pal. lat. 161 (Lactantius, *Institutiones*); Paris, BnF, lat. 2109 (Eugippius, *Excerpta*); Laon, Bibliothèque municipale, 298 (Origen, *Homeliae in numeros*); and Paris, BnF, lat. 2296 (Gelasian Scaramentary, Plate 16.8). The script is characterized by the use of both a small upright minuscule *a* and an open *a*; an *f* that descends well below the line; a short dotted *y*; a small *z*; and by frequent ligatures with *r*. For plates, see *CLA* 6.839 (Troyes, Bibliothèque municipale, 581: Cyprian); *CLA* 9.1237 (Munich, Bayerische Staatsbibliothek, clm 208: Cyprian); *CLA* 1.112 (Vatican City, BAV, Reg. lat. 1040: *Acta Concilii*); *CLA* 10.1478 (Vienna, ÖNB, 418: *Acta Concilii*); *CLA* 10.583 (Leiden, Bibliotheek der Rijksuniversiteit, Voss. Lat. Q 60: *Liber Pontificalis*). Longer texts were copied by groups of ten or more scribes: examples are Bamberg, Staatsbibliothek, Misc. Bibl 40 (Gregory, *Moralia in Job*); Brussels, Bibliothèque Royale, II 2206 (Jerome, *In Matthaeum*); Chartres, Bibliothèque municipale, 6 (Augustine, *In Iohannem*); Cologne, Erzbishöfliche Diözesan- und Dombibliothek, 75 (Augustine, *De Civitate Dei*); Munich, Bayersiche Staatsbibliothek, clm 14527 (Augustine, *De libero arbitrio*); Ghent, Universiteitsbibliotheek, 224 (*Vita s. Amandi*); Vienna, ÖNB, 765 (Ambrose, *in Lucam*: *CLA* 10.1489).

In the mid ninth century, Saint-Amand made several copies of the Gregorian Sacramentary; these are now Le Mans, Bibliothèque municipale, 77; New York, Pierpont Morgan Library, G 57; Paris, BnF, lat. 2290 and lat. 2291; Saint-Petersburg, Russian National Library, Q v I 41; and Stockholm, Kunglige Biblioteket, Holm A 136.

EASTERN FRANCIA

Metz

The earliest manuscripts from the Metz scriptoria were copied for Archbishop Angilram (768–91): Bern, Burgerbibliothek, 289 (*CLA* 7.861: Chrodegang of Metz, *Regula canonicorum*); Metz, Bibliothèque municipale, 7 (*CLA* 6.786: Bible) and 134 (*CLA* 6.788: Ephraem, *Sermones*). A richly illuminated sacramentary (now Paris, BnF, lat. 9428) and a Gospel book with superb monumental capitals (now Paris, BnF, lat. 9388, Plate 16.9) were copied for Bishop Drogo, as were the Gospels in Veste Coburg.

Cambrai

The earliest copy of a Gregorian Sacramentary, Cambrai, Bibliothèque municipale, 164, was made for Hildoard of Cambrai in 811/812. The script is an even minuscule; a distinctive characteristic is the abbreviation of *orum* by *or* with a cross stroke having a dot and line above it. Cambrai, Bibliothèque municipale, 295 (Bede, *in Lucam*) is in the same script, while 299 (Jerome, *in Danielem*), 350 (Augustine, *De Civitate Dei*), and 541 (Hilarius, *De Trinitate*) date from the mid-century.

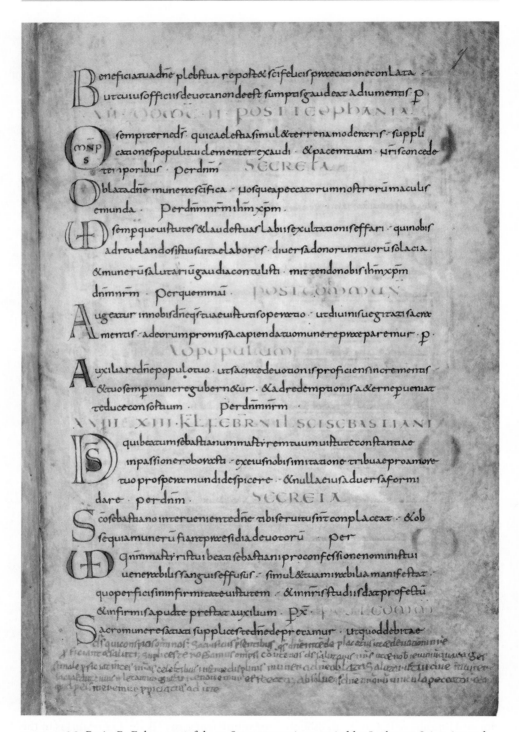

PLATE 16.8 Paris, BnF, lat. 2296, fol. 4r: *Sacramentarium* copied by Lothar at Saint-Amand.

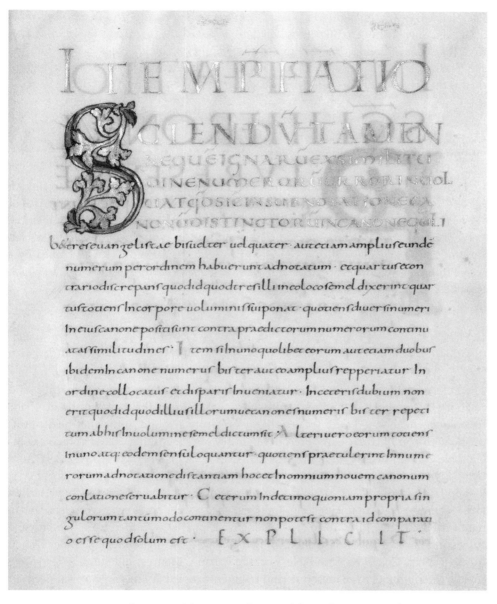

PLATE 16.9 Paris, BnF, lat. 9388, fol. 3r, Gospels copied for Bishop Drogo of Metz (823–55).

MAINZ

The archbishopric of Mainz and the monastery of St. Martin started by using an Insular minuscule to copy texts in both Latin and German. The largest number are now in the Vatican and in Munich, including Vatican City, BAV, Pal. lat. 577 (Canons);

Pal. lat. 578 (*Decretales*); Pal. lat. 1447 (*Computistica*); Munich, Bayerische Staatsbibiliothek, clm 8104 (Gregory, *Moralia in Iob*); clm 8107 (Augustine, *Varia*); clm 8112 (*Epistulae* of Boniface); and Berlin, Staatsbibliothek zu Berlin-Preussischer Kulturbesitz, Theol. Lat. Fol. 283 (Gospels). Mainz script uses a distinctive *Q* followed by a triangle of dots as the abbreviation for *quae*. Mainz books are commonly copied on calf.

TRIER

In Trier the monasteries of St. Maximin and St. Mathias had substantial Carolingian libraries though only three manuscripts can be shown to have been copied at St. Maximin. The scribe *Harduinus presbyter* signed Berlin, Staatsbibiliothek zu Berlin-Preussischer Kulturbesitz, Lat. Fol. 741. And in Vatican City, BAV, Pal. lat. 1448 there is a calendar with references to two feasts of Maximin. It was copied by a scribe found in fragmentary copies of Bede's *De temporum ratione* and Priscian which have been preserved in bindings from St Maximin.

BAVARIA AND AUSTRIA

The chief scriptoria of Bavaria and Austria, at Freising, Regensburg, Tegernsee, and Salzburg, were expertly studied by Bischoff. At Freising, the Northumbrian scribe Peregrinus collaborated with local scribes who wrote a round, somewhat heavy minuscule with *r* in ligature. Early Freising manuscripts are Munich, Bayerische Staatsbibliothek, clm 6279 (*CLA* 9.1259), clm 6282 (*CLA* 9.1260), clm 6239 (*CLA* 9.1254), and clm 6305 (*CLA* 9.1269). Several scribes writing at Freising use the insular form of *g*. Bishop Hitto (811–36) was praised for making copies of theological works; his scribes use a compressed script with long and thickened ascenders, long descenders, and a rightward slant (e.g., Plate 16.10).The distinctive capital *Q* is formed from two crossing curves and has two tails; *h* is formed with an ascender starting to the left. Under Bishop Anno (854–75) Gospel books, a Bible, works of Rabanus Maurus, and liturgical texts were copied. Over a hundred manuscripts and fragments copied at Freising have survived.

At Saint-Emmeram in Regensburg, insular script was adapted under the influence of manuscripts from Verona, and a well-proportioned minuscule which resembles the script used by Godescalc at the Carolingian court was employed in the 790s. A variety of ligatures, as well as straight and uncial *d*, and round as well as minuscule *a* were widely used in Bavaria. Early manuscripts from Regensburg are Munich, Bayerische Staatsbibliothek, clm 14197 (*CLA* 9.1292) and clm 14425 (*CLA* 9.1297). Under Bishop Baturich (817–47) clerics and notaries wrote a stylized script with only *N* as a majuscule letter, and with few ligatures (see Plate 16.11). Some 60 surviving manuscripts were copied at Regensburg in the first half of the ninth century, only ten in the second half.

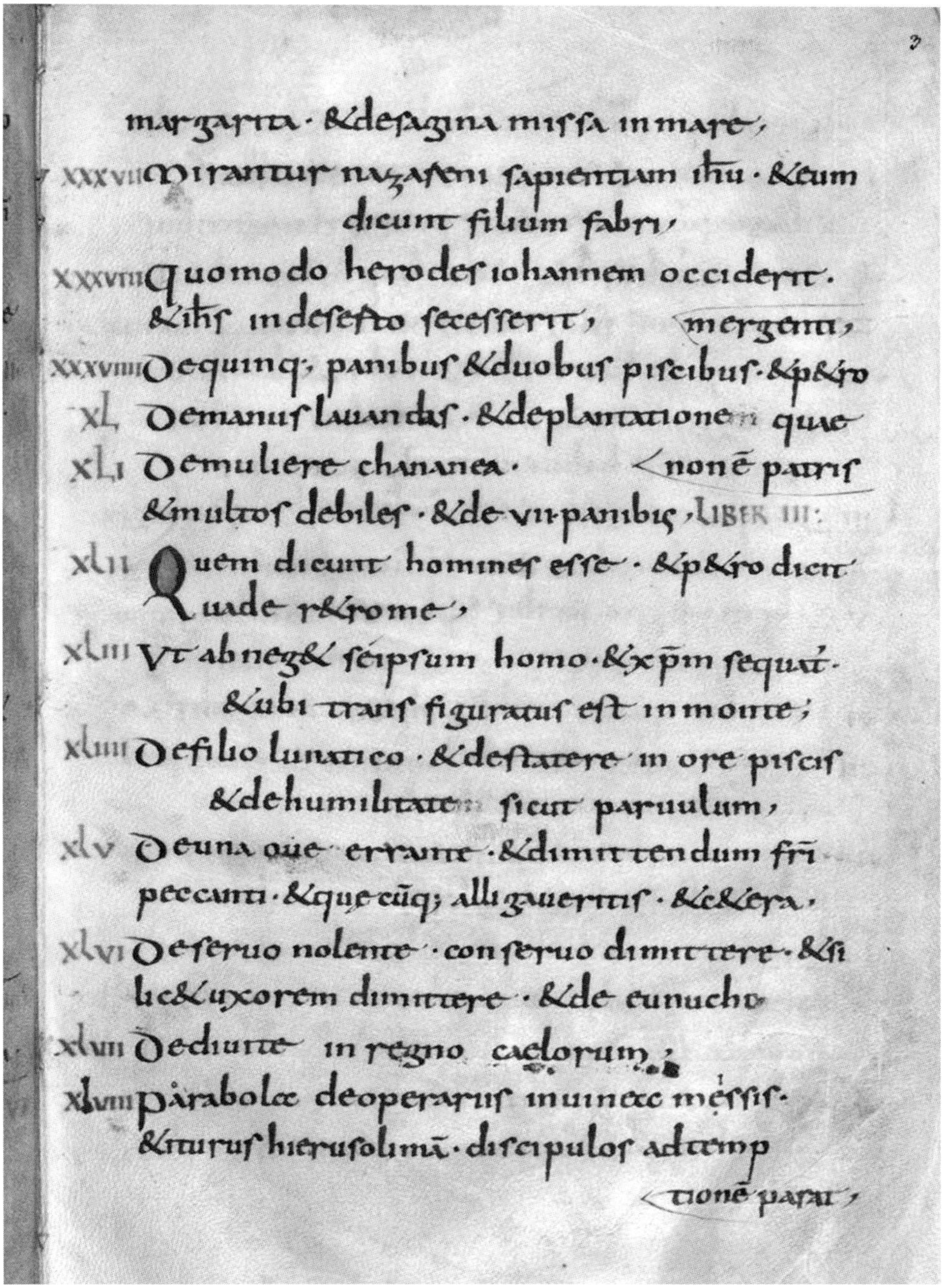

margarita · &defagina miffa in mare,

xxxvii Mirantur nazareni fapientiam ihu · &cum dicunt filium fabri,

xxxviii quomodo herodes iohannem occiderit. &itis in deferto feceflerit,   mergenti,

xxxviiii De quinq; panibus &duobus pifcibus. &p&fo

xl, De manus luandas · &de plantatione que

xli, De muliere chananea ·   <non e patris &multos debiles · &de vii panibus, LIBER III.

xlii, Quem dicunt homines efe · &p&fo dicit Quade regrome,

xliii, Vt abneg& feipfum homo · &x pm fequat · &ubi tranffiguratur eft in monte;

xliiii, De filio lunatico · &de ftatere in ore pifcis &de humilitate ficut paruulum,

xlv, De una oue errante · &dimittendum fri peccanti · &que cuq; alligauerit · &&eta ·

xlvi, De feruo nolente · con feruo dimittere · &fi lic&uxorem dimittere · &de eunucho

xlvii, De diuite in regno caelorum;

xlviii, parabolae de operarus in uinea meffis · &iturus hierufolima · difcipulos adtemp <tione patri,

PLATE 16.10   Munich, Bayerische Staatsbibliothek, clm 6272, fol. 3r, *Hieronymus in Evangelium Matthaei*, Freising, 811–36.

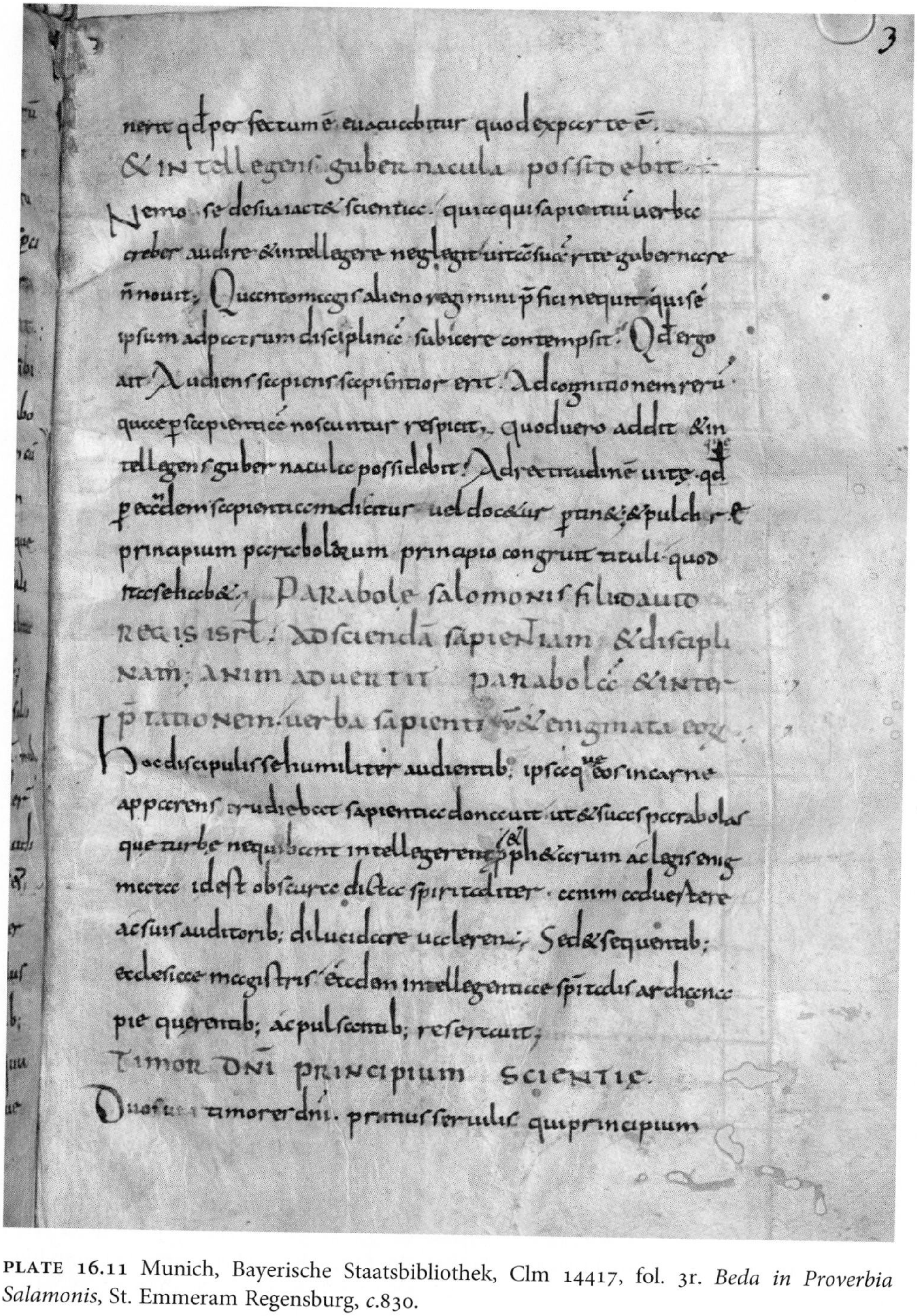
nerit qd per factum ē. euacuabitur quod expertae ē.
& intellegens gubernacula possidebit.
Nemo se desuia iactet scientiae. quia qui sapientium uerba
crebro audire & intellegere neglegit uitae suae rite gubernare
n̄ nouit; Quanto magis alieno regimini p̄ficere nequit qui se
ipsum ad paterum disciplinae subicere contempsit. Qd ergo
ait Audiens sapiens sapientior erit. Ad cognitionem reru̅
quae p sapientiae noscuntur respicit. quod uero addit & in
tellegens gubernacula possidebit. Ad rectitudinē uitę qd
p eādem sapientiam dicitur uel docetur ptinet. & pulchre
principium parabolarum principio congruit tituli quod
praefixa habet. PARABOLE salomonis filii dauid
regis isrl. ad sciendā sapientiam & discipli
nam; animaduertit parabolae & inter
pretationem. uerba sapientium & enigmata eoz.
Hoc discipulis se humiliter audientib; ipse q̄ue dns in carne
apparens erudiebat sapientiae docendo ut & sua per parabolas
quae turbae nequibant intellegere & pphetarum ac legis enig
mata idest obscure dicta spiritaliter eorum aduertere
ac suis auditorib; dilucidare uelerent. Sed & sequentib;
ecclesiae magistris eadem intellegentiae spiritalis archana
pie quaerentib; ac pulsantib; reserauit;
TIMOR DNI PRINCIPIUM SCIENTIAE.
Duo sunt timores dni. primus seruilis qui principium

PLATE 16.11 Munich, Bayerische Staatsbibliothek, Clm 14417, fol. 3r. *Beda in Proverbia Salamonis*, St. Emmeram Regensburg, *c.*830.

REIMS

There are some surviving manuscripts from the end of the eighth century that were copied at Reims, but the finest Reims manuscripts were copied for Archbishop Hincmar, 845–82. These include Reims, Bibliothèque muncipale, 1 and 2 (a two-volume Bible) with distinctive punctuation; Paris, BnF, lat. 12132 (Hilary, *De Trinitate*); Cambridge, Pembroke College, 308 (Rabanus Maurus, *in Epistolas Pauli*); Bamberg, Staatsbibliothek, Hist. 162 (*Vita Remigii*); and The Hague, Koninklijke Bibliotheek, 10 D 2 (*Capitularia*). The script has an *s* with the head over the following letter and the uncial form of *N* when it begins a word (see Plate 16.12). Works of Hincmar surviving in contemporary Reims copies include *De cavendis vitiis*, in Oxford, Bodleian Library, E Mus. 157; *Ad simplices* in Leiden, Bibliotheek der Rijksuniversiteit, BPL 141; *Contra Godescalcum* in Brussels, Bibliothèque Royale, 1831–3, and *Epistula ad Hardwicum* in MS 5413–22 of the same library. Illuminated manuscripts from Reims are described by Koehler and Mütherich (1930–2013).

LORSCH

The monastery of Lorsch used a round minuscule which has similarities to the script employed by Godescalc at Charlemagne's court. Manuscripts produced at Lorsch include Vatican City, BAV, Pal. lat. 170 (Hegesippus), Pal. lat. 188 (*CLA* 1.82: Augustine, *De Doctrina Christiana*), and Pal. lat. 207 (Augustine, *In Evangelium Iohannis*, Plate 16.13). Features of the script include three forms of *a* (the double *c*, Half-uncial, and minuscule forms); round and straight *d*; *r* with a large shoulder; the bowl of *g* extended to the right; and clubbing of ascenders. The *Nt* ligature is common, as are the *ae*, *ri*, and *re* ligatures. There is assimilation of some insular elements both in the decorated initials with interlace and in the use of Insular Half-uncial for opening lines. Greater regularity is found in the script used in the 820s and 830s, in which one finds limited use of ligatures *et*, *st*, and *re*. Most Lorsch manuscripts are now in the Vatican and in the Laudian collection in the Bodleian library in Oxford: the library has been reconstructed on the Bibliotheca Laureshamensis website.

FULDA

At Fulda the scriptorium used Insular script until the 840s, when it was replaced by a rather clumsy version of Caroline minuscule with squarish letterforms. Notable Fulda manuscripts include Basel, Universitätsbibliothek, AN. IV. 18 (*Aratea*); Florence, BML,

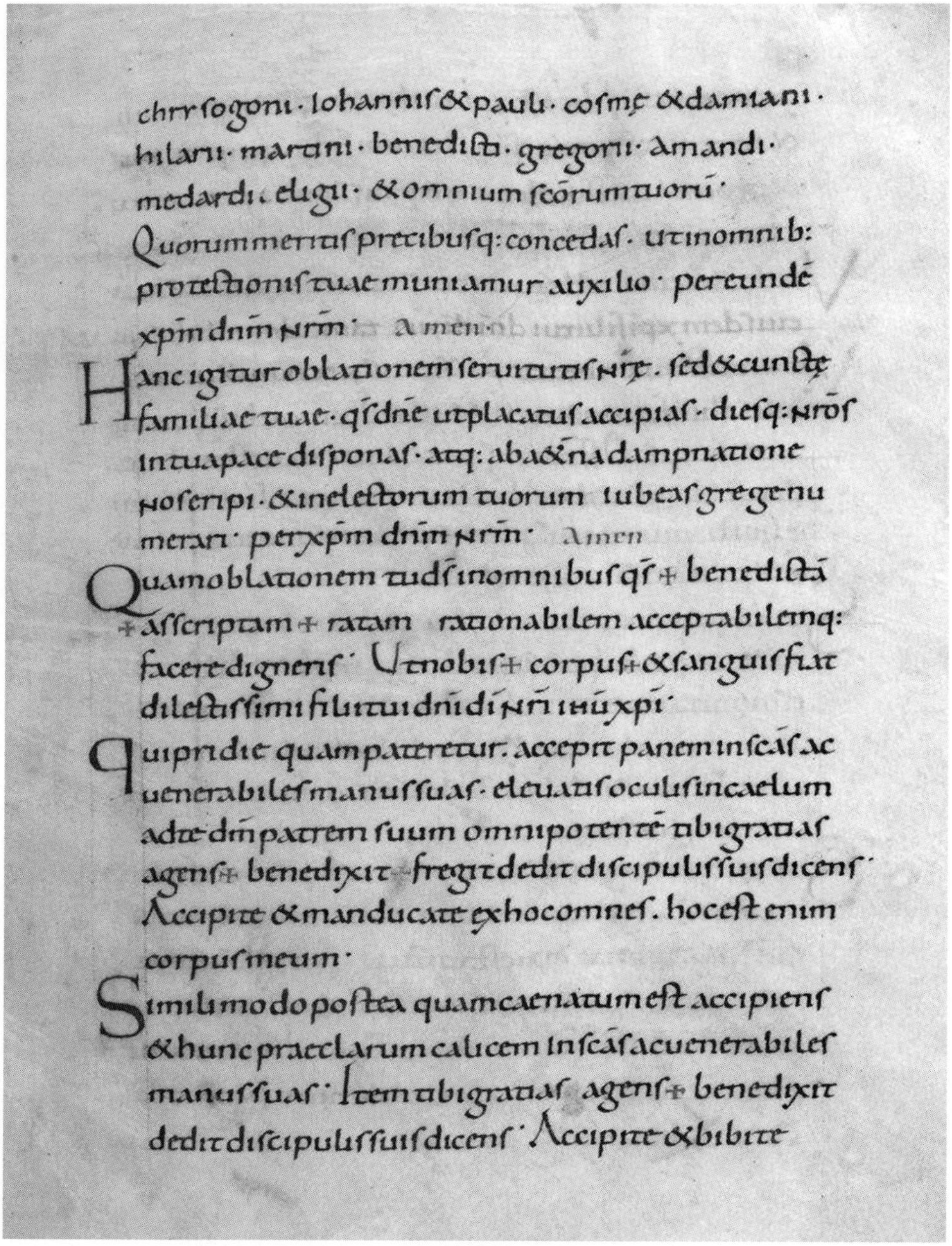

chrysogoni · Iohannis & pauli · cosme & damiani ·
hilarii · martini · benedicti · gregorii · Amandi ·
medardi · eligii · & omnium scorum tuorum ·
Quorum meritis precibusq; concedas · ut in omnib:
protectionis tuae muniamur auxilio · per eunde
xpm dnm nrm · Amen

Hanc igitur oblationem seruitutis nre · sed & cuncte
familiae tuae · qs dne ut placatus accipias · diesq; nros
in tua pace disponas · atq; ab aeterna dampnatione
nos eripi · & in electorum tuorum iubeas grege nu
merari · per xpm dnm nrm · Amen

Quam oblationem tu ds in omnibus qs + benedicta
+ ascriptam + ratam rationabilem acceptabilemq:
facere digneris · Ut nobis + corpus & sanguis fiat
dilectissimi filii tui dni di nri ihu xpi ·

Qui pridie quam pateretur · accepit panem in scas ac
uenerabiles manus suas · eleuatis oculis in caelum
ad te dnm patrem suum omnipotentem tibi gratias
agens + benedixit · fregit dedit discipulis suis dicens ·
Accipite & manducate ex hoc omnes · hoc est enim
corpus meum ·

Simili modo postea quam caenatum est accipiens
& hunc praeclarum calicem in scas ac uenerabiles
manus suas · Item tibi gratias agens + benedixit
dedit discipulis suis dicens · Accipite & bibite

PLATE 16.12 Reims, Bibliothèque municipale, 213, fol. 15r: *Sacramentarium*, showing the characteristic long *s* and the uncial *N* (Nrm line 6 and Nre line 7).

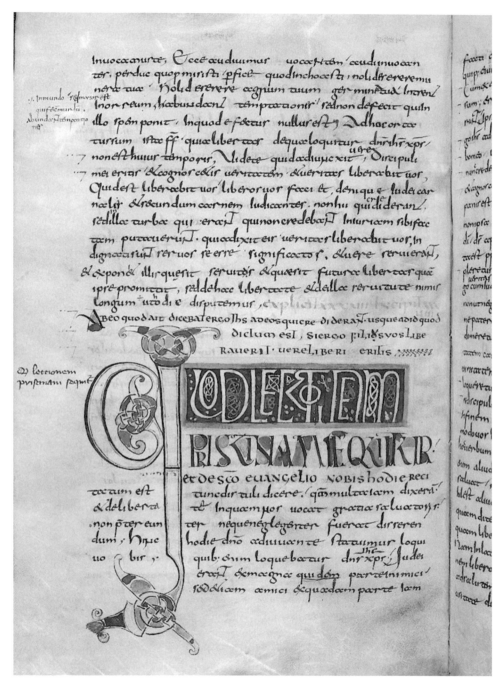

PLATE 16.13 Vatican City, BAV, Pal. lat. 207, Augustine, *In Evangelium Iohannis*, fol. 61v, showing Insular initials and early Lorsch minuscule.

Plut. 38.2 (Tacitus, *Historiae*); Kassel, Landesbibliothek, 2° Ms theol. 23 (Jerome, *in Ezechielem)*; 2° Ms theol. 25 (Bede, *in Apocalypsin*); 2° Ms theol. 49 (Origen, *in Epistolam ad Romanos*); Erlangen, Universitätsbibliothek, 9 (Gospel book); and Milan, Biblioteca Ambrosiana, I 85 sup. (Columella). Many copies of the works of Rabanus Maurus, especially of his biblical commentaries, survive in Fulda scripts: Darmstadt, Hessische Landes- und Hochschulbibliothek, 4108 (*In Genesim*); Karls-ruhe, Badische Landesbibliothek, Aug. Perg. 208 (Jerome, *in Danielem*); Princeton, Princeton University Library, Garrett 72 (*In Matthaeum*); Munich, Bayerische Staats-bibliothek, clm 14210 (*De institutione clericorum*); Stuttgart, Württembergische Land-esbibliothek, VII 45 (*In librum Sapientiae*); Paris, BnF, lat. 2440 (*De institutione clericorum*) and lat. 2443 (*Ad Drogonem*). The following manuscripts include Rabanus' acrostic poem *De Laudibus Sanctae Crucis*: Vienna, ÖNB, 652; Vatican City, BAV, Reg. lat. 124; Paris, BnF, lat. 2422 (Plate 16.14) and lat. 2423; Amiens, Bibliothèque municipale, 223; and Turin, Biblioteca Nazionale, K II 20.

Würzburg

At Würzburg, Anglo-Saxon script was used into the first third of the ninth century and was replaced by a Caroline minuscule with clubbed ascenders, ligatures of *st* and *ct*, and a distinctive abbreviation stroke (see Plate 16.15). Under Abbot Hunbert (832–42) a more balanced and calligraphic script was developed, influenced by the Caroline minuscule at Fulda with a breaking of the shafts. Under Hunbert's successor Gozbald, discipline was less strong and the scribes share fewer common features. Most Würz-burg manuscripts have survived in the cathedral library or in the Laudian collection in the Bodleian Library in Oxford.

Breton

Breton manuscripts were probably copied in the monasteries of Redon and Land-évennec and in the Breton bishoprics located at Vannes, Rennes, Dol, Quimper, Saint-Pol, Alet and Nantes. Save for Rennes and Nantes these centres resisted the claims of Tours to metropolitan status over Brittany. With the exception of the few manuscripts copied at the monastery of Landévennec, no place of origin can be suggested for any manuscript, though we know of libraries at the monastery of Redon (founded in 832) and Alet. The province was subject to frequent Viking invasions.

An important group of Breton Gospel books has survived: Alençon, Bibliothèque municipale, 84; Angers, Bibliothèque municipale, 24; Baltimore, Walters Art Gallery, W 1; Bern, Burgerbibliothek, 85; Boulogne, Bibliothèque municipale, 8; Cambridge, Fitzwilliam Museum, 45-1980; Douai, Bibliothèque municipale, 13; London, BL,

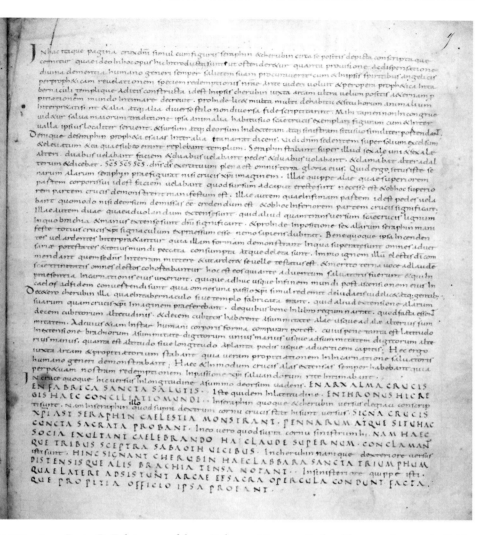

PLATE 16.14 Paris, BnF, lat. 2422, fol. 7r, Rabanus Maurus, *De laudibus sanctae crucis*. Fulda 830–47.

Add. 9381; Egerton 609; Cotton Otho B IX; Harley 2823; and Royal 1 A xviii; Montpellier, Bibliothèque de la Faculté de Médecine,153; New York, New York Public Library, de Ricci 115; Oxford, Bodl. Library, Auct. D 2 16; Auct. D 5 3; Laud Lat. 26; Oxford, St. John's College, 194; Paris, BnF, nouv. acq. lat. 1587; and Troyes, Bibliothèque municipale, 960(15).

Five copies of the Irish *Collectio Hibernensis* copied in Brittany survive: Orléans, Bibliothèque municipale, 221, copied by the scribe Junobrus, who uses an insular *g*; London, BL, Royal 5 E XIII and Cotton Otho E XIII; London, Lambeth Palace Library, MS 1231 (fragment); and Cambridge, Corpus Christi College, 279 (excerpts). Many Breton manuscripts have important vernacular glosses. A full list of Breton manuscripts is given by Deuffic (1985).

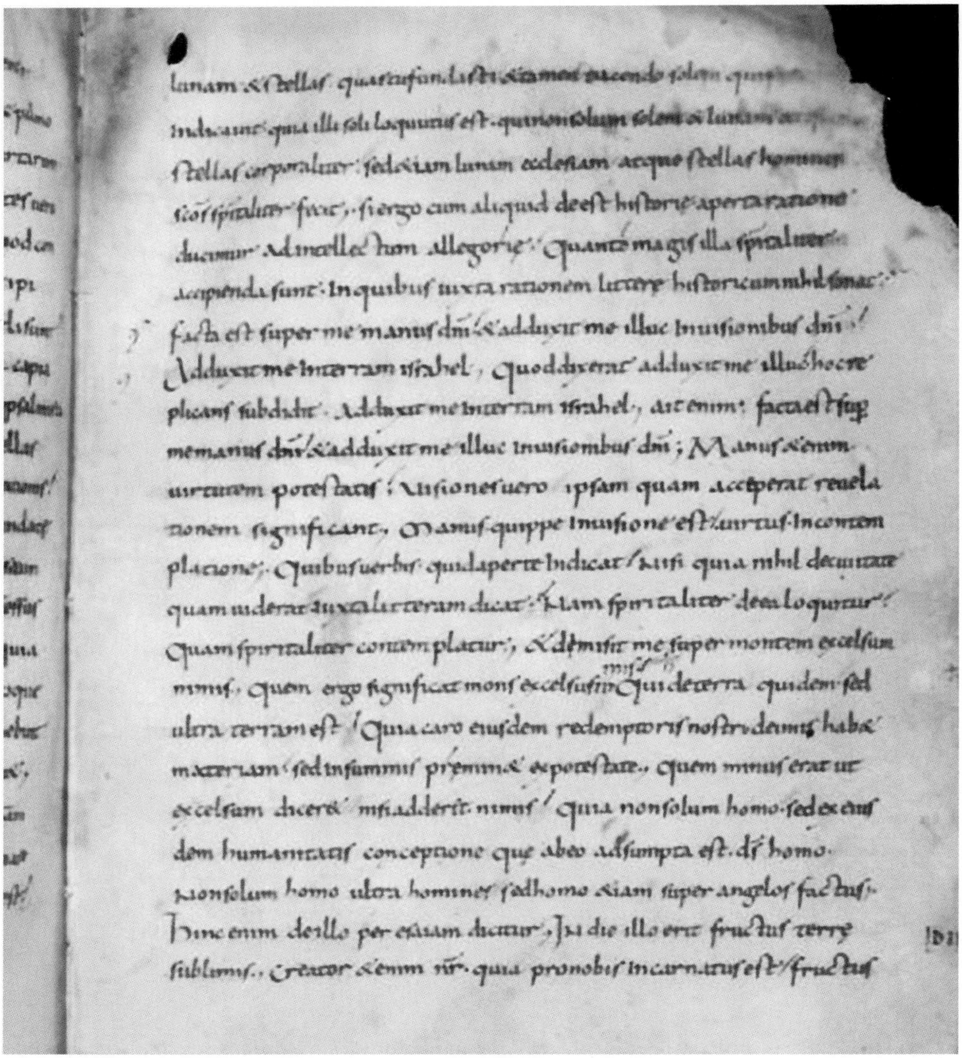

PLATE 16.15 Würzburg, Universitätsbibliothek, M. p. th. f. 6, fol. 4r. Gregory, *Moralia in Iob*, with *st* and *ct* ligatures and the slanting abbreviation stroke.

Notes

1. The list of names of scripts in Berlin, Staatsbibliothek zu Berlin-Preussischer Kulturbesitz, Diez B Sant. 66, fol. 346r.
2. Mordek(†), Zechiel-Eckes(†), and Glatthaar (2012).
3. Plates of these are in Alverny, et al. (1964).

Bibliography

A comprehensive catalogue of all surviving manuscripts and fragments in Caroline minuscule can be found in Bernard Bischoff's *Katalog der festländischen Handschriften des neunten Jahrhunderts (mit Ausnahme der wisigotischen) Teil I Aachen-Lambach* (Wiesbaden, 1998), *Teil II Laon-Paderborn* (Wiesbaden, 2004), and *Teil III Padua-Zwickau* (Wiesbaden, 2014).

The Court of Charlemagne

Holter, K. 1980. *Der goldene Psalter Dagulf-Psalter*. Graz: Akademische Druck u. Verlagsanstalt.

Laffitte, M. P. 2007. "L'Évangéliaire de Charlemagne et les débuts de la Renaissance artistique à la cour de Charlemagne." *Art de l'enluminure* 20: 4–17.

Reudenbach, B. 1998. *Das Godescalc Evangelistar, ein Buch fur die Reformpolitk Karls des Grossen*. Frankfurt: Fischer-Taschenbuch-Verlag.

Saint-Denis

Duval, Y.-M. 1984. "Un Triple Travail de copie effectué à Saint-Denis au IXe siècle et sa diffusion à travers l'Europe carolingienne et médiévale. À propos de quelques *Commentaires sur les petits prophètes* de saint Jérôme." *Scriptorium* 38: 3–49.

Nebbiai dalla Guarda, D. 1985. *La Bibliothèque de l'abbaye de Saint-Denis en France du IXe au XVIIIième siècle*. Paris: Éditions du Centre national de la recherche scientifique.

Vezin, J. 1979. "Hincmar de Reims et Saint-Denis. À propos de deux manuscrits du *De trinitate* de Saint Hilaire." *Revue d'histoire des textes* 9: 289–98.

Vezin, J. 1981. "Les Manuscrits copiés à Saint-Denis en France pendant l'époque carolingienne," *Paris et Île-de-France* 32: 273–87.

Saint-Germain-des-Prés

Alverny, M.-T. d' et al. 1964. *Catalogue des manuscrits en écriture latine portant des indications de date, de lieu ou de copiste*, 3. Paris: CNRS.

Bischoff, B. 1965. "Die Handschrift." In *Der Stuttgarter Bilderpsalter. Bibl. Fol. 23. Württembergische Landesbibliothek Stuttgart*, 15–30. Stuttgart: Schreiber.

Tours

Koehler, W. 1930–3. *Die karolingischen Minaturen*, Band I, *Die Schule von Tours*. Berlin: Deutscher Verein für Kunstwissenschaft.

Rand, E. K. 1929. *A Survey of the Manuscripts of Tours*. Cambridge, MA: Mediaeval Academy of America.

Rand, E. K. 1934. *The Earliest Book of Tours: Studies in the Script of Tours* 2. Cambridge, MA: Mediaeval Academy of America.

Rand, E. K. and G. Howe. 1917. *The Vatican Livy and the Script of Tours*, Memoirs of the American Academy in Rome, 1: 19–57. New York: University Press Association.

Mainz

Hanselmann, J. 1987. "Das Cod. Vat. Pal. Lat. 289." *Scriptorium* 41: 78–87.

Ladner, P. 1979. "Karolingische Sakramentarfragmente aus Freiburg in der Schweiz. Ein Beitrag zum Mainzer Skriptorium des 9. Jahrhunderts." In *Palaeographica, Diplomatica et Archivistica Studi in onore di Giulio Battelli*, ed. Università di Roma. Scuola speciale per archivisti e bibliotecari, 99–104. Rome: Edizioni di storia e letteratura.

Lindsay, W. M. and P. Lehmann. 1925. "The (Early) Mayence Scriptorium." *Palaeographia Latina* 4: 15–39.

Ottermann, A. 1998. "Das Beda Fragment Hs. Frag I in der Stadtbibliothek Mainz. Ein Beitrag zum Mainzer Skriptorium des 9 Jahrhunderts," *Philobiblon* 42: 301–7.

Trier

Knoblich, I. 1996. *Die Bibliothek des Klosters St. Maximin bei Trier bis zum 12. Jahrhundert* Trier: Wissenschaftlicher Verlag Trier.

Bavaria and Austria

Bischoff, B. 1940. *Die südostdeutschen Schreibschulen und Bibliotheken in der Karolingerzeit 1 Die bayerischern Diözesen*. Leipzig: Harrassowitz [2nd ed. Wiesbaden: Harrassowitz, 1960].

Bischoff, B. 1980. *Die südostdeutschen Schreibschulen und Bibliotheken in der Karolingerzeit 2 Die vorwiegend österreichischen Diözesen*.Wiesbaden: Harrassowitz.

Lorsch

Bischoff, B. 1989. *Die Abtei Lorsch im Spiegel seiner Handschriften*. Lorsch: Heimat- und Kulturverein Lorsch mit Unterstützung der Stadt Lorsch.

Gorman, M. 1982. "The Lorsch 'De Genesi ad Litteram' and two fragments in the Script of Luxeuil." *Scriptorium* 36: 238–45.

Fulda

Gugel, K. 1995. *Welche erhaltene mittelalterlichen Handschriften dürfen der Bibliothek des Klosters Fulda zugerechnet werden? Teil 1: Die Handschriften*, Fuldaer Hochschulschriften. Frankfurt: Knecht.

Spilling, H. 1978. "Angelsächsische Schrift in Fulda." In *Von der Klosterbibliothek zur Landesbibliothek*, ed. A. Brall, 47–98. Stuttgart: Hiersemann.

Spilling, H. 1982. "Das Fuldaer Skriptorium zur Zeit des Hrabanus Maurus." In *Hrabanus Maurus, Lehrer Abt und Bischoff*, ed. R Kottje and H. Zimmermann, 165–81. Wiesbaden: Steiner.

Spilling, H. 1996. "Die frühe Phase Karolingischer Minuskel in Fulda." In *Kloster Fulda in der Welt der Karolinger und Ottonen*, ed. G. Schrimpf, 249–84. Fuldaer Studien 7 Frankfurt: Knecht.

Würzburg

Hoffman, J. and B. Bischoff. 1952. *Libri Sancti Kyliani. Die Würzburger Schreibschule und die Dombibliothek im VIII und IX Jahrhundert*. Würzburg: Kommissionsverlag Ferdinand Schöningh.

Breton

Deuffic, J.-L. 1985. "La Production manuscrite des scriptoria Bretons (VIII–XI siècles)." In *Landévennec et le monachisme Breton dans le haut Moyen Age*, 289–321. Landévennec: Association Landévennec.

McGurk, P. 1987. "The Gospel Book in Celtic Lands before A.D. 850: Contents and Arrangement." In *Irland und die Christenheit: Bibelstudien und Mission*, ed. P. Ní Chatháin and M. Richter, 165–89. Stuttgart: Klett-Cotta .

Morey, C. R. 1931. *The Gospel Book of Landevennec (the Harkness Gospels) in the New York Public Library*. Cambridge, MA: Harvard University Press.

Wormald, F. 1977. *An Early Breton Gospel Book : A Ninth-Century Manuscript from the Collection of H. L. Bradfer Lawrence, 1887–1965*, ed. Jonathan Alexander. Cambridge: Printed for presentation to the members of the Roxburghe Club.

Further bibliography

Bischoff, B. 1981a. *Kalligraphie in Bayern. Achtes bis zwölftes Jahrhundert*. Wiesbaden: Reichert.

Bischoff, B. 1981b. "Die karolingische Minuskel." *Mittelalterliche Studien* 3: 1–4.

Bischoff, B. 1981c. "Panorama der Handscriftenüberlieferung aus der Zeit Karls des Grossen" *Mittelalterliche Studien* 3: 5–38.

Ganz, D. 1987. "The Preconditons for Caroline Minuscule." *Viator* 16: 23–44.

Ganz, D. 1995. "Book Production in the Carolingian Empire and the Spread of Caroline Minuscule." In *The New Cambridge Medieval History II c.700–c.900*, ed. R. D. McKitterick, 786–808. Cambridge: Cambridge University Press.

Koehler, W. and F. Mütherich. 1930–2013. *Die karolingischen Miniaturen*, 8 vols. Berlin and Wiesbaden: Deutscher Verein für Kunstwissenschaft.

Mordek(†), Hubert, Klaus Zechiel-Eckes(†), and Michael Glatthaar, eds. 2012. *Die Admonitio generalis Karls des Großen*, MGH Fontes iuris Germanici antiqui in usum scholarum separatim editi. Hanover: Hansche Buchhandlung.

CHAPTER 17

EARLY CAROLINGIAN
Italy

SIMONA GAVINELLI

THE TRANSITION TO CAROLINE SCRIPT

ACCORDING to Bernhard Bischoff's definition, Caroline minuscule is a "general term for a situation that was reached as a result of related tendencies and changes of forms."[1] In Italy under Charlemagne, following the Frankish conquest of 774, the slow formalization and consolidation of Caroline script had a non-linear chronological and geographical development. We find accordingly a panorama of multiple minuscule scripts with variegated letter forms, all more or less close to Caroline on the basis of greater or lesser resemblance to a unitary canon that Giorgio Cencetti placed not earlier than the beginning of the tenth century.[2] The only dated manuscript is an Isidore, *Chronicon* of 801 (Modena, Archivio Capitolare, O.I.11, fols. 1r–21r: *CLA* 3.368; *Kat.*, II 2795). The semi-cursive script, perhaps Modenese and rather irregular, has no relation to the graphic style of the minuscule of Nonantola, which reached its full development at that monastery a few kilometers from Modena within the first third of the ninth century[3]. Points of contact with the pre-Caroline scripts of southern Italy and with proto-Beneventan impose caution, however, with regard to the localization of Isidore's manuscript to Modena. Localizing manuscripts requires convergent lines of analysis, among them study of text transmission. The Nonantola minuscule constitutes the only standardization of a minuscule book hand in northern Italy: in the initial period it has a peculiar *ductus*, heavy and with a tendency to roundness and larger, strongly clubbed shafts, open cursive *a* or single shaped like two contiguous *c*'s, two-tiered *c*, Uncial *d* with the shaft heavily sloping to the left, *r* with the second stroke curled upwards, majuscule *Q* shaped like a *2*. Common ligatures, among them *ri* in the shape of a pointed arch and *ti* in the form of an *8*, the *i* descending below the line, become less frequent in the latest phase, in the second quarter of the ninth century; at the same time the shafts become longer and less clubbed. Under the influence of Caroline script, which became dominant from the mid-century, Uncial-type *a* becomes established, *g* tends to close its upper bow, and round *r* in the form of *2* appears in the group *or*, and also barred in the abbreviation for *orum*. Yet Nonantola, an avant-garde and notably productive scriptorium, also used in parallel with this script a precocious and primitive Caroline minuscule in the oldest witness of the *Liber diurnus Romanorum Pontificum* (Vatican City, Archivio Segreto Vaticano, Misc., Arm. XI, 19, s. $IX^{1/4}$; *Kat.*, III 6409), the papal formulary used in the monastery as a sourcebook for study.[4] In the same region, toward the end of the ninth century further affinities with Nonantola are noticeable in two law books made at Modena cathedral; the episcopate was in fact becoming markedly more important in northern Italy during this period. The minuscule of Nonantola influenced one of the scribes of the pseudo-Isidorean *Decretales* (Modena, Archivio Capitolare, O.I.4, fols. 13r–36v, 65r–88v, s. $IX^{3}/_{4}$: *Kat.*, II 2793), and it appears in consciously calligraphic form in a rare illustrated collection of *Leges* and *Capitularia* (Modena, Archivio Capitolare, O.I.2, s. $IX^{4}/_{4}$), ruled four bifolia at a time.[5] As regards the preparation of manuscripts, in fact, in the eighth and ninth centuries, Gregory's rule that like pages should face like—flesh side against flesh side, hair side against hair side—is observed throughout the peninsula (with very rare exceptions, e.g., Modena, Archivio Capitolare, O.I.11, fols. 1r–21r; *Kat.*, III 2795; Vatican City, BAV, Pal. lat. 1547, *Kat.*, III 6581; Cesena, Biblioteca Malatestiana, S.XXI.5, *Kat.*, III 855). In the first half of the ninth century, the ruling is done two or four bifolia at a time, with an increasing tendency toward the latter, the predominant form in the second half of the century (Milan is an exception, where liturgical books alone continue to be ruled four bifolia at a time throughout the ninth century); during the tenth century in Piedmont and Lombardy two bifolia at a time, at Bobbio one bifolium at a time.

In northern Italy the semi-cursive script of the eighth and ninth centuries is characterized by a general verticality, which continues to be seen as Caroline script. Shafts are clubbed and not extended very much, and a variety of letter forms appear: three sorts of *a* (an open cursive type; a closed, Semi-uncial type, sometimes with a flattened top; and Uncial), *c* short or two-tiered, *e* Semi-uncial or tall and broken with an upper loop and a lower bow, *g* with the lower bow only open, *m, n, o* in the later Caroline forms, *t* sometimes 8-shaped in ligature; in some cases, in ligatures, the second letter is small and written below the line; occasional ligatures such as *li, ct, st*, and ampersand *&* even within a word.

The process of formalizing Caroline script was slow and was often affected by the conservative instincts of the scribes. In the first third of the ninth century, some calligraphic and regular semi-cursive scripts were still in use. For north-central and northern Italy, Bischoff lists a number of witnesses to scriptoria at Aosta, Ivrea, Vercelli, Novara, Milan, Bobbio, Aquileia and Cividale del Friuli, Nonantola, Lucca, and the abbey of S. Salvatore on Monte Amiata.[6] The situation in the south and in south-central Italy is more fluid.[7] At Rome in the first half of the ninth century, Uncial script was still in use for liturgical and non-liturgical books alike. The additions made to the *Homeliary* of Agimundus (Vatican City, BAV, Vat. lat. 3836: *CLA* I.18b) in fact date from around 800; a luxury *Evangeliary* received illumination (Rome, Biblioteca Vallicelliana, B.25.II, s. IX$^{1/4}$: *CLA* 4.430); of the same period are the additions made to the *Acta* of the Sixth Ecumenical Council held at Constantinople (Vatican City, BAV, Reg. lat. 1040, written at Saint-Amand, s. VIII–IX: *CLA* 1.112).[8]

In the scribal area of the northeast, at Novara, there is a detectable influence of neighboring Rhaetia on the script, at times angular, in a group of three legal and patristic manuscripts written for the cathedral toward the end of the eighth century (Milan, Biblioteca Trivulziana, 688: *CLA* 3.366; Karlsruhe, Badische Landesbibliothek, Aug., CCLIV, fols. 72r–213r: *Kat.*, I 1735; Novara, Biblioteca Capitolare di S. Maria, LXXXIV [2]: *CLA* 3.406), the last of which has a section (fols. 40v–51v) in contemporary Semi-uncial.[9] Part of Isidore's *Etymologiae*, I 9.3–VI 10.2, was presumably written at Vercelli (Vercelli, Archivio e Biblioteca Capitolare, CCII, s. IX$^{1/3}$: *Kat.*, II p. 154), known as the *Apollo Medicus* for the lively miniature that decorates it. At Ivrea a static and archaic pre-Caroline was employed for a substantial *Evangeliary* in two columns (Ivrea, Biblioteca Capitolare, XCIX [32], s. IX$^{1/4}$; *Kat.*, II 1581) at a time when other copyists of the same scriptorium were already using Caroline script.

The pre-Caroline script of Seneca, *De beneficiis* and *De clementia* (Vatican City, BAV, Pal. lat. 1547, *Kat.*, III 6581), copied around the year 800, and of the contemporary *rex palimpsestorum*, St. Gall, Stiftsbibliothek, 908 (*CLA* VII 953–65) derive from the area of Milan.[10]

In these developments the writing of the area of Verona appears specially advanced. Here the local minuscule took on a well-proportioned, calligraphic appearance as early as the second half of the eighth century, a style it kept into the tenth. The first standardization of the Caroline hand got under way during the episcopacies of Egino (796–9), who came from Reichenau, and Ratoldus (799–840).[11] In this phase, under the influence of the transalpine centres of Reichenau and St. Gall, it adopted the characteristic large-face letters and rounded *ductus* of the Alemannic minuscule, alongside forms and abbreviations of Irish derivation (e.g., the *Orationale-Obituarium*, Verona, Biblioteca Capitolare, CVI [99], s. IX$^{1/4}$, *Kat.*, III 7071; or the Cassiodorus, *Expositio Psalmorum* of similar date, Oxford, Bodleian Library, Add. C. 152: *Kat.*, II 3767). In this process the persistence of the Semi-uncial tradition, well attested and still very much alive alongside the pre-Caroline hands, was also decisive (Verona, Biblioteca Capitolare, LV [53], *CLA* IV 507: s. VIII^2). Complete formalization came about after 840 thanks to the intense production coordinated by the archdeacon Pacificus (†848): besides the clubbed shafts, Semi-uncial *g* with both bows open (like a *3*) stands out, along with phenomena shared with the Italian pre-Caroline such as the alternation between Uncial and cursive, open *a*, Uncial *d* and one with a straight shaft, capital *N* and *R* within a word, and the majuscule ligature *NT*. A peculiar abbreviation, and one useful for localization, is *ma* = *misericordia*, as opposed to the regular *mia*. The precociousness of the handwriting in any case answers to larger movements for reform, in the liturgical field among others. The production of the scriptorium was rich and distinctive throughout the course of the ninth century. It was at Verona in the first quarter of the ninth century that the text of the Franco-Carolingian *Sacramentary* was copied for the first time in Italy (Verona, Biblioteca Capitolare, XCI [86], *Kat.*, III 7066), and it remained alone of its kind for an entire generation; an elegant *Pontifical* (Verona, Biblioteca Capitolare, XCII [87], s. IX$^{1/4}$, *Kat.*, III 7067) was written somewhat later.[12]

In northeast Italy, in the area of Aquileia and Cividale del Friuli, the influence of Bavaria on the local minuscule is clear, with mixed letter forms, both Caroline and cursive, in the contemporary historical work of Paul the Deacon, *Historia Langobardorum* (Cividale del Friuli, Museo Archeologico, XXVIII, s. IX in.: *Kat.*, I 926).

From Emilia, around the Po, there remain two manuscripts, both dated to the first third of the ninth century s. IX$^{1/3}$: Isidore, *Etymologiae* (Cesena, Biblioteca Malatestiana, S.XXI.5: *Kat.*, I 885) and *Praedicationes* (Kraków, Archiwum Kapituly Metropolitanej, 140 [43]: *Kat.*, II 2006).[13]

At Lucca the local minuscule, in the course of formalization between the first and second quarters of the ninth century, is still marked by ostentatious ligatures and Visigothic influences. Its character is seen in a block of patristic manuscripts containing Ambrose, *De fide, De spiritu sancto*, and Augustine, *De civitate Dei* and *Tractatus in evangelium Iohannis* (Lucca, Biblioteca Capitolare, 13, 19, 21: *Kat.*, II 2517, 2519, 2520).[14]

THE TRIUMPH OF CAROLINE

The spread of Caroline minuscule in Italy was doubtless closely tied to imperial projects for institutional reform. In the revived cathedral and monastic chapters there was a need for books suitable for performing divine service and pastoral care. But the fundamental impulse was the program of studies and the re-establishment of public teaching enjoined by the Capitulary of Corteolona in 825 and assigned to nine principal seats of learning. At Pavia, the capital of the kingdom and nodal point of the Italian northwest, the teaching was done by the Irishman Dungal, who came from the abbey of Saint-Denis, in concert with the archbishop of Milan Angilbert II (824–59) and with the monastery of Bobbio, to which he left his own books, which he had brought from France. High-quality Caroline seems indeed to begin with Dungal's own working copy of his *Responsa contra Claudium*, (Milan, Biblioteca Ambrosiana, B 102 sup. *Kat.*, II 2629; Plate 17.1). Finished in 827, the transcription of the work was given under the author's supervision to two scribes, one of them with a French hand showing a delicacy of line and a pronounced slope to the right, as well as the Irish abbreviation for *est* which later spread throughout northern Italy. The style of the Italian hand at the beginning (perhaps Pavian) has more emphatic strokes with scarcely any inclination to the right (shafts not extended and strongly clubbed, *a* always Uncial, oscillation between Uncial *d* and one with a straight shaft, *r* in the ligatures *re, rt* sometimes taking the 2-form after *o*, the ampersand *&* also found within words, and the terminal ligature of majuscule *NT*; abbreviations *b;* and *q;* for *bus* and *que*); *ur* written as a superscript 2 is also encountered, an abbreviation of French origin and more developed hac specie quauer suf indicant.

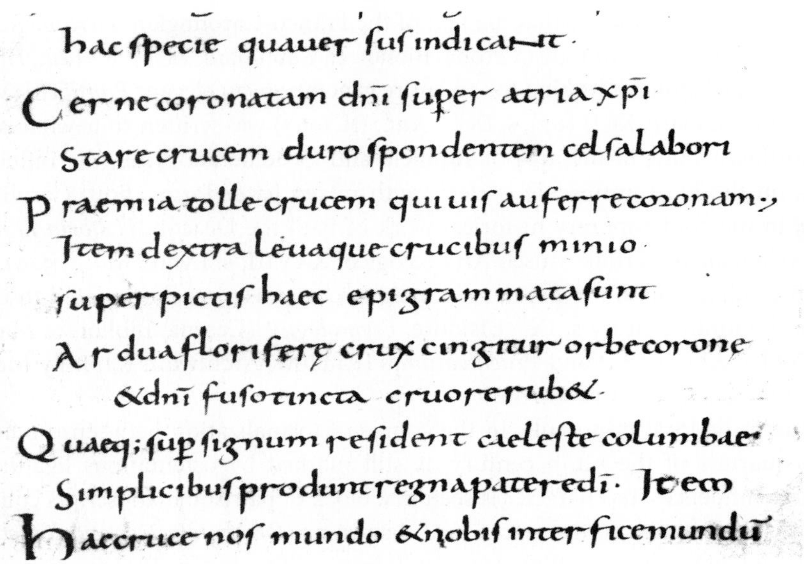

Cerne coronatam dni super atria xpi

Stare crucem duro spondentem celsalabori

Praemia tolle crucem qui uis auferre coronam;

Item dextra leuaque crucibus minio

super pictis haec epigrammata sunt

Ardua florifere crux cingitur orbe corone

&dni fuso tincta cruore rub&.

Quaeq; sup signum resident caeleste columbae

Simplicibus produnt regna patere di. Item

Haec cruce nos mundo &nobis interficemundu

PLATE 17.1   Milan, Biblioteca Ambrosiana, B 102 sup., fol. 22r. Dungal, *Responsa*, c.827, Pavia.

than the *t* with apostrophe for *tur* that was still practiced in the Milan–Pavia area in this period. From this same educational milieu, probably at Pavia again, come the Quintilian and the *Brutus* of Cicero (Milan, Biblioteca Ambrosiana, E 153 sup., and Cremona, Archivio di Stato, Fondo Comunale, n° 295, s. IX$^{2/3}$: *Kat.*, I 968; II 2633). Connected as it was with the court of the kingdom of Italy and its organizational and judicial needs, Pavia became the center for the recovery and circulation of civil and ecclesiastical law. Two law books may be associated with that environment: the first is a collection of *Capitularia* and *Leges Langobardorum*, which combines more cursive elements with a more Caroline section (fols 1r–56v), where *t* with apostrophe for *tur* is still found (Ivrea, Biblioteca Capitolare, XXXIV [5], s. IX$^{2/4}$: *Kat.*, I 1561); the second is a rich *Collectio canonum* of the same period (Vercelli, Archivio e Biblioteca Capitolare, CLXV, *Kat.*, III 7010), introduced by some leaves illustrated by ink drawings (fols. 2r–5r), with captions in Uncials (Plate 17.2). The harmonious script has ascenders only slightly clubbed, alternation of cursive open *a* with the Uncial form, of two-bow *e* with Semi-uncial, the fused diphthong *ae*, *g* with both bows open, the cursive ligatures *fi*, *li* (with *i* sinking below the line), *re*, *r* in the 2 shape after *o*, and sinking below the line when it has a bar through it to indicate *orum*, capital *R* with a bar for *runt* and the ligatured majuscule *NT* at the end of words; abbreviations *b; q;* or *b₇ q₇; ur* as a superscript 2. The localization to Pavia is based on some verses in honor of St. Syrus, patron of the city, written by the scribe of the text himself in the lower margin of fol. 53v.[15]

The imitation of models from France is clearly visible in an Augustine, *De Trinitate* (Vercelli, Archivio e Biblioteca Capitolare, CIV, s. IX$^{1–2/4}$, *Kat.*, III 6996). The scribes, who

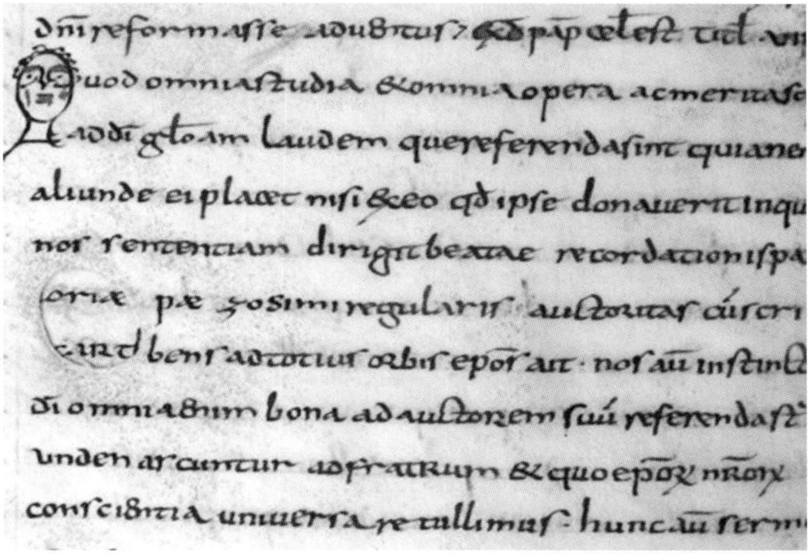

PLATE 17.2 Vercelli, Archivio e Biblioteca Capitolare, CLXV, fol. 171v. *Collectio canonum*, s. IX second quarter, presumably Pavia.

were active in a high-grade scriptorium, perhaps at Pavia, made an effort to adapt themselves to the style of Tours that they found in the first, elaborately decorated gathering.[16]

At Milan, too, the first attempt to move away from local scribal tradition, without arriving at Caroline, is a school encyclopedia commissioned by the archbishop Angilbert II, the *Liber glossarum* (Milan, Biblioteca Ambrosiana, B 36 inf., s. c. IX$^{2/4}$: *Kat.*, I 2602).[17] Put together by a team of scribes, it shows a harmonious script with marked fluctuations in the characters between more cursive forms and Caroline, and different abbreviations.

In general, decoration in the manuscripts is limited to initials and to the use of display scripts, in rustic or epigraphic capitals and Uncial. For scholastic books the prevalent format is medium-small, tending to be square in shape and written in long lines. Collections of *Canones* and Bibles, in particular, were written in two columns, often very large books. The Bible was available in various different textual recensions, such as the edition of the Vulgate prepared by Theodulf of Orléans († 821) contained in Vercelli, Archivio e Biblioteca Capitolare, XI (s. IX$^{1-2/4}$, *Kat.*, III 6979), executed by several contrasting hands in the characteristic pale vegetable ink widely used in northern Italy.[18]

An exemplary case of rapid formalization of Caroline script is seen in the episcopal seat of Ivrea between the second and third quarters of the ninth century, during the episcopate of Joseph (*c.*829–62), an arrival from northern France and arch-chaplain of the young Louis II (†875). Besides the presence of transalpine models in the episcopal library, the fundamental impulse came from an able *magister scriptorii*. In preparing a rare *Epitome* of Gregory the Great's *Moralia in Job* (Ivrea, Biblioteca Capitolare, LXV [41]), he increasingly strove to shape the local minuscule to the Franco-Carolingian

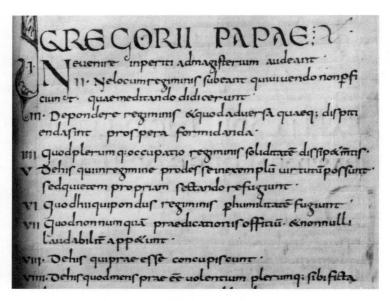

PLATE 17.3 Ivrea, Biblioteca Capitolare, XXI (68), fol. 28r. Gregorius Magnus, *Regula pastoralis*, s. IX, second quarter or middle, Ivrea.

model offered by a manuscript of Saint-Amand, including its runic cryptograms and display scripts. The scribal activity of the *magister*, now brought to perfection, is recognizable in two other scholastic manuscripts containing patristic and computistical texts (Ivrea, Biblioteca Capitolare, XXI [68] and XXXII [3], *Kat.*, III 1559).[19] The localization of the group to Ivrea is confirmed chiefly by the presence of Gregory's *Regula pastoralis* in Ivrea, Biblioteca Capitolare, XXI [68] (Plate 17.3): it is a direct copy of the *Regula pastoralis* written about 680 in Luxeuil minuscule for Bishop Desiderius of Ivrea (Ivrea, Biblioteca Capitolare, I [1]; *CLA* III 300)).

After the middle of the ninth century, in almost all of northern Italy as far as Tuscany, the scribes together consolidated a canon of Caroline minuscule whose general characteristics have been indicated by Petrucci, Bischoff, Cencetti, and Cherubini and Pratesi.[20] Thereafter, a harmonious script becomes established, of medium size and free of contrived, artificial features, with a tendency to separate the words, few abbreviations, progressive elimination of majuscules (though the ligature *NT* remains) and of cursive forms (the ligature for the diphthong *ae* and *e caudata* remain) and ligatures, with the exception of *ct*, *st*, and *&*; open *a* tends to disappear entirely, Semi-uncial *a* remains, sometimes with a flattened top, along with Uncial *a* with a gradual development to an upright shaft, the latter then becoming the sole form in the tenth century; *g* is preponderantly found with the lower bow only open, *m* and *n* elongate the last curved stroke along the line, and then make little serifs to complete the letter. Ascenders become less clubbed and sometimes take on a wedge-shaped form. There are various abbreviations for *bus* and enclitic *que*, with *b* and *q* followed by a middle point, a colon, a semicolon, or a large comma.

The Piedmontese and Lombard centers of Bobbio, Brescia, Milan, Novara, and Tortona produce manuscripts. One that is dated is Claudius of Turin's *Expositio in epistulas ad Corinthios*, commissioned in 862 by Theodulf of Tortona for the monastery of Bobbio (Vatican City, BAV, Vat. lat. 5775 dated to 862, *Kat.*, III 6926). This is the scribal and chronological context in which to place such witnesses to the monastic scriptorium of Bobbio as Augustine, *Enarrationes in Psalmos* (Milan, Biblioteca Ambrosiana, D 547 inf., s. c. IX$^{3/4}$: *Kat.*, II 2617; Plate 17.4) and the interesting contemporary Bible, copied from different exemplars, in which the presence of a *magister scriptorii* is manifest (Milan, Biblioteca Ambrosiana, E 26 inf.: *Kat.*, II 2618). There is notable manuscript production under Abbot Agilulf of Bobbio (887–c.896), with the creation of two different scribal styles. In at least five deluxe copies of patristic and liturgical texts, which are enriched by illuminated initials within panels, the handwriting imitates the Caroline minuscule of Tours with great exactness, only with the ascenders beginning to be wedge-shaped (e.g., Gregory the Great, *Moralia in Job*, Turin, Biblioteca Nazionale Universitaria, F I 6, *Kat.*, III 6293; the *Lectionary*, Milan, Biblioteca Ambrosiana, C 228 inf. or the slightly later *Missal*, Milan, Biblioteca Ambrosiana, D 84 inf., *Kat.*, II 2610 and 2616).[21] The writing is more simple in the unpretentious *Canones* and *Concilia* (Milan, Biblioteca Ambrosiana, M 67 sup. and S 33 sup.: *Kat.*, II 2648 and 2655; Vatican City, BAV, Vat. lat. 5748 and 5749, *Kat.*, III 6906 and 6907).[22]

A mature and settled style of Caroline script was also in use at Milan during the second half of the ninth century, morphologically similar to that of Bobbio:

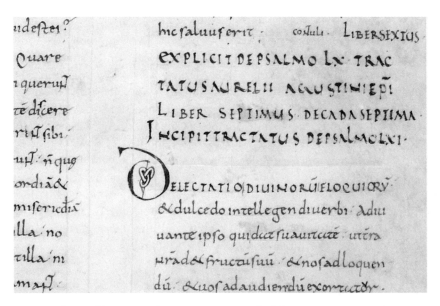

PLATE 17.4 Milan, Biblioteca Ambrosiana, D 547 inf., fol. 95r. Augustinus, *Enarrationes in psalmos*, s. c. IX$^{3/4}$, Bobbio.

well-proportioned letter forms, the *ductus* more or less heavy, and very little sloping of the letters (the shaft of *a* is almost upright); abbreviation *mia* for *misericordia*. It was employed for liturgical books, such as the *Evangelistary* of Busto Arsizio, Biblioteca Capitolare, M.I.14 (s. IX²: *Kat.*, II 2594), and in books for study. In these manuscripts a particular localizing feature is the characteristic *ei* with a horizontal stroke over it (a *titulus*) for *eius*, seen in an Ambrosian *Sacramentary* (Bergamo, Curia Vescovile, Archivio Vescovile, S.N., s. IX²/³: *Kat.*, I 335); in a *Lectionary* (Milan, Biblioteca Ambrosiana, A 28 inf., s. IX³/₃: *Kat.*, II 2594) with a script larger in face for greater legibility, as well as a graphical layout which is recalled, in an archaizing manner, by a *Lectionary* of the following century (Milan, Biblioteca Ambrosiana, C 187 inf., fols. 17r–152r, s. X²: *Kat.*, p. 152); in a patristic manuscript (Milan, Biblioteca Ambrosiana, S 55 sup., s. IX³/₄: *Kat.*, II 2656); and in two copies of Cassiodorus, *Historia tripartita*, which are also tied together textually (Vercelli, Archivio e Biblioteca Capitolare, CI, s. IX²/³ and Milan, Archivio Capitolare della Basilica di S. Ambrogio, M 7, s. IX⁴/₄: *Kat.*, III 6993 and II 2661). Two miscellanies of much the same date were made for the medical school that was perhaps based in the monastery of S. Ambrogio in Milan (Milan, Biblioteca Ambrosiana, G. 108 inf. and Florence, BML, 73.1, s. IX med. or IX³/₄: *Kat.*, II 2620 and I 1238). More emphatic is the *ductus* of Symeon, a monk at S. Ambrogio in the time of Abbot Petrus II (859–99), in the Greco-Latin *Psalter*, Berlin, Staatsbibliothek zu Berlin-Preussischer Kulturbesitz, Hamilton 552 (*Kat.*, I 360).

An overall compactness in the writing, sometimes broken up by features of the system of abbreviation, unites the mature Caroline of the metropolitan territory of Milan. The influence of Frankish models is clear, as at Bobbio and Milan, which use the abbreviation *mia* = *misericordia*. The scriptorium of Novara forms part of this scribal catchment area toward the last third of the ninth century, with production of patristic texts and collections of canons, e.g., Isidore, *Sententiae* (Novara, Biblioteca Capitolare di S. Maria, XLIII [14], s. IX²: *Kat.*, II 3628); there is an interesting collection of *Canones* (Novara, Biblioteca Capitolare di S. Maria, XXX [15], s. IX³/³: *Kat.*, II 3627), which includes a direct copy of the *Collectio canonum Novariensis* in Novara, Biblioteca Capitolare de S. Maria, LXXXIV [2] mentioned in Section 17.1 above; Eusebius-Rufinus, *Historia ecclesiastica* (Novara, Biblioteca Capitolare de S. Maria, LXXVI [13] + the guard leaf of Milan, Biblioteca Trivulziana, 688, about s. IX³/⁴: *Kat.*, II 3633), and Augustine, *Quaestiones* and *Locutiones in Heptateuchum* (Novara, Biblioteca Capitolare de S. Maria, LXXXII [6], s. IX³/³: *Kat.*, II 3634). Some manuscripts presumably written at Monza are also close to the Milanese style of the time: Flavius Josephus, *Antiquitates*, Monza, Biblioteca Capitolare, b-20/136 (*Kat.*, II 2880; Plate 17.5); Ambrosiaster, Monza, c-2/62 (*Kat.*, II 2885); and the *Liber glossarum*, Monza, h-9/164 (*Kat.*, II 2895), a direct copy of Milan, Biblioteca Ambrosiana, B 36 inf. mentioned earlier in this section.

At Brescia, Hildemar of Corbie was active in teaching and monastic reform in the monastery of SS. Faustino e Giovita toward the middle of the ninth century. Caroline models were fully absorbed in the famous *Liber Vitae* of the monastery of S. Salvatore-S. Giulia (Brescia, Biblioteca Civica Queriniana, G VI 7), written by the principal

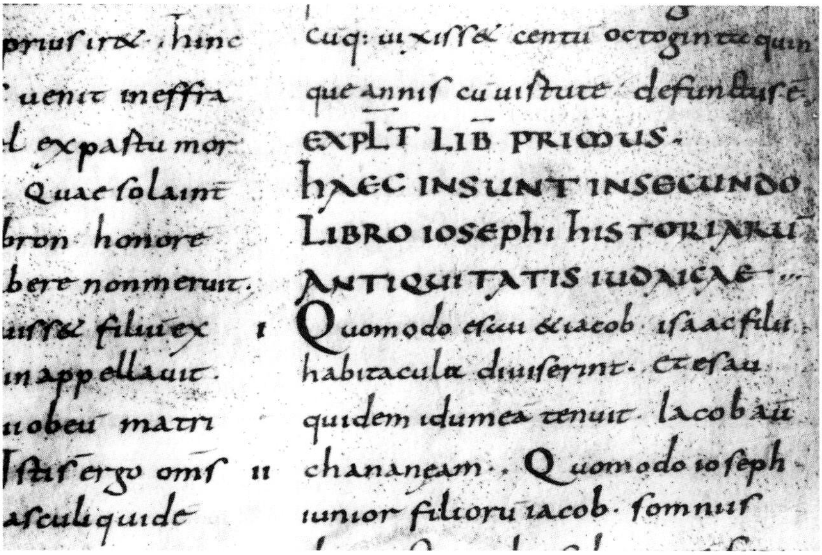

PLATE 17.5 Monza, Biblioteca Capitolare, b-20/136, fol. 27r. Flavius Josephus, *Antiquitates*, s. IX middle, presumably Monza.

copyist about 857 and localizable by the presence in the *Sacramentary* at the end of the local saints Faustinus and Iovita (*Kat.*, I 685). The consolidation of the Caroline canon took place here too in the last third of the ninth century, probably under the influence of Milanese circles. Guided by an able *magister scriptorii*, three large-format books were copied for the cathedral school: Seneca, *Epistulae morales*, Florus of Lyons, *Collectanea in epistulas Pauli*, and Augustine, *De civitate Dei* (Brescia, Biblioteca Queriniana, B II 6, G III 2, G III 3: *Kat.*, I 680, 683, 684). From the middle of the ninth century, numerous manuscripts were copied in northern Italy in this uniform Caroline script with its French influences. Many, however, remain difficult to assign to a precise scriptorium, even if they are preserved in the same chapter libraries which have certainly housed them since the Middle Ages (Ivrea, Novara, Vercelli, Bergamo, Monza, Lucca, and Modena).

Examples of such manuscripts include two copies of Gregory the Great, *Moralia in Job*, I–V (Bergamo, Biblioteca Capitolare, 1046 and Intra, Archivio Capitolare di S. Vittore, 14 [12], s. IX med.: not registered in *Kat.*, I); or an Augustine, *De civitate Dei* (Vercelli, Archivio e Biblioteca Capitolare, LXXI, s. IX$^{4/4}$, *Kat.*, III, p. 461) with display scripts similar to a glossed *Psalter* (Vercelli, Archivio e Biblioteca Capitolare, LXII, fols. 19r–165r, s. IX$^{4/4}$, *Kat.*, III 6986): here the liturgical additions with Vercelli saints (fols. 165v–177v) by a hand different from that of the scribe, but contemporary with it and very similar, perhaps place both manuscripts there.[23]

In the area of Aquileia, two passionaries and a patristic manuscript were written in the last quarter of the ninth century (Graz, Universitätsbibliothek, 412: *Kat.*, I 1456; Cividale del Friuli, Museo Archeologico Nazionale, XXII; *Kat.*, I 925; Paris, BnF, lat. 9531, *Kat.*, III 4597).[24]

The preparation of *Collectiones canonum* for ecclesiastical jurisdictions was a special characteristic of the ninth and tenth centuries. The way they were made is striking. Their shared codicological features seem to indicate that they were all the product of a single center in the metropolitan area of Milan, perhaps connected with Bobbio: several scribes collaborated by dividing up the work into sections, using different styles of Caroline script, often far from calligraphic. These *Collectiones canonum* generally bring together the *Collectio Dionysio-Hadriana*, an ancient Italian compilation, the pseudo-Isidorean *Decretales*, drawn up in France about the middle of the ninth century but here in the shortened form common in northern Italy, and sometimes also rare *excerpta* of Roman law. The scribal community to which they belong is the one in which the same materials were used to compile the *Collectio canonum Anselmo dedicata* for the archbishop of Milan Anselm (882–96), the high point of Lombard canon law. Toward the end of the ninth century examples of this method of compilation are found in Vercelli, Archivio e Bibliteca Capitolare, LXXX (*Kat.*, III 6988); Monza, Biblioteca Capitolare, h-3/151 (*Kat.*, II 2894); Milan, Biblioteca Ambrosiana, G 58 sup. (*Kat.*, II 2635), written at Bobbio and one of the two surviving witnesses of the rare *Excerpta Bobiensia*, the other being the contemporary Livorno, Biblioteca Comunale Labronica F.D. Guerrazzi, Sez. XVI n. 12 (Inv. 476); a little later there are Brescia, Biblioteca Civica Queriniana, B II 13 (s. IX–X, *Kat.*, I 681) and Bamberg, Staatsbibliothek, Can. 5, of the tenth century.[25]

In the tenth century the evidence for book production is drastically reduced. In northwest Italy a uniform Caroline holds sway, still harmonious but more rigid than before, and written in a characteristic ochre ink. The shafts are slightly slanted and of uniform thickness (or they thicken with an oblique wedge at the top), or in less calligraphic contexts the tops of ascenders become claw-shaped, or later, at the end of the tenth century, fully wedge-shaped; *a* is now always Uncial, with a straight shaft, upper bow of *g* tends to close, the minims end in serifs, ligatures are limited to *ct*, *st*, and *&*; in the abbreviation *orum*, the barred 2-shaped *r* following *o* sinks below the line.[26] At Monza at the beginning of the tenth century, there are good examples of regular Caroline script in a portion of the Bible (Books of Solomon, Monza, Biblioteca Capitolare, a-2/4, fols. 136r–261v) or in miscellanies with Isidore and books of computus in Monza, Biblioteca Capitolare, b-10/70 (fols. 1r–77v) and c-9/69.

At Bobbio the first third of the tenth century is particularly distinguished by its liturgical production, with at least six books decorated in the style of Abbot Agilulf, but less richly (e.g., the *Homeliary*, Turin, Biblioteca Nazionale Universitaria, F II 20, the two copies of the *Vita Columbani*, Turin, Biblioteca Nazionale Universitaria, F III 15 and F IV 12).[27] Almost nothing survives from the second half of the tenth century.

At Vercelli, during the episcopate of the Milanese Atto (924–60), four manuscripts stand out. Three make up an elegant liturgical ensemble in which can be seen the most elaborate calligraphic style of the scribes of the *Collectio canonum Anselmo dedicata* (Vercelli, Archivio e Bibliteca Capitolare, XV), which was of Milanese origin and given by Atto himself: the *Orationale-Rituale* (Vercelli, Archivio e Biblioteca Capitolare, CLXXVIII), written at Vercelli between 931 and 947, and two copies of

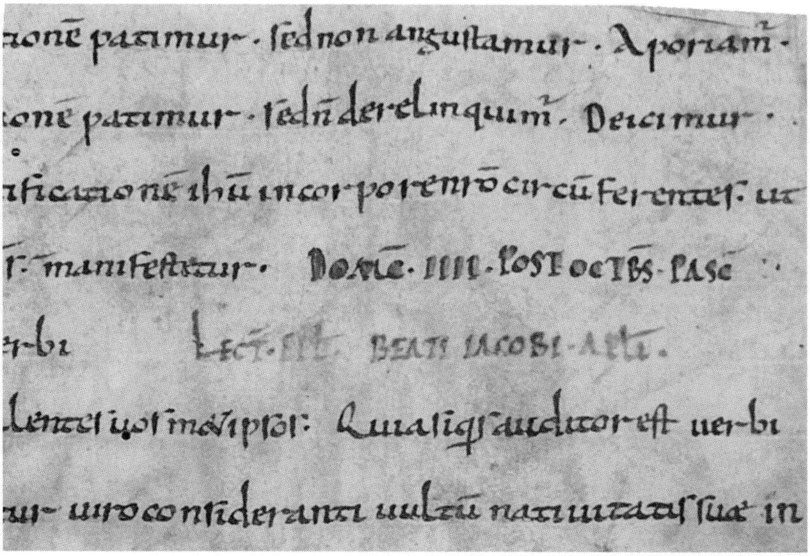

PLATE 17.6 Vercelli, Archivio e Biblioteca Capitolare, CX, fol. 134r. *Lectionary-Evangelistary*, s. X second quarter, Vercelli.

the *Lectionary-Evangelistary* (Vercelli, Archivio e Biblioteca Capitolare, CX [Plate 17.6] and CXV) of the same period, marked by use of the abbreviation *miscdia = misericordia*. The handwriting of the volume with Atto's works, done by Vercellinus and Teutbertus at the author's own request, is more everyday (Vercelli, Archivio e Biblioteca Capitolare, XXXIX).

An awareness of different registers of handwriting, albeit within a stable set of letter forms, is a regular feature of well-organized scriptoria. About the year 1000 the phenomenon is seen again in exemplary form at Ivrea, thanks to the munificent patronage of the bishop Warmund (*c*.969–1005). Its production of liturgical books is unparalleled in Lombardy outside the metropolitan seat at Milan. Finely illustrated with iconographic cycles framed by captions, they culminate in a *Sacramentary* (Ivrea, Biblioteca Capitolare, LXXXVI (31)), and a *Psalter* (Ivrea, LXXXV (30)): the script is a large and solemn upright Caroline, the shafts short with their tips sometimes wedge-shaped, almost devoid of cursive links, with majuscule *S* at the ends of words, and use of majuscule *N*, e.g., in the ligature *NT*. Even under Warmund the writing of manuscripts for study is minute in size and more cursive. The scribal and cultural leadership of an anonymous *magister scriptorii*, an avid reader and annotator, is manifest. He arranged the manufacture of, or personally completed, a handful of classical and patristic manuscripts such as Ivrea, Biblioteca Capitolare, XVI (65), LIII (37), LXX (24), and LXXXVII (54), including out-of-the-way authors like Martial and Optatianus Porphyrius.

ROMAN CAROLINE AND THE
DAWN OF "ROMANESCA"

At Rome specimens of Caroline script were absorbed in a range of different ways, but only from the second half of the ninth century.[28] Perhaps in connection with the papal court, a strain of pure Caroline writing managed to establish itself, though so far witnessed only by two collections of canons (Rome, Biblioteca Vallicelliana, A 5, s. IX², *Kat.*, III 5349, by foreign scribes, and the similar Düsseldorf, Universitätsbibliothek, E 1: *Kat.*, I 1070, of the same period).

The influence of Roman Uncial, bound up with the initial diffusion of the works of Gregory the Great (†604), remained persistently strong, and was a determining factor in the earliest standardization of Caroline script in the area of Rome. Besides the use of majuscule *R M N T* within a word, the terminal forms *NS* and *US*, and a small *u* in the shape of a pointed *v* placed interlinearly between *q* and the following vowel, all letters derive from Uncial. The style of the initial period, as yet not fixed, is attested in a few manuscripts of the last third of the ninth century: Vatican City, BAV, Vat. lat. 4965, *Kat.*, III 6900, a working copy of Anastasius bibliothecarius (815–78), executed under the direction of the author in 870–1, with the *Acta* of the Ecumenical Council of Constantinople; Tours, Bibliothèque municipale, 1027, *Kat.*, III 6148, with the recently finished (873–6) *Vita Gregorii* of John Immonides, copied by Iohannes, priest of S. Peter's (one of the four principal basilicas of Rome); Vatican City, BAV, S. Maria Maggiore 43, *Kat.*, III 6810, a *Regula pastoralis* of Gregory the Great, with a subscription of 'Hermenulfus peccator'; finally Munich, Bayerische Staatsbibliothek, Clm 14008, *Kat.*, III 6810, a *Collectio canonum* to which were added, about 880, glosses in proto-Slavonic.[29]

The "Romanesca" script was to be formalized at a later stage, the oldest witness being a *Homeliary* (Vatican City, BAV, S. Maria Maggiore 104), copied in 938–9 for the female monastery of S. Bibiana.

DOCUMENTS

Caroline in Italy, then, was at first essentially a book hand. Following the tradition of their professions *notarii, iudices*, and *tabelliones* for their part continued to employ the later Roman cursive throughout the ninth and tenth centuries. The occasional Caroline element sporadically appears in these hands. At Asti in Piedmont, a document of 832 has a semi-cursive hand in which open and Semi-uncial *a* alternate (*ChLA²* LVI 2). This uniformity of the notarial cursive, however, is disrupted by a number of documents, concerning in particular the great monasteries and certain bishops, where the intervention of ecclesiastics accustomed to book hands is apparent. In these the turn toward Caroline, with a special preference for Uncial *a*, was more prominent.

The *subscriptiones* of ecclesiastics demonstrate this at Brescia and Novara from the beginning of the ninth century, at Milan from mid-century, and at Novara after 867 (*ChLA²* LVII 2).[30] Entirely in Caroline are, for example, the Bobbio deed of lease of 844 (*ChLA²* LVII 16), the *Abbreviationes* (i.e. fiscal declarations) of 862 and 883 written at the same monastery (*ChLA²* LVII 19, 21), and a document of the same sort, the *Polittico* made for the monastery of S. Salvatore-S. Giulia at Brescia, perhaps about 904 (Milan, Archivio di Stato, Museo Diplomatico, *Capsa* V n° 225).

At Rome, on the other hand, no private documents survive dating from the eighth to the tenth centuries: hence the early medieval Roman notarial script is not attested. Meanwhile, at the papal chancery the *curialis* script remained in use until the eleventh century, a stylized descendant of later Roman cursive attested from 788 and employed by the *scriniarii*, that is, clerics in minor orders.[31]

Notes

1. Bischoff (1990, 108).
2. Cencetti (1993, 129).
3. Palma (1983).
4. Palma (1980); Bischoff (1994, 46).
5. Not registered in *Kat.*, II; see the studies in the facsimile edition, *Leges Salicae Ripuariae* (2008).
6. Bischoff (1994, 45–50).
7. Bassetti and Ciaralli (2005, 99–116).
8. Bischoff (1994, 45, 51, 54).
9. Bischoff (1994, 47–8, 54).
10. Bischoff (1994, 48, 129, 147).
11. Santoni (2009, Plates. III–VI).
12. Bischoff (1994, 45, 48 n. 139).
13. Bischoff (1994, 46–8); Bellettini (2009, Figs. 1–3, Plates. 4–10, 12–13).
14. Bischoff (1994, 5, 50).
15. Gavinelli (2007, 51, 66–7).
16. Gavinelli (2009, 399–400, Plate. 2).
17. Ferrari (1986, 247–50, Plates I–II).
18. Gavinelli (2009, 398).
19. Ferrari (1998, 520–2).
20. Petrucci (1968, 1118); Bischoff (1990, 112–15); Cencetti (1997, 172–9); Cherubini and Pratesi (2010, 397–400).
21. Crivello (2001, Plates I–XL).
22. Gavinelli (2007, 73–4, Plates XXIX–XXXIII).
23. Gavinelli (2009, 401–2, 404 n. 63).
24. Pani (2009, 412–25, Plates I–III); in earlier studies they had been dated to s. IX–X.
25. Gavinelli (2007, 59–78, Plates XXIV–XXVII).
26. Petrucci (1968, 1119–20).
27. Crivello (2001, Plates XLII–LXV).

28. Petrucci and Supino Martini (1978); Supino Martini (2001, 950–3, 961–2); Cherubini and Pratesi (2010, 390, Plate 81).
29. See the complete manuscript at http://daten.digitale-sammlungen.de/~db/0003/bsb00032665/images/, accessed January 4, 2020.
30. Cau (1971–4, 16 n. 29, 35–6, Plates II, Xa); Valsecchi (1995, 316).
31. Radiciotti (1999).

BIBLIOGRAPHY

ChLA² LVI = *Chartae Latinae Antiquiores. Facsimile-Edition of the Latin Charters.* 2nd Series. *Ninth Century*, ed. G. Cavallo and G. Nicolaj, vol. 56, *Italy* 28, *Piemonte* I, *Asti*, ed. G. G. Fissore, Dietikon-Zürich: U. Graf, 2000.

ChLA² LVII = *Chartae Latinae Antiquiores. Facsimile-Edition of the Latin Charters.* 2nd Series. *Ninth Century*, ed. G. Cavallo and G. Nicolaj, vol. 57, *Italy* 29, *Piemonte* II, *Novara, Torino*, ed. G. G. Fissore. Dietikon-Zürich: U. Graf, 2001.

Kat., I, Kat., II, and Kat., III = B. Bischoff, *Katalog der festländischen Handschriften des neunten Jahrhunderts (mit Ausnahme der wisigotischen)*, vol. 1, *Aachen-Lambach*; vol. 2, *Laon-Paderborn*; vol. 3, *Padua-Zwickau*. Wiesbaden: Harrassowitz, 1998–2014.

Bassetti, M. and A. Ciaralli. 2005. "Scritture e libri nella diocesi di Perugia." In *La Chiesa di Perugia nel primo millennio. Atti del Convegno di studi. Perugia, 1–3 aprile 2004,* ed. A. Bartoli Langeli and E. Menestò, 85–149. Spoleto: Centro italiano di studi sull'alto medioevo.

Bellettini, A. 2009. "Testi e scrittura." In *Biografia di un manoscritto. L'Isidoro Malatestiano S. XXI.5,* A. Bellettini, P. Errani, M. Palma, and F. Ronconi, 11–31. Rome: Viella.

Bischoff, B. 1990. *Latin Palaeography,* trans. D. Ó Cróinín and D. Ganz. Cambridge: Cambridge University Press [tranl. of *Paläographie des römischen Altertums und des abendlandischen Mittelalters*. Berlin: E. Schmidt, 1986].

Bischoff, B. 1994. *Manuscripts and Libraries in the Age of Charlemagne.* Cambridge: Cambridge University Press.

Cau, E. 1971–4. "Scrittura e cultura a Novara (secoli VIII–X)." *Ricerche medievali* 6–9: 1–87.

Cencetti, G. 1993. "Postilla nuova a un problema paleografico vecchio: l'origine della minuscola 'carolina'." In *Scritti di paleografia*, ed. G. Nicolaj, 111–34. Dietikon-Zürich: U. Graf [repr. of *Nova Historia* 7 (1955), 1–24].

Cencetti, G. 1997. *Lineamenti di storia della scrittura latina. Dalle lezioni di paleografia (Bologna a.a. 1953–54),* ed. G. Guerrini Ferri. Bologna: Patron.

Cherubini, P. and A. Pratesi. 2010. *Paleografia latina. Storia dell'avventura grafica nel mondo occidentale.* Vatican City: Scuola Vaticana di paleografia diplomatica e archivistica.

Crivello, F. 2001. *La miniatura a Bobbio tra IX e X secolo e i suoi modelli carolingi.* Turin: Allemandi.

Ferrari, M. 1986. "Manoscritti e cultura." In *Milano e i milanesi prima del Mille. Atti del 10° Congresso internazionale di studi sull'alto medioevo (Milano 26–30 settembre 1983),* 241–75. Spoleto: Centro italiano di studi sull'alto medioevo.

Ferrari, M. 1998. "Libri e testi prima del Mille." In *Storia della Chiesa di Ivrea dalle origini al XV secolo,* ed. G. Cracco, 511–33. Rome: Viella.

Gavinelli, S. 2007. "Testi agiografici e collezioni canoniche in età carolingia attraverso codici dell'Ambrosiana." In *Nuove ricerche sui codici in scrittura latina dell'Ambrosiana. Colloquio organizzato dall'Università Cattolica del Sacro Cuore, dalla Biblioteca Ambrosiana, dall'Istituto Centrale per il Catalogo Unico delle biblioteche italiane e per le informazioni bibliografiche, Milano, 6-7 ottobre 2005*, ed. M. Ferrari and M. Navoni, 53-78. Milan: Vita e Pensiero.

Gavinelli, S. 2009. "Transiti di manoscritti attraverso le Alpi occidentali in epoca carolingia: gli episcopati di Ivrea e Vercelli." In *Le Alpi porta d'Europa. Scritture, uomini, idee da Giustiniano al Barbarossa. Atti del Convegno internazionale di studio dell'Associazione italiana dei Paleografi e Diplomatisti. Cividale del Friuli (5-7 ottobre 2006)*, ed. L. Pani and C. Scalon, 381-407. Spoleto: Centro italiano di studi sull'alto medioevo.

Leges Salicae Ripuariae 2008. *Leges Salicae Ripuariae, Longobardorum, Baioariorum, Caroli Magni. Archivio del Capitolo della Cattedrale di Modena, O.I.2. Commentario all'edizione in facsimile*: G. Vigarani, P. Golinelli and G. Z. Zanichelli; *Testi*: G. Nicolaj, Saggio storico-critico. Modena: Il Bulino.

Palma, M. 1980. "L'origine del codice Vaticano del *Liber Diurnus*." *Scrittura e civiltà* 4: 295-310.

Palma, M. 1983. "Alle origini del 'tipo di Nonantola': nuove testimonianze meridionali." *Scrittura e civiltà* 7: 141-9.

Pani, L. 2009. "Transiti di manoscritti attraverso le Alpi orientali in epoca carolingia: il Patriarcato di Aquileia." In *Le Alpi porta d'Europa. Scritture, uomini, idee da Giustiniano al Barbarossa. Atti del Convegno internazionale di studio dell'Associazione italiana dei Paleografi e Diplomatisti. Cividale del Friuli (5-7 ottobre 2006)*, ed. L. Pani and C. Scalon, 409-47. Spoleto: Centro italiano di studi sull'alto medioevo.

Petrucci, A. 1968. "Censimento dei codici dei secoli XI-XII. Istruzioni per la datazione." *Studi medievali* s. III, 9: 1115-26.

Petrucci, A. and P. Supino Martini, 1978. "Materiali ed ipotesi per una storia della cultura scritta nella Roma del IX secolo." *Scrittura e civiltà* 2: 45-101.

Radiciotti, P. 1999. "Attorno alla storia della curiale romana." *Archivio della Società Romana di Storia Patria* 122: 105-23.

Santoni, F. 2009. "Scrivere documenti e scrivere libri a Verona." In *Le Alpi porta d'Europa. Scritture, uomini, idee da Giustiniano al Barbarossa. Atti del Convegno internazionale di studio dell'Associazione italiana dei Paleografi e Diplomatisti. Cividale del Friuli (5-7 ottobre 2006)*, ed. L. Pani and C. Scalon, 173-211. Spoleto: Centro italiano di studi sull'alto medioevo.

Supino Martini, P. 2001. "Aspetti della cultura grafica a Roma fra Gregorio Magno e Gregorio VII." In *Roma nell'Alto Medioevo, [Spoleto], 27 aprile-1 maggio 2000*, vol. 1, 921-68. Spoleto: Centro italiano di studi sull'alto medioevo.

Valsecchi, B. 1995. "La scrittura carolina nei documenti notarili milanesi: proposta e ricezione di un modello (sec. IX-X)." *Aevum* 69: 311-45.

CHAPTER 18

···

LATE CAROLINGIAN
Italy

···

MIRELLA FERRARI

AFTER the year 1000, the number of scriptoria increased and so did the quantity of manuscripts produced; the typologies of the books are more varied, particularly, compared to the earlier period, in areas not tied to religious life. The increase in activity led to modifications taking place more quickly than had been the case in the tenth century, especially from the second half of the eleventh century onward. About the middle of the twelfth century, new types of books from the university milieu introduce pronounced innovations in the layout, added to which toward 1170–80 the handwriting takes on an increasing rigidity: the general appearance is much altered, paving the way for Gothic script. In southern Italy very few centers are of interest for the history of Caroline, and then only for limited periods, since in most of the region and for most of the period Beneventan script was dominant. The local characteristics of the script across the areas of Italy where Caroline was practiced allow distinction of "writing provinces": the Northwest (Piedmont, Lombardy, Emilia; Plate 18.1); the Northeast (the "Tre Venezie": Trentino-Alto Adige, Friuli-Venezia Giulia, and the Veneto proper; Plate 18.2); and the Center. The scripts of the district around Modena and Bologna and in the Romagna are for the most part closer to those of central Italy than to those of the north: in such cases the term North-Central can be used. Within central Italy a distinction is drawn between the scripts of Tuscany (Plate 18.3) and those of the "Umbro-Roman" area.[1] At Rome itself, and in the Umbro-Roman area, two styles of handwriting were employed: one that fits into the general category of Italian Caroline (Plate 18.4), and a stylized script called "Romanesca" or "Farfa-type" (Plate 18.5). The scriptoria of western Piedmont show affinities with those of France, while northeast Italy shares many characteristics with Austrian and Bavarian writing centers. Some monasteries may follow the practice of a distant mother house and diverge from that of their immediate surroundings.

In setting out the elements which may enable one to date the manuscripts, Bischoff cautions against too rigid an application of rules; Petrucci stresses that in the period

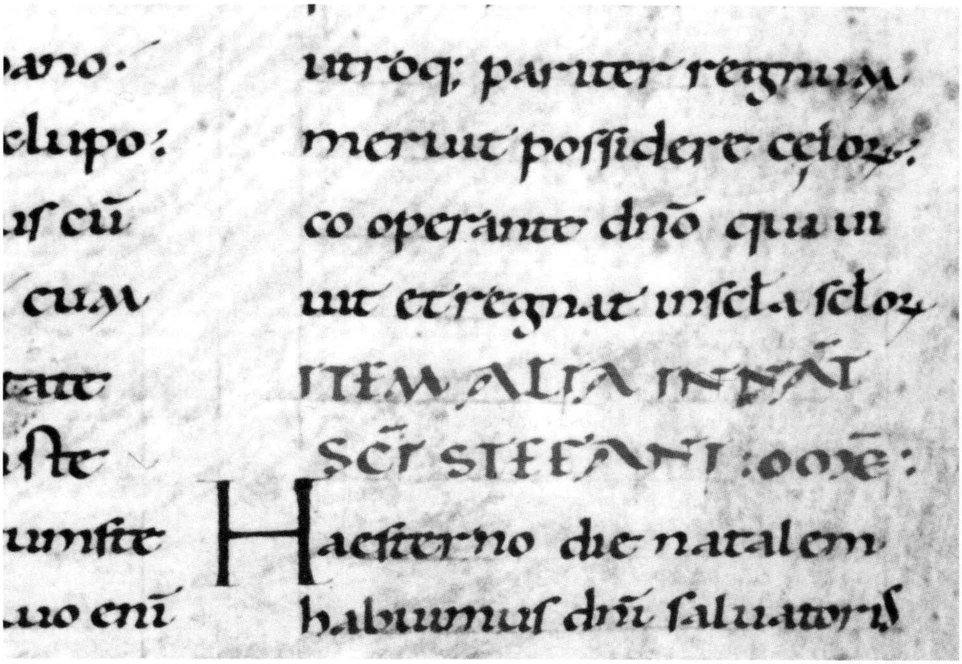

PLATE 18.1 Milan, Archivio della Basilica di S. Ambrogio, M 39, fol. 154r. *Homiliary*, s. XI², Milan.

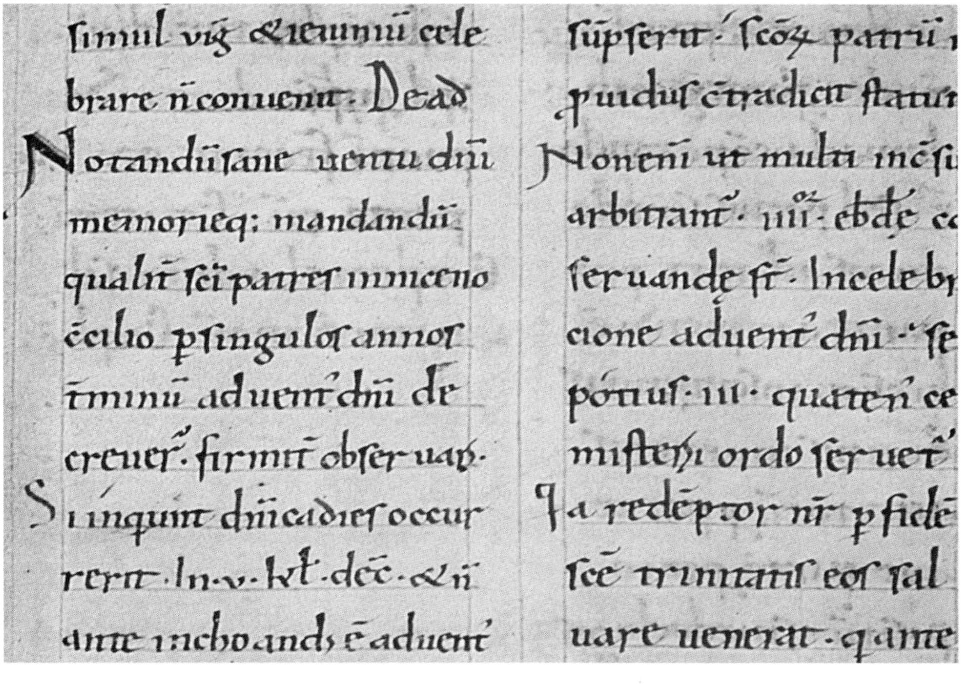

PLATE 18.2 Verona, Biblioteca Capitolare, XCIV (89), fol. 8r. Stephanus cantor, *Carpsum*, s. XI med. or XI ³/⁴, Verona.

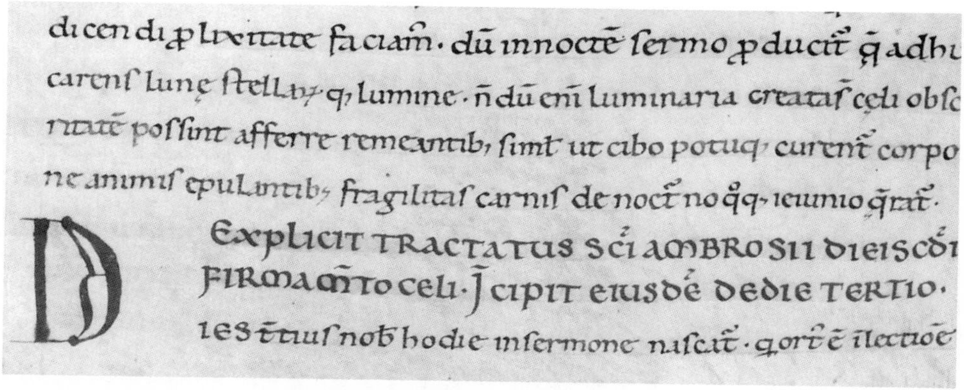

PLATE 18.3 Milan, Biblioteca Ambrosiana, R 82 sup., fol. 18r. Ambrosius, *Exameron*, s. XI ³/³, Vallombrosa.

PLATE 18.4 Milan, Biblioteca Ambrosiana, B 47 inf., fol. 170r, *Giant Bible*, c.1100, Roman area.

970–1050 the distinctions between different classes of books become sharper: luxury books, library books, schoolbooks; and that the grander codices show less advanced graphic features than those found in more workaday manuscripts.[2] The frequency of abbreviations can be a good dating criterion, in that in the course of the two centuries under consideration their use gradually but constantly increased; but it depends on the category of book. In the best liturgical manuscripts between the mid-eleventh and mid-twelfth centuries, for example, abbreviations using interlinear marks are often almost

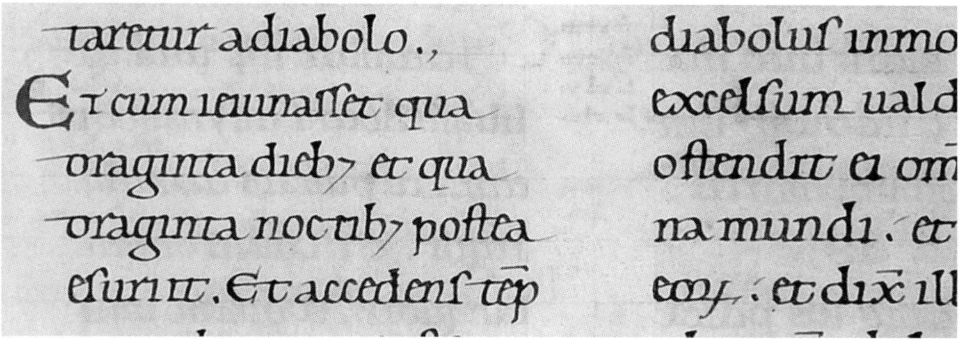

taretur adiabolo.,   diaboluſ inmo
Et cum ieiunaſſet qua   excelſum uald
oraginta diebȝ et qua   oſtendit ei om̄
oraginta noctibȝ poſtea   na mundi. et
eſuriit. Et accedenſ tep   eoɥ: et dix̄ ill

PLATE 18.5 Cesena, Biblioteca Malatestiana, Piana 3.210, fol. 7v. *Evangeliary*, AD 1104, written in "Romanesca" script, Roman area.

entirely absent, except *nomina sacra*; those that involve marks of abbreviation more or less embraced within the height of the minim strokes (e.g., the sign for *orum*) are found sparingly; the interlinear space is preferably reserved for marks of accentuation to help in reading aloud in public, something for which all liturgical books were designed.

Bischoff furnishes criteria for comparing Italian Caroline hands with the European background, and Petrucci gives a list of general characteristics, and I refer the reader to them.[3] Here I give some chronological details specific to Italy and offer some points of distinction between the various regions mentioned above; but these are mere tendencies rather than hard and fast rules.

1000–1110

Ascenders take on a triangular form towards the top; the tops of minims may form small triangles, buttons, or hooks, increasingly so in the second half of the eleventh century.

The dominant form of the letter *d* has a vertical shaft. The two-stroke round form with sloping shaft is frequent in the more everyday and hurried level of script (*currens*), e.g., in drafts of scientific or legal texts; it is rare in more formal script until the third quarter of the eleventh century, but increasingly common thereafter (Fig. 18.1.1). In Romanesca the *d* is flattened (Fig. 18.1.2).

Both bowls of *g* tend to close, a process that was in general complete by the end of the eleventh century; in liturgical manuscripts at Milan the lower bowl remains open until well into the twelfth century; about 1080, in northern Italy especially, there appears a *g* in which the first stroke takes the form of an *s* comprising the left side of the upper bowl and the right of the lower one (Fig. 18.1.3).

Two short strokes begin to be added above double *i* in the second half of the eleventh century.

FIG. 18.1 *c*.1000–1110: *quid, d, g, quia, eos.*

FIG. 18.2 *c*.1000–1110: Different abbreviations for -*que* and -*bus.*

FIG. 18.3 *c*.1110–80: *m,* two different shapes for –*bus, sp.*

The group *or* with the *r* in the form of a 2, within a word, is fairly frequent in the more everyday and documentary hands; in formal handwriting it appears later than elsewhere in Europe, beginning at the end of the eleventh century and becoming widespread only in the twelfth; the same group *or* with 2-shaped *r* and an abbreviating bar through it for terminal -*orum* is, on the other hand, commonplace throughout the period. The use of the *rum* abbreviation after *a* as well takes place sporadically from about the middle of the eleventh century, becoming more frequent in the twelfth.

A majuscule *s* appears first at the end of lines and in the *nomina sacra* (s. XI med.), and then also at the end of words (s. XI²); in certain scriptoria (e.g., Vallombrosa, s. XI³/⁴) a double *s* within a word may occasionally be majuscule. An *s* at the end of a word appears as a sinuous superscript marking in the second half of the eleventh century, a usage that markedly increases in the twelfth.

The diphthong *ae* is rendered either by *e caudata* (*ę*) or by the ligature *æ*, the use of the latter declining from the beginning of the twelfth century.

The ampersand ligature *&* is used both as the conjunction and at word ends; the use of the shorthand sign 7 for *et* makes an intermittent appearance toward the end of the eleventh century, becoming commoner in the following century, when it alternates with both the ampersand and *et* written in full.

Some cursive ligatures are almost canonical in Romanesca but very seldom found elsewhere; *ri* persists in Romanesca and to some degree also in central Italy and the

FIG. 18.4 Romanesca: *a*, *mi*, *n*, *ri* ligature, *ti* ligature, and abbreviation for *-arum*.

Romagna, where it is found till at least 1100 and above all in everyday hands, but also later and in deluxe manuscripts (e.g., Tuscany, s. XII: London, BL, Yates Thompson 40).

There is very occasional use of the Insular *est*, which begins to increase from the second half of the eleventh century onward, when the gradual adoption of the Insular *enim* also begins to appear; from the second half of the eleventh century, the abbreviation for *quia* becomes common (Fig. 18.1.4). The *q* with a bar through the descender for *qui* is in regular use (Fig. 18.1.1).

At the end or in the body of a word a sign in the form of a superscript apostrophe or curled stroke does service for both *s* and the abbreviation *us*:[4] common in everyday and notarial hands throughout Italy during the tenth to the twelfth centuries, it is also used in formal texts only in Romanesca, in central Italy and the Romagna, as far as Nonantola and occasionally at Polirone, at least from the mid-eleventh century till the mid-twelfth (Fig. 18.1.5); it is extremely rare elsewhere.

The abbreviations for *bus* and *que* are expressed by *b* and *q* respectively joined to a sign that evolves from its simplest and most primitive forms (a dot, two dots, 7) into multiple variants: a dot (for *bus* it disappears already from the middle of the eleventh century; for *que* it is in retreat from the second half of the eleventh century, tending to disappear in the twelfth), two dots (disappears around the middle of the eleventh century), a semicolon (particularly used in northern Italy), a small comma or a long rounded comma (especially in central Italy), a sinuous oblique stroke in the form of an *s*, a curved stroke like a reversed *c* (especially in the *littera antiqua* of central Italy and Tuscany), or 7 (especially in central Italy and in particular Rome) (Fig. 18.2.1–6). The same copyist may even use two different forms on the same page, and it is also normal for a scribe to differentiate *bus* from *que* by using different signs after their respective letters.

Ruling is normally done a bifolium at a time on the hair side; ruling two bifolia at a time, old style, is still found in Lombardy around the year 1000, but not after 1020, while in some northeastern centers (e.g., Verona) it continues to 1050 and beyond. In Roman productions of the mid- and late eleventh century, but not always and inconsistently, two bifolia are ruled at a time (predominantly two bifolia at a time, old style, for the horizontal lines only, one at a time on the hair side for the vertical lines). From about 1100–10 it is usual to rule one bifolium at a time, on the hair side.

Full word separation begins to take place after the middle of the eleventh century (later than in other parts of Europe) and is complete by the first quarter of the twelfth century or a little later;[5] in the twelfth century the hyphen starts to come into use.

Around the middle of the eleventh century catchwords appear at the end of gatherings, but the alternative system of marking Roman numerals (less often letters) in the lower margin of the verso of the last leaf continues for a while; use of the catchword becomes general only in the twelfth century.

1110–70/1180

There is a progressive diminution of the space between lines and of the length of ascenders and descenders (except in chancery hands); the thickening of the tops and bottoms of minims becomes very marked.

One finds an increasing (more so in north Italy) use of rubrics for headings in a minuscule like that of the text, except for the red ink of the rubrics. The red tends to be a ruby color rather than the orange that predominated in the preceding centuries. The brown-black ink for the text tends towards a gray-green shade at the end of this period as opposed to the light or dark brown of the earlier period.

In northern Italy opening words tend not to be differentiated from the rest in color or script, except perhaps for a first word of mixed capitals and Uncials in brown ink; a small Uncial for a few words of the incipit continues to be generally used in central Italy; in some parts, especially in the area around Bologna, there develop incipits in alternating red and blue elongated Gothic majuscules.

In central Italy (and Bologna) the *littera antiqua* becomes standardized, large and round, with the last stroke of *m* and *n* spaced out and curved (Fig. 18.3.1). The *littera antiqua* preserves the æ ligature (which tends to disappear elsewhere), alongside the *e caudata*; in the second half of the twelfth century simple *e* prevails.

Use of & becomes very rare (it survives somewhat better in north Italy) in favor of the shorthand sign 7 and *et* in full (the dominant form in *littera antiqua* in particular).

The use of the "Insular" abbreviations for *est* and *enim* increases.

About the middle of the twelfth century, beside the signs long in common use, an apostrophe or curled stroke above the *b*, a form normal north of the Alps, comes into use for the abbreviation *bus*. For *bus* and *que* the forms *b3* and *q3* appear around 1070 (Fig. 18.3.2–3).

The shorthand sign for *con* spreads only after the middle of twelfth century (with some very occasional appearances in the third quarter of the eleventh).

In the last decades of this period, features of Gothic script are found in the more innovative types of texts, principally manuscripts of higher education.

North Italy has a pronounced tendency to develop more vertical and compact writing compared to that of central Italy, which is much larger and rounder, even before the stylization of the *littera antiqua*. In central Italy, the Romanesca, the origins of which are still debated, had a separate development, but the criteria for dating it are essentially the same as for Caroline script: it is found fully formed a little before 1000 and continues as far as the middle of the twelfth century (Plate 18.5). Its distinguishing marks are a flattening of the round letters, the development of horizontal linkage between letters, a slope to the right; long final strokes of *a*, *m*, *n*; *i* with little horizontal strokes at top and bottom (Fig. 18.4.1–3); *d* for the most part in round form, flattened (Fig. 18.1.2); *g* with upper bowl flattened and the lower sometimes opened in a flourish when it is on the bottom line; *r* sloping, the shoulder stroke wavy; majuscule forms of *N, R* occasionally appear. The majuscule round *s* appears earlier than that in Italian Caroline: at least as early as the beginning of the eleventh century at line endings and a little later at the end of words; the cursive ligatures *ri* (Fig. 18.4.4) and *rt* are kept, and in smaller measure also *mi, ni, rm,* and *rn*; exceptionally *ti* in the shape of an 8 sinks below the line to indicate the assibilated pronunciation (Fig. 18.4.5). Occasionally, one finds an *m* in the form of a superscript 3, typical of Beneventan. Characteristic is the abbreviation for *arum* made up of the letter *a* alone with the second stroke barred (Fig. 18.4.6). Romanesca was practiced at Rome, where scriptoria are attested in the great basilicas (the Lateran, St Peter's, S. Maria Maggiore, S. Paolo), in Latium south of Rome, as far as Velletri and S. Scolastica at Subiaco, on the border with Beneventan, and to the north as far as Umbria, in the monasteries of Farfa and S. Eutizio in Val Castoriana near Norcia.[6]

Central Italy is also notable for producing a particular sort of book: giant Bibles ("*Bibbie atlantiche*"), which have been much studied in the last fifty years (Plate 18.4).[7] These Bibles are connected with the birth of the movement to reform the Church and apparently date from the reign of Leo IX but certainly by the third quarter of the eleventh century, above all under Gregory VII. They were produced at Rome in a Caroline script that Bischoff called "reformed"[8] and are to be connected with the birth of the movement to reform the Church. We continue to localize them as Umbro-Roman, even if it is now believed that they were made in the city itself. At Rome, Caroline was not in fact the dominant script (though it should be remembered that under the German pope Leo IX a script based on Caroline had been introduced in the documents of the papal chancery);[9] the models seem to have been the transalpine Bibles of the ninth century that were then present in Rome, the Bible of S. Paolo fuori le Mura for example. Copied by numerous scribes who usually divided the text into sections and made their stints coincide both with quire ends and the ends of the biblical books, they are characterized by their large format, about 550/650 × 360/380 mm, in two columns of some 50–9 lines. The decoration—and often the illustration too—is very important; the highly uniform and stylized handwriting tends to lean to the right; common use of the abbreviations *b7, q7,* and tall *s*, with the top part flat rather than rounded (Fig. 18.3.4); round *d* and majuscule *s* at word ends occur sporadically. Generally disposed in two volumes, they provide evidence of major production for large-scale export throughout Europe in the eleventh and twelfth centuries, just as with the Bibles of Alcuin, but in much greater numbers. Manufacture of the Bibles went on alongside production of patristic texts, likewise in large format and very similar in layout. Copies of such texts are found scattered throughout virtually all the monastic and chapter libraries of Italy, from the Alps to the Beneventan area, for example in the cathedrals of Novara (Novara, Biblioteca Capitolare, IX [23]), Milan (Milan, Biblioteca Ambrosiana, E 45 inf.), and Troia in Apulia (a group of manuscripts, s. XII[1]).[10] From about the beginning of the twelfth century, giant Bibles modeled on the Roman ones were being written in Tuscany in *littera antiqua* (e.g., Florence, BML, Edili 125–6; Conv. Soppr. 630, dated 1140); these too were exported in large numbers to northern Italy. The imported giant Bibles sometimes generated imitations, as in the handsome Bibles of Modena cathedral (Modena, Biblioteca Capitolare, O.III.1; O.III.2, s. XII med.). At times the imitation is so close that the distinction between model and copy is difficult to draw.

In northern Italy, on the other hand, many local Bibles were produced in which the format and *mise-en-page*, the *titulationes* and style of the capitals of the major headings may variously derive from those of central Italy, but not the other features (e.g., Intra, Biblioteca Capitolare di S. Vittore, 15, s. XII in.; Udine, Archivio di Stato, fragm. 58, fragm. 163, fragm. 237, all three of s. XII^1;[11] Piacenza, Biblioteca Capitolare, 68 and 69, s. XII$^{4/4}$); there are, in contrast, Bibles in a large, but not giant format and wholly local in style, such as those from the cathedral of Milan (Milan, Biblioteca Ambrosiana, A 263 inf., s. XI^2), the monastery of Leno (Brescia, Biblioteca Queriniana, A. I. 11, s. XI med.), and Brescia cathedral (Brescia, Biblioteca Queriniana, G.III.1, s. XI^2; A.II.8, s. XII med.). It is noteworthy that in this period there is no production of Bibles in either Romanesca or Beneventan. The direct influence of central Italian styles on northern Italy through these Bibles is enormous; yet the influence of Rome and the rest of central Italy took other routes as well.

Matilda of Canossa, countess of Tuscany (1046–1115) was a supporter of the papacy and a great promoter of the cultural currents connected with the reform of the Church. She was the protectress of the jurist Irnerius and of the canonist Anselm, bishop of Lucca; many books came from Rome to the Po valley in these years. Anselm represented the cultural bridge between Tuscany and the Po valley. A number of churches and monasteries gravitated into Matilda's orbit. The principal one was S. Benedetto di Polirone (near Mantua), the library with the greatest number of surviving eleventh- and twelfth-century manuscripts in north Italy, more than 100, and many of those were certainly produced by the monastic scriptorium there. Polirone was open to many foreign influences, as can be seen in its miniatures; as far as its script is concerned, it was rooted in the traditions of Lombardy but with Tuscan influences.

The influence of Tuscany on Italy as a whole was greatly enhanced by the spread of the Vallombrosan order. It had had a very active scriptorium in the mother house from the mid-eleventh century, but from the early decades of the twelfth the order expanded, with foundations from the Alps to the sea: volumes were written at Vallombrosa for the use of its dependent houses.[12] Vallombrosan production did not involve very high-quality manuscripts, nor did it have a uniform style (Plate 18.3); the books are predominantly medium-small in format, written in long lines, with headings often in minuscule already in the eleventh century; the abbreviations *q7*, and *b*, *n*, and *m* followed by wavy lines for *bus*, *nus*, and *mus* are common.

Imitation of the central Italian style penetrated into some of the mid-Po valley scriptoria: for example, the cathedral of Modena from the middle of the twelfth century, and Cremona from the third quarter of the century for more than 50 years (e.g., Cremona, Biblioteca Statale, Gov. 115; Cremona, Archivio di Stato, Fr. Com. 2 [ex 217]: s. XII$^{3/4}$).[13]

Compared with the situation 40 years ago, the number of known manuscript witnesses has radically increased with the identification and cataloguing of fragments preserved as pastedowns or (much more commonly) archive bindings. These have allowed us to reconstruct the activities of scriptoria of which scarcely a single manuscript has survived entire. There was a very large number of scriptoria, some of which were already active in earlier centuries: those of the important cathedrals, the greater palaeo-Christian churches, monasteries of Lombard or Carolingian foundation. To these may be added the numerous monasteries of recent origin, erected in the eleventh century (e.g., the group connected with Fruttuaria in Piedmont, initially closely tied to France), cathedrals of new episcopal seats or of small towns, and collegiate churches.[14] Liturgical manuscripts are those most easily traced back to a particular scriptorium, since the text nearly always shows local elements (feasts, saints): it was on the basis of the names of saints that Garrison made progress in such localizations. The greatest range in the development of locally distinctive traditions is found in musical manuscripts, whose systematic production in Italy began in the eleventh century; musical notations with their own distinctive and localized character are very numerous.[15]

Rooted in the scribal traditions of north Italy but heavily influenced by both Swiss and French models, Aosta produced manuscripts in the eleventh century at the cathedral and in the collegiate church of Saint-Ours. From Piedmont there survive manuscripts written in the ancient abbey of Novalesa and in a circle of minor centers, monastic and collegiate.[16] Robust and individual scriptoria, already famous in the pre-Carolingian period, were in the cathedrals of Ivrea (at least 17 manuscripts were written in Caroline at Ivrea in the eleventh and twelfth centuries), Vercelli, and Novara (at least 15 manuscripts); at Novara a numerical check is afforded by an inventory of 1175 with a score of liturgical manuscripts and some 60 books in the library *armarium*.[17] In Lombardy Brescia stands out, with its cathedral, churches, and monasteries, as does Monza. Milan develops its own peculiar characteristics, finding itself in some degree isolated because of its different liturgy (the Ambrosian rite), which hindered the circulation and use of liturgical books written elsewhere: the color of its ink, for example, is fairly characteristic, a reddish ochre. In the eleventh century a series of Ambrosian sacramentaries was made there, some modest, others deluxe items such as the Sacramentary of S. Satiro (Milan, Biblioteca del Capitolo Metropolitano, II. D.3.2, ante 1045).

In Emilia and Romagna there are flourishing centers of production in the cathedrals at Piacenza, Parma, Reggio, Modena, Ravenna, Rimini, and in the monasteries, including Bobbio, which at this time no longer has the central importance it had in the early Middle Ages, and which from its early connections with Pavia moved in the course of the twelfth century to a closer affinity with the centers and style of Emilia. Nonantola, on the other hand, was greatly reinvigorated under the abbot Rodulfus (r. 1002–35), who is credited with having commissioned 39 manuscripts, of which 11 have been identified. The letter of the cleric Heinricus tells us of the activities of the abbot of

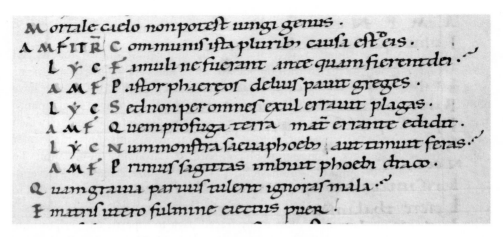

PLATE 18.6 Florence, BML, 37.13, fol. 8r. Seneca, *Tragoediae*, s. XI ex. (ante 1093), Pomposa.

Pomposa, Hyeronimus, in enriching the library between 1078 and 1093 with more than 60 manuscripts, of which at least five are extant. Important, and unusual, is the presence at Pomposa of classical manuscripts, not treated as modest objects of study but as decorous books for the library. From Pomposa, a Seneca survives (Florence, BML, 37.13, Plate 18.6), outwardly extremely similar to an Augustine (Oxford, Bodleian Library, Canon. Pat. lat.134).

In Tuscany, Pisa and Lucca, and, in the twelfth century, Florence are particularly important for their high levels of output and for illumination. The monastery of S. Salvatore at Monte Amiata was very active in the eleventh century.

In northeast Italy, the production of Verona seems scanty in comparison to its extraordinary Carolingian antecedents, but, as in that period, it continues to maintain contact with, and so receive influence from, the German lands (Plate 18.2). In nearby Padua it is difficult to identify local products with assurance before the *Evangelistarium* copied by Ysidorus in 1170 (Padua, Biblioteca Capitolare, E.1). There is good production in the Trentino and Friuli, in both cases characterized by strong influence from neighboring German areas, so much so that there is still debate as to whether a fine group of manuscripts from the abbey of S. Gallo of Moggio is local work or an import from Hirsau, from which Moggio was founded. In the twelfth century, the patriarchal scriptorium of Cividale and the district of Aquileia show connections with German lands, but also with the Slavic and Adriatic regions. There are two highly interesting Passionaries in the cathedral of Cividale (mss. XXII and XXIII, s. XII [2/4]), written by 16 and 13 scribes respectively, with perhaps only two hands shared between the two manuscripts, which seem to be the fruit of a scholastic exercise. Modest in their aesthetic level, they yet bear witness to the organization of a school, doubtless the capitular school; and many of the hands seem almost German.[18]

Classical texts and grammars used in the schools are not in general assignable to recognizable scriptoria, which up to the twelfth century are very largely tied to ecclesiastical institutions. Like the schoolbooks, law books cannot be traced to institutional

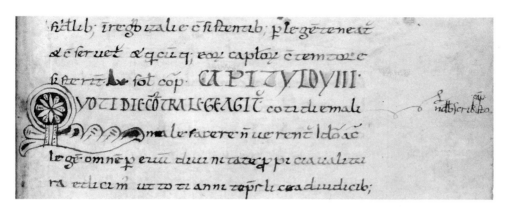

PLATE 18.7 Milan, Biblioteca Ambrosiana, O 55 sup., fol. 34r, *Leges Longobardorum*, c.1019–24, presumably Pavia.

scriptoria: they are more difficult to localize because, unlike liturgical texts, they lack useful internal information, and then again because they belonged to people (teachers, notaries, and judges) whose professional activities made them itinerant. It is also the case that the same educational texts were used all over Europe, and those for learning the law were beginning to have success on a vast scale. They therefore circulated widely and were less open to adopting local styles. The scripts of these texts are on a lower level and rather personal, and not uniform. In the context of the *palatium* (the seat of administration originally at Pavia, then itinerant) and on their travels around the courts of Italy, notaries and judges—laymen and professionals, used to writing documents—studied the law as they had for centuries. Notaries and judges produced manuscripts which were of medium to small size and portable, modest in appearance, and probably made by themselves, and written in a book hand with separate and basically uniform letters, but very everyday and rapid, full of abbreviations and of certain features derived from documents: already at the beginning of the eleventh century round *d* and the group *or* with 2-shaped *r* sometimes appear (Milan, Biblioteca Ambrosiana, O 53 sup., and O 55 sup., written presumably at Pavia, c.1019–24, Plate 18.7). The study of the law took place at Pavia but also in the area of Rome (e.g., Bamberg, Staatsbibliothek, Iur. 1, s. XI in.) and in the north-central region between eastern Tuscany, Perugia, and Emilia-Romagna (e.g., London, BL, Add. 5411, s. XI[2], with almost contemporary glosses in a small *currens* hand). The role of Bologna, so impressive at the height of the twelfth century, is before that date very unclear.[19] The handwriting of juridical texts, and especially of their glosses, represents the most developed and advanced stage of the script of the age.

The intensive textual study of law in the course of the eleventh century (the "juristic revival") also led judges and notaries to give themselves a good grammatical foundation. As well as learning the trade "on the job," from father to son, they now frequented the grammar school, perhaps attached to the cathedral, where, according to the most plausible theory, they learned and consequently adopted a script different from the minuscule cursive hitherto used in documents (the "later Roman cursive"). In this way

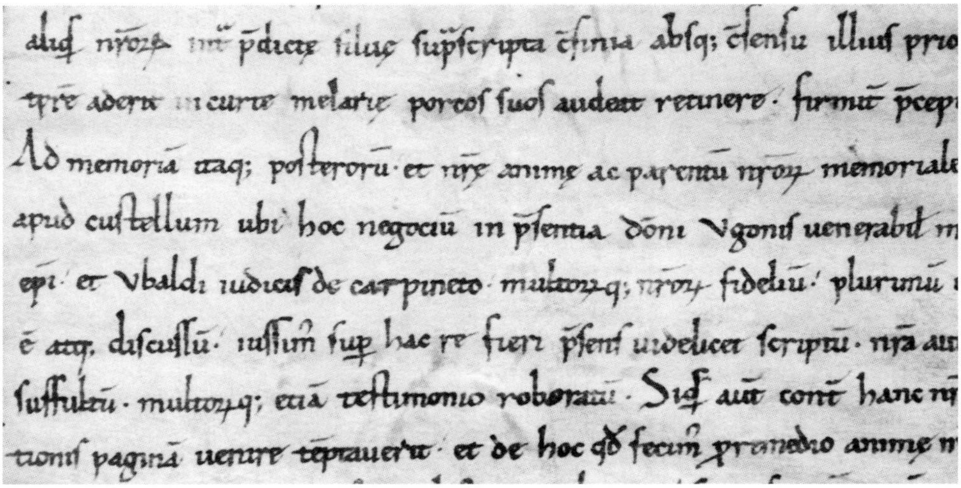

PLATE 18.8 Milan, Istituto Toniolo–Università Cattolica del S. Cuore, Biblioteca Negri da Oleggio, Matildina. Notification by Matilda of Tuscany, AD 1106 January 9, Quistello (near Mantua).

the script of the schools, Caroline minuscule, began to spread even into private documents. In its new documentary role Caroline underwent some adaptation: shafts a little more extended than in books, a general use of the round *d* with a long sloping shaft, and the persistence for some decades of a number of peculiar cursive ligatures and abbreviations. The spread of this Caroline in the hands of notaries, which makes the scripts of documents and books similar and—with all due caution—comparable, can help to date and localize the manuscripts. The handwriting of the imperial chancery (the "diplomatic minuscule") had been for a long time based on Caroline, with some features peculiar to the chancery style, such as long and curled ascenders, flourishing in the ligatures *ct* and *st*. In eleventh-century Italy this script was imitated to give documents a solemn appearance; so it was in the Pavia chancery of the kings of Italy, in the chancery of the Canossa (Plate 18.8), in the episcopal documents of various cities. As had happened sporadically well before 1000, a Caroline book hand continued to be used in some episcopal and monastic documents, probably written by ecclesiastics accustomed to copying out manuscripts. A general change happened at the hands of practitioners dealing with legal documentation. The chronology of this change differs a good deal in different parts of Italy, as between cities, between the city and the countryside, even according to the notaries' membership of progressive or more traditional social groups, depending in turn on their relationship with the bishop or the local political authorities and the social prestige they had managed to acquire. At Pavia and Milan, in the documents of the *iudices sacri palatii*, the change had already taken place in the opening decades of the eleventh century.[20]

The case of Genoa is emblematic, where the development of the maritime republic and the growth of trade hugely increased the demand for notarial deeds. The work of the notaries increased along with their importance; their handwriting came to be based on a good Caroline script only toward the end of the eleventh century, but it then evolved with great rapidity; soon after the middle of the twelfth century there arose both a new system of documentation (the *imbreviature*) and a new style, a quick and cursive hand of a Gothic type (API, II, 83–6; XI, 11; XII, 35–46). At Arezzo, Caroline had already begun to be employed by 1001 and the process was complete by the third decade of the century;[21] it is known at Pistoia in the second half of the eleventh century. In some cities of north Italy, the change takes place around the year 1000. At Nonantola, Caroline script is already in use at the beginning of the eleventh century. At Milan, the passage from cursive to notarial Caroline begins to take effect in private documents shortly after the beginning of the eleventh century and concludes about 1050; at Verona, it happens at the end of the eleventh century (API, III, 9–12, 18–21, 27, 31–3); at Bologna, the process gets under way in the 1070s and concludes in the third decade of the twelfth century (API, XII, 16–34; XIII, 17–18, 20, 22, 24–6). At Ravenna and the Romagna, the traditional cursive survives much longer than in any other part of Italy, right up to the end of the twelfth century (API, I, 27–33, 41–6, 50; III, 46, 58–64, 83; VII, 11–19, 45–8, 61, 67–71, 84–5; XIII, 19, 21, 23).

In the papal chancery, the old Roman "curialis" was employed until the middle of the eleventh century; the chancery script based on Caroline minuscule ("diplomatic minuscule") takes root during the pontificate of Leo IX (1048–54), but does not supplant the "curialis," which remains in use as an alternative script until the pontificate of Pasquale II (1099–1117) (API, VI, 1–8, 11–12); the practice in private documents of the Roman notaries falls into line after some delay (API, II, 2, 16–17, 20–4, 71–2; VI, 56–76, 80–8).

In the south, in Beneventan territory, there was little room for diplomatic minuscule or chancery script based on Caroline. Alien to the tradition of *Longobardia minor* are the documents of the Norman counts of Italy (in Sicily and the south), and later of the royal chancery of Roger II: from at least 1065, by virtue of political choice and the link to the land of their origin, the Normans use the script and style of northern France. The highly polished chancery script based on Caroline in the royal documents (API, III, 45; XIV, 1–12, 18–19, 27–38) finds an echo, later and in a limited but deliberate manner, in the adoption of "Norman" Caroline in the *Liber capituli* of the abbey founded by them at SS. Trinità of Venosa in Apulia (Montecassino, Archivio e Biblioteca dell'Abbazia, 334, dating from 1154–6), in some manuscripts of the abbey of Cava, and in various very beautiful and luxurious products made in Sicily from about the middle of the twelfth century (before 1153: London, BL, Harley 5786, a trilingual Psalter in Greek, Latin, and Arabic; c.1154–60: Paris, BnF, Nouv. acq. lat. 1772); this Caroline is directly related to northern French models. In the Norman kingdom, strong links with France were also kept up by Cistercian foundations, where, however, scriptoria only begin to show signs of life (and not many) toward the end of the twelfth century. The activities of the Cistercians in the north and center of Italy (Staffarda, Morimondo, Casamari) were much more energetic and influential: they produced a notable series of manuscripts in faithful adherence to the models of their mother houses. Cistercian manuscripts, and parallel to them those of the glossed Paris Bible, brought a strong French influence into Italy in the third quarter of the twelfth century.

NOTES

1. These two regions were distinguished by Garrison (1953–62).
2. Bischoff (1990, 121); Petrucci (1968, 1116, 1120).
3. Petrucci (1968); Bischoff (1990, 119–30, esp. 125–6, 129–30); Battelli (1999, 176–84); Cherubini-Pratesi (2010, 397–403).
4. Vezin (1967, 17–18).
5. Saenger (1993).
6. Supino Martini (1987).
7. Maniaci (2000).
8. Bischoff (1990, 126).
9. Cherubini-Pratesi (2010, 408 n. 12); API, VI, 4-5.
10. Maniaci (2000, 87–90).
11. Scalon (1987, 138–9, 222–3, 270–1).
12. Frioli (1999).
13. Cremona (2007, 133–7).
14. An excellent bibliography on Italian scriptoria, region by region, even if selective and designed in the first place for the study of illumination, is given by Augustyn (2007); later works: Gavinelli (2007); Scappaticci (2008); Zanichelli (2008). Other bibliography, of a strictly palaeographical character, is found in Cherubini-Pratesi (2010).
15. Baroffio (2003), (2006), (2009).
16. Segre Montel (1994).
17. A survey of surviving inventories of Italian libraries in Nebbiai Dalla Guarda (2001); copious notices in Fiesoli and Somigli (2009–).
18. Scalon (1998, 139–43).
19. Nicolaj (2005); Radding (2007).
20. Petrucci (1989, 35–7).
21. Nicolaj (1986); on the episcopal documents, see API, XIII, 33–46.

BIBLIOGRAPHY

API = *Archivio Paleografico italiano*, vol. I–XIV, fasc. 1–75. 1882–1984. Rome: Istituto di Paleografia dell'Università di Roma.

Augustyn, W. 2007. "Italien." In *Geschichte der Buchkultur*, vol. 4/2: *Romanik*, ed. A. Fingernagel, 9–79, 379–80. Graz: Akademische Druck und Verlaganstalt.

Baroffio, G. 2003. "La vita musicale a Nonantola." In *Lo splendore riconquistato: Nonantola nei secoli XI e XII*, ed. M. Parente and L. Piccinini, 63–98. Modena: Panini.

Baroffio, G. 2006. "Manoscritti liturgici e musicali a Novalesa e in Italia nord-occidentale." In *Carlo Magno e le Alpi. Viaggio al centro del medioevo*, ed. F. Crivello and C. Segre Montel, 187–235. Milan: Skira.

Baroffio, G. 2009. "Notazioni neumatiche (secoli IX–XIII) nell'Italia settentrionale: inventario sommario", *Aevum* 83: 529–79.

Battelli, G. 1999. *Lezioni di paleografia*, 4th ed. Vatican City: Libreria Editrice Vaticana.

Bischoff, B. 1990. *Latin Palaeography*, transl. D. Ó Cróinín and D. Ganz, Cambridge: Cambridge University Press [trans. of *Paläographie des römischen Altertums und des abendländischen Mittelalters*. Berlin: E. Schmidt, 1986].

Cherubini, P. and A. Pratesi. 2010. *Paleografia latina. Storia dell'avventura grafica nel mondo occidentale*. Vatican City: Scuola Vaticana di paleografia, diplomatica e archivistica.

Cremona. 2007. *Cremona, una cattedrale, una città: la Cattedrale di Cremona al centro della vita culturale, politica ed economica dal Medio Evo all'Età Moderna. Mostra documentaria*. Milan: Skira.

Fiesoli, G. and E. Somigli (eds.). 2009–. *RICABIM: Repertorio di inventari e cataloghi di biblioteche medievali dal secolo VI al 1520/Repertory of Inventories and Catalogues of Medieval Libraries from the VIth Century to 1520*, vol. I–. Florence: SISMEL/Edizioni del Galluzzo

Frioli, D. 1999. "Lo scriptorium e la biblioteca di Vallombrosa." In *L'Ordo Vallisumbrosae tra XII e XIII secolo. Gli sviluppi istituzionali e culturali e l'espansione geografica (1101–1293)*, ed. C. Monzio Compagnoni, 505–68. Vallombrosa, Ed. Vallombrosa.

Garrison, E. B. 1953–62. *Studies in the History of Mediaeval Italian Painting*. vols. I–IV. Florence: L'Impronta [repr. London: Pindar Press, 1993].

Gavinelli, S. 2007. "Cultura e scrittura a Brescia in età romanica." In *Società bresciana e sviluppi del romanico (XI-XIII secolo)*, ed. G. Andenna, 31–83. Milan: Vita e pensiero.

Maniaci, M. and G. Orofino. 2000. *Le Bibbie atlantiche: Il libro delle Scritture tra monumentalità e rappresentazione*. Milan: Centro Tibaldi.

Nebbiai Dalla Guarda, D. 2001. "Bibliothèques en Italie jusqu'au XIIIe siècle. État des sources et premières recherches." In *Libri, lettori e biblioteche dell'Italia medievale (secoli IX–XV). Fonti, testi utilizzazione del libro: Atti della tavola rotonda italo-francese (Roma 7–8 marzo 1997)*, ed. G. Lombardi and D. Nebbiai Dalla Guarda, 7–129. Rome and Paris: ICCU–CNRS.

Nicolaj, G. 1986. "Alle origini della minuscola notarile italiana e dei suoi caratteri storici." *Scrittura e civiltà* 10: 49–82.

Nicolaj, G. 2005. "Documenti e 'libri legales' a Ravenna: rilettura di un mosaico leggendario." In *Ravenna da capitale imperiale a capitale esarcale: Atti dell'XVII Congresso internazionale di studio sull'Alto Medioevo, Ravenna 6–12 giugno 2004*, 761–99. Spoleto: Cisam.

Petrucci, A. 1968. "Censimento dei codici dei secoli XI–XII, Istruzioni per la datazione." *Studi medievali* s. III, 9: 1115–26.

Petrucci, A. and C. Romeo. 1989. "Scrivere 'in iudicio.' Modi, soggetti e funzioni di scrittura nei placiti del 'Regnum Italiae' (secc. IX–XI)," *Scrittura e civiltà* 13: 5–48 [repr. in "*Scriptores in urbibus.*" *Alfabetismo e cultura scritta nell'Italia altomedievale*, 195–236. Bologna: Il Mulino, 1992].

Radding, C. M. and A. Ciaralli. 2007. *The Corpus iuris civilis in the Middle Ages. Manuscripts and Transmission from the Sixth Century to the Juristic Revival*. Leiden: Brill.

Saenger, P. 1993. "The Separation of Words in Italy." *Scrittura e civiltà* 17: 5–41.

Scalon, C. 1987. *Libri, scuole e cultura nel Friuli medievale. "Membra disiecta" dell'Archivio di Stato di Udine*. Medioevo e umanesimo 65. Padua: Antenore.

Scalon, C. and L. Pani. 1998. *I codici della Biblioteca Capitolare di Cividale del Friuli*. Florence: SISMEL.

Scappaticci, L. 2008. *Codici e liturgia a Bobbio: testi, musica e scrittura (secoli X ex.–XII)*. Vatican City: Libreria Editrice Vaticana.

Segre Montel, C., S. Castronovo, and A. Quazza. 1994. "La miniatura." In *Piemonte romanico*, ed. G. Romano, 286–392. Turin: CRT.

Supino Martini, P. 1987. *Roma e l'area grafica romanesca (sec. X-XII)*. Alessandria: Dell'Orso.

Vezin, J. 1967. "Observations sur l'emploie des réclames dans les manuscrits latins." *Bibliothèque de l'École des Chartes* 125: 5–33.

Zanichelli, G. Z. 2008. "Biblioteche e *scriptoria* a Reggio Emilia in età medievale: la strategia della memoria." In *Matilde e il tesoro dei Canossa: tra castelli, monasteri e città*, ed. A. Calzona, 68–83 and descriptions of manuscripts. Milan: Silvana.

CHAPTER 19

....

TIRONIAN NOTES

....

DAVID GANZ

ACCORDING to a tradition recorded by Isidore, Latin shorthand was developed by Marcus Tullius Tiro, the slave (freed in 53 BCE) and secretary of Cicero. Shorthand was mentioned by Manilius, who was writing before AD 22 (*Astronomica*, 4.197–9); and Martial also praises a *notarius* (*Epigrammata*, 14.208). In Late Antiquity shorthand was used by imperial and ecclesiastical bureaucracies for the transcription of speeches, sermons, and the proceedings of church councils; and a lexicon of some 13,000 signs was assembled, the *Commentarium notarum Tironianum*, which has survived in 15 Carolingian manuscripts (see Plate 19.1). It gives signs for the names of Roman emperors (ending with Antoninus Pius), lists of cities and provinces, and much pagan religious terminology. But there are also signs for *episcopus, papa, diaconus, monasterium, abba*, and many biblical names. It includes important descriptions of some of the signs *pressum, acutum*, (tapering), *volutum* (rounded), *longum, latum*, and *excussum*. In the ninth century, Heiric of Auxerre used shorthand to record the teachings of Lupus of Ferrières, and Abbot Hilduin of Saint-Denis dictated to secretaries.

Seven psalters in Tironian notes have survived. Other complete texts are the *Rule of Chrodegang* (Leiden, Bibliotheek der Rijksuniversiteit, Voss. Lat. F 94); the collection of patristic texts and imperial formulae (Paris, BnF, lat. 2718); the commentary on Vergil's *Eclogues* written at Tours (Bern, Burgerbibliothek, 165); and glosses to Vergil (Bern, Burgerbibliothek, 172 and 184; Einsiedeln, Stiftsbibliothek, 365, Oxford, Bodleian Library, Auct. F. 2. 8). Glosses to Priscian are found in manuscripts from Tours, glossed by Ermengarius, from Reims, Ferrières, and Fleury.[1] Tironian notes are used for recording variant readings (*aliter*) in Angers, Bibliothèque municipale, 148, for *antiquus* in Boulogne, Bibliothèque municipale, 45; Florence, BML, Plut. XXIX.20; and Paris, BnF, lat. 7230 A. The Tironian symbols for *hic* and *usque hic* are used as excerpting marks in the margins of patristic texts. In addition to the elaborate system of Tironian notes recorded in the *Commentarium notarum Tironianarum* the first-century tablets from Vindolanda use symbols which await decipherment. Syllabic notes were used at Verona and Ravenna in the sixth century, and later at Bobbio.

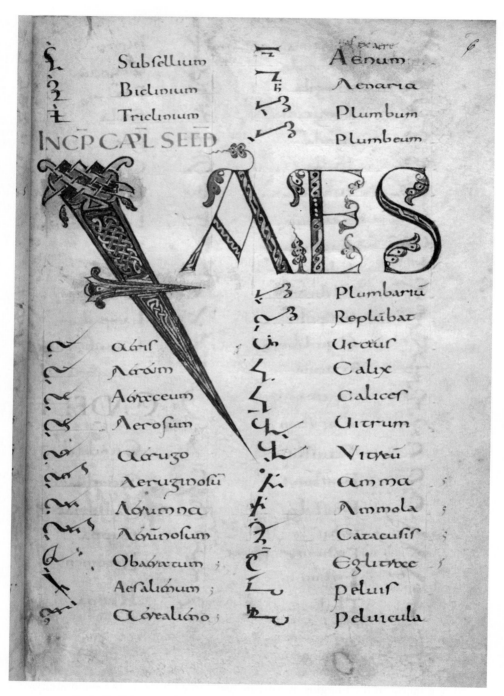

Subsellium

Biclinium

Triclinium

INCP CAPL SEED

Aenum

Aenaria

Plumbum

Plumbeum

Aes

Plumbariū

Replūbat

Urceus

Calix

Calices

Uitrum

Vitreū

amma

Ammola

Caracusif

Eglietxe

Pelius

Pellicula

aeris

Aeram

Aoreceum

Aerosum

aerugo

Aeruginosū

Aerumna

Aerunosum

Obaeratum

Aesalianum

Aerealiano

PLATE 19.1 Paris, BnF, lat 190, fol. 6r *Commentarii notarum Tironianarum*, Western France.

Tironian notes were used in the Merovingian and Carolingian chanceries by the *referendarius* to authenticate royal charters; and a set of imperial charters and capitularies from the reign of Louis the Pious was transcribed in Tironian notes, together with several patristic texts. Shorthand subscriptions were used by Visigothic and Italian notaries.

NOTE

1. Autun, Bibliothèque municipale, 40 (cf. also Hellmann, 2000, 37–41); Reims, Bibliothèque municipale, 1094; Paris, BnF, Latin 7496; and Paris, BnF, Latin 7503, respectively.

BIBLIOGRAPHY

Chatelain, É. 1900. *Introduction à la lecture des notes tironiennes.* Paris: Published by the author.

Ganz, P. 1990. *Tironische Noten*, Wolfenbütteler Mittelalter Studien 1. Wiesbaden: Otto Harrassowitz.

Hellmann, M. 2000. *Tironische Noten in der Karolingerzeit am Beispiel eines Persius-Kommentars aus der Schule von Tours.* Hanover: Hahnsche Buchhandlung [this text has the fullest list of Carolingian manuscripts containing Tironian notes].

Schmitz, W. 1882. *Monumenta Tachygraphica codicis Parisiensis latini 2718.* Hanover: Bibliopolio Hahniano.

Schmitz, W. 1893. *Commentarii notarum Tironianarum* Leipzig: Teubner.

I . 5

GOTHIC

CHAPTER 20

....

THE NOMENCLATURE
OF GOTHIC SCRIPTS

....

ALBERT DEROLEZ

"IN scholarly communication, and in particular in a catalogue of manuscripts...one could replace a definition [i.e. the name of a script] with as many reproductions as possible, along with a free description of the handwriting, based on the competence provided by the education of the paleographer and the state of the discipline."[1] This gentle disinclination toward palaeographical nomenclature, recently expressed by a well-known Italian palaeographer, is a far cry from the outright condemnation of the subject by no less renowned specialists, including Armando Petrucci and Giorgio Cencetti. The former declared that the use of palaeographical nomenclature "often hides a lack of understanding and errors in valuation and perspective; it is always the symptom of imperfect knowledge of the available documents."[2] Cencetti claimed that "terminology and classification cannot be precise and arbitrary constructions, suggested by nothing other than empirical observations; rather they must reflect real and historical articulations in the development of writing, to be established by a substantial study and not by the abstract combination of mere external data."[3] Years earlier François Masai had already written that palaeographical nomenclature would best be replaced by a collection of numbered reproductions, whereby the various numbers should be used to indicate the various types of script.[4] Recently, the late Emmanuel Poulle once again repeated his dislike for a nomenclature of book scripts, "because it is only interested in the result of the graphic activity, not in its genesis; and because that activity is seen as fixed within a predefined framework, that in turn is a confirmation of the nomenclature established by the palaeographer." Like Cencetti and many others, Poulle believed that much more study is needed to form sound views of the historical types of script, their evolution, and their mutual relationships.[5]

Whatever the validity of the statements with which the previous paragraph begins (as well as many similar statements not mentioned here), there is still much to say on the other side of the question. Those who propose to replace a script name with one or more reproductions are no doubt right in arguing that the easiest and most reliable way to indicate how a handwritten text looks is with a photographic reproduction (at life size, it should be added). Gumbert's *Illustrated Inventory of Medieval Manuscripts* (Gumbert 2009)[6] and the more and more common practice of adding to a catalogue of manuscripts a reproduction of all items described are testimonies to the soundness of this approach.[7] For comparative purposes, however, the examination of reproductions requires skills that only an accomplished palaeographer commands. Referring to a plate in the *Catalogues de manuscrits datés* in order to characterize a given script sample is not as simple a process as some scholars would have us believe.[8] In order to do this accurately, one needs to know which features to take into account when comparing two, let alone numerous, examples of handwriting. And this knowledge can only be obtained from years of experience. The alternative to acquiring a professional level of expertise is to adopt a framework for classification and a nomenclature appropriate to it. This has the undeniable advantage of being accessible to novices; and it need not be rejected by experts, as will be shown in the following pages.

Every scholarly discipline needs names for the categories it deals with. In the case of palaeography and codicology, a well-founded nomenclature is especially needed for cataloguing purposes, for teaching, and for quantitative studies. If cataloguers inform the readers about the nomenclature they are using, a very few words will suffice to give the users an idea of the appearance of a given hand and guide them directly to manuscripts featuring the same type of script. Students need well-defined categories when beginning the study of palaeography. And for the specialists of codicology and quantitative manuscript studies, the application of script names that always describe the same script type is essential.

The palaeographers who investigate the history and evolution of scripts, on the other hand, will generally consider the application of a detailed nomenclature unnecessary or even harmful. They consider it contrary to the essence of handwriting, which is a constantly changing, free-flowing, unpredictable and unclassifiable human activity. The static categories on which nomenclature is based conflict with the dynamism of the evolution of Latin script with its uninterrupted continuity. A focus on nomenclature takes us back to the unfruitful classifications of the eighteenth century and ignores the fundamental renewal of palaeographical studies initiated by Jean Mallon. But if nomenclature is given its proper (and modest) place as an aid in palaeographical research and communication, there is no need to suppose that the acceptance of a "static" nomenclature should impede research into the genesis of script forms, their mutations and evolution.

Some modern trends in palaeographical research see handwriting essentially as a cultural phenomenon and replace "the history of script" with "the history of written culture."[9] No serious scholar will deny that studying the theoretical, philosophical, cultural, anthropological, communicative, social, economic, and political aspects and functions of handwriting is a legitimate field of research, and one that may lead to highly interesting results. However, in many cases such studies no longer concentrate on the script itself, but instead resort to sociological reasoning, jargon, and the use of abstractions that risk turning the new palaeography into a hermetic science. It is understandable that this approach does not need—indeed has an aversion for—formal classifications and rigid nomenclatures.

Palaeography as I envision it is, so far as is possible, the *objective* study of handwriting in itself and more precisely of the result of the graphic activity—not because "la scrittura nel suo farsi" would be uninteresting, but because the examination of "script in its making," in its *ductus* or "tratteggio," in the human faculties involved in writing, in the physiology of the writing act, the preparation of the scribe, and his mood during the process of writing, etc.[10] either are very difficult to determine or cannot easily be subjected to a scientific approach. Although absolute objectivity in this field is impossible, the scientific character of palaeography requires that elements of subjectivism should be avoided as much as possible. In a now famous statement, Bernhard Bischoff lamented that palaeography, which he considered "an art of seeing and comprehending," was "in the process of becoming an art of measurement."[11] Seeing is, of course, essential in the study of script;[12] and for great masters like Bischoff, intuition is no doubt a priceless faculty. But for students and for the mutual understanding between scholars—as well as for the progress of the discipline—an approach less dependent on personal elements within the personality of the researchers is needed.

"Measuring" and "counting" have for some decades been essential tools of strict objectivity in codicology. In spite of the existence of some more or less successful experiments in quantitative palaeography,[13] objectivity in the discipline is not always based on a mathematical approach and on quantification of the observed data. But the forms of the letters and signs as they are visible on the page can be observed objectively in so far as they ostensibly differ from other forms of the same letters and signs. This does not mean that the way these are traced, the speed and care of their execution, the shape of the pen that was used, and other features are not taken into account; it means that morphology, as the script element that is the most suitable to an objective and unproblematic observation, is used as a major criterion for the distinction of the primary types within an historical group of scripts.

It will at once be clear that only more or less calligraphic scripts, especially those in which almost every letter is traced in several strokes ("constructed letters") can easily be studied in their morphology. "Cursive" scripts, by contrast, executed at high speed without frequent lifting of the pen from the writing surface, lend themselves far less to a morphological description. In spite of the fundamental role that cursive scripts have, at all times, played in the development, evolution, and transformation of scripts, and in spite of Françoise Gasparri's view that cursive scripts are the "real" and "spontaneous" forms of writing, while canonized calligraphic types are dead ends,[14] cursive handwriting must remain outside the field of application of a method based on morphology. It requires another approach, as the promising ongoing research on cursivity shows.[15]

Book scripts are almost always more or less of a calligraphic nature, and almost never executed in a fully cursive technique. Even if book scripts are seen as less "interesting" than cursive scripts, it is still the case that books, especially those of the Late Middle Ages, the period of Gothic script with which we are concerned here, have survived in extremely large numbers; and they constitute a phenomenon worthy of investigation from many perspectives, including their handwriting.

In the following discussion, only book scripts will be addressed. Documentary scripts are left out of consideration (aside from the example in Plate 20.7). The formal ones among them—charter hands, chancery hands, court hands—are often, like book scripts, calligraphic; but their use is generally limited to more or less narrow geographic or administrative boundaries and within these to special kinds of documents. Since chanceries are accustomed to developing individual forms for the documents they issue in order to assure their authenticity, the number of different formal documentary scripts to be found in Europe is too large to be brought into a system. The informal documentary hands as seen in accounts, letters, notes, etc. are generally of too personal a nature to allow classification on a morphological basis. Their scribes often lack the training which a professional scribe would have undertaken.

It has been observed that in the last centuries of the Middle Ages many individuals copied books for their own use and did this in their own personal hand. They often executed the script in a more calligraphic style than they would regularly employ in their letters and annotations. But such volumes are exceptions to the rule that during this period books were mostly copied by professional scribes; and the exceptions should not be the basis for condemning the study of book scripts as something separate from the field of documentary scripts, as Cencetti and others do.[16]

The professional scribes of the Late Middle Ages, whether writing books in universities, cities, or ecclesiastical environments, were working in an age in which a commercial spirit had invaded the world of book production, replacing the spirit of the monastic scriptorium, which had dominated book production until roughly the end of the twelfth century. As long as the producers of books in the monasteries were working *ad maiorem Dei gloriam*, there was generally no pressure to finish a book within a given time limit, and there was no need to apply standardized techniques and methods in order to save time. This contributes, no doubt, to the fancifulness that marks many aspects of the early medieval manuscript. But when the role of monasteries was taken over by secular workshops, scribes, decorators, and miniaturists, efficiency and the search for time-saving and labor-saving devices and methods became essential for transforming book production into a profit-making enterprise. Especially in the fourteenth and fifteenth centuries, strict standardization is visible in the sizes and hierarchy of initials[17] and in the standardization and hierarchy of border decorations.[18] Standardization in the decoration of manuscripts was generally given up after printing became the normal way of producing books, as seen, for example, in the manuscripts of the so-called Ghent-Bruges school.

The existence of standardized forms of decoration shows that scribes (who had to reserve spaces for initials), decorators, and illuminators were fully conscious of well-defined categories of decoration that could be utilized. In the application of these, their personal taste or individual preference was not to play a role. There is no doubt that the scribes were also aware of the existence of a variety of script types (whether or not they were themselves able to execute more than one type), and that normally there was very little scope for introducing individual features into their handwriting.

It is interesting to note, in passing, that Gothic script originated in the most glorious period of the monastic scriptorium, before the advent of the economic changes that are at the core of the above-mentioned introduction of standardized procedures and forms. So it seems that economic circumstances did not play a significant role in the generation of the new script. Of the various explanations that have been given for the transformation of Carolingian script into Gothic, a change in esthetic taste probably comes closest to the reality; the parallelism with Gothic architecture cannot be entirely fortuitous.[19]

A palaeographical nomenclature can be developed in different ways. One option is to adopt the historical names found in medieval sources—such as the placards of the writing masters, writing manuals, and catalogues and inventories of books—and to investigate which script types correspond to each of them. This method has been applied with varying degrees of success by several palaeographers. It was the basis for the "Latin palaeographical nomenclature" planned at the first International Colloquium of Palaeography in Paris (1953) but eventually abandoned in light of the difficulty of the undertaking.[20]

A second and more promising methodology for creating a palaeographical nomenclature is to identify all the different types that can be distinguished from one another and to give them names, either historical names or neologisms. The thousands of excellent reproductions now at our disposal in the various *Catalogues de manuscrits datés* make the identification of the extant varieties of medieval script possible (it is unfortunate that there are no such catalogues for some important areas, including the Iberian Peninsula, and that some palaeographers are curiously reluctant to admit that dated manuscripts constitute useful milestones for research in Late Medieval palaeography).[21] So the starting point for a nomenclature is a classification of scripts, comprising as far as possible all the types that can be distinguished, and applying names to them. If possible, these names would ideally be those that are in use in present-day palaeographical research. The advantages of this approach would be (1) the entire field would be covered, with the exception of the rare examples that are too deviant to be included ("hors système" scripts); (2) individual script names would be subordinated to the main classes or types, so that no overlap occurs and so that the names of any types that are, in fact, subcategories of other types are not treated on the same basis as the names of the main types; (3) order would be imposed on the confusing multitude of names, and an end would be brought, at least to some extent, to the national biases that have been so detrimental to the discipline and to scholarly exchanges between researchers across the Western world.

The internationalization of our discipline—particularly fostered after World War II by Charles Samaran, the founder of the Comité International de Paléographie Latine (in 1957, after preparatory proceedings started in 1953), and by François Masai, who founded the journal *Scriptorium* (1946)—requires that names of script types that are used only in one country be avoided, unless they point to types peculiar to that country, for example, *anglicana*, *cancelleresca*, and *mercantesca*.

Generally speaking, I think that a palaeographical nomenclature should adhere to the following requirements in its main subdivisions:

(1) It should use a universally acceptable language; in this case Latin has the advantage of being absolutely neutral.
(2) It should be based on a classification with a limited number of subdivisions, in order to keep it manageable; the inevitable "hors système" scripts should form a relatively small group.
(3) It should be founded on objectively definable criteria. These should be the forms of signs and letters, not their size, rapidity of execution, or the general appearance of the page, and not the use or destination of the script, etc.
(4) It should correspond to actual historical script names, as far as it is possible to ascertain these;[22] and it should, as far as possible, include all the types that palaeographers have hitherto identified.

These requirements mean that certain names cannot be maintained in the system, either because the scripts they indicate are not sufficiently defined or for other reasons: so *écriture scolastique* (especially when the term is used for French vernacular texts),[23] university hand, book hand, *scrittura dei dotti*,[24] *gotichetta*, *gotica francese*, *gotische Buchschrift*, even *notula* or *Glossenschrift*, as it seems probable that the small size of the last two types is the only cause of their different forms.[25]

Various nomenclatures of Gothic script have been proposed in the last half-century, mostly as a help for cataloguing manuscripts. But none has met with such a widespread response—both positively and negatively—as the system and nomenclature devised by Gerard I. Lieftinck (1902–94) and afterwards systematized by J. Peter Gumbert and further developed by myself in *The Palaeography of Gothic Manuscript Books* (Derolez 2003). Although originally formulated in sometimes badly chosen and confusing terms, the "Lieftinck" system (as far as a system can do this) answers all the requirements outlined above.[26]

This is not the place to describe once again this system. In its original form, it made a distinction between three main categories that can be observed in the script of the Low Countries and adjoining areas.[27] More recently, in Derolez (2003), three further, mostly minor categories were added in order to cover the book scripts in use in the whole of Europe. The main categories are based on the morphology of no more than three letters or groups of letters: *a* (in one or in two compartments),[28] *f* and its companion tall *s* (standing on the baseline or descending below the baseline) and *b*, *h*, *k*, and *l* (with looped or unlooped ascenders). The choice of such a narrow basis for classifying all the scripts appearing in many thousands of manuscripts has justly been criticized.[29] There is no doubt that other variables could be chosen. Including more variables in the criteria on which a classification is based would allow more refinements to the system. But doing so would probably also have undesirable consequences for the clarity of the system. It is essential to remember that the system seeks, in the first instance, to establish basic, objectively definable main categories.

These main categories have been given Latin names: *textualis, semitextualis, cursiva antiquior, cursiva (recentior), hybrida, semihybrida.*[30] For reasons of consistency, it has been suggested that the northern and southern versions of *textualis* be called, respectively, *textualis septentrionalis* and *textualis meridionalis* (Dominique Stutzmann 2005–, in his review of Derolez 2003, nos. 31 and 37).

The names of the main categories are followed in the modified Lieftinck system by a qualification describing the level of execution of a given example. In these qualifications, the subjective impression of the viewer necessarily plays an important part (along with the examination of certain details and of the *ductus*, as far as the examination of the latter is possible), and it is often a matter of debate whether a given hand will be called *formata* (very carefully executed), *libraria* (*media* in the version of Julian Brown, an intermediate level as judged normal for a book script), or *currens* (rapidly written, with a more or less cursive technique). If there is hesitation as to which qualification should be applied, one can write *formata/libraria, libraria/currens*, etc.[31]

After the qualification of the level of the script, it is often desirable to add as a third element the name of a subtype (generally a traditional or historical name) that falls under the main type, at least if it can be ascertained that the added name is pertinent. An example: French *bâtarde* can be described as *gothica cursiva formata* (*bastarda*).[32] In this name, *gothica* is used for one of the main classes of scripts, as distinct from such classes as Merovingica, Carolina, and humanistica; *cursiva* stands for a script type, marked by single-compartment *a*, by *f* and tall *s* descending below the baseline, and by *b, h, k,* and *l* with looped ascenders (the term is distinct from *cursive*, which refers to a writing *technique*); *formata* indicates a very careful, calligraphic execution (versions more rapidly written may be qualified *libraria*); *bastarda* is the name for a universally recognized canonized subtype with unmistakable features that is referred to as *bâtarde* in numerous Late Medieval French sources. In a similar way the scripts proper to the various European countries and areas can be incorporated into the system.

The double or triple name proposed above is normally sufficient for describing a given script specimen. It can be followed, in order to make the description more precise, by a note on the forms that are special to the given example, or are related to other script types, or by whatever observations one thinks useful for characterizing the hand on the page. In this way a terminology that may seem oversimplified, coarse, and unrefined becomes a framework in which even the most subtle features of a script can be described.

Plates 20.1–20.16 and their descriptions demonstrate how the system works. The examples, chosen at random from one collection, do not cover the entire range of the nomenclature. A full list of alternative names has not been included. In his review of Derolez (2003), Dominique Stutzmann (2005–) provides an ample but not exhaustive list of the names applied to Gothic book scripts in palaeographical literature. Their incredible multitude is the best argument in favor of a simple and manageable nomenclature for Gothic book scripts (the "Lieftinck system" or another) that will allow us to escape from the swamp of confusion which makes discussion of this period in the history of handwriting so difficult.

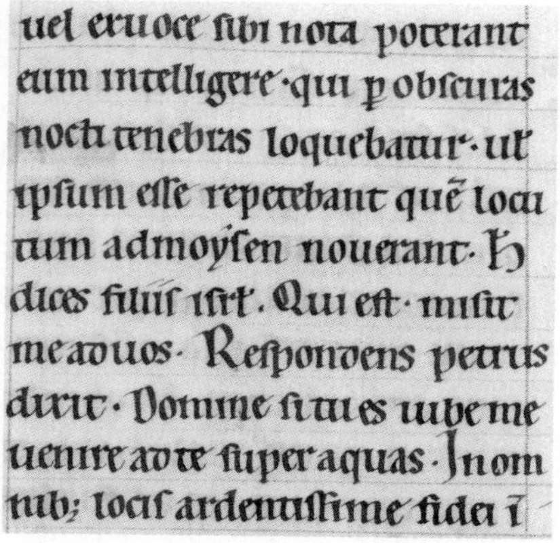

> uel eruoce subi nota poterant
> eum intelligere·qui p obscuras
> nocti tenebras loquebatur· ut
> ipsum esse repetebant que loca
> cum admoysen nouerant· Ꜧ
> dices filius isrł. Qui est· misit
> meaouos· Respondens petrus
> dixit· Domine si tu es iube me
> uenire ao te super aquas· Jn om
> nib; locis ardentissime fidei ī

PLATE 20.1 Hieronymus, *Explanatio in Matthaeum et Marcum*, Southern Low Countries, s. XII². Ghent, University Library, MS 132, fol. 48r.

Praegothica

Praegothica is the name given to the many transitional forms between Carolingian script and Gothic. Level indications are normally not necessary for the handwriting found in most of these carefully executed twelfth-century manuscripts.

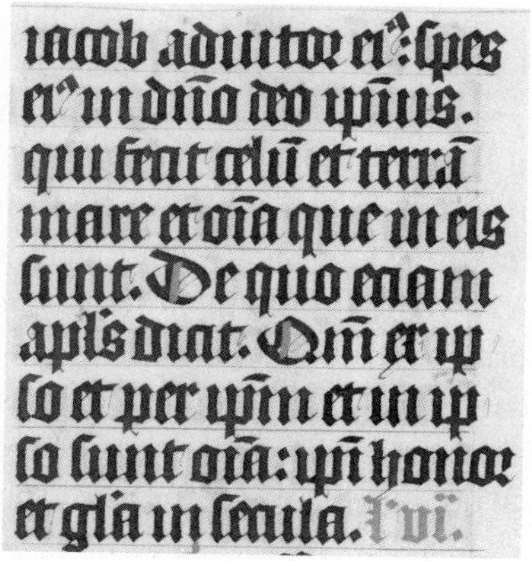

> iacob adiutor eᵈ:spes
> eᵘ in dño deo ipsius.
> qui fecit celū et terrā
> mare et oīa que in eis
> sunt. De quo etiam
> apłs dicat. Oīn et ip
> so et per ipsm et in ip
> so sunt oīa: ipsi honor
> et gła in secula. Uī.

PLATE 20.2 *Lectionarium officii*, Holland, s. XV. Ghent, University Library, MS 105, fol. 29r.

Northern gothica textualis formata (textus quadratus)

The typical forms of *textualis* are *a* in two compartments (here in two different shapes, the "double bow *a*" and the "box-*a*"), *f* and tall *s* not going beneath the baseline, *b*, *h*, *k*, and *l* without loops on their ascenders. There is no doubt that the qualification *formata* should be applied to the highly calligraphic script reproduced here. *Textus quadratus* or *textus fractus* are the names traditionally given to a form of *textualis formata* that is at the top of the hierarchy of Gothic scripts; it is marked by extreme angularity and by the diamond-shaped serifs or quadrangles at the top and foot of the minims and at the foot of the ascenders.

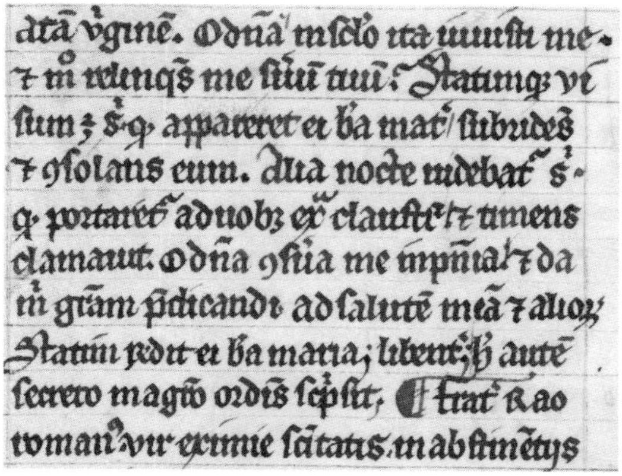

PLATE 20.3 Gerardus Lemovicensis, *Vitae Fratrum Ordinis Praedicatorum*, Germany, s. XIII. Ghent, University Library, MS 534, fol. 6v.

Northern gothica textualis libraria

The execution in this example is careful, but not as calligraphic as in Plate 20.2. Hence the qualification *libraria*.

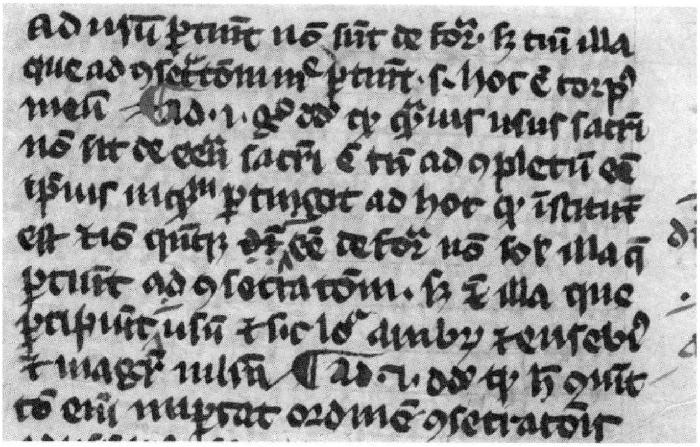

PLATE 20.4 Thomas Aquinas, *Commentum in quartum sententiarum*, Paris, s. XIII/XIV. Ghent, University Library, MS 117, p. 161a.

Northern gothica textualis currens (littera Parisiensis)

The extremely rapid execution (hence the qualification *currens*) and the relatively small module in combination with the use of a pen with a rather wide nib, apart from affecting the form of *s* (round *s* is not used), have induced the scribe of this example to use single-compartment *a* in addition to the two-compartment *a* that is normal for *textualis*. Strictly speaking, this script, which has the characteristics of the university script known as *littera Parisiensis*, should be called *northern gothica textualis/semitextualis currens* (see Plate 20.6).

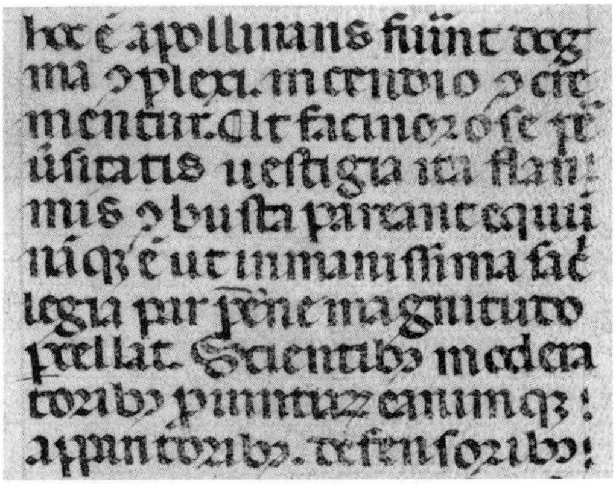

PLATE 20.5 *Codex Iustiniani*, Italy (Bologna), s. XIII. Ghent, University Library, MS 22, fol. 23v.

Southern gothica textualis libraria (littera Bononiensis)
The southern form of *textualis* differs from its northern counterpart by the roundness of many letterforms and by a series of additional features, such as the *d* with a nearly horizontal ascender, the *con-* abbreviation, and the *–bus* abbreviation. The specific form of the script in this example is typical of the manuscripts produced at the university of Bologna. Whether the level indication should be *libraria* or *formata* is open to discussion. *Rotunda* is a name commonly used for this type of script.

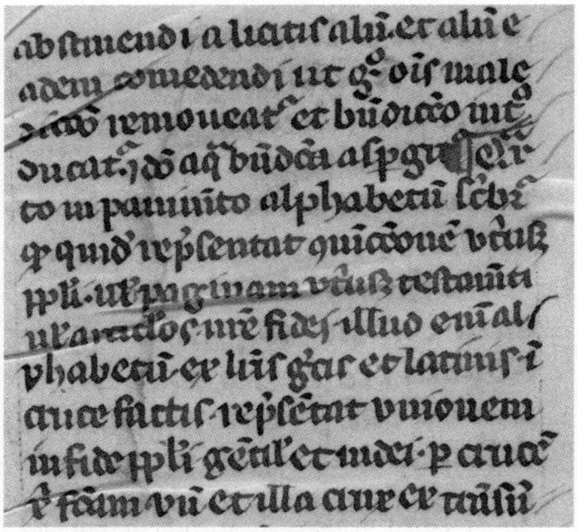

PLATE 20.6 Iacobus de Voragine, *Legenda aurea*, France, s. XIV. Ghent, University Library, MS 405, fol. 341r.

Gothica semitextualis libraria
Semitextualis is the name proposed for a *textualis* consistently using one-compartment *a*. Its typical features are thus one-compartment *a*, *f* and tall *s* standing on the baseline, and *b*, *h*, *k*, and *l* without loops on their ascenders. Although frequently used in Italy and linked by some scholars to the person of Petrarch, it is also seen in other countries as a minor variant of *textualis*. Alternative names are *semigotica*, *AS-textualis* (the latter name, proposed by Julian Brown, refers to the typical *a* and the so-called trailing-*s* often used in final position.

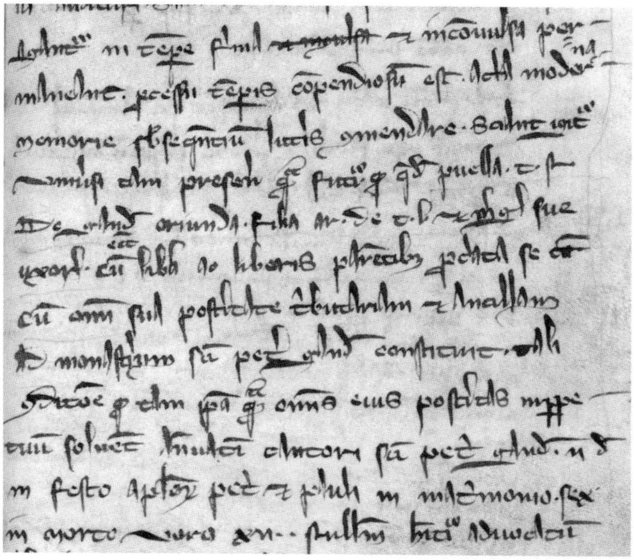

PLATE 20.7 *Formularium*, Ghent, s. XIII. Ghent, University Library, MS 267, fol. 38r.

Gothic documentary cursive

This example of a rapid script, with features rarely or never seen in books (the bold strokes obtained by exerting pressure on the pen—as we see here, for example, in *d* and *V*—recur in reduced form in *anglicana*, see Plate 20.8), illustrates that a separate nomenclature of book hands is justified.

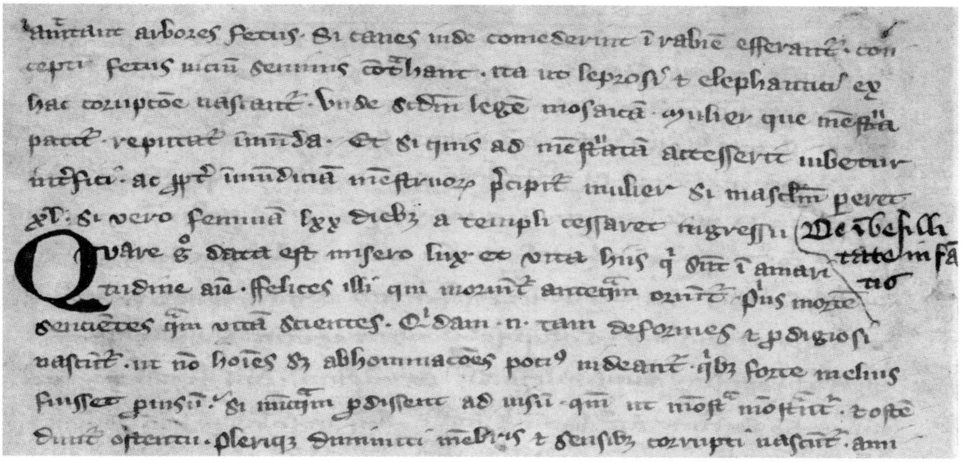

PLATE 20.8 Innocentius III, *De miseria humanae conditionis*, England, s. XIII/XIV. Ghent, University Library, MS 317, fol. 2v.

Gothica cursiva antiquior libraria (anglicana)

The term *cursiva* in the Lieftinck system describes a type of script, not the use of a cursive technique. The typical features of this "older" *cursiva* are two-compartment *a*; *f* and tall *s* descending below the baseline; *b*, *h*, *k*, and *l* with loops on their ascenders. As a book script, it is especially typical of Late Medieval England.

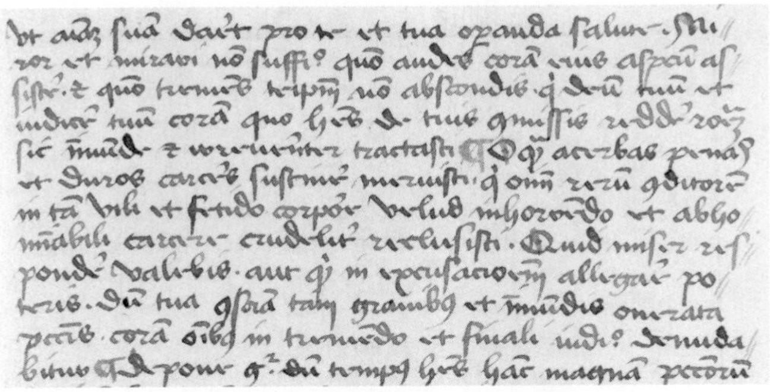

PLATE 20.9 *Tractatus ascetici*, Ghent, 1474. Ghent, University Library, MS 1186, fol. 9r.

Gothica cursiva currens

Cursiva (or *cursiva recentior*, as opposed to *cursiva antiquior*) is a script using single-compartment *a*; *f* and tall *s* descending below the baseline; *b*, *h*, *k*, and *l* with looped ascenders. The qualification *currens* points to the very rapid, "cursive" execution of this example.

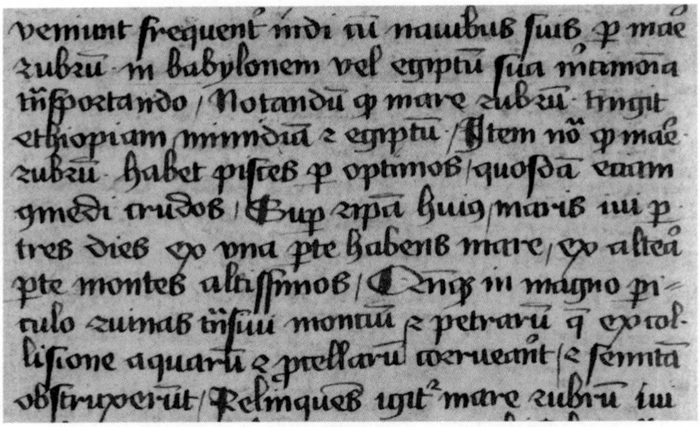

PLATE 20.10 Thietmarus, *Iter in Terram Sanctam*, Western Germany, s. XV. Ghent, University Library, MS 486, fol. 112v.

Gothica cursiva libraria

A less rapid, more "bookish" execution of the script than that shown in Plate 20.9.

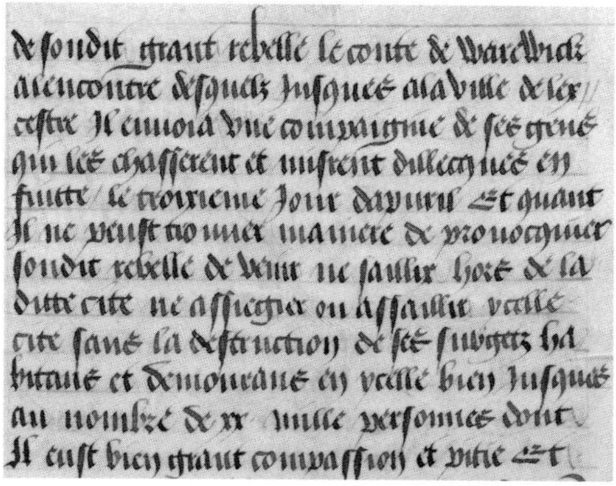

PLATE 20.11 *Histoire de la rentrée victorieuse du roi Edouard IV en son royaume d'Angleterre,* Southern Low Countries, *c.*1471. Ghent, University Library, MS 236, fol. 3v.

Gothica cursiva formata (bastarda)
Calligraphic execution of *cursiva* (with the same basic features as in Plate 20.9), in the style which is known as *bâtarde*.

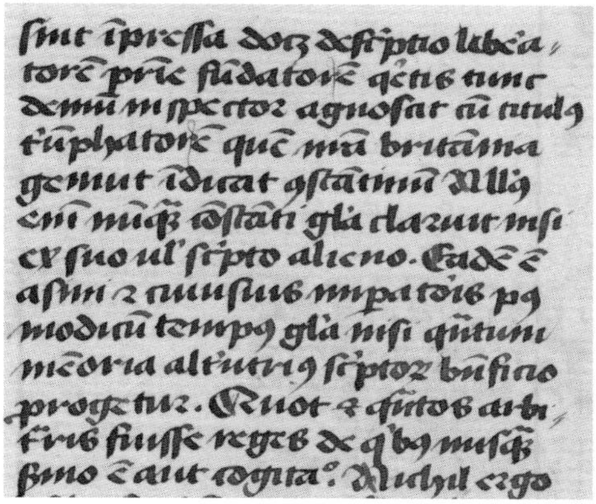

PLATE 20.12 Iohannes Saresberiensis, *Policraticus,* Western Germany, 1470. Ghent, University Library, MS 533, fol. 2v.

Gothica hybrida libraria
Hybrida is an intermediate form between *textualis* and *cursiva*; its typical features are: single-compartment *a*; *f* and tall *s* descending below the baseline; *b, h, k,* and *l* with unlooped ascenders.

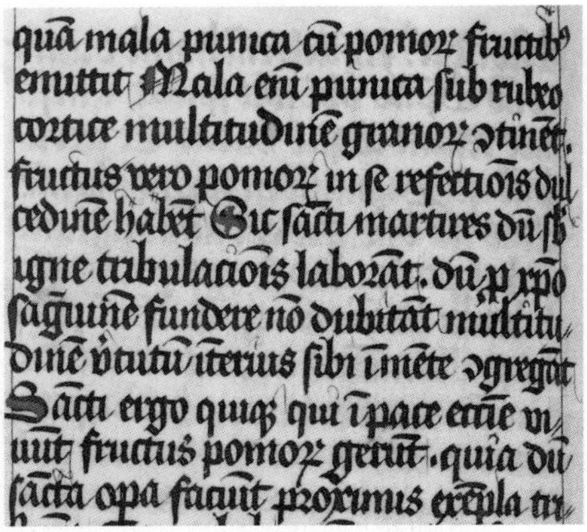

PLATE 20.13 Gregorius Magnus, *Expositio in Cantica Canticorum*. Western Germany, 1500. Ghent, University Library, MS 242, fol. 64v.

Gothica hybrida formata (fractura)

This example of a calligraphic execution of *hybrida* has the typical features of the subtype known as *Fraktur*, for example, the spiky forms and the *o* in the shape of a pointed oval.

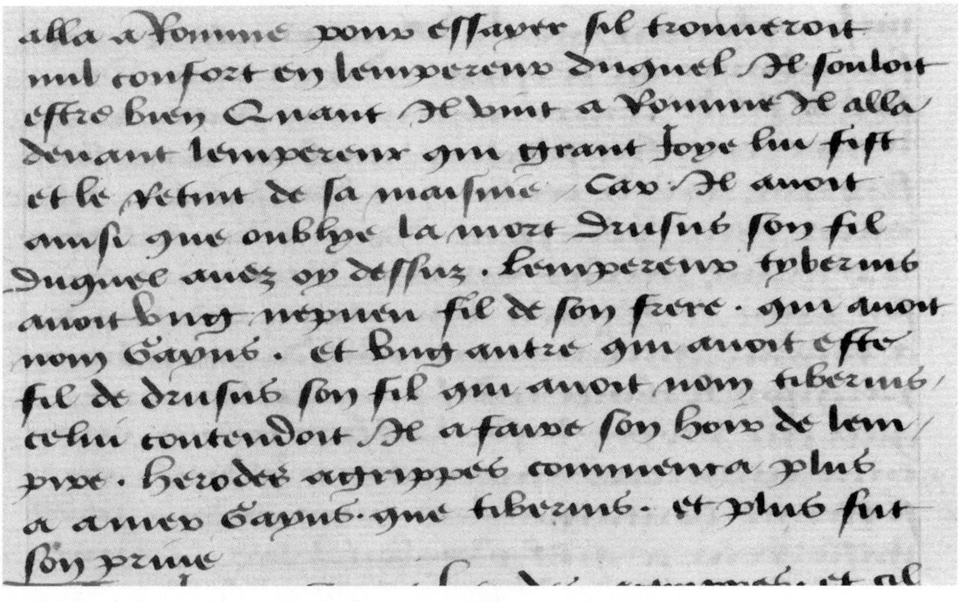

PLATE 20.14 Baudouin d'Avesnes, *Le Trésor des histoires*, Southern Low Countries, s. XV². Ghent, University Library, MS 415 II, fol. 14v.

Gothica semihybrida formata (bastarda)

There are many examples of *cursiva* or *hybrida*, especially in Germany, in which *b*, *h*, *k*, and *l* are found with looped as well as with unlooped ascenders. For these scripts Gumbert has proposed the name of *semihybrida*. The calligraphic version seen here has the features of *bâtarde*, so that the term *bastarda* applies here just as it does in the *cursiva* shown in Plate 20.11.

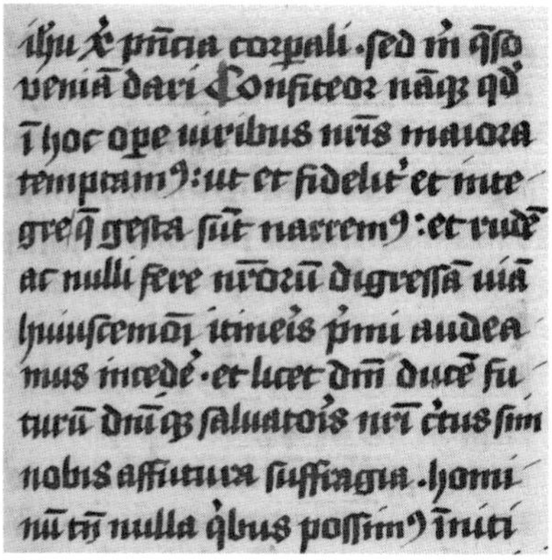

PLATE 20.15 Eusebius-Rufinus, *Historia ecclesiastica*. Southern Low Countries, s. XV. Ghent, University Library, MS 113, fol. 2r.

Gothic "hors système" script, libraria
This example looks *textualis*, but *f* and tall *s* descend below the baseline and *a* is sometimes of the single-compartment type (not visible on the plate). It is consequently intermediate between *textualis* and *hybrida*.

PLATE 20.16 Diogenes Laertius, *De vitis philosophorum*, Latin transl., France, s. XV². Ghent, University Library, MS 148, p. 4.

Gothic "hors système" script, libraria
A most idiosyncratic Gothic script, betraying influence of Italian models but probably created by a scribe who tried to adapt his hand to a content at that time scarcely circulating in Northern Europe.[33]

NOTES

1. Translated from Palma (2010, 193).
2. Translated from Petrucci (1969).
3. Cencetti (1954–6, 479). The translation is by Gumbert (1976, 45). Nicolaj (2007, 27) also expresses reservations about what she calls "tourments terminologiques."
4. Masai (1956, 294); reprinted in Gruys and Gumbert (1976, 46).
5. Poulle (2004, 572).
6. The first volume of the *Illustrated Inventory of Medieval Manuscripts* (*IIMM*) published, after a series of preliminary *Precursors*, is volume II: *Leiden, Universiteitsbibliotheek, BPL*.
7. The author is not able, and it is perhaps too early, to evaluate the effect on palaeographical studies of the immense possibilities now created by the digitization of manuscripts.
8. Lemaire (1989, 162).
9. A few names among the many protagonists of this trend: Armando Petrucci, the founder of the journal with the significant title *Scrittura e Civiltà* (1977–2002); see, for example, Petrucci (1996); Alessandro Pratesi, defender of the social history of handwriting against Attilio Bartoli Langeli, who believed palaeography is in crisis due to the "progressiva penetrazione della problematica storico-sociale" (Pratesi 1992, 90); Castillo Gómez and Sáez (1999).
10. Gasparri (1994, 9) sees handwriting as an activity involving all human faculties; Nascimento (2005) is an example of all the elements that according to some authors should be taken into account when studying handwriting, from the physiology and mechanism of writing to the education of the scribe and the ritual character of the writing act.
11. Bischoff (1990, 3). At the invitation of Armando Petrucci a selection of palaeographers discussed the phrase in *Scrittura e Civiltà* in the years 1995–8; see Derolez (2003, 8, n. 18) and J. Peter Gumbert's indispensable conclusive note in Gumbert (1998).
12. See the quotation from T. Julian Brown, used as a motto by Fabio Troncarelli in Boyle (1999, ix), and the "Editor's Introduction" in Bately, Brown, and Roberts (1993, 14).
13. Derolez (2003, 8–9). See also Derolez (2004) and the important contributions in Ornato *et al.* (1996).
14. Gasparri (1994, 81).
15. A real advance in the study of palaeography thanks to the adoption of appropriate methods may be expected from the "Séminaire permanent 'Écritures cursives'" promoted by Marc Smith in collaboration with a select group of young palaeographers; see Marc H. Smith in the preface to the volume of palaeographical studies, most of them devoted to cursive handwriting, collected in Smith (2007 [2008], 7–8).
16. Cencetti (1993, 278).
17. Derolez (2003, 40–2); Stirnemann and Smith (2007, 92–3).
18. Hindman and (1977, 72–5).
19. See Derolez (2003, 68–71). For an important new viewpoint in the discussion of the origin of Gothic script, see Smith (2004, 277).
20. Derolez (2003, 18–19); Bischoff, Lieftinck, and Battelli (1954, 4); Muzerelle (1988, 151–2).
21. In the recent handbook by Cherubini and Pratesi (2010, 479–80), following in the footsteps of Paola Supino Martini, the authors remain very suspicious of the validity of dated manuscripts as a basis for the study of Late Medieval handwriting. The arguments are (1) scribes in the Late Middle Ages travelled a lot; (2) there are manuscripts that are

much more typical of a given period and a given area than dated manuscripts. However, (1) every manuscript scholar knows that scribes traveled and takes this into account when dealing with dated manuscripts; (2) the second argument may very well be true, but how do we know to what period and area these manuscripts belong, if they are not dated? For the author's controversy with Cherubini and Pratesi, see now A. Derolez, "The Import-ance of the Catalogue of Dated Manuscripts for Palaeographical and Codicological Studies, and a Reply to Recent Criticisms". *Catalogazione, storia della scrittura, storia del libro. I manoscritti datati d'Italia vent'anni dopo*, ed. Teresa De Robertis and Nicoletta Giovè Marchioli. Firenze: Sismel. Edizioni del Galluzzo 2017, 61–74.

22. Smith (2004) rightly points to the fundamental weakness of this point, which resides in the assumption that the "Lieftinckian" categories are indeed historical script types.

23. Gasparri (1994, Plates 30–2).

24. Cencetti (1978, 30).

25. This is also the opinion of Stiennon (1999, 99).

26. The system was extended and modified to be applied to the entire field of Latin palaeography by Julian Brown; his terminology has become more widely known in a somewhat adapted form through the work of Michelle Brown (1990, 2).

27. The best description of the system is provided by Gumbert (1988, 23–32); see also Derolez (2003, 20–3).

28. The expression '*a* in two compartments' does not necessarily mean that the upper compartment is closed.

29. E.g. in Poulle (2004) and Smith (2004).

30. The validity of these classifications is a fundamental point of debate and cannot be treated here. Most of the proposed terms are neologisms. Their introduction has been considered a further complication of an already confused matter. Recently Cherubini and Pratesi (2010, 479, n. 1), have once again argued that these terms only add to the confusion of the system. This criticism, repeatedly uttered during the last half century (see Derolez 2003, 22), is the result of a misunderstanding, as the new terms indeed are not *added* to the ones already in use, but *superimposed* on them in order to bring clarity and simplification into a world of confusion, largely based on national prejudices. The "Lieftinck" system is not "extremely complicated" or "una macchinosa classificazione", as is claimed by Petrucci (1984, 58–9).

31. This solution was already proposed by Julian Brown; see n. 26.

32. An example is in Plate 20.11.

33. This chapter is a postscript to Derolez (2003). I thank Dr. Sylvia Van Peteghem, Director of Ghent University Library, for generously providing me with the photographs illus-trating the present text; I also thank Prof. Robert G. Babcock for editing the present chapter and Dora Vandenbroucke for translating from the Portuguese Nascimento's review of my book.

BIBLIOGRAPHY

Autenrieth, J. 1963. "Paläographische Nomenklatur im Rahmen der Handschriftenkatalogi-sierung." In *Zur Katalogisierung mittelalterlicher und neuerer Handschriften*. Zeitschrift für Bibliothekswesen und Bibliographie, Sonderheft, ed. C. Köttelwesch, 98–104. Frankfurt am Main: Klostermann.

Barker, N. 2005. "Script and its Names." *The Book Collector* 2005–02: 171–94.

Bately, J., M. P. Brown, and J. Roberts, eds. 1993. *A Palaeographer's View. The Selected Writings of Julian Brown*. London: Harvey Miller.

Bell, N. 2004. "Review of *The Palaeography of Gothic Manuscript Books*." *Times Literary Supplement*, April 30.

Bischoff, B. 1990. *Latin Palaeography. Antiquity and the Middle Ages*, trans. Dáibhí ó Cróinín and David Ganz. Cambridge: Cambridge University Press.

Bischoff, B., G. I. Lieftinck, and G. Battelli. 1954. *Nomenclature des écritures livresques du IXe au XVIe siècle*. Colloques Internationaux du C.N.R.S., Sciences Humaines 4. Paris: Centre national de la recherche scientifique.

Boyle, L. E. 1999. *Paleografia latina medievale. Introduzione bibliografica*, trans. Maria Elena Bertoldi. Rome: Quasar.

Brown, M. P. 1990. *A Guide to Western Historical Scripts from Antiquity to 1600*. London: British Library.

Castillo Gómez, A. and Sáez, C. 1999. "La eliminación de lo 'social': A propósito del concepto y destino de la paleografía." *Scrittura e Civiltà* 23: 439–43.

Catalogues de manuscrits datés, http://www.palaeographia.org/cipl/cmd.htm, accessed March 3, 2020.

Cencetti, G. 1954–6. *Lineamenti di storia della scrittura latina*. Bologna: Pàtron [new enlarged edition by Gemma Guerrini Ferri. Bologna: Pàtron, 1997].

Cencetti, G. 1978. *Compendio di paleografia latina*, 2nd ed. with a supplement by Paola Supino Martini. Rome: Jouvence.

Cencetti, G. 1993. "La paleografia del bibliotecario." In *Giorgio Cencetti. Scritti di paleografia*, ed. Giovanna Nicolaj, 273–8. Zurich: Urs Graf Verlag.

Cherubini, P. and A. Pratesi 2010. *Paleografia latina. L'avventura grafica del mondo occidentale*. Littera antiqua 16. Vatican City: Scuola Vaticana di Paleografia, Diplomatica e Archivistica.

Colker, M. L. 2005. "Review of *The Palaeography of Gothic Manuscript Books*." *Medievalia et Humanistica* new ser., 31: 147–9.

Derolez, A. 2003. *The Palaeography of Gothic Manuscript Books: From the Twelfth to the Early Sixteenth Century*. Cambridge Studies in Palaeography and Codicology 9. Cambridge: Cambridge University Press.

Derolez, A. 2004. "Possibilités et limites d'une paléographie quantitative." In *Hommages à Carl Deroux* 5, ed. Pol Defosse, 98–102. Brussels: Latomus.

Doyle, A. I. 2005. "Review of *The Palaeography of Gothic Manuscript Books*." *Medium Aevum* 74: 119–20.

Dutschke, C. W. 2006. "Review of *The Palaeography of Gothic Manuscript Books*." *Speculum* 81: 171–2.

Gasparri, F. 1994. *Introduction à l'histoire de l'écriture*. Reference Works for the Study of Mediaeval Civilization. Louvain-la Neuve: Brepols.

Gavinelli, S. 2005. "Review of *The Palaeography of Gothic Manuscript Books*." *La Bibliofilia* 107: 291–2.

Gumbert, J. P. 1976. "A Proposal for a Cartesian Nomenclature." In *Essays Presented to G. I. Lieftinck*, IV, ed. J. P. Gumbert and M. J. M. de Haan, 42–52. Amsterdam: A .L. van Gendt.

Gumbert, J. P. 1988. *Manuscrits datés conservés dans les Pays-Bas. Catalogue paléographique des manuscrits en écriture latine portant des indications de date*, vol. 2. Leiden, New York, Copenhagen, and Cologne: North-Holland.

Gumbert, J. P. 1998. "Commentare 'Commentare Bischoff.'" *Scrittura e Civiltà* 22: 397–404.

Gumbert, J. P. 2009. *Illustrated Inventory of Medieval Manuscripts*, vol. II: *Leiden, Universiteitsbiblioteek, BPL*. Hilversum: Verloren.

Hindman, S. and J. D. Farquhar. 1977. *Pen to Press: Illustrated Manuscripts and Printed Books in the First Century of Printing*. College Park, MD: The University of Maryland and Baltimore, MD: The Johns Hopkins University.

Kalinke, M. E. 2005. "Review of *The Palaeography of Gothic Manuscript Books*." *Journal of English and Germanic Philology* 104: 273.

Lemaire, J. 1989. *Introduction à la codicologie*, Université catholique de Louvain. Publications de l'Institut d'études médiévales. Textes, Études, Congrès 9. Louvain-la-Neuve: Université catholique de Louvain.

M. M. 2004. "Review of *The Palaeography of Gothic Manuscript Books*." *Deutsches Archiv für Erforschung des Mittelalters* 60: 699.

Masai, F. 1956. "La paléographie gréco-latine, ses tâches, ses méthodes." *Scriptorium* 10: 281–302 [repr. in A. Gruys and J. P. Gumbert, eds. 1976. *Codicologica*, I. *Théories et principes*, 34–53. Leiden: E. J. Brill].

Muzerelle, D. 1988. "Un siècle de paléographie latine en France." In *Un secolo di paleografia e diplomatica (1887–1986)*, ed. Armando Petrucci and Alessandro Pratesi, 131–58. Rome: Gela.

Nascimento, A. A. 2005. "Review of *The Palaeography of Gothic Manuscript Books*." *Euphrosyne*, new ser. 33: 555–7.

Nicolaj, G. 2007. "Questions terminologiques et questions de méthode. Autour de Giorgio Cencetti, Emanuele Casamassima et Albert Derolez." *Bibliothèque de l'École des Chartes* 165: 9–28.

Ornato, E., *et al.* 1996. *La face cachée du livre médiéval. L'Histoire du livre vue par Ezio Ornato, ses amis et ses collègues*. Rome: Viella.

Overgaauw, E. 1994. "Die Nomenklatur der gotischen Schriftarten bei der Katalogisierung von spätmittelalterlichen Handschriften." *Codices Manuscripti*, 17: 100–6.

Palma, M. 2010. "La definizione della scrittura nei cataloghi di manoscritti medievali." In *La catalogazione dei manoscritti miniati come strumento di conoscenza: esperienze, metodologia, prospettive. Convegno internazionale di studi, Viterbo, 4–5 marzo 2009*, 183–93. Rome: Istituto Storico Italiano per il Medio Evo.

Petrucci, A. 1969. "Review of *Chartae Latinae Antiquiores*." *Gnomon* 41: 771.

Petrucci, A. 1984. *La descrizione del manoscritto. Storia, problemi e modelli*. Aggiornamenti 45. Rome: La Nuova Italia Scientifica.

Petrucci, A. 1996. "Au-delà de la paléographie: histoire de l'écriture, histoire de l'écrit, histoire de l'écrire." *Académie Royale de Belgique. Bulletin de la Classe des Lettres et des Sciences Morales et Politiques*, 6th ser. 7: 123–35.

Poulle, E. 2004. "Review of *The Palaeography of Gothic Manuscript Books*." *Bibliothèque de l'Ecole des Chartes* 162 : 571–4.

Pratesi, A. 1992. *Frustula palaeographica*. Florence: I. S. Olschki [originally published in *Scrittura e Civiltà* 3, 1979].

Rushforth, R. 2004. "Review of *The Palaeography of Gothic Manuscript Books*." *The Library*, 5: 204–6.

Smith, M. H. 2004. "Review of *The Palaeography of Gothic Manuscript Books*." *Scriptorium* 58: 274–9.

Smith, M. H. 2007 [2008]. "Avant-propos." *Bibliothèque de l'École des Chartes*, 165: 5-8.

Soler, A. 2004. "Review of *The Palaeography of Gothic Manuscript Books*." *Studia Lulliana*, 44: 163–4.

Stiennon, J. 1999. *Paléographie du Moyen Âge*, 3rd ed. Paris: A. Colin.

Stirnemann, P. and M. H. Smith. 2007. "Forme et fonction des écritures d'apparat dans les manuscrits latins (VIIIe–XVe siècle)." *Bibliothèque de l'École des Chartes* 165: 67–100.

Stutzmann, D. 2005–. *Nomenklatur der gotischen Buchschriften: Nennen? Systematisieren? Wie und wozu?* http://www.iaslonline.lmu.de/index.php?vorgang_id=995, accessed January 5, 2020.

Vandamme, L. 2008. "Review of *The Palaeography of Gothic Manuscript Books*." *Handelingen van het Genootschap voor Geschiedenis te Brugge*, 145: 171–4.

CHAPTER 21

···

GOTHIC SCRIPT IN FRANCE IN THE LATER MIDDLE AGES

(XIIIth–XVth centuries)

···

MARIE-HÉLÈNE TESNIÈRE
(Translated by Frank T. Coulson)

DURING the last three centuries of the Middle Ages, France saw the development of what is commonly called Gothic script. Derived from a late Latin term *gothicus* which means "related to the Goths," the term Gothic appears for the first time around 1440 under the pen of Lorenzo Valla to designate a script considered in some way "barbaric."[1] Today, one uses the term Gothic script to designate a script which from the morphological perspective is neither a Caroline script nor a humanistic script. In the French domain, one places it between the end of the twelfth century and the beginning of the sixteenth century.

In fact, Gothic script includes several types of script. Albert Derolez's new study, *The Palaeography of Gothic Manuscript Books from the Twelfth to the Early Sixteenth Century* (Derolez, 2003), is a fundamental and indispensable reference tool.[2] Reworking the nomenclature of scripts established by Lieftinck and his students, Derolez, who was Curator of Manuscripts of the library of the University of Ghent, classified the scripts into five types which henceforward are recognized as authoritative.[3] For France, one retains in particular:

Littera textualis of the North or *textualis*
Littera textualis of the South or *rotunda*
Littera cursiva
Littera hybrida
Littera semihybrida or *Bastarda*

To each of these types of scripts is also applied a term, sometimes a bit subjective, which takes into account the level of calligraphic execution, and particularly the degree of elaboration of the upper and lower finishing strokes:

- *formata* describes a script perfectly executed, written with particular care, and which gives an impression of order.
- *libraria* describes a script of a good workmanship for ordinary books.
- *currens* describes a rapidly written script with a certain carelessness of execution and one that gives an impression of disorder.

Thus, *littera textualis formata* designates a Gothic script that is perfectly calligraphic.

A page which appears black, a script written close together laterally, with a narrow space between the lines, an impression of closeness, sometimes of roughness, this is the image which a page written in Gothic script gives at first glance. It is totally opposed to the sense of space, readability, and execution which, up to the end of the twelfth century, a page written in Gothicizing Caroline gives.

In their investigation of the emergence of Gothic script, palaeographers have posited a totality of new technical, socio-economic, and cultural factors which help to explain its appearance:[4]

- the sharpening on a beveled edge of the tip of the pen, which begins in England at the end of the twelfth century and expands into Normandy, then toward the Paris basin, spreading a Gothicizing tendency (the Gothic break with its thick and thin strokes).[5] It is in Normandy where one finds, toward the beginning of the thirteenth century, the oldest witness of calligraphic Gothic script.[6]
- the development of royal administrations, particularly at Paris, and the establishment of schools and then universities at Bologna (1158), Oxford (1214) Paris (1215), Toulouse (1229), Salerno (1231), Montpellier (1289), increased exponentially the need for books as instruction developed. The rapid development in the production of manuscripts, in the second quarter of the thirteenth century, took place at the same time as the establishment of the Gothic script. Gothic script goes hand in hand with the development of secular workshops which, in taking the place little by little of the monastic scriptoria, brought about a new division of work between the craftsmen of the book.[7]
- Gothic script comes out of the "Gothic" style, a term which not only covers artistic work but encompasses an entire thought system. The art historian Erwin Panofsky (1957) drew a link between scholasticism and the birth of Gothic cathedrals: in the same way as scholastic teaching structures texts by a succession of divisions and reordering of its smallest elements, so Gothic architecture, beginning with the crossing of the ribs of the vault, divides and reorders each of the elements which makes up a cathedral. Several years later, the palaeographer Robert Marichal (1963, 199–247, esp. 233–43) showed that the appearance of Gothic script worked on a similar system: he posited that the serif at the base of the ascenders of letters led in the script to an angular imbalance which was balanced by the breaking which divided the round letter into basic angles. The analogy between the Gothic style in architecture and the Gothic script (see Plate 21.1) is continued in the link one can make between the flamboyant Gothic style and the Gothic *Bastarda* script (see Plate 21.2).

PLATE 21.1 Window in the Gothic Rayonnant style and a Psalter, written in Aisne between 1245 and 1272 (cf. CMDF, vol. I, p. 357 and Plate XIV, manuscript Paris, Bibliothèque Sainte-Geneviève 2689, fol. 20v), from Marichal (1963, 234).

PLATE 21.2 Window in the Gothic Flamboyant style and the *Decameron* of Boccaccio in French, written at Grammont (Belgium) around 1432 (cf. CMDF, vol. I, p. 173 and pl. XCIV, manuscript Paris, Bibliothèque de l'Arsenal 5070, fol. 395), from Marichal (1963, 242).

- the organization and formalism particular to the thirteenth century, with its encyclopedias and its dictionaries, equally affected script. While the number of Gothic scripts multiplies, one notices during the thirteenth century a sort of "international" standardization in the *ductus* of each type of script.

The expansion of Gothic script was helped by the circulation of men, works, and models throughout Europe, especially through the networks of the religious orders, but the University of Paris, by its power of attraction, played a fundamental role in this area.

Each script evolved following a different time frame, and so we shall approach this study of Gothic script following a division which reflects the evolution of manuscript production in France, and particularly in Paris, which played a dominant role at least up to the first quarter of the fifteenth century:

- from the end of the twelfth century/beginning of the thirteenth century to the first quarter of the fourteenth century
- from the second quarter of the fourteenth century to the first quarter of the fifteenth century
- from the second quarter of the fifteenth century to the first quarter of the sixteenth century.

One finds good examples of all these scripts in the plates transcribed and commented on in Thomson (1969, Plates 6–28).[8] For the *ductus* of the letters, one may consult Brown and Lovett (1999, 127). One may also read with profit the review of the research on Gothic script conducted over the last 50 years in Steinmann (2004, 399–415).

FROM THE BEGINNING OF THE THIRTEENTH CENTURY TO THE SECOND QUARTER OF THE FOURTEENTH CENTURY

The urbanization of the city, the centralization of power, and the renewal of scholarship which took place in the last third of the twelfth century made Paris in the thirteenth century the book capital of Europe. Around 1208, teachers and students joined in a *Universitas* which received statutes in 1215, and in the middle of the thirteenth century it numbered four faculties (arts, theology, law, and medicine). The first secular workshops produced large quantities of books, developing notably in Paris around 1210–30. The name of one of these bookshops has been preserved, Master Alexander, who inscribed his name in gold lettering on a Bible dated to 1220–30 (see Plate 21.3). From 1260, a system of renting out collections of works for copying, known as *pecia*, was put into place at the Convent of the Paris Dominicans.[9]

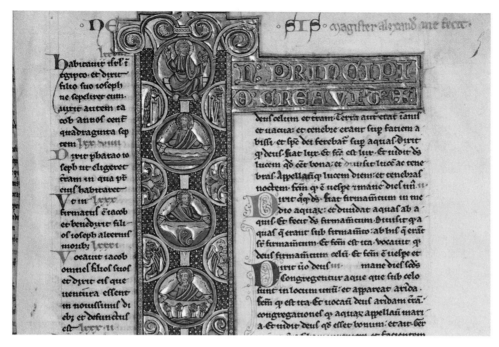

PLATE 21.3 The so-called Bible of Master Alexander, MS. Paris, BnF, lat., 11930, fol. 5. Paris, *c*.1220–30, one of the oldest examples of Parisian secular production at the beginning of the thirteenth century.

Example of *littera praegothica*.

- Note: the reference in gold letters: "Magister Alexander me fecit"; the incipit [I]n principio creavit: in capitals with an Uncial *e* and *a*; small-scale pre-Gothic script with a *d* with a disproportionate and inclined shaft; upward ascenders of *b*, *l*, and *h* are short and forked; the lower ascenders of *p* and *q* are also short and end with a finishing stroke; no fusion; *ct* ligature.

Littera textualis formata

The finest Gothic script is the *littera textualis formata*, namely the script used for the copying of Bibles (*textus* means the Bible). It is according to this script that one defines the three elements which characterize a Gothic script: the breaking, the lateral compression, the vertical flattening.

- Breaking transforms imperceptibly in the course of the twelfth century the form of letters: the *o*, which had the shape of a circle, takes the form of rounded diamond-shape (Fig. 21.1); the bow of the *e* breaks in successive strokes. The breaking is accompanied by contrast between full and heavy strokes and strokes which are slender and fine. The script sometimes becomes more angular. But the development of hooks at the end of the downstrokes in the letter *m*, which seems to link the downstrokes to one another and to give an impression of cursivity, makes up for this angular character (Fig. 21.2):

o

FIG. 21.1

m

FIG. 21.2

- The lateral compression of the letters entails the phenomena of overlapping, of fusion or elision. So, very quickly the double letters *bb*, *pp*, for example, have a tendency to overlap (Fig. 21.3). Then the bows, henceforth broken in straight strokes, in some letters have a tendency to fuse (Wilhelm Meyer's rule): firstly, the groupings of *de*, *do*, and then *da* with *a* in the form of a box, but also *be*, *bo*, *pe*, and *po* or again *oc* and *od* (Figs. 21.4 and 5). Sometimes the fusion entails three successive letters, *doc* or *hoc*.[10] Similarly, in order to ensure that a curved form does not find itself in contact with a straight stroke, it is always a round form of the *r*, derived from the old *or* ligature, which is placed next to letters with a round form, such as *b*, *d*, or *r*. One also notes the elision of certain approach strokes of the *i* or the *h*, after *c* or *t* (Zamponi's rule), *c+i* appears as an *a* (Fig. 21.6).

FIG. 21.3   FIG. 21.4   FIG. 21.5   FIG. 21.6

- the vertical compression of the script, by reducing the height and depth of the ascending and descending ascenders, has made the letters with ascenders and tails difficult to differentiate from the other downstrokes. In order to make them stand out, one accentuates ascending ascenders (*b*, *l*, *h*) with serifs or with forked strokes (Fig. 21.7); one underlines the tails (*q*, *p*) with a quick stroke to the right (Fig. 21.8).

FIG. 21.7   FIG. 21.8

Littera textualis formata, moreover is remarkable for the development of certain letters:

- the letter *a*: The uncial *a* of the Caroline minuscule stood notably upright during the Romanesque period. Its upper approach stroke developed little by little into a hook (Fig. 21.9), then into a large crook, which closes on the lower bow (Fig. 21.10). Toward 1300, the *a* is made with a double bow. It will close truly into the form of a box in the fourteenth century.

FIG. 21.9   FIG. 21.10

- the letter *d*: The semi-uncial *d* with the straight upward ascender (Fig. 21.11) disappears little by little to be replaced by an uncial *d* with an inclined upward ascender (Fig. 21.12). This phenomenon was completed at Paris around 1300.

FIG. 21.11   FIG. 21.12

The straight *f* and *s* are written above the writing line (Figs. 21.13 and 21.14). At the end of lines, the round *s* is generally used (Fig. 21.15).

FIG. 21.13   FIG. 21.14   FIG. 21.15

- ligatures: All ligatures have disappeared, except for the group *ct*, which is still found throughout the thirteenth century (Fig. 21.16), and the group *st*, which will last up to the end of the Middle Ages (Fig. 21.17). The ampersand & disappears to be replaced by *et* written in full or as a sort of crossed *7* (Fig. 21.18).

FIG. 21.16   FIG. 21.17   FIG. 21.18

The *littera textualis formata* originates in Paris during the second quarter of the thirteenth century. It is well established by the middle of the thirteenth century at the time of the dedication of the Sainte-Chapelle (1248) (See Plate 21.4).

Pregothic script (Plate 21.5) or *littera praegothica* designates a script written between the second half of the twelfth century and the first quarter of the thirteenth century which shows only some elements of Gothic (Plate 21.6).

Southern *littera texualis* or *littera rotunda*

In the south of France and in the centers closely linked with Italy, such as Lyons, *littera textualis formata* competes with a script which is called Southern *littera textualis* or

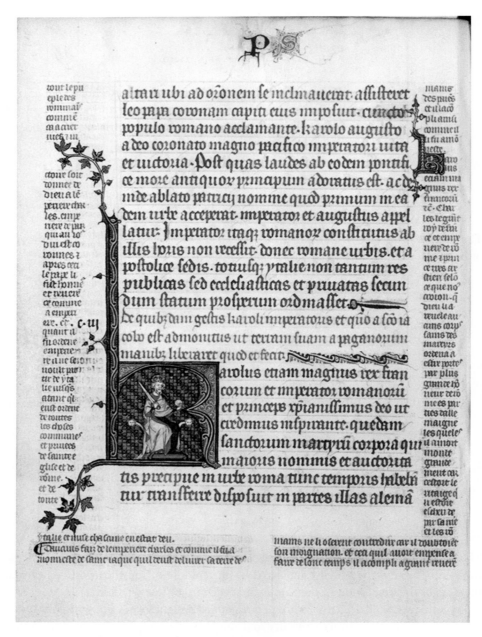

PLATE 21.4 Yvo de Sancto Dyonisio, *Gesta regum Francorum*, MS. Paris, BnF, lat. 13836, fol. 34v made at Saint-Denis-en-France (near Paris), in 1317 (cf. CMDF, vol. III, p. 339).

Example of *littera textualis formata*.

- Note: a script giving the impression of roundness because of the hooks at the ends of the downstrokes of *m* and *n*; the *a* whose upper bow is marked by a slender stroke which closes the upper part of the *a*; upper ascenders of *d* and *l* relatively tall in comparison with the smaller downward ascender of the *p*; the *d* with a sloping downstroke and ending in a finishing stroke; ligatures of *st* and *ct*; fusion in *po, od, do, de*, but also *da*.

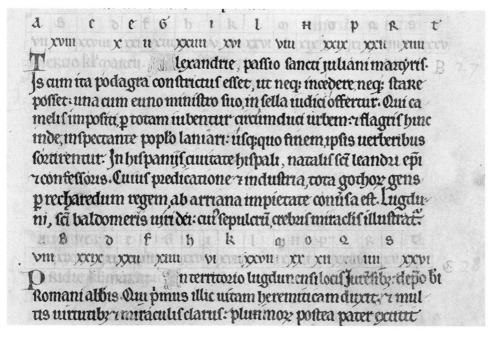

PLATE 21.5 An example of Pregothic script or *littera praegothica*: Usuardus, *Martyrologium*, Paris, 1216–20, Paris, BnF, lat. 12833, fol. 36r.

- Particular features: the *a* with one bow; the overlapping of the two *bb* of *abbati*s (line 15); several forms of *r*: Uncial *r* after *o*, but also after *a* (cf. *martyris* line 3); capital *r* (*stare* line 4); capital *n* still in Uncial form (line 1).
- Transcription: Tercio Kalendas Marcii. Alexandrie Passio sancti Juliani martyris. / Is cum ita podagra constrictus esset ut neque incedere neque stare / posset una cum Euno ministro suo in sella iudici offertur. Qui ca/melis impositi per totam iubentur circumduci urbem et flagris hinc / inde inspectante populo laniari usquequo finem ipsis uerberibus / sortirentur. In Hispaniis ciuitate Hispali natalis sancti Leandri episcopi / et confessoris cuius predicatione et industria tota Gothorum gens / per Recharedum regem ab arriana impietate conuersa est. Lugdu/ni sancti Baldomeris uiri Dei cuius sepulcrum crebris miraculis illustratur.

littera rotunda, since it is derived from *littera bononiensis*, a script which originated at the University of Bologna and which was used especially in legal manuscripts. In fact, the *littera rotunda* is frequently used to copy works of law and medicine.

Littera rotunda is a script which has a rounded appearance, but is compressed laterally, and is written in a relatively large space between the lines (Plate 21.7). The following elements characterize the script:

- the circular or semi-circular form of certain letters *e*, *o*, *q*, *d*, *b*, *h* (Figs. 21.19, 20, and 21) which form a contrast with the straight endings of the first two down-strokes of the *m* (Fig. 21.22) and the first downstroke of the *n* (Fig. 21.22).

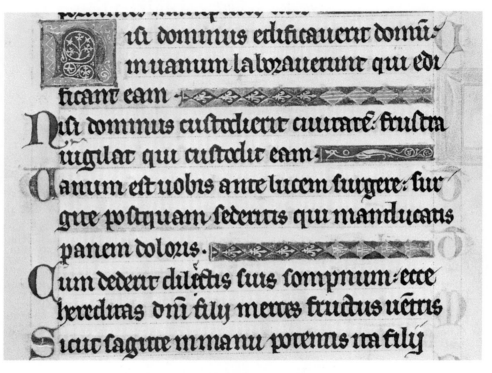

e   **od**   **b**   **m**

FIG. 21.19    FIG. 21.20    FIG. 21.21    FIG. 21.22

- the *a*, consisting of a downstroke and a lower bow with a triangular shape, with a full stroke curving up in a slender stroke which outlines the upper bow (Fig. 21.23).

a

FIG. 21.23

PLATE 21.6 Example of Gothic script or *littera textualis formata*: *Psalterium ad usum Sanctae Capellae Parisiensis*, Paris, [1258–70], BnF, MS. lat. 10525, fol. 228v, cf. CMDF, vol. III, p. 185 and Plate LXXXV.

- Particular features: the *a* with a double bow, the upper bow being closed with a crook formed with a thin stroke; the fusions *do* (*domum*, line 1), *bo* (*laborauerun*t with an Uncial *r* after *o*, line 2), and *od* (*custodierit*, line 4); the ligatures *st* (*custodit*, line 5) and *ct* (*dilectis*, line 8); short, forked ascenders of the *d* (*edificauerit*, line 1) and *b* (*uobis*, line 6); two forms of *d*, sometimes upright (*edificauerit*, line 1) and sometimes Uncial (*domum*, line 1).
- Transcription: Nisi Dominus edificauerit domum / in uanum laborauerunt qui edi/ficant eam. / Nisi Dominus custodierit ciuitatem frustra / uigilat qui custodit eam. / Vanum est uobis ante lucem surgere sur/gite postquam sederitis qui manducatis/ panem doloris. / Cum dederit dilectis suis sompnum. Ecce / hereditas Domini filii merces fructus uentris / sicut sagitte in manu potentis ita filii.

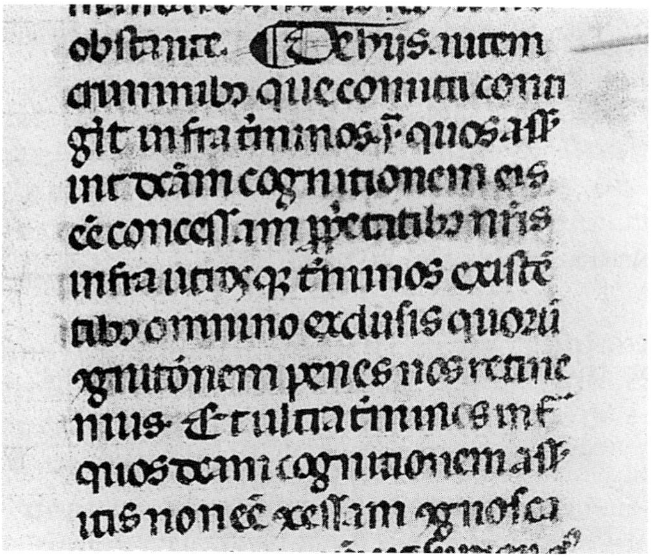

PLATE 21.7 Example of *littera rotunda*: *Consuetudines urbis Tholosae cum glossa*, Toulouse, 1296, MS. Paris, BnF, lat. 9186, fol. 32, cf. CMDF, vol. III, p. 103.

- Particular features: the round *d* with a ascender leaning to the left on the horizontal line (*dcam=dictam*, line 4); the *a* with a lower bow in a triangle (*infra*, line 3); the *g* in the form of an *8* (*cognitionem*, line 4); the abbreviation *us* in the form of a semicircle after *b* (*criminibus*, line 2); the abbreviation for *con* in the form of a *9* (*cognitionem* line 8); several types of *r*, trailing *s*.[11]

- Transcription: De hiis autem / criminibus que comita conti/gerit infra terminos infra quos asser/int dictam cognitionem eis / esse concessam proprietatibus nostris / infra utrosque terminos existen/tibus omnino exclusis quorum / congnitionem penes nos retine/mus, et ultra terminos infra / quos dictam cognitionem asser/itis non esse concessam cognosca...

- the *d* often having a very short ascender and turned practically on the horizontal toward the left (Fig. 21.24)

FIG. 21.24

- at the end of words, the *s* is generally round (Fig. 21.25) or trailing (Fig. 21.26).

FIG. 21.25    FIG. 21.26

- the abbreviation *us* after *b* takes the form of a semicircle (Fig. 21.27); the abbreviation *con* looks like a *9* (Fig. 21.28).

FIG. 21.27   FIG. 21.28

- the *z* is sometimes replaced by a *c cedilla*.

Remarks on the different forms of *littera textualis*

The *littera textualis formata* is the script used to copy liturgical manuscripts, paraliturgical manuscripts, constitutions, customaries, sacred manuals, and quite simply books with an "official" character. In particularly luxurious liturgical books, one uses a particular form of the script called *littera textualis praescissa* (from the Latin *praescindere* which means "to cut"), for the downstrokes of the *m* and *n* appear to have been cut straight.

For ordinary books of good workmanship one uses *littera textualis libraria*, a less carefully executed script than *textualis formata*, and whose angle and incline are less constant, whose alignment is less rigorous, and whose regularity of layout is less strict. It is often characterized by an *a* which exceeds the body of the writing and by a *d* whose ascender to some extent lies to the left, overflowing into the margin. Frequently under the influence of documentary script, the first line of the page has *litterae elongatae*, that is, letters whose ascenders extend into the upper margin.

On the lowest rung of the calligraphic hierarchy one finds *littera textualis currens* or *littera parisiensis* (Plate 21.8), used for the copying of university manuscripts at Paris from the second half of the thirteenth century to the third quarter of the fourteenth century. It is a script which seems to dance between the lines. Its full strokes are thick, with a rather large number of finishing strokes in the *e* and the *t*. The ascenders are especially short. The Uncial *u* take the form of a rounded *v* whose first ascender is higher than the second: it may be confused with the *b*. The *a* is now simplified into an *a* with only one compartment, sometimes with a double bow. The final *s* is sometimes straight, resembling a capital *C*, sometimes round. The lower bow of the *g* is closed by a slender stroke. The ligature *&* is noted by a crossed *7*.[12] The script is rapidly executed and is highly abbreviated (the abbreviations can be found in Capelli (1966). One may also consult the list of abbreviations at http://www.menestrel.fr.

From the second quarter of the thirteenth century till the end of the thirteenth century Parisian booksellers produced bibles of a very small size (a maximum of 150 mm high by 110 mm wide) which one usually calls "pocket bibles." They are generally equipped with new chapter numberings by Stephen Langton and they end with the *Interpretatio nominum hebraicorum*. They are copied on very fine parchment. The script is so tiny that the succession of letters gives the impression of a string of pearls threaded on the line of writing (see Plate 21.9).[13]

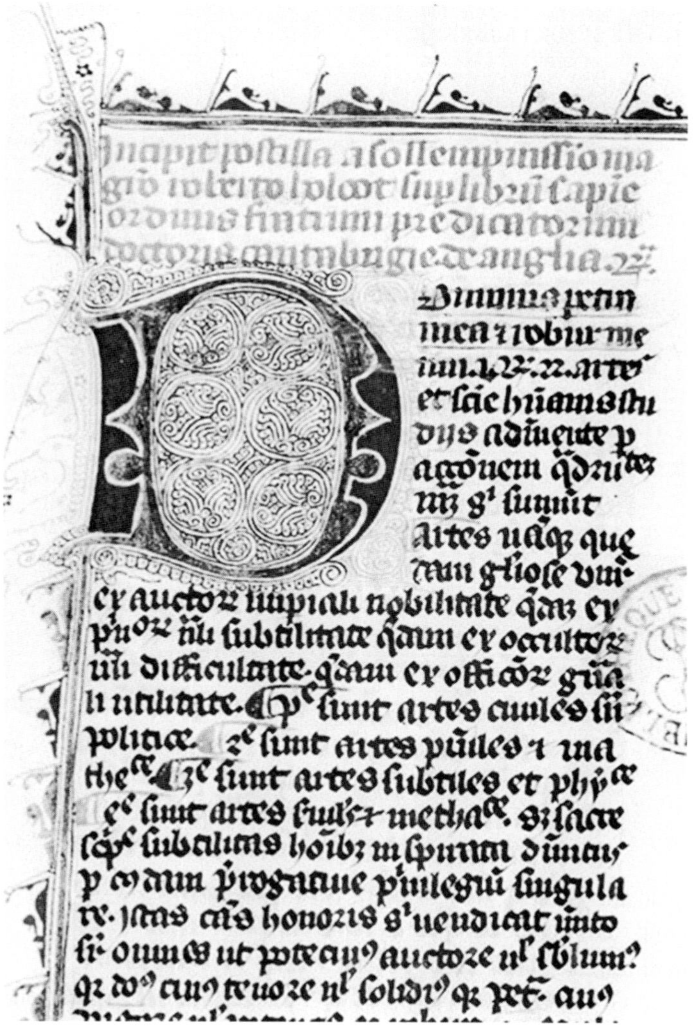

PLATE 21.8 Example of *littera parisiensis*: Robertus Holcoth, *Expositio in librum Sapientiae*, [Paris] 1353, MS. Paris, BnF, lat. 15885, fol. 1, CMDF, vol. III, p. 461.

- Particular features: the difference between the rubricated title written in *littera textualis libraria* and the body of the text written in *littera textualis currens* or *littera parisiensis*; finishing strokes on certain letters at the end of the line but also on *h* and *x*; the trailing *s* at the end of line (*artes*, line 7) or in abbreviated words (*serviles*, line 20), but round *s* elsewhere; very numerous abbreviations, especially the *z* in the form of a *3* marking the *m* of the accusative (*materiam*, line 11).

- Transcription: Incipit Postilla a sollempnissimo ma/gistro Roberto Holcot super librum Sapientie / ordinis fratrum predicatorum / doctoris Cantabrigie de Anglia. Rubrica. / *Dominus petra* / *mea et robur me/um*. 2 Reg. 22. Artes et scientie humanis stu/diis adinuente per / accionem quadruplicem / materiam sibi sumunt. / Artes namque que/ dam gloriose uidentur / ex auctorum imperiali nobilitate quedam ex / principiorum naturali subtilitate quedam ex occultorum / materiali difficultate quedam ex officiorum genera/li utilitate. Prime sunt artes ciuiles siue / politice. Secunde sunt artes pueriles et mathematice. Tertie sunt artes subtiles et physice. / Quarte sunt artes seruiles et mechanice. Sed Sacre / Scripture subtilitas hominibus inspirata diuinitus / per cuiusdam prerogatiue priuilegium singula/re istas causas honoris sibi uendicat merito / super omnes utpote cuius auctore nihil sublimius / quam *Dominus*, cuius tenore nihil solidius quam *petra*, cuius...

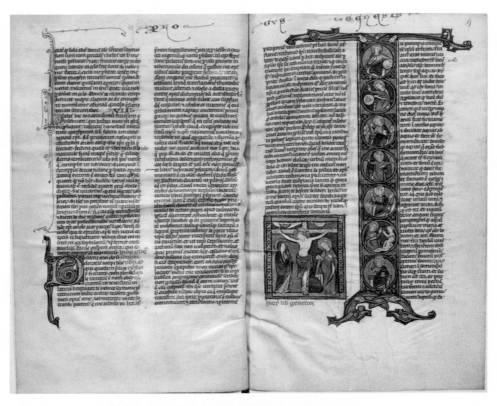

PLATE 21.9 Small pocket Bible, MS Paris, BnF, lat. 16265, fols. 3v–4r, 137 × 101 mm, very fine parchment, dating from the second quarter of the thirteenth century.

Example of *littera textualis libraria*

- Note: the running title in the upper margin "Prologus Genesis"; small-scale script whose upper and lower ascenders are very short, but forked; a single *d* whose downstroke extends into the left margin, but elsewhere *d* whose downstroke is straight or inclined; the *a* has a single bow with a prominent beginning stroke.

Not infrequently, one finds several types of script on the same page. In glossed manuscripts, particularly bibles, the primary text, in this case the Bible, is copied in large format *littera textualis formata* written between two double lines, whereas the commentary, that is to say the text of the *Glossa ordinaria*, is copied in a script of smaller format, the two texts intercalated one with the other according to a page layout particular to Parisian manuscripts of the thirteenth century (Plate 21.10).[14] Thus, one may compare the difference of script arising from the use of a different format.

Such an organization of the different levels of script is also found in university manuscripts, and more specifically in the canonical commentaries on the works of Aristotle (see Plate 21.11).

The script in vernacular manuscripts has to date not been the object of a palaeographical study. For this, see Careri, Fery-Hue, Gasparri, *et al.* (2001) for transcribed

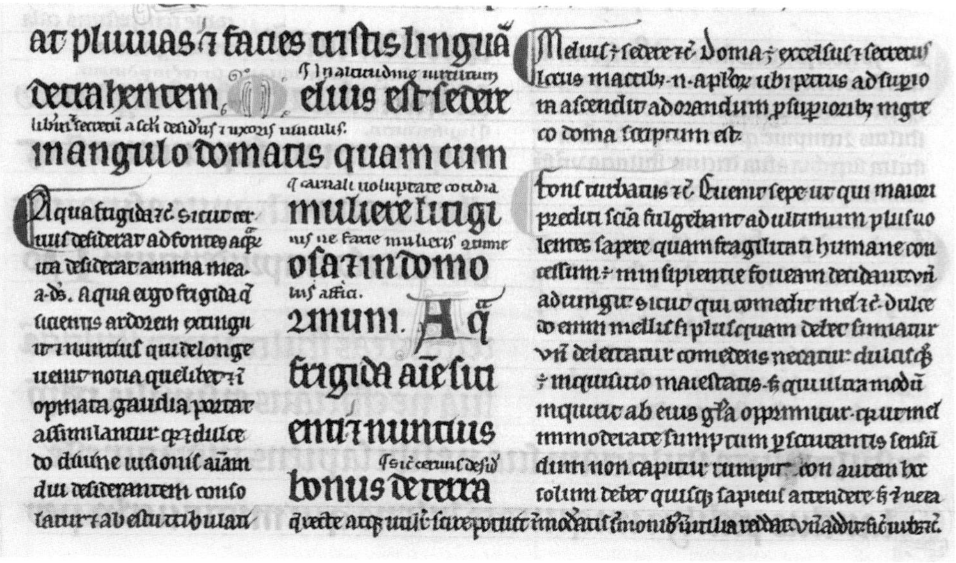

PLATE 21.10 Bible (Proverbs), copied for the bishop Gui de Clermont at Paris, between 1250 and 1260, MS. Paris, BnF, lat. 466, f. 34.[15]

- Special features for script copied in *littera textualis praescissa*: the feet of the downstrokes of *m* and *n* seem cut; the *d* has a downstroke to the left in the form of a hook (*detrahentem*, line 2); the sign for con (*communi*, line 6) resembles a 2.
- Special features for the *Glossa ordinaria*, right column: the script of the commentary seems to dance on the line; Tironian abbreviation sign (two points with a stroke through the middle) for *est*; ligatured *&* and *also* in the form of *7* with a stroke (*etc.*, line 1); fusion of *oc* (*locus*, line 2).
- Special features for the interlinear gloss: the last downstroke of the *m* is longer (*uirtutum*, line 1).
- Transcription: Proverbs XXV, 23–5: at pluuias et facies tristis linguam detrahentem. Melius est sedere in angulo domatis quam cum muliere litigiosa et in domo communi. Aqua frigida anime sitienti et nuntius bonus de terra.
- *Glossa ordinaria*, right column, Melius est sedere etc. Doma est excelsus et secretus locus. In Actibus enim apostolorum (X,9) ubi Petrus ad superiora ascendit ad orandum pro superioribus in greco doma scriptum est.
- Interlinear gloss: In altitudine uirtutum liberum et secretum a seculi desideriis et uxoris uinculis.

plates and commentary, and, in particular, the introduction (pp. xxv–xxx).[16] The authors define thus the current French script of the thirteenth century:

a small script with the appearance of Gothic, but as a general rule much less broken than the latter, and remaining closer to the Caroline script which evolved from 12th-century glosses as well as from non-book script (*notula*), not codified, . . . often more running and rapid than *textualis*, which was influenced more or less by documentary script.

(Careri, Fery-Hue, Gasparri, *et al.* 2001, xxvi)

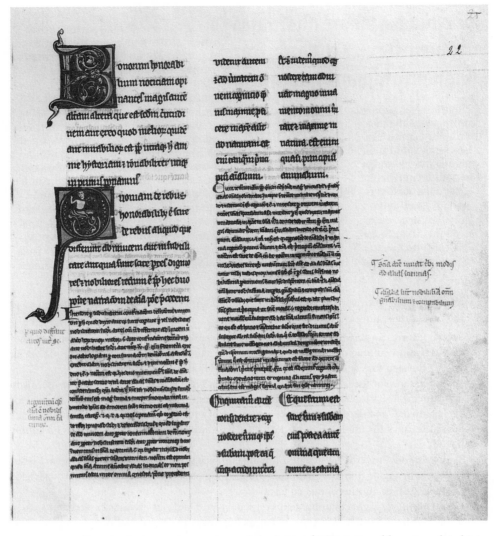

PLATE 21.11 *Commentarium magnum Averrois in Aristotelis De Anima libros*, translated into Latin by Michael Scot, MS. Paris, BnF, lat. 16151, fol. 22r, copied at Paris during the third quarter of the thirteenth century.

Example of *littera textualis formata*.

- Note: the two translations of the *De anima* of Aristotle, placed either one following the other (left column) or one next to one another in the same column (right column); the commentary of Michael Scot is smaller in scale; in both cases, a script whose body is relatively stretched toward the vertical, with an *a* formed from two bows which surpasses the body of the script.

It is thus a script which to a degree takes into account the secondary character attributed to writings in the vernacular.

From the Second Quarter of the Fourteenth Century to the First Quarter of the fifteenth Century

The period which extends from the second quarter of the fourteenth century to the first quarter of the fifteenth century corresponds to the full flowering of book production in Paris, and, in particular, to the development of books in the vernacular intended for the aristocracy. Fine ecclesiastical and princely libraries are built up, witnesses to the vitality of intellectual exchange and of book circulation. The library of the College of the Sorbonne held nearly 1,200 volumes in 1339. The library of Charles V, installed in the tower of the Hawk House in the Louvre, held 917 volumes at the death of Charles V in 1380, of which two-thirds were in French. Paris at the beginning of the fifteenth century was an influential center of illuminated manuscripts. A small circle of scholars centered round Jean de Montreuil were particularly interested in the transmission of classical texts and in the material quality of their copies.[17]

The evolution of *littera texualis formata*

Littera textualis formata continued to be used during the fourteenth century and at the beginning of the fifteenth for official books whether they were liturgical, paraliturgical, or royal. The script is, however, more angular and of a larger format. For bibles of large format and expensive liturgical books, one used a squarer script, *littera textualis quadrata* (Plate. 21.12): the strokes of the letters in this script on the upper and lower lines were finished with thick strokes in the form of a diamond or square (Fig. 21.29), which makes all the letters appear the same, as we find, for example, in the Gospel of the Sainte-Chapelle, manuscript Paris, Bibliothèque de l'Arsenal 161 (see Plate 21.13).

FIG. 21.29

In the French sphere, a particular form of *textualis quadrata* develops marked by:

- a rounded form of the feet of the downstrokes for *m* and *n* and straight *s* which is joined to the following letter by a thin upstroke (Fig. 21.30)

m

FIG. 21.30

- the evolution of the form of *a*: the form of the *a* of *textualis quadrata* (*a* with a double bow whose upper bow is formed with a crook ending in a thin stroke) is replaced little by little by an *a* in the form of a box, at first only after *d*, *b*, and *h* (the fusion of *da*, *ba*), then also after *c*, *t*, *v*, and *g*; at the beginning of the fifteenth century, only the *a* at the beginning of the word retains the form of the *textualis quadrata*, and this form will also disappear by the middle of the fifteenth century.

The scribes of Charles V, particularly Henri de Trevou and Raoulet d'Orléans, used a rounded script of a smaller type derived from *textualis formata*. This script will become the canonical one for texts in French. It is characterized by an elegant balance between the lateral compression and readability (Plate 21.14).[18]

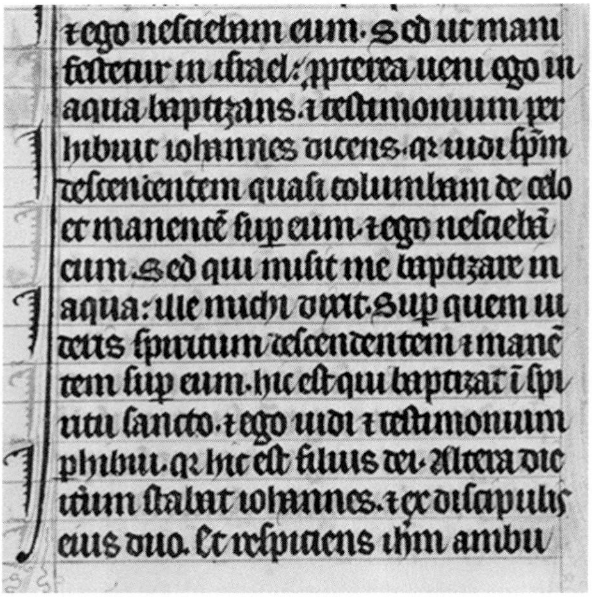

PLATE 21.12 Example of *littera textualis quadrata*: Bible, called the Bible of Robert de Bylling (Paris) April 30, 1327, MS. Paris, BnF, Latin 11935, fol. 557v; see CMDF, vol. III, p. 261.

- Particular features: very short ascenders of *d* and *b*; the rounded feet of the downstrokes of *m*, *n*, and *s*; the *a* in form of a box after *b* (*nesciebam*, line 1 and *baptizans*, line 3) and after *h* (*Johannes*, line 4), but elsewhere with an upper bow in the form of a crook.
- Transcription Joh. I, 31–5: Et ego nesciebam eum sed ut mani/festetur in Israel propterea ueni ego in / aqua baptizans. Et testimonium per/hibuit Johannes dicens quia uidi Spiritum / descendentem quasi columbam de celo / et manentem super eum. Et ego nesciebam / eum sed qui misit me baptizare in /aqua ille michi dixit super quem ui/deris Spiritum descendentem et manen/tem super eum. Hic est qui baptizat in Spi/ritu sancto . . .

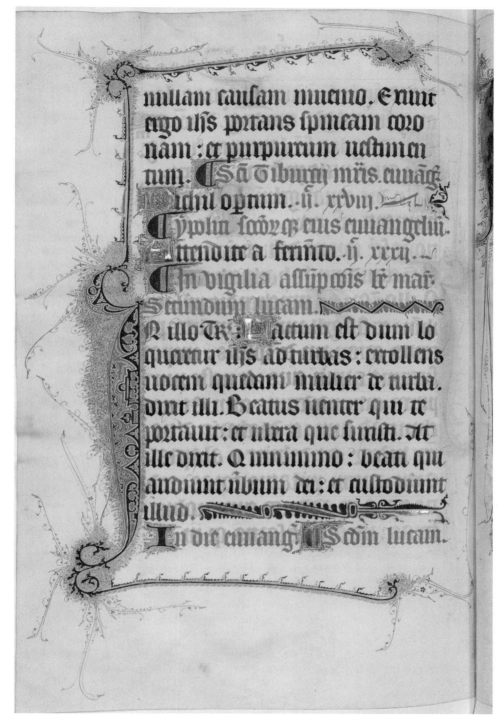

PLATE 21.13 Gospel of the Sainte-Chapelle, MS. Paris, Bibliothèque de l'Arsenal 161, fol. 210v, made at Paris, *c.*1345–50, the filigree work is that of Jacquet Maci.

Example of *littera textualis quadrata*.

- Note: the strokes of the *m* and *n* end with little diamonds giving a square appearance to the script; end strokes particularly on the final letters such as *r*, *t*, or *s*; an *a* whose double bow is formed by a slender stroke which joins the opening top stroke and the vertical stroke which forms the lower bow.

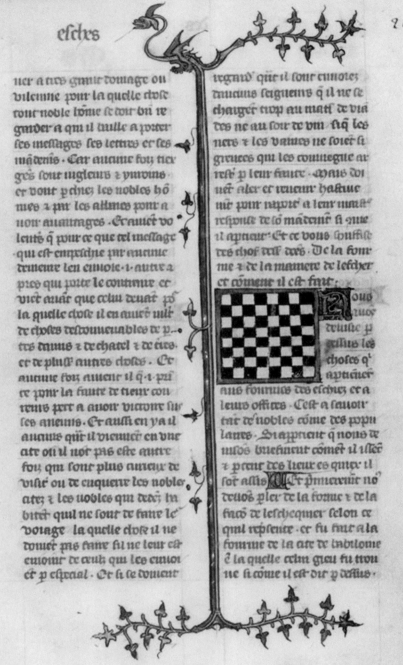

PLATE 21.14 Translation of the *Liber super ludo scaccorum* of Jacques de Cessoles by Jean de Vignay, copied by Henri du Trévou for Charles V, MS. Paris, BnF, Fr. 1728, fol. 210r.

An example of *littera textualis quasi formata*.

- Note: small scale writing written entirely in a space between the lines, with ascenders barely going above the body of the text, final *s* in the form of a *13*; the *i* has a tick; finishing strokes complete the *h*.

In the south of France, *textualis rotunda* becomes more angular during the four-teenth century: the script seems more square than round, as one finds in the Pontifical of the bishop of Fréjus which comprises one part copied in *textualis quadrata* and the other copied in *littera rotunda* (Plate 21.15), or in the Breviari d'amor of Matfre Ermengau, MS. Paris BnF, Fr. 857, fol. 84v) copied at Toulouse in the second quarter of the fourteenth century (*c*.1340) (see Plate 21.16).

Littera cursiva formata

The burgeoning of commerce, which increased the use of script in all commercial transactions, contributed to the development of cursive script in the course of the thirteenth century in documents related to trade. Cursive script was also employed in manuscripts, where, because of its rapid writing, it was often used to take down sermons. But since its characteristics varied from one individual to another, we will not study it here.

Rather we shall take up the study of Gothic cursive script or *littera cursiva formata*, a formal and stylized cursive script which appears in manuscripts of the second half of the fourteenth century. *Littera cursiva formata* is the heir to the documentary script of the royal chancellery, on which one may consult Brunel (2005).

Contrary to *littera textualis*, which was vertically and horizontally compact, *littera cursiva formata* fills up the entire limits of the space between the lines. But if the ascending ascenders take up a great deal of space in height, the body of the text remains, in comparison, relatively small. As in charters, the incipit of the text is often noted in *littera textualis formata* whose large letters are copied with a thick stroke.

The following letters are characteristic:

- the *a* with a single compartment (Fig. 21.31)

FIG. 21.31

- the ascenders of the *b* and *l* form a loop (Figs. 21.32 and 21.33), which is sometimes reduced to a simple triangle, whereas the base of the letter is thicker (Figs. 21.34 and 21.35).

| FIG. 21.32 | FIG. 21.33 | FIG. 21.34 | FIG. 21.35 |

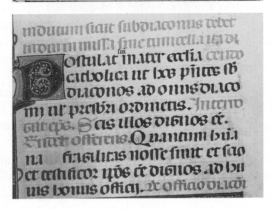

PLATE 21.15 Examples of *littera textualis quadrata* and *littera rotunda*: Pontificale ad usum archiepiscopatus Arelatensis, France (Toulouse?), 1371–8, MS. Paris, BnF, lat. 9479, fol. 38v quadrata and fol. 33v rotunda; cf CMDF, vol. III, p.123. François Avril (1981, n° 309) attributes the illumination to a workshop in Toulouse.

- Compare the phrase "*Postulat mater Ecclesia*" in the two scripts: *a* with a triangular bow, round *o* and *e* in the *rotunda*, *a* in the form of a box with thin stroke separating the two bows, *o* almost in the form of a diamond, *e* formed with two strokes in the *textualis quadrata*.
- Transcription: ... Et presentantibus eum atque ducen/tibus duobus diaconibus usque ad / presbiteros et dextera leuam tenentibus / duo presbiteri deducant eum usque / ad sedem pontificis et diaconus / dicit. Postulat mater Ecclesia ut supra in ordinatione diaconi et / ipse se erigens interrogens si dignus / sit. Ille autem atestantibus eundem / dignum et iustum esse Dei gratia / episcopus sedendo cum mitra dicat.
- Note in *littera rotunda* script: the lower bow of the *a* in the form of a closed triangle with a thin stroke and the stroke at the top lightly closed with a thin stroke (*ad*, line 5); the *h* made with a ascender and a semicircle (*catholica*, line 4); the *g* which takes the form of a capital *G* (*dignos*, line 7).
- Transcription: indutum sicut subdiaconus debet / indui in missa sine tunicella ita dic / endo. / Postulat [*interlinear addition* sancta] mater Ecclesia catholica ut hos presentes sub/ diaconos ad onus diaco / ni uel presbiteri ordinetis. Interro/gat episcopus. Scis illos dignos esse. / Respondet offerens. Quantum huma / na fragilitas nosse sinit, et scio / et testificor ipsos esse dignos ad hu / ius honus officii. De officio diaconi.

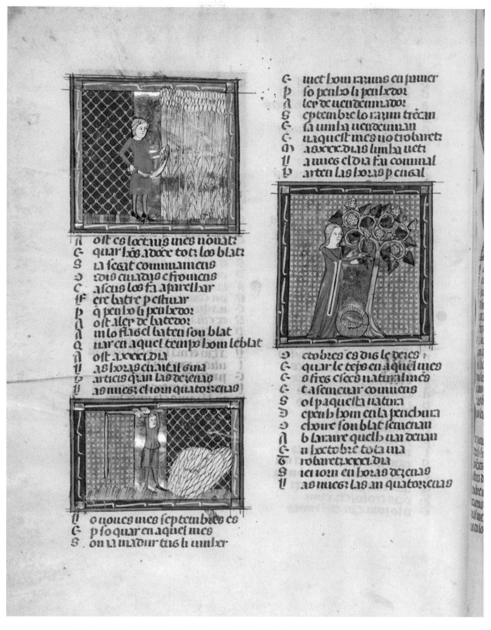

PLATE 21.16 Matfré Ermengau, *Breviari d'amor*, MS. Paris, BnF, Français 857, fol. 54v, copied at Toulouse in the second quarter of the fourteenth century (*c.*1340).

Example of Southern *littera textualis*.

- Note: capital letters at the beginning of verses; the *a* with a small triangular bow marked by a simple finishing stroke; the *e* with a small loop, made with a semicircle; the *o* and the bow of the *d* made from two vertical half-circles; the *g* which looks like our capital *G*.

- the ascender of the *d* sometimes has a loop which allows it to be linked with letters (Fig. 21.36); the lower part of the *d* is often bigger and more angular (Fig. 21.37).

FIG. 21.36    FIG. 21.37

- straight *f* and s descend below the line (Figs. 21.38 and 21.39).

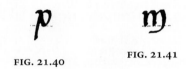

FIG. 21.38   FIG. 21.39

- the beginnings of certain letters have approach strokes (Fig. 21.40); the last stroke of the *m* and *n*, placed at the end of the word, is longer (Fig. 21.41).

p   *m*

FIG. 21.41

FIG. 21.40

- the final *s* has the form resembling *13* (Fig. 21.42).

ß

FIG. 21.42

- *r* has the form of a sort of *v* which may equally be open in a *u* (Fig. 21.43); the capital *R* is frequent (Fig. 21.44).

FIG. 21.43   FIG. 21.44

- *v* at the start of a word has a first stroke disproportionately large, so much so that it is sometimes confused with the *b* (Fig. 21.45).

FIG. 21.45

- *c* is made with two strokes of the pen, which gives it an angular look and sometimes allows it to be confused with the *t* (Fig. 21.46); in contrast, the *e*, which is made from two disjointed strokes (Fig. 21.47), is similar to a *c*.

FIG. 21.46    FIG. 21.47

- the tail of the *g* closes up and on the upper part it often has two horns.
- *st* and *ct* ligatures are frequent.

The level of stylization of *littera cursiva formata* varies. We provide two different examples (Plates 21.17 and 21.18). In the first, the script is quite clearly close to the script of the chancellery; in the second, the script has already undergone changes which foreshadow *Bastarda*. See also Plate 21.19.

Littera Hybrida

In the fifteenth century throughout Europe, with the exception of England, a script developed which mixes cursive and *textualis* and which one calls *littera hybrida* (Plate 21.20). It has long divided palaeographers.

From the *littera cursiva*, it has the following essential characteristics:

- *a* in a single compartment
- straight *s* and *s* descend below the line
- round *s* at the end of the word

From *littera textualis* the script has:

- ascenders on the *b*, *l*, and *d* without loops
- a precise manner of writing where the letters are detached

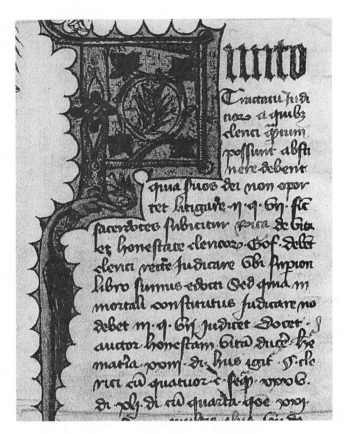

PLATE 21.17 Example of *littera cursiva formata*: Johannes Andreae, *Commentaria novella in tertium et quintum librum Decretalium*, France (Vendée), 1391–2, MS. Paris, BnF, lat. 4014, fol. 1, cf. CMDF, vol. II, p. 203.

- Note: the incipit *Finito* (line 1) written in large-scale *littera textualis formata*; the ascenders of *b*, *h*, *l*, and *d* have loops; s descends below the line; the *u* of *ubi* (line 11) is very open, with the first part of the letter disproportionate in comparison with the second; opening strokes on the *p* (*possunt*, line 5), *n* (*non*, line 7), and *r* (*recte*, line 11); capital *R* for *rubrica* (line 9).
- Transcription: Finito tractatu iudi/ciorum, a quibus clerici quantum / possunt abstinere debent / quia seruos Dei non oportet litigare 2 q. 7 [*sic*] sicut sacerdotes subicitur. Rubrica. De vita / et honestate clericorum Gof. debent / clerici recte iudicare vbi superiori / libro sumus edocti sed quia in / mortali constitutus iudicare non / debet 3 q. 7 iudicet docet auctor honestam vitam ducere…

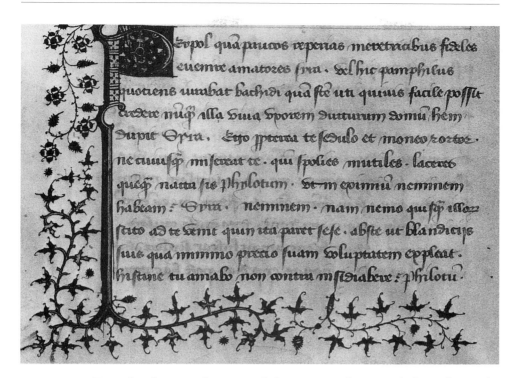

PLATE 21.18 Example of *cursiva formata* with humanist tendencies, which prefigures the *Bastarda*:[19] Terentius, *Comoediae*, [Paris, beginning of the fifteenth century], MS. Paris, BnF, lat. 8193, fol. 128v.

- Note: the unclosed loops of *l*, *h*, and *b*; ascenders of *q* and *s* which descend like a spindle; *s* is thicker than other letters (*ste = sancte*, line 3); opening strokes of *m* and *n* and of the ligature *et*; the *v* and *u* (*viva uxorem*, line 4); the rather thick base of *b* and *d* (*Bachidi*, line 3; *credere*, line 4); the *g* carrying two small horns with a tail ending in a fleeting stroke (*Ego*, line 5).
- Transcription: Per Pol quam paucos reperias meretricibus fideles /euenire amatores Syra. Vel hic Pamphilus / quotiens iurabat Bachidi quam sancte uti quiuis facile possit /credere numquam illa viua vxorem ducturum domum. Hem / duxit. Syra. Ego propterea te sedulo et moneo et ortor/ ne cuiusquam misereat te qui spolies mutiles laceres/.

Research by French humanists on script

Hostile to the calligraphic mannerisms of Gothic script, Italian humanists, particularly Petrarch, (1304–74) dreamed of a careful and clear script which "of itself penetrates the eye and respects the laws of orthography."[20] It will be up to his successor, Coluccio Salutati (1331–1406), chancellor of the Florentine republic, to invent "a new script, close to Caroline minuscule of the eleventh century, whose readability reflected, in his eyes, the purity of ancient writing."[21]

United in a common taste for Latin rhetoric and the search for manuscripts of ancient authors, Parisian scholars tried in their turn to adopt a script which was in

PLATE 21.19 Guillaume de Lorris and Jean de Meun, *Roman de la Rose, ex libris* artistically written by Jean Flamel, secretary of the Duc de Berry, MS. Paris, BnF, Fr. 389, fol. A, made in Paris at the end of the fourteenth century.

An example of *cursiva formata*, with the incipit, for the most part, in large scale *textualis formata*.

- Note the extensively elongated and lavishly decorated ascenders.
- Transcription: Ce Rommant de la rose / est a Jehan, filz de roy de France, duc de / Berry et d'Auvergne, conte de Poitou, d'Estampes, / de Bouloingne et d'Auvergne. / J Flamel.

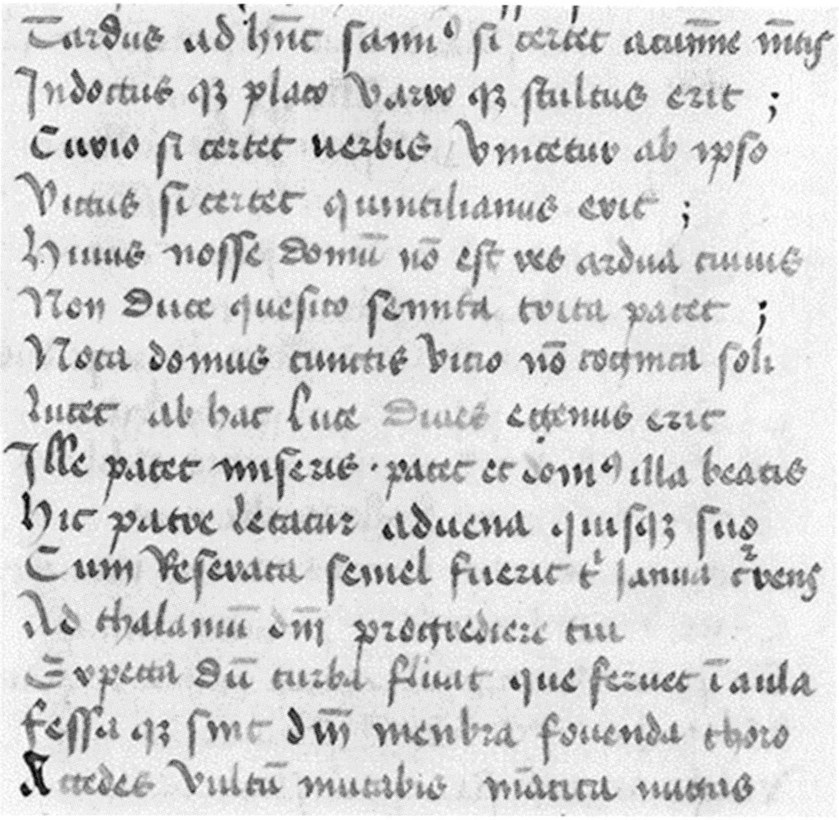

PLATE 21.20 Example of *littera hybrida libraria*: Johannes Saresberiensis, *Entheticus in Policraticon*, Paris, 1380, Paris, BnF, lat. 6416, f. 1; cf. CMDF, vol. II, p. 339.

- Note: straight *s* descending below the line, at the beginning or middle of a word, but *s* in the form of *13* at the end of the word and sometimes a trailing *s* (*mentis*, line 1); capital *v* and *r* (*vincetur*, line 3; *reserata*, line 11); several types of *r*, figure 2 *r* and straight *r* successively in *Varro* (line 2); ascenders of *b*, *h*, and *d*, generally straight, however with some loops; *g* with a single horn and a very short tail; a firm writing, sometimes discontinuous.

- Transcription: Tardus ad hunc Samius si certet acumine mentis / Indoctusque Plato Varroque stultus erit. / Curio si certet uerbis vincetur ab ipso; / Victus si certet Quintilianus erit. / Huius nosse domum non est res ardua cuiuis / Non duce quesito semita trita patet. / Nota domus cunctis vicio non cognita soli / Lucet ab hac luce diues egenus erit. / Ille patet miseris patet et domus illa beatis / Hic patre letatur aduena quisque suo / Cum reserata semel fuerit tibi ianua currens / Ad thalamum domini progrediere tui. / Expecta dum turba fluat que feruet in aula / Fessaque sint domini menbra fouenda thoro / Accedes vultum mutabis mantica nugas.

greater conformity with their search: Jean de Montreuil (1354–1418) introduced a prehumanistic Italian script into France;[22] Nicolas de Clamanges (1363–1437) adopted at the end of his life a Gothic-humanistic script with round forms, entirely Italianate, a *littera antiqua renovata* (Plate 21.21) which recalled the script of Poggio Bracciolini (1380–1459).[23] For these individuals, as for Jean Gerson (1363–1429) in the *De laude scriptorum*, the copying of a manuscript involves more than the process of writing; it is a spiritual act, a work of salvation.[24]

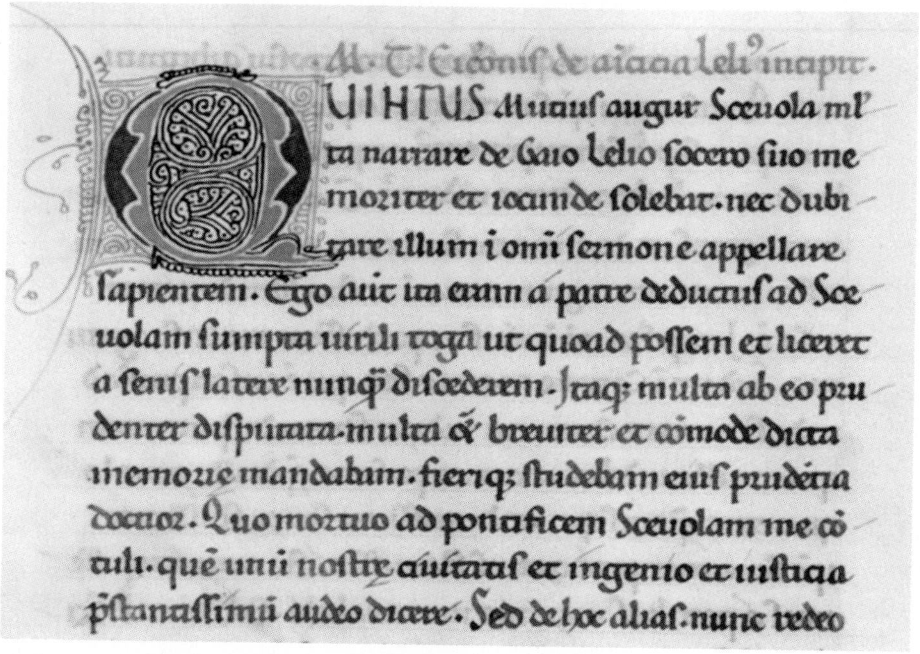

PLATE 21.21 Cicero, *De amicitia*, copied by Nicolas de Clamanges, Paris, *c*.1415–25, MS. Paris, BnF, lat. 15138, fol. 112.

- The round, small, regular script imitates the Caroline minuscule of the twelfth century. The initials sometimes imitate Rustic Capital (*S* and *N*), sometimes Uncial (*E* and *N*, line 1). Note the ampersand (*etiam*, line 9) and the *e caudata* (*nostre*, line 12). Also note the accent on the *a* of *a patre* (line 6).
- Transcription: M. T. Ciceronis De amicitia Lelius incipit. / Quintus Mutius augur Scevola mul/ta narrare de Gaio Lelio socero suo me/moriter et iocunde solebat nec dubi/tare illum in omni sermone appellare / sapientem. Ego autem ita eram a patre deductus ad Sce/uolam sumpta uirili toga ut quoad possem et liceret / a senis latere nunquam discederem. Itaque multa ab eo pru/denter disputata multa etiam breuiter et commode dicta / memorie mandabam fierique studebam eius prudentia / doctior. Quo mortuo ad pontificem Sceuo-lam me con/tuli quem unum nostre ciuitatis et ingenio et iustitia/ prestantissimum audeo dicere.

From the Second Quarter of the fifteenth Century to the Beginning of the sixteenth century.

The end of the Middle Ages marks a time of profound changes. Paris loses the preeminent position it had attained in manuscript production: regional centers like Rouen, Tours, Bourges, and Lyons take up the torch. At the same time, manuscripts reach a wider and wider public and particularly the bourgeoisie. The first Parisian printing press, set up in the library of the College of the Sorbonne in 1470, at first only published works for a small circle of well-read individuals. It was the printing press at Lyons which gave momentum to the development of printed books, particularly Books of Hours, which were bestsellers. It was not until the end of the fifteenth century that printing truly supplants the hand-copied manuscript.[25]

Bastarda script

In the second quarter of the fifteenth century, an artificial deluxe script appeared, particularly used in vernacular manuscripts, combining roundness and angularity, which one calls Bastarda (Plates 21.22, 21.23, 21.24, and 21.25). It is a pseudo-cursive which mixes the formalism of Gothic script with the characteristics of cursive script: in other words, it imitates cursive forms but traces them in a discontinuous manner, as in a well-executed script. *Bastarda* script is noteworthy for the contrasts between thick and thin strokes, between short ascenders and large-bodied letters.

Here are the characteristics:

- Straight *f* and *s* have tails which are tapering, and are sloped notably to the right; a *ductus* which ascends from bottom to top and descends from top to bottom often gives them a form that is heavy and thick; the shafts of the *p* and *q*, also pointed, are written like the straight *f* and *s*.
- The upper bow of the *g* is adorned with one or two horns; the tail of the *g* may take on different forms: often it is written with a trailing stroke.
- The shaft of the *t* extends so that one no longer confuses it with the *c*.
- The *v*, whose first downstroke is very developed, opens visibly.

The finest examples of *Bastarda* script are found in the beautiful volumes in French which enriched the library of the dukes of Burgundy, particularly Philippe le Bon, hence the name *Bastarda bourguignonne* given to the script. Particularly noteworthy in this regard are the volumes copied at Brussels by David Aubert (Plate 21.26).

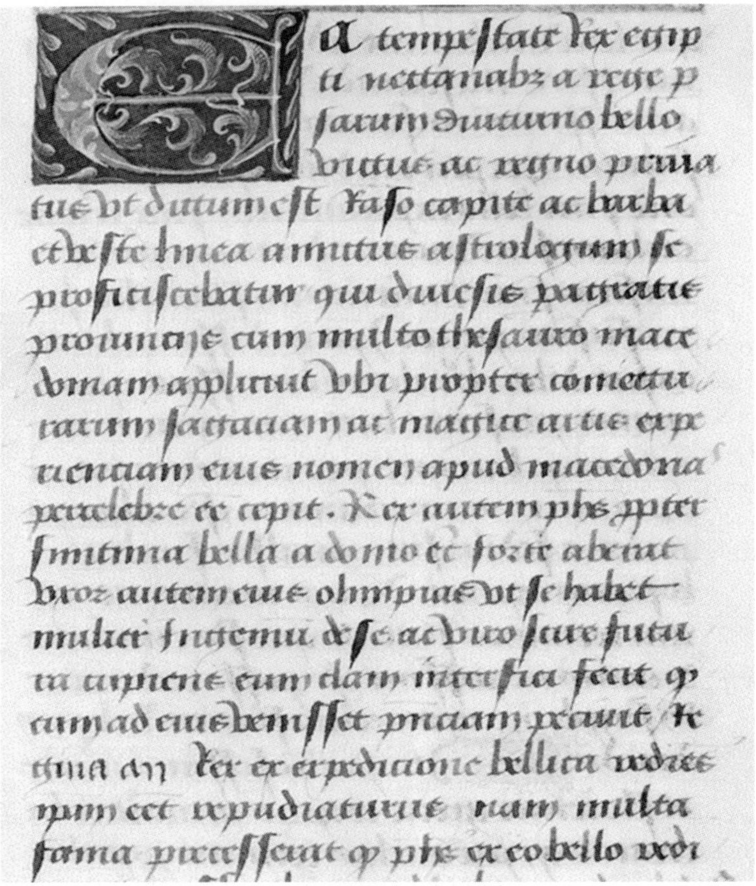

PLATE 21.22 Example of a fine and regular *Bastarda*: Johannes de Columna, *Mare historiarum*, France. Loire valley, 1448, MS. Paris, BnF, lat. 4915, fol. 82, CMDF, vol. II, p. 245.

- Note: the *s* with a thick body but slender points lightly leaning to the right; the descending ascender of the *q* in the same incline as the *s*; on the other hand, the *d* inclines to the left; the first stroke of the *v* is enlarged and very open (*victus*, line 4); the letter *g* is finished with a very light finishing stroke; the *us* abbreviation in the form of a *z* (*Nectanabus*, line 2); the form of final *s* in a trident (*provinciis*, line 8); the form of capital *r* (*raso*, line 5)
- Transcription: Ea tempestate rex Egi/pti Nectanabus a rege Per/sarum diuturno bello / victus ac regno priua/tus ut dictum est, raso capite ac barba / et veste linea amictus astrologum se / proficiscebatur qui diuesis [*sic*] peragratis / prouinciis cum multo thesauro Mace/doniam applicuit vbi propter / coniecturarum sagaciam ac magice artis expe/rienciam eius nomen apud Macedonas / percelebre esse cepit. Rex autem Philippus propter / finitima bella a domo et forte [*sic*] aberat. Vxor autem eius Olympias ut se habet / mulier ingenii de se ac viro scire futu/ra cupiens eum clam interfici fecit quod...

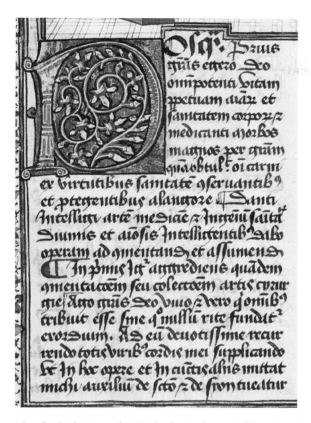

PLATE 21.23 Example of a thick *Bastarda*: Guido de Cauliaco, *Collectorium in parte chirurgicali medicinae*, [Paris] December 10, 1461, MS. Paris, BnF, lat. 6966, fol. 4.

- Note: the script is written with a black and thick stroke; two kinds of *d*, one with the downstroke inclined to the left in a rounded form; the other with a loop and an open bow.
- Transcription: Postquam prius / gratias egero Deo / omnipotenti vitam perpetuam anima-rum et / sanitatem corporum et / medicanti morbos / magnos per gratiam / quam obtulit omni carni / ex virtutibus sanitatem conseruantibus / et protegentibus a langore. Danti / intelligi artem medicine et ingenium sanitatis / diuinis et animosis (?) intelligentibus dabo / operam ad commentandum et assumendum /In primis igitur aggrediens quamdem / commentacionem seu colectionem artis cyrur/gie. Ago gratias Deo viuo et vero qui omnibus / tribuit esse sine quo nullum rite fundatur / exordium.

Even though the author does not deal with script, one will find an important collection of full-page reproductions of manuscripts in Smeyers (1998, esp. 288–416).

Regional diversity

Up to this point, we have not mentioned the regional variations in French Gothic script, since these scripts have not been studied to date. But one may say that in the case

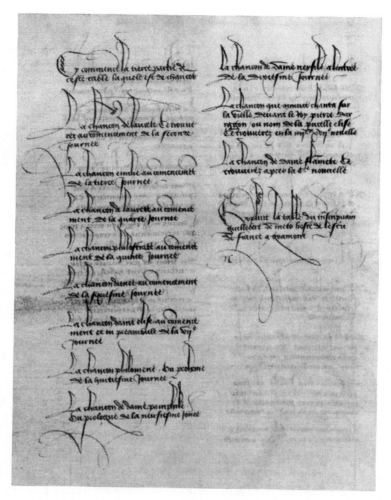

PLATE 21.24 Boccaccio, *Decameron* translated by Laurent de Premierfait, (Explicit la table du transcripvain Guillebert de Mets, hoste de l'escu de France a Gramont), MS. Paris, Bibliothèque de l'Arsenal, 5070, fol. Dv.

Example of *bâtarde* script.

- Note: *s* with a thick stroke finishing on the top with a slender stroke; the *e* with a feather; multiple forms of *d*; large loops on *h, l, b,* and *g*.

of script, as in other areas, the West of France often reflects an English tradition, the East a Germanic tradition, the South Italian and Spanish traditions. Until about the first quarter of the fifteenth century, Paris is the main center for the production of manuscript books. This is less true for the later period. Many of the great noblemen of the second half of the fifteenth century had manuscripts copied in the provinces which they later entrusted to Parisian artists. Such is the case with Jacques d'Armagnac, who employed scribes of La Marche, and of Louis de Laval who paid those of Troyes.[26]

PLATE 21.25 *Grandes Heures d'Anne de Bretagne*, MS. Paris, BnF, lat. 9474, fol. 55 Tours, 1503–8, painted by Bourdichon, MS. 300 × 195 mm.

Example of a *bâtarde* script with rounded and upright letters, perhaps influenced by printed books.

- Note: the *d* with a stroke to the right; the very short lower ascender of p; the very similar forms of the *u* and *v* (cf. *ubique*, line 14).

In fact, such a study of regional diversities in Gothic script is difficult to undertake since men and books circulated so much in the Middle Ages: such and such a scribe who worked in the north might, for example, have had his apprenticeship at Paris or vice versa. In any case, such a study should rely on a perusal of the *Catalogues des Manuscrits datés* (Samaran and Marichal 1959–850, particularly for those manuscripts

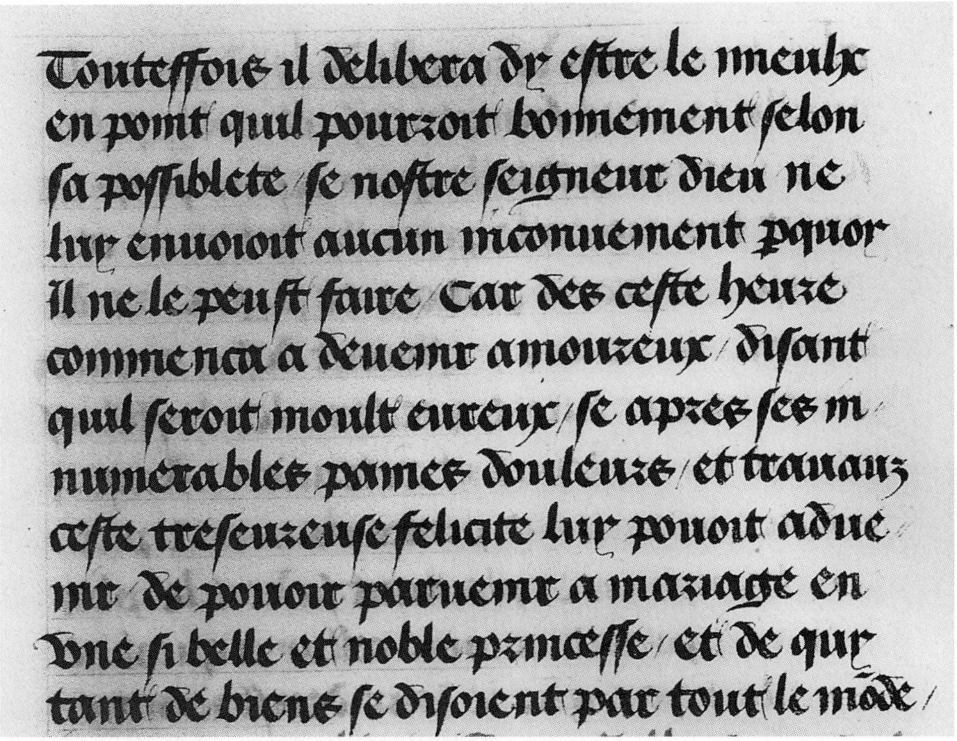
Touteffois il delibera dy estre le mieulx
en point quil pourroit bonnement selon
sa possiblete se nostre seigneur dieu ne
luy envoioit aucun inconvenient pquoy
il ne le peust faire / Car des ceste heure
commenca a devenir amoureux / disant
quil seroit moult eureux / se apres ses in
numerables paines douleurs / et travauz
ceste treseureuse felicite luy povoit adve
nir de povoir parvenir a mariage en
une si belle et noble princesse / et de quy
tant de biens se disoient par tout le mōde /

PLATE 21.26 Philippe Camus, *L'Histoire d'Olivier de Castille et Artus d'Algarbe*, copied by David Aubert [Brussels, a little before 1467], MS. Paris BnF, Français 12574, fol. 38.

- An example of a *Bastarda* script whose ascenders without loops aligns it with the *littera hybrida*.
- Note: the horns on the *a*, *e*, and final *s* (*Touteffois*, line 1); the finishing strokes on the *t* and the *d*.
- Transcription: Touteffois il delibera d'y estre le mieulx / en point qu'il pourroit bonnement selon / sa possibleté se Nostre Seigneur Dieu ne / luy envoioit aucun inconvenient par quoy / il ne le peust faire. Car des ceste heure / commença a devenir amoureux disant / qu'il seroit moult eureux se aprés ses in/numerables paines douleurs et travauz / ceste tres eureuse felicité luy povoit ad/venir de povoir parvenir a mariage en / une si belle et noble princesse et de quy / tant de biens se disoient par tout le monde.

preserved in the East of France (*CMDF*, vol. V, 1965), in Burgundy, the Center, Southeast and Southwest of France (*CMDF*, vol. VI, 1968), and in the West and the Loire (*CMDF*, vol. VII, 1984). One may also find some details on regional workshops in three exhibition catalogs on the history of art: Avril (1981, 276–362), (1998, 256–334), and Avril and Reynaud (1993). One should be cautious of positing a regional workshop for illumination, which can only be applied to script.

The printed book

The first printers, who had often been copyists of manuscripts, illuminators, or librarians, naturally used in their incunables characters which reproduced the script of manuscripts.[27] Derived from the *littera texualis formata*, the "block letter" was used for copying the Bible and liturgical texts. "Block letter" was used in the 42-line Bible published by Gutenberg in 1454–5. The Italic of Italian origin—one may compare it to the *textualis rotunda*—was used in the printing of theological and philosophical texts, particularly at Lyons and in the South of France. It appeared for the first time in the *Catholicon*, published at Mainz, in 1460. Lastly, the *littera cursiva formata* gave birth to the *Bastarda* script, a script which was used above all in vernacular printed books, as, for example, in the edition printed at Lyons of the *Abuzé en court* in 1485. Inspired by humanistic Italian script, Roman character was used for printing classical texts. The first books printed in Paris in 1470 at the College of the Sorbonne, were printed in "Roman" and particularly the very first amongst them, the *Epistolae* of Gasparino Barzizza.

NOTES

1. Wartburg (1928–70, vol. 16, 105, n. 6); Valla (1471–2, Preface to Book Three):

   Nam postquam hae gentes [i.e. Gothi et Vandali] semel iterumque Italiae influentes Romam ceperunt, ut imperium eorum ita linguam quoque, quemadmodum aliqui putant accepimus, et plurimi forsan ex illis oriundi sumus. Argumento sunt codices gothice scripti, quae magna multitudo est; quae gens si scripturam Romanam depravare potui, quid de lingua praesertim relicta sobole putandum?

2. See Smith (2004, 274–9) and Muzerelle (2005, 381–4).
3. See also Lieftinck (1954, 15–34); Gumbert (1974, 204–6).
4. Boyle (1970, 175–83).
5. Boussard (1951, 238–64).
6. This concerns a Missal copied at the abbey of Saint-Pierre de Jumièges (Seine-Maritime), MS. Rouen, Bibliothèque municipale, MS 299; fol. 31r is reproduced and commented upon in Derolez (2003, Plate 29); fol. 265v, reproduced in CMDF, vol. VII, pl. 54.
7. Gasparri (1994, 106–7).
8. See also Kirchner (1966).
9. De Hamel (1994, 108–41).
10. Cf. MS Paris, BnF, lat. 15875, fol. 110, right column, line 16, reproduced in CMDF, vol. III, p. 457 and pl. XCII, or MS Paris, Bibliothèque Sainte-Geneviève, 1829, fol. 167v, left column, line 6, reproduced in CMDF, vol. I, p. 345 and Plate 37.
11. Other examples of *littera rotunda*: CMDF, vol. III, Plate 67 (MS Paris, BnF, lat. 11019, p. 75, *Varia opuscula ad historiam monasterii Sancti Martialis Lemovicensis spectantia*, Saint-Martial de Limoges, *c*.1284) ; CDMF, vol. II, Plate 40 (MS Paris, BnF, lat. 875, fol. 3v, *Missale ad usum ecclesiae Arelatensis*, [1308–11]) and CMDF, vol. II, Plate 44 (MS Paris, BnF, lat. 365, f. 2, Dominicus Grima, *Lectura in Bibliam*, Toulouse, 1319).

12. Cencetti (1954, 220–1).

13. De Hamel (2001, 112–32).

14. De Hamel (1984) and also Powitz (1979, 80–9, esp. 84).

15. This concerns one of five volumes in large format (470/450 mm × 325/300 mm) of a glossed Bible which contained eleven, ordered by Bishop of Clermont Gui de la Tour from the Parisian Bookseller Nicolas Lombard, and which, according to the agreement struck between them, should have been written by a single hand (*de una manu*), between 1250 and 1260. The preserved volumes reveal the work of three scribes. Scribe I is responsible for MSS Paris, BnF, lat. 370 (Genesis, Exodus), and lat. 388 (Leviticus, Deuteronomy). Scribe II wrote MSS Paris, BnF, lat. 398 (Kings, Chronicles, Oratio Manasse) and lat. 395 (Joshua-Maccabees). Scribe III wrote MS Paris, BnF, lat. 466. The overall impression is the same, but one may note the rather apparent differences in the characteristics of the breaking, the thick and thin strokes, the lateral compression, the feet of the downstrokes and the Tironian form of *et*. See Rouse and Rouse (2000, 50–71).

16. Note, in particular, the following dated French manuscripts: from 1237, Paris, Bibliothèque de l'Arsenal, 3340 (*Roman de Troie*), pp. 3–5 ; from 1267–8, Paris, Bibliothèque de l'Arsenal, 3516 (*Vie de saint Jean-Baptiste*), pp. 139–41; from 1273–4, Paris, BnF, Français 24276 (*Livre des nativités*), pp. 195–7; from 1274, Paris, BnF, Français 342 (*Lancelot en prose*), pp. 131–3; from 1285, Paris, BnF, Français 412 (*Légendier*), pp. 147–9; from1298, Paris, BnF, Français 24368 (*Auberi le Bourguignon*), pp. 71–3.

17. De Hamel (1994, 142–67).

18. Oeser (1996, 395–418).

19. Another example of writing which imitates a string of pearls, Sallust, *Bellum Iugurthinum*, [Paris] beginning of the fifteenth century, MS Paris, BnF, lat. 5747, CMDF, vol. II, p. 498.

20. In one of his *Epistolae familiares* (*ep.* 33) to Boccaccio:

   non vaga quidem ac luxurianti littera, qualis est scriptorum seu verius pictorum nostri temporis, longe oculos mulcens, prope autem afficiens et fatigans quasi ad aliud quam ad legendum sit inventa [. . .] sed alia quadam castigata et clara seque ultro oculis ingerente, in qua nichil orthographum, nichil omnino grammaticae artis omissum dicas!
      not in this indistinct and luxuriant script which is that of the writers or rather of the artists of our time, charming the eye from afar but close up injuring it and tiring it, as though it were invented for something else than to be read [. . .] but rather in a refined and clear script, jumping out to the eyes and which respects scrupulously the laws of orthography and of grammar.

See also Gasparri (1994, 119–26).

21. De la Mare (1973), especially, Petrarch, pp. 1–16, Salutati, pp. 30–43, Poggio, pp. 62–84.

22. Ouy (1976, 53–61).

23. Ouy (1988, 1–12).

24. See Gerson (1973, 423–34).

25. De Hamel (1994, 168–99).

26. Avril and Reynaud (1993, 164 and 152).

27. Labarre (1983, 195–215, esp. 205–9). See also Morison (1981, I, 22–294, esp. 270–3 and Carter (1969).

BIBLIOGRAPHY

Avril, F. 1981. "Manuscrits." In *Les Fastes du gothique: le siècle de Charles V* (Galeries nationales du Grand Palais, 9 octobre 1981–1er février 1982), 276–362. Paris: Réunion des Musées Nationaux.

Avril, F. 1998. *L'Art au temps des rois maudits, 1285–1325*, Paris: Réunion des Musées Nationaux.

Avril, F. and N. Reynaud. 1993. *Les Manuscrits à peintures en France, 1440–1520*. Paris: Flammarion–Bibliothèque Nationale.

Boussard, J. 1951. "Influences insulaires dans la formation de l'écriture gothique." *Scriptorium* 5: 238–64.

Boyle, L. 1970. "The Emergence of Gothic Handwriting." In *The Year 1200*, vol. II, *A background survey*, ed. Florens Deuchler, 175–83. New York: Metropolitan Museum of Art [repr. in *Journal of Typographic Research* 4, 1970, 307–16 and in Leonard Boyle, *Integral Palaeography*, Turnhout: Brepols, 2001, 27–31, Plates 1–4].

Brown, M. P. and P. Lovett. 1999. *Historical Source Book for Scribes*. London: British Library.

Brunel, G. 2005. *Images du pouvoir royal: les chartes décorées des Archives nationales, XIIIᵉ–XVᵉ siècles*. Paris: Somogy.

Capelli, A. 1966. *Dizionario di abbreviature latine ed italiane*, with a supplement by A. Pelzer, 2nd ed. Louvain: Publications universitaires; Paris: Béatrice-Nauwelaerts.

Careri, M., F. Fery-Hue, F. Gasparri, *et al.*, eds. 2001. L'*Album de manuscrits français du XIIIᵉ siècle: mise en page et mise en texte*. Rome: Viella.

Carter, H. 2002. *A View of early Typography up to about 1600*, 2 ed. London: Hyphen.

Cencetti, G. 1954. *Lineamenti di storia della scrittura Latina*. Bologna: R. Pation.

De Hamel, C. 1984. *Glossed Books of the Bible and the Origins of the Paris Booktrade*. Woodbridge: D. S. Brewer.

De Hamel, C. 1994. *A History of Illuminated Manuscripts*, 2 rev. ed. London: Phaidon Press.

De Hamel, C. 2001. *The Book. A History of the Bible*, London and New York: Phaidon Press.

de la Mare, A. 1973. *Handwriting of Italian Humanists*. Oxford: Oxford University Press.

Derolez, A. 2003. *The Palaeography of Gothic Manuscript Books: From the Twelfth to the Early Sixteenth Century*. Cambridge Studies in Palaeography and Codicology 9. Cambridge: Cambridge University Press.

Gasparri, F. 1994. *Introduction à l'histoire de l'écriture*. Turnhout: Brepols.

Gerson, J. 1973. *Œuvres complètes*, ed. Palémon Glorieux, vol. IX, *L'Œuvre doctrinale*. Paris: Desclée.

Gumbert, J. P. 1974. *Utrechter Kartäuser und ihre Bücher im frühen 15. Jahrhundert*. Leiden: Brill.

Kirchner, J. 1966. *Scriptura gothica libraria a saeculo XII usque ad finem Medii Aevi*. Munich and Vienna: R. Oldenbourg.

Labarre, A. 1983. "Les Incunables: la présentation du livre." In *Histoire de l'Édition française*, vol. I, *Le Livre conquérant du moyen-âge au milieu du XVIIᵉ siècle*, ed. H.-J. Martin and R. Chartier. Paris: Promodis.

Lieftinck, G. I. 1954. "Pour une nomenclature de l'écriture livresque de la période dite gothique: Essai s'appliquant spécialement aux manuscrits originaires des Pays-Bas méridionaux." In *Nomenclature des écritures livresques du IXᵉ au XVIᵉ siècle*, Actes du premier colloque international de paléographie latine, Paris, 1953, ed. B. Bischoff, G. Lieftinck, and G. Battelli, 15–34. Paris: Service des publications du Centre national de la recherche scientifique.

Marichal, R. 1963. "L'Ecriture latine et la civilisation occidentale du Ier au XVIe siècle." In *L'Écriture et la psychologie des peuples*, XXIIe semaine de synthèse, 199–247. Paris: Armand Colin.

Morison, S. 1981. *Selected Essays on the History of Letter-Forms in Manuscript and Print*, vol. 1, ed. David McKitterick, 22–294. Cambridge: Cambridge University Press.

Muzerelle, D. 2005. "Gothique." In *Dictionnaire encyclopédique du livre*, vol. II, ed. P. Fouché, D. Péchoin, and P. Schuwer, 381–4. Paris: Éditions du cercle de la Librairie.

Oeser, W. 1996. "Raoulet d'Orléans und Henri du Trévou, zwei französische Berufsschreiber des 14. Jahrunderts und ihre Schrift." *Archiv für Diplomatik, Schriftgeschichte, Siegel- und Wappenkunde* 42: 395–418.

Ouy, G. 1976. "Jean de Montreuil et l'introduction de l'écriture humanistique en France au début du XVe siècle." In *Essays Presented to G. I. Lieftinck*, vol. IV, ed. J. P. Gumbert and M. J. M. de Haan, 53–61. Amsterdam: A .L. van Gendt.

Ouy, G. 1988. "Nicolas de Clamanges (ca. 1360–1437), philologue et calligraphe: imitation de l'Italie et réaction anti-italienne dans l'écriture d'un humaniste français au début du XVe siècle." In *Renaissance- und Humanistenhandschriften* (Schriften des historischen Kollegs, 13), ed. Johanne *Autenrieth, 1–12. Munich: R. Oldenburg.*

Panofsky, E. 1957. *Gothic Architecture and Scholasticism.* New York: Meridian Books.

Powitz, G. 1979. "Textus cum comment." *Codices manuscripti* 5: 80–9.

Rouse, R. H. and M. Rouse. 2000. *Manuscripts and their Makers: Commercial Book Producers in Medieval Paris.* London: H. Miller.

Samaran, C. and R. Marichal. 1959–85. *Catalogue des manuscrits en écriture latine: portant des indications de date, de lieu ou de copiste.* 7 vols. Paris: CNRS.

Smeyers, M. 1998. *L'Art de la miniature flamande, du VIIIe au XVIe siècles.* Tournai: La Renaissance du livre.

Smith, M. H. 2004. "Review of *The Palaeography of Gothic Manuscript Books.*" *Scriptorium* 58: 274–9.

Steinmann, M. 2004. "Aus der Forschung zur gotischen Schrift in den letzten fünfzig Jahren: Ergebnisse und offene Fragen, *Actes du XIVe colloque du Comité international de paléographie latine*, Enghien-les-Bains, 2003," *Archiv für Diplomatik*, 50: 399–415.

Thomson, S. H. 1969. *Latin Book Hands of the Later Middle Ages, 1100–1500.* Cambridge: Cambridge University Press.

Valla, L. 1471–2. *Elegantiarum latinae linguae libri sex.* Paris: Ulrich Gering, Martin Crantz, and Michael Friburger.

Wartburg, W. von. 1928–70. *Französisches etymologisches Wörterbuch: eine Darstellung des galloromanischen Sprachschatzes.* 20 vols. Bonn: F. Klopp.

CHAPTER 22

··

THE EMERGENCE OF
FORMAL GOTHIC SCRIPT
IN ENGLAND

··

RICHARD GAMESON

IN England the emergence of formal Gothic book hands, characterized by a rectilinear matrix, angular elements, and a dense application to the page, is essentially a phenomenon of the twelfth century. We shall first examine the morphological changes that were involved and their chronology; we shall then review possible reasons for the developments in question, and consider their implications.

Alongside the conservative minuscule, generously proportioned with various elegantly rounded forms, that was current in many English scriptoria in the late eleventh century, certain scribes already practiced more angular hands. Sometimes demonstrably of Norman origin or training, such individuals were prominent, for example, at Durham in the north and Canterbury in the south. In the prickly script that is found first at Christ Church, Canterbury (emerging in the 1080s, maturing by the 1090s), subsequently at St. Augustine's Abbey and nearby Rochester, strokes that were hitherto curvilinear were broken into several separate, differently angled lines, the general impression of spikiness being enhanced by triangular, often-slanting serifs and rising feet. Angled serif and rising feet, along with a tendency to compress the bowls of *b*, *d*, *g*, *o*, and *p*, were likewise features of the angular, yet fluid writing practiced by some scribes at Durham. An illustrated Life of St. Cuthbert (Oxford, University College, 165), datable to between 1080 and 1104, and the authorial manuscript of Symeon of Durham's Tract on the Church of Durham (Durham, University Library, Cosin V. ii.6),[1] datable to between 1104 and 1115 (or possibly 1107), are calligraphic examples of the manner in question (Plate 22.1).

While elements of the rounded Anglo-Caroline survived in certain centers (especially in the west of England) into the third quarter of the twelfth century, lateral compression is observable in most English hands long before this. By the second quarter of the century the general matrix of much script had become more rectilinear,

PLATE 22.1 Durham University Library, Cosin V.ii.6, fol. 11r (page size: 292 × 185 mm).

and letters regularly touched their neighbor at foot and/or head level; this is true even in the writing of more conservative scriptoria such as those of Bury St. Edmunds and Worcester. Widespread developments of the second and third quarters of the twelfth century, affecting the stately script of grand volumes such as giant bibles and fine psalters as well as that of lesser books, were the tendency to form round letter shapes as ovoids and to break the "bridges" of *m*, *n*, and *r* into two straight strokes, the first rising, the second falling. As the squeezing process continued during the second half of the twelfth century, the linking and coalescing of adjacent letters became more frequent and pronounced; simultaneously, the space between words was reduced. In books of the third quarter of the twelfth century—such as those from Cirencester that are conveniently datable to the time of Abbot Andrew (1147–76)[2]—the sharply rising feet not only linked letters but formed a semi-continuous corrugation at the bottoms of the words, matching that created by the angled serifs and broken minim bridges at their heads.

The prominence or otherwise of these last details, and hence the strength of the impression of angularity, often related to the care lavished on the process of writing, which in turn tended to reflect the status of the project. In less formal work, where scribes tried to create the letter shapes with fewer separate strokes and pen lifts and were sometimes influenced by contemporary documentary scripts, feet and serifs were more restrained and the letter forms themselves more heterogeneous. Such was variously the case, for instance, in the authorial copy of Clement of Lanthony's *In Epistolas canonicas* (London, Lambeth Palace Library, 239) written at Lanthony Secunda (Gloucs.) before 1174, in the authorial copy of Nigellus de Longchamp's *Contra curiales* (Cambridge, Gonville and Caius College, 427/427) written at Canterbury between 1193 and 1194, in the authorial copy of Richard of Devizes' *Chronicon* (Cambridge, Corpus Christi College, 339, vol. i) written at Winchester between 1192 and 1198, and in a Canterbury letter collection of *c*.1201–5 (London, Lambeth Palace Library, 415). Thus, by the later twelfth century there was a fairly clear divide between, on the one hand, the more formal book hands with their rectilinear matrix, fractured strokes, spiky finishing touches, and corrugated head and baselines and, on the other, their less regimented, more varied, often less angular, lower-grade counterparts.

Around 1200 two further developments characterized the highest grade book hands. The first was the full rectilinearization of forms such as *c*, *e*, and the bowl and tail of *g*: having been rounded in Caroline minuscule and become multi-angular during the course of the twelfth century, these were now effectively rectangles, wholly assimilated to the vertically orientated aesthetic of the other letters. The phenomenon is clearly visible in, for instance, a missal of Cistercian use (London, BL, Harley 1229), perhaps from Waverley, datable to 1192–1202. The second development concerned the way downstrokes were terminated, an upward turn to the right being replaced with a separate straight stroke rising at 45°; alternatively a splayed foot was used (script with this feature may be qualified as "quadratus"), or nothing at all—the downstroke simply being squared off at the bottom (a type qualified as "prescissus"). Together these elements completed a radical transformation. Whereas the graphemes of Caroline

minuscule had articulated the individuality of each letter form, the incremental modifications during the twelfth century slowly but surely assimilated the shape of the different
characters to each other. Thus, by the beginning of the thirteenth century elegance was
achieved not via a balance of different forms, rounded and rectilinear, but by the
homogeneity of the letters and hence the regularity of words: lines of writing were turned
into runs of parallel bars complemented by oblique angles and spiky head- and baselines.
Stylish at the expense of legibility, such writing in its canonical form was Textualis, the
archetypical Gothic script of northern Europe. Fine datable early English specimens
include the Lesnes Missal (London, Victoria and Albert Museum, 404-1916), probably
produced sometime between 1197 and 1220, and the Psalter (London, Society of Antiquaries, 59) that belonged to Robert of Lindsey when abbot of Peterborough (1214–22).

That legibility was indeed being compromised is suggested by the restriction of the
most formal and extreme manifestations of the type (Textura) to the highest-grade
books with the largest script and the best-known texts, where familiarity with the
content could inform and support the visual recognition of words which were, in any
case, boldly written. The more commonly used formal Gothic scripts, deployed for
"library" as opposed to service books, generally in Latin, sometimes in French, retained
more curvilinear elements, had longer ascenders and descenders, and made less use of
unifying serifs, thereby preserving clearer distinctions between individual letters: a
copy of Wace's metrical French Life of St. Nicholas (Oxford, Bodleian Library,
Douce 270) that was made at Durham in 1225/6 and the Latin Chronicle (London,
College of Arms, Arundel 30) written at Bury St. Edmunds in 1285 may serve for the
enormous range of such writing. The same was true *a fortiori* of the script used in
humbler "working" books: the ill-disciplined hands responsible for a commentary on
the Sentences of Peter Lombard of Worcester provenance that is dated to 1231
(London, BL, Royal 9 B. v), for example, though densely applied to the page, heavily
abbreviated, and often untidy, preserve a heterogeneity of letter forms that makes each
individual character easier to recognize.

Defining and explicating the many grades and shades of early English Gothic book
hands are impossible in the present context. What should, however, be added to the
summary above is that tiny script (typified by that in a Bible of 1228–34 (London, BL,
Arundel 131) and a dictionary dated 1278 (Cambridge, University Library, Dd.15.1),
whose scale tended to rule out angled serifs and sharp breaks within strokes, generally
retained greater distinctions between characters, whatever its quality. Similarly, while
some of the writing used for texts in English could echo qualities of Textualis (for
instance, that of an *Ancrene Riwle* manuscript of *c.*1225 [London, BL, Cotton Titus
D. xviii] and the London copy of *The Owl and the Nightingale* [London, BL, Cotton
Caligula A. IX]), it generally displayed a graphic variety typical of less formal hands, the
visual diversity being further accentuated by the additional letters "eth," "thorn," "wyn,"
and "yogh." In documentary script, with its greater cursive tendencies, the progress of
lateral compression was generally slower and less extreme, while the elongation of
ascenders, descenders, and tildes that characterizes many such hands created new
calligraphic permutations that could offset the growing homogeneity of other elements.

What is most striking about the early development of English Gothic book hands is not the variations in the rate of evolution during the twelfth century and in the interpretation of forms (numerous though they are), but rather the fact that the main script types that emerged by the early thirteenth century were relatively universal. This is all the more noteworthy given that, far from there having been a unified central authority (such as a dominant "court school" or chancery) to define and promulgate a system of writing styles with Textualis at the top, scribal production had been scattered across a plethora of essentially independent ecclesiastical scriptoria and chanceries, further diversification resulting from the unmeasurable but steadily growing contribution of paid professionals.

No really satisfactory explanation for the birth of Gothic script has yet been advanced; but then as it evolved in different ways and at different rates across a large area of northern Europe during the course of a century rather than being the result of focused reformulation (in contrast, for instance, to the Humanistic scripts), no single cause can be at issue. Clearly elucidation should embrace the parallel developments immediately across the Channel in northern France and Flanders, regions with which England had extensive bibliographical, scholarly, and scribal intercourse; however, within the structure of the present volume, their story is treated elsewhere.

One general point that has often been made is that it is faster to form script with broken strokes and easy links between letters than with carefully rounded forms and multiple pen lifts. In England in the aftermath of the Norman Conquest, when many religious foundations were embarking on ambitious programs of copying often substantial patristic texts and biblical commentaries, most scriptoria, even those of old Benedictine houses, will surely have wanted to optimize the speed of transcription. A second point is that lateral compression offered the advantage of saving space and hence economizing parchment. Again, given the length of many of the works then being copied, this may have been an appreciable consideration for major centers as well as minor ones. Thirdly, the personnel and books that came from Normandy after 1066 practiced and displayed more compressed and angular interpretations of late Caroline minuscule than was then customary on the other side of the Channel. Moreover, if their arrival marks a first stage in the move toward Gothic handwriting in England, their influence represents a second. Exemplars for the sort of texts that were newly in demand were in short supply in post-Conquest England. Canterbury and Durham were highlighted above for their precocious prickly or angular script; significantly, they were also major centers for the supply of exemplars to other scriptoria—thus circulating examples of new styles of writing along with sought-after texts.

Toward the middle of the twelfth century a further impulse was provided by the vogue for glossed books of the Bible which, becoming in their turn the sine qua non of any significant collection, were widely disseminated principally from northern France, subsequently being imitated in some English scriptoria. Their basic design (fixed quantities of biblical text and commentary slotted into parallel columns) favored lateral compression of script both in order to keep space-hungry volumes to manageable proportions and as a device to help the scribe with the challenging task of synchronizing main text and gloss. They also provided models for setting down on the page blocks of text which were more solid than hitherto. Furthermore, some glossed books reinforced the tendency toward a bifurcation of formal writing styles, the script used for the primary texts inevitably being grander, and sometimes more calligraphic, than that of the gloss. This is clearly echoed, for instance, in a glossed psalter (Oxford, Bodleian Library, Auct. D.4.6) that was made at Reading Abbey between 1154 and 1164, whose glossing script is not only smaller but also less formal than that used for the psalm text.

By the later twelfth century the now prevalent rectilinear book hands will doubtless have been perceived as "fashionable"—especially since they were reinforced by the norms and practices on the other side of the Channel. Evidently appreciated, their characteristic parallelism, angularity, and density on the page were then further enhanced—largely, it would seem, for aesthetic effect. The growth around 1200 of broader bases of patronage for books (in the form of university students and other lay clienteles) and the concomitant rise of professional scribes based in urban centers may also have helped to crystallize the situation. It made commercial sense for scribes (and purchasers) to perpetuate a broad range of scripts that extended from the artificially formal to the economically compact and current, with appropriately varied costs—and a corresponding ability to broadcast clear messages about the relative value of projects and the status of their patrons. The increasing "professionalization" of the trade will also have facilitated the diffusion of the forms, as the work of a limited number of centers was distributed to an extensive hinterland. A couple of early thirteenth-century psalters that were written in a fine Textualis, probably at Oxford, one for Holy Rood Abbey in Edinburgh (Durham, University Library, Bamburgh Select 6, Plate 22.2), the other for the Augustinian nunnery on Iona (Edinburgh, National Library of Scotland, 10,000), exemplify this phenomenon.

In conclusion, two changes that were correlatives of the emergence of Gothic script in England may be highlighted. In the first place, there were now clearer distinctions between the letter forms used for different grades and types of writing. At the beginning of the twelfth century a calligraphic late Caroline minuscule (be it a generously proportioned English version or a more angular Norman one) would be deployed for a high-status project, and a less spacious, less carefully formed interpretation of exactly the same script for a lower-status one. In the early thirteenth century, by contrast, the most formal and rectilinear Textualis ("Textura") was employed for high-status work, a range of less stylized, more flowing and rounded types ("libraria") for lesser ones, with different versions again used for "working" books and for texts in English, while beyond this was a diversity of documentary hands. Grade and type of script (and not just the quality of scribal performance) now reflected—and projected—the importance of the work and its sponsor.

Secondly, it brought England scribally into step with a large area of Europe for the first time in her history. Whereas up to c.1100 Englishmen working abroad and continental personnel in English centers are readily recognizable by their handwriting, a century later this was no longer the case. The same types of script with closely similar

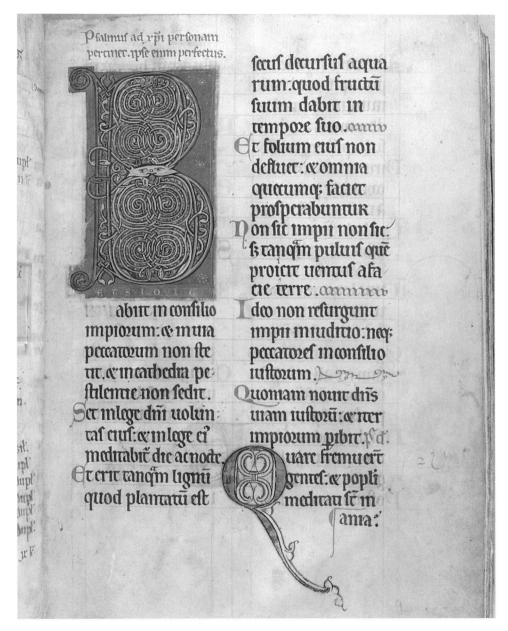

PLATE 22.2 Durham University Library, Bamburgh Select 6, fol. 9r (page size: 296 × 205 mm).

letter forms were now widely current across north-west Europe as a whole. Consequently, it is only thanks to the information in their colophons that we can perceive
that the Manerus who wrote a great Bible in France (probably at Troyes) in the late
twelfth century (Paris, Bibliothèque Sainte-Geneviève, 8, 9, and 10) was from Canterbury, and that the John who transcribed a lectionary at Mons (now Belgium) in 1269

(London, BL, Egerton 2569) was from Salisbury. Correspondingly, it is difficult as never before to localize many books, even to identify their country of origin, on grounds of script alone.

NOTES

1. Facsimile plates of most of the examples cited are readily available in the English volumes of the *Manuscrits datés* (Dated and Datable) series.
2. e.g. Oxford, Jesus College, 52, 53, 63, 67, 68, and 70.

CHAPTER 23

....

GOTHIC SCRIPT IN ENGLAND C.1300–1500

....

PAMELA ROBINSON

GOTHIC IN ENGLAND 1300–1400

....

THE term "Gothic" can be misleading. As recently stated, "It refers (or should refer) not
to a group of scripts, or even a category of script, but to a prevailing attitude towards what
constituted elegance in handwriting, and the features of style that produced it."[1] Now
often loosely applied to all handwriting of the so-called "Gothic period" (1200–1500), it
originated among the early Italian humanists as a derogatory term and was introduced
into English by the diarist John Evelyn (1620–1706). In the not so recent past "Gothic,"
when applied to handwriting, was often taken to specify the script known as *Textura* (as
it still does on the website of Digital Scriptorium, http://www.columbia.edu). *Textura* or
text hand (from the Latin *texere*, "to weave," because the letters look as if woven
together), had evolved from the twelfth-century set book hand ("Protogothic") and by
the first quarter of the fourteenth its letterforms were fully developed.

The most obvious features of *Textura* are the angularity of its letterforms and its lateral
compression. This angularity can be seen in the pointed arches at the tops of the minims,
m and *n*, in the lozenge shape of the letter *o*, and in the stem of *t*, which instead of curving
at the foot was broken where the pen changed direction on the page. The space between
letterforms was much reduced. This was achieved by the fusion or "biting" of adjacent
bow strokes wherever they occurred, so that we find the linking together of letters such as
be, pa, de, and **do**. Although **d** with an upright ascender was maintained in this script for a
long while, it was gradually abandoned in favor of the round-backed form, since it was
difficult to make bitings with an upright ascender. Other characteristic features of *Textura*
are the two compartment *a*, and the use of a two-shaped *r* after the letters *b*, *d*, *h*, and *p*
as well as *o*. The space between lines was greatly reduced, with shortened ascenders
and descenders, *g* hardly coming below the line. Plate 23.1 (Columbia University Rare
Book and Manuscript Library, Plimpton MS 028A recto),[2] a single leaf from a mid-
fourteenth-century Bible, written perhaps for the nuns of the convent of St. Radegund,

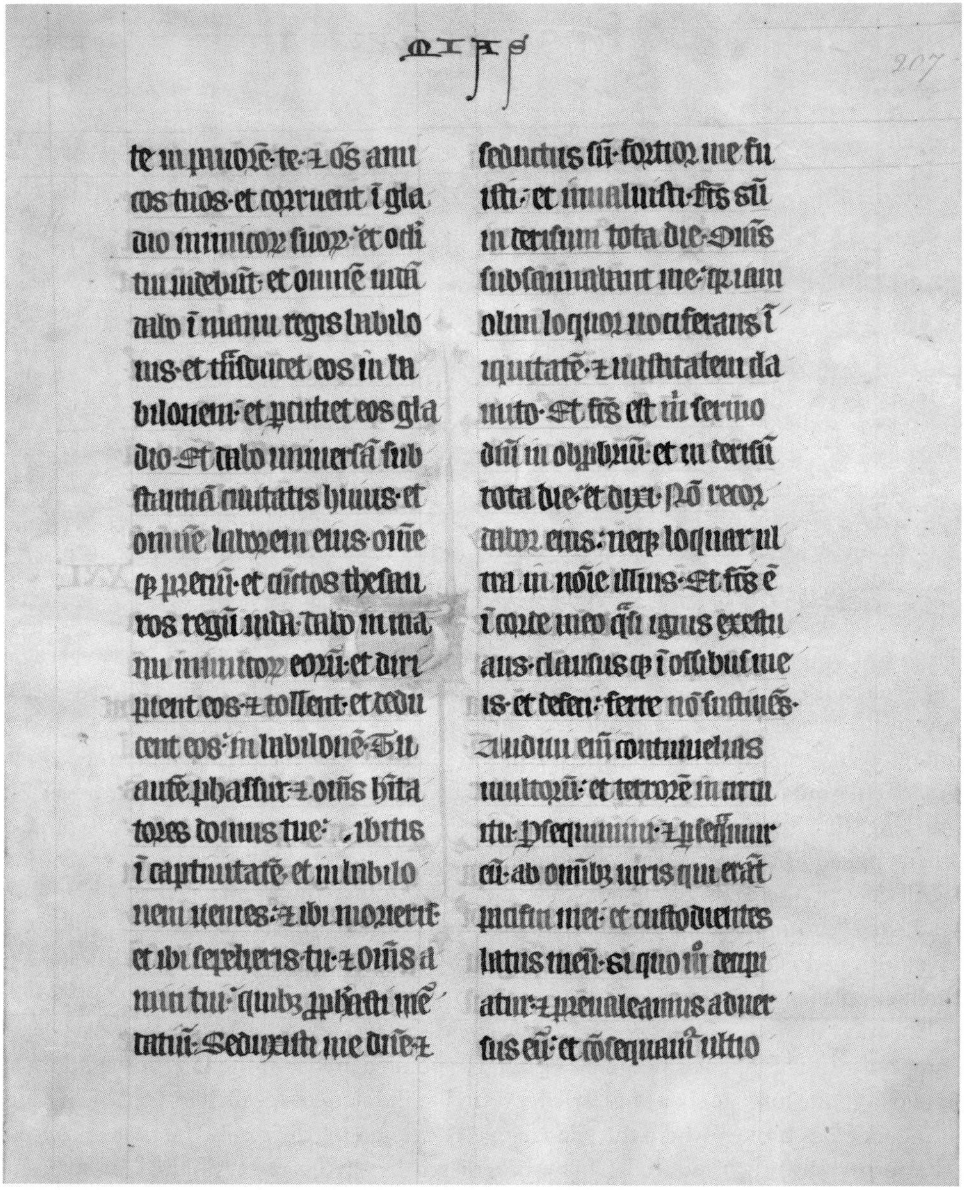

PLATE 23.1 Columbia University Rare Book and Manuscript Library, Plimpton MS 028A recto.

Cambridge, provides an example of a typical page. Note "**b**ellator" (col. 1, line 2), "ca**d**ent" (col. 1, line 3) "obpro**b**rium" (col. 1, line 6), and "egressus" (col. 2, line 8).

The appearance of a page written in *Textura*, a script where letterforms were pointed and broken wherever possible, thus looked completely different from one written in the round and open "Protogothic." The *ductus* (a combination of the angle at which the nib was cut, the quill was held, and the sequence of strokes making up a letter) led to a regular alternation in *Textura* of thick and thin strokes producing a graphic image which remained fashionable until the end of the Middle Ages. Four different grades of *Textura* existed, distinguished by their different treatment of the feet of the minims. The fragmentary remains of a poster displayed by an early fourteenth-century Oxford writing master exhibits each of these grades, although it gives no names to them.[3] The adjectives used today to qualify the term *Textura*, *prescissus*, *quadrata*, *semi-quadrata*, and *rotunda*, are derived from fifteenth-century continental writing masters.

The oldest and most prestigious grade was *prescissus* ("cut off") or *sine pedibus* ("without feet") in which the minims have no serifs at their feet but end flat on the writing line. This variety, seen in a number of psalters produced in East Anglia, reached its apogee in the famous Luttrell Psalter (London, BL, Add. 42130), commissioned sometime in the second quarter of the fourteenth century by Sir Geoffrey Luttrell, a wealthy Lincolnshire landowner (d. 1345).[4] It was time-consuming and expensive to produce a volume in this script and *quadrata* ("square") came to be preferred, although it too could be costly. It took the scribe Thomas Preston two years to copy a missal for Abbot Litlyngton of Westminster (d. 1386) and cost the abbot £4 for Preston's board and lodging over that time. In *quadrata* the minims are finished with diamond-shaped serifs, as in the recently discovered Macclesfield Psalter, also produced in the second quarter of the fourteenth century.[5] During the century *prescissus* was gradually replaced by *quadrata*, the grade which survived into the age of the early English printed book as "black letter" type. The third variety was known as *semi-quadrata* ("semi-square") where some of the minims had lozenge-shaped feet and others did not; this was often used for academic texts for much of the century,[6] but the increasing number of longer texts to be copied led to its deterioration. Finally, one encounters *rotunda* ("round"), where the minims were finished with a simple upward flick of the pen. Texts in Middle English were written in one of these last two varieties before *Anglicana* came to be widely adopted.[7]

In the course of the fourteenth century English scribes increasingly began to employ a script to copy books that had evolved from the everyday "business" or cursive handwriting of twelfth- and thirteenth-century documents. Until the twelfth century there had been no difference in the script of books and documents, but with the increasing bureaucracy of the Norman state, the growth of towns and trade, and the rise of the legal profession, the pressure was on copyists to produce documents much more quickly than before. The work rate demanded of them led to a modification of letterforms such that by about 1230 many documents and registers were being written in a fully developed documentary script, for which the palaeographer Neil Ker adopted the name *Anglicana*.[8] Medieval people did not attempt to categorize different models of handwriting in the analytical terms that some modern scholars do, but they did recognize different national hands. Thus, for them, *Anglicana* or "English letters" denoted different scripts at different times. Among the books Cardinal Guala Bicchieri, papal legate in England 1216–18, left to S. Andrea, Vercelli, in 1227 were a Bible and homiliary both in "littera Anglicana."[9] Given the date and the contents of these volumes, they must have been in the monumental set book hand of an age Ker characterized as the "greatest in the history of English book production."[10] On the other hand, when Joan de Walkingham of Ravensthorpe, Yorkshire, (d. 1346) left "quemdam librum scriptum littera Anglicana," as distinct from a psalter "cum littera grossa," she surely referred in the first instance to a book in the cursive book hand we today call *Anglicana*.

The key features of *Anglicana* are two-compartment *a, d* with a looped ascender, an "8"-shaped two-compartment *g*, long *r* whose stem descended below the general level of the letterforms, and the cursive capital form of final *s*.[11] The *Statuta Vetera*, a collection of ancient statutes from Magna Carta (1215) to the end of Edward II's reign in 1327, was an essential text for a lawyer to own. A copy dating from around the turn of the fourteenth century is written in the characteristic hand of the period (Plate 23.2, Plimpton MS 272, fol. 73v), with elaborate forked ascenders (*l* in "Gloucestr," line 6; *b* in "pa-ciebantur," line 8), *r* with a pronounced shoulder stroke ("regno," line 7), and the heavy oblique downstroke of the looped ascender of *d* ("apud," line 6). The limb of the letter *h* (as in "exheredacionem," line 7) barely descends below the level of the other letters. The features of this type of handwriting changed frequently, and hence it proves much easier to date than *Textura*. In a copy of the Wycliffite New Testament from Norwich Cathedral Priory (Plate 23.3, Plimpton MS 03, fol. 3), written around the end of the century or beginning of the fifteenth, the elaborate forked ascenders have disappeared, the letter *r* has lost its shoulder stroke but the connecting stroke between its descending

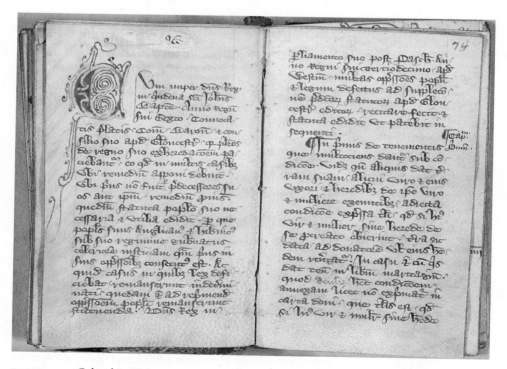

PLATE 23.2 Columbia University Rare Book and Manuscript Library, Plimpton MS 272, fols 73v–74.

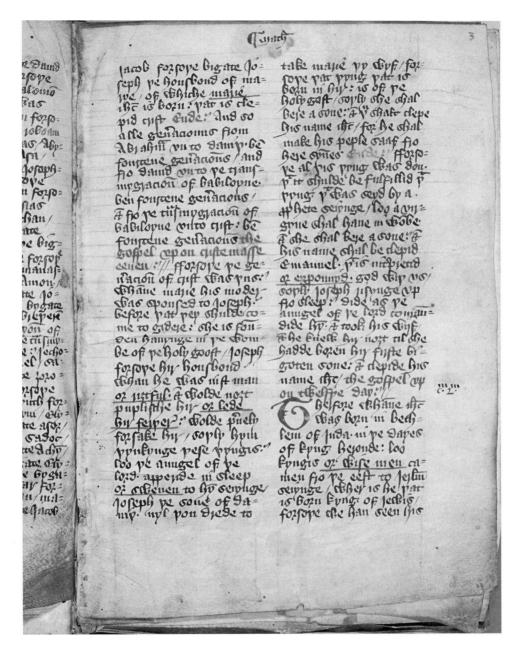

PLATE 23.3 Columbia University Rare Book and Manuscript Library, Plimpton MS 03, fol. 3.

stroke and the following letter is prominent ("marie," col. 2, line 1, "crist," col. 1, line 5), and the limb of *h* now descends well below the level of other letterforms to avoid any possible confusion with the letter *b* ("housbond," col. 1, line 2, "whiche," col. 1, line 3). And at the turn of the century the shaft of *t* is just beginning to protrude above the head stroke (compare "þat," col. 1, line 4 with "vnto," col. 1, line 7).

The adoption of *Anglicana* as a script in which books could be copied reflects the growth of literacy among the laity.[12] This was the current handwriting (written with a running pen so that letterforms were joined up) that merchants and lawyers had become accustomed to in the course of conducting their day-to-day business, both as readers and writers. While reading and writing are separate skills, it is possible (as Michael Clanchy has suggested)[13] that medieval children learned to read and write from their primers. The primer, a book which Chaucer's "little clergeon" studied at school, opened with the sign of the cross and was followed by the letters of the alphabet, the Lord's Prayer, the Hail Mary, and Creed (the basic articles of faith that every Christian should know). When a child had mastered the alphabet and learned to read and memorize the following prayers, he could use his primer as a copybook, learning to make his letters in imitation of the alphabet at its beginning. The survival rate of primers is poor, as they were read until worn out, but one that does survive, a rare late-fourteenth-century example with the prayers written in Middle English, is written in *Textura*.[14] Whether or not at some stage primers provided copy for children to learn to write from, wax tablets would presumably have been used to practice one's letters, as they were at Lübeck, Germany.[15] While no such tablet with practice alphabet is known to have survived from England, a twelfth-century slate with the alphabet incised on one side and the Lord's Prayer on the other has survived from Hastings, Sussex, and early fifteenth-century slates from medieval Scotland also contain examples of someone practicing the formation of letters.[16] In scratching one's letters into wax or incising them onto slate, it would be impossible to write a set hand like *Textura* – much easier to use the cursive hand that documentary scribes used. The clumsy way that some scribes, such as the London alderman Arnald Thedmar (d. 1275), or the scribe of a late-thirteenth-century compilation of Latin, French, and Middle English texts stab at their letters seems to reflect scribes accustomed to writing on wax.[17]

Scribes soon began to feel the need to produce a more dignified version of the script than basic *Anglicana* when copying books. As with *Textura* there were different grades of *Anglicana* depending on the degree of formality with which it was written. In the basic grade the letter *m* was formed with a single multiple stroke, but in the more formal grade, "formata," the pen was lifted between strokes and the minim often furnished with feet. The distinction between these two grades arose from that made between the enrolling hand (that is, the more hurried and less careful handwriting used in writs and office copies of documents issued) and the engrossing hand (employed for more important documents such as charters or letters patent).[18] As once scribes had deployed a hierarchy of scripts to distinguish titles, chapter divisions, and other divisions in a text, so now scribes deployed these different grades of *Anglicana* to distinguish titles or quotations within a text. A page from a late-fourteenth-century copy of a Latin translation of Euclid's *Elements* with the commentary of Campanus of Novara (d. 1296) shows how the different sizes of the handwriting helped the reader to distinguish immediately between Euclid's text and Campanus's commentary (Plate 23.4, Plimpton MS 160, fol. 10), as today we might use different sizes of font. In the *formata*, the larger square hand, the short *s* does not protrude above the general

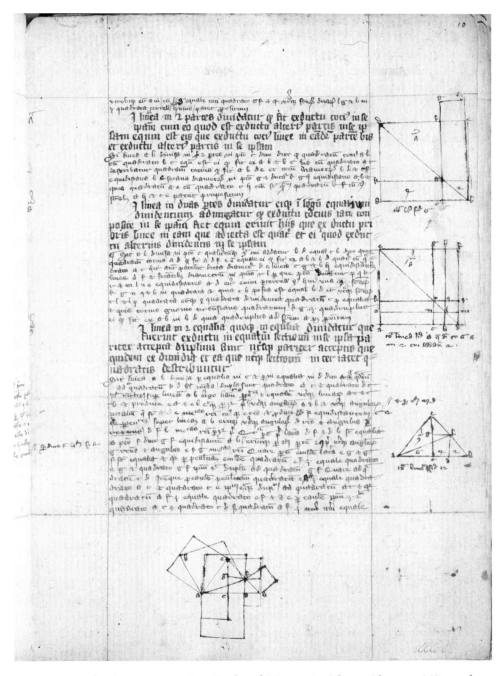

PLATE 23.4 Columbia University Rare Book and Manuscript Library, Plimpton MS 160, f10.

level of the other letters ("partis," line 6) and the minims are furnished with feet (*m* in "ipsam," line 6) in contrast to these letterforms in the commentary. An even more formal grade of *Anglicana*, Bastard *Anglicana*, emerged in the middle of the century, better spaced and with greater attention to calligraphic details. It is called a "Bastard" hand because it incorporates features derived from a "noble" script, that is *Textura* (with "bitings"and a straight-sided two-compartment *a*) and a "base" cursive script, *Anglicana*.[19]

Toward the end of the fourteenth century, scribes began to use a third script, called Secretary after its descendant, the Tudor and Stuart "secretary hand," published in the first writing manual printed in England, 1571.[20] Secretary was also a cursive hand but, unlike *Anglicana*, it had not evolved from a native script but was imported from France. There it had developed from the version of the Italian "scrittura cancelleresca" used by scribes employed at the Papal Chancery at Avignon. The influence of French cultural models helped the new script's diffusion throughout Europe.[21] It was adopted by English messengers on business in France, and first appears in episcopal registers and in documents issued under the Royal Privy Seal because most Privy Seal documents were written in French during the fourteenth century.[22] The introduction of Secretary brought a new style of penmanship to England. Instead of the curved strokes of *Anglicana*, Secretary had broken ones traced in different diagonals: as seen in the diamond-shaped single compartment *a*, the broken lobes of the letters *d*, *q*, and *o*, and the stems of *c* and *e*. Key features of Secretary are the form of *a*, a single compartment *g* with a lobe traced like *a* and a tail stroke, short *r* with a thin shoulder stroke rising from the bottom of the stem (sometimes *r* could almost be mistaken for a "v"); and a kidney-shaped final *s* at the end of words. It was not, however, until the fifteenth century that it began increasingly to be used by those who copied books as well as those who copied documents. As with *Anglicana* the emergence of Secretary was an important development in the history of English book production, promoting the emergence of less expensive books for the growing reading public among laymen and women in the fifteenth century.

GOTHIC IN ENGLAND 1400–1500

In the fifteenth century, English scribes basically had the choice of three different scripts, *Textura*, *Anglicana*, and Secretary, depending on the kind of text they copied. *Textura*, the most imposing in appearance, was employed in copies of the Bible, liturgical manuscripts, and Books of Hours. It was also used where text was on display in the public arena, such as the lettering on monumental brasses, inscriptions in stained glass windows, and on posters. A petition by John Elvet, archdeacon of Leicester 1392–1405, complains that one John Belgrave had defamed his official, Walter Barnack, by fixing "priuement et maliciousement vn bille escript de mayn de texte" to the door of St. Martin's church, Leicester. The petition itself, however, is written in the new Secretary script.[23]

Fifteenth-century *Textura* was written with "almost mechanical precision."[24] Letter-forms were taller and stiffer than in the previous century such that a page consisted of lines of writing with letterforms consisting of upright heavy thick strokes. This resulted in a pattern on the page of "chiaroscuro" (light and shade).[25] The serifs at the tops of letters and the feet of the minims bound letters together within a word and helped to discourage the reader from skipping inadvertently from one line of text to the next (eye-skip is a common cause of textual error). Already in the fourteenth century scribes had begun to link the head and feet of letters (as is very evident on monumental brasses). The ornamental nature of the script was further emphasized by adding otiose hairline strokes to letters at the end of words.

Since *Textura* is a calligraphic script that had become so stylized and uniform, the decoration of a manuscript can be a more helpful indicator in assigning a date to it than its handwriting. Few medieval manuscripts were precisely dated by their scribes, so unless content provides internal evidence as to when a book was written or there is some external evidence (for instance, an owner's coat of arms), the scholar has to make an educated judgment based on a manuscript's script or decoration. Along with greater scribal precision in writing *Textura* had come a greater interest in the appearance and layout of the page. While *Textura* had crystallized, artistic style had not, and art historians can discern change and development in the decorative style of miniatures and the use of motifs in the borders that frequently decorate manuscripts written in *Textura*.[26]

Textura, deemed the most prestigious of the three available scripts, was the script thought appropriate for copies of the Bible. In the late fourteenth century the first complete English translation of the Bible emerged, attributed to the theologian and religious reformer, John Wyclif (d. 1384), or to his followers. Despite the later prohib-ition by Thomas Arundel, archbishop of Canterbury (d. 1414), against this translation, some 250 copies of the Wycliffite Bible survive. In several manuscripts of the early version of the text the scribes preferred to use *Anglicana* (Plate 23.3, Plimpton Add MS 03, fol. 3),[27] but for the later version *Textura* became standard.[28] The choice of the latter, the script of Latin bibles, presumably was preferred in order to make a suspect text look authoritative. Hence a copy of the later version of the Wycliffite New Testament written *c.*1420 (Plate 23.5, New York, New York Public Library, NYPL MA 066, fol. 260v). In both specimens, as well as the letters of the Latin alphabet, the scribe has used the Runic letter þ ("thorn") in words like "þe" (Plate 23.3, col. 1, line 2; pl. 5, col 1, line 4) and "þat" (col 1, line 7).

When writing English, as well as "thorn" for "th" many scribes also used "yogh" (descended from the Insular form of *g* used by Anglo-Saxon scribes) for both "g" Plate 23.5, col. 1, line 8 "ȝeue") and "gh" (Plate 23.5, col. 2, line 9 "siȝt"). Because of these orthographic alternatives an early fifteenth-century compiler of a concordance to the Wycliffite New Testament felt it necessary to explain to the reader that he would find words beginning with þ in his copy under "th" in the concordance, while words beginning with yogh, since it is "figured lijk a zed," were under *z*.[29]

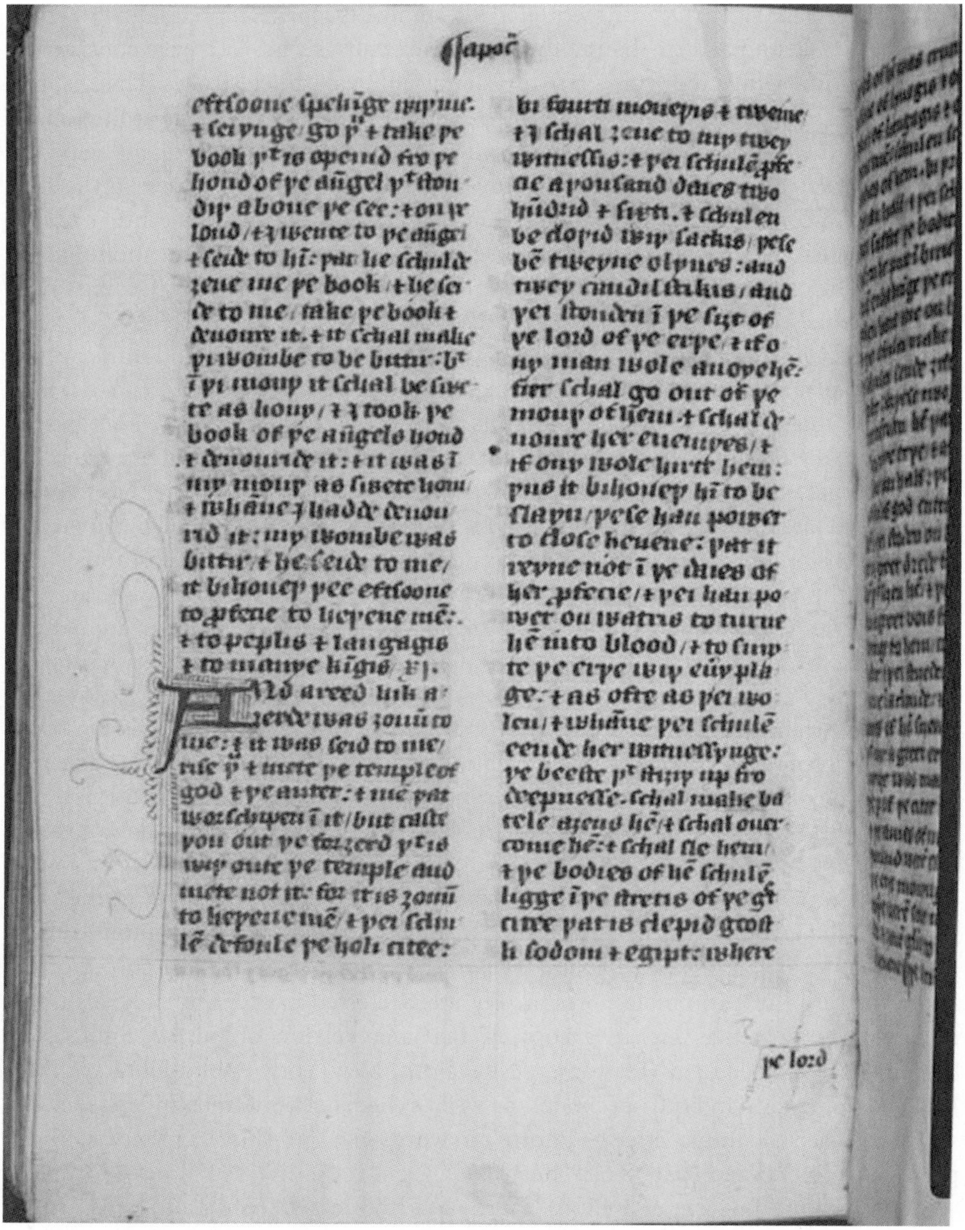
Apoc.

eftsoone spekinge wiþ me.
& seiynge. go þou & take þe
book þat is opened fro þe
hond of þe aungel þat ston
diþ aboue þe see: & on þe
lond / & I wente to þe aungel
& seide to hym: þat he schulde
ȝeue me þe book / & he sei
de to me / take þe book &
deuoure it. & it schal make
þi wombe to be bitter: but
in þi mouþ it schal be swe
te as hony / & I took þe
book of þe aungels hond
& deuouride it: & it was in
my mouþ as swete hony
& whanne I hadde deuou
rid it: my wombe was
bitter / & he seide to me /
it bihoueþ þee eftsoone
to prophecie to heþene men:.
& to peplis & langagis
& to many kyngis. xj.
And a reed lijk a
ȝerde was ȝouun to
me: & it was seid to me /
rise þou & mete þe temple of
god & þe auter: & men þat
worschipen in it / but caste
þou out þe forȝerd þat is
wiþ oute þe temple and
mete not it: for it is ȝouun
to heþene men / & þei schu
len defoule þe holi citee:

bi fourti monethis & tweine
& I schal ȝeue to my tweye
witnessis: & þei schulen prophe
cie a þousand daies two
hundrid & sixti. & schulen
be cloþid wiþ sackis / þese
ben tweyne olyues: and
tweye candilstikis / and
þei stonden in þe siȝt of
þe lord of þe erþe / & if o
ny man wole anoye hem:
fier schal go out of þe
mouþ of hem. & schal de
uoure her enemyes / &
if ony wole hirte hem:
þus it bihoueþ him to be
slayn / þese han power
to close heuene: þat it
reyne not in þe daies of
her prophecie / & þei han po
wer on watris to turne
hem into blood / & to smy
te þe erþe wiþ euery pla
ge: & as ofte as þei wo
len / & whanne þei schulen
ende her witnessynge:
þe beeste þat stiȝeþ up fro
depnesse. schal make ba
tele aȝens hem / & schal ouer
come hem: & schal sle hem /
& þe bodies of hem schulen
ligge in þe stretis of þe gre
te citee þat is clepid goost
li sodom & egipt: where

þe lord

PLATE 23.5 New York, New York Public Library, NYPL MA 066, fol. 260v.

It was not only in *Textura* manuscripts that the appearance of the page was important. From the late fourteenth and in the first half of the fifteenth century scribes frequently employed *Anglicana Formata* in vernacular manuscripts, which were increasingly in demand as a result of rising literacy among the laity. Several copies of John Gower's *Confessio amantis* were produced in the early fifteenth century by the same scribe, who seems to have been a full-time copyist, since he also copied Chaucer's *Canterbury Tales, Piers Plowman*, and John Trevisa's translation of Bartolomaeus Anglicus' *De proprietatibus rerum*.[30] He wrote a careful and disciplined hand (Plate 23.6, Plimpton MS 265, fol. 135) that shows some influence of the recently introduced Secretary script in the broken lobe strokes of letters such as *d* and *o* and in the use of kidney-shaped final *s* ("answerd," col. 1, line 3; "goode," col. 2, line 3; "þis" and "Manachas," col. 1, line 2). The shaft of *t* now protrudes above the headstroke (that is, *t* is now written with a cross bar), and in this larger squarer version of *Anglicana* the round-backed *d* has acquired a more upright back ("deþ," col. 2, line 1). The layout is carefully planned to help the reader find his or her way around the text with filled lombards at minor divisions of the text and the Latin gloss in the second column (lines 5–7) and the marginal commentary written in red.

In another copy of the text (Cambridge, Trinity College, MS R.3.2) the scribe worked with four others, including the scribe who copied both the Ellesmere manuscript of the *Canterbury Tales*, illustrated with portraits of the pilgrim-narrators, and the more workaday Hengwrt manuscript of the text . He too employs *Anglicana Formata*.[31] The lack of coordination between the different scribes' stints and the absence of any evidence of overall supervision in the Trinity manuscript provides important evidence for our understanding of the organization of the medieval book trade. The scribes are likely to have been independent craftsmen living in the same neighborhood (in London this was Pater Noster Row, near St. Paul's Cathedral) who could call on one another's help in producing a volume, rather than working together in a single scriptorium or workshop.

Anglicana was increasingly influenced by Secretary script. A copy of Trevisa's translation of the popular encyclopedia, *De proprietatibus rerum* by Bartholomaeus Anglicus, owned by Sir Thomas Chaworth, M.P. for Nottinghamshire (d. 1459) is one of three surviving books shown to be Chaworth's by the presence of his coat of arms (Plate 23.7, Plimpton MS 263, fol. 299v). They are all professional and expensive productions, but whereas the "Wollaton Antiphonal," as a liturgical book, is written in *Textura*, his Trevisa, being in the vernacular, is in *Anglicana Formata*, dating from the second quarter of the century.[32] Secretary influence can be seen here in the angular broken strokes of letters such as *d* and *o*, the simplified form of *w* ("what," line 3 and "when," line 6, as opposed to the more complex form in "ichewed," line 6), the use of short *r* ("first," line 1), and the horns (small projecting strokes) that occur where the pen changes direction on the page (for example, *e* in "lasse," line 4 or *g* in "restynge," line 2). Sir Thomas's will survives and mentions several other books, some for his chapel and others in English, but they cannot now be identified.

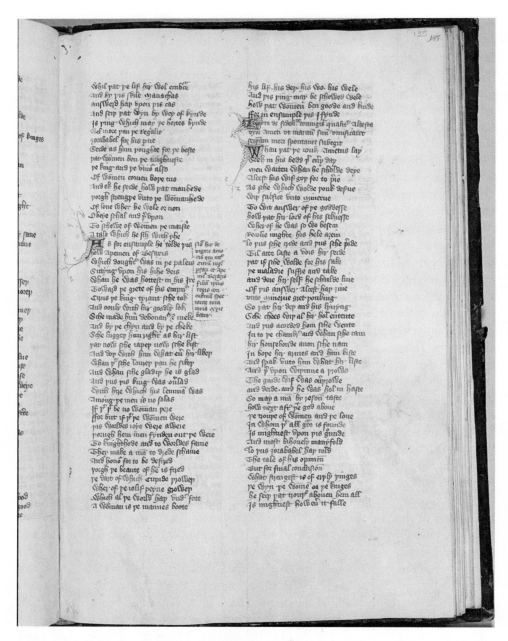

PLATE 23.6 Columbia University Rare Book and Manuscript Library, Plimpton MS 265, fol. 135.

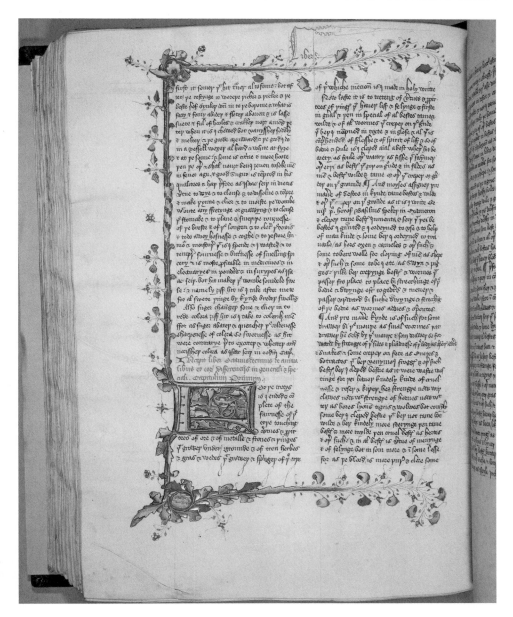

PLATE 23.7 Columbia University Rare Book and Manuscript Library, Plimpton MS 263, fol. 299 v.

Toward the end of the century the handwriting of scribes writing *Anglicana* can often convey an impression of irregularity. A page from a commonplace book (Plate 23.8, Plimpton 259, fol. 39v) presumably written for his own use by the scribe is not written with any concern for calligraphy, although it is provided with a fine strapwork initial. The writing sprawls across the page, and the size and proportion of

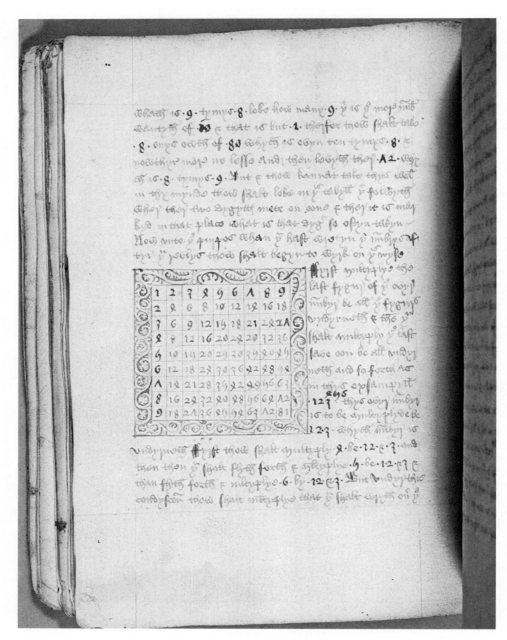

PLATE 23.8 Columbia University Rare Book and Manuscript Library, Plimpton MS 259, fol. 39 v.

individual letters vary (compare *w* in "whan" with that in "two," line 6), while descenders frequently trail into the letters of the line below (as *r* in "fowre," line 4, "numbrys," line 6; *y* in "wretyn," line 15).

By the middle of the fifteenth century Secretary had been adopted for copying vernacular texts. Already the poet Thomas Hoccleve had produced a volume of his poetry in it for presentation to Joan, Countess of Westmorland, sometime between 1422 and 1426.[33] Hoccleve, as an official in the Privy Seal Office, was accustomed to writing documents in French and so this script would come naturally to him. However, it would not make sense to give Joan a book copied in Secretary, although his hand is firm and clear, if she or someone in her household had not also become accustomed to it, perhaps through checking accounts or receiving incoming missives.

Malcolm Parkes has called attention to the importance of the influence of fashion on later medieval handwriting.[34] By the time a copy of Lydgate's *Fall of Princes* (Plate 23.9, Plimpton MS 255, fol. 25v) came to be copied in the mid- to later fifteenth century English scribes and readers had become familiar with the kind of current handwriting found in French books through manuscripts brought back home by those returning from the English occupation of France. An awareness of French attitudes to style and decorum in books "initiated new trends in fashion among English scribes and their patrons . . . . Commercial scribes seem to have regarded handwriting influenced by *Lettre courante* as an economical, yet stylish book hand particularly appropriate for copies of vernacular texts, and used it throughout the rest of the century."[35] A more up-market variety was influenced by *Lettre bastarde*, as seen in this copy of the *Fall*. The hand splays across the page, the forward slant indicating the speed with which it was written. French influence is seen in the short curved ascenders finished with small loops (for example, *k* in "took," and *h* in "him" col. 1, line 1) and the long, tapering descenders (*p* in "pepill," col.1, line 2, *f* in "deifei," col. 2, line 2, and long *s* in "rehersith" col.1, line 5). A distinctive form of the letter *g* with its tail ending in a crescent-shaped curve enables the identification of this scribe in two other copies of the text, as well as a copy of the *Canterbury Tales*.[36] Although this copy has many leaves missing, those that remain are eye-catching, with gold initials marking major divisions in the text.

However, many scribes in the later fifteenth century adopted a more "pick and mix" approach to handwriting, that is, graphs appropriate to *Anglicana* and Secretary could be employed together within an individual's repertory of letterforms. A scribe's decision to use one form rather than another was a matter of choice; hence the composition of such mixed hands varied. A copy of the *Nova Statuta* (containing the Statures of the Realm from the reign of Edward III and continued up to various dates in various copies) was a required volume for lawyers. Although one's initial impression is that the copy seen here dating from the second quarter of the fifteenth century (Plate 23.10 Plimpton 273, fol. 53v) looks as if it were written in Secretary with the pronounced spiky appearance of the hand, apart from a pronounced preference for the single compartment Secretary *a* ("cas," line 1, "hastiment," line 4) as opposed to the *Anglicana* form ("contrarie," line 11), other letterforms belong to *Anglicana*: long *r* (line 5 "remedie"), *g* ("ordeigner" lines 4–5, "beignent," lines 10–11), and sigma-shaped final *s*

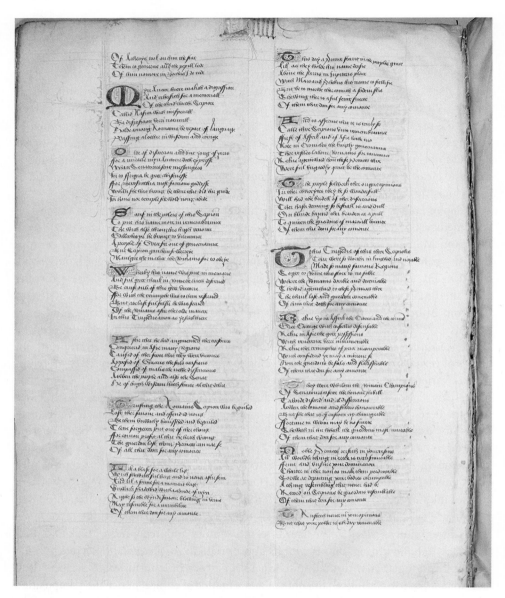

PLATE 23.9 Columbia University Rare Book and Manuscript Library, Plimpton MS 255, fol. 25v.

("freres," line 3). An *Index to the Statutes of the Realm* (Plate 23.11 Plimpton Add MS 03, fol. 4v), on the other hand, appears written in small neat Secretary typical of the mid-fifteenth century with small looped ascenders, though on closer inspection it can be seen that both Secretary and *Anglicana* features occur. Thus the scribe uses the Anglicana long *r* ("caried," line 3; "from" line 5) alongside Secretary short *r* ("Chauncerye," line 1; "caried," line 2); *Anglicana* two-compartment *g* ("alleggyd," line 10)

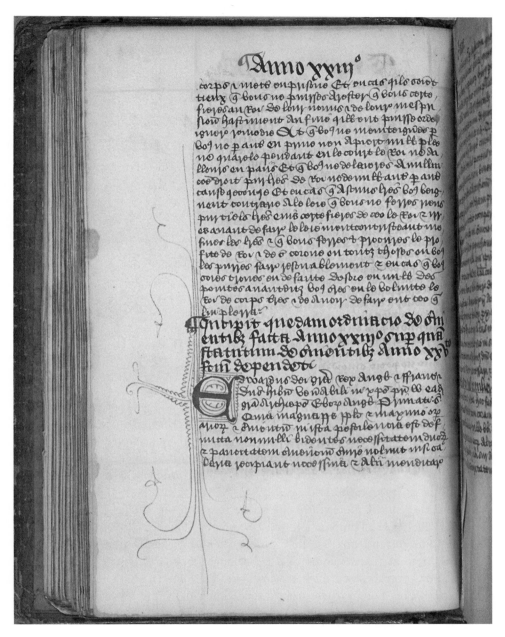

PLATE 23.10 Columbia University Rare Book and Manuscript Library, Plimpton MS 273, fol. 53v.

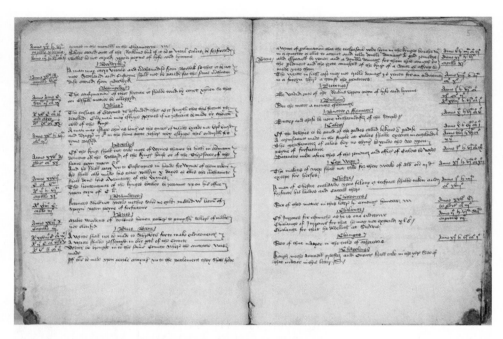

PLATE 23.11 Columbia University Rare Book and Manuscript Room, Plimpton Add MS 03, fol. 4v.

alongside a Secretary *g* that looks like a "y" with a flat top and protruding horns ("passage," line 12). However, he appears consistently to use the Secretary form of *a*. The letter *v* has a heavy approach stroke both initially and in the middle of a word ("vitail," line 2; "avauntage," line 24).

Toward the end of the century the scribe of a copy of Walter Hilton's *Scale of Perfection* (Plate 23.12 Plimpton 257, fol. 25v) employs Secretary *g* ("regarde," line 2), *r* ("sauter," line 6), and final *s* ("þus," line 6), but consistently prefers *Anglicana a* ("regarde," line 2). The ascender of *d* is no longer looped ("shuld," line 3), the tall shaft of *t* now protrudes well above the cross bar ("hit," line 1, "prophete," line 8), and *v* is written with a heavy approach stroke ("voce," line 10). By now þ looks like a "y" ("þat þei" line 2), and the scribe still uses yogh ("ȝeueþ," line 3). The Latin quotation or lemma is written in a rather clumsy *Textura*.

However, handwriting was becoming increasingly idiosyncratic, and after William Caxton's introduction of the printing press to England in 1476 hand-written books gradually ceased to be the normal method of producing and disseminating texts. In the sixteenth century, while Secretary remained in use as the principal script for letters, documents and the occasional book, *Anglicana* tended to survive only within government offices and the law.[37]

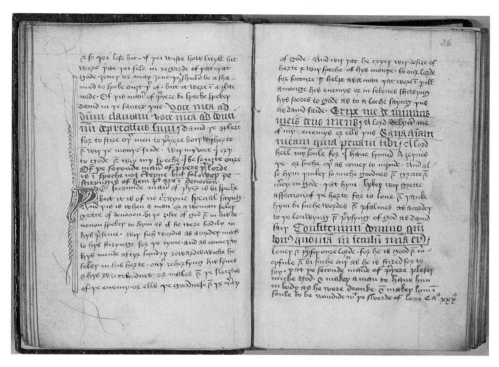

PLATE 23.12 Columbia University, Rare Book and Manuscript Room, Plimpton 257, fol. 25v.

NOTES

1. Parkes (2008b, 103 and n. 5).
2. Henceforth manuscripts at Columbia will be cited by shelfmark only.
3. Van Dijk (1956).
4. Brown (2006).
5. Panayotova (2008).
6. Destrez (1935, Plates 27–8).
7. See for instance Roberts (2005, Plate 35); Wright (1960, Plates 10-11); Pearsall and Cunningham (1977).
8. Ker (1969, xi). The development of *Anglicana* can be traced in the plates in Johnson and Jenkinson (1915, Plates xiv–xix) and Hector (1966, Plates iv (b), v (a), vi–vii (a)).
9. Hessel and Bulst (1932–3, items 4 and 43 in their list of his manuscripts).
10. Ker (1960, 3). The suggestion that the homiliary was the famous Vercelli Manuscript of Old English verse and prose (see most recently Vincent 1996, lx) is unlikely, since the cardinal kept the book in his chapel. See further Swanton (1987, 3–4). Bicchieri had previously been legate in France, where he acquired books in "Parisian letters."
11. The essential text book for what follows is Parkes (2008a).
12. Parkes (2008a).
13. In a paper given to the XVIth Colloquium of the Comité International de Paléographie Latine, London 2008.

14. For Glasgow University Library, Hunter MS 472 (V.6.22), see http://special.lib.gla.ac.uk/exhibns/chaucer/learning.html, accessed January 12, 2020.

15. Cf. Lalou (1992, 262–3).

16. Whittick (1993); Caie (2000). It would, however, be impossible to rub off incised letters from slate.

17. Tschann and Parkes; for Thedmar's handwriting, see Robinson (2003, Plate 27).

18. Chaplais (1971, Plates 4 (a) and (b)) illustrate the distinction.

19. See Parkes 2008a, xvii–xviii and Plate 7(i) and (ii). I prefer to use Parkes's terminology for the grades of Anglicana rather than that advocated by Roberts (2005, 161) because too rigid a description of letterforms denies the complexity of the human factor in forming the shapes of letters.

20. Baildon and Beauchesne (1571).

21. Smith (2008).

22. Parkes (2008a, Plates 9–10); Chaplais (1971, Plates 16(c), 17(c), 19(a), 21(a)).

23. Kew, TNA, C1/68/63. For Elvet's dates, see Le Neve (1962, 12) and (1967, 15).

24. Johnston (1906/1969, 13).

25. Parkes (2008b, 105 and Plate 28).

26. See Freeman Sandler (1986); Scott (1996), (2002).

27. Cf. Peikola (2006); Alexander, Marrow, and Sandler (2005, no. 14).

28. Peikiola (2008); cf. Alexander, Marrow, and Sandler (2005, nos 15–17); Roberts (2005, Plate 39).

29. British Library, Royal MS 17.B.i, fols 4v-5. Printed Kuhn (1968); McIntosh (1965).

30. Doyle and Parkes (1978). I am unpersuaded that this scribe can be identified with John Marchaunt, Common Clerk of London's Guildhall, as suggested by Mooney and Stubbs (2013, 38–65).

31. Both manuscripts can be seen in facsimile, i.e., Woodward and Stevens (1995), published with companion volume Stevens and Woodward (1997); and Ruggiers (1979). I am unconvinced that this scribe is Chaucer's Adam (i.e. Adam Pinkhurst: see Mooney and Stubbs (2013, 67–85).

32. For the Wollaton Antiphonal, see Scott (1996, no. 69 and ills 275–80); Marks and Williamson (2003, no. 312, with colour plate).

33. Durham University Library, Cosin MS V.iii.9, for which, see Burrow and Doyle (2002).

34. Parkes (2008b, 101–25).

35. Parkes (2008b, Plate 40); Roberts (2005, Plates 55–6).

36. Mooney and Mosser (2004); Parkes (2008b, 41).

37. Jenkinson (1927).

BIBLIOGRAPHY

Alexander, J. J. G., J. H. Marrow, and L. Freeman Sandler, eds. 2005. *The Splendor of the Word: Medieval and Renaissance Manuscripts at the New York Public Library*. New York: New York Public Library.

Baildon, J. and J. de Beauchesne. 1571. *A Booke Containing Diuers Sortes of Hands as Well the English as French Secretarie* . . . . London: Thomas Vautrouillier.

Brown, M. P. 2006. *The Luttrell Psalter: A Facsimile*. London: British Library.

Burrow, J. A. and A. I. Doyle. 2002. *Thomas Hoccleve: A Facsimile Edition of the Autograph Verse Manuscripts* (EETS SS 19). Oxford: Early English Text Society and Oxford University Press.

Caie, G. 2000. "The Inscribed Paisley Slates." In *The Monastery and Abbey of Paisley,* ed. John Malden, 199–203. Renfrew: Renfrewshire Local History Forum.

Chaplais, P. 1971. *English Royal Documents: King John–Henry VI 1199–1461.* Oxford: Clarendon Press.

Derolez, A. 1996. "Observations on the Aesthetics of the Gothic Manuscript." *Scriptorium* 50: 3–12.

Derolez, A. 2003. *The Palaeography of Gothic Manuscript Books from the Twelfth to the Early Sixteenth Century.* Cambridge: Cambridge University Press.

Destrez, J. 1935. *La Pecia dans les manuscrits universitaires du xiiie et xive siècle.* Paris: Éditions Jacques Vautrain.

Doyle, A. I. and M. B. Parkes. 1978. "The Production of Copies of the *Canterbury Tales* and the *Confessio Amantis* in the Early Fifteenth Century." In *Medieval Scribes, Manuscripts and Libraries: Essays presented to N. R. Ker,* ed. M. B. Parkes and A. G. Watson, 163–210. London: Scolar Press.

Freeman Sandler, L. 1986. *Gothic Manuscripts 1285–1385* (Survey of Manuscripts Illuminated in the British Isles, 5). London: Harvey Miller.

Hector, L.C. 1966. *The Handwriting of English Documents,* 2nd ed. London: Edward Arnold.

Hessel, A. and W. Bulst. 1932–3. "Kardinal Guala Bichieri und seine Bibliothek." *Historische Vierteljahrschrift* 27: 772–94.

Jenkinson, H. 1927. *The Later Court Hands in England from the Fifteenth to the Seventeenth Century.* Cambridge University Press.

Johnson, C. and H. Jenkinson. 1915. *English Court Hand A.D. 1066-1500.* Oxford: Clarendon Press.

Johnston, E. 1906. *Writing & Illuminating, & Lettering* [repr. London: Pitman, 1969]. London: John Hogg.

Ker, N. R. 1960. "Introduction." In *Facsimile of MS Bodley 34,* EETS OS 247.

Ker, N. R. 1963. "Introduction." In The Owl and the Nightingale reproduced in Facsimile, EETS OS 251.

Ker, N. R. 1969. *Medieval Manuscripts in British Libraries,* I. Oxford: Clarendon Press.

Kuhn, Sherman M. 1968. "The Preface to a Fifteenth-Century Concordance." *Speculum* 43: 258–73.

Lalou, É. 1992. "Inventaire des tablettes médiévales." In *Les Tablettes à écrire de l'antiquité à l'époque moderne,* 262–3. Turnhout: Brepols.

Le Neve, J. 1962. *Fasti Ecclesiae Anglicanae 1300–1500,* I: *Lincoln Diocese,* ed. H. P. F. King. London: Athlone Press.

Le Neve, J. 1967. *Fasti Ecclesiae Anglicanae 1300–1500.* XII: *Introduction, Errata and Index,* ed. Joyce M. Horn. London: Athlone Press.

Marks, R. and P. Wiliamson, eds. 2003. *Gothic: Art for England 1400-1547.* London: V and A Publications.

McIntosh, A. 1965. "Some Linguistic Reflections of a Wycliffite." In *Franciplegius: Medieval and Linguistic Studies in Honor of Francis Peabody Magoun, Jr,* ed. J. B. Bessinger Jr. and R. P. Creed, 290–3. New York: New York University Press.

Mooney, L. R. and D. W. Mosser. 2004. "Hooked-g Scribes and Takamiya Manuscripts." In *The Medieval Book and a Modern Collector: Essays in Honour of Toshiyuki Takamiya,* ed. Takami M., R. A. Linenthal, and J. Scahill, 179–96. Cambridge: D. S. Brewer and Tokyo: Yushodo Press.

Mooney, L. R. and Estelle Stubbs. 2013. *Scribes and the City: London Guildhall Clerks and the Dissemination of Middle English Literature, 1375–1425.* New York: Boydell Press.

Morison, S. 1981. "'Black-Letter' Text." In *Selected Essays on the History of Letter-Forms in Manuscript and Print*, ed. David McKitterick, 2 vols., I: 177–205. Cambridge: Cambridge University Press.

Panayotova, S., ed. 2008. *The Macclesfield Psalter.* London: Thames and Hudson.

Parkes, M. B. 2008a. *English Cursive Book Hands 1250–1500*, 2nd ed., repr. Aldershot: Ashgate.

Parkes, M. B. 2008b. *Their Hands before Our Eyes: A Closer Look at Scribes.* Aldershot: Ashgate.

Pearsall, D. and I. C. Cunningham. 1977. *The Auchinleck Manuscript.* London: Scolar Press.

Peikola, M. 2006. "Lollard (?) Production under the Looking Glass: The Case of Columbia University Plimton Add. MS 3." *Journal of the Early Book Society* 9:, 1–23.

Peikola, M. 2008. "Aspects of mise-en-page in Manuscripts of the Wycliffite Bible." In *Medieval Texts in Context*, ed. Denis Renevey and Graham D. Caie, 28–67. London and New York: Routledge.

Roberts, J. 2005. *Guide to Scripts Used in English Writings up to 1500.* London: British Library.

Robinson, P. R. 2003. *Dated and Datable Manuscripts c.888-1600 in London Libraries.* London: British Library.

Scott, K. L. 1996. *Later Gothic Manuscripts 1390–1490* (Survey of Manuscripts Illuminated in the British Isles, 6). London: Harvey Miller.

Scott, K. L. 2002. *Dated and Datable English Manuscript Borders c.1395–1499.* London: Bibliographical Society.

Smith, M. H. 2008. "L'Écriture de la chancellerie de France au xive siècle. Observations sur ses origines et sa diffusion en Europe." In *Régionalisme et internationalisme. Problèmes de paléographie et de codicologie du Moyen Âge, Actes du XVe Colloque du Comité International de Paléographie Latine (Vienne, 13–17 septembre 2005)*, ed. Otto Kresten and Franz Lackner, 279–97. Vienna: Verlag der Österreichischen Akademie.

Stevens, M. and D. Woodward, eds. 1997. *The Ellesmere Chaucer: Essays in Interpretation.* San Marino, CA: Huntington Library.

Swanton, M.. ed. 1987. *The Dream of the Rood.* Manchester: Manchester University Press.

Tschann, J. and M. B. Parkes. 1996. *Facsimile of Oxford, Bodleian Library, MS 86* (Early English Text Society, Supplementary Series 16). Oxford: Early English Text Society and Oxford University Press.

Van Dijk, S. J. P. 1956. "An Advertisement Sheet of an Early Fourteenth Century Writing Master at Oxford." *Scriptorium* 10: 47–64.

Vincent, N., ed. 1996. *The Letters and Charters of Cardinal Guala Bicchieri.* Woodbridge: Canterbury and York Society.

Whittick, C. 1993. "A Didactic Slate." *Sussex Archaeological Collections* 131: 106–9.

Woodward, D. and M. Stevens, eds. 1995. *The Canterbury Tales, by Geoffrey Chaucer. The New Ellesmere Chaucer Facsimile (of Huntington Library MS EL 26 C 9).* Tokyo: Yushodo Co and San Marino, CA: Huntington Library Press.

Wright, C. E. 1960. *English Vernacular Hands from the Twelfth to the Fifteenth Centuries.* Oxford: Clarendon Press.

CHAPTER 24

···

GOTHIC SCRIPT
IN GERMANY

···

KARL-GEORG PFÄNDTNER

THE TRANSITION FROM CAROLINGIAN
TO GOTHIC SCRIPT

···

GOTHIC script did not begin in Germany with a significant break from Caroline minuscule. The change to a new script was a slow development over a long period of time. The new forms and style of the Gothic script—used both for Latin and for vernacular texts—spread step by step, at different times, in the various politically independent regions of Germany. From the second quarter of the twelfth century until the first quarter of the thirteenth, a number of different types of transitional Gothic scripts are found in this area. These transitional scripts are variously named in the paleographical literature: "Romanesque minuscule" (Bruckner), "*Carolina-gotica*" (Kirchner), "Carolingian-Gothic mixed-script" (Mazal). The two last names signal that in these scripts only a few of the new Gothic characters occur in scripts that continue to exhibit many of the older Caroline forms. This mixture of characters peculiar to each script is found even within single documents or books copied by the same scribe. The main change that occurs during this phase is in the overall appearance of the script. More elongated forms and narrower characters become the norm, and there is a new emphasis on, and exaggeration of, the contrast between the thick and thin strokes within letters, especially evident in the increased use of hairline strokes. A good example of this mixed script is seen in Plate 24.1 (BSB, Cgm 39, fol. 101r)[1], a hand from western Bavaria, dating to the fourth quarter of the twelfth century. The minims of *b, c, e, g, h, o,* and *p* are somewhat pointed at the shoulder, are unbroken, and remain essentially curved. Adjacent curves do not overlap. The individual strokes that comprise the letters *m* and *n* are slightly pointed at the shoulder, unbroken, and not all identical. An important modernization is that the shafts of *f* and tall *s* end on the baseline.

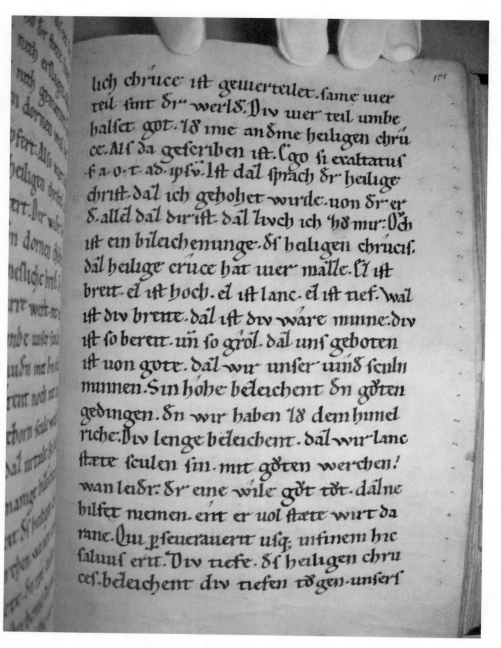

PLATE 24.1 BSB, Cgm 39, fol. 101r.

EARLY GOTHIC MINUSCULE

In early Gothic minuscule, in addition to the increasing narrowness of the shafts and the emphasis on the vertical strokes, one also notes a tendency, which had already begun in the Carolingian minuscule, toward a greater stress on the intermediate zone. This may be seen in Plate 24.2 (BSB, Cgm 5256, fol. XXIra; first quarter of the thirteenth century).[2] This hand generally has simple upward turns of the shafts at the baseline, and also, sporadically, the older forms of *f* and tall *s* which extend below the baseline. The tops of the shafts are generally forked, and the forking frequently forms a triangle. The ascenders can also begin with small introductory strokes from the left (Plate 24.2, line 5: *behaltet*). Newer forms are the bow of *h*, which is increasingly extended under the line, and the shorter lower bow of *g*, which connects securely to the upper bow, so that the whole assumes a broken, complex, angular appearance, with a pointed top. Slashes over single *i* become more frequent. Round *d*, including in the *de*-ligature (Plate 24.2, line 5: *den*), and round *s* become more common (Plate 24.2, line 3: *si*), although the straight *d* (Plate 24.2, lines 2/3: *dise*) continues to be used throughout the thirteenth century as a higher-quality calligraphic form. Typical for this period is the consistently increasing adornment of letters: in addition to the long-established extension of the termination of the shoulder of the *r*, decorative strokes can now appear on the *v* and *w* (Plate 24.2, line 2: *ware*). The interiors of the majuscules receive ornamental curves and strokes, and the shaft of *J* gets a row of hairline strokes.

For archival material in codex form, rental agreements, memorial books, annals, and not infrequently for German-language texts, especially secular literature, much simpler chancery scripts were used, in addition to the calligraphic broken book script. These displayed very few of the more up-to-date characteristics of the emerging Gothic style. They are generally written with little differentiation between thick and thin strokes, and the shoulders of the curved strokes remain round and unbroken. The shafts of the *f*, tall *s*, and *r*, are characterized by long descenders below the baseline, frequently curving to the left, a feature taken over from documentary and business scripts. At the same time, the ascenders are notably extended and increasingly have introductory strokes placed lower and lower on the shaft; toward the middle of the century this could lead to looping of the ascenders. It is likely that many of the scribes whose scripts bear similarities to documentary forms were active in chanceries.

TEXTURA (TEXTUALIS FORMATA)

The Gothic script spread through the German-speaking world from the west. The transition to the new script was completed in the Rhineland before the middle of the thirteenth century, and nearly everywhere else by around 1275. The most formal type

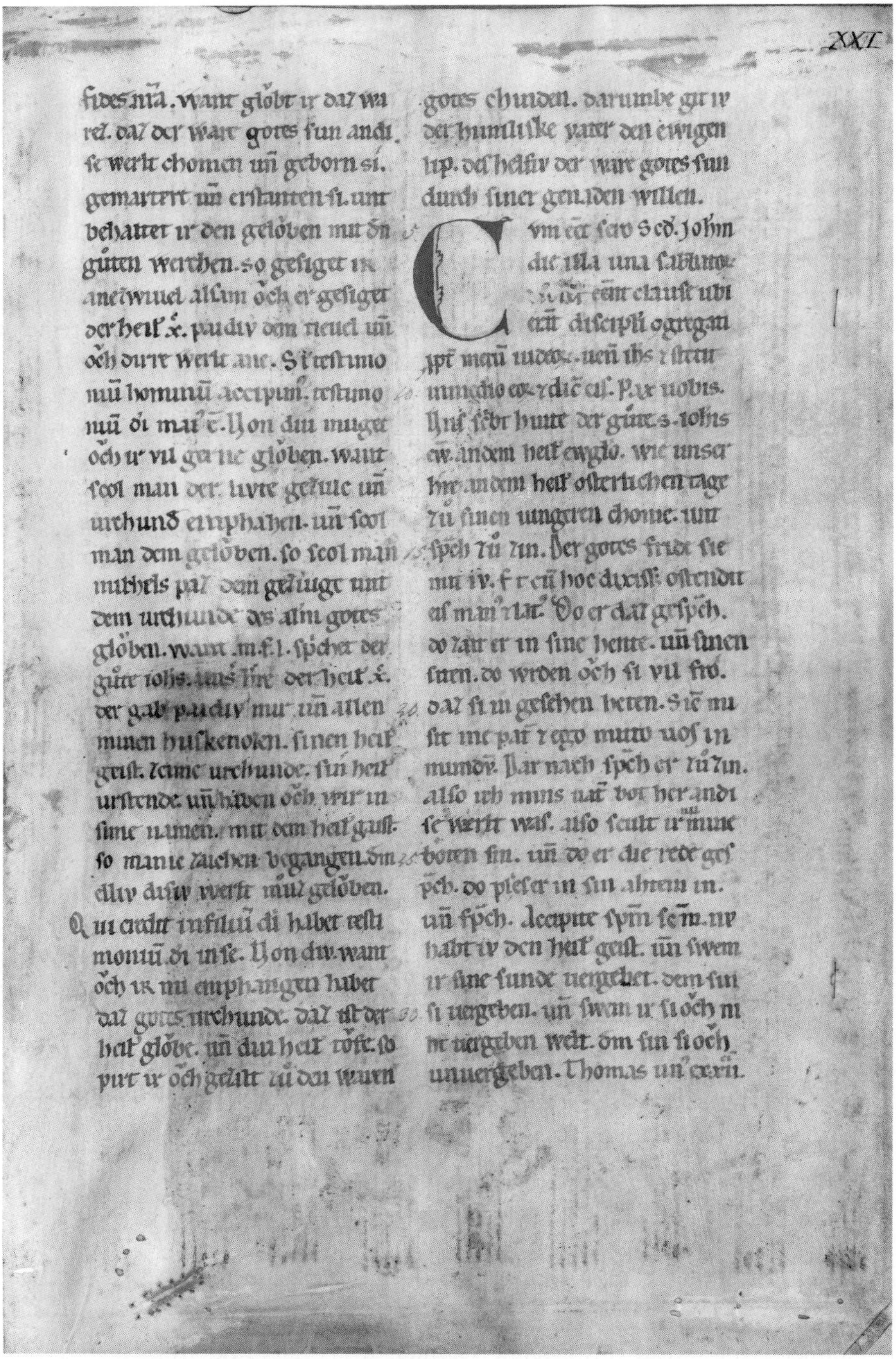

XXI

PLATE 24.2 BSB, Cgm 5256, fol. XXIr; Bavaria, first quarter of the thirteenth century.

(*textura*) employed as consistently as possible the double breaking of minims and the identical formation of all shafts, as well as the fusion of adjacent curves. And it carefully differentiated between the thick and thin strokes within individual letters. Because of its difficulty and because of the time it took to write it, *textura* was employed only for high-quality codices, especially for Latin liturgical texts, for bibles, and for legal statutes. It was also used in more simply written texts as a display script for noteworthy lemmata, a practice that continued into the fifteenth century. In the course of time, *textura* developed diverse and sometimes highly individualized or mannered styles. These were particularly cultivated, and subsequently named, by the writing masters of the fifteenth century.

At its calligraphic peak in the first half of the fourteenth century, *textura* exhibits nearly everywhere the regular fusion of adjacent curves; *a* with a closed upper bow; and round *r* after curved letters. It also regularly employs various ornamentations through hairline serifs. When *t* appears at the end of a word or at the end of a line, its horizontal stroke sometimes ends with a purely ornamental vertical serif which may also be beveled. This same detail is seen on *f* and *g* in final position. A few changes occur in the second quarter of the fourteenth century. At the high end of the calligraphic scale, a new method of double breaking develops through the placing of elongated diamond-shaped strokes at the tops of shafts and bows.

This mannered style was used, for instance, in a Bamberg evangelistary of the second third of the fourteenth century (Plate 24.3, Bamberg, Staatsbibliothek, Msc. Bibl. 100, fol. 2).[3] The breaking of the shafts is further enhanced as the technique is extended to the bows of *a*, *b*, *d*, *g*, *h*, etc. The diamond at the top of the shafts and of the bows is curved, as it takes on the shape of a concave lozenge between short oblique strokes (Plate 24.3, line 2/3: see the third shaft of the *m* in *iherosolimis*.) The inward curve in the diamond makes the breaks more prominent. From roughly 1320 onward this style of writing is found in the west, as well as in Bavaria and Austria.

Another new development of calligraphic *textura* is that the shaft and its foot meet at a right angle at the baseline. The first examples of this angularity can be dated to shortly before the middle of the fourteenth century. Such rectilinear letters become frequent after the middle of the century and sometimes also appear in the simpler *textualis*. Additionally, curved hairline strokes occur on final *t* (Plate 24.3, line 3: *uenisset*), hooks on *final-s* (Plate 24.3, line 5: *discipulos*), and a hook or curve instead of a slash or a point on the *i* (Plate 24.3, line 4: *misit*). From the second half of the fourteenth century onward, a characteristic of the highest calligraphic level of *textura* is the heavy emphasis on the intermediate zone, whereby the individual letters within words are closely connected to each other at the top of the minims. A connected, horizontal band forms in this intermediate zone from the fully identical formation of all minims. These are singly or doubly broken, both at the top and bottom, and are written as quadrilaterals (i.e., diamond shapes are placed at the ends of the shafts). In extreme cases, all the minims are attached to one another, above and below; and they are also connected at the baseline to the feet of the ascenders, which are relatively short. In this way lattice-like bands of writing developed, making it very difficult to read this style of script.

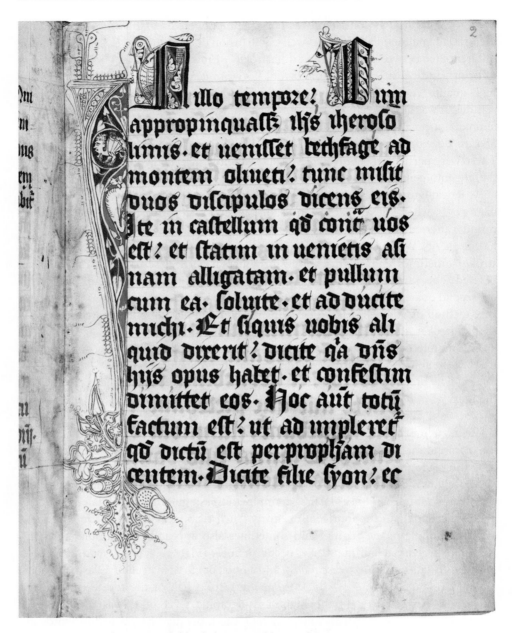

PLATE 24.3 Bamberg, Staatsbibliothek, Msc. Bibl. 100, fol. 2r.

TEXTUALIS

The *textualis* script was used when the goal was not prestigious calligraphy but rather a clear, easily readable script that was also relatively simple and quick to write. The basic *textualis* is the most frequently used book hand from the middle of the thirteenth century to the middle of the fourteenth, and is distinguished from *textura* by a reduction in formality and precision. Its relative informality permits a wide range of different grades of scripts. The faster the hand is written, the simpler the letterforms necessarily become. During the periods of its use as a book hand, *textualis* underwent changes and developments of certain letterforms and letter groups. These, along with the degree to which the script has transitioned to pure Gothic, can be useful criteria for dating the manuscripts.

In the second half of the thirteenth century, the fusion of adjacent curves increases. During this same period, the double-bowed *a* also emerges, and it becomes a hallmark letter of the fourteenth century. It appears sporadically in a simplified form around 1250 in west German scripts; and in the course of a generation, its use extends nearly everywhere that German was spoken. It is used at first, however, in *textura* at a high level of calligraphic quality and in documentary scripts. The *a* in simpler *textualis*, even as late as the first quarter of the fourteenth century, often still has the old-fashioned, single-bowed form which was faster to write. Initially, the *a* appears in a transitional form in which the top of the shaft arches or bends more or less extensively over the lower bow, but does not yet fully connect to it (see Plate 24.4, line 4: *abte, daz*; BSB, Cgm 91, fol. 5r, east Bavaria, 1270s).[4] Around 1300 a new, ligatured form of double *t* emerges in which the shaft of the second *t* is taller. This feature becomes more common during the fourteenth century (Plate 24.3, line 13: *dimittet*).

In the third quarter of the thirteenth century more formal scripts are increasingly ornamented with hairline serifs. Horizontal strokes or hooks are attached to the top or bottom of the ascenders of *b*, *h*, *l*, and *k* (Plate 24.4, line 1, *tumbe*; line 3: *losestu*). Adjacent ascenders, such as *ll*, *lb*, *lh*, can be connected with horizontal strokes (Plate 24.3, line 8: *pullum*). The traditional extension of the termination of the shoulder of *r* as well as the stroke over the *i*, which was becoming more frequent, can appear as hooks by the end of the fourteenth century. At the same time, the ornamentation of the end of the vertical of final *t* spreads from the southeast (Plate 24.3, line 3: *uenisset*). A little later, the cross stroke of *f* also gets an ornamental addition, and the letter further develops a long vertical stroke or a bow to the right at the top of the ascender. From the second quarter of the fourteenth century onward, the double-bowed *a*, with a closed upper bow, is increasingly extended above the intermediate zone, extending eventually to the height of the ascenders. Another dating criterion emerges in the 1320s, namely the placement of points over the *i*; for a while, these are employed alongside the more customary hairline slashes over the *i*. Hyphens to divide words broken between two lines, which formerly had consisted of a single slash, become in the 1320s two diagonal parallel lines.

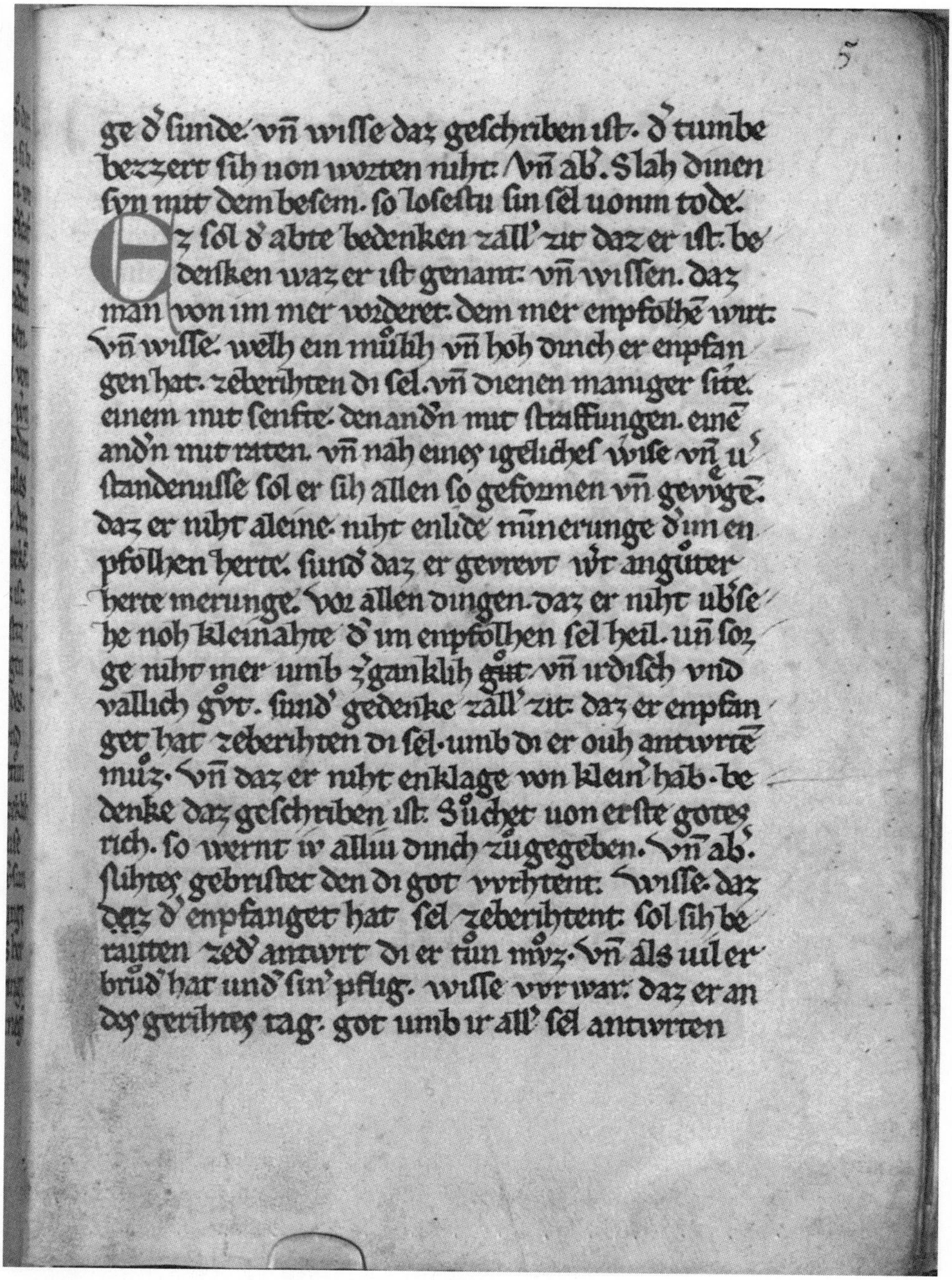

5

ge d sunde vñ wisse daz geschriben ist. d tumbe
bezzert sih non worten niht /vñ ab. Slah dinen
syn mit dem besem. so losestu sin sel uonm tode.
Ez sol d abte bedenken zall' zit daz er ist. be
denken waz er ist genant: vñ wissen. daz
man von im mer voderet. dem mer enpfolhe wirt:
vñ wisse. welh ein mulih vñ hoh dinch er enpfan
gen hat. zeberihten di sel. vñ dienen maniger site.
einem mit senfte. den andn mit straffungen. eine
andn mit ratten. vñ nah eines igeliches wise vñ u'
standenusse sol er sih allen so geformen vñ gevuge.
daz er niht aleine. niht enlide minerunge dim en
pfolhen herte. sund daz er gevrevt wr anguter
herte merunge. vor allen dingen. daz er niht ubse
he noh kleinahte d im enpfolhen sel heil. un sor
ge niht mer umb z ganklih gut. vñ irdisch vnd
vallich gvt. sund gedenke zall' zit. daz er enpfan
ger hat zeberihten di sel. umb di er ouh antwrte
muz. Vñ daz er niht enklage von klein hab. be
denke daz geschriben ist. Suchet uon erste gotes
rich. so wernt iu alliu dinch zu gegeben. Vñ ab.
suhtes gebristet den di got vrhtent. Wisse. daz
daz d enpfanger hat sel zeberihtent. sol sih be
ratten zed antwrt di er tun muz. Vñ als uil er
brud har und sin pflug. wisse vvr war: daz er an
des gerihtes tag. got umb ir all' sel antwrten

PLATE 24.4 BSB, Cgm 91, fol. 5r, east Bavaria, 1270s.

Cursive Scripts

··

Already at the end of the thirteenth century, some of the simpler and more quickly written book hands show evidence of the transition to cursive. In the second half of the fourteenth century, *textualis* began to lose to cursive its former status as the everyday book hand. Cursive scripts moved from their former spheres of administration and commerce into the realm of the book hand. As a result, the use of the calligraphic *textura* was restricted to a few narrowly defined purposes, and *textualis* was more or less completely ousted by the end of the fourteenth century. In order not to break the flow of the script, in cursive writing the pen is not lifted from the writing surface as the scribe moves from one letter to the next. This was the origin of the connecting lines between letters and also of the loops on the ascenders, which, at least in documentary scripts, were written starting from the right. The shaft of *d* usually ends in a loop; and loops are also added to *b*, *h*, *l*, and *k*. On some descenders as well, a loop extends from the end of the shaft back to the top.

In the cursives of the fourteenth century, it is possible to distinguish two consecutive stages of development. The "older Gothic cursive" (Plate 24.5, BSB, Cgm 2150, fol. 10v, region of Munich, shortly after the middle of the fourteenth century)[5] was primarily in use during the second and third quarters of the fourteenth century. Like the contemporary simple *textualis*, it developed an *a* with a closed upper bow which was often extended above the intermediate zone, sometimes almost reaching the height of the ascenders. Characteristic of this script is also a short *g* in the form of an *8*, which is often set slightly above the baseline and integrated into the intermediate zone. The final strokes of *h*, *y*, and *z*, and also often of *m* and *n*, are usually curved to the right under the line. In some calligraphic book cursives, the tops and ascenders of *f* and tall *s* are thickened. The loops on the ascenders can also be thickened and triangular. The increasing differentiation between thick and thin strokes develops from highly stylized chancery scripts. The use of the "older Gothic cursive" as a book hand was limited to the German-speaking world and bordering areas.

As a consequence of simplifications, and with the increasing connection of letter groups, the cursive which had formerly been common in German-speaking regions lost its unique, mannered, ornamental appearance. In the last quarter of the fourteenth century, the documentary as well as the book cursive developed a new, more efficient character. The old *a* with a closed upper bow is replaced by the simpler, single-bowed form, the short *g* is written with an open descender extending far to the left under the line (Plate 24.6, line 3: *gantz*; BSB, Cgm 424, fol. 232va, southwest Germany, 1398),[6] the thickening disappears from the ascenders, and their loops are now drawn more rounded than triangular. The "new Gothic cursive" retains from the older form the descenders on *f* and tall *s*, the looped ascenders, and the writing of letters with a single stroke of the pen. An innovation which begins in the last quarter of the fourteenth century in the "new Gothic cursive" is the practice of writing initial *v* and

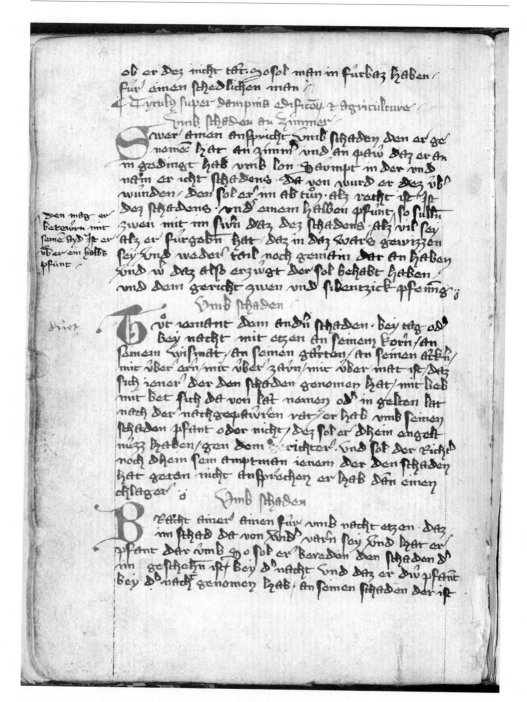

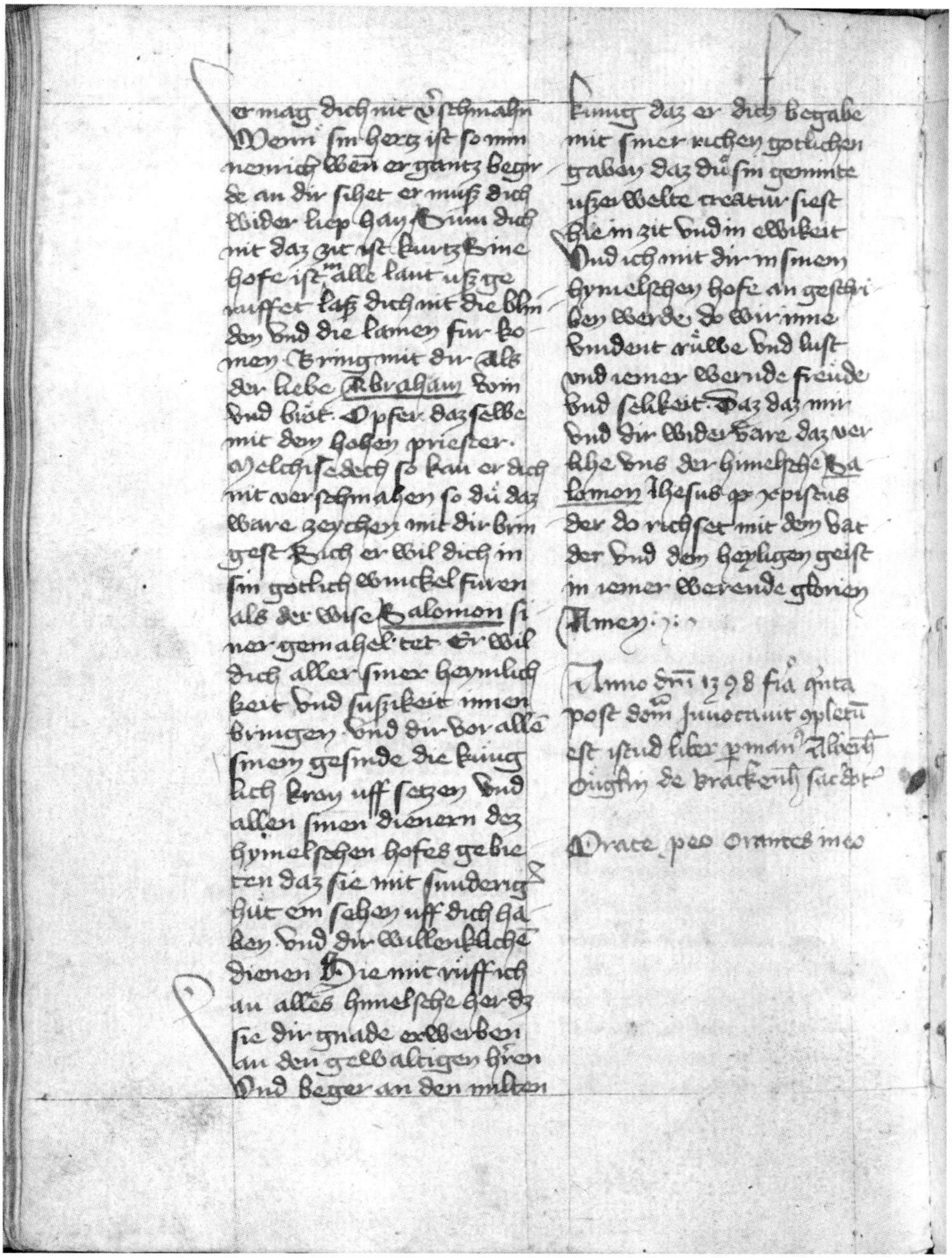

PLATE 24.6 BSB, Cgm 424, fol. 232v, southwest Germany, 1398.

w with, respectively, one or two loops (Plate 24.6, line 5: *wider*; line 9: *und*). This characteristic is found also in the *bastarda* script in the German-speaking world until the second quarter of the fifteenth century. The "new Gothic cursive" continues in use into the third decade of the fifteenth century.

BASTARDA

The *bastarda* script develops in the German-speaking world from the early phases of the "new Gothic cursive" around the end of the fourteenth century. This script combines the advantages of both cursive and *textualis*. From cursive, *bastarda* retains the typical extension of the shafts of *f* and tall *s* below the line (these long shafts and the simple, single-bowed *a* fundamentally distinguish it from *textualis*) and, at least initially, also the cursive loops on the ascenders of *b*, *h*, *l*, and *k*, as well as on the shaft of *d*. The *bastarda* hand was elevated to a higher calligraphic level through the inclusion of individual elements from *textualis*; these could be adopted in a wide variety of ways. Some letters could appear in their *textualis* form, constructed from a number of individual pen strokes (for example, *m*, *n*, and *r* in Plate 24.7, BSB, Clm 14675, fol. 139r, Regensburg, St. Emmeram, Konrad Peystainer, a St. Emmeram library catalogue of the middle of fifteenth century);[7] the simple breaking of the rounded strokes can be reintroduced, and the shafts that end on the line can be broken or bent above the line. At a higher calligraphic level, distinctions between thick and thin strokes are emphasized or ornamentation with fine strokes or hooks is introduced.

Bastarda reached the German-speaking world through the Prague chancery of the Holy Roman Emperor Charles IV (1355–78). It initially became common as a book hand in Austria and Bavaria. More or less at the same time, there are also *bastarda* scripts used as book scripts in western and southwestern Germany, probably developed under the influence of the French *lettre bâtarde*. Until the 1420s, the *bastarda* scripts in the German regions all have the continuous loops on the ascenders of *b*, *h*, *l*, and *k* and on the shaft of *d*, features that emerged with the book cursives of the fourteenth century. They share many characteristics with the "new Gothic cursive" and appear in countless transitional forms.

One of the most noticeable changes in *bastarda* is the gradual development of ascenders without loops. These are written, as in *textualis*, either as straight upright strokes or with a small serif (Plate 24.8, BSB, Clm 14675, fol. 1r, Regensburg, St. Emmeram, *c*.1500).[8] The *bastarda* without loops first appears in isolated examples shortly before 1420. Its use becomes more frequent during the 1420s, and gains particular popularity in the Netherlands and in northwest Germany, where it is used more widely and in more important contexts than it is in other regions. It developed especially in the centers of the Windesheim reform movement, but it was also culti-vated in some south German Augustinian communities associated with that reform. In the remainder of the German-speaking world, however, *bastarda* without loops was

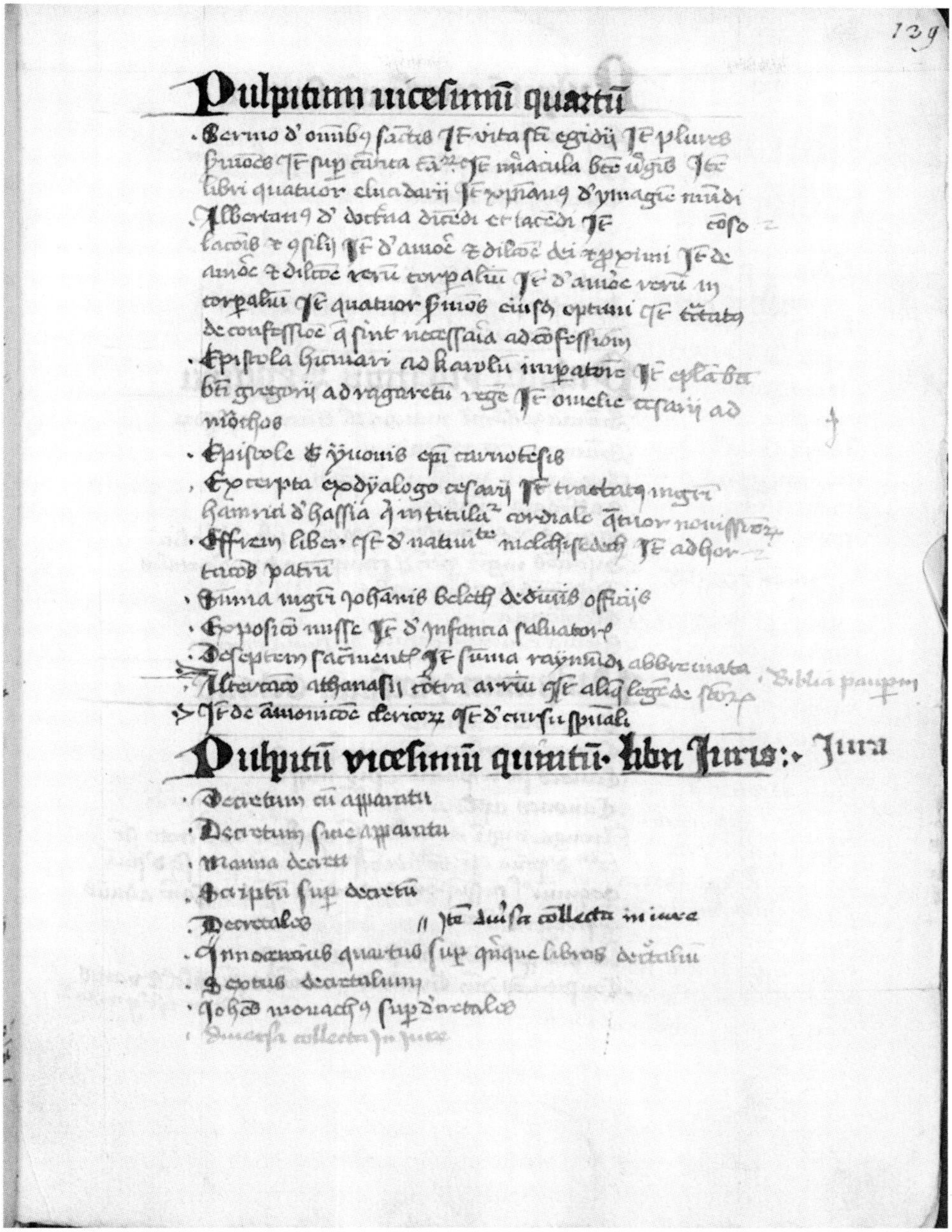

139

Pulpitum uicesimū quartū

[Manuscript text in Gothic cursive script, largely illegible medieval Latin book list]

Pulpitū uicesimū quintū · libri Iuris ·: Iura

[Manuscript text list]

PLATE 24.7 BSB, Clm 14675, fol. 139r, Regensburg, St. Emmeram, Konrad Peystainer.

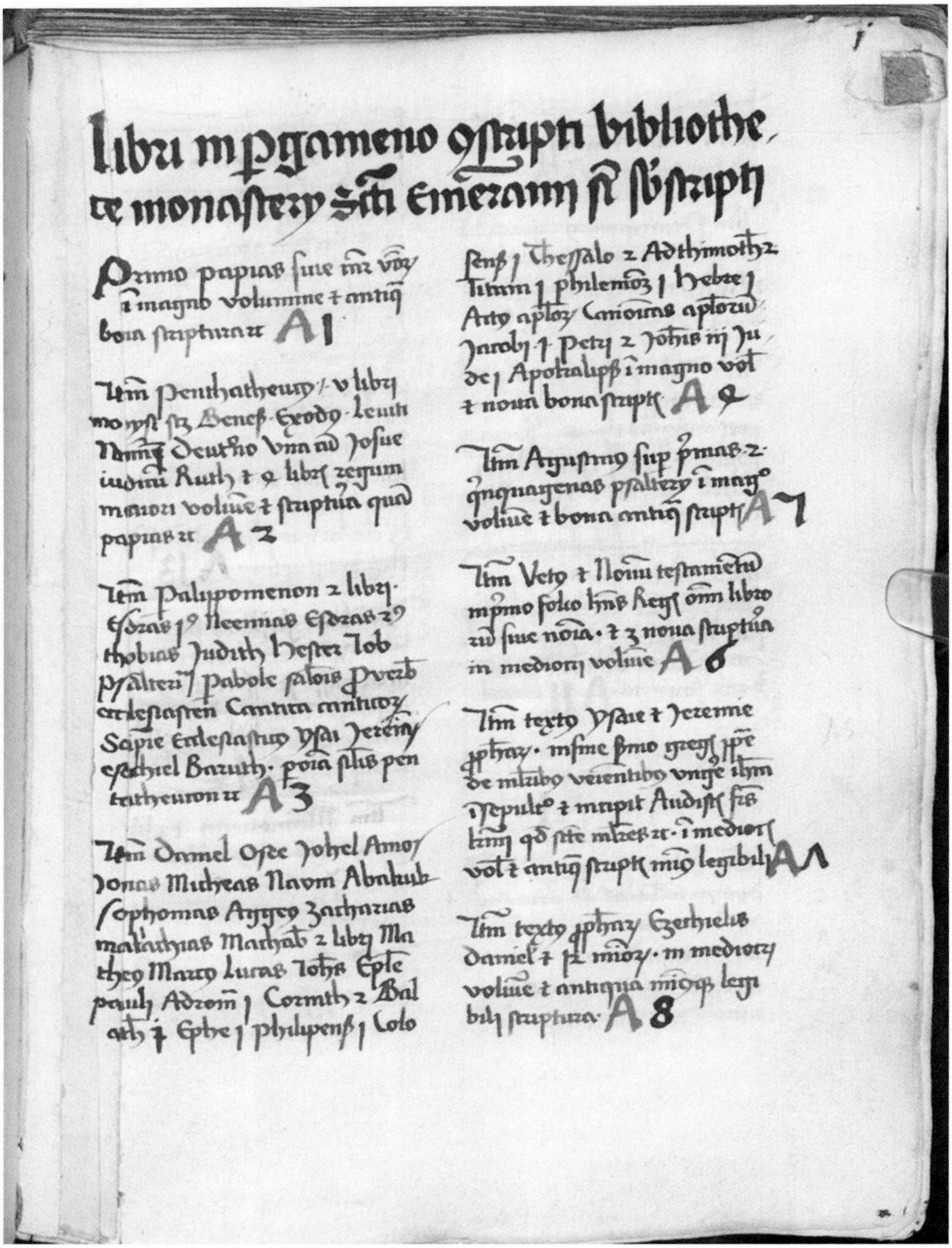

PLATE 24.8 BSB, Clm 14675, fol. 1r, Regensburg, St. Emmeram, *c.*1500.

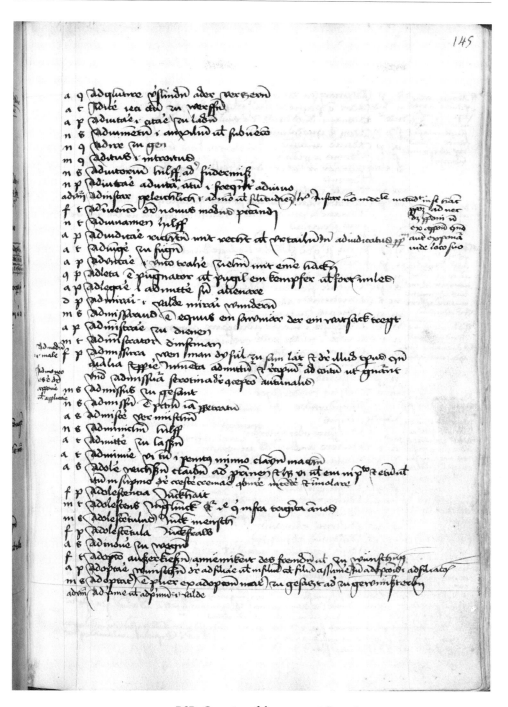

PLATE 24.9 BSB, Cgm 651, fol. 145r, east Bavaria, 1444.

only sporadically employed. Around the middle of the century, looped *bastarda* hands were still in the majority; and even after 1450 this was the prevalent form, at least in southern Germany. An example of looped and straight shafts occurring together in a single hand appears in Plate 24.9 (line 15: *l* with and without loops in *pugil* and *miles*, BSB, Cgm 651, fol. 145r, east Bavaria, 1444).[9]

Among the countless simpler and more or less idiosyncratic everyday scripts included under the heading *bastarda*, the book bastarda attains a higher calligraphic level identical with, or influenced by, chancery hands. Specimens of the documentary hand which was developed and cultivated in the imperial chancery, for instance, were disseminated throughout the realm in the fifteenth century. Chancery hands are generally slanted rightward. They have a preference, observable, for example, in the imperial chanceries of Friedrich III and Maximilian I, for looped ascenders; and they cultivate overhanging introductory strokes on many capitals, the so-called elephant's trunk (Plate 24.9, line 1: *A* and *v*, line 3: *z*), as well as terminal flourishes at the ends of some words. Especially typical are the elongated descenders of *f* and tall *s*, which regularly extend into the following line. The shafts of these same letters can also be extended at the top and end in a sharp point.

FRAKTUR

From the ceremonial documentary script of the chanceries, *Fraktur* develops into a highly calligraphic book hand around the middle of the fifteenth century. It is a highly stylized *bastarda* in which the *f* and tall *s* are particularly elongated and spindle-shaped, and have shafts with prominent swelling and thinning. *Fraktur* exhibits clear contrasts between thick and thin strokes, ascenders that begin from the right or with loops, and fine ornamentation through flourishes and serifs. The Viennese chancery scribe Wolfgang Spitzweg employed *Fraktur* for the schoolbooks of the young Maximilian I (see, e.g., http://daten.digitale-sammlungen.de/~db/0001/bsb00013106/image_11). Sometimes it is employed as the principal script in particularly precious illuminated prayer books from the end of the fifteenth century and the beginning of the sixteenth; but more often it is used as a display script, for example as an alternative to the usual *textura* in the rubrics.

HUMANIST AND ITALIANATE SCRIPTS

Humanist and Renaissance scripts, which have increasingly become a major focus in the field of paleography, are reserved for Latin literature, rarely appearing in German manuscripts. These scripts entered the German-speaking world through humanist circles in the middle and at the end of the fifteenth century, for example via the Viennese manuscripts of the immediate circles of Kaiser Friedrich III, Georg Peuerbach, and Wilhelm von Reichenau. A type of *bastarda* used around and after 1450, especially by a few scribes at Augsburg, and heavily influenced by Italian *rotunda*, was an Italianate script, but not a humanist one.[10] We also occasionally find a pure *rotunda* used in Latin books at Augsburg as well as in the monasteries of Melk and Tegernsee, especially, but not only, in manuscripts written by the Augsburg scribe and illuminator Heinrich Molitor.[11]

KURRENT

One of the new writing styles which developed from chancery *bastarda* in the early sixteenth century was *Kurrent* script. It is used for German-language manuscripts. The writing master Jakob Egloff demonstrated for each individual letter stroke how this fluid, even, and broadly traced cursive script (a script "which flows," "die correnndt"), was written (Plate 24.10, BSB, Cgm 4200, fol. 13r, Bavaria, c.1510).[12] It is a rightward slanting script with loops on the ascenders and with highly extended shafts on *f* and tall *s* taken over from chancery *bastarda*. But it also has many cursive letters, for example *g*, *p*, and round *s*. The *h* and the *z* have continuous loops on the descenders; *a* and *r* are formed of two parts connected by fine serifs, and the *e* has a characteristic form, seen in lines 3 and 4. For German texts, *Kurrent* is the basis for later scripts of the seventeenth through nineteenth centuries.

DOCUMENTARY AND COMMERCIAL SCRIPTS

In the second half of the thirteenth century, documentary and commercial scripts—distinguished from book hands by their lack of differentiation between thick and thin strokes, by their general avoidance of breaking of shafts, and by the extension of *f* and *s* below the line—developed in new ways. From the middle of the century onward, the cursive style of writing of letters in a single stroke began to increase. At the same time, the ascenders, especially those on *b*, *d*, *l*, *h*, and *k*, increasingly developed loops. Such continuous cursive loops were, in isolated cases, already adopted in the simpler book hands around the end of the thirteenth century.

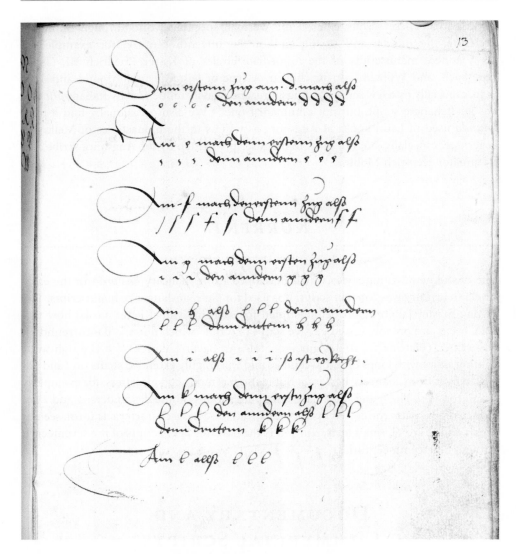

PLATE 24.10 BSB, Cgm 4200, fol. 13r, Bavaria, c.1510.

NOTES

1. Schneider (2009, 32, Plate 4).
2. From the Rothsche Predigstammlung: see Schneider (2009, 35, Plate 5).
3. On this manuscript, see Pfändtner, Westphal, and Suckale-Redlefsen 2015, cat. No. 23).
4. Schneider (2009, 43, Plate 7).
5. Schneider (2009, 61, Plate 13).
6. Schneider (2009, 64, Plate 14).

7. I owe thanks to Dr. Julia Knödler, BSB Munich, for knowledge of this manuscript. The entire manuscript is digitized at http://daten.digitale-sammlungen.de/~db/0006/bsb00064855/images/index.html?id=00064855&fip=eayayztssdasyztswwyztseayaewqen&no=16&seite=293, accessed January 13, 2020.

8. This is the first part of the manuscript referenced in n. 7, and is another library catalogue from St. Emmeram. It is available in digital scans at https://daten.digitale-sammlungen.de/~db/0006/bsb00064855/images/index.html?seite=13, accessed January 13, 2020.

9. Schneider (2009, 75, Plate 17).

10. Schneider (1995, 17–19).

11. A good example is his script in Munich, BSB, clm 18075, *Codices Manuscripti* 48/49 (2004): 55–72, Tafelband, fig. 1.

12. Schneider (2009, 85, Plate 19).

BIBLIOGRAPHY

Pfändtner, K.-G., S. Westphal, and G. Suckale-Redlefsen. 2015. *Die Handschriften des 13. und 14. Jahrhunderts der Staatsbibliothek Bamberg mit Nachträgen von Handschriften und Fragmenten des 10. bis 12. Jahrhunderts* (Katalog der illuminierten Handschriften der Staatsbibliothek Bamberg, 3). Wiesbaden: Harrasowitz.

Schneider, K. 1995. "Berufs- und Amateurschreiber. Zum Laien-Schreibbetrieb im spätmittelalterlichen Augsburg." In *Literarisches Leben in Augsburg während des 15. Jahrhunderts* (Studia Augustana 7), ed. J. Janota and W. Williams-Krapp, 8–26. Tübingen: Max Niemeyer.

Schneider, K. 2009. *Paläographie/Handschriftenkunde für Germanisten. Eine Einführung.* 2nd ed. Tübingen: DeGruyter [This account summarizes portions of his groundbreaking account].

Fraktur

Bruckner, A. 1935–78. *Scriptoria medii aevi helvetica* vol. 8: 49–51. Geneva: Roto-Sadag.

Haidinger, A. 2004. "Schrift und Zieralphabete." *In Das ABC-Lehrbuch für Kaiser Maximilian I. Vollständige Faksimile-Ausgabe des Codex 2368 der Österreichischen Nationalbibliothek Wien. Kommentar,* ed. Karl-Georg Pfändtner and Alois Haidinger, 17–28. Graz: ADEVA.

Kirchner, J. 1966. *Scriptura gothica libraria.* Munich and Vienna: Oldenbourg.

Humanistic script in Vienna

Autenrieth, J. 1963. "Paläographische Nomenklatur im Rahmen der Handschriftenkatalogisierung," in *Zur Katalogisierung mittelalterlicher und neuerer Handschriften. Zeitschrift für Bibliothekswesen und Bibliographie. Sonderheft,* ed. Clemens Köttelwesch, 98–104. Frankfurt am Main: Klostermann.

Bischoff, B. 1986. *Paläographie des römischen Altertums und des abendländischen Mittelalters.* 2nd edn. Berlin: E. Schmidt.

Bischoff, B., G. I. Lieftinck, and G. Batelli, 1954. *Nomenclature des écritures livresques du IXe au XVIe siècle.* Paris: Centre national de la recherche scientifique.

Crous, E. and J. Kirchner. 1928. *Die gotischen Schriftarten.* Leipzig: Klinkhardt & Biermann.

Derolez, A. 2006. *The Paleography of Gothic Manuscript Books from the Twelfth to the Early Sixteenth Century*. Cambridge: Cambridge University Press.

Gumbert, J. P. 1975. "Nomenklatur als Gradnetz. Ein Versuch an spätmittelalterlichen Schriftformen," *Codices manuscripti* 1: 122–5.

Mazal, O. 1975. *Handschriftenbeschreibung in Österreich. Referate, Beratungen und Ergebnisse der Arbeitstagungen in Kremsmünster (1973) und Zwettl (1974)*. Vienna: Verlag der Österreichischen Akademie der Wissenschaften.

Pfändtner, K.-G. 2007. "Eine spätmittelalterliche Wiener Gelehrtenbibliothek: die Büchersammlung des Hofastronomen Georg Peuerbach (1423–1461)?" *Mitteilungen des Instituts für Österreichische Geschichtsforschung* 115: 121–33.

Powitz, G. 1976. "Datieren und Lokalisieren nach der Schrift." *Bibliothek und Wissenschaft* 10: 124–39.

Schneider, K. 1995. "Berufs- und Amateurschreiber. Zum Laien-Schreibbetrieb im spätmittelalterlichen Augsburg." In *Literarisches Leben in Augsburg während des 15. Jahrhunderts* (Studia Augustana 7) ed. J. Janota and W. Williams-Krapp, 8–26. Tübingen: Max Niemeyer.

CHAPTER 25

....

GOTHIC SCRIPT IN ITALY

....

STEFANO ZAMPONI
(Translated by Consuelo Dutschke)

THE transition in Italy from Caroline minuscule to *littera textualis*[1] and the diffusion of the new script (already acknowledged by thirteenth-century witnesses as an opposition between a *littera antiqua* and a *littera nova* or *moderna*) do not occur in a single linear movement. Deep political fractures and the complex cultural geography of the Italian peninsula had already emerged as factors during the process of diffusion of Caroline minuscule; this script had only imposed itself completely (in equal use for books and for documents) during the eleventh century in the cities of northern and central Italy,[2] while in southern Italy Caroline minuscule remained in limited use until the political unification of the area in 1091 under the Normans[3] (the Duchy of Benevento and Byzantine and Arab dominions had until then ensured the coexistence of Beneventan script and the various scripts in the Greek, Arabic, and Hebrew alphabets).

Along the length of the peninsula, books of a similar nature (such as the codices of religious houses, copied in a formal *littera antiqua*, of medium or large size) in the third quarter of the twelfth century present minuscules of Caroline origin that vary greatly in execution and style;[4] for example, there is a significant difference between the manuscripts produced in Veneto, Emilia and Tuscany, and those of the south of Italy, whose minuscule is essentially that of Northern France, already well advanced on the road towards *textualis*. This graphic panorama splinters even more as we move from manuscripts of highly controlled production to manuscripts for schools and scholars, in medium to small format, that respond in a varied manner to the processes of simplification and disambiguation of letterforms.

The script that we call *rotunda*[5] is the Italian *littera textualis* par excellence, holding as it does the position of an exemplar and the status of an original script in the history of handwriting in the late Middle Ages. Its origin certainly lies in the solid, airy, and rounded *littera antiqua* used in the valley of the Po River and in central Italy, where by the first half of the twelfth century the division between book and documentary hands was least pronounced. This *rotunda* script, characterized by a precise selection of forms and by stylistic unity, stands out unequivocally from the *litterae textuales* of northern Europe, unlike the other Italian *litterae textuales*; we cannot view the latter as similar to *rotunda*, and yet, justifiably, they too constitute part of the graphic panorama of the Duecento in Italy (differences between them do not affect graphic structures, but rather aspects of production and style, which vary also according to the purpose of the individual books).

The decision to discuss the origin and diffusion of *littera textualis* in Italy in a chapter that closes with the end of the thirteenth century is justified by the history of this script and by the overall panorama of book scripts in Italy (for a discussion of Italian *textualis* of the later period, through the Cinquecento, see Chapter 26 of this volume). In first place, by the end of the thirteenth century many of the levels of execution and style that define the script during the course of its history will have come into being; secondly, from the beginning of the Trecento onward, *littera textualis* in its various applications is no longer the sole choice in scripts for book production, as other scripts of documentary origin parallel *rotunda*, and become associated with the transmission of certain texts (consider, for example, the close relationship between Dante's *Divine Comedy* and the bastard script[6] in which it circulated).

In Italy, as in all of Europe, the transition to a *textualis* script depends only marginally on the relationship between morphology and the *ductus* of the single letters, since the letters remain essentially unchanged in the number, direction, and succession of their basic strokes. The forms of only a few letters of late Caroline minuscule stand out as precursors, with significant alteration, of the new graphic environment: the *a* whose first stroke traces a low and flattened bowl; the *g* whose lower bowl is pulled up close to the body of the letter; the *h* whose second and rounded stroke closes in toward the first; the Tironian *et* constructed of a horizontal bar, usually wavy, and of an oblique descender; the abbreviations for *–b(us)* and for *–q(ue)* made with a comma that can be more or less ample and round; the round *s* at the end of the word that can be narrowed, lengthened, and trailing (Fig. 25.1).

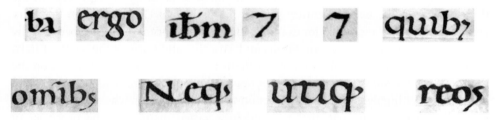

FIG. 25.1 Typical letters of late Caroline minuscule.

Textualis in its entirety (letters, abbreviation marks, punctuation) organizes itself into compact, broken and angular forms (the breaking especially affects arched and rounded strokes);[7] letters, compressed laterally and with short or very short ascenders and descenders that permit minimal interlinear space,[8] are associated with heavy vertical strokes, emphasized by a decidedly black ink; the so-called minims (vertical strokes analogous to the letter *i*) are strongly similar to one another; in the progressive movement toward a 2-line script, the body of the letters rests more clearly on a baseline and holds itself below an idealized upper line (with the consequent disappearance of the forms of *f*, *r*, *s*, and *x* extended below the baseline and that still remained visible during the third quarter of the twelfth century), while continuous repetition of the same standardized strokes of the pen shaped many letters in a similar fashion, resulting very visibly in the shapes of *c*, *e*, *t*, and the right side of *x*.

By the time the process came to a conclusion, in the mid-Duecento, we may observe that the forms of the letters in Italian *textualis* do not justify the judgment of complete novelty that is implied by the opposition of the terms, *littera antiqua* and *littera moderna*. Aside from specific matters of execution (greater weight, angularity, and compression), this script distances itself from the preceding century especially in the standardization of the approach and finishing strokes, and in the frequent or even exclusive use of graphic variants already present in *littera antiqua*: round *d*, round *r* after a curved shape, *s* in majuscule form at the end of a word, and the Tironian *et*.[9]

Once it becomes clear that the differences between the two scripts do not lie in the basic form of the letters, it will be necessary to pinpoint the nature of the change represented by the Italian *littera textualis* compared to the *littera antiqua* of the twelfth century. As occurs, for that matter, in all of Europe, the change is twofold. In the first place, the change affects the manner of execution: by classifying letterforms, rendering them similar to one another, and finally by reducing similar strokes to a few essential elements, the new script achieves for its practitioners an economy of learning and writing that, to use terminology from linguistics, can be called a "second articulation," in that the new script depends upon the existence of minimal functional units, in and of themselves without meaning (i.e., the constitutive strokes), but which combine to differentiate minimal meaningful units.[10] Secondly, the change is also a structural matter, in that it reorganizes relationships between the letters in favor of a flow of text that will distinguish words graphically. In the system of *littera moderna*, in fact, to learn to write means to learn to trace a series of strokes that, in varying combinations, constructs first the individual letters and then the individual words.

A first innovation of the Italian *littera textualis* with respect to Caroline minuscule is the broken execution of all the letters, reduced to a few essential strokes that, repeated in varying positions and order of occurrence, permit the construction of all the graphic and paratextual signs. This phenomenon occurs generally; in Italy, with *rotunda*, it assumes specific characteristics. It has often been underlined how this script, when compared to the *litterae textuales formatae* of France, England, and the Germanic countries, is distinguished by large and rounded forms, without or almost without the breaking of strokes. Although the passage from *antiqua* to *textualis* also involves in Italy a reduction of the height of the ascenders and the length of the descenders, as well as a lateral compression of the letters, it cannot be denied that Italian scripts present a less angular aspect than do the scripts of central and northern Europe. This is due to the absence in Italy of the rhomboid or diamond shape of the approach and finishing strokes that in scripts north of the Alps puts into such strong relief the baseline and the idealized upper line which together define the body of the letters. The seeming simplicity of *rotunda*, often described (wrongly) as a "natural" manner of execution of the letters, is instead the conscious result of a stylistic choice that utilizes a considerable amount of breaking of strokes: all the ascenders and descenders (*b, d, h, k, l, p,* and *q*) and all the vertical strokes that stop at the baseline (the first stroke of *f, h, k, n, r,* and *s*; the first and second strokes of *m*, as well as the second and diagonal stroke of the Tironian *et*) are brought into a shared uniformity by means of a small added stroke. At the same time, the approach and finishing strokes, when they form a wide curve, are often made with an independent lift of the pen with respect to the descending stroke; this break in the execution mainly affects the approach strokes of *i, m, n, r,* and *u*, the second and third stroke of *m*, the second stroke of *a* and *n*, the baseline strokes of *b* and *l* (Fig. 25.2).[11] In short, the simplicity of Italian *rotunda* resides entirely in choices of style, in the choice to employ secondary strokes that finish the vertical strokes of the letters without visible breakings; with regard to the technique of writing, the *rotunda* of Italy contains as much breaking as the *littera textualis formata* of all other European countries.

FIG. 25.2 Straight strokes finished by small added strokes (*p, l, n, b, s*) and broken curved strokes (*a, n*).

By means of a stylistic interpretation that completes the shape of the main strokes by means of small accessory strokes, by avoiding lozenge-shaped tops and bottoms of minims (which would provoke a thick and undifferentiated ribbon of text) and by diversifying the letters *i, m, n,* and *u*, the Italian *rotunda* distinguishes letters very readily and thus facilitates reading. The individual strokes of *i, m, n,* and *u* begin and end with such variation that, for example, *i + n* cannot be read as *n + i*, or as *m*, or as *u + i*, or as *i + u*,[12] and so forth for all possible similar combinations, which, instead, are occasions for error in the *littera textualis formata* of central and northern Europe.[13]

The second fundamental and new characteristic of Italian *littera textualis* with respect to Caroline minuscule lies in the elimination of blank spaces within graphic words and in the normalized presence of spaces between words. This is achieved by the ever wider use (at least until well into the thirteenth century) of functional devices that tie the letters together, namely approach and finishing strokes, that throw a bridge from one letter to the next, and that organize the succession of one letter after another along the top of the baseline and under the idealized line that contains the body of the letters on their upper limit: the fusion of contrary convex curves; the use of round *r* after a curve; the elision of approach strokes on the letters *i, m, n, p, r, t,* and *u*; the closing of *c, e, t,* and *x* against the following letter even when the latter begins with a round or a straight stroke (for example, concordia, clementia).[14] A similar function, among the several strategies for linking letters to one another, is performed by the varying use of round or straight *d* (round *d* before *a, e,* and *o*, round *r* so as to allow for fusion of the contrary curves; straight *d* before *i, u, m, n,* and *r*, but also after *e, g,* and *r* and in fusion with preceding round *d* or *o*). This alternation of the two shapes of the letter *d* never systematizes itself into a rule, and it tends to lose coherence in the final decades of the Duecento as round *d* becomes prevalent (Fig. 25.3).

(1)   (2)   (3)   (4)

FIG. 25.3 (1) approach and finishing strokes; (2) fusion of contrary convex curves, and closing of the letter *c* upon the following letter; (3) elision of approach stroke of the letter *n* and round *r*; (4) elision of approach stroke of the letter *r* and presence in one word of both forms of *d*.

These are known and well-studied phenomena that in Italy take on specific characteristics as they conform to the graphic nature of *rotunda*. Since in Italy curves never disintegrate into a series of short rectilinear strokes (as happens, for example, with the *littera textualis formata* north of the Alps), fusions come into being always and only by means of a partial, even minimal overlapping of two contrary convex curves; such fusions are far less frequent than the theoretical 90 cases that Meyer had foreseen (it is quite rare in Italy at the end of the Duecento for an expert copyist to use more than *c.* 20 fusions).[15] Round *r* occurs not just after the letters *b*, *h*, *o*, and *p*, but in manuscripts of the late thirteenth century, it can be found after any vowel (thus returning to a capital form when positioned after *i* and *u*). Again, in the mid-thirteenth century elision of the approach strokes of *i*, *m*, *n*, *p*, *r*, *t*, and *u* is usually present after *f*, *g*, *r*, and *t*; its occurrence is uncertain after *c*, *e*, and *x* (and the same scribe may elide the *c* more than the *e*, with a diversifying function possibly intended to distinguish two very similar letters). Overall, elisions are more frequent and more regular in Italian manuscripts than in their northern counterparts, where the diamond- or lozenge-shaped approach stroke of their *litterae textuales formatae* resists this kind of suppression.

In conclusion, *rotunda* is a book script whose letters are strung together, ribbon-like, and yet are dissimilar one from the other; thus, as a script it is eminently readable. It was probably this legibility that determined *rotunda*'s hegemony in Italy for the copying of liturgical books and determined its extensive use in university books (especially law, theology, and medicine) as a choice over other models of book scripts that are instead characterized by approach and finishing strokes that look almost the same for many letters and that produce a band of undistinguishable forms.

In this presentation of the changes in book scripts from the twelfth to the thirteenth century, we have focused exclusively on matters of structure (the syntactical relationships between letters) and of execution (Casamassima's "second articulation" of graphic materials). Among these various issues of execution, we have not discussed the new method of cutting the quill (with an oblique nib, angling to the left, with the consequent change in the angle of writing that would derive from this change); this change in the angle of the quill was supposedly diffused across northern Europe (the Anglo-Saxon kingdom, Belgium, the north of France) during the course of the eleventh century, and ultimately reached Italy as well. A good half century ago, inspired by thinking that overestimated the effects of the angle of writing (which depends on several factors, and not only on the cutting of the quill, which in any case cannot be reconstructed after the fact by an examination of the letterforms), Jacques Boussard hypothesized that the new left angle to the quill was the determining factor in the transition from *littera antiqua* to *littera nova*;[16] many scholars accepted his assertion without objection.[17] Even admitting that a new manner of cutting the quill came into use in northern Europe (although the demonstration offered by Boussard is wrong), we must state categorically that no script is modified by a single change in execution, that *littera textualis*, whatever national shape it may take, can easily be written with a flat-nibbed pen, and that the pen with a nib angled to the left, at most, might have found success once the system of *textualis* was in place, in order to produce with less effort the letterforms that had already been fully accepted.

In the absence of a body of specialized studies on the graphic panorama of Italy from the twelfth century onward (when traditional monastic scriptoria were joined by important urban centers for book production, especially in the cathedral chapters and in the episcopal centers), we can only reconstruct provisionally the process that *rotunda* followed to achieve a consolidated shape and dispersal throughout almost all the peninsula.

We can assert that clear examples of the new script exist from the second quarter to the middle of the thirteenth century; however, in order to track the dates and the means through which late Caroline minuscule transitions to *littera textualis* and accepts the choices that will characterize it as *rotunda*, we must examine various phenomena that obviously do not appear all at the same time, but that instead come into being in an asynchronic distribution over a period of one hundred years.

To begin, we can point to easily seen evidence, such as the use of specific variants of letterforms (round *d*, round *r*, majuscule *s* at the end of a word, and Tironian *et*); from the third and fourth decades of the twelfth century these variants occur regularly and as a group in the scripts of notarial documents and in charters copied in a formal minuscule of Carolingian origin, and they do so in significant advance on the scripts of books, where these same variants, during the period in question, are more irregularly attested. The forms appear with increasing frequency in book hands that date from the second half of the twelfth century until their general acceptance at the beginning of the thirteenth century, when, together, they contribute to the production of a compact and yet distinguishable graphic chain.[18]

In Italy the evolution from late Caroline minuscule to *littera textualis* is not linear; instead, it is defined (as happens normally in many parts of Europe) within an area of opposing tensions, between the requirements of legibility, on the one hand, and the tendency towards increasing assimilation of letters and strokes, on the other.

The execution of the letters with broken strokes and the organization of the word as a graphic unit do not have a simultaneous origin as new features. The first achievement, already realized in the third quarter of the twelfth century and in a script still within late Carolingian tradition, is the breaking of the strokes; this takes place as part of a standardization of both primary and secondary strokes, including those secondary strokes that render vertical strokes similar to one another at the baseline (Fig. 25.4).

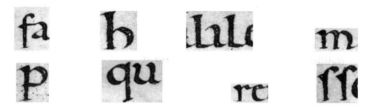

FIG. 25.4 Broken execution of letters in late Caroline minuscule.

The method of forming the individual letters in late Caroline minuscule already exhibits all the single touches of the pen that will continue into the later book scripts, albeit according to different shapes, weight, width.

During this time frame, the new script had not yet organized itself into a succession of graphic words whose letters are placed in close proximity to one another; such organization will only be achieved later. But already by the middle of the twelfth century, in a script that remains essentially Carolingian, the new script had achieved a constant presence of approach and finishing strokes (with the ribbon-like graphic stream that derives from it), and the closing of letters open to the right (*c*, *e*, *t*, and *x*) onto the letters that follow them. At the same time other characteristics remain sporadic and uneven: the fusion of contrary convex curves; the round *r* after a round letter (excluding the omnipresent case ending *–orum*); and, instead of the elision of approach strokes, we notice the overlapping of the final stroke of the preceding letter onto the approach stroke of the following letter (for example, *gi*). At least in Tuscany, Emilia, and in the flatlands of the Veneto, it is clear that writing according to graphic words, with letters regularly bound together, takes place initially in documents produced by notaries, who constituted a renewed professional class, practicing grammar and *ars dictaminis*, and possessing a Latin imbued with rhetoric. In the handwriting of notaries, innovations in the graphic stream seem to precede by a good 30 years analogous shifts in book hands; this starts with wide usage of variant letterforms, arrives at frequent use of fusions and of round *r*, and then, in the final decades of the twelfth century, we come to an organization of script that is essentially *littera moderna*.[19] Not by chance is one of the first examples of Italian *littera textualis* attributed to a notary from Verona, at the end of the twelfth century, in AD 1199.[20]

We must wait until the early years of the thirteenth century before we see in book production the actual organization of the signs and words that will display all the phenomena of compression, breaking of strokes, and ordering and joining of letters according to the forms that belong specifically to Italian *textualis*. Some 30 to 40 years will need to pass before out of the variety of scripts that characterize the thirteenth century in Italy, one will settle on those choices of style discussed above (especially in the handling of minims) that pinpoint *rotunda*.

This script, ordered, concatenated, and compact, with the regular presence of pronounced vertical strokes, and with letters of standardized appearance but always legible, will come into being with extraordinary coherence in the period between the

PLATE 25.1 Pistoia, Archivio Capitolare, C.154, f. 82r. *Rotunda*, c. 1270–80.

last decades of the thirteenth century and the first half of the fourteenth; it will continue, essentially unvaried in its more monumental forms, until the Cinquecento (Plate 25.1). Other than its general appearance, as discussed above, it will be useful to point out some peculiarities of individual letters: *a* can be open or it can close its second stroke down onto the first with a thin line (in the open variant, the second stroke may look like the final stroke of *n* and *m*), but it can also have a simplified form, apparently round, after letters like *f*, *g*, and *t* that elide the upper portion of the second stroke; round *d* has a small ascender, sometimes almost perfectly horizontal, which in the compression of the graphic stream can provoke misunderstanding (when round *d* is preceded by a letter that ends in a stroke similar to an *i*, it generates the false perception of a straight *r* + *o*); *g* offers two main forms, made either by reducing the original first and third strokes to one stroke or by a similar reduction to a single stroke of the original second and third strokes; the second stroke of the *h*, similar to the second part of the *o*, closes in with an added stroke at the baseline toward the ascender; round *r*, perceived during the last quarter of the Duecento as a simple allograph of straight *r*, is often used after letters that are not round (not just vowels, but also after *c* and straight *r*), and it may lengthen its first stroke below the baseline with a thin line; round *s*, especially if space is lacking (for example, at the end of line) may present itself in a narrow and lengthened form that can be fused with a preceding curve; *x* has two forms, because it can be constructed as the crossing of two straight strokes, or, more commonly, as the overlapping of two contrary convex curves, of which the first descends below the baseline with a fine line; *z* is often expressed as a *c* with a cedilla (*ç*); the mark that indicates truncation in the endings –*b(us)* and –*q(ue)* is essentially the same as the second part of an *o*;[21] also almost identical to an *o*, with the first stroke interrupted and missing the lower part, is the shorthand note for *con*. As to the abbreviations, one should point out that a thin, almost invisible cross bar cuts across the descender of *p* and *q* (this last giving the typically Italian form of the abbreviation for *qui*) (Fig. 25.5).

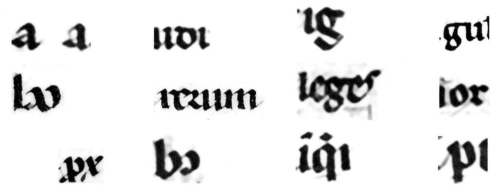

FIG. 25.5 Letters and marks typical of *rotunda*.

This script is recognizable in three ways: for its rounded strokes that visually predominate over all other strokes and that justify the traditional name of *rotunda* (cf. the letters *b, c, d, e, g, h, o, p, q*, round *s*, the abbreviation mark for *con*, and the endings for –*bus* and –*que*); for its relatively few angled forms (*a*, Tironian *et*); and for its readily distinguishable minims. Alternation between thick and thin strokes, common to all the *litterae textuales* of Europe, is particularly noticeable (for example, the last stroke of *e* is often almost invisible); the script, with its short or very short ascenders and descenders, avoids all sense of verticality and seems wider and less compressed than it is in reality; the very strong concatenation of letters internal to a graphic word (by means of fusion, round *r*, elision, closing of one letter against the following one, or approach and finishing strokes) results in a sort of compact 2-line ribbon, which is emphasized in professional texts by an extremely reduced space between words.

Together with the development of the new script, the canons of legibility are modified (or rather, vice versa: new canons of legibility render the existence of a new script understandable) according to a widespread phenomenon that seeks a more intense utilization of the space of the page. With university texts, one now practices silent reading that demands solid knowledge of professional writing. Various factors aid in this endeavor, such as a layout in two columns (already common in books of medium size) to allow seeing the entire line at once, and thus the reading of a line one at a time. Other factors include the highly developed system of abbreviations that aids in legibility, by replacing a less legible series of minims with clearly legible abbreviations (e.g. the six minims in "anima" are disambiguated in the abbreviation "aīa"); letters that are linked and bound together to identify the graphic word and encourage the use of standardized spaces between the words; clear divisions of the text that reference one another. All this takes place in a script whose very short ascenders and descenders allow for narrow interlinear spacing, and thus for pages that are very rich in text.

We have examined how script in Italy is transformed between the twelfth and thirteenth centuries; it now becomes necessary to touch upon those extra-graphic factors which, even though they did not directly influence evolution of the script, certainly encouraged the acceleration and then the conclusion of the process, culminating in general diffusion of the new script. *Littera textualis*, in all its many forms, is the script of a renewed and vigorous urban society that, especially in central and northern Italy, developed into free communes; this script was incubated in the chapter and episcopal schools of the twelfth century, but rapidly passed into the hands of lay people, of those who copied books as a profession (the figure of the scribe for hire is reborn). This script sees the foundation of the great libraries of religious houses (in particular for the new mendicant orders), and it accompanies the organization of the new structures of higher learning, the universities (Bologna, Padua, and Naples are particularly important in Italy during the thirteenth century). The universities demand a conspicuous production of manuscripts copied to an agreed-upon standard, sustaining development of scholarly reading in which books multiply without cease in the ongoing relationships between text and ever new commentaries.

The presence in Italy of important universities demands that we face the problem of the so-called *litterae scholasticae*, i.e., of those book scripts that are supposedly typical of specific universities according to the theory of Jean Destrez, who attempted to define four types of *littera* (*Parisiensis*, *Bononiensis*, *Oxoniensis*, and *Neapolitana*).[22] While there is by now long-standing agreement that there is no script specific to the university of Naples (the examples that Destrez cites are no different in execution or style from other book scripts of Italy and northern Europe),[23] the script of Bolognese and Paduan law books is well documented and very recognizable; it is in wide use already by the second half of the thirteenth century (although the best-known and most-cited examples date from the fourteenth);[24] geographically, it had a large diffusion throughout Europe, thanks to the number of foreign students in both Bologna and Padua.

It should be stated clearly that the name of *littera bononiensis* has been applied to a type of *rotunda* that is tied to the production of a specific kind of manuscript, but that this script remains always and only a *rotunda* in terms of its morphology and structure.[25] Differences are almost imperceptible: essentially the *rotunda* of these juridical codices displays slightly greater compression both horizontally (less space between words, and greater use of fusions and of closings between letters) and vertically (shorter ascenders and descenders with the goal of a denser layout); so far as variant letterforms are concerned, law manuscripts prefer round *d* and the angular *u* at the end of a word and especially at the end of a line. As is normal with professional texts, abbreviations are used extensively; for many juridical terms, they have the additional function of clearly disambiguating series of minims. Well into the thirteenth and then in the fourteenth century, when Bolognese law books have assumed their canonical form, the dense gloss that frames the main text is copied in the same script, albeit in a smaller module (the x height of the body of the letters of the main text is $c.3.5-4$ mm, and that of the gloss is $c.2.7-3$ mm). Use of the same script is not a given; it contradicts the traditional and much older opposition between text and gloss already witnessed in manuscripts of the Carolingian era[26] and surviving into the first half of the thirteenth century in many codices, including codices of the law, whereby the gloss presents a noticeable difference in size, morphology, and style compared to the main text.

Although we have spoken only of *rotunda* until now, in keeping with the tradition of studies on book scripts in Italy, we must call attention to the existence of a much more varied and nuanced graphic panorama in the Italy of the thirteenth century. Above all, at least in the first half of the century, many books of medium size and careful production display choices in execution and style that are foreign to the model of *rotunda*; books for study and for the professions, even those of small size ("pocket" books are a characteristic of this century), often use simplified scripts (usually a smaller size implies a less broken execution and imposes the use of taller ascenders and longer descenders). In books intended for personal use or at any rate for reduced circulation, the script of the text may move toward the general deconstruction of the individual letters due to the rapidity of the copying, or it may produce results that resemble the more formal style of contemporary documentary scripts.

Within this panorama, it will be pertinent to remember that Sicily and the kingdom of Naples retain their own cultural identity. Until the early decades of the thirteenth century, both in the cultivated circles of the Norman (and later Swabian) courts[27] and in the Cistercian monasteries in rapid expansion throughout the kingdom, we discover script models of French origin; these models are characterized by compressed letter-forms, rapid shifts from thick to thin in curved strokes, sporadic use of crossed Tironian *et*, and especially by the presence of finishing strokes at the baselines and of triangular additional strokes or forkings (as "swallows tails") on the tops of the ascenders. Even during the full flourishing of the Swabian period, as graphic models from central and northern Italy circulated in the southern kingdom (the founding of the university of Naples in 1224 accelerated the movement of books and men), the script of distinguished codices did not model itself on *rotunda*: consider the *De arte venandi cum avibus* (Vatican City, BAV, Pal. lat. 1071) with its small, simplified, rounded, and spacious script, or consider the *De balneis* of Peter of Eboli (Rome, Biblioteca Angelica 1474), whose minims are formed with broken strokes and whose wide finishing strokes are typical also of the letters *f, r,* and *s* common to scripts from north of the Alps.

Alongside this reality limited geographically to southern Italy, which in any case is destined to interact increasingly with examples of *rotunda* as the thirteenth century moves forward,[28] we find in central Italy and in the Po Valley, already in the early decades of the century, law books of good or high quality, potentially with excellent levels of decoration, that employ a book script of small size (with average height of $c.2$ mm). This script, thin and necessarily simplified, displays uneven baselines and reduced similarity of the strokes of individual letters (imperfections that were probably neither intended nor desired), while at the same time it quite noticeably adds separate touches of the pen (for example on the tops of ascenders); if a contemporary gloss is present, it is very small (hardly more than 1 mm high), and it often binds the letters tightly to one another (Plate 25.2).[29] Within these same first 30 years of the thirteenth century, we have examples both of small-format book scripts (where the x height of the letter remains less than 2 mm), where the letters are mutually and tightly bound by approach and finishing strokes, and with similarly constructed minims that are not dissimilar to those of northern Europe,[30] and of small-format book scripts that are wide and rounded.[31]

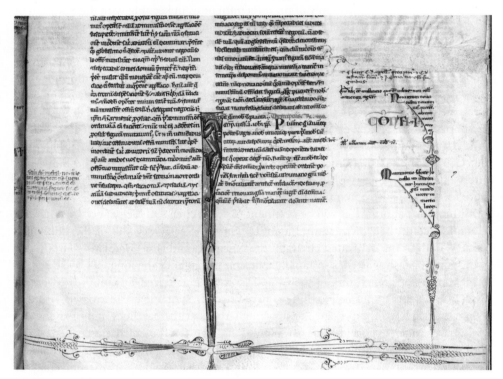

PLATE 25.2 Pistoia, Archivio Capitolare, C.131, f. 19r. Simplified *littera textualis*, first quarter of the thirteenth century.

Throughout the thirteenth century *litterae textuales* in Italy appear in a multiplicity of forms that lie outside the canon of *rotunda*: not infrequent are the cases in which in a codex of medium to small size, a moderately sized (even decidedly narrow) pen,[32] and a restricted letter module (under 2.5 mm) will produce only a modest thick–thin alternation. In these situations the script can be comparatively angular and compressed,[33] or comparatively rounded and wide,[34] usually with a breaking of the minims that is not found in the rigid thick–thin alternation of *rotunda*.

Already by the early years of the thirteenth century, the overall sober appearance of the script may acquire a simplified form of the *a* (with a reduced second section, otherwise always present in an Italian *littera textualis*)[35] which occurs with a certain regularity even in modest books for study, where the individual strokes of the letters present a variety of forms, angles, and alignments that appear more clearly when the script size is even slightly larger.[36]

Some aspects of simplification that have already been discussed (rounded script, rather small and slight, and widened) emerge by the end of the century even in codices of high-end production and considerable importance for the cultural history of Italy, i.e., in the poetry collections in Provençal copied in northern Italy (e.g., Paris, BnF, fr. 854 and fr. 12473; Modena, Biblioteca Estense, lat. 45 (a.R.4.4)) or in the *Canzoniere Rediano* (Florence, BML, Redi 9);[37] these books document the continuity and the harmonious script solutions already present throughout the Duecento. Books produced in university environments may break with *rotunda* as a model, as we see in a pocket Bible[38] and in a copy of the *Summa* of Monaldus, where the minims are rendered with very similar approach and finishing strokes.[39]

Much more radically altered is the *littera textualis* in working books of scholars (theologians, philosophers, jurists, and preachers) when in the form of notes or drafts; here hurried writing does not result in an increased number of ligatures, but in the greater or lesser deconstruction of the letterforms that disaggregate into individual strokes. The most famous and extreme examples (not necessarily only among the Italians) are those of Thomas Aquinas and his copyists.[40]

To move on to books intended for a wider circulation, yet another form of simplified *littera textualis* is found in scripts that have received and reproduced with only minor amounts of standardization a formal documentary script clearly of notarial origin (Plate 25.3).[41]

The panorama of scripts in the Italian Duecento must be integrated with at least a mention of the distinctive majuscules (used for titles, text divisions, closing formulas), where the following forms can be found in varying degree: capital *A*, possibly with a bar across the top; *D*, *E*, and *T* in both uncial and capital forms; a rounded *G*; *h*, *n*, and *u/v* possibly in minuscule form; uncial *M*. All these letters, as well as those that reproduce a model originally in capitals, as the century moves onward, are often written in strokes that mix straight and round lines, gradually acquire hairlines, and generate potentially closed forms.

With some exceptions, such as southern Italy at the beginning of the century, it does not seem possible in the current state of knowledge to identify production or stylistic aspects that point with certainty to the *littera textualis* of a specific region or territory. Copyists and models move; patrons determine the level or quality of the single codex. We are not capable today of discerning a sure geography in the *littera textualis* of thirteenth-century Italy; instead, its wide varieties are refracted across issues of execution and style.

From what has been said, it is clear that we face a widely varying panorama, in which *rotunda* plays only one role: beginning from a common graphic base, scripts in Italy achieve highly diversified forms, and such variety will continue to present itself during the course of the Trecento. At the uppermost level of production, in the books that are both the most monumental and the most conservative, during the final 30 years of the

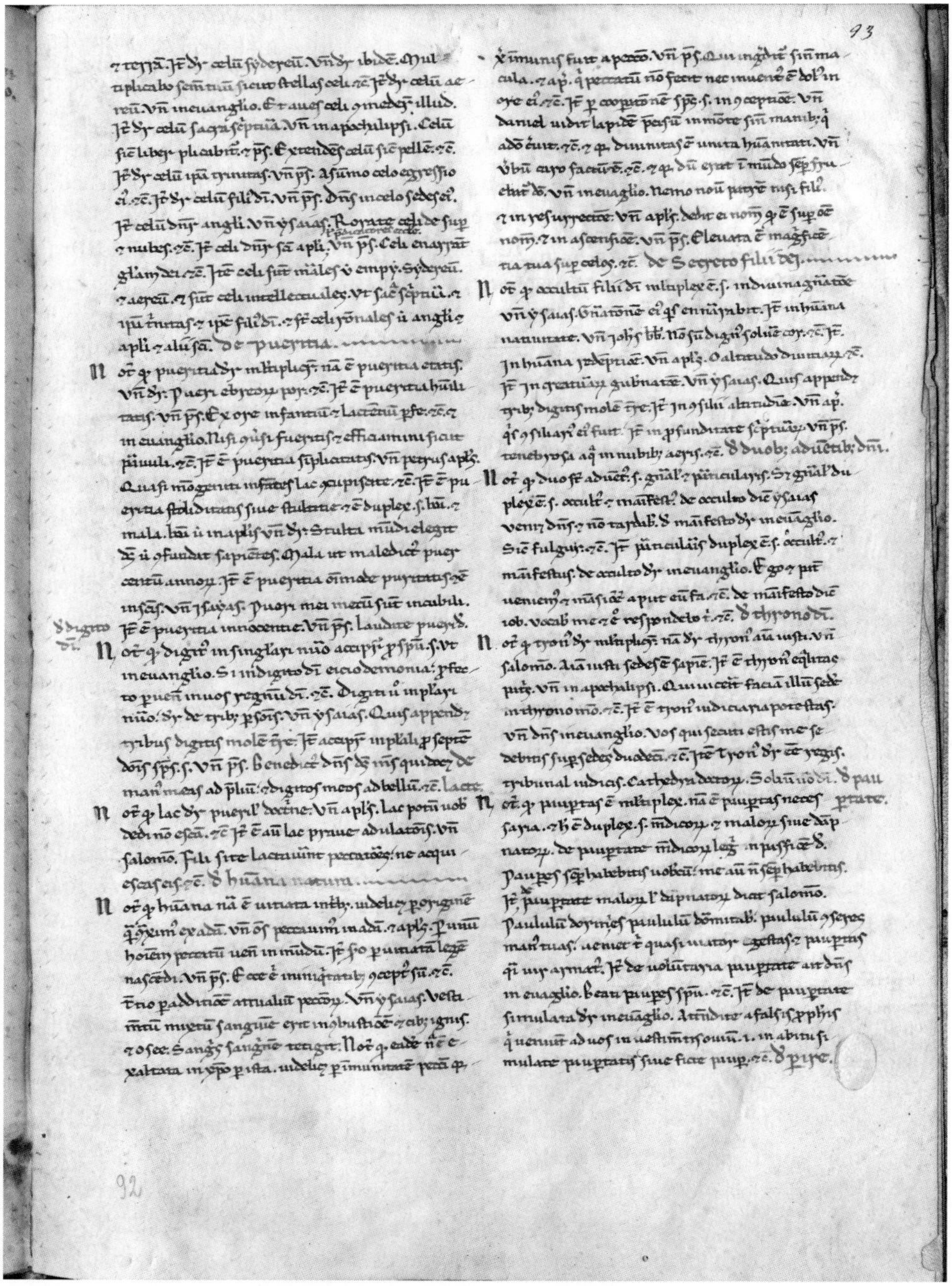

PLATE 25.3 Pistoia, Archivio Capitolare, C.108, f. 92r. *Littera textualis* of notarial origin, first quarter of the thirteenth century.

century, we can identify the place in which *rotunda,* as the principal interpretation of Italian *littera textualis,* becomes stable and immobile with canonical strength: the deluxe law books of Bologna and Padua; the choir books—antiphonaries and graduals—whose rigid and ever more majestic script reaches a height of 8 to 15 mm; the liturgical books, such as missals; the statute books of the free communes and of the urban guilds.

NOTES

1. In the present chapter I avoid the term "Gothic script," which has no historical foundation, although it is in wide use; see Casamassima (1964).
2. For this, see Ferrari, Chapter 18 of this volume, pp. 278–94; only in certain cities did the high-medieval cursive script survive in document production through the late twelfth century.
3. Pratesi (1992, 317–18) lists codices of definitely southern Italian origin that were copied in Caroline minuscule (all are datable to the mid- or late twelfth century).
4. By execution I mean the angle of the script, the size, and the weight; by style I mean the assimilation or the distinguishing (i.e. the intention to make the strokes appear in a uniform fashion or the intention to distinguish them visually) of elementary or complementary strokes, and the emphasized execution of analogous strokes.
5. *Rotunda* is the only Italian textualis examined by Derolez (2006, 103–11).
6. I use the term "bastard" as in Casamassima (1988); see also Zamponi (1997).
7. Note, for example, the obvious alternation of thick and thin strokes in the letter *a,* which tends to take on a closed form.
8. Restricted interlinear space also affects the letter *g*: the upper body of the letter grows and acquires the dimensions of an *o,* while the lower section, tightened up against the body of the letter, becomes smaller.
9. In Italian *textualis,* the angular *u/v* at the beginning of a word occurs only rarely.
10. For the concept of second articulation in a graphic system, see the ample discussion by Casamassima (1988, 104–16).
11. In the case of elision of an independent approach stroke, for example in the sequence *tu,* we incur thereby an actual graphic saving, by eliminating one stroke in the execution of the letter.
12. The sequence *i + n* differentiates itself from *n + i* by the separation of the first and the second stroke, from *m* by the separation of the first stroke, from *u + i* by the separation of the second stroke; from *i + u* by the separation of the second stroke.
13. Meyer (1897, 97–8). Because of consistent distinguishing of letters in *rotunda,* I take Steinmann's classification of the script as *textus praescisus* to be wrong (see Steinmann 1979, 318–19).
14. On this matter, see Zamponi (1989); on fusions and round *r,* see Meyer (1897); on elisions, see Zamponi (1988).
15. The most common fusions are *ba, be, bo, da, de, do, ds, ha, hc, he, ho, oc, od, oe, og, oq, os, pa, pc, pd, pe, po,* and *ps,* the abbreviation for *con + c, g,* and *d;* and finally, the fusions *bb* and *pp,* which are already found in the twelfth century.
16. Boussard (1951).
17. In Italy, see for example, Petrucci (1992, 128); Supino Martini (1994, 351); Cherubini and Pratesi (2010, 434).

18. There are vast numbers of examples of documents from the mid-twelfth century on the website of the Archivio di Stato di Firenze; for example, see the documents from Firenze, San Frediano in Cestello, San Giovanni Battista, Santa Maria della Badia (Badia fiorentina); from Pistoia, San Zenone; from Prato, Santo Stefano (http://www.archiviodistato. firenze.it/nuovosito/); see also Orlandelli (1963).

19. As will have become evident in this chapter, I consider the breaking of strokes to be a stylistic choice, a result, and certainly not the cause of the series of transformations that eventually led to *littera textualis*.

20. Verona, Biblioteca Civica, 2004 (Kirchner 1966, Plate 8).

21. This round sign alternates with the mixed-line mark, 3, usually used for the abbreviation *s(ed)*, but often also for the ending *–q(ue)*.

22. Destrez (1935, 43–61, Plates 1–36).

23. Destrez (1935, Plates 32–6).

24. Destrez (1935, Plates 22–6).

25. The two manuscripts, Padua, Biblioteca Antoniana, 51 and Arras, Bibliothèque municipale, 525, cannot be said to have been copied in *littera bononiensis* since their script is not in *rotunda* (Destrez 1935, Plates 19–21 was led into confusion by the fact that both were copied in Bologna). It will not be superfluous to insist that, even conceding validity to the term *littera bononiensis*, it cannot be applied to everything that was copied in Bologna: execution and style only and always are the determinants.

26. In Carolingian glosses we may find round *a* and *d*, ascenders of even considerable height, as well as *f*, *r*, and *s* descending below the baseline.

27. Norman domination ended in 1194; the Swabian dynasty of the Hohenstaufen held sway until 1266.

28. It is not possible in the context of this chapter to bring up the uncertain and complex graphic situation of the first decades of Angevin rule in southern Italy; on this matter, see Supino Martini (1993, 43–87).

29. Pistoia, Archivio Capitolare, C.131 and (for the text alone) Florence, BML, Plut. 6 sin. 2 (the two manuscripts are datable to the first quarter of the century).

30. Oxford, Bodleian Library, Laud. Misc. 646, dated 1228 (Watson 1984, Plate 100), and Tours, Bibliothèque municipale, 1, dated 1223–4 (Garand *et al.* 1984, Plate 56b).

31. Cambridge, Fitzwilliam Museum, McClean 24, dated 1204 and Paris, Bibliothèque nationale de France, lat. 7731, dated 1226 (Thomson 1969, 61and 62).

32. Paris, BnF, lat. 6963, dated Modena 1257 (d'Alverny 1962, Plate 29b).

33. Florence, BML, Plut. 3 sin. 9, dated 1239; Paris, BnF, lat. 15453, dated 1243 (Thomson 1969, 63).

34. Dijon, Bibliothèque municipale, 253, dated 1252 (Garand *et al.* 1968, Plate 22b); Florence, BML, Plut. 5 sin. 2, dated 1258; Vatican City, BAV, Vat. lat. 1465, dated 1262 and Pal. lat. 1611, dated 1268 (Katterbach *et al.* 1928, Plates 15 and 19); the hand of a notary from Pistoia is particularly dilated; see Pistoia, Bibl. Fort. A.53, dated 1278 (Murano *et al.* 1998, n. 185, Plate 200).

35. A late example in which this *a* is the only form in use is in Florence, BNC, Conv. Soppr. C.VI.209, dated 1285 (Bianchi *et al.* 2002, n. 59, Plate 3; Thomson 1969, 66).

36. Vatican City, BAV, Pal. lat. 324, dated 1284 (Ehrle and Liebaert 1912, Plate 42b); Vienna, Österreichisches Staatsbibliothek, 2281, dated 1300 (Unterkircher 1969, Plate 59).

37. Such forms are obviously also found in Latin manuscripts such as Vatican City, BAV, Pal. lat. 1611 (dated 1268) and Cortona, Biblioteca comunale 23.

38. Bamberg, Staatsbibliothek, Theol. 5, dated 1263 (Thomson 1969, 65).

39. Padua, Biblioteca Antoniana, 51, dated Bologna 1293 (Cassandro 2000, n. 49, Plate 7; Destrez 1935, 96–7, Plates 19–20, where the script is erroneously classified as *littera Bononiensis*).
40. Dondaine, *Sécretaires*, Plates 1, 2, 9, 28, 30, 33, 34, 37, 38.
41. Pistoia, Archivio Capitolare, C.108, ff. 91–6; C.138, ff. 52–5.

BIBLIOGRAPHY

Bianchi, S., A. Di Domenico, R. Di Loreto, G. Lazzi, M. Palma, P. Panedigrano, S. Pelle, C. Pinzauti, P. Pirolo, A. M. Russo, M. Sambucco Hammoud, P. Scapecchi, I. Truci, and S. Zamponi. 2002. *I Manoscritti datati del fondo Conventi Soppressi della Biblioteca Nazionale Centrale di Firenze.* Florence: SISMEL Edizioni del Galluzzo.

Boussard, J. 1951. "Influences insulaires dans la formation de l'écriture gothique." *Scriptorium* 5: 238–64.

Casamassima, E. 1964. "Per una storia delle dottrine paleografiche dall'Umanesimo a Jean Mabillon." *Studi medievali* (ser. 3) 5: 525–78.

Casamassima, E. 1988. *Tradizione corsiva e tradizione libraria nella scrittura latina del Medioevo.* Rome: Gela.

Cassandro, C., N. Giovè Marchioli, P. Massalin, and S. Zamponi. 2000. *I Manoscritti datati della provincia di Vicenza e della Biblioteca Antoniana di Padova.* Florence: SISMEL Edizioni del Galluzzo.

Cherubini, P. and A. Pratesi. 2010. *Paleografia latina. L'avventura grafica del mondo occidentale.* Vatican City: Scuola Vaticana di Paleografia, Diplomatica e Archivistica.

d'Alverny, M. T. 1962. *Catalogue des manuscrits en écriture latine portant des indications de date, de lieu ou de copiste.* II: *Bibliothèque nationale, fonds latin (Nos 1 à 8000), Notices établies par M. C. Garand, M. Mabille and J. Metman*, vols. 1–2. Paris: Centre National de la Recherche Scientifique.

Derolez, A. 2006. *The Paleography of Gothic Manuscript Books from the Twelfth to the Early Sixteenth Century.* Cambridge: Cambridge University Press.

Destrez, J. 1935. *La Pecia dans les manuscrits universitaires du XIIIe et du XIVe siècle.* Paris: Éditions Jacques Vautrain.

Dondaine, A. 1956. *Sécretaires de saint Thomas.* Rome: Editori di S. Tommaso.

Ehrle, F. and P. Liebaert. 1912. *Specimina codicum Latinorum Vaticanorum.* Bonn: A. Marcus and E. Weber.

Garand, M. C., M. Mabille, and J. Metman. 1968. *Catalogue des manuscrits en écriture latine portant des indications de date, de lieu ou de copiste.* VI: *Bourgogne, Centre, Sud-Est et Sud-Ouest de la France* vols. 1–2. Paris: Centre National de la Recherche Scientifique.

Garand, M. C., G. Grand and D. Muzerelle. 1984. *Catalogue des manuscrits en écriture latine portant des indications de date, de lieu ou de copiste.* VII: *Ouest de la France et pays de Loire*, vols. 1–2. Paris: Centre National de la Recherche Scientifique.

Katterbach, B., A. Pelzer, and C. Silva-Tarouca, 1928. *Codices Latini Saeculi XIII.* Vatican City: Biblioteca Vaticana.

Kirchner, J. 1966. *Scriptura gothica libraria a saeculo XII usque ad finem Medii Aevi.* Munich and Vienna: Oldenbourg.

Meyer, W. 1897. *Die Buchstaben-Verbindungen der sogenannten gothischen Schrift*. Berlin: Weidmannsche Buchhandlung.

Murano, G., G. Savino and S. Zamponi.1998. *I manoscritti medievali della provincia di Pistoia*. Florence: Regione Toscana - SISMEL, Edizioni del Galluzzo.

Orlandelli, G. 1963. *Il sindacato del podestà. La scrittura da cartulario di Ranieri da Perugia e la tradizione tabellionale bolognese del secolo XII*. Bologna: Pàtron.

Petrucci, A. 1992. *Breve storia della scrittura latina*. Rome: Bagatto Libri.

Pratesi, A. 1992. "La scrittura latina nell'Italia meridionale nell'età di Federico II." In *Frustula palaeographica*, 315–24. Florence: Olschki.

Steinmann, M. 1979. "Textualis formata." *Archiv für Diplomatik, Schriftgeschichte, Siegel- und Wappenkunde* 25: 301–27.

Supino Martini, P. 1993. "Linee metodologiche per lo studio dei manoscritti in *litterae textuales* prodotti in Italia nei secoli XIII–XIV." *Scrittura e civiltà* 17: 43–101.

Supino Martini, P. 1994. "Il libro nuovo." In *Il gotico europeo in Italia*, ed. V. Pace and M. Bagnoli, 351–9. Naples: Electa.

Thomson, S. H. 1969. *Latin Bookhands of the Later Middle Ages, 1100–1500*. Cambridge: Cambridge University Press.

Unterkircher, F. 1969. *Die datierten Handschriften der Österreichischen Nationalbibliothek bis zum Jahre 1400*. Vienna, Verlag der Österreichischen Akademie der Wissenschaften.

Watson, A. G. 1984. *Catalogue of Dated and Datable Manuscripts c. 435–1600 in Oxford Libraries*, vols. 1–2. Oxford: Clarendon Press.

Zamponi, S. 1988. "Elisione e sovrapposizione nella *littera textualis*." *Scrittura e Civiltà* 12: 135–76.

Zamponi, S. 1989. "La scrittura del libro nel Duecento." In *Civiltà comunale: libro, scrittura, documento. Atti della Società Ligure di Storia Patria*, n.s. 29/2: 315–54.

Zamponi, S. 1997. "Bastarda." In *Der neue Pauly Enzyklopädie der Antike*, II, ed. H. Cancik, M. Landfester, and H. Schneider, cols. 485–7. Stuttgart-Weimer, J. B. Metzler.

CHAPTER 26

··

LATE GOTHIC

Italy (XIVth–XVIth centuries)

··

STEFANO ZAMPONI
(Translated by Consuelo Dutschke)

As we saw in Chapter 25 of this volume, during the period from the end of the thirteenth century through the early years of the fourteenth, Italian *littera textualis* displays varying executive and stylistic levels that correspond to differing books and functions. At the highest level of canonization we place the steady script of large liturgical books (and also of statute books). On a different functional level is the *rotunda*, as it is commonly called; it is written with notable graphic competence by professional copyists, and characterizes university production, especially in law books, but it is also used to a lesser degree for classical and medieval Latin literature, and for the new literature in the vernacular. We then have scripts for texts that attest to a high and coherent graphic level, although they cannot be classified within the canon of the *rotunda* script. Finally, we encounter a number of scripts that alter and simplify, sometimes significantly, the graphic arrangement of the *litterae textuales* used in Italy; they remain, however, witnesses to the fundamental organization of that script.

These differing realizations of a single graphic substance are destined to produce varied results between the fourteenth and the sixteenth centuries, because in Italy from the early fourteenth century new scripts reduce the areas of use available to *littera textualis*. Alongside cursive scripts that reject specific typologies as book hands,[1] a stylized and steady notarial script comes into use; it occurs from the second quarter of the fourteenth century in literary texts, especially in the vernacular, and is executed stroke by stroke; usually termed *cancelleresca* (in fact, it is a canonized Italian *bâtarde*), it occurs widely, for example, in the oldest manuscripts of the *Divine Comedy* of Dante Alighieri and in many books of high graphic level.[2] Not long before the middle of the same century we see the diffusion of *mercantesca*, a cursive script, ligatured, produced with a narrow pen; originating in Tuscany, it is in ample use not only in merchant and banking circles, but also in the intermediate and lower levels of the urban population, in a varied group of writers who do not know Latin and who produce on their own books in the vernacular (usually on paper and executed in a very simple manner).[3] During the course of the fourteenth century, we also see the use of actual *bâtarde* scripts, i.e., scripts originating in the documentary world but used for literary texts, more or less steadily or rapidly, that regularly present *a* in its cursive form, *s* and *f* that descend below the baseline, and a closed final *s*. These *bâtarde* scripts stand outside the canon of *cancelleresca* and may also be executed with a rather narrow pen that allows for—but does not imply—the presence of ligatures; these scripts are used widely for books of university and religious culture as well as for literary texts.[4]

The graphic panorama of book production in Italy is yet further complicated in the early fifteenth century, as the various *litterae textuales* are used in an increasingly specialized manner: *cancelleresca*, whose style was already less coherent by the end of the fourteenth century, diminishes and passes away; *mercantesca* which will remain in use for vernacular texts until the sixteenth century, continues and indeed consolidates its presence; the use of *bâtarde* scripts (especially for religious and university texts) is reinforced. One adds to this that the cultural renewal promoted by Italian humanism intentionally distinguishes itself from university culture (theology, law, and medicine) and expresses this distinction in new scripts: *littera antiqua,* cursive script "all'antica" and capitals, as used especially for classical authors, Church Fathers, and the new humanistic literature. This graphic reform also reorganizes the book with respect to its Gothic tradition: beyond script, it also innovates certain aspects of book production such as the quality of the parchment, the ruling, the means of indicating quires, and the decorative apparatus.[5]

Within this continuous flux of new graphic experience, the highest level of textual scripts remains stable, or rather it consolidates itself and becomes inflexible: I refer to the script that characterizes, from the end of the Duecento onward, both liturgical manuscripts and large format statute books (as an example, I point out a gradual that originated in San Domenico in Perugia, datable to the early years of the fourteenth century: 701 × 420 mm, i.e., 27.6 × 16.5 inches).[6] Between the early years of the fourteenth century and those of the sixteenth, the script used for graduals and antiphonals takes on an ever more solid and monumental aspect, assimilating itself to the large format of the volumes; it rigidifies into a canon and proves with the greatest clarity its respect for the organization of the graphic chain and the production choices typical of Italian *textualis.* We find, therefore, a succession of letters that within the graphic word completely fulfills the four syntagmatic rules (overlapping of contrary curves; use of round *r* after a curve; elision of the attaching stroke of *i, m, n, p, r, t,* and *u* when after *c, e, f, g, r, t,* or *x*; closing of *c, e, t,* and *x* onto *a, b, c, d, e, f, g, h, l, o, q, s,* and *x*). In so far as the executive choices are concerned, we continue to observe a differing treatment of the attaching and the detaching strokes of the letters *i, m, n,* and *u* so that the so-called minims should never generate doubts in reading (the sequence *–ini–* can only be read *ini* and not *iui, im, mi, nn, nu, un* or *uu*); in the same manner, we always observe the equalizing of all the descending strokes that end on the line of the writing base (*f*, *h*, *k*, *r*, and *s*) or just below it (*p* and *q*) (Fig. 26.1). The size of letters in these books presents considerable dimensions and easily reaches some 22 mm (0.86 inches).[7] In the phase of its final canonization, this script becomes the object of the erudite geometrical constructions of Sigismondo Fanti (who calls it "fermata moderna"), and of the teaching "per pratica e per ragione" ("through practice and reasoning") of Giovanbattista Verini, who in fact sings the heart-wrenching dirge of the "littera moderna."[8]

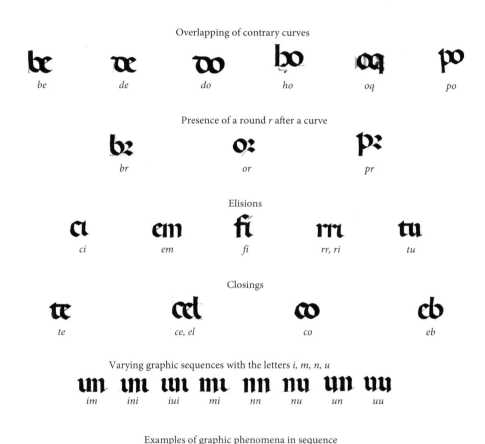

FIG. 26.1 Graphic structures of the Italian *littera textualis*.

From the gradual B.1 of the Archivio Capitolare of Pistoia, dated 1457.

Rotunda is characterized by a much smaller size, which accompanies the lesser evidence and definition of accessory strokes (such as the attaching and detaching strokes, and the equalizing strokes; it is a professional script that maintains full adherence to the canons of *textualis* in Italy in the forms of the letters, syntagmatic rules, and executive choices. The graphic tradition that begins in the second half of the Duecento continues uninterrupted and especially in the ample production of university law books during the first half of the Trecento the *rotunda* script offers results of considerable homogeneity.[9] Equally high levels are attested to by many manuscripts in Italian[10] (the written tradition of Italian literature begins in the final decades of the Duecento, and includes both original works as well as translations of Latin texts). In the first half of the Trecento, vernacular literature shows a firm preference for *littera textualis* in its various realizations;[11] in the Trecento, *rotunda* is widely used also for classical and medieval authors, Church Fathers, and religious literature in general.[12] The plague of 1348, however, had as a consequence a drop in the production of new books, and an ample circulation of second-hand books (this situation is amply documented, for example, for law books). In particular, from the final 20 years of the fourteenth century and through the fifteenth, the space occupied by *rotunda* was significantly reduced, because books of traditional culture (especially texts for law, theology, philosophy, and also books of sermons and of religious literature in general) were produced more commonly in *litterae textuales* that lie outside the canon of *rotunda* and in bastard scripts of different and varying organization, and of greater or lesser formality;[13] at the same time, humanistic scripts see to the diffusion of classical texts and the new literature in Latin and in the vernacular. During the fifteenth century, therefore, the most typically Italian *littera textualis* is restricted to the ecclesiastical arena; as well as in the monumental forms in the large antiphonals, graduals, and psalters, *rotunda* appears in the scripts of high-class codices (the most famous example is the Bible of Borso d'Este),[14] and in liturgical or devotional books of smaller, even tiny sizes; it thus becomes the "*lettera moderna*" specific to Books of Hours, breviaries, psalters, lectionaries, monastic rules and, to a lesser degree, religious literature (Fig. 26.2).[15]

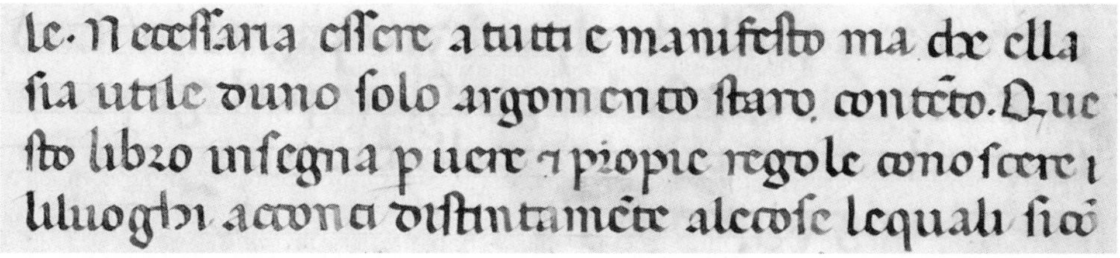
le. Necessaria essere a tutti e manifesto ma che ella
sia utile duno solo argomento stato contecto. Que
sto libro insegna p uere 7 proprie regole conoscere i
liluoghi acconci distintamente alecose lequali sico

FIG. 26.2 Florence, BML, Plut. 43.13, f. 1r. *Rotunda*, sec. XIV second quarter.

As has already been mentioned, in the later years of the thirteenth century, i.e., during a period of solid affirmation of the *rotunda* script, we also see the use of *litterae textuales* of considerable formal coherence, written with full attention to the "rules," which adopt, however, certain executive and stylistic choices that differ from *rotunda*:[16] e.g., round *a*; opening and closing strokes that make it difficult to recognize the letters *i*, *m*, *n*, and *u* when in sequence with one another; ample ascenders and descenders; generally, a less compressed and concatenated aspect. Such distancing from the canon of *rotunda* script does not imply an inferior graphic level; we cite as excellent examples of the script of the Trecento the following manuscripts: Florence, BML, Plut. 44.28 (s. XIV in), where the round *a* is accompanied by larger spacing between the letters, by more ample ascenders, and by a pen that is slightly narrower; Florence, BNC, Naz., II.IX.13 (s. XIV med), where regular use of round *a* is inserted into a completely formal aspect of the script (Fig. 26.3); Florence, BNC, Conv. Soppr. C.VI.1651, dated 1395, with a script of equally weighted letters with long ascenders and descenders that clearly distinguish the graphic words; for the fifteenth century, we mention only Florence, BNC, Conv. Soppr. A.III.871, dated 1444, whose heavy flattened script includes a round *a*, a final *s* that is usually wavy and lengthened; and with attaching and detaching strokes of *i*, *m*, *n*, and *u* that do not always follow the models of *rotunda*.[17]

FIG. 26.3 Florence, BNC, Naz. II.IX.13, fol. 75v. *Littera textualis*, middle of sec. XIV.

Already in the Trecento and throughout the entire Quattrocento we find numerous scripts that, even though they have an evident and undeniable root in the graphic tradition of *littera textualis*, display clear levels of simplification, but with a large difference in results, whether in Latin or in vernacular texts, whether works originating in the universities or in classical and medieval literature, both in verse and in prose. This simplification comes about most frequently in scripts of medium or small size, executed with a narrow (or at least not a wide) pen, with an inconsistent application of the rules that construct the graphic chain of the *littera textualis*, with variant letter-forms (such as the round *a*; the final *s* that is flattened and descends below the baseline),[18] and it assumes various forms: the script shows up in 1346 in the competent hand of an Augustinian friar, with an absence or very reduced use of complementary strokes (a fact that implies strong assimilation of all the strokes like the *i* and encourages the use of abbreviations to distinguish words in the graphic chain).[19]

In the same year, simplification can present opposite effects in a textual script that displays movement, is not always compressed or perfectly aligned, and makes ample use of detaching strokes along the baseline of the script, even for letters that normally in Italy are without them (*f*, *r*, and *s*).[20] Still during the Trecento, we also find *litterae textuales* that descend into a light, enlarged script of uncertain style (Fig. 26.4).[21] In the advanced Quattrocento we could mention a textual script that is closely written but light and in movement, simplifies minims and seems to feel reflections of the contemporary bastard hands of university circles in the height of its ascending strokes;[22] at the opposite pole of these executive and stylistic choices, we find a steady script with ample spacing between the letters of a word which is clearly a *littera textualis* influenced by contemporary rounded *antiqua*.[23]

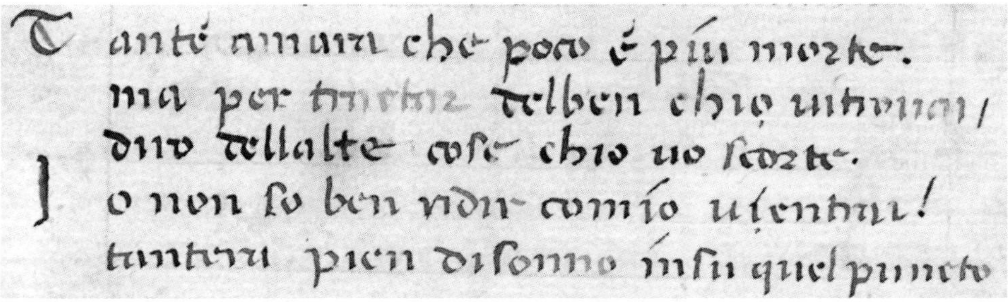
Tante amara che poco e piu morte.
ma per tractar delben chio uitrouai
diro dellaltre cose chio uo scorte.
Io non so ben ridir comio uentrai!
tantera pien disonno insu quel puncto

FIG. 26.4 Florence, BML, Plut. 26 sin. 1, f. 1r. Filippo Villani.
Simplified *littera textualis*, end of the fourteenth–early fifteenth century.

Still within the Trecento in cultural circles dedicated to the rediscovery of the Latin classics, and animated by literary men, functionaries of lay and ecclesiastical chanceries, and high-level prelates, one may follow the processes of simplification of *littera textualis* that find their theoretical justification in the thinking of Petrarch on the writing of his time, and on its sometimes difficult legibility.[24] These exceptional copyists, who with their friends, collaborators, and students launch the erudite tradition of Italian humanism, exhibit a handwriting that does not detach itself from any of the mechanisms of simplification that we have just mentioned. Petrarch's formal script, although it may be rather airy,[25] remains coherent to the graphic organization of *littera textualis* that is rendered more legible by its pronounced ascenders and descenders.[26] The " *littera castigata et clara*" (as Petrarch praised the script) that we observe in the Vatican Canzoniere copied by Giovanni Malpaghini[27] is also a script that fully respects the rules of the *littera textualis* while nevertheless achieving a different visual impact: it acquires legibility through the ample height of the ascenders and the length of the descenders that distinguish as well as possible the individual words, and via the existence of a decidedly enlarged graphic chain[28] in which individual letters offer full individuality in spite of juxtapositions, overlaps, and elisions. The incessant and well-documented experience of Boccaccio as a *scriptor* through fifty years of activity oscillates between simplified results in his collection of classical and medieval Latin texts (Fig. 26.5a)[29] (sometimes in an undifferentiated minuscule that shows only an occasional element of *littera textualis*)[30] and his regular *textualis* that even in cases of assured calligraphic commitment remains light, airy, and with tall ascenders (Fig. 26.5b).[31]

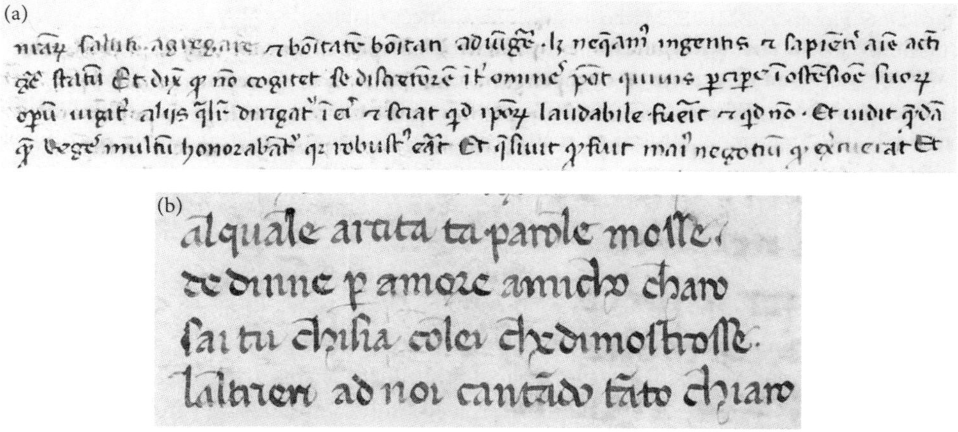

FIG. 26.5 Giovanni Boccaccio. (a) Florence, BML, Plut. 29.8, fol. 35r. Highly simplified script based on a *littera textualis*, c.1330. (b) Florence, Biblioteca Riccardiana, 1035, f. 4r. Simplified *littera textualis*, c.1360–70.

Equally varied, within the circle of simplified textual scripts (a constant is the form of the final *s*, both flattened and lengthened below the line) is the script of Coluccio Salutati, who accounts for several graphic registers: a sober *littera textualis* with well-spaced letters;[32] a regular script, orderly and of small size, of Petrarchan imprint (Fig. 26.6),[33] a more decided simplification in a rapid script that rejects clear contrasts between heavy and light strokes, as well as all calligraphic normalization, very close to the writing of his marginal notes.[34] During the final decades of the fourteenth century, in the circle of Salutati, but also in northern Italy, classical Latin texts and those of the new humanistic literature are frequently copied in textual hands, generally widened and simplified, into which are inserted, as if erudite citations, forms that derive from manuscripts in late Caroline minuscule of the eleventh and twelfth centuries (the ampersand; the *e caudata*) that will later characterize the restoration of the *littera antiqua*.[35] At the origin of this phenomenon is Salutati himself, who experiments with these forms in autograph manuscripts of the 1370s and 1380s.[36] With his collaborator and student Iacopo Angeli, the first humanist who learned Greek in Constantinople, we can follow a series of experiments from 1391 until c.1406 which, still within the tradition of the *littera textualis*, manage to bestow on the script a feeling of antiquity: in a clearly open arrangement, rounded and simplified, we see within words the letters *s* and *f* that sometimes descend below the baseline of script, a final straight *s*, an ample *g* that is articulated into two sections, an *e* and a *q* both with a *cauda*.[37]

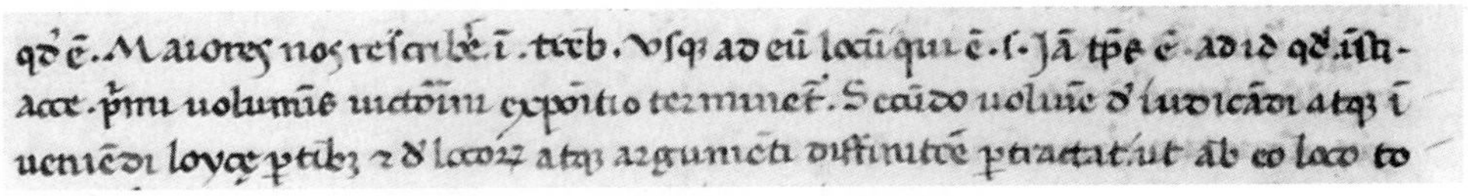

FIG. 26.6 Florence, BML, S. Marco 165. fol. 1r. Coluccio Salutati. Simplified *littera textualis* according to Petrarchan models, *c*.1375.

In the same cultural line that extends from Petrarch and Boccaccio to Salutati and his students, the traditional system of majuscules for the *littera moderna* (made of capitals, uncials, and minuscules characterized by swellings, ornamental elements, and ample optional strokes) is modified by the acceptance of letters from the ancient capital script that appear alongside or sometimes even instead of traditional uncial or minuscule forms (*A*, *E*, *H*, *M*, *N*, *T*, and *V*); eventually one arrives at a selection of majuscules that are essentially capital letters, realized by Iacopo Angeli several years in advance of similar experiments by Poggio Bracciolini, who, however, worked within the context of a restored *littera antiqua*.[38]

Facing a highly diversified panorama of simplified scripts that originate in highly differentiated environments and cultural projects, and that therefore cannot be circumscribed or classified within a single graphic type, many Italian scholars in the past 50 years have used the term "semi-Gothic" to define these varied experiences, finding that the term is adequate to account for this complexity. The term "semi-Gothic," however, is not used in this chapter and I will pause briefly to explain the reason. When Cencetti correctly registers in fourteenth-century Italy the diffusion of a "simplified Gothic script"[39] and he defines it with the term "semi-Gothic" taken as a loan word from bibliography, he means with this definition to include a variety of graphic situations that are not opposed to the so-called "Gothic" script via consistent and specific characteristics. The relationship between "Gothic" and "semi-Gothic," to stay with the terminology proposed by Cencetti, is not similar to the relationship between uncial and half-uncial (the only other case in which a definition of a more recent script was coined from a more ancient script): if half-uncial is a graphic system that is deeply different from uncial, the so-called "semi-Gothic" is not an autonomous graphic system compared to its named parent, the "Gothic" script.[40] Therefore, it seems preferable to us to use the expression "simplified *littera textualis*" (suggested by Cencetti with "simplified Gothic script"), and to try to specify each time the elements of the simplification that we analyze within the script.[41] The actual historiographical challenge is to invert our perspective for observation; we should not examine the reality of Italian *litterae textuales* by departing from *rotunda*, and thus considering everything that does not match this canon as an anomaly (if we are faced with well-formed scripts) or as a decay (if the script before us is simplified). Instead, we should bear in mind the large varieties of textual scripts in the Duecento and the Trecento as a mainstream in which the *littera textualis* is formed, seeing in *rotunda* only the one aspect in which the canon stabilizes itself.

Equally absent from this analysis of book hands during the fourteenth and fifteenth centuries is the term "*semitextualis*" recently proposed by Derolez, taking as his point of departure the definition of "*semi-Gothic*."[42] The essence of *semitextualis* is defined by a single fact of simplification: the round *a* instead of the uncial *a* occurring within a normal *littera textualis*. Once we point out that this form of the letter *a* was always present in Italian book hands, starting in the early thirteenth century,[43] it does not seem that this fact should force us to consider it a distinctive aspect of script between the late Duecento and the Quattrocento, nor does it seem necessary to us to employ a specific term to signal only a shared presence of variant forms. In cases such as this, one must always ask what the essence of the discontinuity is, and whether single graphic changes are sufficient to constitute a new script. It would seem to me that *littera textualis* remains true to itself even if it presents an occasionally different form of a letter, such as the form of the round *a*; the only graphic realities relevant for judging this script are represented by the organization of the graphic chain and the absence of specific markers for cursivity (such as a regular presence of *s* and *f* descending below the baseline, a closed final *s*, both of which normally refer to the tradition of bastard hands).

As I presented the various realizations of *littera textualis* in the Trecento, I had occasion to point out phenomena that persisted into the following century, and occasionally through the early years of the Cinquecento. In particular we see multiple traditions of *litterae textuales* produced in the circles of university and ecclesiastical cultures, albeit with lesser frequency of attestations, because the books of professors, students, theologians, and preachers are by now copied chiefly in bastard or humanistic hands that can be both rapid and unstructured. In looking, however, at textual hands there are several novelties that generally have to do with scripts of good executive level, often used for Latin classical texts or for the Church Fathers; in these scripts, which show influence from the new humanistic script, it is sometimes difficult to understand what the copyist intended, whether a humanistic script for which he does not fully follow the canon given his own education in Gothic scripts, or whether a *littera textualis* updated according to the model of the *littera antiqua*. To cite examples only from the first decades of the Quattrocento, we find in the first case the latest witness known to us today of the handwriting of Iacopo Angeli, that is, his autograph translation of the Pseudo-Aristeas, *Epistola de LXX interpretibus* (Fig. 26.7),[44] completed when Poggio, Niccoli, and Luigi di ser Michele Guidi had already produced and diffused the first solid models of *littera antiqua*. A phenomenon attested to in northern Italy (especially in Lombardy and in the Veneto) from the second decade of the century seems of another origin; this is the period when the restored *littera antiqua* is certainly known outside of Tuscany. In these regions to copy classical Latin authors one uses a *littera textualis*, often simplified, that accepts single humanistic forms: this is not the uncertain experiment of a novelty that has yet to define and diffuse itself, but the intention to write in the "old style" but within the Gothic tradition. I cite two cases, located within a graphic panorama already delimited by recent research, which, for Lombardy, point to the exclusive presence of *litterae textuales* for at least the first two decades of the century. In Oxford, Bodleian Library, Canon. Class. Lat. 193, Sallust, *De coniuratione Catilinae*, dated 1411–12,[45] the overall appearance of the page is still predominantly what we find in the fourteenth century. But it is tempered by an enlarged graphic chain, by ample spacing between the words, well-defined tall ascenders, and especially by the forms of the straight final *s*, and by the ampersand. In an example dating from two decades later (Ferrara, Biblioteca Ariostea, Cl. II. 97, dated 1431), only the straight final *s* and the majuscules in Greek style (according to the tradition of Venice) are designed to impart an air of ancientness to a traditional *littera textualis*.[46]

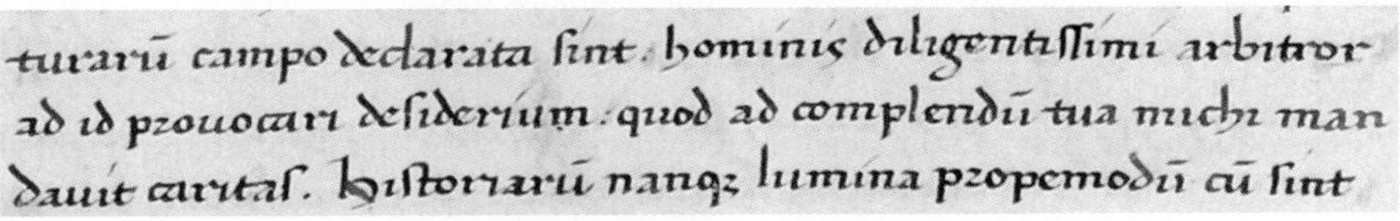

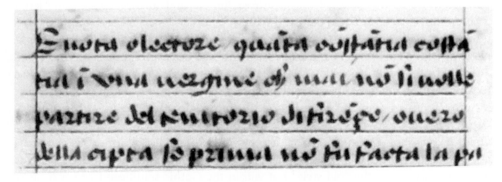

FIG. 26.7 Florence, BML, Plut. 25 sin. 9, fol. 1r. Iacopo Angeli.
A script "all'antica" based on a *littera textualis*, first decade of the fifteenth century.

Alongside these achievements, the Quattrocento presents a phenomenon of which isolated attestations are already present in the preceding centuries, namely, a greatly simplified *textualis* (Fig. 26.8); this book hand derives its simplification not from a conscious choice, or quickness, or sobriety, but from the difficulty of writing in coherent forms. This *littera textualis,* destined for the copying of traditional works of devotion and popular piety, lies within the prerogative of priests, friars, nuns, and members of the third orders with small culture and modest graphic competence, who, while intending to copy the traditional model of a book, occasionally imitated the large two-column book of the Trecento,[47] but certainly with very modest results.[48] We encounter rough hands, often of a rather large size, heavy, struggling, and irregular, that bear witness to the relative cultural marginality of both the writers and their

FIG. 26.8 Florence, Biblioteca Riccardiana, 1291, fol. 141v. Suor Checha of the monastery of Ripoli (Florence). Simplified and unstructured *littera textualis*, 1468, April 26.

readers, lagging behind in a culture that is substantially deprived of "grammar" (meaning good awareness of Latin) that contemporary humanists looked down upon.[49]

By the end of the fifteenth century, in the last period of use of *littera textualis*, a quick check allows us to verify the presence of this script especially in liturgical books and in religious texts; this speaks to the essentially marginal position held by the script at this late date, rather than to its specialization.

Suggested Reading

For the study of the *littera textualis* in Italy between the fourteenth and sixteenth centuries, see Giorgio Cencetti, *Lineamenti di storia della scrittura latina*. Bologna: Patron, 1997, 229–35 [1st ed. 1954–6]; Albert Derolez, *The Palaeography of Gothic Manuscript Books from the Twelfth to the Early Sixteen Century*. Cambridge: University Press, 2003, 102–11, 118–21, 176–80; Paolo Cherubini and Alessandro Pratesi, *Paleografia latina. L'avventura grafica del mondo occidentale*. Vatican City: Scuola Vaticana di Paleografia, Diplomatica e Archivistica, 2010, 549–59. These three manuals offer accounts that differ widely from the historical outline presented in this chapter.

Notes

1. See the manuscripts: Florence, BNC, II.IV.323 (s. XIV in; Bertelli 2002, n. 25, Plate 32), II.III.330 (s. XIV med; Bertelli 2002, n. 13, Plate 19) and Conv. Soppr. A.IX.20, dated 1376 (Bianchi *et al.* 2002, n. 17, Plate 16). I should point out that in this chapter all the cited manuscripts should only be understood as examples to give a first idea of that very rich variety of codices reproduced in print and online; many more deserve to be cited as well.
2. Milan, Biblioteca Trivulziana, 1080, dated 1337 (Pontone 2011, n. 71, Plate 3) and Florence, BML, Gadd. 110, s. XIV second quarter (Bertelli 2011, n. 83, Plate P and 126).
3. Florence, BNC, Magl. VIII.1416^{IV}, dated 1343 (Marchiaro and Zamponi 2018, n. 65, Plate 9) and Biblioteca Riccardiana, 1315, dated 1378–79 (De Robertis and Miriello, 1998, n. 58, Plate 6).
4. Florence, Biblioteca Riccardiana, 1356, dated 1372 (De Robertis and Miriello 1998, n. 68, Plates 4–5); Florence, BNC, Conv. Soppr. da ord. Vallombrosa 40, dated 1374 (Bianchi *et al.* 2002, n. 140, Plate 14); Conv. Soppr. F.VIII.1299, dated 1375 (Bianchi *et. al.* 2002, n. 95, Plate 15); Vatican, BAV, Ottob. lat. 1738, dated 1386 (Ruysschaert, Marucchi, and de la Mare 1997, n. 388, Plate 18a), Barb. lat. 1410, dated 1392 (Ruysschaert, Marucchi, and de la Mare 1997, n. 64, Plate 19b); Chig. E.V.161, dated 1401 (Ruysschaert, Marucchi, and de la Mare 1997, n. 179, Plate 21c).
5. A script- and codicology-based panorama of Quattrocento Italy is offered by De Robertis (2008, 505–22). For humanistic script, see De Robertis, Chapters 31 and 32 of this volume.

6. Perugia, Biblioteca Comunale Augusta, 2789. This book has imposing dimensions: in the early Trecento, graduals and antiphonals usually oscillate at measurements around 550 mm in height, while these numbers easily go up to 620/650 mm during the second half of the Quattrocento (i.e. from 21.5 inches to c.24–25.5 inches).

7. This number refers to the medium height of the letters as measured on *m* and *o*.

8. Fanti (1514, ff. DIr–FIIr); Verini (c. 1527, ff. IIv–XVIv). This is the statement of Verini, ff. 2v–3r (with spelling and punctuation slightly adapted to modern usage):

> questa litera nominata Moderna è la più difficile litera di tutte le altre et quanto maggiore si fa, tanto più è difficile a ffare, perché meglio si vede li diffetti de lo scrittore che l'ha scritta. Usasi questa litera Moderna a ffare Graduali et Antiphonarii; già più tempo fa era di bono e grandissimo guadagno, ma al presente mi pare se usi pocho; et la causa si è per questa benedetta stampa, che ha guasta sì nobile et sì bella virtù. Et Dio voglia che io non dichi la verità, che mi dubito che non passi cinquanta anni che non si troverà chi sappi fare uno graduale.

> This letter called "modern" is the most difficult letter of all of the others, and the bigger you make it, the harder it is, because the defects of the scribe who wrote it show up all the more. This letter is used to make graduals and antiphonals; a while ago it was of good and even great earning, but now it seems to me that it's used very little; and the reason is this blessed [!] print, which has ruined such a noble and beautiful virtue. And may God forbid that I speak the truth, because I doubt if in fifty years we will find anyone who will know how to make a gradual.

9. Vatican City, BAV, Urb. lat. 161 and Paris, BnF, lat. 14339 (Destrez 1935, Plates 23 and 24); Vatican City, BAV, Vat. lat. 1393, dated 1316 (Caldelli 2007, n. 117, Plate 6) and Vat. lat. 1388, dated 1342 (Caldelli 2007, n. 116, Plate 10). At mid-century: Vatican City, BAV, Vat. lat. 1456, c.1453 (Steffens 1910, 106).

10. Florence, BNC, Banco Rari 18 and 19 (Bertelli 2002, n. 38, Plate F, 48 and n. 39, Plate G, 49); BML, Plut. 43.13 and Ashburnham 415 (Bertelli 2011, n. 15, Plate 23–24 and n. 53, Plate G, 89).

11. Research by S. Bertelli on the manuscripts of Italian literature from the origins to c.1350 held by the Biblioteca Nazionale Centrale and the Biblioteca Medicea Laurenziana of Florence shows that *littera textualis* is used in 55% of the codices in the vernacular, that a bastard hand or *cancelleresca* occurs in 39%, and that *mercantesca* is used in 6% (see Bertelli 2011, 22 graph 13).

12. See Milan, Biblioteca Trivulziana, 691, dated 1373 (Lucan; Pontone 2011, n. 39, Plate 5); Vatican City, BAV, Vat. lat. 1647, dated 1391–2 (Seneca; Caldelli 2007, n. 134, Plate 21), Vat. lat. 588, end of the XIVth century (Gregory the Great; for which, see Cherubini and Pratesi 2004, Plate 103).

13. As examples of steady bastard hands in Italy during the fifteenth century of quite differing styles, I cite: Florence, BNC, Conv. Soppr. F.VI.855 (two treatises on confession dated 1432; Bianchi *et al.* 2002, n. 93, Plate 39) and B.III.2875 (a *Summa de vitiis et virtutibus* by Guilelmus Peraldus dated 1434; Bianchi *et al.* 2002, n. 35, Plate 42). From the environs of the university or from *studia theologica*, in simplified bastard hands that display more movement, I cite: Padua, Biblioteca Antoniana, 163 (Pietro da Candia on the Sentences dated 1420; Cassandro *et al.* 2000, n. 55, Plate 19) and Florence, BNC, Conv. Soppr. C.VIII.794 (Michele da Massa on the Sentences dated 1467; Bianchi *et al.* 2002, n. 65, Plate 103).

14. Modena, Biblioteca Estense Universitaria, lat. 422–3.

15. Vicenza, Biblioteca Civica Bertoliana, 25 (Book of Hours, dated 1433; Cassandro *et al.* 2000, n. 1, Plate 27); Florence, Biblioteca Riccardiana, 284 (breviary, dated 1471; De Robertis and Miriello 1997, n. 9, Plate 69), Forlì, Biblioteca Comunale, Piancastelli Sala O. I/40 (psalter, dated 1475; Errani and Palma 2006, n. 5, Plate 60).

16. In Chapter 25 of this volume I cited the example of Padua, Biblioteca Antoniana, 51, dated Bologna 1293 (Cassandro *et al.* 2000, n. 49, Plate 7; Destrez 1935, Plates 19–20).

17. See, respectively, Bertelli (2011, n. 16, Plate C, 25); Bertelli (2002, n. 35, Plate E, 45); Bianchi *et al.* 2002, n. 60, Plate 19 and Bianchi *et al.* 2002, n. 7, Plate 56.

18. I will not repeat these graphic characteristics that can be found in the examples cited below.

19. Florence, BNC, Conv. Soppr. G.V.1217; Bianchi *et al.* 2002, n. 106, Plate 7.

20. Florence, BNC, Conv. Soppr. I.I.34; Bianchi *et al.* 2002, n. 110, Plate 8.

21. Florence, BML, Plut. 26 sin. 1, copied by Filippo Villani; see the reproduction in De Robertis *et al.* (2008, 76–7).

22. Padua, Biblioteca Antoniana, 402 dated 1448; Cassandro *et al.* 2000, n. 73, Plate 37.

23. Padua, Biblioteca Antoniana, 24 dated 1471; Cassandro *et al.* 2000, n. 43, Plate 73.

24. The main positions taken by Petrarch are against copying divided into several steps that leads to incorrect copies (*Fam.* XVIII 5, 4–6), against the ignorance of copyists (*De remediis* I XLIII, 12), against small, compressed, and assimilated scripts (*Sen.* VI, 5); on the other hand, he shows appreciation for a large codex of Augustine copied in a late Caroline minuscule (*Fam.* XVIII 3, 9).

25. Examples of Petrarch's hand, which is never compressed, are offered in some of his autograph manuscripts: Berlin, Staatsbibliothek zu Berlin-Preussischer Kulturbesitz, Hamilton 493 (*De ignorantia*); Florence, Biblioteca Riccardiana, 972 (*Sen.* IX.1), Vatican City, BAV, Vat. lat. 3358 (*Bucolicum carmen*), and Vat. lat. 3359 (*De ignorantia*); reproductions are available in Feo (2003, 428, 431, 277, 429).

26. On this, see Derolez (2004, 3–19).

27. Vatican City, BAV, Vat. lat. 3195. Closer to textual models (especially for the more reduced height of the ascenders) is the copy of Homer by Malpaghini, Paris, BnF, lat. 7880 I/II; reproductions in Feo (2003, 490, 491). I keep the traditional identification of the copyist of Petrarca with Giovanni Malpaghini, while aware of the reasonable doubts expressed by Berté (2015).

28. On fol. 37r of Vatican City, BAV, Vat. lat. 3195, one can easily see how the script of Malpaghini is less compressed, and more airy than that of Petrarch; Cherubini and Pratesi (2004, Plate 118).

29. The originally single manuscript is now divided into two codices: Florence, BML, Plut. 29.8 (Zibaldone Laurenziano) and 33.31(Latin miscellany); reproductions in De Robertis *et al.* (2013, 292–7, 300–4).

30. The greatest reduction to the most essential elements of the single letters is found in the writings of his youth (Plut. 29.8, f. 36v, reproduced in De Robertis *et al.* 2013, 300) but the graphic chain is distended and well distinguished even in his later writings.

31. As is visible in Boccaccio's three autograph copies of the *Divine Comedy* of Dante: Toledo, Archivo y Biblioteca Capitulares, Zelada 104.6; Florence, Biblioteca Riccardiana, 1035; Vatican City, BAV, Chig. L.VI. 213, reproduced in De Robertis *et al.* (2013, 249–74).

32. London, British Library, Add. 11987; reproduction in De Robertis *et al.* (2008, 20, 318).

33. Florence, BML, S. Marco 165; reproduction in De Robertis *et al.* (2008 320).

34. Florence, BML, Plut. 23 sin. 3, reproduction in De Robertis *et al.* (2008, 21, 321–3).

35. On all this, see De Robertis (2016).

36. The two manuscripts are cited in nn. 32–3 above.

37. Zamponi (2010).

38. Examples of the majuscules of Iacopo Angeli are in De Robertis *et al.* (2008, 233 [Paris, BnF, lat. 7942] and 303 [Oxford, Bodleian Library, Ital.e.6]).

39. Cencetti (1997, 233 [1954–6, 264]): "scrittura gotica semplificata."

40. The intrinsic homogeneity of the graphic system between *littera textualis* and the simplified *littera textualis* must be underlined, because sometimes it seems as though the so-called "semi-Gothic" acquires the status of a self-standing graphic system; for example, Cherubini and Pratesi (2004, 108, n. 116) (Vatican City, BAV, Vat. lat. 11559), speak of a "semi-Gothic script of the origins," in reference to a simplified book hand of 1305 (from their definition one might think that we are presented with an autonomous script that exhibits various phases—origins, full development, decadence– according to the biological model dear to palaeography of the late nineteenth century).

41. On the other hand, an expanded use of the definition of "semi-Gothic" includes for certain Italian scholars even bastard or various cursive scripts.

42. Derolez (2003, 118–21).

43. See Zamponi, Chapter 25, Plate 25.3, in this volume.

44. This is the first section, fols. 3–24, of Florence, BML, Plut. 25 sin. 9; see the reproduction in Zamponi (2010, Plate 6).

45. Watson (1984, 32, Plate 266).

46. De Robertis (1998, 72, Plate 2).

47. This is the situation of the nuns of the Florentine monastery of the Paradiso, who copy books between the last two decades of the Quattrocento and the mid-Cinquecento; on them, see Miriello (2007).

48. Among the possible examples are Vicenza, Biblioteca Civica Bertoliana, 366, dated 1447 (Cassandro *et al.* 2000, n. 29, Plate 36); Florence, Biblioteca Riccardiana, 357, dated 1449 (De Robertis and Miriello, 1997, n. 12, Plate 34); Florence, BNC, Conv. Soppr. B.II.1719, dated 1498 (Bianchi *et al.* 2002, n. 28, Plate 150).

49. Even a truly believing humanist such as Bartolomeo Fonzio in one of his letters blames the barbarianisms of the *fraticelli*; see Fonzio (2008, *Ep.* I, 4: 10; commentary on 218–24).

BIBLIOGRAPHY

Berté, M. 2015. "Giovanni Malpaghini copista di Petrarca?" *Cultura Neolatina* 75: 205–16.

Bertelli, S. 2002. *I manoscritti della letteratura italiana delle origini. Firenze, Biblioteca Nazionale Centrale.* Florence: SISMEL Edizioni del Galluzzo.

Bertelli, S. 2011. *I manoscritti della letteratura italiana delle origini. Firenze, Biblioteca Medicea Laurenziana.* Florence: SISMEL Edizioni del Galluzzo.

Bianchi, S., A. Di Domenico, R. Di Loreto, G. Lazzi, M. Palma, P. Panedigrano, S. Pelle, C. Pinzauti, P. Pirolo, A. M. Russo, M. Sambucco Hammoud, P. Scapecchi, I. Truci, and

S. Zamponi. 2002. *I Manoscritti datati del Fondo Conventi Soppressi della Biblioteca Nazionale Centrale di Firenze*. Florence: SISMEL Edizioni del Galluzzo.

Caldelli, E. 2007. *I codici datati nei Vaticani Latini 1–2100*. Vatican City: Biblioteca Apostolica Vaticana.

Cassandro, C., N. Giovè Marchioli, P. Massalin, and S. Zamponi. 2000. *I Manoscritti datati della provincia di Vicenza e della Biblioteca Antoniana di Padova*. Florence: SISMEL Edizioni del Galluzzo.

Cencetti, G. 1997. *Lineamenti di storia della scrittura latina*. Bologna: Patron [1st ed. 1954–6].

Cherubini, P. and A. Pratesi. 2004. *Paleografia latina. Tavole*. Vatican City: Scuola Vaticana di Paleografia, Diplomatica e Archivistica.

De Robertis, T. 1998. "Motivi classici nella scrittura del primo Quattrocento." In *L'ideale classico a Ferrara e in Italia nel Rinascimento*, ed. Patrizia Castelli, 65–79. Florence: Olschki.

De Robertis, T. 2008. "Aspetti dell'esperienza grafica del Quattrocento italiano attraverso i *Manoscritti Datati d'Italia*." *Aevum* 82: 505–22.

De Robertis, T. 2016. "I primi anni della scrittura umanistica. Materiali per un aggiornamento." In *Palaeography, Manuscript Illumination and Humanism in Renaissance Italy: Studies in Memory of A. C. de la Mare*, ed. R. Black, J. Kraye and L. Nuvoloni, 55–85. London: Warburg Institute.

De Robertis, T., and R. Miriello. 1997. *I Manoscritti datati della Biblioteca Riccardiana di Firenze, vol. I (mss. 1–1000)*. Florence: SISMEL Edizioni del Galluzzo.

De Robertis, T., and R. Miriello. 1998. *I Manoscritti datati della Biblioteca Riccardiana di Firenze, vol. II (mss. 1001–1400)*. Florence: SISMEL Edizioni del Galluzzo.

De Robertis, T., G. Tanturli, and S. Zamponi. 2008. *Coluccio Salutati e l'invenzione dell'Umanesimo* (Catalog of the Exhibition "Florence, Biblioteca Medicea Laurenziana, 2 November 2008–30 January 2009"). Florence: Mandragora.

De Robertis, T., C. M. Monti, M. Petoletti, G. Tanturli, and S. Zamponi, eds. 2013. *Boccaccio autore e copista* (Catalog of the Exhibition "Florence, Biblioteca Medicea Laurenziana, 11 October 2013–11 January 2014"). Florence: Mandragora.

Derolez, A. 2003. *The Palaeography of Gothic Manuscript Books from the Twelfth to the Early Sixteen Century*. Cambridge: Cambridge University Press.

Derolez, A. 2004. "The Script Reform of Petrarch: An Illusion?" In *Music and Medieval Manuscripts: Paleography and Performance. Essays Dedicated to Andrew Hughes*, ed. J., Haines and R., Rosenfeld, 3–19. Aldershot: Ashgate.

Destrez, J. 1935. *La pecia dans les manuscrits universitaires du XIIIe et du XIVe siècle*. Paris: Éditions Jacques Vautrain.

Errani, P. and M. Palma. 2006. *I Manoscritti datati della provincia di Forlì-Cesena*, con il contributo di D. Gnola, A. Menghi Sartorio, D. Savoia, V. Tesei, P. Zanfini. Florence: SISMEL Edizioni del Galluzzo.

Fanti, S. 1514. *Theorica et pratica*, Venice: Ioannes Rubeus Vercellensis.

Feo, M. 2003. *Petrarca nel tempo. Tradizione, lettori e immagini delle opere* (Catalog of the Exhibition "Arezzo, Sottochiesa di San Francesco, 22 November 2003–27 January 2004"). Pontedera: Bandecchi & Vivaldi.

Fonzio, B. 2008. *Bartholomaei Fontii Epistolarum libri I*, ed. Alessandro Daneloni. Messina, Centro interdipartimentale di studi umanistici [*Letters to Friends*, ed. A. Daneloni, trans. M. Davies, Cambridge, MA: Harvard University Press, 2011].

Marchiaro, M. and S. Zamponi. 2018. *I manoscritti datati della Biblioteca Nazionale Centrale di Firenze. IV. Fondo Magliabechiano*, con la collaborazione di S. Bertelli, M. Boschi Rotiroti, R. Bruni, S. De Lucchi, E. Giusti, P. Massalin, R. Miriello, B. Rigoli e G. Stanchina. Florence: SISMEL Edizioni del Galluzzo.

Miriello, R. 2007. *I manoscritti del monastero del Paradiso di Firenze*. Florence: SISMEL Edizioni del Galluzzo.

Pontone, M. 2011. *I Manoscritti datati dell'Archivio Storico Civico e Biblioteca Trivulziana di Milano*. Florence: SISMEL Edizioni del Galluzzo.

Ruysschaert, J., A. Marucchi, with the collaboration of A. C. de la Mare. 1997. *I codici latini datati della Biblioteca Apostolica Vaticana, 1. Nei fondi Archivio S. Pietro, Barberini, Boncompagni, Borghese, Borgia, Capponi, Chigi, Ferrajoli, Ottoboni*. Vaticano City: Biblioteca Apostolica Vaticana.

Steffens, F. S. 1910. *Paléographie latine*, trans. Remi Coulon. Trèves and Paris: Schaar & Dathe and H. Champion.

Verini, G. c.1527. *Luminario*. Toscolano sul lago di Garda: Alessandro Paganini.

Watson, A. G. 1984. *Catalogue of Dated and Datable Manuscripts c.435–1600 in Oxford Libraries*, vols. 1–2. Oxford: Clarendon Press.

Zamponi, S. 2010. "Iacopo Angeli copista per Salutati." In *Coluccio Salutati e l'invenzione dell'Umanesimo*. Atti del convegno internazionale di studi, Firenze, 29–31 ottobre 2008, ed. Concetta Bianca, 401–20. Rome: Edizioni di Storia e Letteratura.

CHAPTER 27

....

LATE GOTHIC SCRIPT

The Netherlands

....

†J. P. GUMBERT

THE late medieval script of the Netherlands is rather like that of its eastern and southern neighbours. The northern Netherlands, however, do have some particularities which warrant a separate treatment.

As elsewhere in Europe at the start of the fourteenth century, script is divided into two main script types: *textualis* and *cursiva*.

TEXTUALIS

....

The proper book script is the *textualis*. This is generally written with a broad-nibbed pen cut fairly wide in relation to the intended letter height, which makes for a black appearance; also, the letters tend to be rather high in relation to the line distance, which gives them a narrow appearance and leaves little light between the lines. There also is a tendency to place the letters close together. The result is a dark and dense page, which does not please modern eyes attuned to the aesthetics of the humanistic tradition, and contributes to the reputation of illegibility that *textualis* has.

The pen is stiff and does not react to pressure with a noticeable amount of spreading; it discourages pushed strokes: in principle only pulled strokes, toward the scribe, are allowed, ranging in direction roughly between southwest and northeast, with the thickest strokes more or less southeast (depending on the angle at which the nib is cut and that at which the pen is held), strokes being thinner in the measure they diverge from this direction. (In more calligraphic varieties subtle variations are possible by turning the pen; very thin short lines can be drawn in any direction with the corner of the nib.)

Apart from the clear distinction between Northern (French, German, etc.) and Southern (Italian, Spanish, etc.) *textualis*, there are few marked differences within

Northern *textualis*, either related to region of origin or to date; this makes dating and localizing very difficult.

Two features can be considered characteristic of *textualis*. The *a* has a two-compartment shape, with the upper compartment closed (there are at least three current varieties [Figs. 27.1–3, All illustrations are original size],[1] of which the box-shaped *a* is the most common); the form with the upper compartment reduced to a mere vestige, so that it is in effect a one-compartment *a*, and even the form with an open upper compartment (Figs. 27.4–5), are already old-fashioned or obsolete in the fourteenth century. The *f* and long *s* end on the line with a little foot pointing to the right, just like the feet of the minims of *i*, *m* and *n*.

Some other letters have variant forms worthy of notice. Of *d*, the round-backed or Uncial form is now the norm; the straight-backed *d* has virtually disappeared (except in some liturgical manuscripts). The *e* with a pronounced tongue (most easily seen at word end) is being replaced by the easier form with the head stroke curling inward, not a tongue (Figs. 27.6–7). Of *g* there are two structures: the old one, with the right side of both the upper and the lower part forming one sinuous or bent stroke, and the newer form, with the upper right and lower left strokes made as one (Figs. 27.8–9); no correlation of these forms with time or place of origin is evident. Of *i* there are (mainly) two forms, a short one and a longer, tailed form; the latter is properly used for the last of two or more *i*, as in *alij*, *clxiiij* (it is the root of the modern Dutch digraph *ij*). The round *r*, originally the half of a ligature OR (or, in the abbreviation of *-o/arum*, of AR), had become usual after any letter with a rounded right side, and by the end of the Middle Ages could be found in any position, even at word beginnings. The distribution of the two forms of *s*, the long and the round, is generally simple: round *s* is found at word endings, long *s* elsewhere, although it can still be found at word ends in the fourteenth century (especially in the Dutch word *als* it has a long life). For round and pointed *u* the distribution is equally simple: the pointed form (*v*) appears at word beginnings, the round form elsewhere; but this rule is applied with less rigor than the

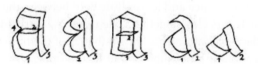

FIGS. 27.1–5 Forms of the letter *a*.

FIGS. 27.6–9 Forms of the letters *e* and *g*.

s-rule. (Note that the Dutch word *nu*, because of its four minims, is conventionally written *nv*.)

Two general phenomena should be mentioned. One is breaking. Writing taller but not wider letters with a heavier nib makes for sharper bends; from this, a conscious element of style can be developed, and so *textualis* got its reputation of being a broken script. For most hands this is hardly or only partially true. But many curves are indeed executed with abrupt, instead of gradual changes in direction; and in the upper reaches of calligraphy the whole script may be executed as an array of straight strokes. For an *o* this leads to a form built up of four straight lines (Fig. 27.10); the heads and the feet of the minims (and the feet of *f*, *l*, and tall *s*) may become small diamonds (Fig. 27.11). (The other highly calligraphic type, with the feet being made to end flat on the line, is rarely seen in the Netherlands.) Another feature is biting: grown naturally in the late twelfth century from the fusion of the last curve of *d* with the first of *e* or *o*, it developed into a system where every pair of meeting curves could, or should, fuse; and if the strokes did not permit a true fusion, the curves were instead made to overlap (Figs. 27.12–13). In many hands, especially in the vernacular, the bitings remain restricted to *de* and *do*; but at the high end of the spectrum the system could be carried to extremes, producing some very surprising digraphs.

The heads of the ascenders *b*, *h*, and *l* are formed in a variety of ways, generally implying an approach stroke from the upper left. If two ascenders come together, simple hands may connect their tops with a thin horizontal stroke.

Within this material, several styles can be distinguished more or less clearly.

At the lower end of the scale, there are hands that only write the strokes essential to making the letters, and write them in the simplest way available. The minims end with the barest short feet or short thin upward strokes (Plate 27.1). Script of this type becomes rare after the early fifteenth century, when other scripts become available for this level of work.

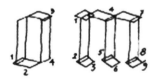

FIGS. 27.10–11 Forms of the letter *o* and of the minims of the letter *m*.

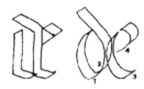

FIGS. 27.12–13 Phenomenon of biting of adjacent curved strokes.

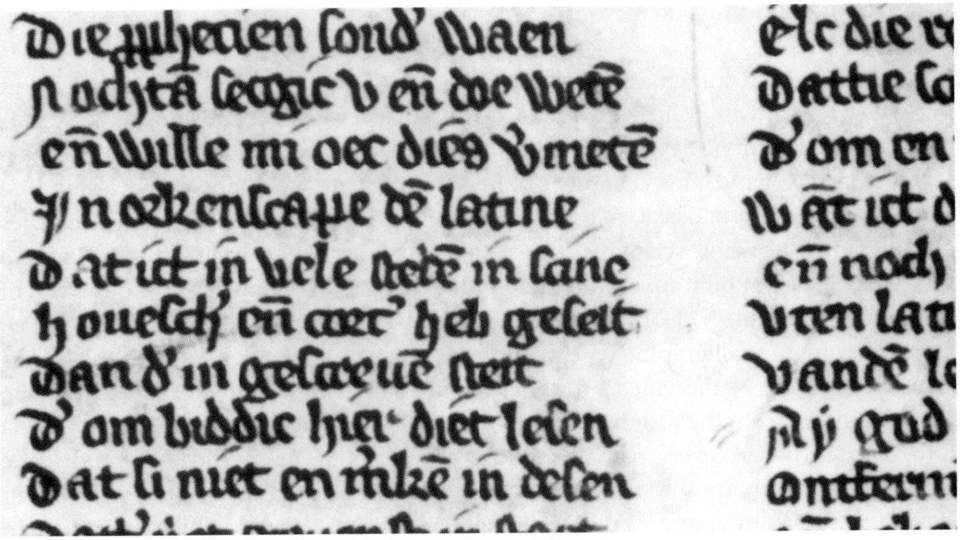

PLATE 27.1 "Minimal" *textualis*, Brabant *c*.1320 (Leiden, University Library, BPL 14 E fol. 87v: Lod. v. Velthem, *Spiegel Historiael*, 5th part).

Textus rotundus is the contemporary name for the medium class, "round" because the minims begin with an approach stroke that either describes a rounded curve into the downstroke, or makes so narrow a curve that it is virtually a break; similarly, the minims end with a foot in the form of a curve or a thin stroke sharply upward; in either case there is no particular calligraphic skill or complication of rhythm required. But within the spectrum of *textus rotundus* there is room for styles. Until far into the fourteenth century one finds many full-bodied, well-rounded hands, with relatively wide letters, and some sway in the verticals (Plate 27.2). Toward the end of the century taste shifts to narrower script with really straight minims and ascenders (Plate 27.3); that is the dominating mood until the end.

Textus quadratus is the highest level of *textualis*, where the minims begin and end with a broken curve which has taken the form of a quadrangle, a square on its point; this takes a good control of the pen, and an extra beat in movement, so that an *m* becomes a nine-stroke letter instead of a three-stroke one (Plate 27.4). There may also be precise rules for minims following letters that end top right, such as *ci*, *gu*.

At the end of our period one can find techniques that we would be tempted to class as degenerations: feet of minims at excessively steep angles, or script where the shafts are made with two parallel strokes of the pen, because the pen could not make that width in one stroke (Plate 27.5). But at the same time script can also be found that conforms perfectly to the norms of the fifteenth century.

As elsewhere, the place of *textualis* in the whole spectrum of script diminishes in the course of time. But it seems that, especially in the northern Netherlands and especially for the vernacular, it declines more slowly than in other regions.

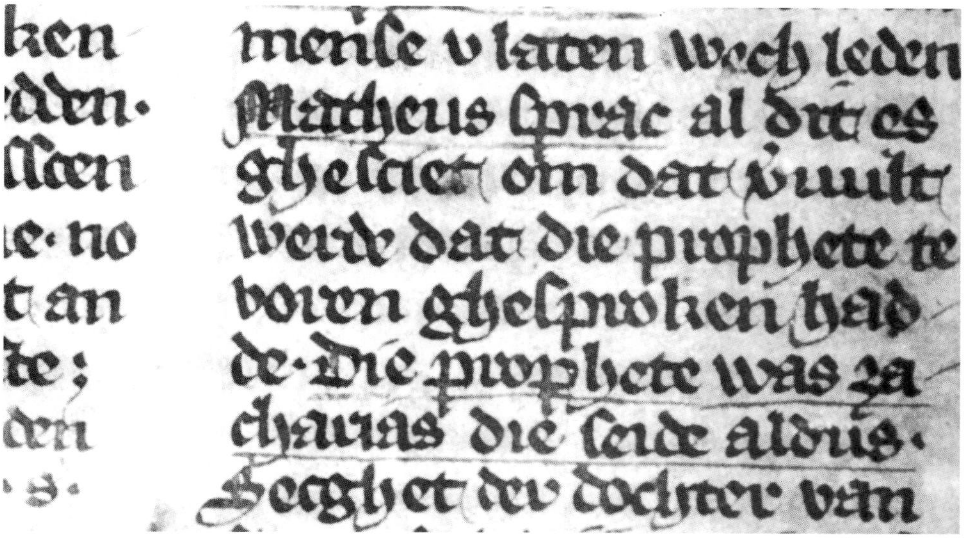

PLATE 27.2 *Textus rotundus*, round style, Flanders 1348 (Amsterdam, Bibliotheek der Universiteit, Allard Pierson, University of Amsterdam, hs. I G 41. fol. 1r: Evangelien ende epistelen).

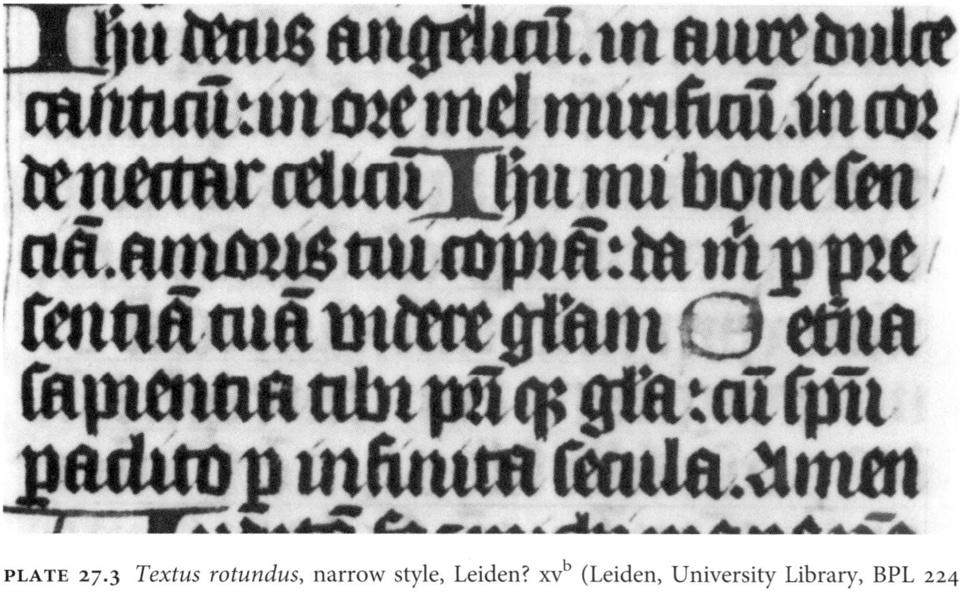

PLATE 27.3 *Textus rotundus*, narrow style, Leiden? xv[b] (Leiden, University Library, BPL 224 fol. 21r: Book of Hours).

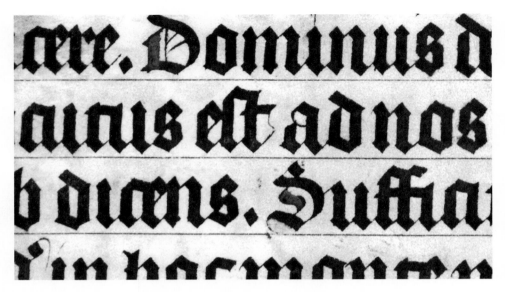

PLATE 27.4 *Textus quadratus*, Zwolle *c*.1465 (Utrecht, Catharijneconvent, ABM h fragm 45c [part of Utrecht, Bibliotheek der Rijksuniversiteit, 31 I fol. 195r]).

PLATE 27.5 "Degenerated" *textualis*, xvi (Utrecht, Catharijneconvent, ABM h fragm 45b: *graduale*).

CURSIVA

In the thirteenth century new scripts had been developed, principally for administrative uses. These scripts were written with a relatively narrow pen, producing letters which are much less black than *textualis* letters; this pen is also more supple and reacts to pressure by spreading, which can cause lines to swell and shrink without changing direction. Also, for some reason this pen allows the scribe to write pushed lines, so that he does not need to lift his pen when he moves from the end of one stroke to the beginning of the next, and so parts of the letter movement that should have been executed in the air can, in fact, be traced in ink; this provides linking strokes and, most strikingly, loops (Figs. 27.14–15). Furthermore, these scripts were generally written with a generous line distance, with the body of the letter occupying only a small part of it, and in long (sometimes excessively long) lines.

In the Netherlands two distinct strains of *cursiva* were in use. One is the type current in the German regions, where it is known as the "older cursive," because it went out of fashion and disappeared by the end of the fourteenth century. (This type has some similarities with the English type of *cursiva*, the *anglicana*.) The other is the type usual in France (ultimately it has Italian roots).

The characteristic features of *cursiva* are two. One is the use of *f* and long *s* with descenders ending below the line, instead of on the line with a little foot. The second is the use of loops, especially on the ascenders of *b*, *h*, and *l*, on the round *d* (straight *d* is virtually absent), and on final *s* (Figs. 27.16–19). Loops may also occur in other places, wherever a link between strokes is called for, or where a stroke changes direction abruptly. And the minims normally have no feet, so they can be linked to the next minim or the next letter without interruption.

FIGS. 27.14–15 Linking stroke that produces a loop in the letter *l*.

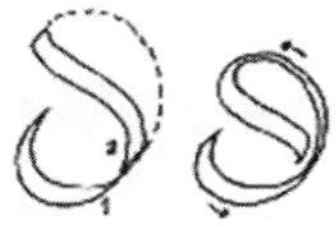

FIGS. 27.16–17 Forms of the cursive round *d*.

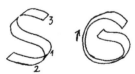

FIGS. 27.18–19 Forms of the final *s*.

PLATE 27.6 "Old" *cursiva*, xiv^m (Leiden, University Library, BPL 2429 fol. 6or: Guido de Colonna, *Liber de casu Troie*).

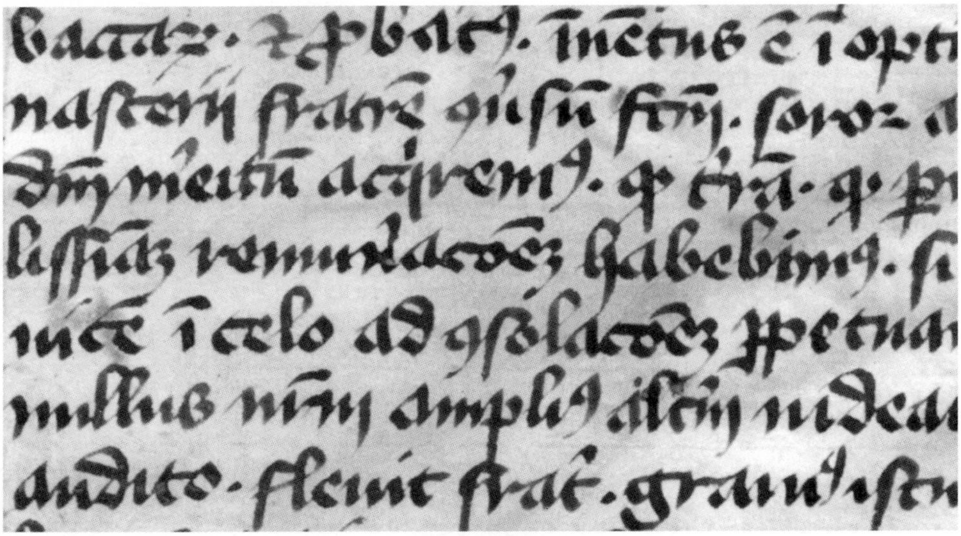

PLATE 27.7 *Cursiva*, xv^1 (private coll.: Thomas Cantipratensis, *Bonum universale de apibus*.)

The differences between the two types mainly concern the *a* and the *g*. The older type uses a two-compartment *a*, often in structures like those of low-grade *textualis*, but there is also a looped form. It also generally uses a *g* with the fairly complicated structures of *textualis* (Plate 27.6). The French *cursiva*, on the other hand, uses a one-compartment *a* and prefers simplified structures of *g* (Plate 27.7). Also, the older type tends to be straighter, less rounded than the other.

FIGS. 27.20–1 Forms of the letters *b* and *s*.

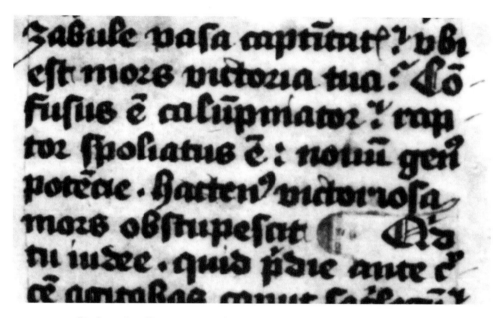

PLATE 27.8 "Reformalized" *cursiva*, Doesburg 1422 (Utrecht, Bibliotheek der Rijksuniversiteit, 151 fol. 1r: Bernardus, *Sermones*.

In the course of the fourteenth century these administrative scripts began to gain a place in books as well, first in books that are not proper library books, but climbing upward to ever higher levels. But in this development the need was felt to make the *cursiva* behave more as a book script ought to: a broader, stiffer pen was used to get the required blackness, minims were given little feet and lost the capacity of continuous writing, bitings were introduced, and loops, which no longer could be executed as pushed strokes, were reconstructed as pulled strokes. The loop of *b* became artificial, the *-s* became a backed *-s* (Figs. 27.20–1; Plate 27.8). (There is also a change in the *a*: since the original form tends to be a rather narrow triangle, a form with a broken back was devised, which gave the letter a more generous eye [Figs. 27.22–3].)

Such a script, reformalized after the pattern of the *textualis*, is no longer "cursive" in the sense of being written fluently and quickly, but it is still a "*cursiva*" in the sense that it still obeys the same rules: it has a single-compartment *a* (the older cursive having in the meantime disappeared before ever going through the full process of reformalization),

FIGS. 27.22–3 Forms of the letter *a*, the second showing the broken back.

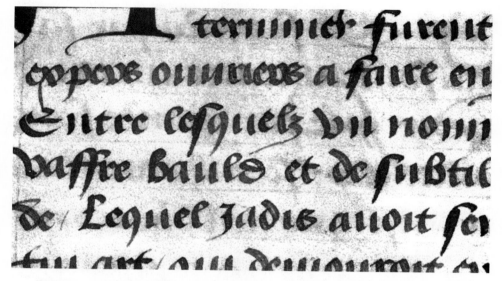

PLATE 27.9 *Lettre bourguignonne* (*cursiva*), xv[d] (Leiden, University Library, BPL 2552:16/2: Guill. Caoursin, *Siège de Rhodes*).

tailed *f* and *s*, and loops. (It also still tends to be somewhat airier than *textualis*, and to tolerate longer lines.)

In the northern Netherlands reformalization rarely achieved the highest levels. But in the southern Netherlands very calligraphic forms are found, of the type that the French call *lettre bâtarde*. The summit is reached (if not passed) in the very heavy script called *lettre bourguignonne*, because the Burgundian court used it in the large and thick books that were to express their wealth and power (Plate 27.9).

HYBRIDA

The loops, which had allowed *cursiva* to be easily and quickly written, had a drawback: they tended to give *cursiva* pages a cluttered look. At the time when *cursiva* was formed, many scribes used loops sparingly; even later, when *cursiva* was recognized and even while it was being reformalized, scribes would now and then hit upon the idea

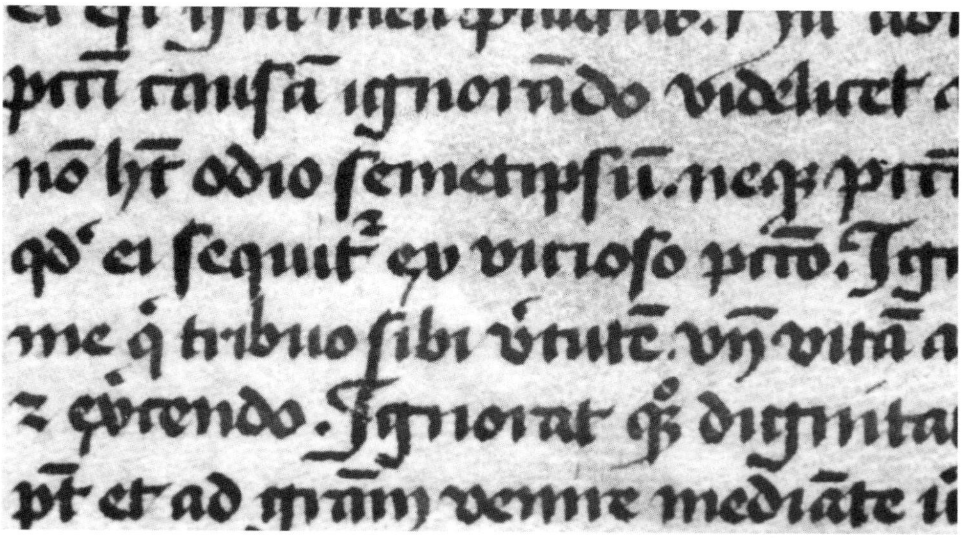

PLATE 27.10 *Hybrida*, Utrecht 1438 (Utrecht, Bibliotheek der Rijksuniversiteit, 180 fol. 103v: Catherina de Senis, *Liber divine doctrine*).

of avoiding loops; in Spain and Italy loopless or partly loopless *cursiva* hands were not rare in the fourteenth century. Early in the fifteenth century the idea took hold in northern countries (perhaps stimulated by contact with Italian loopless hands during the Council of Constance); from *c*.1425 on a loopless *cursiva*, generally well reformalized (with the ascenders treated like those of *textualis*), was common in the Netherlands (although less in the francophone regions) and parts of western and northern Germany (Plate 27.10). (It may be no accident that these are the regions where the movement of the Modern Devotion took hold, although a direct connection probably does not exist.) When Lieftinck in 1953 first presented this script, he called it by its contemporary name of *bastarda*; but, on the French protest that this was not what they called a *bâtarde*, he rebaptized it *hybrida*.

Since the difference between *cursiva* and *hybrida* is merely the presence of loops, it is not difficult to cross that border. Accordingly, next to scribes who took a firm decision either to write or not write loops, we always find scribes who changed their decisions, sometimes back and forth several times, and scribes who simply did not bother to decide: they unconcernedly mix looped and unlooped forms, in what has been called *semi-hybrida* (Plate 27.11). For most French or German scribes, loopless forms are simply a permitted variety within *cursiva*. This freedom even extends to the *lettre bourguignonne*: one finds it with 100% loops, 0% loops, or any percentage in between. But in the northern Netherlands and adjacent regions pure *hybrida* quickly became dominant, and was much better separated from pure *cursiva* (with writers of *semi-hybrida* in a minority). What elsewhere is only a mode within an extended and modernized *cursiva*, in the northern Netherlands is clearly a separate script, and its position is such that it might be called our national hand.

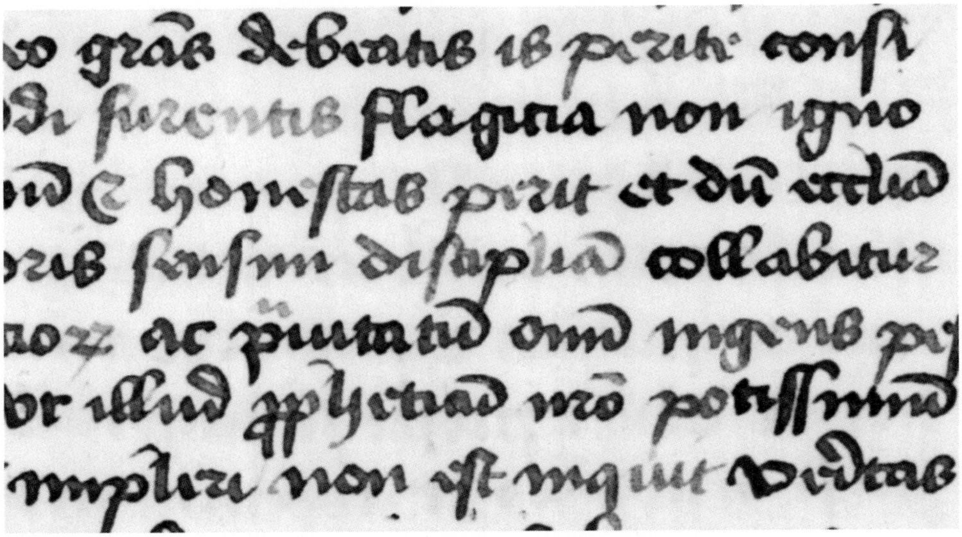

PLATE 27.11 *Cursiva/hybrida* (*semi-hybrida*) [cf. looped *flagitia* line 2, *honestas* 3, loopless *disciplina* 4, *prophetiam* 6], Brabant 1462 (Leiden, University Library, Abl. 39 fol. 73r: Julianus Toletanus, *Prognosticon futuri seculi*).

OTHER SCRIPTS

This survey of book script in the Netherlands would not be complete without pointing out that there are other scripts to be found.

In the first place, there are hands that systematically make a selection from the possibilities that are not one of the three canonical ones. For instance, they may write *hybrida* but with a *textualis s*, which could as well be described as a *textualis* with a *cursiva a*. There are also, in the early fourteenth century, *textualis* hands with *cursiva* traits, especially some loops. (*Textualis* with a tailed *f s* later became the standard script for the printing of Dutch for popular consumption, until the eighteenth century)

In the second place there are always scribes who simply do not bother, or are not able, to conform to any rule.

Then there is a substantial amount of "Italian" script, or rather script written more or less precisely in the style of Italian *textualis*, particularly in numerous Flemish Books of Hours.

There is also some influence of Humanistic script. Some scribes use (presumably as a souvenir of a period of study in Italy) some Humanistic traits in their script; some others actually write what is unequivocally Humanistic script, but these are late and rare (Plate 27.12).

And finally the Netherlands were not immune to the vogue of "neoromanic" scripts, composed by scribes who (undoubtedly after the model of Humanistic script, which

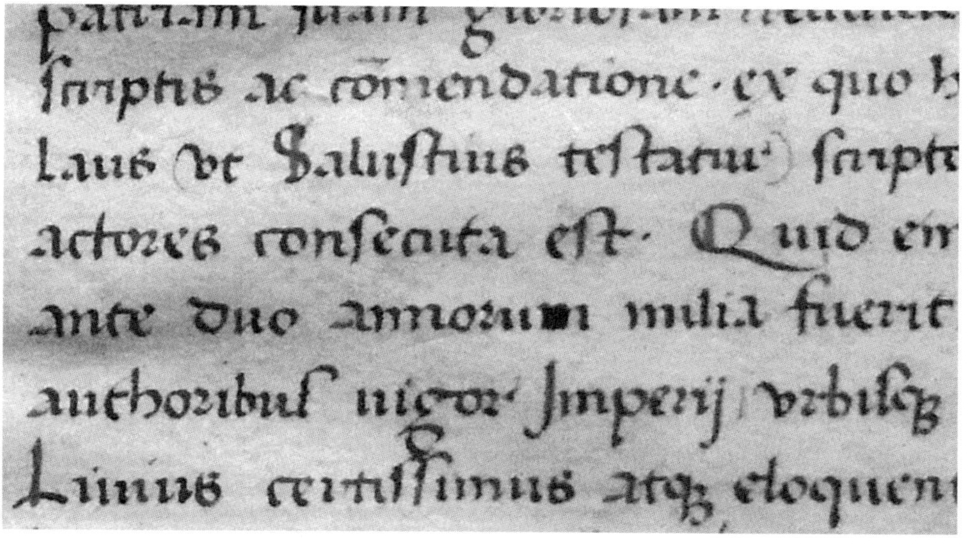

PLATE 27.12 Humanistic, Maastricht *c*.1485 (Brussels, Bollandists, 618 fol. 2r: Matthaeus Herbenus, *De Traiecto instaurato*, autograph).

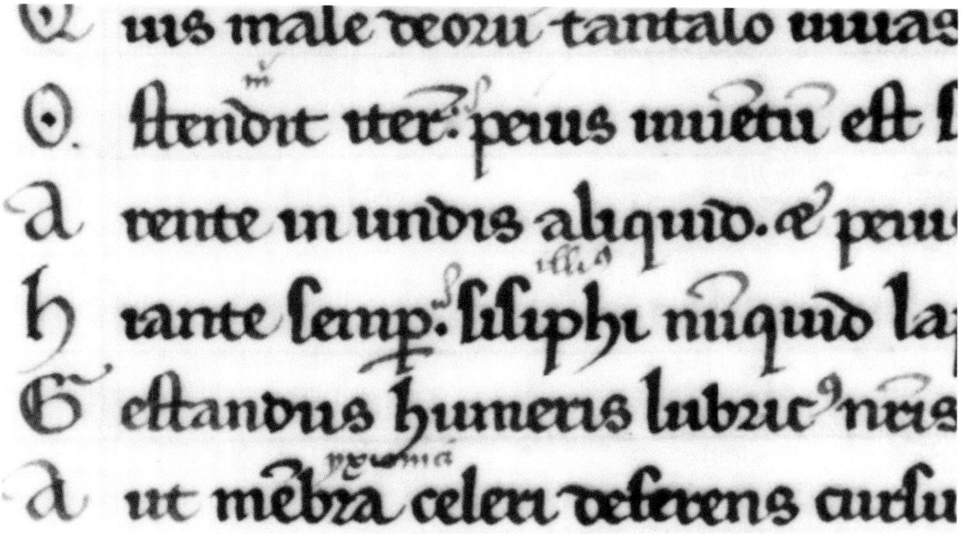

PLATE 27.13 Imitation of pre-Gothic [note the *&* in line 3], Flanders 1477 (Leiden, University Library, BPL 45 A fol. 27r: Seneca, *Tragoediae*).

imitates Italian script of the eleventh and twelfth centuries) imitated script of earlier times, but not that of Italy but of the cultural heritage of their own region. Such scripts can be found in Germany, in France, and in England; and there is at least one case in the Flemish Cistercian abbey of Ter Doest, where at least two monks produced a respectable reinterpretation of the abbey's own script of *c*.1200 (Plate 27.13).

NOTE

1. In the figures the order of the strokes is indicated by numbers placed near the end of the stroke.

BIBLIOGRAPHY

Plates

Deschamps, J. 1970 (1972). *Middelnederlandse handschriften uit Europese en Amerikaanse bibliotheken*. Brussels: Koninklijke Bibliotheek Albert I.
Lieftinck, G. I., ed. 1988. *Manuscrits datés conservés dans les Pays-Bas*, especially II: *Les Manuscrits d'origine néerlandaise (XIVe–XVIe siècles)*, by J. P. Gumbert. Amsterdam: North-Holland Publishing Company.
Masai, F. and Wittek, M., eds. 1968–90. *Manuscrits datés conservés en Belgique*, 6 vols. Brussels and Ghent: E. Story-Scientia.

Older atlases

Brugmans, H. and O. Oppermann. 1910. *Atlas der Nederlandsche Palaeographie*. The Hague: De Jager.
Hulshof, A. 1918. *Schrift in den Niederlanden* (Tabulae in usum scholarum, 9). Bonn: A. Marcus und E. Weber.
van den Gheyn, J. 1908. *Album belge de paléographie*. Brussels: Van-damme et Rossignol.

Script

Biemans, J. A. A. M. 1997. *Onsen Speghele Ystoriale in Vlaemsche* I, 189–95. Leuven: Peeters.
Gumbert, J. P. 1988. *Les Manuscrits d'origine néerlandaise (XIVe–XVIe siècles)*, vol. II of *Manuscrits datés conservés dans les Pays-Bas*, ed. G. I. Lieftinck. Amsterdam: North-Holland Publishing Company, 22–35.
Lieftinck, G. I. 1954. "Pour une nomenclature de l'écriture dite gothique, Essai s'appliquant spécialement aux manuscrit originaires des Pays-Bas médiévaux." In *Nomenclature des écritures livresques du IXe au XVIe siècle,* ed. B. Bischoff *et al.*, 15–34. Paris: Centre national de la recherche scientifique.

CHAPTER 28

GOTHIC WRITING IN BOHEMIA AND MORAVIA

HANA PÁTKOVÁ

THE medieval Czech state, which corresponds only in part to the modern area of the Czech Republic, was centered in Bohemia and Moravia. In the thirteenth, fourteenth, and fifteenth centuries, the neighboring regions of Germany, as well as France and Italy, exerted important influences on the development of scripts in this region. At the end of the fifteenth century, influences from Hungary are also perceptible. The nomenclature of the Gothic script in Bohemia and Moravia was created by Jiří Pražák, who followed, in general, the system of Lieftinck, with the exception of his treatment of the bastarda script.[1]

In the thirteenth century, the script of our region began gradually to change from one in which late Caroline features predominate to one with mostly Gothic characteristics. In this same period, there is also a sharp increase in the number of surviving documents. The earliest extant script samples are documentary (e.g., land rolls), not literary.[2] The thirteenth century also saw the introduction more generally of the Gothic style in the fine arts into this area.[3] Changes were underway in the organization of the church as well, including the diminution of the role of the sovereign in church matters and the creation of more complex administrative structures within the church hierarchy. A network of parishes was added in the thirteenth century to the previously existing bishoprics of Prague (Bohemia) and Olomouc (Moravia), and to the archdeaconries created in the mid-twelfth century.[4] New religious communities also appeared in our region at this time: first the Dominicans and the Franciscans, but also the Augustinian Hermits. The older communities (Premonstratensians, Cistercians, and Benedictines) extended their activities as well. There was no university in the region in the thirteenth century. Students from the Czech lands apparently sought out, for the most part, the universities in Paris and in northern Italy, especially those specializing in the teaching of law. Through the returning students, the opportunities for contacts with non-native forms of written culture and script increased. A further factor that influenced written culture was the increasing urbanization of the region during the Gothic period. Schools grew up in the towns to address the educational needs of the new city dwellers.

There is a serious lack of information about Bohemian and Moravian scriptoria in the thirteenth century, even though there were certainly codices being produced during this period. There must have been a functioning scriptorium within the Prague Cathedral chapter, where, in the period after 1241, Deacon Vitus was responsible for copying many liturgical books.[5] A scriptorium was probably in operation at the Benedictine convent of St. George, which was situated in Prague Castle.[6] It was at St. George that the daughters of the most important noble families of the Přemyslid dynasty were educated. From the point of view of the development of writing, the scriptorium of this convent is particularly interesting because of the possibilities it offers of researching the hands of professional scribes, and also of female scribes. Marginalia in the hands of the nuns who belonged to this community are preserved in their manuscripts. But surviving manuscripts provide only a partial and discontinuous record of the development of the scriptorium, which apparently reached its qualitative high point at the end of the thirteenth and the beginning of the fourteenth century. The community of canons of St. George, which is mentioned in sources from the second half of the thirteenth century onward, also participated in the production of manuscripts. Already in the second half of the twelfth century, there was probably also a scriptorium at the Premonstratensian monastery at Strahov near Prague.[7]

Written culture outside of Prague is even less well documented. It is likely that the Cistercian monastery of Plasy was an important center in western Bohemia.[8] And some books may have been produced at the Premonstratensian monastery of Teplá; but a copy of the *Vita fratris Hroznatae* (Prague, Národní knihovna, Teplá MS b4), the founder of the monastery, is the only manuscript preserved.[9] There are no direct sources about the scriptorium of the Cistercian monastery of Nepomuk; but Robert, bishop of Olomouc, who was active in the chancery of kings Přemysl Ottokar I and Wenceslas I, was originally a monk at Nepomuk.[10] The *Annales* of the Cistercian monastery of Žďár, near the border between Bohemia and Moravia, were written in the second half of the thirteenth century;[11] and manuscripts of the Bible were copied in the Cistercian house in Osek in northern Bohemia.[12] For Moravia, we can only hypothesize the existence of scriptoria in the more important monasteries, e.g., in the Benedictine house in Rajhrad, and in the monasteries of the Premonstratensians in Hradisko (near Olomouc) and in Louka (near Znojmo).[13]

In addition to the local production of books, there were also books made elsewhere that were brought into the country, their scripts reflecting the styles employed in their region of origin. The founding monks of the newly created monastic houses will have brought with them the most important manuscripts needed for their communities.[14] Books were also purchased abroad. For example, in the mid-twelfth century Daniel I, bishop of Prague, bought manuscripts in Bologna.[15] Students returning from foreign schools also brought books with them. The books imported from northern Italy, especially the law books that were written in Rotunda script, were very different in terms of script from the products of the local scribes.

From the second half of the twelfth century, there is a marked increase in the number of surviving manuscripts. The script of these books is a late form of Caroline minuscule.[16] Gothic elements begin to penetrate into the script gradually during the thirteenth century. An important monument of the Gothic book hand at the end of the thirteenth century is the copy of the *Vita fratris Hroznatae*, founder of the monastery of Teplá (Prague, NK, Teplá, b 4). It is written in a fully developed Gothic minuscule with rounded feet on the shafts and with the upper bowl of the *a* not yet closed.

From the first half of the fourteenth century we have two significant guides to the book hands of Bohemia and Moravia.[17] The first is the group of liturgical manuscripts donated by Elisabeth Richenza, the wife of the kings Wenceslas II and Rudolf of Habsburg, to the Cistercian monastery in Staré Brno (Moravia). They are written in a fully developed Gothic minuscule, but the region of their origin is unknown.[18] Our second touchstone is the scriptorium of St. George, which remained the most important writing center in the region during the first half of the fourteenth century.[19] The so-called *Passionale* of Abbess Kunigunde (NK XVI A 17, before 1321, when the abbess died) was written there.[20] This manuscript is written in a fully developed Gothic minuscule. The illumination at the beginning of the book preserves the image of the scribe Beneš, a canon of St. George.

John of Dražice, bishop of Prague, became familiar with the culture of southern France during his stay in Avignon. Manuscripts in the monastery of the Augustinian canons in Roudnice, created by the bishop in 1333, are written in a type of minuscule that is reminiscent of the script of southern France.[21] This is the first appearance of this style in our region. At the beginning of the fourteenth century, the Cistercian monastery in Zbraslav (near Prague) acquired manuscripts from Paris.[22] This monastery was probably an important regional center of written culture. And it is likely that the houses of the Augustinian Hermits at St. Thomas in Prague and that of the Carthusians in Smíchov (near Prague), founded by King John of Luxemburg in 1342, were also influential centers. The variations in the hands of the manuscripts in this relatively late period do not allow us to characterize with any precision the different scriptoria. On the other hand, some evidence for localizing the products of this period is provided by colophons. For example, colophons inform us about the scribal work of the Cistercian monks of Nepomuk, Gotzwin, and Bobellin;[23] and they allow the identification of manuscripts written in the Cistercian monastery in Vyšší Brod.[24] It is, additionally, very likely that manuscripts were written by the canons of Prague Cathedral.

The court during the rule of King John of Luxemburg was international in character; especially prominent were its ties to France. It is a reasonable supposition that the court's interest in written culture was oriented toward France as well. The movements of the court, in particular its long absences from the country, did not create conditions that were favorable to the development of a local writing style. On the other hand, the interaction with other centers was fruitful for the introduction of foreign developments in script. During the reign of Charles IV, the conditions were probably similar to what obtained under John. The literacy of Charles, as well as his interest in literary work, surely stimulated the production of manuscripts.[25] An important advance in writing apparently took place in the reign of Wenceslas IV. Some of the surviving manuscripts make it possible to identify the work of several scribes and illuminators of good quality. Significant figures in manuscript production were John of Neumarkt,[26] chancellor of King Charles IV and bishop of Olomouc, and Ernest of Pardubice, the first archbishop of Prague (1344–64).[27] The *textualis* we find in their manuscripts is of a generic sort; it lacks characteristic elements that would allow any definite conclusions about where these manuscripts originated.

In the course of the fourteenth century, there was a decline in the importance of monastic and cathedral scriptoria. This same period saw the rise of professional scribes, craftsmen working alone or for commercial establishments. These scribes, often called "*cathedrales*" or "*cathedratici*" appear sporadically in the sources of pre-Hussite Bohemia. The majority of the roughly 30 such scribes recorded in this period worked in Prague, but some were active in smaller towns.[28] Students returning from foreign universities continued to be an important factor in the book culture of the region, for they brought home with them from abroad books copied in the latest styles.[29] Writing was not necessarily a full-time profession for scribes, and copying for pay was also undertaken by priests and students.[30] The professional scribes employed a wide range of different scripts. The oldest known scribal pattern book from Bohemia and Moravia was probably written at the beginning of the fifteenth century. It contains five types of script, all of them variations of Gothic minuscule book hand.[31]

The creation of the University of Prague in 1348 had an enormous impact on the written culture of the region. Previously there had been schools operated by some of the monastic orders (Dominicans, Franciscans, and Augustinians), and the teachers from these schools provided the first faculty of the newly founded university. In the 1360s, the first college (the Carolinum) was created; it had a substantial library.[32] A pragmatic, quick, and relatively simple writing style was practiced in the schools; and scholars themselves were often responsible for copying the texts they needed for their studies. There were also schools operating in the fourteenth and fifteenth centuries in small towns, and some of these town schools maintained high standards (e.g., those at Plzeň[33] and Český Krumlov[34]). Ownership of books was probably also increasing to new heights, but this applied for the most part only to specific types of books. For example, every deacon or priest was expected to have his own breviary.[35] And schoolbooks were produced not only at the university, but also in the numerous town schools where written materials were required.[36]

During the second half of the fourteenth century, the cursive script began to be intensively employed in the writing of Bohemian and Moravian manuscripts. The cursive script was especially favored for texts read in the university, where the quick and inexpensive production of manuscripts was paramount. In the same context, we also find a hybrid script, combining the elements of both minuscule and cursive scripts. It is a rather broader script, characterized by the use of the cursive form of *a* and by the shafts of *s* and *f* standing on the line.[37]

The long period of the Hussite wars, the exile of some of the clergymen, and the destruction of many of the monasteries had a major and negative impact on the written culture of the region. From the 1430s, conditions in the country generally became quieter and more stable. Since many of the monasteries were destroyed, monastic scriptoria were not major producers of books in this period, and manuscripts from their libraries began to appear on the market.[38] The production of books, especially luxurious ones, declined; but the market for books was lively.[39] The consolidation after the wars eventually provided the conditions for an increase in the manufacture of books.

As in the fourteenth century, in the fifteenth the monasteries and cathedral chapters were of secondary significance as producers of manuscripts. At the same time, the role of professional scribes was increasing. There were still some functioning monastic scriptoria, including that of the Augustinian canons in Třeboň. Here the canons compiled and copied texts in the second half of the fifteenth century, but mostly for the internal use of the members of their community.[40] There is some limited evidence for copying in other monasteries as well, e.g., in the Franciscan house in Bechyně.[41]

The university played an important part in the gradual stabilization of the country after the Hussite wars.[42] The number of students began to increase in the 1440s, and even foreigners started enrolling at the University of Prague. At the end of the 1450s, the conflict between Catholics and Utraquists embroiled the university and resulted in the widespread adoption of Utraquism in the university community. Some of the graduates of the university became priests and teachers, and others municipal servants, especially members of municipal chanceries.

In spite of the rise of the University in Prague, many students from Bohemia and Moravia continued to pursue their studies abroad, not only in the nearby universities in Krakow, Vienna, Leipzig, or Erfurt, where the situation for Catholics was more favorable, but also in Paris. There was an additional impulse for going abroad in this period. In the wake of the wars, the archbishopric of Prague remained vacant for some time, and going abroad offered the only opportunity for priestly ordination, both for Utraquists and Catholics. The Catholics could turn to the neighboring dioceses of Olomouc, Regensburg, Passau, or Meissen; but the Utraquists had to travel to remote bishoprics in Italy, where no precise information about the conditions in the Czech countries could hinder their ordination.

The major development in this period as far as book hands are concerned is the common use of the *bastarda* script for writing luxurious manuscripts. After the Hussite wars, the production of luxurious books, especially manuscripts of the Bible or of its parts (e.g., Vienna, ÖNB, 1175, Vatican City, BAV, Reg. lat. 87, etc.), gradually increased; and it appears that Prague was the principal center for this activity. Another important center was Plzeň, a purely Catholic town, which seems not even to have had an Utraquist minority within its territory. The *bastarda* script was used both for Czech and for Latin versions of the Bible, as well as for secular texts such as the *Chronicle of Dalimil* (Vienna, ÖNB, ser. nov. 44), or the story of Tristan and Isolde (Prague, Strahov, D 6 III 7). *Bastarda* was also employed for scholarly and scientific texts

(Prague, KNM, Křivoklát I d 36) as well as for law books (Prague, AHMP, 1864). In addition to the *bastarda* script, cursive was also used as a book hand. It differed from the *bastarda* principally in its greater tendency to connect one letter to the next (e.g., Prague, NK, III G 6; Prague, KNM, II F 8). Gothic minuscule, more and more petrified in its form, remained in use for liturgical books, especially for missals and graduals, but also for breviaries.[43]

Notes

1. Pražák (1966).
2. See the relevant chapters in Šebánek, Fiala, and Hledíková (1984).
3. For basic information, see the relevant chapters in Chadraba (1984).
4. For basic information and bibliography, see Hledíková, Janák and Dobeš (2005, 172–202).
5. Kosmowi Pokračovatelé (1874, 321–2). Spunar (1957).
6. For general information about the scriptorium, see Sádlová (2004).
7. Pražák (1990).
8. Hlaváček (1981, 157).
9. Ibid., 156.
10. Hlaváček (2001, 400).
11. Zaoral (1970, 79).
12. Hlaváček (2001, 400).
13. Cf. Dokoupil (1972, 6, 24).
14. e.g. the Cistercians from Wilhering brought books to Vyšší Brod. Cf. Friedl (1965, 5).
15. The bishop was even Italian-speaking. Cf. Vincenciův Letopis (1874, 442, 445).
16. Cf. Dokoupil (1972, 6, 24).
17. A basic overview of sources about medieval books and libraries is given by Hlaváček (1966).
18. Friedl (1930, esp. 27–9), on scribes. There were three or four scribes working on this group of manuscripts.
19. In addition to the work of Sádlová (2004), see Plocek (1990); Hledíková (1990).
20. On this manuscript, see the recent contribution of Toussaint (2003).
21. See Hledíková (2007); Kadlec (1981); Kadlec suggested specific influence from the monastery of St. Rufus in Avignon.
22. Hlaváček (1990, 6).
23. Hlaváček (1981, 158); Friedl (1928–30).
24. See Hejnic (1972, 9 note 18). Hejnic identifies five monks as scribes in the period from 1392–1415: Jan (MS XXXIV, 23 and 92, 1392–1402), Přibík (MS 22, 42, 80, 104, 1402–11), Vavřinec (MS LXXIV, 1411), Jan Stajč (MS 49, 1415), Mikuláš of Hořice (MS LXIII, beginning of the fifteenth century).
25. Although the library of Charles IV is not preserved, his autograph is known. He had a good scribal hand that combines elements of both the cursive and the minuscule book hands, e.g., he uses the cursive *a*; the shafts of *s* and *f* stand on the baseline; and there are no loops on the ascenders.

26. Among his manuscripts is the *Liber viaticus* (KNM XIII A 12). It was written *c*.1360 in a very calligraphic Gothic minuscule of the type known as *textus rotundus*. On the other hand, his missal (APH, KMK Cim. 6, before 1380) was written in Gothic minuscule of the type called *textus sine pedibus*.

27. Cf., e.g., the *Orationale Arnesti* (KNM XIII C 12), a manuscript written after 1360. It was written in the type of Gothic minuscule called *textus rotundus*.

28. Hlaváček (1981, 163, 165) and the list on pp. 11, 19–21. Petr of Čáslav worked in the early 1430s in Klatovy.

29. Hlaváček (1981, 163).

30. On late medieval Augsburg, see Schneider (1995). Among the 32 lay scribes (including one woman) she finds not only "*cathedrales*," but also merchants, a member of the municipal council, the administrator of the town hospital, the mayor, etc. The conditions in Bohemia might have been similar.

31. Hoffmann (1995–6).

32. Cf. KNM, 1 Da 1. Spunar (1986, 350).

33. Hejnic (1979).

34. Hejnic (1972).

35. According to the synodal resolution of 1368; cf. Polc (1994, 38).

36. Cf. Boockmann (1986, 337).

37. Cf. the copy of the *Communiloquium* of John of Wales from 1373 (NK ČR, V B 4; Spunar 1986, 348), where the scribe depicted on fol. 1r writes the text using a fully developed cursive that includes loops on the ascenders and the typical forms of *s* and *f*. The main text of the manuscript is written in a hand that uses some cursive elements (cursive *a*, broader letters) and some elements of the minuscule book hand (shafts of *s* and *f* stand on the baseline; occasional use of minuscule *a*; no loops).

38. Hlaváček (1990, 13–14) considers the possibility that books were preserved during the destruction of the ecclesiastical institutions because of the possibility of later sale.

39. In the year 1423 a parchment missal from the Benedictine monastery of Kladruby was sold in Stříbro for a mere 1 ss. gr. SOA Plzeň–Státní okresní archiv Tachov, Archiv města, Stříbro, kniha soudnictví nesporného od roku 1409, fol. 71v.

40. Kadlec (2004, 126–32).

41. Cf. Beneš (2004, 10–11), for a manuscript of the life of St. Francis (SOA Třeboň, RA Černínů, rkp. č. 2) written at the beginning of sixteenth century by Egidius of Ratiboř for Ladislav of Sternberg, the supreme chancellor of the Kingdom of Bohemia.

42. Cf. Svatoš and Čornejová (1995, 207–15).

43. The research for this chapter was undertaken within the framework of the MSM 0021621927 research project conducted by the Faculty of Philosophy of the Charles University in Prague, and supported by the Ministry of Education, Youth, and Sport of the Czech Republic.

BIBLIOGRAPHY

Beneš, P. R. 2004. *Historia Franciscana*. Prague: Provincie bratří františkánů.

Boockmann, H. 1986. *Die Stadt im späten Mittelalter*, 2nd ed. Munich: Beck.

Chadraba, R., ed.1984. *Dějiny českého výtvarného umění* 1. Prague: Academia.

Dokoupil, V. 1972. *Dějiny moravských klášterních knihoven ve správě Univerzitní knihovny v Brně.* Brno: Muzejní a vlastivědná společnost.

Friedl, A. 1928–30. "Graduál bratra Gotzwina, mnicha kláštera nepomuckého." *Památky archeologické* 36: 15–46.

Friedl, A. 1930. *Malíři královny Alžběty.* Prague: Aventinum.

Friedl, A. 1965. *Iluminované rukopisy vyšebrodské.* České Budějovice: Krajská knihovna.

Hejnic, J. 1972. *Českokrumlovská latinská škola v době rožmberské* (Rozpravy ČSAV 82/2). Prague: Nakladatelství ČSAV.

Hejnic, J. 1979. *Latinská škola v Plzni a její postavení v Čechách (13.–18. století)* (Rozpravy ČSAV 89/2). Prague: Nakladatelství ČSAV.

Hlaváček, I. 1966. *Středověké soupisy knih a knihoven v českých zemích. Příspěvek ke kulturním dějinám českým. AUC–Phil. et hist. Monographia* 11. Prague: Charles University.

Hlaváček, I. 1981. "Středověká knižní kultura v západních Čechách, zejména v Plzni." *Minulostí západočeského kraje* 17: 153–67.

Hlaváček, I. 1990. "O výrobě a distribuci knih v Praze do rozšíření knihtisku." *Documenta Pragensia* 10/1: 5–22.

Hlaváček, I. 2001. "Zisterziensische Bibliotheken Böhmens in der vorhussitischen Zeit (Mitte des 12. Jh.–1420)." In *Mediaevalia Augiensia,* ed. J. Petersohn, 375–406. Stuttgart: Thorbecke.

Hledíková, Z. 1990. "Poznámka ke svatojiřskému skriptoriu kolem roku 1300." *Documenta Pragensia* 10: 31–49.

Hledíková, Z. 2007. "Die südeuropäische Schrift im böhmischen Umfeld des 14. Jahrhunderts unter besonderer Berücksichtigung des Einflusses der bolognesischen Schrift auf die Handschriftenproduktion für Raudnitz." In *Régionalisme et internationalisme: problèmes de paléographie et de codicologie du Moyen Âge. Actes du XVe Colloque du Comité international de paléographie latine (Vienne. 13–17 septembre 2005),* Veröffentlichungen der Kommission für Schrift- und Buchwesen des Mittelalters, Reihe IV: Monographien, 5, ed. Otto Kresten and Franz Lackner, 139–51. Vienna: Österreichische Akademie der Wissenschaften.

Hledíková, Z., J. Janák, and J. Dobeš. 2005. *Dějiny správy v českých zemích od počátků státu po současnost.* Prague: NLN.

Hoffmann, F. 1995–6. "Vzorník gotického písma z 15. století." *Studie o rukopisech* 31: 27–34.

Kadlec, J. 1981. "Začátky kláštera augustiniánských kanovníků v Roudnici." *Studie o rukopisech* 20: 65–86.

Kadlec, J. 2004. *Klášter augustiniánů kanovníků v Třeboni.* Prague: Karolinum.

Kosmowi Pokračovatelé. 1874. Příběhy krále Přemysla Otakara II (*Fontes Rerum Bohemicarum* 2). Prague: Museum Království českého.

Plocek, V. 1990. "Svatojiřské skriptorium." *Documenta Pragensia* 10: 23–9.

Polc, J. V. 1994. "Kapitoly z církevního života Čech podle předhusitského zákonodárství." In *Pražské arcibiskupství 1344–1994,* ed. Z. Hledíková and J. V. Polc, 30–57. Prague: Zvon.

Pražák, Jiří. 1966. "Názvosloví knižních písem v českých zemích 2." *Studie o rukopisech* 5: 1–30.

Pražák, Jiří. 1990. "K existenci strahovského scriptoria." *Documenta Pragensia* 10: 51–8.

Sádlová, R. 2004. "Svatojiřský klášter ve světle jeho nekrologických přípisků: jeden z méně užívaných pramenů ke klášterním dějinám." Dissertation. Prague.

Schneider, K. 1995. "Berufs- und Amateurschreiber. Zum Laien-Schreibbetrieb im spätmittelalterlichen Augsburg." In *Literarisches Leben in Augsburg während des 15. Jahrhunderts*

(Studia Augustana 7), ed. Johannes Janota and Werner Williams-Krapp, 8–26. Tübingen: Niemeyer.

Šebánek, J., Z. Fiala, and Z. Hledíková. 1984. *Česká diplomatika do roku 1848*. Prague: Univerzita Karlova.

Spunar, P. 1957. "Das Troparium des Prager Dechans Vít (Prag, Kapitelbibliothek, Cim. 4)." *Scriptorium* 11: 50–62.

Spunar, P. 1986. *Česká středověká kultura*. Prague: Odeon.

Svatoš, M. and I. Čornejová. 1995. *Dějiny Univerzity Karlovy* 1. Prague: Karolinum.

Toussaint, G. 2003. *Das Passional der Kunigunde von Böhmen. Bildrhetorik und Spiritualität*. Paderborn, Minich, Vienna, and Zurich: Ferdinand Schoeningh.

Vincenciův Letopis. 1874. *Fontes Rerum Bohemicarum* 2, ed. Josef Emler. Prague: Museum Království českého.

Zaoral, P. 1970. "Příspěvek ke knihovně a skriptoriu kláštera ve Žďáře v 15. Století." *Studie o rukopisech* 9: 79–100.

CHAPTER 29

LATE MEDIEVAL WRITTEN CULTURE IN THE REALM OF KING ST. STEPHAN

Gothic and later script in Hungary and Slovakia

JURAJ ŠEDIVÝ

(Translated by Anna A. Grotans and Robert G. Babcock)

THE kingdom of Hungary unified a large portion of the area around the Danube River in the Middle Ages. As a result of political changes after World War I, the kingdom collapsed, and, after World War II, the region became very strongly divided according to ethnic groups. What was once a political unity became several modern states, including Hungary and Slovakia; other parts were inherited by Poland, the Ukraine, Romania, former Yugoslavia, and Austria. Even in the Middle Ages the kingdom was made up of several cultural and economic regions, of which the most important were found in the center (around cities like Buda, Esztergom, Székesfehérvár, and Veszprém). The cities in the western borderlands (Bratislava, Trnava, Nitra, Sopron, Moson, and Szombathely) had strong connections to Austria. Other important regions included the mining area in present-day middle Slovakia (Banská Štiavnica, Kremnica, and Banská Bystrica), eastern Slovak Spiš (Levoča, Spišská Kapitula) and the area around Košice and Prešov, which had contacts with *Polonia Minor*. An important region in the western part of present-day Romania was Transylvania (around Alba Iulia, Cluj Napoca, Oradea, and Sigisoira), and a further region was found in the south (Kalocsa, Pécs, Szeged). The areas of Croatia, Slavonia, and Dalmatia were always a separate part of the kingdom.

One can divide the medieval script culture of this heterogeneous area into three principal topics. *Book culture* encompasses the copying of literary manuscripts in local scriptoria and the reception of local as well as imported manuscripts. *Pragmatic writing* deals with the products of scribal chancelleries (diplomatic writing such as charters and administrative books). The third element of script culture concerns inscriptions, *epigraphic culture*. In all three areas, one must look at both official and unofficial texts (e.g., in the case of manuscripts one must consider individual glosses; in the case of charters, one must look at drafts; as regards inscriptions, it is necessary to include graffiti). Furthermore, one must keep in mind that throughout the entire Middle Ages alongside the scribal culture there also flourished an oral culture. Its importance varies with the social class and the period one is studying. In accordance with the focus of this handbook, this chapter deals only with the first two of these topics, epigraphic culture falling outside the present survey.

On the basis of the reciprocal relationship between oral and written culture, one can distinguish three main periods in the history of the Hungarian kingdom. Following the retreat of the Roman legions (*c.*430) and after the relatively short period of missionary activity in connection with the Great Moravian Empire (*c.*833–906), we have the first written texts, which we owe to missionaries from the end of the tenth and the beginning of the eleventh centuries. However, until the beginning of the thirteenth century, only a fraction of the monks and canons were literate (hence the period may be referred to as that of "*ilitterati*-culture"). The thirteenth century was characterized by an advance in book culture and an upsurge in diplomatic activity (royal chancery, the establishment of the so-called "places of authentication"—the *loci credibiles*—which performed the same function as the public notary in Southern Europe). The majority of the populace, though aware of the power of the written word (witness the exponential increase of charters), remained illiterate. Many had only a basic command of reading, without being able to write (= "*semi-litterati*-culture"). A growth in literacy and a general proliferation of written culture among the noble and middle classes began in the fourteenth century thanks to chapter and city schools (= "*litterati*-culture"). This process went hand in hand with the diffusion of vernacular texts (in German, Czech/Slovak, and Hungarian[1]), with the substitution of parchment by less expensive paper, with the spread of Arabic numerals, and above all with the growth in lay scribes and notaries. The palaeographically important process of adopting the Gothic style falls in the second period of book culture in our region, while the high and late Gothic works belong to the third period.

METHODOLOGICAL PROBLEMS AND SUMMARY OF RESEARCH

Within the territory of present-day Hungary there are only about 1,000 extant manuscripts, and there are even fewer in Slovakia (*c.*200). The number of surviving charters from the area of the entire kingdom is much greater—up to 250,000 items (in the Slovak archives alone there are 35,000 charters).[2] The disproportion in the survival of these different types of written material is reflected in the scholarly literature: the book culture of the region has been almost completely described;[3] the history of pragmatic script culture is less fully studied, but already dozens of good preliminary investigations have been completed.[4]

The authors of the earliest modern manuscript catalogues deal with book scripts, e.g., Emma Bartoniek and László Mezey from Hungary and Július Sopko from Slovakia.[5] The true founder of Latin palaeographical studies in Hungary was István Hajnal.[6] Modern-day research in palaeography and codicology is associated with the name of László Veszprémy and with the group *Fragmenta codicum* (a combined effort of the Hungarian Academy of Sciences and the Széchényi-National Library) comprised, in particular, of András Vizkelety, Edit Madas, Gábor Sarbak, Judit Lauf, and Edina Zsupán.[7] In Slovakia, palaeographical studies have a center at the Institute for Archival Studies and Ancillary Historical Sciences of the University of Bratislava (Juraj Šedivý),[8] and also one within a group studying manuscript fragments (Eva Veselovská, Rastislav Adamko, Janka Bednáriková),[9] albeit their focus is exclusively on fragments containing neumes.

Studies devoted to the palaeography of diplomatics, mostly of local charter scripts, notaries, and chancelleries are relatively numerous. András Kubínyi and Lajos Bernát Kumorovitz from Hungary and Darina Lehotská with Richard Marsina from Slovakia have described the general framework and the functioning of the documentary landscape.[10] More particularly focused on charter scripts are various publications of István Hajnal, Zsikmond Jakó, Richard Marsina, and Juraj Šedivý.[11]

A fairly basic synthesis of the general development of Latin script, which also serves as a university textbook on the subject, is the work of the Slovak scholar Alexander Húščava; this was followed by the books of László Mezey and, most recently, that of Zsikmond Jakó and Radu Manolescu.[12] Juraj Šedivý has tried to combine epigraphical and palaeographical investigations, in order to provide a more complete picture of the development of script culture in the region.[13]

THE BEGINNINGS OF GOTHIC SCRIPT
IN THE HUNGARIAN KINGDOM

The earliest signs of a change toward Gothic script forms appear in local charters (last third of the twelfth century), then a bit later in manuscripts (*c.*1200). Three phases of the development of the Gothic style are observable, in book scripts as well as in documentary scripts: a Carolingian-Gothic transition script, an early Gothic script, and the fully developed high and late Gothic scripts.

A movement toward the use of a Gothic script type is evident in the imperial chancery of Frederick Barbarossa. The charters that were formerly of large format become smaller, and the older characteristics change (e.g., wide line spacing and the extremely long ascenders with figure 8 loops). Instead, we find narrower line spacing, angular and more closely spaced letterforms and an alternation of thick and thin strokes. Some of the other older characteristics eventually disappear altogether (e.g., the writing of proper names in an elongated script, the so-called *Elongata*, or in small capitals). Whereas the Gothic minuscule of charters used in the imperial chancery developed out of the diplomatic minuscule, in Hungarian charters a "pure" charter script first had to develop in opposition to a script type that was influenced by book scripts (so, for example, the charters of Stephan III. /1147–72/, e.g., MOL DL 39 417, dated 1165; MOL DF 290939, 24 October 1166; or MOL DF 208422, from 1171). However, if we examine the charters of Bela III (1172–96), which were written by professional notaries in the chancery (e.g., MOL DL 22 from 1181, or MOL DF 248601, from 1186), we find a Gothicized charter script characterized by the consistent formation of shafts, a contrast of thick and thin strokes, and an incipient tendency toward breaking of the shafts.

Examination of various scribal hands in local manuscripts from the second half of the twelfth century, for example those in the Commentary to the Song of Songs (Esztergom, Erzbischöfliche Bibliothek, MS III) or in the Codex Albensis (Graz, Universitätsbibliothek, 211), reveals that the scribes of these manuscripts are still employing typical twelfth-century (post-)Carolingian minuscule scripts. Their features include a balanced module, no elongation of shafts, inconsistent formation of shafts, and no breaking. In the Commentary manuscript, we still find the *et* ligature, *e caudata*, majuscules borrowed from *capitalis*, a separation of the bowls of *g*, and other conservative characteristics.

The hands of other manuscripts from the same period (for example, in the Ernst-Codex [Budapest, OSzK, Clmae 431] or in the Hartwik Legend [OSzK, Clmae 17]) already exhibit some Gothic characteristics. The script of both books has a vertical orientation (particularly that of the Hartwik Legend is very regular), the shafts begin to stretch in height, there is a clear tendency toward breaking and toward a consistent organization of the shafts, and the connecting strokes become more prominent. Because of such characteristics we can categorize these transitional scripts as Carolingian-Gothic minuscule.

More striking changes in the script of local manuscripts can be seen only in the last third of the thirteenth century. They are no doubt tied to the transition in Hungarian society from an illiterate to a semi-literate culture: the royal chancery began to function systematically at the end of the twelfth century; the *loci credibiles* ("places of authentication") began to be the authoritative producers of written records for the region from the first third of the thirteenth century. The number of charters increased from a few to hundreds. László Veszprémy already noticed an increasing differentiation in the script of local charters and manuscripts beginning with this period.[14] Before this many charters were written with forms similar to those used in books (and some continued to be written like this until shortly after 1250).

The adoption of the Gothic style should be treated not just as an aesthetic change. Rather, the process was greatly accelerated by other social changes. Through canon law the belief was spreading in Central Europe at this time that written witnesses had more worth than verbal agreements. For this reason it was deemed necessary to have one's property and privileges recorded, which, of course, led to an enormous rise in charter production. This, in turn, had an effect on the format of charters: chanceries could no longer afford to produce documents in a wasteful, large format; the former uneconomical line spacing, which was filled with elongated ascenders, was abandoned. Instead charters were produced in small format with narrow margins, cramped line spacing, compressed letters, and greater use of abbreviations. The new intellectual who was born at this time contributed to the spread of the Gothic script culture, which, unlike the preceding Romanesque script, was not meant solely for clerics, but for a larger body of nobles as well as for city folk of varying social backgrounds and status.

Book Writing: From Early to Late Gothic

In accord with the distinctions formulated by B. Bischoff and G. I. Lieftinck,[15] one can differentiate two major periods of Gothic script in the large area of the former kingdom of Hungary: the early Gothic period (when both a minuscule and a gloss script were in use); and the high and late Gothic period (when three different scripts were employed: minuscule, cursive, and *bastarda*). The early Gothic minuscule (*Gothica primitiva*) is characteristic of the first half of the thirteenth century. The script has regular and fixed forms, the letters are horizontally compressed and vertically extended, and the minims and shafts are consistently executed. Simple breaking is noticeable. However, joining of adjacent curved strokes is not yet found.

The hand of a codex from Zagreb serves as an example of this script (Güssing, Klosterbibliothek, Ms. I 43; Plate 29.1). László Veszprémy found parallels to this script in charters from the 1220s.[16] The connecting strokes are prominent, and breaking is present. As for individual letterforms,: the *a* is nearly vertical; both the round *d* and the upright *d* are found; the ascenders are thicker and either forked or broken; the tall-s is still used at the end of words. The horizontal stroke of *t* is shifted to the right of the shaft, so that the letter appears almost like a *c*. The *ę* and *ct* ligatures are no longer used. The Tironian *et* sign characteristic of Gothic scripts is used throughout (and the old ligature does not appear). In comparison with the older scripts, one also finds a more frequent use of the round *r*, which better accommodates the typical Gothic preference for uniform organization of shafts and bows. At the end of the twelfth century a new symbol appears, the oblique hairline stroke over the *i*. This becomes the norm in the thirteenth century. Although this feature was occasionally used even earlier north of the Alps (e.g., in Normandy *c.*1030),[17] it first appears in our lands in the Zagreb Codex, where it is employed only over double-*i*. The use of abbreviations slowly becomes more widespread than it had been in the previous period. The script type of the

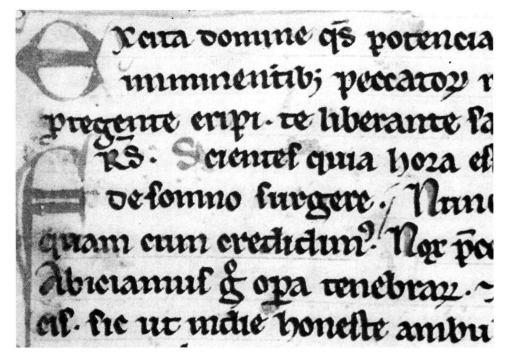

PLATE 29.1 Early Gothic minuscule from the Zabreb Codex (1220s, Güssing, Klosterbibliothek, Ms. I 43, fol. 15v).

Zagreb Codex is also found in a manuscript of Boethius' *Arithmetica* (Vienna, ÖNB, Cod. Lat. 2463).

After the second half of the fourteenth century the complete form of the three main script types gradually emerges: the Gothic minuscule (*Gothica textualis*—used from the second half of the thirteenth century until around the beginning of the sixteenth), the Gothic cursive (*Gothica cursiva*—from around the middle of the fourteenth century until the beginning of the sixteenth), and the Gothic *bastarda* (*Gothica bastarda*—from around 1370/80 until the beginning of the sixteenth century). For each of these three types one can further distinguish three main aesthetic variants: the highest calligraphic form (*formata*), the simple or "normal" form (*libraria*), and the quickly written form, which was produced without complexity or any calligraphic ambition (*currens*).

In medieval Hungary, as elsewhere, it was an unwritten rule that the content and the intended use of a manuscript influenced the choice of script. In the hierarchy of medieval books, the most valued were the liturgical codices through which a man "spoke to God." For these the scribes usually chose Gothic minuscule in its most calligraphic form, *Gothica textualis formata*. Bibles or other important texts could be written in a simpler type of minuscule, *Gothica textualis libraria*. The lowest—casual—type of minuscule script, *Gothica textualis currens*, was used for a brief period (in the second half of the thirteenth century and the first half of the fourteenth) for less important texts. *Bastarda* (*Gothica bastarda*) was the script for "second-tier" liturgical books (private prayer books such as breviaries or Books of Hours), but also for standard secular texts such as chivalric poems or chronicles. Cursive (*Gothica cursiva*) became the prevailing script for texts intended either for personal use or for a restricted circle of well-educated readers (for example, collections of sermons or scientific treatises—but also for writing personal reader's notes in a manuscript's margins).

The oldest of the three script types is undoubtedly the Gothic minuscule. Just as elsewhere in Europe, the variant of the minuscule written in the medieval kingdom of Hungary was characterized by separately written letterforms, each of which was complexly formed out of several strokes. In addition to the features that were already found in early Gothic script (letters that are horizontally compressed and vertically extended, contributing to the movement toward a consistent treatment of the shafts), are now added double breaking of the vertical strokes, the contrast of thick and thin strokes, and above all the "Meyer-type" of joining of adjacent curved strokes (in the case of two successive letters with bowls, these are often overlapped). The main characteristics of individual letterforms are a complex form of *a* and *g*; long *s* and *f* that do not extend below the writing line; and ascenders that are neither slanted nor looped (the finials are either blunt or forked). As far as regional variants are concerned, the Central European minuscule type was used throughout the kingdom of Hungary. The Southern type (*rotunda*) is found only in the regions of Dalmatia and Croatia and was then in the late fifteenth century adopted in other parts of the kingdom (as a sign of the Renaissance).

The oldest example of well-formed Gothic minuscule is found in the so-called Hungarian Psalter (Wolfenbüttel, Herzog August Bibliothek, Cod. Guelf. Helmst. 52; Plate 29.2), which can be dated after 1255 and before 1261.[18] The form of this script remains stable until the first third of the fourteenth century: the *a* is usually two-tiered with an open upper bowl; in addition to the round *d* typical of Gothic script, the *d* with a straight shaft also occurs; the *ct* ligature, per se, is not used, but if the letters are written consecutively, the shaft of the *t* extends vertically and is often curved to the left; unlike in early Gothic scripts, only the round *s* is used at the end of a word. Representative of this stage of Gothic minuscule are, e.g., the scripts of the now dispersed Bratislava Missal I (Pressburg/Bratislava, Archív mesta Bratislavy, EC Lad. 3, EL 18; Múzeum mesta Bratislavy, A/9; Trnava, Spolok sv. Vojtecha, s.n.), the Bratislava Breviary (Pressburg/Bratislava, Múzeum mesta Bratislavy, A/13), the Processional of Michael of Buda written perhaps 1309–14 in Transylvania (Budapest, OSzK, Clmae 69). A compendium with grammatical and poetic texts (Munich, Bayerische Staatsbibliothek, Clm 9684), which can only be approximately dated to the first half of the fourteenth century, also belongs to this group.[19]

Roughly in the second third of the fourteenth century, changes occur in the local minuscule. The ascenders and descenders become shorter as the emphasis shifts towards the zone between the headline and the baseline. The contrast of thick and thin strokes is more intense, and final letters or free-standing abbreviations are often decorated with hairline strokes. Breaking can already be curved like a flame. In addition to the older

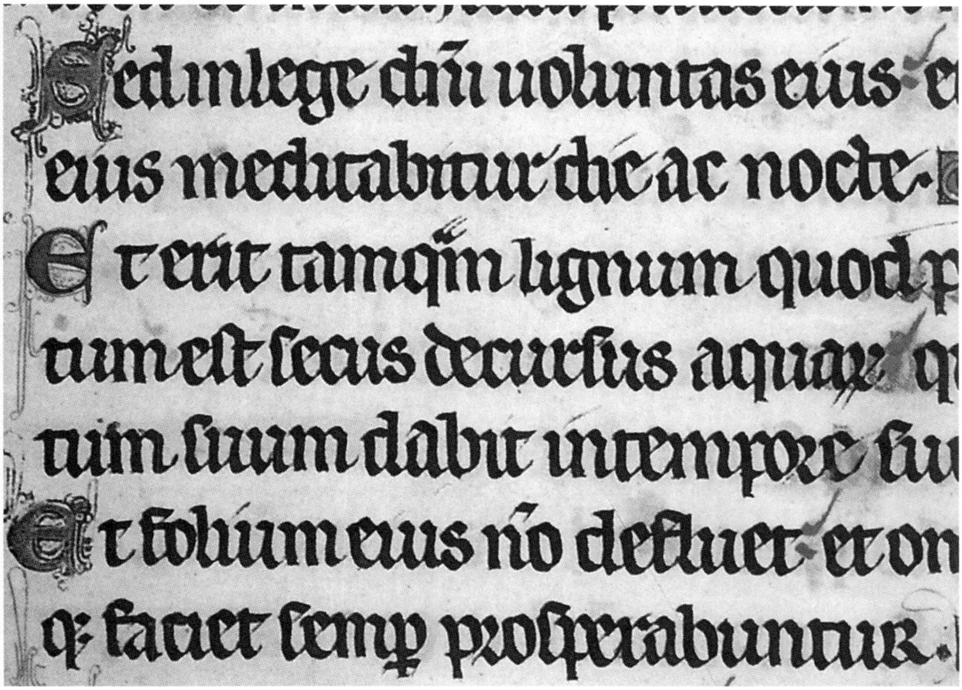

PLATE 29.2 Gothic Minuscule (the so-called Hungarian Psalter, 1255–61, Wolfenbüttel, Herzog August Bibliothek, Cod. Guelf. Helmst. 52, fol. 15r).

form of breaking, we also now find the placement of diamonds on the shafts. There are also new letterforms: the two-tiered *a* usually has a closed upper bowl, only round *d* is found, the hairline stroke over the *i* becomes shorter and rounder, and the *-rum* abbreviation usually has a very complicated form (with embellishment of the second shaft). Examples of this script are found in the Bratislava Missals and the *Missale itinerantium* (Budapest, OszK, Clmae 214, 215, 220, 94, 435). Some of the characteristics of the Demeter Nekcsei Bible (Washington, Library of Congress, MS Pre-Accession 1) appear only a bit older than the Pressburg group. Although Tünde Wehli considers the script and decorations to be the work of the Bologna school, the minuscule has no *rotunda* characteristics and clearly reflects the usual script of Central Europe.[20] One of the latest examples of this script type is the somewhat inconsistent minuscule employed in the longer explicit of Bartolomeus de Sancto Concordio's *Summa casuum conscientiae* (Bratislava, SNA, Kapitulská knižnica 47, fol. 237v) from the year 1386.

A generation before and after 1400 we find box-shaped letters in the local minuscule (this is evident above all in the bowls of *a*, *d*, *g*, *p*, and *u* and also in the square form of *-rum*). The script in the Missal copied by Heinrich from Veľké Tŕnie is a good example (Alba Iulia, Batthyaneum, R II 134) from the year 1377. One also finds box-form letters in the Bratislava Missal VI (Bratislava, Archív mesta Bratislavy, EC Lad. 2/34 and Múzeum mesta Bratislavy A/2) from *c*.1403 (Plate 29.3); more developed forms appear

PLATE 29.3 Gothic Minuscule with typical box-shaped letters *c.*1400 (Bratislava Missal VI, 1403, Archív hl. mesta Bratislavy Lad. 2/34—fragment).

in the Bratislava Missal D (Budapest, OszK, Clmae 216) from the 1420s and in the Bratislava Psalter (Budapest, OSzK, Clmae 128).[21]

The minuscule of the second third of the fifteenth century begins to change once again, as can be seen in the script of the Bratislava Missal E, the Kremnitz City Book, Missal 92 from the Széchényi Library, or the Bratislava Antiphonals I, IIa, and IIb, as well as the Pressburg Missals III, IV, F, G, and I, dating from 1426 to 1488.[22] This minuscule can be characterized as late Gothic and is used in this form until the beginning of the sixteenth century. Breaking often appears in the form of squares placed on the ends of the shafts, the *g* is often open at the bottom even in the calligraphic script, the more modern form of *con-* similar to an Arabic numeral 2 is more common than the older form shaped like an inverted *c*, the Tironian *et* has only a short cross stroke. A new form of *a* is striking with its open upper bowl. The form may have been borrowed from Italy where it occurs as early as the second half of the fourteenth century.

The gradual adoption of a humanistic and Italian aesthetic appears to have been an engine for change, especially in the last third of the fifteenth century. The vernaculars (in the kingdom of Hungary, first German, then later Czech with or without Slovakian influence, as well as Hungarian) were used more often for written communications, and this resulted in the creation of a few special symbols. The cosmopolitan atmosphere of the fifteenth century—with its councils, *devotio moderna*, and European-wide exchange of correspondence between intellectuals—had a globalizing influence, so the development of script in Hungary did not lag behind developments in Germany and

France. On the contrary, the spread of the Renaissance can be dated earlier at the court in Buda and among the highest prelates in Gran—beginning in the 1460s—than in the lands to the north or the west. The ascenders in the local minuscule script from the period around 1500 once again get longer, the straight *d* reappears, and a two-tiered *a* with a large upper bowl is borrowed from the *rotunda*. The minuscule is clearly assimilating characteristics of the Italian *rotunda* and as a result breaking is slowly discarded. One can refer to the process as "de-Gothizing" and regard it as the mirror process to "Gothizing" in the thirteenth century. The Gothic minuscule lost its place especially due to the quick spread of printing, although one still finds it occasionally in handwritten liturgical manuscripts from the second half of the sixteenth century.

Writing in the more formal types of Gothic script was a laborious and time-consuming process, so for manuscripts of less importance or for manuscripts intended for private use, scribes began in the second half of the thirteenth century using a more quickly written form of minuscule (*Gothica textualis currens*). The forms of letters were generally the same as those found in the more calligraphic scripts, but the method of writing them changed: for example, the letter *g* is no longer formed from five or seven strokes, but with only three. In the middle of the fourteenth century, the simple Gothic minuscule was increasingly replaced by the cursive script (especially for manuscripts of basic scientific works or practical theology) and by *bastarda* forms (for small prayer books intended for private use). Simple forms of the minuscule are still found in the script of the Gran Capitulary (Budapest, OSzK, Clmae 408) or the Kaschau Missal A (Budapest, OSzK, Clmae 395)—both written shortly before 1389—and the Bratislava Missal V (Bratislava, SNA, KK s.n.) from the end of the fourteenth century.

From the middle of the thirteenth century, an increase in literacy in the kingdom of Hungary encouraged greater differentiation in the employment of the various Gothic scripts. The search for faster and less elaborate scripts led to experimentation in the second half of the century. As a result some scribes not only gave up the overall form of the Gothic *textualis* (for example by using *textualis currens*), but also began to use simplified letterforms. The new semi-cursive Gothic (*Gothica semicursiva*, end of the thirteenth century–middle of the fourteenth century) stands between minuscule and cursive (Plate 29.4). The mixed script sacrificed basic aesthetic elements of the Gothic style in favor of speed, retaining the majority of the minuscule shapes, but modifying certain letters. For example, *f*, *r*, and long *s* extend beneath the baseline, the letter *a* can be nearly cursive in form, and the ascenders can slant to the right (but they do not have loops). The minuscule used in the Anonymous Chronicle (Budapest, OSzK, Clmae 403), probably written in the last third of the thirteenth century, already reveals a simplification of the overall style: lineation is not always even and the height and spacing of letters fluctuate. The St. Elizabeth Legends (Budapest, OszK, Clmae 40) also have simplified forms: a single-tiered *a*, and tall-*s* and *f* extending beneath the baseline. Even further simplification can be found in the Leuven Codex with the Old Hungarian *Planctus Mariae* from the end of the thirteenth century (Budapest, OSzK, MNY 79); it has a simple, single-tiered *a*, and the tall-*s* and *f* consistently descend below the baseline. The first sermon collection written in Hungary (Alba Iulia, Batthyaneum,

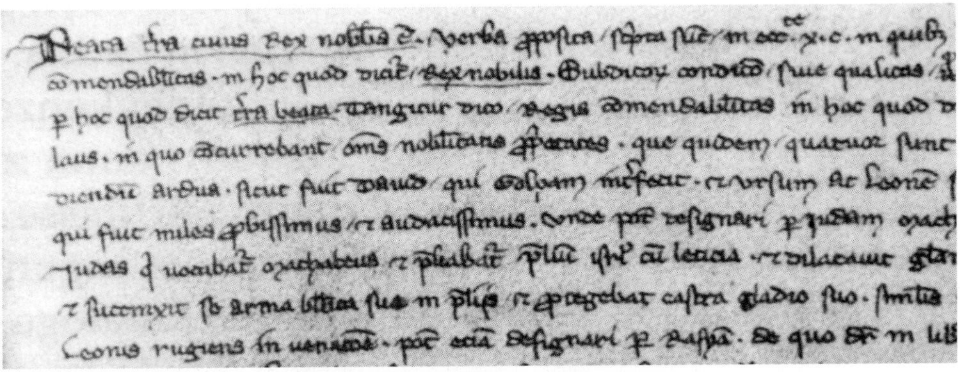

PLATE 29.4 An example of semi-cursive from *c*.1300 (Vienna, Österreichische Nationalbibliothek, Cod. lat. 1062, fol. 110r).

R III 89), which was produced around 1320, reveals clear cursive characteristics in its tendency to join letters to one another.[23]

It is interesting to note that the scribes from Hungary and Slovakia do not use the older form of cursive (the equivalent of Heinemeyer's "Trecento I").[24] By the end of the first third of the fourteenth century, semi-cursive had developed into a quickly written script with an even more simplified *ductus*, namely Gothic cursive (*Gothica cursiva*, second quarter of the fourteenth century until the beginning of the sixteenth). This new script abandoned the aesthetic elements of Gothic minuscule: missing are the consistent organization of the shafts, the breaking, and the complex and carefully constructed letterforms. Instead we find the tendency to connect letters and to write them with fewer strokes; letterforms are relatively round, without any breaking, and with no contrast of thick and thin strokes (which can still be found to some extent in the fourteenth century). The *a* is single-tiered, the *g* has a distinctive loop or is even open at the bottom, tall-*s* and *f* extend below the baseline, the *r* is written without lifting the pen from the writing surface, and there are loops on the ascenders. The mixed script of Alba Iulia, Batthyaneum, R III 89 (*c*.1320) is well on its way to cursive; clearly written in cursive are most of the locally copied sermon manuscripts such as Alba Iulia, Batthyaneum, R I 105.

One can discern a new development in cursive scripts around 1370/1380: the letters *i, m, n,* and *u,* when written in succession, are connected and as a result resemble the teeth of a saw. The loops on ascenders no longer appear in the shape of a sail, but become narrower. Breaking and contrast of thick and thin strokes is abandoned. A good example of this younger cursive is the hand of Johann Rheinensis, who copied Bartolomaeus de San Concordio's *Summa casuum consciencie* (Bratislava, SNA, Kapitulská knižnica 47) for the Provost of Bratislava in 1386 (Plate 29.5).

Further significant changes to the Gothic cursive were made a generation later when the late Gothic cursive developed (Plate 29.6). The general form remained the same, but there is a noticeable bifurcation of the finials on the shafts of some letters, e.g., the *a* can have a form similar to a fork at the top of its shaft, and the bottom of the shaft

PLATE 29.5 Younger Gothic Book Cursive, (1386, *Summa casuum consciencie*, Bratislava, SNA, Kapitulská knižnica 47, fol. 7a).

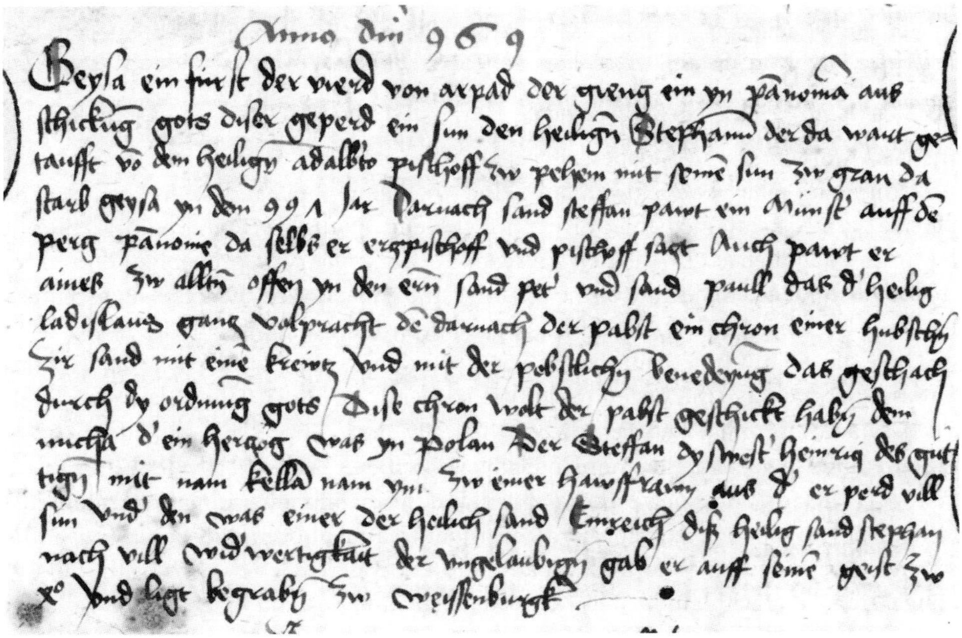

PLATE 29.6 Late Gothic Book Cursive in the *Weltchronik* of Johannes of Utino (1480s, Slovenská národná knižnica—Literárny archív, J 324, fol. 49r).

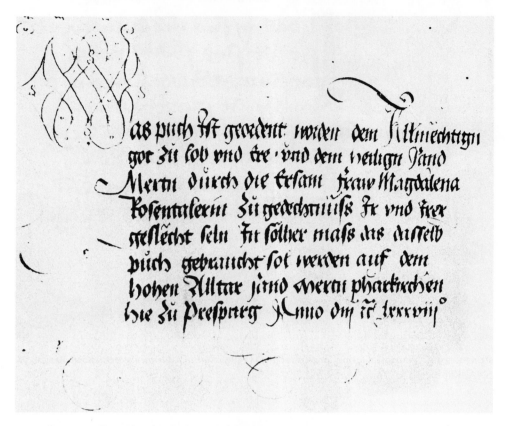

PLATE 29.7 Calligraphic *bastarda* in the dedication of the Bratislava Antiphonary IV (1488, Bratislava, Archív hl. mesta SR Bratislavy, EC Lad. 2, fol. 1v).

of *r* can have a similar form at the bottom of its minim. In the cursive script of the *Gesta Romanorum* (Budapest, Egyetemi Könyvtár Cod. Lat. 25), for example, we find that the *g* has open lower bowl and that loops appear less frequently. The cursive script maintained this form until the end of the fifteenth century when it began to be influenced by the new Humanist script types. It is probably the result of this same influence that some of the cursive scripts abandoned the loops on ascenders (noticeable especially in the last third of the fifteenth century).

There are relatively few fourteenth-century examples of Gothic *bastarda* (*Gothica bastarda*, *c.*1370/80—the beginning of the sixteenth century). This script was developed as a compromise between the aesthetically more impressive, but more slowly written minuscule and the more quickly written, yet aesthetically less impressive cursive (Plate 29.7). The new *bastarda* borrowed the manner of writing from minuscule (a tendency to separate letterforms, a consistent treatment of minims, breaking, and a strong contrast of thick and thin strokes) and the concrete letterforms of the cursive (single-tiered *a*; *g* with an open lower bowl; tall-*s* and *f* descending below the baseline; and occasional loops on the ascenders, although these are not always present).

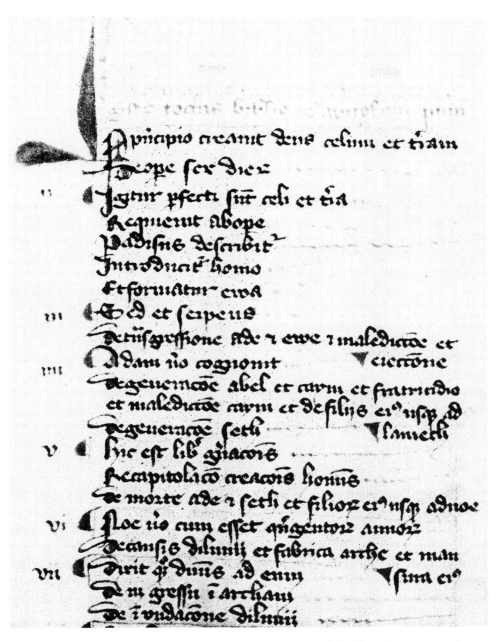

PLATE 29.8 Simple *bastarda* in a biblical register (beginning of the fifteenth century, Budapest, OSzK, Clmae 78, fol. 515r).

Sometimes it can be difficult to distinguish between less calligraphic *bastarda* scripts (Plate 29.8) and more calligraphic cursives. Scribes often employ *bastarda* for vernacular texts.[25] *Bastarda* was used from the last third of the fourteenth century until the beginning of the sixteenth (e.g., in the St. Gerhard Legend, Vienna, ÖNB, Cod. Lat. 3662, and in the sermons of Michael of Hungary, Budapest, OszK, Clmae 336). The script changes very little throughout the period of its use, although a gradual disappearance of loops on ascenders is observable in the second half of the fifteenth century.

Gothic Script in the Diplomatic Field

In the eleventh and twelfth centuries, charters in the kingdom of Hungary were written almost exclusively at important ecclesiastical institutions, although they could also be issued by the king and by certain other members of the elite. The scribes of these documents were more experienced at copying manuscripts than notarial texts. As a result, the establishment of professional chanceries during the thirteenth century is closely tied to the spread of professional notaries and of a proper documentary script.

The adoption of Gothic norms for documents is already observable at the end of the twelfth century. At the beginning of the thirteenth century, most of the important documents of the royal court or of ecclesiastical production were written in Gothic documentary minuscule (in use from the beginning of the thirteenth century until the middle of the fourteenth) (Plate 29.9). The overall appearance of the script is similar to that of the book minuscule: there is breaking of the shafts and curves, and contrast of thick and thin strokes. But the individual letters are not written as close together as in the book script, so there is less attention paid to harmonizing of shafts. As in the book minuscule, in the documentary minuscule, the joining of curved strokes is found (approximately a generation earlier than in the book script). The principal differences, however, are in the concrete letterforms: in the documentary minuscule the ascenders are strikingly long, and they are normally curved to the right (but without loops). The descenders, on the other hand, are variously treated; they often curve to the left. In contrast to the book script, in the documentary minuscule tall-*s* and *f* extend below the baseline. Almost all charters were written in Gothic documentary minuscule in the first third of the thirteenth century; approximately half of them after the middle of the century; but only the most important charters in the fourteenth century. In the second half of the fourteenth century, the documentary minuscule was replaced by documentary *bastarda*.

A rapid increase in documentary literacy took place in Hungary about two generations later (the first half of the thirteenth century) than in the most developed regions of Italy or Western Europe. The increase is closely tied to the implementation of the canon law principle that written witness took precedence over oral witness. The increased need for written documents resulted in the search for a new script that was less demanding and could be used for less important documents. Just as with book scripts, one can observe a period of experimentation in documentary scripts

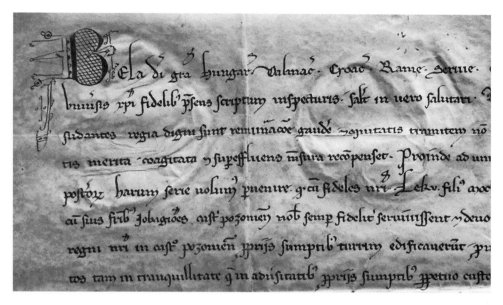

PLATE 29.9 Gothic Documentary Minuscule of the royal Chancery of Bela IV (1245, Bratislava, Archív mesta Bratislavy, Zbierka listín 1).

throughout the thirteenth century. This experimentation resulted in the development of several semi-cursive scripts.

Within the span of a single generation, a Gothic documentary cursive (in use from the first or second third of the thirteenth century until the beginning of the sixteenth) spread through the chanceries of the entire Hungarian kingdom (Plates 29.10–12). In the process of becoming a cursive, this new script type lost the horizontal compression of the book script, and thus the tendency to harmonize the shafts of the letters. The individual letters become shorter and broader, and there is no Meyer-type of joining of bowls. The contrast of thick and thin strokes and the breaking of shafts disappear only c.1370/1380. Until this time there are usually still loops shaped like sails on the ascenders, the letter *a* can be two-tiered, and *g* can be contorted and occasionally is still written with an additional loop far to the left on the lower bowl (attached to the end of the lower horizontal stroke of the lower bowl). From c.1370/1380, the last remnants of a contrast between thick and thin strokes disappear; only a single-tiered *a* is used; the *g* is simple, with a loop or open at the bottom; small loops are found on the ascenders; and, above all, the shafts develop the sawtooth appearance (particularly when the letters *i*, *m*, *n*, and *u* are found in succession). The cursive *r* is distinctive: whereas the minuscule form is clearly comprised of two strokes, the cursive *r* appears to be formed without lifting the quill from the writing surface. The early period of Sigismund of Luxemburg also marks an important breakthrough in Hungary for book and epigraphic scripts. In the realm of palaeography, this breakthrough can be associated with the relatively quick replacement of parchment by paper.

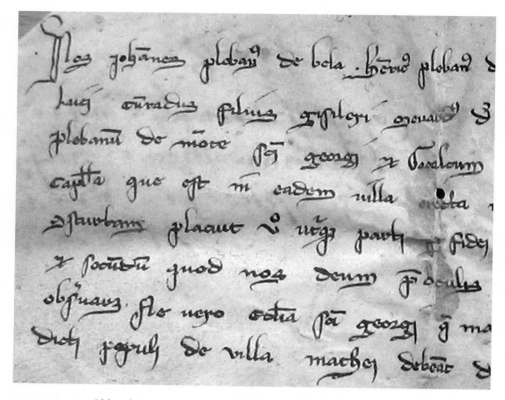

PLATE 29.10 Older documentary cursive from the region of Spiš (1287 Spišská Kapitula, Archív biskupského úradu, arch. fond Hodnoverné miesto Spišská Kapitula, 9-2-10).

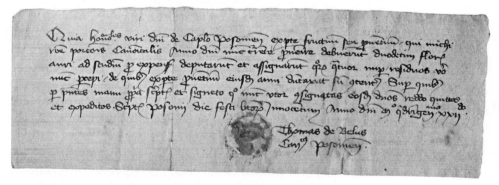

PLATE 29.11 Younger documentary cursive of the Bratislava canon Thomas de Belus (1422, Bratislava, Slovenský národný archív, arch. fond Hodnoverné miesto Bratislavská kapitula, H-3-33).

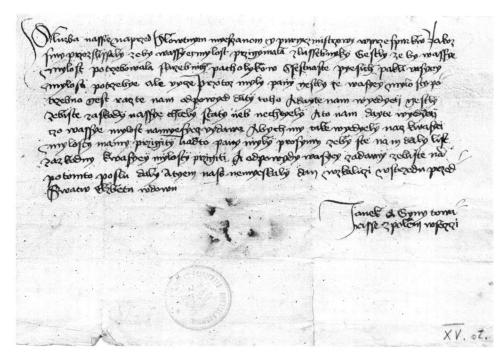

PLATE 29.12 A typical late Gothic documentary cursive in a Czech text for Pressburg/Bratislava (mid-fifteenth century, Bratislava, Archív mesta Bratislavy, Zbierka listín 2588).

In the years after 1430 the same process begins to take place in the documentary cursive as had taken place in book cursives: bifurcation can be observed in the upper part of the shaft on the letters *a* and *r*, sometimes only on the bottom part of the shaft in the letter *r* (a bifurcation of shaft finials). The process is typical for local cursive scripts from the second third of the fifteenth century until the first third of the sixteenth. After this period the shafts are now bifurcated, a characteristic that is typical for the early modern *Kurrentschrift*.

The third documentary script type, the Gothic documentary *bastarda*, is found in local documentary materials after the middle of the fourteenth century. As was the case in manuscripts, this script was often preferred for copying vernacular texts. German documents appear first (in the western part of the kingdom after 1319, in the remainder of the kingdom after 1350) (Plate 29.13); Czech documents follow (in the area of present-day Slovakia after 1430), and Hungarian documents appear last (in the last third of the fifteenth century, above all in the central region of the kingdom and in Transylvania). The *bastarda* form tended to separate individual letterforms, although not consistently (the more calligraphic the style, the more consistently). Just as in neighboring countries, the *bastarda* in Hungary is marked by a single-tiered *a*, the simple *g*, and by loops on the ascenders (though the loops partially disappear in the second half of the fifteenth century).

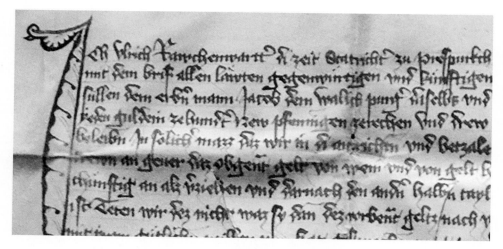

PLATE 29.13 A documentary *bastarda* in a German document from Bratislava (1411, Bratislava, Archív mesta Bratislavy, Zbierka listín 796).

EARLY RENAISSANCE WRITTEN CULTURE IN THE REALM OF KING ST. STEPHAN: HUMANISTIC SCRIPT IN HUNGARY AND SLOVAKIA

For a generation before and after 1500, the culture of the written word in the central Danube area (i.e., the area of present-day Slovakia, Hungary, Western Romania, Croatia, and Slovenia), is characterized by the parallel existence of conservative late Gothic as well as new humanistic elements. Sometimes these even occur within the same text. In the kingdom of Hungary, the early Renaissance spread largely through two channels: the royal court and a few ecclesiastical prelates such as Johannes Vitez and Johannes Pannonius. The spread of classical works, and with these the new Humanistic script, was facilitated both by local intellectuals, who corresponded with Italian humanists, and by universities in neighboring countries (above all those in Vienna and Cracow). Between 1465 and the 1490s there was even a local university in Bratislava (*Universitas Istropolitana*). Nonetheless, the late Gothic scripts still flourished in many regional centers (e.g., in Bratislava until the end of the fifteenth century).[26]

In the late fifteenth and the early sixteenth centuries, new impulses appeared which led to drastic changes in the local script culture. First of all, the printing press began to provide competition for the scribes (the first printed books appeared in Hungary in the 1470s). Secondly, at the end of this period (after 1520), Protestantism—which was closely tied to a culture of vernacular texts and late Gothic and early modern writings—played an important role. Literacy reached a level that would not be surpassed until the second half of the eighteenth century (when general schooling first became compulsory in the Hungarian kingdom). The main reason for the increase in literacy was, no doubt, the cheaper price of books made possible thanks to the printing press. The first printed books entered the region via Italy (mostly from Venice), from Germany (above all from Nuremberg and Strasbourg), and to a lesser degree also from Switzerland.[27]

Hungarian codicologists have been interested primarily in the period between the middle of the fifteenth and the middle of the sixteenth century. The principal thrust of their research has been the early Renaissance at the court of King Matthias Corvinus (1458– 90). Several significant catalogues and dozens of seminal studies have been devoted to this topic.[28] The extant manuscripts and incunables of the former Corvinian Library have been digitized and are accessible online.[29] Recent studies have moved into the next generation; for example, an exemplary catalogue was published with studies devoted to the early sixteenth century.[30] There have also been important modern inventories of incunables: for Hungary, a catalogue of early printing was compiled by Csaba Csapodi and Klára Csapodiné-Gárdonyi; for Slovakia, by Imrich Kotvan and Eva Frimmová.[31] Interestingly, only a few scholars have investigated diplomatic and epigraphic scripts of the period.[32]

Book scripts

The new Humanist script forms affected the late Gothic minuscule. The influence of Humanistic scripts is probably responsible for the lengthening of the ascenders on the local Gothic minuscule letterforms. The earlier emphasis on the middle zone of the line of writing is no longer as pronounced; and, in general, the script has a lighter and rounder appearance. Instead of the earlier exclusive use of round *d*, it becomes more common to employ also the upright *d*, imported from Italy. The *a* with a smaller lower bowl is modeled on the Italian *Rotunda*. This type of minuscule occurs, for example, in the Bratislava Antiphonary III (end of the fifteenth century, AMB, EC Lad. 6; Plate 29.14) and in the Antiphonary of Buda (from the 1510s, Budapest, OSzK, A 23/3). We can call this mixed minuscule from the period around 1500 (*c.*1470–1520) a Gothic-Humanistic minuscule. A certain number of the lavishly decorated manuscripts of Esztergom from the time of Ladislaus von Jagello were written in this script. Manuscripts copied in the late Gothic or Gothic-Humanistic minuscule could not keep pace with the mass production of books printed in *antiqua* or Schwabacher type. Nonetheless, we still find it in the sixteenth century in elaborately produced conservative liturgical manuscripts. The Graduale of the Bratislava Chapter (no. 67) was produced in 1581 and is no doubt one of the latest examples of the script.

Mixed Gothic-Humanistic scripts also appeared in the domain of the cursive and *bastarda* scripts (Plates 29.15 and 29.16). The individual forms remained the same, but

PLATE 29.14 The Italian-influenced minuscule at the end of the Middle Ages (The Bratislava Antiphonary III, *c.*1500, Bratislava, Archív hl. mesta Bratislavy, EC Lad. 6, fol. 135r).

the general impression changed: the mixed scripts appear much lighter, because the letterforms are further separated than in Gothic script; they are also much rounder and written almost without breaking. A beautiful example is the Gothic-Humanistic *bastarda* which Matheus de Stara used for his copy of the *Historia Troiana* in 1475 (Budapest, Egyetemi Könyvtár, Cod. Lat. 71).

The first phase of the development of Humanistic scripts, namely the imitation of the Caroline minuscule, is evident also in the kingdom of Hungary in the second half of the fifteenth century. One of the few examples of this imitation is the manuscript of the *Commentarii in Ciceronis Librum de inventione* (Budapest, OSzK, Clmae 70), which was produced before 1462 in the Transylvanian city of Sibiu. The *i* is not yet dotted, as in Humanistic minuscule (Plate 29.17), but rather finished with a stroke, just as in the post-Caroline minuscule; furthermore, the round *s* has not yet appeared.

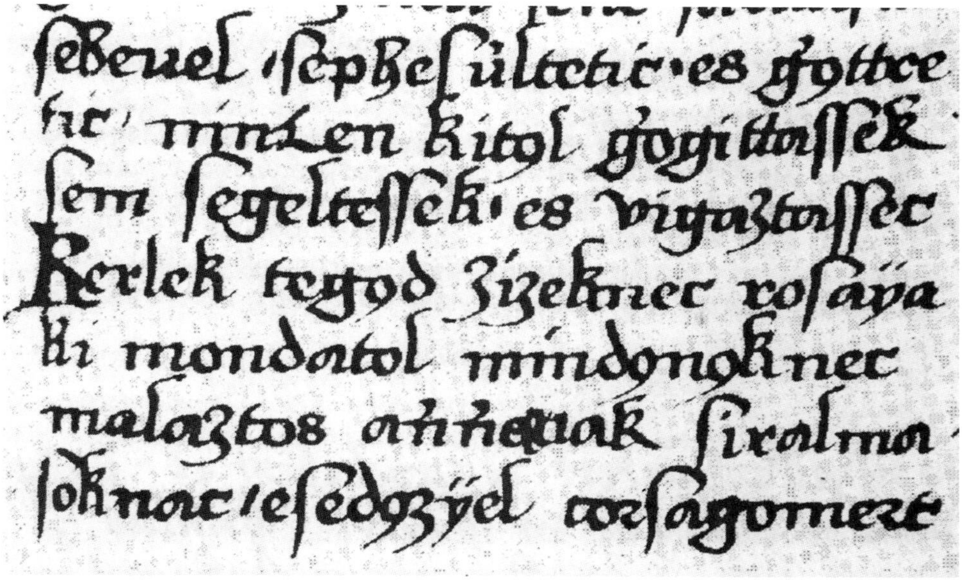

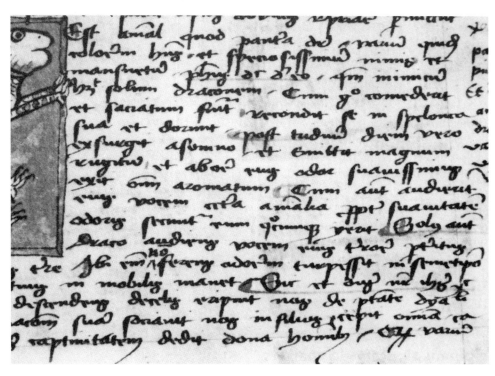

PLATE 29.15 Gothic-Humanistic book *bastarda* (Nádor kódex, 1508, Budapest, Egyetemi Könyvtár, Cod. Hung. 1, pag. 703).

PLATE 29.16 Gothic-Humanistic book cursive (Bestiary, end of the fifteenth century, Budapest, OSzK, Clmae 506, fol. 286r).

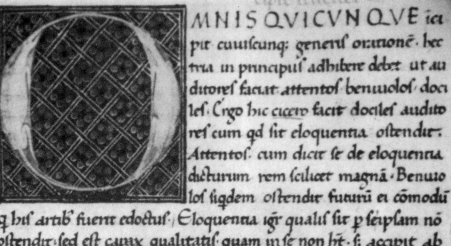

PLATE 29.17 Humanistic minuscule in a manuscript produced in Sibiu before 1462 (Budapest, OSzK, Clmae 379, fol. 1r).

Many manuscripts in developed Humanistic minuscule were produced in Italy for Hungarian patrons, especially for King Matthias Corvinus. There was also an Italian *bodega* at the king's court in Buda between *c.*1470 and 1490 (see, for example, the philosophical texts in Budapest, OSzK, Clmae 422 or the *Aristeas* in Munich, BSB, Clm 341) (Plate 29.18). Other manuscripts copied for Matthias Corvinus were written in Humanistic cursive (as, for example, Wolffenbüttel, Herzog August Bibliothek, Cod. Guelf. 43 Aug. 2°)—all the scribes, however, were Italians. This is also true for the manuscript written by Antonio Surriano, written in Humanistic cursive in the period from 1513–14 in Buda for Corvinus' successor—King Vladislavs Jagello (Budapest, OSzK, Clmae 371). The least calligraphic script type, Humanistic Kurrent, was rarely used in the copying of books; it occurs more commonly in the personal notes of scholars of this period.

Humanistic script in charters

Humanistic charter scripts are first found at the court of the king. Already in the last decade of Matthew Corvinus' reign (1458–90), we find Humanistic capital forms in

PLATE 29.18 *Capitalis* and Humanistic Minuscule (workshop of Buda, 1470–90, Munich, Bayerische Staatsbibliothek, Clm 627, fol. 1r).

PLATE 29.19 Humanistic charter minuscule used in the royal chancery (1494 V 14, Bratislava, SNA, arch. fond HMBK 11-2-24).

PLATE 29.20 *Fraktur* script used in the first line of a charter written at the royal chancery (1496 IV 18, Bratislava, SNA, arch. fond HMBK 12-2-5).

charters. In the chancery of Ladislaus Jagello (1490–1516) capital letters were used in display text for the *intitulatio* formula, and Humanistic minuscule (Plate 29.19) or cursive was used for the text itself. The use of Humanistic forms was, however, reserved for more important charters, often for letters with coat of arms. Most charters were still written in late Gothic cursive. Around 1500, notaries in the provincial chanceries of the *loci credibiles* and in the cities began to use majuscule Humanistic forms only with a few letters (above all with the letter *M*). Complete texts written in Humanistic forms are found only a generation later in the provinces.

In addition to humanistic forms, there are in this period also traces of the development that eventually resulted in *Fraktur* script. Just as with the Humanistic scripts, the first *Fraktur* forms appear in majuscule letters issued by members of the royal chancery or by the king himself (from the 1470s onward) (Plate 29.20). Interestingly, one also finds *Fraktur* majuscule letters in provincial chanceries at almost the very same time.[33]

NOTES

1. On the expansion of vernacular written texts, see Madas (2003, 154–67).
2. The majority of these are accessible through the Portal of the Hungarian Central Archives: http://mol.arcanum.hu/dldf/opt/a091002.htm?v=pdf&a=start, accessed September 1, 2015.
3. On book culture in the kingdom of Hungary, see Madas and Monok ([1999]); also very useful is Vizkelety (1985a). On the situation in the territory of present-day Slovakia, see Kuzmík (1987) and Sopko (1974, 47–80). On illuminated manuscripts Berkovits (1968).

4. e.g. Hajnal (1921), (1943), (1954); Veszprémy (1998), (2000), (2003); Marsina (1974), (1989), (1991).

5. Bartoniek (1940); Mezey (1961); Sopko (1981), (1982), (1986). Also Radó (1973).

6. Hajnal (1921), (1954).

7. Mezey (1983).

8. Buran and Šedivý (2003a, 161–81), (2003b, 513–27); Šedivý (2007c), (2008, 151–640, Šedivý (2009a, 279–89).

9. Veselovská (2002), (2006), (2008), (2011); Adamko, Veselovská, and Šedivý (2008).

10. Eckhart (1915, 395–558); Kumorovitz (1960, 3–38); Kubínyi (1977, 299–324); Lehotská, (1958, 222–74); Marsina (1974), (1989).

11. Hajnal (1921); Jakó (1958); Marsina (1991, 21–35); Šedivý (2007a, 81–115), (2009b, 483–520).

12. Húščava (1951); Mezey (1962); Jakó and Manolescu (1987). See also: Šedivý (2005, 78–97). On the current state of palaeographical research in Hungary, see Veszprémy (2003, 33–51).

13. Šedivý envisions the codicological, diplomatic, and epigraphic aspects of written culture as parts of a single entity.

14. Veszprémy (1998, 222–30).

15. Bischoff, Lieftinck, and Batelli (1953).

16. Veszprémy (1998, 229).

17. Hajnal (1954, Fig. 3).

18. Vizkelety (1985b, 97).

19. Šedivý (2015, 413–30).

20. Wehli (1985, 106).

21. Šedivý (2007c, 110–11, 145–50).

22. Bratislava Missal E (BP, OSzK, Clmae 218); Kremnitz City Book (Kremnica, Štátny archív v Banskej Bystrici—pobočka Kremnica, liber civitatis); Missal 92 (BP, OSzK, Clmae 92); Bratislava Antiphonal I (Bratislava/BA, Archív hl. mesta SR Bratislavy/ AMB, EC Lad. 3); IIa (BA, AMB, EC. Lad. 6) IIb (BA, Slovenský národný archív/SNA, Kapitulská knižnica/KK, no. 4 + AMB, EC Lad. 4) III (BA, AMB, EL13); IV (BA, AMB, EC Lad. 2); F (BP, OSzK, Clmae 222); G (BP, OSzK, Clmae 219); I (Esztergom, Prímasi Könyvtár, MS I. 20).

23. Madas (2003, 154–67) does not use the term "semicursiva." She prefers "*minuscule with cursive elements.*"

24. Heinemeyer (1962).

25. Madas (2003, 154–67).

26. Rusina (2009).

27. Detailed statistics for the Region of Spiš, e.g., in Selecká (1974, 22–6).

28. Csapodi (1973); Csapodi and Csapodiné-Gárdonyi (1976), (1990), Karsay (2002); Milano (2002); Maillard *et al.* (2009).

29. See http://www.corvina.oszk.hu/, accessed January 16, 2020.

30. Réthelyi *et al.* (2005).

31. Csapodi (1988–94); Kotvan(1979); Kotvan and Frimmová (1996)

32. Ludiková (2002); Várady (2002); Šedivý (2007c, 220).

33. Šedivý (2007c, 217–21).

Bibliography

Manuscripts cited

Austria

Graz, Universitätsbibliothek, Codex 211 ("Codex Albensis")
Güssing, Klosterbibliothek, MS I 43
Vienna, ÖNB, Cod. Lat. 2463
Vienna, ÖNB, Cod. Lat. 3662

Germany

Munich, Bayerische Staatsbibliothek, Clm 9684
Munich, Bayerische Staatsbibliothek, Clm 341
Munich, Bayerische Staatsbibliothek, Clm 627
Wolfenbüttel, Herzog August Bibliothek, Cod. 43 Aug. 2°
Wolfenbüttel, Herzog August Bibliothek, Cod. Guelf. Helmst. 52 ("Ungarischer Psalter")

Hungary

Budapest, Egyetemi Könyvtár, Cod. Hung. 1
Budapest, Egyetemi Könyvtár, Cod. Lat. 25
Budapest, Egyetemi Könyvtár, Cod. Lat. 71
Budapest, OSzK, Clmae 17 ("Hartwik Legend")
Budapest, OSzK, Clmae 40
Budapest, OSzK, Clmae 69 ("Prozessionale Michaels von Buda")
Budapest, OSzK, Clmae 70
Budapest, OSzK, Clmae 94 ("Bratislava-Missale H")
Budapest, OSzK, Clmae 128 ("Bratislava psalter")
Budapest, OSzK, Clmae 214 ("Bratislava-Missale A")
Budapest, OSzK, Clmae 215 ("Bratislava-Missale B")
Budapest, OSzK, Clmae 216 ("Bratislava-Missale D")
Budapest, OSzK, Clmae 220 ("Bratislava-Missale C")
Budapest, OSzK, Clmae 336
Budapest, OSzK, Clmae 371
Budapest, OSzK, Clmae 403 ("The Anonymous Chronicle")
Budapest, OSzK, Clmae 422
Budapest, OSzK, Clmae 431 ("Ernst-Codex"),
Budapest, OSzK, Clmae 435 ("Missale itinerantium")
Budapest, OSzK, MNY 79
Esztergom, Erzbischöfliche Bibliothek, Ms. III ("Kommentar zum Hohen Lied")

Romania

Alba Iulia, Batthyaneum, R I 105
Alba Iulia, Batthyaneum, R II 134
Alba Iulia, Batthyaneum, R III 89

Slovakia

Bratislava (Pressburg/Pozsony), Archív mesta Bratislavy, EC Lad. 2/34; Múzeum mesta Bratislavy A/2

Bratislava, Archív mesta Bratislavy, EC Lad. 3, EL 18; Múzeum mesta Bratislavy, A/9; Trnava, Spolok sv. Vojtecha—sine numero ("Bratislava-Missale I")

Bratislava, Múzeum mesta Bratislavy, A/13("Bratislava-Brevier")

Bratislava, SNA, Kapitulská knižnica 47

Bratislava, SNA, Kapitulská knižnica 67

USA

Washington, Library of Congress, MS Pre-Accession 1 ("Demeter Nekcsei Bibel")

Secondary Sources

Adamko, R., E. Veselovská, and J. Šedivý. 2008. *Spišský antifonár* [The Antiphonary of Spiš]. Ružomberok: Katolícka univerzita.

Bartoniek, E. 1940. *Codices latini medii aevi. Codices manu scripti latini I.* Budapest: Országos Széchényi Könyvtár.

Berkovits, I. 1968. *Illuminierte Handschriften aus Ungarn vom 11.–16. Jahrhundert.* Hanau: Dausein.

Bischoff, B., G. I. Lieftinck, and G. Batelli. 1953. *Nomenclature des écritures livresques du IX. au XVI. siécle.* Paris: CIPL.

Buran, D. and J. Šedivý. 2003a. "Písmo a knižné maliarstvo: objednávatelia, umelci a adresáti" ["Writing and Illumination: Sponsors, Artists and Recipients"]. In *Gotika. Dejiny slovenského výtvarného umenia,* ed. Dušan Buran, 161–81. Bratislava: Slovart.

Buran, D. and J. Šedivý. 2003b. "Listiny a knižné maliarstvo na sklonku stredoveku" ["Illumination of Charters and Books at the End of the Middle Ages"]. In *Gotika. Dejiny slovenského výtvarného umenia,* ed. Dušan Buran, 513–27. Bratislava: Slovart.

Csapodi, C. 1973. *The Corvinian Library. History and Stock,* Budapest: Centre for Renaissance Research.

Csapodi, C. 1988–94. *Bibliotheca Hungarica. Kódexek és nyomtatott könyvek Magyarországon 1526 előtt* ["Bibliotheca Hungarica. Manuscripts and Printed Books in the Kingdom of Hungary before 1526"]. Vols. I–III. Budapest: Magyar Tudományos Akadémia.

Csapodi, C. and K. Csapodiné-Gárdonyi, eds. 1976. *Bibliotheca Corviniana.* Budapest: OSzK.

Csapodi, C. and K. Csapodiné-Gárdonyi, eds. 1990. *Bibliotheca Corviniana 1490–1990.* Nemzetközi corvinakiállítás az Országos Széchényi Könyvtárban Mátyás király halálának 500. évfordulójára 1990. április 6.–október 6. Budapest: OSzK.

Debae, M. 1987. *La Librairie de Marguerite d'Autriche. Europalia Österreich.* Brussels: Bibliotheque royale Albert Ier.

Eckhart, F. 1915. "Die glaubwürdigen Orte Ungarns im Mittelalter." *Mitteilungen des* Instituts für Österreichische Geschichtsforschung. Ergänzungsband 9: 395–558.

Engel, P., P. Lővei, and L. Varga. 1981. "A tornagörgői, egy bazini és egy ismeretlen helyről származó sírkőről" ["About Tombstones from Hrhov, Pezinok, etc.]. *Műveszettörténeti Értesítő* 30: 255–9.

Fabian, C. and E. Zsupán. 2008. *Ex Bibliotheca Corviniana. Die acht Münchener Handschriften aus dem Besitz von König Matthias Corvinus.* Budapest: OSzK.

Hajnal, I. 1921. *Írástörténet az írásbeliség felujulása korából* ["History of Writing since the Restoration of Writing (in Hungary)"]. Budapest: Budavári Tudományos Társaság.

Hajnal, I. 1943. *Vergleichende Schriftproben zur Entwicklung und Verbreitung der Schrift im 12. und 13. Jh.* Budapest, Leipzig, and Milan: Danubia.

Hajnal, I. 1954. *L'Enseignement de l'écriture aux universités médievales.* Budapest: Maison d'édition de l'Académie des Sciences de Hongrie [2nd ed., 1959].

Heinemeyer, W. 1962. *Studien zur Geschichte der gotischen Schrift.* Münster and Cologne: Böhlau Verlag.

Húščava, A. 1951. *Dejiny a vývoj nášho písma.* Bratislava: SAVU.

István, Pusztai, ed. 1994. *Nádor-kódex 1508. A nyelvemlék hasonmása és betűhű átirata,* közzéteszi Pusztai István, bevezetés Pusztai István és Madas Edit. Budapest: OSzK, 1994.

Jakó, Z. 1958. *Az oklevélirások fejlödése Erdélyben a XII–XV században* ["Writing Charters in Transylvania, XIIth–XVth Centuries"] Budapest: Levéltári Híradó.

Jakó, Z. and R. Manolescu. 1987. *A latin írás története* ["History of Latin Writing"]. Budapest: Európa Könyvkiadó.

Karsay, O., ed. 2002. *Uralkodók és corvinák/Potentates and Corvinas. Az Országos Széchényi Könyvtár jubileumi kiállítása alapításának 200. évfordulóján/ Anniversary Exhibition of the National Széchényi Library.* Budapest: OSzK.

Kotvan, I. 1979. *Inkunábuly na Slovensku* ["Incunabula in Slovakia"]. Martin: Matica slovenská.

Kotvan, I. and E. Frimmová. 1996. *Inkunábuly zo slovenských knižníc v zahraničných inštitúciách* ["Incunabula from Slovak Libraries in Foreign Institutions"]. Martin: Matica slovenská.

Kubínyi, A. 1977. "Königliche Hofkanzlei und Hofkapelle in Ungarn um die Mitte des 12. Jahrhunderts." In *Friedrich Hausmann. Festschrift,* ed. Herwig Ebner, 299–324. Graz: Akademische Druck- und Verlagsanstalt.

Kumorovitz, L. B. 1960. "Die erste Epoche der ungarischen privatrechtlichen Schriftlichkeit im Mittelalter (XI–XII. Jahrhundert)." *Studia Historica Academiae Scientiarum Hungaricae* 21: 3–38.

Kuzmík, J. 1987. *Knižná kultúra na Slovensku v stredoveku a renesancii* ["Book Culture in Slovakia in the Middle Ages and Renaissance"]. Martin: SNK.

Lehotská, D. 1958. "Vývoj bratislavskej mestskej kancelárie do roku 1526" ["Development of the City Chancery in Bratislava"]. *Historické štúdie* 4: 222–74.

Lővei, P. 1996. "Mittelalterliche Grabplatten und Grabsteine in Pannonhalma." *Acta Historiae Artis Hungariae* 38: 89–96.

Ludiková, Z. 2002. "Niekoľko príkladov náhrobných pamiatok humanistov zo západného Slovenska (Tumba Ladislava Kubínskeho)" ["Some Examples of Sepulchral Monuments of Humanists from Western Slovakia"]. *Ročenka Slovenskej národnej galérie–Galéria:* 123–36.

Madas, E. 2003. "Die Entwicklung der Buchkursive in Ungarn im Spiegel der Predigthandschriften vom Ende des 13. bis zum Anfang des 16. Jahrhunderts." In *The History of Written Culture in the "Carpatho-Danubian" Region I,* ed. H. Pátková, P. Spunar, and J. Šedivý, 154–67. Prague and Bratislava: Chronos.

Madas, E. 2009. *"Látjátok feleim . . . ": Magyar nyelvemlékek a kezdetektől a 16. század elejéig* ["You see, my fellows . . . " The Text Monuments in the Hungarian Language from Beginnings to the Beginning of the 16th Century]. Budapest: Országos Széchenyi Könyvtár.

Madas, E. and I. Monok. [1999]. *A könyvkultúra Magyarországon. A kezdetektől 1730-ig* ["Book Culture in Hungary. From the Beginnings up to 1730"]. Budapest: Balassi Kiadó [2nd edition 2003].

Maillard, J.-F. *et al.*, eds. 2009. *Matthias Corvin, Les Bibliothèques princières et la genèse de l´état moderne,* Budapest: OSzK.

Marsina, R. 1974. *Štúdie k slovenskému diplomatáru* ["Studies of the Slovak Diplomatarium"] I. *Historické štúdie*, no. 16. Bratislava: SAV.

Marsina, R. 1989. *Štúdie k slovenskému diplomatáru* ["Studies of the Slovak Diplomatarium"] II. Bratislava: Veda.

Marsina, R. 1991. "Vývoj listinného písma v stredoveku na Slovensku" ["Development of Documentary Script in Slovakia"]. *Slovenská archivistika* 26: 21–35.

Mezey, L. 1961. *Codices latini medii aevi Bibliothecae Universitatis Budapestinensis*. Budapest: Akadémia Kiadó.

Mezey, L. 1962. *Paleográfia. A latin írás története* ["Palaeography. History of Latin Writing"]. Budapest: ELTE.

Mezey, L. 1983. *Fragmenta latina codicum in Bibliotheca Universitatis Budapestinensis*. Budapest: OSzK.

Milano, E. 2002. *Nel segno del Corvo. Libri e miniature della biblioteca di Mattia Corvino re d'Ungheria (1443–1490)*, Modena: Bibliotheca Estense Universitaria.

Radó, P. 1973. *Libri liturgici manuscripti bibliothecarum Hungariae et limitropharum regionum*. Budapest: MTA.

Réthelyi, O., et al., eds. 2005. *Mary of Hungary, The Queen and Her Court 1521–1531*. Budapest: Budapest History Museum.

Rusina, I., ed. 2009. *Renesancia. Umenie medzi neskorou gotikou a barokom.* ["The Renaissance. Art between the late Gothic and Baroque"]. Bratislava: SNG a Slovart.

Šedivý, J. 2002. "Vývoj gotického písma na príklade bratislavských misálov z Krajinskej Séčéniho knižnice" ["The Development of Gothic Writing: The Missalia from Bratislava, Today in the Széchényi Library"]. Zborník Filozofickej fakulty Univerzity Komenského–Historica 45: 187–95.

Šedivý, J. 2005. "Stredoveká latinská paleografia vo 'východnej' Európe a medzinárodná paleografická spolupráca" ["Mediaeval Latin Palaeography in 'East' Europe and International Palaeographic Cooperation"]. *Slovenská archivistika* 38: 78–97.

Šedivý, J. 2007a. "Die Anfänge der Beurkundung im mittelalterlichen Pressburg (Bratislava)." In *Wege zur Urkunde, Wege der Urkunde, Wege der Forschung*, ed. Karel Hruza and Paul Herold, 81–115. Vienna: Böhlau.

Šedivý, J. 2007b. "Epigrafické písma z územia Slovenska medzi neskorou gotikou a renesanciou" ["Epigraphic Scripts from the Slovak Territory between Late Gothic and Renaissance"]. *Zborník FF UK–Historica* 47: 7–26.

Šedivý, J. 2007c. *Mittelalterliche Schriftkultur im Pressburger Kollegiatkapitel*. Bratislava: Chronos.

Šedivý, J. 2007d. "Stredoveké uhorské pečate a ich písmo. K datovaniu pečatí analýzou písma" ["Medieval Seals from Hungary and Their Script. Dating with Help of Epigraphic Analysis]. In *Pečate a ich používatelia*, ed. J. Ragačová, 129–45. Bratislava: Archívna správa.

Šedivý, J. 2008. "Italienische Einflüsse im Grenzgebiet des mittelalterlichen Ungarn. Gedanken über einige gotische Handschriften aus Bratislava (Slowakei)." In *Régionalisme et internationalisme. Problèmes de paléographie et de codicologie du Moyen Âge*, ed. Otto Kresten and Christian Lackner, 151–64. Vienna: Verlag der ÖAW.

Šedivý, J. 2009a. "Gotische Minuskel in Handschriften aus dem Königreich Ungarn." In *Magistrae discipuli: tanulmányok Madas Edit tiszteletére*, 279–89. Budapest: Argumentum.

Šedivý, J. 2009b. "Stredoveká písomná kultúra na Spiši" [Medieval Written Culture in the Spiš Region]. In *Historia Scepusii I*, ed. Martin Homza and Stanisław A. Sroka, 483–520. Bratislava and Cracow: Comenius University.

Šedivý, J. 2015. "Handschriftenproduktion im mittelalterlichen Pressburg/Bratislava. Gab es dort ein Scriptorium?" In *Scriptorium. Wesen—Funktion—Eigenheiten.* Comité international de Paléographie latine, XVIII. Internationaler Kongress St. Gallen 11.–14. September 2013. ed. Andreas Nievergelt *et al.*, 413–30. Munich.

Šedivý, J. and H. Pátková. 2008. *Vocabularium parvum scripturae latinae.* Bratislava: Published by authors.

Selecká, E. 1974. *Stredoveká levočská knižnica* ["Medieval Library from Levoča]. Martin: Matica slovenská [also published in Hungarian: *A középkori Lőcsei könyvtár.* Szeged: Scriptum, 1997].

Sopko, J. 1974. "Die Kodexliteratur aus der Slowakei des Mittelalters." *Zborník FF UK Graeco-orientalia* 6: 47–80.

Sopko, J. 1981. *Stredoveké latinské kódexy v slovenských knižniciach* ["Medieval Latin Manuscripts in Slovak Libraries"]. Martin: SNK.

Sopko, J. 1982. *Stredoveké latinské kódexy slovenskej proveniencie v Maďarsku a Rumunsku* ["Medieval Latin Manuscripts of Slovak Provenance in Hungary and Romania"]. Martin: SNK.

Sopko, J. 1986. *Kódexy a neúplne zachované rukopisy v slovenských knižniciach* ["Manuscripts and Fragments in Slovak Libraries"]. Martin: SNK.

Várady, Zoltán. 1999. *Gótikus minuscula feliratok a Dunántúlon* ["Inscriptions in Gothic Minuscule from the Transdanubia Region"]. Szekszárd: IPF kiskönyvtár.

Várady, Zoltán. 2000. *Románkori, korai gótikus és gótikus maiuscula feliratok a Dunántúlon* ["Inscriptions of the Romanesque and (early) Gothic Periods in Gothic Majuscule from the Transdanubia Region"]. Szekszárd: IPF kiskönyvtár.

Várady, Zoltán. *Humanista capitalis feliratok a Dunántúlon* ["Inscriptions in Humanistic *Capitalis* from the Transdanubia Region"]. Szekszárd: IPF kiskönyvtár.

Veselovská, E. 2002. *Mittelalterliche liturgische Kodizes mit Notation in den Archivbeständen von Bratislava.* Bratislava: Slovenské národné múzeum–Hudobné múzeum.

Veselovská, E. 2006. *Mittelalterliche liturgische Kodizes mit Notation in den Archivbeständen von Bratislava II.* Bratislava: Ústav hudobnej vedy SAV.

Veselovská, E. 2008. *Catalogus fragmentorum cum notis musicis medii aevi e civitatibus Modra et Sanctus Georgius.* Bratislava: Ústav hudobnej vedy SAV.

Veselovská, E. 2011. *Catalogus fragmentorum cum notis musicis medii aevi e civitate Schemnitziensi.* Bratislava: Ústav hudobnej vedy SAV.

Veszprémy, L. 1998. "A 12. századi Magyar kódexírás alakulása" ["The Origins of Book Writing in 12th-Century Hungary"]. *Századok* 132: 222–30.

Veszprémy, L. 2000. "On the Margins of Book and Charter Paleography. The Dating of Some Hungarian Manuscripts from the Eleventh to the Thirteenth Century." In *Dating Undated Medieval Charters,* ed. M. Gervers, 193–205. Woodbridge: Boydell and Brewer.

Veszprémy, L. 2003. "Zum Stand der paläographischen Forschung in Ungarn." In *The History of Written Culture in the "Carpatho-Danubian" Region 1,* ed. H. Pátková, P. Spunar, and J. Šedivý, 33–51. Bratislava and Prague: Chronos.

Vizkelety, A., ed. 1985a. *Kódexek a középkori Magyarországon* ["Manuscripts in Mediaeval Hungary"]. Budapest: OSZ.

Vizkelety, A. 1985b. "Magyarországi Psalterium." In *Kódexek a középkori Magyarországon* ["Manuscripts in mediaeval Hungary"], ed. A. Vizkelety, 97. Budapest: OSzK.

Wehli, T. 1985. "Nekcsei Demeter Biblája." In *Kódexek a középkori Magyarországon* ["Manuscripts in Mediaeval Hungary"], ed. A. Vizkelety, 106. Budapest: OSzK.

CHAPTER 30

··

EARLY PRINTING AND
PALAEOGRAPHY

··

PAUL NEEDHAM

In Mainz in the early 1450s the inventor of European typography, Johann Gutenberg, had no reason to create printed books different in appearance, whether by lettering or layout, from the books familiar to German readers of the mid-fifteenth century, that is, from manuscript books typically written in Gothic script of varying degrees of formality. In the first years of printing, therefore, each newly made printing font was comprised of a wide range of metal types, each character responding to a specific convention or requirement of high-quality Gothic writing. The challenge of creating, in metal, types that adequately model the subtle pen strokes of well-trained scribes is revealed strikingly in perhaps the earliest surviving fragment of typographic printing, a portion of a single leaf of a Middle High German verse text, the *Sibyllenbuch*, printed in Gutenberg's shop in Mainz in the early 1450s. The *Sibyllenbuch* fragment is valuable precisely because its typographic execution falls so short of the goal it was trying to attain. In particular, this first printing font, commonly known as the DK (Donatus-and-Kalendar) type, attempted to obey the letter-combination conventions of high-grade *Textualis* that palaeographers think of as the "Meyer rules" and the "elision rule." The majority of the font's minuscule characters were designed and cast in two forms, a primary form with whatever thorns and spurs were part of the left side of the character, and an "abutting" form, with smooth left sides, which the compositors would set when the preceding letter had a rightward projection (*c, e, f, g, r, t, x*). Thus, by selecting the appropriate types for the context, the compositors in principle could produce the same result that a trained scribe would achieve by penwork: the maintenance of an even rhythm of vertical strokes across the long line of text. In the earliest state of the DK font the rhythm was further maintained by casting certain letter combinations, *ff, pp*, long *ss*, and long *s + t*, as digraphs, with two characters on a single piece of type. The rule of fusion of the right stroke of *d* with the left stroke of *o* or *e* was achieved by a makeshift solution: a selection of the *d* types were heavily filed on their right side, so that the *o* and *e* types sat directly against them, their left strokes serving at the same time as the missing right strokes of the *d*s.

In the *Sibyllenbuch* fragment, the typography is undisguisedly crude. Letter by letter, the typesetting closely follows the Gothic rules, and yet the result is very irregular. The letters do not keep to an even baseline, and various of them are skewed from the vertical. Many letters do not print cleanly. Similar irregularities appear in scattered vellum fragments of the *Ars minor* of Donatus printed with the DK type. To judge only from these early fragments, one might suspect that typographic printing would have been seen by critical eyes of the time as intrinsically an unsatisfactory substitute for the work of trained scribes. Yet it is doubtful if early readers held this opinion. The *Sibyllenbuch* leaf is hand-rubricated, indicating that the pamphlet from which it derives had been a completed work, fully finished for reading. Presumably many dozens of other now entirely lost copies were likewise marketed successfully. The argument holds even more strongly for the Donatuses printed in the DK type. The various surviving fragments can be shown to belong to numerous different editions, and these fragments too are remnants of fully rubricated copies. Thus, we can say with confidence that schoolmasters in the region around Mainz were satisfied to buy copies of the printed *Donatus*, and that when one edition was sold out, Gutenberg found it worth his while to print another edition, and then another, in response to this continuing market. There is no point in the history of early printing where we find evidence that readers were resistant to printed texts because of a preference for written versions.

Experimentation with printing processes continued intensively in Mainz in the mid- to late 1450s, and within a few years great improvements in the typemaking and printing process were achieved. Two technological milestones, one reflected in a small printing job, the other in a major enterprise, were reached in the fall of 1454. The former is a printed broadside indulgence issued for the defense of the island of Cyprus from Ottoman attack. The indulgence itself was promulgated in 1453 by Pope Nicholas V. In the fall of 1454 papal commissaries in Germany must have seen the advantage of having in hand a supply of indulgence forms preprinted by Gutenberg's new process, rather than having to write out the forms one by one as each purchaser came forward. This printed indulgence, commonly called the 31-line Indulgence, survives in 50 copies, a remarkably large number for an intrinsically ephemeral item and one that implies a very substantial print run. Some 21 titling words of the indulgence are printed with the DK type, while the text proper is printed with a much smaller type, unique to this indulgence. The three paragraphs are begun with metalcut initials closely based on documentary penwork initials. In contrast to the *Sibyllenbuch* and early Donatus fragments, the DK-type printing of the indulgence is extremely sharp, regular, and clean. By measures invisible to us, great improvements in typemaking had been achieved. The text type of the 31-line Indulgence is likewise notably sharp and clean, and even elegant in its design. Palaeographically, it corres- ponds to what Albert Derolez (2003, 118) has distinguished as *Semi-textualis*, with "single-compartment *a*, all other features being those of Textualis." This suggests an Italian influence that may have been transmitted with the text of the indulgence itself, but the type also shows elements more characteristic of German Gothic script, such as Tironian *et* with a cross-stroke, and bifurcation of the ascenders of *b* and *l*. Overall, the

31-line Indulgence is an exceptionally successful piece of printing. There are about 20 known manuscript copies of the same indulgence, but these are mostly rapidly written in cursive hands on unruled lines. The printed 31-line Indulgence form would undoubtedly have been seen as the physically superior record.

The massive printing enterprise likewise underway in Mainz in the fall of 1454 was the production of a two-column, large-format Vulgate Bible in an edition of approximately 180 copies which could be purchased either on vellum or on paper. Today this is commonly known as the Gutenberg Bible, but it is best seen as the joint production of Johann Gutenberg and a well-off Mainz citizen, Johann Fust, whose funding would have supported a significant staff of workers. The Bible was probably completed in 1455; yet a letter written by the humanist Aeneas Sylvius reveals that sample gatherings of the forthcoming work were exhibited in late 1454 at nearby Frankfurt am Main during the time of an Imperial diet, and then again a few months later at Wiener Neustatt. Palaeographically, the significant aspect of the Gutenberg Bible is that its type, *Textualis formata* (*Quadrata*) like the DK type, is in every way an improvement on the latter; the "knitting" of letters is now close and precise. The distinguishing feature of the font is the great number of digraphs, particularly those that fuse vowels with preceding "round" consonants: not just *da*, *de*, and *do*, but also similar series based on *b*, *h*, *p*, and *v*. In essence, the font follows the "Meyer rule" of fusion even to an exaggerated degree. In all, the Gutenberg Bible font contained about 270 distinct characters (sorts). Similarly to the 31-line Indulgence, one can argue that the Gutenberg Bible was a book superior in precision, sharpness, and blackness of letterforms, to what almost any scribe could produce. This is suggested by Aeneas Sylvius' report, which is highly enthusiastic. There is no trace of the disdain that an eminent Italian humanist might be expected to feel for a German literary product.

In early 1455, another Mainz printed work appeared that is of considerable palaeographical significance: a broadside reprint of the Cyprus indulgence, now set to 30 lines. The typographical materials are all different from those of the 31-line Indulgence from which it was copied. The titling words are set with the Gutenberg Bible font, the text proper with a small font different in every character from the 31-line Indulgence font (and again, unique to this indulgence), and with different cast-metal initials. Almost all recorded copies of the 31-line Indulgence were sold within the sprawling archdiocese of Mainz, whereas most copies of the 30-line Indulgence were sold within the archdiocese of Cologne, four within the city of Cologne. It can hardly be a coincidence that the text font of the 30-line Indulgence corresponds precisely to the script that Gerard Lieftinck (1954) called (Netherlandish) *Hybrida*, a script whose origin and widest dissemination was within this region. Through some channel the papal commissaries must have been aware of the appropriateness of this script for the intended market, and have ordered a font of type that corresponded to it.

In the second half of the 1450s the business partnership of Gutenberg and Fust broke up. Fust set up another printing shop together with Peter Schöffer, who is recorded as an accomplished scribe. Their first major projects were large-format Psalters of 1457 and 1459, printed with magnificent *Quadrata* fonts and with two-part initials (a letter plate and a surrounding filigree plate) printed in two colors that substituted for the hand-finishing that would ordinarily have been supplied by individually hired rubricators. After this, large-size *Quadrata* fonts stopped being made in Mainz. Gutenberg apparently sold his DK type to a printer in Bamberg, and both he, at the so-called Catholicon Press, and Fust and Schöffer made new, smaller fonts heavily influenced by Italian *Rotunda* script. Printing spread and expanded relatively gradually in the 1460s, to Strasbourg, Bamberg (where no new types were made), Cologne, Eltville near Mainz (briefly, with types from Mainz), Augsburg (where the first font was again an Italian *Rotunda*), and Vienna (perhaps); to an unidentified north Italian town, briefly to the monastery of Subiaco (where a Roman font was used), and then to Rome (where both Roman and *Rotunda* fonts were made). In the late 1460s and early 1470s the tempo of the printed-book trade increased considerably, printing was introduced to many towns in Italy, France, the Low Countries, and Spain, and a large number of new fonts were created. During the same years Venice grew to special prominence as a printing town, and no other city marketed its printed wares so broadly across all of Europe.

Scholarly study of early printing fonts has proceeded more or less independently of the world of palaeographers, partly because until recent decades the study of late medieval palaeography itself was a neglected field of study. Nevertheless, a palaeographical method has played a powerful role in the study of the earliest Mainz fonts, beginning in the 1890s with the work of Karl Dziatzko, librarian of Göttingen University. Dziatzko studied and compared the DK and Gutenberg Bible fonts, character by character, by a method that corresponds closely with the palaeographer's study of scripts. He determined for each character the rules that compositors were to follow in selecting it rather than some other character, and in so doing arrived at the "Meyer rules" of Gothic writing seven years before Meyer published them. Put another way, Dziatzko's result was to show that the early compositors followed particular selection rules for combining types, and these rules corresponded to scribal practice. He saw deeply enough into the nature of the DK type to point out that it ought to have had a *b* with a spur on its shaft, although no example was known to him. Later, as other fragmentary examples of DK printing came to light, such a *b* was indeed found.

Dziatzko and other early investigators were especially puzzled by a seemingly bizarre *a*-form that showed up sporadically in early DK printing: what is now known as box-*a*. Incunabulists treated it as an unorthodox and unsuccessful "trial" letter that disturbed the success of the font. In fact, it is a letterform with a long history in Gothic handwriting and so found a natural place when the first European printing font was designed. Yet the puzzlement of early incunabulists is easy to understand, for it was only in the 1970s and after that palaeographers began to give close attention to this letterform. Other palaeographically derived features of the early fonts help us to understand better the original purposes for which the fonts were made. For example, both the DK and Gutenberg Bible fonts contain designated abbreviation characters representing the demonstrative pronouns *hic*, *haec* and *hoc*. These respond specifically to the text of the frequently printed *Ars minor* of Donatus, dozens of whose paradigms used the three pronouns as indicators of the three genders of Latin. And indeed, the Gutenberg Bible font was used like the DK type for printing numerous, now fragmentary editions of Donatus, including several which were almost certainly marketed before the Gutenberg Bible itself.

The goal of incunabulists has been more pragmatic: the accurate identification of all the fonts used in the fifteenth-century printing shops. The four "founding fathers" in this area, each successively enlarging the scope of the task, were J. W. Holtrop (1806–70), Henry Bradshaw (1831–86), Robert Proctor (1868–1903), and Konrad Haebler (1857–1946). Type identification has provided the fundamental tool for the correct assignment to cities and shops of the large quantity of early printed books that lack colophons identifying printer and date; or, in some cases, that have colophons misstating the printer, city, or date, either intentionally or by careless direct copying of some other printed edition. In the simplest case, a printer may possess a very distinctive font, used both in one or more editions with colophons providing his name and in one or more editions lacking his name. Their common type font brings them together to a single workplace. At this level of detail, the palaeographical background of the fonts becomes a matter of minor concern. Thus, in most of the literature on early printing, fonts are typically classed only as either Gothic or Roman, with a relatively small additional category, *Bastarda*. Yet, as noted, even in the earliest years of typemaking in Mainz, distinct fonts were made that palaeographers would specify more closely, and the palaeographical subdivisions relate intimately to the uses or markets the types were meant to serve: *Quadrata*, *Rotunda*, Netherlandish *Hybrida*. Fonts that can be classed as Netherlandish *Hybrida* were subsequently used in printing shops in Cologne, Brussels, Ghent, and Louvain.

The most revealing palaeographical distinction to be made in the incunabulists' "Gothic" is between *Quadrata* and *Rotunda*. Only a relative handful of fonts, including the mentioned Netherlandish *Hybrida*, do not fit comfortably in one or the other class. When typographic "Gothic" is so broken down, a significant difference becomes clear. On the one hand, the Italian printers (including, that is, the large numbers of German printers who brought their trade to Italy) had no need at all for *Quadrata* fonts: all early printing fonts used in Italy can be classed as either Roman or *Rotunda*. On the other hand, *Rotunda* fonts based historically on Italian Gothic writing spread widely to all regions of Europe with the exception of the northern Netherlands. The broad reception of the script style began before printing, especially via the large numbers of German students who studied law in northern Italian universities and became thoroughly familiar with the "littera Bononiensis." With printing, *Rotunda* became an international style, and the process began in Mainz years before the printing technology itself had migrated to Italy. When turned into types, the "Bologna letter" became even more widely known as the "Venetian letter." In the colophon of one of the first books printed in Alost, in 1474, the printer, Thierry Martens, referred to himself as having brought the skill of the Venetians to Flanders, and the type of the Alost books is very close in design to a font used in Perugia in the early 1470s by the northern printer Conrad of Paderborn.

The first printing fonts were closely modeled on the current book hands because there would have been no advantage to printers, who needed a market of willing readers, to proceed in any other way. All early printing fonts, beyond the few that are highly imperfect, may be seen as corresponding to the highest grade of writing, what palaeographers call the *formata* level, for, when properly made, the multiply cast printing types were unambiguous representations of the desired letters. The product of good printing may be seen as equivalent to the work of a scribe who both traced letters with absolute regularity and used an ink considerably darker and denser than the typical inks of other scribes. The latter feature was emphasized in various early colophons of Fust and Schöffer in Mainz, which stated that their books were "not made with ink, quill or stylus" (as, e.g., Boniface VIII, *Liber sextus Decretalium*, 17 December, 1465, f.141r: *non atramento, plumali canna neque erea*), a formulation that Schöffer made less paradoxical in a 1468 colophon stating that the book was made "not with ordinary ink" (*Corpus iuris civilis, Institutiones*, 24 May, 1468, f.103v: *non atramento communi, non plumali canna neque erea*). It is a reasonable supposition that the styles of the earliest fonts were modeled on the hands of specific scribes, and in the case of the first Augsburg printer, Günther Zainer, Carl Wehmer (1938) made a strong argument that at least one of his fonts was based on the hand of the well-known Augsburg scribe, Heinrich Molitor. Peter Schöffer is an equally strong candidate as the designer of several of the early Mainz fonts, perhaps including that of the Gutenberg Bible. Two examples of his calligraphic writing in *Quadrata* and *Rotunda*, dated 1449 and 1472, are preserved in facsimile reproductions, their originals having been destroyed in battles of the Franco-German War and of World War II. Both give evidence that Schöffer was a scribe of considerable ability and versatility.

However, from the earliest years of printing, there are continual evidences that printing fonts, both in their making and in their handling by compositors, moved toward increasing independence from scribal conventions and practices. For example, the DK font, when used to print the Mainz *Sibyllenbuch*, would ideally have included a majuscule *W*, to be set at the beginning of verses beginning with *w*. But the font, made primarily for printing the *Ars minor* of Donatus, had no such letter. In the 22 lines preserved in the small *Sibyllenbuch* fragment, the compositor encountered this situation once. As a substitute for the non-existent *W*, he set minuscule *w* preceded by a raised point. In principle the rubricator would notice the point and respond by drawing a red stroke through the *w*, as he did with the majuscule letters. However, in this particular copy the rubricator either overlooked the point or failed to understand it as a "majuscule marker," leaving the relevant *w* untouched. No scribe, of course, would have been incapable of writing a majuscule *W*, and so would have been compelled to find a workaround every time that letterform was required.

There are also frequent instances where a font had a necessary character, but in setting a given page the compositor emptied the box, and so had to find some substitute. There are various examples within the fragmentary Donatuses of the 1450s set in the DK type. In one, the frequent paradigms beginning with the word "Preterito" were regularly set with a single abbreviation character for *Pre*, but when all the available types of that character had been drawn and set, the compositor reverted at the bottom of the page in question to spelling out P-r-e in full. After that page was printed, its types would be cleaned and put back into the typecase, and the *Pre* character would become available again for setting following pages. Similarly, the frequent word "vel" was typically spelled in the Donatuses as *vł*, using a barred-*l* character. But in one edition, the v-box apparently became depleted, so that in the final lines of the page in question, the compositor indicated "vel" simply with the *ł* character, a convention that would have been very familiar to readers. In another Donatus edition, the compositor at one point depleted the box containing the 9-shaped *–us* character. For the remainder of the page *–us* endings were not, however, spelled in full. Instead the compositor set the "trailing" final *s* as a substitute abbreviation for *–us*, a use the character did not have in the handwriting of the time. Readers had to make their own interpretation.

It is almost impossible to estimate the rate at which printed books came to supersede handwritten books. We have no idea of the ratio of surviving manuscripts of the second half of the fifteenth century to the number originally written. We have a much firmer grasp of how many printed books of the period survive, but still can make only crude estimates of the numbers originally printed of each edition; documentation of original print runs is quite rare. Nonetheless, the growing records of dated manuscripts of the period, provided by the various "Dated Manuscripts" projects, show that the numbers of explicitly dated manuscripts fell off sharply in the last three decades, from the early 1470s onward. It is reasonable to suppose that the chief cause was the ever increasing availability of printed versions of the texts that were most widely read. As printed books spread in use, their readers, probably for the most part unconsciously, adjusted their own expectations of what reading matter should look like.

In particular, readers became satisfied with printing types that in letter shapes responded closely to familiar book hands, but they did not demand of type a close adherence to the rules of "abutting" forms and fused letters that the best scribes followed. Rudolf Juchhoff (1935) traced the slow but steady disappearance of digraph types to represent fused letter combinations in Italian *Rotunda* fonts, and it is clear that a similar process developed over time with *Quadrata* fonts. Thus, whereas the Gutenberg Bible's typecases needed roughly 270 boxes to hold all the differently used characters, certain Paris *Quadrata* fonts of the 1490s, extremely handsome in their cutting and so by no means makeshift fonts, had only 90 or so distinct characters.

Another feature of fifteenth-century typemaking draws even more clearly a line between the scribal hand and the compositor's typecases. As early as the 1460s, when the printing trade was still growing slowly, we begin to see new type fonts that were based not on scribal hands, but on other printing fonts. The first clear examples are the *Rotunda* fonts of the first printer of Cologne, Ulrich Zel, in 1466 and after. It is more than probable that Zel's introduction to the printing trade began a few years earlier in Mainz, in the shop of Fust and Schöffer, and his first types, which in turn became models for other early Cologne printers, are unmistakably modeled on Fust and Schöffer's types. In Venice, a decade later, the prestige of Nicolas Jenson's Roman and *Rotunda* fonts was even greater, and the wording of his 1481 testament indicates that in his mind the punches and matrices he had created were monuments that would outlive him. Since Roman type designs today continue to be influenced by Jenson's design, his ambitions were fulfilled to a degree he could hardly have imagined. The process of typemaking itself encouraged and allowed the wide transmission of particular types beyond the towns where they were originally made. From a single set of punches, duplicate (and more) sets of matrices could be made, which then could be supplied for typefounding distant in time and space from where and when the punches were originally engraved. The closest analysis of the phenomenon has been carried out by W. and L. Hellinga (1966) in their pathbreaking study of the printing types of the Low Countries. As regards printing in England, a relative backwater in the fifteenth century, it has long been recognized that various fonts used by English presses had their origins not in England but in Bruges, Cologne, and Paris.

To come full circle, it should be noted that before long scribes were influenced by printing, and illuminators were influenced by printed images. In the last decades of the fifteenth century, it was common for manuscripts to be copied from printed editions, for the obvious reason that a printed work might well be the easy and available source. (Similarly, hundreds of times over, and beginning with the Gutenberg Bible, printed editions were copied from other printed editions.) Regarding manuscripts dating to the late fifteenth and early sixteenth centuries, scholars must always consider whether the text in question had already come into print and, if so, whether the scribe's exemplar might have been a printed edition. As noted by M. D. Reeve (1983, 12–13) there have been instances where philologists, overlooking this, have treated as independent witnesses to a text multiple late manuscripts that all derive from a single printed source. It is not unusual in such manuscripts to find clues to the printed source copy not only in the textual readings, but also in the layout and script. We may say that at least in some cases, the standard, even for a scribe, of what a book ought to look like had become the printed edition.

ABBREVIATIONS

Note: The majority of fifteenth-century printing types are reproduced and commented on in one or more of three works commonly cited as BMC, GfT, and TFS:

BMC   *Catalogue of Books Printed in the XVth Century Now in the British Museum [British Library]*, I–X, London: Trustees of the British Museum, 1908–71; XI, 't Goy-Houten: Hes & De Graaf, 2007; XII, London: British Library, 1985; XIII, 't Goy-Houten: Hes & De Graaf, 2004.

GfT   *Veröffentlichungen der Gesellschaft für Typenkunde des XV. Jahrhunderts. Band 1–33 (Taf. 1–2460)*. Leipzig: Gesellschaft für Typenkunde, 1907–39 (repr. Osnabrück: Otto Zeller, 1966, with Typenregister zu Tafeln 1–2460, ed. R. Juchhoff and E. von Kathen). The types of the GfT plates are numbered according to K. Haebler, *Typenrepertorium der Wiegendrucke. Abteilung*, I, Halle, Rudolf Haupt, 1905; II, Leipzig And New York: Rudolf Haupt, 1908; III, Leipzig: Rudolf Haupt, 1909; IV, Leipzig: Otto Harrassowitz, 1922; V, Leipzig: Otto Harrassowitz, 1924.

TFS   *Type Facsimile Society. Specimen of Early Printing Types*, ed. R. Proctor [et al.], Fascicles 1–10, Index ed. K. Burger. Oxford: Type Facsimile Society, 1900–13.

BIBLIOGRAPHY

Bühler, C. F. 1960. *The Fifteenth-Century Book: The Scribes, the Printers, the Decorators.* Philadelphia, PA: University of Pennsylvania Press.

Carter, H. 1969. *A View of Early Typography.* Oxford: Clarendon Press.

Derolez, A. 2003. *The Palaeography of Gothic Manuscript Books: From the Twelfth to the Early Sixteenth Century.* Cambridge: University Press.

Dziatzko, K. 1890. *Gutenbergs früheste Druckerpraxis.* Berlin: Sammlung Bibliothekswissenschaftlicher Arbeiten, 4. Heft.

Gumbert, J. P. 1974. *Die Utrechter Kartäuser und ihre Bücher im frühen fünfzehnten Jahrhundert.* Leiden: Brill.

Hellinga, W. and L. Hellinga. 1966. *The Fifteenth-Century Printing Types of the Low Countries,* 2 vols. Amsterdam: Menno Hertzberger.

Juchhoff, R. 1935. "Das Fortleben mittelalterlicher Schreibgewohnheiten in den Druckschriften des 15. Jahrhunderts. I: Italien." *Beiträge zur Inkunabelkunde* neue Folge 1: 66–77.

Lehmann-Haupt, H. 1950. *Peter Schoeffer of Gernsheim and Mainz with a List of his Surviving Books and Broadsides.* Rochester, NY: Printing House of Leo Hart.

Lieftinck, G. 1954. "Pour une nomenclature de l'écriture livresque de la période dite gothique." In *Nomenclature des écritures livresques du IXe au XVI siècle,* 15–34. Paris: Colloques Internationaux du C.N.R.S., Sciences Humaines, 4.

Meyer, Wilhelm. 1897. "Die Buchstaben-Verbindungen der sogenannten gothischen Schrift." *Abhandlungen der königlichen Gesellschaft der Wissenschaften zu Göttingen, Philologisch-historische Klasse,* neue Folge 1 no. 6: 00–0.

Needham, P. 1983. "The Compositor's Hand in the Gutenberg Bible: A Review of the Todd Thesis." *PBSA* 77: 344–71.

Needham, P. 1988. *The Bradshaw Method: Henry Bradshaw's Contribution to Bibliography.* The Seventh Hanes Lecture. Chapel Hill, NC: Hanes Foundation, Rare Book Collection, University Library, University of North Carolina.

Needham, P. 1990. "Paul Schwenke and Gutenberg Scholarship: The German Contribution, 1885–1921." *PBSA* 84: 242–64.

Needham, P. 1993. "Palaeography and the Earliest Printing Types." In *Johannes Gutenberg — Regionale Aspekte des frühen Buchdrucks,* ed. H. Nickel and L. Gillner, 19–27. Wiesbaden: Reichert.

Reeve, M. D. 1983. "Manuscripts Copied from Printed Books." In *Manuscripts in the Fifty Years after the Invention of Printing,* ed. J. B. Trapp, 12–20. London: Warburg Institute.

Schwenke, P. 1903. *Die Donat- und Kalender-Type.* Mainz: Veröffentlichungen der Gutenberg-Gesellschaft, II.

Schwenke, P. 1923. *Johannes Gutenbergs zweiundvierzigzeilige Bible. Ergänzungsband zur Faksimile-Ausgabe.* Leipzig: Insel-Verlag.

Wehmer, C. 1938. "Augsburger Schreiber aus der Frühzeit des Buchdrucks. II: Heinrich Molitor." *Beiträge zur Inkunabelkunde* neue Folge 2: 108–27.

Zedler, G. 1913. *Die Mainzer Ablassbriefe der Jahre 1454 und 1455.* Mainz: Veröffentlichungen der Gutenberg-Gesellschaft, XII–XIII.

I . 6

HUMANIST

CHAPTER 31

···

HUMANISTIC SCRIPT

Origins

···

TERESA DE ROBERTIS
(Translated by Consuelo Dutschke)

DURING the final years of the Trecento and the early years of the Quattrocento, in Italy, in certain identifiable environments of humanistic culture (the Florentine circle of Salutati; the circles of Guarino or of Francesco Barbaro in the Veneto), a new or rather an ancient script came into use.

The innovation consisted in the conscious return to a script of the past, the *littera antiqua* or (if we choose the paleographic term) Caroline minuscule, to which, already from Petrarch's time, were attributed qualities of formal balance, sobriety, and legibility; in part these qualities were intrinsic to the script, and in part they acquired emphasis through the ideological perspective from which they were viewed. Above all, *littera antiqua* was, in the eyes of the humanists, the script that identified the most ancient transmission of the texts that were re-emerging through humanistic search and discovery. Nor is this view incorrect: if we examine the *stemma codicum* of a classical Latin text, we see how the earliest stages are almost always occupied by manuscripts datable to the period from the ninth to the twelfth century. In short, *littera antiqua*, until the subsequent discovery of the late antique codices of Vergil copied in capitals, was the script par excellence for classical texts; it was the script closest to an ideal antiquity that was otherwise impossible to achieve.

It would be wrong, however, to think that in restoring *littera antiqua* Niccoli, Poggio Bracciolini, or Guarino Veronese believed it to be a truly ancient script, of the Roman era. In spite of uncertain opinions about dates of scripts, and in spite of some contradictions about the meaning of the term *littera antiqua*, about the exemplum to imitate, about the very significance of the work that they were accomplishing, the humanists were conscious that the revivified Caroline minuscule was, yes, an old script, but a medieval one.[1] When Salutati in 1395 writes to Jean de Montreuil saying that he would prefer a codex of Abelard's works *de antiqua littera*, he is certainly aware that

that script so pleasing to his eye cannot be more than a few centuries old.[2] Again, Salutati in a famous letter that he wrote in 1397 (in reference to a mythical copy of Livy, complete in all the Decades, "in littera tam antiqua" that it would require a "lector ideoneus"), expresses himself with absolute clarity on the distance separating the script of the ancients and that of the moderns:

> The letters or the shapes of the letters have changed to such a degree over the course of so many centuries that in comparing the present letters with the ancient ones we do not recognize a similarity between them, so that it is necessary to habituate the mind and the eye to them with diligence.[3]

Yet more compelling is Ponticus Virunius (in 1508–9), who, while insisting upon the impossibility of recognizing in the script of his day a similarity with the script of the ancients, manages to hypothesize the existence during classical times of a script in daily use alongside the monumental script legible in epigraphic inscriptions and on ruins.[4]

Thus, reasons of an aesthetic, philological, grammatical, and orthographic nature lie at the base of what was an actual restoration of a graphic system.[5] In contemporary sources, these multiple reasons are tightly interconnected and seem to carry equal weight. Such references to script are hardly ever as explicit and rich in information as during this period.[6] In the correspondence of the humanists, news of discoveries of rare or lost texts is accompanied by judgments on the greater or lesser correctness of the codices, on their actual or assumed antiquity, on the quality of the scripts.[7] In requesting a transcription, they give precise and detailed indications of the type of script to use, the capabilities of the copyists to hire, and the physical characteristics of the copies to be made.[8]

Recuperation of the *littera antiquae formae* is a phenomenon that initially only pertains to books, or rather, only to certain categories of books. Only classical authors and the Church Fathers are copied in the new manner, with "litterae quae sapiunt antiquitatem";[9] liturgical texts, "modern" authors of university materials, technical works, and vernacular literature (with the partial exception of Dante[10] and Petrarch,[11] who were soon put on a par with ancient authors) were excluded. In spite of an occasional precocious but isolated experiment,[12] humanistic script made its way into notarial, administrative, and chancery practice only uncertainly and later in the century (it must said that this area has received very little study).[13] Much more rapid, on the other hand, is the diffusion of *littera antiqua* in the correspondence of the humanists, in inscriptions, and in the *tituli picti*.

In Florence the model for the characteristics that we recognize as typical of the humanistic manuscript takes shape in the study codex of the twelfth century: medium format; ample margins for notes; sober decoration, usually limited to one major initial with interlace and void design (the 'vine-stem' or 'bianchi girari' pattern); and orthography that retains use of the diphthong (see Plates 31.1a and 31.1b). In the Veneto and in areas influenced by it, the models are sometimes older, and not only Latin or only books, but also Greek and epigraphic.

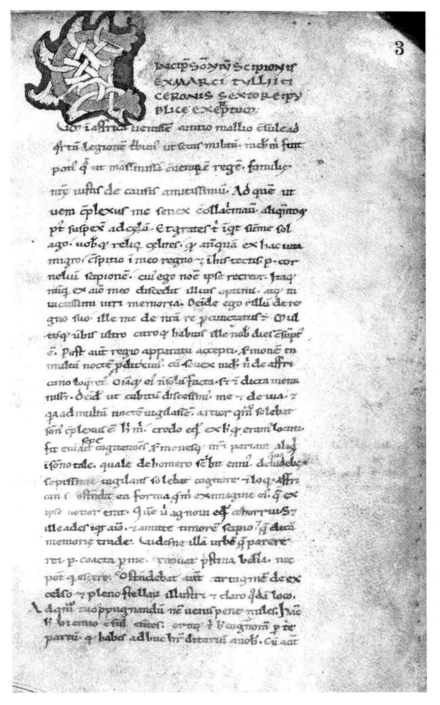

PLATE 31.1a Possible model for the humanist codex: Florence, Biblioteca Riccardiana, 716 (fol. 3r), saec. XII².

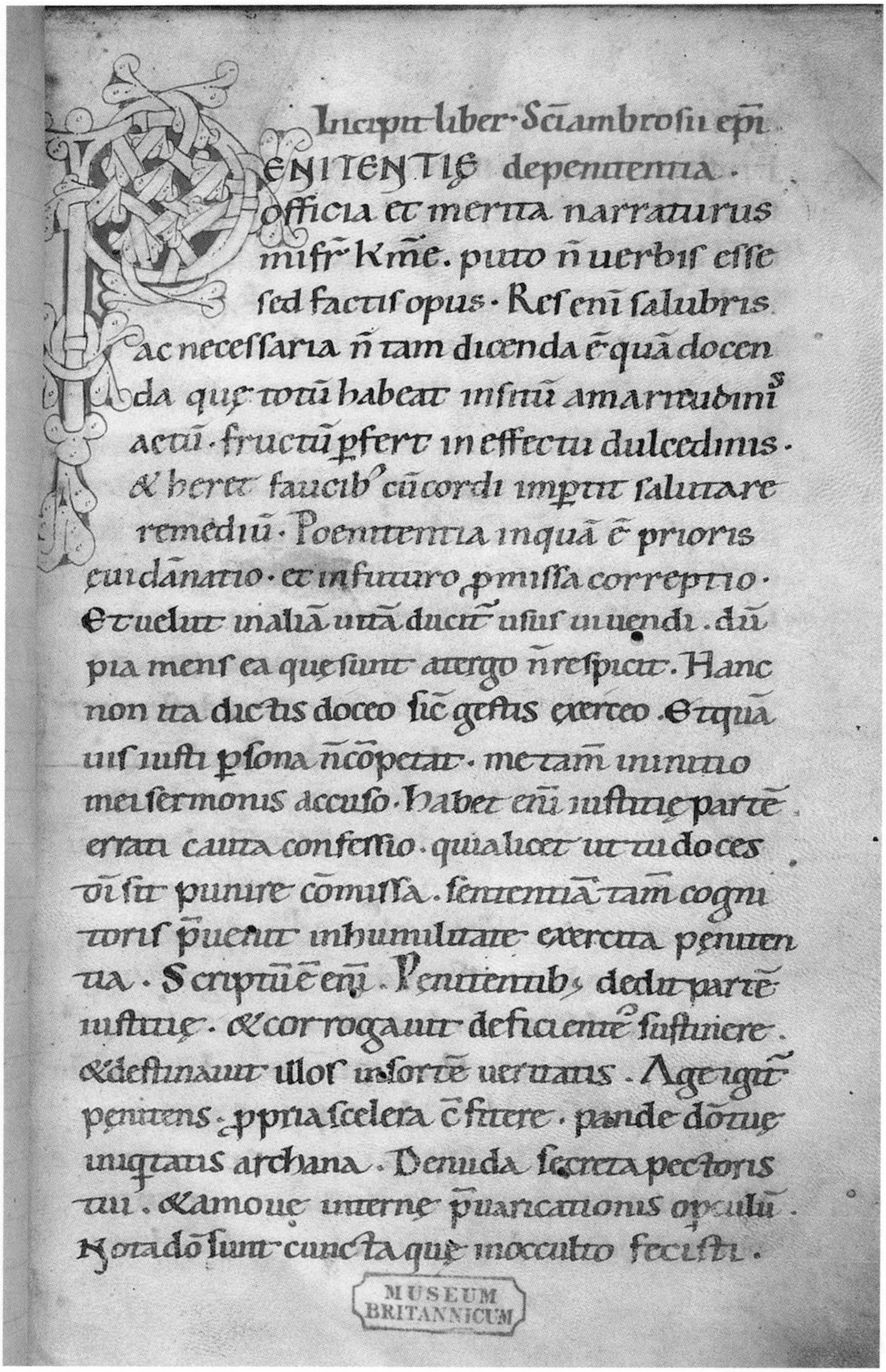

Incipit liber·Sci ambrosii epi
ENITENTIE de penitentia·
officia et merita narraturus
mifr kme. puto n̄ uerbis esse
sed factis opus· Res eni salubris.
ac necessaria n̄ tam dicenda ē qua docen
da que̅ totū habeat insitū amaritudinis
actū· fructū pfert in effectu dulcedinis·
& heret faucib' cū cordi imptit salutare
remediū· Poenitentia inquā ē prioris
cuidanatio· et in futuro pmissa correptio·
Et uelut in alia uitā ducit usus uiuendi. dū
pia mens ea que sunt atergo n̄ respicit. Hanc
non ita dictis doceo sic gestis exerceo. Et quā
uis iusti psona n̄copetat. me tam in initio
mei sermonis accuso· habet eni iustitie parte̅
errati cauta confessio. quia licet ut tu doces
oi̅ sit punire comissa. sententia tam cogni
toris p̅uetur in humilitate exercita peniten
tia· Scriptū ē eni. Penitentib, dedit parte̅
iustitie· & corrogauit deficiente̅ sustinere·
& destinauit illos insorte̅ ueritatis· Age igit̄
penitens· ppria scelera c fiteri· pande docue̅
iniqtatis archana· Denuda secreta pectoris
tui· & amoue interne p̅uaricationis opculū·
Notado su̅nt cuncta que inocculto fecisti·

MUSEUM BRITANNICUM

PLATE 31.1b Possible model for the humanist codex: London BL, Burney 281 (fol. 1r), saec. XII².

The first occasions for experiments with *littera antiqua* may have resulted from small restorations of missing sections. In Florence, BML, San Marco 284 (Apuleius and Pliny, middle of the eleventh century, Plates 31.2a and 31.2b), Salutati utilized the last leaf for the addition in a script that is unusual for him, in ancient style, to minimize differences from the preceding pages.[14] Niccolò Niccoli occasionally does the same in the margins of manuscripts of the twelfth century or on added leaves[15]; in one manuscript, damaged by water, he rewrites in *littera antiqua* the parts of the text that had been ruined, in perfect imitation of the original script.[16] In a Vergil of the eleventh century (Holkham Hall 303), one can hardly distinguish the replacement quire added by Poggio Bracciolini.[17] Occasionally inspiration may arise from the exemplar that the copyist has on his desk: such is the case in Rome, Biblioteca Vallicelliana, C.54 (*Somnium Scipionis*, end of the fourteenth century), *descriptus* and a faithful copy, almost to the level of photography, of Florence, BML, San Marco 287 (twelfth century).[18] More often, the copyists seem to refer to a model that exists more as an idea than in reality, to an abstract or mediated concept of a book in the ancient style.

Such differences in the point of departure (various models; differing ways of looking at the model) and possibly variations in the goal one was attempting to reach inevitably influence the results, as do personal capabilities and inclinations. There is, nevertheless, a shared characteristic that binds the experiences of all the first protagonists of the so-called humanistic graphic reform. Imitation is not restricted to script alone, but touches all aspects of the book, even the most detailed: decoration, format, layout, physical structure (the well-formed codex *all'antica* is always on parchment; paper can only be a fallback, and is permitted strictly for private or temporary copies), ruling techniques, the paragraphemic system (punctuation and abbreviation), the system for cross-referencing between text and notes, *nota bene* signs, orthography (diphthongs reappear, sometimes in the form of hypercorrections, first as *e caudata*, then by means of the ligature æ, and finally in the extended form; the spellings *mihi* and *nihil* are brought back in place of the medieval forms, *michi* and *nichil*). In short, it is clear that *littera antiqua*, as it was termed by its contemporary users, who defined in the same way both the model and the resulting imitation, is only one of the ways in which the book reveals its virtues— legibility, cleanliness, level of correction of the text, its philological and orthographic viability—qualities that, as Petrarch lamented, had been lost in the scripts of his day so fraught with the stylistic excesses of scribes who were technically capable but who had abandoned the sense of their craft and the function of script, or written by ignorant copyists who were barely able to hold a pen in their hands. Petrarch castigated the first for their execution of a *littera* that was a "spreading luxuriant lettering, fashionable at [our] time when scribes are painters, that pleases but tires the eyes, as if it were invented for anything else than reading";[19] he spoke with great harshness of the second group, emphasizing the damage they caused to the text:

> Thus anyone who has learned to scribble something upon parchment and to hold a pen in his hand is thought to be a scribe, although he has no knowledge whatsoever, no mind, and no skill. I do not look anymore for orthography, nor

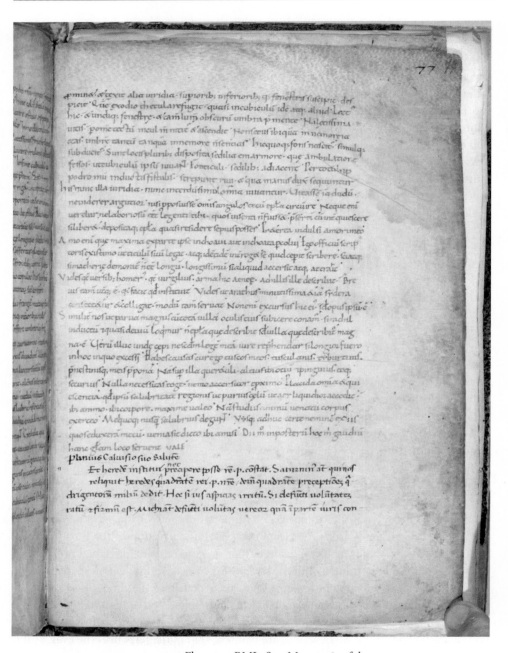

PLATE 31.2a Florence, BML, San Marco 284, fol. 77r.

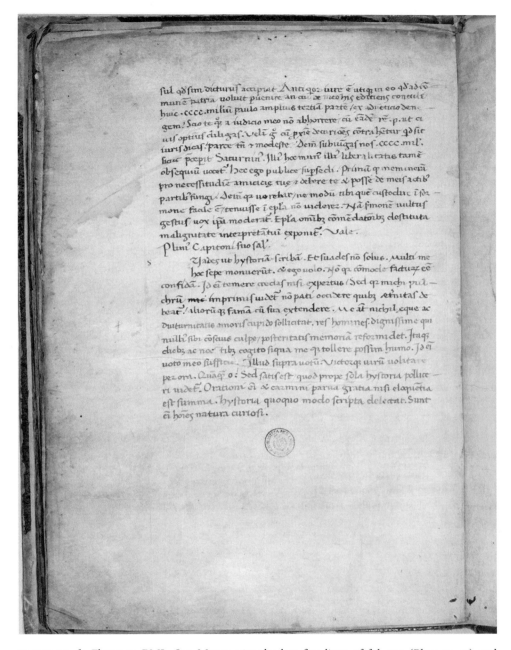

PLATE 31.2b Florence, BML, San Marco 284: the last five lines of fol. 77r (Plate 31.2a) and fol. 77v (Plate 31.2b) are written by Coluccio Salutati in imitation of the preceding script (Apuleius and Pliny, middle of the eleventh century).

do I complain that it has perished long ago. If only they would write what they are told to write . . . Now, with the confused copies and drafts, they promise to write one thing but write another, so that you do not recognize what you yourself dictated.[20]

The historical awareness, even if uncertain and naive, that lies at the base of the graphic reform of the humanists (script, as with all human endeavor, did not remain immutable throughout time) would not have been sufficient to instigate change if not for the presence of two conditions: a notable technical ability on the part of the first protagonists of the reform due to the fact that most earned their living with jobs based on writing (almost all are notaries); the possession of extraordinary personal libraries (according to Poggio Bracciolini, the libraries of Salutati and of Niccoli counted some 800 manuscripts each) or the possibility of access to significant public collections (in Florence available libraries were those of the Franciscans of S. Croce, of the Dominicans of S. Maria Novella, of the Augustinians of S. Spirito, where the books that had belonged to Boccaccio were held, and many others). Observers so capable of judging a book in all its aspects were aware that these libraries, together with a very large variety of authors and texts, offered a rich sampling of script. The new *littera antiqua* and of the book produced *all'antica* proved to be an instant success: in Florence, production of books in the ancient style had passed into the hands of professional scribes already by the end of the second decade of the century, while in northern Italy, this took place by the end of the third decade. But scripts of the modern or Gothic tradition were not jettisoned, nor were the many stylistic versions of *littera textualis* nor the cursives of notarial usage or *mercantesca* abandoned. Throughout the fifteenth century, in humanist circles and those outside of humanistic culture, these scripts continued in use for the transcription of medieval philosophers and theologians, for books of law, medicine, and general science, for liturgical books, and for a considerable segment of vernacular literature. In Quattrocento Italy, therefore, we are confronted with a sharply defined bipartite graphic system, i.e., a cultural, aesthetic, and functional opposition between *littera moderna* and *littera antiqua*, between "Gothic" books and books *all'antica*— an opposition that will be canonized in the fonts of typography. Only partially, and much later (and due to the effects of print) will the rest of Europe experience an analogous situation.

SUGGESTED READING

For humanistic thinking on script, see Emanuele Casamassima. "Per una storia delle dottrine paleografiche dall'Umanesimo a Jean Mabillon," *Studi medievali* 5 (1964) 525–78 and Silvia Rizzo, *Il lessico filologico degli umanisti* (Rome: Edizioni di Storia e Letteratura, 1973). For the ideological climate in which the restoration of script operated by the humanists matured, see B. L. Ullman, *The Origin and Development of Humanistic Script*. (Rome: Edizioni di Storia e Letteratura 79, 1960) 11–19; Armando Petrucci, "Le antiche e le moderne carte: imitatio e renovatio nella riforma grafica umanistica," in *Renaissance- und Humanistenhandschriften*, ed. Johanne Autenrieth and Ulrich Eigler (Munich: Oldenburg, 1988) 1–12.

Notes

1. Casamassima, (1964, 547).

2. "Interim te rogatum velim, quod epistolas Petri Abailardi, si non habes, inquiri facias, et ex tuis vel repertis studeas meo nomine quanto correctius poterit exemplari. Sed si de antiqua littera haberi possent, libentius acciperem; nulle quidem littere sunt meis oculis gratiores" (Salutati, *Ep.* III 76).

3. "Mutate autem sunt littere sive litterarum figure iam tot seculis, quod presentes cum priscis illis antiquissimis conferentes minime inter eas similitudinem deprehendant, ut oporteat diligenter et mentem et oculos illis assuefacere litteris" (Salutati, *Ep.* III 76).

4. "Cum autem nusquam in marmoribus antiquis nisi maiusculae reperiantur, erant tamen certo et aliae formae litterarum, ita ut si manus Maronis, Ciceronis, et Ovidii, et illorum temporum nunc essent, non cognoscerentur, et si inter vivos reverterentur illi beati manes, litteras istas non cognoscerent quantum vis venustas, ut nec nos illorum" (Guarino Veronese, 1509, 13).

5. Casamassima (1964, x).

6. Rizzo (1973).

7. "[Giovanni Corvini] habet Macrobium, ut audio, litteris antiquis, fidelem, emendatum" (Guarino Veronese, 1915–19, *Ep.* 223, 52).

8. "Video quod librum 'De viris illustribus' in papyro facies exemplari, ut scribis; sed per religiosum virum Tedaldum de ordine Minorum michi relatum fuit te in hoc mutasse consilium. De quo, si scriptorem habes qui possit in pergameno conscribere, longe magis contentor, ne ex nova exemplatione dolo, mendaciis et inconstantie fraudibus scriptorum quorum more, quid dixi mores?, imo vitia te novisse reor, quasi mancipium dedar. Si igitur in una potes transcriptione me expedire, ne ex altera pendeam, te totis affectibus rogo." (Salutati, *Ep.* I 330–1).

9. Poggio Bracciolini, *Ep.* II 27.

10. Rome, Fondazione Caetani *s.n.* (the same scribe as in Florence, BML, 90 sup. 132) and Florence, Biblioteca Nazionale, Banco rari 215 (the scribe is Luigi di ser Michele Guidi); reproduced in Bertelli (2007, Plates i, vii, viii, 31, and 63).

11. Florence, BML, 41.10, *Canzoniere*, direct and faithful copy of Vat. lat. 3195, which is in part autograph by Petrarch (De Robertis, Tanturli, and Zamponi 2008, 304–6).

12. Already during the second decade of the fifteenth century, Giovanni Aretino (Petronio 1981 and Davies 1988) and some Venetian notaries (Barile 1994, 49–66).

13. The only systematic study pertains to the Roman curia: Frenz (1973).

14. Ullman (1960, 16–19); de la Mare (1973, 35–8, Plate viii*h*); De Robertis, Tanturli, and Zamponi (2008, 22 and 325–8).

15. For example, Florence, BML, Fiesol. 12 and 13, Augustine, *De civ. Dei* with plates in Gentile (1973 *i*, 162–4); for the manuscripts, Paris, BnF, lat. 6798 (Pliny, *Nat. hist.*) and Oxford, Bodleian Library, Canon. Ital. 131 (Augustine), cf. de la Mare (1994, 100, 107, and Plate 28).

16. Vatican City, BAV, Vat. lat. 2026, Ptolemy, *Almagest* (De Robertis, Tanturli, and Zamponi 2008, 272–4).

17. Private communication of A. de la Mare (1999). See now Reynolds (2015, 163–64, 337). Another restoration made by Poggio in Vatican City, BAV, Barb. lat. 65 has been reported by Cursi (2012).

18. Caldini Montanari (2009, 133–54).

19. "Vaga quidem et luxurians littera, qualis est scriptorum seu verius pictorum nostri temporis, longe oculos mulcens, prope autem afficiens ac fatigans, quasi aliud quam ad legendum sit inventa" (*Fam.* XXII 19, 8; the English paraphrase is from Ullman 1960, 12–13). Against this script, Petrarch places the *littera textualis* of his preferred copyist, Giovanni Malpaghini, "castigata et clara...in qua nichil ortographicum, nichil omnino grammatice artis omissum dicas."

20. "Quisquis itaque pingere aliquid in membranis manuque calamum versare didicerit, scriptor habebitur, doctrinae omnis ignarus, expers ingenii, artis egens. Non quero iam, nec queror, orthographiam, quae pridem interiit, qualitercumque utinam scriberent quae iubentur...Nunc, confusis exemplaribus et exemplis, unum scribere polliciti, sic aliud scribunt, ut, quod ipse dictaveris, non agnoscas" (*De remediis* I xliii 12; the English translation is by Rawski 1991, 1:140–1).

BIBLIOGRAPHY

Barile, E. 1994. *Littera antiqua e scritture alla greca: Notai e cancellieri copisti a Venezia nei primi decenni del Quattrocento.* Venice: Istituto veneto di scienze, lettere ed arti.

Bertelli, S. 2007. *La commedia all'antica.* Florence: Mandragora.

Bracciolini, P. 1984. *Lettere*, ed. Helene Harth. Florence: L. S. Olschki.

Caldini Montanari, R. 2009. "Un codice protoumanistico del Somnium Scipionis." *Medioevo e Rinascimento* 23: 133–54.

Casamassima, E. 1964. "Per una storia delle dottrine paleografiche dall'umanesimo a Jean Mabillon." *Studi medievali* 5: 525–78.

Cursi, M. 2012. "Un'*ars poetica* di mano di Poggio Bracciolini (Barb. lat. 65)", *Miscellanea Bibliothecae Apostolicae Vaticanae,* 19: 205–27.

Davies, M. C. 1988. *An Enigma and a Phantom: Giovanni Aretino and Giacomo Languschi.* Leuven: Leuven University Press.

de la Mare, A. 1973. *The Handwriting of Italian Humanists.* Paris: University Press for the Association internationale de bibliophilie.

de la Mare, A. 1994. "A Paleographer's Odyssey." In *Sight & Insight : Essays on Art and Culture in Honour of E. H. Gombrich at 85*, ed. John Onians, 89–108. London: Phaidon.

De Robertis, T., G. Tanturli, and S. Zamponi. 2008. *Coluccio Salutati e l'invenzione dell'umanesimo.* Florence: Mandragora.

Frenz, T. 1973. *Das Eindringen humanistischer Schriftformen in die Urkunden und Akten der päpstlichen Kurie im 15. Jahrhundert.* Cologne: Böhlau.

Gentile, S. 1997. *Umanesimo e padri della Chiesa: manoscritti e incunaboli di testi patristici da Francesco Petrarca al primo Cinquecento.* Rome: Rose.

Guarino Veronese. 1509. *Erotemata, cum Multis Additamentis et cum Commentariis Latinis.* Ferrara: Joannes Mazochus.

Guarino Veronese. 1915. *Epistolario di Guarino Veronese*, ed. Remigio Sabbadini. Venice: R. Deputazione veneta di storia patria.

Petronio, N. 1981. "Per la soluzione di un enigma: Giovanni Aretino copista, notaio e cancelliere." *Humanistica Lovaniensia* 30: 1–12.

Petrucci, A. 1988. "Le antiche e le moderne carte: imitatio e renovatio nella riforma grafica umanistica," In *Renaissance- und Humanistenhandschriften*, ed. Johanne Autenrieth and Ulrich Eigler, 1–12. Munich: Oldenburg.

Rawski, C. H. 1991. *Petrarch's "Remedies for Fortune Fair and Foul": A Modern English Translation of "De Remediis utriusque Fortune," with a Commentary.* Bloomington, IN: Indiana University Press.

Reynolds, S. R. 2015. *A Catalogue of the Manuscripts in the Library at Holkham Hall. Manuscripts from Italy to 1500. Part 1. Shelfmarks 1–399.* Turnhout: Brepols.

Rizzo, S. 1973. *Il lessico filologico degli umanisti.* Rome: Edizioni di Storia e Letteratura.

Salutati, Coluccio. 2010. *Epistolario di Coluccio Salutati,* ed. Francesco Novati. Rome: Forzani e C., Tipografi del Senato (1st ed. 1891–1911).

Ullman, B. L. 1960. *The Origin and Development of Humanistic Script.* Rome: Edizioni di Storia e Letteratura 79: 11–19.

CHAPTER 32

HUMANISTIC SCRIPT

Italy

TERESA DE ROBERTIS

(Translated by Consuelo Dutschke)

THE FIRST GENERATION
IN FLORENCE

PRIMACY in the rediscovery of *littera antiqua* goes to Florence, where, about the year 1400 (in any case before 1403), eight manuscripts destined for the library of Niccolò Niccoli were produced according to the new style: seven are on parchment, only one on paper; all eight are of medium to small dimensions, in long lines, ruled in dry point, formed of quinternions, and copied in imitation of the Caroline minuscule of small size used in books for private study during the twelfth century.[1] The imitation is produced by systematic use of letters that because of their morphology and their position in the word are identified as "ancient" (see Fig. 32.1): the conjunction handled via the ampersand (&) in place of the tironian *et*; tall *s* not only internally to the word but also at the end; *d* with a straight ascender instead of the Uncial variant with oblique ascender; straight *r* after a curve in place of the so-called round *r*; *g* formed of two circular sections connected to one another by a short vertical stroke; *e* with a cedilla or cauda (ę) and sometimes the nexus *æ* to indicate the diphthong; majuscules with origin in *capitalis* in the text.

The two copyists at work are Niccolò Niccoli himself (1364/5–1437) and Poggio Bracciolini (1380–1459).[2] The eight prototypes are well advanced, but not yet complete: the script is already *all'antica*, but it still lacks the characteristics that will mark the fortune of the humanistic codex in Florentine style: decoration with white vine stem (it, too, an imitation of manuscripts of the twelfth century from central Italy), titles in capital letters, and, when necessary, Greek that is graphically and orthographically perfect (blank spaces were reserved for such complements to the text).

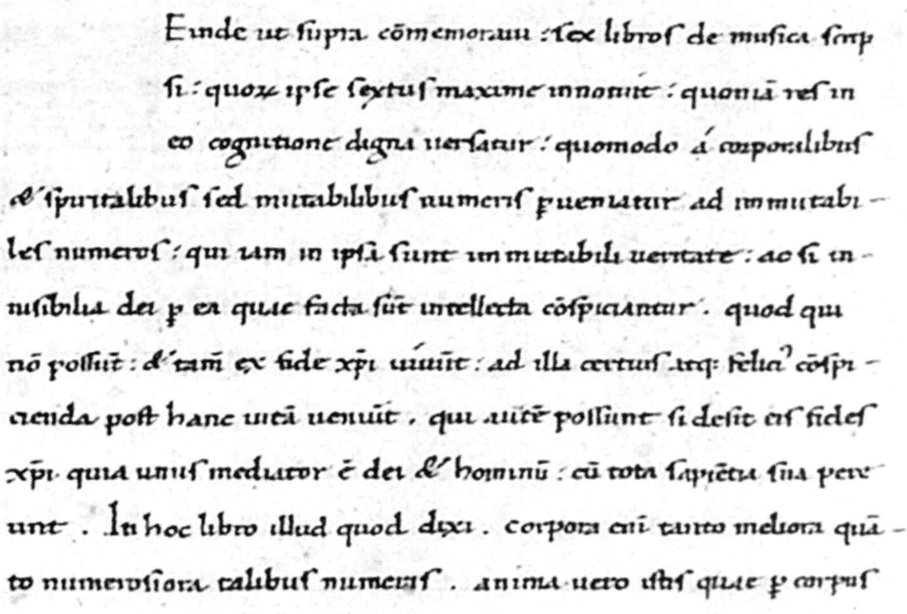

FIG. 32.1 Florence, BML, San Marco 649 (fol. 1r): Niccolò Niccoli.

It is hard to tell the hands of Niccoli and Poggio apart. But while the young Poggio shows some uncertainties and oscillations, typical of someone who is learning a new manner of writing,[3] the hand of the older Niccoli is consistent and sure of itself. For Niccoli, the moment of first experimentation has passed, and it had taken place during the fourteenth century: in the manuscript, Florence, Biblioteca Riccardiana, 264 (Lactantius, *Divinae institutiones*), copied perhaps before 1397, we have the good luck of seeing the moment in which Niccoli transforms his hybrid script into the new *littera antiqua*, substituting bit by bit those letterforms that belong to the modern (or Gothic) script with the corresponding "antique" forms.[4]

Niccoli was the pioneer and the apostle of the new script: *littera antiqua*, in the form that dominated the entire century and made its way into the roman font of typography, was born under his pen and owes much to his popularizing, at times so pedantic as to irritate his contemporaries. At the end of the Trecento, however, there are other experiments that move or seem to move in the same direction: independently of actual results, these experiments show agreement of certain ideas or directions in matters of script. Dating from 1397 are a Valerius Maximus copied by an anonymous scribe who worked in the circle of Salutati[5] and a codex of Lucan signed by one "Matheus filius ser Iohannis olim Cechi ser Totti de Imola";[6] at least three manuscripts by the hand of Iacopo Angeli da Scarperia,[7] a student and colleague of Salutati, go back to the end of the century. In these codices, copied in formal or semi-cursive scripts of a traditional or "Gothic" nature, "ancient" variants appear in an irregular manner, often in alternation with those typical of *littera moderna*. For that most visible marker of *littera antiqua*, the

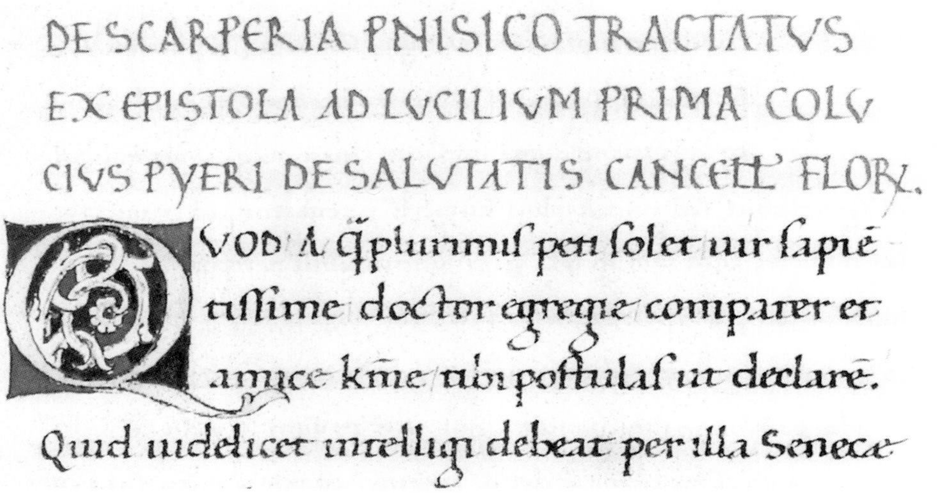

DE SCARPERIA PNISICO TRACTATVS
EX EPISTOLA AD LVCILIVM PRIMA COLV
CIVS PYERI DE SALVTATIS CANCELL' FLOR.
VOD A q̃plurimis peti solet uir sapiē
tissime doctor egregie comparer et
amice kme tibi postulas ut declarē.
Quid uidelicet intelligi debeat per illa Senece

FIG. 32.2 Florence, BML, Strozzi 96 (fol. 28r): Poggio Bracciolini.

ampersand, we can go back farther still, as it was used by Salutati *c.*1370 in the manuscript, London, BL, Add. 11987 (Seneca, *Tragoediae*);[8] isolated majuscules in the form of capitals can be found in the autograph manuscripts of Petrarch (for example, in Vatican City, BAV, Vat. lat. 3358, *Bucolicon carmen*, copied in 1357)[9] and in those of Boccaccio (in the last part of his *Zibaldone*, Florence , BML, 29.8, dating from the end of the 1340s)[10]. Nevertheless, in the handwriting of Petrarch and Boccaccio the presence of an occasional "ancient" majuscule has the value of a simple quotation: the "Gothic" substance of their handwriting remains intact.

Matters are different, at least in part, for Coluccio Salutati (1332–1406) whom Ullman has long since designated as the inspiration of the graphic reform.[11] Salutati, where books are concerned, has decidedly traditional tastes, both as a copyist and as an owner.[12] Nevertheless, in old age, he gave in to the "new" script, asking or accepting that Poggio copy his *De verecundia* (Florence, BML, Strozzi 96, Fig. 32.2) in the ancient style, and attempting some restoration in *littera antiqua* in Florence, BML, San Marco 284.

The first dated codices in which we find initials decorated with white vine stem and titles in capital letters date to 1404 (Florence, BML, 34.55, Juvenal and Persius), to 1405 (Florence, BML, Conv. soppr. 111, Sallust and Justinus), and to 1406 (Florence, BML, Conv. soppr. 131, Cicero, *De finibus* and *Academica priora*); the first was transcribed by Luigi di ser Michele Guidi (1391–1461), who, in the course of some ten years copied another seven codices,[13] many of which are decorated with initials of extraordinary quality (his is the first humanistic codex with a frame of white vine stem);[14] the manuscripts Florence, BML, Conv. soppr. 111 and 131 are by the same scribal hand (Antonio Corbinelli?) that also copied the contemporary Florence, BML, 51.4 (Varro, *De re rustica*).[15] The series of letters used in the titles and colophons are not yet fully consistent (majuscule letters are mixed with minuscule, Gothic variants with capitals; the design is free-form, the proportions not always correct), but the intention is clear:

innovate with respect to current practice by returning to an ancient model, as was done with the script of the text. In these, as with other manuscripts of the first period, decorated initials are in all likelihood produced by the copyists themselves. Certainly, contemporary sources (Poggio, Bruni) point to Niccoli as the person to seek out to obtain initials that are decorated "vetusto more"; Bartolomeo Facio will remember Niccoli as the "librorum exornandorum inventor."

Similar combinations of script, titles, and/or decoration may be observed in Florence, BML, Strozzi 96 (Fig. 32.2), with corrections in the hand of Salutati, and in Venice, Biblioteca Nazionale Marciana, lat. XII 80 [4167] (Catullus) formerly attributed to Poggio[16], both manuscripts dating before 1406. Between 1403 and 1408, in Florence or in Rome, Poggio copied four codices (Berlin, Staatsbibliothek zu Berlin-Preussischer Kulturbesitz, Hamilton 125, Caesar; Hamilton 166, Cicero, *Epistulae ad Atticum,* etc., signed and dated 1408; Florence, BML, 48.34, Cicero, *Philippicae*; Florence, BML, 76.1, Cicero, *De finibus, Tusculanae quaestiones, De senectute, De amicitia, Paradoxa Stoicorum*).[17] The manuscript Pistoia, Biblioteca Comunale Forteguerriana, A.26 (Juvenal) dating from 1410 is the first codex in *antiqua* by Sozomeno da Pistoia (1387–1458);[18] Vatican City, BAV, Pal. lat. 1496 (Cicero, *Epistulae ad familiares*), with the same date, is the oldest of the some 30 manuscripts copied by Giovanni di Cenni Aretino.[19]

Within ten years, in Florence, *littera antiqua* and the new model of the humanistic book took on the formal characteristics and the cultural and social function that were to remain essentially constant for the entire century. In the following 20 years, the number of copyists capable of writing *all'antica* multiplied; we do not know the names of many of them; others were intellectuals with profile and interests similar to those of Niccoli or Poggio (for example, Traversari, Guglielmino Tanagli); yet many others were professional scribes already trained to write in the new script. We know that Poggio, when he returned from Rome after the Council of Constance and his mission to England, was obliged to teach *littera antiqua*—sometimes with disheartening results—to copyists of varied origin (including Neapolitan and French scribes), since he was not personally able to satisfy the numerous requests for copies of texts discovered in his explorations of Swiss, German, and French monasteries. Traversari taught *antiqua* to the monks of S. Maria degli Angeli, a monastery that already during the lifetime of Salutati was famous for its scribes and miniaturists. *Littera antiqua* thus passed from the hands of able scholars driven by deep philological passion to the hands of scribes-for-hire who perhaps had never seen an ancient codex, transforming *littera antiqua* into a production-line instrument of extremely high quality (Plate 32.1). The greater part of the 30 or so manuscripts copied by Giovanni Aretino is concentrated between 1410 and 1423; Antonio di Mario (*c.*1388–1461), the most gifted and prolific copyist of *littera antiqua* during the first half of the fifteenth century (A. C. de la Mare counted more than 50 manuscripts by him),[20] began working in 1417; the Genoese Giacomo Curlo, who will become the court scribe in Naples from 1446 to 1458, began his work in Florence for Cosimo de' Medici in 1423.[21] A decisive factor in the success of *littera antiqua* and of the book *all'antica* was certainly the prestigious patronage of

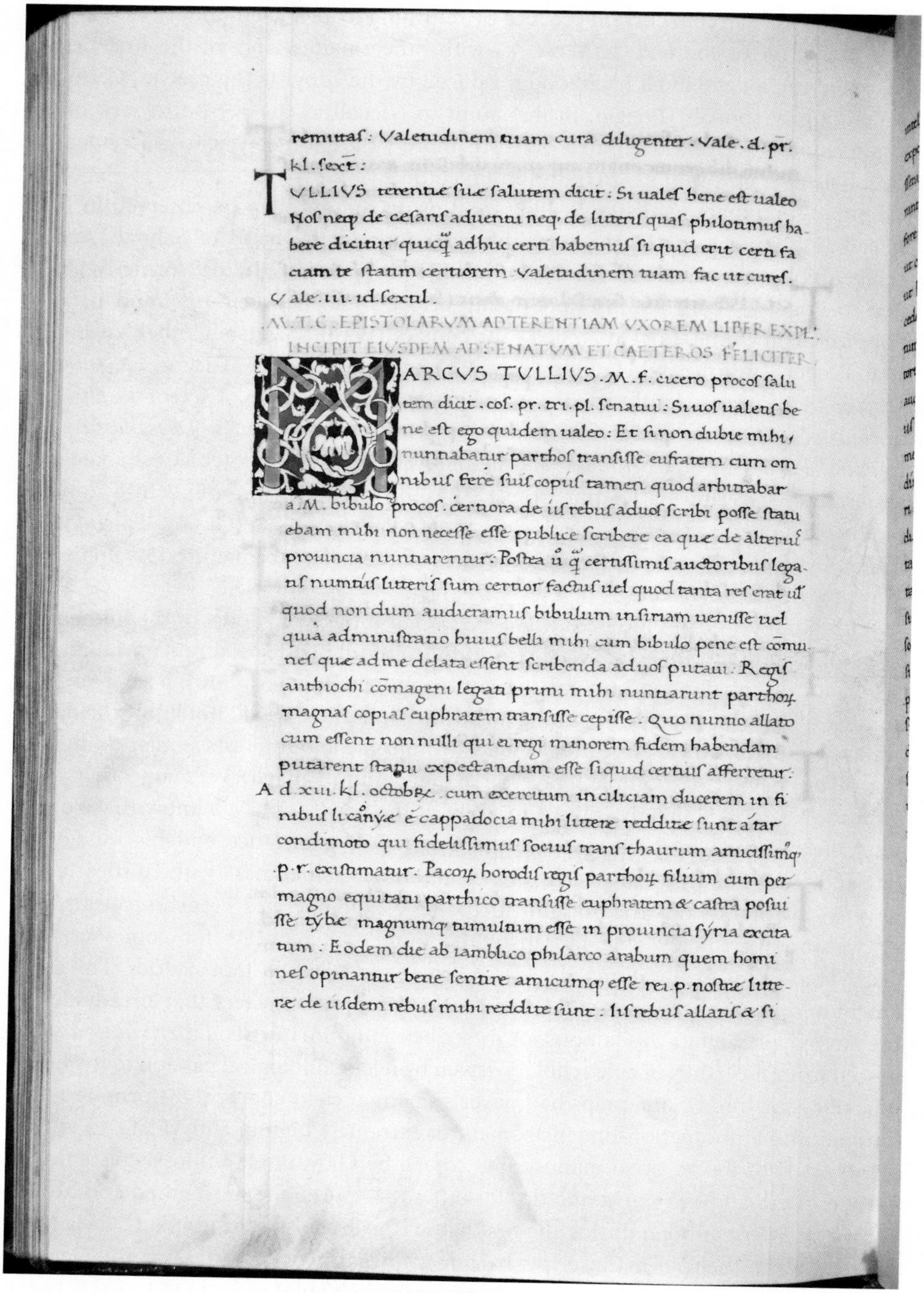

remittas· Valetudinem tuam cura diligenter· Vale· d· pr·
kl· sext·

TVLLIVS terentie sue salutem dicit· Si uales bene est ualeo
Nos neq de cesaris aduentu neq de litteris quas philotimus ha
bere dicitur quicq̃ adhuc certi habemus si quid erit certi fa
ciam te statim certiorem· valetudinem tuam fac ut cures·
Vale· iii· id· sextil·

M·T·C· EPISTOLARVM AD TERENTIAM VXOREM LIBER EXPL·
INCIPIT EIVSDEM AD SENATVM ET CAETEROS FELICITER·

MARCVS TVLLIVS·M·f· cicero procos salu
tem dicit· cos· pr· tri· pl· senatui· Si uos ualetis be
ne est ego quidem ualeo· Et si non dubie mihi
nuntiabatur parthos transisse eufratem cum om
nibus fere suis copiis tamen quod arbitrabar
a·M· bibulo procos· certiora de iis rebus ad uos scribi posse statu
ebam mihi non necesse esse publice scribere ea que de alterius
prouincia nuntiarentur· Postea u q̃ certissimis auctoribus lega
tis nuntiis litteris sum certior factus uel quod tanta res erat ut
quod non dum audieramus bibulum in siriam uenisse uel
quia administratio huius belli mihi cum bibulo pene est comu
nes que ad me delata essent scribenda ad uos putaui· Regis
antiochi comageni legati primi mihi nuntiarunt parthoru
magnas copias euphratem transisse cepisse· Quo nuntio allato
cum essent non nulli qui ei regi minorem fidem habendam
putarent statu expectandum esse si quid certius afferretur·
A·d· xiii· kl· octobr· cum exercitum in ciliciam ducerem in fi
nibus licaonie e cappadocia mihi littere reddite sunt a tar
condimoto qui fidelissimus socius trans thaurum amicissimq̃
p·r· existimatur· Pacory horodis regis parthoru filium cum per
magno equitatu parthico transisse euphratem & castra posui
sse tybe magnumq̃ tumultum esse in prouincia syria excita
tum· Eodem die ab iamblico philarco arabum quem homi
nes opinantur bene sentire amicumq̃ esse rei p· nostre litte
re de iisdem rebus mihi reddite sunt· iis rebus allatis & si

PLATE 32.1 Florence, BML, 49.06, Cicero (fol. 168v). Copyist in the first generation: Antonio di Mario (Florence, 1420): *littera antiqua*, white vine-stem initials and titles in capital script.

Cosimo de' Medici (1389–1464):[22] Giovanni Aretino began working for him perhaps as early as 1412 (Florence, BML, 63.6; Livy, *Decades* IV) and became Cosimo's main purveyor of codices *all'antica* during the second decade of the century; he was later replaced by Antonio di Mario.

In the period that extends from 1420 until shortly after 1433, in many notes and in a group of 12 codices,[23] all on paper and without decoration, Niccoli uses a cursive hand that has been modified *all'antica*. His experiment is part of the active tradition of cursive scripts adapted to book use (the great acquisition and novelty of the Trecento in Italy and more generally in Europe). A comparison between the normal script of letters in his own hand[24] and the *antiqua* of the first years of the century shows that the transformation takes place according to a single procedure: the "ancient" elements (straight *d*; ampersand; *g* in two compartments; straight *r* even after a curve; straight *s* in final position, albeit with many exceptions; simple ascenders on *b*, *h*, *l*, that are no longer looped) replace the letter-forms that came into use in the cursive script during the thirteenth-century while retaining its continuous movement, rich in ligatures from the baseline upward (see Fig. 32.3). Use of this script (long believed to be the only one Niccoli employed)[25] can be associated with transcriptions done rapidly, from exemplars that were available only for a few days or even done under dictation (Florence, Biblioteca Nazionale Centrale, Conv. soppr. J.6.26);[26] these manuscripts, in any case, are visibly intermediary copies; they are work accomplished with the plan of future and final preparation on parchment.

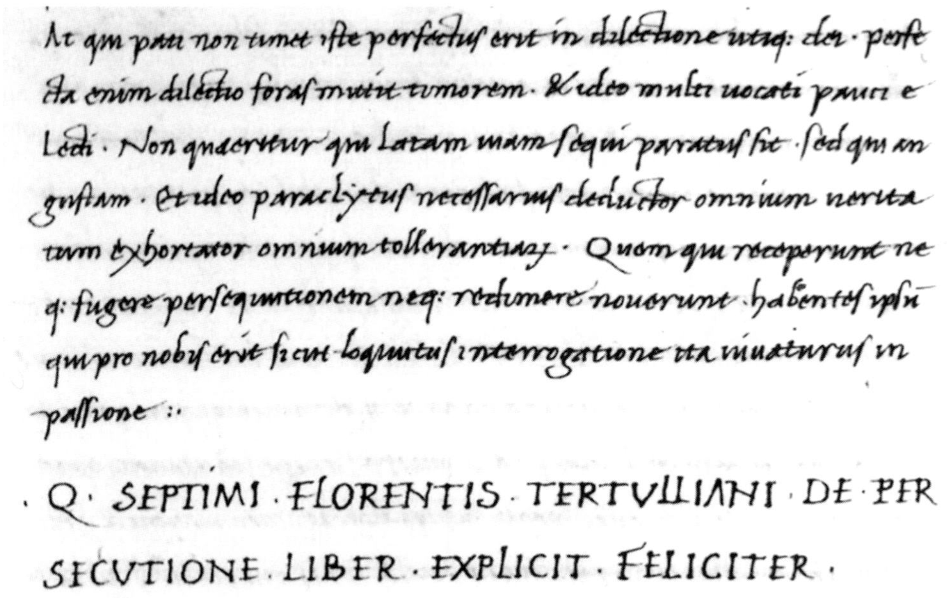

FIG. 32.3 Florence, Biblioteca Nazionale Centrale, Conv. soppr. J.6.11 (fol. 124v): Niccolò Niccoli.

Together with the formal *littera antiqua*, which is a script with historical plausibility in its imitation of late Caroline codices, we also have a cursive script *all'antica*, a script of pure invention, with no concrete model or historical precedent; with the exception of occasional grafted "ancient" variants, this cursive *all'antica* remains deeply "modern" or, if we prefer the term, "Gothic," in so far as the deep essence of cursivity, i.e., in the dynamics of its ligatures. At the same time we see that the typical opposition during the late Middle Ages between the tradition of *textualis* (represented by *littera antiqua*) and the cursive tradition (represented by cursive *all'antica*) resurfaces.[27]

The novelty of Niccoli's cursive script should not be denigrated simply because, before him, Poggio had also occasionally used a script which was basically cursive with "ancient" graftings (e.g., Madrid, BN, 8514, Valerius Flaccus, dated 1416):[28] the results are very different in consistency, quality, and functionality. The cursive experiments of Niccoli apparently remain in isolation; the only one to follow him down this road, and who in reality imitated Niccoli almost to the point of forgery, was Ambrogio Traversari (in the manuscript Florence, Biblioteca Nazionale Centrale, Conv. soppr. J.6.16,[29] works of John Chrysostom translated by Traversari, the two hands interact and it is difficult to distinguish them). The cursive script of Sozomeno da Pistoia, modified *all'antica* possibly according to a lesson learned from Guarino,[30] also remains confined to a strictly private and scholarly environment. Nor was greater fortune enjoyed by the experiment carried out by Giovanni Aretino, also during the second decade of the century but with different purposes: working in the opposite direction to Niccoli, he attempts to incorporate into the *antiqua* of some of his codices[31] letters of cursive form (*f* and *s* with narrowing descenders that push below the baseline, *m* with its final stroke lengthened and curved). There is a clear intention to propose an alternative of equal dignity to the now codified forms of *antiqua* (all the manuscripts copied in this manner are on parchment and have decorated initials), but the results of this attempt are an artificial script that is "soltanto in apparenza leggera e rapida, in realtà non meno laboriosa a scriversi della lettera antica,"[32] which explains its rapid decline.

The First Experience in the Veneto and in Lombardy

A few years after the first experiments of Niccoli and of Poggio, *littera antiqua* comes into use by the humanists and scribes of northern Italy, especially in the Veneto and Lombardy, although with characteristics that are sometimes similar and more often extremely original (Plate 32.2). For some of these humanists contact with Florence is proven and decisive for their knowledge and choice of the new, ancient script; for others a tie with Florence is less certain or only indirect, raising the possibility of polygenesis in independent creation of the *littera antiqua* (which could be explained in light of identical points of departure and a shared ideological climate).

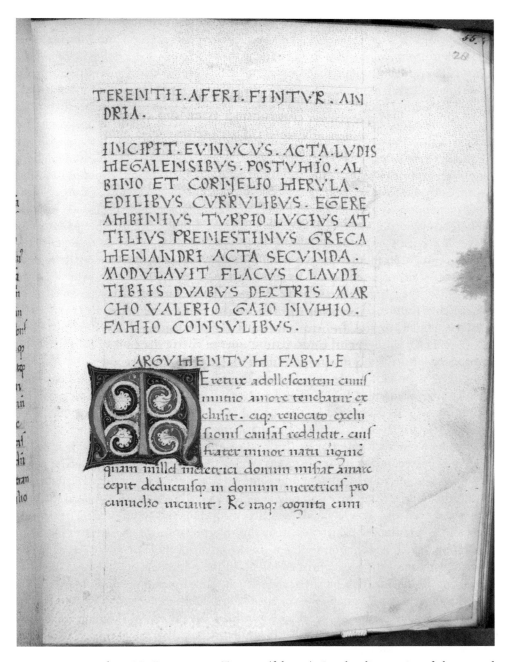

TEREINTII.AFFRI.FINTVR.AIN
DRIA.

IINCIPIT. EVINVCVS . ACTA.LVDIS
HEGALEIMSIBVS . POSTVHIO . AL
BIINO ET CORIMELIO HERVLA .
EDILIBVS CVRRVLIBVS . EGERE
AHBIINIVS TVRPIO LVCIVS AT
TILIVS PREIMESTIIMVS GRECA
HEIINAINDRI ACTA SECVINDA .
MODVLAVIT FLACVS CLAVDI
TIBIIS DVABVS DEXTRIS MAR
CHO VALERIO GAIO IMVHIO .
FAHIO COIMSVLIBVS .

ARGVHEINTVH FABVLE

E retur adollescentem cuius
mutuo amore tenebatur et
chisit. eiqz renocato exclu
sionis causas reddidit. cuis
frater minor natu uigine
quam milles meretrici domini misat amare
cepit deductusqz in domum meretricis pro
eunuclio meauit. Re itaqz cognita cum

PLATE 32.2 London, BL, Burney 263, Terence (fol. 28r). Lombardic copyist of the second quarter of the fifteenth century: *littera antiqua*, white vine-stem initials and mixed capital script.

We recognize the Florentine model (adopted en bloc: script, majuscules, decoration in white vine stem) in the manuscripts copied by the Venetian Girolamo Donato for his uncle Pietro, who will be bishop of Padua from 1428 until 1447 (Bologna, Biblioteca Universitaria, 2621, Catullus, dated 1411; Milan, Biblioteca Trivulziana, 661, Cicero, *De officiis*, dated 1412); in the manuscripts of the Ferrarese Rodolfo de Misotis (Paris, BnF, lat. 8537, Cicero, *Epistulae ad Atticum*, dated 1415);[33] in those of Niccolò Schiaffini da Camogli (London, BL, Harley 3551, Plato, translated by Leonardo Bruni, copied in Caffa, on the Black Sea, in 1416);[34] in those of the Lombard notary Ambrogio de Marudis, who worked in Florence for Matteo di Filippo Strozzi (Florence, Biblioteca Nazionale Centrale, Magl. VI 185, Cicero, *De oratore*, dated 1418; London, BL, Add. 24913, Suetonius, dated 1419;[35] Siena, Biblioteca Comunale, H XI 65, Cicero, *Tusculanae quaestiones*, dated 1419); and in those of Marco "Quartarius" of Parma (Florence, Biblioteca Nazionale Centrale, Conv. soppr. J.7.19, John Chrysostom translated by Traversari, *c*.1418–20).[36] Although we cannot exclude awareness of models of the twelfth century, all these copyists seem to hold as their reference the contemporary book that is *all'antica* and not actual old codices. Yet another scribe who looks to Florence is the Roman Cencio dei Rustici (Berlin, Staatsbibliothek zu Berlin-Preussischer Kulturbesitz, lat. fol. 609, Cicero, *Epistulae ad familiares*, *c*.1413).[37]

In the script *all'antica* of other manuscripts from the Veneto and especially of those from Lombardy during the second decade of the century, even while it is evident that the general principles of the transformation to the old style are the same as those embraced by the Florentines (substitution of variant letterforms, definition of a new paradigm of majuscules, and a new repertoire of decoration), we also notice great continuity with the present tradition, whether it is termed "moderna" or "Gotica." This continuity is displayed in the use of a rather large pen producing a line that is rich in contrast between thick and thin strokes (while in Florence, once the first experimental phase had passed, one tended to use a pen with a thinner point) or in the technique of writing that is, in essence, still that of the *littera textualis* (with assimilated strokes that have turned into stereotypes, repeating in all letters; with a finishing stroke at the base of all the descenders; with letters written closely together and compacted). The tie with the Gothic tradition is evident even in the interpretation of the white vine stem decoration, which is sometimes present in the initials of these manuscripts, or in the tenacious fondness for pen-flourished initials in the traditional colors of red, blue, or purple. As examples of this northern style which, while innovating, never quite cuts its ties with the "modern" system, we can cite Oxford, Bodleian Library, MS Laud Lat. 70 (Seneca, *Epistulae morales*, dated 1409[38]); in the same library, MS Canon. Class. Lat. 193 (Sallust, dated 1411–12)[39] and MS Canon. Class. Lat. 96 (Terence, copied in Florence in 1419 by one "presbiter Guilierimus," who, not managing to sustain the effort of the new script, returns in the second part of the manuscript to his more natural *rotunda*);[40] London, BL, Egerton 2909 (Terence, copied near Ferrara in 1419 by Giovanni Bergognini from Asti);[41] Oxford, Bodleian Library, MS Canon. Pat. Lat. 224 (Jerome, *Epistolae*, copied in 1420 by Ruggero Cataldo);[42] Vatican City, BAV, Barb. lat. 684 (Ramon Llull, copied in Rome in 1425);[43] Brussels, BR, 14873 (Cicero,

De officiis, dated 1428, in the hand of the Milanese Bartolomeo Sachella);[44] dubious, on the other hand, is the date of 1400 (derived from the exemplar?) for the manuscript, London, BL, Burney 208 (Valerius Maximus),[45] datable perhaps to the third decade of the century, a typical example of this Gothicizing line of *antiqua*, decorated with splendid initials in white vine stem by a Lombard miniaturist.

Completely independent of the Florentine models, and of greater interest than the number of surviving witnesses might suggest, is the experiment attempted by Guarino Veronese (1374–1460) in 1406 during his stay in Constantinople, while ignorant of what was happening in Florence. In Vatican City, BAV, Pal. gr. 116 (Aristophanes)[46] Guarino inscribed his ownership note in *littera antiqua*, using, alongside the "ancient" variants already identified by the Florentines, completely different letterforms that will mark in a permanent way the fifteenth-century graphic experience of the Veneto and more generally that of the entire valley of the Po River. These spot letters are so particular that they can serve to signal the origin of copyists, or the origin of their schooling: the letter *r* with its first stroke pulled below the baseline and curved to the left (a form that is found in documents of the twelfth century), and majuscules of Byzantine derivation. A few years later, in 1414, in the dedication copy prepared for Francesco Barbaro of his translation of the Life of Dio by Plutarch (Oxford, Bodleian Library, MS Bywater 38),[47] Guarino uses a script that is certainly *all'antica*, but that cannot be linked to Florentine models: produced with a narrow pen, more inclined, with descenders below the baseline, not fully purified of the "modern" markers (round *r*, normally required after a curved letter and carefully avoided by the Florentines, appears with great frequency); above all, his script is interwoven with ligatures and with letters produced by a single movement of the pen. It was thought that some of the characteristics of Guarino's *antiqua* could derive from a different and older model (*f*/*s* with descenders below the baseline and slanted *ductus* are found in the Caroline minuscule of the ninth century).[48] It seems more likely that Guarino's point of departure is different (he was educated as a notary): a bastard script which could be used either in books, in correspondence, and in the production of documents, with greater or lesser rapidity, written with pens of greater or lesser width.[49] Different kinds of the same adaptable *antiqua* are used during the second and third decades of the century by Michele Selvatico, a Venetian notary of German origin, in five codices datable to the years 1414–18, almost all with corrections and notes by Guarino (Florence, BML, 78.25, Francesco Barbaro, *De re uxoria*; Florence, Biblioteca Riccardiana, 1221/3, Plutarch, *De liberis educandis* in the translation by Guarino; Florence, Biblioteca Nazionale Centrale, Conv. soppr. J.10.44, Plutarch, *Vitae*, translated by Barbaro, Fig. 32.4a; Vatican City, BAV, Pal. lat. 1364, Letters and orations by Barbaro; Venice, Biblioteca Nazionale Marciana, Z 483, Nonius Marcellus).[50] Eight other scribes attest to this script as well: Giovanni Campofregoso (Holkham Hall, Misc. 36, Propertius, copied in 1421);[51] Biondo Flavio (Vatican City, BAV, Ottob. lat. 1592, Cicero, *Brutus*, dated 1422),[52] Giovanni Aurispa and Iacopo Languschi (Vatican City, BAV, Ottob. lat. 1984, Cicero, *De finibus, Academica posteriora*, dated 1422);[53] Giovanni de Canonicis (Oxford, Bodleian Library, MS Canon. Class. Lat. 121, dated 1420);[54]

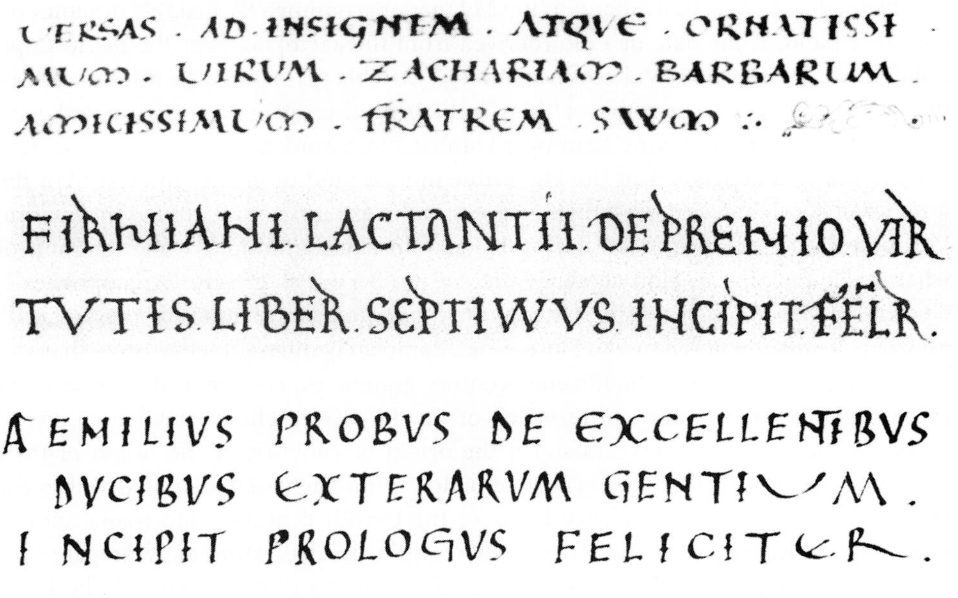

*ERSAS · AD INSIGNEM · ATQVE · ORNATISSI ·
MUO · UIRUM · ZACHARIAO · BARBARUM ·
ADOICISSIMUO · FRATREM · SUOO ·.

FIRMIANI LACTANTII DE PREMIO VIR
TVTIS LIBER SEPTIWVS INCIPIT FELR.

AEMILIVS PROBVS DE EXCELLENTIBVS
DVCIBVS EXTERARVM GENTIVM.
INCIPIT PROLOGVS FELICITCR.

FIG. 32.4 Examples of *variatio*: (a) Florence, Biblioteca Nazionale Centrale, Conv. soppr. J.10.44 (fol. 105r): Michele Germanico; (b) Florence, BML, 21.6 (fol. 158r), AD 1432; (c) Florence, Biblioteca Riccardiana 631 (fol.1r): Milano Borri, AD 1444.

"Oddo Mazolinus" (Oxford, Bodleian Library, MS Lat. class. d.5, of 1420–1);[55] Giorgio Begna da Zara (Paris, BnF, lat. 6106, Caesar, Frontinus, and Vegetius, copied between 1425 and 1435);[56] "Franciscus Viglevius de Ardiciis" (in a note dated 1425 in Vatican City, BAV, Ottob. lat. 2057).[57]

But the aspect that best exemplifies the difference between the early Florentine tradition and that of Lombardy and the Veneto is found in the letters used in titles or with a display function (Fig. 32.4). If the paradigm of the majuscules of Niccoli, Poggio, and their followers tends to consistency, i.e., to an orderly recovery of the alphabet of capitals (deduced rather than imitated; Romanic rather than Roman) that permits only minimal variations rather than variants (*A* with or without the middle stroke, *M* with the first and final strokes straight or angled, and so forth[58]), the majuscules used in codices of northern Italy (even assuming that one may speak of paradigms in this case) depend on *variatio*, from the short note by Guarino in 1406 onward, i.e., on a combination of letters of diverse matrix and antiquity: Latin and Greek-Byzantine majuscules (especially *A*, *B*, *C*, *E*, *M*, and *O*), Capital and Uncial letters, of book or epigraphic tradition, often produced with acrobatic fusions or interlaces.[59]

Once the taboo that enforced consistency had been violated, the use of *variatio* contaminated the script of the text as well. In the codices of Michele Selvatico (already by the second decade, but in growing measure in the following decades), in the codex copied in Pisa in 1419 by the aforementioned Niccolò Schiaffini (Brussels, BR, IV 719, a compilation of short works translated by Bruni),[60] and in the codices of another Venetian notary, Sebastiano Borsa (El Escorial, Real Biblioteca de San Lorenzo, T III 19, Cicero, *De officiis* and Paris, BnF, lat. 6761, both dated 1424),[61] we can observe an intense use of Capital and Uncial letters in the body and at the end of words, of epigraphic fusions, in forms of unexpected *ductus*, more often extravagant and picturesque. These scripts constitute the immediate precedent to the hand of Ciriaco d'Ancona (1391–1452) that so impressed his contemporaries (and so impresses us) for its daring and inventive solutions, for its continuous allusions to graphic realities that were distant in time and space and, at the same time, for the casual naturalness of its results.[62] The first codex by this inventor of *litterae* "copulatae et colligatae et invicem connexae atque contextae" dates from 1427 (Vatican City, BAV, Vat. lat. 10672, Ovid):[63] the script, still fairly disciplined, is a semi-cursive in the vein of Guarino with inlays at the end of the lines of letters deriving from capitals and uncials. In the 1430s and 1440s a passion for the antique explodes: the script of Ciriaco, who knew Greek and collected inscriptions, is transformed into a pastiche of letters and ligatures taken from Byzantine minuscules, of majuscules within the body of words, of epigraphic fusions (Fig. 32.5). His experiment is very personal and bizarre, but it is not born in a void: it can only be explained as continuity with the script of Guarino and as amplification of the ideas and styles that had been circulating in humanistic circles in the Veneto since the first appearance of the *litterae antiquae formae*. This continuity explains the persistence of some of Ciriaco's inventions, within that same environment, into the second half of the century.

The experience in the Veneto and in Lombardy in the first half of the century appears, in many ways, different from that of Florence. Not only is there no one model shared by many copyists, but the copyists themselves behave with considerable liberty with respect to what functions as their own model, sometimes committing themselves to precise imitation and sometimes taking from the model isolated stylistic characteristics that may prove useful to give a patina of antiquity to scripts that remain, in their

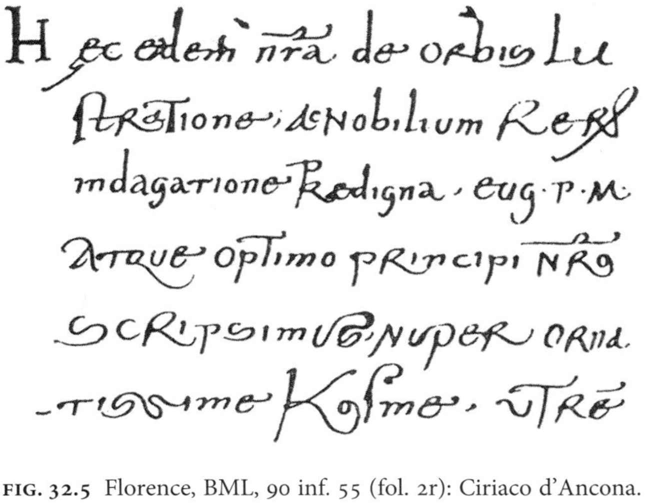

FIG. 32.5 Florence, BML, 90 inf. 55 (fol. 2r): Ciriaco d'Ancona.

essence, "modern" or Gothic. The absence, during the first half of the century, of production in series of codices *all'antica* accentuated the variations and occasional anarchies of the experiences in the Veneto and in Lombardy. What was missing was the leveling action exerted upon *antiqua* by professional copyists such as occurred early on in Florence. Before Lombardy can lay claim to copyists with a comparable level of activity to that of the Florentines, even though quantitatively much reduced, we must wait at least until the fourth decade of the century: for Bartolomeo Sachella (eight manuscripts copied between 1428 and 1438);[64] for Milano Borri (ten manuscripts between 1433 and 1449);[65] for Antonio Crivelli or Balzaride (11 manuscripts copied between 1433 and 1458);[66] and for Pagano da Rho (32 manuscripts *all'antica* between *c.*1440 and 1468).[67] No one, however, exceeds the Venetian Michele Selvatico (more than 40 codices, datable between 1416 and about 1456).[68]

THE SECOND HALF OF THE CENTURY

By 1440 *littera antiqua* as restored by the humanists imposes itself on a much larger public, sometimes remote from the cultural reasons and ideals that lie at the root of its "invention"; this public, however, recognizes the script as a distinctive component of luxury books (and ownership of these books is a symbol of social prestige). The presence of copyists (even foreigners) capable of writing the new script spreads to all parts of Italy, not only in cities hosting temporarily or permanently a well-to-do and international clientele, attentive to the novelty of a book *all'antica* (Rome),[69] but also in cities where the large court libraries are coming into being, sometimes from zero (Naples, Urbino, Cesena, Rimini, Mantua, Bologna, and Ferrara) (Plate 32.3). But the centers in which *littera antiqua* was developed and put into precocious use (Florence, the Veneto, and to a lesser degree Milan) do not thereby lose importance; on the contrary, for various reasons their position is reinforced: Florence by becoming the seat of a book industry on an international scale,[70] and the Veneto as the seat of elaboration of a new variation on the *antiqua*.

   In the book as copied in Florentine style in the second half of the Quattrocento (both within and outside of Florence), the script presents differences essentially only of execution with respect to the forms of the first 20 years: generally, preference goes to a thinner pen; the size of the letters is larger; the ascenders of *b*, *d*, *h*, and *l* and the descenders of *p* and *q* thicken or divide into forking at their terminations (in Neapolitan codices, analogous thickening occurs at the base of every vertical stroke); the lower bowl of *g* lengthens noticeably downward in a more flowing and sinuous movement; round *s* reappears at the end of words, and one sees again the fusion of contrary convex curves (which, for that matter, had never completely disappeared). The major differences reside in the non-script aspects of the book, especially in the decoration: the white vine stem becomes more complicated by incorporating animals, flowers, and putti; even the lowest level of a good codex *all'antica* demands an opening page with decorated initial and a two- or three-sided border, or else a full border and a solemn

PLATE 32.3 Bloomington, Indiana University, Lilly Library, Ricketts 222, Cicero (fol. 173r). Copied by Leonardus Job (Rome, third quarter of the fifteenth century): *littera antiqua*, frieze with white vine stem.

inscriptio (with the name of the author, title of the work, etc.) in majuscules in gold or in colored inks, sometimes with letters alternating various colors (other initials and titles may appear at the lesser text divisions). Given their cost, these are books destined for a highly select clientele, perhaps more interested in the book as an object than in its content.

Obviously, books continue to be copied for personal use with results that are not necessarily of inferior quality. Within this more private dimension in Florence in the 1440s, we see the beginning (or the return) of a cursive script *all'antica*. By the 1460s, almost all professional copyists possess a repertory that includes both scripts (one name will suffice to stand for many: Antonio Sinibaldi); others use only the cursive with notable elegance (e.g., Bartolomeo Fonzio or Tommaso Baldinotti; Plate 32.4). It is difficult to say whether we are dealing with a reflowering of the cursive used almost 30 years earlier by Niccoli that had then sunk below the surface, or whether this is a new, autonomous development brought about by the same principle. Compared to the minute, dense, and rapid cursive of Niccoli, with its undeniably Gothic flavor (remember that Niccoli learned to write in the 1370s), this new humanistic cursive (whether its base lies in notarial or even in merchant scripts) asserts itself in an environment strongly conditioned by the aesthetic model of *antiqua*, and thus offers forms that are straighter and round, with fewer ligatures. In varying levels of formality, this cursive is employed for notes, letters, and owner copies of texts, but it is also the script in which the humanists published their own writings.

Throughout the second half of the fifteenth century, therefore, Florence retains its central role in the production of books *all'antica*: numerous copyists ply their trade in that city (A. C. de la Mare counts more than one hundred scribes whose hand is known in at least three manuscripts, for a total of over 1,500 codices).[71] In that city we also find numerous shops of "cartolai" (Vespasiano da Bisticci, Zanobi di Mariano, Girolamo di Giovanni Parigi, Francesco di Neri, Benedetto di Giovanni, Antonio di Filippo Ventura, Bartolomeo d'Agnolo Tucci, and Gherardo and Monte di Giovanni) who coordinate the activities of copyists, miniaturists, and bookbinders, and thus satisfy all kinds of requests (not only for codices *all'antica*) in relatively short spans of time. Vespasiano asserts with ill-concealed pride that in 22 months he oversaw the production of 200 manuscripts for the library of the Badia Fiesolana ordered by Cosimo de' Medici by putting to work 45 scribes. Verification by A. C. de la Mare has slightly changed these numbers (some manuscripts were not copied *ex novo*, but acquired in the second-hand market; some manuscripts were not procured by Vespasiano but by other booksellers). Nevertheless, the main part of the library was, in fact, put together between 1462 and 1464, and among the "new" manuscripts procured by Vespasiano we recognize the hands of 38 copyists.[72] Orders from high-ranking figures arrived in Vespasiano's bookshop and were executed by Florentine copyists; their books were gifts to popes and kings. The list of names is impressive: the Medici, obviously, and all the richest and most influential families of Florence; the Aragonese of Naples; the Montefeltro; the Sforza of Milan and those of Pesaro; Matthias Corvinus, king of Hungary; Louis XI, king of France; Manuel, king of Portugal; Pius II, Paul II, Sixtus IV, the cardinal

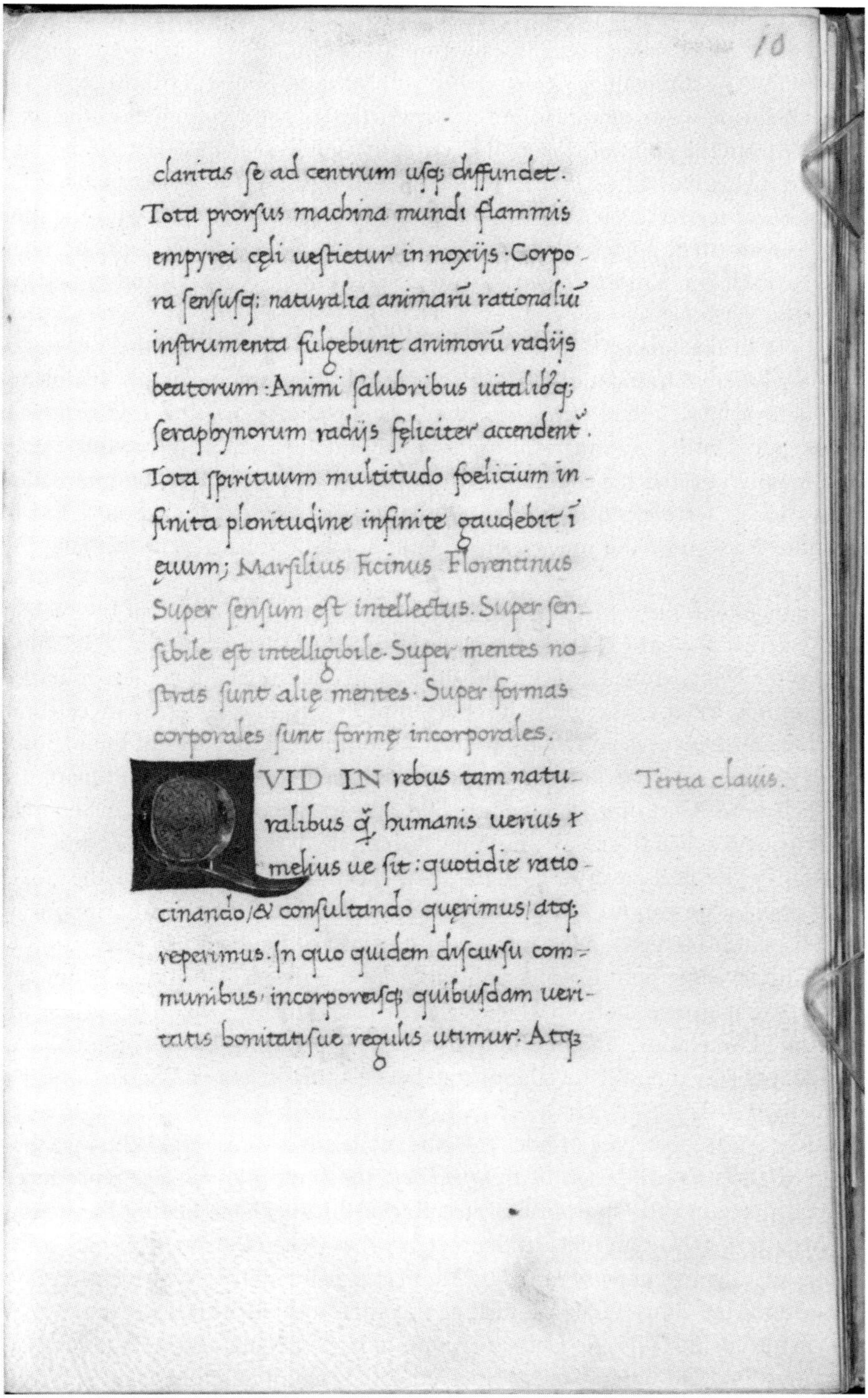

claritas se ad centrum usq; diffundet.
Tota prorsus machina mundi flammis
empyrei celi uestietur in noxijs ·Corpo
ra sensusq; naturalia animaru rationaliu
instrumenta fulgebunt animoru radijs
beatorum ·Animi salubribus uitaliboq;
seraphynorum radijs feliciter accendent.
Tota spirituum multitudo foelicium in
finita plenitudine infinite gaudebit i
euum; Marsilius Ficinus Florentinus
Super sensum est intellectus. Super sen
sibile est intelligibile·Super mentes no
stras sunt alie mentes·Super formas
corporales sunt forme incorporales.

QVID IN rebus tam natu
ralibus q̃ humanis uerius r
melius ue sit :quotidie ratio
cinando/& consultando querimus/atq;
reperimus·In quo quidem discursu com ‐
munibus· incorporeisq; quibusdam ueri‐
tatis bonitatisue regulis utimur·Atq;

Tertia clauis.

PLATE 32.4 Ithaca, Cornell University Library, Rare B. F. 44, Marsilio Ficino, *Claves Platonicae Sapientiae* (fol. 10r). Copied by Tommaso Baldinotti (Florence, 1478–80) in cursive *alla antica*.

Jean Jouffroy, the bishop Janos Vitez; the marquis of Santillana; Robert Fleming, and so on. Florentine copyists were celebrities with pay scales to match; they were sometimes scooped up by the competition (as happened with Antonio Sinibaldi from 1460 to 1480).

Nevertheless, if we examine Florentine production of the second half of the century exclusively from the point of view of the script, this golden age reveals itself partially as an illusion. Once Florentine *littera antiqua* passed into the hands of capable artisans who had never seen a *codex vetustus*, the script—having lost contact with the models and the ideals that guided the first experiments—repeats itself without change: faithful to itself for almost 50 years, impeccable, but impersonal and closed to all renewal.

The myth of the "ancient" continues to renew itself, however, in the Veneto, on a profoundly different foundation and with an entirely different meaning.[73] If, during the early Quattrocento, it had been left to philology to nourish the myth, now it is archaeology or, rather, antiquarianism; if, during the first half of the century, graphic change mainly affected the minuscule script, now it is the turn of the majuscules; if the first models were exclusively (or in large preponderance) from books and from the Middle Ages, now the models are epigraphic and truly ancient, actually of the Roman era.

The change took place in Padua, Verona, and Venice. It is here that between 1450 and 1465 actual ancient capital letters derived from stone inscriptions of the imperial age make their appearance not only in titles or in the initials of codices, but also in panel painting, frescoes, sculpture, architectural details, and funerary or celebratory inscriptions. Precedences and debts among the various occurrences of the majuscules have not yet been clarified, in part because the people involved in this antiquarian shift (Felice Feliciano, Giovanni Marcanova, Bartolomeo Sanvito, Francesco Squarcione, and Andrea Mantegna) are all in some fashion tied to one another, and are all implicated in the rediscovery of epigraphy: Feliciano is the copyist of the *Collectio antiquitatum* of Marcanova[74] (Plate 32.5) and of other collections of inscriptions; with Marcanova and Mantegna, Feliciano is a protagonist of the boat trip in 1464 on Lake Garda on a scavenger hunt for epigraphic inscriptions (the tale is told in an autograph manuscript that also contains the *Vita Kyriaci Anconitani*);[75] Sanvito has access to the *exemplaria* of Marcanova and he will transcribe the epigraphic *Sylloge* of Fra Giovanni Giocondo a full six times;[76] the relationship between Mantegna and Squarcione is well known.

From the start, the degree of fidelity to the models is astonishing. When we look at the work of artists the effect is of *trompe l'oeil*: the "new" capitals are reproduced in correct proportion, with appropriate variation of thickness, simulating the furrow of the stonecutter or the high relief of the metalworker (when the letter mimics casting): consider the *Judgment of Saint James* by Mantegna, painted in 1451 (which reproduces the inscription of Titus Pullius Linus, at the time located near Este, and which is also known to us through the *Collectio antiquitatum* of Marcanova) or the initials of the manuscripts, Deventer, Stadsarchief en Athenaeumbibliotheek, 11.D.4.Kl (one of the first works of Bartolomeo Sanvito, c.1454-5);[77] Paris, BnF, lat. 17542 (Ptolemy,

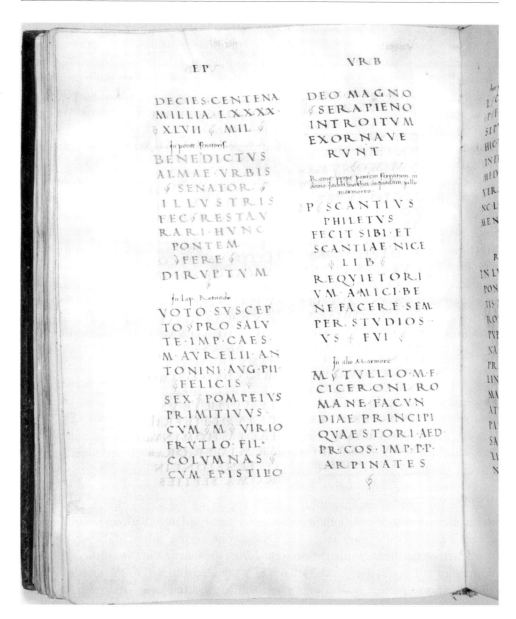

PLATE 32.5 Modena, Biblioteca Estense, Estense lat. 992 (alpha. L.5.15), Giovanni Marcanova, *Collectio antiquitatum* (fol. 76v). Square capitals in the hand of Felice Feliciano (Bologna, 1465).

*c.*1456–7);[78] and Albi, Médiathèque Pierre-Amalric (formerly Bibliothèque Roche-gude), 4 (Strabo, 1459),[79] produced with such three-dimensionality as to seem as if objects were placed on the book.

The appearance of epigraphic initials in books is accompanied by the arrival of new decorative motifs: opening pages are framed by architectural structures that are at times very complex (in an inventory of the early sixteenth century[80] these frames are termed "a casamento"), embellished with columns, aediculae, inscriptions, coins, cameos, medals, panoplies, garlands, cornucopias, and inhabited by putti, satyrs, centaurs, dwarfs, mermaids, and sphinxes. At the same time ancient book production techniques, or ones imagined so, were rediscovered, such as the use of purple parchment (also tinted blue, green, or yellow)[81] that required lettering in gold or silver; another high medieval or Byzantine habit reappeared: the use of a frontispiece that placed a page containing the title or the dedication of the work (often decorated and laid out as if an epigraphic inscription) to face the opening page of the text.

The visibility, the variety, and the high quality of antiquarian quotations in the areas of the book controlled by the miniaturist risk overshadowing the work of the copyist, which is of equal significance and which, at least in part, derives from the same sources. Beginning in 1450, copyists begin to use in titles and with display functions the same repertory of epigraphic capitals, produced obviously in freer and simpler forms (the letters are written, not drawn), but nonetheless correct in their proportions and layout, as we can see in the manuscript Venezia, Biblioteca Nazionale Marciana, Marc. lat. IX 1 [3496] (Eusebius-Jerome, *Chronicon*),[82] copied in 1450 by Biagio Saraceno and in the 12 manuscripts of his first Paduan period (1453–9) by Bartolomeo Sanvito (1437–1511), the longest-lived and most prolific copyist of the century (A. C. de la Mare identified 124 manuscripts in his hand; Plate 32.6).[83] Capitals of equal quality are used by Felice Feliciano of Verona (c.1433–c.1480; Plate 32.5) in all his autograph manuscripts and in many codices in which he functioned only as decorator. We owe to Feliciano the first treatise on geometric construction of capitals according to the norms of epigraphy (Vatican City, BAV, Vat. lat. 6852, copied in 1460).[84] From epigraphic inscriptions they took not only the forms of the letters, but also the manner in which the letters combined together: titles and colophons reproduce the forms of classical layout, using fusions, *litterae inclusae* or diminished size, *interpuncta*, etc.

At the moment when epigraphic capitals appear on the scene, alphabets of mixed majuscules are abandoned, both in codices in *antiqua* and in codices copied in the most informal and varied cursive scripts *all'antica*; gone are the mixed alphabets that had characterized northern Humanistic scripts during the first half of the century with their majuscules in Greek style, Uncial letters, minuscules promoted to the level of majuscules. In almost perfect synchronicity with diffusion of the "new" ancient majuscules, the minuscules accept normalization and stylization in both the *antiqua* and in the cursive *all'antica*.[85]

As had already occurred with the Florentine model, normalization plays out mainly in the execution of the script: here, too, a narrower pen is preferred, the bodies of the letters tend to a squarish shape, there is more space between the letters, and the sequence of strokes within the letters is also more spacious. There is, however, one important difference, which is the conclusion of a tendency active in the Veneto during the first half of the century and which now surfaces, encouraged by the presence of the new epigraphic capitals in the titles: the use of majuscules (now exclusively capitals)

PLATE 32.6 Austin, University of Texas, Harry Ransom Humanities Research Center, HRC 35, Horace (fol. 56r). Copied by Bartolomeo Sanvito (Padua, active 1460–1): text in *littera antiqua*, gloss in cursive; title, first verse ("Humano capiti cervicem pictor equinam") and beginning of verses in square capitals.

within and at the end of words, liberated from any distinguishing purpose; the most frequent are *R* and *T* (especially at the end of words), *S* (at the end of and within words), and *Q*; but we also find the letters *A*, *D*, *M*, *H*, and *V*.

In the 1450s the "minuscule" capitals are used by Bartolomeo Sanvito in some of his manuscripts in *antiqua* (e.g., Deventer, Stadsarchief en Athenaeumbibliotheek, 11.D.4. Kl, Propertius; Milan, Biblioteca Braidense, AC XII 34, Vergil; Venice, Biblioteca Nazionale Marciana, lat. XII 153 [4453], Tibullus and Catullus; Evanston, Illinois, Northwestern University, McCormick Library, Western MS 12, Statius). In the 1460s we find analogous insertions of capital letters in the *antiqua* of Felice Feliciano,[86] in the 1470s in the *antiqua* of the copyist Iohannes de Nydenna ("Io. Ny."), originally from Koblenz, but active in the Veneto.[87] In Lombardy we point out the very peculiar case of the manuscript Milan, Biblioteca Ambrosiana, I 86 sup., copied by Pagano da Rho between 1450 and 1452, where, as well as the majuscules already listed, are *F*, *G*, *L*, and *P*.[88] The example given here is from London, BL, Harley 2511, dating from 1464, by an anonymous scribe (Fig. 32.6).[89]

From the 1460s certain stylistic variants *alla greca* already used by Ciriaco d'Ancona and Michele Selvatico enter the script of Sanvito with new calligraphic visibility (Fig. 32.7): the tall variant of *t* in the form of a *tau* (used also by Feliciano), sometimes in ligature; the ligature *ho*, with the *o* contained within the *h*; the ligature *sp* in at least two forms; the letter *c* enlarged sufficiently to contain the following vowel *o*.

Stylistic variants in Greek mode and capitals cross over into Sanvito's calligraphic and regular cursive during these same years; this is the script tied to his fame as a most elegant *scriptor*; it can be defined, not inappropriately, as *cancelleresca* (or even, according to the terminology of the calligraphers of the early Cinquecento, italic *cancelleresca*). These features, namely the essential morphological identity of the letters (only *a* and *r* are, in fact, different, being cursive in form), and the technique of writing (the letters are produced in the same manner stroke by stroke without actual ligatures), make *cancelleresca* and *antiqua* by now two grades of a single script (Plate 32.6).

Some forms move from Sanvito's *cancelleresca*, which quickly became a model, almost a new archetype, into the more calligraphic and professional cursives of copyists in the Veneto (e.g., Antonio da Salla)[90] or in Rome (where Sanvito spent long periods of time); these forms also influenced the occasional Florentine (e.g., Antonio Sinibaldi

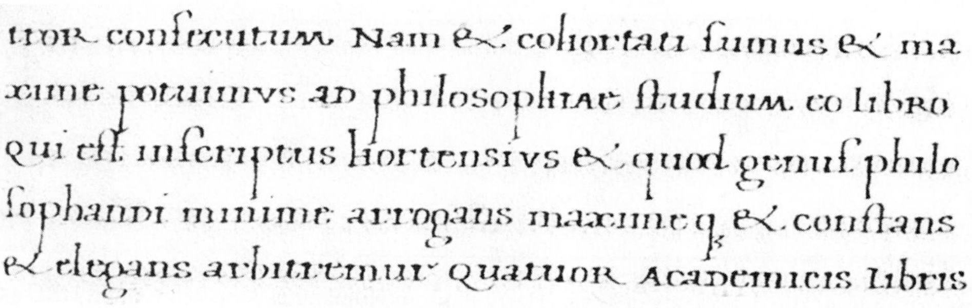
tior consecutum. Nam et cohortati sumus et ma
xime potuimus ad philosophiae studium eo libro
qui est inscriptus Hortensius et quod genus philo
sophandi minime arrogans maximeque et constans
et elegans arbitraremur quatuor Academicis libris

FIG. 32.6 London, BL, Harley 2511 (fol. 122r): AD 1464 (Padua).

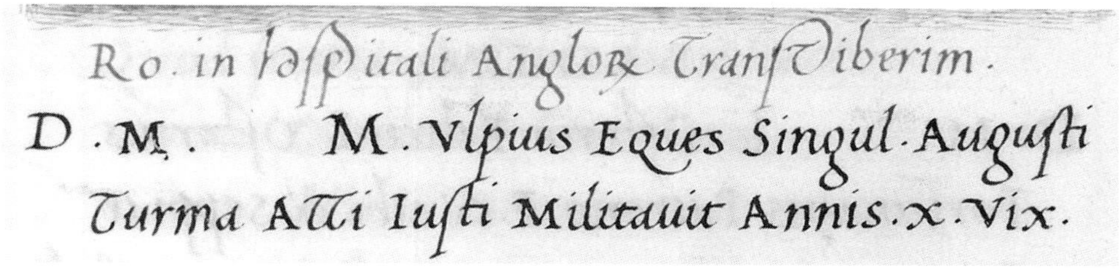

FIG. 32.7 London, BL, Stowe 1016 (fol. 133r).

and Alessandro da Verrazzano)[91] and they survived into the Cinquecento (Fig. 32.8), mainly thanks to the treatises of the early writing masters (see the *mostra* of "litere cancellaresche" of Giovanni Antonio Tagliente, *Lo presente libro insegna la vera arte delo excellente scrivere*, 1524; Fig. 32.9). It is a well-known fact that the series of cursive characters adapted for Aldus Manutius by the punch cutter Francesco Griffo derive from a *cancelleresca* of the Veneto in the Sanvito mode.

But the lesson learned from Ciriaco and the genealogy that goes from him back to Guarino (and from Guarino to the very origins of the graphic reform) are not exhausted in the exalted, sometimes frigid forms of Sanvito's script. Greek and majuscule forms (tall *t* in the form of a *tau*; the conjunction handled as a ligature *epsilon–tau*; the more unusual *theta* for the group *th*; *G* within the body of the word) and references to high medieval scripts surface in varying combinations in the hands of several humanists (Pomponio Leto, Pontano, Politian, and their students), in particular for those who also copied Greek or who studied the philology of ancient texts. The true heir to Ciriaco is, however, Felice Feliciano, active throughout the third quarter of the century, in locales also frequented by Sanvito (the Veneto, Bologna, Florence, and

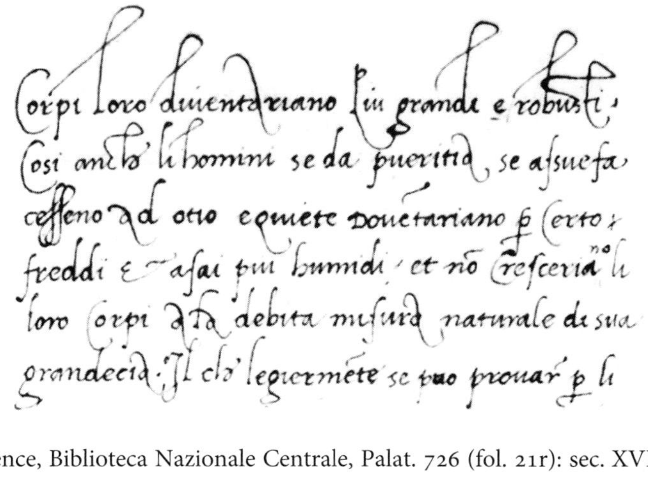

FIG. 32.8 Florence, Biblioteca Nazionale Centrale, Palat. 726 (fol. 21r): sec. XVI in.

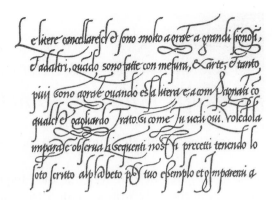

FIG. 32.9 Giovanni Antonio Tagliente, *Lo presente libro insegna la vera arte delo excellente scrivere*, [Venezia] 1524 (fol. A4v).

Rome). The production of Feliciano is so varied and eclectic (and not only in terms of its scripts) that each codex essentially stands alone. The range of his scripts goes from an elegant *littera antiqua* in the best tradition of the Veneto (Verona, Biblioteca Comunale, 2845, or Florence, Biblioteca Riccardiana, 794)[92] to a frankly old-fashioned cursive (e.g., Oxford, Bodleian Library, MS Canon. Ital. 56, Giusto dei Conti, *La bella mano*, 1465),[93] to a cursive *all'antica* not terribly far from Sanvito's own (Florence, Biblioteca Nazionale Centrale, Magl. XXIII 17, Cato, *De re militari*),[94] to an *antiqua* chock full of quotations from Ciriaco or at least of inventions that only make sense if Ciriaco is their source (Trento, Buonconsiglio, 1659 or Vatican City, BAV, Vat. lat. 5641),[95] and finally to a capital used as the main script of the text as in Padua, Biblioteca Civica, B. P. 1099 (*Hercules in bivio* translated by Sassolo da Prato, *c.*1463);[96] this experiment of a text in all capitals does not seem to have been attempted by any other copyist of the Italian Quattrocento, with the exception of the short space of a frontispiece. Thus, with the experiment of Feliciano, who imagined a book as written by the ancient Romans, the backward-looking initiative of Poggio and Niccoli reached its ultimate goal: from the *litterae quae sapiunt antiquitatem* one arrived at the *litterae Romanae*.

SUGGESTED READING

Berthold L. Ullman. *The Origin and Development of Humanistic Script*. Rome: Edizioni di Storia e Letteratura, 1960; James Wardrop, *The Script of Humanism: Some Aspects of Humanistic Script 1460–1560*. Oxford: Clarendon Press, 1963; Emanuele Casamassima. "Literulae Latinae. Nota paleografica." In Stefano Caroti and Stefano Zamponi. *Lo scrittoio di Bartolomeo Fonzio umanista fiorentino*, ix–xxxii. Milan: Il Polifilo, 1974. For the first Florentine generation: Albinia C. de la Mare. *The Handwriting of Italian Humanists. I, 1:*

Francesco Petrarca, Giovanni Boccaccio, Coluccio Salutati, Niccolò Niccoli, Poggio Bracciolini, Bartolomeo Aragazzi of Montepulciano, Sozomeno da Pistoia, Giorgio Antonio Vespucci. Oxford: Association Internationale de Bibliophilie, 1973. For an update, see Teresa De Robertis. "I primi anni della scrittura umanistica. Materiali per un aggiornamento." In Palaeography, Manuscript Illumination and Humanism in Renaissance Italy: Studies in Memory of A. C. de la Mare, ed. Robert Black, Jill Kraye, and Laura Nuvoloni, 55–85. London: Warburg Institute, 2016. For the tradition in the Veneto (other than Wardrop and Casamassima): Elisabetta Barile. "Littera antiqua" e scritture alla greca. Notai e cancellieri a Venezia nei primi decenni del Quattrocento. Venice: Istituto veneto di scienze, lettere ed arti, 1994; Teresa De Robertis. "Motivi classici nella scrittura del primo Quattrocento." In L'ideale classico a Ferrara e in Italia nel Rinascimento, ed. Patrizia Castelli, 65–79. Florence: Olschki, 1998. For humanistic majuscules: Millard Meiss. "Toward a More Comprehensive Renaissance Paleography." The Art Bulletin 42 (1960) 97–112; Stefano Zamponi. "Le metamorfosi dell'antico: la tradizione antiquaria veneta." In I luoghi dello scrivere da Francesco Petrarca agli albori dell'età moderna, ed. Caterina Tristano, Marta Calleri, and Leonardo Magionami, 37–68. Spoleto: Centro Italiano di Studi sull'Alto Medioevo, 2006. For the miniatures: The Painted Page. Italian Renaissance Book Illumination 1450–1550, ed. Jonathan J. G. Alexander. Munich and New York: Prestel, 1994. Ample bibliography, including all the more important studies until 2003, in Stefano Zamponi. "La scrittura umanistica." Archiv für Diplomatik 50 (2004): 485–92.

ABBREVIATIONS

CMDB   François Masai and Martin Wittek, eds. 1968–. Manuscrits datés conservés en Belgique. Brussels and Ghent : Éditions scientifiques Story-Scientia.

CMDLond   Andrew G. Watson. 1979. Catalogue of Dated and Datable Manuscripts c.700–1600 in the Department of Manuscripts, the British Library. London: British Library.

CMDOx   Andrew G. Watson. 1984. Catalogue of Dated and Datable Manuscripts c.435–1600 in Oxford Libraries. Oxford: Clarendon Press.

CMDVat   I codici latini datati della Biblioteca Apostolica Vaticana. 1997–. Vatican City: Biblioteca Apostolica Vaticana.

NOTES

1. Florence, BML, S. Marco 230 (Plautus); S. Marco 262 (Cicero); S. Marco 690 (Propertius) (scriptio inferior); S. Marco 635, S. Marco 643, S. Marco 649, and S. Marco 665 (Augustine); S. Marco 612 (Origen); see de la Mare (1973, 77 and 1977, 94–6, fig. 2); De Robertis (1995, 497–503, Plates 1–2); Butrica (1984, 226).
2. Niccoli copies Florence, BML, S. Marco 612 and 649; Poggio copies Florence, BML, S. Marco 230, 262, 635, 643, and 665, and 690.
3. Especially in Florence, BML, S. Marco 635: see Gentile (1997, 166).
4. De Robertis (1990, 111–17, Plates 5–7).

5. Vatican City, BAV, Pal. lat. 903 (Billanovich (1981, 128–40; De Robertis, Tanturli, and Zamponi 2008, 290).

6. Bologna, Biblioteca Universitaria 2340; by the same hand are Bologna, Biblioteca Universitaria 2278 (Ovid), 2279 (Valerius Maximus), 2340 (Lucan), Cremona, Archivio di Stato, Framm. 83 (Seneca, *Thyestes*), Florence, BML, 37.5, Vatican City, BAV, Vat. lat. 1645 (both with Seneca, *Tragoediae*, not dated or signed; see *Seneca*, pp. 100–1 and 150–1 and Buonocore (1996, 311–13) and possibly Rome, Biblioteca Corsiniana, Cor. 1717 (Boccaccio, *De casibus*; see Cadei, 139). The only other signed manuscript is Florence, BML, 78.16 (Boethius). See Orsino (2018, 1–24).

7. Paris, BnF, lat. 7942 (Vergil); Oxford, Bodleian Library, MS Ital.e.6 (Dante); Florence, BML, Ashb. 1049 (*Rhetorica ad Herennium* and Cicero, *De inventione*): descriptions and images in De Robertis, Tanturli, and Zamponi (2008, 232–3, 302–3, 332–4); see also Zamponi (2010).

8. Ullman (1960, Plate 6); de la Mare (1973, 40 and Plate viie–*f*); De Robertis, Tanturli, and Zamponi (2008, 318–19).

9. Petrucci (1967, Plates xxii–xxvi).

10. *Boccaccio autore e copista* (2013, 300–5, with several plates.

11. Ullman (1960, 16–19).

12. De Robertis and Zamponi (2008, 345–51); De Robertis (2010).

13. De Robertis (2006, 113–26). For biographical information, see Miglio (2009).

14. London, BL, Harley 2648 (Juvenal and Persius, dated 1410; *CMDLond*, 16, Plate 325).

15. De la Mare (1977, 96–7, Plates 3–4).

16. De la Mare and Thomson (1973). The attribution is under discussion: see McKie (1989); de la Mare (1992, 120); De Robertis (2006, 126–8).

17. Ullman (1960, 27, Plate 15); de la Mare (1973, 75–7, Plates xve–*g* and xvi*f*.

18. De la Mare (1973, Plate xx*a*); for his script, see also Casamassima and Savino (1995).

19. De la Mare (1992, 120).

20. De la Mare (1985a, 482–4 and 595).

21. Ullman (1960, 96–8).

22. De la Mare (1992).

23. To the 12 codices listed by de la Mare (1973, 56–7), now add Florence, Biblioteca Nazionale Centrale II.IX.125 (Butrica (1981) and Florence, Biblioteca Riccardiana, 136 (De Robertis (1990, 105–10, Plates 1–3).

24. De la Mare (1973, Plate xiii*a*).

25. Ullman (1960, 73, 77).

26. Ullman (1960, 67–8).

27. Casamassima (1974, xiii–xiv); Zamponi (2004, 475).

28. Ullman (1960, 48, Plate 27); de la Mare (1973, 78, Plate xivc–*d*).

29. *MDI*, V 108, Plate 41.

30. For example, Pistoia, Biblioteca Comunale Forteguerriana, A.7 (Cicero, *Epistulae*), A.14 (Cicero, *De natura deorum*), A. 34 (Antonio Loschi, *Inquisitio super XI orationes Ciceronis*), all of the third decade (de la Mare 1973 100, 104; Ceccherini 2016, 267–72, 313–6).

31. Vatican City, BAV, Vat. lat. 9491 (Plato and Plutarch translated by Bruni and Guarino, 1414); Florence, BML, 78.24 (Barbaro, *De re uxoria*, 1416), Florence, BML, 46.13 (Quintilian, 1416–18), Florence, Biblioteca Nazionale Centrale, Conv. soppr. J.7.18 (John Chrysostom, *c*.1418; *MDI*, V 142, Plate 174) and Florence, Biblioteca Centrale,

Conv. soppr. J.9.35 (Juvencus and Faltonia Proba, *c.*1418; *MDI*, V 145, Plate 175); Oxford, Bodleian Library, MS D'Orville 78 (Cicero, *Orationes*, after 1417; *CMDOx*, 70, Plate 281).

32. "Only apparently light and rapid; in reality not less laborious to write than the *littera antiqua*," for which, see Casamassima (1974, xxiii).

33. *CMDF*, III 63, Plate 190.

34. *CMDLond*, 136–7, Plate 347.

35. *CMDLond*, 67, Plate 355.

36. *MDI*, V 142–3, Plate 186.

37. Lombardi (1983, 31–2, Plate 1).

38. *CMDOx*, 96, Plate 261.

39. *CMDOx*, 32, Plate 266. I point out that the original ms. also included a sections with Cicero (Canon. Class. Lat. 230). By the same scribe also Canon. Class. Lat. 110 (Albertino Mussato, *Ecerinis*).

40. *CMDOx*, 29, Plate 282.

41. *CMDLond*, 116, Plate 357.

42. *CMDOx*, 65, Plate 288.

43. *CMDVat*, I 26–7, Plate 32.

44. *CMDB*, II 40, Plate 317–18.

45. *CMDLond*, nr. 503, Plate 303.

46. De Robertis (1998a, 65, 69–70, Plate 1).

47. *CMDOx*, 26, Plate 270.

48. Casmassima (1974, xvii), followed with some caution by de la Mare (1977, 107–8).

49. Casmassima (1974, xvi–xvii); Zamponi (2004, 476 and Plate 5).

50. Barile (1993, 92–101); De Robertis (1994).

51. *CMDOx*, 86, Plate 299.

52. *CMDVat*, I 165–6, Plate 29.

53. *CMDVat*, I 182, Plate 28.

54. *CMDOx*, 30, Plate 284.

55. *CMDOx*, 88, Plate 291.

56. *CMDF*, II 313, Plate 90.

57. *CMDVat*, I 186–7, Plate 29.

58. But Antonio di Mario is the exception.

59. Morison (1952); Petrucci (1991); Barile (1994) ; De Robertis (1998a).

60. *CMDB*, II 28, Plates 268–9.

61. Barile (1994, 17–32) (for the manuscript of El Escorial, Plates 3–4); *CMDF* II 373 (for the manuscript of Paris, recognized by Granata (2004–5, 73). Florence, Biblioteca Riccardiana 286 may also have belonged to Sebastiano Borsa (Ephrem and John Chrysostom, Sermons): cf. Plate 7 in De Robertis (1998b).

62. Fava (1944); Wardrop (1963, 14–16, Plate 4); Casamassima (1974, xii, xviii–xx, figs. 5–7); De Robertis (1998a, 74–6, Plate 5); Zamponi (2004, 479–81, Plate 8).

63. Fava (1944, Plate 13).

64. Ferrari (1988, 27–8).

65. Zaggia (1995, 4–9).

66. Zaggia (1995, 12–17), (2007, 353–6).

67. de la Mare (1983, 402); Zaggia (2007, 358–74).

68. To the five manuscripts mentioned above, add those listed by de la Mare (1985b).

69. Caldelli (2006, 48–71).

70. Derolez (1984, 21–4): almost one third of the 1200 humanistic manuscripts studied by him were produced in Florence.
71. De la Mare (1985a, 398 and 479–554) for the census of the copyists.
72. De la Mare (1985a, 440–4 and 555–64).
73. Zamponi (2006a).
74. Modena, Biblioteca Estense, Est. lat. 992 (alpha L.5.15) (*L'antiquario Felice Feliciano*, 1995, Plates xiv–xvi, figs. 9, 86, 89).
75. Treviso, Biblioteca Capitolare, i 138. The story is told in the first redaction in the manuscripts Verona, Biblioteca Capitolare, CCLXIX and Venice, Biblioteca Nazionale Marciana, Marc. lat. x 196 [3766], with a dedication to Mantegna. On the epigraphic collections, see Mitchell (1961).
76. De la Mare and Nuvoloni (2009, nr. 51, 92, 104, 110, 112, 123).
77. De la Mare and Nuvoloni (2009, 108–9).
78. Molli, Canova, and Toniolo (1994, 241–3).
79. Alexander (1994, 87–90).
80. "Plinio de naturali historia, de volume de foglio reale, scripto de littera antica in carta bergamena. Miniato nella prima faza de oro macinato et azuro de uno casamento con la imagine de Vesapasiano in medaglia et con lo cavallo de Theseo alato et altre imagine" (Cherchi and De Robertis, p. 217), describing one of the frontispieces of Valencia, Biblioteca Universitaria, 691 (Alexander 1994, 209–10, reproducing the page with the architectural frame described in the inventory).
81. See, for example, Wolfenbüttel, Herzog-August Bibliothek, Cod. Guelf. 277.4 Extrav.
82. Molli, Canova, and Toniolo (1994, 239–40).
83. De la Mare and Nuvoloni (2009, 104–27).
84. Feliciano (1987). For other treatises, see Mardersteig (1959).
85. Zamponi (2006a, 60).
86. In the manuscripts Glasgow, University Library, Hunter 275, Bartolomeo Cipolla, *De imperatore militum eligendo*, *c.*1458 (Thorp 1987, 144 and Plate 33); Florence, Biblioteca Riccardiana 794, Valturius, of the 1460s (De Robertis 1998a); Verona, Biblioteca Comunale 2845, oracles of the Eritrean Sibyl, possibly done in 1464 (Benedetto 1995, Plate 72). Also to be attributed to Feliciano is the manuscript London, BL, Burney 292, Augustine, *De civitate Dei*, of the 1460s.
87. Alexander and de la Mare (1969 , 121–4); *MDI* , IV 18–19.
88. Zaggia (2007, 364–7, Plate 92).
89. *CMDLond*, nr. 661.
90. See, for example, Florence , Biblioteca Riccardiana 540, Cicero, *Ep. ad familiares*, 1479 (*MDI*, II 28, Plate 78); on distinguishing Pier Antonio Sallando from Antonio da Salla, see Nuvoloni (2008, 169–74).
91. Regnicoli (2005, 167–8) and (2011, 111–17).
92. Di Benedetto, (1992, Plate 72); De Robertis (1998a, Plates i–vi).
93. *CMDOx*, 37, Plate 628.
94. Di Benedetto (1995, 99–103, Plates i and 24).
95. *MDI*, I 71–2, Plate 78; Wardrop (1963, Plate 9).
96. This phenomenon is repeated partially in Vatican City, BAV, Reg. lat. 1388 (fols. 2v–29v, the same text, dated 1463): Zamponi (2006b), with a description of the manuscripts and numerous plates.

BIBLIOGRAPHY

Alexander, J. J. G. 1994. *The Painted Page: Italian Renaissance Book Illumination 1450–1550.* Munich and New York: Prestel.

Alexander, J. J. G. and A. C. de la Mare. 1969. *Italian Manuscripts in the Library of Major J. R. Abbey.* London: Faber & Faber.

Barile, E. 1993. "Michele Selvatico a Venezia, copista e notaio dei Capi sestiere." In, *L'umanesimo librario tra Venezia e Napoli. Contributi su Michele Selvativo e su Andrea Contrario,* ed. G. P. Mantovani, L. Prosdocimi, and E. Barile, 43–103. Venice: Istituto veneto di scienze, lettere ed arti.

Barile, E. 1994. *"Littera antiqua" e scritture alla greca. Notai e cancellieri a Venezia nei primi decenni del Quattrocento.* Venice: Istituto veneto di scienze, lettere ed arti.

Bertelli, S. 2007. *La Commedia all'antica.* Florence: Mandragora.

Billanovich, G. 1981. "Alle origini della scrittura umanistica: Padova 1261 e Firenze 1397." In *Miscellanea Augusto Campana*, I, 125–40. Padua: Antenore.

Buonocore, M., ed. 1996. *Vedere i classici. L'illustrazione libraria dei testi antichi dall'età romana al tardo medioevo,* ed. Rome and Milan: Rose.

Butrica, J. L. 1981. "A New Fragment in Niccoli's Formal Hand." *Scriptorium* 35: 290–2, Plates 15–16.

Butrica, J. L. 1984. *The Manuscript Tradition of Propertius.* Toronto: University of Toronto Press.

Cadei, A., ed. 2003. *Il trionfo sul tempo. Manoscritti illustrati dell'Accademia Nazionale dei Lincei.* Modena: Panini.

Caldelli, E. 2006. *Copisti a Roma nel Quattrocento.* Rome: Viella.

Caldini Montanari, R. 2009. "Un codice protoumanistico del Somnium Scipionis." *Medioevo e Rinascimento,* 23: 133–54.

Casamassima, E. 1964. "Per una storia delle dottrine paleografiche dall'umanesimo a Jean Mabillon." *Studi medievali* 5: 525–78.

Casamassima, E. 1974. "Literulae Latinae. Nota paleografica." In Stefano Caroti and Stefano Zamponi, *Lo scrittoio di Bartolomeo Fonzio umanista fiorentino,* ix–xxxii. Milan: Il Polifilo.

Casamassima, E. and G. Savino. 1995. "Sozomeno da Pistoia: un irregolare della 'renovatio' grafica umanistica." *Medioevo e Rinascimento* 9: 187–95.

Ceccherini, I. 2016. *Sozomeno da Pistoia (1387–1458). Scittura e libri di un umanista.* Firenze: Olschki.

Cherchi, P. and T. De Robertis. 1990. "Un inventario della biblioteca aragonese." *Italia medievale e umanistica* 33: 109–347.

Contò, A. and L. Quaquarelli, eds. 1995. *L'antiquario Felice Feliciano veronese tra epigrafia antica, letteratura e arti del libro.* Atti del convegno (Verona, 3–4 giugno 1993). Padua: Antenore.

Davies, M. C. 1988. "An Enigma and a Phantom: Giovanni Aretino and Giacomo Languschi." *Humanistica Lovaniensia* 37: 1–29.

de la Mare, A. C. 1973. *The Handwriting of Italian Humanists. I, 1: Francesco Petrarca, Giovanni Boccaccio, Coluccio Salutati, Niccolò Niccoli, Poggio Bracciolini, Bartolomeo Aragazzi of Montepulciano, Sozomeno da Pistoia, Giorgio Antonio Vespucci.* Oxford: Association Internationale de Bibliophilie.

de la Mare, A. C. 1977. "Humanistic Script: The First Ten Years." In *Das Verhältnis der Humanisten zum Buch,* ed. F. Krafft and D. Wuttke, 89–108. Boppard: Boldt.

de la Mare, A. C. 1983. "Script and Manuscripts in Milan under the Sforzas." In *Milano nell'età di Ludovico il Moro. Atti del convegno internazionale (28 febbraio–4 marzo 1983)*, 399–408. Milan: Comune-Archivio storico e Biblioteca Trivulziana.

de la Mare, A. C. 1985a. "New Research on Humanistic Scribes in Florence." In *Miniatura fiorentina del Rinascimento, 1440–1525: un primo censimento*, ed. Annarosa Garzelli, 2 vols., I, 395–574 [Florence]: Giunta regionale toscana.

de la Mare, A. C. 1985b. "Preliminary List of Manuscripts Attributed to Michael de Selvaticis." *Lettere italiane* 37: 351–4.

de la Mare, A. C. 1992. "Cosimo and his Books." In *Cosimo "il Vecchio" de' Medici, 1389–1464. Essays in Commemoration of the 600th Anniversary of Cosimo de'Medici's Birth*, ed. F. Ames-Lewis, 115–56. Oxford: Clarendon Press.

de la Mare, A. C. 1994. "A Palaeographer's Odyssey." In *Sight and Insight. Essays on Art and Culture in Honour of E. H. Gombrich at 85*, ed. John Onians, 89–107. London: Phaidon.

de la Mare, A. C. and L. Nuvoloni. 2009. *Bartolomeo Sanvito: The Life & Work of a Renaissance Scribe*. Paris and Dorchester: Association Internationale de Bibliophilie.

de la Mare, A. C. and D. F. S. Thomson. 1973. "Poggio's Earliest Manuscript?" *Italia medioevale e umanistica* 16: 179–95.

De Robertis, T. 1990. "Nuovi autografi di Niccolò Niccoli (con una proposta di revisione dei tempi e dei modi del suo contributo alla riforma grafica umanistica)." *Scrittura e Civiltà* 14: 105–21.

De Robertis, T. 1994. "Contributo per Michele Germanico." *Medioevo e Rinascimento* 8: 241–8.

De Robertis, T. 1995. "Un libro di Niccoli e tre di Poggio." In *Studi in onore di Arnaldo d'Addario*, ed. L. Borgia, F. De Luca, P. Viti, and R. M. Zaccaria, II, 494–513. Lecce: Conte.

De Robertis, T. 1998a. "Feliciano copista di Valturio." In *Tra libri e carte. Studi in onore di Luciana Mosiici*, ed. T. De Robertis and G. Savino, 73–97. Florence: Cesati.

De Robertis, T. 1998b. "Motivi classici nella scrittura del primo Quattrocento." In *L'ideale classico a Ferrara e in Italia nel Rinascimento*, ed. Patrizia Castelli, 65–79. Florence: Olschki.

De Robertis, T. 2006. "I percorsi dell'imitazione. Esperimenti di *littera antiqua* in codici fiorentini del primo Quattrocento." In *I luoghi dello scrivere da Francesco Petrarca agli albori dell'età moderna*, ed. C. Tristano, M. Calleri, and L. Magionami, 109–34. Spoleto: Centro Italiano di Studi sull'Alto Medioevo.

De Robertis, T. 2010. "Salutati tra scrittura gotica e *littera antiqua*." In *Coluccio Salutati e l'invenzione dell'umanesimo: Atti del convegno internazionale di studi, Firenze, 29–31 ottobre 2008*, ed. C. Bianca, 369–87 and Plates 1–12. Rome: Edizioni di storia e letteratura.

De Robertis, T. and S. Zamponi. 2008. "Libri e copisti di Coluccio Salutati: un consuntivo." In *Coluccio Salutati e l'invenzione dell'umanesimo*, ed. T. De Robertis, G. Tanturli, and S. Zamponi, 345–63. Florence: Mandragora.

De Robertis, T., G. Tanturli, and S. Zamponi, eds. 2008. *Coluccio Salutati e l'invenzione dell'umanesimo*. Florence: Mandragora.

De Robertis, T., C. M. Monti, M. Petoletti, G. Tanturli, S. Zamponi, eds. 2013. *Boccaccio autore e copista* (Catalogo della mostra. Firenze, Biblioteca Medicea Laurenziana, 11 ottobre 2013–13 gennaio 2014), Firenze: Mandragora.

Derolez, A. 1984. *Codicologie des manuscrits en écriture humanistique sur parchemin*. Turnhout: Brepols.

Di Benedetto, F. 1995. "Tre schede per Feliciano." In *L'antiquario Felice Feliciano veronese tra epigrafia antica, letteratura e arti del libro. Atti del convegno (Verona, 3–4 giugno 1993)*, ed. Agostino Contò e Leonardo Quaquarelli, 89–108. Padua: Antenore.

Fava, D. 1944. "La scrittura libraria di Ciriaco d'Ancona." In *Scritti di Paleografia e diplomatica in onore di Vincenzo Federici*, 295–305, Plates 13–23. Florence: Olschki.

Feliciano, F. 1987. *Alphabetum Romanum. Cod. Vat. Lat. 6852. Anno 1460*, ed. Rino Avesani. Milan: Jaka Book.

Ferrari, M. 1988. "La *littera antiqua* à Milan, 1417–1439." In *Renaissance- und Humanistenhandschriften*, ed. J. Autenrieth and U. Eigler, 13–29. Munich: Oldenburg.

Frenz, T. 1973–4. "Das Eindringen humanistischer Schriftformen in die Urkunden und Akten der päpstlichen Kurie im 15. Jahrhundert." *Archiv für Diplomatik*, 19 (1973): 287–418; 20 (1974): 384–506.

Gentile, S. 1997. *Umanesimo e padri della Chiesa. Manoscritti e incunabuli di testi patristici da Francesco Petrarca al primo Cinquecento*. Rome and Milan: Rose.

Granata, L. 2004–5. "Renovatio grafica e tradizione antiquaria nell'umanesimo veneto del secondo Quattrocento." Ph.D. diss., Università di Firenze.

Lombardi, G. 1983. "Note su Cencio dei Rustici." In *Scrittura, biblioteche e stampa a Roma nel Quattrocento*. Atti del secondo Seminario (Roma 6–8 maggio 1982), ed. Massimo Miglio, P. P. and A. Modigliani, 23–35. Vatican City: Scuola Vaticana di Paleografia, Diplomatica e Archivistica.

Mardersteig, G. 1959. "Leon Battista Alberti e la rinascita del carattere lapidario romano nel Quattrocento." *Italia medioevale e umanistica* 2: 285–307.

McKie, D. S. 1989. "Salutati, Poggio, and Codex M of Catullus." In *Studies in Latin Literature and its Tradition in Honour of C. O. Brink*, ed. J. Diggle, J. B. Hall, and H. D. Jocelyn, 66–86. Cambridge, Cambridge Philological Society.

Miglio, L. 2009. "Un copista Carneade?" In *In uno volumine. Studi in onore di Cesare Scalon*, ed. Laura Pani, 395–406. Udine: Forum.

Mitchell, C. 1961. "Felice Feliciano Antiquarius." *Proceedings of the British Academy* 47: 197–221, Plates xxvi–xli.

Molli, G. B., G. M. Canova, and F. Toniolo, eds. 1999. *La miniatura a Padova dal Medioevo al Settecento*, Modena: Panini.

Morison, S. 1952. *Byzantine Elements in humanistic script: Illustrated from the Aulus Gellius of 1445 in the Newberry Library*. Chicago: Newberry Library.

Nicolaj Petronio, G. 1981. "Per la soluzione di un enigma: Giovanni Aretino copista, notaio e cancelliere." *Humanistica Lovaniensia* 30: 1–12.

Nuvoloni, L. 2008. "Pier Antonio Sallando o 'il più excellente scriptore credo habia il mondo'." In *Il libro d'Ore Durazzo*, ed. A. De Marchi, 145–88. Modena: Panini.

Orsino, S. 2018. "Matteo di Giovanni Totti da Imola, copista di classici." *Medioevo e Rinascimento* 32: 1–24.

Petrucci, A. 1967. *La scrittura di Francesco Petrarca*. Vaticano City: Biblioteca Apostolica Vaticana.

Petrucci, A. 1991. "Scrivere 'alla greca' nell'Italia del Quattrocento." In *Scritture, libri, e testi nelle aree provinciali di Bisanzio*, ed. G. Cavallo, G. De Gregorio, and and M. Maniaci, 499–517. Spoleto: Centro italiano di studi sull'Alto Medioevo.

Rawski, C. H. 1991. *Petrarch's Remedies for Fortune Fair and Foul*, 5 vols., Bloomington and Indianapolis, IN: Indiana University Press.

Regnicoli, L. 2005. "Antonio Sinibaldi copista di corte." In *Il libro d'Ore di Lorenzo de' Medici*, ed. Franca Arduini, 141–81. Modena: Panini.

Regnicoli, L. 2011. *Il libro d'Ore di Maddalena de' Medici*. Modena: Panini.

Salutati, C. 1891–1911. *Epistolario*, ed. Francesco Novati. Rome: Istituto storico italiano per il Medioevo,.

Thorp, N. 1987. *The Glory of the Page: Medieval & Renaissance Illuminated Manuscripts from Glasgow University Library*. London: Miller.

Ullman, B. L. 1960. *The Origin and Development of Humanistic Script*. Rome: Edizioni di Storia e Letteratura.

Wardrop, J. 1963. *The Script of Humanism: Some Aspects of Humanistic Script 1460–1560*. Oxford: Clarendon Press.

Zaggia, M. 1995. "Copisti e committenti di codici a Milano nella prima metà del Quattrocento", *Libri & Documenti* 21/3: 1–45.

Zaggia, M. 2007. "Codici milanesi del Quattrocento all'Ambrosiana: per il perodo dal 1450 al 1476." In *Nuove ricerche su codici in scrittura latina dell'Ambrosiana*. Atti del convegno (Milano, 6–7 ottobre 2005), ed. M. Ferrari and M. Navoni, 331–84. Milan: Vita e Pensiero.

Zamponi, S. 2004. "La scrittura umanistica. *Archiv für Diplomatik* 50: 467–504.

Zamponi, S. 2006a. "Le metamorfosi dell'antico: la tradizione antiquaria veneta." In *I luoghi dello scrivere da Francesco Petrarca agli albori dell'età moderna*, ed. C. Tristano, M. Calleri, and L. Magionami, 37–68. Spoleto: Centro Italiano di Studi sull'Alto Medioevo.

Zamponi, S. 2006b. "Il paradigma e la fine della scrittura. L'Ercole senofontio del Feliciano." In *La maestà della lettera antica. L'Ercole senofontio del Feliciano (Padova, Biblioteca Civica, B.P. 1099)*, ed. G. P. Mantovani, 9–27. Padua: Il Poligrafo.

Zamponi, S. 2010. "Iacopo Angeli copista per Salutati." In *Coluccio Salutati e l'invenzione dell'umanesimo: Atti del convegno internazionale di studi, Firenze, 29–31 ottobre 2008*, ed. C. Bianca, 401–14 and Plates 1–6. Rome: Edizioni di storia e letteratura.

CHAPTER 33

....

BYZANTIUM AND THE WEST

....

MARIANNE PADE

THIS chapter aims to characterize the early humanist interest in Greek language and culture from the mid-fourteenth century until the fall of Constantinople *c.*100 years later. By that time Greek studies were well established in the West—and Gutenberg had invented printing with movable types, an invention that signaled the end of manuscript culture. The chapter will focus on a number of key figures who were all instrumental in shaping the Greek revival in Early Modern Europe.

PETRARCH AND THE GREEKS

....

It has often been said that the reason why Renaissance humanists were convinced that the study of Greek should be made an integral part of the *studia humanitatis* was that the Latin writers of antiquity had emphasized the indispensability of a knowledge of that language for any serious writer. This also holds true for what we may call the first stage of the assimilation of Greek into Western education, the period when a few single scholars attempted to learn the language from native speakers who for some reason were living in the Latin West (Percival 1988, 75).

Petrarch (Francesco Petrarca, 1304–74), whose influence on the next generations of humanists was immense, became interested in the Greek world through classical Latin writers. He wanted to become acquainted with the orators and the philosophical writers upon whom Cicero had drawn and with Homer, who had inspired Vergil. His admiration, however, was never more than moderate, and he always maintained the superiority of Latin culture:[1]

> Why do I speak of natural ability? Imitation created that one eminent pair, the stars
> of the Latin tongue, Cicero and Vergil, and thus brought about that we yield to the

Greeks no more in any part of eloquence. While Vergil follows Homer and Cicero Demosthenes, the first of them equalled his guide, whereas the second left him behind.[2]

However, Petrarch never read a word of Demosthenes and, at the time he wrote the above to his patron, Cardinal Giovanni Colonna, he probably had not read a line of Homer either. We possess another letter to Colonna in which Petrarch uses the political history of ancient Greece to claim the superiority of modern Italy. Referring to the series of military defeats which in antiquity led to the subjected state of Greece, he concludes that "nobody could deny that it was more glorious to be Italian than to be Greek."[3] There is no doubt that for Petrarch the study of Greek remained first and foremost a means to better his understanding of Latin literature, as would be the case with many of his followers in the fifteenth century. He fervently wished to make a wider range of ancient Greek authors accessible in the Latin West, to make the study of them an integral part of the *studia humanitatis*, but his endeavors were part of his efforts to achieve a better understanding of classical Latin literature and to enhance *litterae latinae*—of which he saw his own writings as an important part.

I shall here examine the way Petrarch approached two specific Greek authors, namely Plutarch and Homer. In the case of Plutarch we see how Petrarch had to content himself, more or less at least, with information culled from Latin literature, but also how he put the little he had to very good use (Pade 2007, I Ch. 2.2). His interest in Homer, on the other hand, led to quite different results; in collaboration with his friend Giovanni Boccaccio he managed to have the Homeric poems made accessible again in the West for the first time since antiquity, and in the process to reintroduce the Greek mythological tradition.

Plutarch

In the Middle Ages Plutarch was known in Western Europe almost exclusively as the teacher of Trajan and author of the spurious *Institutio Traiani* ("The Education of Trajan").[4] This didactic treatise on the theory of government, allegedly written by Plutarch for his imperial pupil Trajan, was quoted by John of Salisbury in books 5 and 6 of his *Policraticus*, completed in 1159.[5]

Petrarch too knew Plutarch as the teacher of Trajan. From the 1340s onward, we find references to Plutarch in Petrarch's work which are often intriguing. In a passage in his *Letter to Seneca* Plutarch is mentioned as comparing Greek and Roman achievement in literature and statesmanship, something not mentioned by John, and this piece of information is combined with his role as the teacher of Trajan:

> When Plutarch, a Greek and teacher of the Emperor Trajan, compared our famous men to those of his own country, he held Marcus Varro up against Plato and Aristotle—the first of whom the Greeks call divine, the second almost

so—Virgil against Homer and Cicero against Demosthenes. In the end he had the courage also to start a contention between generals; not even respect for his exalted pupil held him back. In one instance he was not ashamed to acknowledge the genius of his own as inferior: they do not have anyone comparable to you when it comes to moral philosophy. High praise indeed, especially coming from someone who is biased, someone who compared his own Alexander the Macedonian to our Julius Caesar.[6]

Here and elsewhere we see that Petrarch knew more about Plutarch than he could have learned from John's *Policraticus*. However, rather than postulate a now lost written source, I believe we may assume that Petrarch's source was contemporary and oral. By August 1, 1348, when the *Letter to Seneca* was written, Petrarch had known the Greek bishop Barlaam for six years and studied Greek with him in Avignon. In January of that year he had, moreover, made the acquaintance of Nicholas Sigeros, the learned Byzantine ambassador who was later to present him with a manuscript of Homer. Petrarch would have had ample opportunity to discuss matters of literature either with Barlaam or with Sigeros, as he did some years later with the Calabrian Leontius Pilatus (see Section 33.1.2 below).[7] And some conversation, dimly remembered, may also explain the imprecise nature of Petrarch's information: although in the *Letter to Seneca* he does mention two pairs of lives which exist in the Plutarchan corpus, those of Demosthenes and Cicero, and Alexander and Caesar, he also lists lives that do not, e.g., Plato, Aristotle, Homer, and Virgil. However that may be, these passages show Petrarch's curiosity toward the Greek world, a curiosity, however, that was always governed by his wish to draw the Greek writers into and evaluate them against Latin culture. And alongside his evident wish to find out more about the Greek author, he, as everybody else, kept thinking about him as the teacher of Trajan.

Homer

Petrarch's evident interest in Plutarch is one instance where we see him concerned with parts of the Greek cultural heritage which had not played a significant role in the Latin West during the Middle Ages. In the centuries before Petrarch, the few Western scholars who knew Greek had produced Latin translations of primarily philosophical and scientific texts, and of related commentaries, whereas Greek literary texts had been largely ignored (Dionisotti 1992).[8] Considering Petrarch's fervent admiration for Virgil (Petrarca 2006). it is not surprising that he showed an even keener interest in Homer.

From his earliest years Petrarch collected whatever information he came upon about Homer and his poems. From classical Latin writers he knew that Homer was *pater* or *princeps* of poets and always wanted to be able to read him, a wish unlikely to be fulfilled, since the greater part of Greek literature was completely inaccessible to him, as it was to almost everybody outside the cultural orbit of Byzantium. Upon receiving the Greek codex of Homer from Sigeros in 1348, he lamented:

> With me your Homer is dumb, or rather I am deaf in his company. However, just looking at him I rejoice and I often embrace him, sighing: "Oh great man, how I would wish I could hear you!"[9]

Then in the winter of 1358–9 Petrarch met Leontius Pilatus, a Greek-speaking native of Calabria. Together with Giovanni Boccaccio (1313–75) Petrarch persuaded Leontius to produce a complete translation of the Homeric poems.[10] For more than two years, from 1360 to 1362, Leontius lived in Boccaccio's house in Florence, worked with him on Homer, and taught Greek at the *Studio*.[11] The translations of Homer were not the only result of Leontius' sojourn in Florence. Boccaccio's mythological works, and especially, of course, *The Genealogy of the Pagan Gods* shows the eagerness with which he took advantage of the opportunity to get acquainted with the Greek mythological tradition, and he recalls his many conversations with Leontius on the topic:

> Leontius Pilatus...is a most learned Hellenist, as any inquirer discovers, and a fairly inexhaustible mine of Greek history and myth...For nearly three years I heard him read Homer and conversed with him in terms of singular friendship; but so immense was the measure of all he had to tell that my memory, quickened though it was by pressure of other care, would not have been good enough to retain it, had I not set it down in a notebook.[12]

Petrarch only received copies of Leontius' translations around 1367, from Boccaccio. His manuscripts contain a number of notes which show that he, like Boccaccio, gathered information on Greek mythology from Leontius. Even so, Petrarch was sorely disappointed with Leontius' translations. In his *Letter to Homer*, Petrarch complained that the poet had been translated word for word and moreover into prose, a procedure that rendered the most eloquent of poets almost dumb—as Jerome had put it. All the same, he rejoiced at being able to read the Greek poems (Petrarca 1933–42, XXIV 12, 4).

If Petrarch's interest in Greek literary texts influenced the direction of Greek studies in the next generations of humanists, so his criticism of Leontius' translations may be said to have inaugurated the view on translation which became predominant from the beginning of the fifteenth century. Leontius had followed the word-for-word method used for translation from Greek into Latin in the West during the Middle Ages, a procedure which may assure that the factual contents of the original are rendered, but which cannot do justice to its literary and stylistic qualities. Petrarch deplored the loss of just that in Leontius' translations and thus anticipated the growing concern for the aesthetic qualities of translations which we encounter in fifteenth-century theoreticians: while it, of course, remains important that translators understand the original text, focus is often on how to achieve a beautiful and thoroughly Latin text (Pade 2008b).

COLUCCIO SALUTATI
AND CHRYSOLORAS

Coluccio Salutati (1331–1406) became chancellor of Florence in 1375, a position he held until his death.[13] An ardent admirer of Petrarch, he did much to transmit his ideas to the next generation, and Petrarch's influence may be seen in many aspects of his work, as in his interest in Greek and views on translation. Like Petrarch, Salutati never mastered the language, but was eager to acquire new translations of works of Greek literature. One of them was Simon Atumanus' word-for-word translation of ps.Plutarch's *De cohibenda ira* ("On Controlling Anger," 1373). Abhorring its style, Salutati decided to rework Simon's version into better Latin. He admitted that he had often doubted the meaning of the text before him, but then he had chosen the solution which seemed to make better sense. Moreover, to enliven the prose he had sometimes inserted questions or exclamations where there were none in the original. The result, he believed, was Latin instead of half-Greek.[14] We recognize Petrarch's insistence that a Latin translation should indeed be Latin and aesthetically pleasing.

Salutati also owned copies of Leontius' Homeric versions. Like Petrarch he was highly critical of them. His solution was the same as he adopted with *De cohibenda ira*, but this time he tried to persuade a young disciple, Antonio Loschi, to embellish the rough and unadorned prose version of Leontius by recomposing it in hexameters (Pade 2007, I Ch. 3.2).

However, Salutati's most important achievement within the field of Greek studies was his role in persuading the Greek scholar and diplomat Manuel Chrysoloras (1350/55–1416) to come to Florence.[15] As a high ranking diplomat and intimate of the Emperor Manuel II Palaeologus (1391–1425), Chrysoloras surely hoped that in accepting Salutati's invitation he would become a cultural ambassador for his country and be able to influence the West to help defend Constantinople against the Ottoman Turks. In this he did not succeed, but Chrysoloras held the chair of Greek at Florence from 1397 to 1400, and his tenure marks the beginning of a stable tradition of Greek studies in Italy.[16]

So far, I have described Western interest in Greek as it manifested itself in Petrarchan humanism: Greek studies were always seen as ancillary to the Petrarchan project of a reawakening of *litterae latinae*. Chrysoloras did not change that point of view fundamentally, but his attitude was different, and his voice, due to his immense popularity among his students, was influential. Chrysoloras repeatedly stresses the close community of religion and culture which once existed between Greeks and Romans, a community in which writers like Cicero partook. This theme pervades his Σύγκρισις τῆς παλαιᾶς καὶ νέας Ῥώμης ("Comparison between the Old and the New Rome"), written in 1411 as a letter to the emperor, Manuel II Palaeologus. Here Chrysoloras compared the old and the new Rome, that is, the Italian city and

Constantinople, dwelling at length on the Roman origins of the Greek capital as well as the Greek influences on early Rome.[17]

Chrysoloras' teaching had a lasting effect in a number of ways: not only did he manage to create an enduring enthusiasm for Greek, but he has also been attributed with having introduced what became the humanist method of translation and Byzantine methods of textual interpretation (Botley 2010). As mentioned, Petrarch criticized the traditional method of literal word-for-word translation from the Greek; according to the testimony of his pupils, Chrysoloras taught a different method of translation. He found the results of *ad verbum* literal translation harsh and disagreeable, preferring instead *conversio ad sententiam* ("translation of sense"), which also aimed at reproducing the style of the original. Chrysoloras views on translation became so influential partly because it was central to his pedagogical method to practise translation. The first exercises in translation undertaken by his students would often be literal, perhaps interlinear translations, whose aim was simply to render the words of the Greek text, whereas stylistically satisfactory translations were reserved for a more advanced stage.[18] There is no doubt that Chrysoloras' method of teaching was partly responsible for the great number of translations made by his pupils during the first years of the fifteenth century and for a new conception of how they should ideally be read. All through the fifteenth century, we find humanist translators excusing themselves if they had not managed a *conversio ad sententiam*, if their translations were *ad verbum* and inelegant. But whereas Chrysoloras had emphasized the importance of reproducing the style of the original, many humanists concentrated on achieving the correct Latin style in their translation, a style that showed their ability to imitate the best Latin authors.

Chrysoloras, moreover, imparted to his pupils the traditional methods of Byzantine philology, that is, textual criticism, methods of interpretation, and historical method. He definitely influenced the choice of Greek authors who were read and the order in which they were studied. There was also a very practical reason for this, since he necessarily supplied many of the Greek texts which were copied and used for teaching and translation purposes.

Chrysoloras praised Salutati's interest in Plutarch (Salutati 1891–1911, IV 341–3), and even though the *Lives* were not a central part of the curriculum in Byzantine schools, Chrysoloras used them to bridge the cultural gap between Byzantium and Italy. He successfully made use of the interest in Plutarch we have already noted, and if Plutarch became one of the most widely read Greek authors in Italy, Chrysoloras' teaching was the first cause of this. Chrysoloras' pupils, and eventually their pupils as well, were responsible for most of the translations of the *Lives*: Leonardo Bruni; Iacopo Angeli da Scarperia; Guarino Veronese, who studied with Chrysoloras in Constantinople from 1403 to 1408, and his pupils Francesco Barbaro and Leonardo Giustinian; and Francesco Filelfo, the pupil and eventually son-in-law of Manuel's nephew, Johannes Chrysoloras, with his pupil Lapo da Castiglionchio the Younger.

THE EARLY HUMANIST TRANSLATORS
FROM THE GREEK

Chrysoloras' teaching in Florence was an immense success. Salutati attended some of his lessons but never came to master the language, partly because of old age, partly because his duties in the chancellery took up the greater part of his time. Chrysoloras' most successful pupil from these years was Leonardo Bruni, but a number of others are well known too, such as Roberto Rossi, Palla Strozzi, Iacopo Angeli da Scarperia, Niccolò Niccoli, and Pier Paolo Vergerio. Back in Constantinople, he also taught Guarino Veronese, who achieved an exceptional mastery of Greek as well as a lasting respect for Greek culture. In the following I shall examine the attitudes to Greek studies of Bruni and Guarino respectively.

Leonardo Bruni

Leonardo Bruni (1370–1444) from Arezzo has been seen as the embodiment of the so-called "civic humanist" (Baron 1966). Both his original writings and the quality and Latin style of his translations made him the most widely read contemporary writer in the fifteenth century. As chancellor of Florence from 1427 until his death, Bruni was a humanist who participated actively in the affairs of the state. His choice of the *vita activa* is reflected in the classical texts he worked on. His *Isagogicon moralis disciplinae* ("Introduction to Moral Philosophy") is largely based on Aristotle's *Nichomachean Ethics*. Among his translations proper, an emphasis on matters pertaining to civic virtues is especially evident in the translations of Aristotle's *Politics* and of some of Plutarch's *Lives*.

It has been said that Bruni's Greek scholarship was primarily influenced by Petrarch's humanism and first and foremost intended to restore and renew Latin culture—rather than Greek, as his teacher Chrysoloras would have wished.[19] This is certainly the case if we take note of the conscious aims expressed in Bruni's writings, and it is borne out by several of his translations and by his historical compilation, the *Commentaria de primo bello punico* ("The First Punic War"). The *Commentaria* were based on Polybius, but Bruni supplemented Polybius' text with portions of Zonaras, Thucydides, Strabo, Florus, Eutropius, and possibly Diodorus Siculus in order to correct Polybius' account and make it less anti-Roman.[20] Most of Bruni's translations from Plutarch are of the lives of famous generals and statesmen from the Roman republic: Mark Antony, the Younger Cato, Paulus Aemilius, the Gracchi, Quintus Sertorius, and Cicero in the *Cicero novus,* his adaptation of the *Life of Cicero*. His translation of the life of King Pyrrhus of Epirus was surely motivated by his interest in Roman republican history, even if its eponymous subject is non-Roman. His *Demosthenes* was intended as a foil for the *Cicero novus*, the new life of Cicero aimed at reversing Plutarch's judgment that the Greek orator was to be preferred to the Latin one. Bruni's interest in the target culture and language, Latin, is expressed in his treatise on translation, the *De interpretatione recta* ("On the Correct Way to Translate") and in some of his letters. In the often quoted letter to Niccolò Niccoli on his method in translating Plato's *Phaedo*, Bruni wrote:

> I follow a Plato whom I represent to myself as a man who knew Latin and was able to express his own opinions in it . . . Plato himself asks me to do that, for a man who wore a most elegant aspect among the Greeks surely does not want to appear crude and clumsy with the Latins.[21]

He wanted, so to speak, to pull his Greek author into the Latin world; in Bruni's work translation, rewriting, or adaptation all become a conscious cultural translation, a transfer of the Greek material to a Roman context.

Guarino Veronese

Guarino from Verona (1374–1460),[22] was another pupil of Chrysoloras', whose name he revered until his death more than 40 years after that of his *maestro*. It is tempting to see this lifelong admiration as a symptom of a different attitude towards the Greek world than the one we observed in Bruni's works. In his youth Guarino studied for five years in Constantinople, staying in the Chrysoloras household, an experience he often referred to in later years. Even at the age of 75 he recalled the pure Greek spoken by women and children in Constantinople (Guarino Veronese 1915–19, *ep.* 813, 200–15, AD 1449).

Guarino is remembered as one of the great teachers of the Italian Renaissance. For about 30 years pupils came from all over Europe to study with him at his famous school in Ferrara, where they received an elite education, i.e. an excellent training in both Latin and Greek and the ability to express themselves fluently in humanist Latin. It is thus safe to say that Guarino influenced the language and cultural attitudes of generations of humanists. Guarino was also a prolific translator. Though there is no doubt that he almost invariably read Greek texts with a view to their relevance for contemporary life, it is also true that he did not favor texts relevant for Roman history. He translated 13 of Plutarch's *Parallel Lives*, and though some of them are of Roman public figures, Guarino was the first to produce Latin versions of a larger number of Greek lives, seven in all. He also translated several dialogues of Lucian, some Herodotus, and a large part of Strabo.

Guarino's letters, of which we still possess almost a thousand, bear witness to his relations with the intellectual elite of the time and his ongoing preoccupation with moral and pedagogical issues, among them the importance of Greek studies for *studia humanitatis.* Chrysoloras is frequently mentioned, and on several occasions his extraordinary influence is stressed, not just with regard to Greek studies, but on the general development of those around him:

> Antiquity rightly praised those who educated men of the first rank, because one person transformed the character and way of life of many. This was what Anaxagoras did with Pericles, Plato with Dion, Pythagoras with the Italian princes, Athenodorus with Cato, Panaetius with Scipio, Apollonius with Cicero and Caesar, and, in our time, what Manuel Chrysoloras, a great man and a great philosopher, did with many people.[23]

In this letter of 1419, Chrysoloras is mentioned alongside several of the greatest teachers and philosophers of antiquity—Anaxagoras, Plato, Pythagoras, etc.—and his (Italian) students are on a par with their famous pupils, from Pericles and Dion to Cicero and Caesar. It is striking that all the teachers in Guarino's list are Greeks, whereas the pupils are both Greeks and Romans, and politicians as well as men of letters. The implication must be that without Greek learning, Rome would not have had a Cicero and fifteenth-century Italy would never have experienced the longed-for *renovatio studii.*

Guarino actually planned to edit a collection of letters as a tribute to Chrysoloras, the so-called *Crisolorina.* One of the letters, written in 1452 to his son Niccolò, is an answer to a letter from Niccolò that has not survived. However, it appears that Niccolò had come across some youthful writings of his father's and had been appalled by the poor quality of the Latin. Guarino explains that in his youth there had been a lack of interest in *humanitas,* in good letters, and as a result of this a decline of Roman, or Latin, eloquence. Of course, they now lived in far better times, and a major factor in this, according to Guarino's letter, was Chrysoloras' teaching:

> He [i.e., Chrysoloras] came to Florence almost as a token of the new flowering of learning and as a cherished guest of that magnificent city. His residency, surrounded by many honors, was fruitful in no small measure; from this city, which had always been a second parent of the arts, of elegance and adornment, he began, like a second Triptolemus, to spread the fruits of learning in the minds of Latin-speaking people, to exhort them to cultivate these fruits, whence in a short time they would reap a wonderful harvest. Growing slowly, *humanitas* shed its old skin, like a newborn snake, and recovered its old vigor, which has survived until now and seems to portend a Roman age.[24]

This homage to Chrysoloras is only a relatively short paragraph in a letter that explains how the renewal of Latin letters came about during Guarino's lifetime. What is relevant in this context is that Chrysoloras, a teacher of Greek, brings about a Latin renaissance—and here Guarino fittingly quotes Cicero's *De oratore,* where we hear that Roman eloquence began to flower after the Latins had studied Greek rhetoric, literature, and philosophy:

So what Cicero says about his fellow citizens came about: "When they had heard the Greek orators, studied their books, devoted themselves to their learning, our people burned with an incredible eagerness to express themselves."[25]

Guarino wrote this letter on the eve of the fall of Constantinople. Already Greek scholars were coming to Italy in increasing numbers, if not yet actually exiled, then all the same seeking an escape from the troubled situation of their country and attracted by the hope of obtaining a teaching position. After May 29, 1453 Italy and not least Venice generally welcomed the learned Greeks who fled the Turks. However, the most illustrious Greek scholar to take up residence in Italy was the Basilian Bessarion (1403–72). He had come to Italy as part of the Byzantine delegation already at the "Council of the Greeks"' (1438–9) which aimed at a unification of the Catholic and the Orthodox churches. Bessarion converted to Catholicism, became one of the most eminent cardinals of the Roman Curia, and twice was nearly elected pope. He was a leading figure of Roman intellectual life from the middle of the century, and his household in Rome deserved the name of Academy. Honored by contemporaries for his *humanitas* and described as "the most Greek of the Greeks and the most Latin of the Latins," Bessarion seemed the personification of the union of the two cultures Chrysoloras had hoped for.[26] None of it saved Byzantium, but a second *translatio studii* had been achieved, and Greek studies continued to thrive in the West.

Notes

1. Weiss (1977) 170–1.
2. "Quid de ingeniis loquar? imitatio unum insigne par siderum lingue latine, Ciceronem et Virgilium, dedit, effecitque ne iam amplius Grecis ulla in parte eloquentie cederemus; dum hic Homerum sequitur, ille Demosthenem, alter ducem suum attigit, alter a tergo liquit" (Petrarca 1933–42, VI 4, 12).
3. "Credo neminem negaturum aliquanto clarius italicum esse quam grecum" (Petrarca 1933–42, I 4, 3). For Petrarch's nationalism, see Pade (2012).
4. Cf., e.g., Ziegler (1945, cc. 824–5) and Pade (2007, Ch. 2.1).
5. For literature on the *Policraticus* see the bibliography in Kloft and Kerner (1992, 127–30). The latest edition of the *Institutio Traiani* is by Kloft in Kloft and Kerner (1992, 8–31), based on the edition of Webb in John of Salisbury (1909).
6. "Plutarchus siquidem grecus homo et Traiani principis magister, suos claros viros nostris conferens, cum Platoni et Aristotili—quorum primum divinum, secundum demonium Graii vocant—Marcum Varronem, Homero Virgilium, Demostheni Marcum Tullium obiecisset, ausus est ad postremum et ducum controversiam movere, nec eum tanti saltem discipuli veneratio continuit. In uno sane suorum ingenia prorsus imparia non erubuit confiteri, quod quem tibi ex equo in moralibus preceptis obicerent non haberent; laus ingens ex ore presertim hominis animosi et qui nostro Iulio Cesari suum Alexandrum Macedonem comparasset" (Petrarca 1933–42, XXIV 5,3). The passage is discussed in Momigliano (1949, 189–90).

7. For Petrarch's relationship with Barlaam, Sigeros, and Pilatus, see Pertusi (1964) and Fyrigos (1990).
8. By "literary texts" I mean not only fiction but also genres like biograpy, historiography, and rhetorical writings.
9. "Homerus tuus apud me mutus, imo vero ego apud illum surdus sum. Gaudeo tamen vel aspectu solo et sepe illum amplexus ac suspirans dico: O magne vir, quam cupide te audirem!" (Petrarca 1933–42, XVIII 2, 9). Petrarch's Greek Homer, which contains only the *Iliad*, is now the MS I 98 inf. of the Biblioteca Ambrosiana in Milan.
10. The fundamental study of Leontius' translation is still Pertusi (1964). See also Pertusi (1966); Fyrigos (1997); and Fabbri (1997 100–3).
11. See Ricci (1952).
12. Boccaccio (1998, XV 6, 9), English translation in Osgood (1956). For the influence of Leontius on Boccaccio's writings and the *fortuna* of the Homeric versions, see Pade (2001), (2008a), and (2010), with references to earlier literature.
13. For a comprehensive study of the life and works of Salutati see Witt (1983) and (2000, 292–337).
14. "denique pro semigreca translatione remitto tibi latinum tractatum" (Salutati 1891–1911, II 480–3).
15. For Chrysoloras see now the various contributions in Maisano and Rollo (2002), with earlier bibliography.
16. For the story of Salutati's invitation to Chrysoloras and the circumstances of his appointment see for instance Witt (1983, 303–5).
17. New critical edition in Crisolora (2000a). Renaissance Latin and modern Italian translation in Crisolora (2001); there is another Italian translation in Crisolora (2000b).
18. For Chrysoloras' teaching and views on translation, see Berti (1987), (1988), and (1998); Wilson (1992, 8–12); and Pade (2017).
19. See Hankins (2002) for Petrarch's influence on Leonardo Bruni's Greek studies.
20. Cf. Hankins (2002, 189–90).
21. "Ego autem Platoni adhaereo, quem ego ipse michi effinxi et quidem latine scientem, ut iudicare possit . . . Hoc enim ipse Plato praesens me facere jubet, qui cum elegantissimi oris apud Graecos sit, non vult certe apud Latinos ineptus videri" (Bruni 1741, I 8). English translation by J. Hankins in Griffiths, Hankins, and Thompson (1987, 10). For Bruni's views on translation, see also Hankins (2003) and Pade (2018); for his interest in Plutarch, see Pade (2019).
22. For the life of Guarino, see Verger (1997). For an assessment of Guarino's "application to the Greek legacy," see Wilson (1992, 42–7). For Guarino's translations from Plutarch, see Pade (2011 and 2014a).
23. "Iure itaque illos extollit antiquitas qui primores erudierunt, quoniam una in persona plurimorum mores et instituta reformarentur: ut Anaxagoras Periclem, Plato Dionem, Pythagoras principes italicos, Athenodorus Catonem, Panaetius Scipionem, Apollonius Ciceronem et Caesarem, plurimos etiam hac aetate Manuel Chrysoloras, magnus et vir et philosophus" (Guarino Veronese 1915–19, *ep.* 159, AD 1419).
24. "Is delatus Florentiam quasi reflorescentis eruditionis auspicium et magnificentissimae civitatis delectatus hospitio, ibi sedem habuit multis conditam honoribus nec parvis fructibus laetissimam; ut, quae artium egregiarum munditiarumque ac expolitionis parens altera semper extitisset, ea ex urbe coeperit, sicuti Triptolemus

alter, litterarum fruges per nostrorum ingenia dispertiri et nostrates ad colendum animare, unde germinantia late semina brevi fructus mirificos edidere. Sensim augescens humanitas veteres, ut serpens novus, exuvias deponens pristinum vigorem reparabat, qui in hanc perdurans aetatem romana portendere saecula videtur" (Guarino Veronese 1915–19, *ep.* 862). On this letter and its implications for our understanding of humanist Latin, see Pade (2014b).

25. "Contigit igitur quod de suis civibus Tullius factum affirmat: "Post autem auditis oratoribus graecis cognitisque eorum litteris adhibitisque doctoribus incredibili quodam nostri homines dicendi studio flagraverunt" (Guarino Veronese 1915–19, *de orat.* 1.14).

26. Cf. Wilson (1992, 57–67). Chapters 9–14 give an overview of Greek studies in Italy until the beginning of the sixteenth century.

BIBLIOGRAPHY

Baron, H. 1966. *The Crisis of the Early Italian Renaissance.* Princeton, NJ: Princeton University Press.

Berti, E. 1987. "Alla scuola di Manuele Crisolora. Lettura e commento di Luciano". *Rinascimento* n.s. 27: 3–73.

Berti, E. 1988. "Traduzioni oratorie fedeli". *Medioevo e Rinascimento* 2: 245–66.

Berti, E. 1998. "Manuele Crisolora, Plutarco e l'avviamento delle traduzioni umanistiche". *Fontes* 1: 81–99.

Boccaccio, Giovanni 1998. *Genealogie deorum gentilium* (Tutte le opere di Giovanni Boccaccio VII–VIII), ed. V. Zaccaria. Milan: A. Mondadori.

Botley, P. 2010. *Learning Greek in Western Europe, 1396–1529. Grammars, Lexica, and Classroom Texts* (Transactions of the American Philosophical Society, 100, 2). Philadelphia, PA: American Philosophical Society.

Bruni, L. 1741. *Epistolarum libri VIII*, vol. I–II, ed. L. Mehus. Florence: Paperinus.

Bruni, L. 1996. *Opere letterarie e politiche*, ed. P. Viti. Turin: UTET.

Crisolora, M. 2000a. "Confronto tra 'Antica e la Nuova Roma', a c. di C. Billò." *Medioevo greco* O: 1–26.

Crisolora, M. 2000b. *Roma parte del cielo. Confronto tra l'Antica e la Nuova Roma*, introduction E.V. Maltese, trans. and notes G. Cortassa. Turin: UTET.

Crisolora, M. 2001. *Le due Rome. Confronto tra Roma e Costantinopoli* (RR 2000 Viaggi a Roma 7). With Latin translation by Francesco Aleardi, ed. F. Niutta. Bologna: Patron.

Dionisotti, A. C. 1992. "The Medieval West". In *Perceptions of the Ancient Greeks*, ed. K. J. Dover, 100–27. Oxford: Blackwell.

Fabbri, R. 1997. "Sulle traduzioni latine umanistiche da Omero". In *Posthomerica. Tradizioni omeriche dall'Antichità al Rinascimento I*, ed. F. Montanari and S. Pittaluga, 99–124. Genoa: Dipartimento di archeologia, filologia classica e loro tradizioni.

Fyrigos, A. 1990. "Barlaam e Petrarca". *Studi Petrarcheschi* 6: 179–200.

Fyrigos, A. 1997. "Il fondamento bizantino del Rinascimento italiano". *Studi sull'Oriente Cristiano* 1/1–2: 47–65.

Griffiths, G., J. Hankins, and D. Thompson. 1987. *The Humanism of Leonardo Bruni* (Medieval and Renaissance Texts and Studies 46). Binghamton, NY: Renaissance Society of America.

Guarino Veronese 1915–19. *Epistolario di Guarino Veronese* 1–3 (Miscellanea di storia veneta 8, 11, 14), ed. Remigio Sabbadini. Venice: R. Deputazione veneta di storia patria.

Hankins, J. 2002. "Chrysoloras and the Greek Studies of Leonardo Bruni". In *Manuele Crisolora e il ritorno del greco in occidente* (Atti del Convegno Internazionale Napoli, 26–29 giugno 1997), ed. R. Maisano and A. Rollo, 175–97. Naples: Istituto Universitario Orientale.

Hankins, J. 2003. "The Ethics Controversy". In *Humanism and Platonism in the Italian Renaissance I*, 193–239. Rome: Edizioni di storia e letteratura.

John of Salisbury. 1909. *Joannis Saresberiensis Episcopi Carnotensis Policratici Libri VII*, I–II, ed. C. C. I. Webb. Oxford: Clarendon.

Kloft, H. and M. Kerner. 1992. *Die Institutio Traiani. Ein pseudo-plutarchischer Text im Mittelalter* (Beiträge zur Altertumskunde, 14). Stuttgart: Teubner.

Maisano, R. and A. Rollo, eds. 2002. *Manuele Crisolora e il ritorno del greco in occidente* (Atti del Convegno Internazionale Napoli, 26–29 giugno 1997). Naples: Istituto Universitario Orientale.

Momigliano, A. 1949. "Notes on Petrarch, John of Salisbury and the Institutio Trajani". *JWCI* 12: 189–90.

Osgood, C. G. 1956. *Boccaccio on Poetry*. Indianapolis, IN : Bobbs-Merrill.

Pade, M. 2001. "Un nuovo testimone dell'Iliade di Leonzio Pilato; il Diez. B. Sant. 4 della Staatsbibliothek, Stiftung Preussischer Kulturbesitz, di Berlino". In *Posthomerica. Tradizioni omeriche dall'Antichità al Rinascimento III*, ed. F. Montanari and S. Pittaluga, 87–102. Genoa: Dipartimento di archeologia, filologia classica e loro tradizioni.

Pade, M. 2007. *The Reception of Plutarch's* Lives *in Fifteenth-Century Italy* I–II (Renæssancestudier 14). Copenhagen: Museum Tusculanum.

Pade, M. 2008a. "The *Fortuna* of Leontius Pilatus' Homer. With an edition of Pier Candido Decembrio's *Why Homer's Greek verses are rendered in Latin prose*". In *Classica et Beneventana: Essays Presented to Virginia Brown on the Occasion of her 65th Birthday* (Textes et Études du Moyen Âge 36), ed. F. T. Coulson and A. A. Grotans, 149–72. Turnhout: Brepols.

Pade, M. 2008b. "Niccolò Perotti and the *ars traducendi*." In *Sol et homo. Mensch und Natur in der Renaissance*: *Festschrift zum 70. Geburtstag für Eckhardt Keßler*, ed. S. Ebbersmeyer, H. Pirner-Pareschi, and T. Ricklin, 70–100. Munich: Wilhelm Fink.

Pade, M. 2010. "Boccaccio, Leonzio, and the Transformation of the Homeric Myths". In, *Homère à la Renaissance. Mythe et transfigurations* (Collection d'histoire de l'art, Académie de France à Rome—Villa Médicis), ed. L. Capodieci and P. Ford, 27–40. Paris and Rome: Somogy Éditions/Académie de France à Rome.

Pade, M. 2011 "The Latin Dion: Guarino Veronese's translation of the Plutarchan life (1414)". *Humanistica: an international journal of early Renaissance studies* VI.I, 33–42.

Pade, M. 2012. "Humanist Latin and Italian identity: sum vero Italus natione et Romanus civis esse glorior". In *The Role of Latin in the Early Modern World: Latin, Linguistic Identity and Nationalism, 1350–1800* (Renæssanceforum 8), eds. A. Coroleu, A. Laird & M. Pade, 1–21.

Pade, M. 2014a. "I give you back Plutarch in Latin—Guarino Veronese's version of Plutarch's Dion (1414) and early humanist translation". HYPERLINK "http://muse.jhu.edu/journals/canadian_review_of_comparative_literature" *Canadian Review of Comparative Literature / Revue Canadienne de Littérature Comparé* 41,4: 354–68.

Pade, M. 2014b. "From medieval Latin to neo-Latin". In *Brill's Encyclopaedia of the Neo-Latin World*, eds. P. Ford *et al.*, 5–19. Leiden-Boston: Brill.

Pade, M. 2017. "Chrysoloras on Translation: a note on the meaning of proprietas graeca". In *God latin. Studies in Honour of Peter Zeeberg on the Occasion of his Sixtieth Birthday 21 April 2017* (Renæssanceforum 12), eds. B. B. Johannsen, K. Kryger & K. Skovgaard-Petersen, 53–60.

Pade, M. 2018. "Greek into Humanist Latin: Foreignizing vs. domesticating translation in the Italian Quattrocento". In *Issues in Translation Then and Now: Renaissance theories and translation studies today* (Renæssanceforum 14), eds. A. den Haan, B. Hosington, M. Pade & A. Wegener, 1–23.

Pade, M. 2019. "Leonardo Bruni and Plutarch". In *Brill's Companion to the Reception of Plutarch*, eds. S. Xenofontos & K. Oikonomopoulou, 388–403. Leiden & Boston: Brill.

Pertusi A. 1964. *Leonzio Pilato fra Petrarca e Boccaccio. Le sue versioni omeriche negli autografi di Venezia e la cultura greca del primo Umanesimo* (Civiltà veneziana. Studi 16). Venice and Rome: Istituto per la Collaborazione Culturale [repr. Florence: Olschki, 1980].

Pertusi A. 1966. "Leonzio Pilato e la tradizione di cultura italo-greca". *Byzantino-sicula* (Quaderni dell'Istituto Siciliano di Studi bizantini e neoellenici, 2), 66–84.

Petrarca, F. 1933–42. *Le Familiari*, I–IV, ed. V. Rossi and U. Bosco. Florence: Sansoni.

Petrarca, F. 2006. *Le postille del Virgilio Ambrosiano* (Presentazione di G. Velli, I–II) (Studi sul Petrarca 33–34), ed. M. Baglio, A. Nebuloni Testa, and M. Petoletti. Rome and Padua: Antenore.

Rabil, A., ed. 1988. *Renaissance Humanism: Foundations, Forms, and Legacy*. Philadelphia, PA: University of Pennsylvania Press.

Ricci, P. G. 1952. "La prima cattedra di greco in Firenze". *Rinascimento* 3: 159–65.

Salutati, C. 1891–1911. *Epistolario*, I–IV, ed. F. Novati. Rome: Istituto Storico Italiano.

Verger, J. 1997. "Guarino de Vérone". In *Centuriae Latinae. Cent une figures humanistes de la Renaissance aux Lumières offertes à Jacques Chomarat* (Travaux d'Humanisme et Renaissance CCCXIV], ed. C. Nativel, 409–15. Geneva : Droz.

Weiss, R. 1977. *Medieval and Humanist Greek* (Medioevo e Umanesimo 8). Padua: Antenore.

Wilson, N. G. 1992. *From Byzantium to Italy: Greek Studies in the Italian Renaissance*. Baltimore, MD: Johns Hopkins University Press.

Witt, R. G. 1983. *Hercules at the Crossroads. The Life, Works and Thought of Coluccio Salutati* (Duke Monographs in Medieval and Renaissance Studies 6). Durham, NC: Duke University Press.

Witt, R. G. 2000. *In the Footsteps of the Ancients. The Origins of Humanism from Lovato to Bruni* (Studies in Medieval and Reformation Thought 74). Leiden, Boston, and Cologne: Brill.

Ziegler, K. 1945. "Plutarchos". *RE*, XXI, 1: cc. 636–62.

CHAPTER 34

....

THE WANING OF MANUSCRIPT PRODUCTION

....

GREGORY HAYS

THE PERIOD OF TRANSITION

....

THE introduction in the late 1450s of printing with movable metal type appears in retrospect as a watershed in European culture, and was greeted rapturously even by some contemporaries.[1] Yet the new technology did not instantly make the old obsolete.[2] Script and print coexisted for at least a generation after Gutenberg, and Latin texts continued to be copied by hand well after 1500.[3]

In many ways, the earliest printed books can be regarded as simply an extension of contemporary manuscripts.[4] Early typefaces were naturally modeled on existing script, abbreviations, ligatures, and all.[5] Thus, Italian Humanistic book hand gave rise to the Roman type used by Sweynheym and Pannartz. Humanistic cursive produced the familiar "italic" type popularized by Aldus Manutius, who may have used the hand of the Paduan scribe Bartolomeo Sanvito as his model.[6] Gothic book hands generated the *Fraktur* or "black-letter" preferred for law books, service books, and bibles. In the Low Countries, the Brethren of the Common Life developed a typeface modeled on their distinctive script style. Some familiar conventions of the printed book (e.g., the running head, indexing, tables of contents) can be traced back to late medieval manuscripts. One new development was the title page, which emerged, sporadically and for reasons still unclear, in the first decades of printing.[7] Its occasional adoption by late fifteenth-century scribes shows that print conventions could influence manuscripts as well as vice versa.

The absence at this period of a rigid distinction between script and print holds good for reception also. Fifteenth-century booklists often specify whether a given entry represents a manuscript or a printed book, but typically list them in a single sequence; owners seem to have stored them side by side. Library catalogues do not consistently separate printed books from manuscripts until the later seventeenth century.[8] Indeed, doing so would often have caused serious difficulty, since printed books and manuscripts were frequently bound together.[9]

Print had its limitations, especially in its early stages. Incunabula often include handwritten elements (or space left blank for them): illuminated capitals, penwork, diagrams, illustrations, musical notation, Greek. But the press's repertoire grew rapidly. The technical challenges of non-Roman alphabets were overcome relatively quickly. The first printed book in Greek (an edition of the pseudo-Homeric *Batrachomyomachia*) was published in 1475. Books were printed in Hebrew as early as the 1470s and in Cyrillic by 1491. Still more complicated was the case of music, which required careful alignment and (at least with early techniques) several passes through the press. The obstacles were not insuperable, and printed music was circulating widely by the early sixteenth century.[10] Even so, large liturgical books (antiphonals and graduals) continued to be produced by hand, and hand-copying remained important for musical scores well into the 1700s.[11]

Absent technical issues, the promotion of a text to print depended on at least two factors: the availability of an exemplar at a particular date in a particular place, and the printer's expectation—not always well founded—that the text would find buyers. Works that could not meet both conditions remained in manuscript, at least for the time being.[12] First in line for the press were scriptural texts (Gutenberg's Bible, the Mainz Psalter) and popular works such as Donatus' grammar. Printing also had obvious utility for lengthy reference works like Giovanni Balbi's *Catholicon* and for legal texts, which were much in demand but expensive and time-consuming to copy. In the wake of humanism, classical texts could also look for a fair-sized readership. Most of the major Latin authors had reached print by 1485, though a few had to wait longer (Phaedrus, for example, until 1596). Post-classical writers were more haphazardly served.[13] Many significant medieval texts still await a printed edition.

Yet as late as 1500 readers are still found copying classical texts by hand, even when the work had already made its way into print. Indeed, it is by no means uncommon to find that a late fifteenth-century manuscript has been copied from a printed book.[14] This practice, startling at first glance, becomes explicable in the context of early printing and distribution practices. As we shall see, some such volumes were commissioned by patrons who placed a premium on a handwritten manuscript. In other cases the copyist may not have been able to afford a printed book, or may not have had access to one other than the exemplar. The practice has an important corollary for students of transmission. For most texts, the products of even a small print run are likely to have outnumbered all extant manuscripts. It follows that any manuscript written after the publication of the corresponding *editio princeps* is very likely a copy of a printed book.

MANUSCRIPTS AT THE MARGINS

By the last decade of the century, it was clear that the balance had shifted. The memoirs of the Florentine cartolaio Vespasiano da Bisticci (d. 1498) look back wistfully to a golden age of manuscript production. At Venice the Dominican scribe Filippo della Strada (active into the 1490s) wrote scathing poems against the technology that was eating away at his livelihood.[15] Some of those involved in scribal book production looked for other lines of work. Others made the transition to the new technology successfully. Some of the early printers, including Peter Schöffer, Colard Mansion, and Johannes Mentelin, had in fact begun their careers as scribes.[16] The Brethren of the Common Life, having previously supported themselves by copying, now did so by manufacturing printed books. Hand-copying continued into the sixteenth century (and beyond), but was increasingly restricted to certain types of book.[17]

At the high end are deluxe copies. As contemporaries noted, the new technology had a democratizing effect. It multiplied copies, lowered their price, and spread book ownership further down the social scale. But in the process it enhanced the value of the hand-copied and illuminated volume as a unique object and a status symbol. In the early fifteenth century, for example, Books of Hours were among the most popular scribal productions, turned out by workshops in northern France and Flanders and exported all over Europe.[18] Printed Books of Hours were a natural development, and are found by 1475 in Italy and 1485 in France. Yet individually written and illuminated hours did not disappear; they continued to be produced into the early decades of the sixteenth century. The advantages of printing—economies of scale and low marginal costs—had less weight here. The manuscript-makers already benefited from a degree of mass production, and the cost of illumination could not be reduced without an obvious drop in quality.

When they set out to form a library, wealthy fifteenth-century patrons still turned to scribes and illuminators, commissioning classical and humanistic texts directly or through intermediaries. These bespoke codices are generally on parchment, with heavy illumination and decoration, and bound elaborately. Earlier examples are written in Humanistic *Rotunda*, the script proper to their largely classical content, though after 1480 Humanistic cursive is increasingly common. (As with many deluxe books today, the excellence of the presentation often goes hand in hand with a striking indifference to the accuracy of the text.)

Three such libraries are worth mention here. Starting around 1465, in Urbino, Federigo da Montefeltro (1422–82) built up a major collection (most of which is now in the Vatican), with the aid of his advisor Ottaviano Ubaldini della Casa. Many of the books were deluxe copies commissioned from the Florentine bookseller Vespasiano da Bisticci.[19] Often quoted is Vespasiano da Bisticci's comment: "In that library the books are all beautiful to the highest degree, all written with the pen, and there was not a single printed book—it would have felt embarrassed [i.e., to be numbered among such objects]."[20] This is sometimes taken to imply deliberate exclusion of print.[21] In reality Federigo did own at least a handful of incunabula, and his heirs certainly had no reservations about acquiring them.[22]

A great mythology has grown up around the library of the Hungarian monarch Matthias Corvinus (reigned 1458–90).[23] Employing Italian scribes and illuminators, Matthias established on the frontiers of Christendom the second-largest library then extant. His successors were less intellectually inclined: individual volumes were sold or wandered off, and what remained of the library was plundered by the Turks in 1526. Some 200 extant volumes have been identified, a fraction of the original total.

Yet a third example is the library of Raphael de Marcatellis (1437–1508), illegitimate son of Philip the Good, duke of Burgundy, who became abbot of St. Bavon in Ghent (while managing to spend most of his time in Bruges).[24] Over 50 manuscripts survive from his personal library: they are large, specially commissioned volumes, many copied from printed books (which the library resolutely excluded). Their contents reflect humanist interests, but their main purpose was clearly to serve as "exponents of their owner's sense of grandeur."[25]

In the early decades of the sixteenth century there was still work for professional scribes. They were needed to produce personal or presentation copies, of the sort written in England by Peter Meghen (d. 1540) for John Colet, or in Italy by Ludovico Arrighi (1475–1527) for Machiavelli and others.[26] The tradition of the deluxe illuminated codex generated late masterpieces like the Psalter of Paul III (1542) or the Farnese Hours (1546).[27] Italian chanceries, and especially the papal curia, needed scribes to generate briefs and bulls. In the process, Humanistic cursive acquired a new life as a documentary script, cancellaresca.[28] The need for training in the script was filled by a succession of writing manuals, notably Arrighi's *Operina* (1522).[29] Yet such works also indicate a weakening of traditional training; handwriting is now an artificial skill to be acquired from a (printed) book, rather than taught in a scriptorium or mastered in the course of an apprenticeship. And, of course, it was print, and the skill of engravers, that allowed the writing masters to reach a broad audience rapidly.

For secular patrons like Corvinus or de Marcatellis, the manuscript had value as an object, to be desired and possessed like a painting or piece of silver. For others, the manuscript's meaning lay at least as much in the process that generated it as in the product itself. This is the case with monastic copying, which remained important in some areas through the end of the fifteenth century and even into the sixteenth. Its persistence may owe something to a continuing need (not yet met by printers) for specialized service books. But it also represented an ideological commitment to writing as a part of monastic discipline. There is evidence of continuity in training and scribal practice at various houses of the Melk Congregation, including Melk itself, Kremsmünster, and Augsburg.[30] Manuscript production also continued in the northern monastic houses of the Windesheim and Bursfeld reforms.

A key document for this movement is the 1492 treatise *De laude scriptorum* of Johannes Trithemius (1462–1516), abbot of Sponheim, whose intellectual interests ranged from ecclesiastical bibliography to cryptography and the occult.[31] Trithemius defends the practice of hand-copying on pragmatic grounds: printed books are subject to problems of availability and cost; not everything has yet been printed. He draws qualitative distinctions: printers are often careless, and books written on parchment are more durable than printed books on paper. But he also emphasizes the spiritual benefits to be gained from copying Scripture and devotional works. It is easy and tempting to take the work as a kind of rearguard action. But other facts complicate this picture. Trithemius was no hidebound conservative. He speaks admiringly of the new technology in other contexts and acquired printed books for the Sponheim library. He had many of his own works printed—among them, in 1494, the *De laude scriptorum*. For Trithemius copying retained its value as instrument of monastic discipline, even in the age of print. The same symbiosis is found elsewhere. SS. Ulrich and Afra at Augsburg, for example, housed both a thriving scriptorium and an active printing operation.

A notable characteristic of late fifteenth- and early sixteenth-century scribes is their versatility. Professional scribes were prepared to write a variety of hands, depending on their patrons' expectations and the type of work being copied. A good example is the fifteenth-century Dutch scribe Theodericus Werken, active in Cologne, Italy, and England, whose known manuscripts are so diverse in style that they might be mistaken for the work of several different men.[32] We also see a nascent historical sense and an interest in reviving earlier scripts. Leonhard Wagner (1454–1522) a monk of SS. Ulrich and Afra, Augsburg, was responsible (by his own account) for at least 50 manuscripts. Of these, one of the most interesting is the *Proba centum scripturarum una manu exaratarum*, an album of palaeographical samples, intended for presentation to the Emperor Maximilian I.[33] It includes attempts at the reproduction of older hands dating back to the twelfth century. Such experiments had a practical as well as an antiquarian side. A scribe might be called on to supply material missing from an older, fragmentary manuscript; such "supply leaves" sometimes employ an archaizing script. In a monastic context there might be an attempt to preserve or revive a "house style"; such imitation of twelfth- and thirteenth-century script is found in English monasteries such as Christ Church, Canterbury, in the years immediately preceding the Dissolution.[34] Scribes were even prepared to imitate the productions of the press. An early printed edition of Jean Gerson's opuscula in the Huntington Library includes an additional treatise copied by hand; the scribe has made an effort to reproduce the style and layout of the printed text.[35]

At the other extreme from the work of professional scribes are what we might call "subprint" manuscripts—those copied by occasional or nonprofessional scribes and containing texts whose nature or content made printing unnecessary, economically unfeasible, or problematic in other ways. This does not necessarily imply a lack of interest or readership. Works of an ephemeral or topical nature—political satires, for instance—might be widely read without ever achieving print publication; they circulated virally, like the ubiquitous email forwards of the early 2000s. Works might be individually too short or collectively too miscellaneous to fill a printed volume: hence the manuscript anthologies of lyric poems (especially in the vernacular) or epigraphic texts that persist well into the early modern period.[36]

Other texts presupposed a readership too small to make a print run worthwhile: copies of letters, for instance, or local and family histories. Some types of material were meant primarily for the writer's own use: a teacher's lectures, a student's notes, a gentleman's commonplace book. Early modern scholars transcribed and collated the manuscripts of classical authors. Antiquarians might copy documentary texts, such as English monastic charters, many of which circulated in manuscript well into the seventeenth century.[37] Transcripts of this kind shed light on early modern scholarship; they can also be valuable witnesses to manuscripts now lost or subsequently damaged.[38] To this group we can add texts of a less rarefied sort: calendars, recipes, medical notes, and the like, accumulated or compiled for daily use.

Yet another subcategory is constituted by prohibited or dangerous texts: works on the Index (in Catholic areas), or Catholic service books (in post-Reformation England). Early modern regimes had little success in suppressing printers (who could simply move across the nearest political or religious border), but somewhat more in confiscating printed copies or stopping them at the frontier. When printed texts were unavailable, such works circulated in manuscript, which also had the advantage of being less identifiable to a cursory inspection.

Sometimes several of these factors were at work. In the early years of the sixteenth century there had been a substantial informal trade in the natal charts of well-known individuals, which were collected and exchanged by astrologers.[39] Such *geniturae* were a natural candidate for manuscript circulation: they were relatively short, were generated on an ongoing basis, and often existed in multiple versions. They involved figures and diagrams that were time-consuming to engrave and typeset. They were of intense interest to a specialist community, but required considerable knowledge to interpret. Their formal publication could potentially cause offense to living subjects. It is scarcely surprising, then, that no printed collection appeared before the publication of Girolamo Cardano's *Libelli* in 1538.

Physically, such sub-print manuscripts are at the other extreme from the opulent codices of a Corvinus or Montefeltro. They typically employ more casual scripts: *bastarda*, secretary, or various kinds of cursive. Apart from basic rubrication they are usually undecorated, and written on paper, not parchment. Formats are generally smaller; for some of these books, portability was a major consideration. Their late date and lack of art-historical appeal have left most little studied, except as vehicles for the texts they contain. As a group they would repay more detailed investigation.

Digital Scriptorium
Illustrations

PLATE 34.1 New York Public Library, Spencer Collection, NYPL Spencer 027, fol. 1 "Corvinus Livy." http://images.nypl.org/?id=427402&t=w.

PLATE 34.2 Huntington Library, HM 64, ff. 154v–155. Astrological and Medical Compilation, s. XVex. Recipes and charms; ownership note of John Wallton. http://dpg.lib.berkeley.edu/webdb/dsheh/heh_brf?Description=&CallNumber=HM+64.

Notes

1. For contemporary reactions, see Widmann (1973).
2. The revolutionary impact of print on all areas of European life is the central theme of Eisenstein (1979). Others see the transition from a scribal to a print culture as more gradual: McKitterick (2003).
3. General treatments of this period: Bühler (1960); Lülfing (1981, 17–26); Petrucci (1995).
4. See "Scribal Tradition and Innovation in Early Printed Books" in Hirsch (1978, no. XV); Smith (1994). As Smith emphasizes, it is misleading to speak of incunables as "imitating" manuscripts. Incunables were not designed to look like manuscripts, but to look, simply, like books.
5. Mazal (1984); Needham (1993). Another relevant influence is the lettering of inscriptions: see Morison (1937).
6. Wardrop (1963).
7. "The Earliest Development of Title Pages," in Hirsch (1978, no. XVII); Smith (2000).
8. McKitterick (2003, 12–13).
9. Separation of departments of manuscripts from those of incunabula and early printed books in modern libraries has led to the dismembering of many such hybrid volumes: see McKitterick (2003, 50–1).

10. Fenlon (1995).

11. Chan (2002).

12. For a brief list of *editiones principes* of classical Latin authors, see Sandys (1903–8, vol. 2. 103). More expansive is Mazal (2003). For medieval authors, see Goldschmidt (1943), including a sample listing for "Mystical Writers" at 122–38.

13. Of the works of the sixth-century allegorist Fulgentius, for example, two (the *Mitologiae* and *Sermones antiqui*) were printed as early as 1498, and their manuscript tradition effectively ceases at that point. By contrast, his *Expositio Virgilianae continentiae* had to wait until 1589, and at least three sixteenth-century manuscripts are extant (Milan, Biblioteca Ambrosiana, D 498 inf., Vatican City, BAV, Vat. lat. 3898, 5216). A fourth work (*De aetatibus mundi et hominis*) first saw print in 1694.

14. Bühler (1960, 15–16, 34–9); Lutz (1975, 129–38); Reeve (1983).

15. Haye (1997).

16. Mertens (1977).

17. Cf. the typology in Nebbiai (1978) based on material from the Biblioteca comunale Augusta at Perugia.

18. De Hamel (1983).

19. Clough (1966); Tocci (1986); de la Mare (1986); Simonetta (2007).

20. "In quella libreria i libri tutti sono belli in superlativo grado, tutti iscritti a penna, e non ve n'è ignuno a stampa, che se ne sarebbe vergognato."

21. e.g. Clough (1966, 103), "Vespasiano tells us that Federigo did not consider printed books worthy of a place in his Library"; Bischoff (1986, 237), "Von Federigo...hatte Bisticci geschrieben, daß er sich geschämt hätte, in seine erlesene Bibliothek ein gedrucktes Buch aufzunehmen." Vespasiano's wording is not unambiguous.

22. Davies (2007).

23. Csapodi (1973); Rady (2004).

24. Derolez (1979), (2002).

25. Derolez (1979, 9).

26. Petrucci (1995, 516–23). On Meghen, see Trapp (1975), (1983), (1991, 15–29). On Arrighi, see Casamassima (1962).

27. Paris, BnF, lat. 8880 (Psalter of Paul III); New York, Pierpont Morgan Library, M. 69 (Farnese Hours). See further Alexander (1994).

28. Wardrop (1963, 36–49).

29. Casamassima (1966); Osler (1972); Morison (1990).

30. Steinberg (1941).

31. On Trithemius, see Brann (1981); Arnold (1991). The *De laude scriptorum* has been edited with an English translation by Arnold and Berendt (1974). See also Howie (1976); Embach (2000).

32. Mynors (1950).

33. See the facsimile edition of Wehmer (1963).

34. Parkes (1997).

35. Haselden (1939).

36. Manuscript circulation remained common for vernacular literature until an even later date. See Love (1993).

37. Crick (2004).

38. Even much more recent transcriptions can sometimes prove unexpectedly valuable. The glossary compiled by Ainardus of Saint-Èvre survived in a single manuscript, destroyed at

Metz in 1944. Extracts had been published in Goetz's *Corpus Glossariorum Latinorum*, but the complete text was presumed lost until the recent discovery of a transcript made in 1879 by Gustav Loewe. See Gatti (2000, xviii).
39. Grafton (1999, 73–4).

BIBLIOGRAPHY

Alexander, J. J. G., ed. 1994. *The Painted Page: Italian Renaissance Book Illumination 1450–1550*. New York: Prestel.

Arnold, K. 1991. *Johannes Trithemius*, 2d ed. Würzburg: Kommissionsverlag F. Schöningh.

Arnold, K., ed. Berendt, R. tr. 1974. *Johannes Trithemius. In Praise of Scribes (De laude scriptorum)*. Lawrence, KS: Coronado.

Bischoff, B. 1986. *Paläographie des römischen Altertums und des Abendländischen Mittelalters*, 2d ed. Berlin: Erich Schmidt.

Brann, N. 1981. *The Abbot Trithemius (1462–1516): The Renaissance of Monastic Humanism*. Leiden: Brill.

Bühler, C. 1960. *The Fifteenth-Century Book*. Philadelphia, PA: University of Pennsylvania Press.

Casamassima, E. 1962. "Ludovico degli Arrighi detto Vicentino." *La bibliofilia* 64: 117–62.

Casamassima, E. 1966. *Tratatti di scrittura del Cinquecento italiano*. Milan: Edizioni Il Polifilo.

Chan, M. 2002. "Music Books." In *The Cambridge History of the Book in Britain, vol. IV. 1557–1695*, ed. Michael F. Suarez SJ and Michael L. Turner, 128–37. Cambridge: Cambridge University Press.

Clough, C. H. 1966. "The Library of the Dukes of Urbino," *Librarium* 9: 101–5.

Crick, J. 2004. *The Uses of Script and Print 1300–1700*. Cambridge: Cambridge University Press.

Csapodi, C. 1973. *The Corvinian Library, History and Stock*. Budapest: Akadémiai Kiadó.

Davies, M. 2007. "'Non ve n'è ignuno a stampa': The Printed Books of Federico da Montefeltro," in *Federico da Montefeltro and his Library*, ed. M. Simonetta, 63–78.

de Hamel, C. 1983. "Reflexions on the Trade in Books of Hours at Ghent and Bruges." In *Manuscripts in the Fifty Years after the Invention of Printing*, ed. J. B. Trapp, 29–34. London: Warburg Institute.

de la Mare, A. 1986. "Vespasiano da Bisticci e i copisti fiorentini di Federico." In *Federico di Montefeltro: lo Stato, le arti, la cultura*, ed. G. C. Baiardi *et al.*, 81–96. Rome: Bulzoni.

Derolez, A. 1979. *The Library of Raphael de Marcatellis, Abbot of St. Bavon's, Ghent, 1437–1508*. Ghent: E. Story-Scientia.

Derolez, A. 2002. "Early Humanism in Flanders: New Data and Observations on the Library of Abbot Raphael De Mercatellis (†1508)." In *Les Humanistes et leur bibliothèque. Humanists and their Libraries*, ed. R. De Smet, 37–57. Leuven: Peeters.

Eisenstein, E. 1979. *The Printing Revolution in Early Modern Europe*, 2 vols. Cambridge: Cambridge University Press.

Embach, M. 2000. "Skriptographie versus Typographie: Johannes Trithemius' Schrift *De laude Scriptorum*." *Gutenberg-Jahrbuch* 75: 132–44.

Fenlon, I. 1995. *Music, Print and Culture in Early Sixteenth-Century Italy*. London: British Library.

Gatti, P., ed. 2000. *Ainardo: Glossario*. Florence: SISMEL-ed. del Galluzzo.

Goldschmidt, E. P. 1943. *Medieval Texts and their First Appearance in Print*. London: Bibliographical Society and Oxford University Press.

Grafton, A. 1999. *Cardano's Cosmos*. Cambridge, MA: Harvard University Press.

Haselden, R. B. 1939. "A Scribe and Printer in the Fifteenth Century." *Huntington Library Quarterly* 2: 205–11.

Haye, T. 1997. "Filippo della Strada: ein Venezianer Kalligraph des späten 15. Jahrhunderts im Kampf gegen den Buchdruck." *Archiv für Geschichte des Buchwesens* 48: 279–313.

Hirsch, R. 1978. *The Printed Word: Its Impact and Diffusion*. London: Varorium Reprints.

Howie, D. I. 1976. "Benedictine Monks, Manuscript Copying and the Renaissance: Johannes Trithemius' *De laude scriptorium*." *RB* 86: 129–54.

Love, H. 1993. *Scribal Publication in Seventeenth-Century England*. Oxford: Clarendon.

Lülfing, H. 1981. "Die Fortdauer der handschriftlichen Buchherstellung nach der Erfindung des Buchdrucks: ein buchgeschichtliches Problem." In *Buch und Text im 15. Jahrhundert. Book and Text in the Fifteenth Century*, ed. L. Hellinga and H. Härtel, 17–26. Hamburg: Hauswedell.

Lutz, C. 1975. *Essays on Manuscripts and Rare Books*. Hamden, CT: Archon Books.

Mazal, O. 1984. *Paläographie und Paläotypie*. Stuttgart: Anton Hiersemann.

Mazal, O. 2003. *Die Überlieferung der antiken Literatur im Buchdruck des 15. Jahrhunderts*, 4 vols. Stuttgart: Anton Hiersemann.

McKitterick, D. 2003. *Print, Manuscript and the Search for Order 1450–1830*. Cambridge: Cambridge University Press.

Mertens, D. 1977. "Eine Mentelin-Handschrift." In *Landesgeschichte und Geistesgeschichte*, ed. Kasper Elm *et al.*, 169–87. Stuttgart: Kohlhammer.

Morison, S. 1937. "The Art of Printing." *Proceedings of the British Academy* 23: 373–400.

Morison, S. 1990. *Early Italian Writing-Books, Renaissance to Baroque*, ed. N. Barker. Verona: Valdonega.

Mynors, R. A. B. 1950. "A Fifteenth-Century Scribe: T. Werken." *Transactions of the Cambridge Bibliographical Society* 1: 97–104.

Nebbiai, D. 1978. "Per una valutazione della produzione manoscritta cinque-seicentesca." In *Alfabetismo e cultura scritta nella storia della società italiana* (Atti del Seminario tenutosi a Perugia il 29–30 marzo 1977), 235–67. Perugia: Università degli Studi.

Needham, P. 1993. "Palaeography and the Earliest Printing Types." In *Johannes Gutenberg— Regionale Aspekte des frühen Buchdrucks*, ed. H. Nickel and L. Gillner, 19–27. Berlin: Staatsbibliothek zu Berlin.

Osler, A. S. 1972. *Luminario. An Introduction to the Italian Writing-Books of the Sixteenth and Seventeenth Centuries*. Nieuwkoop: Miland.

Parkes, M. B. 1997. "Archaizing Hands in English Manuscripts." In *Books and Collectors 1200–1700: Essays Presented to Andrew Watson*, ed. J. P. Carley and C. G. C. Tite, 101–41. London: British Library.

Petrucci, A. 1995. "Copisti e libri manoscritti dopo l'avvento della stampa." In *Scribi e colofoni. Le sottoscrizioni di copisti dalle origini all'avvento della stampa*, ed. E. Condello and G. De Gregorio, 507–25. Spoleto: Fondazione CISAM.

Rady, M. 2004. "The Corvina Library and the Lost Royal Hungarian Archive." In *Lost Libraries*, ed. J Raven, 91–105. New York: Macmillan.

Reeve, M. D. 1983. "Manuscripts Copied from Printed Books." In *Manuscripts in the Fifty Years after the Invention of Printing*, ed. J. B. Trapp, 12–20. London: Warburg Institute.

Sandys, J. E. 1903–8. *A History of Classical Scholarship*, 3 vols. Cambridge: Cambridge University Press.

Simonetta, M., ed. 2007. *Federico da Montefeltro and his Library*. Milan: Foundation for Italian Art & Culture.

Smith, M. M. 1994. "The Design Relationship between the Manuscript and the Incunable." In *A Millennium of the Book*, ed. R. Myers and M. Harris, 23–43. Winchester and New Castle, DE: Oak Knoll Press.

Smith, M. M. 2000. *The Title Page. Its Early Development 1460–1510*. London and New Castle, DE: Oak Knoll Press.

Steinberg, S. H. 1941. "Instructions in Writing by Members of the Congregation of Melk." *Speculum* 16: 210–15.

Tocci, L. M. 1986. "La formazione della biblioteca di Federico da Montefeltro: Codici contemporanei e libri a stampa." In *Federico di Montefeltro: lo Stato, le arti, la cultura*, ed. G. C. Baiardi *et al.*, 9–18. Rome: Bulzoni.

Trapp, J. B. 1975. "Manuscripts Written by Peter Meghen." *The Book Collector* 24: 80–96.

Trapp, J. B. 1983. "Peter Meghen, Yet Again." In *Manuscripts in the Fifty Years after the Invention of Printing*, ed. J. B. Trapp, 23–8. London: Warburg Institute.

Trapp, J. B. 1991. *Erasmus, Colet and More: The Early Tudor Humanists and their Books*. London: British Library.

Wardrop, J. 1963. *The Script of Humanism*. Oxford: Oxford University Press.

Wehmer, C. and L. Wagner. 1963. *Proba centum scripturarum. Ein Augsburger Schriftmusterbuch aus dem Beginn des 16. Jahrhunderts*. Leipzig and Frankfurt: Insel-Verlag.

Widmann, H. 1973. *Vom Nutzen und Nachteil der Erfindung des Buchdrucks—aus der Sicht der Zeitgenossen des Erfinders*. Mainz: Gutenberg-Gesellschaft.

PART II

MATERIAL EMBODIMENT AND TECHNIQUES

CHAPTER 35

STAGES IN MANUSCRIPT PRODUCTION

LUCIEN REYNHOUT

THE CODEX

THE roll, or *volumen*,[1] was the main form of the book in antiquity. During the Late Antique period and the Middle Ages a new form of book developed, the *codex*,[2] the form familiar to us today which can be leafed through. In the first century of the modern era, the term codex designated a joined series of documentary wax tablets; but by the beginning of the third century, the word was used for parchment or papyrus literary notebooks, which until then had been called *membranae* or *pugillares membranei*. The latter were praised by the Latin poet Martial.[3] The codex originated from the polyptychs[4] used throughout antiquity and into the Middle Ages. It is composed of folded sheets assembled in one or more quires and sewn together at the fold (Fig. 35.1). The codex eventually replaced papyrus rolls for most literary texts.

MATERIALS

Writing Surfaces

Parchment

HISTORY

Already in antiquity, Mediterranean civilizations used tanned skins as writing surfaces. These were plunged into tannin baths in order to preserve them from rot and make them more flexible. They were prepared for writing on only one face.[5] In the Greco-Roman world, parchment was used in the fabrication of the "membranae" mentioned above and of the "codex." In the fourth century AD, parchment was still competing with

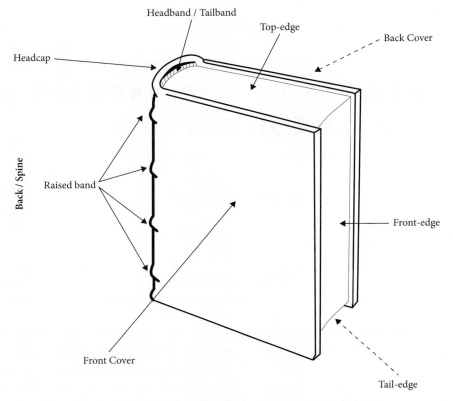

FIG. 35.1 The parts of a codex (after Muzerelle 1985, fig. 301[6]).

papyrus as the principal material for the fabrication of codices, and it did not supplant it until the supply network for papyrus stopped functioning after the seventh century. During the Middle Ages, parchment was prepared in monasteries by craftsmen who either worked for their own needs or acted as subcontractors. The rise of cathedral schools and universities during the twelfth century led to the introduction of some forms of standardized production in the manufacture of parchment in non-monastic contexts. The same development was simultaneously beginning in the manufacture of paper.

PRODUCTION AND USE

In the medieval West, parchment[7] was generally produced from calf-, sheep-, or goatskin which was plunged into a lime bath. The craftsmen defleshed and dehaired it by scraping. It was then washed and rubbed down in order to give it a texture conducive to ink penetration. It was eventually stretched on a frame and dried (Fig. 35.2). The process could take from six to twelve weeks.[8]

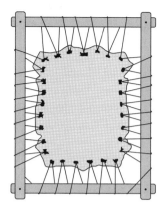

FIG. 35.2 Parchment drying frame (from Muzerelle 1985, fig. 17).

Ancient civilizations employed more than one kind of parchment, which could be distinguished according to the animal skin used, and the nature of treatments applied. For instance, there is "abortive" or "uterine" vellum, which is the high-priced, thin, and flexible parchment produced from the skin of a stillborn calf (or manufactured to imitate the same). In contrast to that made from the finest calfskin, the parchment made from the skins of sheep or goats was rougher and less flexible. Parchment is not a low-cost material. But, in the beginning, it was not prized as much as papyrus. The making of a parchment manuscript could require as many as 500 skins.[9]

Paper

In contrast to parchment, paper (*charta papiri*), like papyrus, is a plant material. Paper pulp was prepared from cellulose (plant) fibers, often of textile origin (linen, hemp, cotton, or old fabrics).

HISTORY

Invented in China in the first century BC, paper has been used as a writing material since about AD 150. In AD 751, Chinese prisoners transmitted their knowledge of the manufacturing process of paper to Arabs in Samarkand. While still imported in the seventh century AD, it seems to have been produced in Samarkand from the second half of the eighth century. Craftsmen then substituted linen and hemp for the traditional raw materials (tree bark), and developed a process for mechanical crushing of the fibers in stone mills. During the eighth and ninth centuries, the production of paper spread to Syria, Palestine, Egypt, the Byzantine Empire, and the western Muslim areas (the Maghreb and Al-Andalus). In the Christian West, it appeared at the end of the eleventh century, initially as an import. In Játiva (Spain), a factory already existed in 1054.[10] In the thirteenth century, paper began to be made in Fabriano (Italy). It spread then from Spain and Italy to the rest of Europe. As a commercial product, paper could be used relatively far from its place of production. An industrialized production process became widespread at the end of the fourteenth century.

MANUFACTURE AND USE

Paper was made in paper mills (Fig. 35.3). Rags, previously reduced to shreds, were steeped and putrefied for several weeks, then beaten in a stone trough (therefore called a "beating trough," an engine which appeared in Italy during the thirteenth century) and thereby reduced to pulp. The "sizing"[11] of the pulp allows a greater cohesion of the fibers and prevents the paper from becoming too absorbent. After sizing, the pulp was poured into a mold that allowed water to flow out while the cellulose fibers were retained and formed into sheets (Fig. 35.4). The mold was made of two parts: the frame and the deckle. Metal threads called wirelines were strung in lines parallel to the long sides of the frame. In order to prevent them from flexing under the pulp's weight, they were held up by chain supports, triangular pieces of wood inserted parallel to the short sides of the frame. The wirelines were interwoven with an additional series of wires running perpendicular to them, and spaced farther apart. These perpendicular wires are called chain lines. The complete web of wires is called the grid. Once the pulp that was poured into the mold had dried enough to form a thin layer or sheet, this was removed from the mold and stacked between felts, squeezed under a press, dried on a drying rack, then smoothed.

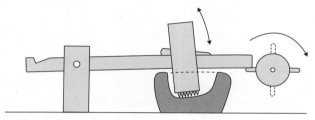

FIG. 35.3 Beating trough of a medieval paper mill (from Muzerelle 1985, fig. 19).

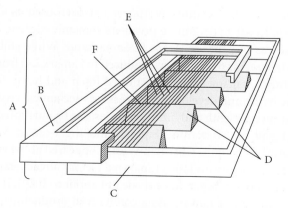

FIG. 35.4 Paper mold: framework (A), deckle (B), frame (C), chain support (D), grid (E–F) (from Muzerelle 1985, fig. 21).

FIG. 35.5 Watermark in the shape of a unicorn ("Van Hulthem" Manuscript, Brussels, Royal Library, MS 15589–623, fifteenth century, fol. 157, © KBR).

Shortly before 1300, Italian paper makers began marking their paper with watermarks (Fig. 35.5), an imprint made by a wire design sewn onto the grid (in the shape of letters, animals, tools, etc.). These marks make it possible to identify, to a greater or lesser extent, the place and date of manufacture of the paper, so they are an important aid in dating and localizing manuscripts written on paper. For each vat in a papermill, two molds were normally used; their watermarks were quite similar and therefore are called "twin" watermarks. In addition to the watermark, the grid could be outfitted with a smaller mark called a countermark; these largely consisted of letter shapes.

Papyrus (Medieval Uses)

In spite of the widespread adoption of parchment, and later of paper, for making books, some codices on papyrus are known, dating from the sixth to the eighth centuries. Papyrus continued to be used into the eleventh century for documents from royal and pontifical chanceries, perhaps until the papacy of Gregory VII (1072–85).[12] Papyrus was produced in Egypt until the Muslim era—when it was replaced by paper of Chinese origin—and perhaps also in Sicily. In the seventh century, it began to be a common practice for notaries to add seals to charters. Since papyrus is too weak to support the additional weight of the seals, it became obsolete, and parchment began to replace papyrus also for documents.[13]

Inks

Although their color may vary, medieval inks are now generally called "black inks." From antiquity onward, two kinds of ink were known: carbon inks and iron-gall inks. The first are made of black pigment derived from calcinated matter or soot mixed with a binding agent (gum Arabic, honey, egg white, oils, etc.). While they do not harm the written support, in general they adhere badly to it. The second type of ink, the iron-gall inks, are tannin-based; they are produced from substances such as oak galls.[14] After the oak galls are boiled or macerated and filtered, they are mixed with iron sulfate or copper sulfate. The blend is then made more viscous by adding a binding agent. Iron-gall inks adhere well to parchment and paper, but if there is excessive iron in them, they can cause corrosion, damaging the parchment or paper.

Until the twelfth century in Europe, ink recipes describe only carbon inks. Iron-gall inks have systematically been used only since the thirteenth century. From the Carolingian era onward, other kinds and colors of ink—most frequently a red minium-based ink—were used in order to highlight specific elements of a text.[15] In the twelfth and thirteenth centuries, scribes frequently alternate ink colors (red, blue, green, yellow, etc.) on the same page. From antiquity onward, luxury books were produced with gold and silver inks applied on red- or purple-dyed parchment, but the technique was seldom used in the late Middle Ages.

Preparing the Writing Surface for Copying

In rolls (*volumina*), the columns of written text were not always evenly spaced. In contrast, the layout of "codices" was generally more careful and regular. The process of laying out the page, that is, delimiting the area to be written on the surface, is called justification (see Fig. 35.6a). The portion of the page that is to be inscribed is called the writing frame and is usually a quadrilateral formed by four lines running parallel to the four sides of the page. The writing frame could be divided into two or more columns. The techniques which were used to define and draw writing frames are pricking and ruling.

Ruling

The term "ruling" is used for vertical or horizontal lines drawn on the page to guide writing (see Fig. 35.6b). The choice of which ruling pattern to employ for a given manuscript was determined by the typology of texts, the format of the manuscript, and by local traditions. Ruling can be applied using the relief technique (scratching or incising the parchment or paper with a dry point), or through the application of color from graphite, carbon ore-based lead, or ink (black or colored). Ruling can also be achieved by folding to create crease marks on the writing surface.

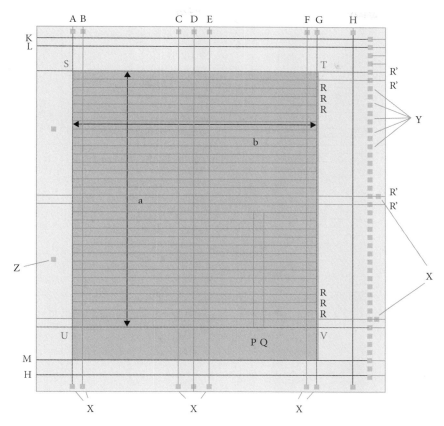

FIG. 35.6a Basic page layout: Writing frame (STUV); Frame lines (ST, UV, SU, TV); Top line (ST); Bottom line (UV); Bounding line (SU, TV); Intercolumn (C, D, E); Occasional intercolumn (PQ); Double, Triple, Quadruple ruling (AB, FG); Marginal lines (KL + H + MN) (from Muzerelle 1985, fig. 63b).

The relief technique was used from the early Middle Ages through the twelfth century, graphite from the twelfth century to the end of the medieval period, and inks from the thirteenth century onward. Italian Humanistic manuscripts, at the very beginning of the fifteenth century, reintroduce the use of dry point ruling (the relief technique) in imitation of Carolingian manuscripts.[16] Dry point ruling could be produced with a stylus that was used to score the surface of the writing material. This created a furrow on one side (the side that the stylus touched), and a ridge on the other side. Parchment can be dry-ruled a single sheet at a time, or several sheets at once. For the latter process, the sheets are stacked one on top of the other, and, by applying greater pressure to the stylus, they can all be scored simultaneously with a single pass of the stylus across the surface of the uppermost sheet. We thus speak of "direct ruling" when the stylus was in direct contact with the writing support, and of "transmitted ruling" when the furrow was imprinted through multiple layers of writing material.

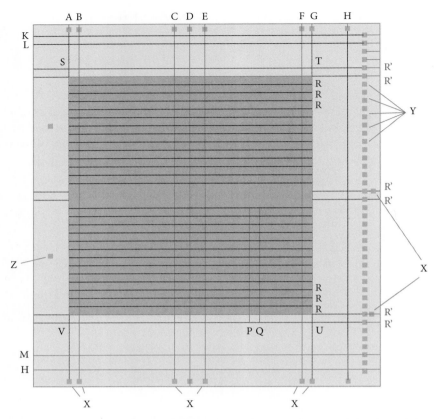

FIG. 35.6b Basic page layout: Horizontal lines (R + R'), Line of writing (R), Through line (R') (from Muzerelle 1985, fig. 63d).

Before a stylus could be used to score the writing surface, guide marks for the scoring lines had to be applied to the surface. These are called "prickings," and are discussed in Section 35.2.3.2 below.

Some medieval written sources speak of a tool called a *tabula ad rigandum* or *postis ad rigandum* which imprinted—manually or with a press—the ruling onto the writing surface, an entire sheet at one pass. These devices may have resembled the Arabic ruling board (or *mastara*, as it is sometimes called following Arabic terminology).[17] But not a single example of a ruling tool has been preserved from the West from the Middle Ages. Alternatively, the board might have been a template to guide the ruling; this is sometimes called a frame pattern. It consisted of a quadrangular wooden frame, with a series of strips attached at regular intervals on opposing sides. It was placed on top of the leaves to be ruled, and the strips of wood served as guides for applying ink or hard point ruling.[18] One further type of mechanical device for ruling was the so-called ruling rake, a tool equipped with a variable number of nibs or points which could be used for tracing a predetermined number of horizontal lines, or for ruling the entire page at one pass.[19] However, the most frequently used techniques were probably the simplest ones: a straightedge with which the drawing of the first line of writing (perhaps obtained by folding) was transferred from line to line to the bottom of the justification.[20]

Pricking

All rulings, other than those produced with a board, require a set of "prickings" consisting of rows of regularly spaced holes or slits made in the parchment. For ruling the writing lines, two columns of prickings were made from top to bottom of the sheet, generally in the outer margins on the right and left side of the surface of the sheet. Then a straightedge was laid between the corresponding prickings in each column, and the writings lines were impressed into the parchment with a stylus, following the straightedge. Similarly paired prickings, placed in the upper and lower margins of the writing surface, guided the making of the bounding lines. In fifteenth-century manuscripts, one occasionally finds single, isolated prickings in manuscripts that were ruled with a rake.[21] The pricking in these manuscripts may have been produced in the same way as the register marks that are found on sheets of paper that were run through a printing press. A register mark allows the proper alignment of the sheet within the frame, so that the text is correctly matched up on the front and the back of the sheet (and for other operations that require multiple passes of a single sheet through the press). Some scholars have hypothesized the use of a pricking wheel[22] or a nail-board for producing prickings, but the application of such devices raises technical problems that argue against their having been widely employed.[23] Although various more elaborate procedures for applying prickings may have been used from time to time, it seems the most frequent method of pricking was the simplest: an awl or knife which, when used in conjunction with a ruler to guide the placement of the holes, permitted piercing multiple layers of the writing material at one go.

TRANSCRIPTION OF TEXTS

Writing Process

The composition of a text begins when the author establishes a draft on wax tablets or on loose pieces or fragments of parchment or paper. The production of a final copy might be the work of the authors themselves or of *amanuenses*, copyists working under the authors' supervision. A limited number of authors dictated their works to scribes; and in some medieval universities, a peculiar transcription method called *reportatio* was employed for writing down a speech (sermon, lecture, etc.) delivered in public.[24] Although copies made on the basis of the authors' recitation implicate the authors in the production process, only when the text of a work was copied in the author's own hand is the manuscript properly called an autograph.

During the early Middle Ages, the individual quires from an unbound exemplar might be distributed by the head of a monastic scriptorium to several different scribes, who would simultaneously copy the various sections of the work. This allowed making a copy of the entire work in less time. Although this was a time-saving technique, it was not a labor-saving technique. It required the same effort to produce a book, but it allowed the book to be produced more quickly. The goal might have been to produce more books in a shorter period of time (for example, for building a new library, or for rapidly disseminating multiple copies of a specific text), or it might have been related to the limited term of availability of an exemplar for copying (see Section 35.3.3.2 below).

When the main text had been copied, the rubricator, who may or may not be the same person as the copyist, added further elements, for example colored initials or paragraph marks to divide the text into discrete sections; rubrics or headings to call attention to specific parts of the text; and titles. Finally, corrections were made to the text by a professional reviser, who might be the head of the scriptorium, the copyist, or even the author.

Some changes in basic copying and layout techniques are observable in different periods and regions. So, for instance, before the twelfth century, scribes began copying a page on the first ruled line—"above top line," as (Ker 1960) has named this method.[25] From the thirteenth century onward, they began copying on the second ruled line ("below top line"), the top line serving then as a bordering frame for the written space on the page. In the fifteenth century, scribes of Humanistic manuscripts in Italy reintroduced the "above top line" method, in imitation of pre-Gothic models.[26]

The posture of scribes when they were transcribing a text varied considerably from period to period, and the changes may have been related to the different writing materials and writing implements in common use. In the ancient world, scribes commonly wrote sitting down, with the writing material (papyrus or wax or wooden tablets) resting on their knees. Their writing instrument was a reed. During the Middle Ages, a lectern (reading or writing desk) supported the writing material (parchment or paper), and a stripped quill was the typical writing instrument. The quill pen was held with the thumb and the two adjacent fingers, which were stretched or slightly curved. The two remaining fingers were folded against the palm, and the hand was only supported on the desk by the little finger.[27]

Colophons and Subscriptions

Sometimes, copyists added a colophon (from Greek κολοφών, "top," "summit," "completion of an undertaking or of a text") at the end of their work. According to Denis Muzerelle, a colophon is "a final formula in which scribes mentioned the place and date of copying, or both."[28] Sometimes in a rigidly formulaic fashion, sometimes more spontaneously, colophons supply important information: the copyist's, commissioner's, recipient's, or, more rarely, the illuminator's name; the social status, age, and other

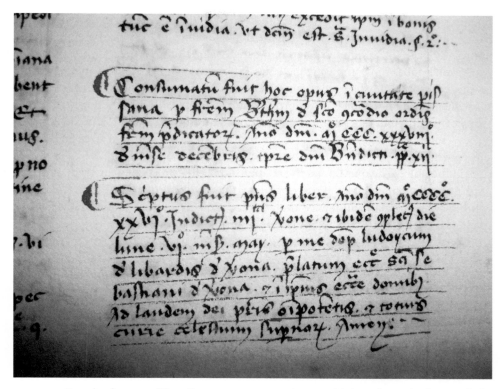

FIG. 35.7 Sample from a fifteenth-century manuscript combining the colophons of the model and of the copyist (Brussels, Royal Library, MS IV 449, fol. 179vb, Bartolomeo da San Concordio, *Summa de casibus conscientiae*, 1338 [work], 1426 [copy], © KBR).

prosopographical details about any of the parties involved; the origin and state of conservation of the model manuscript; the date, hour, and duration of the transcription, etc.[29] A colophon is normally linked to the manuscript which carries it; but it may also have been copied from the exemplar, its direct model (see Fig. 35.7). It can even go back to the autograph. Therefore, one should be extremely wary about the information supplied by colophons unless the manuscript has been subjected to a thorough analysis, including palaeographical, codicological, and textual examination.[30]

Peculiarities

Imposition

Once a manuscript has been ruled, transcription can begin. This was normally achieved page by page on folded bifolia. But some scholars have proposed—on the basis of a few more or less direct surviving examples, mainly small-sized fifteenth-century, manuscripts—that the process of imposition employed by printers was also used in the hand-copying of books. Imposition is a method of laying out text quire by quire instead of page by page (or bifolium by bifolium). Instead of cutting a sheet of parchment or paper into bifolia, and composing the quires before copying, imposition applies writing to the entire, uncut sheet (first on one side, then on the reverse side) that will subsequently be folded and cut to form a quire. To copy a book by imposition would require that different blocks of text be positioned on the uncut sheet at predetermined places (some of them upside down in relation to one another), such that when subsequently folded and cut, the blocks of text would each fall on the appropriate page in the quire. The question of the relationship of this practice to the birth of the art of printing remains unclear: did scribes copy the method from printers, or did a pre-existing scribal practice influence the printers? Equally unclear is the practicality or usefulness of the process in a manuscript culture.[31]

"Pecia"

The transcription of manuscripts was generally made from one complete copy to another. However, in the late Middle Ages, a new system of manuscript production was introduced in the largest universities, including Paris, Bologna, Naples, and Oxford, called the "pecia system." It allowed for a faster multiplication of copies from a smaller number of exemplars. During the thirteenth and fourteenth centuries, universities officially controlled the texts used in lectures. An official copy of a text was registered at the bookshop of an appointed *stationarius*, and it was divided into several units, called *peciae* (pieces).[32] An individual pecia usually consisted of two folio-sized bifolia written in two columns, each of them supplied with a sequential number on the first leaf which defined its place within the complete text.[33] Students, or professional scribes employed by them, rented out each pecia one at a time, not necessarily—indeed probably not often—in sequential order. The text was to be reproduced in the same format as the exemplar, so that the individual pieces of the exemplar could be transcribed non-sequentially, it being clear in advance what portion of text would appear on each page (or within each piece). Copying in this manner did not increase the average speed of transcription—it was not a labor-saving technology—but allowed multiple copies of a given text to be produced simultaneously by different scribes, all of them using only a single exemplar. Production of manuscripts by pecia disappeared in the fifteenth century. Although the system seems to have been employed for the production of many copies of the most popular university texts, there are relatively few surviving examples of pecia manuscripts (that is, of the original exemplars belonging to the stationers). The manuscripts were often made with low-cost but sturdy parchment, and they were heavily worn by use.

Palimpsests

Another practice, not part of the normal production process, has, nevertheless, played a decisive role in the history of the transmission of texts: palimpsests (from Greek παλίμψηστος, "scraped again"), i.e. papyrus or parchment manuscripts from which

FIG. 35.8 Palimpsest (Brussels, Royal Library, MS II 1069, fols. 86v–87r; twelfth century, upper script/eighth century, lower script, © KBR).

one text was removed by washing or scraping it off in order to allow the reuse of the writing material for the transcription of a new text (Fig. 35.8). The impetus for this practice was the scarcity and high cost of the raw materials used for the transcription of books, combined with the fact that some types of books became obsolete as a matter of course (for example, texts that were revised or superseded by later books). Many texts may have been palimpsested simply because they had fallen out of fashion in a later period. Palimpsesting, regardless of how the earlier text was removed, results in an inferior writing material, and this limited the practice. There is little or no evidence that it was ever employed as a method of censorship aimed at destroying prohibited works. Palimpsests have played important roles in the rediscovery of many classical, patristic, and medieval texts.

ASSEMBLING THE BOOK

The *membranae* from antiquity could consist of a single gathering of bifolia. The longer a text, the more pages were needed, and, at least theoretically, it was possible to endlessly increase the number of bifolia. But assembling too many bifolia into a single quire (that is, around one central fold) made the book unwieldy to produce and difficult to handle. From this constraint arose the practice of making multiple group-ings of *membranae*, and this process evolved into the medieval production of multiple joined quires. A quire[34] is a set of leaves which have been sewn together. This is the building unit of any sewn book.

Quires

Quires are named according to the number of leaves they contain: a binion is 2 bifolia or 4 leaves (8 pages); a ternion, 3 bifolia or 6 leaves (12 pages); a quaternion, 4 bifolia or 8 leaves, (16 pages); a quinion, 5 bifolia or 10 leaves (20 pages); a sexternion, 6 bifolia or 12 leaves (24 pages), etc.

Quires can be produced according to a variety of formulas (see Section 35.4.2 below), and they may be regular or irregular. A regular quire is comprised of folded bifolia. An irregular quire may be produced from single leaves or from a combination of bifolia and single leaves. To add a single leaf to a quire (e.g. for the sake of thrift, in order to make use of all the available fragments of parchment), stubs or guards were employed (Figs 35.9a and 35.9b). A fragment that was large enough for a single leaf of the book, but too small to be folded into a bifolium, was folded near one edge, so that a full-sized sheet appeared on one side of the fold, and a stub on the other. This allowed inserting

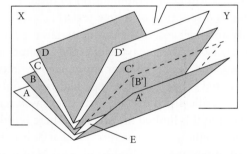

FIG. 35.9a Quire containing a singleton with a stub (E) (from Muzerelle 1985, fig. 38).

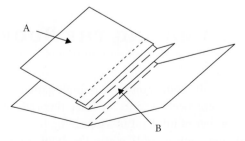

FIG. 35.9b Part of a quire consisting of a bifolium and a singleton attached to a guard (B) (from Muzerelle 1985, fig. 48).

the leaf into a quire, and sewing at the fold. If a fragment was large enough to make a single sheet, but not large enough even to accommodate folding to make a stub, the individual leaf was attached to a guard. This unit was then inserted into the quire in the same way as the sheet with a stub.

The arrangement of parchment leaves within a quire was not haphazard. Generally, they were arranged so that at each opening a hair side faced a hair side and a flesh side faced a flesh side. The arrangement of the leaves in this manner is referred to as the "Rule of Gregory," from the name of the German scholar who called attention to it at the end of the nineteenth century.[35]

Folding Formulas

To construct a regular quire, bifolia are fitted together, most often by folding the parchment skins or paper sheets once (to produce a folio-sized volume), twice (for a quarto), or three times (for an octavo), etc. After folding, the quire was cut before being written on (except in cases where imposition was employed). Folding could be done in different ways. The most common formula for producing a quarto involved making the first fold perpendicularly to the long side of the skin or sheet. Folding one more time perpendicularly to the first fold produced a binion (2 bifolia, 4 leaves, 8 pages; Fig. 35.10). The quaternion was then produced by embedding two binions, one inside the other, after having folded them (see Fig. 35.11). Alternatively, a quaternion could be made by superimposing two parchment skins or paper sheets before folding them. This formula is less frequently observed in manuscripts (Fig. 35.12).

Octavo folding of a single skin or sheet produces an entire quaternion. There are principally four theoretical formulas (Fig. 35.13a–d), which are more or less commonly found in medieval manuscripts: **A** and **B**, in which the first fold is made in parallel to the long side of skin or sheet; **C** and **D**, in which the first fold is made perpendicularly to the long side of skin or sheet (the same method as for quarto folding). Several

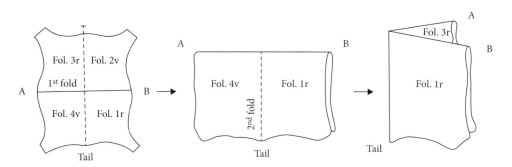

FIG. 35.10 Construction of a parchment binion (after Lemaire 1989, figs. 18, 19, & 20).

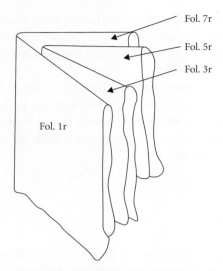

FIG. 35.11 Construction of a quaternion by embedding two binions (after Lemaire 1989, fig. 24).

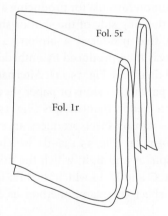

FIG. 35.12 Construction of a quaternion by superimposing skins or sheets before folding (after Lemaire 1989, fig. 25).

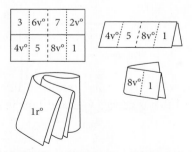

FIG. 35.13a Octavo folding, formula **A** which leads to 1 quaternion (after Muzerelle 1985, fig. 45a).

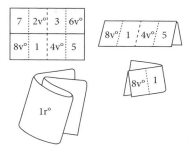

FIG. 35.13b Octavo folding, formula **B** which leads to 1 quaternion (after Muzerelle 1985, fig. 45b).

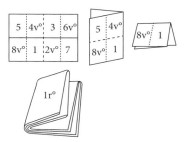

FIG. 35.13c Octavo folding, formula C which leads to 1 quaternion (after Muzerelle 1985, fig. 45c).

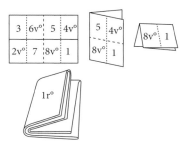

FIG. 35.13d Octavo folding, formula D which leads to 1 quaternion (after Muzerelle 1985, fig. 45d).

alternate orientations and directions are possible for the second and third folds. The method employed influences the manner in which the leaves are cut, because it determines the cohesiveness of folios along the top edge and/or along the front edge of the quire. The different folding formulas result in differing arrangements of the bifolia within the quire, and this is especially important in cases where imposition is used, that is, cases in which the transcription occurs before folding and cutting. This is because the order and the direction of the pages to be written are not the same from one formula to another.

Signatures, Catchwords, Foliation, and Pagination

After the pages were inscribed, the quires needed to be assembled in appropriate order before binding the volume. In order to ensure that the proper sequence of the text was maintained from quire to quire, marking techniques were introduced, namely "signatures" and "catchwords" applied to the quires, as well as the numbering of individual folios (foliation) or pages (pagination).

Foliation and Pagination

Foliation was already known in antiquity. Derived from the numbering of text columns (*paginae*) in rolls, pagination sporadically appears in older Greek "codices," for instance in the *Codex Vaticanus* of the Bible (Vatican City, BAV, Vat. gr. 1209; fourth century AD). In Latin manuscripts, foliation is frequently indicated by Roman or Arabic figures placed in the upper outer corner of the leaf or in the margin (Fig. 35.14). It may be executed in the same ink as the text, in colored ink, in graphite, or with dry point. From the twelfth century onward, the continuous numbering of pages, columns, or

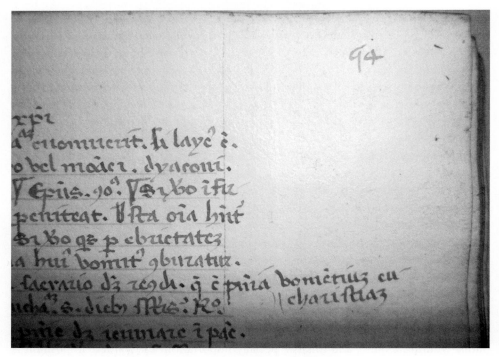

FIG. 35.14 Sample of foliation, medieval Arabic figures for "54"

(Brussels, Royal Library, MS II 7324, fol. 54r : Guido de Monte Rocherio, *Manipulus curatorum*, dated 1463, © KBR).

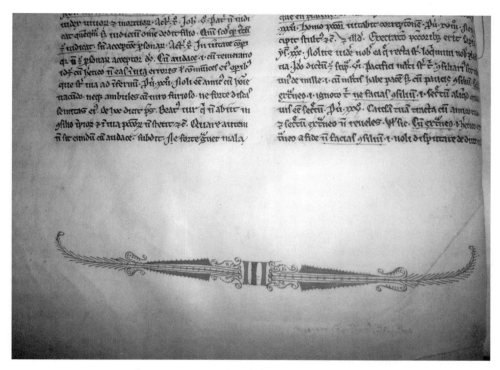

FIG. 35.15 Signature with Roman numeral and decorative flourishes (Brussels, Royal Library, MS II 1093, fol. 24v, thirteenth century, © KBR).

even lines began to appear, especially in university texts. This facilitated locating specific passages.

Signatures

Applying numbering or signatures to quires ("quire signatures"), or to bifolia ("leaf" or "bifolia signatures"), is much more common than foliation or pagination. The location of the signatures within a quire may vary, and so may their place on the page and their form. Signatures may consist of Roman or Arabic figures, of letters or other signs (short strokes, circles, etc.), or sometimes even of decorative elements (Fig. 35.15). In the West, bifolia signatures, already used as early as the Carolingian era, became widespread in the thirteenth century.

Catchwords

Catchwords are words written at the end of a quire, providing the first word or words of the text on the following quire. They have the same function as quire signatures. Frequently, both systems are employed together. Already in the tenth and eleventh

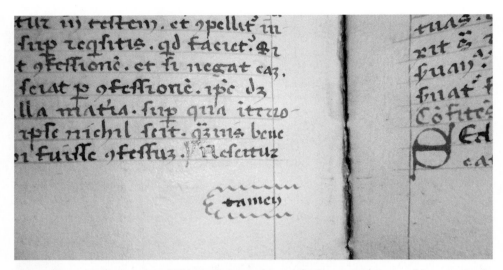

FIG. 35.16 Sample of catchword *"tamen"* (Brussels, Royal Library, MS II 7324, fol. 120v: Guido de Monte Rocherio, *Manipulus curatorum*, 1463, © KBR).

centuries, catchwords are found in Visigothic manuscripts (from Spain); they spread to France and Italy in the following century, and became widespread thereafter.[36] Catchwords may be written horizontally, vertically, or diagonally, and they are usually in the lower margin on the last page of a quire. They may be near the gutter, in the middle of the lower margin, or more rarely, near the outer edge of the leaf (Fig. 35.16).

Methods for Sewing Quires

When the quires have been written in their entirety, they are assembled and sewn together. This process is generally but not necessarily undertaken by the copyists themselves. In the late Middle Ages, books which were trade products sometimes circulated in unbound quires. The most frequently used technique for joining quires was "sewing on cords." The cords were made from tawed or leather straps, which were attached to wooden binding boards. The quires were connected to the cords with a sewing thread (Fig. 35.17). Quire sewing was simplified by the invention, perhaps in the twelfth century, of the sewing frame, a machine which holds the cords in a vertical position.

Scrolls (Medieval Uses)

In addition to the "codex," a book in the form of a scroll also existed during the Middle Ages, the so-called *rotulus*, written parallel to the short edge and vertically unrolled.

FIG. 35.17 The sewn quires of a "codex," evidenced from an Ethiopian manuscript (Brussels, Royal Library, MS IV 725, © KBR).

Made of parchment or paper, *rotuli* are thin and long, from a few centimeters wide to many meters long. They are nearly always written on one side only. The constituent leaves of which the scroll was made were often sewn together with a piece of string or a parchment strip, though they could also be pasted or pinned together.[37] There were many different uses for this type of book: liturgy (including the famous *Exultet* rolls used in the Easter liturgy), synodal decrees, lists of bishops and abbots, mortuary rolls, pilgrimage guides, chronicles, Rolls of Arms, rolls of guilds, lists of goods, copies of legal acts, etc. (Fig. 35.18). Literary rolls, though the standard form for books in antiquity, are very rare in the Middle Ages. Lyric and epic poems circulated from the

FIG. 35.18 Chronicle and Genealogy of the Kings of England to Henry VI (Brussels, Royal Library, MS IV 739, *c*.1480, © KBR).

thirteenth century onward in the form of singer's rolls. Theater rolls were used by actors to learn their roles in dramatic performances. The roles were distributed amongst the actors by giving each of them a roll that contained only their lines.[38]

Owners and Readers
(Material Evidence)

The "codex" was also provided with reference tools and finding aids. For instance, place markers or leaf tabs (Fig. 35.19) allow for quickly locating a passage within a volume. There are also column markers or line markers, small parchment wheels which slid along a piece of string and bear figures corresponding to the columns. Such devices, which survive from the thirteenth, fourteenth, and fifteenth centuries, provide evidence of new ways of reading introduced during the late Middle Ages.[39]

When books entered libraries, they could also be provided with title labels or classification numbers on the front cover, on the spine, on the inside cover, on the edges (at the top, bottom, or fore-edge), or on the back cover. In the late Middle Ages, some libraries allowed public browsing. In such a library, the books might be chained (*libri catenati*) to a desk, table, or reading stand. The chain was usually attached to one of the boards of a book's binding by a staple (Fig. 35.20).

Several other identifying marks, relating to their possession or use, might be added to books in libraries. Owners, for instance, might add an *ex libris*, a short text or image (for example, a coat of arms) declaring their ownership. Curses (anathemas) were also sometimes added in the early Middle Ages, generally before the twelfth century, threatening with divine wrath anyone who damaged or stole the book. The so-called *ex dono* inscription, on the other hand, recorded the lawful gift of a book by one individual or legal entity to another.[40]

Amongst the less formalized paratextual elements encountered in books are pen-trials (Fig. 35.21) They consisted of words, letters, figures, or scribbles written by scribes to test whether their pen was properly cut (or their ink properly mixed).[41]

Readers could, in their turn, add commentaries or glosses to the text. Glosses, for instance–called "interlinear" if they were written between the lines of the text and "marginal" if they were written in the margins–are explanations added by a reader to a word or passage of a text in a particular copy (Fig. 35.22). They were not necessarily intended to be transmitted with the text in further copies, but they could become a constituent part of the text in which they were transmitted, and so might influence the page layout in subsequent copies.[42] In many manuscripts, glosses were copied at the same time as the text.

FIG. 35.19 Place markers called "tabs" (Brussels, Royal Library, MS 5648, sixteenth century, © KBR).

FIG. 35.20 Chained book (*Liber catenatus*; Brussels, Royal Library, Imp. III 68045C, Alexander de Imola, *Consilia*, Trino, 1515, © KBR).

FIG. 35.21 Pen-trials (Brussels, Royal Library, MS 1682, fol. 1r, fifteenth century, © KBR)

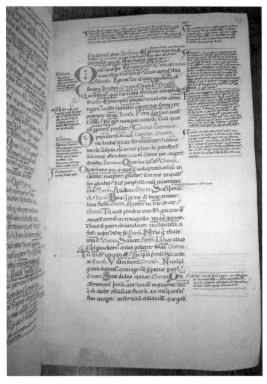

FIG. 35.22 Marginal and interlinear glosses (Brussels, Royal Library, MS 5328–9, fol. 58r, Terence, *Comoediae*, twelfth century, © KBR).

Abbreviations

OED   J. A. Simpson and E. S. C. Weiner, eds. 1989. *The Oxford English Dictionary*, 2nd ed., 20 vols. Oxford: Clarendon Press.

Notes

1. For a general introduction to book forms in antiquity, see Bülow-Jacobsen (2009).
2. A later spelling of the ancient Latin word *caudex*, "the trunk of a tree, a wooden tablet, a book, a code of laws"; cf. the entry "Codex" in the *OED* 3: 429.
3. AD 40–*c*.104; cf. Mart., *Epigr.* 1.2.
4. A writing support composed of more than two wax tablets.
5. Sirat (1988, 22).
6. The illustrations from Muzerelle 1985 are now available on the website of the Institut de Recherche et d'Histoire des Textes, *Codicologia*, 2011, http://codicologia.irht.cnrs.fr/, accessed January 23, 2020.
7. The term derives from Middle English, through Ancient French *parchemin*, adapted from Latin *pergamena*. The Latin term is derived from *Pergamena*, the feminine form of the adjective *Pergamenus*, meaning 'belonging to Pergamum,' a city in Asia Minor; cf. the entry "Parchment" in the *OED* 11: 216.
8. Géhin (2005, 15–16).
9. Bischoff (1995, 10).
10. Valls i Subira (1978–80, Vol. 1: 5).
11. The action of spreading a coat of glue (size) on a paper sheet in order to allow it to receive ink without absorbing it; Muzerelle (1985, 135.02).
12. Agati (2003, 52–3).
13. Sabbe (198, 140).
14. Oak galls are tumoral growths on oak leaves caused by an insect bite (galls also occur on some other trees). A dye is produced from dried gall. Oak gall is also used as a tanning agent; Muzerelle (1985, 241.03).
15. Minium is a lead oxide which is made into an orangey-red pigment; cf. Muzerelle (1985, 234.09).
16. Derolez (1984, I: 70–1).
17. On ruling boards in Eastern and Western manuscript culture, see Dukan (1986).
18. Agati (2007). This was a quadrangular wooden frame, with strips of wood or some other material attached from one side to the opposite side in regular rows to form a matrix. The contraption was placed on top of a sheet of paper or parchment and the wooden strips (serving the same function as the straightedge in the simplest ruling technique) then guided the stylus or knife in impressing blind ruling onto the sheet.
19. Gumbert (1986); cf. Derolez (1984, I: 77).
20. Muzerelle (2008).
21. Derolez (1984, I: 77–8).
22. A tool comprised of a spiked wheel that revolved around an axis and was fixed on a handle; it is rolled along the parchment and the spikes make a series of holes or prickings; Muzerelle (1985, 215.10).
23. Dane (1996, 13); Muzerelle (1997, 22).
24. For a discussion of *reportatio*, see Rusconi (1989) and Hamesse (1986), (1988).

25. Ker (1960); cf. Bischoff (1995, 22).
26. Derolez (1984, I: 83–4).
27. Bischoff (1995, 38).
28. Muzerelle (1985, 435.03).
29. For a general introduction to colophons of Western manuscripts, see Reynhout (2006).
30. As is the case, for instance, of the *Summa de casibus conscientiae* by Bartolomeo da San Concordio, whose colophon was copied in many later manuscripts, as for example, Brussels, Royal Library, MS IV 449, fol. 179vb. The first part of the Brussels colophon ([a–a]) goes back to the original exemplar, whereas the second one ([b–b]) was added by a later copyist:

   [a]Consumatum fuit hoc opus in civitate pissana per fratrem Bartholomeum de sancto concordio ordinis fratrum praedicatorum. Anno domini. M°. ccc. xxxviij° de mense decembris. tempore domini Benedicti papae. xij.[a] [b]Scriptus fuit presens liber Anno domini m°cccc°.xxvj°. Indictione iiii[ta] verone et ibidem completus die lune vj° mensis may per me dompnum ludoycum de libardis de verona prelatum ecclesie sancti sebastiani de verona et in ipsius ecclesie domibus Ad laudem dei patris omnipotentis et totius curie celestium supernorum Amen.[b]

31. Irigoin (1992, 88). See also Gilissen (1972) and Vezin (1990).
32. The word *pecia* does not appear in Classical or Patristic Latin, but its probable Celtic origin, its great spread, and its general use in Romanesque languages (pièce, pezza, pezzo, pieza) and indirectly in English (piece) probably indicate that it is an ancient term of Vulgar Latin, used to designate the pieces or parts of something; cf. Bataillon (1989, 206–7).
33. The numbering typically has the form *p(ecia) I, p(ecia) II, p(ecia) III,* etc.
34. From a hypothetical word *quaternum* in Vulgar Latin (cf. medieval Latin *quaternus*, related to Old Latin *quaterni*, derived from *quattuor*, "four"); cf. the entry "Quire" in *OED* 13: 39. See "quaternion" as deriving from Late Latin *quaternio*, also from *quaterni*; entry "Quaternion" in *OED* 12: 1004 and Muzerelle (1985, 313.05).
35. Gregory (1885).
36. Bischoff (1995, 23).
37. Lalou (1991, 53).
38. The word derives from Latin *rotulus*, through Old French and Middle English; cf. Klein (1967, 2: 1354); Onions (1966, 771).
39. See Destrez (1935a) ; Samaran (1935).
40. Muzerelle (1985, 435.05 and 435.20).
41. This practice is different from pen exercises employed for the purpose of learning to write; see Muzerelle (1985, 435.21a).
42. Muzerelle (1985, 434.02, 434.07, 434.05, and 434.08).

BIBLIOGRAPHY

Agati, M. L. 2003. *Il libro manoscritto: introduzione alla codicologia* (Studia archaeologica 124). Rome: "L'Erma" di Bretschneider.

Agati, M. L. 2007. "Qualche riflessione relativa agli strumenti di rigatura: solo un problema di terminologia?" *Gazette du Livre Médiéval* 51: 30–36.

Bataillon, L. J. 1989. "*Exemplar, pecia, quaternus.*" In *Vocabulaire du livre et de l'écriture au Moyen Âge*. Actes de la table ronde, Paris, 24–26 septembre 1987 (Comité international du vocabulaire des institutions et de la communication intellectuelles au Moyen Âge) (Études sur le vocabulaire intellectuel du Moyen Âge 2), ed. O. Weijers, 206–19. Turnhout: Brepols.

Bischoff, B. 1995. *Latin Palaeography: Antiquity and the Middle Ages*, trans. Dáibhí Ó Cróinín and David Ganz. Cambridge: Cambridge University Press.

Bülow-Jacobsen, A. 2009. "Writing Materials in the Ancient World." In *The Oxford Handbook of Papyrology*, ed. R. S. Bagnall, 3–29. Oxford: Oxford University Press.

Boyle, L.E. 1988. "*Peciae, apopeciae, epipeciae.*" In *La Production du livre universitaire au Moyen Âge: exemplar et pecia* (Actes du symposium tenu au Collegio San Bonaventura de Grottaferrata en mai 1983), ed. L. J. Bataillon, B. G. Guyot, and R. H. Rouse, 39–40. Paris: Centre National de la Recherche Scientifique.

Briquet, C. M. 1968. *Les Filigranes: dictionnaire historique des marques du papier dès leur apparition vers 1282 jusqu'en 1600*, ed. A. Stevenson. 4 vols. Amsterdam: Paper Publications Society.

Cavallo, G., G. Orofino, and O. Pecere. 1994. *Exultet: rotoli liturgici del medioevo meridionale (Bimillenario di Cristo).* Rome: Istituto poligrafico e Zecca dello Stato, Libreria dello Stato.

Condello, E. and G. De Gregorio, eds. 1995. *Scribi e colofoni: le sottoscrizioni di copisti dalle origine all'avvento della stampa* (Atti del seminario di Erice, X Colloquio del Comité international de paléographie latine [23–28 ottobre 1993]). Spoleto: Centro Italiano di Studi sull'Alto medioevo.

Dane, J. A. 1996. "On the Shadowy Existence of the Medieval Pricking Wheel." *Scriptorium* 50: 13–21.

Declercq, G., ed. 2007. *Early Medieval Palimpsests: Handelingen van het contactforum "Vroegmiddeleeuwse palimpsesten—Early medieval palimpsests" (Brussel, 8 februari 2002)* (Bibliologia 26). Turnhout: Brepols.

Derolez, A. 1984. *Codicologie des manuscrits en écriture humanistique sur parchemin* (Bibliologia 5–6). Turnhout: Brepols.

Destrez, J. 1935a. "L'Outillage des copistes du XIIIe et du XIVe siècles." In *Aus der Geisteswelt des Mittelalters*, ed. A. Lang, 1: 19–34. Münster: Aschendorffsche Verlagsbuchhandlung.

Destrez, J. 1935b. *La Pecia dans les manuscrits universitaires du XIIIe et du XIVe siècle.* Paris: J. Vautrain.

Dukan, M. 1986. "De la difficulté à reconnaître des instruments de réglure: planche à régler (mastara) et cadre-patron." *Scriptorium* 40: 257–60.

Fossier, F. 1980–1. "Chroniques universelles en forme de rouleau à la fin du Moyen Âge." *Bulletin de la Société nationale des Antiquaires de France.* 162–182.

Géhin, P., ed. 2005. *Lire le manuscrit médiéval* (Collection U, Histoire). Paris: Armand Colin.

Gilissen, L. 1972. "La Composition des cahiers, le pliage du parchemin et l'imposition." *Scriptorium* 26: 3–33.

Gilissen, L. 1977. *Prolégomènes à la codicologie: recherches sur la construction des cahiers et la mise en page des manuscrits médiévaux* (Les Publications de Scriptorium 7). Ghent: Story-Scientia.

Gregory, C. R. 1885. "Les Cahiers des manuscrits grecs." *Comptes rendus des séances—Académie des Inscriptions et Belles Lettres*, 4. sér., 13: 261–8.

Gumbert, J. P. 1986. "Ruling by Rake and Board: Notes on Some Late Medieval Ruling Techniques." In *The Role of the Book in Medieval Culture* ed. P. Ganz, (Bibliologia 3), I, 41–54. Turnhout: Brepols.

Gumbert, J. P. 1989. "Quelques remarques autour de la pecia." *Gazette du Livre Médiéval* 15: 8–11.

Hamesse, J. 1986. "*Reportatio* et transmission de textes." In *The Editing of Theological and Philosophical Texts from the Middle Ages* (Studia Latina Stockholmiensia 30), ed. M. Asztalos, 11–34. Stockholm: Almqvist and Wiksell International.

Hamesse, J. 1988. "*Collatio* et *reportatio*: deux vocables spécifiques de la vie intellectuelle au Moyen Age." In *Terminologie de la vie intellectuelle au Moyen Âge* (Actes du Colloque, Leyde/La Haye 20–21 septembre 1985), ed. O. Weijers, 78–87. Turnhout: Brepols.

Irigoin, J. 1992. "Manuscrit imposé ou copie sur carnet." *Scriptorium* 46: 88–90.

Ker, N. R. 1960. "From 'above top line' to 'below top line': A Change in Scribal Practice." *Celtica* 5: 13–16.

Klein, E. 1967. *A Comprehensive Etymological Dictionary of the English Language,* 2. Amsterdam; London; New York: Elsevier Publishing Company.

Lalou, E. 1991. "Les Rolets de théâtre: étude codicologique." In *Théâtre et spectacles hier et aujourd'hui. Moyen Âge et Renaissance,* 51–71. Paris: Ministère de l'Éducation Nationale.

Lemaire, J. 1989. *Introduction à la codicologie* (Publications de l'Institut d'Études Médiévales—Textes, Études, Congrès 9). Louvain-la-Neuve: Université catholique de Louvain.

Mallon, J. 1949. "Quel est le plus ancien exemple connu d'un manuscrit latin en forme de codex?" *Emerita* 17: 1–8.

Maniaci, M. 2002. *Archeologia del manoscritto: metodi, problemi, bibliografia recente.* Rome: Viella.

Marichal, R. 1990. "Du volumen au codex." In *Mise en page et mise en texte du livre manuscrit,* ed. H. J. Martin and J. Vezin, 45–54. Paris: Éditions du Cercle de la Librairie-Promodis.

Muzerelle, D. 1985. *Vocabulaire codicologique: répertoire méthodique des termes français relatifs aux manuscrits* [Hypertext edition, Version 1.1, 2002–3]. Paris: Editions CEMI.

Muzerelle, D. 1997. "La Machine à rouler . . . les codicologues." *Gazette du Livre Médiéval* 31: 22–30.

Muzerelle, D. 2008. "Un Instrument de réglure inattendu: la règle." *Gazette du Livre Médiéval* 52–3: 79–85.

Onions, C. T., ed. 1966. *The Oxford Dictionary of English Etymology.* Oxford: Clarendon Press.

Polastron, L. X. 1999. *Le Papier: 2000 ans d'histoire et de savoir-faire.* Paris: Imprimerie nationale.

Pollard, G. 1978. "The Pecia System in the Medieval Universities." In *Medieval Scribes, Manuscripts and Libraries: Essays Presented to N. R. Ker,* ed. M. B. Parkes and A. G. Watson, 145–61. London: Scolar Press.

Reed, R. *The Nature and Making of Parchment.* Leeds: Elmete Press.

Reynhout, L. 2006. *Formules latines de colophons* (Bibliologia 25). Turnhout: Brepols.

Roberts, C. H. and T. C. Skeat. 1985. *The Birth of the Codex.* Oxford: Oxford University Press.

Rouse, R. H. 1982. "Roll and Codex: The Transmission of the Works of Reinmar von Zweter." In *Paläographie 1981.* (Münchener Beiträge zur Mediävistik und Renaissance-Forschung 32), ed. G. Silagi, 107–123. Munich: Arbeo-Gesellschaft.

Rusconi, R. 1989. "Reportatio." *Medioevo e Rinascimento* 3: 7–36.

Sabbe, E. 1981. "Papyrus et parchemin au haut Moyen Âge." In *Miscellanées Étienne Sabbe* 3, 135–41. Brussels: Archives Générales du Royaume.

Samaran, C. 1935. "De quelques instruments de copistes." *Bibliothèque de l'école des chartes* 96: 194–6.

Samaran, C. 1940. "Manuscrits 'imposés' à la manière typographique." In *Mélanges en hommage à la mémoire de Fr. Martroye*, 325–36 and Plates XVIII–XX. Paris: Société Nationale des Antiquaires de France.

Shooner, H. V. 1988. "La Production du livre par la pecia." In *La Production du livre universitaire au Moyen Âge: exemplar et pecia* (Actes du symposium tenu au Collegio San Bonaventura de Grottaferrata en mai 1983), ed. L. J. Bataillon, B. G. Guyot, and R. H. Rouse, 17–37. Paris: Centre National de la Recherche Scientifique.

Sirat, C. 1988. "Le Parchemin." In *Le Livre au Moyen Âge*, ed. J. Glénisson, 22–3. Paris: Centre national de la recherche scientifique.

Smith, D. 2003. "Plaidoyer pour l'étude des plis: codex, mise en page, transport et rangements." *Gazette du Livre Médiéval* 42: 1–15.

Turner, E. G. 1977. *The Typology of the Early Codex*. Philadelphia, PA: University of Pennsylvania.

Valls i Subira, O. 1978–80. *La historia del papel en Espana*. 2 vols. Madrid: Empresa Nacional de Celulosas.

Van Balberghe, E. 1981. "Repères de mise en place pour l'insertion d'un feuillet à l'intérieur d'un cahier." *Scriptorium* 35: 294–5.

Van Haelst, J. 1989. "Les Origines du codex." In *Les Débuts du codex: actes de la journée d'étude organisée à Paris les 3 et 4 juillet 1985*, ed. A. Blanchard, 13–35 (Bibliologia 9). Turnhout: Brepols.

Vezin, J. 1967. "Observations sur l'emploi des réclames dans les manuscrits latins." *Bibliothèque de l'École des Chartes* 125: 5–33.

Vezin, J. 1990. "Manuscrits imposés." In *Mise en page et mise en texte du livre manuscrit*, ed. H.-J. Martin and J. Vezin. 422–5. Paris: Éditions du Cercle de la Librairie-Promodis.

Zerdoun Bat-Yehouda, M. 1983. *Les Encres noires au Moyen Âge jusqu'à 1600* (Documents, études et répertoires 25). Paris: Centre National de la Recherche Scientifique.

Zerdoun Bat-Yehouda, M. 1989. Les Papiers filigranés médiévaux: essai de méthodologie descriptive (Bibliologia 7–8). Turnhout: Brepols.

Zerdoun Bat-Yehouda, M. 1998. *Le Papier au Moyen Âge: histoire et techniques*. Colloque international organisé par l'IRHT, Paris 23–25 avril 1998 (Bibliologia 19). Turnhout: Brepols.

CHAPTER 36

··

STAGES IN DIPLOMATIC PRODUCTION

··

OLIVIER GUYOTJEANNIN
(Translated by Robert G. Babcock and Frank T. Coulson)

THE study of the evolution of administrative documents in the medieval period confronts the researcher with questions both old and new. Since the beginning of the discipline, editors have focused their attention on the numerical evaluation of documents—both those preserved and those thought to have been produced but which are no longer extant. This emphasis is particularly evident in studies of sovereign documents (those of pontifical, imperial, and royal origin). Initial assessments, with scarcely a trace of nuance, privileged the unstoppable forces of progress, postulating that writing declined during the "dark ages" of the barbarian kingdoms and the brutal feudal system only to resurface in the later Middle Ages, a period marked by the rapid development of schools, towns, and monarchies.

In the last 30–40 years, studies on literacy and alphabetism inaugurated by Michael Clanchy (1979) and Hagen Keller (1992, 2002) have prompted students of diplomatics to pose new and more refined questions. While earlier research stressed the opposition between lack and overabundance of sources, between the written and the oral, between literate and illiterate, more recent approaches take account of a broader spectrum of complementary and overlapping competencies in regards to writing, and no longer retain such an irenic vision of the progress of the written word.

Students of diplomatics, therefore, undertake both qualitative and quantitative studies for which the data is incomplete, making only partial enquiries possible. Their inquiries are further complicated by a clearer realization of how problematic it is to evaluate the existing mass of material and to reconstitute the tally of lost materials.

DOCUMENTATION IN THE EARLY
MIDDLE AGES

The first centuries of the Middle Ages are particularly problematic for students of diplomatics. It is difficult to break down the early Middle Ages into particular periods and regions given the paucity of preserved documents: we have about 100 authentic documents (37 of which are original) for the rulers of Merovingian Gaul from the late sixth to the middle of the eighth century (and no documents survive from the fifth century); about 1,500–1,800 Anglo-Saxon documents; virtually no evidence for the non-Romance part of continental Europe; and only partial information in the other areas. Attempts to differentiate periods are problematic. In some respects, the early Middle Ages, when one speaks of documents, may extend to the tenth, the eleventh, or even the twelfth century, depending on whether one takes into account the universal scarcity of material, the continuity of earlier forms of reception and preservation of writing, or the very significant impetus given by the royal chancelleries. From the tenth to the twelfth century, secular archives appeared which supplanted the Church monopoly. A true break occurs in the thirteenth century, which witnessed the methodical recording of royal acts that provided a written memory of the decisions adopted. During the thirteenth century, there was a notable increase in the use and archiving of documents. This had formerly been a very elitist act, but it now occurred at many other strata of the social body—what Clanchy calls the "documents at village level."

The central portion of our time span also fails to present a unified picture. Certainly, we may single out the documents from the Carolingian period (AD 750–900), giving us about 2,800 documents (of which 980 are original) for all the kings of the dynasty who reigned before the tenth century. But generalization for Europe as a whole is not possible: border countries like Ireland, Scotland, the Scandinavian kingdoms, and Poland begin diplomatic production only in the twelfth century, often under heavy outside pressure. We can say the same for non-Romanized Germany four centuries earlier under the influence of missionaries, French kings, and also Italy in so far as it concerns Bavaria, beginning with isolated ecclesiastical structures. In the heart of the former Roman Empire, diplomatic features are quite varied. In the south, writing remains diffused and non-centralized, in part rural; and it is taken over and expanded by the Lombards and the Visigoths. In the north, writing and archiving decline but are supported by relatively rigid norms and by sophisticated practices that frequently rely on orality; and, more than in the south, the Church plays a greater role in gathering, transmitting, and reconstituting ancient forms.

If one may suppose that Rome endured thanks to the veneer of ancient practices which continued through the early Middle Ages, there can be no doubt that the decline in city structures and royal power entailed a similar decline in archival practices, made all the more acute with the decline of palace archives so important to antiquity (and to the cities of Baghdad and Constantinople). Confronted with few written records, characterized by ancient topoi, one has the impression during this period of fleeting and very selective structures which supported ad hoc inquiries and which had recourse to oral memory. At a time when the counts of Barcelona began to accumulate a dynastic archive and the last Anglo-Saxon kings had established only a rudimentary written fiscal record, the last Carolingian and the first Capetian kings, as well as the Ottonians, inhabited a world with a strong and prestigious liturgical and diplomatic written record. Yet it is as if they had no archives at all, or scarcely any other than the most important ones. The aristocracy continued to rely on wills and dower charters, and they put down in writing only exceptional situations, here a plea, there a grant—largely created at the initiative of, and always preserved by, the Church. In the south, the situation is quite different; for example, an individual named Alahis, a rich Lombard landowner in Tuscany, possessed some 80 charters before the Frankish invasion.

If there is any common characteristic throughout the Christian West—other than the more or less customary recourse to the written word, other than a varying emphasis on written versus oral (the latter especially in the form of appeals to the memory of the community), other than the varied profiles of the redactors of the documents (semi-professional or lay judges, secular clergymen of a parish, members of religious houses)—it is the predominant role played by the Church in training the redactors of written documents, and the nearly exclusive role of the same institution in the preservation of those documents. Henceforth, one may assume that the increase and decrease in preserved documents may be credited less to an improbable oscillation of written culture than to an evolution in the documentary and archival practices of Church institutions, themselves influenced by successive reforms. This is evident for royal documents, particularly in the case of the Carolingian kings whose intense concern about their own new privileges entailed the loss of the privileges of their predecessors, the Merovingian sovereigns. It is conceivable, if not necessarily demonstrable, that the same is true for a broad swath of the documentation of private individuals.

The principal flaw with the concentrated role of the Church lies in the contrast between, on the one hand, the innumerable houses that have bequeathed us only fragments and, on the other, the isolated institutions in which the documentation runs to the hundreds or even thousands of charters, transmitted in original documents or compiled in cartularies: St Gall with 839 charters before AD 920; Redon and its cartulary; Marmoutier, whose resources are now dispersed; Saint-Victor of Marseille—to say nothing of the Italian resources.

Exacerbated at times by other factors (such as the recourse to fragile papyrus through the seventh and even the first half of the tenth century), the lack of documentation could have worsened in the tenth to twelfth centuries: this was a period in which, more than previously, the inconsistency of archival methods and the complete monopoly of the Church over written documents coalesce. But the activities of certain reformed abbeys produced an increase in written production and compensated for these weaknesses. Some monasteries scrupulously preserved all their written documents: Cluny, for example, has left us 3,650 documents dating between its foundation in 910/911 and the year 1090. Most monasteries, however, only preserve a few royal or pontifical documents (which often enough are forgeries) judged to be fundamental in establishing their rights and their patrimony. Documents considered no longer essential were often discarded, not only documents of daily administration, but also documents which no longer had a useful purpose (direct or symbolic, real or imagined). Fragments of accounts of the revenues paid to Saint-Martin of Tours during the Merovingian era—expertly published by Pierre Gasnault and Jean Vezin (1975)— were preserved by pure luck (they were reused as binding material). Martina Stratmann (1991), through her meticulous research of surviving evidence and of disparate references, was able to reconstitute the complex documents which reveal how Hincmar, the archbishop of Reims, administered his diocese.

From the end of the eleventh century, the Church reorganized its administrative structures (religious, political, and social), increasing its practice of writing and archiving; this was supplemented in the twelfth century by the great secular individuals, such as the king and territorial princes, as well as by the communes, and in the thirteenth by the lesser princes and certain members of the bourgeoisie, and by more modest rural communes. Diplomatic production was further spurred by appeals to higher authorities for the regulation of conflicts, by the greater circulation of men and goods, and by the more punctilious reading practices of the jurists who evaluated the documents. All of these factors powerfully contributed to an increase in the production of written records, to a greater unity in the formulas employed and in the methods of validation, and to placing a higher value on archival conservation.

The first effects of this phenomenon can be read in the tally of original documents written before 1120 that are now preserved in public depositories in France (ARTEM Nancy, since 2009 the Centre de médiévistique Jean-Schneider) (Table 36.1):

Table 36.1 Original acts preserved in France (public archives) up to 1120 (tally by Benoît-Michel Tock.)

Date	Genuine Acts	False or Suspect Acts	Total
500–700	40	7	47
701–800	71	21	92
801–900	333	44	377
901–1000	661	48	709
1001–1100	2350	135	2485
1101–20	1169	32	1201
Total	4624	287	4911

A similar picture emerges from the original documents up to 1250 conserved in German-speaking countries; Table 36.2 additionally highlights the role of different authorities (Lichtbildarchiv of Marburg an der Lahn):

Table 36.2 Original Acts preserved in Germany, Austria, and Swizerland to 1250 (tally by Frank M. Bischoff)

Date	Total	Papal and Legates	Bishops and Chapters	Kings and Emperors
Without date	237	–	–	–
–1000	939	35	43	749
1001–50	575	22	52	392
1051–1100	487	35	147	182
1101–50	1410	215	635	211
1151–1200	3067	319	1358	328
1201–50	3198	399	775	457
Total	9913	1025	3010	2319

Church officials lead the way: beginning in the eleventh century (and continuing until the eighteenth, but more slowly after the thirteenth and fourteenth centuries), they eagerly compile collections of copies of the original documents in their possession. These collections, or cartularies, transmit a colossal documentation, incomparably more numerous than the originals. As yet they have not been inventoried in total, but the initial French repertory, published a century ago (Stein 1907), numbered around 4,000, for Church documents alone. The admirable catalogue of G. R. C. Davis (1958) for Great Britain, which provided a more refined analysis, listed 1,125 cartularies for religious houses and 158 for secular. The Church cartularies alone from the ecclesiastical province of Reims (in the northeastern portion of the French kingdom) transmit the text of around 180,000 documents written prior to 1300.

The eager pursuit of legal standards and of their day-to-day implementation lies behind an explosion of writing, even if orality continues to play an important role before the tribunals. There is an increase in the recording (at this stage still slow) of sentences and in the multiplication of written proceedings. A lawsuit of the High Middle Ages is usually known to us, in the best of circumstances, by a formal document mentioning it. If the document is lost, the suit must be judged again. By contrast, for nearly a decade between 1252 and 1261, a lawsuit of only modest importance, in which two religious houses of Noyon battled one another over the ownership of the skull of St. Eloi, who had died six centuries earlier, resulted in the writing of nearly 250 documents on behalf of one of the parties involved. What was true of the Church and the secular tribunals also applied to the new regulatory bodies which came into being with newly created state structures (such as feudalism, the police, taxation, and bureaucracy), namely, written documents linked the central power to its numerous representatives, who were often far distant and difficult to oversee.

This geographical remoteness and the desire to combat it in a world that was more unified, where new diplomatic developments spread as quickly as any other innovations, were the greatest spur to the explosion in the production of documents by the sovereigns (for this could hardly have been the result of some deliberate policy).

This phenomenon better explains the temporary gulf separating the Plantagenet and Capetian kings of the twelfth century: 45 documents survive for each year of the reign of Henry II of England, an average that was barely reached by Philippe Auguste (the annual averages for his predecessors in the twelfth century, Louis VI and Louis VII, were only 14 and 22, respectively). The gulf separating the Plantagenets and the Capetians is even greater if one considers the spread of royal documents of financial administration and of legal written procedures (which may be studied by means of the first financial rolls and the fragments of judiciary archives), which would raise to between 4,000 and 4,500 the hypothetical annual average of diplomatic production in the Plantagenet "empire". The delicacy of its control and its uniform features imposed upon this empire an unprecedented management through formulaic writs and standardized accounting. The Capetian kingdom adopted the same solutions less than a century later, clearly in imitation of the Plantagenets, when it was confronted with an unparalleled expansion of its dominion.

This dominant model, which multiplied the written word and lent weight to preserving it in archives, also affected small and mid-sized private landowners in the countryside and villages. Merchants too preserved many documents, though this happened much later in France than in Italy, where as early as 1410 Francesco de Marco Datini, a merchant of some means, left at his death 150,000 letters and some 500 registers. Around 1110, documents concerning a courtesan of the king of France, Henry of Lorraine, are known to us through the archives of a Parisian monastery, Saint-Magloire, to which his goods were bequeathed; from 1257 to 1289, a bourgeois of Provins (of Italian origin) accumulated a minimum of 546 documents concerning his purchases of property and feudal rights. These documents are known to us through a cartulary, for from this period onward secular individuals also compiled cartularies.

This unprecedented need to write led the authorities not only to multiply their own production (e.g., the chancellery of Pope Boniface VIII sent up to 50,000 letters a year, and that of the king of France around 1330 sent about 20,000 documents and letters a year) but also to regulate and control the production of documents between private citizens. Church institutions, secular courts, and public notaries all vied with one another to produce documents, which were archived by the parties involved. The authors of these documents—at least the public notaries—also kept traces of them in their registers. Notaries expand their innovations through vague powers, from their epicenter in Italy, northward throughout Europe (with lessening force in the north). The archival tally is gigantic, even if the first century is not well documented, to judge from the first preserved registers: 1154 in Italy (Genoa); 1248 in France (Marseilles). The notaries of Lucca, in the central decades of the thirteenth century, produced a theoretical average of 10,000 acts yearly. The southeast of France (Dauphiné, Savoy, Provence, and Comtat), where practices were most directly under Italian influence, has left us, after many thirteenth-century losses, something like 4,000,000 notary acts of the fourteenth and fifteenth centuries. The number and proximity of notaries in a town (evidence suggests that in Italy there was one notary for every hundred households), but also in the neighboring countryside, provided that individuals had immediate and regular access to the practitioners.

At times, factors which are strictly political come into play. For example, the people of the communes of northern and central Italy, from the middle of the thirteenth century onward, show a particular fondness for the multiple production and organized preservation of documents. This applied especially to registers, which, alongside statutes and accounts, provided a guarantee of readability and of the transparency of the practices of power—the very antithesis of aristocratic secrecy. At the same time, such documents as fiscal registers, records of deliberation, and court registers gave powerful tools for controlling adversaries and subjects.

This development, though unstoppable, was subject to slowdowns. There are many indications that it became necessary—obligatory—after the pressure placed upon the seigneurs by ecclesiastical houses in the twelfth century, to issue sealed documents and to preserve autographs. The progress of writing accompanied and reinforced the control of society.

The exponential increase in the number of formal documents, which continued to be written on parchment, a symbol of permanence, went hand in hand with a change in the typology of administrative documents. From the fourteenth century, these were more and more written on paper, and the writing was adapted for mass production, as evidenced by its quality. These administrative documents, often in the form of booklets and registers, less often on parchment rolls, reveal an administration (of the State, of cities, of the collective and individual patrimonies) which is more and more refined, and also more concerned with careful preservation. Accounts (including descriptive documents of land holdings and payments owed by tenants [*censiers* and *terriers*], manorial registers, descriptive documents of fiefs [oaths and tallies], descriptive documents of movable property, documents of taxation [*pouillés* and *compoix*] and the imposition of diverse levies, registers of legal proceedings and inquiries of all sorts, registers of daily deliberations of religious communities or city organizations, etc.) total, before 1500, tens of thousands. For the southeast of France, the only area to have been properly inventoried, we have about 1,100 land registers (*terriers*) and 40,000 accounts between the thirteenth to the fifteenth century.

In sum, these great numbers, even though approximate, tell of the dizzying disproportion that exists between the archival sources of the two periods. On the one hand, the written records of the High Middle Ages are rare, dispersed, difficult to find and to evaluate, but rich in information. For these reasons, these documents have fascinated historians since the seventeenth century, and they have served as the basis of training in the fields of diplomatics and palaeography. On the other hand, the production during the last three centuries of the Middle Ages is massive. It calls for examination of the whole as well as of discreet subsections. For this material the traditional practices of classification and editing are impractical, and the studies to date are inadequate. We have incomplete censuses, and our editions and studies are unequally distributed and few and far between.

BIBLIOGRAPHY

Regional Studies

Adamska A., and M. Mostert, eds. 2004. *The Development of Literate Mentalities in East Central Europe* (Utrecht Studies in Medieval Literacy 9). Turnhout: Brepols.

Cammarosano, P. 1992. *Italia medievale, struttura e geografia delle fonti scritte* (Studi superiori N.I.S., Storia, 109). Rome: La Nuova Italia Scientifica [5th repr. 1998].

Clanchy, M. T. 1979. *From Memory to Written Record: England 1066–1307*. London: Edward Arnold [new eds. 1993 and 2000].

Davis, G. R. C. 1958. *Medieval Cartularies of Great Britain: A Short Catalogue*. London, New York, and Toronto: Longmans, Green and Co.

Fichtenau, H. 1971. *Das Urkundenwesen in Österreich vom 8. bis zum frühen 13. Jahrhundert*, Vienna, Cologne, Graz (*M.I.Ö.G. Ergänzungsband*, 23).

Stein, H. 1907. *Bibliographie générale des cartulaires français ou relatifs à l'histoire de France*. Paris: Alphonse Picard.

More Specialized Studies

Anheim, É. and P. Chastang, eds. 2009. *Pratiques de l'écrit* = *Médiévales* 56: 1–114.

Bertrand, P. 2015. *Les Écritures ordinaires: sociologie d'un temps de révolution documentaire, entre royaume de France et Empire, 1250–1350* (*Histoire ancienne et médiévale*, 138). Paris: Publications de la Sorbonne.

Bertrand, P. 2019. *Documenting the Everyday in Medieval Europe: The Social Dimensions of a Writing Revolution, 1250–1350* (*Utrecht Studies in Medieval Literacy*, 42). Turnhout: Brepols.

Gasnault, P., and J. Vezin, eds. 1975. *Documents comptables de Saint-Martin de Tours à l'époque mérovingienne* (Collection de documents inédits sur l'histoire de France, série in-4°). Paris: Bibliothèque nationale.

Guyotjeannin, O., L. Morelle, and M. Parisse, eds. 1997. *Pratiques de l'écrit documentaire au XIᵉ siècle* = *Bibliothèque de l'École des chartes* 155: 1–349.

Heidecker, K. 2000. *Charters and the Use of the Written Word In Medieval Society* (Utrecht Studies in Medieval Literacy 5). Turnhout: Brepols.

Keller, H., K. Grubmüller, and N. Staubach, eds. 1992. *Pragmatische Schriftlichkeit im Mittelalter: Erscheinungsformen und Entwicklungsstufen* (Münstersche Mittelalter Schriften 65). Munich: Wilhelm Fink and Leiden: Brill.

McKitterick, R. 1989. *The Carolingians and the Written Word*. Cambridge: Cambridge University Press [esp. p. 77–134 on the *charters de Saint-Gall*].

Meier, C., V. Honemann, H. Keller, and R. Suntrup, eds. 2002. *Pragmatische Dimensionen mittelalterlicher Schriftkultur* (Münstersche Mittelalter-Schriften 79). Munich: Wilhelm Fink and Leiden: Brill.

Melville, G., ed. 1996. *"De ordine vitae": Zu Normvorstellung, Organisationsformen und Schriftgebrauch im mittelalterlichen Ordenswesen* (Vita regularis 1). Münster: LIT.

Stratmann, M. 1991. *Hinkmar von Reims als Verwalter von Bistum und Kirchenprovinz*, Sigmaringen: J. Thorbecke.

CHAPTER 37

THE *MISE-EN-PAGE* IN WESTERN MANUSCRIPTS

MARIE-HÉLÈNE TESNIÈRE
(Translated by Frank T. Coulson)

THE *mise-en-page* is "the general placement of the different elements which make up a page."[1] It is composed of the ratio of the written and decorated surface of the page to its support and the manner in which this surface is structured. At the confluence of several disciplines (such as codicology, paleography, and history of texts) the *mise-en-page* is rarely studied for itself, and its history in Western medieval manuscripts remains to be written.

The *mise-en-page* of manuscripts is rarely described in the catalogues of libraries. Rather, they are content to list a certain number of elements which, placed in context one with another, could readily define it: these are the support material, the page size, the margins, the ruling, the type of writing, the titles, the initials, the paragraph signs, the decoration, etc.

Likewise, codicological manuals do not generally have a chapter on the *mise-en-page* of manuscripts, but study in a minute fashion each of the individual elements of which it is composed, taking into account the way in which the artist has placed them successively in place.[2] They limit themselves to recalling the formula for the *mise-en-page* (margins and lines) noted in a manuscript of the ninth century, Paris, BnF, lat. 11884. Léon Gilissen, in the very technical chapters on the *mise-en-page* of manuscripts in his *Prolégomènes à la codicologie,* provided a commentary: "The formula seems to guide the craftsman in the rather exact construction where the column corresponds to the superimposing of two golden rectangles (one speaks of a golden rectangle when, in dividing the large side of a rectangle by the small one, one obtains the quotient 1.6)."[3]

The *mise-en-page* in a manuscript follows a program prescribed by the head of a workshop: it may be based on an existing model or it may be an original creation, more or less luxurious according to the financial limits of the person commissioning the manuscript; often the *mise-en-page* is determined by the type of text. It is established before the copying of the text; it defines and establishes the written space at the heart of the page, anticipates the elements of its readability, and develops the program of illustrations.

(1) The organization of the space written in the center of the page is contingent
upon
  (i) the format of the support, i.e., the dimensions of the page. These evolve
according to economic indicators and the clientele.[4]
  (ii) the relationship between the parameters of the justification (i.e., the dimensions in height and width of the written surface) and the margins.[5] Wide
margins are a sign of a deluxe manuscript and the wealth of the person
ordering the manuscript.
  (iii) the structure of the written space, which may be in long lines or in several
columns. Gothic manuscripts show a preference for a two-column layout,
whereas humanistic manuscripts prefer long lines. The lines may be of
variable spaces.

The structure of the written space is defined by the ruling, which contains
the outline of the *mise-en-page* at the same time as it serves as a guideline
for the copy. The establishment of the scheme for the ruling is the first
thing to do in describing the *mise-en-page*. The ruling may be done with
dry point, lead point, or ink.[6]
  (iv) the special case of text with commentary. Texts with commentary have
complex *mises-en-page* (Plate 37.4). Antiquity had two types of commentary: the marginal commentary in the form of scholia transmitted in the
manuscript of the classical author, and the autonomous commentary with
lemmata. The novelty of the early Middle Ages is that the text that
functions as commentary will be copied according to a layout that attempts
to associate the authoritative text with the commentary text; the layout will
vary according to whether one sees it primarily serving the goals of the
authoritative text or of the commentary text.[7]

Created at the end of the eleventh and beginning of the twelfth century, the
glossa ordinaria further developed the organization of the *mise-en-page*.
Text and commentary were welded together little by little on the page.
The hierarchy between the Bible and its commentary was established by the
contrast between the scripts and their interlinear placement: the text of the
Bible filled one interline in two; the intermediary line remained empty.
There were three sizes of writing: the largest for the biblical text, the middle
for the *glossa ordinaria*, and the smallest for the interlinear gloss.

Often, particularly in legal manuscripts, the commentary encircled the
authoritative text, and the different modules of script indicated the level
of importance accorded each text.

(2) The degree of "readability" of the page takes into account:
  (i) all the aspects of writing: its form (Caroline minuscule, Gothic, cursive,
bastarda); its module; its position vis-à-vis the space between the lines; its
degree of leaning. For example, the readability of Caroline minuscule has
often been praised (Plate 37.3). That is one of the reasons for which its later
form was imitated by the humanists in the fifteenth century.

(ii) the separation of words.

(iii) the punctuation.

(iv) abbreviations which render the page more dense.

(v) all the elements which organize into a hierarchy and structure the text to facilitate the reading and comprehension (Plate 37.2): the hierarchy of scripts; the colors (red ink for chapter titles and biblical lemmata) and their variation (blue and red, or black and red, violet and red); underlined words; decorated or filigree letters cutting into or separating the text; the succession of paragraph marks (which are called in French *pieds de mouche*).

(vi) anything which makes the page more spaced out, and in particular the ends of line which suppress empty spaces.[8]

(3) The relationship of text and image

The placement of the image in the text and of its relationship with the text is governed by multiple constraints: it should be precisely determined before copying the text.

The illustration (miniature or drawing) was for a long time inserted in the columns of text, the space it occupied in ancient rolls. A good example is provided by the illustration of the *Comedies* of Terence, from the Carolingian period (Paris, BnF, lat. 7899, fol. 31r, dated to the second half of the ninth century). Associated with a decorated letter and sometimes with a rubricated title, the miniature becomes, from the thirteenth century, a guide indicating the beginning of books or chapters. From this moment, the miniature often enters into a relationship with other elements of the decoration: side panels or full-frame vegetation. The last-mentioned will invade the pages of French manuscripts in the fifteenth century, in an abundance of acanthus leaves and small flowers, around the entire written text. Consequently, depending on the importance given to the illustration, the miniature may spread out through the two columns of text.

Freeing itself from the antique model, the illustration sometimes occupied the margins, particularly in Italian regions.

The title page in its true sense does not exist in medieval manuscripts. Nevertheless, the picture inscribed on the first page of the deluxe manuscript, often illustrated with a portrait of the author, a dedicatory scene, or a symbolic synthesis of the work, will serve in the final centuries of the Middle Ages as a title page.

Although one usually studies the *mise-en-page* on a single folio, one must remember that the esthetic and artistic norm for the medieval page is in reality the double page of an open book (Plates 37.5 and 37.6).

The *mise-en-page* is one of the elements on which researchers rely to reconstruct the output of scriptoria or of copying workshops. Sometimes they allow one to reassemble parts of manuscripts dispersed to various places. Placed in relation to the text or the illustration, it may also give much information on the norms of reading or the medieval esthetic codes.[9]

SOME EXAMPLES OF *MISE-EN-PAGE*

A Codex of the Fifth Century Modeled on the Ancient Roll

Livy wrote a Roman history in 142 books going from the foundation of Rome to the death of Drusus. Only a small part is extant, Books 1–10, and 21–45. In the Roman period, each book was preserved in a papyrus roll called a volume. Today, we have only a fragment of the first decade conserved at Oxford in a papyrus from Oxyrhinchus.[10] The *mise-en-page* of the oldest codices on parchment reproduced the succession of columns of the *volumina*. This is the case with manuscript BnF, lat. 5730, which contains the third decade (Plate 37.1). It was written in Italy, probably at Naples, in the fifth century. At the beginning of the Carolingian age it was transported to the abbey at Lorsch and then to Tours; Alcuin, who was abbot at the monastery of Saint-Martin of Tours from 796 to 804, allowed it to be freely copied. In the seventeenth century, the scholar Claude Dupuy revealed it to the scholarly world, whence its name *Puteanus*.[11]

Note the almost square format of the page: 280 × 245 mm; dry-point ruling; writing surface: 180 × 173 mm. Note the narrowness of the text columns: 73 mm. Written in Capitals mixed with Uncials, in *scripta continua*, i.e., with no word separation. The beginning of Book 26 is noted in red. Running title: *Titi Livi Lib(er) XXVI*.

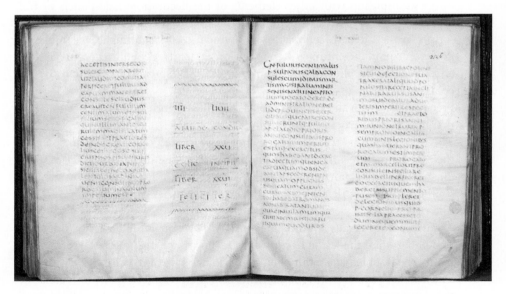

PLATE 37.1 Livy, *Ab urbe condita*, manuscript of the fifth century in mixed Capitals and Uncials. Paris, BnF, lat. 5730, fols, 225v–226r: end of Book 25 and beginning of Book 26 of Livy's *Ab urbe condita*.

Reading Aids and Editorial Work in a Manuscript of the Fourteenth Century

(Continued)

PLATE 37.2 Paris, BnF, lat. 5690, fol. 142r, beginning of Book 9 of Livy's *Ab urbe condita*

Copied for Landolfo Colonna from a manuscript preserved at the cathedral of Chartres, at Rome between 1300 and 1306, the manuscript went next to his nephew Giovanni Colonna, then to the Dominican Bartolomeo Papazurri, before being bought by Petrarch in Avignon in 1351.

Page measurements: 365 mm × 235 mm; ruled in lead; justification: 262 × 165. Written in two columns of 49 lines, in Italian Gothic. Note the reading aids such as capitalization, with chapter numbering and chapter summaries. These have been attributed to Donato degli Albanzani, a friend of Petrarch. Several readings different from the main text are noted in red. Rubricated title, miniature (knights before Pontius, general of the Samnites) and a historiated initial (with an individual) *S(equitur)* trailing in the margin with a frame and decoration of grotesques (a knight attacking a griffon) serving as a visual marker to note the beginning of Book 9 in the manuscript volume.

Hierarchy of Scripts and Inks in a Manuscript of the Ninth Century

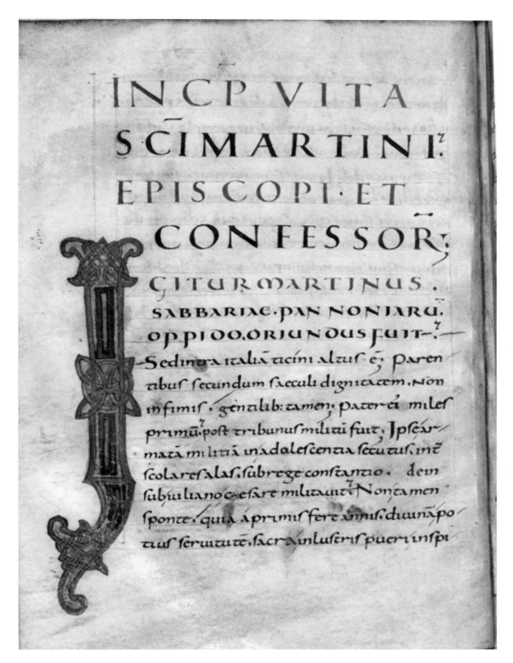

PLATE 37.3 Paris, BnF, lat. 10848, fol. 5v.

Elegant use of the hierarchy of script to construct the first page of the *Vita Martini* of Sulpicius Severus dating to the second quarter of the ninth century: *mise-en-page* where the writing goes in "diminuendo," as in Irish manuscripts. Page measurements 230 × 177 mm; dry-point ruling; justification: 177 × 125 mm. Title in Capitals (7 mm) written on every other line, with alternating black and red; the beginning of the text is marked by a large ornamented initial jutting out in the margin; copied in Capitals mixed with Uncials (5 mm) every other line in red ink and then in a black ink; the text in Caroline minuscule follows.

PLATE 37.4 Paris, BnF, lat. 12593, fol. 232r: *De anima* of Aristotle (*translatio vetus*), Paris, third quarter of the thirteenth century, with a historiated initial portraying the two intellects of the soul.

Page measurements 330 × 218 mm; text justification: 166 × 90 mm; written in long lines, 26 lines to the page.

The text of Aristotle is written in the central part corresponding to the third column; the commentary is written in a cursive script by at least two, perhaps three hands.

Eleven vertical lines (that is to say, five double lines + 1) delineate six columns of writing, as well as the right margin; beginning at the left: first column (text partially obscured by the binding): 20 mm; second column: 20 mm; third column: 90mm (authoritative text); fourth column: 15 mm; fifth column: 20 mm; sixth column: 30 mm. The double lines, which derive from Caroline models where the first letters of a text were carried outside the justification, serve in the thirteenth century to inscribe the paragraph markers, thus placing them in relief.

Note the paragraph signs alternating in blue and red which determine the paragraphs, as well as the title running along the top margin.

Double Page in a Manuscript of the Ninth Century

PLATE 37.5 AND 37.6 Paris, BnF, lat. 1979, fols. 11v and 12r: Augustine, *Enarrationes in Psalmos*, first half of the ninth century.

Page measurements 400 × 275 mm. Note the name of the person who commissioned the manuscript in the rounded frame: "Landulfus ovans hunc libellum fieri iussit pro quo funde preces carmina qui legis et dic: ipsius post obitum tu miserere Christe" and in the gold lettering: "Landulfo sit vera lux" (fol. 12r). Note the decorative use of different Capitals, the play of color, and the enclosed letters to mark the beginning of a Bible text.

PLATE 37.5 AND 37.6 Continued

SUGGESTED READING

Some important books and reference articles

Mise en page et mise en texte du livre manuscrit under the editorship of Henri-Jean Martin and Jean Vezin, Paris, 1990. This very complete work is structured as a series of descriptive articles; some treat the case of unusual manuscripts, such as the Bible of Rorigon (Paris, BnF, lat. 3, by P. Petitmengin, pp. 78–83), or the Psalter of Otbert (Boulogne-sur-mer, Bibliothèque municipale, MS 20, by G. Lobrichon, pp. 174–77); others provide a synthesis of a particular theme, such as the *mise-en-page* of the Canon of the Mass and Breviary by Father P.-M. Gy, pp. 113–20), or that of concordances and indices (by Richard and Mary Rouse, pp. 219–28); still others study the *mise-en-page* by genres: lyric poetry (by Pascale Bourgain, pp. 164–68), translations and commentaries. The work treats the *mise-en-page* of mainly Latin and French manuscripts, but also Greek and Hebrew, and it provides several outlines for the *mise-en-page*.

Mise en page et mise en texte du livre français. La naissance du livre moderne (XIVe–XVIIe siècle), under the editorship of Henri-Jean Martin, Paris, 2000. The work shows how the *mise-en-page* of printed books up until the sixteenth century is profoundly influenced by the *mise-en-page* of medieval manuscripts.

Album des manuscrits français du XIIIe siècle. Mise en page et mise en text by Maria Careri, Françoise Fery-Hue, Françoise Gasparri, Geneviève Hasenohr, Gilette Labory, Sylvie Lefèvre, Anne-Françoise Leurquin, and Chrisine Ruby, Rome: Viella, 2000. This work, which deals with French manuscripts, may serve as a model. It investigates the *mise-en-page* of a booklet in *c.*50 French manuscripts from the thirteenth century.

Three short articles related to quantitative codicology attempt to provide syntheses and to raise questions:

- Carla Bozzolo, Dominique Coq, Denis Muzerelle, and Ezio Ornato, "Noir et blanc, premiers résultats d'une enquête sur la mise en page dans le livre médiéval," in *Il Libro e il Testo* (Atti del Convegno internazionale, Urbino 20–23 settembre 1982), ed. C. Questa and R. Rafaelli,Urbino 1984, pp. 195–221, reprinted in *La Face cachée du livre médiéval*, pp. 473–508. The article studies the coefficient of replacement of black in relationship to white, i.e., the relationship of the written surface (not comprising the space between the columns) to the total surface of the leaf.
- Carla Bozzolo, Dominique Coq, Denis Muzerelle, and Ezio Ornato, "Page savante, page vulgaire: étude comparative des livres en latin et en français écrits ou imprimés en France au XVe siècle," in *La Présentation du livre*, Paris, 1987, pp. 121–33.
- Carla Bozzolo, Dominique Coq, Denis Muzerelle, and Ezio Ornato, "L'Artisan médiéval et la page: Peut-on déceler des procédés géométriques de mise en page ?" in *Artistes, artisans et production artistique au Moyen-Âge* (Actes du colloque, Rennes, 2–6 mais 1983), ed. X. Barral i Altet, vol. III, pp. 295–305. Reprinted in Ezio Ornato, *La Face cachée du livre médiéval. L'histoire du livre vu par Ezio Ornato, ses amis et ses collègues*, Paris, 1997, pp. 447–56.

NOTES

1. Muzerelle (1985); see http://codicologia.irht.cnrs.fr/theme/liste_theme/331#tr-431, accessed March 26, 2020.
2. See, in particular, Lemaire (1989).
3. This ratio was published in 1934 by Rand (88–9). It is explained by Gilissen (1977, 216–22):

   Taliter debet fieri quaternionis forma, quinta parte longitudinis, quarta latitudinis. Quintam partem da inferiori vel anteriori margini, et ipsam quintam partem divide in .III. et dabis .II. superiori, subtracta .I. Rursus ipsas .II. partes divide in tres, dabisque duas posteriori margini subtrahendo unam. Huic compar erit si media interfuerit. Lineas vero juxta rationem scripturae divides, quia major scriptura latioribus, minor autem strictioribus lineis indiget.

4. Bozzolo and Ornato (1980).
5. Gilissen (1977, 134–45).
6. See Muzerelle (1999) and the slideshow the same author made in 1994, available at http://www.palaeographia.org/muzerelle/reglure.htm, accessed February 20, 2020. Basing himself upon Leroy (1977), Muzerelle established a simple codification for the description of the schemes for ruling. See, in particular, Muzerelle (1999, 167–70) on types of ruling schemas from the seventh to the fifteenth century. See also Derolez (1984), especially the chapter on rulings, vol. 1, 65–123.
7. Holtz (2000).
8. On the question of readability, defined as "the qualities which favor at the same time the integrity of the text and the comfort of reading," see Bergeron and Ornato (1990).
9. Derolez (1996).
10. A fragment with the shelf mark, Oxford, Bodleian Library, lat. class. f. 5 (P). P Oxy. Xi 1379. See *CLA* II, 247.
11. On this topic, see, Van Büren (1996).

BIBLIOGRAPHY

Bergeron, R. and E. Ornato. 1990. "*La Lisibilité dans les* manuscrits et les imprimés de la fin du moyen-âge, préliminaires d'une recherche." *Scrittura e civiltà* 14: 151–98 [repr. in Ezio Ornato, *La Face cachée du livre médiéval. L'histoire du livre vu par Ezio Ornato, ses amis et ses collègues*, 52–4, Paris, 1997.

Bozzolo, C., and E. Ornato. 1980. "Les Dimensions des feuilles dans les manuscrits français du moyen-âge." In *Pour une histoire du livre manuscrit au moyen-âge : trois essais de codicologie quantitative*, 317–51. Paris: Éditions du Centre national de la recherche scientifique.

Derolez, A. 1984. *Codicologie des manuscrits en écriture humanistique sur parchemin*, 2 vols. Turnhout: Brepols.

Derolez, A. 1996. "Observations on the Aesthetics of the Gothic Manuscript." *Scriptorium* 50: 3–12.

Gilissen, L. 1977. *Prolégomènes à la codicologie: Recherches sur la construction des cahiers et la mise en page des manuscrits médiévaux*. Ghent: Story-Scientia.

Holtz, L. 2000. "Le Rôle des commentaires d'auteurs classiques dans l'émergence d'une mise en page associant texte et commentaire (Moyen Âge occidental)." In *Le Commentaire, entre tradition et innovation* (Actes du colloque international de l'Institut des traditions textuelles, Paris et Villejuif, 22–25 septembre 1999), ed. Marie-Odile Goulet-Cazé, 101–22. Paris: Vrin.

Lemaire, J. 1989. *Introduction à la codicologie*. Louvain : Université catholique de Louvain, Institut d'études médiévales.

Leroy, J. 1977. *Les Types de réglure des manuscrits grecs*, Paris: Éditions du Centre national de la recherche scientifique.

Muzerelle, D. 1999. "Pour décrire les schémas de réglure: une méthode applicable aux manuscrits latins (et autres)." *Quinio, International Journal of the History and Conservation of the Book* 1: 123–70.

Van Büren, A. 1996. "Livy's Roman History in the Eleventh-Century Catalogue from Cluny: The Transmission of the First and Third Decade." In *Medieval Manuscripts of the Latin Classics: Production and Use*, ed. Claudine A. Chavannes-Mazel and Margaret M. Smith (Proceedings of the Seminar in the History of the Book to 1500, Leiden, 1993), 57–73. Los Altos Hills, CA: Anderson-Lovelace.

CHAPTER 38

···

FORMATS OF BOOKS

···

†J. P. GUMBERT

THE word "format" is used, in relation to manuscripts, with a variety of meanings. Some of these are briefly discussed below.

Most manuscripts have lost material along the edges through trimming, sometimes repeatedly. Yet it is likely that in most cases these losses are modest, not more than one or two centimeters on each edge, so discussing dimensions and proportions becomes imprecise but not meaningless.

"FORMAT" = SIZE
···

Parchment manuscripts come in all sizes, which are mainly determined by practical considerations (such as the desire for portability, the length of the text, or the need for easy reading in a dark church), or by the wish to express wealth and power, or on the contrary modesty. Most are between 20 and 40 cm in height. Books of Hours and similar books are generally smaller, down to about 10 cm. Even tinier books (the smallest is perhaps a ninth-century Psalter of 37×31 mm) probably served as curiosities or as amulets rather than as books. There seems to be a natural upper limit at about 55 cm; few books are taller; it is mainly late Italian and Spanish choir books that tend to measure 70 or 80 cm. The biggest known book is the thirteenth-century Bohemian *Codex Gigas* (Stockholm, Kungliga Biblioteket, A 148) of 90×49 cm.

Paper manuscripts show a different pattern. Paper is, at least since it started to be manufactured in Italy in the thirteenth century, made in four standard sizes, of which the two most current are Common (or Chancery) paper, with sheets of about 44×31 cm (or somewhat smaller), and Royal paper, of double that size, 61×44 cm, whereas Median, 49×35, and especially Imperial, 73×50, are much rarer. And virtually all paper manuscripts consist (as can easily be seen by the watermarks) of bifolia which are whole sheets, half-sheets, or quarter sheets. The effect is that almost all paper manuscripts have sizes close to (but generally a bit smaller, owing to trimming) these (Table 38.1):

Table 38.1 Standard sizes of paper manuscripts

paper	sheet	folio	quarto	octavo
(Imperial	73 × 50	50 × 36	36 × 25	25 × 18)
Royal	61 × 44	44 × 30	30 × 22	22 × 15
(Median	49 × 35	35 × 24	24 × 17	17 × 12)
Common	44 × 31	31 × 22	22 × 15	15 × 11

(On the notions of folio, etc., see Section 38.3 below.)

"FORMAT" = PROPORTION

If one can speak about the "size" of manuscripts on the basis of the spine height alone, it is because not only are all codices (with the exception of some heart- or circle-shaped curiosities) rectangular, but most of them have approximately the same proportion of width to height: the width is generally close to 0.71 of the height.

Now 0.71 is half of the square root of 2, and that is the famous proportion that has the property that a rectangle with this proportion, divided along its short axis, produces two rectangles that have the same proportion (so that sheet, half-sheet, and quarter sheet all "look alike"). It is the proportion of our DIN-formats, which were designed with this property in view. But it probably developed spontaneously (and not by design) in the early Middle Ages as an acceptable approximate mean of all possible shapes.

So, if a book is 30 cm high, it is very likely to be between 19.5 and 22.5 cm wide (= a proportion of 0.65–0.75). The paper sizes are tailored to the same tradition. Within this similarity there are subtle variations, which await further study (Italian books, for instance, appear to be often slightly narrower).

Clearly wider proportions, around 0.8–0.9 (called "square," although they are not really square) are found in some manuscripts of antiquity, and—presumably in emulation of those—in many Carolingian books. Books with proportions over 1.0, *oblong* books, are a rare exception in the Middle Ages.

Some books have narrower proportions. Manuscripts of Latin poetry of the thirteenth century may be as slender as 0.5; tenth-century tropers can be 0.4; a certain type of late medieval book, known as a "holster book" and having a tall material format (see Section 38.3 below), is only 0.35.

It may be pointed out that there is no evidence that the so-called golden section (giving a proportion of about 0.62), often believed to have played an important role in all sorts of classical and medieval arts and crafts, actually was ever used in book design.

MATERIAL FORMAT

In the earliest times of the codex, the bifolia for a future book were simply cut to the desired size and proportion out of the available skins. This process would not always use the whole skin; but pieces that remained could be used as singletons (the use of pairs of singletons in lieu of "real" bifolia being a common practice), or for another, smaller book, or for documents; anyway, some current ideas about the extreme parsimoniousness of medieval scribes, or the extreme expensiveness of parchment, are exaggerated.

Dividing skins (or paper sheets) economically, into two or four equal parts, was a later discovery; this was best done by folding the skin and dividing it along the folds. From this point on one can, if it is possible to determine which part of a sheet the bifolium is, speak of *material format* (Figs. 38.1 and 38.2):

folio = the bifolium is a whole skin/sheet (and therefore the leaf is half a sheet),

quarto = the bifolium is a half-sheet (and the leaf is a quarter-sheet),

octavo = the bifolium is a quarter-sheet (and the leaf is one-eighth-sheet).

To this list should be added plano = the bifolium is two sheets glued together (found in the tallest books, such as Italian choir books), and at the other end sedecimo = the bifolium is an eighth of a sheet (rarely found, and probably not before the fifteenth

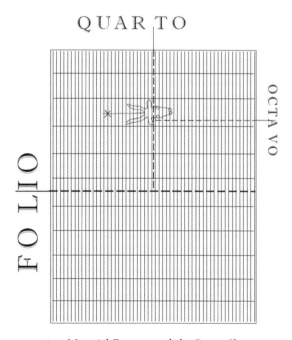

FIG. 38.1 Material Format and the Paper Sheet

QUARTO

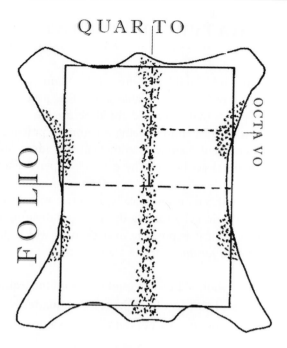

FIG. 38.2 Material Format and the Parchment Skin

century; duodecimo, a frequent format of small printed books, does not seem to be medieval at all). There is also tall folio = the bifolium is a whole sheet but folded along its long, not its short axis, and, similarly, tall quarto and tall octavo.

How can one see which part of the sheet a bifolium is? For paper this is (in most cases) easy, by observing the direction of the chain lines and the position of the watermark. (Therefore, it should always be given when describing a paper manuscript.) For parchment it is difficult, but sometimes possible; the most helpful features are the dorsal stripe, which is often strikingly evident, particularly in Italian goat parchment, and certain structures at the edges of the skin that correspond to the "groins" of the animal.

In paper the material format is, through the standard sheet sizes, immediately related to the size of the book (see Section 38.1 above), leaving a margin for variations in sheet size and for trimming. For parchment this is less clear, because skins have no standard sizes. But conversely it is possible, from a sample of parchment manuscripts where the material format could be observed, to get an idea of skin sizes. And it turns out that these are rather smaller than is often thought (and smaller than modern parchment makers produce, from modern animals). Skins commonly used north of the Alps (or, more precisely, the largest rectangles which can be cut from them) range from about 80 × 56 cm (which, used folio, produce books of 55 cm tall, which are the largest common size) down to 44 × 30; skins used in Italy tend to be smaller, down to 38 × 28. (The smallest skins are surely goat, the largest, calf; but the identification of the species of skin is still a problem.) Larger skins can be found. But for a choir book of 80 × 60 it is necessary to glue two (quite large) skins together to make one bifolium (the material format is plano).

It is evident that the "material format", in this technical sense, is related to the "library format" as commonly used, where "folio" means "so big that it has to go on the bottom shelf" and "duodecimo" means "quite small." It is, however, not at all identical to it; and one should not be misled by format indications in many shelf marks of manuscripts. For instance, the Leiden Vossiani Latini are divided into Folio (47–28 cm tall), Quarto (28–22), and Octavo (23–13), but many Quartos really are material folio or octavo.

Working on Undivided Sheets

Sometimes it can be seen (thanks to surface marks such as stipple patterns [= groups of hair follicles], or ancient repairs) that two bifolia were originally adjoining parts of the same skin (Plates 38.1 and 38.2). Sometimes these are found in the same quire; and

PLATES 38.1 AND 38.2 The ancient repair of a tear, and the follicle pattern on the hair sides, prove that these bifolia were once adjoining parts of the same skin. (Leiden, UL, BPL 99 fol. 17v+18 [France xii]; Leiden UL, BPL 105A fol.7v+8 [Italy xv.])

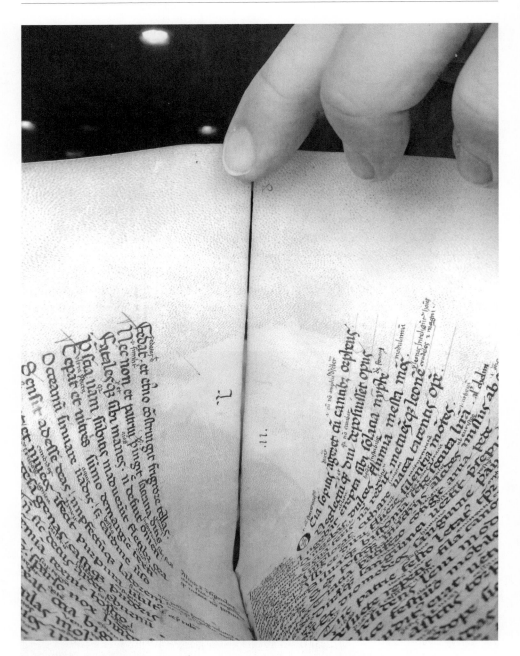

PLATE 38.1 AND 38.2 Continued

sometimes they are found in the position they would have if the quire had been made by folding the skin(s). This has been taken as proof that the quire was indeed formed by folding one skin (octavo), or folding two skins (quarto) and nesting them; but it is not proof: it is quite possible to cut a skin into bifolia, and form the quire out of loose bifolia, and still have "bridge marks" in the "correct" positions.

Yet it was discovered (it is not known when; but there is no firm evidence before about the eleventh century) that various ulterior processes could be executed while the skin was still entire and not divided into bifolia. It could be ruled. And after that, even the quire could indeed be formed out of one or two folded skins, and tacketed (= fixed with tiny loops of string or parchment; writing in tacketed quires was a fairly normal procedure up to the thirteenth century). Evidently the scribe would have to open the top (and front) folds as he progressed; near the spine fold a narrow "bolt" might remain, still connecting the bifolia that were part of one skin.

Another possibility (known, somewhat improperly, by the printers' term of "imposition") was to do the writing on the undivided and unfolded sheet; the scribe—who wrote in sense order, not (as has been supposed) first the one, then the other side of the sheet—would have to turn and rotate his "quadrifolium" in various ways in order to place the text on the correct pages (Plate 38.3). The opening of the folds would be left to the binder, or to the reader (who might leave blank leaves uncut) (Plate 38.4). It is difficult to prove that a given manuscript was written in this fashion (the best proof being that the first and *third* leaf of the quire are signed a1, *a*2, etc.); yet it is probable that this method was fairly common from the fourteenth century on (and so was well known to printers when they started to print small books).

Work on undivided sheets will produce "even" quires: quaternions, senions, and so on. But it is not suitable for making quinions, which may be the reason why it does not seem to be attested for Italy (where quinions are dominant).

Non-Codex "Formats"

Not all manuscripts are "codices" in the sense that they consist of bifolia, nested in quires and sewn (or tacketed) through the fold. Some are constructed in fundamentally different ways.

A very important book form is the roll (inherited from antiquity; but, whereas classical rolls are generally written as a *horizontal roll* (with lines parallel to the length of the roll and grouped in columns), the medieval roll is almost always a *vertical scroll* (with lines perpendicular to the length and forming one continuous column). Rolls generally consist of sections, which have the length, but most often not the width, of the sheet out of which they are made; any desired number of sections can be added (glued or sewn) to the end; but many rolls consist of only one section.

The roll is well known as an administrative form; but for other texts it also plays an important and often underrated role. There are numerous chronicles and genealogies

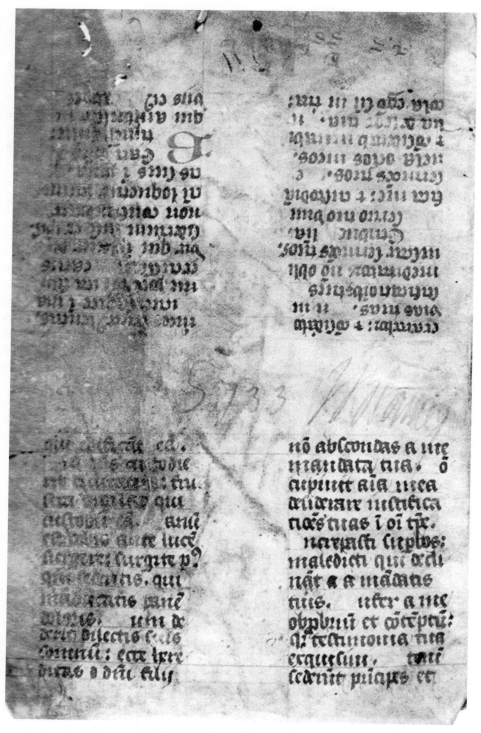

PLATE 38.3 An "imposed" quadrifolium (Cambridge UL, Oates 2998; s. xv; after Smith [1995, 149]).

PLATE 38.4 An "imposed" book, never fully opened because it was never completely read; there actually is text on the inaccessible pages (Chicago, Newberry Library MS 37.4, fols. 101+102; xv).

(of the world, of English kings, etc.) in roll form; the liturgical Exultet-rolls of Southern Italy are famous; but there are countless rolls with other contents: prayers, saints' lives, classical texts, heraldry, poetry, theatre (the "roles" of actors!), music, law, medicine, pilgrims' guides, cookery books, etc. There are, even now, far more rolls, and fragments of rolls, in our libraries than most scholars realize; in the Middle Ages they must have been quite frequent. Probably they were used particularly often for rather short texts, which in codex form would have made a very thin booklet.

A continuous strip can be rolled, but it can also be folded ("concertina" fashion). This seems to be rare, at least in the West; but some chronicle "rolls" were made for that form (as is clear by the fact that there are breaks in the column of text where the folds are); and then the inner folds may be sewn in some fashion (Plate 38.5). The result looks rather like some codices containing similar texts, where the lines are written parallel to the spine.

The folded strip (but, in a clever way, provided with fold-out flaps) is also the basis of a type of very small pocket almanac.

Another completely different structure consists of leaves (not bifolia) that are folded into six or eight compartments; each leaf has a tab at its lower edge, and the tabs are gathered by stab-sewing; the bundle of folded leaves is designed to be carried, upside down, on the girdle, and when required the relevant leaf can be unfolded (I propose calling them "bat books"). Invented in the thirteenth century as an attempt to make a book that is inwardly big but outwardly small, it only survived for portable almanacs (Fig. 38.6).

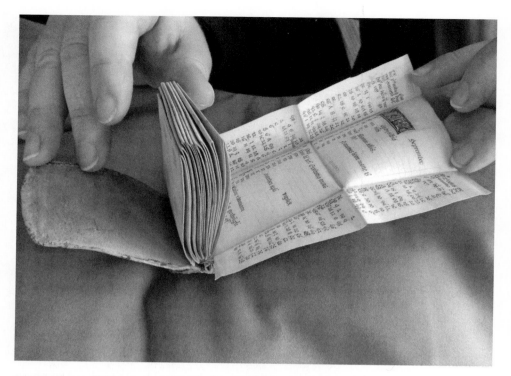

PLATE 38.5 A "fold-out concertina" calendar (Ljubljana, NUL 160 [Utrecht 1415]).

PLATE 38.6 A "bat-book" almanac (Leiden, UL, Vulc. 100 C [France c.1430]).

BIBLIOGRAPHY

On size and format

Bozzolo, C. and E. Ornato. 1980. *Pour une histoire du livre manuscrit au Moyen Âge*. Paris: Éditions du Centre national de la recherche scientifique, esp. pp. 217–332.

Gilissen, L. 1972. "La composition des cahiers, le pliage du parchemin et l'imposition." *Scriptorium* 26: 3–33 [reworked in L. Gilissen, *Prolégomènes à la codicologie: Recherches sur la construction des cahiers et la mise en page des manuscrits médiévaux*. Ghent: Story-Scientia, 1977, pp. 14–122].

Gumbert, J. P. 1993. "Sizes and Formats." In *Ancient and Medieval Book Materials and Techniques*, ed. M. Maniaci and P.F. Munafò, I, 227–63.Vatican City: Biblioteca Apostolica Vaticana.

Needham, P. 1994. "Res papirea; Sizes and Formats of the Late Medieval Book." In *Rationalisierung der Buchherstellung im Mitelalter und in der frühen Neuzeit*, ed. P. Rück et al., 123–45. Marburg: Institut für Historische Hilfswissenschaften.

On imposition

Bozzolo, C. and E. Ornato. 1980. *Pour une histoire du livre manuscrit au Moyen Âge*. Paris: Éditions du Centre national de la recherche scientifique, pp. 125–212.

Gilissen, L. 1977. *Prolégomènes à la codicologie: Recherches sur la construction des cahiers et la mise en page des manuscrits médiévaux*. Ghent: Story-Scientia.

Obbema, P. F. J. 1978. "Writing on Uncut Sheets." *Quaerendo* 8: 337–54 [replaced by his "Een bijzondere manier van schrijven," in P. F. J. Obbema, *De middeleeuwen in handen: Over de boekcultuur in de late middeleeuwen*, Hilversum: Verloren, 1996, pp. 48–68].

Smith, M. M. 1995. "Imposition in Manuscripts: Evidence for the Use of Sense-Sequence Copying in a New Fragment." In *Making the Medieval Book: Techniques of Production*, ed. L. L. Brownrigg, 145–56. London: Anderson-Lovelace.

On tackets

Gullick, M. 1996. "From Scribe to Binder." In *Roger Powell, The Compleat Binder*, ed. J. L. Sharpe, 240–9. Turnhout: Brepols, Bibliologia.

Gumbert, J. P. 2011. "The Tacketed Quire; An Exercise in Comparative Codicology," *Scriptorium* 65: 299–320.

On rolls

There is, regrettably, no useful study on rolls at all.

On folded almanacs

Gumbert, J. P. 1994. "Über Faltbücher, vornehmlich Almanache." In *Rationalisierung der Buchherstellung im Mitelalter und in der frühen Neuzeit*, ed. P. Rück et al., 111–21. Marburg: Institut für Historische Hilfswissenschaften.

Gumbert, J. P. 2016. *Bat Books: A Catalogue of Folded Manuscripts Containing Almanacs or Other Texts*.Turnhout: Brepols.

CHAPTER 39

··

THE FORMAT OF
DOCUMENTS

··

OLIVIER GUYOTJEANNIN
(Translated by Robert G. Babcock and Frank T. Coulson)

THE question of the format of documents has only recently attracted the attention of scholars in the field of diplomatics, inspiring a handful of studies which are as full of promise as they are rare. This situation makes it impossible to sketch even a slightly detailed picture of the topic. Indeed, until the beginning of the twentieth century, the question had no place in the manuals (even if no one would declare it impossible to discuss), since the medieval practices in this area seemed so confused and disorganized. The first scientific efforts to establish a corpus and to produce editions, starting with the pontifical, imperial, and royal documents, began slowly to gather data in the nineteenth century. These had the sole object of furnishing an additional argument for critiquing forgeries in those cases where the forger had followed the practices of his own time rather than the norms employed in the purported chancery of origin. Since the late 1920s (with the establishment at Marburg of the *Lichtbildarchiv* for the documents of German-speaking countries before 1250), the creation and exploitation of large collections of photographs of original documents, combined with a new interest in the materiality of documents, have increased tenfold the resources available for research in this field.

Yet these resources require careful examination, guided by an historical curiosity. The groundwork for the exploitation of this material was established, after a series of exploratory studies, by the late Peter Rück; it was then further developed by some of his students. Rück, the director of the *Lichtbildarchiv*, was a diplomatist; but he was open to all of the new approaches in codicology, in the history of typography, and in semiology. These led him, in the last stages of his career, to explore the multifaceted aspects of the "visual rhetoric" of medieval documents. His explorations, which were more readily and more easily undertaken in the domain of formal sovereign documents issued by the papal Curia or by the royal/imperial court, were valuable not only in making new discoveries and in proposing keys to the understanding of this or that aspect of the "form" of the documents. They also brilliantly (re)read the sovereign document as a system in which all aspects of the "form" were conceived and work effectively in correspondence with the content of the documents in a visual and rhetorical dance, accompanying, prolonging, and legitimizing the initial message.

Conceived in this way, the study of the format of documents is not limited to the measurement of the height and width of the support used, nor is it merely a question of assigning the documents to some deceptively simplified categories: a document taller than it is wide (that is, short lines of writing running parallel to the shorter dimension of the support; called in Latin *carta transversa*, in German *Hochformat*); a document wider than it is tall (Latin *carta non transversa*, German *Querformat*); a nearly square document (German *Quadrat*). Rather, this study makes sense when connected to other data: the ratio of width to height (this is more meaningful because of the differences in length of texts, revealed by the overall surface dimension), the relation of empty margin to written surface, and additionally, in the case of parchment, the regularity of the cut edges, the thickness of the support, the height of the fold to which the seal is attached, etc. Once this data has been tabulated in order to identify patterns, other questions arise which allow one to add nuance to the interpretation and to make progress in comprehending intentionality (on the part of the producer) and reception or decoding (on the part of the person at whom the document is directed, or among the public associated with the promulgation of the document). Such questions are: Do the rules generated in a chancellery tolerate deviations? Do they move in the direction of normalization and regularity which for a long time largely elude written rules? Further, do they betray influences, a desire to imitate which goes beyond the chance arrival of a new redactor?

Appropriately, the early results indicate a fascinating playfulness and strong currents of imitation in sovereign chancelleries (traits that had already been observed in regards to the seal, the language, and the spelling). In the domain of private documents, they reveal variations that often cannot be ascribed to a simple evolution. These early results also allow us to discern a variety of tendencies and of abrupt changes; they suggest few certainties but offer strong insights on problems with broad implications, e.g., working methods, supervision, susceptibility to the innovations of "professional" scribes, diffusion and reception of fashions, and status and functions of writing. It is also true that anachronism and overinterpretation are constant hazards in analyzing a body of material so limited, so isolated, in a domain which mixes—as do all products of medieval writing—secular traditions, abrupt or progressive discontinuities, constraints imposed by the writing support, the desire to communicate, etc.[1]

Along with papyrus, the early Middle Ages inherited and followed a series of ancient traditions, some of whose conventions are linked to the format of documents. Papyrus, which is more amenable to use than parchment, yet is constrained in one of its dimensions by the methods employed in its manufacture and marketing, accommodates long texts and makes use of two radically opposed formats: one where the width of the written space is expanded (the very elongated format of Merovingian royal precepts, whose layout is derived from documents executed by the provincial civil servants of the empire), the other where the elongation is in the height of the written space (seen, for example, in pontifical privileges, in Byzantine practice, and in the private documents from Ravenna). The period of the "barbarian" kingdoms, for the most part limited to the Merovingian kingdoms, is well explored and suggestive, in spite of the limited number and the chronological imbalance of the surviving examples; nonetheless, the 38 original documents that are preserved allowed Irmgard Fees (1992) to make some subtle observations. When parchment abruptly replaces papyrus in the 670s, there is an immediate change. Minor royal documents (notices of judgment, *tractorie*, regarding fiscal exemptions) announce their limited and practical character in a systematic fashion by a format that is taller than it is wide. On the other hand, precepts, which are solemn and enduring documents, recapture their traditional format from the age of papyrus only gradually and with some detours along the way.[2] See the diagrams in Fees, 1992, 226–7. Once they became kings, the descendants of Pepin and then the Carolingians adopted once again this format (elongated in width), denoting majesty, a clear proof of the existence of an implicit code in the formatting of documents.

This code changes progressively in the course of the long tenth century, though the precise chronological and geographical distinctions have yet to be studied in detail. The evolution, inaugurated under the Ottonians, apparently spreads to the popes in their first use of parchment (in 967, but far from Rome), and from there it influences episcopal documents. It also spreads to royal chanceries, where the format that is taller than it is wide, but only slightly taller (that is to say, almost square), by the beginning of the twelfth century denotes majesty and solemnity (it does so in association with an increase in overall dimensions of the documents, an increased effort at symmetry, an increase in graphic ornamentation, extensive use of blank space, greater emphasis placed on the seal and the monogram, etc.) These are all traits which characterize, until their disappearance in the fourteenth century, precepts, privileges, and other diplomas (passing also, in the course of the twelfth century, to charters and other letters), which had been characterized originally by a format wider than it is tall, signaling the everyday govern-ment. In sum, the code has radically changed from that in force in the early Middle Ages.[3]

In contrast, the field of private documents from the fifth to the twelfth century, which is vast and only now beginning to be addressed, is marked by an insurmountable diversity, resulting from several factors: local or regional traditions; personal habits or the habits of a scriptorium; economic constraints, which often led to the use of informal scraps of parchment (Fig. 39.1), until some Italian notaries and princely chanceries, such as that of Savoy, intentionally played up the natural irregularities in the shape of the parchment (Plate 39.1). The same context, between the eighth and the eleventh centuries, in Catalonia and in Rhetia, resulted in multiple legal documents being transcribed on the same uncut sheet. A different study by Irmgard Fees (1991), on private documents from the archives of St Gall, demonstrates clearly that there is no regularized practice: from 719 to 919 the production of eight redactors (among the best documented) are divided between 643 parchments wider than they are tall, 25 taller than they are wide, and 20 that are square. The tendency, which is exacerbated through the influence of model letters and of "writs" of all kinds, continues to reinforce the predominance of the wide format, wherever, as in royal chancelleries, a sliding scale of

FIG. 39.1 Document of a public scribe, region of Toulouse, 1192 (Paris, Arch. nat., J 304, n° 27, repr. École nat. des chartes, lithographie AF 405).

signification associates the very wide format with the daily domain, with the injunction, and associates the format that is, relatively speaking, elongated in height with solemnity of discourse (with the princely decision and the notarial report). Definitively in place in the fourteenth century, this code has continued to influence practices up to the present day. As Peter Rück (personal communication) remarked, the professional patent placed by his barber on the wall of his shop has the exact format of the royal charters of the fourteenth century. Even more frequently encountered are the checks and banknotes which preserve the format of the commands and receipts produced in abundance from the twelfth century. (Plate 39.2)

The importance of these shifts, which still have not been studied in detail, entails, as do the other aspects of the presentation and the text of documents, a progressive normalization (at work apparently in the twelfth century and noteworthy in the thirteenth century) from one producer to another as well as within a single chancery. This implicit, even spontaneous normalization is illuminated in a celebrated passage from Conrad de Mure (1275) dealing with the cutting of parchment by the redactor: *ne latitudo nec longitudo modum debitum excedant et mensuram sicut archa Noe . . . jussu Dei artificialiter et proportionaliter composita fuit et compacta* (Let neither the width nor the height exceed the appropriate size and measure, just as the ark of Noah . . . by God's command was constructed and fashioned artfully and proportionally). The recipes that were followed in the workshops for establishing the formats, in any case, can only be flushed out by a systematic campaign of measurement in the archives (Bischoff 1996).

Finally, it should be pointed out that the close of the Middle Ages, at least from the fourteenth century, witnessed the complete triumph of the great medieval inventions in the realm of authenticating documents, the seal and the notarial sign. These allowed, in response to the elongation of texts, an exceeding of the constraints previously imposed by the size of the skin (constraints which made parchment written on one side of a

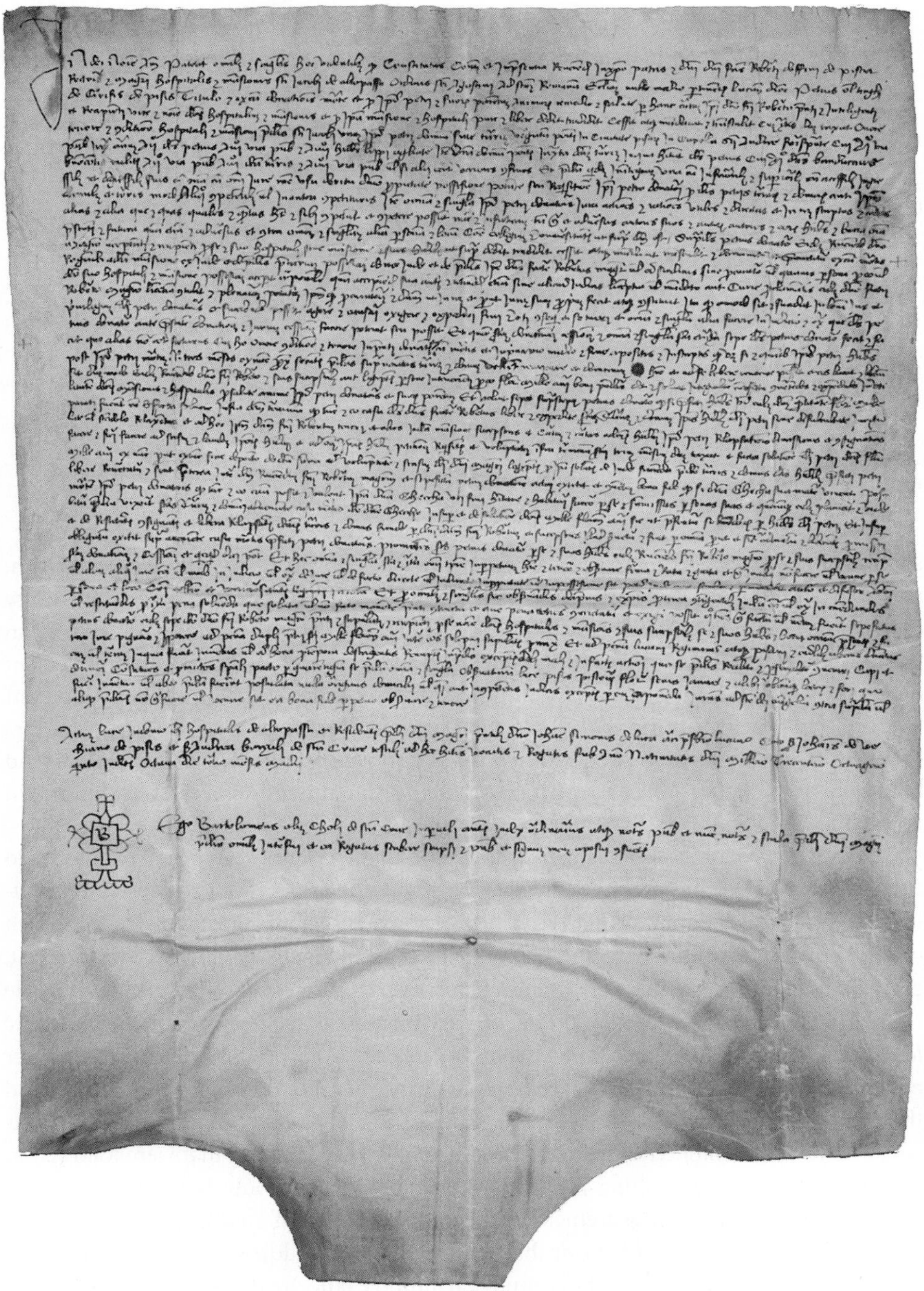

PLATE 39.1 Document of an Italian imperial notary, diocese of Lucca, 1385 (New York, Columbia University, Rare Book and Manuscript Division, Smith 157).

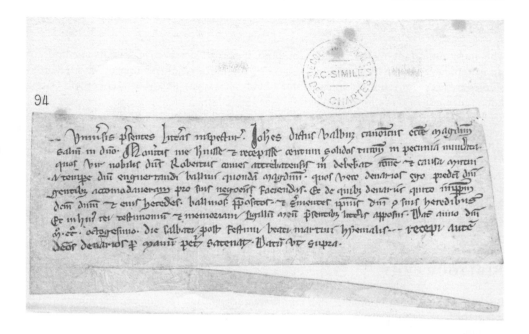

PLATE 39.2 Bill of Acquittal granted to the comte d'Artois, 1280 (Arch. dép. Pas-de-Calais, repr. Musée des Archives départementales, Paris, 1888, n° 94); contemporary banknote (private collection).

single sheet the close cousin of ancient inscriptions). For at that time, documents begin to be written on several pieces of parchment glued or sewn from head to foot, a practice taken over from the realm of libraries and administrative archives. This practice had previously been rare, but from this time onward each passage on a new sheet was authenticated by a seal or a marginal signature. Additionally, longer documents were written in booklets (authenticated by a seal made possible by the passage of the fastener through the bottom or the center of the quire). Although they remained limited, these practices had an influential posterity.

Suggested Reading

The most important modern study, for both its broad perspective and its methods of measurement and statistical analysis, is that of Bischoff (1996). Among other specialized studies are Fees (1991, esp. 83–4) and (1992), Lübbecke (1992), and Martín López and García Lobo (2012, esp. 99–153 for deeds).

Notes

1. See, e.g., Bischoff 1996, 78.
2. See the diagrams in Fees, 1992, 226–7.
3. See the diagrams in Bischoff, 1996, 55 and 66.

Bibliography

Bischoff, F. M. 1996. *Urkundenformate im Mittelalter: Grösse, Format und Proportionen von Papsturkunden in Zeiten expandierender Schriftlichkeit (11.–13. Jahrhundert)* (Elementa diplomatica, 5). Marburg an der Lahn: Institut für Historische Hilfswissenschaften.

Fees, I. 1991. "Die Pergamente des St. Galler Urkunden (8.–10. Jahrhundert): ein praktischer Versuch zur Bestimmung von Tierhäuten." In *Pergament: Geschichte, Struktur, Restaurierung, Herstellung* (Historische Hilfswissenschaften, 2), ed. P. Rück. Sigmaringen: Jan Thorbecke.

Fees, I. 1992. "Die Matrix der abendländischen Herrscherurkunde: Format und Layout der Merowingerdiplome." In *Mabillons Spur, Zweiundzwanzig Miszellen aus dem Fachgebiet für Historische Hilfswissenschaften der Philipps-Universität Marburg zum 80. Geburtstag von Walter Heinemeyer*, ed. P. Rück, 213–29. Marburg an der Lahn: Institut für Historische Hilfswissenschaften.

Lichtbildarchiv älterer Originalurkunden, Marburg: http://lba.hist.uni-marburg.de/lba/, accessed January 29, 2020.

Lübbecke, I. 1992. "Formate lothringischer Grafenurkunden 1091–1250." In *Mabillons Spur, Zweiundzwanzig Miszellen aus dem Fachgebiet für Historische Hilfswissenschaften der Philipps-Universität Marburg zum 80. Geburtstag von Walter Heinemeyer*, ed. P. Rück, 247–51. Marburg an der Lahn: Institut für Historische Hilfswissenschaften.

Martín López, M. E. and V. García Lobo, eds. 2012. *Impaginatio en las inscripciones medievales*. León: Universidad de León.

Rück, P. 1991."Die Urkunde als Kunstwerk." In *Kaiserin Theophanu: Begegnung des Ostens und Westens um die Wende des ersten Jahrtausends*: Gedenkschrift des Kölner Schnütgen-Museums zum 1000. Todesjahr der Kaiserin, ed. Anton von Euw and Peter Schreiner, vol. 2, 311–33. Cologne: Das Museum [= *Ausgewählte Aufsätze zum 65. Geburtstag von Peter Rück* (Elementa diplomatica, 9), ed. Erika Eisenlohr and Peter Worm, 117–39. Marburg an der Lahn: Institut für Historische Hilfswissenschaften, 2000].

CHAPTER 40

THE APPLICATION OF QUANTITATIVE METHODS TO THE HISTORY OF THE BOOK

EZIO ORNATO

(Translated by Robert G. Babcock and Frank T. Coulson)

IN the expression "quantitative codicology," coined by me and Carla Bozzolo, it is questionable which of the two terms is more ambiguous, since in my opinion both, in their commonly accepted meaning, are incomplete and restrictive. Although the term "codicology" is usually reserved for the study of the manuscript, I believe that this discipline should apply to all material aspects of all types of books, regardless of their form (codex, roll, or otherwise), their purpose (literary or documentary), or their method of reproduction (handwritten, xylographic, or typographic).[1] As to the term "quantitative," it is necessary to stress that it should be understood in its broadest sense: it should be applied not only to strictly numerical data but to everything which can be measured in a book. The concept of "measurement" is itself very broad. It may imply the metrical value of a parameter (e.g., a folio measures 200 × 150 mm; a page has 35 written lines), but the term may also be applied to a qualitative characteristic in an established system of classification, which may or may not be hierarchical. Thus, the measurement of a property such as "the color of the binding" may yield such results as "yellow," "green," "violet," etc., whereas that of "the type of initial" may be classified as "historiated," "painted," or "filigree," which is directly related to a hierarchical scale of richness.

This enlarged definition of the concept of measurement implies that everything in a book is theoretically measurable, or, better yet, that each characteristic observed in a book may be formalized to extract measureable data from it, provided it is worth the effort. Even a piece of information as complex and discursive as that which we derive from the colophons of the copyists may be split up into formal data: the date is of utmost importance, but its degree of precision (mention of the year, month, day) and the manner of expressing it (modern, Roman, or liturgical calendar) are not without interest if the objective is not only to take note of the year the book was written, but to examine closely, in a systematic manner, the behavior of the copyist in relation to the dating of the manuscript.

These operations of measurement often require a considerable initial effort of conceptual elaboration, and their results are never perfect—what should be measured, how should the measurement be made? They also require long and detailed surveys, either by autoptic examination or by combing through catalogues (when they exist and the descriptions are sufficiently detailed and trustworthy). But contrary to what one may think, it is not the numerical character and the application of more or less refined statistical techniques that lie at the heart of the quantitative approach. Its salient traits are rather the nature of the survey and of the problems tackled, as well as the specificity of the procedures employed to answer the questions posed.

It is true that the novelty of this approach was not immediately obvious. Codicology is a relatively recent discipline, and it is even more recently that it has attained a status of relative autonomy. Earlier scholars relegated the study of the material aspects of the book (when it was not willfully ignored) to the sphere of "auxiliary disciplines." Codicology was thus subordinated to the primary goal of dating and localizing a volume. In this context, even an innovation as revolutionary as the computer, far from thwarting this vision of things, could only strengthen it. It was hoped that computers would allow us instantly to bring together data, previously unobtainable because of the slowness of the human brain, for establishing more impressive and more objective criteria for dating and localizing. This prospect was illusory. The know-how of the medieval craft being too uniform at any given time and its evolution too slow across time, the attempt to come up with better results by this method than those that could be obtained from the intuition of a skillful observer proved fruitless. Even if it is true that new issues and practices could not emerge in the absence of the technological tools necessary to make use of them (the organ often creates the function and not the reverse), it is also true that the presence of these tools was not sufficient to ensure the development.

However, all the ingredients came together at once to produce change. On the one hand, the necessity, imposed by the "stupidity" of the machines, of dealing with strictly formalized data, i.e., data that is rigorously classified and uniformly codified; and on the other hand, the need to focus our attention on vast quantities of objects and not solely on certain individual ones chosen for their distinctive qualities. It was, therefore, inevitable that a new way of looking at books would lead sooner or later to our asking questions which we could now answer. For example, it was only when dated manuscripts were catalogued in sufficient numbers that we could think of tallying them up year by year to establish curves of production.[2] Similarly, it was only when we could deal simultaneously and rapidly with the characteristics of several hundred manuscripts that we could see that the volumes with a two-column layout were in general bigger than those with a single-column format, written in long lines.

In spite of their apparent simplicity, these two examples reveal the profound essence of the quantitative approach, so different in every respect from the methodology of connoisseurship or of traditional scholarly methods, namely, (1) the collection of data which is, in and of itself, very uninformative—and thereby totally devoid of interest when taken singularly—but which we encounter again and again in all, or nearly all, of the volumes; and (2) the absence of any hierarchy within the material studied, the great monuments of cultural history having the same anonymity as the most modest documents. But above all, the quantitative approach takes into account problems which the traditional scholarly method shows itself intrinsically inadequate to address, and it asks questions that aim not at constituting facts and establishing relationships between them but at revealing unknown phenomena or at organizing observations of known phenomena so as to disclose the factors that influenced them. In other words, it is less a question of establishing the "who," "when," "where," and "how" and more of establishing the "why".

This aspect, which could rightly be called "sociological,"[3] is at the heart of the quantitative approach. Just as sociology studies people collectively and under diverse perspectives in their roles as members of a society so as to reveal the roots and the dynamic of their behavior, quantitative codicology studies collectively and under diverse perspectives the "behavior" of books as functional objects destined to transmit a message. To study means first of all to describe in a systematic manner the results of observations. However, if one is to study the "why," it is obvious that the tabular or graphic description of a phenomenon, perhaps accompanied by a verbal paraphrase, only constitutes a first step and has nothing to do, in spite of its usefulness, with the profound philosophy of the approach, a philosophy which is necessarily strategic and "experimental." This last term should be taken in its weakest sense: it is not possible to experiment physically on the remnants of the past to test a hypothesis, and it is even less possible to go back in time to study the surviving books as they existed in the past. It is possible, however, and indeed necessary, to change the light we shine on a body of material, and therefore our perspective, with the aid of more or less elaborate filters. When we study the forms of appearance of any specific characteristic to determine its frequency in a population of books, the simplest procedure is to divide the material being studied on the basis of some other characteristic. We may then see if this division engenders a significant variation of the characteristic being studied. If no such division appears to be meaningful, we must conclude that the characteristic being studied is the product of free will, associated with coincidental phenomena such as fashion, or that it depends on restrictive factors but ones that are exterior to the process of the making of the book, or perhaps even of the cultural sphere. If, however, the division proves meaningful, we may suppose that the two characteristics are linked.

In reality, things are much less clear, for even at its simplest level this type of procedure is full of booby traps. The fact that the behavior of one characteristic varies contingent upon that of another does not mean that one depends *uniquely* on the other, nor that one depends *directly* on the other, nor even that the two characteristics are in reality linked. One example will suffice to show how slippery the ground is in this respect and to underline the need to proceed with caution.

If the layout of the text in long lines or in two columns is correlated to the dimensions of the pages, this certainly reveals that the factor of size is what we call a "contributing factor." But are we, in fact, dealing with the real "guilty" party or at least a single "guilty" party? Nothing is less certain, for numerous characteristics of the page, including the script, are scaled to the size of the page. Thus, the height of the ruled writing space—which depends to a large degree on that of the page—might be a more adequate "guilty party," for it is one of the major elements of the layout. However, it is also the case that even when the height of the ruled writing area is short, the volumes may tend toward the two-column format—which seems to contradict the hypothesis. This happens when there are many lines and the writing is small. So, in the end, it is necessary to ask what the purpose of this layout is: since the two-column layout divides in half the length of the lines of writing, it is likely that its purpose is to preserve the legibility of the page.[4] This raises another question: what is legibility? Or rather, how can we translate the abstract and subjective concept of legibility into concrete and measureable terms, in other words, into pertinent and efficient "indicators?"[5] It is clear that as we investigate the problem more deeply, the situation becomes more and more nuanced and complex.

But that is not the worst of it: we must constantly be aware of the possibility that the results obtained through statistical analysis and the investigation of explanatory factors may be wrong in a more or less subtle manner due to what are commonly called "structural effects." There are cases in which the statistical analysis is not defective and the numbers are exact, but the interpretation is wrong because the connections made between one parameter and another only appear to be relevant.

In the quantitative study of written culture, the effects of structure are omnipresent. Often, however, and contrary to what we might think, they do not arise from faulty sampling on the part of the historian. Rather they flow objectively from the selective character of the centuries-long process of dispersion and loss of the book patrimony, a process whose forms and conditions we must understand. If we agree that most loss is due to negligence and not to intentional destruction or natural disasters, it follows that the survival of books is strictly linked to their sale value. This cannot be separated from the aesthetic evaluation of the object.[6] But, if it is relatively easy to detect the direct effects of this non-egalitarian process (even if it is impossible to correct them), their secondary effects are more difficult to apprehend. The loss of the poorest manuscripts does not just reverberate only on parameters like price,[7] which depend directly on the richness of execution, but also on phenomena seemingly more distant.

Here is an example related to book size: If we observe in the course of the fifteenth century an increase in the relative percentage of liturgical manuscripts, we should be suspicious of the result. The processes of destruction and loss disproportionately affected volumes on paper—which had become, little by little, the principal writing support—and resulted in an overrepresentation of surviving manuscripts on parchment, which was the material used almost exclusively for liturgical manuscripts.[8]

Likewise, we should be suspicious of assessments of the increased use of paper in the book production of Italy, for the calculations are based on the catalogues of dated manuscripts, and these have been for a long time systematically biased. Until quite recently there were few volumes in the Italian series of catalogues of dated manuscripts, so the calculations concerning Italy were based on the books conserved in foreign libraries, libraries which, because of pillaging and the activity of collectors, are filled with volumes on parchment whose qualitative level is excellent.[9]

From the preceding, it appears that the essence of the quantitative approach does not lie in the precision of the observation and measurement, nor in the massive application of statistical tests of validation, though both are necessary. Rather, it lies in the imagination we employ in choosing strategies for achieving unequivocal answers and in ferreting out the artifacts which might, otherwise, insidiously skew the results. These are, relatively speaking and *mutatis mutandis*, the same principles which govern research in the universally recognized experimental disciplines.

The few examples which follow are intended to illustrate various problems confronted by a quantitative codicologist and the procedures adopted to resolve them, as well as the difficulties, often insurmountable, which impede the researcher's curiosity. They also demonstrate the absolute necessity of knowing in detail the world of the medieval book, in its material aspects as well as its historic and cultural environment. It is intentional, in light of the unifying principle of quantitative research on the book, that one of the examples involves the printed book.

Quantifying Medieval Book Production

In theory, what could be simpler than quantifying the level of book production in Western Europe?[10] We need only count up, year by year, the number of dated volumes to produce very detailed graphs; and these—even if we take into account that the number of volumes does not acquire statistical significance until the later Middle Ages—extend over nearly two centuries. This operation does not require detailed statistical manipulations: if the annual tally is too small, we may regroup the data in periods of five or ten years. Similarly, chance fluctuations may easily be smoothed over, should the occasion arise, by calculating moving averages.

The idea, elementary as it is, of calculating the annual level of manuscript production is impossible without one reliable tool, namely the repertory of dated manuscripts. Fortunately, by the 1970s, the number of catalogues published since the inauguration of the project in 1953 had reached a sufficient level that it became possible to make such a calculation, at least for certain countries.[11] However, behind the simplicity of the statistical apparatus hides a complex historical reality, the central problem being: how representative is the corpus of dated manuscripts available to the researcher?

It is necessary to take into account that the extant manuscript patrimony is but a small fraction of the quantity of volumes produced; that the volumes having a date are only a small part of the extant patrimony; that neither the general cataloguing of the extant patrimony nor that of the dated manuscripts is exhaustive at the present time. This multistage filter created by the destructive work of time and by the inevitable gaps in reporting would not be significant if the reduction of the population at each step was uniform relative to the initial state. But this is not the case. We know for a fact—in part from the study of incunables where we can count the remaining copies of an edition and compare that to the press run (when known)—that losses varied in severity as a result of the type of text (and, therefore, of the intended audience). Moreover, as we have seen, comparison between the inventories of old libraries and the surviving books demonstrates that the losses were much heavier for less expensive volumes. Finally, soundings taken at regular intervals in certain catalogued collections demonstrate that the percentage of dated manuscripts varies in accordance with both chronology (it increased over time) and geography.

These important distortions make it difficult to interpret the collected data. The trick is to understand what we can reasonably expect to get from the data and what, on the contrary, might lead to erroneous extrapolations. Thus, it would be very hazardous to compare for one particular period the level of production in different countries because the tendency to record a date in a manuscript is geographically sensitive.[12] One may, on the contrary, but with great prudence, sketch the underlying or cyclical trends of production within the same country, if one takes into account the fact that the rate of dating may quickly increase in time—which will lead to an overestimate—or that the percentage of manuscripts on paper—which have been destroyed in great numbers—also increases in time, which leads, on the contrary, to an underestimate. In other words, it is imperative that this type of analysis avoid venturing too far into detail and losing sight of the fact that quantitative studies always presuppose an excellent knowledge of the historical background and of its development.

Typographical Composition
in the Early Printing Shops

We commonly assume that, as with the majority of manuscripts, ancient editions were composed and printed page by page in the "natural" sequence of reading.[13] In fact, the reality is more complicated. For reasons of productivity, the text to be printed was often divided into parts and distributed to two or more teams working simultaneously. Even so, we might still suppose that, within each working group, each signature was composed following the natural order. But this was not always the case. It has been established that in certain German editions printed between 1460 and 1470, the pages of the recto were systematically set up before the pages of the verso.[14] From the middle of the following decade, what had earlier been an exception became the rule: the signatures were never put together and printed in the order of reading. Two phenomena combined to produce this result. Firstly, the invention of the "two-strike" press allowed the near simultaneous printing of two pages of a folio edition, (or four of a quarto edition, etc.). These pages appeared side by side on the folded sheet, but did not follow the sequence of reading.[15] Secondly, the quantity of characters available was not sufficient to allow composing all the pages of a book before the printing of the first forms commenced. Each form, once printed, had of necessity to be disassembled, so that the characters could be reused immediately. Thus, in the case of a folio printing, pages 1 and 16 of a quire—far apart in the text—had to be set at the same time.

The discovery of these disturbances in the work of composition were made by observation of macroscopic phenomena: irregularities in the number of lines on a page and/or in the leading; systematic variations in the composition of the form (certain characters are systematically present on some pages and not on others). But how can we identify the sequence of composition when, as is nearly always the case, we do not have this type of information? To answer this question, it is necessary to analyze the procedures of the typesetters. When pages are set in the sequence of reading, the setters have considerable freedom. When not, they must take into account the already printed pages, which establish inviolable boundaries. To reduce to a minimum the risk that a text being composed would turn out too long or too short relative to the available space, the typesetters needed to make advance calculations of the length of the text and, above all, make adjustments as the work proceeded to ensure that the estimate corresponded to reality.

The simplest means of adjustment involved the use of abbreviations. If the text being set was too long for the space available, the number of abbreviations employed was increased. In the opposite case, it was reduced. Since the parameter "number of abbreviations" is sensitive to the slightest error of calculation, it follows that the variations in the number of abbreviations—represented statistically by the variance—are a reliable witness to the sequence of the composition of the text, even when the typesetter encountered no real difficulty. The pages where variation is significantly more than the average are those which precede pages that had already been printed. The counting of abbreviations in several quires is necessary to assure that the pages where the variations are more significant are systematically the same, and that it is not a question of accidental influences.[16]

THICKNESS OF PARCHMENT AND THE ORGANIZATION OF QUIRES IN A MANUSCRIPT BOOK

The thickness of parchment can only be correctly determined by a measuring instrument, since touching only provides data that is useable—at a very rudimentary level—when the differences between the bifolia of a single quire or of a single book, or between the leaves of several books, are macroscopic.[17] Measuring the thickness allows, first of all, an assessment of the variations of this parameter in space and time, as well as in respect to other characteristics of the volumes (dimensions and number of pages, qualitative level). It can also allow the lifting of the veil on certain practices related to the formation and organization of quires. More particularly, it may answer the following question: did the artisans pay attention to this material aspect while they were making books (even though they did not have precise instruments for measuring the thickness of parchment)? If so, to what end? In principle, their awareness could be revealed in two ways: within quires, by modulating differences in thickness vis-à-vis the order of the bifolia, and within the volume by enforcing a uniformity of thickness on the bifolia belonging to the same quire.

Given the irregularities which affect the surface of a skin (especially close to the spine of the animal), the measurement of the thickness should be taken at several points on each bifolium, and should be repeated on a large number of bifolia belonging to a large number of manuscripts. The answer to our question about the artisans of books is easiest to answer when we are dealing with folio volumes, for in this case each bifolium corresponds to a skin. The calculation does not require a complex procedure. It will be observed that there is a tendency—but not always and not everywhere[18]—to place the thickest bifolia at the outside of the quire. This technique should not surprise us. It has the same purpose as another practice which is visible to the naked eye and which gives rise to manuscripts which are called "mixed," where the outside bifolia are made of parchment, while the inner ones are paper. The goal is to place the sturdiest material on the outside of the quire, which is exposed to the most wear and tear.

The verification of the internal homogeneity of quires, on the other hand, is more complicated. One must determine if the bifolia of the same quire are more like one another than they are like those of different quires belonging to the same volume, and if the quires belonging to the same volume resemble one another more than they do those belonging to another volume.

Several procedures allow us to answer these questions. These are all founded on the measure not of the resemblance but, on the contrary, of the variability whose statistical indicator is the variance.[19] One relatively elegant method involves creating fictive quires by randomly mixing real bifolia from other quires of the same volume (in the same way that we shuffle a deck of cards). The comparison between the "artificial" quires and the real quires shows that the variance is significantly larger in the first. The experiment may be repeated in a more elaborate fashion to demonstrate that the variance increases proportionately when one, two, or several bifolia are replaced in a real quire, with bifolia from another quire. And this increase is even greater if the replacement bifolia come from quires that belong to a different manuscript.

It appears, then, so far as parchment is concerned, that the artisanal practice aimed at producing a high degree of homogeneity. The making of a manuscript involved the choice of a "set" of skins which were as homogeneous as possible, and within each manuscript, even more homogeneous subsets were selected to make up each quire.

Finally, where the level of professionalism was the highest, the bifolia within each quire were arranged according to their thickness.

On the methodological level, this type of research contradicts in part the received notion that the quantitative approach in the social sciences differs radically from that in physics, chemistry, or biology, where one can alter at will the conditions of the experiment. Here, the mixing of bifolia is assuredly virtual, but it is certainly an experimental procedure.

RECIPES OR FORMULAS FOR CALCULATING THE PAGE LAYOUT IN MEDIEVAL MANUSCRIPTS

Everyone who leafs through medieval manuscripts is aware that their layout is substantially the same as that of modern-day books, that is, it contains a frame intended to enclose the lines of writing (perhaps divided into two columns) within a four-sided border of margins.[20] One difference, however, is that the division of the written space in the manuscripts is achieved through a series of perpendicular lines traced with the aid of various instruments, as well as by prickings which allow the identical layout to be reproduced on every page of the quire.

The construction of the layout was of necessity the product of prior planning, if only because the degree to which the page is filled and used determines the number of pages needed for a copy, and thus the quantity of parchment or paper needed to produce it. That said, we may wonder how the base parameters were chosen and what the construction methods were.

In answer to these questions, it is possible to hypothesize that, at least in rather carefully worked out instances, the layout resulted from applying elaborate aesthetic canons based on the construction of rectangles with "remarkable" proportions (the golden rectangle, the Pythagorean rectangle, etc.).[21] But the documentary evidence, namely a very small number of medieval recipes, suggests that the procedure followed was much less ambitious. And, surprisingly, in none of the recipes are the dimensions of the frame of writing even mentioned. Determining the dimensions of the frame is done solely with reference to the relative size of the various margins.[22] The focus on the margins is so complete that the dimensions of the frame of writing constitute only a byproduct. This is the case, notably, in two of the oldest recipes: one called "the recipe of St. Remi" (ninth century) and the other "the recipe of Munich" (fifteenth century).[23]

Be that as it may, the question arises: what is the real impact of these recipes? In theory, there are two possible answers to the question. They could be theoretical reflections, imposed after the fact, based on observation of the independent choices made by a great number of different artisans. Or they could just as well be the result of an isolated process, conforming to artificial geometric principles and situated outside of actual practice.

An answer to this question can be obtained from a quantitative analysis conducted on a large group of manuscripts from different geographical areas and periods. The possibility of undertaking such a study is hindered by the fact that catalogues almost never provide the dimension of margins, but there are also immense methodological difficulties stemming from a simple fact. The margins are, without a doubt, the most elusive parameter of the book, given that the outer margins were likely to be trimmed during each successive rebinding, and because the inner margins are hard to measure because of the sewing of the quires. Furthermore, when we compare the margins we have measured to what we find in the recipes, we must also take into account the lack of precision which characterizes the craftsmanship of the medieval book. These difficulties are all the more formidable because we must evaluate the relationship between two sizes. In this context, even the smallest alteration in the base parameters—regardless of their origin—has a considerable impact on the value of the derived parameter.

So, the only solution is to test the validity of the recipes by determining for each of the four margins a range of uncertainty (in absolute terms and in percentage). If all the margins of the volume fall within the range, we may conclude that its layout is compatible with one or the other of the recipes. By applying this methodology, it becomes clear that there is a close match between the recipe of St Remi and the layout of Byzantine manuscripts, and that there is an ever closer match between Western manuscripts and the recipe of Munich as one advances in time.

Without the introduction of a margin of error, very few manuscripts would have successfully passed the test and one could have concluded that the recipes had no link with the real practice of the artisans. This type of investigation reveals one of the basic principles of quantitative studies, namely, that one should not confuse statistics with mathematics. Sometimes precision is not synonymous with better understanding, and sometimes it is quite the contrary.

The Rhythms of the Scribe: The Gospels of Henry the Lion

Palaeographical studies which concentrate on the morphological evolution of scripts pay scant attention to a whole range of phenomena related to what one might call "the conquest of space," that is, the devices employed by the scribes to modify their work plan in relation to the available space: the segmentation of the text in quires, pages, and lines; the relationship of text and illustration or of text and gloss.[24] These mechanisms of adaptation are numerous and varied. One of them consists simply in compressing or expanding the plan by making the size of each letter or graphic sign smaller or larger, or by compressing/enlarging the amount of blank space between the individual signs or words. Sometimes, these adjustments are macroscopic—which leads the observer to attribute them to a lack of professionalism—but in other cases they are not evident to the naked eye.

The scribe Herimann—who, in the second half of the twelfth century, transcribed the text of the Gospels of Duke Henry the Lion—certainly did not suffer from a lack of professionalism. However, in this sumptuous manuscript, the adjustments of the work plan are everywhere evident. Is this a question of accidents along the way, or is it rather the coherent result of a conscious effort on the part of the scribe vis-à-vis a predetermined "road map"? To answer this question—and above all to uncover the motivations and the goals of the scribe's behavior—we should not be content with a visual assessment, which will of necessity be imprecise and subjective.

If it is a question of predetermined adjustments, we may suppose that their nature is in part cyclical, in the sense that they come round at regular intervals. But measuring these possible fluctuations is not simple. They are generally muted and, additionally, they overlap. Let us consider, as a point of comparison, climate variations: the temperature measurements evolve according to a general "trend" (at the present time, heating-up) that is part of the regular seasonal variations that are, in turn, influenced by daily fluctuations, the whole being subject to the vagaries of inter-annual variations of daily averages which constitute, in some way, a background noise. One can say the same for economic variables (industrial production, unemployment) whose values are constantly corrected according to seasonal variations.

Statistical techniques provide a means for addressing this difficulty but, in this instance, they are not easy to employ. In the case of writing, in particular, there is a major obstacle: since it is impossible to measure the width of every letter in the entire manuscript, we must instead take broader measurements of the "density" of the writing, that is, the number of letters within a certain amount of space (centimeters, lines, etc.). But, since the width is not the same for every letter of the alphabet, the density can vary considerably vis-à-vis the frequency of each letter in a passage of a given text, and this occurs all the more if a passage is short. In longer passages, however, the frequency of occurrence of individual letters moves toward the average (for the language in question). We should, therefore, count the number of letters in a group of lines of writing, page by page, quire by quire, each sampling of lines being long enough to reduce to a minimum the background noise. Preliminary experiments indicate that samplings of four to five lines suffice to reduce to a minimum the sampling fluctuations.

The calculations made on the basis of these samplings show the great flexibility of Herimann's work plan. In addition to the gradual expansion of the writing which is obvious up to quire 18, and the ad hoc adjustments related to the amount of ornament, we may observe the presence of an "intra-page" cycle (the writing is denser at the beginning of the page). Moreover, two other cycles are overlaid, though they are less pronounced. An "inter-page" cycle between the rectos and versos, mixed with an "inter-face" cycle between the sides of the skin.[25] In fact, the writing of Herimann is denser at the beginning of a page when it is found on the recto of a folio and on the "flesh" side of the skin. In addition, there are non-cyclical fluctuations which correspond to the frequency of certain sections of the text. Thus, the irregularities which might have been attributed to blunder, to negligence, or to fatigue demonstrate, on the contrary, an unwavering attention and a sagacious mastery of the plasticity of handwriting.

THE USE OF A RAKE AS AN INSTRUMENT FOR RULING

The number of lines per page is a piece of data that is found in nearly every modern catalogue description of a medieval manuscript.[26] Unfortunately, in the manuscripts in question, this parameter is often subject to considerable variation, which the catalogues address only imperfectly. If a single value is supplied, we can never be sure that it is really unique. If, on the other hand, a variable range is given, we cannot know whether we are dealing with systematic fluctuations between two values or, on the contrary, with the application of a norm within which there might be a certain number of exceptions. That said, when one knows the height of the frame of writing—a parameter which appears nowadays frequently in catalogues—this number indicates the "unit of ruling" (the distance between two ruled lines) and contributes, therefore, to measuring the degree of exploitation of the written page.

Since the calculation of the unit of ruling requires only a simple division, the use of the number of lines per page is common in quantitative procedures and does not entail a complex manipulation of data. A less obvious use of this parameter, and one that is somewhat roundabout, is however imaginable. It consists of correlating it with other characteristics which, at first sight, do not seem to have anything to do with it: the method of ruling (in relief, with lead, with ink) and the patterns of ruling (presence of "major" prickings above and/or below the frame of writing).

This type of approach is founded not on the potential irregularities of the statistical distribution of the number of lines, but on the probability that this will be a prime number (which is not divisible) or a multiple of 2, 3, 4 ... n.[27] One may then compare this probability, in a great number of manuscripts, with the frequencies actually observed; in this case, in the several thousand volumes catalogued by Albert Derolez in his work on parchment manuscripts in Humanistic script.[28]

The results of this comparison are particularly significant in the case of ruling in ink, which in the fifteenth century could be accomplished by means of rakes with a variable number of teeth.[29] In fact, when a rake is used, the number of lines should of necessity correspond to a multiple of the number of teeth (which excludes the possibility that it might be a prime number). It will always be a question of an even number if the comb has an even number of teeth. If the number of teeth is odd, the number of lines will be odd one time out of two, with the result that the total of evenly ruled pages will represent 75% of the cases.

The results obtained coincide with the theoretical predictions. This allows the supposition that the use of the rake was very widespread in the fifteenth century, at least in Italy. This is, of course, a global finding and cannot replace direct examination if one wants to know whether a particular volume was ruled with the aid of a rake. The existence on the page of concrete evidence for the use of a rake is far from common, so a study founded solely on such evidence would result in an underassessment of the extent of this practice.

These examples sufficiently demonstrate the vast expanse of the horizon potentially covered by quantitative codicology and, at the same time, the enormous gulf which separates it from traditional approaches, both in the nature of the problems it addresses, and in the procedures of scientific induction it employs. Indeed, this gulf is very difficult to breach, and its existence explains the limited enthusiasm the new approach has aroused in the scholarly community, both in daily practice and in teaching. This attitude, which might be called "abstention," is regularly justified by the claim that quantitative codicology is not problematic per se, but it is a very specialized field, reserved for those well versed in mathematics. It appears to many that it is a daunting mountain, too difficult to scale.

In reality, there are sometimes deep ideological roots to this resistance, which may be imbued with a hierarchy that values the spiritual realm over the material, the prototype more than the replica, the rare over the common, the famous more than the anonymous, the flamboyant more than the modest, the unexpected more than the expected.

However, this effort to point out the radical differences between the two approaches does not imply that they are contrary one to another: far from it. Just as certain questions cannot be treated without having recourse to quantitative methods, there are others which require the deep and direct examination of the book as object. And we must not forget that the quantitative approach benefits from information acquired through expertise (dating, localization) and scholarly method, and above all from the irreplaceable documentation which the latter alone grants us. Lastly, we must insist on the fact that in the absence of a solid base of philological and historical knowledge, any use of tables, graphs, or factorial axes is fumbling in the dark and may give rise to serious misunderstandings. From this perspective, whatever may be the differences and fears, the quantitative codicologist is much closer to his colleagues in the humanities who avoid numbers than to computer scientists.

That said, quantitative codicology must avoid becoming too narrowly focused—only studying the object to know how it was made—thus reducing it to a simple branch of the history of technology, aimed solely at making restoration techniques more successful and more respectful of the object. We must, instead, enlarge our perspective as much as possible and view the materiality of the book as a double mirror: on the one hand, a reflection of economic, technological, and sociological factors, on the other, a reflection of its own purposes; some of these, like readability, are inextricably tied to its function, and others vary according to changes in cultural needs.

This is the only way to go beyond the history *of books*, or even of isolated parts of books (text, script, decoration, binding) and arrive at a history *of the book* which would be something more than a juxtaposition of monographic studies. We should aim at a *global* study, with the goal of understanding how the world of the book—defined as the ensemble formed by the object, its producers, and its consumers—functions; and above all why it functions as it does, caught between the hammer of innovation and the anvil of tradition. This history would also be *unitary*, inasmuch as all the complex and contradictory mechanisms which exert influence on the book would, in spite of everything, respect its primary function. Thus, regardless of the variety of forms of the object adopted in various times or places, and regardless of the technique of manufacture, its function—to ensure the proper transmission of a text—never varied, and it is this fact which allows us to undertake comparative studies, embracing multiple periods and cultural zones. And finally, this history would be *open*, for a study of an object so rich in connotations as the book is inseparable not only from that of the texts which it transmits and the authors who created them, but also that of the materials from which it is constructed, the tradesmen who fabricated it, the artists who illustrated it, the silent partners or entrepreneurs who financed it, the bookshops that sold it, the readers who consulted it, and the libraries that preserved it. This wide range of information, entered into specific databases but sufficiently standardized, would form a powerful network that the historian of written culture could consult and link with the greatest profit.

Notes

1. For an excellent overview of the genesis and evolution of codicology, see Gumbert (2004).
2. See Section 40.1.
3. See, in particular, Bozzolo and Ornato (1982).
4. On the functional aspects of text layout, see Bozzolo, Coq, Muzerelle, and Ornato (1984).
5. On this problem, see Bergeron and Ornato (1990).
6. See Bozzolo and Ornato (1981, 76–9 and 373–75), with reference to the very selective nature of the survival of manuscripts in the medieval library of the Sorbonne.
7. This is why the average price of a book differs significantly depending on whether it is based on medieval inventories or on the notations on the flyleaves of surviving volumes; see Bozzolo and Ornato (1981, 79–80).
8. For the great loss of paper manuscripts see Bozzolo and Ornato (1989).
9. The publication of the new series *Manoscritti datati d'Italia* (20 volumes published since 1996 ; for the list, see http://www.manoscrittidatati.it/, accessed January 30, 2020) allows us to correct the tally: from the end of the fourteenth century onward, most dated manuscripts conserved in Italian libraries are on paper.
10. For this topic, see Bozzolo (1994); Bozzolo, Coq, and Ornato (1984); Bozzolo and Ornato (1979), (1981); Coq and Ornato (1988); Ornato (1997).
11. For the list of volumes published to date see http://www.palaeographia.org/cipl/cmd.htm, accessed January 30, 2020.
12. It is usually higher in German countries.
13. See Coq and Ornato (1987).
14. See Jenkinson (1927, 56–8).

15. Except, of course, in the central two pages of each quire.

16. Such as the forced reinsertion of omitted pages discovered in correcting the proofs.

17. On this problem, see Bianchi *et al.* (1993); Bischoff (1993), (1994); Bischoff and Maniaci (1996).

18. One finds this practice in certain liturgical manuscripts of the eleventh century and law manuscripts of the thirteenth and fourteenth centuries.

19. The variance is the sum of the squares of the deviations from the mean divided by the size of the population.

20. On recipes, see Maniaci and Ornato (1993); Muzerelle (2009); Muzerelle *et al.* (1993).

21. See Gilissen (1977). For a critique of this type of approach, see Bozzolo, Coq, Muzerelle, and Ornato (1990b).

22. Software for word processing also requires us to define the layout of a document according to the margins.

23. Paris, BnF, lat. 11884 ; Munich, Bayerische Staatsbibliothek, clm 7775.

24. See Bischoff (1996).

25. In general, according to the so-called "law of Gregory ", the leaves within a quire of a medieval manuscript are disposed such that, on any given opening, a flesh side faces a flesh side or a hair side faces a hair side.

26. See Muzerelle (1989).

27. The probabilities depend on a well-known mathematical law, the binomial law, which allows one to calculate the probability that an event will occur *N* times in a series of repeated trials.

28. See Derolez (1984).

29. On the use of the comb, see Gumbert (1986); Casagrande Mazzoli (1997); Derolez (2000).

BIBLIOGRAPHY

Bergeron, R. and E. Ornato. 1990. "La Lisibilité dans les manuscrits et les imprimés de la fin du Moyen Âge. Préliminaires d'une recherche." *Scrittura e Civiltà* 14: 151–98 [republished in *La Face cachée*, pp. 521–54].

Bianchi, F., D. Buovolo, M. G. De' Caterina, M. Maniaci, L. Negrini. E. Ornato, M. Palma, and A. Pannega. 1993. "Facteurs de variation de l'épaisseur du parchemin italien du VIIIe au XVe siècle." In *Ancient and Medieval Book Materials and Techniques: Actes du colloque international, Erice, 18–25 septembre 1992*, ed. P. F. Munafò and M. Maniaci, 2 vols., I, 95–184. Vatican City: Biblioteca Apostolica Vaticana [republished in *La Face cachée*, pp. 275–345].

Bischoff, F. M. 1993. "Observations sur l'emploi de différentes qualités de parchemin dans les manuscrits médiévaux." In *Ancient and Medieval Book Materials and Techniques: Actes du colloque international, Erice, 18–25 septembre 1992*, ed. P. F. Munafò and M. Maniaci, 2 vols., I, 57–94, Vatican City: Biblioteca Apostolica Vaticana.

Bischoff, F. M. 1994. "Systematische Lagenbrüche: Kodikologische Untersuchungen zur Herstellung und zum Aufbau mittelalterliche Evangeliare." In *Rationalisierung der Buchherstellung im Mittelalter und in der frühen Neuzeit: Ergebnisse eines buchgeschichtlichen Seminars der Herzog August Bibliothek Wolfenbüttel 12.–14. November 1990*, ed. P. Rück and M. Boghardt, 83–110. Marburg an der Lahn: Institut für Historische Hilfswissenschaften.

Bischoff, F. M. 1996. "Le Rythme du scribe. Analyse sérielle de la densité de l'écriture dans les évangiles d'Henri le Lion." *Histoire & mesure* 11: 53–91.

Bischoff, F. M. and M. Maniaci. 1996. "Pergamentgröße, Handschriftenformate, Lagenkonstruktion. Anmerkungen zur Methodik und zu den Ergebnissen der jüngeren kodikologischen Forschung." *Scrittura e civiltà* 20: 277–319.

Bozzolo, C. 1994. "La Production manuscrite dans les pays rhénans au XVᵉ siècle à partir des manuscrits datés." *Scrittura e civiltà* 18: 183–242.

Bozzolo, C. and E. Ornato. 1979. "Les Fluctuations de la production manuscrite à la lumière de l'histoire de la fin du Moyen Âge." *Bulletin philologique et historique (jusqu'à 1610) du Comité des travaux scientifiques et techniques*: 51–75 [republished in *La Face cachée*, pp 179–96].

Bozzolo, C. and E. Ornato. 1981. *Pour une histoire du livre manuscrit au Moyen Âge. Trois essais de codicologie quantitative*. Paris: Éditions du Centre national de la recherche scientifique [2nd ed. 1983].

Bozzolo, C. and E. Ornato. 1982. "Pour une codicologie expérimentale." *Scrittura e Civiltà* 6: 263–302 [republished in *La Face cachée*, pp 3–32].

Bozzolo, C. and E. Ornato. 1989. "Les Bibliothèques entre le manuscrit et l'imprimé." In *Histoire des bibliothèques françaises*, I. *Les bibliothèques médiévales du VIᵉ siècle à 1530*, ed. A. Vernet, 333–47. Paris: Promodis–Éditions du Cercle du librairie [republished in *La Face cachée*, pp. 245–72].

Bozzolo, C. and E. Ornato. 1997. "Les Lectures des Français aux XIVᵉ et XVᵉ siècles. Une approche quantitative. " In *Ensi firent li ancessor. Mélanges de philologie médiévale offerts à Marc-René Jung*, 2 vols., ed. L. Rossi, 713–62. Alessandria: Edizioni dell'Orso.

Bozzolo, C., D. Coq, D. Muzerelle, and E. Ornato. 1984. "Noir et blanc. Premiers résultats d'une enquête sur la mise en page dans le livre médiéval." In *Il libro e il testo* (Actes du colloque international, Urbino, septembre 1982), ed. C. Questa and R. Raffaelli, 195–221. Urbino: Pubblicazioni dell'Università di Urbino [republished in *La Face cachée*, pp. 473–508].

Bozzolo, C., D. Coq, D. Muzerelle, and E. Ornato. 1987. "Page savante, page vulgaire: étude comparative de la mise en page des livres en latin et en français écrits ou imprimés en France au XVᵉ siècle." In *La Présentation du livre* (Actes du Colloque de Paris X–Nanterre, 4–6 décembre, 1985), ed. E. Baumgartner and N. Boulestreau, 121–33. Nanterre: Centre de Recherche du Département de Français de Paris X [republished in *La Face cachée*, pp. 509–18].

Bozzolo, C., D. Coq, D. Muzerelle, and E. Ornato. 1990a. "Les Abréviations dans les livres liturgiques du XVᵉ siècle: pratique et théorie." In *Actas del VIII Coloquio del Comité internacional de paleografía latina*. Madrid–Toledo, 29 setiembre–1 octubre 1987, ed. M. C. Díaz y Díaz, 17–28. Madrid: Joyas Bibliográficas [republished in *La Face cachée*, pp. 555–66].

Bozzolo, C., D. Coq, D. Muzerelle, and E. Ornato. 1990b. "L'Artisan médiéval et la page: peut-on déceler des procédés géométriques de mise en page?" In *Artistes, artisans et production artistique au Moyen Âge*, Actes du Colloque (Rennes, mai 1983), 3 vols., ed. X. Barral i Altet, III, 295–305. Paris: Picard [republished in *La Face cachée*, pp. 447–56].

Bozzolo, C., D. Coq, and E. Ornato. 1984. "La production du livre en quelques pays d'Europe occidentale aux XIVᵉ et XVᵉ siècles." *Scrittura e Civiltà* 8: 129–59 [republished in *La Face cachée*, pp. 197–226].

Casagrande Mazzoli, M. A. 1997. "Foratura, rigatura e *pectines* in codici italiani tardomedievali." *Aevum* 71: 423–40.

Casagrande Mazzoli, M. A. and E. Ornato. 1999. "Elementi per la tipologia del manoscritto quattrocentesco dell'Italia centro-settentrionale." In *La Fabbrica del codice*, ed. P. Busonero, M. A. Casagrande Mazzoli, L. Devoti, and E. Ornato, 207–87. Rome: Viella.

Coq, D. and E. Ornato. 1987. "Les Séquences de composition du texte dans la typographie du XVe siècle: une méthode quantitative d'identification." *Histoire & mesure* 2: 87–136 [republished in *La Face cachée*, pp 397–444].

Coq, D. and E. Ornato. 1988. "La Production et le marché des incunables. Le cas des livres juridiques." In *Le Livre dans l'Europe de la Renaissance* (Actes du XXVIIIe Colloque international d'études humanistes, Desrousilles, Tours, juillet 1985), ed. P. Aquilon, H. J. Martin, and F. Dupuigrenet, 305–22. Paris: Promodis–Éditions du Cercle de la librairie [republished in *La Face cachée*, pp. 227–44].

Derolez, A. 1984. *Codicologie des manuscrits en écriture humanistique sur parchemin*, 2 vols. Brepols: Turnhout.

Derolez, A. 2000. "Ruling in Quattrocento Manuscripts: Types and Techniques." In *Septuaginta Paulo Spunar oblata (70+2)*, ed. J. K. Kroupa, 284–94. Prague: Koniasch Latin Press.

Gilissen, L. 1977. *Prolégomènes à la codicologie. Recherches sur la construction des cahiers et la mise en page des manuscrits médiévaux*. Ghent: Éditions scientifiques Story-Scientia.

Gumbert, J. P. 1986. "Ruling by Rake and Board. Notes on Some Late Medieval Ruling Techniques." In *The Role of the Book in Medieval Culture* (Proceedings of the Oxford International Symposium, 26 September–1 October 1982), ed. P. Ganz, 41–54. Turnhout: Brepols.

Gumbert, J. P. 1993. "Sizes and Formats." In *Ancient and Medieval Book Materials and Techniques*, ed. M. Maniaci and P.F. Munafò, I 227–63. Vatican City: Biblioteca Apostolica Vaticana.

Gumbert, J. P. 2004. "Fifty Years of Codicology." *Archiv für Diplomatik, Schriftgeschichte, Siegel- und Wappenkunde* (Actes du XIVe colloque du Comité international de paléographie latine, Enghien-les-Bains, septembre 2003) 50: 505–26.

Jenkinson, F. 1927. "Ulrich Zell's Early Quartos." *The Library*, 4e série, 7: 46–66.

Maniaci, M. 1995. "Ricette di costruzione della pagina nei manoscritti greci e latini." *Scriptorium* 49: 16–41.

Maniaci, M. 1997. "Alla fine della riga. Divisione delle parole e continuità del testo nel manoscritto bizantino." *Scriptorium* 51: 189–233.

Maniaci, M. 2000. "La pergamena nel manoscritto bizantino dei secoli XI e XII: caratteristiche e modalità d'uso" *Quinio* 2: 63–92.

Maniaci, M. 2002. *Costruzione e gestione della pagina nel manoscritto bizantino (secoli IX–XII)*. Cassino: Edizioni dell'Università degli studi di Cassino.

Maniaci, M. 2006. "*Problemi di mise en page dei manoscritti con commento 'a cornice'. L'esempio di alcuni testimoni dell'*Iliade." *Segno e testo* 4: 211–98.

Maniaci, M. and E. Ornato. 1993. "Che fare del proprio corpus? I. Costituzione e descrizione di una popolazione di libri a fini statistici." *Gazette du livre médiéval* 22 (Spring): 7–37; II. "L'osservazione 'sperimentale' e l'interpretazione dei risultati." *Gazette du livre médiéval* 23 (Autumn): 18–27 [republished in *La Face cachée*, pp. 67–84].

Maniaci, M. and E. Ornato. 1995. "Intorno al testo. Il ruolo dei margini nell'impaginazione dei manoscritti greci e latini." *Nuovi Annali della Scuola Speciale per Archivisti e Bibliotecari* 9: 175–94 [republished in *La Face cachée*, pp. 457–71].

Muzerelle, D. 1989. "Normes et recettes de mise en page dans le codex pré-carolingien." In *Les Débuts du codex* (Actes de la journée d'études organisée à Paris les 3 et 4 juillet 1985), ed. A. Blanchard, 125–256. Brepols: Turnhout.

Muzerelle, D. 2009. "Les Propriétés arithmétiques de la linéation dans les manuscrits humanistiques." *Gazette du livre médiéval* 55 (Autumn): 20–30.

Muzerelle, D., F. Bianchi, P. Canart, C. Federici, E. Ornato, and G. Prato. 1993. "La Structure matérielle du codex dans les principales aires culturelles de l'Italie du XIe siècle." In *Ancient and Medieval Book Materials and Techniques: Actes du colloque international, Erice, 18–25 septembre 1992*, ed. P. F. Munafò and M. Maniaci, 2 vols., II, 363–452. Vatican City: Biblioteca Apostolica Vaticana.

Muzerelle, D. and E. Ornato. 2004. "La terza dimensione del libro. Aspetti codicologici della pluritestualità." *Segno e testo: International Journal of Manuscripts and Text Transmission* 2: 43–74.

Neddermeyer, U. 1998. *Von der Handschrift zum gedruckten Buch. Schriftlichkeit und Leseinteresse im Mittelalter und in der frühen Neuzeit. Quantitative und qualitative Aspekte*, 2 vols. Wiesbaden: Harrassowitz.

Ornato, E. 1991. "La Codicologie quantitative, outil privilégié de l'histoire du livre médiéval." *Historia instituciones documentos* 18: 375–402 [republished in *La Face cachée*, pp. 41–65].

Ornato, E. 1997. *La Face cachée du livre médiéval. L'histoire du livre vue par Ezio Ornato, ses collègues et amis*. Rome: Viella.

Ornato, E. 2003a. "Libri e colofoni: qualche considerazione." *Gazette du livre médiéval* 42 (Spring): 24–35.

Ornato, E. 2003b. "Tra ostentazione e reticenza: i colofoni nel libro a stampa." *Gazette du livre médiéval* 43 (Autumn 2003): 34–46.

Ornato, E. 2004. "Un esperimento di datazione tramite le filigrane: le 'lettere p' negli incunaboli dei Paesi Bassi." In *Paper as a Medium of Cultural Heritage: Archaeology and Conservation* (Actes du 26e Congrès de l'IPH (Roma–Verona, août 2002), ed. R. Graziaplena and M. Livesey, 225–43. Rome: Istituto centrale per la patologia del libro.

Ornato, E. 2010. "Division du travail et pratiques de composition dans l'atelier de Günther Zainer (Augsbourg, 1469)." In *Le Berceau du livre imprimé. Autour des incunables*, ed. P. Aquilon and T. Claeer, 57–105. Brepols: Turnhout.

Ornato, E., P. Busonero, P. F. Munafò, and M. S. Storace. 2000. "Variations de l'épaisseur et du degré de blancheur dans six exemplaires d'une édition vénitienne de 1495." In *Science and Technology for the Safeguard of Cultural Heritage in the Mediterranean Basin* (2nd International Congress, Paris– Nanterre, 11–17 July 1999), 2 vols., II, 949–59. Paris, Amsterdam, New York, Shannon, and Tokyo: Editions scientifiques et médicales.

Ornato, E., P. Busonero, P. F. Munafò, and M. S. Storace. 2001. *La carta occidentale nel tardo Medio Evo. I. Aspetti qualitativi, tipologia, struttura delle forme*, 2 vols. Rome: Istituto centrale per la patologia del libro.

CHAPTER 41

....

COMPARATIVE
CODICOLOGY

....

MALACHI BEIT-ARIÉ

THE emergence of codicology in the domain of medieval manuscript studies in the middle of the twentieth century gradually stimulated the awareness that codicological empirical and theoretical inquiries should not be confined to the scribal practices and the social contexts of handwritten codices produced in a specific script (or sometimes in the Greco-Latin book culture), but should also be expanded to include by juxtaposition and comparison other codices that were written in other scripts within the orbit of the codex civilizations around the Mediterranean basin and further north and east.

Whether written in Latin, Greek, Arabic, Hebrew, Syriac, Coptic, Armenian, Glagolitic, or Cyrillic script, medieval codices shared the same anatomy, the same materials and therefore similar proportions and formats, a molecular structure of quiring achieved by folding a certain number of bifolia, and the employment of means for ensuring the right sequence of the quires or the bifolia and folios within the quires, located on the margins. Almost all of them were prepared for copying by designing the *mise-en-texte*—the disposition of the written space and its placement within the page—and ruling its grid in a variety of techniques. All scribes introduced into the copied text parascriptural and peritextual elements in order to enhance the legibility and transparency of its hierarchical structure and improve its searchability. Most of them applied various traditional line management devices to achieve justified written space. Some manuscripts were decorated and illuminated in the margins or within the written space. This common inherent structural setting—which often displayed equivalent technical manifestations, not infrequently temporal, interdependent, or independent, such as the composition of quires, various ruling techniques, and layout of the copied text—was indeed universal as far as the codex civilizations are concerned. Furthermore, this structural model remained, despite its multiple and transformational representations over time and space, remarkably stable, without any rupture, even with the beginning of mechanical printing; in many aspects it was inherited and implemented by the printers. This structural configuration of the codex book lasted to a large degree until our own time, despite the restoration of scrolling on our computer screens—which should be compared not to the ancient horizontal book form of a scroll unfolded horizontally but to a vertically written roll described in Latin sources as written "*transversa charta*," known now by the term *rotulus*.

The powerful regularity and continuity of the basic structure, technical construction, social and intellectual functionality, and aesthetic principles inscribed in all medieval codices by unexplained osmosis justify comparative study, not just as sheer intellectual and cultural pursuit of this common codex "grammar," but because it may and does yield a better understanding of the production processes of medieval books and their ergometric and socioeconomic conditioning. Comparative study of similar and even disparate codicological features, styles of book script, and their changes in different, similar, opposing, or self-contained cultures can offer us explanations of phenomena pertaining to a specific book culture. Different practices may be the consequence of factors other than technological ones, such as aesthetic conventions or economic or scholarly needs.

Similar practices in different circumstances would prove that they were not conditioned by social, economic, or cultural context, but were universally inherent in the making of a codex. Similar practices in similar circumstances would prove that they were conditioned by those circumstances, as in the case of the late introduction of the ruling plummet in Franco-German Hebrew manuscripts in comparison to Latin ones, a fact which contributes to our understanding of the reason for the shift of the ruling techniques in both book cultures. Hebrew scribes in Europe (particularly in northern France and Germany) started to adopt plummet as a ruling instrument only in the middle of the thirteenth century, at least a century and a half after Latin scribes had started to employ it. At the beginning of the Hebrew codicology study it seemed that this chronological difference could be explained with reference to Jewish Halachic considerations. Upon the appearance of plummet in Europe in the twelfth century, Jewish scholars rejected its employment in ruling ritual biblical scrolls (mostly Pentateuch) designed for reading aloud during ceremonies in the synagogues. According to the Talmudic law those scrolls had to be ruled, and because in Talmudic times they had been ruled by blind ruling, Halachic scholars in Germany, France, and Provence dismissed the new instrument and disapproved of colored ruling for ritual scrolls. The late adoption of plummet in Hebrew codices was ascribed to the psychological impact of that rejection, which lasted about 150 years. Later on, by comparing Hebrew and Latin composite and glossed texts it became obvious that the reason for the chronological gap in the employment of plummet must have been different. The visual presentation of those texts with commentaries, glosses, and scholia in both Hebrew and Latin manuscripts required variable and changeable layout. The development of flexible *mise-en-texte* necessitated a shift in ruling technique from blind or relief to colored ruling. While ruling with hard point imposed and guaranteed the uniform layout of at least two sides of each bifolium (or leaf), or even two or more bifolia (or leaves) which are ruled together, the use of plummet and later ink, which had to be applied on each page or each side of the unfolded bifolium separately, enabled flexibility within the inner structure of the text design. The emergence of a variable configuration of texts in Latin glossed Bibles was generated by scholarly developments and methods of reading and studying in Christian societies. Thus, the employment of the plummet as a ruling instrument followed the requirement of conveniently flexible ruling. Similar intellectual circumstances in Jewish society in northern Europe a century and a half later led to the same technological shift and to the adoption of plummet. When Jewish Halachic creativity declined from the second half of the thirteenth century onward, and compilations, abridgements, glosses, scholia, and marginalia replaced coherent works, a similar flexible layout was introduced into glossed books of Halachic corpora. As in Latin glossed books, this integration encouraged the manipulation of decorative configurations, the use of different scripts, and the splitting of columns. We can conclude from the comparison of Hebrew with Latin codices that plummet was introduced by scribes employing either Latin or Hebrew script as a ruling instrument, replacing hard point, because of the growing demand for complex glossed books, rather than being adopted by scribes for some other technological or aesthetic reason which subsequently encouraged the development of variable layout. To clarify the many other questions raised while attempting to understand the history of book production one would have indeed to resort to comparative codicology.

A comparative study of book production in societies which employed the codex form should focus first on common technical problems and the ways different cultures resolved them. Different solutions to identical necessities, and diverse technical procedures achieving the same goals, would require us to re-examine traditional assertions and question basic assumptions and premises. For instance, different quiring practices in different cultures sharing the same writing materials may refute certain explanations of format and quire construction by folding. A comparison of corresponding functional needs and scholarly developments with concomitant changes in styles of script, design, and manufacture of codices would illuminate the dependence or independence of the changes. Only comparative study of different traditions of book production will enable us to judge whether social or intellectual circumstances entailed those changes, whether they were generated by inherent deterministic technical permutations, or were the outcome of artistic creativity.

Comparative study of different book scripts would concentrate on common structural elements of writing rather than on shapes of letters, as defined, for example, by Jean Mallon (1952) with regard to the Roman script system: the *ductus*–the dynamic aspect of executing characters; angle of writing; proportions of height and width of letters, "relative module" (following the modification suggested by Léon Gilissen 1973, 21–32), and "weight"—the relationship between the width of horizontal and vertical strokes. It should also examine and compare the relationship between book format and text layout and the modular proportions of scripts, and attempt to determine whether letter proportions dictated certain formats and layouts or were influenced by them. Comparative study of scripts may expose common styles of different scripts, and by so doing enrich our ability to analyze and characterize particular scripts.

The necessity for a comparative approach in the study of Hebrew codices which were produced in almost all the zone of the codex civilizations and were interwoven with other major and minor traditions of book production is self-evident. Any presentation of the diversified types of the Hebrew script, as well as the making of medieval Hebrew manuscripts, is bound to be related to and shaped by the division of the main civilizations within which Jewish scribes and producers of books were active. Any attempt to classify the various styles and characteristics of Hebrew handwritten books turns out to correspond geographically to the territorial zones of the host religions, cultures, and scripts at the time of the formation and crystallization of the Hebrew codex. The affinities between the script and scribal practices employed in Jewish book production and those employed in Christian book production in each geocultural area which encompassed Jewish population may contribute tangible evidence in measuring the degree of acculturation or segregation of the usually oppressed Jewish communities contained within Christian societies and in clarifying the direct symbiotic or indirect osmotic nature of the contacts between Hebrew and Latin scribes. The distinctive calligraphic and codicological Hebrew traditions cluster in accordance with the three main literate medieval civilizations which flourished around the Mediterranean basin— Islam and its Arabic script, Western Christendom and its Latin script, and Byzantine Christianity and its Greek script. The geographical distribution of those distinctive characteristics corresponds to the geopolitical orbits of Islam, the Latin West, and the Greek East in the formation periods of the Hebrew codex. The division of the Jewish traditions generally persisted until the end of the Middle Ages, notwithstanding major changes in the encompassing geopolitical structure and cultural domination.

No doubt the practice of comparative presentation of codicological historical typology began with the inception of Hebrew codicology in the 1960s. Bridging East and West, Islam, Eastern and Western Christianity, Hebrew handwritten books as cross-cultural agents may indeed serve as a useful means for comparative codicology and palaeography.

The study of the principal codex cultures will surely also benefit from such an approach, for it may reveal cross-cultural influences and borrowings. This is particularly likely to be the case in the border regions and polygraphic societies around the Mediterranean, such as those of Spain, southern Italy, and the Near East. Alternatively, such an approach may simply provide us with information contained in one culture's records but pertaining to the history of the book of another culture. For instance, Jewish commercial letters written in the Middle East in Arabic rendered in Hebrew characters in the middle of the eleventh century present the earliest authentic evidence of the disputable date of the beginning of paper production in Muslim Spain, while a Hebrew legal source written in Germany in the early fifteenth century testifies to the practice of German courts of verifying documents' authenticity by examining their watermarks.

In recent years interest in comparative codicology has indeed grown, as witnessed by scholarly conferences and their published proceedings, as well as by publications dedicated to it or the inclusion of comparative data in codicological handbooks.

BIBLIOGRAPHY

Agati, L. M. 2009. *Il libro manoscritto da Oriente a Occidente: Per una codicologia comparata.* Rome: "Erma" di Bretschneider.

Bausi, A. *et al.* eds. 2015. *Comparative Oriental Manuscript Studies: An Introduction.* Hamburg: Tradition.

Beit-Arié, M. 1993a. *Hebrew Manuscripts of East and West: Towards a Comparative Codicology* (The Panizzi Lectures, 1992). London: British Library.

Beit-Arié, M. 1993b. "Why Comparative Codicology?" *Gazette du livre médiévale* 23: 1–5.

Beit-Arié, M. 2002. "Towards a Comparative Typology of Italian Hebrew and Latin Codices." In *Libri, documenti, epigrafi medievali: Possibilità di studi comparativi* (Atti del Convegno internazionale di studio dell'Associazione Italiana dei Paleografi e Diplomatisti, Bari, 2–5 ottobre 2000), ed. F. Magistrale, C. Drago, and P. Fioretti, 377–96. Spoleto: Centro italiano di studi sull'Alto Medioevo.

Beit-Arié, M. 2020. Hebrew Codicology: Historical and Comparative Typology of Hebrew Medieval Codices Based on Documentation of the Extant Dated Manuscripts Using Quantitative Approach. Updated preprint, Internet version 0.4 (February 2020). http://web.nli.org.il/sites/NLI/English/collections/manuscripts/hebrewcodicology/Documents/Hebrew-Codicology-continuously-updated-online-version-ENG.pdf, accessed July 21, 2020.

Condello, E. and G. De Gregorio, eds. 1995. *Scribi e colofoni: Le sottoscrizioni di copisti dalle origini all'avvento della stampa: Atti del seminario di Erice, X Colloquio del Comité international de paléographie latine (23–28 ottobre 1993)* (Biblioteca del "Centro per il collegamento degli studi medievali e umanistici in Umbria" 14). Spoleto: Centro italiano di studi sull'Alto Medioevo.

Gilissen, L. 1973. *L'Expertise des écritures médiévales. Recherche d'une méthode avec application à un manuscrit du XIe siècle: Le lectionnaire de Lobbes. Codex Bruxellensis 18018.* Ghent: E. Story-Scientia.

Hoffman, P., ed. 1998. *Recherches de codicologie comparé au Moyen Âge en Orient et Occident* (Collection Bibliologie), ed. P. Hoffmann. Paris: Presses de l'École normale supérieure.

Mallon, J. 1952. *Paléographie romaine.* Madrid: Consejo Superior de Investigaciones Científicas, Instituto Antonio de Nebrija, de Filología.

Maniaci, M. 2002. *Archeologia del manoscritto: Metodi, problemi, bibliografia recente.* Rome: Viella.

Rosenfeld, R. 2008. "Early Comparative Codicology: Late-Medieval Western Perceptions of Non-Western Script and Book Materials." In *Classica et Beneventana: Essays Presented to Virginia Brown on the Occasion of Her 65th Birthday* (Textes et Études du Moyen Âge, 36), ed. F. T Coulson and A. A. Grotans, 173–200. Turnhout: Brepols.

CHAPTER 42

··

PEN-FLOURISHED
DECORATION

··

ALISON STONES

THE term "pen-flourished" refers to decoration in colored ink, drawn with a pen, and used to embellish an initial letter or a border.[1] Pen-flourishing is a type of embellishment, used for initial letters, that was current from the twelfth century to the end of the Middle Ages in Western Europe. Called *litterae parvae* in Vatican City, BAV, Vat. lat. 6443, fol. 204v, they complement another type of initial present in that manuscript, called *litterae partitae*, referring to larger initials whose bars are done in two colors like a puzzle.[2] Another Latin term for pen-flourished initials is *litterae florissae*.[3] And in the devotional miscellany, Porto, Biblioteca Municipal 619 (made for use in Verdun *c*.1260–70), notes in French for the decorator distinguish between *dor champie de color* for the two-line gold initials on a pink and blue field, commonly referred to as "champie initials" and *de penne*, a term that seems (somewhat inconsistently) to refer to the pen-flourished initials.[4]

The usual colors were red (minium) and various shades of blue (woad or more usually cobalt, though little technical analysis of the pigments has been done), alternating so that red initials had blue flourishing and vice versa. Green and yellow were less frequently used in France, England, and Italy, although green was common in the Netherlands, especially in the fourteenth and fifteenth centuries, and yellow is often found in Germany, while mauve became popular in southern France during the second half of the thirteenth century, replacing blue in the flourishing, and its use spread during the fourteenth century. Pen-flourished initials could include gold, a mark of greater expense, costing more to produce but adding value to the book. Pen-flourishing left the parchment background plain to create a silhouette effect in which the pen-drawn motifs, geometric, foliate, or figured, leave blank (in reserve) the white of the parchment on which they are outlined.

In books containing miniatures or historiated initials, pen-flourished initials were considered as minor decoration, used to mark paragraphs or stanzas, whereas fully painted initials or miniatures mark text openings and important textual breaks, while capitals without flourishing occupy a lower place than pen-flourished initials in the decorative hierarchy of medieval manuscript illustration. In the manuscript of Papias preserved in Valenciennes, Bibliothèque municipale, 396–7, each letter of the alphabet is singled out for special decoration, and the range includes historiated initials, foliate initials with hybrid components, and pen-flourished initials.[5] Pen-flourished initials can be as small as one or two lines high and the flourished component mainly limited to the inside of the initial bar; but they can also be the only decorative component in a manuscript and form a substantial part of the book's embellishment and a focus for sophisticated and beautiful work. It was also common for there to be a hierarchy of use even among pen-flourished initials, whereby versals or paragraphs would begin with a small (1–5 line) pen-flourished initial, and major textual divisions would be marked with a larger pen-flourished initial (5–10 or more lines high). Party-bar or puzzle initials were still more important and were often accompanied by a pen-flourished border extending from the initial, sometimes enclosing the entire text block, especially in southern France, Italy, and Spain. Many decorative motifs were invented by the flourishers—"frogspawn," spirals, curlicues, palmettes, aubergines, and many other motifs. Distinct regional and personal styles evolved, so pen-flourished initials can provide useful criteria for establishing the chronology and geography of a manuscript and complement what can be deduced from the script and major illustration, as recognized by L. M. J. Delaissé in his concept of the "archéologie du livre."[6] The examples given here are drawn from French manuscripts, but much work remains to be done on French regional styles.[7] Similar types of initials are also found in England,[8] the Netherlands,[9] Germany,[10] Spain,[11] Portugal,[12] Italy,[13] Slovenia,[14] and further afield in central Europe from the early twelfth century onward, and the studies listed give representative reproductions of this type of decoration alongside historiated initials and miniatures.[15]

The Cistercians particularly favored the simplicity of initials that avoided historiation and painted decoration. In the constitutions of the Cistercian order, article LXXX/82, approved in 1152, stated that letters should be of a single color.[16] Red was the preferred color in the twelfth century (Plate 42.1, Périgueux, Archives départementales de la Dordogne, MS 171 fol. 14 from Cadouin). By the thirteenth century, however, a wider color range and a greater profusion of decorative elements is found in manuscripts owned by the Cistercians, of which striking examples are the *De civitate dei* of St. Augustine owned by Notre-Dame du Val-des-Choux (Dioc. Langres), where the pen-flourishing, based on multifoil rose motifs, encircles the text block on the opening folio (Plate. 42.2, Paris, BnF, lat. 2068, fol. 1),[17] and the Minnesota copy of the *Speculum historiale* and *Speculum naturale* by Vincent of Beauvais from Cambron which contain a variety of decorative motifs including castles, cinquefoil flowers, palmettes, and teardrops alongside frogspawn (Plate 42.3, Minneapolis, University of Minnesota, James Ford Bell Library, MS B1280fVi, vol. IV fol. 10v).[18] Recent studies of Cistercian manuscripts in France have focused on the holdings of particular monastic libraries: Cadouin, Cîteaux, Chaalis, La Charité, Cheminon, Montier-en-Argonne, Clairvaux, Faize, Fontenay, Haute-Fontaine, Igny, Pontigny, and Vauluisant.[19] Key questions about production and circulation remain to be answered: which abbeys made the

PLATE 42.1 Périgueux, Archives départementales de la Dordogne, 171, Gregory the Great, *Homilies on Ezechiel*, fol. 14v (photo: author).

books and how widely did they circulate? Analysis based on decoration will play an important part in determining the answer.

Pen-flourished initials may occupy a large proportion of the page and constitute a significant component of the decoration of a book, as the Val-des-Choux and Cambron manuscripts demonstrate. Pen-flourished decoration was not limited to Cistercian books, however. Three manuscripts written, noted, and signed by Philip, priest of

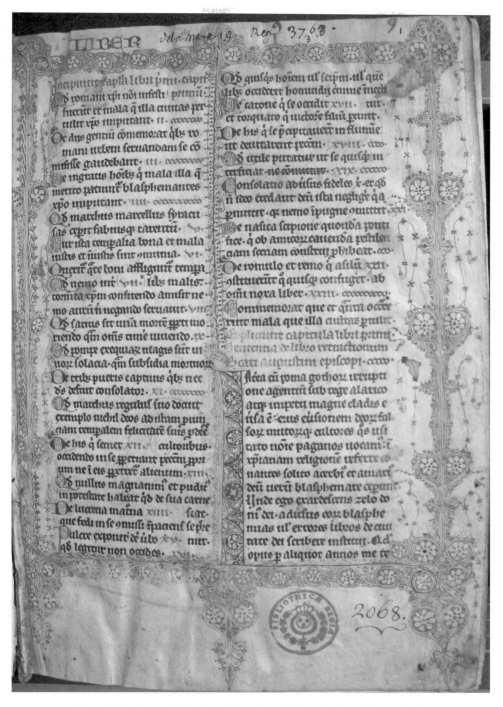

PLATE 42.2 Paris, BnF, lat. 2068, St Augustine, *De civitate dei*, fol. 1 (photo: BnF).

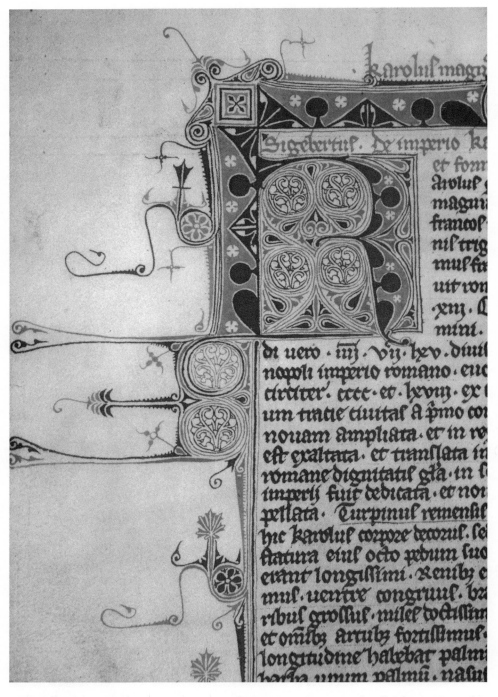

PLATE 42.3 Minneapolis, MN, University of Minnesota, James Ford Bell Library, B1280fVi, Vincent of Beauvais, *Speculum historiale*, vol. IV, fol. 10v.

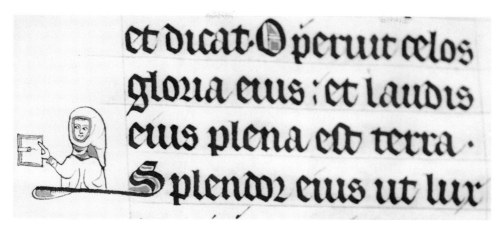

PLATE 42.4 Oxford, New College 3, Bible, fol. 8v (photo: author, reproduced by permission of the Warden and Scholars of New College, Oxford).

Troyes, at the end of the thirteenth century, are especially noted for their pen-flourishing. In the four-volume Bible, Oxford, New College, 3–6, which he wrote in 1290, the penwork ranges from decoration of text letters (Plate 42.4, New College 3, fol. 8v) to elaborate flourishing used for major initials (Plate 42.5, New College, 3, fol. 13, Genesis). Philip wrote and noted an Office for the feast of St. William of Bourges, inserted into Troyes, Bibliothèque municipale, 1148, fols. 282–90, and he also wrote a Missal, now preserved as a fragment in Paris, Bibliothèque Sainte-Geneviève 98, which is also noted, though Philip does not mention the notation in his colophon.[20] Nor does he mention the pen decoration in his books, which suggests that for him, writing and noting of sacred texts and music were more important activities than decorating. The Sainte-Geneviève Missal, the Office of William of Bourges, and the New College Bible all show Philip's distinctive writing, full of humorous motifs drawn in ink as part of the ascenders and descenders of the letters. The Missal and the Bible both contain the same distinctive large and small pen-flourished initials, which leads one to wonder whether Philip might not have executed them as well—the decoration of his lettering certainly shows him to have been a very competent draftsman—but he does not claim to have done the pen-flourished decoration, so nothing can be proven. A further manuscript by the same decorator—perhaps Philip himself—has recently come to light in Brussels, BR 4, a late thirteenth-century copy of the *Grandes chroniques de France*, the first part of which ends with the death of Philip Augustus in 1223.[21] Whether Philip of Troyes was also one of the scribes is an open question as this time; the script is much smaller in scale than in the liturgical books and lacks their decorated ascenders and descenders. At all events, Philip's work and that of his decorator are of the very highest quality, putting him/them at the center of debate about pen decoration, its makers, and its relation to script on the one hand and illumination on the other. Was he operating only in Champagne, or also in Paris? A reflection of his initials is to be found in the *Bible historiale*, Paris, BnF, fr. 160, whose major illustration is by the

PLATE 42.5 Oxford, New College 3, Bible, Genesis, fol. 13 (photo: author, reproduced by permission of the Warden and Scholars of New College, Oxford).

PLATE 42.6 Paris, BnF, lat. 16260, Bible, fol. 359v (photo: Bibliothèque nationale de France).

artist known as the "Papeleu Master," a principal participant in the *Bible historiale*, Paris, Bibliothèque Arsenal 5059, written by Jean Papeleu in 1317. Here too, further investigation is called for.

Pen-flourished decoration may on occasion be combined with fully painted image components. For instance, in the Bible, Paris, BnF, lat. 16260 (*c*.1260–70, probably from Cambrai), pen-flourished initials are mostly reserved for the prologues while the books of the Bible each open with a historiated initial (Plate 42.6, Paris, BnF, lat. 16260, Jeremiah, fol. 359v), but on occasion both techniques are found in a single initial (Plate 42.7, Paris, BnF, lat. 16260, Numbers, fol. 64), which suggests that the (anonymous) artist was responsible for the pen-flourishing as well as for the painted work. There are also instances where motifs drawn in pen contain figures or animals that reappear in painted initials or miniatures, another likely indication that an artist was responsible for the pen-flourishing, as in the Seneca from Arras (*c*.1300) (Plate 42.8, Paris, BnF, lat. 15377, fol. 215).

If the question whether Philip of Troyes decorated his books as well as writing and noting them is unresolved, several names of individuals who were certainly pen-flourishers are known from French manuscripts of the thirteenth and fourteenth centuries. The best-known is Jacobus Mathey, brought to attention by François Avril in 1971.[22] Jacobus signed the pen-flourishing in a copy of the Letters of St. Augustine made for Frater and Magister Gregory of Rimini, Vatican City, BAV, Rossi 259, in 1345, and Avril has attributed to Jacobus Mathey a large corpus of decoration. Mathey

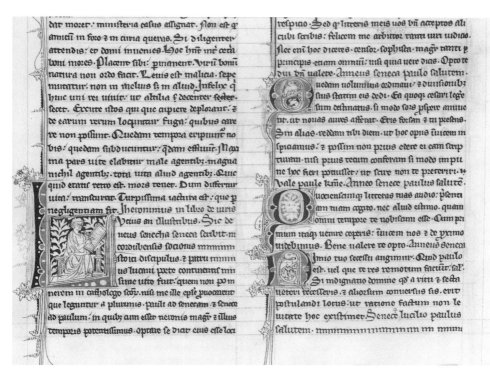

PLATE 42.8 Paris, BnF, lat. 15377, Seneca, *Opuscula*, fol. 215r (photo: Bibliothèque nationale de France).

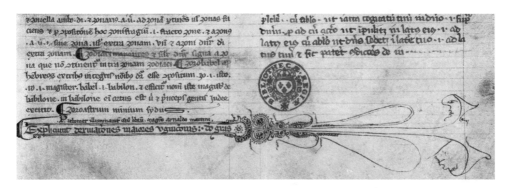

PLATE 42.9 Paris, BnF, lat. 7622, Huguccio, *Derivationes*, fol. 141r (photo: Bibliothèque nationale de France).

was Parisian. A southern French pen-flourisher who also signed his work in the same mauve ink as the pen-flourishing, incorporating his name into the flourishing itself, was P. de Bonier, decorator of the *Vocabularium* and *Derivationes* of Huguccio of Pisa, with glosses in Occitan (Plate 42.9, Paris, BnF, lat. 7622, fol. 141r), who probably worked in Sarlat.[23] He uses the term "illuminavit": the book has only pen-flourished

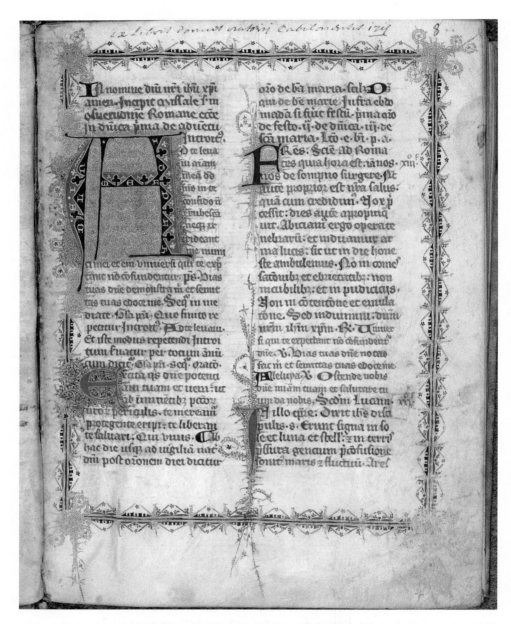

PLATE 42.10 Carpentras, Bibl. Inguimbertine, 91, Missal, fol. 8r (photo: IRHT, reproduced by permission of the Bibliothèque Inguimbertine).

decoration. Two lesser-known French decorators, both working *c.*1300, are Belin, probably working in Burgundy, who signed his name in the opening initial of the Roman Missal, Carpentras, Bibliothèque Inguimbertine, MS 91 (fol. 8r), "Belin me fit P. F. H." (Plate 42.10),[24] and Johannes Reth, named in the Missal of Digne in the Bibliothèque municipale of Marseilles, MS 104 (f. 2r). A half-length portrait, showing

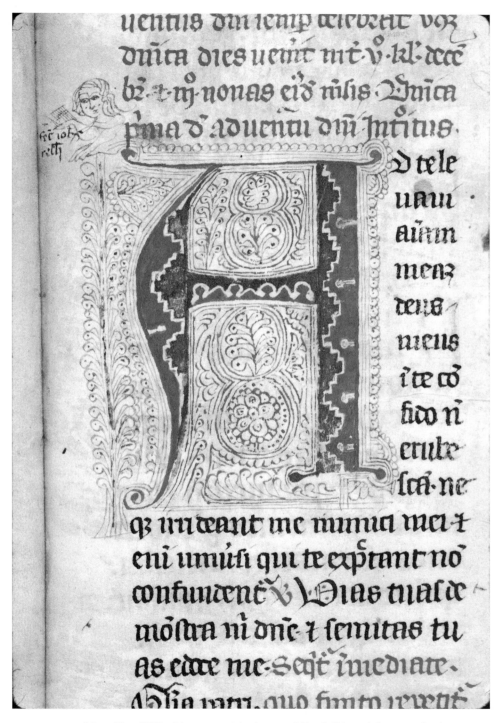

PLATE 42.11 Marseilles, Bibliothèque municipale, 104, Missal, fol. 2r (photo: author).

him holding a set of pens, is drawn in the mauve ink of the opening flourished initial above which is it placed and identified, "fec[it] Johannes Reth" (Plate 42.11).[25] Were Belin and Johannes Reth also the scribes, and do the words "fit" and "fecit" refer to the book as a whole, or just the pen-flourished initials?

The importance of this level of decoration has been slow to achieve general recognition, and even in current scholarship pen-flourished decoration is less frequently reproduced than illumination. The *Manuscrits datés* series, so fundamental for dating and placing medieval handwriting, did not adopt a consistent stance regarding pen-flourishing, with the result that some examples include pen-flourished initials, while most do not.[26] The websites of the Institut de Recherche et d'Histoire des Textes, Enluminures (http://www.enluminures.culture.fr/documentation/enlumine/fr/) and Initiale (http://initiale.irht.cnrs.fr/) have adopted a broader policy toward pen-flourished decoration and are now offering a wide selection alongside miniatures and painted initials. These and the works cited in the Notes and Bibliography for this chapter have paved the way for future research on this neglected aspect of the medieval book.

Notes

1. One of the first scholars to mention pen decoration was Guillaume de Jerphanion, SJ, writing in French, who used the term "décoration calligraphique" in his analysis of the Sainte-Chapelle Missal in Lyons (Jerphanion 1944). The term "calligraphique" has more recently been replaced by "filigranée," unfortunate in French because of its close similarity to the French for watermark in paper, which is "filigrane," as in Briquet (1907).
2. Cited by Avril (1971, 257 and n. 4). Avril characterized these party-bar initials as "puzzles," and the term "puzzle initials" has been much used by P. Stirnemann (especially Stirnemann 1990).
3. Alexander (1978, 21). See also Muzerelle (1985), under "lettre" with its various categories.
4. These notes went unrecorded in the published catalogues, Nascimento and Meirinhos (1997, 350–3, Santa Cruz no. 87 [no. general 619]) and Cepeda (2001, 177–8, no. 327). I base my Verdun attribution on the presence in the litany of saints Sanctinus and Vitonius, patrons of Saint-Vannes de Verdun. See Stones (2010, 244 and n. 24), (2014, Part II, vol. 1, Cat. no. IV-0).
5. Stones (2010).
6. Delaissé (1967).
7. For small-scale pen-flourishing in dated manuscripts from Paris, see Stirnemann (1990).
8. The Windmill Psalter, New York, the Pierpont Morgan Library, MS M.102, is the most notable example, fully reproduced, with bibliography, on Corsair: https://www.the morgan.org/manuscript/77025, accessed March 5, 2020. For pen-flourishing in England, see also Avril and Stirnemann (1987) and Scott-Fleming (1989).
9. See especially Lieftinck (1953) and Korteweg (1992).
10. Beer (1959), (1965); Avril and Rabel with Delaunay (1985).
11. Avril *et al.* (1982).
12. Cepeda and Ferreira (1994); Cepeda (2001).
13. Avril and Załuska (1980); Avril and Gousset with Rabel (1984); Avril and Gousset with Aniel (2005); Avril and Gousset (2012).

14. Golob (1996).

15. Gerhard Schmidt was a pioneer in the domain of pen-flourishing and was responsible for launching the series of publications sponsored by the Österreichische Akademie der Wissenschaften under the direction of Otto Krestner, which include material from Hungary, former Czechoslovakia, and Poland as well as Austria; see Fingernagel and Roland (1997); Fingernagel, Hranitzky, and Pirker-Aurenhammer (2002); Hranitzky *et al.* (2012).

16. *Litterae unius coloris fiant et non depictae.* For the monochrome style to which this interdict gave rise, see especially Załuska (1989, Ch. V, "Le style monochrome," 149–67). For further Cistercian abbeys and their holdings, see n. 19 below.

17. Samaran and Marichal (1959, I, 103, Plate CXCVI, ff. 33, 134).

18. Stones (1977). Similar volumes of Vincent of Beauvais' works once in the Collège de Bonne Espérance at Vellereille-lez-Brayeux (Belgium) as MSS 1, 2, and 3, are now at the Séminaire de Tournai.

19. http://patrimoine.bm-dijon.fr/pleade/subset.html?name=sub-citeaux (Cîteaux, Pontigny, Paris, Mazarine, Arsenal, BnF); Bondéelle-Souchier (1991). Cadouin: Stones *et al.* (2015); Chaalis: Bondéelle-Souchier and Stirnemann (2009); La Charité, Cheminon, Montier-en-Argonne: Turcan-Verkerk (2000); Cîteaux: see n. 16 above and http://patrimoine.bm-dijon.fr/pleade/subset.html?name=sub-citeaux; Clairvaux: Vernet and Genest (1979), Bouhot and Genest (1997), Genest *et al.* (2006); Faize: Darricau (1984), Garde (1964); Fontenay: Stutzmann (2002); Haute-Fontaine: Turcan-Verkerk (1991); Igny: Masson (1998); Pontigny: Peyrafort-Huin (2001): Vauluisant: Bougard *et al.* (2012).

20. Colophons in two of the four volumes of the New College Bible give his name and the date 1290: MS 5, fol. 435v and MS 6, fol. 411r; see Temple and Alexander (1986, 69). For the missal, see Leroquais (1924, II, 162–3, no. 344); Samaran and Marichal (1959, I, 323, Plate CLXXVII); Bernard (1965, 91); Bénédictins du Bouveret (1965–82, VI, no. 16112).

21. Kindly drawn to my attention by François Avril and Marguerite Debae.

22. Avril (1971).

23. ibid., 257. The colophon reads, "*P. de Bonier illuminavit istum librum magistro Arnaldo Martini. Factum fuit in uilla Sarl[ati?]*" added over an erasure (f. 141r) together with the date *MoCCoXCoVIIo* (f. 141).

24. Mély (1913, 69); Leroquais (1924, II, 223 -4, no. 397); Fyot (1918, 13–16), kindly drawn to my attention by M.-F. Damongeot; Stones, (2014, Cat. VI-14, p. 150). Fyot expanded P.F.H. as *Post finem hoc.*

25. Billioud (1924, II, 3–19, Tableau des manuscrits utilisés); Leroquais (1924, II, 284–5, no. 461).

26. Begun in 1959, fully listed on http://www.palaeographia.org/cipl/cmd.htm, accessed January 31, 2020).

BIBLIOGRAPHY

Alexander, J. J. G. 1978. *The Decorated Letter.* New York: Braziller.

Avril, F. 1971. "Un ornemaniste parisien de la première moitié du XIVe siècle: Jacobus Mathey (Jacquet Maci?)." *Bulletin Monumental* 129: 249–64.

Avril, F., J.-P. Aniel, M. Mentré, A. Saulnier, and Y. Załuska, eds. 1982. *Manuscrits enluminés de la péninsule ibérique* (Manuscrits enluminés de la Bibliothèque nationale de France). Paris: Bibliothèque nationale de France.

Avril, F. and M.-T. Gousset. 2012. *Manuscrits enluminés d'origine italienne. 3, XIVe siècle. II, Émilie-Vénétie* (Manuscrits enluminés de la Bibliothèque nationale de France). Paris: Bibliothèque nationale de France.

Avril, F. and M.-T. Gousset, with J.-P. Aniel. 2005. *Manuscrits enluminés d'origine italienne, 3, XIVe siècle. I, Lombardie-Ligurie* (Manuscrits enluminés de la Bibliothèque nationale de France). Paris: Bibliothèque nationale de France.

Avril, F. and M.-T. Gousset, with C. Rabel. 1984. *Manuscrits enluminés d'origine italienne. 2, XIIIe siècle* (Manuscrits enluminés de la Bibliothèque nationale de France). Paris: Bibliothèque nationale de France.

Avril, F. and C. Rabel, with I. Delaunay. 1985. *Manuscrits enluminés d'origine germanique. Tome I, Xe-XIVe siècle* (Manuscrits enluminés de la Bibliothèque nationale de France). Paris: Bibliothèque nationale de France.

Avril, F. and P.D. Stirnemann. 1987. *Manuscrits enluminés d'origine insulaire VIIe-XXe siècle* (Manuscrits enluminés de la Bibliothèque nationale de France). Paris: Bibliothèque nationale de France.

Avril, F. and Załuska, Y. 1980. *Manuscrits enluminés d'origine italienne. 1, Vie–XIIe siècles* (Manuscrits enluminés de la Bibliothèque nationale de France). Paris: Bibliothèque nationale de France.

Beer, E. J. 1959. *Beiträge zur Oberrheinischen Buchmalerei in der ersten Hälfte des 14. Jahrhunderts unter besonderer Berücksichtigung der Initialornamentik.* Basle and Stuttgart: Birkhäuser Verlag.

Beer, E. J. 1965. *Initial und Miniatur, Buchmalerei aus neun Jahrhunderten in Handschriften der Badischen Landesbibliothek* (Jubiläumsausstellung, 1965). Karlsruhe: Badische Landesbibliothek.

Bénédictins du Bouveret (1965–82). *Colophons de manuscrits occidentaux des origines au XVIe siècle,* (Spicilegii Friburgensis subsidia 2–7), 6 vols. Fribourg: Éditions universitaires.

Bernard, M. 1965. *Répertoire de manuscrits médiévaux contenant des notations musicales, I: Bibliothèque Sainte-Geneviève.* Paris: CNRS.

Billioud, J. 1924. "Manuscrits à enluminures, exécutés pour des bibliothèques provençales (890–1704)." In *Encyclopédie Départementale des Bouches-du-Rhône,* ed. P. Masson, 2: 1–42. Marseilles: Barlatier.

Bondéelle-Souchier, A. 1991. *Bibliothèques cisterciennes dans la France médiévale. Répertoire des abbayes d'hommes,* Paris, CNRS.

Bondéelle-Souchier, A. and P. Stirnemann. 2009. "Vers une reconstitution de la bibliothèque ancienne de l'abbaye de Chaalis: inventaires et manuscrits retrouvés." In *Parva pro magnis munera. Études de littérature tardo-antique et médiévale offertes à François Dolbeau par ses élèves,* ed. M. Goullet, 9–73. Turnhout: Brepols.

Bougard, F., P. Petitmengin, with P. Stirnemann et al. (2012). *La Bibliothèque de l'abbaye cistercienne de Vauluisant: Histoire et inventaires* (Documents, études et répertoires, Institut de recherche et d'histoire des textes 83). Paris: CNRS.

Bouhot, J.-P. and J.-F. Genest. 1997. *La Bibliothèque de l'abbaye de Clairvaux du 12e au 18e siècle.* vol. 2. *Les manuscrits conservés. 1. Manuscrits bibliques, patristiques et théologiques.* Paris: CNRS and Turnhout: Brepols.

Briquet, C.-M. 1907. *Les Filigranes: dictionnaire historique des marques du papier dès leur apparition vers 1282 jusqu'en 1600,* 4 vols. Geneva: A. Julien [repr. 1985, New York: Hacker].

Cepeda, I. V. 2001. *Inventário dos códices iluminados até 1500, vol. II, Distritos de Aveiro, Beja, Braga, Bragança, Coimbra, Evora, Leiria, Portalegre, Porto, Setúbal, Viana do Castelo e Viseu. Apêndice distito de Lisboa.* Lisbon: Ministério da cultura.

Cepeda, I. V. and A. S. D. Ferreira. 1994. *Inventário dos códices iluminados até 1500, vol. 1, Distrito de Lisboa.* Lisbon: Secretaria de estado da cultura: Instituto da Biblioteca nacional e do livro.

Darricau, R. 1984. "La Bibliothèque de l'abbaye de Faize." In *Mélanges Anselme Dimier, 2. 4 Histoire cistercienne. Abbayes*, ed. B. Chauvin, 639–44. Arbois-Pupillin: B. Chauvin.

Delaissé, L. M. J. 1967. "Towards a History of the Mediaeval Book." In *Miscellanea André Combes.* 2 vols., 2, 27–39. Rome: Libreria editrice della Pontificia Università Lateranense and Paris: Vrin.

Fingernagel, A., K. Hranitzky, V. Pirker-Aurenhammer. 2002. *Die illuminierten Handschriften und Inkunabeln der Österreichischen Nationalbibliothek: Mitteleuropäische Schulen 2, ca. 1350–1410: Österreich, Deutschland, Schweiz* (Veröffentlichungen der Kommission für Schrift- und Buchwesen des Mittelalters. Reihe 1), 2 vols. Vienna: Verlag der Österreichischen Akademie der Wissenschaften.

Fingernagel, A. and Roland, M. 1997. *Die illuminierten Handschriften und Inkunabeln der Österreichischen Nationalbibliothek: Mitteleuropäische Schulen 1, ca. 1250–1350* (Veröffentlichungen der Kommission für Schrift- und Buchwesen des Mittelalters. Reihe 1), 2 vols. Vienna: Verlag der Österreichischen Akademie der Wissenschaften.

Fyot, E. 1918. "L'Enlulminure en Bourgogne." *Revue de Bourgogne* 7: 5–32.

Garde, J. A.-A. 1964. "Bibliothèque de l'abbaye de Faise." *Revue historique et archéologique du Libournais* 32: 85–7.

Genest, J.-F. *et al.* 2006. *Les Manuscrits de Clairvaux de Saint Bernard à nos jours*, Troyes: Association Champagne historique.

Golob, N. 1996. *Twelfth-Century Cistercian Manuscripts: The Sitticum Collection.* London: Harvey Miller.

Hranitzky, K., V. Pirker-Aurenhammer, S. Rischpler, M. Roland, M. Schuller-Juckes *et al.* 2012. *Die illuminierten Handschriften und Inkunabeln der Österreichischen Nationalbibliothek: Mitteleuropäische Schulen V (ca. 1410–1450)* (Veröffentlichungen der Kommission für Schrift- und Buchwesen des Mittelalters. Reihe 1), 2 vols. Vienna: Verlag der Österreichischen Akademie der Wissenschaften.

Jerphanion, G. de. 1944. *Le Missel de la Sainte-Chapelle à la Bibliothèque de la ville de Lyon* (Documents paléographiques, typographiques, iconographiques, fasc. XIII). Lyons: Les Amis de la Bibliothèque de Lyon and Mâcon: Protat.

Korteweg, A.S. 1992. *Kriezels, aubergines en takkenbossen: randversiering in Noordnederlandse andschriften uit de vijtiende eeuw.* Zutphen: Walburg Pers.

Kresten, O. 1997, 2010– *Veröffentlichungen der Kommission für Schrift- und Buchwesen des Mittelalters.* Vienna: Verlag der Österreichischen Akademie der Wissenschaften.

Leroquais, V. M. 1924. *Les Sacramentaires et les missels manuscrits des bibliothèques publiques de France*, 3 vols. Mâcon: Protat.

Lieftinck, G. I. 1953. *De Librijen en Scriptoria der Westvlaamse Cisterciënser-abdijen Ter Duinen en Ter Doest in de 12e en 13e eeuw en de Betrekkingen tot het Atelier van de Kapittelschool van Sint Donatiaan te Brugge.* Brussels: Paleis der Academiën.

Masson, M.-G. 1998. "L'Ancienne Bibliothèque d'Igny. Témoignage et inventaires (XVIIe– XVIIIe siècles." *Cîteaux. Commentarii Cistercienses* 49: 259–307.

Mély, F. 1913. *Les Primitifs et leurs signatures. I, Les miniaturistes.* Paris: Geuthner.

Muzerelle, D. 1985. *Vocabulaire codicologique: répertoire méthodique des termes français relatifs aux manuscrits.* Paris: CEMI.

Nascimento, A. A. and J. F. Meirinhos, eds. 1997. *Catálogo dos Códices da Livraria de Mào do Mosteiro de Santa Cruz de Coimbra na Biblioteca Pública Municipal do Porto*. Porto: Biblioteca pública do Porto.

Peyrafort-Huin, M. with P. Stirnemann. 2001. *La Bibliothèque médiévale de l'Abbaye de Pontigny, XIIe–XIXe siècles*. Paris: CNRS.

Samaran, C. and R. Marichal. 1959. *Les Manuscrits en écriture latine portant des indications de lieu, de date ou de copiste, Paris, 1959–1. Musée Condé et bibliothèques parisiennes*. 2 vols. Paris: CNRS.

Schmidt, G. 1997. *Veröffentlichungen der Kommission für Schrift- und Buchwesen des Mittelalters*. Vienna: Verlag der Österreichischen Akademie der Wissenschaften.

Schwarz, M. V. 2010. *Die illuminierten Handschriften und Inkunabeln in Österreich ausserhalb der Österreichischen Nationalbibliothek* (Veröffentlichungen der Kommission für Schrift- und Buchwesen des Mittelalters. Reihe 5), Vienna: Verlag der Österreichischen Akademie der Wissenschaften.

Scott-Fleming, S. 1989. *The Analysis of Pen Flourishing in Thirteenth-Century Manuscripts*. Leiden: E. J. Brill.

Stirnemann, P. 1990. "Fils de la vierge, l'initiale à filigranes parisienne: 1140–1314." *Revue de l'art* 90: 58–73.

Stones, A. 1977. *The Minnesota Vincent of Beauvais Volumes and Cistercian Thirteenth-Century Book Decoration* (James Ford Bell Lectures, University of Minnesota). Minneapolis, MN: James Ford Bell Library.

Stones, A. 2010. "Les Prières de Gautier de Coinci, leur distribution et leur réception d'après la tradition manuscrite." In *Le Recueil au moyen âge. Le moyen âge central*, ed. Yasmina Foehr-Janssens and Olivier Collet (Texte, Codex et Contexte VIII), 237–68. Turnhout: Brepols.

Stones, A. 2013. *Gothic Manuscripts 1260–1320*, Part I, 2 vols. (A Survey of Manuscripts Illuminated in France). Turnhout: Harvey Miller and Brepols.

Stones, A. 2014. *Gothic Manuscripts 1260–1320*, Part II, 2 vols. (A Survey of Manuscripts Illuminated in France). Turnhout: Harvey Miller and Brepols.

Stones, A. and T. Falmagne, with C. Cazaux-Kowalski, M.-F. Damongeot, M. Etchechoury, B. Reviriego, Y. Załuska. 2015. *Les Manuscrits de Cadouin* (exhibition catalogue). Périgueux: Archives départementales de la Dordogne.

Stutzmann, D. 2002. *La Bibliothèque de l'abbaye cistercienne de Fontenay (Côte-d'or): constitution, gestion, dissolution (XIIe–XVIIIe s.)*, 4 vols. (Thèse d'archiviste-paléographe). Paris: École nationale des chartes.

Temple, E. and Alexander, J. J. G. 1986. *Illuminated Manuscripts in Oxford College Libraries*. Oxford: Clarendon.

Turcan-Verkerk, A.-M. 1991. "La Bibliothèque de l'abbaye de Haute-Fontaine aux XIIe et XIIIe siècles: formation et dispersion d'un fonds cistercien." *Recherches augustiniennes* 25: 223–61.

Turcan-Verkerk, A.-M. 2000. *Les Manuscrits de la Charité, Cheminon et Montier-en-Argonne, collections cisterciennes et voies de transmission des textes, IXe–XIXe siècles* (Documents, études et répertoires, Institut de recherche et d'histoire des textes 59). Paris, CNRS.

Vernet, A. and J.-F. Genest. 1979. *La Bibliothèque de l'abbaye de Clairvaux du XIIe au XVIIIe siècle*. vol. 1: *Catalogues et répertoires* Paris: CNRS.

Załuska (1989), *L'Enluminure et le scriptorium de Cîteaux au XIIe siècle*, (Cîteaux, Commentarii cistercienses, Studia et Documenta, vol. IV). Brecht: Abbaye de Cîteaux.

PART III

CULTURAL SETTING

CHAPTER 43

....

ORALITY AND VISIBLE
LANGUAGE

....

PAUL SAENGER

In antiquity, the earliest texts that have come down to us were auditory, that is, they were composed orally and retained in memory to be performed orally. The *Iliad* and *Odyssey* of Homer were thus poems that were composed and then preserved solely in the memory of the generations of bards who performed them. Centuries later, perhaps as late as the early fifth century BC, these epics were set down in written form, but the ancient papyrus scrolls that initially preserved them and early works of Greek poetry, including theatrical dramas and philosophy, served principally as supports for oral performance. The teaching of Socrates was preserved in Plato's dialogues, which implied oral and quasi-theatrical presentation. Aristotle's corpus, focusing on logic and science, was "more prosaic," but it too was intended for oral, peripatetic inter-action. For these texts, there is no evidence of any graphic accommodation in the *mise-en-page* of ancient papyri to facilitate the individual study of logical texts such as was to become common a millennium later in the parchment leaves of medieval codices, when Aristotelian logic was studied in Latin translation in northern European monasteries and nascent universities.

In general, ancient writings, including the books of the Hebrew Old Testament, were intended to be read aloud continuously from the beginning to the end. The papyrus and leather scrolls on which these texts were written were ill-suited to intrusive reference consultation. Tables of content were very rare, and there existed no material divisions to which such an index might refer. A few grammatical and medical manuals disseminated in papyri scrolls were divided into chapters. A single commentator on the orations of Cicero, Asconius Pedianus Quintus, referred to a line number (*versus*) as an approximate point in a text so as to identify a particular passage, but without strict conventions for the standardized replication of papyrus scrolls, such a precocious use of materially defined reference loci within Greek and Roman prose was not replicated.

At the end of the fourth century, the parchment codex increasingly supplanted the scroll, but it too, at least in the elite world of pagan *belles lettres*, served primarily to support oral presentation. In both Greek and Latin, the texts contained in codices—as in scrolls—were written without spaces between words and without graphic marks of punctuation. In Greek codices, numbered pages sometimes were present, but these were apparently used only for assembling a codex and never as points of cross reference within a book or to refer from one book to another. Ancient Greek and Latin codex books at the end of antiquity were essentially phonographic transcriptions of a text. Although prefaced with large illuminations for visual display, the text of the deluxe codices containing Vergil's *Aeneid*, like the papyri texts they supplanted, was meant to be received by an aural audience. The full realization of such literary works with their highly variable word order could be achieved only through the intercession of an oral reader, whose task it was to delineate with his voice words and larger units of syntax. Only in a decorous performance, with appropriate inflections and pauses, was meaning fluidly communicated by the reader to his listener.

Because ancient scribes provided neither ancient Greek nor Latin with interword spaces, or with graphic signs of punctuation or diacritical marks, reading aloud with the appropriate intonation required a rehearsal or preparatory examination of the text, a process which Quintilian and other Roman grammarians referred to as *praelectio*. It was customary for wealthy Greeks and Romans to employ a well-educated slave whose task it was to rehearse an oral reading in private of a literary work prior to a public performance. A satisfactory oral performance required the reader to keep his eyes well ahead of his voice, a daunting task in a syntactically complex text written continuously in *scriptura continua*. For the reader of Vergil's Latin verse, only the contextual space that delineated metrical poetic lines offered rudimentary cues for correct enunciation. Because of the profound ambiguity of the ancient *mise-en-page*, even an experienced reader was obliged to rely on his memory of a familiar text, previously read aloud and heard, to ensure satisfactory enunciation. In the classroom, masters placed points between words to aid young readers in reading and memorizing the standard corpus of classical texts, but such supplementary paratextual devices, personally added on an ad hoc basis, were intended only to help schoolboys to master the art of reading ancient poetry and prose. They had no place in a fully confected formal codex of a literary text.

At the end of antiquity the codex, the very leaves of which invited intratextual consultation, began to incorporate new and more exclusively visual elements to facilitate the reading process. The corpus of Roman law, an important component of which was termed "the Codex," was divided into numbered sections readily identified by incipits that protruded into the margins accompanied by marginal Roman numerals in red ink. Practical manuals in codex form were similarly divided into chapters preceded by tables of *capitula*. Codices divided into chapters prefaced with tables of *capitula* won special favor among early Christians, both in Greek and in Latin. In the third century, Ammonius of Alexandria divided the Greek Gospels into short numbered paragraphs, and in the early fourth century Eusebius of Caesarea devised a set of ten concordance tables, inserted as a preface into Gospel codices, that referred the reader to the Ammonian numbers, several of which were written in the margins of virtually every Gospel page. The primary function of the *Canons of Eusebius*, the decoration of which enhanced ready access, was doubtless to aid the private study of scholars and particularly to assist priests in preparation of homilies and sermons for the public narration in church of the life of Jesus. Such an apparatus of marginal numbers was without antecedents in the extensive corpus of Greek and Roman classical literature. The Eusebian concordance tables, whose use presupposed the codex format, quickly migrated into Latin Gospel books where added marginalia enhanced their reference function. In Latin codices the Eusebian apparatus was both consistently more present and far more widely disseminated than it had been in Greek. Jerome in the early fifth century incorporated the Eusebian apparatus and marginal numbers as intrinsic components of the *mise-en-texte* of his new Vulgate translation. He also recognized that Christian readers with whom he corresponded might divide their codex books with marginal subject—i.e., chapter—headings.

Peter Brown (1971, 86) has brilliantly described early Christians of the late Roman Empire as middlebrow, that is, they were not part of the upper class that constituted the principal aural audience of pagan literary texts. The prevalence of the codex among Christians is readily comprehensible in this context. Jerome, to aid the anticipated simple readership of his Vulgate Bible, which was always copied in codex format, drew inspiration from the graphically defined liturgical sections and versification that were in the course of evolving in the Hebrew Bible of his day. He divided his new Latin translation into fixed lines of sense, *cola et commata*, analogous to the fixed verses of the Hebrew Bible. These fixed syntactic divisions in Latin Bibles, replicated from codex to codex, aided the relatively unsophisticated Christian Latin reader to grasp the meaning of sacred Scripture. The set word order that Jerome observed in emulation of Hebrew (and in defiance of Ciceronian eloquence) complemented the graphic distinctions and simplified the reader's task.

Even prior to Eusebius and Jerome, Greek-speaking Christians of the second century, drawing inspiration from the Jewish graphic liturgical divisions for the annual (or triannual) Sabbath readings of the Torah, had divided the Gospels graphically, first in Greek and later in Latin codices, into numbered chapters according to a variety of systems. These chapters facilitated the liturgical reading of the Gospel narrative of the life of Jesus during the course of a year on each successive Sunday. Toward the very end of antiquity, most of the books of the Old Testament in Christian codex Bibles evinced similar signs of division into chapters. As in the Gospels, these chapter divisions were often denoted and numbered in red ink. However, whereas the liturgical divisions of the Jewish tradition (of which a few early examples have been found among the Dead Sea Scrolls, also marked with red ink) had been from an early date relatively standardized, Christian biblical chaptering in late antiquity was highly variable and remained so throughout the early Middle Ages both in Latin and in Greek, until the introduction of the standardized chaptering that first emerged during the last two decades of the twelfth century in England and among English scholars in Paris.

Among the Latin Fathers, Augustine, likely inspired by the chapter division present in Scripture and particularly the Gospels, composed lists of *capitula* or chapter headings for his own compositions. His list of subject headings for the *City of God* initially circulated separately, but likely within his lifetime, the headings and the apposite numbers of these divisions were inserted into the body of his text. There they served to help guide the inexpert reader through Augustine's elegant and syntactically complex prose, which, written in *scriptura continua*, was especially difficult to parse. Eugippius (*c.*465–533) completed the task of dividing most of Augustine's extensive corpus into numbered chapters with summary headings, and in his own *Excerpta ex operibus Augustini*, Eugippius cited most of Augustine's works by both book and *titulus*, i.e., chapter number. This peculiarly Christian penchant for embracing chapter division, consistently evinced in the exegetical works of Jerome, culminated in Quodvultdeus' *Liber promissionum et praedictorum Dei*, which was divided into 153 chapters in emulation of Jesus's miraculous catch of 153 fishes described in the Gospel of John (John 21:1–11) and in Cassiodorus' *Institutiones*, of which the 36 numbered chapters of Book II symbolized the age of Jesus when he was crucified. In the *Institutiones*, Cassiodorus cited both Augustine and Josephus by book and chapter number.

Jerome, Cassiodorus, and subsequently Isidore also commended—and in their tracts made abundant use of—critical graphic signs placed in the margin of codex pages to facilitate the rapid interpretation of Scripture. Cassiodorus notably introduced marginal Hebrew characters (which in Hebrew had the value of numbers) into his *Expositio Psalmorum*, thus enhancing the verisimilitude of the Latin incipits of the acrostic Psalms (present in the *lemmata*) to the original Hebrew. Since these Hebrew characters were de facto numbers, their marginal presence in the acrostic passages of the *Expositio*, or in transliteration in Jerome's Vulgate, constituted the beginning of graphic numbering of biblical verses, a Latin practice that, while inspired by the Hebrew custom of acrostic versification, was a unique Western innovation. Vatican City, BAV, Vat. lat. 5704, the sole securely identified codex to survive from Cassiodorus's proto-monastery of Vivarium, contained a Latin translation of the Song of Songs in which each verse was numbered in red ink. The tendency toward numbered subdivisions of chapters and verses in biblical codices, evident in the volumes produced by and for Cassiodorus, was emulated and expanded in the seventh century at the Northumbrian Benedictine abbey of Wearmouth-Jarrow, notably in the *Codex Amiatinus*, almost every book of which was prefaced by a table of *capitula* and divided into correspondingly numbered chapters. In the acrostic passages, the Hebrew names were written in red ink in the margins of the leaves. For Lamentations, the acrostic enumeration of chapters 1–4 in Lamentations was expanded by using Greek letters to number the verses of chapter 5, which in Hebrew was not acrostic, an enumeration sometimes replicated in English Bibles of the twelfth century.

Such tendencies of division, subdivision, and enumeration in the Bible and other texts reached their fruition in the central Middle Ages as the primary function of the Latin codex radically shifted from one of exclusively serving as a phonographic transcription that ensured the accurate oral recreation of an aural opus to a vehicle which also facilitated a direct visual access. The new graphic innovations of the medieval codex made simpler the oral reading of liturgy and also provided direct access to the information and complex ideas hidden within a text, unmediated by audible or subvocal pronunciation. The dramatic shift rendering the codex into an instrument of visible language, incipient at Vivarium, expanded in Ireland in the seventh century as Celtic monastic scribes introduced the regular separation of words by readily visible quantities of space. As has been noted, word separation (more usually by points than by space) had existed as a pedagogic tool for beginning readers in the Roman and Greek classroom. Outside of the classroom, traces of the efficacy of inserting occasional interword and intersyllabic spaces into Latin writing can be detected in funerary epitaphs, which on Christian tombs were intended to be readily legible to the "middlebrow" adherents of the new faith. Simple soldiers of the Roman legions (who were notably present among the early adherents to Christianity) formed part of the unsophisticated readership that developed in the Roman Empire at levels of society largely hidden to later scholars by the luxurious veneer of the elite world of pagan *belles lettres*. The ephemeral notes of ordinary soldiers written on wooden fragments, discovered during the last century in the excavation of Roman military camps in Vindolanda in northern England, evinced occasional interword and intersyllabic spaces.

After the collapse of Rome, the quest to make sacred texts accessible to Irish and Anglo-Saxon monks, whose native language was not derived from Latin and who therefore confronted written Latin as an entirely foreign tongue, gave impetus to elevating the occasional insertion of interword and intersyllabic space current in restricted contexts in the late Empire into the confection of formal codices. In the British Isles, interword space became an intrinsic element of the formal sacred page of the Irish and Anglo-Saxon Bibles by the end of the seventh century, notably in Saint Cuthbert's copy of the Gospel of John. When Celtic and Anglo-Saxon missionaries went to evangelize large sections of the Continent, they brought with them from the British Isles word-separated Gospel books, Bibles, and biblical commentaries. Within these tomes, interword space created signs for words that were physiologically readily perceptible to the reader in peripheral vision. Thus, each written Latin word came to have its own distinct profile or, in the parlance of cognitive psychology, Bouma shape. For the first time the verbs *videre* and *inspicere*, with their implicit visual emphasis and implication of silent perusal, became alternatives for *legere*, the ancient Latin verb regularly used to denote reading aloud. The new medium of word-separated script, and the new physiological process of reading that it implied, rapidly spread from Ireland to the Anglo-Saxon realms of England and Scotland, all lands exterior to the frontiers of the late Roman Empire where the linguistic knowledge of the natives was of scant aid in deciphering a Latin page, particularly when written in unseparated script.

The Venerable Bede was an early heir of Irish monastic scribal practices, and all his works were composed (and in Britain always diffused) in word-separated script. The new word-separated script was exemplified by the *Codex Amiatinus*, the word-separated rendition of the Latin Vulgate Bible transcribed at Bede's abbey of Wearmouth-Jarrow. Anglo-Saxon monastic scribes in reworking a now lost exemplar (which had been transcribed at Vivarium in *scriptura continua* and brought to Britain) introduced word separation of sufficient quantity to aid readers of the Vulgate. Irish and especially Anglo-Saxon missionaries, including the eminent Saint Boniface and Saint Willibrord, introduced word separation by space to the Continent, particularly to the Low Countries, Germany, and Switzerland, where the new recruits to the Order of Saint Benedict spoke Teutonic vernacular dialects. However, only at the Benedictine abbeys of St. Gall and Einsiedeln was the newly imported medium of word-separated script received and consistently emulated in the course of the tenth century. Elsewhere on the Continent a new kind of writing developed that was intermediate between the *scriptura continua* of Jerome, Cassiodorus, and ancient pagan literature and the new word separation of the Insular Christian Bible. This new text format, current on the Continent until the late tenth century, may be designated as *aerated script*. In *aerated script*, major units of space separated some words to form word blocks. These often varied between ten and twenty characters in length, and within a block some words and syllables were separated by lesser quantities of space.

Separated script in the British Isles and aerated script on the Continent constituted the principal text formats of the early medieval book until the late tenth or early eleventh century (depending on locality); in general the closer a monastic center was located to the Mediterranean, the longer the tradition of aerated script prevailed. The panoply of paratextual marginal and interlineal signs that originated in word-separated script in Britain, however, was imperfectly transferred to the aerated script of the Continent even before word separation itself won general acceptance. The marginal symbols that Bede had employed in his codices to identify the four principal patristic sources for his commentaries on the Gospels either entirely vanished or were highly truncated in the Continental transcriptions of these works. Nevertheless, many of the graphic signs of syntactic punctuation formed by clusters of points and comma-like marks, which had originated in Ireland and migrated to England, spread widely in Continental aerated writing. At St. Gall, such marks evolved into neumes, the earliest graphic mode of melodic transcription. Whether serving as simple punctuation or as indication of musical inflection and pitch, such paratextual signs constituted increasingly important visible cues to the oral reader, and as such facilitated rapid comprehension and a more fluid oral performance of Scripture, both in *lectio divina* and in chant.

In addition, early books present in England provided new and entirely visual aids in the form of liturgical tables for the reader in quest of the appropriate readings. The New Testament volume, Fulda Codex 1 (Fulda, Hessische Landesbibliothek, Bonifatianus 1), written in the sixth century in unseparated script in southern Italy and brought to Britain, where it belonged to Saint Boniface, contained a table of lessons with numerical references that rapidly led the eyes of a monk to the appropriate daily reading of the Epistles. Such relatively rare reader prefatory aids, suitable for silent perusal before commencing the oral performance of liturgy, multiplied in the British Isles. English scribes created new liturgical tables for the Gospels that first appear in eighth-century Gospel books (written in word-separated script). Present in numerous codices, these tables guided readers to the appropriate lessons by providing them with the apposite Eusebian section number. Also, in early medieval word-separated Irish and Anglo-Saxon Gospel books (under the influence of certain late antique antecedents) the function of the Eusebian tables (sometimes no longer present) was assumed by the clusters of direct marginal cross references (extracted from the information contained in the Eusebian tables). These marginal concordance notes rapidly led the reader's eyes to concordant passages identified by their marginal Eusebian *capitulum* numbers. The reader was thus freed from the obligation of flipping the leaves first to consult the tables themselves and a second time to find the indicated concordant passages.

In addition, early medieval codices under Insular influence, whether in separated or aerated script, made frequent use of illuminated diagrams and incorporated lavish multicolored decoration. These visible enhancements served to convey historical information and to communicate subtly encoded messages of awe and piety directly to the eyes of the monastic readers, with an intensity that had almost no antecedent in either pagan or Judeo-Christian scrolls and codices. In antiquity, graphic tables and diagrams, including primitive maps, may have been used (rarely) in the classroom, but they were scarcely, if ever, incorporated within the continuously written text of a formal scroll or codex.

The enhanced emphasis on visible language that initially characterized word-separated manuscripts produced in Ireland, England, Brittany, and Insular monastic centers of the early Middle Ages endured in the British Isles into the Central and late Middle Ages. However, until the early eleventh century Anglo-Saxon and Celtic culture's graphic innovations were reflected in most of Germany, France, and Italy only in codices copied in aerated script replete with a new and, in respect to antiquity, entirely unprecedented repertoire of visible marks of punctuation. This "semi-separated" Continental script was most firmly entrenched as a mode of textual display in France, Iberia, and Italy, lands that had formerly constituted the core of the Roman Empire, where vernacular speech was derived from ancient Latin. As a consequence, there emerged an important palaeographic frontier between word-separated writing in Insular scripts in Britain and aerated writing in Caroline letterforms on the Continent.

This division progressively disappeared in the course of the late tenth and early eleventh century due to a variety of causes. An underlying and profoundly significant factor leading to the reception of full word separation throughout Western Europe was the evolution of the Romance tongues away from their Latin roots into discrete languages that were increasingly recognizable as languages distinct from Latin. The first crude attempts to transcribe Romance text using Latin characters commencing in the tenth century with the *Serments de Strassbourg* constituted palpable recognition of a new perceived distinction between the spoken tongue and written Latin. Although only a smattering of written Romance texts antedate the year 1100, their very existence demonstrates the growing awareness of a disjuncture between the Romance vernacular and written Latin that had come to parallel that which had already existed in the British Isles since the sixth century. The more that graphic Latin on the Continent was perceived to be a foreign tongue, the more attractive word separation and the new "visible" Latin became as a mode of mastering it. At the end of the tenth century, the new movement of Benedictine monastic reform embraced word-separated Caroline script, spread it in northern France, and brought word-separated Caroline writing to Britain.

In addition, intellectual changes within the world of monasticism in the late tenth century gave impetus to the wide adoption of word separation in Western Europe. The first of these changes was the renewal of interest in logic and science which was accompanied by the reception and translation into Latin from Arabic of hitherto unavailable mathematical and astronomic texts. In Latin, these translations replicated the word separation of their Arabic exemplars. The new medium of word-separated script was employed for the newly received expanded corpus of the Aristotelian *logica vetus*. The complexities of such difficult texts were rendered more transparent by their presentation in word-separated format. Gerbert of Reims introduced the abacus, and he and his followers introduced graphic Arabic numerals into Latin in tracts explaining its use. These exotic characters appeared within texts disseminated across northern Europe exclusively in word-separated script. At the abbey of Fleury, Abbo also embraced the abacus and composed original writings on logic inspired by Aristotle that incorporated at once word separation, emblematic abbreviations, and special spacing and ordering of words for the visible expression of syllogisms, graphically making them readily comprehensible. Under Abbo and his successors, the use of tree diagrams mushroomed in the scriptorium of Fleury as a paratextual format for displaying complex logical and scientific relationships that in antiquity had been communicated only orally and verbally. The use of highly complex tree diagrams to illustrate texts in word-separated script rendered the written page into a transparent vehicle for the communication of Aristotelian logic that Aristotle and his Peripatetic disciples of the previous millennium could never have anticipated.

In the course of the twelfth century new interest in Oriental models provided an increasing impetus to innovation in text format, particularly in the British Isles. Whereas in earlier centuries Eusebian division of the Gospels had been used virtually exclusively for cross references within a single Gospel book, Senatus of Worcester used them in an *Epistle* as fixed loci for reference citation. In an attempt to correct discrepancies in numeration that had crept into Gospel books, Senatus created a table of incipits that provided the initial words for each section, thus encouraging uniformity for these points of textual division in different copies of the Gospels. In the East among the Jews, analogous tables or incipits for insuring the uniformity of liturgical sections had long existed as part of the Mesorah, the apparatus for the Hebrew Bible. However, before the late twelfth century no equivalent tool for ensuring standardized divisions had existed in the tradition of the Latin Vulgate. In about 1180 at the royal abbey of Saint Albans, in keeping with a new monastic interest in fixed loci based on uniformity of text distinctions, a scribe placed the appropriate numbers of the Eusebian chapters in the margins of the abbey's copy of Rupert of Deutz's *De officiis ecclesiasticis* (Oxford, Christ Church, MS 97) to aid the reader in identifying Rupert's citations from the Gospels using any Bible with a correctly written Eusebian apparatus. In the early thirteenth century, in England and France, marginal concordances based on a variety of chapter schemas extended the principle of marginal Eusebian cross references to the entirety of the New and Old Testaments.

The earliest occurrences of the fully developed modern chapter divisions for both the Old and New Testament of the Bible also transpired at Saint Albans, where they are to be found in a small group of Vulgate Bibles. For the Five Books of Moses, these modern chapter divisions corresponded to a remarkable extent to the *sederim,* the graphically defined numbered divisions of Palestinian tradition placed in the margins of the earliest surviving Hebrew codex Bibles, by means of which the entire Torah had been divided to facilitate its liturgical reading in Sabbath services over the course of three years. Cognizant of Hebraic antecedents, reformed monks, first at Saint Albans and then at Cîteaux, and soon thereafter regular canons at the abbey of Saint Victor in Paris adopted a fixed uniform chapter division to facilitate the *lectura divina* of the entire Bible over the course of a single year. The first Bible in which the new chapter divisions (which two generations later were identified with Stephen Langton) were present was Cambridge, Corpus Christi College, MS 48, a codex written *c.*1180 that exemplified a number of aspects salient to Jewish tradition. This moderately large volume was written in three columns, like contemporary larger Hebrew Bibles copied in England, Yemen, and Sephardic Spain, where the *sederim* (that is the triannual liturgical divisions) were regularly denoted with Hebrew numbers in the margins. Also in Corpus 48, a scribe, likely a Sephardic Jew, wrote the Hebrew alphabet (whose characters had the values of numbers) in the margins of the acrostic verses of Lamentations.

In a New Testament copied at Saint Albans, Oxford, Bodleian Library, Finch e.25, the new chapters for the Gospels, Acts, and the Apocalypse were marked with Arabic numbers in precisely those forms employed by late twelfth-century scribes in Hereford and western England. (Sephardic Jews played an important role introducing to the court of Henry II the Arabic numerical characters then current in the Islamic world which provided some of the models for the specific set of graphic forms for Arabic numbers that emerged in England.) No longer confined to the abacus, the newly received English versions of Arabic symbols were used for calculation on parchment, and within arithmetic and astronomical tables. They were also employed to number chapters in scientific works and to number chapters and eventually graphic lines in English Bibles. In England these forms of Arabic numbers were firmly linked to the new biblical chapter division. The new set of Arabic numbers (a unique hybrid molded from a synthesis of Arabic forms and Insular signs) served to disambiguate the new chapter division from various unstandardized biblical chapter schemas in current use, which were invariably denoted by Roman numerals.

The Oriental reception in late twelfth-century England of selected elements of Eastern *mise-en-page* from Hebrew and Arabic provided a foundation for the scholastic books that in many ways culminated the millennium-long evolution from the aurally received book of late antiquity to the highly legible "visible" codices of the medieval university, the use of which was increasingly solitary, private, and silent. In Hebrew, the liturgical divisions of Sabbath readings were from late antiquity onward divided into seven parts for seven male readers. This sevenfold Jewish division inspired in early thirteenth-century Latin Bibles a *graphic* division of modern biblical chapters into septants for ease in reference citation. In about 1215, a scribe divided the new chapters of Genesis in Oxford, Oriel College, MS 77 with the letters A through G written in red ink. This mode of subdividing chapters provided an effective alternative to our citation by verse number for the rapid intrusive consultation of the Bible until the end of the Middle Ages. Thomas Gallus, an Insular scholar residing at Saint Victor, who had an English cure near Cambridge, used chapter and letter for reference citation in his *Commentary on Isaiah* composed in 1218. By *c.*1230 the septant mode of marginal letter subdivision had spread to Oxford; the English scribes who prepared Paris, BnF, lat. 10417 divided every chapter in the margin with the red letters A–G. The great verbal concordance composed in the mid-thirteenth century (credited to Richard of Darlington but which the French attributed to Hugh de Saint-Cher), called by the English *Concordanciae Anglicae,* employed the modern chapter and alphabetical subdivision for all its references. In the fourteenth century the Lollards regularly embraced marginal alphabets A through G in their vernacular Bibles, and they referred to book, chapter, and alphabetical letter in liturgical tables both for Gospel readings and readings from the Epistles.

While graphic marginal alphabets won limited acceptance in English Vulgate Bibles and very wide acceptance in English vernacular Bibles, other systems of numbered subdivisions may trace their origins to the fecund graphic milieu of England in the late twelfth and early thirteenth centuries. Building on the antecedents (including the *Codex Amiatinus*) of graphic numbering of acrostic verse, the scribe of an early thirteenth-century Vulgate Bible, Oxford, Bodleian Library, Kennicott 15, substituted Roman numerals in the margins for the names of the Hebrew letters, creating the earliest example of verse numbering within modern chapter divisions based on canonical Hebraic versification. The first medieval text in which Arabic numbers were used to number verses was likely a Latin translation of Ps.-Ptolemy's *Centiloquium*, of which the earliest copy is Berlin, Staatsbibliothek zu Berlin-Preussischer Kulturbesitz, Hamilton 557, transcribed in Italy in the first half of the thirteenth century. It contains verses numbered with "fossilized" Arabic numbers, i.e., in the forms current in the twelfth-century Islamic world. In about 1230, a single copy of an anonymous commentary on the Psalms, contained in Paris, BnF, lat. 14251 and 14252, denoted each verse with Arabic numbers in the forms current in Paris after *c.*1215. While no subsequent copies of this text transcribed in France contained such verse numbers, the practice of using Arabic numbers for the entire Psalter won favor among English Dominicans. Nicolas Trevet used them in his personal diglot Psalter (Oxford, Corpus Christi College, MS 12) to link his Latin version to the Hebrew original, and he subsequently integrated the use of verse numbers into the *mise-en-page* of his *Commentary* on Jerome's *Iuxta Hebraicum* version of the Psalter. Another English Dominican, Thomas Waleys, also integrated verse numbers into his *Commentary on the Gallican Psalter* (with its slightly variant versification), and Waleys composed a subject index to his work that referred explicitly to chapter and verse, the earliest such table to use the modern mode of biblical reference citation.

The evolution toward intensive citation of the Bible by visible distinctions was paralleled in canon law and theology. The same scholastics, beginning with contemporaries of Stephen Langton, who cited Scripture by book, chapter, and sometimes by alphabetical distinction (where we moderns would refer to verse number) also cited civil and canon law by numbered distinctions and subdistinctions. In the summae of penance and theology composed in France in the early thirteenth century, we see in contemporary manuscripts traces of the introduction of numbered chapters and chapter tables that palaeographically and codicologically replicate the introduction of standard chapter divisions into Bibles. By 1250, texts like the *Sentences* of Peter Lombard had been divided into a standard format that facilitated rapid consultation and citation. The new summae of the mid-thirteenth century assumed a structure of parts, distinctions, and *quaestiones* and responses as a quintessential part of their *mise-en-texte*. The judicious application of rubrication as a marker for these textual distinctions facilitated swift, visual, silent consultation. By the year 1400, virtually every attribute of the page that was later to characterize the privately and silently read printed volumes of the fifteenth and sixteenth century had been created.

BIBLIOGRAPHY

Bowman, A. K. and J. D. Thomas. 1983. *Vindolanda: The Latin Writing Tablets* (Britannia Monograph Series 4). London: Society for the Promotion of Roman Studies.

Brown, P. 1971. *The World of Late Antiquity: AD 150–750*. New York: Harcourt Brace Jovanovich.

Courcelle, P. 1948. *Les Lettres grecques, en occident de Macrobe à Cassiodore*. Paris: Éditions de Boccard.

Gorman, M. 2001. *The Manuscript Tradition of the Works of Saint Augustine* (Millennio medievale, Reprints, 2). Florence: SISMEL.

Gorman, M. 2002. "Source Marks and Chapter Divisions in Bede's Commentary on Luke." *Revue Benedictine* 112: 246–90.

Graux, C. 1878. "Nouvelles recherches sur la stichometrie." *Revue de philologie* 2: 97–143.

Klauser, T. 1935. *Das Romische Capitulare Evangeliorum: Texte und Untersuchungen zu seiner ältesten Geschichte*. Münster: Aschendorff.

Lambot, C. 1939. "Lettre inédite de saint Augustin relative au *De civitate Dei*." *Revue Benedictine* 51: 109–21.

Marrou, H.-I. 1951. "La Division en chapitres des livres de la *Cité de Dieu*." In *Mélanges Joseph de Ghellinck, S.J.*, 235–49. Gembloux: J. Duculot.

Martimort, A. G. 1992. *Les Lectures liturgiques et leurs livres*. (Topologie des sources du moyen âge occidental 64). Turnhout: Brepols.

Meyvaert, P. 1995. "Bede's *Capitula lectionum* for the Old and New Testament." *Revue Bénédictine*, 105: 348–80.

Morin, G. 1910. "Le Plus Ancien *Comes* ou lectionnaire de l'église romain." *Revue Bénédictine* 27: 41–74.

Morin, G. 1911. "Liturgie et basiliques de Rome au milieu du VIIIe siècle, d'après les listes d'Évangiles de Würzburg." *Revue Bénédictine* 28: 296–30.

Palmer, N. F. 1989. "Kapitel und Buch. Zu den Gliederungsprinzipien mittelalterlicher Bücher." *Fruhmittelalterliche Studien* 23: 43–56.

Parkes, M. B. 1982. *The Scriptorium of Wearmouth-Jarrow* (Jarrow Lecture, 1982). Jarrow: Parish of Jarrow P.C.C.

Parkes, M. B. 1993. *Pause and Effect: An Introduction to the History of Punctuation in the West*. Berkeley, CA: University of California Press.

Petitmengin, P. 1985. "Les Plus Anciens Manuscrits de la Bible latine." In *Le Monde latin antique de la Bible*, ed. Jacques Fontaine and Charles Pietri, 89–123 and Plates I–IV. Paris: Beauchesne.

Petitmengin, P. 1997. "Capitula païens et chrétiens." In *Titres et articulations du texte dans les œuvres antiques: Actes du Colloque International de Chantilly, 13–15 décembre 1994*, ed. J. C. Fredouille, M. O. Goulet-Cazé, P. Hoffmann, P. Petitmengin, and S. Deléani, 491–507. Paris: Institut d'Études Augustiniennes.

Rouse, R. H. and M. A. Rouse. 1974. "The Verbal Concordance to the Scriptures." *Archivum Fratrum Praedicatorum* 44: 5–30.

Saenger, P. 1997a. "Separated Script at Fleury and Reims at the Time of Gerbert and Abbo." In *Le Livre et l'historien: études offertes en l'honneur du Professor Henri-Jean Martin*, ed. F. Barbier, A. Parent-Charon, F. Dupuigrenet-Desroussilles, C. Jolly, and D. Varry, 3–22. Geneva: Droz.

Saenger, P. 1997b. *Space between Words: The Origins of Silent Reading*. Stanford, CA: Stanford University Press.

Saenger, P. 2005. "The British Isles and the Origin of the Modern Mode of Biblical Citation." *Syntagma, Revista de Historia del Libro y de la Lectura* 1: 77–123.

Saenger, P. 2008. "The Anglo-Hebraic Origins of the Modern Chapter Division of the Latin Bible." In *La fractura historiográfica: las investigacions de la Edad Media y Renacimento desde el tercer milenio*, ed. Javier San José Lera et al., 177–202. Salamanca: Seminario de Estudios Medievales y Renacentistas.

Saenger, P. 2012. "Jewish Liturgical Divisions of the Torah and the English Chapter Divisions of the Vulgate attributed to Stephen Langton." In *Pesher Nahum: Texts and Studies in Jewish History and Literature from Antiquity to the Middle Ages Presented to Norman Golb* (Studies in Ancient Oriental Civilization 66), ed. Joel L. Kraemer and Michael G. Wechsler, 107–202 and Plates 15.1–15.4. Chicago: Oriental Institute of the University of Chicago.

Saenger, P. 2013. "The Twelfth-Century Reception of Oriental Languages and the Graphic Mise-en-Page of Latin Vulgate Bibles Copied in England." In *The Late Medieval Bible: Form and Function*, ed. Laura Light and Eyal Poleg, 31-66 and Plates I–III. Leiden: Brill.

Verey, C. D. 1980. "Description of the Manuscript." In *The Durham Gospels together with Fragments of a Gospel Book in Uncial, Durham Cathedral Library, MS A.II.17* (Early English Manuscripts in Facsimile 20), ed. Christopher D Verey et al., 15–35. Copenhagen: Rosenkilde and Bagger.

Vezin, J. 1985. "La Division en paragraphes dans les manuscrits de la basse antiquité et du Haut Moyen Âge." In *La Notion de paragraphe*, ed. Jean Châtillon et al., 41–51. Paris: Éditions du CNRS.

Vezin, J. 1987. "Les Divisions du texte dans les Évangiles jusqu'à l'apparition de l'imprimerie." In *Grafia e interpretazione del latino nel medioevo*, ed. A. Maieru, 53–68. Florence: Olschki.

CHAPTER 44

WHO WERE THE SCRIBES OF LATIN MANUSCRIPTS?

ALISON I. BEACH

WHO were the scribes of Late Antiquity and the Middle Ages? Broadly defined, scribes were individuals who were able to write, either for themselves or for others. Scribes produced a broad range of written "objects," including charters, letters, records of financial or legal transactions, manuscripts of original literary texts, and copies of sacred Scripture. A scribe might specialize in a particular kind of writing. He or she might, for example, offer a fine calligraphic book hand, a serviceable documentary hand, or shorthand useful for taking dictation (Gamble 1995, 91). Most scribes worked anonymously. Some, however, identified themselves in colophons, inscriptions that might also record the date of the work, the place it was copied, or the name of the person for whom the copy was made. Such colophons, which became more common in the later Middle Ages, sometimes even include a line or two expressing the joy of the scribe at the completion of the task, or a complaint about its difficulty.

The status of the scribe varied dramatically from antiquity through the end of the Middle Ages, changing in parallel with the social, intellectual, and religious changes that influenced attitudes toward the use of the written word. While the scribes of the ancient Near East enjoyed considerable social prestige, their counterparts in the Greco-Roman world were more likely to be drawn from the lowest levels of society. Most were slaves, male and female, educated by masters who needed literate workers, or freedmen and women (Gamble 1995, 91; Haines-Eitzen 1998, 639). Still, a scribe in Republican Rome might use his skill to rise socially, as was the case of Cn. Flavius, who seems to have used his ability to write to rise from the status of official clerk (*scriba*) to aedile by carefully exploiting a social context in which the written word was growing in importance (Harris 1989, 155). Although it was a given in the Greco-Roman world that the elite would engage, for reasons of social necessity, in a variety of written interactions (Harris 1989, 248), many did so by proxy, relying on the scribal work of their slaves, a fact that may have contributed significantly to low levels of literacy among the freeborn population of the late Roman Republic and High Empire (Harris 1989, 259).

There is also evidence of a professional book trade in Rome in the first century BC, and in the Roman provinces by the first century AD, which may have provided a context for non-servile scribes to market their skills. It was also possible for an independent scribe to earn a living in the employ of a particular author, for a library, in a governmental office, or on a contract basis (Gamble 1995, 91).

The emergence of Christianity, particularly after the legalization and spread of the religion within the Roman Empire in the fourth century, contributed to an increased demand for books. In 332, the Emperor Constantine (*c.*272–337) sent a letter to Eusebius (*c.*263–339) ordering 50 copies of the "divine Scriptures" to facilitate religious education. These were to be "written on well-prepared parchment by copyists most skillful in the art of accurate and beautiful writing"—a formulation that seems to suggest that the emperor had professional scribes in mind and that he was willing to pay for their expertise (Gamble 1995, 79–80). Eusebius claimed that when Origen (*c.*185–254) needed copyists to help him with his scriptural commentaries, he tapped into a traditional system of patronage, using the labor of "girls trained in beautiful writing" made available to him by a certain Ambrose of Milan (Haines-Eitzen 1998, 631).

Copying sacred texts rapidly came to be seen as an act of religious devotion in the context of Christianity—a particularly significant shift in view of inherited ideas about copying as a difficult and menial form of manual labor. The rise of Christian monastic institutions in the course of late antiquity and the early Middle Ages provided a new social location for the work of the scribe. Melania the Younger (d. 439), a woman of high social status, is said to have embraced the low-status work of the scribe in her religious community, diligently working every day to produce texts (Parkes 2008, 6). In an intentional inversion of the antique paradigm of the servile copyist, Melania's devotion to writing raised her standing by signaling her pious humility (Haines-Eitzen 1998, 642). The abbess Caesaria the Younger (d. 529) is said by the slightly later author of the life of her brother, Caesarius of Arles (d. 543), to have taught the nuns in her charge at Arles to "copy out the holy books" (Haines-Eitzen 1998, 642). When Cassiodorus (d. 585) founded the monastic community of Vivarium as a place of spiritual and intellectual refuge on his family estate in Calabria, he took care to establish an extensive library comprising both Christian and non-Christian authors. While he brought a number of his own books with him, he also attempted to procure others from booksellers in North Africa—a hint that there were still professional scribes at work there in the middle of the sixth century (Bischoff 1994, 3). Book One of his *Institutions of Divine and Secular Learning* is peppered with references to gaps that needed filling in the library:

> But I trust that by the mercy of the Lord I shall shortly locate these commentaries of Jerome in the various regions where I have directed inquiry ... and so if any of you come on them by chance before they arrive here, take care to have them carefully transcribed and added to the aforesaid commentators.
>
> (*Institutions* 1:14; trans. Halporn 2004, 130)

Cassiodorus assumed that the high-status men whom he expected to congregate at the Vivarium would have the means and the inclination to engage the services of copyists rather than to copy texts themselves. Given the central place of books and sacred study at Vivarium, however, it is not surprising that the men who worked as scribes within the community were highly valued (Bischoff 1994, 7). Cassiodorus devoted a full chapter of the *Institutions* (30) to the work of scribes within the community:

> Still, I have to admit that of all the tasks that can be achieved among you by physical labour, what pleases me most (not perhaps unjustifiably) is the work of scribes if they write correctly...A blessed purpose, a praiseworthy zeal, to preach to men with the hand, to set tongues free with one's fingers and in silence to give mankind salvation and to fight with pen and ink against the unlawful snares of the devil. For Satan receives as many wounds as the scribe writes words of the Lord.
>
> (*Institutions* 30:1; trans. Halporn 2004, 163)

The *Rule of the Master* (sixth century) also assumed the presence of copyists, naming them among the craftsmen of the monastery (Parkes 2008, 7). Although Benedict was silent on the subject of book production in his *Rule* (sixth century), his insistence on reading as spiritual practice at various points in the monastic day, as well as the extent and complexity of the liturgy, clearly assumed some access to books, either copied on site or procured from external sources.

The spiritual value attached to the production of books is also clear in the letters of St. Boniface (*c.*673–754), the great missionary to the Germanic peoples, who received gifts of books from nuns, monks, and clerics back in England. Boniface thanked Eadburga, abbess of the Benedictine monastery of Minster-in-Thanet, for a gift of books that had "consoled [him] with a spiritual light" (Letter 22; trans. Emerton 1940, 60–1) and sent her the materials necessary to make him a copy of the Epistle of Peter in gold letters (Letter 26; trans. Emerton 1940, 64–5). He also requested books from abbots Nothelm (Letter 24) and Duddo (Letter 25), and from Bishop Daniel of Winchester (Letter 51), although these letters refer to procuring, rather than copying, particular texts.

The combination of the humility implicit in taking on what was traditionally considered a menial task and the spiritual value assigned to the act of producing texts for sacred study and liturgical use was powerful and had profound implications for the history of book production and of the institution of monasticism. During the period from around 600 to 1100, the monastery dominated book production in the Latin West. The presence of trained scribes with the space and materials they needed to work was the norm among well-endowed monasteries of this era. A monastery might house a single scribe, or a community of scribes who might work singly or in teams. In many communities this work was overseen and coordinated by a supervisor (*armarius* or *armaria*) who assigned work to his or her copyists (Bischoff 1986, 41). Team-copying, by which two or more scribes collaborated to produce a single text or set of texts, was common at many houses (McKitterick 1992, 33; Beach 2000, 57–75). If a monastic community operated an internal school, its student scribes might progress, through experience and practice, from the least delicate tasks to work on liturgical and biblical texts for which the most skilled copyists were preferred. Such an established school could yield a particular house style, which could survive the transfer between one or more generations, and gain a reputation for producing manuscripts of great beauty or accuracy. This was also true of the scribal centers associated with some of the great cathedral schools, whose book production, and consequently whose libraries, rivaled those of the most prominent monastic centers of the period. That a team of at least eight nuns from the monastery of Chelles in Francia made a three-volume copy of Augustine's *Commentary on the Psalms* (Cologne, Dombibliothek MS 63, 65, and 67) for Archbishop Hildebald of Cologne (784–818) suggests that the reputation of a particular writing school might extend beyond a monastery's own region, and that, like Eadburga and her nuns, later monastic copyists might put their skills to use in the service of, or under contract for, others (McKitterick 1992, 2). This connection between the monastery of Chelles and the archdiocese of Cologne bears witness to the kind of exchange that could take place between schools and institutions of various sorts when books were needed.

In some cases, a scribe might develop his or her own personal reputation. The work of the scribe Otloh of Regensburg (*c*.1010–70), for example, can still be identified among the surviving manuscripts from St. Emmeram, one of the monasteries with which he was associated. Otloh was not only a skilled scribe, but also an author, and through his writings he reveals interesting details about his scribal career. He explains that he taught himself how to write, and although he was later punished for the way he held his pen (Joyce 2005, 98), he was already in great demand as a scribe when he was still a young cleric. He was sent to a number of monasteries to work as an expert copyist even before he became a monk (Joyce 2005, 101). Otloh's non-monastic scribal training is yet another reminder of the presence of medieval scribal cultures beyond the confines of a single monastery. Monks and nuns, but also cathedral clerics, lay craftsmen, and notaries worked as scribes throughout the Middle Ages (McKitterick 1994, 236–7; Parkes 2008, 39). Even during the great age of monastic book production, monastic communities might employ cleric or lay scribes when no competent internal personnel were available for a particular job (Diringer 1982, 208).

In contrast to Otloh, who took clear pride in his scribal abilities (Joyce 2005, 98), Diemut, a prolific female scribe of the dual-sex Benedictine monastery of Wessobrunn in the eleventh century, copied anonymously. Like the great majority of medieval scribes down to the fifteenth century, she did not sign her name to any of her work. Her community, however, considered her individual contribution to the intellectual and spiritual life of the monastery to be so significant that they compiled two lists of the books she had copied, the first around the time of her death and the second in the thirteenth century, and established a yearly commemoration in her honor in 1221 (Beach 2004, 60–1).

The new religious orders that emerged in the eleventh and twelfth centuries evalu-ated book production within their communities in ways that reflected their spiritual values. For the strongly eremitical Carthusians, for example, book production was seen as a form of pastoral care (Parkes 2008, 13). From the seclusion of the individual cell, furnished with all of the necessities for book copying, a Carthusian monk could, like one of Cassiodorus' monk scribes, engage in the "active life" of the pastor. The Dominicans, on the other hand, saw scribal work as an unnecessary distraction from study, preaching, and other forms of pastoral care. Instead of producing their own books, the friars normally purchased or obtained them through networks of friends and relatives (Parkes 2008, 27). The increased availability of lay scribes from the thirteenth century on may have been a factor that facilitated the greater reliance of some religious communities on external sources of books, or increased demand from these houses may have stimulated the market for lay scribes.

A new wave of reform movements in the late Middle Ages also contributed to a marked increase in monastic book production in the fourteenth and fifteenth centuries. In the wake of the Observant Reform at the monastery of Ebstorf, for example, the women worked diligently to produce the new liturgical books they needed—of which 51 volumes survive (Winston-Allen 2004, 170). At the Dominican community of St. Katharine in St. Gall, the sisters were permitted to use some of their free time to copy books—as long as they did not neglect their other duties—and to sign their names to their work—as long as this was not done out of vanity (Winston-Allen 2004, 174).

The rise of the university, beginning at the end of the twelfth century, was naturally significant for the history of medieval book production. Students and masters needed books, and universities such as Paris, Oxford, Bologna, and Naples took care to organize and control copying through the *pecia* system. This system depended upon a new group of middlemen, the stationers, who let out sections of university-approved exemplars to copyists against a fee and supplied needed materials (Bischoff 1986, 42; Brown 1994, 97 and 118; Bataillon 1988; Destrez 1935)). University students, many of whom were destined to become secular priests, might thus make their own copies, or hire a professional scribe to do the work. It was also possible for a student to market his skills as a part-time copyist to augment his income (Parkes 1998, 46).

Finally, the changing needs of secular government also generated work for scribes who specialized in drawing up documents. From the twelfth century, clerks begin to appear in lists of the king's officers. From 1228, the documents for the City of Oxford were prepared by a town clerk, and by the fifteenth century there was a Common Clerk and a staff of clerk-assistants in the City of London (Parkes 2008, 33).

Who, then, were the scribes? They were slaves trained to write in the service of masters, educated religious women engaged in supporting the work of distant missionaries, secular priests in need of liturgical texts, cathedral canons expanding libraries, professional "freelancers" making a living through their ability to write, authors interested in circulating their own writings, university students in need of texts for study, reformed nuns with new liturgies to master and community histories to record, and town clerks with records to keep. Many worked anonymously in settings as varied as an upper-class household in late antiquity, a Benedictine scriptorium, a hermit's cell, or an urban workshop in a growing university town. What all of these men and women had in common was the ability to produce written objects—texts and documents that bear witness to the social, intellectual, economic, legal, and religious contexts of their production.

BIBLIOGRAPHY

Bataillon, L. J., B. G. Guyot, and R. H. Rouse. 1988. *La Production du livre universitaire au Moyen Âge. Exemplar et Pecia.* Paris: Institut de recherche et d'histoire des textes.

Beach, A. 2000. "Claustration and Collaboration between the Sexes in the Twelfth-Century Scriptorium." In *Monks and Nuns, Saints and Outcasts: Religion in Medieval Society,* ed. Sharon Farmer and Barbara H. Rosenwein, 57–75. Ithaca, NY: Cornell University Press.

Beach, A. 2004. *Women as Scribes: Book Production and Monastic Reform in Twelfth-Century Bavaria.* Cambridge: Cambridge University Press.

Bénédictines de Bouveret. 1965. *Colophons de manuscrits occidentaux des origines au XVIe siècle.* Fribourg: Éditions universitaires.

Bischoff, B. 1986. *Latin Palaeography: Antiquity and the Middle Ages.* Cambridge: Cambridge University Press.

Bischoff, B. 1994. *Manuscripts and Libraries in the Age of Charlemagne,* trans. and ed. Michael Gorman. Cambridge: Cambridge University Press.

Brown, M. P. 1994. *Understanding Illuminated Manuscripts: A Guide to Technical Terms.* Malibu, CA: J. Paul Getty Museum.

Destrez, Jean. 1935. *La pecia dans les manuscrits universitaires du XIIIe et du XIVe siècle.* Paris: Éditions Jacques Vautrain.

Diringer, D. 1982. *The Book before Printing: Ancient, Medieval and Oriental.* New York: Dover Publications.

Emerton, E., trans. 1940. *The Letters of St. Boniface.* New York: Columbia University Press.

Gamble, H. Y. 1995. *Books and Readers in the Early Church: A History of Early Christian Texts.* New Haven, CT: Yale University Press.

Haines-Eitzen, K. 1998. "'Girls Trained in Beautiful Writing': Female Scribes in Roman Antiquity and Early Christianity." *Journal of Early Christian Studies* 6/4: 629–46.

Harris, W. V. 1989. *Ancient Literacy.* Cambridge, MA: Harvard University Press.

Heinzer, Felix. 2008. *Klosterreform und mittelalterliche Buchkultur im deutschen Südwesten.* Leiden: Brill.

Joyce, E. 2005. "Scribal Performance and Identity in the Autobiographical Visions of Otloh of St. Emmeram (d. 1067)." *Essays in Medieval Studies* 22: 95–106.

McKitterick, R. 1992. "Nuns' Scriptoria in England and Francia in the Eighth Century." *Francia* 19/1: 1–35.

McKitterick, R. 1994. "Script and Book Production." In *Carolingian Culture: Emulation and Innovation,* ed. Rosamond McKitterick, 221–47. Cambridge: Cambridge University Press.

Parkes, M. B. 2008. *Their Hands before our Eyes: A Closer Look at Scribes.* Aldershot: Ashgate.

Winston-Allen, A. 2004. *Convent Chronicles: Women Writing about Women and Reform in the Late Middle Ages.* University Park, PA: Pennsylvania State University Press.

CHAPTER 45

BOOK TRADE

Antiquity and the early Middle Ages

GUGLIELMO CAVALLO
(Translated by Robert G. Babcock)

In examining Latin book production from the first centuries of the empire onward, a production that survives almost entirely on papyrus, it becomes clear that the extant specimens exhibit a diversity of technical levels. This is manifested above all in the quality of their writing. It is possible to get an idea of this diversity from the surviving fragments of a few papyrus rolls. P. Qasr Ibrîm 78-3-11/1, the papyrus with verses from the elegies of Cornelius Gallus (first century BC– first century AD) found at Qasr Ibrîm in southern Egypt, is an example of Latin *Capitalis* of high quality. This may be deduced not only from the studied and accurate contrast between the thick and thin strokes of the letters, but also from the layout and from the use of diacritical signs employed to separate words and to separate the poems one from another. In contrast, P. Mich. 430a (first–second century AD),[1] fragments of uncertain content (maybe a philosophical work), found at Karanis in the Fayum in Egypt, presents a form of writing executed with minimal contrast in the thickness of the strokes and with a *ductus* that is somewhat free, characterized by the prolongation of some of the vertical strokes in a manner recalling the technique of incised writing (on wax or metal)—a *Capitalis*, in short, less formal than that of the papyrus of Cornelius Gallus. Finally P. Oxy. XVII 2088 (second century AD),[2] a fragment of a historical narrative about Servius Tullius, also of Egyptian provenance, and more precisely from Oxyrhynchus, offers an informal style of writing modeled on the typical forms of incised writing. It is executed, therefore, with a rapid *ductus*, albeit one lacking in ligatures. The script is characterized by strokes that at times are broken or prolonged and by a few cursive forms. This is, in fact, a *Capitalis* of second quality.

We do not know with any precision who the intended audience was for the books mentioned here. But no doubt, if they *were* books made for the commercial market, they must have been offered for sale, and eventually purchased, at quite different price levels: high for the Cornelius Gallus, in the middle for the philosophical treatise, somewhat lower for the historical work. To be sure, we have very little information on book prices in antiquity. For the period of Diocletian (that is, between the third and fourth centuries), a price difference between writing of the first quality and writing of the second quality is precisely established by the *Edictum de pretiis rerum venalium*, issued by that Emperor in AD 301: 25 denarii for 100 lines of writing of the first quality and 20 denarii for the same number of lines of the second quality (1 denarius = 16 asses).[3] It is clear, therefore, that the quality of writing directly influenced the cost of the book. If we calculate the cost of writing materials and take into account that, in general, every line of writing corresponds roughly to the length of a hexameter, we find that a book of average size—especially if it is of the highest quality in writing style and in the materials of manufacture—ought to cost several hundred denarii. Its price, therefore, was considerably more than the daily wage of a mason, a carpenter, or a smith, these being fixed by the same edict at 50 denarii (plus meals).[4]

For the period before the economic crisis of the third century—that is to say in an entirely different economic environment, before devaluation and inflation accelerated from the time of Emperor Aurelian (270–5)—a few scattered references may be extracted from Latin authors, showing that the prices of books varied considerably. At the end of the first century AD, for instance, we have the testimony of Martial. He was preoccupied by his concern that the reading public on whom he depended for his success might consider his books too expensive when they circulated not in *tabellae* (modest booklets), but rather in copies of a different and higher quality. A change of publisher's clothing, in fact, implied an increase in price. This price, if related to the salaries of the period or to the cost of essential commodities like bread, wine, or oil, proved to be somewhat unstable. The first book of the *Epigrams* of Martial, in a deluxe edition, cost 5 denarii,[5] approximately a week's pay for a legionary soldier at that time. But some books were less expensive, such as the thirteenth book of the *Epigrams* (entitled *Xenia*), which was sold at a maximum price of 4 asses[6] at a time when roughly half a liter of wine cost 5 asses. In the same period, a *libellus* of good quality could be had for 10 asses according to the report of Statius, who is perhaps referring to one of the books of his *Silvae*.[7] The extremely modest price Martial cites for the *Xenia* may suggest that he is trying to assure his audience, in a general way, that his verses were within the means of every pocketbook. In fact, a centurion, or *faciles puellae,* or the colorful collection of individuals who participated in the *ludi Florales*, all of whom Martial records as members of his reading public,[8] did not have the economic means to acquire expensive books. And the same may be said of the farmers and the artisans (*agricolae* and *opificum turbae*) who were the regular readers of works of technical literature.[9] In sum, the books that were produced—and the fragments of book rolls mentioned above demonstrate this also—were not all of the same quality. And no doubt, the price varied according to the quality.

What are the origins of the commercial book trade in the Greco-Roman world? It must be stated immediately that the concept of a "commercial book trade" cannot be understood in the modern sense. In antiquity the prevailing system of production was always private. Sometimes it was managed by the authors themselves, who, employing secretary copyists from among their domestic slaves, arranged for the transcription and dissemination of their own works. Sometimes it was the work of slaves within aristocratic households and was assigned to those competent at writing and at book manufacture. Sometimes it was accomplished through the private commissioning of freelance copyists, who were paid according to the number of lines completed. Evidence for the last of these methods derives not only from the *Edictum de pretiis* of Diocletian, but also from the so-called "stichometric notations" that are found in many papyrus rolls. These notations record the total number of lines of writing on the roll. All the same, there is evidence for a true and proper commercial book trade, at least in some periods.

In the fifth and fourth centuries BC, in the classical period of Greek civilization, Plato tells us that it was possible to buy the books of Anaxagoras at a place in Athens called the "orchestra." The price was a drachma at the most, a rather moderate sum considering that at that time a sheep cost between 12 and 17 drachmas.[10] We will immediately wonder whether these books of Anaxagoras were new or secondhand. Plato does not say. There are other references, also from Athens, which speak of *biblia* being sold along with other merchandise, or of *bibliopolai*, sellers of *biblia*, who crowded the marketplace. But in these cases it is not possible to say whether the books in question contained writing or were simply rolls of uninscribed papyrus (in other words, raw materials for writing) that were sold for a variety of purposes. Further, from a passage of Xenophon we learn that among the flotsam from grounded ships that was sold on the coasts of the Black Sea there were "written rolls."[11] These "written rolls" may have been intended for the commercial market, but their contents cannot be established. We know, in addition, that there were book merchants who sold the forensic speeches of Isocrates;[12] and it seems that Plato was able to procure from Sicily the works of the philosopher Philolaus, though at a very high price.[13] It is also recorded that when the philosopher Speusippus died, Aristotle acquired his books.[14] In sum, a trade in books clearly existed during the classical period of Greece, but it must be considered a relatively modest one.

From the Hellenistic age onwards there is ample evidence for a commercial book trade. Zeno, the founder of Stoicism, decided to dedicate himself to philosophy after hearing a bookseller reading the second book of the *Memorabilia* of Xenophon in his bookshop.[15] We must ask, however, what purposes a commercial book trade would have served in the Hellenistic age. On the one hand, the philosophical or medical schools had no need for such a trade because the writings of the leaders and disciples of the schools would have been composed, transcribed, and disseminated, for the most part, within the schools themselves. On the other hand, the foundation of great private and public libraries (at Alexandria, at Pergamum), and likewise the increased number of readers, both individuals and groups (such as symposiastic groups), may have contributed to an expansion of the production of books destined for the open market or fashioned in some way to satisfy particular sorts of customers.

It was at Rome and in the Greco-Roman world from the first century BC onward, but especially between the first century and the late second century AD, that a relatively high social diffusion of alphabetism—the highest documented in antiquity—brought about ever more pressing demands for reading material, and thus a commercial book trade that was more consistent in the quantity of supply and more differentiated in quality than had previously existed. Surely the foundation of public libraries and the furnishing of private ones—whether created out of genuine scholarly or didactic interests, or as a luxurious but pointless status symbol, or from the capricious passion of bibliophiles and bibliomaniacs—contributed to the further expansion of book production at Rome and in the Roman world. It is no accident that at this period, in particular in the second century AD, we find bibliographical treatises designed to orient readers to the books that they could acquire on the book market and to give suggestions on the preparation and organization of a library. The Latin authors up to the time of Cicero had disseminated their works in copies prepared by scribes who worked in the service of wealthy and cultivated individuals. One of these was Atticus, the friend of Cicero and editor not only of the latter's writings, but also of other literary works. Atticus, however, should not be considered a merchant but rather an "amateur" of literary texts and of books, which he was able to get copied and disseminated thanks to his substantial means and to the *plurimi librarii* ("numerous book-makers") who operated in his *domus*.[16] In the Imperial period, however, the authors, as a result of the increased demand for reading, entrusted what they had written to *librarii* or *bibliopolae*, true and proper publisher-booksellers, in order to achieve a greater multiplication of copies and thereby an ever greater diffusion of their writings.

At Rome the first writers to document bookshops are Catullus, who speaks of *librariorum scrinia*,[17] and Cicero, who mentions a *taberna libraria*.[18] Later, in the Imperial age, we find more publisher-booksellers—individuals of very low social rank, usually freedmen—who appear to be engaged in the production and sale of books. Among these may be mentioned the Sosii, known not only as editors from the *Epistles* of Horace, but also from a papyrus (P. Mil. Vogl. I, 19) that contains grammatical questions of Apollodorus of Athens related to book 14 of the *Iliad*;[19] Dorus, who had copies of the writings of Cicero and of the historical work of Livy;[20] Trifo, who was editor of the *Institutio oratoria* of Quintilian and also sold the *Epigrams* of Martial;[21] Atrectus and Secundus, who likewise offered the books of Martial's *Epigrams* for sale, the former in a deluxe edition, the latter in the form of *breves tabellae* ("parchment booklets");[22] and Valerius Quintus Pollio, yet another bookseller from whom one could acquire Martial's verses.[23] The name of another *bibliopola*, Sextus Peducaeus Dionysius, is known from a funerary inscription.[24] We do not know how the bookshops of these booksellers operated. The *librarius* or *bibliopola* could himself be a copyist, and he may have also had, at times, assistance from others. But in certain cases it is possible that multiple scribes copied from dictation, transcribing the same work at the same time, in order to achieve a more rapid multiplication of copies. The copyists certainly had a variety of graphic expertise, since the quality of the books they produced was varied. There were expert calligraphers (one thinks of a script like the highest quality *Capitalis Rustica*) as well as scribes accustomed to less precise graphic forms or to rather informal writing styles. We do not know how high the profits of the booksellers might have been, but it is clear that authorial copyrights did not exist; and there is no documentation that the bookseller returned to the author any sum of money, although such an arrangement cannot be entirely ruled out.

Martial puts us in contact with what we might call a true revolution in the history of the book: the change in the form of the book from the roll to the codex. This revolution began, more or less, in the late first century AD and was completed around the end of the fourth century. At the beginning of this period, however, as we may deduce from the testimony of Martial, the commercial book trade produced both rolls and codices. In this same time period, additionally, parchment was beginning to replace papyrus as a writing material. The codices of which Martial speaks, containing works by Homer, Vergil, Cicero, Livy, Ovid, as well as his own *Epigrams*, were, in fact, on parchment.[25] It is possible that codices were more attractive to customers—either because papyrus was a writing material imported from Egypt, and therefore made books more expensive, or because a codex could include a quantity of text equal to that of several, and sometimes many, rolls. A greater quantity of text on the same amount of writing material could also be obtained from papyrus codices, since these could be inscribed on the recto as well as the verso, while normally a roll was only inscribed on the recto. For authors like Martial who were rather lacking in money, consigning their works to the market in copies in codex format, especially if the codices were made of parchment, meant promoting the dissemination of their works, since this resulted in a lower cost to the buyer.

Books put on sale, as is shown once again by the example of the *Epigrams* of Martial, were customarily presented in a specific editorial package: there were modest editions as well as deluxe ones. The latter, as the previously mentioned papyrus of Cornelius Gallus allows us to glimpse, offered not only a calligraphic script, but also a careful layout, writing material of better quality, even elegant and sometimes precious refinements such as *umbilici* (rods around which one wound the roll), boxes, and ties. However, these books destined for the market could be distinguished not only by their editorial dress; they also differed from one another as regards their level of textual accuracy. In a limited number of cases, there were copies written correctly and perhaps even further revised by a *grammaticus*, a *corrector*, or a professional *diorthotes*. Indeed, Gellius and Galen testify that *grammatici* were sometimes involved in the commercial book trade. But, in general, copies offered for sale in the book market must have been full of errors because they were written or corrected badly, or not corrected at all. This sorry state of affairs is clear from references to that effect in authors such as Strabo (who is referring particularly to this issue in Alexandria and Rome), but also Cicero, Martial, and Seneca.[26] Quintilian recommends to the editor of his *Institutio oratoria*, Trifo, that the books be appropriately corrected;[27] and sometimes, as in the case of Pliny, it is even the author himself who undertakes the duty of correcting copies of his works that have already been acquired by friends.[28]

At Rome, the shops of the editor-booksellers are concentrated in well-trafficked areas of the city. The Sosii plied their trade at the *Vicus Tuscus*.[29] Atrectus sold books on the Argileto, opposite the Forum of Caesar, in a shop whose doors were covered by advertisements for the books one might acquire there.[30] Secundus had a *taberna* behind the Temple of Peace and the Temple of Minerva in the Forum of Nerva.[31] Other booksellers operated in the *Vicus Sandaliarius*,[32] itself not far from the Temple of Peace, and in the quarter of the *Sigillari*.[33] The *tabernae* for books, as we learn from the entertaining vignettes offered by Gellius and Galen, were sometimes the settings for erudite discussions and served more generally as social spaces. A particularly expert grammarian identifies an error in a commercial copy of the *Annales* of Fabius Pictor which had been guaranteed by the bookseller to be *sine mendis*.[34] Another grammarian, seated in a bookshop and boasting that he could elucidate the *Menippean Satires* of Varro, becomes an object of ridicule to those present when he fails to explain a passage put to him.[35] A learned man by the name of Sulpicius Apollinaris embarrasses a pseudo-connoisseur of the *Histories* of Sallust by asking him to interpret a passage that the latter proves incapable of explicating.[36] Or, again, a scholar discovers, by reading only the first two lines, that a book attributed to Galen, offered for sale in a *taberna* in the *Vicus Sandaliarius*, is a forgery.[37]

Especially in the first and second centuries AD a book trade can be documented in various cities of Roman Italy and in the provinces, even if this trade did not, perhaps, flourish to the same extent elsewhere as it did at Rome. At the port of Brindisi one could purchase, at a small price, since they were rather worn out and damaged, books containing "extraordinary material, fabulous, unheard of, and incredible":[38] books to while away the hours in reading during a sea voyage. Outside of Italy, *bibliopolae* and *tabernae* for books are recorded at Lyons and Vienne in Gallia.[39] Because the book trade provided a reliable means of distribution, works of authors of the period could be disseminated to the ends of the known world: Horace is convinced of this and thinks that his verses can be read in Spain and even in Roman Africa;[40] Ovid boasts of a reading public *in toto orbe* ("throughout the world") and extending from east to west;[41] Martial is elated by imagining his books circulating through the whole Roman Empire, from Britain to Thrace;[42] and the Elder Pliny says that the *Imagines* of Varro were spread abroad "into every land" (*omnes terras*).[43] In Greco-Roman Egypt in the second century AD a trade in books (of Greek works) is demonstrated by at least two witnesses. A private letter from Oxyrhynchus (P. Oxy. XVIII, 2192) records the name of a *bibliopoles*, Demetrios, from whom one could buy rare and learned works. Another letter (P. Petaus 30) speaks of books—*membranai*, that is to say, parchment books—which a certain Deios, some kind of traveling book peddler, offers for sale door to door. Demetrios and Deios were vendors of Greek books; but in Greco-Roman Egypt many books by Latin authors were also in circulation, as the papyrus and parchment fragments that have emerged from the excavations there demonstrate. The enthusiastic pronouncements of the Latin authors about the vast distribution of their books contain, we may suppose, some measure of exaggeration. But certainly the circulation of literary works was achieved in the first centuries of the Roman Empire largely by means of books, and this would have been impossible without the support of businessmen, shops, and, especially, traveling salesmen who were active in book production and distribution. Nevertheless, it should also be recognized that there were other channels of distribution—as was indicated above—such as privately produced copies.

There was also a trade in used books. Here it is necessary to make a distinction between, on the one hand, secondhand books that could be acquired by anyone who was interested in reading the works contained in them, and, on the other hand, antiquarian books, considered precious because they were old and/or rare. In the latter category there were even autographs—or, at any rate, books described as such. Of the first type of used book there are few examples: Statius mentions a book devoured by worms and rotted by mold that contained the writings of the Elder Brutus, which was acquired at a risible price from a poor vendor.[44] There is also evidence of the acquisition of complete, preexisting libraries, and these would obviously be collections of secondhand books. On the other hand, antiquarian books, whether authentic or otherwise, are well attested by Aulus Gellius. In the second century AD, in a shop in the quarter of the *Sigillari*, a roll containing Book 2 of the *Aeneid* was sold at an enormous price, 20 *aurei*, because it was believed that it had formerly been the property of Vergil himself. Books "of good and true age" (*bonae et sincerae vetustatis*) of the *Annales* of Fabius Pictor were sold in a *libraria* of this same quarter. The rhetor Antonius Julianus, a rather erudite fellow, paid an exorbitant price to rent an ancient manuscript of the *Annales* of Ennius in order to examine a single verse for the sake of verifying a reading.[45] And there was no lack of forgeries: Dio Chrysostom reports that the booksellers, knowing that ancient books were more in demand because they were written better and on papyrus of better quality, coated new books in ground meal so that they would acquire the same patina, and therefore the same value, as ancient books; and then they sold as ancient books those that had been artificially aged and distressed.[46]

The third century AD witnessed the beginning of a crisis in the commercial book trade that accelerated between the fourth and the sixth centuries. This was part and parcel of the broader institutional and economic crises of the period, including the collapse of urban structures, the decline of schools, and the decrease in alphabetism as well as in the practices of writing—all factors that resulted in an ever-shrinking demand for books and, consequently, a continuing disappearance of bookshops. Furthermore, with the spread of Christianity, the dissemination of Christian writings—whether of texts of sacred Scripture, or of patristic works, or of other genres of writing—was not achieved through commercial channels, but came about rather through private initiatives. For producing and propagating copies of the texts of interest to the new religion, there were numerous Christian communities dispersed far and wide, which, thanks to their close web of relationships, were able to create effective avenues for the exchanges and loans that allowed for the circulation and transcription of books. Bookshops and the commercial trade as it had existed earlier came then, over time, to be replaced by the activity of copyists, whether paid or not, in the service of private individuals or allied with the new Christian community and its institutions: churches, episcopal seats, and monasteries, especially when there were important Christian figures working within a particular institution (e.g., Ambrose,

Augustine, or Jerome). It is significant that in fifth-century Gaul the term *bibliopola*, which in Greece and Rome at the time of Martial and Pliny had been applied to a seller of books or to the manager of a bookshop, came instead to have the meaning of "scribe for hire." Such scribes labored in the service of intellectuals or wealthy aristocrats for whom they produced editions of new writings or for whom they transcribed copies of preexisting works.

In this regard, mention should be made of the renewal of the system of book production in the households (*domus*) of wealthy individuals. This is documented at Rome from the end of the Republic, and it re-emerges in Late Antiquity for the manufacture of books, both pagan and Christian, which are, so far as their production and distribution are concerned, increasingly less differentiated from one another. From this period on, in short, book production is divorced almost entirely from a commercial trade in the true and proper sense. Meanwhile, in the fifth and sixth centuries, the two systems which were described above were defined and developed. These continued, though to different extents, into the High Middle Ages. The first consists, as various sources attest, of the commissioning of books—whether by private individuals, or by ecclesiastical or monastic institutions, or by bishops or abbots—from professional scribes, i.e., paid scribes. We apparently have the name of at least one of these scribes preserved in the codex of Hilary, *In Psalmos*,[47] in Uncial script of the fifth century. Its colophon reads, "*scribit antiquarius Eutalius*" (fol. 327r). This system of production continued, though within restricted boundaries, through the centuries of the High Middle Ages. Around the turn of the first millennium, Gerbert of Aurillac wrote in a letter to a monastic friend, "*nosti, quot scriptores in urbibus ac in agris Italiae passim habeantur* ("you know how many scribes might be found here and there in the cities and in the countryside in Italy"). By *scriptores* he is referring to copyists working for hire, who wrote books in the cities and villages of Italy in the late tenth century.[48] Another letter of Gerbert reports to Eberhard, abbot of Tours, that he has shipped to him parchment and money for scribes, who were to prepare for him copies of authors and works included on an accompanying list.[49] Nonetheless, this does not constitute a true commercial book trade. The other system of book production was centered within the monasteries, cathedrals, and smaller city churches, where individuals in monastic orders or attached to the secular clergy within the churches dedicated themselves to the copying of books. We are talking here of the preparation and transcription of books which was, for the most part, undertaken by members of the community within monastic or episcopal—or, at any rate, ecclesiastical—scriptoria. This was the system of book production that prevailed throughout Western Europe in the High Middle Ages, a system sustained economically by the internal resources of the monasteries or ecclesiastical institutions, or also by wealthy lay or religious people of high social stature, including even the emperors themselves, able to furnish the necessary means. In this regard, it is perhaps opportune to call attention to the significant difference that existed between the East and the West. Within monasticism, from its origins, and among the ancient Fathers of the desert, the work of copying was seen as a means for providing sustenance and other resources to support the economy of the cenobitic community as well as that of individual monks. Therefore, we may find in literary sources references to the economic value of books (one *abba* Gelasios, for example, had a Bible worth 18 golden *solidi*); and, moreover, many books were written by monastic hands on commission and were intended for sale. In the East, this practice continued through the entire Byzantine era. On the contrary, we have a variety of testimonies (some of them inspired by contacts with the East) demonstrating that, in the West, this practice was limited to the Late Antique period, not extending beyond the end of the fifth century. In the monastery of Marmoutier, founded by Martin of Tours, the art of writing, which was restricted to the younger members of the community, may have been pursued with the intention that at least a portion of the books produced would be placed for sale.[50] In the *Institutiones* of John Cassian, it is assumed that the monks will dedicate themselves to writing in order to acquire money (*compendia lucrave*).[51]

Although it is a matter of isolated cases, there is evidence from the period between the end of the Late Antique era and the beginning of the Middle Ages that some commercial books were in circulation. Between the fourth and fifth centuries, it appears that the *Vita Martini* of Sulpicius Severus, which was introduced to Rome by Paulinus of Nola, spread joy among the *librarii* by increasing their business, since the reception of the work by the public was already extremely favorable everywhere, even in far-off lands.[52] This report—and we are in no position to ascertain its veracity—must be considered an exceptional one. In some important cities where a certain level of book circulation and certain habits of reading still persisted, it is possible that professional copyists spent their lives in some sort of bookshop and therefore in some sort of commercial activity. At Ravenna this seems to be the case of the *statio* of the Goth Viliaric, in which, at the beginning of the sixth century, copies in Uncial script of Orosius (Florence, BML. 65.1)[53] and of Jerome's *Tractatus in librum Psalmorum* (Paris, BnF, lat. 2235)[54] were apparently produced. At Rome, approximately in the sixth century, a certain Gaudiosus had a shop *ad vincula Sancti Petri*, as is shown by Angers, Bibliothèque municipale cod. 24, a medieval copy of a book of the Gospels from the Late Antique period. In Rome, through the seventh century it was still possible to purchase books, even if it is not entirely clear when those books were produced, or in which specific circles, or by which scribes. In any case, there is evidence from the *Historia abbatum* of Bede that in the late seventh century Benedict Biscop, abbot of the Anglo-Saxon monastic foundation of Wearmouth-Jarrow, made several trips to Rome and bought there for his twin monasteries "*libros . . . omnis divinae eruditionis non paucos*" ("no small number of books of every sort of divine learning") as well as a codex of marvelous workmanship containing cosmographical texts.[55] And, again, in the tenth century, Gerbert of Aurillac reports that he has acquired books *multitudine nummorum* ("for a great deal of money") at Rome, in other parts of Italy, and also in Germany and Belgium.[56] These are, however, exceptional cases. Bookshops and a true and proper book trade were only reborn and again flourishing in the Late Middle Ages.

Notes

1. *CLA* 11.1644.
2. *CLA* Suppl. 1714.
3. *Edictum Diocletiani et collegarum de pretiis rerum venalium*, 7, 39–40, ed. Marta Giacchero (Geneva, 1974) vol. 1, p. 152.
4. Ibid., 7, 2–3 and 10–11 (Giacchero, vol. 1, p. 150).
5. Martial, 1, 117, 16–17.
6. Martial, 13, 3, 1–4.
7. Statius, *Silv.* 4, 9, 7–9.
8. Martial, *Epist.* 14–15; 3, 69, 5; 11, 3, 4.
9. Pliny, *Nat. hist., praef.*, 6.
10. Plato, *Apol.*, 26d.
11. Xenophon, *Anab.*, 7, 5, 14.
12. Dionysius of Halicarnassus, *Isocr.*, 18.
13. Diogenes Laertius, 3, 9; Aulus Gellius, 3, 17, 3.
14. Diogenes Laertius, 4, 5; Aulus Gellius, 3, 17, 3.
15. Diogenes Laertius, 7, 2–3.
16. Nepos, *Att.*, 3, 13.
17. Catullus, 14, 17–18.
18. Cicero, *Phil.*, 2, 21.
19. Horace, *Epist.*, 1, 20, 2; 2, 3, 345.
20. Seneca, *Benef.*, 7, 6, 1.
21. Quintilian, *Inst., praef.*, 1–3; Martial, 13, 3, 1–4.
22. Martial, 1, 117, 13–17; 1, 2.
23. Martial, 1, 113.
24. *CIL* 6, 9218.
25. Martial, 14, 184; 14, 186; 14, 188; 14, 190; 14, 192; 1, 2.
26. Strabo, 13, 1, 54; Cicero, *Ad Quintum fratrem*, 3, 5, 6; Martial, 2, 8, 1–4; Seneca, *Dialogi*, 4, 26, 2.
27. Quintilian, *Institutio oratoria, praef.*, 3.
28. Pliny, *Epistulae*, 4, 26, 1.
29. Horace, *Epistulae*, 1, 20, 1–2.
30. Martial, 1, 117, 9–12.
31. Martial, 1, 2, 7–8.
32. Aulus Gellius, 18, 4, 1; Galen, *Libr. prop.*, prol., 1 (ed. V. Boudon-Millot, Paris, 2007, p. 134).
33. Aulus Gellius, 2, 3, 5; 5, 4, 1.
34. Aulus Gellius, 5, 4, 1–5.
35. Aulus Gellius, 13. 31, 1–13.
36. Aulus Gellius, 18, 4, 1–9.
37. Galen, *Libr. prop.*, prol., 2 (ed. V. Boudon-Millot, p. 134).
38. Aulus Gellius, 9, 4, 1–10.
39. Pliny, *Epistulae*, 9, 11, 2.
40. Horace, *Odes*, 2, 20, 13–20; *Epistulae*, 1, 20, 9–13.
41. Ovid, *Tristia*, 4, 9, 19–24; and 4, 10, 128.
42. Martial, 7, 88, 1–4; 8, 3, 4–8; 11, 3, 3–5.
43. Pliny, *Naturalis Historia*, 35, 11.

44. Statius, *Silvae*, 4, 9, 20–3.

45. Aulus Gellius, 2, 3, 5; 5, 4, 1; 18, 5, 11.

46. Dio Chrysostom, *De pulchritudine*, 12.

47. Verona, Biblioteca Capitolare XIII (11) = *CLA* 4.484.

48. Gerbert of Aurillac, *Epistulae*, 130 (ed. F. Weigle, *MGH, Die Briefe der deutschen Kaiserzeit*, 2, Weimar, 1966, pp. 157–8).

49. Gerbert of Aurillac, *Epistulae*, 44 (ed. Weigle, p. 73).

50. Sulpicius Severus, *Vita Martini*, 10, 6 (ed. J. Fontaine, vol. 1, Paris, 1967, *Sources chretiennes*, 133, p. 274).

51. John Cassian, *Institutiones*, 4, 12 (ed. M. Petschenig, Prague, Vienna, and Leipzig, 1888, *CSEL*, 17, pp. 54–5).

52. Sulpicius Severus, *Dialogi*, 1, 23 (ed. C. Halm, Vienna, 1866, *CSEL*, 1, pp. 175–6).

53. *CLA* 3.298.

54. *CLA* 5.543.

55. Bede, *Historia abbatum*, 4 and 15 (ed. C. Plummer, vol. 1, Oxford, 1896, pp. 367 and 380).

56. Gerbert of Aurillac, *Epistulae*, 44 (ed. Weigle, p. 73).

SUGGESTED READING

On the book trade in the ancient world, see F. Reichmann, "The Book Trade at the Time of the Roman Empire," *The Library Quarterly* 8 (1938) pp. 40–76; T. Kleberg, *Bokhandel oc bokförlag i Antiken* (Stockholm: Almqvist and Wiksell, 1962); G. Mastromarco, "Commercio librario e testi teatrali attici nel quinto secolo a.C.," in *Storie di cultura scritta. Studi per Francesco Magistrale*, ed. P. Fioretti (Spoleto: Fondazione CISAM, 2012) pp. 585–604; M. Caroli, "Il commercio dei libri nell'Egitto greco-romano," *Segno e Testo* 10 (2012) pp. 3–74. In particular on the commerce of secondhand and antiquarian books, see T. Kleberg, "Antiquarischer Buchhandel im alten Rom," *Annales Academiae Regiae Scientiarum Upsaliensis* 8 (1964) pp. 21–32; R. J. Starr, "The Used-Book Trade in the Roman World," *Phoenix* 44 (1990) pp. 148–57. On the relationship between authors, the diffusion of literary works, and the book market, see P. Fedeli, "I sistemi di produzione e diffusione," in *Lo spazio letterario di Roma antica*, ed. G. Cavallo, P. Fedeli, and A. Giardina, vol. 2 *La circolazione del testo* (Rome: Salerno Editrice, 1993) pp. 343–78; J. W. Iddeng, "*Publica aut peri!* The Releasing and Distribution of Roman Books," *Simbolae Osloenses* 81 (2006) pp. 58–84; P. White, "Bookshops in the Literary Culture of Rome," in *Ancient Literacies. The Culture of Reading in Greece and Rome*, ed. W. A. Johnson and H. N. Parker (Oxford: Oxford University Press, 2009) pp. 268–87; O. Pecere, *Roma antica e il testo. Scritture d'autore e composizione letteraria* (Rome and Bari: Editori Laterza, 2010). On the social position of *librarii* and *bibliopolae*, see N. Brockmeyer, "Die soziale Stellung der "Buchhändler" in der Antike," *Archiv für Geschichte des Buchwesens* 13 (1973) pp. 238–47. On qualitative differences in ancient Latin books, see P. Fioretti, "Libri d'uso e scritture informali in età romana," in *Bibliothèques, livres et culture écrite dans l'empire romain de César à Hadrien. Actes du Colloque International de la Société Internationale d'Études Neroniennes* (Paris, 2–4 October 2008), *Neronia*, 8, ed. Y. Perrin (Brussels: Éditions Latomus, 2010) pp. 91–9; in particular on the papyrus of Cornelius Gallus, see M. Capasso, *Il ritorno di Cornelio Gallo. Il papiro di Qasr*

Ibrîm venticinque anni dopo. Con un contributo di P. Radiciotti (Naples: Graus, 2003). On the price of books in Antiquity, see J. J. Phillips, "Book Prices and Roman Literacy," *Classical World* 79 (1985) pp. 36–8. On the erudite discussions in the bookshops and on the bibliographic guides of the period, see C. Esposto, "Poligrafi e bibliografi nel II–III sec. d. C.: la figura del grammatico 'consulente' librario e la manualistica bibliografica," *Seminari romani* 7 (2004) pp. 99–115. On the production and circulation of books in the Christian community and in Christian institutions, see E. Dekkers, "Des Prix et du commerce des livres à l'époque patristique," *Sacris erudiri* 31 (1989–90) pp. 99–115; H. Y. Gamble, *Books and Readers in the Early Church*, (New Haven, CT: Yale University Press,1995); S. Mratschek, "*Codices vestri nos sumus*. Bücherkult und Bücherpreise in der christlichen Spätantike," in *Hortus litterarum antiquarum. Festschrift für Hans Armin Gärtner zum 70. Geburtstag*, ed. A. Haltenhoff and F.-H. Mutschler (Heidelberg: C. Winter Universitätsverlag, 2000) pp. 369–80. On the evolution of the term *bibliopola*, see S. Santelia, "Sidonio Apollinare e i *bybliopolae*," *Invigilata lucernis* 22 (2000) pp. 1–23. On the last bookshops and on the system of book production in late antiquity, see G. Cavallo, "Libro e pubblico alla fine del mondo antico," in *Libri, editori e pubblico nel mondo antico*, 4th ed., ed. G. Cavallo (Rome and Bari: Laterza, 2004), pp. 83–132. Some evidence about the acquisition of books in the Middle Ages is provided in W. Wattenbach, *Das Schriftwesen im Mittelalter*, 3rd ed. (Leipzig: Hirzel, 1896); M. Passalacqua, "Perlege, scribe, reduc," in *Venuste noster. Scritti offerti a Leopoldo Gamberale*, ed. M. Passalacqua, M. De Nonno, and A. M. Morelli (Hildesheim, Zurich, and New York: Olms, 2012) pp. 509–21; M. Caroli, "Circolazione e vendita della 'Syngraphe' di Anassagora (Plat., Apol., 26d–e)", *Elenchos* 34 (2013) pp. 373–98; and M. Caroli, "Il papiro in una lista di spesa dell'agora e nella commedia greca", *Quaderni di storia* 84 (2016) pp. 151–61.

CHAPTER 46

···

THE BOOK TRADE IN THE MIDDLE AGES

The Parisian case

···

KOUKY FIANU

Discussing the book trade in the Middle Ages not only means looking at the object—the codex—from a commercial perspective, but also keeping in mind its cultural and social functions. For specialized artisans, trading in books could provide privileges which testified to their participation in more than simple trading activities. Book commerce, by virtue of dealing with the written word, brought to medieval craftsmen a distinctive character and an increased social status.[1] As M. T. Clanchy points out, "by elaborating the sacred page of Scripture, monks had sanctified writers as much as books."[2] The medieval book trade and its actors are well researched for cities like Paris, which will provide the case study of this essay.

From Monasteries to Universities

···

Western culture and its emphasis on Scripture first reserved book production for the monk: the rule of Saint Benedict designated *lectio* as a divine service, while prominent abbots devoted energy to the developing of scriptoria in their abbeys. So it is no surprise that, according to the research of C. Bozzolo and E. Ornato for northern France, the growing production of books starting in the tenth century mainly concerned religion (Latin biblical, patristic, theological, and hagiographical manuscripts represented 80% of all books produced).[3] Until the early thirteenth century, the growth in the number of books was a response to the multiplication of monastic foundations and not to a diversification of subject matter. After 1200 the typology of manuscripts changed to reflect cultural evolution: Latin religious texts declined to a proportion of 50%, giving way to a multiplication of university manuscripts (philosophy, law, medicine) and lay vernacular works (romances, history, etc.).

Educational institutions, and especially universities, multiplied in thirteenth-century Western Europe, feeding a need for more books. As the number of students and masters steadily grew, so did the demand for writing and reading materials. This phenomenon was accompanied by the development of an urban culture which saw, by the end of the century, the written word spread—both in Latin and in the vernacular—to new social groups. A new type of urban-based book trade emerged in response to the needs of scholars and aristocrats.

Teaching created an exploding demand for multiple copies which was met by an original mode of book production, the *pecia* system. As first described by Jean Destrez in 1935, this system allowed medieval colleges and universities to offer manuscripts for copy by multiple scribes at the same time.[4] The time involved in copying was indeed the main obstacle to fast production. According to best estimates, a 200-folio bound manuscript would have taken a lonely scribe almost 7 months to complete.[5] Under the *pecia* system, universities authorized booksellers—generally called *stationarii*—to keep copies of unbound manuscripts (*exemplaria*) in the form of a series of inspected quires or pieces of manuscript (*peciae*) and to rent them at a fixed price (*taxatio*). The stationer entered his prices in a taxation list and rented the quires one by one to potential scribes who would copy a quire, bring it back, rent the next one, etc. The copy was not necessarily made in the original order of the *peciae*, but the scribe kept a note of his progress by indicating in the margins of his work which *pecia* he copied, or by leaving space to write later the content of a quire used by some other scribe. Once all the quires were copied, a new manuscript was created. Although it required care and good planning from the scribe, the advantage of such a system was obvious: it allowed as many scribes to work on a book as there were quires composing it. In the case of a 200-folio work composed, for example, of 17 *peciae* of 12 leaves each (the standard format for a *pecia* in most universities), the copy would still take almost 7 months for each individual copy, but in that time period 17 scribes could work simultaneously to produce 17 different copies of the original *exemplar*. The pecia system was implemented under the control of universities for their members, starting c.1250, mainly in Italian cities like Bologna, Padua, Perugia, Naples, or Florence, but also in Paris, Orleans, Toulouse, Montpellier, and Salamanca. It declined after a century of existence, when the demographic collapse removed the pressing need for more scholarly books and when the multiplication of libraries, either personal or in colleges and convents, gave access to books previously individually owned. By the mid-fourteenth century, a large number of what we would call "secondhand" books were circulating and feeding the university book trade. It did not, however, stop universities from keeping a more or less careful eye on suppliers of books.

Controlling the Book Trade

The production and sale of books in Paris involved a variety of craftsmen, including parchment or paper makers, illuminators, bookbinders, booksellers, and scribes. The latter are difficult to identify, since many academics and clerics copied books for themselves and were occasionally paid to do so for others without being designated as professional book writers. Only in some exceptional late medieval cases is it possible to recognize an *écrivain* mentioned several times as a scribe working for another person, a patron or a bookseller. By the early fifteenth century, there lived in Paris and London specialized book copyists, distinct from scribes writing deeds and other legal or administrative documents. They identified themselves differently, as *écrivains de lettres de forme* (text writers) who worked on the production of manuscripts, as opposed to the *écrivains de lettres de cour* (writers of court letters or scriveners) who were working for various tribunals and administrations.

In 1275, the University of Paris took a first step in regulating the book trade in order to protect masters and students from allegedly greedy merchants. University officials pleaded for "just and legitimate prices," limiting the profit made from the sale of a book to 1.7% of its selling price and establishing the renting price of *peciae*. Two decades later, parchmenters were invited to demonstrate honest practices when selling skins to university members. The university did not attempt to control illuminators or bookbinders whose activities were not as essential to university members as was access to books and parchment. Booksellers and parchmenters, on the other hand, had to take an oath of obedience and to swear to respect university regulations to be allowed to do business with masters and students. Refusal to comply was met with boycotts, fines, and loss of clients from the university. In exchange for their oath, these craftsmen were designated as university members (*suppositi*), a status which permitted them during the whole of fourteenth century to benefit from a series of fiscal exemptions.

University rules which dealt with *librarii* and *pergamenarii* of Paris at the end of the thirteenth century were in fact targeting all members of the book trade. The first privilege granted in 1307 addressed only booksellers and parchmenters, but it released every book craftsman from future fiscal records. Under the term *librarii* the whole trade was therefore understood, which suggests the prominent role of the bookseller among the other crafts and the strong link existing between them.

The university certainly had a powerful tool in hand at the beginning of the fourteenth century to impose its rule on the selling and production of manuscripts. Punishments for disobedience were real threats to craftsmen of books. In 1313 booksellers went on strike, refusing to swear the oath. They complied after only a few weeks, when they successfully negotiated more autonomy. Their protest led to the creation of four masters of the trade (*magni librarii*) in charge of inspecting the *exemplaria* and of making booksellers obey university rules. By the beginning of the fifteenth century, however, in spite of extended fiscal privileges which set these artisans apart from

Parisian craftsmen, and in spite of threats of losing their advantageous situation, the university was no longer able to impose its control. Numerous reminders of the regulations, along with vain attempts to exclude offending artisans from the university ranks, suggest that booksellers and parchmenters were not always faithful to their oath. Book producers and merchants no longer feared the university, for they also served the growing needs of a widening literate population, lay or clerical, in Latin and in the vernacular.

At the dawn of the fifteenth century the university was unable to claim an oath from booksellers as it had done for decades. Moreover, the University of Paris was unable to convince royal authorities that those artisans—some of whom were illiterate, some of whom abused their position by exercising various other trades, while most did not care about university regulations and on whom the university could impose nothing because they did not work mainly for university members—were legitimately exempt from taxation in the name of their academic status. After almost a century of debate between the university and royal officials, in a context of a contested institution with declining authority, the king decided to limit the number of book craftsmen benefiting from university privileges. After 1489 in Paris, the only artisans with academic status were 24 booksellers, 4 parchmenters, masters of their trade (*maistres jurez*), 4 paper venders, 7 paper makers from outside the city, and 3 trade masters each for the illuminators, the bookbinders, and the book writers. All the others were to fall back under the authority of the royal provost in charge of all trades and crafts in the capital, and to bear normal fiscal burdens. The royal ordinance put an official end to university control over booksellers and parchmenters.

A TIGHTLY BOUND COMMUNITY

Research of the last 20 years has demonstrated that university rules could be misleading if taken at face value. Since booksellers could also be bookbinders or illuminators, since parchmenters could become *stationarii*, or writers be illuminators and booksellers, there was clear evidence that many more crafts were affected by those regulations than had been thought in the past. The need to examine all members of the trade became obvious. It led in turn to a new understanding of the organization of crafts and finally to new hypotheses on book production.

A study of the location of book craftsmen in medieval Paris reveals concentrations which evolved over time, a phenomenon also visible in London.[6] In Paris, the earliest archival records indicate the presence of a book trade on Notre Dame cathedral's square at the beginning of the thirteenth century.[7] Notre Dame was then surrounded by episcopal schools that needed books for their students and masters. No doubt, the presence in this area of the royal residence and of wealthy aristocrats, both lay and ecclesiastical, also provided some patrons for artisans able to produce richly ornate manuscripts (Plate 46.1). Nevertheless, the long-established ecclesiastical use of books,

PLATE 46.1 Woodcut featuring the Parisian bookseller and printer Antoine Vérard presenting to King Charles VIII of France *Jardin de plaisance et fleur de rhétorique*, by the French poet François Villon, Paris. Public Domain (BnF, Gallica scans.). Vérard had a shop on Notre-Dame Bridge and another one at the *Palais* in 1485. Several of his prints represent him offering a book to a patron.

the clerical status of students and masters in schools, the Church's claim to censorship of ideas and knowledge, and the high symbolic value of medieval script associated books with the Church. It is, therefore, not surprising to see the book trade concentrating both in Paris and in London around the cathedral. Since more precious manuscripts have been better preserved than the quickly written, more utilitarian, undecorated, school manuscripts, it is impossible to measure the relative weight of each category. But the absence of book craftsmen on the Right Bank, a part of the city where princes and high nobles had their Parisian residences, tends to indicate that the location of schools and the proximity of the cathedral played the main role in the settlement of the book trade. When schools multiplied and expanded on the Left Bank, book craftsmen followed: In the mid-thirteenth century there were parchmenters, illuminators, and booksellers under the *dominium* of the abbey Sainte-Geneviève, where new schools were established outside of the bishop's authority. Rapidly the Left Bank became the stronghold of the "University" with its colleges, nations, masters' houses, and students' residences.

Two streets in particular accommodated Parisian book artisans. Most of the late thirteenth-century inhabitants of the *rue des Écrivains* were parchmenters, a situation that persisted and that explains why that street changed name around 1400 to become *rue de la Parcheminerie* or *rue des Parcheminiers* ("Parchmenters Street"). Crossing it was the *rue Érembourg-de-Brie*, where the vast majority of Parisian illuminators were established, along with most of the bookbinders. Both illuminators and bookbinders dominated the number of taxpayers on this street to the extent that we could see it as a book production street. Booksellers, on the other hand, present a very different pattern of settlement. Half of those identified in late thirteenth-century Paris were established in several parts of the Left Bank, beside convents or colleges, sometimes accompanied by one other trade. The others concentrated in the Cité, on the street starting at Notre Dame's cathedral (*rue Neuve-Notre-Dame*), which they shared with a few illuminators, bookbinders, and parchmenters, but also with many seal makers and poultrymen. Fiscal documents become silent after the tax exemption of all book craftsmen in 1307, but archival material suggests that the two former main areas of the book trade (the Left Bank and the Cité) remained the same during the fourteenth century and that isolated booksellers were scattered on the Left Bank.

At the turn of the fifteenth century, traces of book trade activities appeared on the Right Bank, in the main Parisian cemetery. What little information we have on that trade suggests the sale of small, inexpensive used books rather than the production of manuscripts. During that century, book artisans settled in new parts of the capital. On the Left Bank a new street (*rue Saint-Jacques*) developed into a concentrated zone of booksellers. It became after 1470 the street of printers and publishers, and around 1550 the main artery for the book trade.[8] In the *Cité*, the Palace (*Palais*), a former royal residence now hosting the crown's courts of justice and the chancery, attracted booksellers specializing in legal books for the many jurists using the various tribunals in the area. The Palace was in the sixteenth century one of the most active centers for the Parisian book trade. Finally, book artisans had shops on the bridges linking the *Cité* to the Left Bank, and especially on Notre-Dame Bridge connecting the *Cité* to the Right Bank. Illuminators and bookbinders had established themselves on the bridge since 1421, followed by booksellers, along with professional writers specializing in the writing of books (*écrivains de lettres de formes*) rather than of charters or letters. As clients diversified and multiplied, the book trade adapted, and this fact explains the expansion outside the traditional areas of concentration of the trade near the schools and the episcopal quarter. But the settlement of book artisans within the same areas of the city suggests their close ties, a fact confirmed not only by professional links but also by many social and family relationships.

In London, as in Paris, book craftsmen were concentrated in certain parishes, more specifically on the north, northwest, and east sides of St. Paul's Cathedral. Their physical proximity fostered personal ties between neighboring book artisans. In London, as in Paris, they married their children within the trade; they pledged for each other; they were last will executors for a deceased peer, etc. Above all, they belonged to the same fraternity under the authority of the booksellers (in Paris since 1401) or stationers (in London since 1403), who were therefore acknowledged as responsible for the whole trade and for every step in the production of a book. Such a responsibility provided these individuals with a prominent status among book artisans. When printing developed in Paris in the late fifteenth century it did so in the Left Bank, where booksellers had been established for two centuries. Moreover, it grew among booksellers, the only craftsmen socially and economically prominent enough to get involved in the new techniques.

BOOK PRODUCTION UNDER THE CONTROL OF BOOKSELLERS

Parisian *libraires* distinguished themselves from other artisans involved in the making and selling of books. Not only were they geographically scattered, while other crafts were concentrated, but they also figured as masters of the whole trade either through their financial situation or through their dominant position in the fraternity.

In Paris, late thirteenth-century tax records clearly show the booksellers as the wealthiest of all book craftsmen, since 85% of them belonged to the medieval fiscal category of the *gros*, which meant they were taxed more than 5 *sous parisis* per year.[9] Only 44% of the parchmenters or of the illuminators, and 28% of the bookbinders were in that category. Book craftsmen's fiscal standing resembled that of modest and average merchants and artisans. Moreover, their distinctive fiscal position corresponds to the general picture of Parisian taxpayers: merchants were taxed substantially higher than artisans. Booksellers can be associated with merchants, whereas illuminators, bookbinders, parchmenters (or later paper makers), and scribes were artisans producing the material and realizing the various steps of the making of a book. Even when a bookseller mastered one or several of the artisanal skills necessary for producing a book (as is obvious when some artisans became *libraires*, or when individuals were designated alternatively as bookseller and illuminator, scribe, or bookbinder), the term *libraire* (or *stationaire*) implied more than merely selling books.

The commercial activities of booksellers meant they had to understand, to foresee, and to answer the needs of their clients. Such functions explain their scattered settlement near schools or palaces, or later even the cemetery. A bookseller like Marguerite de Sens, a member of a family of university *stationarii* established between *c.*1270 and *c.*1340 on Saint-Jacques street next to the convent of the Dominicans in Paris, could supply the bookish Mendicants with the volumes they required for their studies and work.[10] In the early fifteenth century, Petrus de Verona, a former Parisian university master, was selling very expensive books to rich customers in the royal entourage, proposing manuscripts to English ambassadors in Paris, receiving them in his house on Saint-Jacques street to show them his stock, selling two books to the Prince Louis of Orléans for *c.*£340 and providing the library of the abbey Saint-Victor with 12 books in a single year (1422–3).[11] Records, however, never use the term "libraire" to qualify Petrus de Verona's activity. The same is true for all kinds of people who knew of bibliophile aristocrats. By the late Middle Ages, authors, secretaries, or prominent merchants like the Italian brothers Rapondi could offer their services to enrich expanding princely libraries.[12] The book trade of the fifteenth century was animated by a greater variety of actors than thirteenth-century clergy and university members. Yet production of new manuscripts remained over the centuries the prerogative of qualified booksellers.

Since most late-thirteenth century booksellers (*librarii*) were also *stationarii* holding university *exemplaria* and *peciae* for scribes to copy, their involvement in the production of new manuscripts is beyond doubt. For centuries to come, Parisian booksellers would act as entrepreneurs and coordinators of book production and trade. These functions explain why some thirteenth- and fourteenth-century bookbinders and illuminators were established near booksellers, even outside of their concentration areas. In those cases, the merchant (*libraire*) controlled the making of manuscripts for his clients, while providing work to artisans in his neighborhood. Some well-documented cases show booksellers having copies made at the request of a patron. Such was the case of André le Musnier, designated as illuminator (1443) established on Notre-Dame Bridge, by the cathedral, son of Guyot le Musnier, an illuminator and bookseller, brother-in-law to another illuminator.[13] In 1450, André was called *libraire*, while in 1458 he was registered as bookbinder in a college account, before he became one the four main booksellers of the university (1461), which vainly attempted on two occasions to exclude him from its ranks for disobedience (1467 and 1474). André had apprentice illuminators, worked in close cooperation with other illuminators, and had a scribe outside of Paris whom he supplied with work and material to write quires of manuscripts. When he died in 1475, his widow inherited their house and remarried twice to booksellers, presumably pursuing the activities of her first husband. Such booksellers had existed in Paris for many decades. Another example was Thévenin Langevin (1368–98), known as a university bookseller and scribe (*écrivain*), who received money from Louis, duke of Orléans, in order "to pay the scribes, illuminators and other craftsmen to make for milord of Orléans the book entitled *Mirouer historial*."[14] These men were wealthy enough to bear the cost of making new books, they were intermediaries between artisans and patrons, and they had responsibilities toward and privileges from the university. In other words they were the official masters of the trade and of the various crafts involved in the making of books. When paper makers appeared in the late fourteenth century, or when printers multiplied after 1470 (Plate 46.2), they did not alter the socio-professional organization set in place for decades, leaving the bookseller as the entrepreneur in charge of coordinating the printing and decoration of books. In medieval Paris being a *libraire* meant, as it still does, selling books, but it especially meant being able to provide used and newly made books, and having them made by others as the need arose.

The patterns of the Parisian book trade were not unique. In Barcelona, for example, research in notarial contracts indicates that professionals of the fourteenth- and

PLATE 46.2 Dedication miniature showing the bookseller Antoine Vérard giving his book to Anne de Bretagne. Illumination on parchment from *Le trésor de l'âme* by Robert de Saint-Martin, c. 1491–1500. Paris, Bibliothèque Nationale de France, Vélins 350, fol. 6r.

fifteenth-century book trade were closely linked, their activities complementary, and that the *libraterius* was the one coordinating the production of books. Exercised mainly by Jewish or converted craftsmen, the *arte librarie* was transmitted within families, giving birth to dynasties of *libraterii* who trained apprentices, sold paper and other writing materials, bound books, appraised manuscripts, imported and exported them, and had them written and decorated. They were also gathered in a fraternity under the protection of the Holy Trinity. In Barcelona, booksellers contracted into temporary associations for a specific production and shared profits. Such society contracts integrated printers when they first settled in Barcelona in the late fifteenth century: the printer contributed his work and material, while the *libraterius* provided the necessary capital. In Barcelona, as in Paris, booksellers were clearly acting as entrepreneurs in the making of both manuscripts and printed books.

In England, communities of book craftsmen grew first in university towns, Oxford and then Cambridge, and in London around St. Paul's Cathedral in the late twelfth century. Other urban centers such as Lincoln, Norwich, and York also witnessed the establishment of different types of medieval book artisans, including scribes, illuminators, and parchment makers. The cultural needs and intellectual life of these centers determined the size of the communities, which were usually located in specific quarters or streets, as in Paris. In Oxford, book artisans worked in Catte Street, while in London late medieval records point to Paternoster Row as the street concentrating makers and sellers of books near the cathedral. By 1403, London had a fraternity of "writers of text-letters, limners, and others who bind and sell books" under the authority of two wardens, one illuminator, and one text writer. After being designated by several names (Limners and Textwriters, Limners and Stationers) the fraternity became the Stationers' Company in 1441. The London stationer occupied the same position as the Parisian *libraire*, dominating the other book crafts and coordinating their work in the making of books, while mastering one or more of these crafts.

In Bologna, book artisans were early on under the control of the university which in 1317 required an oath from *omnes scriptores, miniatores, correctores et minorum repositores atque rasores librorum, ligatores, cartularii et qui vivunt per universitatem et scolares*. Craftsmen not involved with university members did not have to swear the university oath, but stationers and their shops were still subjected to town authority. San Geminiano parish had a concentration of book artisans in the late thirteenth century; the *stationarius* was a scribe or a coordinator of written works.

The emphasis placed here on professional book makers and sellers certainly does not reflect all cases of book production and circulation. Lack of documentation makes it difficult to identify all the occasional actors of the medieval book trade, but they should not be dismissed, for they animated the book trade for centuries. Various princes were active patrons, keeping copyists and illuminators among their retainers, ordering the making of specific books, or accepting lavish copies authors gave them in exchange for a stipend (Plate 46.2). Students copied books to support their studies. Monks copied for monastic libraries. Books were precious goods because of their high cost and their symbolic function. They were, therefore, transmitted from one generation to the next and used as bequests, gifts, pawns, or guarantees. They attracted thieves and crossed centuries. By the late Middle Ages, specialized craftsmen had multiplied all over Europe to answer a growing need for more varied books well before the appearance of printing. In important cultural centers like Paris the book trade extended after 1350 beyond its original university sphere of influence but always under the dominant figure of the bookseller.

Notes

1. Morsel (2000).
2. Clanchy (2007, 196).
3. Bozzolo and Ornato (1980, 85).
4. Destrez (1935).
5. Schooner (1988).
6. Fianu (2006); Christianson (2007).
7. "Paravisus est locus ubi libri scolarium venduntur," said Jean de Garlande at the beginning of the thirteenth century. See Géraud (1837, 608).

8. Parent-Charon (1974).
9. Fianu (1992).
10. Rouse and Rouse (1988).
11. Mirot (1900); Laborde (1849–52, III, no. 5800).
12. Buettner (1988); Cockshaw (1969).
13. Couderc (1918).
14. Laborde (1852, III, nos. 5678, 5682, 5709, 5725).

BIBLIOGRAPHY

Bozzolo, C. and E. Ornato. 1980. *Pour une histoire du livre manuscrit au Moyen Âge. Trois essais de codicologie quantitative.* Paris: C.N.R.S.

Buettner, B. 1988. "Jacques Raponde, marchand de manuscrits enluminés." *Médiévales* 14 (spring): 23–32.

Christianson, P. C. 2007. "Evidence for the Study of London's Late Medieval Manuscript-Book Trade." In *Book Production and Publishing in Britain 1375–1475*, ed. Jeremy Griffiths and Derek Pearsall, 87–108. Cambridge: Cambridge University Press.

Clanchy, M. T. 2007. "Parchment and Paper: Manuscript Culture 1100–1500." In *A Companion to the History of the Book*, ed. Simon Eliot and Jonathan Rose, 194–206. Oxford: Blackwell Publishing Ltd.

Cockshaw, P. 1969. "Mentions d'auteurs, de copistes, d'enlumineurs et de libraires dans les comptes généraux de l'État bourguignon (1384–1419)." *Scriptorium* 23/1: 122–44.

Couderc, C. 1918. "Fragments relatifs à Andry le Musnier libraire-juré de l'Université de Paris au XVᵉ siècle." *Bulletin de la Société de l'Histoire de Paris et de l'Île-de-France* 45: 90–107.

Destrez, J. 1935. *La pecia dans les manuscrits universitaires du XIIIᵉ et du XIVᵉ siècle.* Paris: Éditions Jacques Vautrain.

Fianu, K. 1992. "Les Professionnels du livre à la fin du XIIIe siècle: l'enseignement des registres fiscaux parisiens." *Bibliothèque de l'école des chartes* 150/2: 185–222.

Fianu, K. 2006. "Métiers et espace: Topographie de la fabrication et du commerce du livre à Paris (XIIIe–XVe siècles)." In *Patrons, Authors and Workshops. Books and Book Production in Paris around 1400*, ed. Godfried Croenen and Peter Ainsworth, 21–45. Louvain: Peeters.

Géraud, H. 1837. *Paris sous Philippe le Bel d'après des documents originaux.* Paris: Crapelet [repr. Tübingen: Max Niemeyer, 1991].

Laborde, L. de. 1849–52. *Les Ducs de Bourgogne. Études sur les lettres, les arts et l'industrie pendant le XVᵉ siècle et plus particulièrement dans les Pays-Bas et le duché de Bourgogne.* Paris: Plon frères.

Mirot, L. 1900. "Le Procès de maître Jean Fusoris, chanoine de Notre-Dame de Paris, (1415–1416): Épisode des négociations franco-anglaises durant la guerre de Cent ans." *Mémoires de la Société de l'histoire de Paris et de l'Île-de-France* 27: 137–287.

Morsel, J. 2000. "Ce qu'écrire veut dire au Moyen Âge . . . Observations préliminaires à une étude de la scripturalité médiévale," *Memini. Travaux et documents de la Société des études médiévales du Québec* 4: 3–43.

Parent-Charon, A. 1974. *Les métiers du livre à Paris au XVIe siècle (1535–1560).* Geneva: Droz.

Rouse, R. H. and M. A. Rouse. 1988. " The Book Trade at the University of Paris ca. 1250–ca. 1350. " In *La Production du livre universitaire au Moyen Âge. Exemplar et pecia*, ed. Louis J. Bataillon, Bertrand G. Guyot, and Richard H. Rouse, 41–114. Paris: Éditions du C. N. R. S.

Rouse, R. H. and M. A. Rouse. 2000. *Manuscripts and their Makers. Commercial Book Producers in Medieval Paris, 1200–1500*. London: Harvey Miller.

Schooner, H. 1988. "La Production du livre par la pecia. " In *La Production du livre universitaire au Moyen Âge. Exemplar et pecia*, ed. Louis J. Bataillon, Bertrand G. Guyot, and Richard H. Rouse, 17–37. Paris: Éditions du C. N. R. S.

PART IV

SELECTED SCRIPTORIA AND LIBRARIES

CHAPTER 47

···

SCRIPTORIA AND LIBRARIES

An overview

···

DONATELLA NEBBIAI
(Translated by Frank T. Coulson)

THROUGHOUT the Middle Ages, integral ties exist between the place of copying and the conservation of texts. This chapter will study them. The research mainly concerns religious foundations, which in the period taken into consideration preserved an almost complete monopoly on book production. Here were born and developed the scriptoria, the places where books were written and decorated. This same term "scriptorium" also applies to the particular style of writing and the decoration which was elaborated there.

The physical isolation which in the beginning characterized religious foundations favored the establishment of a cultural model which, integrating both the classical and Christian heritage, united closely the scriptorium, the library, but also the treasure house and the archives. This close unity tended to loosen from the late eleventh century in favor of a rising spread of the practice of writing, a practice over which the universities successively will exercise control through the intermediary of accredited artists. Even if numerous monasteries, churches, and convents continue to make books *in situ*, or at least part of them (often the case, as we shall see, up to the fifteenth century), one can no longer speak of a scriptorium, but only of a writing office. The sources of supplies for the library diversify. Having become a place of consultation and no longer only a place of conservation, the library reflects the cultural and spiritual program of the institution it houses.

Chronicles, catalogues, literary works, and legal documents help us in reconstituting this process. Often they provide only indirect and fragmentary evidence. However, it turns out that an analysis of the terminology provides a wealth of information, even if the word scriptorium is not always openly mentioned. As to library, the Latin word most often found in the sources seems to have been *armarium* (medieval French *aulmaire*; *bibliotheca* appears only in literary sources, indeed later ones). A term of many meanings, as was often the case in the Middle Ages, *armarium* designates both the place and the piece of furniture where the books were kept. As a noun in the masculine form *armarius* or *armararius*, the term designates the function of the librarian, and this meaning lasts at least until the fourteenth century. The term is also of interest because it refers to a utilitarian and concrete approach to the book, specific to the medieval mentality. For these men, and particularly for the most learned among them, the ideal book is sober and modest, as is the case for those Gospels, copied in the fifth century, now at the Abbey of St. Gall (*CLA*, VII, 984). What counts above all is the text which it contains: "Let us not look for beautiful books but correct books," Saint Jerome reminds us. Its primary aim is to help in spreading the faith. In the twelfth century, the famous dictum "claustrum sine armario est quasi castrum sine armamentario" designates the library under a metaphor borrowed from the feudal world. Similarly, in the thirteenth century, the Dominican master Humbert of Romans recalls his militant view of culture by writing "Books are our weapons."

THE TRADITION

The history of libraries and centers of writing in the West begins in the third century with the disruption of the structures of the Roman Empire. The cultural unity which had characterized the territories up to that point is broken and the system of education dissolves, entailing a lessening in the practice of writing. In the course of the fifth and sixth centuries, secular establishments for book production are replaced definitively by centers situated near religious institutions. The book in the form of the codex becomes dominant: the material used in its fabrication is parchment.

In addition to the material changes, a new vision of books henceforth prevails. The message transmitted in the book is buried now in the mysteries of allegorical exegesis. Gregory the Great speaks thus of the "liber involutus." This interpretation appears even in the iconography of mosaics and Roman frescoes. Indeed, up until the fourth to fifth century, books are generally shown opened. In contrast, after the sixth century, one encloses them in rich bindings which are held for the most part against the chest of the person represented.

READING AND WRITING IN
RELIGIOUS COMMUNITIES

In religious communities, usually located in rural areas with little contact between them, illiteracy was widespread. Few people mastered reading and writing at the same time. If Cassiodorus, the founder of the monastery at Vivarium, can read with ease, the majority of his monks were barely capable of deciphering a text. In his *Institutiones*, the learned senator excuses their ignorance; for him writing can be likened to prayer, and, according to allegorical interpretation, the *antiquarii* copying books followed God's example, who wrote the law with his own fingers. For his part, Caesarius of Arles reminds the faithful that not knowing how to read did not excuse them from knowing God's laws.

It was thanks, therefore, to the initiative of several important individuals in these early Christian environments that measures were adopted to facilitate the approach, the reading, and the memorization of sacred texts. In the fourth century, in the Coptic community of Egypt, miscellanies appeared which united several texts of the same author or on the same subject. Jerome had introduced into the text of the Gospels segments (*cola* and *commata*) to facilitate the memorization of passages read in the divine office. Indices of the Gospels written inside the Canon tables were also drawn up.

But these innovations remained isolated. Early monastic life developed in rural areas where scriptoria and libraries were rare. For the Rule of St. Benedict (ch. 55) writing is manual work. The lawmaker reminds us that he gave to his followers the tools to write and copy, "graphium et tabulae," in the same way he conferred the tools necessary to work the abandoned fields, namely the plough and the spade. Even though he goes on to say that writing serves to preserve the treasures of knowledge, scribes in his view have a purely passive and repetitive task. They need not understand the text they are copying. And this is why one often gives writing to monks who are little gifted for study. This still took place in the tenth century at St. Gall according to Abbot Ekkehard.

One writes, therefore, above all to reproduce books necessary for worship. Thus, this activity, which during antiquity was considered an *opus servile*, the work of a slave or freedman, finds itself advanced to the rank of pious work. The *Institutiones* of Cassiodorus already bear witness to this fact. Later, in the eighth and ninth centuries this new conception appears in colophons. Monks of high rank, abbots, and bishops who commission books underline by the formula "Scribi et feci scribere" their personal involvement in the act of copying. This is the case with Froumond, a monk and later master of the abbey school at Tegernsee in the tenth century. As for the monks who copied, they offer their work to God and do not address their readers except to ask for their piety and prayers. Rare are the formulae where they call upon the critical sense of readers, inviting them, if need be, to check, even to correct, the text they present.

SPACES AND CUSTOMS

According to preserved sources, the scriptorium is generally situated close to the library and the church. This is the case with the abbey of St. Gall, as the ninth century plan attests. That the work carried on there was considered a sacred act is confirmed at the end of the eighth century by a liturgical collection coming from the monastery of Gellone, where, among other prayers prescribed for the monks, one finds an

Oratio de scriptorio. Even in the largest abbeys, the priority of the scriptoria was to enrich the collections of the host institution. Only a few among them, those that were particularly important, are set apart for having engaged in "copying campaigns," so to speak, so as to enrich the libraries of other centers. In the tenth century, for example, Saint-Amand-en Pévèle, in response to an order from the emperor, made a series of remarkable sacramentaries.

It is more difficult, however, to identify the placement of the library and to describe its functioning. In monasteries, books are generally placed in the same places as where they are used. So they can be found just about everywhere, and especially in the church, in the refectory, and in the chapter house, where the community unites in prayer. Here, only the *lector* is entitled to read, under the control, moreover, of the cantor or the *armarius* (librarian). The other monks only listen or repeat the passage chanting.

In the treasury are kept some particularly important and precious manuscripts. These are usually liturgical manuscripts, but one may also find there manuscripts related to the tradition of the monastery. From the ninth century the treasury of St. Denis, for example, housed a precious Greek copy of the works of a Syrian mystic which a tradition identified with the first bishop of Paris and the founder of the abbey.

Whatever their content, the manuscripts in the treasury were venerated; they are assimilated to relics. Enclosed in bindings of ivory enhanced with precious gems, these books, with their imposing beauty, written in gold lettering on purple parchment, draw their decorative inspiration from classical models. This is the case with a Bible made about 800 at the suggestion of the Bishop of Orléans, Théodulf (760–821), at Saint Maximin of Micy. To complete this project, Théodulf employed several monks from the monastery at Aniane. The scribes, who used purple parchment, had recourse to a learned hierarchy of scripts (Caroline minuscule, Uncial, Capitals) which look to Roman customs.

Because of their value, the books of the treasury sometimes serve as collateral for the religious community, or rather for monarchs. At the end of the ninth century, King Eudes removed a series of very expensive objects, among which was a precious copy of the Gospels, from the treasury of the abbey of St. Denis. Books also disappeared during raids. The splendid Sacramentary of Christ Church, Canterbury, today in the Royal Library of Stockholm, was thus stolen by pirates. An English civil servant of the ninth century, Aelfred, recovered it and offered it immediately by devotion to the cathedral, as the long note inscribed on the first folio bears witness.

The first libraries are kept in a room situated near the church, sometimes in the sacristy itself, in a niche hollowed in the wall, even in a locked chest. These collections, dominated by copies of the Rule, bibles, *Vitae patrum,* and the works of Church Fathers, are given to the care of the cantor or librarian. According to the customary of Cluny, the cantor at the beginning of Lent each year distributed volumes for the benefit of the monks.

At the end of the eleventh century, the abbey of Moissac provides an eloquent testimony to the division of books in different pieces of furniture, indeed in different rooms. The *armarium* counts in all 60 books, of which 11, dedicated to the liberal arts, were used in the school of the monastery. There was also, no doubt in the sacristy, a *theca librorum*, containing a collection of 26 works exclusively of religious import: bibles, patristic texts, and theological works. On the other hand, liturgical books needed for the offices are not enclosed in a particular room so that they may be more accessible to monks.

Networks of Men and Books in the Carolingian Era

Besides the libraries of religious orders, the Carolingian period also saw the development of secular collections. Some witnesses of these collections survive, mainly of lords and princes. But it remains difficult to define the composition of these libraries and to ascertain the cultural level of their owners. Dhuoda, for example, the unfortunate wife of Duke Bernard of Septimania, has left us an important witness in the work she dedicates to her son William. However, with the exception of the Bible and major authors such as Gregory the Great or Donatus, the works comprising the library are not explicitly stated. It is likely that, following the example of many scholars of her period, Dhuoda knew her sources by heart. She, therefore, did not necessarily have the book she was citing at hand. She also probably relied upon collections of extracts whose structure we no longer know.

The contents of the library of Count Eccard of Mâcon, who lived at the time of King Pepin of Aquitania and who established the priory of Perrecy in Burgundy, is more readily identifiable since it is described in an inventory of goods made at the time of his will, around 875. There are 23 volumes which contain principally liturgical texts and lives of saints, but also works on law and ecclesiastical history, particularly by Paul the Deacon and Gregory of Tours. This lord also owned a book on military tactics (the title is not specified but it is probably the work of Vegetius), a treatise on farming, and two books on medicine. Heccard also owned Gospels in German.

In spite of their variety, which allows one to assume the high cultural level of the owner, it is probable that Heccard considered his books above all a heritage. Eager to keep them in the family, he left the most precious to his wife Richilde, namely the liturgical books from his chapel, to which were added the chalices and other liturgical facings. He left his other books to certain important clerics, Walda, bishop of Auxerre, Raganfridus, bishop of Meaux, Gautier, bishop of Orléans, Anségise, archbishop of Sens, and the Abbess Bertrade of Farmoutiers. Heccard probably did not wish to spread culture; rather, for him it was a question of showing devotion to powerful religious institutions.

The Carolingian age is characterized by the establishment of a fundamental reform in writing which led to the adoption in nearly all the territory of the empire of the Caroline minuscule. This writing spread all the more readily and was well received, since it is close to the script then taught at the elementary level in the Church and secular schools. In the last decades of the eighth century, the reform gave rise to a book production of a very high level, which references Charlemagne's court. One of its first witnesses is the Gospel of Godescalc (781–3).

The *Capitularies* issued by the emperor insisted upon the promotion of studies and the necessity to have good-quality copies made of the Holy Scripture. In a passage of the *Admonitiones generales* (March 23, 789) Charlemagne reiterates his command to reproduce carefully the "libros catholicos": "Correct well Catholic books. Truly, at times those who wish to pray to God do so badly as the books are not correct." One may credit to these measures a splendid series of manuscripts of the Bible which the scholar Alcuin, bishop of York and advisor to the emperor, had made at the monastery of Saint-Martin of Tours.

Charlemagne was above all responsible for the creation at the palace of Aix-la-Chapelle of the most famous library of the period. This exceptional collection, unique of its kind, was open to scholars, who corrected books herein preserved by comparing them with exemplars that the emperor had transported for from the great Italian monasteries. Thus, reference works were compiled which were worthy of being copied and diffused throughout the entire empire. The copies of these texts which we have preserved bear the note "ex authentico exemplari." Charlemagne's library was, therefore, public (or rather semi-public, given that access to it was accorded to a limited number of scholars). It is the expression of a cultural program and, more, a cultural policy. Yet in spite of these characteristics, the library remains legally a private one, and the emperor thus decided in his will to have it sold to do good works.

It is from the Carolingian period that new cultural foundations of Europe were put in place. The libraries of the largest abbeys, like Corbie and Fleury, become richer and richer thanks to outside contributions. Established networks link several important individuals who pass through monasteries and schools, visit libraries, write to each other, and exchange books. The works of these scholars bear witness to the intensity and depth of their reading. Their mastery of writing is evident, as can be seen from the margins and spaces between the lines of their books. These spaces are full of under-linings, reminder signs, and insertions and annotations. Undoubtedly, these individuals read while writing or wrote immediately after reading. Lupus of Ferrières, for example, customarily finished and commented upon the texts contained in his own manuscripts, he made *indices*, he collated exemplars, referring to the oldest. For his models of script, he looked to the principal scriptoria: thus, he asked for examples of Capital letters from Tours in order to reproduce them. Florus, bishop of Lyons, made use of commas and parentheses so as to isolate in the works he was reading the extracts he would reuse later in his own works.

Many witnesses attest to the assiduous frequenting of libraries. Alcuin thus enjoins one to bind those volumes which his contemporaries have not hesitated to dismember in order to transfer them from one library to another and consult them more readily. Rather of Verona calls to mind with nostalgia the time when, far from his administrative and political obligations, he had the time to work in the library where he "turned and turned again" the books. At about the same time, in 993, Abbot Adson of Montier-en Der, departing from his monastery to go to Jerusalem, leaves in a trunk his personal library, a rich and varied collection of philosophical, literary, and grammatical works. Lastly, Rabanus Maurus, abbot of Fulda, recounts in his *De universo* the story of these deposits from antiquity to the sixth century. For him, this process concludes ideally in the Bible, which constitutes the ideal library.

For these indeed exceptional individuals reading and writing are henceforward two complementary and mastered activities. Thus, we see emerge the figure of the author. One of the most accomplished expressions of this figure of the author will be summed up some centuries later by Gilbert of Nogent (1053–1124), for whom the "perpetuitas legendi" and the "continuatio scribendi" are on the same level.

As far as the organization of the libraries is concerned, the Carolingian age marks the end of the model uniquely centered on conservation, what G. Cavallo (1988, x–xiii) had defined with the suggestive expression "library without a public." The rise in the increase of the written word, found equally in books and in administrative documents, is therefore the basis for profound modifications in the supply and organization of collections.

RENEWAL

From the middle of the eleventh and throughout the twelfth century, religious institutions undergo major reforms. The Cistercian order, founded in 1098, preached the return to a stricter observance of the rule and advocated a rigorous model of life where time dedicated to study was reduced. On the other hand, communities of regular canons, like the Premonstratensian order or the Victorines, insist on the necessity to train themselves so as to involve themselves with the faithful. Consequently, their statutes reconcile the search for contemplation and the exercise of preaching.

NEW BOOKS, NEW TEXTS

In this context, the traditional structure of monastic schools evolves. Benedictine spirituality advocated the rejection of the professorial function, which is judged to be a useless screen between the soul and Christ. Thus, many monasteries reduced the activity of their outside schools, where children not belonging to the community received instruction. At St. Martin of Tours, for example, the school moved from the monastery to the cathedral, and Bouchard took on the administration of it. In the abbeys of the Cistercian order and in the Carthusian order, one no longer admitted a child not belonging to the community. One thus entered the monastery later and one received there an ascetic formation founded on the *lectio divina*, on spiritual instruction, and on meditation.

These reforms, whose effect proved salutary for the quality of religious life, also left a profound imprint on intellectual life. Far from folding in on themselves, the communities rethought their state and mission. The new vision they had for their own past bears witness to this. In the twelfth century, while reorganizing their libraries and archives, the monastic communities also take part in a drafting of important historical works.

Annals represent the simplest and most ancient form of this production. They are composed of simple listings of deeds and names in the margin of calendars, obituaries, and tables. At Saint-Évroult, for example, the monks draw up at the end of the eleventh century a computus table covering the period from the birth of Christ onward. The side columns are used for the listing of the annals. Numerous notices are inscribed therein during the first half of the twelfth century, at the same period as the scholar Ordericus Vitalis, an active member of the scriptorium of the Norman monastery, was working on the composition of his *Ecclesiastical History*.

More developed than the annals, chronicles proposed to tell the story of the religious institution on a wider canvas. Thus, for example, Abbot Arnaud of Saint-Pierre le Vif of Sens had assembled at the beginning of the twelfth century an ample dossier composed of diplomatic acts and stories so that the monks might know not only the history of their monastery but more generally that of the Christian world. Arnaud, a great lover of books, himself composed the chronicle, and he also no doubt copied it in part. We know that he kept watch over the upkeep of the library, punishing monks who sold or damaged books, and promoting the copying of new volumes. He cut the parchment and furnished the *scriptores* with manuscripts to transcribe.

The chronicle of Sens contains also a list of books which this pious bibliophile offered to the abbey at the end of his tenure (Plate 47.1). Let us note in passing that the presence of such a list is not unusual in historical compilations and monastic cartularies of the twelfth century. Several other examples may be mentioned. The chronicle of the Benedictine abbey of Saint Peter and Paul at Bèze (in Burgundy) contains a list of the books ordered by Abbot Stephen (d. 1125). The cartulary of Simon, who was a monk and historian of Saint-Bertin, now lost, contained a catalogue of the library of the abbey classified in alphabetical order. Let us also recall the historical collection of Guimann, monk of Saint-Vaast of Arras, who supplied, inter alia, a description of the abbey church and a presentation of objects and books which were conserved in the treasury.

Thanks to the new institutional networks, the circulation of books increased. The Cistercian order thus prescribed that the mother abbeys supply their daughter houses with books. This clause did not exist in the statutes of the Premonstratensian order. One pointed out, however, the books whose presence was deemed necessary in each monastery. The libraries of the Premonstratensians received gifts of books from the outside. The abbey of Cuissy, for example, obtained from the Cistercians at Vauclair two manuscripts of scriptural commentary (Laon, Bibliothèque municipale, MSS 61

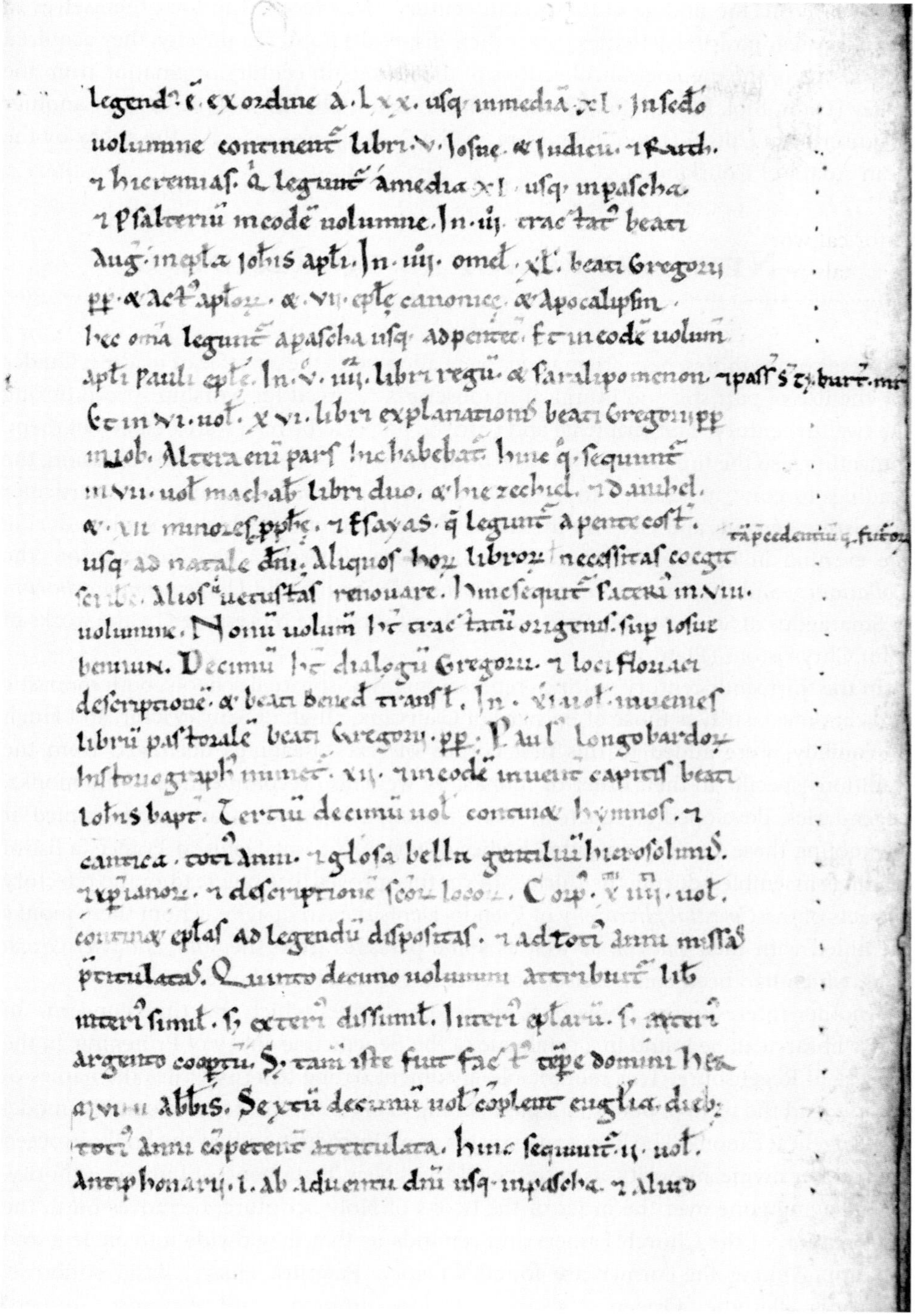

legend̄ e̅ ex ordine a·l·xx· usq̄ in media xl· In secd̄o
uolumine continent̄ libri·v· Iosue·& Iudicu̅·1 Ruth·
1 hieremias· a legun̄ amedia xl· usq̄ in pascha·
1 Psalteriu̅ in eode̅ uolume. In·iij· erac tac̄ beati
Aug· in epla Iohīs apli. In·iiij· omel·xl· beati Gregory
pp·& act apior·& vij· eplē canonice·& Apocalipsin·
hec oma legun̄ a pascha usq̄ ad pentec̄· & in eode̅ uolum
apli Pauli eplē· In·v·iiij· libri regu̅·& Paralipomenon·1pass̄ s̄ rz bur̄ m̄r
& in vi·uol·x vi· libri explanationб beati Gregory pp
in Iob· Altera em̄ pars hic habebat̄ hin̄c q̄ sequun̄t
in vii·uol machab̄ libri duo·& hie zechiel·1 danihel·
& xii minores pptē·1 Esayas· q̄ legun̄ a penticost̄·
usq̄ ad natale dm̄· Aliquos hoz librox necessitas coegit
serib̄· Alios uerustas renouare· huic sequen̄t ficeri in·viii·
uolumine· Nonu̅ uolu̅ hc erac tau̅ originis·sup Iosue
bennux· Decimu̅ hc dialogu̅ Gregoru·1 loci flouuer
descriptione̅·& beari Benedicti transit· In·xi uol·inuenies
libru̅ pastorale̅ beati Gregory pp· Paul longobardoz
historiographi nunc̄·xij· in eode̅ inueni capies beati
Iohīs bapt· Tertiu̅ decimu̅ uol·coninac hymnos·1
cantica· totci anni·1 glosa bella genitlui Iherosolimi·
1xpianoz·1 descriptione scoz loco· Coip·x iiij·uol·
coninac eptas ad legendu̅ dispositas·1 ad toci anni mïssaб
priculaceб·Q̄uinto decimo uolumin̄ attribut̄ lit
interi simit·h̄ exteri diffinit· Interi eptaru̅·f̄· exteri
argento coopru·S̄ tan̄ iste fuit fact̄ tpē domini Her̄
a...u abbis· Sexcu̅ decu̅u̅ uol copleur euglia dieb̄
toci anni coperen̄ articulata· huic sequun̄t ij·uol·
Antiphonary·1·ab aduentu dm̄ usq̄ in pascha·1 aliud

PLATE 47.1 Books offered by Abbot Arnaud to Saint-Pierre Le Vif, Sens, from the chronicle of Sens, twelfth century: Auxerre, Bibliothèque municipale, MS 212, fols. 91v–92r.

and 70). From the middle of the twelfth century, the canons who took themselves to Laon for their pastoral activities had at their disposal a house. In the city, they acquired books: one of the theological collections of the thirteenth century originating from the abbey (Laon, Bibl. Mun., MS 43) was copied at Laon. The same is the case for another manuscript of Cuissy (Laon, Bibl. Mun., MS 20) which was gifted to the abbey by the dean Adam of Courlandon.

NEW APPROACHES TO READING

In these communities, new orientations were adopted to the practice of reading. Guides for the use of patristic and liturgical manuscripts reserved for worship spread during the twelfth century. The scriptural and patristic books to be read were detailed in them, indicating also the time of day or of the liturgical year. Depending on the occasion, the readings foresaw, in addition to the Bible, extracts from patristic authors, in particular Augustine, Jerome, and Gregory the Great. During gatherings which took place during the evening in the cloister, models for life were also read; the *Vitae patrum*, the *Collationes*, and the *De institutis coenobiorum* of Cassius, the *Diadema monachorum* of Smaragdus of Saint-Mihiel. Patristic Greek authors were represented by the works of John Chrysostom (Plate 47.2).

In the thirteenth century writings representing new spiritual schools, both monastic and canonical, such as those of Bernard of Clairvaux, Hugh of Saint-Victor, and Hugh of Fouilloy, were added to this first corpus of texts. Readings borrowed from the traditions specific to their order or monastery were also recommended to the monks. Legendaries, developed as much by the Cistercians as by the Carthusians, aimed at assembling these newly constituted bodies of texts. At Saint-Denis in France, a list of readings assembled during the thirteenth century proves that one read in the refectory extracts of the *Celestial Hierarchy* of Pseudo-Denis the Areopagite, whom these monks identified with their patron, as well as some passages from the *Vita Ludovici Grossi regis*, which had been composed in the twelfth century by Abbot Suger.

Another interesting example of these reading guides which this time concerns an entire library can be found in a catalogue of the Benedictine abbey of Prüfening, in the diocese of Regensburg. This remarkable document dating to 1165 writes the names of authors and the titles of books in a page setting of six columns, reproducing the model of evangelical canons. The librarian explains as an introduction that the books proceed from either divine authority, as with the Old and New Testament, or human authority. After having gone over the order of the books of Holy Scripture, he moves on to the presentation of the Church Fathers and reminds us that they divide into ancient and modern. Among the former are found Gregory, Paterius, Hilary, Basil, Ambrose, Augustine, Jerome, Origen, Caesarius, Isidore, Ephrem, and Ambrose Autpert. Among the latter are included Bede, Alcuin, Rabanus Maurus, Ivo of Chartres (d. 1116), Haymon of Auxerre, Anselm of Canterbury, Hugh of Saint-Victor (d. 1141), Gratian

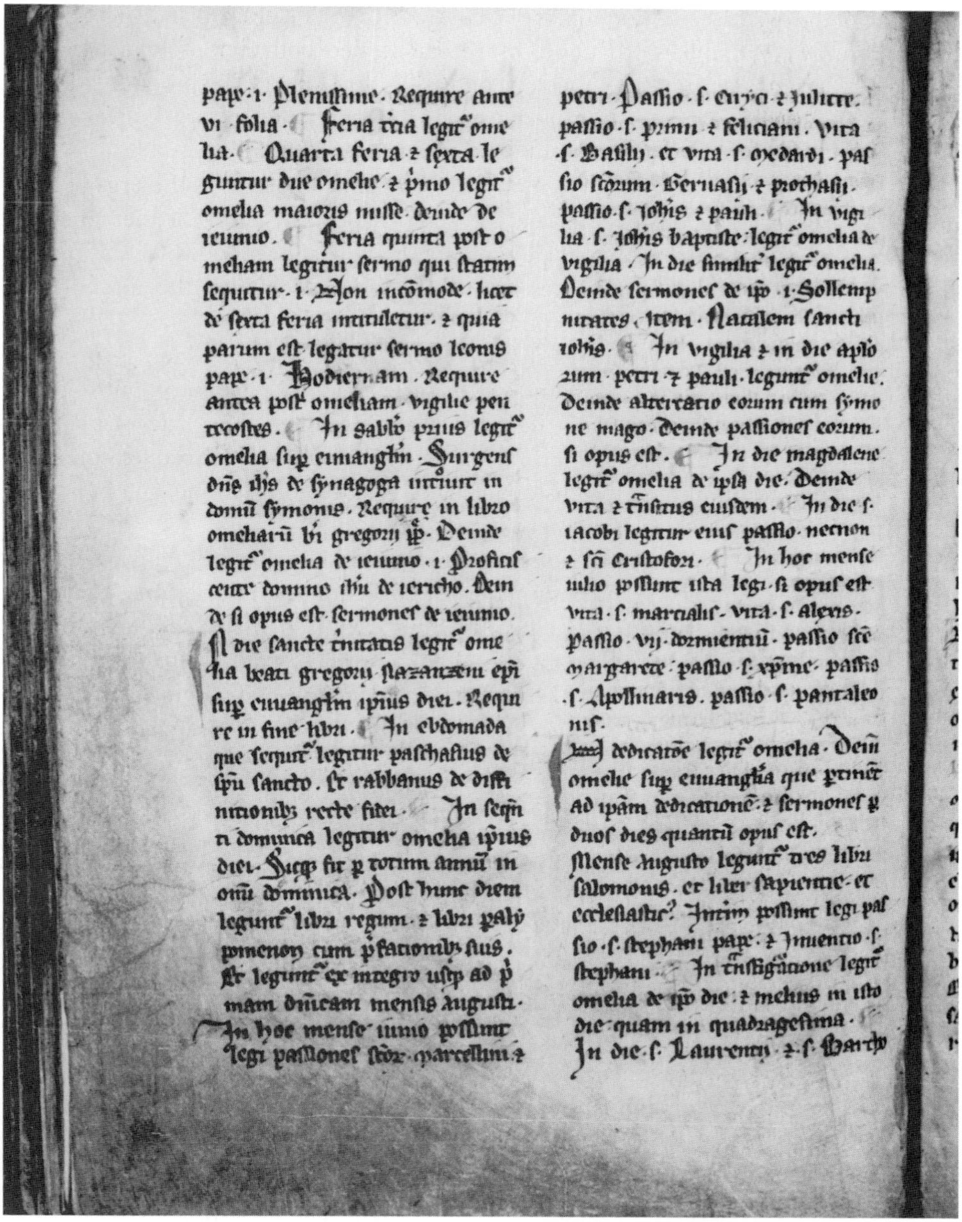

pape·1· Plenitume· Require aut
vi folia· ¶ Feria tria legit' ome
lia· ¶ Quarta feria ⁊ sexta le
guntur due omelie ⁊ p̅mo legit'
omelia maioris misse· deinde de
ieiunio· ¶ Feria quinta post o
meliam legitur sermo qui statim
sequitur·1· Non incomode hec
de sexta feria intituletur· ⁊ quia
parum est· legatur sermo leonis
pape·1· Hodiernam· Require
antea post omeliam· vigilie pen
tecostes· ¶ In sab̅o p̅mus legit'
omelia sup eumangtm· Surgens
dns ihs de synagoga intunt in
domu symonis· Require in libro
omeliaru ubi gregori̇ i̇p· Deinde
legit' omelia de ieiunio·1· Profins
cetur domino ihu de ieriche· Dein
de si opus est· sermones de ieiunio·
Si die sancte tnitatis legit' ome
lia beati gregorii nazanzeni epi
sup eumangtm ipius diei· Requi
re in fine libri· ¶ In ebdomada
que sequit' legitur paschasius de
spu sancto· Er rabbanus de disti
nationibus recte fidei· ¶ In sec̅n
ti dominica legitur omelia ipius
diei· Sic̅q fir p totum annum in
omi dominica· Post hunc diem
legunt' libri regum· ⁊ libri pali
pomenon cum prefationibus suis·
Er legunt' ex integro usq ad p
mam dnicam mensis augusti·
In hoc mense iunio possunt
legi passiones sc̅o marcellini ⁊

petri· Passio s· cirici ⁊ iuliete·
passio s· primi ⁊ feliciani· vita
s· Basilii· et vita s· medardi· pas
sio sc̅oum Geruasii ⁊ prothasii·
passio s· iohis ⁊ pauli· ¶ In vigi
lia s· iohis baptiste legunt omelia de
vigilia· In die similit legit' omelia·
Deinde sermones de ipo·1· Sollemp
nitates· item· Natalem sancti
iohis· ¶ In vigilia ⁊ in die aplo
um petri ⁊ pauli· legunt omelie·
deinde altercatio eorum cum symo
ne mago· Deinde passiones eorum·
si opus est· ¶ In die magdalene
legit' omelia de ipsa die· Deinde
vita ⁊ tnsitus eiusdem· In die s·
iacobi legitur eius passio· necnon
⁊ sn cristofori· ¶ In hoc mense
iulio possunt ista legi· si opus est·
vita· s· marcialis· vita s· alexis·
passio· vii· dormientiu· passio s̅e
margarete· passio s· xpine· passio
s· apollinaris· passio s· pantaleo
nis·
¶ In dedicatoe legit' omelia· Dein
omelie sup eumangtia que pnt
ad ipam dedicatione ⁊ sermones p
duos dies quantu opus est·
Mense augusto legunt tres libri
salomonis· et liber sapientie· et
ecclesiastes· Interim possunt legi pas
sio s· stephani pape· ⁊ Inuentio s·
stephani· In tnsfiguratione legit'
omelia de ipo die· ⁊ melius in isto
die· quam in quadragesima·
In die s· Laurentii ⁊ s· Barthol

PLATE 47.2 Liturgical readings at Marchiennes, thirteenth century: Douai, Bibliothèque municipale, MS 540, fol. 94v.

(first half of the twelfth century), Rupert of Deutz (d. *c.*1130), Peter Damian, Peter Abelard (d. 1142), and Peter Lombard (d. 1160). One recognizes here both the Carolingian masters as well as the great interpreters of theology of the twelfth century. The program does not mention Bernard of Clairvaux, but his omission is probably due to forgetfulness, as his writings are reproduced in the catalogue.

The *libri communes* are one of the innovations which characterizes the organization of religious libraries in the twelfth century, and particularly those of the abbeys of regular canons. These are the books of worship and patristic works which are read in common. In several cases, the sources underline the specificity and the autonomy of this collection of books vis-à-vis the others available in the abbeys.

The oldest attestation of the existence of one of these collections is probably furnished by the *Liber ordinis* of Saint-Victor of Paris. This customary, put together in the time of Abbot Gilduin (first decades of the twelfth century) devotes a large chapter to the duties of the librarian. From Saint-Victor, these directives spread to other canonical communities; the customary of Arrouaise, for example, takes up again the instructions in almost the same terms.

At Saint-Victor, these *libri communes* comprise anthologies for the divine offices and the chant, homiliaries, bibles, and commentaries, collections of lives of saints and of the Church Fathers. It is specified that because they are used in prayers and for the edification of the canons, these books must remain always available to them. It was the responsibility of the librarian to display them ("common books, which one should handle daily . . . ; common books which are displayed"), and then to watch over them to make sure they were replaced after use in the "commune servatorium." This was probably a piece of furniture in the sacristy, but the term could also, in an important abbey like Saint-Victor, designate a specific room.

If the customary of Saint-Victor only supplies general indications, we know precisely the holder of one of these collections thanks to a catalogue of the second half of the twelfth century It comes from another abbey of Premonstratensians canons, Arnstein, in the diocese of Trier. In addition to liturgical books (the Bible, passionaries, legendaries) the *libri communes* contain here commentaries and biblical aids, lists of patristic citations, summae, and encyclopedias. One notices, in particular, the *Etymologies* of Isidore of Seville, an Augustinian florilegium of Eugippius, and even the *Sentences* of Peter Lombard (d. 1160), who is the most recent author mentioned in the catalogue. While reassembling the writings of different periods, these common books form a coherent whole which appears to have been defined according to their use: these were truly reference collections for prayer and for the training of canons.

DIRECTED ACQUISITIONS

Library catalogues reflect the concern to master and direct the accumulation of books, as well as practical documents. The drawing up of these catalogues was sometimes left to the archivist. In the middle of the twelfth century, the Chancellor Hamon classified the library of Lincoln Cathedral. In an inventory made at the end of the twelfth century, the librarian of the abbey of les Vaux de Cernay (a Benedictine foundation of the beginning of the twelfth century, which became Cistercian in 1147) assumes the role of a chronicler when he claims to have registered the titles of the books to transmit their memory to future generations.

During the same period, the librarian of Saint-Aubin of Angers seems to have similar preoccupations. Indeed, he writes the following verses in the margin of his inventory: "Here are written the names of our books so the company of monks may guard the memory." The catalogue of the library of the Abbey of Saint-Évroult sometimes lists the names of former owners of the volumes described. Some decades later, the author of the catalogue of the library of Saint-Amand-en Pévèle mentions them beside the bibliographical items (Plate 47.3).

This exceptional document thus becomes a true chronicle of the library, as it allows one to distinguish its original kernel, which comprised about a hundred volumes principally biblical and patristic, and successive contributions coming from the monks (nearly 70 volumes) which cover roughly four centuries. One thus sees the evolution of the contents of a collection which in the ninth and tenth centuries conforms to the traditional profile of monastic book collections. Though strongly oriented toward patristics, liturgy, and ecclesiastical history, it also seems to include works from the school tradition. The 18 manuscripts gifted by the scholar Hucbald, a known author of musical treatises, bear witness to this fact. Several volumes contain liberal arts treatises. On the other hand, during the years 1120–50, the library of Saint-Amand acquires books on Church history (as is the case with the books donated by the Abbot Gautier the First), several works on philosophy, for example a manuscript of the *Consolation of Philosophy* of Boethius, donated by the monk Hellinus, future abbot of Saint-Thierry of Reims, and, above all, biblical tools and collections of sermons.

This new direction can be seen especially in the 93 manuscripts copied between 1160–70 at the instigation of the librarian and author of the catalogue. A detailed list is provided at the end of the document. It contains commentaries on the Bible, glossed Bibles, an impressive collection of the works of Augustine in 17 volumes, and several volumes of recent theological works: those of the canon Hugh of Saint Victor (in six volumes), and of the Cistercians Bernard of Clairvaux, Gautier of Mortagne, and Guerric of Igny. No book of medicine or science is found in this collection: the cultural heritage of late antiquity is found in a single copy of the *Natural History* of Pliny the Elder (Paris, BnF MS lat. 6797).

The catalogue of Saint-Amand confirms that in the middle of the twelfth century this abbey possessed an active and organized writing workshop, as was the case in many monasteries. One chose sometimes to copy texts which one could no longer read in readily available copies. The catalogue of the Benedictine monastery of Civate (in the north of Italy) indicates the presence in the library of books which were no longer legible and which had therefore become useless. In 1093, Jerome, abbot of

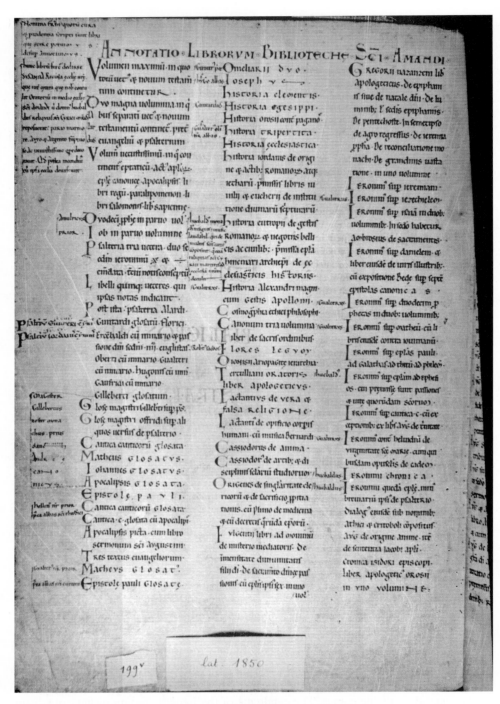

PLATE 47.3 Catalogue of the library of Saint-Amand-en Pévèle, Tournai, twelfth century, second half: Paris, BnF, MS Lat. 1850, fol. 199v.

Pomposa, has copied several manuscripts and integrates them into the library. Cistercian abbeys contain efficient scriptoria, characterized by an easily recognizable style of writing and decoration. To them we owe the establishment of true patristic collections. Such is the case with the magnificent series of ten volumes of the works of St. Augustine produced at Clairvaux (Troyes, Bibl. Mun., MS 40). But the monastic scriptoria of this period do not limit themselves to producing only ecclesiastical works. The heritage of classical antiquity is equally summoned up in a vast movement of *renovatio librorum*, which includes notably the recopying of grammars, works of rhetoric, and even encyclopedias. Thus, in the middle of the twelfth century, an actual edition of the works of Cicero was produced at Stavelot. The *Natural History* of Pliny the Elder was copied in numerous monasteries, for example at Lobbes and Bamberg. The works of Seneca, because of their moral implications, were particularly appreciated in Cistercian monasteries.

The activity of the scriptorium of the Premonstratensian abbey of Bonne-Espérance (diocese of Cambrai) in the first decades of the twelfth century is known thanks to an interesting witness which illustrates as well the systematic production of monumental Bibles in the Mosan region and in the north of France. The Bible of Bonne-Espérance, in two volumes, is noteworthy for its large format (49 × 32 cm). It was made in 1140 by Brother Henry at a time when book production developed considerably in the abbey.

Henry, who calls himself *librarius*, presents himself at the beginning of the manuscript in a text of 30 lines written in red and black ink. Both by the position it occupies and by its style, it cannot be called a colophon. Rather, it belongs to the genre of historical preamble. Adopting a solemn tone, Henry explains that he copied this manuscript "for the use of the brothers of the abbey of Bonne-Espérance" and that it took him nearly three years to complete the work, since he stopped during winter to devote himself to less important work. The manuscript, he writes, comprises two volumes, the first beginning with Genesis, the second finishing with Apocalypse.

Henry also gives a precise date for the beginning and end of his work, recalling the names of the pope, the bishop, the abbot, the emperor, and the count of Hainaut. As a chronicler, he mentions the great works which the abbey undertook during these same years: the laying of the foundation of the basilica and the consecration of the atrium. The text closes with formulas more similar to the usual style of colophons. In particular, one finds the usual curses cast against those who might wish to steal or damage the book, and he asks them to pray for the salvation of his soul.

Not far from Bonne-Espérance, another organized scriptorium is that of the abbey of Saint-Martin of Tournai. Its activity is described in a chronicle, the *Liber de restauratione monasterii Sancti Martini Tornacensis* by Hermann of Tournai (d. *c.*1147). The author narrates that in the time of Abbot Eudes (d. 1105), 12 young men devoted themselves to the copying of patristic and theological works. Their results were of such high quality, he adds, that other monasteries used them as exemplars to correct their books:

> Had you entered into the monastery, you would have been able to see twelve young monks seated on stools and writing with care and in silence on tables constructed for this task. . . . On this account Abbot Eudes had copied all the books of Saint Jerome on the exposition of the Prophets and all that he could find of Saint Augustine, of Ambrose, of Isidore, of Bede and also of Anselm with such great care that if there was a library in the neighboring churches, each sought to borrow our exemplars to correct their own.

The author also cites the books produced for the library of the abbey by one of its copyists, Geoffrey, "scriptor peritissimus," whose script he attests to recognizing.

The *Liber ordinis* of Saint-Victor also contains information on the rooms where books were produced. It details that they are to be found outside those places where the life of the convent takes place but always within its walls so the brothers may work in peace without being bothered by noise. Only the librarian, abbot, and the prior may enter the workroom of the copyists. As at Saint-Martin, the brothers kept silent there; they abstained from conversation and from walking outside. The work was executed under the responsibility of the *armarius*, who had to supply the necessary materials and check regularly what was done. The customary also commands the *armarius* to make sure that the brothers who know how to write but are not to do so do not take upon themselves the task until they have obtained permission from the abbot, who also decided what hours should be devoted to writing.

One of the most important tasks of the *armarius* of Saint-Victor was to manage the quality of the copy and legibility of the liturgical books. He had to correct them and check the punctuation, so as to ascertain that the brothers who were using them on a daily basis for readings or chants encountered no difficulties. In addition, he had to know to perfection the division and use of the books for the Office so as to assist the brothers who did not know how to find the right passage or the right book to read.

In the same spirit, the customary of Prémontré reminds one also that the librarian directs the readings:

> The librarian should preserve and correct the books. . . . He should know all the books which are necessary for the running of the church, such as the Gospels and the Epistolaries so that if one of the brothers who is using them is mistaken or loses his page and cannot find the passage, he can find it without losing time.

The sacristan, the cantor and the sub-cantor watch over the arrangement and distribution of the books of the Office.

These witnesses indicate that what was particularly necessary at this period was correct books of high quality. For if their readers all belong to ecclesiastical and religious ranks, the same cannot be said any longer for the copyists: the use of writing seems henceforth widespread; it extends beyond the walls of the cloister and the cathedral schools. The making of books is handed over in many cases to lay artisans who are paid per accomplished task. The *armarius* of Saint-Victor, for example, must manage the copying activity not only of the monks but also of the commissioned scribes ("eos qui pro precio scribunt"). In the first decades of the twelfth century, the Benedictine abbey of Abingdon also had recourse to outside copyists to enrich its library.

Beyond the general instructions of normative texts, one of the ways the religious authorities had to regulate the quality of copies was notably the production of model exemplars. We referred above to one of these manuscripts, the Bible of the Premonstratensians of Bonne-Espérance. But the Cistercian order, which by the expedient of its institutional network spread manuscripts to all of its offshoots, was equally famous for this type of production. Thus, manuscript Dijon, Bibl. Mun. 114, from the abbey of Cîteaux, is exactly one of these model exemplars, as an inscription, in Capitals and minuscules which encircles the table of contents bears witness:

> In these volumes the books of the Holy Office are contained for which variety is not appropriate in our order. They have been united into a single corpus, principally with the intention of having in this book an immutable exemplar to safeguard the uniformity and correct the variety in the others.

Sometimes authorities were called upon to decide on the examples to copy and on the criteria for establishing new editions. The copyists are in that case sometimes reminded of the need for discretion and good sense. We have preserved the witness to such a case in a manuscript from the library of Clairvaux (Montpellier, Bibliothèque de la Faculté de Médecine, MS 294, twelfth century, on fol. 158, Plate 47.4). This concerns a note recounting the visit made to the monastery of San Martino al Monte Cimino (diocese of Viterbo) by the biblical scholar Nicholas Maniacoria. This former deacon of San Lorenzo in Damaso, who entered the order of Saint Bernard, was then a monk at the abbey of Tre Fontane, near Rome. In the company of Abbot Bernard (1140–5), who would become subsequently pope under the name of Eugene III, Nicholas entered the scriptorium of San Martino. Here a copyist was in the middle of collating two copies of the Bible, an older one and a new one, and was thoroughly correcting the older, incorporating into it many additions. The corrections and the additions were so numerous that they resulted in undermining completely the original text. A lively discussion took place between the two men. The *scriptor* maintained a non-critical viewpoint which gave precedence to the quantity of information over its quality and preferred the new copy which "contained more material," but the learned biblical scholar replied: "In the same way that you consider that the old copy contains less material than the newer, you can also think that in the newer there is a superfluity in comparison with the older." Thus, Nicholas gave weight to the greater quality of the older exemplar and consequently its authority. To conclude, he condemns the imprudent and pretentious attitude of those who, giving short shrift to the source of truth, allow themselves to take out or add to the sacred text passages on the basis of totally arbitrary conjectures.

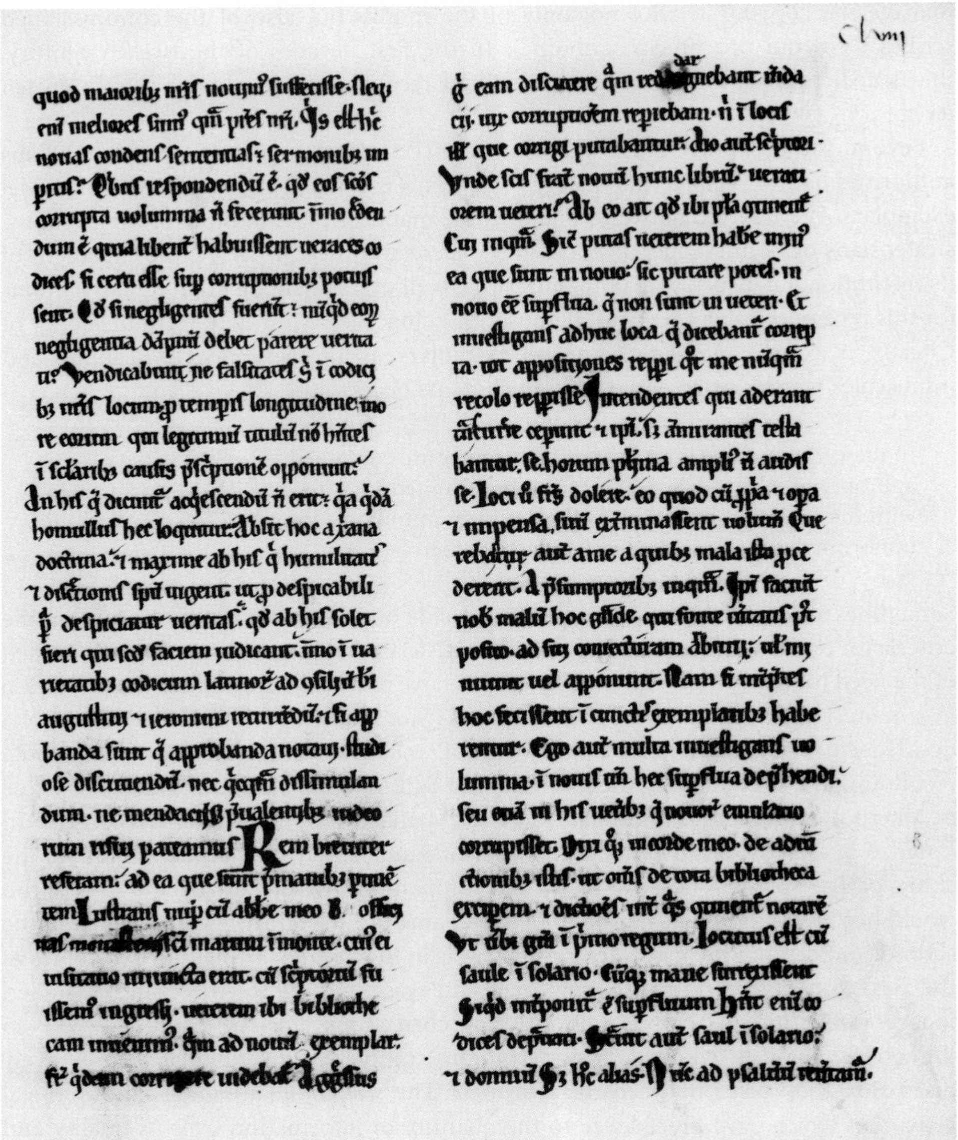

PLATE 47.4 Note recounting the visit made to San Martino al Monte Cimino (Viterbo) by Nicholas Maniacoria, c.1140–5: Montpellier, Bibliothèque Interuniversitaire, Faculté de Médecine, MS 294, twelfth century, fol. 158.

AUTHORITY

The episode of Nicholas Maniacoria is indicative of the attention accorded by the Church authorities henceforth to the indiscriminate and uncontrolled practice of writing. Books circulated more and more without any control over their content. In a letter to William of Saint-Thierry, Bernard of Clairvaux condemns the doctrines defended by the philosopher Abelard. The books of this "reptilian" individual spread so quickly, he observes, that they seem to fly ("Libri volant"). But one can imagine that the learned theologian knows that henceforth it is impossible to forbid copying. Bernard proposes to restrict the practice of writing to authorized places where the contents and even the methods of diffusion can be controlled.

According J. Leclercq (1958, 450), the conflicting relationship this great intellectual had with writing shows up in the representations made of him by his contemporaries in manuscripts. The oldest extant image, no doubt before 1135, shows him writing on tablets, a prop which seems to go back to a frequent and almost spontaneous practice of writing (see Oxford, Bodleian Library, Bodl. 530, fol. 1). In another image, also from the twelfth century but slightly later (Nantes, Musée Dobrée, MS 5, fol. 1v, Plate 47.5), the saint is represented with his head leaning over a desk. He holds a pen in his right hand and in his left an eraser; only the combined and thoughtful use of these two instruments will henceforth guarantee the perfection of the text.

It is in this context that henceforth we must view the activity of the copying centers which, from the second half of the twelfth century, continue on occasion to function in religious communities. The growth of libraries took place there in a regulated manner, and one sought to direct the diffusion of texts and knowledge by a new organization of the collections.

MENDICANT ORDERS

Our most important witnesses for this reconstruction come from the Mendicant orders which, from their foundation in the first decades of the thirteenth century, actively took part in the spiritual renewal of religious life. For these orders, born at the same time as the universities, study is deemed to be one of their principal missions. For them it was not a question of undertaking brilliant academic careers (this refusal will be constantly repeated, particularly by the Franciscans, even at the height of the period of humanism), but to train themselves so as to transmit a religious message, through either teaching or preaching, at a period when heretical and schismatic tendencies multiplied.

Books, indispensable tools for prayer and the acquisition of knowledge, were therefore necessary to them; that is why, while they reject property, the Mendicants justified owning books, if only temporarily and within the confines of institutional structures.

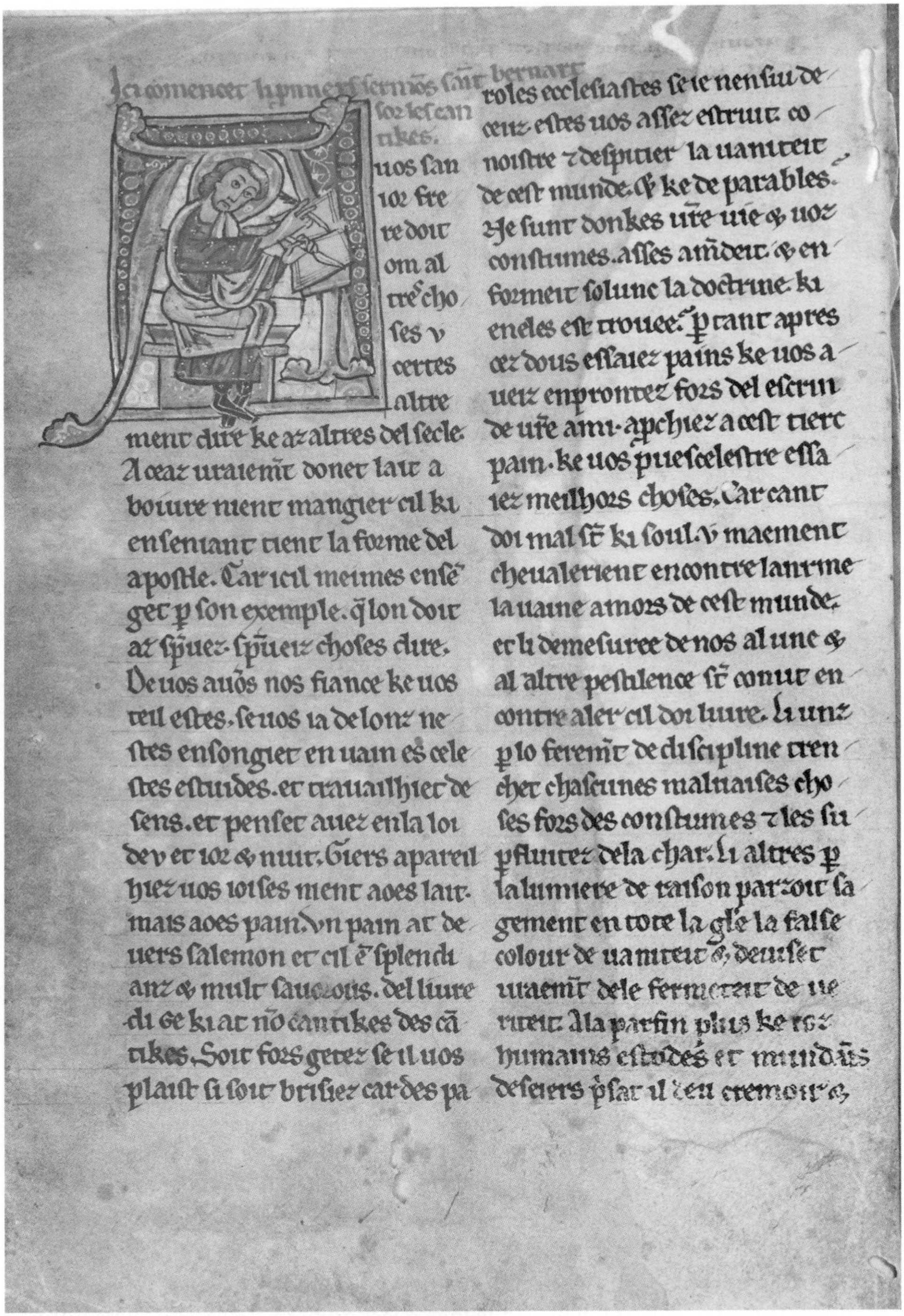
Ci comencet li primiers sermons saint bernart sor les cantikes.
Vos santor frere doit om altres choses v certes altrement dire ke a altres del secle.
A ceaz uraiement donet lait a boivre nient mangier cil ki en seniant tient la forme del apostle. Car icil meimes enseget p son exemple. q lon doit az spiuez spiueiz choses dire.
De uos auons nos fiance ke uos teil estes, se uos la de lonz nestes ensongiet en vain es celestes estuides. et trauailhiet de sens. et penset auez en la loi dev et ior et nuit. Giers apareilhiez uos loises ment a oes lait. mais a oes pain. Un pain at de uers salemon et cil e splendiant et mult saueerous. del liure di se ki at non cantikes des cantikes. Soit fors getez se il uos plaist si soit brisiez car des pa
roles ecclesiastes se ie nen siu deceuz estes uos assez estruit. conoistre et despitier la uaniteit de cest munde. et ke de parables. Ce sunt donkes uite uie et uoz constumes. asses amendeit et enformeit solunc la doctrine ki en eles est trouee. Por tant apres ceaz dous essaiez pains ke uos aueiz enprontez fors del escrin de ulce ami. apchiez a cest tierc pain. ke uos puesceiz estre essaiez meilhors choses. Car tant doi mal st ki soul. u maement cheualerient encontre lanrme la uaine amors de cest munde. et li demesuree de nos al une et al altre pestilence st conut encontre aler cil doi liure. Li unz plo ferment de discipline trenchet chascunes maluaises choses fors des constumes et les superfluitez de la char. Li altres p la lumiere de raison parzoit sagement en tote la gle la false colour de uaniteit et deuiset uraement dele fermeteit de ueriteit. A la parfin plus ke toz humains estodes et mundains deseiers ...

PLATE 47.5 Saint Bernard at his desk, writing and correcting a book: Nantes, Musée Dobrée, MS 5, twelfth century, fol. 1v.

One of their strongest points was to have thoroughly inserted themselves into the urban environment and to have aligned themselves with the laity, who at this period stimulated the economic and cultural revival of society. From the first decades of the thirteenth century onward, convents received private bequests and took charge of the preservation of archives. At the end of the Middle Ages, the Mendicant foundations benefited from the generosity of magnificent patrons. Novello Malatesta chose the Franciscan convent of Cesena to found the town library. Cosimo de' Medici protected the observant Franciscan convent of Mugello (Florence) and richly endowed it with books.

Of the two principal Mendicant orders, the Dominicans seem to have adopted with greater resolution a scholarly vocation. Actively engaged in the diffusion of orthodoxy and taking part through preaching in the control of society, they considered books weapons. The Franciscans, on the other hand, seem to have felt less compelled; yet their adhesion to book culture, influenced by scholastic culture but also by the monastic and canonical tradition of liturgical reading in common, was no less certain and deep. In any case, we are indebted to them for having developed a true policy of the book. Let us look at some of the most significant aspects, which span choices for the growth of collections to methods for the diffusion of works.

To start with, the image that the Mendicants give us of their famous founders provides a glimpse of the importance they accorded books. Legend presents Saint Dominic in the middle of saving a book from the flames burning heretics. Saint Francis affirms that letters, those signs that serve to compose the name of the Lord, are always holy, even in the writings of infidels.

More concretely, one sees that books accompany friars throughout their career. At their entry into the convent, for example, novices receive bibles and breviaries which they often use for the rest of their lives. The terms of these allocations are attested by the *ex libris* found in the manuscripts. But certain more detailed documents on the lines and circumstances of these allocations have also been preserved. We have thus, for example, a register of the allocations of books to novices and brothers for the Dominican convent of St. Catherine of Barcelona which covers the thirteenth and fourteenth centuries.

We know as well that the custodies and the provinces were in a position to provide brothers, on the occasion of their numerous travels, with the necessary tools for preaching and study: sermon collections, commentaries on the *Sentences* of Peter Lombard, and glossaries. These were truly circulating libraries, indeed comprising only a limited number of books, but well designed so as always to answer the needs of the brothers. Some important witnesses are extant, such as the loan register of the Roman province of the Dominican order, covering the entries for the fourteenth and fifteenth centuries.

At the end of the Middle Ages, the brothers even encouraged reading groups, organizing loans of books to brothers of other religious orders and the laity. Such is the case with the Dominican Nicolas Galgani, who lived in Siena in the middle of the fifteenth century and who has left us a book of notes and memoirs. At the same period in Lucca an active group of readers, both clerics and lay people, is centered around the Franciscan convent.

It is in the convent, the central point of the institutional structure of the orders, that we find the most important collections of books. To put them together, the orders adopt the dominant book model of the scholastic milieu, the "libro da banco," in large format. The writing, heavy and closely packed, is, nonetheless, neatly organized on the page with the aid of *signes de renvoi*, punctuation, and secondary decoration designed to aid the reader and help in memorization. But the Mendicants also produced books in a more practical and manageable size in which are found the basic tools of theologians and preachers: sermon collections, tables, concordances, and glossaries.

COPYING AND CIRCULATION

Questions concerning the diffusion and transmission of texts in the confines of the orders and outside are of crucial importance. The Franciscan theologian Bonaventura da Bagnoregio (d. 1274) provides a particularly successful reflection on writing, its stages, and its protagonists at the end of the thirteenth century. He was particularly interested in the role of the author, who was for him the link between the aspects of the copying, composition, and reception of texts. In dealing with the *Modi faciendi libros*, the theologian distinguishes four types of action. The first is the copyist (*scriptor*), who writes the texts of others without adding or modifying anything. The *compilator*, on the other hand, copies the works of others while adding other texts from other authors. Bonaventura mentions next the *commentator*, who writes texts by others while adding his own, which remain secondary material. Finally, the *auctor* writes as much his own texts as those of others, but principally his own. The theologian concludes that it is he alone who may be considered an author ("potest dici auctor").

It was essential to see to the quality of the correction of texts. Their diffusion was thus controlled and guarded by the attentive verification of the quality of the copies. An interesting example comes to us from the Dominican order with the dictionary entitled the *Catholicon* of Giovanni Balbi. Born in Genoa before the middle of the thirteenth century, Giovanni studied liberal arts and entered the order in the 1270s. The *Catholicon*, his major work, was finished on March 7, 1286 in the convent of Genoa, at the same period as other great literary, historical, and religious works, such as the *Speculum maius* of Vincent of Beauvais or the *Golden Legend* of Iacobus de Voragine, were published at the instigation of the Dominican order.

Conceived for the utility of the brothers and for the glory of the Church ("ad utilitatem nostram et sociorum et ad utilitatem meam et ecclesiae sanctae Dei") this encyclopedia comprises notably a dictionary, the true amalgamation of the lexico-graphical tradition. Giovanni Balbi applied to this work for the first time in a strict and rigorous manner the principle of the alphabetical classification of terms, much more efficient for research than the criterion of etymology from *derivatio*. In addition, the diffusion of the *Catholicon* was to rest on a precise choice of editorial principles.

First of all, there was the question of format, which had to stay portable while responding to the needs of consultation in a library, indeed of display. There was a preference for the folio format (34 × 44 cm in height), which would become the standard size for manuscripts of the *Catholicon* during the thirteenth and fourteenth centuries. A selection was also made within the body of the work to answer the needs of readers: in the fourteenth century, the fifth book of the *Catholicon*, the one which contained the dictionary, thus the most appreciated by theologians and preachers, often circulated as a separate work. But above all, Giovanni gave precise instructions for the making of copies, specifying, for example, how to alternate the color of the initials when one moved from one letter to the next of the dictionary. He also, as much for the the copyists as for the readers, gave indications on the use of diphthongs, noting, for example, that those of the type "caelum" were only "diphthongi tacitae" and that it was suitable henceforth to designate them by particular diacritic signs.

Although precise, Giovanni's instructions do not always seem to have been scrupulously followed by the copyists. Sometimes they justify themselves, in the extant manuscripts of the *Catholicon*, for not having used, as the author advised, blue initials and for having preserved, for example, gold. For the majority of these copyists escaped the control of the convent authorities. Only the most important of these continued to have access to a proper copying workshop. Usually there was no more than one *scriptor*, as happened at the end of the thirteenth century in the Franciscan convent of Padua or at Venice. If there were a group of copyists, they only produced a preconceived type of book. In the Dominican convent in Bologna, for example, manuscripts were still copied in the fifteenth century but they were exclusively liturgical.

Consequently the authorities do not shy away from expressing their mistrust of outside *scriptores*. We have a significant witness concerning the Dominican order in the *De officiis ordinis*. This anthology of normative texts was composed around the years 1260–70 by the general of the order Humbert of Romans. Former regular canon of Saint Augustine, the master takes up again in most points the legislation of his original order. Humbert calls to mind that the required payments of the *scriptores* will be paid by the librarian. He recommends that the brothers not mix with these artisans, for their morality is often doubtful. The activity of writing itself is looked upon with suspicion, since Humbert counsels his brothers against the activity. Let them not pass too much time in writing, he says, and let them recall that books are above all tools. It is suitable, therefore, that they be solid and legible: "in legibili lettera et durabili." The Franciscans adopted similar positions, in particular on the question of the use of images. The search for aesthetic fulfillment is condemned, because assimilated to *vana curiositas*, although they also recall that images can be useful, since they allow representing the text more concretely and they aid, therefore, in acquiring knowledge: "Brothers are not discouraged from having the use of books with images, for the image contributes largely to the acquisition of knowledge."

Thus, Franciscan convents encouraged in the course of the thirteenth and fourteenth centuries the finest productions of illumination in northern and central Italy. In the course of the fifteenth century, certain convents of women still distinguished themselves: the Dominican nuns of Unterlinden (Colmar) were acclaimed for their original productions in the fields of liturgy and mystic theology. At the same period, the Clarisses of Monteluce (Perugia, Italy) copy books to enrich not only their own library but also that of the brothers of the convent at Monteripido, seat of a *studium*.

Many witnesses to the copying of books in the heart of the order of Saint Francis have come down to us in the chronicle of Salimbene of Parma (d. 1288). With his usual liveliness, the chronicler shows us several brothers who, among many other activities, are also *scriptores*. He demonstrates in many cases their mobility. Many among them practiced their trade in several places and often in the most distant of regions. Thus, for example, Johannes de Ollis of the convent of Parma worked also in Burgundy, Palestine, and Egypt. John of Parma, general minister of the Order, is presented as a defender of the importance of copying activity as a manual activity, in a spirit which seems to be borrowed directly from the monastic tradition: "Even when he became general, he wanted to write with his own hands to gain by his own work what to clothe himself with. But the brothers did not allow him because they saw him occupied with serving the order and consequently gave him willingly what he needed."

Salimbene himself is a copyist. In 1248, he transcribed in Aix-en-Provence a work of Joachim of Fiore destined for John of Parma. Let us take note that Salimbene did not hesitate, when he deemed it necessary, to correct text which contained a large number of errors, and so professional copyists criticized him. But the Franciscan reiterated the need to control foremost the quality of the text one has before one: "[I corrected] in several places, where I saw a large number of heinous errors, some due to the copyists, who falsify many things, others coming from the first redactors." In the same vein, Salimbene refers to those of his brothers who were in charge of the copyists. Thus, the already mentioned Johannes de Ollis was retained by the Provincial of Bologna to correct its copy of the Bible. Guidolinus Ianuarius, a good copyist and redactor ("bonus scriptor et bonus dictator") played the role of "corrector ad mensam" in the convent in Bologna, that is, the brother who especially oversaw the quality of texts that were read in the refectory.

Probably, one of the most interesting episodes recounted by Salimbene concerns the diffusion of the book of the heretic Gerardo di Borgo San Donnino. While he was studying at the convent of Imola in 1274, the Franciscan was given by the guardian a little book on paper which the brothers had received from a friend of theirs, a notary, on his return from a stay in Rome. Asked his opinion, Salimbene answered that the work of Gerardo was not in agreement with the spirit of the Church Fathers and that it was full of errors; he advises the guardian, therefore, to burn it, aligning himself thus with the decision of the authorities of the Order. In this case Salimbene's severity was probably dictated by the fear that such fiery personalities as Gerardo di Borgo San Donnino could bring into disrepute the Joachimite Doctrines which the Franciscan chronicler adhered to. Whatever the case was, the story reveals a complex and conflicting situation at a period when debates and controversies at the heart of the Order reflect the crisis which overtook the entire Church. It is in this context that we see the rise and the first organization of the Mendicant libraries.

THE ORGANIZATION OF LIBRARIES

In regards to the Dominican order, we have an important witness in the *De officiis ordinis* of Humbert of Romans, which we have already mentioned above. Next, for both orders, the question of the organization of the book collections is regularly dealt with in the general chapters. In addition to these normative documents, we can rely on the testimony of numerous inventories of libraries.

The Mendicants used these inventories both as an evaluative tool and a safeguard for the patrimony and as a scientific tool for the classification and finding of volumes in the library. This last aspect, in particular, seems to have been well integrated into the great Franciscan libraries of Italy during the fourteenth century: one of the most accomplished examples of this is the catalogue of the library of the Sacro Convento of Assisi made in 1381 by Giovanni di Iolo.

We also owe to the Mendicant orders the construction of collective catalogues. One of the most impressive examples is the *Registrum Anglie*, made during the second half of the thirteenth century by the Franciscans of the convent of Oxford. This repertory, describing the content of about 30 libraries and religious institutions in England and Wales (those of the order but also those of a number of cathedrals and abbeys), inventories about 1,400 works of 100 authors, particularly those of the Church Fathers. The entries are followed by references to the libraries analyzed. It is an exceptional document in both its structure and its breath. Indeed its initial aim, which could not be carried out in its entirety, was to investigate the libraries of more than 200 institutions. A list reproduced at the beginning gives evidence of this fact.

At the period of the rise of the universities, the development of libraries in convents is strictly linked to the needs of study. Study is indeed the primary function of the collections reserved for on-site consultation which we find from the middle of the thirteenth century. The *De officiis ordinis* of Humbert of Romans describes in summary fashion their organization, specifying that there should be one or two lecterns where the works necessary for the study and training of the brothers are placed: Bibles, biblical and theological reference works, commentaries on the sentences, dictionaries, sermons, lives of the saints, and chronicles. The text underlines that these books should be quickly accessible to the brothers:

> Also, the librarian should see to it that in a silent and well-suited room there is a large lectern where will be affixed by chains easily readable books, which are, for the most part, lacking to brothers who need them, such as glossed Bibles, unglossed Bibles, canon law summae, books on the vices and virtues, questions, concordances,

interpretations, the decretal, sentences, moral distinctions, sermons for the feast days and the Sundays of the entire year, histories, chronicles, the passions and legends of the saints, ecclesiastical history, and many works of this type so that the community of brothers can quickly make use of them.

The space should also be organized in an efficient manner. These collections, at first only available to the brothers and later, in many cases, to secular masters and students, are, therefore, placed in reading rooms where the lecterns, often with two sides, are arranged in two rows. The books are chained there, guaranteeing that they will stay in place, and above all in order. According to the extant inventories, the placement of volumes on benches often followed an intellectual outline which reproduced the *ratio studiorum* of the Mendicants. Thus, the inventory of the Franciscan convent of Todi, in the first decades of the fourteenth century, opens with the statement of 14 thematic categories found in the collection, from the "libri textuales" and the "libri pertinentes ad textum" to the books on grammar and dictionaries.

Likewise, the inventory of the convent of la Verna in Tuscany, made in 1372 during the tenure of the keeper Stephen de Castro Plebis, details ten categories from "Libri sacri canonis" and "Originalia sanctorum et doctorum" to sermons and breviaries. Within the section reserved for sermons, 40 volumes have a composite shelf mark of one or two letters of the alphabet, which indicates to the readers their placement on one of the desks in the library. The inventory of the library of St. Francis of Bologna (1421), with 539 volumes, is divided into 23 classes. One begins this time with the theologians of the order, followed by the works of St. Augustine, the Bible, biblical reference works, the writings of the remaining Church Fathers, and the *libri naturales*. In 1440, the library of the Dominicans of Cividale del Friuli contains 11 benches where the volumes are placed according to a thematic arrangement, from the Bible to canon law.

Copies aimed at enriching these collections were chosen from the volumes already available in the convent. One should take the best, Humbert of Romans recommends. But one could also commission new copies. The inventory of the library of the convent of Assisi mentions the books in "bona littera" made by Brother Francesco Cioli Pezzini. The libraries also received works donated by important individuals from the order. Sometimes this involves bishops or cardinals, who thus inscribe their legacy in that of the convent.

In 1278, the Franciscan theologian Matteo d'Acquasparta in his will divides his books between the Franciscan convents of Assisi and Todi. Born into a family with affiliations to the latter convent, Matteo leaves to it his personal and working library, whereas the books he acquired as general minister of the order went to the library of the *studium* and of the Franciscan province, that of the convent of Assisi. Several decades later, in the middle of the fourteenth century, the Dominican Pierre de Villers, former confessor of Charles V, elected bishop of Troyes, leaves his books to the Dominican convent of the same city, specifying in a clause in the act of bequest that they should never be sold or dispersed.

Alongside these libraries whose public vocation rapidly increased, one finds in the convent another collection which is used strictly for borrowing and reserved for the members of the community. One finds there duplicate copies but also works not included in the *curriculum studiorum* and therefore less frequently used. Inventories allowing us to evaluate the relative importance of the two collections are not scarce. In general, it appears that the collections reserved for consultation on site contained fewer books than that reserved for lending. Its organization is less well known. It is likely that access to it was reserved to the librarian, who handled the loans and the attributions *ad usum*.

As far as the furnishings are concerned, the documents often refer to armoires equipped with several shelves. The *De officiis ordinis* of Humbert of Romans mentions the presence of labels allowing one to find the content of the works one was looking for:

> The *armarium* where the books are shelved should be in wood so the volumes suffer no damage and they are not subject to too much humidity. And it should have numerous separate compartments where the books are shelved, and these compartments will be marked according to the different subjects so that different books, such as the postil, the summa, and so on are not confused, and these compartments will be marked out by labels so that one may know where to find what one is looking for.

For example, one finds *armaria* of this type equipped with several shelves, or *solaria*, in 1381 in the library of the Franciscan convent of Assisi.

In addition to material devices, libraries also had to be equipped with other work and reference tools. *Tabulae* specifying the intended purpose and use of different books available could be attached to the walls of the library. The one from the convent of Gubbio, dating from the first half of the fourteenth century, has been preserved. It measures 86 × 55 cm. One finds there the books which were to be consulted *in situ* and which, therefore, should remain in place, those for the use of the brothers, and also the duplicate copies, books which had been placed on deposit, and those which been bought or acquired in exchange for other books or merchandise.

Generally, the documents confirm that the Mendicants adopted for the organization of their libraries the model of the double collection, holding on the one hand a stable library to consult *in situ* and on the other hand a loan collection. Much has already been written on the significance and the objectives of this functional division, which at the same time was also adopted by libraries of secular colleges such as the Sorbonne in Paris, for it foreshadows in effect the modern distinction between a reference and lending library.

BIBLIOGRAPHY

As it is impossible to provide an exhaustive bibliography on the subject of scriptoria and libraries, the present bibliography references the most important works consulted during the writing of this chapter. We have placed at the beginning a section devoted to manuals relevant to the subjects here treated, classified according to disciplines or fields of research. An updated bibliography on medieval manuscript studies and codicology is now available in the 2nd edition of Gehin (2005, 2017), see below, Codicology. I'm grateful to Hanno Wijsman (CNRS-IRHT) for his helpful remarks.

Handbooks

Paleography

Battelli, G. 1949. *Lezioni di paleografia*. Vatican City: Pont. Scuola vaticana di paleografia e diplomatica.

Bischoff, B. 1985. *Paléographie de l'Antiquité romaine et du Moyen Âge occidental*, trans. Hartmut Atsma and Jean Vezin. Paris: Picard.

Cencetti, C. 1954. *Lineamenti di storia della scrittura latina*, Bologna: R. Pàtron.

Cherubini, Paolo and Alessandro Pratesi. 2010. *Paleografia latina. L'avventura grafica del mondo occidentale* (Littera antiqua, 16). Vatican City: Scuola Vaticana di paleografia, diplomatica e archivistica.

Gasparri, F. 1994. *Introduction à l'histoire de l'écriture*. Turnhout: Brepols.

Petrucci, A. 1989. *Breve storia della scrittura latina*. Rome: Bagatto Libri.

Codicology

Agati, M. L. 2003. *Il libro manoscritto. Introduzione alla codicologia* (Studia archeologica, 124). Rome: L'Erma di Bretschneider.

Géhin, P., ed. 2005, 2017. *Lire le manuscrit médiéval. Observer et décrire* (Collection U). Paris: Armand Colin. 2nd ed. Paris: Armand Colin, 2017 (with updated bibiliography).

Maniaci, M., trans. 1996. *Terminologia del libro manoscritto* (Addenda 3. Studi sulla conoscenza, la conservazione e il restauro del materiale librario). Rome: Bibliografica.

Muzerelle, D. 1985. *Vocabulaire codicologique. Répertoire méthodique des termes français relatifs aux manuscrits* (Rubricae, 1). Paris: CEMI.

History of Book and Libraries

Nebbiai, D. 2013. *Le Discours des livres. Manuscrits et bibliothèques en Europe, IXe–Xve siècle* (Collection "Histoire"), preface, J. Verger. Rennes: Presses universitaires de Rennes.

Sharpe, R. 2005. *Titulus. I manoscritti come fonte per l'identificazione dei testi mediolatini* (Scritture e libri nel Medioevo, 3), trans. Marco Palma. Rome:Viella.

Vauchez, A. and C. Caby, eds. 2003. *L'Histoire des moines, chanoines et religieux au Moyen Age. Guide de recherche et documents* (Atelier du médiéviste, 9) Turnhout: Brepols.

Wattenbach, W. 1958. *Das Schriftwesen im Mittelalters*, Graz: Akademische Druk und Verlag.

History of Book and Libraries: Websites (Europe, France and Italy)

France

http://blog.pecia.fr/, accessed February 2, 2020.

http://www.libraria.fr/, accessed February 2, 2020.

Other websites for CNRS-IRHT's research projects
http://www.biblissima-condorcet.fr/en, accessed February 2, 2020.
http://www.irht.cnrs.fr/fr/recherche/les-programmes-de-recherche/saint-omer, accessed February 2, 2020.

Italy

http://www.sismelfirenze.it/index.php?option=com_k2&view=item&id=9:biblioteche-medievali-ricabim&Itemid=165&lang=it, accessed February 2, 2020.

Printed Sources

Manuscripts

Bénédictins du Bouveret, *Colophons de manuscrits occidentaux des origines au 16ᵉ siècle*, Fribourg (Swiss), 1965–82.
Grand, G., J. P. Gumbert, D. Muzerelle, and B. M. von Scarpatetti, eds. 1985. *Les Manuscrits datés: Premier Bilan et perspectives* (Neuchâtel, 1983)/*Die Datierten Handschriften: Erste Bilanz und Perspektiven (Neuenburg, 1983)* (Rubricae, histoire du livre et des textes, 2). Paris: CEMI.
Lowe, E. A. 1924–71. *Codices latini antiquiores: A Paleographical Guide to Latin Manuscript prior to the Ninth Century*. Oxford: Clarendon.
Muzerelle, D., ed. 2001. *Manuscrits datés des bibliothèques de France*. Paris: CNRS.
Olsen, B. M. 1982–9. *L'Étude des auteurs classiques latins aux XIe et XIIe siècles*. Paris: CNRS.
Reifferscheid, A. 1865–72. *De latinorum codicum subscriptionibus commentariolum, Index scholarum in universitate Vratislavensis...habendarum*, Vienna: K. Gerold's Sohn.
Samaran, C. and R. Marichal, eds. 1968–84. *Catalogue de manuscrits datés portant des indications de date et de copiste*, Paris: Centre national de la recherche scientifique.

Ancient Libraries

Becker, G. 1885. *Catalogi bibliothecarum antiqui, I. Catalogi saeculo XIII vetustiores*, Bonn: Cohen.
Bondéelle-Souchier, A. 1989. *Bibliothèques cisterciennes de la France médiévale. Répertoire des abbayes d'hommes* (Documents, études et répertoires publiés par l'Institut de recherche et d'histoire des textes, 41). Paris: CNRS.
Bondéelle-Souchier, A. 2000–6. *Bibliothèques de l'ordre de Prémontré dans la France d'Ancien Régime* (Documents, études et répertoires publiés par l'Institut de recherche et d'histoire des textes, 58). Paris: CNRS.
Derolez, A., B. Victor, and W. Bracke, eds. 2001. *Corpus catalogorum Belgii IV. The Medieval Booklists of the Southern Low Countries*. Brussels: Palaeis der Academien.
Genevois, A.-M., J.-F. Genest, and A. Chalandon, 1987. *Bibliothèques de manuscrits médiévaux en France. Relevé des inventaires*. Paris: Éditions du CNRS [revised ed., http://www.libraria.fr/BMF, accessed February 2, 2020].
Gottlieb, T. 1890. *Über mittelalterliche Bibliotheken*, Leipzig: Otto Harassovitz [repr. Graz: Akademische Druck- und Verlagsanstalt, 1955].

Texts

Berthier, J.-J. ed. 1889. *Beati Humberti de Romanis de officiis ordinis.* Rome: A. Befani.

Delorme, F., ed. 1934. *S. Bonaventurae Collationes in Hexaemeron* (Bibliotheca franciscana, VIII). Quaracchi: Editiones Collegii S. Bonaventurae ad Claras Aquas.

Egger, O. H., ed. 1905–13. *Cronica fratris Salimbene de Adam* (Monumenta Germaniae Historica. Scriptores, T. XXXII). Hanover and Leipzig: Hahn.

Grandsen, Antonia, David Knowles, *et al.* 1963–87. *Corpus consuetudinum monasticarum,* 12 vols. Siegburg: F. Schmitt.

Jocqué, L. and L. Milis, eds. 1984. *Liber ordinis Sancti Victoris Parisiensis* (Corpus christianorum. Continuatio medievalis, 61). Turnhout: Brepols.

Lefèvre, P. F., ed. 1946. *Statuts des Prémontrés réformés sous les ordres de Grégoire IX et d'Innocent IV au XIIIe siècle* (Bibliothèque de la Revue d'histoire ecclésiastique, fasc. 23), Louvain: Bureaux de la revue.

Lefèvre, P. F. and W. Grauwen, eds. 1978. *Les Statuts de l'ordre de Prémontré au milieu du XIIe siècle.* Averbode: Praemonstatensia.

Martène, E. and U. Durand, eds. 1736–8 *De antiquis ecclesiae ritibus.* Antwerp: J. B. de La Bry.

Milis, L. and J. Becquet, eds. 1970. *Constitutiones canonicorum regularium ordinis Arroasiensis,* ed. (Corpus christianorum. Continuatio medievalis, 20). Turnhout: Brepols.

Mynors, R. A. B., ed. 1937. *Cassiodori Senatoris Institutiones.* Oxford: Clarendon.

Studies

Manuscripts and texts

Bautier, R. H. and M. Gilles, eds. 1979. *Chronique de Saint-Pierre Le Vif de Sens dite de Clarius.* Paris: Éditions du CNRS.

Bouter, N., ed. 2005. *Écrire son histoire. Les communautés régulières face à leur passé* (Actes du colloque du CERCOR, Saint-Étienne 2002). Saint-Étienne: Publications de l'Université de Saint-Étienne.

Charlier, C. 1945. "Les Manuscrits personnels de Florus de Lyon." In *Mélanges É. Podechard. Études de sciences religieuses offertes pour son éméritat au doyen honoraire de la Faculté de théologie de Lyon,* 71–84. Mâcon: Protat frères.

Charlier, C. 1947. "La Compilation augustinienne de Florus sur l'Apôtre." *Revue bénédictine* 57: 132–86.

Cherubini, P. 2005. *Forme e modelli della traduzione manoscritta della Bibbia* (Littera antiqua 13). Vatican City: Scuola vaticana di paleografia, diplomatica e archivistica.

Garand, M. C. 1995. *Guibert de Nogent et ses secrétaires* (Corpus christianorum. Autographa Medii Aevi, II). Turnhout: Brepols.

Hamesse, J., ed. 1996. *Les Manuscrits des lexiques et des glossaires de l'Antiquité tardive à la fin du Moyen Âge: Actes du colloque d'Erice 1994* (Fidem. Textes et études du Moyen Âge, 4). Louvain-la-Neuve: Oleffe.

Manitius, M. 1934. *Handschriften antiker Autoren in mittelalterlichen Bibliothekskatalogen* (Beiheft zum Zentralblatt für Bibliothekswesen 67). Leipzig: Harrasovitz.

Ricciardi, A. 2005. *L'epistolario di Lupo di Ferrières. Intellettuali, relazioni culturali e politica nell'età di Carlo il Calvo* (Istituzioni e società). Spoleto: CISAM.

Riché, P. and G. Lobrichon, eds. 1984 *Le Moyen Âge et la Bible* (Bible de tous les temps, 4). Paris: Cerf.

Wilmart, A. 1921. "Nicolas Maniacoria cistercien à Trois Fontaines." *Revue bénédictine* 33: 136–43.

Zimmermann, M., ed. 2001. Auctor et auctoritas: *Invention et conformisme dans l'écriture médiévale* (Mémoires et documents de l'École des chartes, 59). Paris: École nationale des chartes.

The Libraries

Bischoff, B. 1966. "Biblioteche, scuole e letteratura nella città dell'alto medioevo." In *Mittelalterliche Studien: Ausgewählte Aufsätze zur Schriftkunde und Literaturgeschichte.* vol I, 122–3. Stuttgart: Anton Hiersemann.

Bourgain, P. and A. Derolez, eds. 1996. *La Conservation des livres et des archives au Moyen Âge: XI colloque du Comité international de paléographie latine, Bruxelles, Bibliothèque royale Albert Ier, 19-21 octobre 1995* (Scriptorium, 2). Brussels: Centre d'étude des manuscrits.

Cavallo, G., ed. 1988. *Le biblioteche nel mondo antico e medievale.* Bari: Laterza.

Cavallo, G. 1990. "La biblioteca monastica come centro di cultura." In *El monasterio como centro de produccion cultural. Tercer seminario sobre el monacato*, 11–22. Aguilar de Campo: Santa María la Réal, Centro de estudios del Romanico.

Cenci, C. 1981. *Bibliotheca manuscripta ad Sacrum conventum Assisiensem*, Assisi.

Clark, J. W. 1901. *The Care of Books. An Essay on the Development of Libraries and their Fittings*, Cambridge: Cambridge University Press [repr. London: Variorum reprints, 1975].

Delisle, L. 1868–81. *Le Cabinet des manuscrits de la bibliothèque impériale [puis nationale].* Paris: Imprimerie impériale.

Francesco d'Assisi. Documenti e archivi.Codici e biblioteche. Miniature (Catalogo della mostra). 1981. Milan: Electa.

Libri, biblioteche e letture dei frati mendicanti (secoli XIII–XIV). 2005. Centro Interuniversitario di studi francescani. Atti del XXXII Convegno internazionale (Assisi, 7–9 ottobre 2004). Spoleto: CISAM.

Lombardi, G. and D. Nebbiai. 2001. *Livres, lecteurs et bibliothèques de l'Italie médiévale. Sources, textes et usages.* Rome and Paris: CNRS.

MacKitterick, R. 1989. *Carolingians and the Written Word*, Cambridge: Cambridge University Press.

Marchioli, N. G. 2001. "Libri sacri, libri preziosi, libri magici. Lo status del libro nell'alto Medioevo." In *Il Vangelo dei Principi*, ed.G. Brunetton, 54–63. Udine: P. Gaspari.

Nebbiai, D. 1994. "Livres et bibliothèques dans les monastères français au XIIe siècle." In *Le XIIe siècle. Mutations et renouveau en France dans la première moitié du XIIe siècle*, ed. Françoise Gasparri, 205–55. Paris: Le Léopard d'Or.

Nebbiai, D. 2002. "Le biblioteche degli ordini mendicanti." In Studium e Studia. *Le scuole degli ordini mendicanti tra XIII e XIV secolo* (Atti del XXIX Convegno internazionale (Assisi, 11–13 ottobre 2001), 221–71. Spoleto: CISAM.

Petrucci, A. 1983. "Le biblioteche antiche." In *Letteratura italiana*, II. *Produzione e consume*, ed. A. Asor Rosa, 527–54. Turin: Einaudi.

Riché, P. 1963. "Les Bibliothèques de trois aristocrates laïcs carolingiens.", *Le Moyen Âge* 69: 87–104.

Rouse, R. H. and M. A. Rouse, eds. 1991. *Registrum Anglie de libris doctorum et auctorum veterum* (Corpus of British Medieval Library catalogues). London: British Library.

Vernet, A. 1989. *Histoire des bibliothèques françaises*, I. *Les bibliothèques médiévales du VIe s. à 1530.* Paris: Éditions du Cercle de la Librairie [repr. Paris: Éditions du Cercle de la Librairie, 2008].

History of Script and Reading

Arns, P.-E. 1953. *La Technique du livre d'après saint Jérôme*. Paris: Éditions de Boccard.

Bartoli Langeli, A. 1994. "I libri dei frati. La cultura scritta dell'Ordine dei Minori." In *Francesco d'Assisi e il primo secolo di storia francescana*, ed. M. P. Alberzoni, A. Bartoli Langeli, G. Casagrande, *et al.*, 283–305. Turin: Einaudi.

Bozzolo, C. and E. Ornato. 1980 –3. *Pour une histoire du livre manuscrit au Moyen Âge. Trois essais de codicologie quantitative*. Paris: CNRS.

Cavallo, G. 1991. "Libri scritti, libri letti, libri dimenticati." In *Il secolo di ferro. Mito e realtà del secolo X* (XXXVIII Settimana di studio del Centro Studi sull'alto Medioevo), 759–802. Spoleto: CISAM.

Cavallo, G. and R. Chartier. 1997. *Histoire de la lecture dans le monde occidental*. Paris: Seuil.

Condello, E. and G. De Gregorio, eds. 1995. *Scribi e colofoni: le sottoscrizioni di copisti dalle origini all'avvento della stampa: Atti del seminario di Erice, X colloquio del Comité International de Paléographie Latine* (Biblioteca del centro per il collegamento di studi medievali e umanistici in Umbria, 14). Spoleto: CISAM.

Hoffmann, P. 1998. *Recherches de codicologie comparée. La composition du codex au Moyen Âge en Orient et en Occident*. Paris: Presses de l'École normale supérieure.

Leclercq, J. 1958. "Aspects littéraires de l'œuvre de saint Bernard", *Cahiers de civilisation médiévale*, 1: 425–50.

Mallon, J. 1982. *De l'écriture: recueil d'études publiées de 1937 à 1981*. Paris: Centre national de la recherché scientifique.

Martin, H.-J. and J. Vezin. 1990. *Mise en page et mise en texte du livre manuscrit*. Paris: Éditions du Cercle de la Librairie–Promodis.

Masai, F. 1967. "Fra Salimbene e la codicologia." *Scriptorium* 27: 91–9.

Nebbiai, D. 1986. "Les listes médiévales de lecture monastiques. Contribution à la connaissance des anciennes bibliothèques bénédictines. " *Revue bénédictine* 96: 271–326.

Pellegrini, L. 1999. *I manoscritti dei Predicatori: i Domenicani dell'Italia mediana e i codici della loro predicazione (secc. XIII–XV)* (Dissertationes historicae, 26). Rome: Istituto storico domenicano.

Petrucci, A. 1973. "Scrittura e libro nell'Italia medievale: La concezione cristiana del libro." *Studi medievali*, 3e série, 14/2: 961–1002.

Petrucci, A. 1984. "Lire au Moyen Âge." *Mélanges de l'École française de Rome, Moyen Age*, 96/2: 603–16.

Rizzo, S. 1973. *Il lessico filologico degli umanisti* (Sussidi eruditi 26). Rome: Edizioni di storia e letteratura.

Roberts, C. H. and T. C. Skeat. 1985. *The Birth of the Codex*, Oxford: Oxford University Press.

Saenger, P. 1982. "Silent Reading: Its Impact on Medieval Script and Society." *Viator* 13: 367–414.

Severino Polica, G. 1978. "Libro, lettura lezione negli Studia degli Ordini mendicanti (sec. XIII)." *Le scuole degli ordini mendicanti, sec. XIII–XIV* (XVII Convegno del Centro di Studi sulla spiritualità medievale,). Todi: Accademia tudertina.

Vezin, J. 1973. "La Répartition du travail dans les *scriptoria* carolingiens." *Journal des savants* (juillet–septembre): 23–44.

Vogüé, A. de. 1989. "La Lecture quotidienne dans les monastères (300–700)." *Collectanea cisterciensia* 5: 241–51.

Weijers, O., ed. 1989. *Vocabulaire du livre et de l'écriture au Moyen Âge*. Turnhout: Brepols.

CHAPTER 48

THE LINDISFARNE SCRIPTORIUM

MICHELLE P. BROWN

THE monastery of Lindisfarne on Holy Island in the Anglo-Saxon kingdom of Northumbria (northeast England) has long been thought to have possessed an important Insular scriptorium during the seventh and eighth centuries. Along with Canterbury and Wearmouth-Jarrow it has been considered one of the few early English centers that can be shown to have made books that still survive. Central to this premise is one of the greatest of early medieval manuscripts—the Lindisfarne Gospels (London, BL, Cotton MS Nero D.iv), which was thought to have been made at Lindisfarne to mark the translation of the relics of St. Cuthbert to its high altar in 698, but which has recently been re-evaluated and dated to *c.*715–20. And yet David Dumville (1999–2007, 1) has felt able to suggest that there was never any such scriptorium. In order to understand such divergence it is useful to review the historiography.

In the hefty commentary accompanying the first full facsimile of the Lindisfarne Gospels (see Plate 48.1), published in 1956–60,[1] Julian (T. J.) Brown discussed the palaeography of the manuscript in full for the first time. Brown was a classicist by training (specializing in Greek vase painting, inter alia) and, as a young curator in the Department of Manuscripts in the then British Museum Library, was allocated to the project and so began his palaeographical career. Working closely with the archaeologist Rupert Bruce Mitford of the Department of Medieval and Later Antiquities in the British Museum and involved in excavating Sutton Hoo, he closely analyzed the relationship between the script and decoration. They determined that the scripts were the work of one hand and that this hand, as stated in the colophon added by the monk Aldred in the mid-tenth century, was that of Bishop Eadfrith of Lindisfarne (698–721). They could not conceive of a busy bishop making time for such work and thus concluded that he must have undertaken it before assuming office in 698 and that it was intended to celebrate the translation of the relics of St. Cuthbert (died 687) to the high altar of Lindisfarne that same year. They also examined the relationship of the manuscript to two stylistically related volumes—the Durham Gospels (Durham,

PLATE 48.1 Lindisfarne Gospels (London, BL, Cotton MS Nero D.iv), fols. 138v–139r, Luke Cross-Carpet Page and Incipit Page.

Cathedral Library, MS A.ii.17) and the Echternach Gospels (Paris, BnF, MS lat. 9389) and concluded that these manuscripts were by the same hand, which they termed the "Durham-Echternach Calligrapher." In order to get round the chronological issues raised by dating the Lindisfarne Gospels as early as 698, which sat uneasily with the broader sequencing of extant Insular manuscripts and the relative stylistic sequencing of the three books in question, they suggested that Eadfrith was a pupil of the Durham-Echternach Calligrapher, but that the latter actually undertook his work on Durham and Echternach after Eadfrith produced Lindisfarne.

Brown argued that (Phase I) Insular attempts to produce a settled, indigenous rediscovered version of Half-uncial script resulted in what he termed a "reformed Phase II Insular half-uncial." This was a heavy, straight-pen script characterized by breadth and rotundity of aspect, by a strict adherence to head and baselines (reinforced by the extension of headstrokes linking words, despite the excellent standards of word separation—a contribution to legibility which he attributed to Insular scribes) and by the inclusion of Uncial lemmata, especially at line ends. He attributed this development to Eadfrith, who in turn influenced the hand of his master in the Durham Gospels. The Echternach Gospels, written in a slightly less formal version of the script, with a slanted pen and with the inclusion of more minuscule letterforms and ligatures, were presented as something of a rushed job by the same hand, writing a "set minuscule," perhaps under pressure to produce a gift for Willibrord's new "Northumbrian" foundation of Echternach (Luxembourg).

Incorporating this thinking into his wider narrative of the development of an Insular system of scripts, Brown, in his as yet unpublished Lyell Lectures and a number of important articles,[2] therefore presented the Lindisfarne Gospels as the fulcrum of an axiomatic shift in Insular palaeography, stabilizing the developments of Phase I which had been led initially by Irish scribes, indebted to selective late Antique influence but free from more recent Roman intervention and working in comparative isolation from wider Continental developments. Irish influence in Northumbria, coupled with more contemporary Roman Uncial, as written in Gregory the Great's time (died 604), transmitted via the Romanizing Northumbrian twin monastery of Wearmouth-Jarrow. These were perceived by Brown to have resulted in the Phase II shift, in which Ireland subsequently partook whilst also perpetuating its Phase I traditions. Brown also perceived a close stylistic relationship between the scripts of the Lindisfarne Gospels and the Book of Kells, which made it difficult for him to accept that the latter could be a product of Iona or Ireland, c. 800. He accordingly suggested that Kells might be earlier in date (perhaps mid-eighth century) and made in an unknown Scottish monastery—a suggestion met with considerable scholarly derision.[3]

In 1980 Brown's student, Christopher Verey, contributed to the commentary to the Early English Manuscripts in Facsimile volume on the Durham Gospels and identified a common, near contemporary correcting hand at work here and in the Lindisfarne Gospels.[4] This reinforced the connection between the two volumes and was presented as the work of a Lindisfarne scribe. Verey, here and in subsequent articles,[5] also explored the textual relationship between these three and other related manuscripts, and strengthened the concept of an influential Lindisfarne scriptorium, active around 700.

Insular Half-uncial was of E. A. Lowe's "majuscule" category, but what of contemporary "minuscule"? Brown saw enough of a relationship between the minuscule "lapses" of the Durham Gospels and the set minuscule script of the Echternach Gospels to suggest that they were the products of the same tradition. He related this minuscule to that of the Vatican Paulinus (Vatican City, BAV, Pal. lat. 235), which he and Tom McKay saw as representative of the Lindisfarne scriptorium's more usual minuscule "library" book production.[6] In 1987, as part of the proceedings of a conference in Durham to mark the anniversary of St. Cuthbert's death, Michelle P. Brown, another of Brown's students, summarized the thinking to date on the Lindisfarne scriptorium.[7]

The monolithic construct of a Lindisfarne scriptorium, built on the substantial foundations of the Codex Lindisfarnensis facsimile study, remained relatively intact until a series of articles by Dáibhí Ó Cróinín launched an attack on the underlying historical assumptions and, in particular, on the place of the Echternach Gospels and related manuscripts within the edifice.[8] He challenged the assumption that Echternach was essentially an English foundation simply because St. Willibrord and his sponsor, Bishop Egbert, were themselves Northumbrian and pointed out that they had been based in Ireland at a monastery named Rath Melsigi (perhaps in Co. Carlow?) prior to launching the mission, which was, therefore, essentially an Irish endeavor. Through his study of the Augsburg Gospels, Ó Cróinín pointed to shared Irish palaeographical features in this and the Echternach Gospels, and to work undertaken in the eighth-century Echternach scriptorium by the Irish scribes Virgilius and Laurentius. In this work, and in subsequent publications by William O'Sullivan,[9] former Keeper of Manuscripts at Trinity College Library, Dublin, criticism was directed at what was presented as an overly pro-English view of the origins and development of Insular (specifically so-called "Hiberno-Saxon") book production. Nancy Netzer, in the Durham St. Cuthbert conference proceedings and in her subsequent monograph on the Trier Gospels from early eighth-century Echternach (Netzer 1989 and 1994), slowed the nationalistic trajectory of the pendulum of debate to a more workable level, analyzing the Echternach scriptorium and presenting it as an Irish-Northumbrian collaborative endeavor which rapidly absorbed more local influences from Merovingian Gaul to form its own distinctive style. The Echternach Gospels were perceived as an early product of this scriptorium, after the foundation of Echternach in 689.

In 1993 a selection of Julian Brown's collected papers was published as a tribute by his colleagues.[10] This stimulated a review in 1999 by David Dumville, in what was essentially an overview of the state of play regarding the study of Insular palaeo-graphy.[11] While allegedly debunking the idea of a Lindisfarne scriptorium in the course of this, Dumville suggested that Wearmouth-Jarrow was actually responsible for the Phase II reform of the Insular system and that—as its distinctive Phase II minuscule seems to have evolved as part of a publishing campaign, identified by Malcolm Parkes,[12] to circulate the works of Bede in the mid-eighth century—the reform of Insular Half-uncial is likely to have occurred there. Such developments are, he would suggest, unlikely to have been protracted.

How then is one to account for the time lapse between the Wearmouth-Jarrow scriptorium's reform of high-grade book script by the introduction of Italianate Uncial around 700 and its completion of the process by a reform of Half-uncial and minuscule around 740–60? I have suggested that it remains equally likely that the Wearmouth-Jarrow campaign of book production employing minuscule script for literary works, commentaries, and the like, rather than the distinctive Romanizing Uncial which it reserved for sacred texts, was itself influenced by the earlier tradition of cursive minuscule scripts. These are found in an Insular milieu from areas as diverse as seventh- to eighth-century Ireland, Continental mission centers such as Willibrord's Echternach and Columbanus's St. Gall, the Canterbury school of Theodore and Hadrian, and Boniface's southwestern England and the Frisian mission field, and are also to be seen as part of the evolution of the genre into what has been termed Phase II. Did Wearmouth-Jarrow need Half-uncial when it had its own Uncial for higher purposes and minuscule for others? If it did, there are—as we shall see—better candidates as examples of what this may have looked like, rather than the Lindisfarne Gospels, which displays little affinity with its codicological and artistic traditions.

A major concern, in the course of these debates, was that the authors of the Codex Lindisfarnensis commentary, and Brown in his subsequent work, had not taken due account of developments in historical research which were demonstrating that Ireland was not as isolated from the late Roman and post-Roman world as had been thought and that the early Insular scripts had not evolved completely separately. A closer reading of Brown, especially his articles on the debt owed by Insular book producers to late antique palaeography and codicology (T. J. Brown 1993, 125–40 and 221–44), shows that this was largely unjustified, but the commentary volume (Kendrick *et al.* 1956–60) certainly failed to take account of the nuanced historical context, a problem enhanced by its adherence to an absolute *terminus ante quem* for the Lindisfarne Gospels of 698.

In 2001 Richard Gameson[13] published an article questioning, as had the aforementioned commentators, whether Aldred's colophon (added in the 950s–960s, after the community had relocated from Lindisfarne to Chester-le-Street) could be taken at face value. It certainly cannot, for Aldred had his own agendas, but the Codex Lindisfarnensis commentary authors had not relied solely on this in their acceptance of a Lindisfarne origin and early dating. Larry Nees (2003) followed with an article questioning the late seventh-century dating, suggesting that a date later in the eighth century would sit more comfortably within the art historical sequencing of Insular manuscripts.[14] At this time a further facsimile (this time in color and a more accurate version from digital photographs, of exact dimensions and carefully color-balanced) and commentary on the Lindisfarne Gospels, authored by myself, was already in press.[15]

In this and a subsequent work,[16] I ascribed the Lindisfarne Gospels a *terminus post quem* of 715, on the grounds of its inclusions of lections being introduced in Rome at that time as part of the Good Friday liturgy and of its probable place in the development of the Cuthbertine cult. The translation of the relics of St. Cuthbert to the Lindisfarne high altar in 698 was not the sort of preplanned event that a complex book like this would have been made for, and the shaping of the cult to fit an eirenic agenda of reconciliation was undertaken by Bishop Eadfrith, with the assistance of Bede, whom he commissioned to rewrite St. Cuthbert's *vita* during the second decade of the eighth century. From around 710 Ripon was also establishing a cult of St. Wilfrid with a book as its focus—a purple codex with chrysography, redolent of Mediterranean culture. This may have inspired the production of a similarly impressive cult book in honor of St. Cuthbert, but one that conflated a wide range of cultural influences and signifiers that stretched from Ireland to the Near East. It is essentially the work of one gifted artist-scribe, which says something about the eremitic spirituality of the place in which it was made, which points to a Columban house, for Columba and his colleague Canice won renown as hero-scribes, writing books singlehandedly. It would probably have taken at least five years for one person to produce, alongside other duties. If its artist-scribe was indeed Bishop Eadfrith, his death in 721 provides a *terminus ante quem*, although work was completed after this hand was out of the picture.

Even if the Durham and Echternach Gospels were not, in fact, by the same hand, which seems likely, they are from a common script background. Lapses at line ends in the Durham Gospels, and to a lesser extent in Lindisfarne, indicate that their scribes were familiar with the sort of cursive and set minuscule scripts that are given fuller rein in the Echternach Gospels. This need be interpreted as no more than the sharing of a common tradition that embraced parts of Ireland, Scotland, Northumbria, and the Continental mission fields at the time. The Vatican Paulinus may have been made at Lindisfarne, and is certainly how we can imagine one of its schoolbooks would have looked, but it need not necessarily have been.

To my mind the development of Insular Half-uncial was a gradual process, evolving in the Columban *parochia* toward a more formal, regular type throughout the seventh century. This script had achieved maturity by the time that the Durham Gospels were written, probably a generation or more prior to the Lindisfarne Gospels,[17] the latter representing a precocious pinnacle within the development of Phase II Half-uncial, rather than its genesis.[18]

The Durham Gospels are somewhat closer to the Columban tradition and exhibit little of the Wearmouth-Jarrow influence apparent in the Lindisfarne Gospels. The same applies to text. The Durham and Lindisfarne Gospels seem to have been in the same center shortly after their production, as the same hand corrects both.[19] His work in Durham formed two campaigns, an initial correction and a later one made with reference to the Lindisfarne Gospels or its exemplar (probably the Lindisfarne Gospels itself, as there appear to be a few corrections by the hand of the Durham-Echternach Calligrapher therein). Durham may have been made in another scriptorium of similar Columban background, such as Melrose, and subsequently joined the Lindisfarne Gospels or, given their similarities, may represent an earlier phase of production at Lindisfarne. In my view, the Echternach Gospels also belong to this earlier generation and were probably written in Echternach, the scriptorium of which was manned by scribes of various origins, trained in the Irish tradition

It therefore seems likely that by *c.*710 there was at least one highly accomplished artist-scribe, probably the head of the community, working at Lindisfarne on its great cult book as a focus of pilgrimage. He was highly creative and technically innovative (inventing the lead pencil and the light box and producing a wide-ranging palette using, as demonstrated by Raman laser analysis, only six locally available mineral and vegetable extracts, handled with the flair of an experimental chemist). He was versed in diverse liturgies, had obtained a Neapolitan textual exemplar via Wearmouth-Jarrow that makes the Lindisfarne Gospels, along with the Ceolfrith Bibles, the most authentic medieval representatives of St Jerome's Vulgate Latin translation, and constructed complex images in which the iconic and aniconic were merged in statements of ecumenical orthodox churchmanship, exegetical insight, and social inclusion. He wrote a well-developed Half-uncial and set minuscule indebted to the Columban tradition from which the monastery sprang and occasionally lapsed into a cursive minuscule indicative of lower-grade book production, such as that embodied in the Vatican Paulinus. The Lindisfarne Gospels were a semi-eremitic endeavor of *opus Dei* conducted by one person, but at least one other hand was present locally and supplied the Eusebian apparatus to complete the work, possibly after Eadfrith's death in 721. A further hand corrected it and the Durham Gospels, with reference to one another.

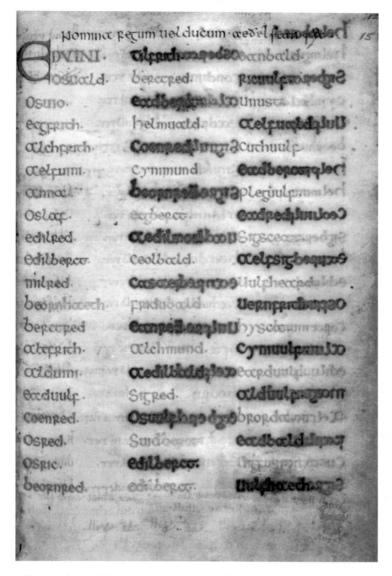

PLATE 48.2 The Durham *Liber Vitae* (London, British Library, MS Cotton Domitian A VII, f. 7v), Lindisfarne or Norham-on-Tweed, 840s onward (the gold and silver script is the earliest).

Whether there was a formal scriptorium, in the manner of more cenobitic monasteries such as Wearmouth-Jarrow, or whether the monks of Holy Island worked separately, it is likely that books were made there and that they merged a Columban background with more recent "Romanizing" influences via Wearmouth-Jarrow and Kent and Near-Eastern elements, to form a distinctive, quintessentially "Insular" style.

The script and artwork of the Lindisfarne Gospels went on to exert an influence throughout the eighth century in works such as the Chad Gospels (Lichfield Cathedral,

MS 1), the Cambridge-London Gospels (Cambridge, Corpus Christi College, MS 197B and London, BL, Cotton MS Otho C.v), the McRegul Gospels (Oxford, Bodleian Library, Auct.D.2.19), and the Book of Kells (Dublin, Trinity College, MS 58). A later example of Lindisfarne's Half-uncial may be the Durham *Liber Vitae* (London, BL, Cotton MS Domitian A.vii; see Plate 48.2),[20] which was probably the community's benefactors' book made soon after 840 either on Holy Island or at its daughter house of Norham-on-Tweed, where the community moved to temporarily in the face of Viking raids.

NOTES

1. Kendrick et al. (1956–60).
2. T. J. Brown (1974), (1982), (1984). These are all reprinted in Bately, Brown, and Roberts (1993).
3. T. J. Brown (1971).
4. Verey et al. (1980).
5. Verey (1989), (1999).
6. Brown and Mackay (1988, 8–9).
7. M. P. Brown (1989). For my more recent thought on the place of the Lindisfarne scriptorium in the Insular system of scripts, see also M. P. Brown (2011).
8. Ó Cróinín (1982), (1984), (1989a). Ó Cróinín continued this line of research publishing, after Julian Brown's untimely death in 1987, Ó Cróinín (1988), (1989b).
9. O'Sullivan (1994a), (1994b).
10. Bately, Brown, and Roberts (1993).
11. Dumville (1999–2007). Dumville suggests many innovative and valuable ways of viewing the earlier stages of development of the Insular system of scripts but becomes somewhat over-dogmatic in the process of his critical analysis of previous work when discussing Phase II.
12. Parkes (1982).
13. Gameson (2001).
14. Nees (2003).
15. M. P. Brown (2002); the commentary was also published as a standalone monograph as M. P. Brown (2003).
16. M. P. Brown (2010).
17. Verey *et al.* (1980); M. P. Brown (2003, 253–71), (2010).
18. M. P. Brown (2003, 253–71).
19. Verey *et al.* (1980); Verey (1989), (1999).
20. Rollason and Rollason (2007).

BIBLIOGRAPHY

Bately, J., M. P. Brown, and J. Roberts, eds. 1993. *A Palaeographer's View: Selected Papers of Julian Brown*. London: Harvey Miller.

Brown, M. P. 1989. "The Lindisfarne Scriptorium." In *St Cuthbert, his Cult and his Community to AD 1200*, ed. G. Bonner, D. Rollason, and C. Stancliffe, 151–63. Woodbridge: Boydell and Brewer.

Brown, M. P. 2002. *The Lindisfarne Gospels*, facsimile with commentary volume. Lucerne and London: Faksimile Verlag and British Library.

Brown, M. P. 2003. *The Lindisfarne Gospels: Society, Spirituality and the Scribe*. London and Toronto: British Library and University of Toronto Press.

Brown, M. P. 2010. *The Lindisfarne Gospels and the Early Medieval World*. London and Chicago: British Library and University of Chicago Press.

Brown, M. P. 2011. "Writing in the Insular World." In *The Cambridge History of the Book in Britain*, ed. R. Gameson, vol. 1, 121–66. Cambridge: Cambridge University Press.

Brown, T. J. 1971. *Northumbria and the Book of Kells*. Jarrow Lecture 1971. Newcastle-upon-Tyne: Jarrow Church [repr. 1972. *Anglo-Saxon England* 1: 219–46].

Brown, T. J. 1974. "The Distribution and Significance of Membrane Prepared in the Insular Manner." In *La Paléographie hébraique médiévale*, ed. J. Glénisson and C. Sirat, 127–35. Colloques Internationaux du Centre National de la Recherche Scientifique 547. Paris: Éditions du Centre national de la recherche scientifique.

Brown, T. J. 1982. "The Irish Element in the Insular System of Scripts to circa A.D. 800." In *Die Iren und Europa im früheren Mittelalter*, ed. H. Loewe, vol. 1, 101–19. Stuttgart: Klett Cotta.

Brown, T. J. 1984. "The Oldest Irish Manuscripts and their Late Antique Background." In *Irland und Europa: die Kirche im Frühmittelalter*, ed. P. Ní Chatháin and M. Richter, 311–27. Stuttgart: Klett Cotta.

Brown, T. J. 1993. *A Palaeographer's View: The Selected Writings of Julian Brown*, ed. Janet Bately, Michelle P. Brown, and Jane Robert. London: Harvey Miller.

Brown, T. J. and T. Mackay. 1988. *Codex Vaticanus Palatinus Latinus 235, an Early Insular Manuscript of Paulinus of Nola*. Turnhout: Brepols.

Dumville, D. N. 1999–2007. *A Palaeographer's Review: The Insular System of Scripts in the Early Middle Ages*, 2 vols. (Kansai University Institute of Oriental and Occidental Studies, Sources and Materials Series 20.2). Suita, Osaka: Kansai University Press.

Gameson, R. G. 2001. "Why Did Eadfrith Write the Lindisfarne Gospels?" In *Belief and Culture in the Middle Ages: Studies Presented to Henry Mayr-Harting*, ed. R. Gameson and H. Leyser, 45–58. Oxford: Oxford University Press.

Kendrick, T. D., *et al.*, eds. 1956–60. *Evangeliorum Quattuor Codex Lindisfarnensis*, facsimile, 2 vols. Olten and Lausanne: Urs Graf Verlag.

Nees, L. 2003. "Reading Aldred's Colphon for the Lindisfarne Gospels." *Speculum* 78: 333–77.

Netzer, N. 1989. "Willibrord's Scriptorium at Echternach and its Relationship to Ireland and Lindisfarne." In *St Cuthbert, his Cult and his Community to AD 1200*, ed. Gerald Bonner, David Rollason, and Clare Stancliffe, 203–12. Woodbridge: Boydell Press.

Netzer, N. 1994. *Cultural Interplay in the Eighth Century: The Trier Gospels and the Making of a Scriptorium at Echternach*. Cambridge: Cambridge University Press.

Ó Cróinín, D. 1982. "Pride and Prejudice." *Peritia* 1: 352–62.

Ó Cróinín, D. 1984. "Rath Maelsigi, Willibrord and the Earliest Echternach Manuscripts." *Peritia* 3: 17–49.

Ó Cróinín, D. 1988. *Evangeliarium Epternacense (Universitätsbibliothek Augsburg Cod. 1.2.4°2), Evangelistarium (Erzbischöfliches Priesterseminar St. Peter, Cod. Ms 25)* (Codices illuminati medii aevi 9). Munich: Helga Lengenfelder.

Ó Cróinín, D. 1989a. "Is the Augsburg Gospel Codex a Northumbrian Manuscript?" In *St Cuthbert, his Cult and his Community to AD 1200*, ed. G. Bonner *et al.*, 189–201. Woodbridge: Boydell.

Ó Cróinín, D. 1989b. "Early Echternach Manuscript Fragments with Old Irish Glosses." In *Willibrord, Apostel der Niederlande*, ed. G. Kiesel and J. Schroeder, 135–43 and 319–22. Luxembourg: Éditions de l'Imprimerie Saint-Paul.

O'Sullivan, W. 1994a. "The Palaeographical Background to the Book of Kells." In *The Book of Kells. Proceedings of a Conference at Trinity College Dublin, 6–9 September 1992*, ed. F. O'Mahony, 175–82. Aldershot: Scolar Press.

O'Sullivan, W. 1994b. "The Lindisfarne Scriptorium: For and against." *Peritia* 8: 80–94.

Parkes, M. B. 1982. *The Scriptorium of Wearmouth-Jarrow*. Jarrow Lecture 1982. Newcastle-upon-Tyne: Jarrow Church.

Rollason, D. and L. Rollason, eds. 2007. *The Durham Liber Vitae*. London: British Library.

Verey, C. D. 1989. "The Gospel Texts at Lindisfarne at the Time of St Cuthbert." In *St Cuthbert, his Cult and his Community to AD 1200*, ed. G. Bonner *et al.*, 143–50. Woodbridge: Boydell.

Verey, C. D. 1999. "Lindisfarne or Rath Maelsigi? The Evidence of the Texts." In *Northumbria's Golden Age*, ed. J. Hawkes and S. Mills, 327–35. Stroud: Alan Sutton.

Verey, C. D. *et al.*, eds. 1980. *The Durham Gospels* (Early English Manuscripts in Facsimile 20). Copenhagen: Rosenkilde and Bagger.

CHAPTER 49

SCRIPTORIA AND LIBRARIES OF NORTHERN ITALY

(VIth–VIIIth centuries)

PAOLO CHERUBINI

A discussion about the scriptoria and libraries in northern Italy during the most mature phase of the Lombard Kingdom is arduous because of the scarcity of written testimonies and the uncertainty of information.[1] Most of the reconstruction is possible only thanks to circumstantial evidence. The areas to be focused upon are naturally the cities that still experienced some political activity, tied in some cases to the past existence of a royal court (Verona, Milan, Pavia, and, to some extent, Ravenna), and sometimes those cities where a more or less important public school had existed; the most relevant bishoprics which had a particularly significant tradition of studies (Novara, Ivrea, Vercelli, Monza, Aquileia, Lucca, etc.); and at a later time (at the threshold of the Carolingian era) the Benedictine monasteries, anticipated by the Irish foundation of Bobbio.

Although from the end of the sixth century the commissioning of books is almost exclusively Christian, the role of monasticism in the copying of the works of antiquity is somewhat ambiguous. While the Rule of John Cassian entrusted the monks with the instruments of a scribe to copy manuscripts in their cells ("intra cubilia sua"), the Rule of St. Benedict expressly prohibited the possession by a monk of either a manuscript or tablets or pen "nec codicem neque tabulas neque graphium" (XXXIII, 3); even access to books (kept in a simple chest: *arca*)[2] was limited, and the codices that were borrowed had to be returned at the end of the day. Only during Lent did the Benedictine Rule concede that monks "receive individual manuscripts from the library which they should read in their entirety" ("accipiant omnes singulos codices de bibliotheca [*naturally the Bible*] quos per ordinem ex integro legant").[3] Secondly, the notion itself of scriptorium in the sixth through the eighth century loses one of its main distinguishing features due to the fact that "*scriptorium* and writing school coincide or at least that each *scriptorium* can more or less easily be seen as referring to a school" (Cencetti 1977, 82). In other words, teaching, involving rules to be respected and a well-defined writing style, was absent from writing centers, so that the few elements that products of the same center have in common may only be sought in physical production techniques and in specific abbreviation practices.[4] This decline resulted in the poor execution of Uncial that characterizes most of the manuscripts produced in the kingdom in the seventh and eighth centuries.[5] Thirdly, the information we have about schools in Italy in the period extending from the Lombard invasion to full Carolingian domination is scarce and not always easy to interpret because of the difficulty of assigning a constant and precise value to terms such as *schola, magister*, and *grammaticus*, as the existence of rudimentary teaching does not necessarily imply actual teachers until the ninth century, and because of the semantic uncertainty of the terms *grammaticus* and *magister grammaticae artis*, which should often be understood as simply "scholar" or "learned man".[6] Undoubtedly, one encounters the use of a writing instrument only from the second generation of Italy's invaders, and it is not until the end of the seventh century that a considerable cultural awakening took place at the court of Pavia, at the time of the reigns of Cunipert (688–700) and Liutprand (712–44).[7]

Uncial, Half-uncial, and more or less orderly adaptations of new cursive were used for the copying of the few manuscripts that have survived to our day from Italian writing centers of the sixth to the eighth century. They present local differences without showing actual types or graphical styles. Moreover, in Italy (unlike Northern Europe) the close relationship between the type of writing and the type of text, which had characterized Late Antiquity, is soon lost: this is particularly true for Uncial, which is used ever more often to copy works on diverse subjects and no longer just for biblical and liturgical texts.[8] In Lombardy, cursive normally used in documents could also be employed in book hands, while in Romanized areas (such as Rome and Ravenna) the script type used for *tabelliones* and *forenses* was never adapted for books.

By the end of the seventh century, the codex of the *Regula pastoralis* (Ivrea, Biblioteca Capitolare, 1 (I), *CLA* III.300), written in Luxeuil, was in Ivrea, although it may have arrived at the city from a Burgundian center or have been copied by a scribe educated across the Alps. It bears a dedication in capital letters to Desiderius, the city's bishop from 679 to the end of the century;[9] the greatest uncertainty reigns over other manuscripts, at least until the second quarter of the ninth century. Even the attribution of a biblical codex (a fragment of *Jeremiah*, Ivrea, Biblioteca Capitolare, XCII (94), *CLA* III.302) to the transitional period between the eighth and the ninth century is uncertain, though it displays all the characteristics of northern Italian writing.[10]

The tradition of a scriptorium in Vercelli, a city of strategic importance because of its situation on the route that crossed the Alps (it had been hit by the plague during the first half of the sixth century, destroyed by Alboin's Lombards during the second half, and had experienced a weak revival in the first half of the eighth century) has its roots in the fourth century. The *Vangeli* codex (Vercelli, Biblioteca Capitolare, S. N.

(*CLA* IV.467), in fact, can be traced to the time of St. Eusebius;[11] the manuscript presents liturgical marginalia of the seventh–eighth century. Otherwise, codices assigned to this time period are nearly nonexistent: merely two manuscripts, in cursive, may be traced to around the time of Liutprand's reign or a little after (Milan, Biblioteca Ambrosiana, C 98 inf. and M 77 sup. [fol. 93] [from Bobbio], *CLA* III.**322 and Vercelli, Biblioteca Capitolare, CLXXXIII [fols. 3–104], *CLA* IV.469). The city's situation worsened because of the rupture between the last Lombard kings and Pope Adrian I, but under Bishop Gisus (788–95) we have news of a copyist by the name of Bebo, whose subscription ("Bebo presbiter scripsit") was transcribed, by then in Carolingian, in a copy of the following century.[12]

A codex in Uncial (Rome, Biblioteca Nazionale Vittorio Emanuele II, Sessoriano 13 (2094), *CLA* IV. 418) and two codices of canonistic interest from the second half of the eighth century written in minuscule of the early Middle Ages are definitely from Novara; the first, an *Epitome* of Julian from the last 20 years of the century (Milan, Archivio Civico Storico Trivulziano, 688, *CLA* III.366), was signed by a certain Titus, identified as "Titus Levita," the only prelate by this name in an episcopal list of the city at the end of the eighth century; the second is contemporaneous or is slightly earlier than the first (Novara, Biblioteca Capitolare, 2 [LXXXIV], *CLA* III.406).[13] Other codices, assigned by Bischoff to the Piemontese scriptorium on the basis of palaeographical evidence, have been studied by Ettore Cau (Einsiedeln, Stiftsbibliothek, 369 [285] [fols. 1–2], *CLA* VII, 881; Shaffhausen, Stadtbibliothek, Min. 80 and Zurich, Staatsarchiv, A. G. 19, no XLII [fol. 67], *CLA* VII.1003; and Carlsruhe, Badische Landesbibliothek, Aug. CCLIV [fols. 72–213], *CLA* VIII.1110).[14]

In Milan, where Uncial[15] and probably Half-uncial[16] were used until the end of the sixth century, an important grammar school, reinvigorated in the seventh and eighth centuries by the Irish presence and by an animated cultural exchange with Bobbio, remained in existence from late antiquity through the early Middle Ages. The composition at the end of the Lombard era of the *Versus de Mediolano civitate* (*c.*738/739), is a testimony of the existence, at the time, of a Milanese school of rhetoric.[17] But in general, information about this period is unclear and uncertain: liturgical elements of the Ambrosian Rite may be recognized with any degree of certainty only in a small number of manuscripts.[18]

The situation in Pavia is even more discouraging: according to the story told by Paul the Deacon, at the time of King Cunipert, the grammarian Felix and his nephew Flavianus[19] taught in the kingdom's capital; we also know of the grammarian Stephanos, perhaps a monk at Bobbio, and even of the teachings of Peter of Pisa, who (in 767) was a renowned teacher of grammar in the palace "in palatio ... grammaticam docens claruit."[20] In 924 the city was sacked and set ablaze by the Magyars: this caused the complete destruction of its book collections. According to Bischoff, however, the *Edictus Rothari*, written in minuscule, today in St. Gall (St. Gall, Stiftsbibliothek, 730, *CLA* VII.949),[21] was almost certainly written at Pavia; two other liturgical codices of the same period are probably from Pavia: the *Epistulae of St Paul* (Vatican City, BAV, Reg. lat. 9, *CLA* I.100) and a *Sacramentarium* (Budapest, Széchényi Nationalbibliothek, Clmae 441, *CLA* XI.1590).[22]

Local tradition has it that a library had existed in Monza since Queen Theodelinda took residence there, between the end of the sixth and the beginning of the seventh century; Pope Gregory the Great had given her a copy of his *Dialogi*; the most ancient document relating the existence of a library in Monza, however, dates back to the tenth century, when Subdeacon Adalbert added a catalogue as an appendix to the *Sacramentarium* known as Berengar's.[23]

Of much more dependable nature is the information we have on Verona, another extremely important center, not only because it had been the seat for a short time first of the Goths, then of Alboin's Lombards, but especially because of its location along the route leading to the Brenner Pass and through it to Rhaetia, Alamannia, and Bavaria. More than one scriptorium was active in Verona, above all, the one attached to the cathedral, where the tradition of using Half-uncial for the copying of liturgical books but also for works of clerical-political and cultural interest tied to the Three-Chapter - Controversy continued throughout the sixth and seventh centuries and earlier. Ursicinus, lector of the Veronese Church, for example, copied the lives of monastic saints and of St. Martin of Tours by Sulpicius Severus in a codex in Half-uncial script finished on August 1, 517 (Verona, Biblioteca Capitolare, XXXVIII [36], *CLA* IV.494);[24] there were also other scriptoria in Verona, including one (perhaps at Theodoric's palace) where it can be assumed that not only liturgical, patristic, and canonistic works were copied but also texts of the Arian faith.[25] Uncial and several minuscules of the cursive type, such as those used for documents, though clearer and more orderly, were also used in Verona until the end of the eighth century. These may have been influenced by Merovingian and Insular scripts as well as, at a period closer to the adoption of Carolingian, by Rhaetian and Alemannic:[26] the most significant examples are a codex of Claudian's *Carmina* (Verona, Biblioteca Capitolare, CLXIII [150], *CLA* IV.516) and one of the *Concordia canonum* by Cresconius (Verona, Biblioteca Capitolare, LXII [60], *CLA* IV.512).[27]

Aquileia and Cividale del Friuli must be considered together as far as the eighth century is concerned, considering that Cividale, from the time of Bishop Calixtus (730–56), was itself seat of the neighboring patriarchate. It may be presumed, in fact, that a school existed in this eastern part of Friuli if Paulinus, who became patriarch of Aquileia in the 780s, declares himself "artis grammaticae magister."[28] In addition, a codex, today in Carinthia, presenting, among other things, undoubted Insular influence similar to other manuscripts from the region, is traced back to the city by Bischoff, and a fragment of Genesis from the eighth century, today in Gorizia, must in all probability be attributed to Aquileia (not to Aosta, as Bischoff himself believed after initially assigning it to the Friulian Patriarchate); finally, some notes written on the Evangeliary known as St. Mark's were almost certainly added in the seventh–eighth century in the nearby Benedictine monastery of St. Mark at Beligna.[29]

Further south we come to Bobbio, where Italian and foreign copyists (mainly Irish but also Frankish, given the strong ties to Luxeuil) were certainly active and where a cursive minuscule for book use with its unique characteristics developed for the first time in Italy, as can be clearly seen in the mid-eighth-century manuscript of Isidore of

Seville's *Etymologiae* (Vatican City, BAV, Vat. lat. 5763, *CLA* I.39).[30] Most importantly, a remarkably large collection of books was gathered in Bobbio, reaching about 700 codices at the time of its greatest splendor under Abbot Agilulf (887–96). In the year 625 or somewhat earlier, the *Commentarium in Isaiam* of St. Jerome was copied in the cenobium using washed and erased sheets of the famous Bible in the Gothic language by Ulfilas (unless the codex was copied in Milan and brought to the monastery soon afterward); it was written in a minuscule with a very strong Irish, if not outright Insular, influence (Milan, Biblioteca Ambrosiana, S 45 sup., *CLA* III.365) before the death of Abbot Atala (628), as a later note bears witness: "liber de arca domni Athalani". The note refers to the place where the manuscript was kept: similar references tell us, indeed, that codices in Bobbio were kept in different *archae*, each marked with the name of an abbot.[31] In fact, however, it is difficult to identify the distinguishing characteristics of the Bobbian minuscule with absolute certainty, as only Gregory the Great's *Dialogi*, transcribed by a copyist named George for Abbot Anastasius around the year 750 (Milan, Biblioteca Ambrosiana, B 159 sup., *CLA* III.309), may be assigned with certitude to the monastery's scriptorium. Lowe listed about 30 manuscripts and fragments which he believed originated in Bobbio, although he classed only 17 as "written doubtless at Bobbio"; Mirella Ferrari added a few others; of these, a fragment stands out: the *De reditu suo* by Rutilius Namatianus, narrating the author's journey from Rome to Gaul.[32]

The monastery of Nonantola was founded between 751/752 and 756 by the Lombard Anselm, duke of Friuli. From the third quarter of the eighth century an important writing school with its own characteristics developed there; the style, similar to the first Beneventan, is already recognizable in a fragment of the *Translatio sancti Benedicti* narrating the displacement of the mortal remains of St. Benedict and St. Scholastica from Montecassino to Fleury (*CLA, Addenda,* 1823), probably dating back to Abbot Silvester (*c.*758–74), as well as in other more recent manuscripts, including the typical study codex of a monastic school of the early Middle Ages containing the Isidorian *Etymologiae,* whose format and workmanship are very similar to the Vatican's specimen of the *Liber diurnus Romanorum pontificum* (Vatican City, Archivio Secreto Vaticano, Misc., Arm. XI 19). The latter belongs to the first half of the ninth century (if not to the last years of the eighth) and already displays the symptoms of Carolingian minuscule, while marginal and interlinear notes are by a hand of the time of Abbot Ansfrid (825–38) which uses a cursive minuscule of the type employed in the cenobium during the previous century;[33] the nucleus of the library was surely formed at the time of its founder, who was exiled for a short time to Montecassino and who "lived blessedly at the aforementioned place and acquired many manuscripts" ("apud prefatum locum Casinum beate vixit et multos codices adquisivit"), as is reported in the ninth-century *Catalogus abbatum Nonantolanum.*[34]

Little is known, finally, of Ravenna, where the episcopate had a library at least from the end of the sixth century, when Bishop John received a copy of the *Regula pastoralis* as a gift from Gregory the Great and where, perhaps in the same period or a few decades earlier, some richly decorated evangeliaria on purple parchment and the chrysographic fragment of the Gospel of Luke[35] were produced. At the time, the tradition of Half-uncial was still perpetuated in the city, perhaps through an actual writing school at the cathedral, as the activity of the two copyists who transcribed the St. Ambrose codex, discovered by Angelo Mercati and studied by Augusto Campana (Ravenna, Archivio Arcivescovile, S.N. [fols. 1–135], *CLA* IV.410a; Ravenna, Archivio Arcivescovile, S.N. [fols. 136–41], *CLA* IV.410b; and Ravenna, Archivio Arcivescovile, S.N., *CLA* 4.412), seems to prove; until the end of the eighth century, Uncial also continued to be used, at times imposing in size (*uncialis gigantea*), as in the codex *Arcerianus A* of the Agrimensores (Wolfenbüttel, Herzog-August Bibliothek, Aug. 2° 36.23 *CLA* IX, 1374a–b); occasionally even an early minuscule with no particular distinguishing features was used, for instance in a biblical fragment containing a few chapters of *Daniel* (Ravenna, Archivio Arcivescovile, S.N., *CLA* IV.414) and in the so-called *Homiliarium Alani* (Troyes, Bibliothèque muncipale 853, *CLA* VI.840), both from the end of the century.[36]

Notes

1. For a fuller description and a bibliography, see chapters 10, 11, 16, 17, 19, 22, and 23 of Cherubini and Pratesi (2010).
2. Only an "archa cum diversis codicibus, membranis et cartis monasterii" is mentioned in the *Regula Magistri* (Cavallo, 1987), and this was the rule at Bobbio.
3. Victor (1996); Vogüé (2003).
4. Cencetti (1977, 82).
5. Supino Martini (2001, 382–3).
6. Bullough (1964).
7. Cavallo (1984, 635); for the readings by the kingdom's scholars during the eighth century, see Cavallo (2000, 146–7).
8. Bischoff (1964).
9. Ivrea, Biblioteca Capitolare, I (I) f. 1*v*: "DESIDERIUS PAPA VIVAT DIU"; cf. Cherubini, Chapter 12, p. XXX, n. 16 of this volume.
10. Ivrea, Biblioteca Capitolare, XCII (94).
11. On the codex and the *status quaestionis* pertaining to it, see Uggè and Ferraris (2005).
12. Vercelli, Biblioteca capitolare, CLXVII, fol. 189*v*: Levine (1955).
13. Respectively: Rome, Biblioteca Nazionale "Vittorio Emanuele II", *Sessoriano* 13 (2094) (based on observations by Bischoff; see Cau 1971–4), Milan, Biblioteca Trivulziana, 688 (subscription to fol. 246*r*): Steffens (1909, Table 42b); Novara, Biblioteca Capitolare, LXXXIV (2).
14. Einsiedeln, Stiftsbibliothek, 369 (283) (*CLA* VII.881); Schaffhausen, Stadtbibliothek, *Min.* 80 + Zurich, Staatsarchiv, A. G. 19, No. XLII, f. 67 = p. 127 (*CLA* VII.1003); Karlsruhe, Badische Landesbibliothek, *Aug.* CCLIV, fols. 72–213 (*CLA* VIII.1110): Cau (1971–4).
15. For example, St. Ambrose's comment on the *Gospel of Luke*, Zurich, Zentralbibliothek, C. 79*b* (*CLA* VII.1018), and some fragments of the *Prophets*, Fulda, Hessische Landesbibliothek, Aa 1a + Darmstadt, Hessische Landes- und Hochschulbibliothek, 895 + 3140 (*was* 896) + Sankt Paul in Carinthia, Stiftsbibliothek, s. n. + Stuttgart, Württembergische

Landesbibliothek, HB, II. 20, II. 54, VII. 1, VII. 8, VII. 12, VII. 25, VII. 28–30, VII. 39, VII. 45, VII. 64, XI. 30, XIV. 14–15 + Oslo, Schøyen Collection, s. n. (*CLA* VIII.1174 + *CLA* X, p. 4 + *CLA., Addendum*, I, p. 363), all of the fifth century.

16. Juvenal, *Satirae*, Milan, Biblioteca Ambrosiana, *Cimeli* 2 (*CLA* III.305), of uncertain Milanese origin, but almost certainly Italian.

17. Ferrari (1986).

18. Priscian's panegyric to Anastasius dating from the seventh–eighth century (Naples, Biblioteca Nazionale, Lat. 2 [Vindob. 16]) certainly derives from a Milanese codex.

19. *Historia Langobardorum*, V, 7; cf. Bullough (1964, 117–18).

20. Cavallo (1984, 635) and Cau and Casagrande Mazzoli (1987, 188).

21. St. Gall, Stiftsbibliothek, 730: Bischoff (1992, 273) and Nicolaj (2001, 483 and note 33).

22. Respectively: Vatican City, BAV, Reg. lat. 9, and Budapest, Széchényi Nationalbibliothek, *Clmae* 441.

23. Monza, Biblioteca Capitolare, 98 (CXXIII).

24. See also Vatican City, BAV, Vat. lat. 1322 (*CLA* I. 8), *Acta* of the Synod of Chalcedon: Cherubini and Pratesi (2004, Table 19) and, still found today in Verona: Biblioteca Capitolare: LIX (57), Vigilius of Thapsus, Athanasius and the *Acta* themselves transcribed in the previous (*CLA* IV.509); XXII (20), St Jerome-Gennadius, *De viris illustribus* and *Vitae Romanorum pontificum* (*CLA* IV. 490); XXXVII (35), St Clement, *Recognitiones* (*CLA* IV.493: Kirchner (1970, Table 11); LIII (51), Facundus of Hermiane, *In defensione Trium Capitulorum* (*CLA* IV, 506); maybe LV (53), *Didascalia Apostolorum, Canones Apostolorum* and *Fasti consulares* (*CLA* IV.508).

25. Avesani (1976, 240–1). Codices in Gothic language were also copied in Verona beginning with the famous *Codex argenteus* containing Ulfilas' *Bible* (Uppsala, Universitetsbiblioteket, DG 1).

26. Bischoff (1982, 98) and Santoni (2009).

27. For Verona, CLXIII (150), see Carusi, Lindsay (1934, II, Table 38) and Cherubini and Pratesi (2004, Table 52) and Verona, Biblioteca Capitolare, LXII (60). Bartoli Langeli (1995, 90–7) suggests that the copyist of Verona LXII (60) may be the author of the so-called "Veronese riddle" written on fol. 3r of the Mozarabic *Orazionale*, Verona, Biblioteca Capitolare, LXXXIX (84) (*CLA* IV.515); for this, see also Petrucci and Romeo (1998).

28. Bullough (1964, 118).

29. In the following order: Sankt Paul in Lavanttal, *Legeshandschrift* 4.1 (Bischoff 1982, 98); Gorizia, Biblioteca del Seminario, s. n. (Pani 1996, 17, note 11); Cividale del Friuli, Museo Archeologico Nazionale, CXXXVIII: *CLA* III.285 (Pani 1996, 21–2, and 1997, 72).

30. Cf. Cherubini and Pratesi (2004, Table 49). We shall not return here to the age-old matter of genuine or presumed foreign influence, for example in the case of the codex Milan, Biblioteca Ambrosiana, D 268 inf. (*CLA* III,.334); on this, see Bischoff (1982, 97); nor shall we return to the use of Insular abbreviations, which one encounters in almost all of northeastern Italy.

31. Schauman (1978); on Bobbio's library, see also Engelbert (1968) and Cavallo (1987, 357–9).

32. Milan, Biblioteca Ambrosiana, B 159 sup., does not contain the *Moralia in Iob* as suggested by Lowe: see Fioretti (2005). The fragment by Rutilius Namatianus was recovered while restoring the codex Turin, Biblioteca Nazionale, F IV 25: Ferrari (1973, 12–13 and 15–30).

33. The *Translatio* is Eichstatt, Universitätsbibliothek, 477a: Belloni (1984); the codex London, British Library, *Add.* 43460 (*CLA* II.180) is also from the beginning of the ninth century; the Isidore is Vercelli, Biblioteca Capitolare, CCII: Cherubini and Pratesi

(2004, Table 51); the *Liber Diurnus*, Vatican City, Archivio Segreto Vaticano, *Arm. XI*, 19, Palma (1980); Cherubini and Pratesi (2004, Table 74); Bischoff (1982, 99) believes the typical Insular triangles may be identified therein.

34. For Nonantola, see Cavallo (1987, 359–60); Palma (1983), (1979).

35. The *Vangeli* codices known as *Vindobonensis* (*CLA* III.399), *Palatinus* (*CLA* IV.437), *Brixianus* (*CLA* III.281), and perhaps also the *Sarzanensis* (*CLA* IV.436a-b) and, with some doubt, the *Veronensis* (*CLA* IV.481): respectively, Naples, Biblioteca Nazionale, lat. 3; Trent, Castello del Buon Consiglio, Monumenti e Collezioni provinciali, 1589; Brescia, Biblioteca Civica Queriniana, s. n.; Sarezzano, Biblioteca Parrocchiale, s. n.; Verona, Biblioteca Capitolare, VI [6]; the hypothesis was put forward for the first time by Butzmann (1970, 21–2); see also Radiciotti (2001). For the *Gospels* in gold writing (*CLA* IV.407), Perugia, Biblioteca Capitolare, 1, see Bassetti and Ciaralli (2005, 94–9).

36. Campana (1958); in general for codices in Half-uncial from Ravenna, see Cavallo (1984, 633–4); for Ravenna's Uncial, see Cavallo (1978, 220–3).

BIBLIOGRAPHY

Avesani, R. 1976. "La cultura veronese dal sec. IX al sec. XII." In *Storia della cultura veneta* I: *Dalle origini al Trecento*, ed. G. Arnaldi and M. Pastore Stocchi, 240–70. Vicenza: Neri Pozza.

Bartoli Langeli, A. 1995. "La mano e il libro." In "Novità sull' Indovinello veronese," by S. Baggio, G. Sanga, and A. Bartoli Langeli. *Quaderni veneti* 21: 39–97.

Bassetti, M. 2003. "La tradizione grafica nei ducati di Spoleto e Benevento." In *Atti del XVI Congresso internazionale di studi sull'alto medioevo: I Longobardi dei ducati di Spoleto e Benevento. Spoleto, 20–23 ottobre 2002. Benevento, 24–27 ottobre 2002* (*Atti dei Congressi* 16), 383–480. Spoleto: CISAM.

Bassetti, M. and A. Ciaralli. 2005. "Scritture e libri nella diocesi di Perugia." In *La Chiesa di Perugia nel primo millennio: Atti del Convegno di studi. Perugia, 1–3 aprile 2004*, ed. A. Bartoli Langeli and E. Menestò, 85–149. Spoleto: CISAM.

Belloni, A. 1984. "La 'Translatio Benedicti' a Fleury e gli antichi monasteri dell'Italia settentrionale." *Italia medioevale e umanistica* 27: 1–16.

Bischoff, B. 1964. "Scriptoria e manoscritti mediatori di civiltà dal sesto secolo alla riforma di Carlo Magno." In *Centri e vie di irradiazione della civiltà nell'alto medioevo* (*Settimane di studio del CISAM*, XI), 479–504. Spoleto: CISAM [repr. in *Mittelalterliche Studien: Ausgewählte Aufsätze zur Schriftkunde und Literaturgeschichte*, ed. B. Bischoff. Vol. 2, 312–27. Stuttgart: A. Hiersemann, 1966–88, and in *Libri e lettori nel medioevo: Guida storica e critica* (*Universale Laterza* 419), ed. G. Cavallo, 29–47. Bari and Rome: Laterza, 1977].

Bischoff, B. 1982. "Die Rolle von Einflüssen in der Schriftgeschichte." In *Paläographie 1981: Colloquium des Comité International de Paléographie. München, 15–18 September 1981* (*Münchner Beiträge zur Mediävistik und Renaissance-Forschung* 32), ed. G. Silagi, 93–105. Munich: Arbeo-Gesellschaft.

Bischoff, B. 1992. "Paläographie: mit besonderer Berücksichtigung des deutschen Kulturgebietes." In *Deutsche Philologie im Aufriss*, ed. W. Stammler, I/2, Berlin, Bielefeld, and Munich: Schmidt, 1957 [revised in *Paläographie des römischen Altertums und des abendländischen Mittelalters* (*Grundlagen der Germanistik* 24). Berlin: E. Schmidt, 1979. French edition: *Paléographie de l'Antiquité romaine et du Moyen Âge occidental*, ed. H. Atsma and

J. Vezin, 2d ed. Paris: Picard, 1993. English edition: *Latin Palaeography: Antiquity and the Middle Ages*, ed. D. Ó. Cróinín and D. Ganz. Cambridge: Cambridge University Press, 1990. Italian edition, with an updated bibliography and the addition of new plates: *Paleografia latina. Antichità e medioevo*, ed. G. P. Mantovani and S. Zamponi. Padua: Antenore, 1992; cf. the review of P. Supino Martini in *Studi Medievali* s. III, 34 (1993): 253–8].

Bullough, D. A. 1964. "Le scuole cattedrali e la cultura dell'Italia settentrionale prima dei Comuni." In *Vescovi e diocesi in Italia nel medioevo (sec. IX–XIII). Atti del II Convegno di storia della Chiesa in Italia, Roma, 5–9 sett. 1961 (Italia Sacra. Studi e documenti di storia ecclesiastica* 5), 111–43. Padua: Antenore.

Butzmann, H. 1970. *Corpus Agrimensorum Romanorum. Codex Arcerianus A der Herzog August Bibliothek zu Wolfenbüttel (cod. Guelf. 36. 23. A) (Codices Graeci et Latini photographice depicti XXII)*, 13–24. Leiden: A. W. Sijthoff.

Campana, A. 1958. "Il codice ravennate di s. Ambrogio." *Italia medievale e umanistica* 1: 15–68.

Carusi, E. and W. M. Lindsay. 1929–34. *Monumenti Paleografici Veronesi, I. Semionciale di Ursicino (sec. VI e VII), II. Vari tipi di scrittura tra Ursicino e Pacifico (Sec. VII–IX)*. Rome: Biblioteca Apostolica Vaticana.

Cau, E. 1971–4. "Scrittura e cultura a Novara (secoli VIII–X)." *Ricerche medievali* 6–9: 1–87.

Cau, E. and M. A. Casagrande Mazzoli. 1987. "Cultura e scrittura a Pavia (secoli V–X)." In *Storia di Pavia, II. L'alto medioevo*, 177–217. Milan: Società pavese di storia patria–Banca del Monte di Lombardia.

Cavallo, G. 1978. "La circolazione libraria nell'età di Giustiniano." In *L'imperatore Giustiniano. Storia e mito. Giornate di studio a Ravenna 14–16 ottobre 1976 (Circolo toscano di diritto romano e storia del diritto* V), ed. G. G. Archi, 201–36. Milan: A. Giuffrè.

Cavallo, G. 1984. "Libri e continuità della cultura antica in età barbarica." In *Magistra Barbaritas: i barbari in Italia*, ed. G. Pugliese Carratelli, 603–62. Milan: Scheiwiller.

Cavallo, G. 1987. "Dallo scriptorium senza biblioteca alla biblioteca senza scriptorium." In *Dall'eremo al cenobio*, ed. G. Pugliese Carratelli, 331–422. Milan: Scheiwiller.

Cavallo, G. 2000. "La biblioteca longobarda." In *Il futuro dei Longobardi. L'Italia e la costruzione dell'Europa di Carlo Magno. Catalogo della mostra, 18 giugno–19 novembre 2000*, ed. C. Bertelli and G. P. Brogiolo, 146–7. Milan: Skira.

Cencetti, G. 1977. "Scriptoria e scritture nel monachesimo benedettino." In *Libri e lettori nel medioevo: Guida storica e critica (Universale Laterza* 419), ed. G. Cavallo, 73–97. Bari and Roma: Laterza [originally published in *Il monachesimo nell'alto medioevo e la formazione della civiltà occidentale (Settimane di studi del CISAM* IV), 187–219. Spoleto: CISAM. 1957].

Cherubini, P. and A. Pratesi. 2004. *Paleografia latina: Tavole (Littera Antiqua* 10). Vatican City: Scuola Vaticana di Paleografia, Diplomatica e Archivistica.

Cherubini, P. 2010. *Paleografia latina: L'Avventura grafica del mondo occidentale (Littera Antiqua* 15). Vatican City: Scuola Vaticana di Paleografia, Diplomatica e Archivistica.

Engelbert, P. 1968. "Zur Frühgeschichte des Bobbieser Skriptoriums." *Revue bénédictine* 78: 220–60.

Ferrari, M. 1973. "Spigolature bobbiesi." *Italia medioevale e umanistica* 16: 1–41.

Ferrari, M. 1986. "Manoscritti e cultura." In *Atti del 10° congresso internazionale di studi sull'alto medioevo*, 241–75. Spoleto: CISAM.

Ferrari, M. 1998. "Libri e testi prima del mille." In *Storia della Chiesa di Ivrea: Dalle origini al XV secolo (Chiese d'Italia* no. 1), ed. Giorgi Cracco and Andrea Piazza, 511–33. Rome: Viella.

Fioretti, P. 2005. "Litterae notabiliores e scritture distintive in manoscritti 'bobbiesi' dei secoli VII e VIII." *Segno e testo* 3: 157–248.

Kirchner, J. 1970. *Scriptura latina libraria a saeculo primo usque ad finem medii aevi*, 2d ed. Munich: R. Oldenbourg.

Levine, P. 1955. "Historical Evidence for Calligraphic Activity in Vercelli from St. Eusebius to Atto." *Speculum* 30: 561–81 [published in Italian with the title *Lo "scriptorium" vercellese da S. Eusebio ad Attone*. Vercelli: Tip. La Sesia, 1958].

Nicolaj, G. 2001. "Ambiti di copia e copisti di codici giuridici in Italia (secoli V–XII in.)." In *A Ennio Cortese*, ed. D. Maffei, I. Birocchi, et al., 478–96. Rome: Il Cigno Galileo Galilei.

Palma, M. 1979. "Nonantola e il Sud. Contributo alla storia della scrittura libraria nell'Italia dell'ottavo secolo." *Scrittura e civiltà* 3: 77–88 [revised in G. Cavallo, ed., *I luoghi della memoria scritta: Manoscritti, incunaboli, libri a stampa di Biblioteche Statali Italiane*, 43–8. Rome: Istituto poligrafico dello Stato–Libreria dello Stato, 1994].

Palma, M. 1980. "L'origine del codice Vaticano del *Liber diurnus*." *Scrittura e civiltà* 4: 295–310.

Palma, M. 1983. "Alle origini del 'tipo di Nonantola': nuove testimonianze meridionali." *Scrittura e civiltà* 7: 141–9.

Pani, L. 1996. "Elementi insulari nel codice cividalese dell'*Historia Langobardorum* di Paolo Diacono." *Memorie storiche forogiuliesi* 76: 11–23.

Pani, L. 1997. "Scriptoria friulani d'epoca carolingia: sintesi ed ipotesi." *Forum Iulii* 21: 69–89.

Petrucci, A. and C. Romeo. 1998. "L'orazionale visigotico di Verona: aggiunte avventizie, indovinello grafico, tagli maffeiani." *Scrittura e civiltà* 22: 13–30 [revised as "Il laboratorio pisano: problemi di scritture, problemi di lingue" in A. Petrucci and C. Romeo, *Scriptores in urbibus: Alfabetismo e cultura scritta nell'Italia altomedievale*, 109–26. Bologna: Il Mulino, 1992].

Radiciotti, P. 2001. "Codici bizantini di ambiente ostrogoto: osservazioni paleografiche." *Orpheus: Rivista di umanità classica e cristiana* 22: 150–65.

Santoni, F. 2009. "Scrivere documenti e scrivere libri a Verona." In *Le Alpi porta d'Europa. Scritture, uomini, idee da Giustiniano al Barbarossa. Atti del Convegno internazionale di studio dell'Associazione italiana dei Paleografi e Diplomatisti. Cividale del Friuli (5–7 ottobre 2006) (Studi e ricerche 4)*, ed. L. Pani and C. Scalon, 173–211. Spoleto: CISAM.

Schauman, B. T. 1978. "The Irish Script of the MS Milan, Biblioteca Ambrosiana, S. 45 sup. (ante ca. 625)." *Scriptorium* 32: 3–18.

Steffens, F. 1909. *Lateinische Paläographie*, 2d ed. Trier: Schaar and Dathe [repr. Berlin: 1929, 1964. French edition: *Paléographie latine*, trans. R. Coulon, Trier: Schaar und Dathe, Paris: H. Champion, 1910, repr. Rome: Multigrafica, 1982].

Supino Martini, P. 2001. "Cultura grafica della *Langobardia maior*." In *Visigoti e Longobardi. Atti del Seminario (Roma, 28–29 aprile 1997)*, ed. J. Arce and P. Delogu, 371–89. Florence: All'Insegna del Giglio.

Uggè, S. and G. Ferraris, ed. 2005. *Et Verbum caro factum est... La bibbia oggi e la sua trasmissione nei secoli: catalogo della mostra tenuta a Vercelli dal 19 novembre 2005–11 giugno 2006*. Vercelli: Museo del Tesoro del Duomo, 2005.

Victor, B. 1996. "Aux origines de la bibliothèque monastique: la distribution du carême." *Scriptorium* 50: 247–53.

Vogüé, A. de. 2003. "Le regole monastiche e il libro." In *Il monaco il libro e la biblioteca. Atti del Convegno Cassino-Montecassino 5–8 settembre 2000*, ed. O. Pecere, 45–63. Cassino: Edizioni dell'Università degli studi di Cassino.

CHAPTER 50

THE LIBRARY AT MONTE CASSINO

FRANCIS NEWTON

ACCORDING to tradition, it was at Monte Cassino that Benedict of Nursia, founder of the monastery around the year 529, wrote the Rule for monks; in its chapter 48 he enjoined: "In quibus diebus Quadragesimae, accipiant omnes singulos codices de bibliotheca, quos per ordinem ex integro legant; qui codices in caput Quadragesimae dandi sunt" ("For these days of Lent, they are all to receive a book apiece from the library, to read in order from the start; these books are to be handed out at the beginning of Lent"). A miniature in MC 132, the *Encyclopaedia* of Rabanus Maurus (copied under Abbott Theobald, 1022– c.1030) would have been very likely understood in the Middle Ages as representing this Lenten distribution (Plate 50.1). It was on the foundation of this injunction that the great Benedictine monastery libraries of the Middle Ages arose, and not least that of Monte Cassino itself.

Do any volumes from the library of St. Benedict's day survive? MC 150, the so-called Ambrosiaster in Half-uncial, is the oldest manuscript preserved at the abbey today. It was read by the presbyter Donatus at Castellum Lucullanum at Naples and can be dated before AD 570. This means that this ancient monument would be approximately contemporary with Benedict himself. But, given the disasters that have befallen the monastery early and late, beginning with the Longobard invasion of c.580, it is most unlikely that this treasure has been in the possession of the abbey continuously since the sixth century; in this case the manuscript may have been brought to Monte Cassino, perhaps from Naples itself, as a gift in the Desiderian or Oderisian period (1058–1105).

THE CAROLINGIAN AGE

The restoration of the abbey under Abbot Petronax (c.718) laid the foundation for its flourishing culture in the Carolingian period. The most famous man of letters in Italy

PLATE 50.1 MC 132 (Theobaldan, 1022–*c*.1030), the famous Rabanus encyclopedia, p. 94 (NB: All Monte Cassino manuscripts are paginated and so cited in scholarly literature.). A monk draws books from a handsome book chest to distribute to two of his fellows.

in this age was Paul the Deacon, author of the *Historia Langobardorum*, whose home was at Monte Cassino—except for a four-year stay at Charlemagne's court (782–6)—in the last two and one-half decades of the century. Apart from the History, Paul's works included the poetry published by Neff and his commentary on Donatus' *Ars Minor* and abridgment of Festus's *De Verborum Significatu*. The house that was home to this scholar will have had a very considerable library. Those who deny this forget that two factors have conspired to rob us of that library: (1) the disaster of the slaughter of abbot and monks and burning of the monastery by the Saracens in 883; and (2) the success of the monastery that rose again with the return of the monks in 950 and especially in the succeeding century and one-half, when the intense program of manuscript production meant that virtually all the older volumes would have been copied in the splendid new script and the surviving Carolingian volumes discarded.

It is telling that the exceptions that do survive from the eighth and ninth centuries were either manuscripts preserved in the Middle Ages in centers other than Monte Cassino or manuscripts that had subscriptions or other historical significance and were preserved for this reason. A famous example of the former sort spent a sizable part of its medieval life at Benevento; it is now Paris, BnF, lat. 7530, datable to the decennovenal Paschal cycle 779–97 (Plate 50.2). L. Holtz (1975) calls this volume a "Cassinese synthesis of the liberal arts." The book must reflect the learning of Paul the Deacon and

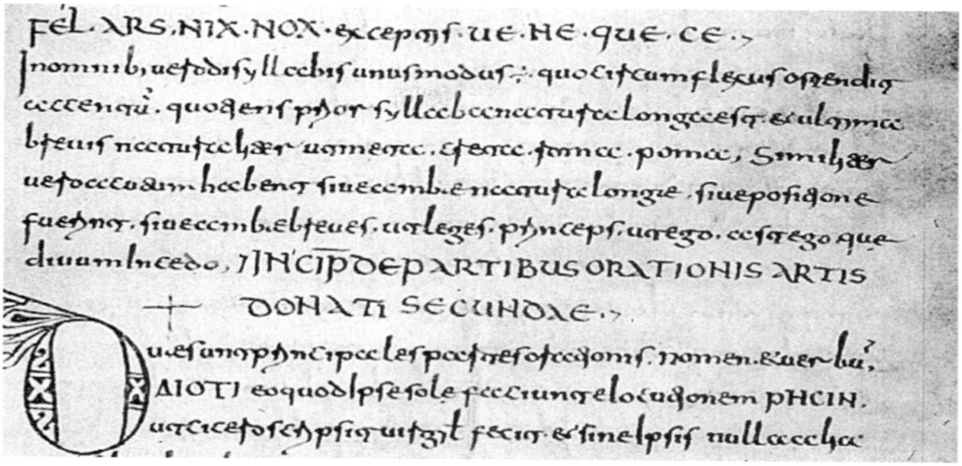

PLATE 50.2 Paris, BnF, lat. 7530 (779–97), fol. 171r. This rich collection of ancient learning presents here (after the stately late Uncial heading) Donatus on the parts of speech. Word separation is rare. The letters a (like 2 c's), which is open, and t, which has loop to left, with loop not extending down to baseline, are characteristic of an early form of Beneventan. Ligatures are especially noticeable: æ on the baseline, ri with long swinging tail, soft ti correctly in "orationis" in line. 9, li., and gi. Especially characteristic of the early form of Beneventan are (l. 4) "te" in "naturaliter" and in particular (l. 5) "tu" in "acutum."

the teaching carried out in the abbey's school in the high Carolingian era. The manuscript is the only one to preserve the *didascaliae* to the lost *Thyestes* of the poet Varius, and the "Anecdoton Parisinum," a text that transmits material from a lost work of Suetonius', this amid a large collection of grammatical works and arithmetical and geometrical texts. The manuscript reflects a rich strain of late ancient learning compatible with Paul's access to the text of Festus, preserved (so far as we know) only in southern Italy. Other manuscripts of Cassinese origin from the Carolingian era are Cava 3, Isidore, also datable to 779–97 by a Cassinese calendar; and perhaps Bamberg, Staatsbibliothek, Msc. Patr. 61, Cassiodorus, Greg. Turon., and Isidore. Rome, Biblioteca Casanatense, 641, pt. 1, Alcuin and calendarial matter, dated 811–12, is clearly Cassinese.

The grammatical treatise of Ildericus preserved in MC 299, the work of Paul's student by that name, was probably faithfully kept because assigned in the Middle Ages to the ninth-century Abbot Hildericus of Monte Cassino. Again, the historical bent of south Italian teachers and students—and local pride—probably accounts for the preservation of this work rich in classical citations.

In addition to the *ars grammatica*, scientific arts and compilations were pursued at Monte Cassino during the ninth century. MC 69, *Medica*, was preserved because of its association with the martyr Abbot Bertharius (856–83). But it is considered that MC 3, containing astronomical drawings, is also Bertharian. Medical treatises are also found in Florence, BML, 73.41 and MC 97, perhaps *Casinenses* as well.

What survives from the Cassinese library of the Carolingian era and down to the Saracen destruction of 883 reflects holdings in the *artes* broadly. It is immediately striking that what is missing is texts of the major Fathers, except where these may be joined in a subordinate role to those handbooks. Otherwise, patristic texts have not survived. And, if, because of the two historical causes mentioned, the disaster that destroyed the Carolingian abbey, and the subsequent brilliant development, the books of the Fathers that Paul the Deacon and Ildericus knew have not survived, it is hardly to be expected that the classical books they consulted would have come down to us.

THE PERIOD OF EXILE IN CAPUA

If certain manuscripts preserved at Monte Cassino today have belonged to the Cassinese community since their origin in the ninth and tenth centuries, that community's interest in the *artes* continued even in exile. To this period belongs (Plate 50.3) MC 332, the *De Nuptiis Philologiae et Mercurii* of Martianus Capella, of the late ninth or early

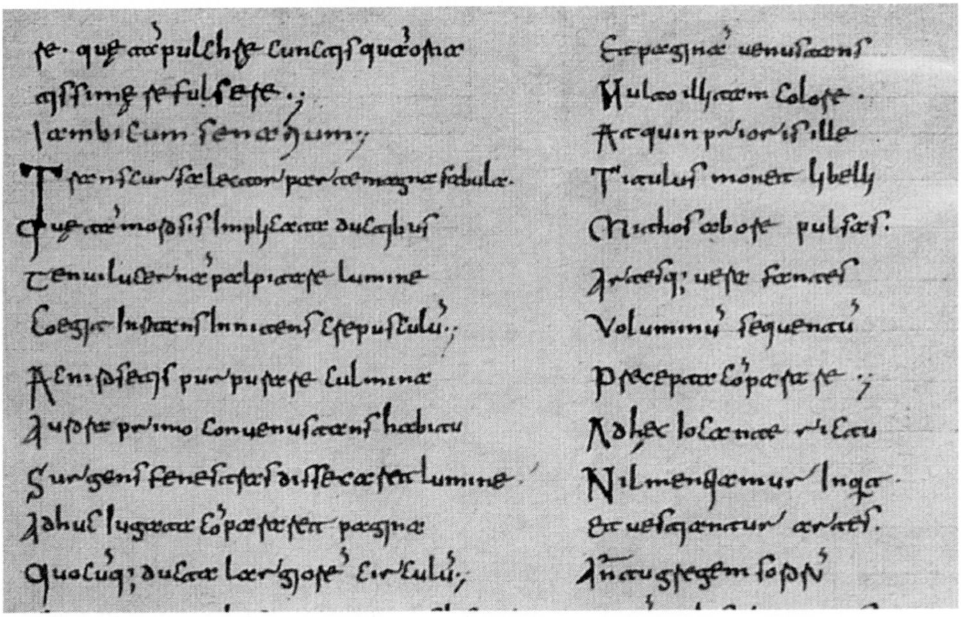

PLATE 50.3 MC 332 (saec. IX ex./X in.), p. 37. Here verses from the end of Book 2 and the opening of Book 3 of Martianus Capella, *The Marriage of Philology and Mercury*. The script is a continuation of the slender variety, with tall ascenders and little or no contrast; it is the ancestor of the later Fine Script. In col. 2, l. 12, the 2-shaped sign over "An" marks the beginning of a question. Arguably, Beneventan gave more aid to the lector in reading aloud than any other medieval script, as Radding and Newton (2003) have proposed.

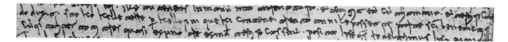

PLATE 50.4 MC, Archivio (969): *Placitum* issued at Capua, 960. The document shows, embedded here, the earliest Italian phrases self-consciously inscribed in a Latin text: "sao ko kelle terre per kelle fini que ki contene trenta anni le possette parte Sancti Benedicti…"

tenth century; though its decoration is "poor and archaizing" (Orofino 1994–2006, vol. 1, 51), the script shows a certain finesse. The *ars grammatica* is represented by the glossaries MC 401 and 402, and historical/scientific interests if Vatican City, BAV, Vat. lat. 3342, Solinus, is to be ascribed to Monte Cassino.

But the fresh energies and recovery of the community are strikingly shown in MC 175, dated to the abbacy of John I (914–34); this is what Dell'Omo (1999, 259) has called "a true, proper *summa* of the liturgical and historical traditions of Monte Cassino." The script has entered a new stage of its development; it is not surprising that a book so deeply imbued with historical feeling and endowed with a portrait of its *committente* John should represent the finest script of the abbey at this moment. It was under the mid-century abbot Aligern that MC 269, Gregory the Great, *Moralia*— finally, a text of a major Father that is preserved—was produced by the community, still then in Capua, and therefore before 1049–50; it is the subscription that attests this. In 1050, Aligern succeeded in re-establishing the community in its home on the mountain at Casinum. Like Rocca Ianula, the fortress that Aligern built there, Monte Cassino still possesses another Aligernian monument, this one also a monument of the Italian language, the *Placitum* issued at Capua in 969 (Plate 50.4) containing the earliest self-conscious attestation of the *volgare* in its contrasting Latin context. The second half of the century sees the copying of other Gregory volumes, e. g., MC 77, signed by its scribe, and of a now lost volume of "Hegesippus"—testimony to the continued interest in history—with subscription of the *committente* Abbot Manso (986–96), whose reign ended tragically with his blinding by his enemies.

THE GOLDEN AGE: THE CENTURY OF ABBOTS THEOBALD, DESIDERIUS, AND ODERISIUS I

Eleventh-century Monte Cassino was marked culturally by three bibliophile abbots. Theobald of Chieti, the red-haired abbot (1022 to, effectively, about 1030) had a program of book-copying already as prior of S. Liberatore alla Maiella; this is documented in his *Commemoratorium* of the year 1019. As abbot, Theobald clearly commanded ample resources for book production; he had his portrait entered in MC 73, another Gregory the Great, *Moralia*, and two other volumes (MC 28 and 57) contain lists of books he had copied; Leo Marsicanus drew on these for the list of Theobaldan books he gives in the *Chronicle*. Most splendid of the books listed there, and one culmination of the monastery's series of handbooks and compilations, is the visually enchanting encyclopedia of Rabanus Maurus (today MC 132, already cited), the earliest surviving copy of this text with illustrations.

Two figures from distant points to north and south illustrate the book culture of Theobald's house. (1) In June 1022 the German Emperor Henry II visited the abbey and arranged the election of Theobald as abbot; in gratitude for a miraculous healing that he experienced there, he presented rich gifts to St. Benedict, among them the handsome Gospel Book now Vatican City, BAV, Ottob. lat. 74, a product of St. Emmeram of Regensburg. (2) Probably in November of the same year a scholar named Leo, of Amalfi, entered the community as a monk under the name Lawrence, the name he is known by in modern literature (he was afterward archbishop of Amalfi). A bilingual polymath (his Greek Psalter with commentary survives as Vatican City, BAV, Vat. gr. 619), he served as technical corrector of the Augustine manuscript MC 28, where he signed in verse at the points at which he began and ended (Plate 50.5). He also compiled the *Handbook of the Liberal Arts*—the recurrent theme at Monte Cassino—surviving as Venice, Biblioteca Nazionale Marciana, Marc. Z. lat. 497, a

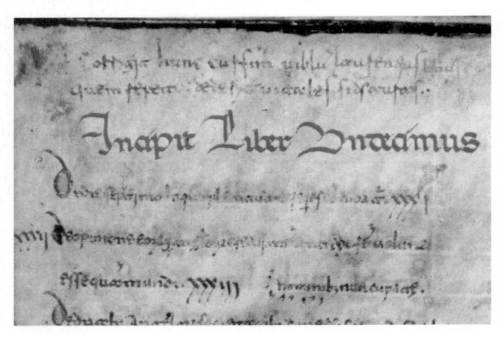

PLATE 50.5 MC 28 (AD 1023), p. 1: Lawrence of Amalfi's hexameter verses on correcting the MS: "+ Corrigit hunc cursim uiblum laurentius imus / Quem repetet, dederit uitales si Deus auras" ("+ Lowliest Lawrence in haste corrects this book; / A task he will resume, if God but grant him breath of life"). Below, the original scribe's hand—a developed early eleventh-century one with very little breaking of minims—on this first page of Augustine's *City of God*, Book 11.

manuscript in Central Italian script manifestly copied from an exemplar in Beneventan script. This volume contains a rich florilegium of excerpts from the classics, the Fathers, and early medieval texts, from Terence down to Paul the Deacon, Theodulf, and Alcuin, which must have been assembled by Lawrence himself. This continues the grammatical/stylistic studies pursued at the abbey since the eighth century. In Lawrence's hagiographical works one can see the scholar making use of extracts from this collection. The wide reading behind the florilegium points to the richness of libraries available to Lawrence, including some exceedingly rare texts, such as the elegist Tibullus.

But it was under the abbots Desiderius (1058–87) and Oderisius I (1087–1105) that the apogee of book production and study was reached. The gifts of generous patrons, such as the German Empress Agnes (a Gospel Book now marked as MC 437), and especially of the new Norman rulers of southern Italy, allowed a bibliophile abbot to indulge his book-collecting and book-copying passion (*studium*). The lists of books preserved in the *Chronicle* of the abbey include only display manuscripts, or texts or forms of texts not held in the Cassinese collection before. Production was, therefore, much more extensive than the *Chronicle's* attestations. At the opening of Desiderius' rule, the master Grimoald (contrary to the traditional Theobaldan date for this scribe) produced *inter alia* his splendid homiliaries MC 104 and 109 (with his own portrait) and the lovely Exultet Roll, now Vatican City, BAV, Vat. lat. 3784. Other superb scribes include the Leo who copied the lectionary MC 99 (AD 1072) with a portrait of another Leo (Leo Marsicanus, the future Chronicler, who oversaw its production), with his uncle Johannes Marsicanus (Plate 50.6). The nephew's hand is seen in Vatican City, Archivio Segreto Vaticano, Regesti Vaticani I, the Register of John VIII, the earliest papal register to survive; and in the draft of his own *Chronicle* (Munich, Bayerische Staatsbibliothek, clm 4623). Another master has been called the Dialectica Scribe, after his logical texts now in Vatican City, BAV, Ottob. lat. 1406, (Plate 50.7), the most splendid classical book ever produced at Monte Cassino; it has been proposed that the volume celebrates the victory of Alberic of Monte Cassino and Desiderius over Berengar of Tours in the climax of the Eucharistic Controversy at the Rome synod of Lent 1079. The same hand produced the handsome Exultet Roll in Beneventan preserved at Pisa as Museo Nazionale di S. Matteo, s.n. (Exultet 2). In this connection, it is clear that the abbey created Exultet Rolls not only for its own use, but to serve as gifts (an example, the Exultet Roll made for Pandulf, bishop of the Marsian church, and still preserved in the Curia Vescovile at Avezzano) and to accompany Cassinese monks chosen as abbots or bishops in other centers (an example, the Exultet of Leo Marsicanus preserved at Velletri in the Archivio Capitolare s.n. [Exultet]). Another master created (Plate 50.8) the celebrated Vatican City, BAV, Vat. lat. 1202 (to be dated to 1075), the third and culminating lectionary for the feasts of Sts. Benedict, Maur, and Scholastica—this one being rich in miniatures illustrating these texts; the texts collected here are the most intimately tied of all books to the central saints of the abbey, and the authors range in time from the eighth century down to the mid-Desiderian period. During the decade preceding this lectionary's production, Cassinese scribes had begun

PLATE 50.6 MC 99 (AD 1072), *Homiliarium*, p. 3. Abbot Desiderius affectionately presents to St. Benedict an older churchman, John of the Marsian church, newly received into the Monte Cassino community. John offers to the saint the book of homilies at the head of which the miniature stands. The verses proclaim that the master scribe of the manuscript was named Leo (his was the *labor*), and that another monk Leo (he was John's brilliant young nephew and the future Chronicler of the abbey), depicted kneeling at the saint's feet with the book's *manutergium* or book cloth in his hands, had supervised (his was the *studium*) the book's production. There is deliberate "specular" parallelism between the faces of John and the saint, and between the monastic habit that John assumes on this day and the rich cloth that young Leo provides for the book; Father Benedict receives, so wrapped, the life that is offered him, and the book.

PLATE 50.7 Vatican City, BAV, Ottob. lat. 1406 (AD 1079 or slightly later), logical texts, fol. 1r. Lady Dialectica, enthroned with her traditional serpent, awards a garland of victory to one of her young protégés before her. Radding and Newton (2003, 109–13) propose that the manuscript, the most elaborate and richest classical manuscript ever produced at Monte Cassino, celebrated Alberic of Monte Cassino's and Desiderius' victory in the debate over the Eucharistic Controversy (ended at the Roman Synod, February 1079 with defeat of Berengar of Tours and his doctrine.)

to create a new style of decorated initial, based upon their own south Italian traditions and upon the strong German influence of the decoration in the Henry II Gospels. At the opening of the lectionary, the Dedication scene and its accompanying poem present a brilliant (and perhaps unmatched in the Latin Middle Ages) instance of the interplay of poetry and visual art, with its subtle "specular" relationship between Alfanus' ode celebrating Desiderius on the left and the renowned miniature on the right, across the opening. The heap of books at Desiderius' feet—most rare in such Dedication scenes— bespeaks the bibliophile abbot and is only part of the visual/verbal pun.

The Monte Cassino monks of the era remembered that the classical Roman poly-math Varro (a primary source for Augustine) had owned a villa at Casinum; the Cassinese hagiographer Guaiferius echoed Cicero and saw his monastic home as a recreation of the villa of the Roman aristocrat, where the Pax Romana, now a Pax Benedictina, made possible study and the pursuit of eloquence. The literary production

PLATE 50.8 Vatican City, BAV, Vat. lat. 1202 (AD 1075), Lectionary for the Feasts of Sts. Benedict, Maur, and Scholastica, fol. 2r. In the year of the dedication of the two tower churches and the chapel of St. Bartholomew (depicted in the upper right background behind St. Benedict, with the great basilica and atrium, already dedicated in 1071, at upper left behind Abbot Desiderius), Abbot Desiderius presents this lectionary and the buildings as offerings to St. Benedict, seated with the Rule on his knee. The dedicatory poem (beginning of col. 1 on 1v) begins with Benedict's founding of the monastery and ends (col. 2) with Desiderius' fulfillment of the promise made to Benedict of its greatness. So the opening 1v–2r moves from the sixth-century founding and promise (col. 1) to the eleventh-century fulfillment (col. 2) and in the facing page mirroring movement from Desiderius (on the left) in his glory to the founder and originator (on the right—a specular effect). The ode and painting mirror each other in other, more complex ways, with verbal/visual plays and allusion across the gutter.

of the Desiderian and Oderisian period is widely varied; we may survey some of the works and some of the contemporary manuscripts that preserve them. Abbot Desiderius himself, in imitation of Gregory the Great, composed his own *Dialogues* (Vatican City, BAV, Vat. lat. 1203). Desiderius' close friend and admirer, Alfanus, archbishop of Salerno, wrote his own hagiographical works in prose, and poetry in a true classical spirit more subtly Horatian than any poet of the age (MC 280). Alfanus' translation of Nemesius' *Peri Physeos Anthropou* was not preserved in Italy, and survives complete in only one manuscript now Paris, BnF, lat. 15078, saec. xii in. The saints' lives of the just-quoted Guaiferius, also of Salerno, bear a striking array of classical *spolia* (preserved in the contemporary manuscript MC 280, with Alfanus). Alberic the *grammaticus* (as Leo's calendar calls him) wrote a series of hagiographical texts, many only recently identified (e.g., a manuscript of Benevento provenance, Monte Cassino, Archivio Privato, Cod. I, containing a saint's life that the young *grammaticus* wrote at the tender age of 14). The *libellus* in which Alberic refuted the teaching of Berengar of Tours on the Eucharist has recently been identified (Radding and Newton 2003) in the late eleventh-century Aberdeen, University Library, MS 106. The same master's rhetorical works included the earliest stage of teaching of *dictamen* (no manuscripts survive in Italy). Leo Marsicanus' *Chronicle* has been mentioned (Munich, Bayerische Staatsbibliothek, clm 4623). In that field, contemporary history was also written; Amatus' *Historia Normannorum* does not survive in Latin, but the Old French version is preserved in Paris, BnF, fr. 688. Cassinese interest in the *artes* continued. Among the books produced in the scriptorium in this period was the remarkably valuable collection of texts on music and musical theory still shelved at the abbey (MC 318). The long fascination with scientific works is unbroken. Pandulf of Capua's little treatise on the abacus, with its newly imported Hindu-Arabic numerals and the earliest European manuscript depiction of a scholar using them on the abacus, survives, alongside grammatical treatises of Alberic, in a single copy (Vatican City, BAV, Ottob. lat. 1354, of the late eleventh or early twelfth century). Most striking of all is the exotic figure of Constantinus Africanus (that is, "of Ifriqiyah," slightly larger than the area of modern Tunisia). Of the 25–30 translations or adaptations of Arabic medical treatises under his name, his masterwork, the *Pantegni*, "The Universal Art [of Medicine]," is dedicated to Abbot Desiderius, and therefore dated before the abbot's assumption of the papal title in 1086 (The Hague, Koninklijke Bibliotheek, MS 73 J 6, in ordinary minuscule but from Monte Cassino).

It is with the Desiderian age that the great series of surviving patristic texts appear, headed by Augustine; a veritable campaign led to the assembling of a total of some 29 Augustinian volumes in this period. Most valuable textually are the volumes of Augustine's sermons (especially MC 17) that transmit the *didascaliae*—information on when and where the sermons were preached. The authentic form of Eugippius' Augustinian handbook is preserved uniquely in a Desiderian manuscript (MC 13), as is the *Expositio libri Iob* (MC 371) of Augustine's opponent, Julian of Eclano; another rare text, Hegemonius' *Acta Archelai*, is preserved in the latter manuscript also. We would not have Hilary's hymns and his Liber *mysteriorum* if the early Desiderian manuscript

(Arezzo, Biblioteca della Città, 405) had not preserved them. The same manuscript is the unique witness to the *Peregrinatio Egeriae*, immensely valuable for the light it throws both upon early Church liturgy and upon Vulgar Latin. The MC manuscript 204 contains the only complete Latin text of the *Passio* of Perpetua and her fellow martyrs. MC 173 uniquely preserves the correct text of a sermon of Quodvultdeus, bishop of Carthage. The presence of a number of rare or unique African texts suggests that the Desiderian and Oderisian scribes had access to a pool of books brought to southern Italy by refugees displaced by the Vandal Invasion. The manuscript of the later, exceedingly rare *Iohannis* of Corippus listed in the Desiderian catalogue is now lost.

In his evocation of the great classics, Amatus, by subtle allusion to Horace's *Odes*, in effect compares the authors to Roman gods, Cicero being the Jupiter among them. This respect is clearer than ever today. Guaiferius' work is splendidly enriched, as Leighton Reynolds (1968) and his successors (e.g., Newton 1999, 96 and 289–90) have shown, by allusions to (among others) Cicero, Seneca—the first time these texts of Seneca had been cited in five hundred years—and the inscription on the arch of Constantine in Rome. The efflorescence of classical manuscripts is stunning. From the early Desiderian period come the unique Tacitus, *Annales* XI–XVI and *Historiae* (Florence, BML, 68.2; the Tacitus was formerly dated before Desiderius' rule, but the evidence supports instead a date in the first half of his era) and the Apuleius, *Metamorphoses* and *Florida* (a separate manuscript bound in the same volume), the somewhat later Seneca, *Dialogi* (Milan, Biblioteca Ambrosiana, C 90 inf.), the unique Oderisian Varro, *De Lingua Latina*, and, with it, the rare Cicero, *Pro Cluentio* (both texts in Florence, BML, 50.10). The same hand as in the Tacitus is seen in MC 71, Gregory the Great, *Register*; and that of the Apuleius in Copenhagen, Kongelige Bibliotek, Gl. Kgl. S. 1653 4°, a fascinating collection of gynecological texts. It can now be asserted that the Bodleian Juvenal with the otherwise unattested "Winstedt Lines" in Satire 6 found only in Oxford, Bodleian Library, Canon. Class. lat. 41 of this period originated at Monte Cassino. The Eton reader (the earliest example of this sequence of Vergil; the *Ecloga Theoduli*; Maximianus, *Elegiae*; Statius, *Achilleis*; Ovid, *Remedia Amoris* and *Heroides*; and Arator) is Desiderian (Eton, College Library, 150). The scriptorium also produced the earliest illustrated ancient history text (Orosius in Vatican City, BAV, Vat. lat. 3340, a Monte Cassino product); and the earliest illustrated Ovid, *Metamorphoses* (Naples, Biblioteca Nazionale, IV F 3), which is also a valuable textual resource for the editor, was a gift to the monastery in this period.

THE LATER PERIOD

At the opening of the twelfth century Alberic's pupil the hagiographer John of Gaeta (d.1119) continued his teacher's work in the study of prose style; he became pope as Gelasius II. Theology was the subject of Abbot Bruno of Monte Cassino, later bishop of

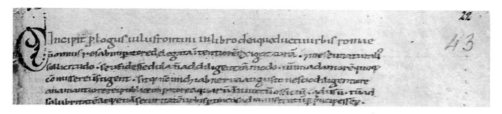

PLATE 50.9 MC 361 (saec. XII²), p. 43. Peter the Deacon's hand, which has preserved here the ancestor of all other manuscripts of Frontinus' treatise *On the Aqueducts of the City of Rome*.

Segni (1107–1111). But the century is dominated by the intriguing figure Peter the Deacon, self-described "cartularius, scriniarius, ac bibliothecarius" of the abbey. Apart from his role in continuing the search for rare texts—it is his hand that copied in MC 361 (Plate 50.9) the *De Aquaeductu Urbis Romae* of Frontinus, on which alone the tradition rests—Peter continued the abbey's *Chronicle* inherited from Leo and the shadowy Guido. Peter was a weaver of hagiographical tall tales and a forger of pious documents, but at the same time it is he who has preserved, alongside the fanciful, many of the facts about the authors of Monte Cassino.

The copying of manuscripts continues, even in Beneventan script, through the thirteenth century and attests a persistent interest in the classics at the abbey; a copy of the Desiderian Apuleius (Florence, BML, 68.2) was made in thirteenth-century Beneventan and survives in the same library with it today (it is Florence, BML, 29.2). As the present-day home of these manuscripts attests, this last of the Beneventan classics of Monte Cassino is close to the age when many of the abbey's books were to be carried off by figures like Zanobi da Strada to cities and communes that were becoming the centers of humanistic learning. In addition, the monks who were guardians of the long tradition were called upon to suffer yet another disastrous destruction, that of the earthquake of 1349.

This survey concludes with brief mention of three critical eras in the subsequent history of the archive of manuscripts and documents of Monte Cassino from the Early Modern period. It was under Pope Paul II (1465–471) that a catalogue (preserved in Vatican City, BAV, Vat. lat. 3961) of the monastery's library holdings was drawn up; and some half a century later that an *ex libris* was entered on the first page of each manuscript (Plate 50.10). The last two archivists of the eighteenth century, the brothers Placido and Giovanni Battista Federici, laid the foundation of a modern catalogue of the manuscripts. Their handwritten *Catalogus Codicum Manuscriptorum* inspired the nineteenth-century published volumes of the *Bibliotheca Casinensis* (1873–94), and Inguanez' *Codicum Casinensium Manuscriptorum Catalogus* (1915–41). For a catalogue of the documents of the abbey, the twentieth century also brought the publication of *I Regesti dell'Archivio* of Leccisotti (1964–77) co-authored by Avagliano from 1974 onward. Alongside these, the monumental volumes of Giulia Orofino (1994–2006) document and illustrate the wealth of art in its manuscripts.

It was the twentieth century that brought the written treasure of the abbey into peril once again (the four destructions are depicted on the modern parts of the basilica's

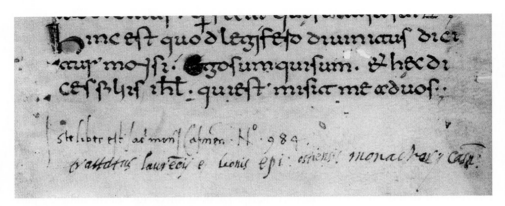

PLATE 50.10 MC 413 (Desiderian; *ex libris* saec. XVI), p. 1. The manuscript, of the early Desiderian period, preserves Lawrence of Amalfi's *Life of St*. Wenceslaus (beginning on this page) and other hagiographical works. At the foot stands the sixteenth-century *ex libris* of the monastery: "Iste liber est sacri monasterii Casinensis numero 984," followed by a still later summary of contents.

bronze doors). In autumn 1943 provident arrangements made by the German officers Captain Becker and Colonel Schlegel and by Abbot Gregorio Diamare removed manuscripts and documents—with other treasure—out of harm's way, taking them first to Subiaco and then to Rome and the Vatican; and so they survived the Allied bombing of February 1944 and could be repatriated after its rebuilding; the evacuation of the treasures is well documented by the photographers attached to the German units.

To return to valuable texts, the last few years have brought fresh discoveries. R. Gyug (1990) has discovered, in the "Compactiones" or binding fragments at the abbey, part of a hitherto unknown liturgical roll in Beneventan script. Radding and Ciaralli (2007, 86–7 and 247) have suggested, with great probability, that leaves of Justinian's *Code* in Beneventan (Rome, Biblioteca Vallicelliana, Carte Vallicelliane XIII, 3) are in the style of the early Desiderian scriptorium. The text has the integral or non-epitomized form of the *Code*, and this volume in its entirety would have been a magnificent monument and fully worthy of the bibliophile passion of Abbot Desiderius. The most recent discovery is the identification of the fair copy of Constantinus Africanus' *Pantegni* (The Hague, Koninklijke Bibliotheek, MS 73 J 6), as produced at Monte Cassino in the late Desiderian period; it bears clear marks of having been revised under the supervision of the translator. Even today, scholars in widely different fields continue to draw treasures out of medieval Monte Cassino's book chest.

BIBLIOGRAPHY

Alfanus. 1974. *I carmi di Alfano I, Arcivescovo di Salerno*, ed. Anselmo Lentini and Faustino Avagliano. Montecasino: no publ. [= *Miscellanea Cassinese* 38].

Anderson, D. W. 2002. "Medieval Teaching Texts on Syllable Quantities and the Innovations from the School of Alberic of Monte Cassino." In *Latin Grammar and Rhetoric. From Classical Theory to Medieval Practice*, ed. C. D. Lanham, 180–211. London and New York: Continuum.

Avagliano, F. 1987. *Montecassino. Dalla prima alla seconda distruzione. Momenti e aspetti di storia cassinese (sec. VI–IX)* (Atti del II Convegno di studi sul Medioevo meridionale, Cassino/Montecassino, 27–31 maggio, 1984). Montecassino: Pubblicazioni cassinesi [=Miscellanea Cassinese 55].

Bloch, H. 1972. "Monte Cassino's Teachers and Library in the High Middle Ages." In *La scuola nell' Occidente latino dell'alto medioevo* (Settimane di studio del Centro italiano di studi sull'alto medioevo 19), 563–613. Spoleto: CISAM.

Bloch, H. 1986. *Monte Cassino in the Middle Ages*, 3 vols. Cambridge, MA: Harvard University Press.

Brown, V. 2005. *Terra Sancti Benedicti. Studies in the Palaeography, History and Liturgy of Medieval Southern Italy* (Storia e letteratura, Raccolta di studi e testi 219). Rome: Edizioni di storia e letteratura.

Cavallo, G. 1975. "La trasmissione dei testi nell'area beneventano-cassinese." In *La cultura antica nell'Occidente latino dal VII all'XI secolo* (Settimane di studio del Centro italiano di studi sull'alto medioevo 22), 357–424. Spoleto: CISAM.

Dell'Omo, M. 1992. "Cultura liturgica e preghiera a Montecassino negli anni dell'abate Desiderio (1058–1087) (con una giunta sulla raccolta di preghiere del cod. Casin. 442)." In *Storia arte e cultura*, ed. F. Avagliano and O. Pecere, 279–361. Montecassino: Pubblicazioni Cassinesi [= *Miscellanea Cassinese* 67].

Dell'Omo, M., ed. 1996. *Virgilio e il chiostro. Manoscritti di autori classici e civiltà monastica*. Rome: Fratelli Palombi.

Dell'Omo, M., ed. 1998. *I Fiori e' Frutti santi. S. Benedetto, la Regola, la santità nelle testimonianze dei manoscritti cassinesi*. Rome: Ministero per i beni culturali e ambientali.

Dell'Omo, M., 1999. *Montecassino. Un'abbazia nella storia* (Biblioteca della Miscellanea Cassinese 6). Milan and Cassino: Silvana.

Dell'Omo, M. 2008. *Montecassino medievale. Genesi di un simbolo, storia di una realtà*, Montecassino: Pubblicazioni Cassinesi.

Gyug, R. F. 1990. "A Fragment of a Liturgical Roll at Montecassino (Compactiones XVI)," *Mediaeval Studies* 52: 268–77.

Gyug, R. F. 1992. "The Pontificals of Monte Cassino." In *Storia arte e cultura*, ed. F. Avagliano and O. Pecere, 413–39. Montecassino: Pubblicazioni Cassinesi [= *Miscellanea Cassinese* 67].

Hoffmann, H. 1965. "Der Kalender des Leo Marsicanus," *Deutsches Archiv* 21: 82–194.

Hoffmann, H. 1973. "Studien zur Chronik von Montecassino." *Deutsches Archiv* 29: 59–162.

Hoffmann, H., ed. 1980. *Chronica monasterii Casinensis*, M.G.H. SS. 34. Hanover: Hahn.

Holtz, L. 1975. "Le Parisinus Latinus 7530, synthèse cassinienne des arts libéraux," *Studi medievali*, ser. 3, 16: 97–152.

Inguanez, M. 1915–41. *Codicum Casinensium Manuscriptorum Catalogus*. Montecassino: no publ.

Inguanez, M. 1941. *Catalogi Codicum Casinensium Antiqui (saec. VIII–XV)*. Montecassino: no publ [= *Miscellanea Cassinese* 21].

Leccisotti, T. 1964–77. (vols. IX–XI with F. Avagliano), *Abbazia di Montecassino. I Regesti dell'Archivio*, vols. I, II, VI–XI. Rome: Ministero per i beni culturali e ambientali [= Ministero dell'Interno, Pubblicazioni dell'Archivio di Stato, vols. LIV, LVI, LXXIV, LXXVIII, LXXIX, LXXXI, LXXXVI, XCV].

Lentini, A. 1988. *Medioevo Letterario Cassinese, Scritti Vari*, ed. F. Avagliano, *Miscellanea Cassinese* 57. Montecassino: Pubblicazioni Cassinesi [= *Miscellanea Cassinese* 57].

Newton, F. 1973a. "Beneventan Scribes and Subscriptions, with a List of Those Known at the Present Time." *The Book Mark* (Friends of the University of North Carolina Library) 43: 1–35.

Newton, F. ed. 1973b. *Laurentius Monachus Casinensis, Archiepiscopus Amalfitanus, Opera*, (M.G., Quellen zur Geistesgeschichte des Mittelalters 7). Weimar: H. Böhlaus Nachfolger.

Newton, F. 1979. "Leo Marsicanus and the Dedicatory Text and Drawing in Monte Cassino 99." *Scriptorium* 33: 181–205.

Newton, F. 1991. "One Scriptorium, Two Scripts: Beneventan, Caroline, and the Problem of Marston 112." *Beinecke Studies in Early Manuscripts (Yale University Library Gazette)* 66: 118–33.

Newton, F. 1999. *The Scriptorium and Library at Monte Cassino, 1058–1105* (Cambridge Studies in Palaeography and Codicology 7). Cambridge: Cambridge University Press.

Newton, F. 2011. "Arabic Medicine and Other Arabic Cultural Influences in Southern Italy in the Time of Constantinus Africanus (Saec. XI²)." In *Between Text and Patient. The Medical Enterprise in Medieval and Early-Modern Europe*, Micrologus Library 39, ed. F. E. Glaze and B. K. Nance, 25–69. Florence: SISMEL.

Oldoni, M. 1978. "Intellettuali cassinesi di fronte ai Normanni (secoli XI–XII)." In *Miscellanea di storia italiana e mediterranea per Nino Lamboglia* (Collana storica di fonti e studi 23), 95–153. Genoa: no publ.

Orofino, G. 1994–2006. *I codici decorati dell'Archivio di Montecassino* 1–3. Rome: Istituto poligrafico e Zecca dello Stato.

Pecere, O., ed. 1994. *Monachesimo benedettino. Profili di un'eredità culturale.* (Pubblicazioni dell'Università degli Studi di Cassino, Sezione Atti, Convegni, Miscellanee, 4). Naples: Edizioni scientifiche italiane.

Petrus Diaconus. 1972. *Ortus et vita iustorum cenobii Casinensis* (University of California Publications: Classical Studies vol. 10), ed. R. H. Rodgers. Berkeley and Los Angeles: University of California Press.

Rabanus Maurus. 1994. *De Rerum Naturis: Cod. Casin. 132/ Archivio dell'Abbazia di Montecassino. Commentari a cura di Guglielmo Cavallo*, 2 vols. Turin: Priuli & Verlucca.

Radding, C. and F. Newton. 2003. *Theology, Rhetoric, and Politics in the Eucharistic Controversy, 1078w–1079. Alberic of Monte Cassino against Berengar of Tours*. New York: Columbia University Press.

Radding, C. and A. Ciaralli. 2007. *The Corpus iuris civilis in the Middle Ages: Manuscripts and Transmission from the Sixth Century to the Juristic Revival*. Leiden: Brill.

Reynolds, L. D. 1968. "The Medieval Tradition of Seneca's *Dialogues*." *Classical Quarterly*, N.S., 18: 355–72.

Spinelli, G., ed. 2006. *Il Monachesimo italiano dall'età longobarda all'età ottoniana (secc. VIII–X)* (Atti del VII Convegno di studi storici sull'Italia benedettina Nonantola (Modena), 10–13 settembre 2003). Cesena: Badia di Santa Maria del Monte, 2006 [Includes essays by Dell'Omo, De Rubeis, Braga, Longo and Palma, Orofino, Branchi, and Fonseca].

Wilmart, A. 1929. "Remarques sur plusieurs collections des sermons de S. Augustin." *Casinensia I*, 217–38. Montecassino: Typographia Casinensis.

CHAPTER 51

THE ABBEY OF ST. GALL

ANNA A. GROTANS

ALTHOUGH the Abbey of St. Gall was dissolved in 1805, its library, or *Stiftsbibliothek* is today still open to scholars and visitors from around the world. It ranks among the top 20 most important repositories of handwritten manuscripts with *c.*2,100 volumes, 400 of them dating before the year 1000. As of 2020, the number of digitized manuscripts is 650. In addition, it also houses 1,650 incunabula and 170,000 printed books. In honor of its prestigious holdings, the *Stiftsbibliothek* was listed as a UNESCO World Heritage Site in 1983.

HISTORY OF ST. GALL

We are extremely well informed about the St. Gall Abbey's history and the accomplishments of its monks, both political and cultural. One of the oldest sources is the monk Ratpert's *Casus St. Galli*, written *c.*884 and extending to the imperial visit of 883. Ekkehard IV (writing *c.*1050) continued the work up until 972. Thereafter follow five separate Latin continuations up until 1232, and a German history by Christian Kuchimaister written in 1335 and covering the years to 1329. Ekkehard's *Casus* is the most animated of the group, full of anecdotes and colorful descriptions that bring to life the daily existence of the monks. A further interesting source is the "Plan of St. Gall," the oldest architectural document of its kind preserved in Europe. It may have been used as a guide in reconstructing St. Gall in the early ninth century, although only in a broad sense. It is more probable that the plan represents an ideal model for a Carolingian monastery. It was probably copied in Aachen in 817/818, based upon a now lost archetype and soon thereafter brought to the Reichenau; the librarian Reginbert gifted it to St. Gall's Abbot Gozbert in 819 and today it is preserved in CSang 1092. More information on the plan and related ninth-century material culture can be found online at "Carolingian Culture at Reichenau and St. Gall" (http://www.stgallplan.org/en/index_plan.html).

The history of the St. Gall Abbey begins in 612, when, in the dense, wild Arbon woods of Alemannia in present-day Switzerland, Gallus retreated as a hermit. According to tradition, Gallus had been en route to Italy with his master, the Irish monk Columban, who eventually went on to found the Abbey of Bobbio. Although in his *vitae* Gallus is associated with Irish descent, recent studies suggest that he actually may have come from the area between Lorraine and Alemannia (Tremp 2007). After Gallus' death, the site of his hermitage was made a pilgrimage and, in 719, a monastery which in 747 accepted the Benedictine Rule. Its first abbot Otmar (719–59) was of local Alemannic heritage and had been trained at the Rhaetian Abbey of Chur. The St. Gall Abbey experienced its first cultural highpoint under Abbot Gozbert (816–37), who had a new church and perhaps monastery built. Gozbert was succeeded by several politically influential abbots who were able to promote the abbey and its interests. The abbey's political and economic position and stability were also strengthened by the fact that it was subject only to the king or emperor and enjoyed independence from local bishops and landowners. Grimald (ruled 841–72) was Grand Chancellor for Louis the German and because of his responsibilities often absent from the abbey. He left in charge his dean Hartmut, who was closely involved with the scriptorium and was eventually made abbot from 872–83. In 883, Emperor Charles III visited St. Gall. Salomon, who was abbot from 890–920, had studied at St. Gall in the external school; he concurrently held the title of Bishop of Constance and was an important advisor to and chancellor for the East Frankish kings Arnulf, Louis IV, and Konrad I. The latter half of the ninth century extending into the abbacy of Solomon is often referred to as St. Gall's "Golden Age," a period in which book production, art, music, and sacred and patristic literature flourished. It was also at this time that St. Gall became an important source for literate administrators and scribes.

The second and third quarters of the tenth century were a difficult time in St. Gall's history. In 926 the abbey was invaded by Hungarians and in 937 ravaged by fire. The library luckily remained intact through both disasters. Upon hearing of the approaching Hungarians, the recluse Wiborada advised the monks to move the library to neighboring Reichenau. She herself remained in her cell and was subsequently murdered by the intruders; later in 1047 she became the first woman to be canonized by the pope and is today the patron saint of libraries and bibliophiles.

The late tenth century through the eleventh century marks another highpoint in St. Gall's cultural output and is often referred to as its "Silver Age." The abbey enjoyed the strong support of the Ottonians with a visit by Emperors Otto I and II in 972. Along with immunity, however, came service to the empire, which included taking part in the Gorze or Lotharingian monastic reform; a commission to undertake this task was sent to St. Gall in 964/66. Key leaders during the "Silver Age" were the abbots Ymmo (976–84), Purchart II (1001–22), and Norpert (1034–72). Many others were either trained at St. Gall or took their vows there and then went on to politically influential positions throughout the kingdom, including those of bishops, cathedral provosts, court chaplains, and royal tutors. It was during this period that the scriptorium produced a large number of liturgical manuscripts, many of them for export. The period after Abbot Norpert's death is commonly referred to as the abbey's "Iron Age," during which St. Gall became embroiled in the contemporary Investiture Controversy. Nonetheless, the scriptorium produced *c*.35 manuscripts in the twelfth century, among them important musical books such as CSang 375 containing an antiphonal with neume notation and the *Processionale* contained in CSang 360.

THE ST. GALL *STIFTSBIBLIOTHEK*

When the monastery was dispersed in 1805, the library fortunately remained intact and *in situ*, and came under the administration of the Catholic diocese of St. Gall. The monastery's archive passed into the control of the state of St. Gall; today the *Stiftsarchiv* houses the monastery's collection of hundreds of charters (mostly originals) as well as a small collection of medieval manuscripts. On the ideal "Plan of St. Gall" the library is situated above the scriptorium next to the church with access to its eastern choir. In the late ninth century, the "Hartmut tower" was built to house the books and remained in place until 1666. A new Renaissance library was eventually built by Abbot Diethelm Blarer, but was soon replaced by the present baroque library hall, which was constructed by Abbot Cölestin and completed in 1766. Today *c*.10,000 visitors a year pass through the ornate entrance marked with the plaque "Sanatorium for the Soul."

The oldest library catalogue, the *Breviarium librorum,* is preserved in CSang 728, pp. 4–21 and dates from *c*.884–8 with 294 entries and 426 separate book titles; the list also contains informative and candid comments, e.g., "ad scolam" ("for school use") and "totum mendacium et inutile" ("full of lies and useless"); some of the comments are by the late ninth-century librarian, historian, and composer, Notker Balbulus (*c*.840–912; Rankin 1991). Four additional book lists from the ninth century also survive in CSang 267 and CSang 614: a catalogue of 53 addenda titles with at least 67 volumes, a list of books copied by order of Hartmut (22 entries with 28 volumes), and lists of books donated by the Abbots Grimald and Hartmut, the latter providing important insight into the collections of private scholars (Lehmann 1918, 66–89).

The *Stiftsbibliothek*'s oldest volume, CSang 1394, was written not at St Gall, but in Rome in the fourth or early fifth century and contains fragments of Vergil's works. CSang 908 contains a palimpsest of poetry and prose by Flavius Merobaudes as well as the only extant copy of Vegetius' guide to veterinary medicine. CSang 730 contains *Rothar's Edicts,* copied in northern Italy in the late seventh century. Fragments of the Vetus Latina version of the Bible copied in Rome are preserved in CSang 1394, and in CSang 1395 fragments of the oldest manuscript of the Vulgate Gospels, probably written in Verona *c*.410–20. The abbey's collection of Irish manuscripts is famous, among them an eighth-century Irish copy of Priscian's *Grammar* with Irish glosses preserved in CSang 904. Thirty other books written in Irish or Anglo-Saxon script are listed on the first page of the CSang 728 catalogue under a section titled "libri scottice scripti." Other manuscripts of Irish cultural importance are the oldest *Vita Columbani* in CSang 553 and the oldest capitulary of Columban's monastic rules in CSang 915. Some of the library's precious volumes were acquired in the early modern and baroque periods, either as gifts by the abbey's benefactors or by purchase. CSang 857, which preserves an important copy of the Middle High German epics, the *Nibelungenlied* and *Lament*, along with Wolfram von Eschenbach's *Parzival* and *Willehalm*, was acquired in 1768 as part of the Aegidius Tschudi collection purchased by the Prince-Abbot Beda Angehrn (1767–96). The same collection contained Walahfrid Strabo's "Vade mecum" (CSang 878) and a compendium of Carolingian laws dating from the beginning of the ninth century (CSang 729). In addition to its manuscripts, the *Stiftsbibliothek* also houses hundreds of incunabula and early printed books. Some of the highlights are the first colored edition of Hartmann Schedel's *Nuremberg Chronicle* and an early "Ptolemy Atlas" which dates from 1486.

Several hundred books originally copied at St. Gall have found their way into libraries and collections throughout the world. On the occasion of attending the Council of Constance in 1416, the humanist Poggio Bracciolini visited St. Gall and absconded with some very important early copies of classical works, including Quintilian's *Institutes of Oratory* and Valerius Flaccus' *Argonautica*. During the War of Toggenburg in 1712 a large number of manuscripts was removed as booty by Zurchoise and Bernese troops; *c.*100 still remain in the Zurich Zentralbibliothek. Other *codices dispersi* are on deposit in the Biblioteca Apostolica Vaticana in Rome, in Cracow, the Pierpoint Morgan Library in New York, and elsewhere.

It is unclear how many scribes were active in the scriptorium at any one time, and the number clearly fluctuated; during Hartmut's abbacy at least 20 scribes can be named; Bruckner (1938, 23) estimated *c.*100 active scribes at the turn of the century, although this number may be a bit high. An overview of various scripts used in the St. Gall scriptorium is found in Chapter 14 of this volume. Books of the highest grade of script were often produced for liturgical use and contain magnificent illuminated initials. This art reached its high point at St. Gall between 860 and 910, examples being the "Folchart Psalter" (CSang 23) with its *c.*200 highly crafted initials and the "Evangelium longum" (CSang 53), calligraphed by the monk Sintram and encased in ivory tablets sculpted by Tuotilo. Futher ivory covers are found on CSang 60 and 359, the latter also known as the "St. Gall Cantatorium" and world-renowned in the history of music. The library possesses a total of *c.*130 original book covers from the Carolingian and Ottonian periods and is an important source for codicologists. The influence of St. Gall book art is also seen on other scriptoria, e.g., in Regensburg, which Abbot Grimald often visited in his role as advisor to the king (Duft 1999, 20).

MEDIEVAL LEARNING AND EDUCATION

The St. Gall school was well known in the early Middle Ages. The internal school was designed for oblates and postulants, who lived and would continue on in the monastery and its daily life. The external school, on the other hand, was a type of boarding school and intended for various types of pupils, including future clerics, abbots, politicians, and others. The rosters of famous teachers and pupils is lengthy, especially in the later part of the ninth and the tenth centuries. Lively accounts of their everyday life can be found in Ekkehard's *Casus*, especially stories of the three young pupils and later teachers, Notker Balbulus, Ratpert, and Tuotilo (chs. 33–46). Works from the seven liberal arts and classical and medieval school authors are well represented in St. Gall manuscripts, e.g., Alcuin (CSang 62, 64, 268, 273, 276, 855, and 878), Boethius (CSang 844, 845, and 825), Cicero (CSang 818, 820, 830, 831, and 854), Donatus (CSang 855, 876, 877, 878, and 882), Horace (CSang 864), Lucan (CSang 864), Martianus Capella (872), and Sedulius (CSang 877). CSang 556 preserves form letters for practice in the *ars dictaminis*; Notker Balbulus' "Formelbuch" may also have been written for this purpose. Examples of metrical compositions assigned to advanced pupils can be found in the *Liber benedictionum* of Ekkehard IV in CSang 393. Ekkehard himself taught at St. Gall and from 1022–31 led the Cathedral School at Mainz. Classroom books from the later part of the tenth and early eleventh century are especially numerous and reflect the new curriculum at this time with its focus on dialectic and practical rhetoric. Noteworthy are the charts and other visual aids found in some of these classroom texts, e.g., CSang 817, 820, and 877, which demonstrate new methods in teaching the curriculum.

St. Gall holds a special place in the history of the German language and its oldest recorded stage, Old High German (OHG). Many St. Gall manuscripts contain lexical glosses in German; a few offer extensive glossing between the lines, called 'interlinear versions'. CSang. 916 contains a ninth-century copy of the *Rule of St. Benedict* with a nearly complete OHG interlinear version up until chapter 67. Another extremely important OHG text preserved in CSang 56 is a bilingual version of the *Diatessaron*, or Gospel Harmony, attributed to the Syrian Tatian. The Latin text appears in the left column, the German translation of over 2,000 words, here written in an East Franconian dialect, in the right column. Scholars believe that the translation, which very closely follows the Latin, was carried out at Fulda under the guidance of Rabanus Maurus, sometime in the second quarter of the ninth century. CSang 911, produced in southwest Germany, contains the oldest German book, an alphabetically organized Latin synonym dictionary with Old High German words and the oldest German version of the *pater noster*. The "Vocabularius Sancti Galli," a missionary's dictionary produced in Germany *c*.790, is today preserved in CSang 913. The most prolific contributor to vernacular writing was the teacher and scholar Notker Labeo (950–1022), who translated several standard Latin classroom texts into his native Alemannic dialect. Notker's corpus covers the whole range of the seven liberal arts: the Psalter (together with the *Cantica* and three catechetical texts; CSang 21), Boethius, *De consolatione philosophiae* (CSang 825), Martianus Capella, *De nuptiis Philologiae et Mercurii* (CSang 872), and Boethius's translations of Aristotle's *De categoriis* (CSang 818 and 825) and *De interpretatione* (CSang. 818, pp. 143–246). Notker also compiled several short Latin treatises on dialectic and rhetoric, some of which are sprinkled with

OHG vocabulary, a Latin "Computus," and a small treatise on music entirely in OHG (CSang 242).

MEDIEVAL LITURGY, MUSIC, AND LITERATURE

The St. Gall scriptorium created texts for various purposes that served the political, economic, spiritual, and intellectual needs of the religious community. The most important documents were religious in nature, as decreed in the *Rule of St. Benedict*. Indeed, CSang 914, copied c.820, most likely at St. Gall, contains the textually most important copy of the *Rule*. It represents a copy of the Reichenau text produced in 817 and based on Charlemagne's exemplar; the last two texts are now lost. Nearly half of the c.500 oldest St. Gall manuscripts contain biblical texts and commentary. Works of the Church Fathers are well represented at St. Gall, particularly the corpus of Augustine's and Jerome's works. Likewise, one finds numerous copies of early Christian writers and early medieval school authors. Hagiographic texts are also found in abundance at St. Gall, and many of the copies here have served as key witnesses in the stemmata of standard editions. Particularly noteworthy are the lives of local saints such as Gallus, Otmar, and Wiborada (cf. CSang 562); on deposit in CSang 553 is also the unique life of St. Ambrose, and in CSang 567 the oldest life of Pope Gregory the Great. The patristic collection at St. Gall is extremely large and contains biblical commentaries, collections of homilies, letters, and excerpts as well as collections of all these. CSang 430, 431, 432, and 434, produced in the mid-ninth century contain homiliaries with readings ordered according to the liturgical year; another ambitious project from approximately the same period is the groups CSang 162, 163, 164, 165, and 166, with a copy of Augustine's *In psalmos* and CSang 200, 201, and 202 with Cassiodorus' *Expositio Psalmorum*.

The abbey also preserves important original Latin compositions from the early Middle Ages, produced either at St. Gall or at neighboring houses. The late eighth-century literary triumvirate Notker, Tuotilo, and Ratpert were particularly productive; all were trained and active at St. Gall. Notker Balbulus (c.840–912) was a prolific writer and composer and penned at St. Gall his *Gesta Karoli magni* c.884-7, a collection of musical sequences known as the *Liber ymnorum* (dedicated in 884 and preserved in hundreds of medieval manuscripts and early printed missals throughout Europe), a metrical life of St. Gall (together with the monk Hartmann), a martyrology, and, c.890, a memorial book, the so-called "Formelbuch" written in honor of the consecration of former pupil Solomo as abbot of St. Gall and bishop of Constance. Finally, he also composed the *Notatio de illustribus viris* written in the tradition of Jerome's *De viris illustribus* and containing a survey of early Christian and medieval literature. Tuotilo is well known for his tropes, a recently new genre at this time; he is also named as the artist of ivory carvings and musical tutor to young noble boys. Ratpert is known for his chronicle of the abbey to 883 and the now lost vernacular version of the *Song of St. Gall* which Ekkehard IV later translated into Latin; he also authored several hymns. Local literature from the "Silver Age" includes the "Life of St. Wiborada" by Ekkehard I (soon reworked by Ekkehard IV), and a later version by Herimannus *c.*1072–6 containing impressive amounts of classical imagery and theological learning; the last-mentioned monk also probably authored glosses to Epistles of St. Paul. Ekkehard IV was a prolific author, penning several works, including the first continuation of the abbey's history up until 972 (CSang 615), and a collection of occasional and school poetry known as the *Liber benedictionum*. The latter survives in an autograph copy in CSang 393; the space in the margins and interlinearly is literally crammed full of Ekkehard's corrections, glosses, and comments and thus preserves for us a unique example of an early medieval "work in progress." Ekkehard also copiously glossed other manuscripts in the library's collection, including the CSang copy of Orosius's *History* in CSang 621. The works of the medieval poet and scholar Walahfrid Strabo are well represented at St. Gall, many in very old and even near contemporary copies, including his "Vita S. Galli" (CSang 562), his "Vita Othmari" (CSang 572), "Visio Wettini" (CSang 573), "De imagine Tetrici" (CSang 869, containing many other poems as well), and various individual poems and other shorter texts and commentaries (CSang 446, 459, and 899), and his Commentary to the Psalms (CSang 167, 313, and 317). CSang 878 may contain Walahfrid's own "Vademecum" written in his own hand.

The early St. Gall manuscripts devoted to music are extremely important for musicologists. The St. Gall *Cantatorium* in CSang 359 preserves the oldest and most complete copy of neumes for the solo parts of the liturgy in the Gregorian tradition. A high point was reached in the third quarter of the ninth century with the three monks Ratpert, Notker, and Tuotilo, whose accomplishments are often referred to as stemming from a St. Gall "School of Song." Hartker's antiphonary preserved in two volumes in CSang 390 and 391 was written *c.*1000 in an elegant script with miniatures, illuminated capitals, and neumes and notations. Also produced at the beginning of the eleventh century is Sang 339, which contains an extensive complete missal. Production of liturgical manuscripts increased again under the rule of Abbot Nortpert of Stablo (1034–72). Important texts from this time are CSang 338, 340, 341, and 376. The liturgical influence of St. Gall reached also to St. Albans in Mainz, whence it emanated to other centers throughout Europe.

BIBLIOGRAPHY

Berschin, W. 1987. *Eremus und Insula. St. Gallen und die Reichenau im Mittelalter: Modell einer lateinischen Literaturlandchaft.* Wiesbaden: Reichert.

Clark, J. M. 1926. *The Abbey of St. Gall as a Centre of Literature and Art.* Cambridge: Cambridge University Press.

Duft, J. 1990. *Die Abtei St. Gallen I: Beiträge zur Erforschung ihrer Manuskripte. Ausgewählte Aufsätze in überarbeiteter Fassung*, ed. Peter Ochsenbein and Ernst Ziegler. Sigmaringen: Thorbecke.

Duft, J. 1991. *Die Abtei St. Gallen II: Beiträge zur Kenntnis ihrer Persönlichkeiten. Ausgewählte Aufsätze in überarbeiteter Fassung*. Sigmaringen: Thorbecke.

e-codices – Virtual Manuscript Library of Switzerland. https://www.e-codices.unifr.ch/en

Eisenhut, H. 2009. *Die Glossen Ekkeharts IV. von St. Gallen im Codex Sangallensis 621*. St. Gallen: Verlag am Klosterhof (*Monasterium Sancti Galli 4*).

Ekkehard IV. 1980. *Casus sancti Galli. St. Galler Klostereschichten*, ed. and trans. Hans Haefele. Darmstadt: Wissenschaftliche Buchgesellschaft.

Grotans, A. 2006. *Reading in Medieval St. Gall*. Cambridge: Cambridge University Press.

Lehmann, P. 1918. *Mittelalterliche Bibliothekskataloge Deutchlands und der Schweiz*. Vol. 1: *Die Bistümer Konstanz und Chur*. Munich: Beck.

King, J. C., ed. 1993. *Sangallensia in Washington. The Arts and Letters in Medieval and Baroque St. Gall Viewed from the Late Twentieth Century*. Berne: Peter Lang.

King, J. C. and Werner Vogler, eds. 1991. *The Culture of the Abbey of St. Gall*. Stuttgart: Belser.

McKitterick, R. 1989. *The Carolingians and the Written Word*. Cambridge: Cambridge University Press.

Ochsenbein, P., ed. 1999. *Das Kloster St. Gallen im Mittelalter. Die kulturelle Blüte vom 8. bis zum 12. Jahrhundert*. Darmstadt: Wissenschaftliche Buchgesellschaft.

Rankin, S. 1991. "Ego Itaque Notker Scripsi." *Revue Bénédictine* 101 (3/4): 268–98.

Ratpert. 2002. *St. Galler Klostergeschichten* (Casus sancti Galli) (MGH Scriptores Rerum Germanicarum in usum scholarum separatim editi 75.), ed. and trans. Hannes Steiner. Hanover: Hahn.

St. Gall Monastery Plan. http://www.stgallplan.org/en/, accessed February 11, 2020.

Tremp, E., J. Huber, and K. Schmuki. 2007. *The Abbey Library of Saint Gall. The History, the Baroque Hall and the Collections of the Abbey Library*. St. Gall: Verlag am Klosterhof.

CHAPTER 52

···

BOOK PRODUCTION
IN PARIS

···

RICHARD H. ROUSE AND MARY A. ROUSE

FROM the mid-twelfth century and before, until the end of the fifteenth century and beyond, the city of Paris was the most important source of manuscript books in northern Europe. We can examine this eminence over some three and a half centuries in documentary records, as well as by means of the books themselves. The majority of the city's book-making past is undocumented, however; and other types of evidence come into play in establishing the early history of Paris as an emerging center of manuscript production. Specifically, we know that literate people lived there and, eventually, that books made there survive. We must begin the history of book-making in Paris by following the implications of these facts.

Roman Paris, Lutetia, was founded on an island in the Seine, an efficient way to bridge the river, which was chosen for its geographic potential as a center of trade, administration, and military governance; and as the Roman frontier pushed north, Paris became the confluence of a series of major roads. Long before the earliest records of a manuscript book or document, one has evidence of a setting auspicious for writing in the form of military and merchant activity that required written records, tax registers, and a courier service. Paris by the second century had an aqueduct, an amphitheater, several thermal baths, and a forum, the physical accouterments of a Roman city. Roman military leaders governed from the administrative center on the Île, including Julian ("the Apostate"), who was proclaimed Roman emperor by the acclamation of his troops in Paris in AD 360. A learned man, Julian had been educated in Athens and read Greek philosophy and mythology; but there is no indication that he had his books copied in Paris.

A more serious milestone for a literate community in Paris was not the arrival of the Roman administration, but rather the arrival of Christianity that came north with the legions. Sparse Christian communities are attested in Paris as early as the late third century, and the adoption of Christianity as the empire's official religion in the fourth century soon led to the building of churches and a cathedral, with Scriptures and written liturgy. The emergence of a series of memorable Parisian saints such as Saint Denis (d. *c.*250) and Sainte Geneviève (d. *c.*500) and bishops of the city such as Saint Marcel (d. *c.*436), and Saint Germain (d. 576) occasioned the composition and dissemination of written legends celebrating their deeds and miracles. Dependable records of fifth-century Paris are almost nonexistent, as the empire inexorably dissolved; but by the era of the Merovingian kings (the sixth through the eighth centuries) there were more than 30 churches in Paris.

The last will and testament of a wealthy matron, a unique document like a small lighted window in the dark, gives evidence of a vital literate Christian community in Paris at the end of the sixth or beginning of the seventh century. Although the will was drafted during the reign of the Frankish king Clotaire II (d. 629) and the testatrix bore the Frankish name of Ermintrude, nevertheless she addressed her witnesses and executors as "my fellow Romans" (*Quirites*); she was literate in Latin and she employed an instrument of the Roman legal system, a written testament, never doubting that her wishes as expressed in writing would have authority after her death. Ermintrude lived near the center of Roman Paris on the Left Bank, but she owned agricultural land complete with buildings, serfs, vines, arable fields, flocks, and herds around the outskirts of the city. After bequests of estates furnished with dependents left to her surviving son and to favored institutions, she was still wealthy enough to free by name 45 serfs, giving each the hut in which he or she lived, together with their gardens, sheds, vineyards, and all the goods that reasonably seemed to belong to them. She left bequests to a number of churches in the city, including Saint-Pierre (later Sainte-Geneviève), Saint-Étienne-des-Grés, Notre-Dame-des-Champs, Saints-Gervais-et-Protais, the cathedral on the Île, and most especially Saint-Symphorien (formerly near the site of the Panthéon), where she had buried one of her sons and on which she lavished gift after gift. Despite all the document tells us about lay literacy, however, it reveals nothing specific about the production of books in Paris. In a family of Erminethrude's status, she would as a girl have been taught by a tutor in the home; but were any of her books produced in Paris? We do not know. Her legacies to churches ranged widely in scale, from "a small gold ring inscribed with my name" bestowed on the Right Bank church of Saints-Gervais-et-Protais, to the substantial *villa* of Lagny "together with the fields, the dependent settlers, the meadows, the pastures, and the forests, ownership in fee simple in perpetuity and in its entirety," as well as its sheep together with the shepherd, its swine together with the swineherd, its draft animals and their keeper, an impressive set of vineyards elsewhere, and countless smaller things, all given to Saint-Symphorien. But frustratingly there is no mention of books.

Our first tangible evidence of book-making in Paris dates from the eighth and ninth centuries, and not surprisingly the important book production of the age here as elsewhere was monastic. The two local centers of learning and of book production in the Carolingian centuries were outside the walls of Carolingian Paris: the Benedictine abbeys of Saint-Germain-des-Prés, not quite a kilometer from the cathedral, and Saint-Denis, some eleven kilometers from the cathedral but still an easy day's walk. Certainly both abbeys were regarded as Parisian by residents of the city in every age. For example,

Erminethrude's will c.600 contains bequests to both Saint-Germain and Saint-Denis, in a sequence of three that includes the cathedral of Paris, while several centuries later the poet Adenet le Roi in the late thirteenth century prefaced no fewer than three of his verse narratives with a fictional stroll from Paris to Saint-Denis, where he found in its library the requisite "old book" that authenticates his story.

From these two, eighth- and ninth-century Saint-Germain-des-Prés and Saint-Denis, we at last have more than inference, in the tangible form of surviving manuscripts made in Paris. A significant proportion, perhaps a fourth, of Saint-Germain's surviving manuscripts of the eighth or ninth century centers on its patron, such as Fortunatus's Life of St. Germain or sermons about the saint. One of the early manuscripts made at Saint-Germain is also the most splendid, the so-called Stuttgart Psalter (Stuttgart, Württembergische Landesbibliothek, Bib. fol. 23) datable between 820 and 830. Its 165 folios are enhanced with 316 miniatures, horizontal in format, extending across the page. The energy captured in the scenes and the invariably strong colors with which they are painted attest the work of a well-trained scriptorium.

It is rare that monastic books, especially at an early date, provide names of any sort—patron, scribe, or illuminator. An eleventh-century book from Saint-Germain-des-Prés proves an exception: the colophon of the lectionary and collected saints' lives in Paris, BnF, lat. 11751 (s. XI med.) says that with the approval of Abbot Adélard (1030–60), and at the command of Prior Sigouin, "the worthy scribe Ingelard decorated it." (The hands of several copyists are present.) With this as a fixed point, five or six other books can be attributed to this time and to the artist Ingelard at Saint-Germain-des-Prés, including the splendid eleventh-century psalter-hymnal Paris, BnF, lat. 11550.

The oldest books unmistakably associated with Saint-Denis were not abbey-made: two fifth- or sixth-century Vergils brought north from Italy. By the eighth century, however, there is clear evidence of both a scriptorium and a library at the abbey itself. In AD 774 Charlemagne gave the monks a forest and all the game therein, with explicit intent that it serve for bookbinding, a forest abounding "with species of wild beasts of both sexes, of deer, of roebucks, with whose hides the books of that holy place [Saint-Denis] may be covered" (MGH, Diplomata Karolingorum, 1.126).[1] A manuscript of Jerome's commentary on Jeremiah (Paris, BnF, lat. 17371) bears a note from the scribe explaining that he wrote at the command of Abbot Fardulf of Saint-Denis (782–806). Two other eighth-century manuscripts are written by the same hand (Cassiodorus on Psalms, Paris, BnF, lat. 15304–5), along with a further two eighth-century manuscripts also probably written during Fardulf's abbacy. The next century saw a much larger number of manuscripts surviving from Saint-Denis; some 41 ninth-century manuscripts are securely attributed to the abbey, with another 45 whose association with Saint-Denis is probable. One does not yet see evidence of the chronicles for which the abbey was later famous.

We do not know what proportion of the manuscripts produced at Saint-Germain-des-Prés and Saint-Denis was made for external consumption, by the court or local nobility. Common sense says that these important Parisian abbeys must to some degree have served demands from outside their walls, but records are lacking.

The physical appearance of the ninth-century Stuttgart Psalter made at Saint-Germain proclaims it to be a book destined for royalty or high nobility rather than for sober monastic use, but the fact is not documented. As for Saint-Denis, written evidence of production for the early manuscripts consists almost entirely of the abbey's thirteenth- and fifteenth-century *ex libris* notes, which restricts our knowledge to those Carolingian books that remained in the abbey library. However, an early ninth-century document provides enlightenment on this point. When the Western emperor Louis the Pious in 827 received from the Eastern emperor a copy of the works of Pseudo-Denis the Areopagite, Louis at once sent the book to Saint-Denis, asking Abbot Hilduin to have it translated from the Greek. Confusion abounds in this situation: the misattribution of the theological works of Pseudo-Denis (late fifth century) to the first-century Denis the Areopagite converted in Athens by St. Paul (Acts 17.34); and the ninth-century misidentification of Saint Denis, the third-century missionary to the Gauls, with this composite predecessor. Despite the compound error, however, Louis was correct to assume that the abbey could deal competently with Greek, and the monks of Saint-Denis provided the original Latin diffusion of the Dionysian corpus.

There must have been other examples, less striking but numerous. Before the end of the thirteenth century, however, Saint-Denis was purchasing books from the exterior, schoolbooks certainly but liturgical texts as well; the principal source of books in Paris had irreversibly changed.

An intermediate stage in Parisian book production emerged in the twelfth century, still quasi-monastic in background but more directly pertinent to scholarship and to urban interests than were the old Benedictine abbeys. Two Augustinian abbeys, Saint-Victor (founded 1108) and Sainte-Geneviève, in the course of the century became closely identified with the increasingly important Paris schools. Almost immediately after its founding Saint-Victor produced renowned scholars of its own, Hugh, Richard, and Andrew of Saint-Victor, and the abbey assumed the task of book production in order to deal with external demand for the writings of the Victorines. Before mid-century the abbey was hiring outside scribes to keep pace with demand; by 1139 it is recorded that the abbey's librarian was responsible for all writing "done inside the abbey or out," and he was charged with "hiring those who write for pay." In documenting the existence of commercial book scribes in the city, this passage suggests that Saint-Victor by employing them played an instrumental role in the origin and growth of commercial book production at Paris. In 1147, at the joint request of church and state, the prior of Saint-Victor was ordered to restore the religious life at Sainte-Geneviève, and (eventually) he effected a virtual refounding of the abbey under the Augustinian Rule. Thereafter, the precincts of these two Left Bank abbeys provided official shelter to which the growing schools of Paris migrated, in order to evade the restrictive oversight of the cathedral chancellor within the city proper. Production of books for the growing schools, which shortly became the University of Paris, was the overriding impetus that expanded the commercial book trade in Paris manyfold, well beyond the works of the Victorines.

Major commercial book production in Paris for the schools antedates the earliest regulations or payment accounts or recorded names of book-makers. Three works, composed at various places at or near the mid-twelfth-century, dominated Parisian book production for the remainder of the century: the Decretum, the most important collection of canons of the Church gathered and organized by the lawyer Gratian; the Sentences, a massive systematized statement of the teachings of orthodox authors on theological subjects organized by Peter Lombard; and the Ordinary Gloss to the Bible. Names of those who first produced these books at Paris are lacking, but the rapid dissemination of these texts and the quasi-uniform appearance of the manuscripts unmistakably indicate commercial production. All three texts were used in the schools in the later twelfth century and continued in use thereafter.

A clear example of the increase is Parisian production of glossed Bibles, which appeared early and continued long. It was probably scholars at the cathedral of Laon, led by Master Anselm and his confrères, who perfected the ordinary gloss, that is, a complete marginal commentary on the biblical text that was widely accepted as authoritative by theologians throughout the West. The center of the text's dissemination, however, was Paris. One of the earliest records of a set of glossed volumes of a multivolume Bible consists of the eight surviving glossed volumes that Prince Henri, third son of King Louis VI, gave to the abbey of Clairvaux when he entered the Cistercian order there as a monk. From their illumination, the making of these volumes has been attributed to Saint-Victor and its hired Parisian workmen, before mid-century (c.1146). By the end of the century the commercial book trade, doubtless in cooperation with the theologians, had worked out the most efficient and useful layout for gloss and text, an intricate page presupposing professional production; and a volume or more of glossed Scriptures, if not a whole glossed Bible, was soon to be found in the libraries of most cathedrals and abbeys.

Although the Ordinary Gloss, like the Decretum, was a masterpiece of systematized learning, in short order the Paris trade was producing deluxe copies for the wealthy, bishops, abbots, and (among the students) wealthy prelates-to-be, books of lectern size meant by their monumentality to serve as fitting appurtenances to a prelate's position. In addition to the many surviving glossed volumes, this phenomenon is amply documented in the record of books left to the abbey of San Andrea in Vercelli by its founder Cardinal Guala Bicchieri (d. 1227), who had studied theology at the Paris schools around 1180, and spent further time there (1208–9) as papal legate. Over half of the 98 books in his bequest were schoolbooks, many specifically described as being written in "littera parisiensis," a script recognizably Parisian; among them, each "in good Parisian script," are a glossed volume of Genesis and Exodus, another of Leviticus, Numbers, and Deuteronomy, the 4 Kings glossed, a glossed volume containing Tobias, Judith, Esther, and Ruth, a glossed psalter, a glossed volume of the Wisdom Books (Proverbs, Ecclesiastes, Song of Songs, Wisdom, Ecclesiasticus), another of Isaiah, another of Jeremiah and Lamentations, another of Ezechiel and Daniel, another glossed volume of all four Gospels with the Gospel canons, as well as two separate glossed volumes, for Matthew and Mark and for Luke and John, respectively, the glossed Pauline epistles, and a single glossed volume containing the Acts of the Apostles, the canonical epistles, and the Apocalypse – 14 glossed volumes of the Bible. This practice of giving glossed Scriptures to a religious house was still in vogue a half-century or more later, when Gui de la Tour du Pin (d. 1286), bishop of Clermont, in 1261 gave a complete set of glossed Scriptures in 11 volumes to the Dominican convent of Lyons, volumes made to Gui's order by the Parisian commercial *libraire* Nicolas Lombard.

Even before the gloss was added, the Bible had customarily been bound in several volumes. By the end of the twelfth century and on through the thirteenth, however, one-volume Bibles were being made at Paris, written on thinner parchment in a tiny abbreviated script. By mid-century Parisian book-makers were producing in large numbers the so-called Paris Bible, small enough for mendicant friars to carry in a pouch or satchel. We know that most of these were produced by the commercial book trade because of the art historical evidence of repetitive images and because faint pencil notes of payment survive on the margins or flyleaves. These same illuminators appeared in the historiated initials of volumes of classical texts like Vergil; one of these, a copy of Ptolemy's Almagest (BnF, lat. 16200), preserves a note stating that the exemplar (the model from which a text was copied) had been rented from the abbey of Saint-Victor—just as similar notes, in glossed Scriptures illuminated by the Almagest artist, show that they were made for Saint-Victor. This reminds us that new methods, and new personnel, in Parisian book production did not necessarily replace, but merely supplemented, the older methods and personnel: book production in or connected to the abbeys of Paris continued, though on a lesser scale than previously, and Saint-Denis in particular was renowned in the thirteenth century as the quasi-official historian of the kings of France, culminating in the massive *Grande chronique de France* composed in Latin at Saint-Denis and then translated into French for courtly use.

We are largely ignorant of the names of those who produced the commercially made manuscripts at the end of the twelfth century and beginning of the thirteenth, roughly 1175–1230, because scribes and illuminators ordinarily did not sign their work. By the 1220s, however, and markedly more frequently as the thirteenth century progressed, we find names of people working in the Paris book trade: names in rental agreements for the typical Parisian residence-cum-workplace, in purchases of property, in tax records, in contracts, in gifts and bequests to religious houses (which were better at preserving their records than were laypeople), and, of course, in the books themselves. Bishop Gui's agreement with the *libraire* Nicolas Lombard around 1260, surviving on a flyleaf of one of the Bible volumes, is a case in point; but by the time of the royal tax rolls of the 1290s one has the names of Paris book trade members in the hundreds, providing a general picture of the size and location of the different specialists working in this trade, parchment sellers, scribes, illuminators, binders, and the *libraires* or publisher/booksellers who controlled the trade.

The *libraires*, the most prosperous segment of the trade, were largely centered on the rue Neuve Notre-Dame, the short straight street that ran west from the front of the new cathedral. This location situated them squarely between two groups of potential patrons, the bishop of Paris and exceptionally wealthy canons of Notre-Dame to the east, the king and his courtiers to the west. But if the most affluent patrons were on the Île de la Cité, the fact remained that the original impetus for the Paris book trade, and for a long time its most numerous, though not its richest patrons, were the students and masters of the Left Bank schools, which by the beginning of the thirteenth century were incorporated into a university. Most of the scribes, parchment sellers, and illuminators resided and worked on the Left Bank, clustered near to the Petit-Pont that crossed to the Île where a majority of *libraires* (source of their employment) were concentrated.

Demand for books by students and masters of the University of Paris led to the adoption of the process of pecia rental. "Pecia" is the Latin for "piece," a word used with regard to land or to cloth; but in reference to books, a pecia meant a quire or gathering. Pecia rental, a procedure pioneered by the Dominicans and perfected at the law university in Bologna, was widely used in Paris in a period dating roughly between 1260 and 1349 (with earlier and later exceptions). Simply put, a specialized *libraire* (called a "stationer," at Paris) made a copy of a book widely in demand and kept it, unbound, with each pecia numbered conspicuously at its head, sequentially through the book. Anyone who wanted a copy of the book could rent, at a modest price regulated by the university, each of the pecias in turn, when pecia 1 was copied exchanging it for pecia 2, and so on until the work was finished. Compared to traditional book production in which the complete book had to be copied before a second copy could begin, pecia rental permitted different copyists to work simultaneously one following after another; in theory, as many copies could be in progress as there were pecias in the book. The earliest Paris stationer on record is Guillaume de Sens (fl. 1254–70), located on the Left Bank next to the Dominican house of Saint-Jacques; he was succeeded in this shop by his widow Marguerite de Sens (known 1292); both Guillaume and Marguerite left significant bequests to Saint-Victor, which perhaps gave them employment early in their careers. Marguerite was succeeded as stationer by their son André (fl. 1296–1304), and he by their grandson Thomas (fl. 1313–42); like all stationers in Paris, they performed the ordinary tasks of a *libraire* as well renting pecias. This family's stationer's shop, from Guillaume's day through his grandson's, was the Dominicans' quasi-official publisher of the works of Thomas Aquinas in rental pecias. The pecia system largely disappeared at Paris with the diminution of the student population from a combination of the Black Death and the Hundred Years War, but in its prime the process was responsible for the rapid dissemination of works by sought-after authors, for the proliferation of standard textbooks, and for the provision of useful alphabetical reference works.

All of the continuing output of the monastic scriptoria and all the stationers' rental pecias for students were in Latin. The fourteenth century brought a major change: for the first time since ancient Rome, books of all sorts began to be produced in the language spoken by the local populace, the vernacular. In Paris, this meant the widespread production of texts in Old and Middle French. These included romances (which at first simply meant "works in French"), such as the tales connected with Arthurian legends and legends surrounding Alexander the Great, or an increasing number of quasi-original stories composed anonymously or by known authors such as

Adenet le Roi or Girart d'Amiens. There can scarcely have been a Parisian *libraire* in the fourteenth century who did not produce at least one manuscript (and probably many manuscripts) of the lengthy narrative poem the Roman de la rose, begun by Guillaume de Lorris and completed in Paris *c.*1274 by Jean de Meun. The Paris book trade turned out volumes of lyric poetry, songs, political verse, and didactic works. Devotional literature was especially centered on French Books of Hours, comprising prayers for laymen and laywomen to turn to at set hours of the day; Paris book-makers produced them in endless numbers. Texts in the vernacular were the bread and butter of the commercial book trade of Paris, from the early fourteenth century onward; and conversely, Parisian manuscript producers, sworn servants of the university, were instrumental in the rapid dissemination of French literature as a bespoke trade for the wealthy lay community.

Works in translation perhaps accounted for the greatest number of pages copied and painted in Paris in the first half of the century. Many, like the Bible historiale, Ovide moralisé, the Grandes chroniques de France, translated or freely adapted from Latin originals, each consumed large amounts of parchment. King Charles V, as regent and then king (1356–80), kept scholars on retainer at his court to translate serious works of history and philosophy from Greek and Latin into French; but he had the manuscripts of the translations made by the Parisian book trade. Charles's younger brother Jean, duke of Berry, a patron of beautiful books, employed in his household famous painters like the Limbourg brothers to illuminate his manuscripts; but he regularly frequented commercial Paris book-makers as well.

The first decades of the fifteenth century were difficult times for those who produced books at Paris, as they were for all Parisians. Beginning in 1407 when the duke of Burgundy's assassins killed his cousin the duke of Orléans, political animosity in Paris became open civil war between armed factions, ending only with the city's occupation by the English (1420–36). The English governors, headed by the bibliophile duke of Bedford, were insufficient in numbers and buying power to replace the French patronage that the book trade lost when the court and the high nobility fled the city. Even after the English were expelled, war continued, accompanied by economic crisis; and the distrustful royal court did not reside in Paris again until well into the sixteenth century, forcing the makers of books in Paris to rely on other patrons. The book trade, therefore, began to serve a more widely varied audience, including the cadre of high royal officials who lived and conducted the affairs of royal government in Paris, the heads of the royal departments or "chambers," the lawyers and judges of the high court of parlement, wealthy canons of Notre-Dame, prelates of various dioceses and abbots of important abbeys who had townhouses in Paris, lesser and higher nobility, wealthy merchants, and financiers. As a result, even with the rise of provincial centers such as Rouen and the Loire châteaux, Paris remained the hub of French book production par excellence, in both quantity and quality, through the century.

The first printing press (manned by German printers) began operation in Paris in 1470, and for a number of years previously the Parisian booksellers had been selling printed works imported from Germany. The adjustment from producing manuscripts to producing printed books was less abrupt than one might expect, but the scale tipped in time. Beginning in the 1480s and 1490s, *libraires* who had made and sold manuscripts began to publish printed books. Some of them were successful; many were not. Scribes, who had never had bargaining power as a profession, dwindled in numbers to the exceptional few, true calligraphers. The illuminators were affected least, initially, by the shift to print. In decreasing numbers, they continued to illuminate printed books for another two centuries.

*   *   *

The emergence of medieval Paris as the major source of manuscript books north of the Alps depended on a reciprocal relation between those who read books and those who produced them, the underlying principle being that no one reads if there are no books, and no one makes books if there are no readers.

The great majority of manuscript books produced in Paris until the late Middle Ages were the Latin texts that served ecclesiastical needs. The great Parisian monasteries of Saint-Germain-des-Prés and Saint-Denis became the producers of the lives and legends of their patron saints in written record, and their libraries from the eighth century on became the custodians of the Christian message in script and image. By the late eleventh century or the beginning of the twelfth the schools nurtured by the cathedral and by the abbey of Saint-Victor were attracting large numbers of ambitious young clerks from across Europe, and before mid-century their need for books had exceeded the ability of the cloister to supply, and had spilled over into the commercial life of the city, a need that increased with the schools' incorporation as a university in 1215. The book trade of Paris furnished the written support for the wandering mendicants trained at the university to teach and to preach to an increasingly literate urban public.

Among literate laymen over the centuries from Erminthrude's day, successive textual communities at Paris gave way, to be joined or replaced by others. A textual community defined by rote familiarity with a classical literary canon centering on Vergil was joined and then supplanted by another centered on the Christian Scriptures. In the vernacular, sung epics about the deeds of warrior heroes were succeeded by romance texts, not sung but composed and transmitted in writing. The city was home not just to provincial bishops and abbots with Parisian residences, but to upcountry nobility, merchants, bankers, royal jurists, and administrators, all of them relying on written records in their daily lives. The demand for Latin texts in church and schoolroom, and the demand by literate laypeople for literature, devotional texts, and scholarly works in the vernacular, by the fifteenth century supported a vigorous commercial book trade with specialist craftsmen who could meet any request: parchmenters, paper sellers, scribes, illuminators, binders, all working for book contractors or *libraires*.

Paris, much the largest city in Western Europe, by the middle of the century offered elements advantageous to a successful introduction of the printing press: a long-established and well-organized system of production by professional bookmen, opportunity for distribution afforded by the Seine, and a large and wealthy book-buying public, both lay and ecclesiastic, whose demand for books seemed insatiable.

NOTE

1. *MGH, Diplomata Karolingorum*, ed. E. Mühlbacher. Hanover: Hahn, 1906, 1:126.

SUGGESTED READING

For geographical and social orientation in medieval Paris, P. Lorentz and D. Sandron, *Atlas de Paris au Moyen Âge* (Paris: Parigramme, 2006). For the books of Saint-Denis from early times to its dissolution, D. Nebbiai-Dalla Guarda, *La Bibliothèque de l'abbaye de Saint-Denis en France, du IXᵉ au XVIIIᵉ siècle* (Paris: CNRS, 1985). Concerning glossed Scriptures in Paris, C. de Hamel, *Glossed Books of the Bible and the Origins of the Paris Booktrade* (Woodbridge, Suffolk, and Dove, NH: D. S. Brewer, 1984); and for the one-volume Bible, L. Light, "French Bibles c. 1200–30: A New Look at the Origin of the Paris Bible," in *The Early Medieval Bible: Its Production, Decoration and Use*, ed. R. Gameson (Cambridge: Cambridge University Press, 1994) 155–76. Regarding rental pecias, J. Destrez, *La Pecia dans les manuscrits universitaires du XIIIe et du XIVe siècle* (Paris: J. Vautrain, 1935). For Parisian manuscript illumination in the thirteenth century, R. Branner, *Manuscript Painting in Paris during the Reign of Saint Louis* (Berkeley and Los Angeles: University of California Press, 1977); in the fourteenth, F. Avril, "Manuscrits: Les ateliers parisiens," in *L'Art au temps des rois maudits: Philippe le Bel et ses fils 1285–1328, exhibit catalog* (Paris: Réunion des musées nationaux, 1998) 256–91; for later illumination, F. Avril and N. Reynaud, *Les Manuscrits à peintures en France 1440–1520* (Paris: Flammarion, 1993), esp. "Paris," pp. 35–69; and for still later illumination, M. Orth, *Renaissance Manuscripts: The Sixteenth Century*, in the *Survey of Manuscripts Illuminated in France* (Turnhout: Brepols, 2015). Regarding commercial manuscript production in Paris from the late twelfth century through the fifteenth, R. H. Rouse and M. A. Rouse, *Manuscripts and their Makers: Commercial Book Producers in Medieval Paris 1200–1500*, 2 vols. (London: Harvey Miller, 2000) and R. H. Rouse and M. A. Rouse, *Renaissance Illuminators in Paris: Artists and Artisans 1500–1715* (London: Harvey Miller, 2019).

CHAPTER 53

THE SCRIPTORIUM AND LIBRARY OF SALISBURY CATHEDRAL

TERESA WEBBER

THE history of the books of Salisbury Cathedral parallels that of many medieval English religious institutions: the creation or amplification of core collections largely through in-house production during the late eleventh and twelfth centuries, maintained thereafter by earmarked revenues but enlarged largely through the vagaries of donation rather than planned acquisition. The books produced for the first canons of Salisbury in the late eleventh and early twelfth centuries have a particular palaeographical significance as somewhat unusual representatives of handwriting, book production, and book collections in post-Conquest England. The majority of the later Salisbury books have yet to receive detailed analysis, but the inscriptions and annotations they contain illustrate the complexities of medieval ownership and use, and the difficulties of interpretation presented by brief inscriptions of donation.

The second edition of N. R. Ker's *Medieval Libraries of Great Britain* and its supplement identified 217 manuscripts as certainly or probably possessed by the pre-Reformation cathedral (182 remain at, or have been returned to, the cathedral).[1] Fourteen of these predate the decision to establish a see at Salisbury in 1075, many of which were presumably transferred from the former see at Sherborne (as is demonstrably the case with London, BL, MS Cotton Tiberius C I [fols. 43–203], a mid-eleventh-century pontifical).[2] At least 78, however, were produced locally by successive groups of scribes working in close collaboration within the first 50 or so years of the see's foundation.[3] Salisbury scribes have since been recognized in two more booklets (Cambridge, Trinity College, MS B.1.37, fols. 46–73, and London, BL, MS Sloane 1122, fols. 9–34).[4]

Such sustained collaboration is evidence of the organized activity that constitutes a scriptorium. As with many identified scriptoria, the activity at Salisbury was limited in duration and undertaken to fulfil a specific need, in this instance to build up the collections of a newly established community in accordance with prevailing attitudes toward their religious and intellectual requirements. An initial phase of intense activity, datable to the 1080s and 1090s, involved to varying degrees at least 17 scribes (Group I), each of whose hands has been identified collaborating with at least one of the others in two or more books. None of the books is datable, but four of the scribes contributed to royal documents, which are the draft return for the southwestern circuit of the Domesday survey (Exon Domesday) and geld accounts for Wiltshire, all of which are datable to 1086.[5] Copying was resumed around or soon after the beginning of the twelfth century, with fewer apparent signs of haste, by a largely new group of at least 13 scribes (Group IIa, which included in the earliest stages one Group I scribe), followed by a smaller group of six (Group IIb), active perhaps into 1120s (the hands of this final group have much in common with that of the Salisbury entry in the mortuary roll of Abbot Vitalis of Savigny, datable to 1123).[6]

In England, as elsewhere on the Continent, the late eleventh and twelfth centuries witnessed a significant level of in-house book production, with a particular focus, observed by twelfth-century chroniclers, upon the copying of liturgical books and the works of the Fathers (although it is only the latter that have survived in any number).[7] Several houses, for example, Christ Church, Canterbury, and St Albans, produced books that reflect in-house training and other conditions conducive to the development of a local tradition of formal handwriting and other common practices in the physical characteristics of the books produced, as well as the resources to produce handsome volumes on good parchment, articulated with elaborate initials and display script. The Salisbury books, however, differ in their handwriting and general appearance. The handwriting is usually smaller, sometimes displaying elements of informality (such as simplified variant forms of *a* and *d*, casually applied serifs, a more frequent use of ligatures, and heavier incidence of abbreviations), more typical of annotations at this date but also, in England, becoming introduced to the handwriting of royal (and subsequently other) documents.[8] In some books, changes of hand occur with unusual frequency, several changes sometimes being present on a single opening. The character of the handwriting and patterns of collaboration are more indicative of urgency than of the alternation of a master-scribe and his pupils. The books are generally smaller than the norm at this date, and most are plain, with little more than simple red initials. The parchment is often poor, the ruling sometimes inexpert, and, in a few books, quires have been cobbled together from discarded bifolia or single sheets.

Despite the fact that books were produced in some number over the course of perhaps four or five decades, no shared tradition in matters of style or scribal practice emerged. The hands reflect training in the different regional traditions of Caroline minuscule distinctive of England, northern France, and the lower Rhineland.[9] It is likely that many of the scribes had received their initial training, and developed their personal hands, before arriving at Salisbury. Few of the hands display consistent features of style. Some exhibit a great deal of variation, especially in the formation of more complex graphs, but nevertheless remain recognizable because of their fluency and the presence of sufficient details that remain consistent. Others, however, are more difficult to identify, and may represent the work of less practised scribes. The early Salisbury books thus provide good evidence that scriptoria do not necessarily produce distinctive palaeographical symptoms, and that, as N. R. Ker demonstrated in his pioneering article on these books, scribal identification and patterns of collaboration are the only secure palaeographical means of localizing and dating.[10]

Despite the highly personal character of the scribes' handwriting, their activity was subject to some direction, especially during the first phase of production. One scribe corrected over 30 of the surviving Group I books, in most instances by checking against the original exemplar, but in one with reference to a second copy. In addition, in eight books he appears to have been responsible for determining the layout, by writing the first few lines of the opening text (in five books or booklets this was his only contribution).[11] Each group shared common ruling practices in all but the lowest grade of books: the late eleventh-century books are ruled with double vertical bounding lines, and with the first two and last two horizontals extended into the margins; the later groups modified this practice by extending the first and third and third last and last horizontals.[12]

More striking evidence of a coherence of approach and deliberate planning is provided by the contents of the books. As elsewhere in England and the Continent at this period, they reflect a special concern with the writings of the Church Fathers, but there is particularly close correspondence with the guidance represented by a corpus of bio-bibliographical texts recording the authentic writings of the orthodox Fathers and those texts most helpful for biblical study (including Augustine's *Retractationes* and the first book of Cassiodorus's *Institutiones*). The corpus was brought together in the Carolingian period, and the imported exemplar that lay behind its circulation in post-Conquest England is a ninth-century Continental manuscript, now Hereford Cathedral, MS O.iii.2.[13] A copy was made directly from this exemplar at Salisbury in the late eleventh century, and the Salisbury books constitute the earliest and arguably the most comprehensive English response to these lists and recommendations. Among the surviving books are 34 of the works listed by Augustine and 31 recommended by Cassiodorus.[14]

The common purpose and communal effort that produced the early books of Salisbury accord with the reassessment of the documentary evidence concerning the cathedral community there, which, as Diana Greenway has demonstrated, led a largely common life, centered around Bishop Osmund (1078–99) and his *clerici*, whom, William of Malmesbury reported, Osmund had attracted from far and wide.[15] Since William also records Osmund himself "not disdaining to copy and bind books," it is likely that other members of the community were involved as scribes.

So comprehensive and collaborative an approach toward book provision appears to have diminished after the early twelfth century, as the community itself began to change. Through a process begun before the end of the episcopacy of Roger Poer (1102/7–39), and complete by the end of the twelfth century, the cathedral community lost much of its communal practice of life with the gradual establishment of individual prebends for the canons, and the introduction of vicars and temporary residency.[16]

This coincided with, and doubtless reinforced, changing practices of book provision. Evidence for in-house production is scant after the first quarter of the century. The surviving books suggest that churchmen, and especially those who were active scholars and pastors, became reliant upon personal book collections rather than communal provision. The emphasis in episcopal and capitular acts is upon repair and correction rather than upon what a modern librarian would call "collection development." Until the early thirteenth century, the bishop could assign revenues (comprising a virgate of land) for such custodianship to whomsoever he chose, but for much of the thirteenth and fourteenth centuries, responsibility lay with the chancellor.[17] From the early thirteenth century, the chancellor also had responsibility for delivering himself or making provision for lectures in theology, and during the mid-thirteenth century, Salisbury become an important center for the teaching of theology.[18] It is impossible, however, to demonstrate whether there was any planned institutional provision of books to support those teaching or studying there. The lectures had to be reinvigorated in the fifteenth century, at the same time as attention was given to the care of books, the two needs being addressed together by a decision taken by the chapter in 1445 to construct a library room for the safe-keeping and consultation of books, incorporating space at the north end for the theology lectures.[19] Although the initiative seems to have prompted a flurry of bequests (mostly small-scale), there is no evidence of any program of acquisition. Only one clear instance of commissioning in response to perceived need is known from medieval Salisbury: in 1389, following a complaint made in chapter that the cathedral had no chronicle, the grammar school master was ordered by the chancellor to make one.[20]

Inscriptions in several of the books and evidence from wills suggest that at Salisbury, as elsewhere, the institutional book collections grew largely through donation, in particular, bequests from canons.[21] Acquisition by donation was necessarily ad hoc, reflecting the means, interests, and decisions of the donors rather than a response to perceived need (although, as in academic institutions, there was inevitably a close correspondence between the interests of former members and those of the community). The earliest known examples from Salisbury date from the late twelfth century, and come from two canons, Robert de Bellofago and Gregory, who gave, respectively, a copy of Peter Comestor's *Historia scholastica* and a glossed copy of John's Gospel.[22] The texts suggest a connection with the schools, a connection reinforced in Robert's case by Gerald of Wales describing him as "magister." The principal component of the donations of the thirteenth and fourteenth centuries remained the textbooks, commentaries, and reference works of higher learning. Three successive chancellors, all university-educated, donated such works: Master Simon de Micham gave a copy of Alexander of Hailes on the *Sentences*; Ralph of York II six (and perhaps nine) glossed books of the Bible, and Henry de la Wyle another four glossed books of the Bible and Aquinas's *Summa theologica* (among other items).[23]

Canons, however, were under no obligation to bequeath their books. Some were pluralists, holding canonries in other cathedrals, and many had connections with academic institutions to which, to judge from the surviving evidence, they appear to have felt a heavier obligation. Wyle's will records the bequest of several books of theology to Merton College, his philosophy books to Balliol, and other books to one Thomas de Bockton.[24] Richard Andrew, who held a succession of prebends between 1441 and 1454, gave a copy of Luke and John with commentaries to the cathedral, but, as the first warden of New College, his closest associations were with Oxford, and he bequeathed 13 volumes to New College and several more to All Souls.[25] William Loring, a residentiary canon at Salisbury at the turn of the fourteenth and fifteenth centuries, amassed a large personal collection of books but appears to have given none of them to the cathedral, instead leaving his volumes of civil law to Cambridge University Library and some of his theological books to Merton College, Oxford, stipulating that the others should be sold by his executors to provide funds for Merton scholars.[26] Erased inscriptions in 2 of the 14 or 15 books donated by Thomas Cyrcetur (a canon from 1431–1453), the largest single bequest surviving from Salisbury, indicate that these (Salisbury Cathedral, MSS 36 and 81, and perhaps also 167) had once been intended for Lincoln College, Oxford.[27]

A brief inscription of donation might give the impression of a straightforward transfer of a book from personal to institutional ownership. Such records, however, may conceal more complex arrangements or even a different history of ownership and use, the circumstances of which can only occasionally be perceived from other, more detailed evidence. It would be reasonable, for example, to speculate that the theological books donated by the chancellors Simon de Micham, Ralph of York, and Henry de la Wyle had originally been procured for their personal use. Nevertheless, Wyle's donation may have included volumes acquired specifically in order to replace books damaged or lost during his term in office, since his will states that he gave certain books "in compensation for books of the church received by me in St Michael's chapel, if the said books have been less well kept, or if by chance some have been lost in my time, which may appear upon examination of receipts and deliveries."[28] Nevertheless, a book in personal ownership could be preassigned subsequent communal ownership long before the owner's death. A detailed inscription in Salisbury Cathedral, MS 153, a Gospel lectionary bequeathed by Bishop Walter Scammel (d. 1286), records a formal ceremony in 1277, in the presence of the precentor, chancellor, subdean, succentor, and penitentiary, at which use of the book was assigned to Scammel (then dean) in the first instance, and after his death to the canons and vicars of the cathedral.[29] In only one instance, however, that of the fifteenth-century canon, Thomas Cyrcetur, is it possible to demonstrate unequivocally that the books bequeathed represented the gradual accumulations of the donor's own working collection. Several contain annotations and longer passages supplied by Cyrcetur that reflect his theological and pastoral concerns, and others contain partially erased inscriptions specifying originally different beneficiaries.[30]

A second complexity that can be concealed by a simple record of donation is the often murky relationship between temporary possession and permanent ownership. Until the fifteenth century, as in most other English ecclesiastical institutions, books were not consulted *in situ* in a library room at Salisbury but were stored in chests and cupboards variously located.[31] The use of the cathedral's books, whether within the precincts or further afield, necessarily involved borrowing. Books in such temporary possession might easily be confused with books in personal ownership, especially by executors. The religious orders stipulated that whilst books might be held by an individual for a specified term for his personal use, ownership remained with the institution; similar provisions were included in the statutes of certain academic institutions, such as Merton College, Oxford.[32] Secular ecclesiastical institutions, where such a principle did not obtain, and in which full ownership of property coexisted with temporary possession, experienced a greater potential for ambiguity and dispute. The issue is neatly illustrated by a series of inscriptions in Salisbury Cathedral, MS 85, a copy of Peter Comestor's *Historia scholastica*.[33] The first comprises a Salisbury *ex libris* and a request for prayer for the soul of Richard Praty, former bishop of Chichester (1438–45), from which one might infer that Richard had some role in donating the book. Another inscription might appear to confirm this, since it states that the book was bought by Praty's executors for 20 shillings. A third, however, firmly dispels any assumption that Praty had owned the book, since it recalls that the book, recovered by the executor, William Swan, was one that the cathedral chapter of Salisbury had allowed Praty to borrow whilst he was chancellor there, together with a copy of Rabanus's *De natura rerum*, also recovered by Swan. A fourth inscription, which, taken on its own, might also mislead, records the book as Swan's benefaction. The recoverable history of this book may help to explain how one of the books produced at (and presumably for) the cathedral in the early twelfth century, Salisbury Cathedral, MS 11, came to be recorded among the books donated by the chancellor Ralph of York II: either the book had come to be regarded as his personal property or he had been responsible in some way for its recovery (or perhaps repair).[34] Still opaque, however, are the circumstances lying behind the transfer of six books in chapter in 1395 from one prebendary, John Turk, to another, Robert Croucheston, including a register of the books kept in the treasury.[35]

The introduction of a library room in the mid-fifteenth century gave physical expression to a communal collection of books as a discrete entity, although we do not know what proportion of the cathedral's books were housed there. Perhaps out of awareness of the potential for books to stray, individual donors who sought spiritual benefit of prayers in return for their gift, took advantage of the additional security afforded by the more permanent library room to stipulate that some or all of their bequests should be not only located but also chained there. Inscriptions in two of Cyrcetur's books (Salisbury Cathedral, MSS 40 and 55) state that these were to be chained in the new library.[36] Earlier donors could only rely upon the diligence of the person charged with the custody of the books, or upon the religious sanction of an anathema, as did the late twelfth- or early thirteenth-century canon Gregory, when seeking prayers for the souls of his father and brother through the gift of Salisbury Cathedral, MS 41.[37] Until at least the fifteenth century, at Salisbury, as elsewhere, the term "library" must encompass something not only less physically discrete but also less stable than its current meaning.[38]

Notes

1. Ker (1964, 171–6); Watson (1987, 60–1).
2. Ker (1959).
3. Webber (1992).
4. Sharpe and Webber (2009); I am grateful to Michael Gullick for drawing my attention to the presence of Group I scribe iii in Sloane 1122.
5. Webber (1989).
6. Webber (1992, 8–30).
7. Ker (1960); Thomson (2006).
8. Webber (2008).
9. Webber (2012, 218).
10. Ker (1976).
11. Webber (1992, 12).
12. Webber (1992, 19–20, 27).
13. Mynors (1937, xv–xvi, xxxix–xlix).
14. Webber (1992, 31–43).
15. Greenway (1991, xxii–xxiv), (1985); Winterbottom and Thomson (2007, vol. 1, 288–9, i.e., book ii. 83, 11–12).
16. Greenway (1991, xxiv–xxxv).
17. Kemp (1999, no. 130); Kemp (2000, no. 358); Edwards (1967, 212–13).
18. Edwards (1967, 191–2, 197–9).
19. Edwards (1967, 201–2); Clark (1901, 115).
20. Edwards (1967, 214).
21. Ker (1964, 303) and (1987, 108–9).
22. Salisbury Cathedral, MSS 42 and 41: Thompson and Lakin (1880, 10). For Robert and for a revised dating for Gregory, see Greenway (1991, 77, 44, and cf. 41 on John the succentor).
23. Ker (1964, 303), listing manuscripts; full details in Thompson and Lakin (1880).
24. Emden (1957, vol. 1, 565–6).
25. Emden (1957, vol. 1, 34–5).
26. Emden, (1957, vol. 2, 1163).
27. Thompson and Lakin (1880, 9, 17, 33); Ball (1986, 210 n. 29).
28. Edwards (1967, 213).
29. Thompson and Lakin (1880, 30).
30. Ball (1986).
31. Gameson (2006).
32. Lucas (2006, 247–9); Lovatt (2006, 156).
33. Thompson and Lakin (1880, 18).
34. Thompson and Lakin (1880, 5).
35. Salisbury Cathedral, Cathedral Muniments, Press II, Chapter Act Book Holmes, p. 29: see Ramsay and Willoughby (forthcoming). I am grateful to Dr. Willoughby for this reference.
36. Thompson and Lakin (1880, 10 and 13).
37. Thompson and Lakin (1880, 10); on Gregory, see also above, n. 22.
38. Leedham-Green and Webber (2006, 1–3).

BIBLIOGRAPHY

Ball, R. M. 1986. "Thomas Cyrcetur, a Fifteenth-Century Theologian and Preacher." *Journal of Ecclesiastical History* 37: 205–39.

Clark, J. W. 1901. *The Care of Books*. Cambridge: Cambridge University Press.

Edwards, K. 1967. *The English Secular Cathedrals in the Middle Ages*. 2nd ed. Manchester: Manchester University Press.

Emden, A. B. 1957–59. *A Biographical Register of the University of Oxford to A.D. 1500*, 3 vols. Oxford: Oxford University Press.

Gameson, R. 2006. "The Medieval Library (to *c.* 1450)." In *The Cambridge History of Libraries in Britain and Ireland, Volume 1: to 1640*, ed. E. Leedham-Green and T. Webber, 13–50. Cambridge: Cambridge University Press.

Greenway, D. 1985. "The False *Institutio* of St Osmund." In *Tradition and Change: Essays in Honour of Marjorie Chibnall*, ed. D. Greenway, C. Holdsworth, and J. Sayers, 77–101. Cambridge: Cambridge University Press.

Greenway, D. 1991. *John le Neve, Fasti Ecclesiae Anglicanae 1066–1300, IV. Salisbury*. London: University of London, Institute of Historical Research.

Kemp, B. R., ed. 1999. *English Episcopal Acta 18: Salisbury 1078–1217*. Oxford: British Academy.

Kemp, B. R., ed. 2000. *English Episcopal Acta 19: Salisbury 1217–1228*. Oxford: British Academy.

Ker, N. R. 1959. "Three Old English Texts in a Salisbury Pontifical, Cotton Tiberius C I." In *The Anglo-Saxons: Studies in Some Aspects of their History and Culture presented to Bruce Dickins*, ed. P. Clemoes, 262–79. London: Bowes & Bowes.

Ker, N. R. 1960. *English Manuscripts in the Century after the Norman Conquest*. Oxford: Oxford University Press.

Ker, N. R. 1964. *Medieval Libraries of Great Britain: A List of Surviving Books*, 2nd ed. London: Royal Historical Society.

Ker, N. R. 1976. "The Beginnings of Salisbury Cathedral Library." In *Medieval Learning and Literature: Essays presented to Richard William Hunt*, ed. J. J. G. Alexander and M. T. Gibson, 23–49. Oxford: Oxford University Press.

Ker, N. R. 1987 *Medieval Libraries of Great Britain: A List of Surviving Books. Supplement to the 2nd edition*, ed. Andrew G. Watson London: Royal Historical Society.

Leedham-Green, E. and T. Webber. 2006. "Introduction." In *The Cambridge History of Libraries in Britain and Ireland, Volume 1: to 1640*, ed. E. Leedham-Green and T. Webber, 1–10. Cambridge: Cambridge University Press.

Lovatt, R. 2006. "College and University Book Collections and Libraries." In *The Cambridge History of Libraries in Britain and Ireland, Volume 1: to 1640*, ed. E. Leedham-Green and T. Webber, 152–77. Cambridge: Cambridge University Press.

Lucas, P. J. 2006. "Borrowing and Reference: Access to Libraries in the Late Middle Ages." In *The Cambridge History of Libraries in Britain and Ireland, Volume 1: to 1640*, ed. E. Leedham-Green and T. Webber, 242–62. Cambridge: Cambridge University Press.

Mynors, R. A. B., ed. 1937. *Cassiodori Senatoris Institutiones*. Oxford: Oxford University Press.

Ramsay, N. L. and J. M. W. Willoughby, eds. Forthcoming. *The Libraries of the Secular Cathedrals of England and Wales* (Corpus of British Medieval Library Catalogues). London: British Library.

Sharpe, R. and T. Webber. 2009. "Four Early Booklets of Anselm's Works from Salisbury Cathedral: Cambridge, Trinity College, MS B. 1. 37." *Scriptorium* 63: 58–72.

Thompson, E. M. and S. M. Lakin. 1880. *A Catalogue of the Library of the Cathedral Church of Salisbury*. London: Spottiswoode & Co.

Thomson, R. M. 2006. *Books and Learning in Twelfth-Century England: The End of "Alter Orbis."* Walkern, Hertfordshire: Red Gull Press.

Watson, A. G., ed. 1987. *Medieval Libraries of Great Britain, a List of Surviving Books: Supplement to the Second Edition*. London: Royal Historical Society.

Webber, T. 1989. "Salisbury and the Exon Domesday: Some Observations Concerning the Origin of Exeter Cathedral MS 3500." *English Manuscript Studies 1100–1700* 1: 1–18.

Webber, T. 1992. *Scribes and Scholars at Salisbury Cathedral c. 1075–c. 1125*. Oxford: Oxford University Press.

Webber, T. 2008 [2007]. "L'Écriture des documents en Angleterre au xiie siècle." *Bibliothèque de l'École des Chartes* 165: 139–65.

Webber, T. 2012. "The Norman Conquest and Handwriting in England to 1100." In *The Cambridge History of the Book in Britain, I: c. 600–1100*, ed. R. Gameson, 211–24, Cambridge: Cambridge University Press.

Winterbottom, M. and R. M. Thomson, eds. 2007. William of Malmesbury, *Gesta pontificum Anglorum: The History of the English Bishops*, 2 vols. Oxford: Oxford University Press.

CHAPTER 54

MANUSCRIPT PRODUCTION IN FLORENCE

XAVIER VAN BINNEBEKE

In the fifteenth century Florence became the principal center of manuscript production in the Latin West. Codices in humanistic script (*litterae antiquae*) conceived by the members of the city's intellectual elite began conquering the domestic market around 1400. Generally containing classics, patristic literature, or humanist compositions they soon acquired renown. By mid-century their innovative script, clear structure, content, and distinctive white vine-stem decoration (*a bianchi girari*—consisting of gracefully meandering branches developing into tendril shoots and buds on particolored grounds), circulated widely in Italy and, subsequently, Europe.

Four scholars in particular have studied this development: Albert Derolez's analyses of the humanist book demonstrated Florence's leading role on the Italian peninsula, and gave a detailed account of the codicological specificities of its products (Derolez 1984). Annarosa Garzelli discussed the development of Florentine Quattrocento illumination in a joint publication with Albinia de la Mare, who in turn compiled a catalogue of 106 Florentine scribes, focusing much of her work on the city's famous bookseller Vespasiano da Bisticci (1422–98) (Garzelli 1985; de la Mare 1985, 1996). Taking up leads formulated by Berthold Ullman in the 1960s and 1970s, de la Mare had, moreover, already examined the late fourteenth- and early fifteenth-century developments of the humanist book, its script, and intellectual background, in several groundbreaking contributions (esp. Ullman 1960, 1972; de la Mare 1973, 1977; cf. de la Mare 1997–2000; De Robertis 2016, 55–56). Continuing philological attention to *recentiores* has, finally, led to an increased understanding of textual transmission within the Florentine Quattrocento, certainly one of the most vibrant scholarly meeting grounds in Italy and Europe (Rizzo 1995; Oakley 2016).

Our understanding of the earlier periods in Florentine history of manuscript manu-facture is, on the contrary, far less comprehensive. Although partly due to insufficient and at times rather impenetrable research, manuscript evidence is, admittedly, scanty. Indeed, up to mid-eleventh century most Tuscan libraries appear to have been poorly stocked compared to their northern European counterparts (Bischoff 1966–81, 3. 70; cf. Gorman 2002): Florence's cathedral clergy probably could not assemble their service books, and manuscripts had to be acquired from other, possibly even non-Italian centers (Tacconi 2005, 12–14, and cf. 25). During the Gregorian reform (from c.1050) and with Peter Damian (1007–72) as guide, production of biblica, patristica, and liturgica grew sharply, initially in the Roman-Umbrian and Cassinese region, but subsequently also in Tuscany (cf. Maniaci and Orofino 2000, 27–37; Gorman 2002, 276–7).

Art historians have proposed chrono-geographical classifications of Tuscan illuminated manuscripts up to c.1200 relying on stylistic developments (in particular of geometric initials), hagiographical content, and (often later) medieval provenance (Garrison 1953–62; Berg 1968). Textual evidence is generally overlooked; palaeographical and codicological analyses are rather inadequate and unsystematic. Several centers of activity are named, including Florence, but identifications of its products are not fully convincing. A case in point is the Corbolinus Bible, AD 1140 (MS 1), said by Berg to have been produced by a Florentine workshop that issued some 15 manuscripts. However, not one contains sufficient evidence for such clear-cut localization. It has recently been suggested that another celebrated Bible was presumably made for the Florentine see (MSS 2–3). But here again attribution of its manufacture to local artisans cannot be substantiated. It is also significant that manuscripts of Camaldolese, or for that matter Vallombrosan pedigree are not uniformly illuminated (Berg 1968, 216). Such is the stylistic diversity that several (inner-city) workshops or itinerant artists may have been involved. But one cannot be sure: there exists an almost total lack of reliable research regarding twelfth-century scriptoria (Frioli 1999, esp. 513 and 554; Gorman 2002, 277). A persistent difficulty for students of this period's manuscripts is, moreover, the absence of subsequent early thirteenth-century volumes of Florentine provenance. Florence could not boast a university and consequently lacked intellectual attraction and the need to innovate. Relatively certain books, mostly liturgical, are known only from the last quarter of the century (Labriola 2004): an unbroken stylistic development is yet to be demonstrated.

The fourteenth century proves more generous. During the first half, for instance, the illuminator Pacino di Bonaguida headed a flourishing workshop (Bollati 2004, 841–3). It continued thirteenth-century practices but was also influenced by pictorial innovations in contemporary Florentine painting. Furthermore, while continual contacts between the cities of the Arno valley proved fecund (Pasut 2006), some Florentine illuminators made headway in more distant centers: the Master of the Codex of Saint George, who worked for the *badia* of Settimo near Florence in 1315–19, was to move on to the papal residence at Avignon from 1309 to 1378 (Bollati 2004, 498–9).

Petrarch (Francesco Petrarca, 1304–74), son of a Florentine exile, spent considerable time in Avignon (de la Mare 1973, 1–16; Feo 2003). As cultural leader of his day, he substantially influenced the circulation of books, their outward features, and reading

and writing practices. This is illustrated by his praise for a Central Italian Augustine of
c.1100 (MS 4) and his criticism of contemporary book hands, but above all by the many
volumes containing venerable texts discovered and handled by him in France, Belgium,
and Italy; works he restored, annotated, and that are often at the heart of Italo-French,
fourteenth-century vulgate traditions (Rizzo 1995, 372–5). What is more, these same
cherished volumes appear center stage when debating the character of his influential
handwriting (Derolez 2003, 119–21, 176).

Several Florentines, including Giovanni Boccaccio (1313–75) and Coluccio Salutati
(1332–1406), maintained ties of friendship with Petrarch, securing Florence a steady
provision of (classical) manuscripts (Rizzo 1995, 375). Boccaccio—like Petrarch a poet,
scholar, and scribe—also possessed a fine library, including texts from Montecassino
and Ravenna (de la Mare 1973, 17–29; Petoletti 2005). But whereas Boccaccio safe-
guarded his collection for the city, eventually leaving it to the Augustinians of Santo
Spirito, Petrarch's passing put his manuscripts initially out of Florentine reach. In 1375,
however, Salutati became Florentine chancellor. Reaping the benefits of this post, he
assiduously pursued (copies of) Petrarch's volumes.

Salutati's library ultimately consisted of c.800 items (De Robertis, Tanturli, and
Zamponi 2008; van Binnebeke 2009). Identified manuscripts date from the ninth
century onward; some are French or English, but most Italian. A few twelfth-century
ones perhaps came from monasteries in or near Florence, and many were produced in
the city during Salutati's lifetime, several in his own *scrittoio* by him or scribes under
his direction. He preferred parchment copies. Though generally modest, some are
finely illuminated, and a handful is possibly decorated by him (MS 5). His correspondence is awash with inquiries concerning manuscripts, urging friends to acquire or
transcribe them, and check readings. This network enabled him to be the first (Florentine) reader of certain classics, most notably Cicero's *Epistolae ad familiares* (MS 6),
and to change classical education in the West by inviting the Byzantine scholar Manuel
Chrysoloras to teach Greek in Florence: he arrived in 1397.

To that very year dates the earliest Florentine book in humanistic script: a Valerius
Maximus written on 19 quaternions ruled in lead point, in a clear, long-line layout
(MS 7). Its white vine-stem initials may, but need not be a later addition (see below).
Salutati and his protégé Poggio Bracciolini (1380–1459) have both been proposed as
the scribe. The latter identification is justly rejected, the former yet to be considered,
even if another attribution to the anonymous professional scribe of Coluccio's late
fourteenth-century Peckham places its manufacture in the chancellor's orbit (MS 8).

The most active promoter of the new book was, undoubtedly, Salutati's friend
Niccolò Niccoli (1364–1437) (de la Mare 1973, 46–61; De Robertis 2006, 119; 2016,
59). His earliest known autograph, a copy of Lactantius on blind ruled paper quinions,
dates to c.1397 and discloses the origins of his *litterae antiquae* (MS 9). In 1400 or
shortly thereafter he assembled the works of several patristic and classical authors using
blind ruled parchment (on the hair side) or paper and adopting for his developed
formal hand long lines within spacious margins (de la Mare 1973, 52–5, 57–9; De
Robertis 2006, 133; 2016, 69). Although their codicological and palaeographical

framework is said to be modeled on eleventh- and twelfth-century, mostly northern European exemplars containing classical texts (de la Mare 1996, 168), the use of quinions, certainly a characteristic of Florentine humanistic manuscripts, is possibly linked to fourteenth-century developments (Casagrande Mazzoli and Ornato 1999, 217).

Niccoli's collaborator was Poggio, a gifted calligrapher and particularly known for his cisalpine discoveries of new exemplars during the next decades (de la Mare 1973, 62–84; Rizzo 1995, 376, 395). Niccoli was often among the first to scrutinize these northern treasures, transcribing them on paper in a rapid humanistic cursive developed by him long before such script became a respected private and commercial book hand in c.1460 (Ullman 1960, 59–77; de la Mare 1973, 50–2, 56; 1985, 444–8; cf. also Böninger 2016; Gentile 2016). At his death he left his extensive collections to form the core of the San Marco library in Florence (Ullman and Stadter 1972; Petitmengin and Ciccolini 2005, 345–51; van Binnebeke 2010–11). They thus remained instrumental to Florentine textual research and manuscript production.

While there is little doubt about Niccoli's technical ability and stimulating attitude, the recent suggestion that he was involved in the creation of Florentine bindings of Islamic inspiration (Hobson 1989, 19) remains unproven. So too the idea that he introduced and possibly even invented the humanistic white vine-stem decoration (de la Mare 1973, 49–50; 1996, 168 n. 7; Ceccanti 1996). True, in a frequently cited letter to Niccoli (AD 1407) Leonardo Bruni (1370–1444) clearly alludes to his friend's active involvement and the early initials do often look homemade. Moreover, the first, certainly original dated specimens appear in a volume (AD 1404) by Luigi Guidi, a humanistic scribe and notary who was his acquaintance (MSS 10–11). Bruni is even less ambiguous about the required approach "vetusto more," effectively equivalent to the colorful but austere style of patristic and biblical eleventh- or twelfth-century models from Tuscany reflected in humanistic ornamentation (de la Mare 1996, 168). Although Niccoli certainly possessed such old books, it is disconcerting that his earliest copies lack both initials and (rubricated) capital headings (De Robertis 2006, n. 24). Moreover, by 1395 bare vine-stem ornamentation had been introduced in an antiphonary written in and for the Camaldolese monastery of Santa Maria degli Angeli in Florence (MS 12). The manuscript's principal illuminator, Lorenzo Monaco, worked in the typical manner of the *Scuola degli Angeli*, a Gothic figure and acanthus style present in numerous Florentine manuscripts of c.1370–1440 (Bollati 2004, 399–401). The liturgical handwriting is, in contrast, embellished with expertly designed vine stems in ink, occasionally set against crosshatched backgrounds colored in yellow wash: scribal intervention is likely. Bicolored penwork initials show comparable approaches, while some subsequent Florentine service books even comprise genuine white vine-stem initials (MSS 13–15). In view of these developments current theories regarding the origin and invention of humanistic decoration are not truly satisfactory.

White vine-stem initials of the first quarter of the century have attracted little attention stylistically (Ceccanti 1996. Cf. De Robertis 2006, 116 n. 17). First, it is worth observing that a wider variety of manuscripts than hitherto acknowledged is concerned: In addition to the humanistic book, certainly their most common vehicle, and antiphonaries, examples can be found in a few vernacular and liturgical codices in humanistic hands (e.g. MS 16; Pächt and Alexander 1966–73, 2 no. 216; De Robertis 2006, 114 and n. 14), classics written in (semi-)Gothic book hands (e.g. MSS 17, 33; de la Mare 1973, 128 no. 46), and early medieval volumes apparently completed in this period (MSS 18–19). Moreover, several styles may be preserved in manuscripts copied out by one humanistic scribe, or, conversely, similarly fashioned initials in apparently unrelated volumes (Plate 54.1; MSS 20–1; Pächt and Alexander 1966–73, 2. no. 214; van Binnebeke 2001, n. 33).

The earliest recorded payments to named artisans for the execution of the ornamentation in manuscripts still extant date to 1422–3; one refers explicitly to "lettere antiche in mino" (van Binnebeke 2001, 221; Levi D'Ancona 2003, 18). Creditors were the companion *cartolai* (stationers) Michele Guarducci and Piero Tornaquinci, but the work may have been done by subcontracted illuminators, apparently the normal practice. The manuscripts in question are the dedication copy of a translation by Leonardo Bruni to Cosimo de' Medici (1389–1464), the most prominent citizen of Florence, and antiphonary B for Santa Maria Nuova (MSS 14, 22; cf. de la Mare 1985, 400 n. 35). Before this date attribution to artistic personalities remains more difficult. Manuscripts can, however, be grouped.

PLATE 54.1 Monreale, Biblioteca Comunale, XXV F. 10, fol. 1 (detail), Aristotle, *Ethics*, translated by Leonardo Bruni. After 1416–17 (see MS 20).

It has been suggested specialists only took over from Niccoli and fellow scholars at the beginning of the second decade at a time when professional amanuenses first appear on the scene (de la Mare 1973, 50; Ceccanti 1996, 13), but the presence of guide-letters accompanying some earlier initials may indicate otherwise. The first professional humanistic scribe may, furthermore, have been active as early as 1397, the date of the Valerius Maximus. Neither size nor indeed quality of design of the *bianchi girari* in this manuscript ought to come as a surprise considering the vine-stem ornament in the 1395 antiphonary. All things considered, Ceccanti's proposal (1996, 15–16) to concentrate on artisans associated with the Angeli seems fully justified.

The Camaldolese monastery was, indeed, to play an important role in the production of humanistic manuscripts. Salutati upheld close ties with the Angeli and Niccoli became a devoted collaborator of Ambrogio Traversari (1386–1439), acclaimed translator of Greek *patristica* and the congregation's most celebrated son (Ullman 1960, 67–8; Ullman and Stadter 1972, 7; Caby 1999, 602, 606; De Robertis, Tanturli, and Zamponi 2008, 346, nos. 34–5). Traversari was the first humanist exponent of a reform movement that by 1400 had awakened historiographical awareness within the order (Caby 1999, 10 and esp. n. 6); by 1414–15 he had mastered a beautiful formal humanistic hand, as, for example, in a copy of Lactantius produced according to the new format (MS 23).

During the 1430s the monastery's scriptorium issued manuscripts in *litterae antiquae* for Traversari's innumerable contacts, including the *Chronicon* of Montecassino for the Venetian abbot Paolo Venier and a Lactantius for Cosimo embellished with one of the earliest four-sided vine-stem borders (MSS 24–5; cf. 26). Traversari also frequently required from his amanuenses copies of his translations, such as the *Vitae philosophorum* by Diogenes Laertius. The script hierarchy of titles, running headings, incipits, and explicits in this work's dedication copy, again made for Cosimo, imitates twelfth-century models (MS 27). Thus, yet another component enhancing the clarity and functionality of the format *all'antica* became fully codified. Although comparison with the actual models is impossible simply because certain material evidence is lacking, Traversari's correspondence is an invaluable source concerning the availability to the scriptorium of early codices and concerning venerable exemplars that reached the congregation from *extra muros*. A copy of the *Vita beati Romualdi* (MS 28) of Peter Damian, the founder of the order, provides a valuable insight not only into the circulation of such exemplars, but also into the dissemination of ideas of the Camaldolese reform, and the seminal—if in this particular instance measured—influence of the scriptorium's humanistic manuscript production.

The *badia fiorentina*, the city's oldest monastery (*c.*970), was also involved in manuscript production. Evidence for a library or scriptorium is lacking for the first centuries of its existence, but from at least 1209 it rented out workshops, and by the end of the fourteenth century *cartolai*, illuminators, binders, and notaries, often acting as scribes, had clustered around the monastery. Scores of surviving documents attest to their wide-ranging activities (Bernacchioni 2002, 262, n. 15). A breviary presumably produced by them even offers a genuine novelty, as it preserves the earliest known European gold-tooled binding (*c.*1400) (MS 29).

The shop area became the humanists' meeting place, in particular the *bottega* of Guarducci and Tornaquinci (van Binnebeke 2001). They sold Gothic codices, classical texts, and contemporary works, and Niccoli, Poggio, Sozomeno (MS 30), and the early Florentine scribe Spina Azzolini (de la Mare 1977, 100–1) were among their customers. Between 1422 and 1425/26 Cosimo and Lorenzo de' Medici enjoyed their services, which included the binding of various volumes and the illumination of works by Bruni (MS 22) and Traversari.

Cosimo's bibliophily, emulated by his sons Piero and Giovanni, and his grandson Lorenzo, evolved under the aegis of humanism: Niccoli advised him, and he was dedicatee of many humanist authors (de la Mare 1992, 127–38, 147–9; 1996, 169). In 1417 his library held about 65 manuscripts, including volumes from Salutati's collection and classical and humanistic novelties copied by Giovanni Aretino, the first really prolific professional humanistic scribe (de la Mare 1985, 397, 425, App. I, 71; 1992, 120–1, n. 29, 128–9; 1996, n. 8). The 1420s, and the early 1430s, were especially rewarding. The German Johannes de Colonia transcribed four manuscripts for Cosimo (de la Mare 1996, n. 11), the Genoese humanist Giacomo Curlo three (de la Mare 2000a, 61–2, 88, App. B. 1–2.), the Florentine notary Antonio di Mario (d.1461) significantly more (de la Mare 1996, n. 35; MSS 31–2). The manuscripts' vine-stem decoration became more colorful and animals and putti were introduced, presumably in imitation of Gothic illumination (de la Mare 1996, 169; MS 31). In 1425–6 he bought Cicero's *Epistolae ad familiares* from Benedetto Strozzi, a member of another illustrious family of collectors (MS 32). Why Benedetto sold the attractive humanistic codex remains unclear, but further examination of Strozzi manuscripts may yield results. Palla Strozzi (1372–1462), undoubtedly the wealthiest Florentine scholar, owned, for instance, about 90 Greek and 240 Latin manuscripts in 1431 (De Gregorio 2002, 109–22). Few of the latter survive, but two are certainly Florentine: a remarkable Cicero, *Epistolae ad familiares*, in a weighty Gothic hand, two columns of 36 dry ruled lines, and with early vine-stem initials (MS 33), and Seneca's *Tragedies* displaying a—for this text—not unusual combination of Gothic script and acanthus decoration (MS 34). Due to rivalry with Cosimo, Palla was exiled from Florence in 1434.

In truth, Cosimo's influence on book culture cannot be underestimated. Backed by his family's rule Florence hosted the curia (1434–6) and the Council of the Reunion (1439–43): seculars and churchmen from all over Europe gathered in the city, stimulating growth of its book market and the spread of humanism (de la Mare 1996). At the same time Cosimo began to direct his bibliophilic patronage toward new libraries at Bosco ai Frati, which has largely escaped scholarly attention, and San Marco (Ullman and Stadter 1972). In these undertakings he could rely on the expertise of the bookseller and biographer of *uomini illustri* Vespasiano da Bisticci.

Books acquired during the Council by the English intellectual Andrew Holes (d.1470) illustrate the market's possibilities and range from canon law to classical oratory, from scholastic theology to humanist epistolography (de la Mare 1996, 175–6). They include volumes from Salutati's library and works in contemporary

PLATE 54.2 Oxford, Bodleian Library, Bodl. 339, fol. 3 (detail), *Somnium viridarii*. Written in 1439 by Io(hannes) Baert and illuminated by Bartolomeo Varnucci. Arms of Andrew Holes.

Florentine Gothic hands decorated with acanthus initials or flower and penscroll illumination (Plate 54.2). Humanistic manuscripts are represented by a Lactantius annotated by the humanist lawyer Guglielmino Tanaglia and a Cicero and a Jerome possibly produced by Vespasiano.

The latter, who apprenticed to the resourceful Guarducci (de la Mare 2000b, 167) and by 1434 had become his assistant, and from 1450 his partner, made his first independent sales during the Council (de la Mare 1985, 401–6, and App. III for much of the following; 1996). Among his earliest clients was Tommaso Parentucelli, later Pope Nicholas V (el.1447). At Cosimo's request Tommaso composed a bibliographic canon for the San Marco library, thus identifying texts lacking in Niccoli's legacy. Guarducci traveled to Siena and Vespasiano to Lucca to obtain these works secondhand; some are still extant (Ullman and Stadter 1972, 16–19; de la Mare 1992, 135–6; 1996, 177).

Manuscripts certainly assembled or sold by Vespasiano are identifiable from documents, autograph guide headings, or *notabilia*, notes of acquisition, or because scribes referred to their work "sub" or "procurante Vespasiano". Several volumes bear his shop inscriptions, and these were invariably for non-Italians. One contains a translation of Chrysostom by Traversari that Vespasiano "fecit transcribi ex originali" by his notary Leonardo da Colle (MS 35; for Leonardo: de la Mare 1985, 435, App. I, 40; 1996, 185).

The French bishop and cardinal Jean Jouffroy, his client since 1446, probably acquired the volume. At the Council of Mantua (1459) he bought another two Vespasiano volumes, testimonies to the bookseller's dealings outside Florence (cf. de la Mare 1996, 201), and shortly afterward the prelate had him prepare several deluxe manuscripts for his king Louis XI (Desachy and Toscano 2010, 114–16, nos. 15, 17). Other foreigners frequenting Vespasiano's shop were the Spanish bishop Juan Margarit, the German scholar Johannes Tröster, and William Gray and Robert Flemmyng from England: All owned various manuscripts produced in Florence (de la Mare 1985, App. I, 28[25–6], 44[11], 49[30], 72[1], 96[11], 83[5]; 1996, 177–80, 201–3).

Overall, Vespasiano's Italian commissions were more numerous. In 1454–5 King Alfonso of Naples paid him for a set of Livy illuminated by Francesco del Chierico. It has the earliest datable humanistic title pages, apparently modeled on a Romanesque exemplar restored by Vespasiano in 1448 (de la Mare 1996, 188, fig. 16, nn. 46, 71; Bollati 2004, 228–32).

He also worked for Piero and Giovanni de' Medici (MSS 36–7) and was commissioned by their father to provide a new library for the *badia fiesolana* (*c.*1461) (Derolez 1984, 2. nos. 258–60; de la Mare 1985, 440–4, App. II; 1996, 190–2). Zanobi di Mariano (de la Mare 1985, 406–7; cf. App. II. i and ii; Levi D'Ancona 2003, 139–44), the monastery's usual *cartolaio*, could not match Vespasiano's organizing skills and Cosimo's man temporarily replaced him, supplying some manuscripts secondhand, but many more *ex novo*. He directed at least 38 scribes and six illuminators and Parentucelli's canon was again his manual. Text typology guided decisions on outward features. Scholastic works present, for instance, "uno principio a 3 facie" in acanthus or flower-scroll style with "una lettera d'oro" (inscr. in Fies. 94, fol. 195[v]) and are copied in Gothic script in two columns. Longer patristic texts are laid out similarly but exhibit (semi-)humanistic handwriting and vine-stem decoration. Manuscripts were foliated and often not ruled in Carolingian styled blind ruling but in ink, more commonly used in Florentine manuscripts than has generally been acknowledged (Derolez 1984, 1. 81; Casagrande Mazzoli and Ornato 1999, 262–4).

The Florentine market was still in full swing during the later 1460s and 1470s. In 1468 Vespasiano prepared several manuscripts for Monte Oliveto Maggiore (e.g., MS 38), apparently as subcontractor to his older colleague Francesco di Neri, who coordinated the bulk of the monastery's commission (de la Mare 1985, 407, App. I, 53[8]; Murano 1993, 230). Sometime earlier he had embarked upon his last grand commission, much vaster in scale than anything done before: a library for Federico da Montefeltro (de la Mare 1985, 448–51, App. III, 20–1, 57–60; 1996, 192–200). Although it included manuscripts from other centers (cf. Derolez 1984, 2. nos. 919–89), the majority came from Vespasiano, initially out of his stock, but subsequently by staging a sector-wide effort. He contracted over 50 scribes, some incredibly productive, and various illuminators, including his shop master of the "pear-shaped putti" and Francesco Rosselli (Bollati 2004, 914–16), between them responsible for more than 150 volumes. The *Urbinati* bear similarities to the *Fiesolani*, but are more elaborate, often with circular title pages. Scholastic texts are usually in (semi-) humanistic handwriting and after *c.*1472 vine stems make way for flower borders; monumental title pages are at times introduced, probably following the Paduan example. The *chef-d'œuvre* of the collection and Vespasiano's last tour de force is Federico's Bible transcribed by Hugo de Comminellis AD 1478, "Vespasiano…procurante." Francesco del Chierico is the principal illuminator. The set is one of the great achievements of Florentine Quattrocento Bible production, a comparatively neglected field of research (cf. *infra*, and Antonio Manfredi in De Robertis, Tanturli, and Zamponi 2008, 224–5), and appears midway between Niccolò Berti's 1452–3 copy (MS 39) and the three volumes for King Matthias Corvinus (d.1490) illuminated by Monte and Gherardo di Giovanni and Attavante (MS 40; Bollati 2004, 258–62, 798–801, 975–9).

This lifelong productivity implies Vespasiano had to secure a large quantity of exemplars. A comprehensive study of their provision and use is lacking (de la Mare 1996, 206–7), but much can be deduced from philological case studies such as Lucia Castaldi's examination of Federico's Bible (Piazzoni 2004–5, 2. 127–205). In assembling the volume, certainly a descendant of the Paris University Bibles, Vespasiano relied on various manuscripts. Rather than turning to the San Marco library which had served Vespasiano excellently on a number of occasions, he may instead have searched for exemplars in Santa Croce, presumably also quite accessible to him (MS 41). The possibility of an intermediate working copy should also be considered. In his shop Vespasiano had access to the so-called Puccini exemplars (Oakley 2016), unpretentious *chartacei* copied in a distinctive humanistic cursive and containing patristic, classical, and contemporary works (Plate 54.3).

At least thirty-nine such manuscripts survive (I owe this information to Stephen Oakley) and among their descendants several were certainly produced by Vespasiano. Although a "Puccini"-Bible has not been identified, comparable paper copies existed in Florence. A "1ª pars bibie bene miniata in papiro et alia in uno volumine et profetia sibille eritre" belonged for instance to the scribe Domenico Pollini (MS 42). Although no proof exists that it ever served Vespasiano as exemplar, it is certain that the bookseller regularly had to rely on his vast network of scribes and scholars to finish and finalize commissions he had taken on, as may be illustrated by the production history of Piero de' Medici's Plutarch (MSS 36–7) or Federico's trilingual Psalter (MS 43). It is worth noting, finally, that printed editions were used as exemplars by Vespasiano and other Florentine bookmen. This happened increasingly from the mid-1470s on (de la Mare 1985, 412–15; 1996, n. 129). If stationers could easily adapt to the new circumstances simply by changing their window display, the new art more seriously affected the livelihood of, in particular, the professional penmen. And although several grand patrons such as King Matthias Corvinus (d. 1490), Lorenzo de' Medici (d. 1492), and King Manuel of Portugal (d. 1521) commissioned lavish manuscripts well into the late 1480s and 1490s, and dedication copies continued to be mostly handwritten, the more common commercial codices, certainly too marginally touched upon in the preceding overview, went into slow and steady decline (Derolez 1984, 1. 21; de la Mare 1985, 466–75; 1996, 188, n. 76; 2000b, 176–81; MSS 44–45). Nonetheless, the fifteenth century had proven one of the most magnificent and prolific periods in the history of Florentine manuscript production.

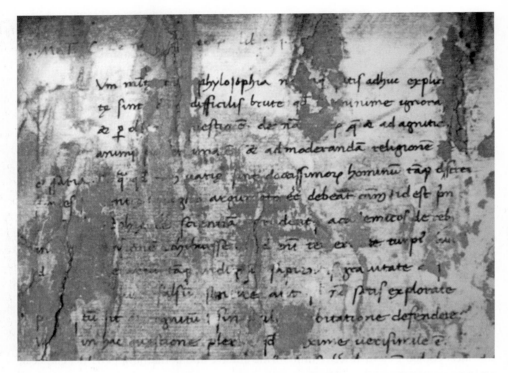

PLATE 54.3 Florence, BML, Plut. 90 sup. 78, fol. 1 (detail), Cicero, *Opera*, beginning with *De natura deorum*. Saec. XV²/⁴. The MS was used as an exemplar by Vespasiano and later belonged to Bernardo Puccini.

ACKNOWLEDGMENTS

Angela Dillon Bussi, Miguel C. Muñoz Feliu, Francesco D'Aiuto, Kate Harris, Antonio Manfredi, Giovanna Murano, Stephen Oakley, Nurit Pasternak, Antonio Rollo, David Rundle, Karl Schlebusch, Jonathan Ungar.

LIST OF MANUSCRIPTS

1. Florence, BML, Conv. Soppr. 630. Signed by Corbolinus Pistoriensis (Berg in Maniaci and Orofino 2000, no. 47; Alidori, Benassai, and Castaldi 2003–6, 1. 101–31). Additional bibliography and references for reproductions of Laurentian manuscripts discussed here are available at http://mss.bmlonline.it/, accessed April 6, 2020.
2–3. Florence, BML, Edili 125–6 (Tacconi 2005, 25, 80–2. Cf. Alidori, Benassai, and Castaldi 2003–6, 2. 10–80).
4. Paris, BnF, lat. 1989/1–2 (Feo 2003, 479; De Robertis 2006, n. 24).
5. Florence, BML, San Marco 165, Boethius (De Robertis, Tanturli, and Zamponi 2008, 351, no. 103).

6. Florence, BML, Plut. 49, 7 (De Robertis, Tanturli, and Zamponi 2008, no. 68).

7. Vatican City, BAV, Pal. lat. 903 (Billanovich 1981; de la Mare 1996, n. 5; De Robertis 2016, 63, 66).

8. Florence, Biblioteca Nazionale Centrale, Conv. Soppr. J. V. 25 (De Robertis, Tanturli, and Zamponi 2008, 349, no. 90).

9. Florence, Biblioteca Riccardiana, 264 (De Robertis 2006, 128–31; 2016, 65).

10. Florence, BML, Plut. 34, 33, Juvenal, Persius (van Binnebeke 2001, 218; 2010–11, 28; De Robertis 2006, 115; 2016, 60–61).

11. Carpentras, Bibliothèque Inguimbertine, ms. 482, Sallust (https://bvmm.irht.cnrs.fr/, accessed April 6, 2020). Scribe: the notary Luigi di ser Michele Guidi. Some notes may effectively be by Niccoli; decoration similar to no. 20.

12. Florence, BML, Cor. 8 (Levi D'Ancona 1994, 39–40, 96, and frontispiece).

13. Douai, Bibliothèque municipale, MS 1171, Antiphonary. Dated 1417. From SS. Annunziata d'Orbatello in Florence. Principal illuminator: Bartolomeo di Fruosino (https://bvmm.irht.cnrs.fr/, accessed April 6, 2020; Bollati 2004, 64–7).

14–15. Florence, Santa Maria Nuova, Antiphonaries B and D. From Santa Maria Nuova. Before 1423. Principal illuminator: Bartolomeo di Fruosino (Levi D'Ancona 2003, figs. 68, 81, 83, 90–1).

16. Florence, Confraternità di Santa Maria della Pietà, s.n., chapters of the confraternity, AD 1413–14. Illuminator: Battista di Biagio Sanguigni (Rolfi, Viti, and Sebregondi 1992, no. 5. 2; Bollati 2004, 67–9).

17. London, BL, Harley 5291, Cicero, *De finibus*, *Acad.* (www.bl.uk, accessed February 12, 2020). From Poggio.

18. Florence, BML, Edili 124, fol. 1, Bible. Saec. XII[1]; cf. Alidori, Benassai, and Castaldi 2003–6, 1. 134. See Plate 54.4.

19. Florence, BML, San Marco 617, Eusebius, Jerome, Gennadius. Saec. XI. The *a bianchi girari* motif (fol. 1) is datable to *c.*1425–35 (van Binnebeke 2001, n. 56; cf. Ullman and Stadter 1972, 117). Annotations by Niccoli and Marsilio Ficino.

20. Florence, BML, Plut. 48, 34, Cicero, *Philippics*. Scribe: Poggio, *c.*1403–8 (de la Mare 1973, 76; cf. nos. 11, 21).

21. Monreale, Biblioteca Comunale, XXV F. 10, Aristotle, *Ethics*, trans. Bruni, with autograph corrections. After 1416–17 (Hankins 2003–4, 235–9). See Figure 55.1.

22. Florence, BML, Plut. 79, 19, Ps.-Aristotle, *Oeconomica*, trans. Bruni (van Binnebeke 2001, 206–8).

23. Florence, Biblioteca Nazionale Centrale, Conv. Soppr. B. IV. 2609 (Pontone 2010, 253–4).

24. Moscow, Rossiiskaia Gosudarstvennaia Biblioteka, Fond 218, N 389, *Chronicon Casinense*; Desiderius, *Dialogi de miraculis S. Benedicti*. Both works revised by Traversari. Scribe: "Nicolaus adolescentus" (Caby 1999, 750 n. 10).

25. Florence, BML, Plut. 21, 5. Scribe: Michele monacus, *c.*1435. Illuminator: Filippo Torelli (de la Mare 1996, 170 n. 12, n. 61; Bollati 2004, 956–8).

26. London, BL, Harley 2648, Juvenal. Scribe: Luigi Guidi, a.1410 (www.bl.uk, accessed February 12, 2020).

27. Florence, BML, Plut. 65, 21. Scribe: Michele monacus, AD 1433 (de la Mare 1992, no. 44).

28. Rome, Biblioteca Vallicelliana, B. 9/1 (https://manus.iccu.sbn.it/opac_viewImmagini Manoscritto.php?ID=16382, accessed April 6, 2020). On paper, two cols., good, formal humanistic hand, Gothic Initials. From Florence, S. Benedetto fuori Porta Pinti, the Angeli's sister house. Saec. XV[2/4], but after 1433, when an ancient copy of the *Vita* was first consulted by Traversari in Faenza (Caby 1999, 750 n. 10).

PLATE 54.4 Florence, BML, Edili 124, fol. 1, Bible. Saec. XII[1]. The *a bianchi girari* initial pictured here is datable to *c.*1410–20. (No. 18 in the List of Manuscripts).

29. Oxford, Bodleian Library, Canon. Liturg. 392, Breviary (Hobson 1989, 24–5).
30. London, BL, Harley 6332, Seneca, *Tragedies* (www.bl.uk, accessed February 12, 2020).
31. Florence, BML, Plut. 45, 32, Seneca, *Letters*. Scribe: Antonio di Mario. Documented by a letter from Niccoli to Cosimo, 1425/26 (de la Mare 1992, no. 42).
32. Florence, BML, Plut. 49, 6. Scribe: Antonio di Mario for Benedetto Strozzi, AD 1420. Guarducci and Tornaquinci acted as middlemen in the sale of the volume (van Binnebeke 2001, 218–19).
33. Warminster, Longleat House, Library of the Marquess of Bath, MS 284ᵃ.
34. Padua, Biblioteca del Seminario, MS 5 (De Robertis and Resta 2004, no. 26). Florentine humanistic manuscripts of the *Tragedies* are rare. Cosimo probably owned one (de la Mare 1992, no. 55; cf. De Robertis and Resta 2004, nos. 24, 27–8).
35. Albi, Bibliothèque municipale, MS 17, Chrysostom, *Adv. vituperatores vitae monasticae* (Desachy and Toscano 2010, 114, no. 11; https://bvmm.irht.cnrs.fr/, accessed April 6, 2020).
36–7. Haarlem, Stadsbibliotheek, 187 C. 9, Plutarch, *Lives* (www.mmdc.nl, accessed February 12, 2020). From Piero. Part of a set with Montpellier, Bibliothèque de la Faculté de Médecine, H. 106 (cf. de la Mare 1996, 183, 188). Scribe: M. Marco Biffoli.
38. London, BL, Add. 14795, Chrysostom, *Homilia in Mattheum*. Two semi-humanistic scribes: Federicus Ray (signed), and the scribe of BML, Fies. 33 (de la Mare 1985, App. II, 24). Vine-stem decoration.
39. San Marino, Huntington Library, HM. 1080, Bible (https://digital-scriptorium.org/, accessed April 6, 2020; de la Mare 1985, App. I, 50¹³). Left in 1459 by the priest Joan Quintá to the monastery of Sant Jeroni de la Murtra in Catalonia.
40. Florence, BML, Plut. 15, 15–17, Bible (Alidori, Benassai, and Castaldi 2003–6, 1. 361–410). Scribe: Alessandro da Verrazzano (cf. de la Mare App. I, 2 and 6⁴⁷). Left unfinished at the death of King Matthias.
41. Vatican City, BAV, Urb. lat. 332, Petrarch, *Rerum memorandum libri*. Scribe: Hugo de Comminellis. A direct copy of Tedaldo Della Casa's BML, S. Croce 26 sin. 9 (Paolo Cherubini in Piazzoni 2004–5, 1. 128–31).
42. Florence, Biblioteca Nazionale Centrale, Magl. VIII, 1282, *Zibaldone* (de la Mare, App. I, 16⁵, and cf. App. II, 87). Pollini listed his books in AD 1454 (fol. 47). His Bible has not yet been identified, but Vatican City, BAV, Barb. lat. 2665 (fols. 1–5ᵛ), on paper, contains the prophecy of the Erithrean Sybil and is signed by him. The revised text by Antonio di Mario referred to in Pollini's colophon is undoubtedly Biblioteca Nazionale Centrale, Magl. VIII, 1503 (fols. 175–83), on paper and signed by Antonio.
43. Vatican City, BAV, Urb. lat. 9. Signed in Hebrew by Aharon ben Gabriel, Florence, AD 1473. The Greek scribe is Iohannes Skutariotes (act. in Florence 1442–c.1494). As exemplar a "Psalterium scriptum in greco, latino et caldeo" may have served, borrowed by Vespasiano from the Certosa in 1472 (Chiarelli 1984, 2. 311 for the document).
44. Genova, Raccolta Durazzo, B. III. 3, Ficino, *Compendium Alcinoi*, etc. Dedicated by Filippo Valori to Lorenzo de' Medici, *ante* February 1492. The script has been attributed to Bartolomeo Paoli (Gentile 2016, 387–93), and to Antonio Migliorotti (unpublished note in Oxford, Bodleian Library, Archive A. C. de la Mare).
45. Florence, BML, Plut. 63, 22, Livy, *Dec.* I. Written by Lorenzo Guidetti in 1464, illuminated by Gherardo di Giovanni, and bound by Zanobi di Mariano. Guidetti, who was unable to sell the fine volume, presented it to Giuliano de' Medici in 1474. For an excellent description see Böninger 2016, 202–6.

BIBLIOGRAPHY

Alidori, L., L. Benassai, and L. Castaldi, eds. 2003–6. *Bibbie minate della Biblioteca Laurenziana di Firenze* (Biblioteche e archivi, 12 and 15). Florence: SISMEL.

Berg, K. 1968. *Studies in Tuscan Twelfth-Century Illumination*. Oslo: Universitetsforlaget.

Bernacchioni, A. 2002. "La bottega di pittura della Badia fiorentina: da Tommaso del Mazza a Masaccio." *Mitteilungen des Kunsthistorischen Institutes Florenz* 46 2/3: 262–9.

Billanovich, G. 1981. "Alle origini della scrittura umanistica. Padova 1261 e Firenze 1397." In *Miscellanea Augusto Campana*, eds. R. Avesani, G. Billanovich, M. Ferrari, and G. Pozzi (Medioevo e Umanesimo, 44 and 45). 2 vols., 1. 125–40. Padua: Antenore.

Bischoff, B. 1966–81. *Mittelalterliche Studien: Ausgewählte Aufsätze zur Schriftkunde und Literaturgeschichte*. 3 vols. Stuttgart: Hiersemann.

Black, R., J. Kraye, and L. Nuvoloni, eds. 2016. *Paleography, Manuscript Illumination and Humanism in Renaissance Italy: Studies in Memory of A.C. de la Mare* (Warburg Institute Colloquia, 28). London: The Warburg Institute.

Bollati, M., ed. 2004. *Dizionario biografico dei miniatori italiani: secoli IX–XVI*. Milan: Sylvestre Bonnard.

Böninger, L. 2016. "The Ricordanze of Lorenzo di Francesco Guidetti: Manuscript Production and Circulation." In Black, Kraye, and Nuvoloni 2016, 199–213.

Caby, C. 1999. *De l'érémitisme rural au monachisme urbain. Les Camaldules en Italie à la fin du moyen âge*. Bibliothèques des Écoles françaises d'Athènes et de Rome, 305. Rome: École française de Rome.

Ceccanti, M. 1996. "Proposte per la storia dei primi codici a bianchi girari." *Miniatura* 5/6: 11–16.

Chiarelli, C. 1984. *Le attività artistiche e il patrimonio librario della Certosa di Firenze (dalle origini alla metà del XVI secolo)* (Analecta cartusiana, 102). 2 vols. Salzburg: Institut für Anglistik und Amerikanistik, Universität Salzburg.

De Gregorio, G. 2002. "L'Erodoto di Palla Strozzi (cod. Vat. Urb. gr. 88)." *Bollettino dei classici* 23: 31–130.

de la Mare, A. C. 1973. *The Handwriting of Italian Humanists, I. 1: Francesco Petrarca, Giovanni Boccaccio, Coluccio Salutati, Niccolò Niccoli, Poggio Bracciolini, Bartolomeo Aragazzi of Montepulciano, Sozomeno da Pistoia, Giorgio Antonio Vespucci*. Oxford: Oxford University Press.

de la Mare, A. C. 1977. "Humanistic Script: The First Ten Years." In *Das Verhältnis der Humanisten zum Buch* (Deutsche Forschungsgemeinschaft, Kommission für Humanismusforschung, Mitteilung, IV), eds. Dieter Wuttke and Fritz Krafft, 89–110. Boppard: Boldt.

de la Mare, A. C. 1985. "New Research on Humanistic Scribes in Florence." In *Miniatura fiorentina del Rinascimento, 1440–1525. Un primo censimento* (Inventari e cataloghi toscani, 18 and 19), ed. Annarosa Garzelli. 2 vols., 1. 393–600. Florence: Giunta Regionale Toscana and La Nuova Italia.

de la Mare, A. C. 1992. "Cosimo and His Books." In *Cosimo "il Vecchio" de' Medici, 1389–1464. Essays in Commemoration of the 600th Anniversary of Cosimo de' Medici's Birth*, ed. Francis Ames-Lewis, 115–56. Oxford: Oxford University Press.

de la Mare, A. C. 1996. "Vespasiano da Bisticci as Producer of Classical Manuscripts in Fifteenth-Century Florence." In *Medieval Manuscripts of the Latin Classics: Production and Use* (Proceedings of the Seminar in the History of the Book to 1500, Leiden, 1993), eds.

Claudine A. Chavannes-Mazel and Margaret M. Smith, 166–207. Los Altos Hills, CA: Anderson-Lovelace.

de la Mare, A. C. 1997–2000. "La produzione del libro umanistico" (Zürich 1997); "Gli inizi della scrittura umanistica" (San Gimignano 1999); "Poggio, the Holkham Vergil and the Origins of Humanistic script" (Leeds 2000); "Il libro umanistico e gli inizi della scrittura umanistica" (San Gimignano 2000); "Scrittura e produzione libraria nel primo Quattrocento" (Florence s.d.). Unpublished lectures. In Oxford, Bodleian Library, Archive A.C. de la Mare.

de la Mare, A. C. 2000a. "A Livy Copied by Giacomo Curlo Dismembered by Otto Ege." In *Interpreting and Collecting Fragments of Medieval Books* (Proceedings of the Seminar in the History of the Book to 1500, Oxford, 1998), eds. Linda L. Brownrigg and Margaret M. Smith, 57–88. Los Altos Hills, CA: Anderson-Lovelace.

de la Mare, A. C. 2000b. "Notes on Portuguese Patrons of the Florentine Book Trade in the Fifteenth Century." In *Cultural Links between Portugal and Italy in the Renaissance*, eds. Kate J. P. Lowe, 167–81. Oxford: Oxford University Press.

De Robertis, T. 2006. "I percorsi dell'imitazione. Esperimenti di *littera antiqua* in codici fiorentini del primo Quattrocento." In *I luoghi dello scrivere da Francesco Petrarca agli albori dell'età moderna* (Atti del Convegno internazionale di studio dell'Associazione italiana dei paleografi e diplomatisti, Arezzo, 8–11 ottobre 2003) (Studi e ricerche, 3), eds. Caterina Tristano, Marta Calleri, and Leonardo Magionami, 109–34. Spoleto: Centro Internazionale di Studi sul Alto Medioevo.

De Robertis, T. 2016. "I primi anni della scrittura umanistica. Materiali per un aggiornamento." In Black, Kraye, and Nuvoloni 2016, 55–85.

De Robertis, T., and G. Resta, eds. 2004. *Seneca. Una vicenda testuale. Mostra di manoscritti ed edizioni* (Cat. exh. Florence, Biblioteca Medicea Laurenziana 2 aprile–2 luglio 2004). Florence: Mandragora.

De Robertis, T., G. Tanturli, and S. Zamponi. 2008. *Coluccio Salutati e l'invenzione dell'umanesimo* (Cat. exh. Florence, Biblioteca Medicea Laurenziana 2 novembre 2008–30 gennaio 2009). Florence: Mandragora.

Derolez, A. 1984. *Codicologie des manuscrits en écriture humanistique sur parchemin* (Bibliologia, 5–6). 2 vols. Turnhout: Brepols.

Derolez, A. 2003. *The Palaeography of Gothic Manuscript Books. From the Twelfth to the Early Sixteenth Century.* Cambridge: Cambridge University Press.

Desachy, M. and G. T., eds. 2010. *Le Goût de la Renaissance italienne. Les manuscrits enluminés de Jean Jouffroy, cardinal d'Albi (1412–1473)* (Cat. exh. Albi, Médiathèque Pierre-Amalric 15 septembre–31 décembre 2010) (Trésors écrits Albigeois, 3). Milan: Silvana.

Feo, M. 2003. *Petrarca nel tempo. Tradizione, lettori e immagini delle opere* (Cat. exh. Arezzo, Sottochiesa di San Francesco 22 novembre 2003–27 gennaio 2004). Pontedera: Bandecchi & Vivaldi.

Frioli, D. 1999. "Lo 'scriptorium' e la biblioteca di Vallombrosa: prime ricognizioni." In *L'Ordo Vallisumbrosae tra XII e XIII secolo. Gli sviluppi istituzionali e culturali e l'espansione geografica (1101–1293)* (II Colloquio vallombrosano, Vallombrosa, 25–28 agosto 1996), ed. Giordano Monzio Compagnoni. 2 vols., 1. 505–68. Vallombrosa: Edizioni Vallombrosa.

Garzelli, A. 1985. "Le immagini, gli autori, i destinatari." In *Miniatura fiorentina del Rinascimento, 1440–1525. Un primo censimento* (Inventari e cataloghi toscani, 18 and 19), ed. A. Garzelli. 2 vols., 1. 1–391. Florence: Giunta Regionale Toscana and La Nuova Italia.

Gentile, S. 2016. "Nuove considerazioni sullo 'scrittoio' di Marsilio Ficino: tra paleografia e filologia." In Black, Kraye, and Nuvoloni 2016, 385–421.

Gorman, M. 2002. "Manuscript Books at Monte Amiata in the Eleventh Century." *Scriptorium* 56. 2: 225–93.

Hankins, J. 2003–4. *Humanism and Platonism in the Italian Renaissance* (Storia e letteratura, 215 and 220). 2 vols. Rome: Edizioni di storia e letteratura.

Hobson, A. 1989. *Humanists and Bookbinders: The Origin and Diffusion of the Humanistic Bookbinding 1459–1559, with a Census of Historiated Plaquette and Medallion Bindings of the Renaissance.* Cambridge: Cambridge University Press.

Labriola, A. 2004. "Aspetti della miniatura a Firenze nella seconda metà del Duecento." In *L'arte a Firenze nell'età di Dante (1250–1300)* (Cat. exh. Florence, Galleria dell'Accademia 1 giugno–29 agosto 2004, eds. Angelo Tartuferi and Mario Scalini, 184–207. Florence: Giunti-Firenze Musei.

Levi D'Ancona, M. 1994. *The Choir Books of Santa Maria degli Angeli in Florence. Vol. 1: The Illuminators and Illuminations of the Choir Books from Santa Maria degli Angeli and Santa Maria Nuova and their Documents.* Florence: Centro Di.

Levi D'Ancona, M. 2003. *I corali dell'Ospedale di Santa Maria Nuova.* Lucca: Maria Pacini Fazzi.

Maniaci, M. and G. Orofino, eds. 2000. *Le Bibbie atlantiche. Il libro delle Scritture tra monumentalità e rappresentazione* (Cat. exh. Montecassino 11 luglio–11 ottobre 2000 and Florence, Biblioteca Medicea Laurenziana 1 marzo–1 luglio 2001. Milan: Centro Tibaldi.

Murano, G. 1993. "La *Summa* Antoniana senese e il convento di San Marco a Firenze." *Archivum Fratrum Praedicatorum* 63: 229–46.

Oakley, S. P. 2016. "The 'Puccini' Scribe and the Transmission of Latin Texts in Fifteenth-Century Florence." In Black, Kraye, and Nuvoloni 2016, 345–64.

Ornato, E. and M. A. Casagrande Mazzoli. 1999. "Elementi per la tipologia del manoscritto quattrocentesco dell'Italia centro-settentrionale." In *La fabbrica del codice. Materiali per la storia del libro nel tardo medioevo*, eds. Paola Busonero, Maria A. Casagrande Mazzoli, and Luciana Devoti, 207–87. Rome: Viella.

Pächt, O. and J. J. G. Alexander. 1966–73. *Illuminated Manuscript in the Bodleian Library, Oxford.* 3 vols. Oxford: Oxford University Press.

Pasut, F. 2006. "Il 'Dante' illustrato di Petrarca: problemi di miniatura tra Firenze e Pisa alla metà del Trecento." *Studi Petrarcheschi* n. s. 19: 115–47.

Petitmengin, P. and L. Ciccolini. 2005. "Jean Matal et la bibliothèque de Saint-Marc de Florence (1545)." *Italia Medioevale e Umanistica* 46: 207–374.

Petoletti, M. 2005. "Il Marziale autografo di Giovanni Boccaccio." *Italia Medioevale e Umanistica* 46: 35–55.

Piazzoni, A. M., ed. 2004–5. *La Bibbia di Federico da Montefeltro. Codici Urbinati Latini 1–2, Biblioteca Apostolica Vaticana.* 2 vols. Modena: Franco Cosimo Panini.

Pontone, M. 2010. *Ambriogio Traversari monaco e umanista. Fra scrittura latina e scrittura greca* (Istituto Nazionale di Studi sul Rinascimento, Miscellanea IV). Florence: Aragno.

Rizzo, S. 1995. "Per una tipologia delle tradizioni manoscritte di classici latini in età umanistica." In *Formative Stages of Classical Traditions: Latin Texts from Antiquity to the Renaissance* (Proceedings of a Conference Held at Erice, 16–22 October 1993) (Biblioteca del "Centro per il collegamento degli studi medievali e umanistici in Umbria," 15), eds. Oronzo Pecere and Michael D. Reeve, 371–407. Spoleto: Centro italiano di studi sull'Alto medioevo.

Rolfi, G., P. Viti, and L. Sebregondi, eds. 1992. *La chiesa e la città a Firenze nel XV secolo* (Cat. exh. Florence, San Lorenzo, 6 giugno–6 settembre 1992). Milan: Silvana.

Tacconi, M. S. 2005. *Cathedral and Civic Ritual in Late Medieval and Renaissance Florence: The Service Books of Santa Maria del Fiore.* Cambridge: Cambridge University Press.

Ullman, B. L. 1960. *The Origin and Development of Humanistic Script.* Rome: Edizioni di Storia e Letteratura.

Ullman, B. L. and P. A. Stadter. 1972. *The Public Library of Renaissance Florence: Niccolò Niccoli, Cosimo de' Medici, and the Library of San Marco* (Medioevo e Umanesimo, 10). Padova: Antenore.

van Binnebeke, X. 2001. "Per la biblioteca di Cosimo e Lorenzo de' Medici e la produzione di manoscritti a Firenze nel primo rinascimento." *Rinascimento* 41: 199–223.

van Binnebeke, X. 2009. "Manoscritti di Coluccio Salutati nella Stadtbibliothek di Norimberga." *Studi medievali e umanistici* 7: 9–26.

van Binnebeke, X. 2010–2011. "Payne & Foss, Sir Thomas Phillipps and the Manuscripts of San Marco." *Studi medievali e umanistici* 8–9: 9–38.

PART V

VARIETIES OF
BOOK USAGE

CHAPTER 55

BOOKS OF HOURS

ROWAN WATSON

FIRST emerging in the thirteenth century, Books of Hours were the preferred prayer book of the northern European and Italian laity by the fifteenth century. They supported a devotional routine that sought to match, in simplified form, the Divine Office followed by clergy in monasteries, cathedrals, and collegiate churches, the Office being the prescriptive set of prayers, hymns, Gospel readings, and other matter recited at each of the fixed times of the day and night known as the Hours (matins, lauds, prime, terce, sext, none, vespers, and compline). Offices were fully recorded for the clergy in a breviary. When Mass and other liturgical actions were involved, priests and other clerics had recourse to a missal and other books. Books of Hours were organized around an abbreviated Office dedicated to the Virgin Mary, often with other minor offices appended and with prayers. Texts relating to the Mass might be included in Books of Hours for the high nobility, who approximated their position to that of a priest (as, for example, in the *Grandes heures* of Duke Philip the Bold of 1376–9, Cambridge, Fitzwilliam Museum, 3-1954); at a later date, elements from the Mass (texts spoken by the priest or sung by the choir) or a Mass dedicated to the Virgin became common in ordinary Books of Hours among a number of accessory texts. In Latin, Books of Hours were generally known as *Horae*, though in Italy as *Officium Virginis Marie*; in English they could be called Primers.

HISTORY

Offices in monastic and other environments had grown enormously since the Carolingian period, the eleventh and twelfth centuries seeing a steady process of accretion. Recital of offices, as of other prayers and the Psalms in particular, became in itself a good work which could gain remission from sin and form part of penitential regimes. Until the fourteenth century, the Psalter was the devotional work most generally owned by lay patrons; many were richly illuminated by the most advanced artists of the day.

Efforts by the laity to emulate clerical practice prompted the addition to the Psalter of calendars, offices, and a variety of prayers. From the mid-thirteenth century, a new kind of manuscript appeared, the Book of Hours, that made devotions to the Virgin Mary their central concern. Their contents were generated by demands from the laity and not by clerical dictat. Female patronage is likely to have been significant. Anselm (c.1033–1109), when at Bec in 1072, had provided Adeleide, daughter of William the Conqueror, with material for devotions based on Psalms, prayers, and mediations, and Jean of Fécamp (c. 990–1078) had done something similar for Agnes, widow of the Emperor Henry III (d.1056). The early-thirteenth century Middle English *Ancrene Riwle* showed a pattern of devotion for women almost identical to that found in later Books of Hours. Over half of the Books of Hours dating from the thirteenth century can be shown to have been made for women (Bennett 1996, 29). The Paris-based author Christine de Pizan in c.1405, describing a mother's role in educating daughters, equated learning the Hours and Office with learning to read, a Book of Hours thus having a teaching role for children (cited in Bell, 1982, 149). In the fifteenth century, such books became the staple of a vastly productive commercial book trade and the link with female patronage less pronounced. Few have indications of ownership.

TEXTS

There was little standardization until the late fourteenth century. This may reflect the bespoke nature of book production in the thirteenth and fourteenth centuries, each patron specifying contents according to family or local tradition. It is most useful to consider texts that made up the conventional fifteenth-century Book of Hours, described in Wieck (1988), against which earlier divergences can be noticed. The edition of the Book of Hours of York Use, *Horae Eboracenses* (Wordsworth 1920), is useful far beyond texts used in the diocese of York.

A standard Book of Hours contains most of the following elements.

Calendar

The most complete have columns giving the Roman "Golden Numbers" and the Dominical Letters, which used together allow the date of Easter to be calculated in any year (Easter is celebrated on the first Sunday after the first full moon of the vernal equinox). Further columns give the Roman calendar (the kalends, nones, and ides), the days of the week, given as the letters A–G, and, finally, the name of the saint or saints or event honored on any day, i.e., the feasts (Wieck, 1988, 157–8, explains how calculations were made). A hierarchy of feasts was often indicated by color: major feasts are frequently given in red letters, or in gold in deluxe manuscripts. Reference to saints connected uniquely or mainly with a specific area can indicate the place where the manuscript was to be used, or an area to which the owner had an attachment, but the cult of many local saints could also be widely distributed. Calendars can be highly unreliable when badly drawn up, with saints misspelt or given the wrong feast days. Calendars are often no more than a quarter full; later additions can be invaluable in indicating ownership or changing usage. In more ordinary Books of Hours, calendars were commonly added as a separate unit, written in a different hand, and with a different page layout from that of the text; saints given prominence in the calendar are often ignored in the litany and other parts of the text. A common calendar is studied by Pedrizet (1933).

Gospel pericopes

Extracts from the Gospels, John 1, 1–14; Luke 1, 26–38; Mathew 2, 1–12; Mark 16, 14–20, the first being the prologue to the major Mass on Christmas Day, and the others recounting the Annunciation, Epiphany and the feast of the Separation of the Apostles

Prayers to the Virgin Mary

Very regular is the *Obsecro te* prayer, a plea for support from the Virgin and for warning of death; included are phrases which indicate whether the user was male or female, eg *Et michi famulo tuo impetres* (Leroquais 1927, II, 346–7; Wordsworth 1920, 66). John Plummer notes almost 2,000 variants in wording which can allow groups and specific textual traditions to be identified (Wieck, 1988, 152). The *O intemerata* prayer, very common despite having "du point de vue littéraire…un faible mérite" ("little merit from a literary perspective"), was addressed to the Virgin Mary and John the Evangelist; issuing from monastic environments before 1200, the prayer emerged in the thirteenth century in two broad families, one characterized by the words *Inclina aures tuas* and the other *De te enim dei filius verus*, both after the initial address to the Virgin. Both prayers were translated into French (Wilmart 1932, 488–95; English translations in Wieck, 1988, 163–4).

Hours of the Virgin

The Hours are the divisions into which the day is divided for purposes of prayer:

Matins (Midnight)
Lauds (Early morning)
Prime (6:00 a.m.)
Terce (9:00 a.m.)

Sext (Midday)

None (3:00 p.m.)

Vespers (Sunset–6:00 p.m.)

Compline (Evening)

The Office for each liturgical hour is made up of a series of Psalms with a hymn, canticle, lessons (matins only), and prayer or collect; these are embedded in versicles, responses, and antiphons, the last a single line recited (in church it would be sung) before and after the Psalm text, intended to identify the fundamental thought of the complete Psalm. The office of matins begins *Domine labia mea aperies; Et os meum annunciabit laudem tuam* (Psalm 50, 17), offices from lauds to vespers begin *Deus in adiutorium meum intende* (Psalm 69, 2); compline begins *Converte nos Deus salutaris noster* (Psalm 84, 5). The elements specified for each hour varied according to the use, that is to say, the particular set of texts followed in any specific diocese or religious order. For the elements making Rome use, see Wieck (1988, 159–61). Tests to identify use devised by James (1895, xxv–xxxviii), and Madan (1920, 39–44), and the notebooks of Leroquais in the Bibliothèque nationale de France (n.a.l. 3157–3173) are now superseded by the website of Eric Drigsdahl, http://manuscripts.org.uk/chd.dk/tutor/index.html, where examples are given of uses of dioceses and religious orders throughout Europe. A number of uses, in particular those of Sarum and Rouen, insert a series of suffrages (see Section 56.2.7) after lauds. The later Middle Ages saw a tendency towards standardization: Sarum use became common all over Britain in the fifteenth century; Rome use became common throughout Europe in the period.

Other Hours

Common are the short hours dedicated to the Cross and the Holy Spirit. Both lack an office at lauds and were frequently appended to the end of each hour of the office of the Virgin. The Hours of the Passion, of the Trinity, or of St Louis are found in some very grand manuscripts whose users probably relied on clerics to aid their devotions.

Penitential Psalms and Litany

These Psalms, asking for forgiveness for sin, are frequently preceded by the antiphon *Ne reminiscaris*.

Ps. 6 Domine ne in furore tuo

Ps. 31 Beati quorum

Ps. 37 Domine ne in furore tuo

Ps. 50 Miserere mei deus

Ps. 101 Domine exaudi

Ps. 129 De profundis clamavi

Ps. 142 Domine exaudi

These are followed by a litany, a series of petitions beginning with those to Christ, God the Father, the Trinity, and the Virgin, followed by the archangels Michael, Gabriel, and Raphael, the twelve Apostles, and saints divided into categories (confessors, martyrs, monks, and hermits, etc., ending with virgins). There are conventional sequences in each category, against which local variants can be noted. The litany ends with a series of appeals beginning with the words *Ab, Per,* and *Ut* (for example *Ab omni malo, libera nos domine; Per gratiam sancti spiritus, libera nos domine; Ut pacem nobis dones, Te rogamus*). The litany is frequently followed by Psalm 69 (*Deus in adiutorium meum*) and a series of collects (short prayers).

Suffrages to Saints

These are intercessory prayers, made up of an antiphon, a versicle and response, and a prayer, dedicated to, for example, the Trinity, the Cross, or the instruments of the Passion, but chiefly to saints. They first appeared in public liturgical services, but were adopted for private devotions in the thirteenth century and later (Bennett, 2003)

Office of the Dead

This is often the longest part of a Book of Hours. It consists of offices for three hours (vespers, matins, and lauds). The first antiphon for vespers begins *Placebo*, that for matins, *Dirige* (hence the word "dirge" in English). Matins includes three nocturnes, each of which has three readings; each reading ends with a response and a versicle. Ottosen (1993) grouped the readings into families and explained the message of each; his catalogue of responses to the nine readings gives numbered sequences peculiar to specific uses which are set out in tables, and can be of major help in establishing the use of any manuscript.

Psalms and abbreviated Psalters

The "Gradual Psalms" (Psalms 119–33), declaring confidence in God's aid, had been recited in monasteries before matins in three groups of five psalms, dedicated to the faithful who were alive, those who were dead and those who had recently died. The abbreviated Psalter of Jerome comprised a hundred verses selected from the Psalms, the first beginning *Verba mea auribus percipe, Domine* (Ps. 5). That of Bernard, said to have been prompted by a competition with the Devil, has verses from seven Psalms, beginning with Psalm 12, 4 (*Illumina oculos meos*); headings for each verse are often "*O bone Iesu*," "*O adonay*," "*O messias*," "*O rex david*," "*O eloy*," "*O emanuel*," "*O christe*," "*O agios*."

Joys of the Virgin

These sequences are made up of five, seven, or fifteen prayers to the Virgin.

- The **Five Corporal Joys** of the Virgin begin *Gaude virgo mater christi que per aurem concepisti*, a series often expanded to seven.
- The **Seven Joys of the Virgin** comprise the Annunciation, Nativity, Presentation of Christ at the Temple, Epiphany, Baptism and First Miracle, Resurrection, and Ascension. One version begins *Primum gaudium virginis Marie. Sancta Maria, domina mea dulcissima, rogo te per illud gaudium quod habuisti quando tibi angelus Gabriel apparuit* (Leroquais 1927, I, xxvii);
- **Seven Celestial or Spiritual Joys** of the Virgin, beginning *Gaude flore virginali / Honoreque speciali / transcendens splendiferum*, each joy ending with the antiphon *O sponsa virgo sancta*. The sequence is commonly attributed to Thomas Becket, instructed by the Virgin in a vision.
- **Seven Earthly Joys**, attributed to Clement IV (1265–8) and said to have been indulgenced by him, begin *Virgo templum trinitatis, deus summe bonitatis*.
- The **Fifteen Joys of the Virgin** add the Visitation, Christ in Womb, Adoration of the Shepherds, Christ Found in the Temple, the Cana Marriage, Death and Passion of Christ, and Pentecost. The sequence, in French, begins with an invocation to the Virgin, *Doulce dame de miséricorde, mère de pitié, fontaine de tous biens... Ave Maria*, followed by fifteen joys, beginning *Tres doulce dame, pour icelle grant ioie que vous eustes quant le saint ange Gabriel vous aporta la nouvelle que le Sauveur de tout le monde vendroit en vous* (Leroquais 1927, II, 310–11).

Devotional sequences

Other common devotional texts added to Books of Hours in the fifteenth century include the following:

- The Fifteen Oes of St Bridget, beginning *O Ihesu christe eterna dulcedo te amantium* (Wordsworth 1920, 76–80), often in English Books of Hours in the vernacular, *O Jesu endless sweetness of loving souls* (see Duffy 1992, 249–56).
- The Seven Requests to Our Lord, beginning typically *Doulz Dieu, doulz Père, sainte Trinité, ung Dieu, biau sire Dieu, ie vous requiers conseil et aide* (Leroquais 1927, II, 309–10).
- The Seven Last Words of Our Lord, beginning *Domine Ihesu christe qui septem verba die ultima vite tue in cruce pendens dixisti* (Wordsworth 1920, 140–2).

Prayers for specific moments of the day were increasingly added in the fifteenth century, most notably those for moments in the Mass relating to the Eucharist (before and after the priest's consecration of the host and Communion, where the celebrant was silent). Prayers such as those against the plague, for safety on journeys, and for the beginning and end of the day also became common, making the Book of Hours a veritable encyclopedia for spiritual health—printed versions added an image of an anatomical man with directions for when bleeding was safe, linking physical with spiritual well-being

ICONOGRAPHY

Images were integral to Books of Hours. Thirteenth- and fourteenth-century manuscripts frequently link scenes from the life of the Virgin with the story of the Passion; by the fifteenth century it was more usual to illustrate the one or the other, the latter being standard in the northern Low Countries. Books of Hours in Dutch associated with the *devotio moderna*, however, regularly omitted all illustration. Typical cycles are as follows:

	Life of the Virgin	Passion of Christ
Matins	Annunciation	Betrayal by Judas
Lauds	Visitation	Christ before Pilate
Prime	Nativity	Scourging of Christ
Terce	Annunciation to Shepherds	Christ carrying Cross
Sext	Adoration of the Magi	Crucifixion
None	Presentation in the Temple	Deposition
Vespers	Flight to Egypt or	Entombment
	Massacre of the Innocents	
Compline	Coronation of the BVM	Resurrection

PENITENTIAL PSALMS (USUALLY ONE OF THE FOLLOWING)

David in Repentance, sometimes with the priest Nathan

David with Goliath

Life of David with Bathsheba, Uriah slain

Last Judgment

OFFICE OF THE DEAD (USUALLY ONE OF THE FOLLOWING)

One or three death figures attacking three living
Job on the Dungheap
Last Judgment
Judgment of Solomon
Raising of Lazarus
Funeral Service

NUMBERS

Calculations rely on numbers of surviving manuscripts. Bennett (1996, 29) recorded 50 Books of Hours dating from the thirteenth century. Nigel Morgan (1991, 72) refers to 12 Books of Hours of thirteenth -century date produced in England, with 11 Psalters to which offices, usually those of the Virgin, had been added. Donovan (1990, 148) calculated that some 35 English Books of Hours survive for the period between the mid-thirteenth and the late fourteenth centuries. From the latter part of the fourteenth century and for the fifteenth century, manuscript Books of Hours survive in very large numbers. Nicholas Rogers (1982) identified 170 imported into England from the Low Countries between the 1390s and the early sixteenth century. De Hamel (1994, 168) estimated that the British Library and the Walters Art Gallery in Baltimore hold about 300 each; the Bibliothèque nationale de France holds over 350. Demand can be calculated more precisely for printed Hours: the Incunable Short Title Catalogue currently lists 422 editions for the period between 1473–1501; Bohatta (1924) shows some 760 editions to have been published between 1485 and 1530, the vast majority of them in Paris. The 1545 inventory of the bookseller Guillaume Godard, a Paris wholesaler, mentioned nearly 150,000 printed Books of Hours in a stock calculated at 263,000 books (Labarrre, 1969, col.420). Working in the Spanish Low Countries, Christopher Plantin printed 63 editions of Books of Hours between 1557 and 1589. Though they were abandoned in Protestant countries at the time of the Reformation, Catholic populations continued to use Books of Hours; Pope Pius V in 1571 set up a commission to reform their contents in the wake of the recommendations of the Council of Trent.

DISTRIBUTION

Centers of production were in France, the Low Countries, and to a lesser extent England. In Germany, Books of Hours were less common than other kinds of prayer book. Manuscripts containing the Office of the Virgin, with calendars, Penitential Psalms and Offices of the Dead and of the Passion appeared in Lombardy in the fourteenth century; the marriages of Blanche of Savoy to Galeazzo II Visconti (1320–78) of Milan, and of Isabel de Valois, sister of Charles V of France, to Gian Galeazzo Visconti (1351–1402), made Books of Hours on the French model popular; such books were produced in Lombardy outside court circles in 1370–1410 (Manzari 2004, 4). The Angevin court of Naples made these works popular, the one made for Queen Jeanne II in 1362/1375 setting a precedent (Vienna, Österreichische National-bibliothek, MS 1921). The devotional routines of Aragonese monarchs of Naples and their barons similarly relied on Books of Hours in the fifteenth century; compact pocket versions were printed in Naples from the 1470s.

LANGUAGE

Latin texts naturally predominate throughout the period when Books of Hours were used. However, French manuscript and, from the mid-1480s, printed Books of Hours regularly include a few prayers in the vernacular, added after the main texts; the same can be said for these works in Italy and England. Rubrics on the other hand were increasingly in the vernacular in the fifteenth century. The followers of the reforming movement known as *Devotio moderna*, and the Brethren of the Common Life, on the other hand, made central to their devotions the translation into Dutch of Geert Grote (1340–84); see Van Wijk (1940). In England, printed Sarum Use Books of Hours began to include prayers in English in the 1520s, but the first full translation, by William Marshall, appeared in 1534 as part of a reforming, Protestant agenda (Erler, 1999, 504)

FORMATS AND SCRIPTS

The earliest Books of Hours were small, as befitted a book carried about the person; most later examples could be called "pocket-size." The hours of Jeanne d'Évreux, datable to 1324–8, measures only 90 × 65 mm. Donovan (1991, 134) noticed the thirteenth-century Salvin Hours (London, BL, Add. MS 48985) as exceptional in its large format, 320 × 218 mm; the celebrated series of Books of Hours made for Jean, duc de Berry between *c*.1384 and 1416 ranged from 210 × 150 mm to 290 × 210 mm, with the *Grandes heures* (Paris, BnF, lat. 919) measuring 400 × 300 mm.

Scripts were those used for book production generally. Thirteenth-century works had large, clear scripts. Gothic scripts begin to be challenged as the preferred style from the mid-fifteenth century, when the Secretary scripts (*lettres bâtardes*) associated with literary texts began to be used for prayer books. In the southern Low Countries, rounded forms of Gothic script, Italian in origin, begin to appear from the 1440s and were used on occasion for Books of Hours from that date. In Italy, Humanistic scripts and ornament are likewise found in Books of Hours increasingly after mid-century.

METHODS OF PRODUCTION

Apart from exceptional commissions, Books of Hours became a staple of the book trade from the late fourteenth century and were produced by the same methods as other books. In the fifteenth century, Books of Hours are likely to have been produced speculatively; positive evidence for this survives from the 1480s, where the Paris *libraire* André Le Musnier had works almost completed ready for sale (Rouse and Rouse 2000, I, 301–2). Among devices to speed production was the use of the outline of border motifs on the recto to guide an identical image on the verso. In the Low Countries, images for Books of Hours were produced separately from the text block to be inserted as singletons. Book-makers in Bruges complained that such sets of images were imported at a price that undercut local production; legislation in 1427 confined import of miniatures to those marked with a registered stamp (Farquhar, 1980). Distinctive sets of miniatures were produced in Delft in the 1440s, some kind of reproductive technique lying behind the uniformity of the images (Renger, 1984)

OWNERS AND MAKERS

The powerful might install book-makers in their households. The Bohun family in fourteenth-century East Anglia famously commissioned a number of works, mostly Psalters, but also Books of Hours, between c.1355 and c.1385, and it seems that they set up a workshop in Pleshy Castle in Essex (Sandler 1986, I, 34–5). By c.1405, such manuscripts might have been had more easily in a commercial environment such as London, where artists like Herman Scheerre and "Johannes" were active. Early examples of works commissioned for royalty include the Book of Hours probably commissioned by Louis X (1294–1328) for Jeanne d'Évreux (1310–71), whom he married in 1324; the Hours were illuminated by Jean Pucelle (d.1333–4), an artist whose compositions and style, unprecedented in the Paris book trade, heralded a phase of copying Italian fashions in northern art generally. The children of king Jean II le Bon (1319–64) adopted his taste for finely produced Books of Hours, Charles V (1337–80) and his brother Jean de Berry (1340–1416) being among the greatest patrons of their day. Books of Hours for Jean de Berry were provided both from the Paris book trade, and by the three Limburg brothers, who moved from the household of Philip the Bold (1342–1404) into that of Jean de Berry, where the *Très Riches Heures* was incomplete at the time of their presumed death in 1416. Operating in the Paris book trade and called on to illuminate Books of Hours were the Boucicaut Master, the Mazarine Master, and the Bedford Master, and their emulators. Books of Hours were the vehicle for major works of art in the fifteenth and sixteenth centuries, examples being the Hours of Catherine of Cleves of c.1440, the Étienne Chevalier Hours of c.1452–60 illuminated by Jean Fouquet (c.1420–c.1480), the Anne of Brittany Hours of c.1503–8 illuminated by Jean Bourdichon (1457–1521), and the series of deluxe works illustrated by Simon Bening (c.1483–1561), Gerard Horenbout (d. before 1541), Lucas Horenbout (c.1490/1495–1544), and their colleagues known today as the "so-called Ghent-Bruges" school. Behind these lay a mass production of ordinary works that was vastly multiplied with the advent of printing. Their power was recognized: the printer John Rastell commented to Thomas Cromwell in mid-1530s England that the devotional habits of the population could be changed if new texts of a reformist nature were introduced into Books of Hours (Erler, 1999, 496–7).

BIBLIOGRAPHY

Bell, S. 1982. "Medieval Women Book Owners: Arbiters of Lay Piety and Ambassadors of Culture." *Signs: Journal of Women in Culture and Society* 7/4: 742–68 [repr. in *Women and Power in the Middle Ages*, ed. M. Erler and M. Kowaleski, 149–87 (Athens, GA, and London, 1988) and in *Sisters and Workers in the Middle Ages*, ed. J. Bennett *et al.*, 135–61 (Chicago and London, 1988)].

Bennett, A. 1996. "A Thirteenth-Century French Book of Hours for Marie." *Journal of the Walters Art Gallery* 54: 21–50.

Bennett, A. 2003. "Commemoration of Saints in Suffrages: From Public Liturgy to Private Devotion." In *Objects, Images and the Word. Art in the Service of the Liturgy*, ed. Coluym Hourihane, 54–78. Princeton: Princeton University Press.

Bohatta, H. 1924. *Bibliographie der Livres d'Heures . . . des XV. und XVI. Jahrhunderts*. Vienna: Von Gilhofer and Ranschburg.

Bowen, K. L. 1997. *Christopher Plantin's Books of Hours: Illustration and Production*. Nieuwkoop: De Graaf.

de Hamel, C. 1994. "Books for Everybody." In *A History of Illuminated Manuscripts*, 2nd edition, 160–85. London: Phaidon.

Dondi, C. 2003. "Books of Hours: The Development of Texts in Printed Form." In *Incunabula and their Readers: Printing, Selling and Using Books in the Fifteenth Century*, ed. Kristian Jensen, 53–70, 212–23. London: British Library.

Dondi, C. 2016. *Printed Books of Hours from Fifteenth-Century Italy: The Texts, the Books and the Survival of a Long-Lasting Genre*. Florence: Leo S. Olschki.

Donovan, C. 1990. "The Mise-en-page of Early Books of Hours in England." In *Medieval Book Production. Assessing the Evidence*, ed. Linda L. Brownrigg, 147–61. Los Altos Hills, CA: Anderson-Lovelace and Red Gull Press.

Donovan, C. 1991. *The de Brailes Hours. Shaping the Book of Hours in Thirteenth-Century Oxford*. London: British Library.

Douglas Farquhar, J. 1980. "Identity in an Anonymous Age: Bruges Manuscript Illuminators and their Signs." *Viator* 11: 371–84.

Erler, M. C. 1999. "Devotional Literature." In *The Cambridge History of the Book in Britain*, vol. III, 1400–1557, ed. Lotte Hellinga and J. B. Trapp, 495–525. Cambridge: Cambridge University Press.

Hindman, S. and J. H. Marrow, eds. 2013. *Books of Hours Reconsidered*. Turnhout: Harvey Miller.

James, M. R. 1895. *A Descriptive Catalogue of the Manuscripts in the Fitzwilliam Museum*. Cambridge: Cambridge University Press.

Labarre, A. 1969. "Heures (Livres d'Heures)." In *Dictionnaire de spiritualité ascétique et mystique* (1935–95), vol. VII, ed. Marcel Viller *et al.*, cols 410–31. Paris: Beauchesne.

Leroquais, V. 1927. *Les Livres d'heures manuscrits de la Bibliothèque Nationale*, vols I–III. Mâcon: Protat frères.

Leroquais, V. 1943. *Supplément aux Livres d'heures manuscrits de la Bibliothèque Nationale*. Mâcon: Protat frères.

Madan, F. 1920. "Hours of the Virgin (Tests for Localization)," *Bodleian Quarterly Record*, 3, 2nd quarter: 39–44.

Manzari, F. 2004. "Les Livres d'heures en Italie: reception et diffusion d'un livre d'origine septentrionale." *Gazette du Livre Médiéval* 45: 1–16.

Morgan, N. 1991. "Texts and Images of Marian Devotion in Thirteenth-Century England." In *England in the Thirteenth Century. Proceedings of the 1989 Harlaxton Symposium*, ed. W. M. Ormrod, 69–103. Stamford: Paul Watkins.

Ottosen, K. 1993. *The Responsories and Versicles of the Latin Office of the Dead*. Aarhus: Aarhus University Press.

Pedrizet, P. 1933. *Le Calendrier parisien à la fin du moyen âge*. Paris: Les Belles Lettres.

Renger, M. 1984. "The Netherlandish Grisaille Miniatures: Some Unexplored Aspects." *Wallraf-Richartz-Jahrbuch* 44: 145–73.

Rogers, N. J. 1982. "Books of Hours Produced in the Low Countries for the English Market in the Fifteenth Century." M.Litt. dissertation, University of Cambridge.

Rouse, R. H. and M. A. Rouse. 2000. *Manuscripts and their Makers: Commercial Book Producers in Medieval Paris, 1200–1500*. 2 vols. Turnhout: Harvey Miller.

Sandler, L. F. 1986. *Gothic Manuscripts, 1285–1385* (Survey of Manuscripts Illuminated in the British Isles vol. 5), ed. J. J. G. Alexander. London: Harvey Miller.

Van Wijk, N. 1940. *Het Getijdenboek van Geert Grote*. Leiden: Brill.

Watson, R. 2020. "Harreteau and his Unfinished Book of Hours." In *Illuminating the Middle Ages. Tributes to Prof. John Lowden*, ed. Laura Cleaver *et al.*, 395–413. Leiden and Boston: Brill.

Wieck, R. 1988. *Time Sanctified. The Book of Hours in Medieval Art and Life*. New York: George Braziller in association with Baltimore: The Walters Art Gallery.

Wieck, R. 2001. "The Book of Hours." In *The Liturgy of the Medieval Church*, ed. Thomas J. Heffernan and E. Ann Matter, 473–513. Kalamazoo, MI: Western Michigan University.

Wilmart, A. 1932. *Auteurs spirituels et textes dévots du moyen âge latin*. Paris: Librairie Bloud et Gay.

Wordsworth, C., ed. 1920. *Horae Eboracenses: The Prymer or Hours of the Blessed Virgin Mary according to the Use of the Illustrious Church of York, with Other Devotions as They Were Used by the Lay-Folk in the Northern Province in the XVth and XVIth Centuries* (Surtees Society, CXXXII). Durham: Andrews & Co.

CHAPTER 56

LAW AT BOLOGNA

SUSAN L'ENGLE

THE University of Bologna celebrated its eighth centenary in 1888 with great fanfare, attributing the founding of this institution to 1088. Nevertheless, there is little to tell us how or by whom law was being taught or studied anywhere in Italy at this date, although there were certainly people who exercised legal functions. The profession of notary had existed since early Roman times, and throughout the Middle Ages these specialized legal scribes continued to use the terminology of Roman law to draft documents such as charters and accounts of lawsuits. Diverse individuals carried out a variety of advisory and officiating functions in courts of law, on behalf of civil and church authorities, such as the judges and advocates who served as legal counselors to Countess Matilda of Tuscany (1046–1115). Clergymen above all were closely involved in a great many administrative and legal institutions and services. However, none of these individuals could have been considered a qualified legal practitioner who could argue a case, analyze problems, and find their solutions.

The emergence and rise to fame of the study of law in Bologna is most closely tied to the medieval recovery of Justinian's texts of Roman law—the *Digest*, the *Codex*, the *Institutiones*, and the *Novellae*—the greater part of which was lost upon the disintegration of the Roman Empire. The *Corpus iuris civilis* represented an important resource for potential legal professionals who faced expanding commercial and judicial requirements of courts, cities, and the commune. After centuries of virtual extinction Roman law made a gradual comeback, initially with brief citations of Justinian's texts in literature of the tenth century, and stronger indications of their diffusion in the eleventh. At Pavia, in the second half of the century, judges and jurists occupied with editing the Lombard laws wrote glosses that made intermittent references to specific Roman law passages. In the late eleventh century a sixth-century Byzantine copy of the complete *Digest* was discovered in Pisa (the *Codex Florentinus*, taken by the Florentines in 1406 as a spoil of war and now Florence, BML, s.n.). Vulgate copies, however, are thought to derive from an earlier-circulating medieval version that broke up the fifty-book work into three separate parts. Copies of the entire *Corpus* of Roman law were probably available by 1125. If there are no documents that preserve the names of masters and pupils of Roman law at this time, the small body of extant late eleventh- and early twelfth-century manuscripts with early glosses and other marginalia provides tangible evidence that their users were engaged in study and exegesis.

The first concrete signs of organized legal studies in Bologna appear in the second quarter of the twelfth century. The renowned Four Doctors—Bulgarus de Bulgarinis (d. c.1166); Martinus Gosia (d. c.1160); Hugo da Porta Ravennate (d. between 1166 and 1171); and Jacobus (d. 1178)—were purportedly the most celebrated pupils of the largely anecdotal figure of Irnerius or Wernerius, usually credited with the revival of law studies in Bologna. The Four Doctors pursued numerous activities in the field of law: they served as judges and legal consultants, composed glosses and other exegetical works on the Roman law texts, and established individual schools of Roman law in Bologna. It is clear from their writings that these early glossators had spent long years studying the newly rediscovered sources, knew them almost by heart, and expected their pupils to memorize them as well. The greatest legacy of the first masters and their successors was the establishment of an intellectual framework within which legal concepts could be analyzed and applied, confronting the growing need for jurists with expertise in interpreting and adapting laws to a particular situation. To this end, the curriculum of the Bolognese *studium* would focus predominantly on Romano-canonical procedure as it related to court cases of the time. Twelfth- and thirteenth-century glossators composed procedural treatises known as *Ordines iudiciorum* or *iudiciarii* in attempts to establish and standardize the order of judicial elements in civil or criminal trials.

In contrast to civil law, disparate collections of canons—the norms and regulations of the Christian Church—had been produced in escalating quantity since the first century, drawing on diverse sources such as the writings of the Church Fathers, the Bible, and papal decrees. New collections compiled in the late eleventh century— particularly those associated with Ivo of Chartres—were aimed at unifying and recon- ciling the many inconsistencies in the existing body of canon law. But this integration would only take place with the compilation of the *Concordia discordantium canonum*, whose earliest recension of around 1140 has been attributed to Gratian, a teacher of canon law at Bologna. Popularly known as the *Decretum Gratiani*, this massive volume was structured dialectically, presenting excerpts from a wide range of texts and directed toward resolving their contradictions and irregularities. A counterpart to Justinian's *Corpus iuris civilis*, it became the first authoritative textbook for the study and teaching of canon law, and was soon analyzed and glossed by decretists. The *Decretum* was followed by a compilation of almost 2,000 subsequent papal decretals, commissioned by Pope Gregory IX and called the *Decretales Gregorii IX* or *Liber extra*. Published in 1234, this new collection was destined to be taught in the law schools as the official law of the Church. Though Roman and canon law were taught separately in Bologna, their instructional methodology followed similar paths, and generated new genres of jurid- ical literature.

In both disciplines classes were conducted by lectures which, before the official establishment of the University of Bologna, would take place in the professor's residence. Thirteenth- and fourteenth-century miniatures and the fourteenth-century Doctors' funerary monuments that survive in Bologna depict the lecturer reading from a pulpit to students arrayed on benches in various positions of attention or distraction, their open books on writing tables before them. These images are misleading for the twelfth century, however, because until book production was expedited by the pecia system, the price of a textbook would be prohibitive. Lessons were primarily oral; students were expected to memorize vast numbers of laws and be able to call them up in order by their opening words. With this in mind, professors proceeded methodically through the textbooks, reading passages aloud and explaining in Latin their meaning and application, citing the opinions of previous glossators and adding their own observations, and identifying locations where a subject was explained more fully. Over time, a growing body of exegetical instruments—various types of glosses—was added to the textbook pages, among them *notabilia* (key phrases summarizing major themes) and *allegationes* (citations of other texts either similar or contradictory to the one being glossed). Individual glossators composed detailed sequences of explanatory remarks called *apparatuses*, which were often published separately as *lecturae* or *commentaria*. Another literary form was the *summa*, a comprehensive summary of subjects treated under individual titles or on entire texts. One of the most prolific Roman law glossators in Bologna was Azo (fl. 1150–1230), whose most influential work was his *Summa Codicis*, a commentary on the titles of the *Codex*.

Marginal glosses had been edited and supplemented over the years, and with each subsequent manuscript copy the signs of individual authors were eliminated and their thematic sequences became disordered. One of Azo's pupils, the brilliant Accursius (*c.*1182–*c.*1263), composed a coherent and consistent body of glosses on the entire *Corpus iuris civilis* that summarized all the work of previous glossators. So valuable was this work that it was soon adopted as the *Glossa ordinaria* and added to new copies of the individual texts. Subsequently, standard glosses were created for the *Corpus iuris canonici*: the first version for the *Decretum Gratiani* composed by the German jurist Johannes Teutonicus (d. 1245) was later revised and expanded by Bartholomaeus Brixensis (d. 1258). The standard gloss to the *Liber extra* was written and revised various times by Bernardus de Botone Parmensis (d. 1266), and the glosses to later canon law volumes (the *Liber sextus* of Boniface VIII and the *Constitutiones Clementinae* of Clement V) taught in Bologna were written by the esteemed Bolognese lay canonist Johannes Andreae (d. 1348).

Classroom lectures at Bologna were supplemented by readings, daily conversation, and debates. Bulgarus, in particular, invented exercises in which two or more students would argue opposing sides of a legal problem as though they were in court, with their professor presiding as judge. Known as the *Quaestiones disputatae*, these debates required an extensive knowledge of the textual sources, and represented a hands-on counterpart to the masters' lectures, an opportunity for students to put theory into practice. The exercise was structured as follows: the professor furnished students with a short description of a hypothetical juridical case and problem prior to the actual debate; next, students would take the positions of prosecutor and defendant and prepare their arguments, armed with one or more passages in the *Corpus* that supported their points of view; finally, the professor would hear the dispute and rule which side had presented the best juridical solution, or present an alternate solution, sustained by his own citations of the sources. The various types of *quaestiones* generated by Bulgarus and successive glossators embody the process by which Roman law was being adapted to the changing contemporary legal environment. They have come down to us in various collections, each preserved in a small number of manuscript witnesses.

Besides the practical exercises, plentiful traces of reader use in twelfth- and thirteenth-century manuscripts reveal early methods of study. In class the master read the text aloud twice, the first time to allow students to make corrections and additions to their textbooks if they had them. An assortment of marginal annotations, some common to other disciplines, indicated difficult or corrupt passages. A cross formed of dots and commas marked a place where the text was very bad; points where the text lacked something that was impossible to add were noted with a letter M (*menda*) surrounded by dots and dashes. *Notabilia* were written in the form of a triangle alongside the text and often decorated with a colored initial. Curved double lines or other markers connecting segments of the text designated passages to be memorized. The twelfth-century glossators also created special signs to identify important concepts and terms that appeared in the texts. Usually transcribed in red ink, they included letters of the Greek and Latin alphabets, signs of the Zodiac, or combinations of marks such as lines and circles. Dots placed at the left or right, top or bottom of each symbol advised the reader that the same expressions could be found at previous or subsequent locations in the manuscript (Plate 56.1).

Further graphic and pictorial material populates the manuscript margins: vegetable matter; profile and frontal human and animal heads; and countless species of creatures, especially birds, fish, and dragons. Some motifs by their nature are particularly effective as pointing devices, such as the beaks of birds, the pointing hand (manicule), or a man's long nose. Rather than being text-specific, they simply draw attention to data that should be studied or memorized. The highest order of marginal activity consists of sketches and pictograms that refer directly to a word or a juridical situation presented in the text, representing locations the reader has bookmarked, to be able to revisit with ease (Plates 56.1 and 56.2). Their negligible artistic quality makes it plain that they were executed by readers, who nevertheless had sufficient ability to portray a recognizable animal and human figures identifiable by profession, as well as tools and equipment in use at the time.

What use could the reader make of these images, whose topical character separates them from the general body of marginal graffiti? For the professor these drawings could represent a visual reminder of points to be brought out in a lecture; for students they could denote key material discussed in class. A third purpose could be to locate supporting references in the textbooks to be argued during the *Quaestiones disputatae*. Whatever the case, it appears that in the early years of the *studium* the selected portions of text represented issues of such juridical import that readers found it essential to record their sites visually. Marginal drawings are rarely seen in manuscripts produced

PLATE 56.1 Cambridge, Sidney Sussex College Library, MS 101, fol. 103v; *Decretum Gratiani*. Author's photo. By permission of the Master and Fellows of Sidney Sussex College, Cambridge.

after mid-thirteenth century, probably because by this time *lecturae, quaestiones,* and other exegetical literature were more readily available in published form.

By mid-thirteenth century, canon and Roman law were taught at the University of Bologna under a critically organized methodology, and the production of its textbooks had become an industry facilitated by the use of the pecia system. This process entailed the division of an unbound exemplar of a given text into a standard number of "pieces" that were rented to scribes in succession. In this way simultaneous copies could be executed, theoretically, as many copies as there were pieces of the text. To guarantee that the exemplar was a faithful copy of the original to be reproduced, university officials selected a reputable individual who would make corrections as necessary, ending his task by writing *cor* (*correctus, correcta*) at the end of each pecia. Now we find contracts that describe the commission of volumes of the *Corpus iuris* by jurists and students, the sale of these textbooks by stationers and private individuals, and the terms under which scribes agree to copy text and gloss. Thereafter, the Bolognese statutes provide detailed information about university administration, courses of study, and the

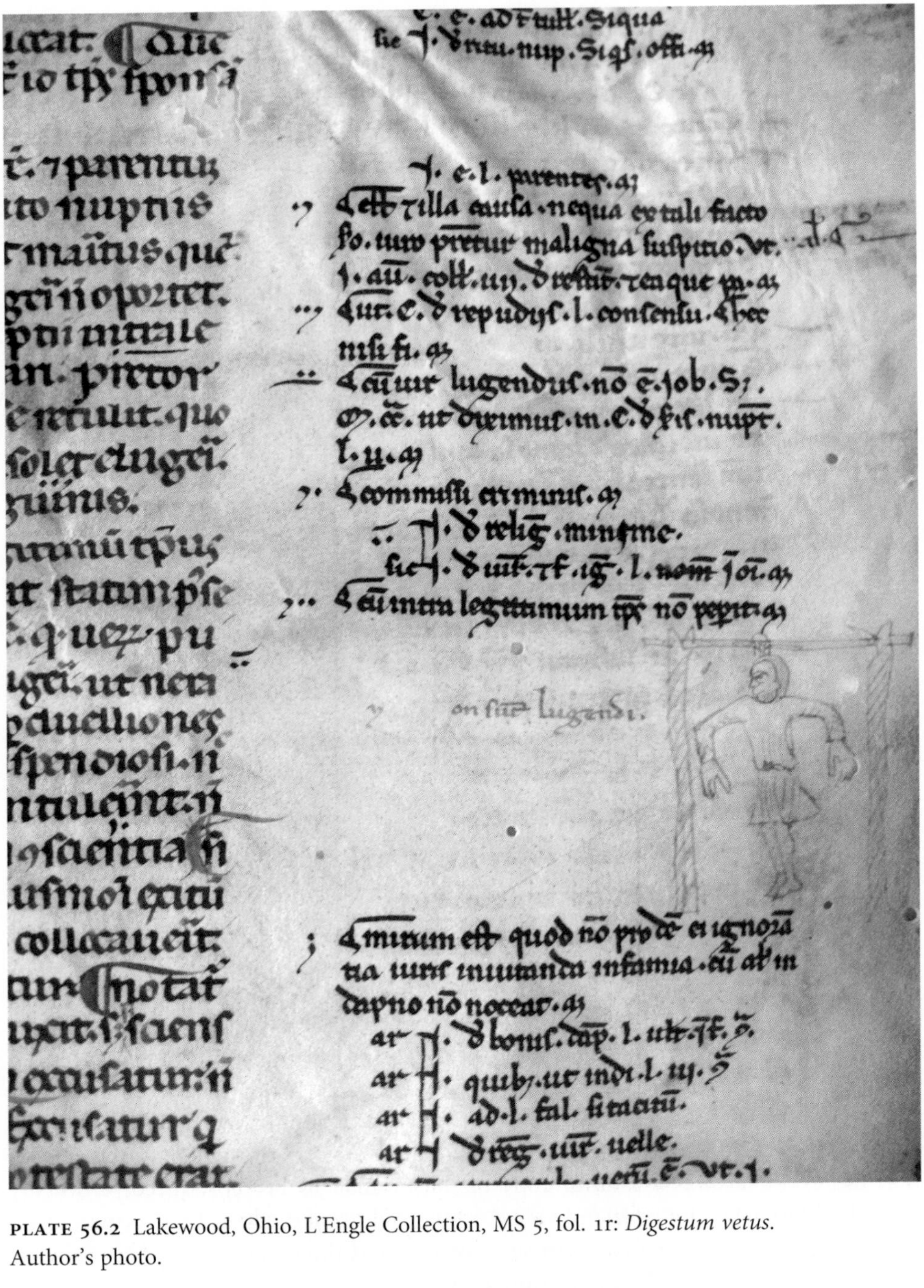

PLATE 56.2 Lakewood, Ohio, L'Engle Collection, MS 5, fol. 1r: *Digestum vetus.* Author's photo.

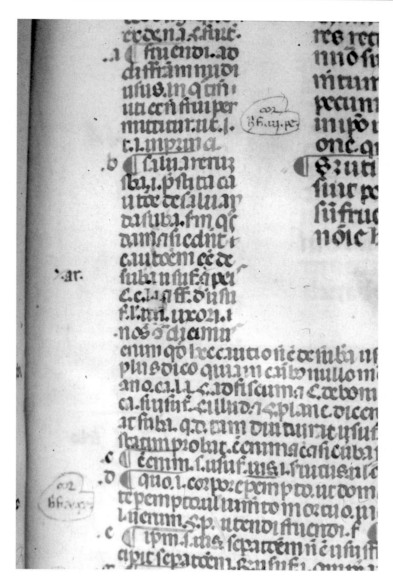

PLATE 56.3 Roermond, Stedelijk Museum, Inv. nr. 1856, fol. 19r: *Volumen parvum.*
Author's photo. By permission of the Stedelijk Museum.

strict control of textbooks and teaching practices. University-produced manuscripts can often be identified by the scribal pecia marks that survive in their margins, recording in numbered sequence the ends of individual pieces, and sometimes giving the name of the stationer from whom they were rented (Plate 56.3). They were also evidence that the scribe had executed the work for which he was paid. By the third quarter of the thirteenth century Bologna had become the most important center for the production of juridical texts, and the *studium* itself drew students from all over Europe.

The codicology of legal manuscripts produced at Bologna also evolves from the twelfth through the fourteenth century. Modifications in layout, dimensions, and articulation were effected to ease readers' navigation through the text and facilitate comprehension and assimilation. In the *Corpus iuris civilis*, each volume comprises a distinct arrangement of texts according to its sources, and its individual characteristics are visually expressed. The *Codex* and the *Digest*, the most important and difficult texts, were from the outset the most clearly articulated. The fifty-book *Digest*—divided in the Middle Ages into three separate volumes, the *Digestum vetus* (Books 1–24.2), the *Infortiatum* (Books 24.3–38) and the *Digestum novum* (Books 39–50)—is composed of excerpts from the writings of the classical jurists. In the oldest medieval copies each excerpt is preceded by a full inscription that indicates the specific bibliographic context from which the passage is extracted: author's name, followed by a book number, and its title, i.e., *Paulus lib. xxx ad edictum*. The earliest medieval witnesses to the *Digestum vetus* are Vatican City, BAV, MS Vat. lat. 1406, attributed to the third quarter of the eleventh century and Paris, BnF, MS lat. 4450, attributed to the last quarter. Both manuscripts are written in a single column of 50/45–50 long lines, leaving space around the text where early glosses were added. Measuring roughly 345 × 215/225 mm, they are minimally but logically organized. Books open with a large vegetal or zoomorphic initial; penwork or white vine initials present titles within books. The inscriptions are introduced by simple two-line initials representing the first letter of the classical jurist's name, for the most part executed in red ink or alternating red and black/dark brown; the one-line capitals that open the first word of the extract are either in black or alternating red and black. These two manuscripts are attributed to northern Italy, but present no features that would identify a specific place of production.

As law became an official university discipline, the format of its textbooks needed to be revised. Early in the twelfth century the single column was supplanted by a two-column layout, which had the twofold advantage of facilitating text legibility—long lines are hard to read on large format books without increasing the size of the script—and making more efficient use of space, since in lengthy texts such as the *Digest* and *Codex* more text per page can be fitted into two columns. In the new arrangement ample space was left around the text to accommodate glosses and reader annotations. With the progressive increase in glosses, the dimensions of the legal page had to expand, and after the composition of the *Glossa ordinaria*, the average size of glossed canon and Roman law manuscripts had grown to around 450 × 280 mm. and the longest texts could run to *c.*300–400+ folios. At this point, the visual profile of manuscripts produced in Bologna had acquired the distinct character by which it would be recognized for centuries thereafter.

The professional craftsmen who wrote and decorated legal manuscripts for the University of Bologna produced volumes with a uniform appearance. We do not know how graphic norms were established for this genre of texts, but they became standardized in the course of the thirteenth century and were widely admired and copied outside Italy, especially in Spain and the south of France. Most often both text and gloss were written in different sizes of the clear, rounded *littera bononiensis*, derived in the second half of the thirteenth century and described in contracts from 1265 on as "littera nova," utilized throughout the most active years of the Bolognese *studium*. The gloss was written in two columns around the text, making use of all four margins. A special criterion was to maintain visual symmetry across each double page opening of verso and recto for both text and gloss. Before the establishment of the *glossa ordinaria* the text could be written from beginning to end in a consistent number of lines per column, but thereafter, maintaining regularity became more complicated. In all legal texts there are passages that were highly commented, and others that were given few or no glosses. It consequently fell upon scribes to adjust the number of lines per text column along openings according to how much gloss was associated with it, obliging each opening to be ruled separately. The most skillful scribes managed to maintain a mirror-image layout of text and gloss throughout the manuscript, whether the text at an opening occupied two columns of twenty lines, or fifty (Plates 56.4 and 56.5).

The glossed university text was an especially important tool, since it presented simultaneously the text and its commentary that would be explicated in the classroom. Beyond a visually consistent format, the reader needed to be able to match up quickly gloss with text. In northern Europe this was achieved by underlining lemmata in the text and in the equivalent marginal gloss, often in red. In Bologna the solution was more succinct: a distinctive graphic sign, known as a tie mark, initiated each gloss passage; a copy of this sign was then placed within the text column at the correct location. The earliest tie marks were composed of dots and dashes (Plate 56.2) but were soon substituted by letters of the alphabet (Plate 56.5). Nonetheless, it seems that readers did not find this system of tie marks absolutely imperative, for we find many glossed manuscripts in which the matching marks were never added to the text.

The system of articulation and decoration also evolved. A penwork composition was created for book divisions, comprising a large red or blue initial for the first letter of the author's name, with rows of alternating red and blue display letters alongside that completed the name and gave the first words of the opening extract. During the twelfth century the ink initials that introduced author and extract fluctuated between red for both and alternating red and blue, but their size continued as two-line for the former and one-line for the latter. Interestingly, complete inscriptions were only transcribed in eleventh- and early twelfth-century manuscripts and had been abandoned by the thirteenth century, retaining only the author's name in abbreviated form, followed by the letter *l* (for *liber*), and then proceeding directly to the text of the extract. This implies, first, that the exemplars from which the earliest medieval copies were made had preserved the textual information furnished in manuscripts produced in Justinian's time and, second, that in the course of readers' growing familiarization with the text (and probably in the interest of expediting the copying process) shortcuts were taken when possible.

In Bologna, it was evidently thought necessary to differentiate visually a glossed canon law manuscript from one of Roman law, probably because they were studied separately. Thus, for texts composed of extracts from multiple sources, their introductory initials were color-coded according to genre. For canon law texts these two-line initials

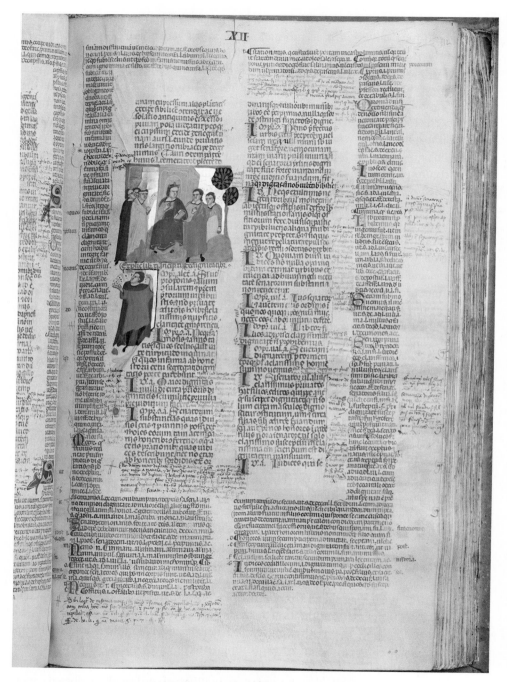

PLATE 56.4 Roermond, Stedelijk Museum, Inv. nr. 1856, fol. 112r: *Volumen parvum.*
Photo Stedelijk Museum. By permission of the Stedelijk Museum.

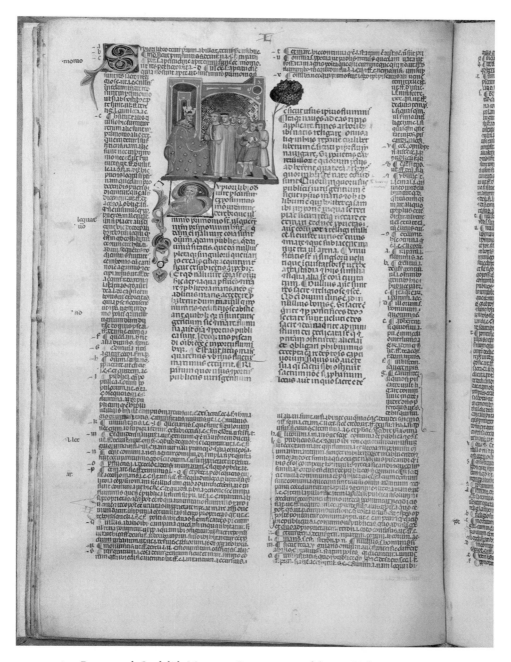

PLATE 56.5 Roermond, Stedelijk Museum, Inv. nr. 1856, fol. 14v: *Volumen parvum.*
Photo Stedelijk Museum. By permission of the Stedelijk Museum.

alternated in red and blue along the page and were flourished in the opposite color; the one-line capitals of the first word also alternated in red and blue. In contrast, for Roman law texts the opening initials were executed in blue only, and penwork flourishing was done in red. The capitals that followed were also in red ink, clearly distinguishing the author's name from his words. The hues of red and blue inks used in Bolognese workshops were particularly intense, making the articulation stand out against the pale vellum. The new visual paradigm for Roman law was most vividly realized in the *Codex*, which embodies a collection of imperial edicts and constitutions, each identified by the name of the emperor who promulgated it, and prefaced by either *Imp.* (*Imperator*) or *Id.* (*Idem*, when succeeding passages have the same author), followed by an abbreviated form of the emperor's name and the edict text. This particular form of text citation makes the *Codex* recognizable at a glance: under the Bolognese system its margins are punctuated by the rich blue initial Is that head the author citation (Plate 56.4).

Painted decoration and articulation began to appear in the thirteenth century as the pecia system accelerated book production and made textbooks more accessible. There were decorative programs for legal texts to fit all pocketbooks. Ink initials could be modestly executed in one color, or elaborately flourished with filigreed extenders reaching up and down the margins and across the *bas-de-page*. The distinction of book divisions could range from a large ink initial to an illuminated initial with display script or to a one- or two-column miniature in the most costly commissions. Individuals with money to spare could have their manuscripts enriched with gleaming gold and colorful narrative pictures (Plates 56.4 and 56.5). The iconography of law began to emerge and, akin to the initials or miniatures that had long illustrated books of the Bible and devotional texts, illuminators created specific compositions to represent the general topic treated in each of the major divisions of each textbook of law.

Pictorial themes were normally derived from the opening words or passage to each book. Book seven of the *Digestum vetus* deals generally with the subject of usufruct, and begins with a definition of the term: *Usus fructus est ius alienis rebus utendi fruendi salva rerum substantia*, "Usufruct is the right to use and enjoy the things of another without impairing their substance" (Dig.7.1.1). Miniatures express this concept by depicting the gathering and use of agricultural products—the picking of fruit from trees and grapes from vines, the milking of a goat or a sheep, and the treading of grapes for making wine. Likewise, Book thirteen, which describes all manner of financial transactions and obligations, commences with the words *In furtive re*, "In relation to stolen things," which prefaces a discussion of actions relating to theft (Dig.13.1.1). The customary illustration for this book features a thief being brought before a judge, usually with hands bound but occasionally holding the object he has stolen: a book or a golden chalice, both representing objects of great value in medieval times.

Unlike the early marginal drawings that reflected classroom practices, the painted decoration and the iconographic content of the miniatures served no didactic purpose beyond locating the reader within his text. Vanity and the desire to display social and financial status probably motivated the most lavish commissions, though numerous costly manuscripts reveal considerable signs of reader use. On the other hand, some of the most splendidly illuminated legal manuscripts are as pristine today as when they were first completed, with no annotations to sully the margins, or darkened page edges to indicate frequent turning. Many were conceived as presentation copies to important individuals that would impart prestige to the recipient and reap credit for the donor. A gift of this sort could be one means for a newly minted lawyer to rise in the profession.

Once the study of law was firmly established at the University of Bologna, its teaching was strictly controlled, as laid out in its statutes of 1252 (surviving in Berkeley, University of California at Berkeley, School of Law, Robbins Collection, MS 22, fols. 140v–141v). A professor was obliged to be punctual in beginning and ending his lectures and was fined for infractions; students were also fined if they lingered in a classroom after the lecture. The strictest regulation was on the schedule of material to be covered during a term. To curb the tendency of masters to spend more time in teaching the first parts of a book and then have insufficient time left to cover the rest of the material, a practical checkpoint system was conceived. Each text was divided up into segments called *puncta*, representing the amount of material expected to be covered by a certain date or within a specified period of time (usually two weeks). The *puncta* were annotated in the margins of a professor's manuscript at the point where each segment of scheduled text terminated, and, much like pecia marks, the *puncta* are usually outlined with decorative patterns or designs to make them more readily visible. The professor would post the *puncta* list before the start of classes, and deposit a sum (25 Bolognese lire, according to the statutes of 1252) with the university officials, from which would be subtracted a fine of three to ten lire every time he failed to meet a deadline. The statutes specify further the exact ranges of the texts that should be lectured upon within each two-week period.

The medieval manuscripts of Roman and canon law produced in Bologna record evolving methodologies in the study of law and the formation of professionals in this discipline. Beyond this, they supply visible evidence of the strong role played by the university in establishing high standards both for quality control of its textbooks and of the curriculum.

BIBLIOGRAPHY

Bellomo, M. 1995. *The Common Legal Past of Europe, 1000–1800* (Studies in Medieval and Early Modern Canon Law, 4), trans. Lydia G. Cochrane. Washington, DC: Catholic University of America Press.

Belloni, A. 1989. *Le questioni civilistiche del secolo XII: Da Bulgaro a Pillio da Medicina e Azzone* (Ius Commune Sonderhefte, Studien zur Europäischen Rechtsgeschichte 43). Frankfurt-am-Main: V. Klostermann.

Brundage, J. A. 2008. *The Medieval Origins of the Legal Profession: Canonists, Civilians, and Courts.* Chicago: University of Chicago Press.

Denifle, H. and F. Ehrle. 1887. "Die Statuten der Juristen-Universität Bologna vom J. 1317–1347, und deren Verhältniss zu jenen Paduas, Perugias, Florenz." *Archiv für Litteratur- und Kirchengeschichte des Mittelalters* 3: 196–397.

Dolezalek, G. and R. Weigand. 1983. "Das Geheimnis der roten Zeichen: Ein Beitrag zur Paläographie juristischer Handschriften des zwölften Jahrhunderts." *Zeitschrift der Savigny-Stiftung für Rechtsgeschichte* 100, Kanonistische Abteilung 69: 143–99.

Fowler-Magerl, L. 1994. *Ordines iudiciarii and Libelli de Ordine iudiciorum.* Turnhout: Brepols.

Kantorowicz, H. 1938a. "The Quaestiones Disputatae of the Glossators." *Tidschrift voor Rechtsgeschiedenis* 16: 1–67. Karlsruhe: C. F. Muller [repr. in H. Kantorowicz, *Rechtshistorische Schriften*, 1970].

Kantorowicz, H. 1938b. *Studies in the Glossators of the Roman Law: Newly Discovered Writings of the Twelfth Century.* Cambridge: Cambridge University Press [repr. Aalen: Scientia Verlag, 1969].

Kuttner, S. and R. Elze, 1986–7. *A Catalogue of Canon and Roman Law Manuscripts in the Vatican library* (Studi e Testi, 322, 328). 2 vols. Vatican City: Biblioteca Apostolica Vaticana.

Lange, H. 1997. *Römisches Recht im Mittelalter*, 1: *Die Glossatoren.* Munich: C.H. Beck.

Lange, H. and M. Kriechbaum. 2007. *Römisches Recht im Mittelalter*, 2: *Die Kommentatoren.* Munich: C.H. Beck.

L'Engle, S. 2000. "The Illumination of Legal Manuscripts in Bologna, 1250–1350: Production and Iconography." PhD Dissertation. New York University.

L'Engle, S. 2011. "The Pro-Active Reader: Learning to Learn the Law." In *Medieval Manuscripts, their Makers and Users: A Special Issue of Viator in Honor of Richard and Mary Rouse*, 51–75. Turnhout: Brepols.

L'Engle, S. and R. Gibbs. 2001. *Illuminating the Law: Legal Manuscripts in Cambridge Collections.* Turnhout: Harvey Miller.

Maffei, D. 1975. "Un trattato di Bonaccorso degli Elisei e i più antichi statuti dello Studio di Bologna nel manoscritto 22 della Robbins Collection." *Bulletin of Medieval Canon Law* 5: 74–101 [repr. in D. Maffei, *Studi di storia delle università e della letteratura giuridica*, 23–51. Keip: Goldbach, 1995].

Müller, W. P. 1990. "The Recovery of Justinian's Digest in the Middle Ages." *Bulletin of Medieval Canon Law* 20: 1–29.

Murano, G. 2005. *Opere diffuse per exemplar e pecia* (Textes et Études du Moyen Âge, 29). Turnhout: Brepols.

Radding, C. M. and A. Ciaralli, 2007. *The Corpus Iuris Civilis in the Middle Ages: Manuscripts and Transmission from the Sixth Century to the Juristic Revival.* Leiden: Brill.

Rouse, R. H. and M. A. Rouse, 1982. "*Statim invenire*: Schools, Preachers, and New Attitudes to the Page." In *Renaissance and Renewal in the Twelfth Century*, ed. Robert L. Benson and Giles Constable, 201–25. Cambridge, MA: Harvard University Press [repr. in M. A. Rouse and R. H. Rouse. *Authentic Witnesses: Approaches to Medieval Texts and Manuscripts*, 191–219. Notre Dame, IN: University of Notre Dame Press, 1991].

Soetermeer, F. 1997. *Utrumque ius in peciis: Aspetti della produzione libraria a Bologna fra due e Trecento.* Milan: Giuffrè Editore.

Weimar, P. 1973. "Die legistische Literatur der Glossatorenzeit." In *Handbuch der Quellen und Literatur der neueren europäischen Privatrechtsgeschichte*, 3 vols., ed. Helmut Coing, 1:129–260. Munich: C. H. Beck.

Winroth, A. 2000. *The Making of Gratian's Decretum.* Cambridge and New York: Cambridge University Press.

Witt, R. A. 2012. *The Two Latin Cultures and the Foundation of Renaissance Humanism in Medieval Italy.* Cambridge and New York: Cambridge University Press.

CHAPTER 57

....

THE MANUSCRIPT
MISCELLANY

....

†GEORGE RIGG

THE object of textual criticism is usually taken to be the restoration of an original text, by the elimination of errors that have entered the manuscript tradition by carelessness, ignorance, or deliberate modification. Its methods and principles have often been debated, but no one disputes its purpose. With miscellanies the focus is almost the opposite: the interest is in the final product. Of course, small errors resulting from inattention can be eliminated, but the resulting text is assumed to be what the compiler (not the author) intended. Deviations from the "original" are not defects but clues for the genesis of the text.

A general account of miscellanies is in principle impossible: each one is unique. It would be like a study of people's basements, attics, desk drawers, garages, or stored boxes in search of a principle of selection. Definitions are dangerous: one person's confusion is someone else's order; what to an outsider appears to be a chaotic jumble of random items may in origin be the result of a carefully planned buying spree in antique shops or of many purchases over several years. When we try to classify the material in miscellanies, we are in danger of imposing our own categories; sometimes our categories arise from modern academic divisions (scientific, medical, literary, historical, etc.); in fact, collectors keep all sorts of things in books—things that they need or think they might need or think interesting. We might compare the diaries of the eighteenth-century antiquary Thomas Hearne, whose "collections" include interesting tomb inscriptions he had seen, major events of the day, college gossip, archaeological finds, and recent book publications (such as the appearance in 1711 of Richard Bentley's brilliantly infamous edition of Horace).

For the purpose of this chapter, I distinguish "miscellanies" from "anthologies," though the terms (and the books themselves) merge into each other. By "anthology" I understand a collection of texts chosen for their variety; "chosen" is the key in this definition, since *anthologia* and *florilegium* both contain the metaphor of choosing or plucking flowers. The element of deliberate selection is seen in the ancient *Anthologia*

Latina and popular models of the twelfth to fourteenth century, in which scribes seem to have aimed at a particular kind of mixture (e.g., poems by Hildebert, Walter of Châtillon, Simon Chèvre d'Or, or poems on Troy, together with moral and morality poems). By "miscellany" I intend to stress the apparent randomness of the process of selection. The terms should never be used definitely, as it is impossible for us to be sure of the motives of the compiler, but the contrast provides us with a paradigm with which to describe some collections.

There are three principal and necessary approaches to the examination. First, physical evidence for the compilation procedure; second, the textual and cultural context in which the collection was made; third, the actual content of the manuscript.

One aim of a physical examination is to see if the manuscript was compiled in booklets. Whereas important books were normally bound between hard covers, personal and ephemeral collections were often in unbound quires or groups of quires, kept loose and separate. A fifteenth-century note in London, BL, Cotton, Titus A.xx (see below) reads "In vinisbery feldis pro lose quuayers et alfabetum," indicating the purchase of "loose quires and an alphabet" in Finsbury Fields in London. Booklets can be detected by the coincidence of common material within a quire or group of quires, together with a common *mise-en-page*, prick-marks, watermarks (in paper manuscripts), and wear and tear on the first and last leaves. It is sometimes difficult to be sure of booklets in paper manuscripts, which are subject to damage from damp and loss of leaves, and where watermarks are not on every page, but sometimes other evidence is helpful: in Oxford, Bodleian Library, Tanner 407 (Robert Reynes's commonplace book) a set of wormholes indicates the beginning and end of a booklet. Sometimes there is other evidence: in Oxford, Bodleian Library, Digby 166, on the first recto folio of each booklet is a figure, ij s. or iij s., indicating that each booklet was for sale at two or three shillings each. In the sale of individual booklets we see the beginning of a practice employed by John Paston's bookseller, William Ebesham, who left it to his customers to specify what collection of texts they would like from his offerings; often it was only after purchase that they would be illuminated.

Books that are made up of several booklets are sometimes by a single scribe: this seems to be true of Tanner 407 (Robert Reynes's book) and Cambridge, Trinity College, O.9.38 (written by a Glastonbury monk in several booklets, though there are some sixteenth-century entries). Very often, however, several scribes are involved over many years. London, BL, Cotton Titus A.xx was built up from eight booklets, by two scribes working in collaboration. One of the most complex is Oxford, Bodleian Library, Bodley 851: the first stage (Part II) was a poetic collection written by two separate scribes; next, another scribe wrote Part I (mainly Walter Map's *De Nugis Curialium*) and filled some blanks in Part II; third, hand X wrote the Z-text of *Piers Plowman*, and had the manuscript (as it was at this point) decorated and supplied with a bookplate, indicating its owner as John Wells, monk of Ramsey; he filled further blank leaves in Parts I and II. In the fifteenth century the text of *Piers Plowman* was completed and other entries made by one Dodsthorp. Later additions such as those in Ty and Bd are themselves informative, as they show that the manuscript was still regarded by its new owners/custodians as a suitable repository for miscellaneous texts. Similarly, just as the main scribe of Ty began his book as an accounts book, so the front flyleaves in Tx contain what is in effect shopping lists for several days in February and March (incidentally indicating that the book came from a large monastic house). Such collections are accretive: not an original large empty "volume" waiting to be filled, but something that grew over time, supplemented by leaves or more whole booklets, sometimes over many decades or even more than a century.

The second approach to such collections is through their cultural and textual context, since their selection of entries is inevitably determined by the availability of texts. Thematic collections are too obvious to need comment: rhetorical anthologies such as Glasgow, Glasgow University Library, Hunterian V.8.14, containing prose treatises on rhetoric and exemplification poems, could have been assembled by a teacher or anyone interested in poetry; class books, such as Cambridge, University Library, Gg.5.35 served an educational function, providing mainly Christian poems (with copious glosses) in ascending order of difficulty. On the other hand, Robert Reynes's commonplace book, Tanner 407, is at a much lower cultural level; it is not primarily literary; its context can best be described as "local" and oral. There is little sign that Reynes had access to a library or other manuscripts, though some of the legal texts must be copies. The English poems, often between two and eight lines long, were almost certainly circulated orally (e.g., apposite tombstone inscriptions, pious prayers, moral advice). Even the "drama" (the *Nine Worthies*) and poems on St. Anne and the Virgin Mary may have been known from oral performance; certainly there are no sure written sources. Reynes's circle seems to have been pious but not clerical.

At a more sophisticated level, anthologies grew in the few communities where anyone could read, i.e., monasteries, cathedral schools, occasionally episcopal houses, and so on. Circulation of manuscripts would be by donations or borrowing. One manifestation of this was the mortuary roll, a kind of invitation to each community to enter a tribute to a deceased monarch, abbot, or noted figure, and this would be copied as it circulated. Collected works of individuals may have travelled in the same way, e.g., the poems of Hildebert of Le Mans, Marbod, Simon Chèvre d'Or, Hugh Primas, Walter of Châtillon, and these might then be divided piecemeal into other collections. Sometimes songbooks might be brought to a community by a visitor: the "Cambridge Songs" (which corresponds to a list by Sextus Amarcius of a German minstrel's repertoire) found its way into Cambridge, University Library, Gg.5.35 (St. Augustine's Canterbury) in the later eleventh century, and an eight-leaf booklet of 35 lyrics, laid out for music, is in Cambridge, University Library, Ff.1.17 (early thirteenth century).

The rise of universities in the twelfth and thirteenth centuries produced communities of very literate students, who were used to copying and to exchanging manuscripts. I have conjectured that D (Oxford, Bodleian Library, Digby 166) was compiled for booklets offered for sale in Oxford, the appropriate place for a mixture of advanced science and lighthearted poetry; it was found by Thomas Allen at Gloucester Hall,

Oxford, the descendant of the Benedictine Gloucester College. This is where textual criticism plays a part. A small group of manuscripts of the immensely popular *De coniuge non ducenda*, London, BL, CottonVespasian E.xii (Ve), Cambridge, Trinity College, O.9.38 (Ty), and Oxford, Bodleian Library, Bodley 851 (Bd), is very closely linked as a textual group, my *alpha²*, Ve was an Oxford manuscript, but Ty came from Glastonbury, and Bd from Ramsey; in fact, their compilers were all at some time students at Oxford, and it must have been there that they copied their texts of the poem. D shares many readings with *alpha²*. The other manuscripts closest to these are *alpha³*, London, BL, Cotton Titus A.xx (Tx) and Rawlinson B.214 (Rb), and a single manuscript Oxford, Bodleian Library, Add.A.44 (the Bekynton, Bk). Rb is from Waltham priory, written by John Wilde; Tx is from some large monastic house near London; Bd belonged to Thomas Bekynton, bishop of Bath and Wells, chancellor of Henry VI (during whose time it acquired a text of the *De coniuge non ducenda*); all these *alpha* manuscripts contain an erroneous shift of stanzas and can safely be said to descend from a common archetype. Although neither Tx nor Rb has any clear Oxford affiliations, their owners were all clearly learned men, and it is quite possible that they had attended the university. Bekynton became a Fellow of New College, Oxford, in 1408, and he remained there for twelve years. These Oxford connections could doubtless be paralleled in all the major European universities.

A distinction between miscellany (or commonplace book) and anthology is visible principally in their contents and is largely a matter of degree: the former is casual, ephemeral, personal, and widely varied in nature; the latter is well planned and has a clear pattern of association with similar collections. We have seen a good example of the commonplace book in Robert Reynes's collection—personal, parochial, practical, not highly educated (e.g., in the Latinity where it seems to be Reynes's own work), mnemonic, and so on. An example of the planned collection is John Wilde's Oxford, Bodleian Library, Rawlinson B.214 (s. xv), from the Augustinian abbey of Holy Cross at Waltham, Essex; this is in parts either a direct copy or close relation of Tx. Its first program is historical, beginning with the Fall of Troy (Thomas Walsingham's text of and commentary on Dictys Cretensis), and Simon Chèvre d'Or's *Ylias*, followed by histories of Britain by Thomas Elmham and John Whethamstede, and then by poems on the wars of Edward III, and then Thomas Elmham's poems to and on Henry V. There is also a calendar, some satirical poems, and finally a mythographic treatise based on Ovid, which is annotated by reference to the commentary on Dictys which began the manuscript. Where Tx is relatively unstructured, Rb is a finely produced "edition" of texts, including many of those in Tx, with pictures and diagrams and fine decoration. It shows how a fine book can be constructed from a more or less random collection.

Naturally, most miscellanies fall between these two extremes. A good example is Cambridge, Trinity College, O.9.38 (Glastonbury, s.xv, after 1438). Its owner has clearly been in Oxford, where he found interesting satires for and against friars and monks (and also shared in the *alpha* branch of the *De coniuge non ducenda*), but he also collects many items of purely Glastonbury interest (a letter from Abbot Nicholas Frome from the Council of Basle 1434, a note about conventual rations by the twelfth-century abbot Henry de Blois, a poem by a Glastonbury monk Stephen Deverell, locally interesting saints (Joseph of Arimathea, St. Uritha of Chittlehampton in Devon). There is a rich mixture of prose and verse and of Latin and English (especially refrain lyrics, satirical and moral): for example, an English account of Henry VI's procession into Paris and an Anglo-Irish poem on gardening; well-known apocrypha (the prose stories of the Holy Cross, Pilate, and Judas Iscariot) alongside humanist Latin (Leonardo Bruni's Latin translation of Boccaccio's tale of Tancred of Salerno and another version of Boccaccio's Wager Story). There is popular satire (the *Apocalypsis Goliae* and *De coniuge non ducenda*) and popular practical verse mnemonics (the date of Easter, the properties of a horse), the satire on Norfolk, and English medical recipes. In short, it contains what seems like a very personal selection from a wide range of materials. It is both local and national, old-fashioned and up-to-date, solemn and frivolous. It also displays, as mentioned above, the sure sign of its status as a commonplace book, the continued use for miscellanea into the sixteenth century: additions include such varied items as love songs (some bawdy), weather lore, a note on currency policy, two poems on the death of Sir Richard Gresham, father of the financier, and various historical events, with regnal lists.

The investigation of miscellanies is in many ways like architectural archaeology. The earliest home of a nineteenth-century Ontario settler was a single-room log cabin (= the first booklet); later this might be expanded by the addition of several rooms with a half-floor upstairs (= additional booklets). In time the wooden building was encased in brick or stone, and the upper story might be extended to cover the whole house (= more booklets, fill, and a title page, as in Bd). In time the original log cabin might become the summer kitchen, and the house might be decorated externally by gingerbread trim and internally with wallpaper (= decoration by colored initials). The summer kitchen might by now have become a storeroom, still available to receive more spare furniture (= renumbering of quires); finally, additional lean-tos might be added (final flyleaves). All stages remain apparent after archaeological investigation, but the overall appearance has changed completely under its many owners.

BIBLIOGRAPHY

I must begin by apologizing for the fact that most of my references are to my own studies; this is simply because I know these texts better than any others. Further, they are exclusively English manuscripts, but I imagine that the same phenomena—the difference between a personal, random miscellany and a planned anthology, the difference between the cultural contexts of a purely local population and of the riches of a monastic or university environment—are found everywhere. Many of the studies have the word "anthology" in their titles (rather than commonplace book or miscellany), but the descriptions of the manuscripts should make it clear where they stand in the continuum.

Specific manuscripts

Brewer, C. and A. G. Rigg. 1994. *Piers Plowman. A Facsimile of the Z-text in Bodleian MS Bodley 851*. Cambridge: Brewer.

Louis, C. 1980. *The Commonplace Book of Robert Reynes of Acle: An Edition of Tanner MS 407*. New York and London: Garland. (Rr).

Lynn, I. P. T. 2001. "A Critical Edition of Latin Poems from Oxford, Bodleian Library, MS Rawlinson G.109. Oxford: MLitt thesis [full introduction on the MS and its relationships; differs in details from Rigg (1981)]. (Rg)

Rigg, A. G. 1968. *A Glastonbury Miscellany of the Fifteenth Century: A Descriptive Index of Trinity College Cambridge, MS O.9.38*. Oxford: Oxford University Press [based on my DPhil thesis (Oxford, 1966), which had editions of many texts]. (Ty).

Rigg, A. G. 1977. "Medieval Latin Poetic Anthologies (I)." *Mediaeval Studies* 39: 291–300 [= London, BL Cotton Titus A.xx, Oxford, Bodleian Library, Rawlinson B.214]. (Tx, Rb)

Rigg, A. G. 1979. "Medieval Latin Poetic Anthologies (III)." *Mediaeval Studies* 41: 468–505 [= Oxford, Bodleian Library, Digby 166, Bodley 603; London, BL, Cotton Vespasian E.xii]. (D, B, Ve).

Rigg, A. G. 1981. "Medieval Latin Poetic Anthologies (IV)." *Mediaeval Studies* 43: 472–97 [= Oxford, Bodleian Library,Rawlinson G.109]. (Rg)

Rigg, A. G. and G. Wieland. 1975. "A Canterbury Classbook of the Mid-Eleventh Century (the "Cambridge Songs" Manuscript)." *Anglo-Saxon England* 4: 113–30 [= Cambridge, University Library Gg.5.35].

Other Works

Bühler, C. F. 1941. "Sir John Paston's *Grete Boke* a Fifteenth-Century 'Best-Seller'." *Modern Language Notes* 56: 345–51 [deals with the "bespoke" book trade, and thus is relevant to booklet compilations].

Doyle, A. I. 1957. "The Works of a Late Fifteenth-Century English Scribe, William Ebesham." *Bulletin of the John Rylands Library* 39: 298–325 [deals with the "bespoke" book trade, and thus is relevant to booklet compilations].

Mantello, F. A. C. and A. G. Rigg. 1996. "Medieval Latin: An introduction and bibliographical guide" In *Anthologies and Florilegia*, 708–12. Washington, DC: Catholic University of America Press [does not deal with the physical makeup of miscellanies].

Rigg, A. G. 1982. "Anthologies." In *Dictionary of the Middle Ages* 1, ed. Joseph Strayer, 317–20. New York: Charles Scribner's Sons [does not deal with the physical makeup of miscellanies].

Rigg, A. G. 1986. *Gawain on Marriage: The Textual Tradition of the* De coniuge non ducenda *with Critical Edition and Translation*. Toronto: Pontifical Institute of Medieval Studies [esp. 29–31 on the relationship of D, TyVeBd, and TxRb (and also the Bekynton MS); also 54–7 on how individual scribes interfered in the text, making their own contribution to the text].

Rigg, A. G. 1992. *A History of Anglo-Latin Literature 1066-1422*. Cambridge: Cambridge University Press [esp. 148–53, 236–8, 303–8, 311–12; deals with literary anthologies only].

Robinson, P. R. 1972. "A Study of Some Aspects of the Transmission of English Verse Texts in Late Medieval MSS." B.Litt. thesis, Oxford University [esp. 17–26 on booklets].

Robinson, P. R. 1980. "The 'Booklet': A Self-Contained Unit in Composite Manuscripts." *Codicologica* 3: 46–69.

CHAPTER 58

FLORILEGIA

JACQUELINE HAMESSE
(Translated from the French by Frank T. Coulson)

THE genre of florilegia was already well established from classical antiquity.[1] One need only mention the doxographical literature, the chains of extracts, and the compendia of citations that date from this period. Witnesses of classical culture and guardians of secular texts, they were equally prized by the Greeks and Romans, and, in certain cases, played an important role in the *translatio studiorum*. Thanks to these works, we can have access, albeit selective and sometimes very limited, to the documentation employed, as much for didactic purposes as for cultural initiation. Moreover, these florilegia are at times the only witnesses which have come down to us of lost texts.[2] The Middle Ages continued this tradition. The success of these anthologies and the use which was made of them in various contexts certainly justifies the contribution devoted to them in this volume.[3]

But how best to approach in a singe chapter the complex questions which may be raised about this secondhand literature? We have just begun to study these research tools, and only collaborative projects will develop our knowledge of the subject. In order to understand the specifics of the transmission of texts through the intermediary of the florilegia, one should first investigate the characteristics of these anthologies and the significance of the terms used to designate them. In effect, florilegia, as well as anthologies, these terms being often confused, are part of a broader "genre" which might be called reference tools. The best definition which can perhaps be applied is the following: "compendia of short citations, easy to memorize, in which the extracts have a certain authority and do not contain personal remarks of the compiler whose work entails only the choice and organization of different citations."[4]

This theoretical definition in many cases does not correspond to reality. In effect, it underlines a series of problems raised by the study of different witnesses which have been recovered: Are the citations really literal or not? How were the criteria used for the selection of extracts put into practice? For whom was the work written? Did those put in charge of selecting the citations always have the required competence to perform the task? Is it only a matter of regrouping a series of phrases taken from original works or did the compiler himself intervene to effect modifications, to suppress important aspects, or, on the contrary, to provide certain added explications?

The above-mentioned questions illustrate well the divergences which exist among modern scholars in establishing a definition of the genre. In fact, everything evolved with the passage of time, and the needs of scholars were not always the same in antiquity and the Middle Ages, all the more so since the latter period covered roughly a thousand years. We must, therefore, supply a more nuanced view in light of chronological criteria and the use made of these documents by their users.

Several significant contributions published in the last 20 years help to understand better the characteristics of florilegia from antiquity and the early Middle Ages.[5] They are principally focused on patristic, religious, and classical authors.[6] It will be sufficient to turn to these works to have a more complete overview of this literary production already flourishing during this period. Later florilegia benefited from this literature, even if they reveal their own peculiarities resulting from different needs. In the later Middle Ages, scholasticism will give rise to an extraordinary development and diversification of these anthologies and thus give birth to a new subgenre: the philosophical florilegium.

In addition, during the last 30 years the study of this secondhand literature has progressed. Several different definitions arising from a colloquium organized in 1981 on the literary genres in medieval philosophical and theological sources have been applied to these anthologies.[7] Even if certain points in common are apparent, a number of divergences also arise due to the peculiarities of the material used and the chronological limits considered by each researcher. To understand exactly the scope of the term, one must take into account the developments the florilegia underwent in the course of the centuries as well as the locales in which they developed. Thanks to the scholarly interest shown in these research instruments over the last 30 years, one may henceforth approach the subject in a more detailed manner, relying on the results of recent research which has given us new elements allowing us to refine our analyses.

THE QUESTION OF TERMINOLOGY

While numerous anthologies of extracts existed for many centuries, the Latin term *florilegium* does not appear in the Latin language before the seventeenth century.[8] How may one explain this anomaly, as scholars have designated several medieval anthologies with the term *florilegium*, a familiar term when one evokes this genre of literature?[9] In reality, the term is a neologism created in modern Latin from the adjective *florilegus* used by Ovid and coming from *flos*, "flower," and *legere*, "to pick" or "to choose."[10] Generally, all titles before 1621 containing *florilegium* to designate an anthology of citations are modern labels proposed by researchers or cataloguers of manuscripts anxious to designate a medieval reality which was referred to by the intermediary of a series of different terms, often metaphorical, that allowed one to express a nuance in regards to the varied contents.[11] These medieval titles are of great interest because they reveal diverse methods put into practice or correspond to techniques of explication and of commentaries on texts practiced in the confines of scholasticism. Likewise, *anthologia* is a transposition from the Greek which appears only in modern Latin.[12]

But even if the abstract term *florilegium* was not used during antiquity and the Middle Ages, the reality which the term designates was indeed present during these two periods, and it is the more concrete term *flores* which was widely used to designate anthologies of citations. This fact is far from exceptional. Technical neologisms often are created after a number of years, when a widespread practice becomes integrated in the general culture of the period. Moreover, since certain florilegia are anonymous and are not always introduced by a prologue or indications that might permit one to give a title to the work, cataloguers have had to employ various tricks in order to divide and identify them in the manuscripts: they use either the place where the florilegium was preserved to distinguish it from another, or the names of the authors who are included, or again the subject matter of the compilation. Thus, the *Florilegium angelicum* takes its title from the fact that one of its manuscripts is conserved at the Biblioteca Angelica in Rome,[13] which distinguishes it from the *Florilegium duacense*, preserved at the library in Douai, which contains different texts. In the case of florilegia dedicated to one or two authors, one may speak, for example, of the *Collectaneum Sedulii Scoti* or of the *Anthologia Valerio-Gelliana*. To designate florilegia systematically, one uses titles such as *Compendium ethicae* or *Flores philosophorum*.

Our modern need for classification does not correspond necessarily to the medieval one, and sometimes it is difficult to perceive specific differences which exist between visible types. In French, the terms "florilège" and "anthologie" may be used interchangeably to designate a "choice or a selection of *flores*," whereas they are not the same in English.[14] In French an anthology brings together "select bits" of one or more works of single or different authors. Anthologies may be distinguished, therefore, rather by the length of extracts assembled therein, whereas in English it would be a question of compilations containing various complete works. In fact, even in French the terms are not completely synonymous. As the definition cited above makes clear, a florilegium normally contains very short extracts, as opposed to an anthology, which has longer passages. The idea of conformity with the sources is assumed in our period, whereas during the Middle Ages compilers were not so careful to copy literally the phrases or chosen passages and to attribute them to their authors. They freely replaced words, cut out sections from the original, or even added brief explanations, including synonyms for technical or rarely used terms or clarifications of the meaning of the author's text. Anthologies usually designate collections of long passages faithfully copied according to the original.

In order to clarify and simplify matters, one could say that the florilegia and the anthologies which are closely related in the Middle Ages arise from the same technique, that of "compilation," and are distinguished from one another normally by the purpose of the compilers.[15] Generally, compilations were made for a "utilitarian," "economic" and "practical" purpose and also were adapted according to the educational level of their intended users as well as the cultural interests of those who commissioned them. They respond primarily to textual referencing and didactic needs. Since they aim to reduce in size and make more accessible in a manageable volume a larger text, the person undertaking the work necessarily imposes a process of selection. Whether it is a question of extracting phrases, abridging longer passages, of shortening the text of an author, or assembling the totality of knowledge in a single volume, the intended purpose is the same, whereas the method used varies and the audience addressed is not the same. Moreover, various methods will be used to attain the same goal: to create indispensable research tools for the era.

To a certain extent the interests of the users can aid in classifying the research tools in question, especially when the borders which separate the different representatives of the genre are not very clear: an encyclopedia, for example, seeks to give the reader access to the totality of knowledge available. An anthology joins together select longer passages from several works written by a single or multiple authors, so as to obtain a collection of relevant references. An abridgment gives the essential points of a work, while a handbook follows a scholarly or university program and is put together from a didactic perspective. Lastly, a florilegium consists of a series of citations, short and easy to memorize, drawn from a single or multiple authors, thus providing easy access to the core of a discipline or a subject. But in the manuscripts, an anthology may be followed by short extracts and a compilation may contain, besides abbreviated sections, a series of literal passages intermixed with citations. One is then speaking of "miscellanies." These research tools are never original works. It is always a question of secondary material, borrowed in one manner or another. The compiler's intelligence will be, therefore, of prime importance in ensuring the quality of work.

Catalogues of manuscripts can distinguish different types of florilegia according to the technical terms used to designate them at the time of their composition for identifying and differentiating purposes. Specific terms are often contemporary with the compositions and express the goals followed by their compilers. The most neutral terms are *flores, dicta, excerpta* or *compendia*, and *collectanea*. Others are more specific, and, in the case of philosophical florilegia, one must above all not confuse *auctoritates* with *summae, axiomata* with *conclusiones,* or *propositiones* with *sententiae*.[16] Each name contains nuances and sheds a different light on the extracts retained. Most of these terms are technical. It is important, therefore, to re-establish them in their context and to apprehend the various meanings they may have before approaching the study of their content. Normally, especially if a florilegium has a prologue—unfortunately, not always the case—the compiler explains his choices and underlines the characteristics of the name used so the reader or user will understand precisely the end followed in choosing the citations. Moreover, one must be certain that the prologue to the work is original and that it is not a question of a borrowing made by the compiler from an earlier compilation, which is sometimes the case. In such instances, one realizes rather quickly that the content of the compilation does not correspond to the information given in the prologue and that the title does not therefore necessarily reflect the character of the chosen extracts.

Another particularity of this genre is that the title does not necessarily always appear at the beginning of the work. One can also find it at the end, as in the case of a philosophical florilegium from the end of the thirteenth century, the *Parvi flores*, where the compiler only gives the title in the explicit of his text.[17] In the first half of the thirteenth century, William of Montague chose the epilogue of his *Liber exceptionum ex libris viginti trium auctorum* to provide his methodological observations, which are usually found in a preface.[18]

Historical Outline

If florilegia have existed from the early Middle Ages to answer the needs of study and to provide access to necessary texts, one notices an evolution in the genre, taking into account over the centuries the progressive increase in literary production in all areas. In addition, in this period intellectuals were more attracted to literary pursuits and the acquisition of a general culture. Thus, a cultured public was drawn above all to classical and Christian authors on whom they were nourished.[19] One is aware also that there is no opposition between literature and Christian doctrine since the anthologies in circulation for the most part are theological.[20] The Latin translations made by Boethius of the Aristotelian works on logic do not pose any problems, nor do the commentaries he composed on them, because the classical heritage did not question the supremacy of Church doctrine. Even logic could not cause offense since it was considered essentially an instrument to improve reasoning and to understand the nuances of the classical and patristic patrimony.

Before the eighth century few manuscripts containing works of classical Latin authors were in circulation, as Munk Olsen well demonstrates.[21] To compensate for this lack, anthologies of citations will become more numerous from the ninth century. To begin with, they were devoted to the Bible, and classical, patristic, and theological authors, following the needs of the intellectual elite and the clerics of the period.[22] Scholars, very cultured for that period and lovers of literature, were intent on making this textual referencing more accessible. One may cite, among others, the initiatives of Lupus of Ferrières or Florus of Lyons.

Scholarly handbooks, in the form of extracts or citations, quickly came into being in an attempt to give first schoolboys, then students, an indispensable source of information for training in the subjects taught in the *trivium* and *quadrivium*. Moreover, the handbooks contained lists of sentences and easily learned proverbs, to complete the didactic material essential to diffuse and to learn.[23] Among these lists, one should mention the *Sententiae philosophorum* attributed to Publilius Syrus, which generally accompanied the citations of classical authors.[24] This work consisted of proverbs classified in alphabetical order which conveyed popular wisdom. One also frequently found the *Disticha Catonis*, which transmitted in short phrases precepts that inculcated rules for an honest and moral life.[25] Other works, such as the *Proverbia philosophorum* of Ps.-Caecilius Balbus, also appeared in anthologies from this period.

At the beginning of the Middle Ages, it was essential to have access to texts of authors deemed suitable for study or general knowledge, whether this had a pedagogical intent or not, though pedagogical concerns most often prevailed.[26] One also tended in reference anthologies to give slightly longer excerpts, sometimes entire passages from works, side by side with short phrases that are easy to memorize, so as to enrich the reading of scholars and allow them to acquire a certain necessary cultural level. Some scholars in this case speak of *libri manuales*, assembling in a single volume the necessary information on a subject.[27]

A very interesting anthology representative of the early Middle Ages, the *Collectio* of Hadoard, who was librarian at Corbie, was composed in the ninth century. This work illustrates perfectly the interests of a compiler and the manner in which he conceived of an anthology of texts during the period. The autograph of the work is preserved in a manuscript at the Vatican Library (Reg. lat. 1762). Unfortunately, *Collectaneum*, the title given by the cataloguer, is different from the one which the compiler himself gave to the work in the incipit, namely *collectio*.[28] Hadoard also provides his name at the end of the prologue: "Hoc opus explicuit, nomen cui est Hadoardus, Ordine presbiteri officioque cluit."

This case demonstrates the problem posed by the titles of these "text anthologies." Whether it is a question of a *collectaneum* or a *collectio*, there is not a great difference in the meaning. These technical terms designate a work of general content and an anthology of disparate components: texts more or less long, extracts from several authors, as well as short citations easily committed to memory. The problem does not reside in the technical meaning of the term used. But it is a shame that modern specialists did not take up the original title given by the author in the incipit to the work and instead substituted an alternative title still used by scholars to the present day. Unfortunately, all modern scholars still continue to speak wrongly of the *Collectaneum* of Hadoard, instead of the *Collectio*.

It is also all the more regrettable that the work of this librarian is not a florilegium in the strictest sense of the term but rather corresponds to an anthology of philosophical texts, as the author informs us.[29] The ensemble reflects the interests of the compiler and contains for the most part long and varied passages from philosophical works (available at that time) of Cicero, to which are joined extracts from Sallust, Macrobius, and Martianus Capella, as well as the *Sententiae* of Publilius Syrus. These works were probably available in the library of St. Peter at Corbie and are representative of the "philosophical" literature of the period. When Hadoard speaks here of "philosophy," it is primarily moral philosophy, to such a degree that many modern scholars have called this anthology a "theological" one.

During this early period, one finds citations from ancient philosophical texts (works of Cicero, Seneca, Lucretius, Apuleius, Plato, Boethius, etc.) in florilegia of classical authors. These anthologies of extracts aimed at making texts available to medieval scholars in condensed form as well as the *auctoritates* from classical authors, whether the extracts were theological, literary, or moral. In this case, as with the *collectio* put together by Hadoard, it is not always possible to differentiate an anthology from a florilegium.[30] One is also aware that the citations with an ethical tenor are very selective.[31] They circulate with other extracts but do not yet constitute a separate literary genre. In the context of the *trivium*, the teaching of ethics became established from the early Middle Ages along with rhetoric and logic. These three subjects aimed at teaching students to live rightly, to express themselves correctly, and to master the rules of reasoning, indispensable to the argument.

The compilation of Hadoard allows for a better understanding of the abridged literature and the compilations which circulated in scholarly circles of his time and which developed over the next two centuries to meet more specific needs. From the eleventh century, there is a development in the content and aim, as Margaret Gibson rightly points out:

> This was the period of the great *compendia*: designed to contain within two covers all that was needed for the study of one subject, as logic, or a related group, as grammar, logic, rhetoric...These *compendia* contain the basic material for the study of the *artes* in the eleventh century. For us they show what was available and what was not, and the passages in the available texts: ideally it offered also the most relevant and up-to-date commentary. It represents a *choice* of texts, moving slowly towards the "right" choice, the non-essential being rejected: and it is the medium for discussion of these texts. The choice and arrangement—often as a marginal gloss—reflects the librarian and the *scriptorium* as well as the teacher. Their *discussion* however is the beginning of new, and finally independent work.[32]

From the twelfth century, the research tools under discussion here became more specialized. In order to meet an ever-growing demand and to make accessible the basics of an expanding literary and scientific production, this "literary genre" quickly diversified, which is clearly seen in the mutiplication of technical terms to designate and distinguish the new "tools" and involving nuances in respect to their content. This evolution entailed a change in mentality as well. One no longer acquired texts for self-improvement, but it was imperative to find documentation essential for study, teaching, writing, and preaching. The Cistercian order, moreover, played a pivotal role in allowing rapid access to information by creating indices and tables which faciliated easy consultation and retrieval of useful passages brought together in an anthology.[33]

Classical Greek and Arabic culture progressively seeped into the West with the influx of texts translated into Latin, and it greatly enriched the cultural Latin patrimony from the eleventh century. New scientific and philosophical texts became available and spread throughout Western Europe, dramatically increasing the amount of literary and scientific production and enlarging the amount of information available. It became more and more difficult, then, for one person to gain command of all the knowledge one needed to know. To respond to the demand and the needs of scholars eager to engage with these works, more and more tools came into being, destined to satisfy the needs of potential users. Complete texts of newly circulated works were few in number and not readily accessible. Manuscripts were expensive, complete copies rare, and the collections of libraries poorly equipped.[34] To circumvent these difficulties, works were abbreviated, cut up into passages deemed indispensable to know, and often reduced to citations or easily memorized extracts. Consequently, from the twelfth century, even the idea of "reading" evolved and one's state of mind changed. Scholars had to be content with piecemeal reading of texts and the monastic *ruminatio* gave way to *utilitas* and also to *brevitas*. Those terms are found in nearly all the prologues to florilegia extant from this period.

In the early thirteenth century with the massive influx of Aristotelian texts in the Latin world, a new "subgenre" rapidly evolved: the philosophical florilegium. The characteristic of these new anthologies, which came into being with the rise of the universities and were based on the newly translated works of Aristotle, was to take into account the totality of available philosophical knowledge. Certain prologues centered on the division of the diverse parts of philosophy well illustrate this concern. Their importance has not been hitherto sufficiently underlined. The number of these texts is so overwhelming that no synthetic study of them exists. Some sparse studies have allowed some insight into the role they played in the scholastic period in medieval intellectual life.[35] However, when one opens a scholarly text of the period, which to a large degree used Aristotle as an *auctoritas* in support of doctrines, one realizes that the majority do not always cite him according to the original Latin version, which was not readily accessible during the period for the reasons discussed above, but from florilegia circulating in university circles or in the *studia* of religious orders. One is left, therefore, with the thorny problem of the exact source of the citations.

Besides philosophical florilegia, the thirteenth and fourteenth centuries also saw the birth of new tools for preachers: anthologies of *distinctiones* and diverse concordances so constructed as to facilitate the retrieval of useful passages. In order to provide easy access to the material, indices and tables were constituted. The majority of these anthologies were Cistercian in origin, as Mary and Richard Rouse have pointed out.[36] The abundance of information available during this period required new techniques to consult them easily. This era also saw the emergence of a new page layout and a more systematic text. Henceforth, one attached titles to texts and divided them into chapters for ease of reading. *Utilitas* and *brevitas* became essential to control the available information.

Florilegia have always been considered, quite rightly, a secondhand literature, and for this reason the majority have remained unedited, researchers preferring to study the original texts rather than their more or less faithful abridgments. Consequently, it is often difficult to find the exact source for certain citations which have undergone numerous changes in the course of their transmission. This contribution is only a preliminary to the consultation of these anthologies, a tool to aid in understanding the dynamics which were responsible for their composition and a guide in assisting their consultation. Though medievalists have recently shown an increasing interest in these tools, the modern researcher still confronts numerous difficulties in consulting them.

Most of them are still unedited, and no inventory exists to give one an easy orientation to this vast domain.

One can situate with some precision the origin and appearance of purely philosophical florilegia. New anthologies came into being in the scholastic era with the arrival of Aristotelianism in university and learned circles and developed to meet specific needs. They represent a defined new category and are separate from the other tools composed from different sources. Easy to recopy and carry, these philosophical tools will rapidly spread through all countries and unversities.

METHOD OF COMPILING

Different methods were employed both in Antiquity and the Middle Ages to compose a florilegium. By chance, we have a useful witness from the early Middle Ages. As we saw in Section 59.2 above, Florus of Lyons left vestiges of his work in a manuscript. To facilitate the collection of material, he himself identifies by certain signs the passages that had been or needed to be copied by the copyist. Florus's work is quite remarkable and represents a very good example from a palaeographical and methodological perspective, as L. Holtz has demonstrated.[37] Florus of Lyons, who had already acquired a personal library of several manuscripts (rare at this time), left his compiler marks in several of them. He isolated in a manuscript of the text of Jerome a series of passages which served as the basis for the florilegium commenting on the letters of Paul.[38] He seems to have done the same thing in another codex assembling the works of Gregory.[39] This very early witness is all the more interesting in that it is rare to have preserved vestiges concerning the diverse stages of a compilation. From the perspective of method, we can thus observe an author of this period at work and see his conception of the choice of passages to be retained. Another point worth underlining is that Florus left in the margins certain glosses and explications in his own hand which we find in the florilegium. Moreover, one can appreciate the care he took while working with a *socius* to prepare the copy which will be made by him. We have preserved the result achieved by these two men, namely the florilegia containing extracts recopied and accompanied by brief comments by Florus.

Florus is not the sole compiler of the Middle Ages who assists us in understanding the method used. Hadoard, his contemporary, explicitly speaks of this in the verses of the preface to his *Collectio*. He explains that inasmuch as he is the guardian (*custos*) of the books in the library, he abbreviated (*contraxit*) the works he read, and then consigned the extracts to wax tablets (*in tabulis*) to assemble them and to reproduce through the expedient of short passages an image (*effigiem*) of the books in question.[40]

In other cases, the compiler worked alone and chose phrases or paragraphs to retain. He was satisfied to make a selection and did not intervene in the original texts either to explain difficult words or to comment on obscure passages. But this was not always the case, and certain compilers did not hesitate to summarize according to their own preferences passages which were too long or to pass over in silence texts which did not seem to them to be in conformity with Christian doctrine. Their interventions thus showed a certain censure.

When earlier florilegia existed, compilers did not refrain either from pillaging or recopying them, adding or not adding supplementary passages. Such is the case with the *Collectanea* of Heiric of Auxerre, who admits in his preface to having recopied in the first part of his compilation the course of his master Lupus of Ferrières *(Haec Lupus, haec nitido passim uersabat in ore / Compensans aptis singula temporibus)*, who had assembled citations from Valerius Maximus and Suetonius. In the second part of the anthology, he takes up again extracts from a course given by another professor, Aimon of Auxerre.[41] Certain compilers did not hesitate to recopy, incorporating changes to the texts they borrowed from their predecessors, as an author admits at the end of the twelfth century in the preface to a florilegium preserved at Heiligenkreuz.[42] He explains how he proceeded: it was essentially a question of the fruit of his scholarly readings, focused especially on ethics, physics, and some theoretical questions *(theorice)*.[43] Likewise, certain authors did not compose their prologues, but sometimes borrowed them from other introductions or from *accessus* which did not correspond to the content of their work, without realizing the incomprehensibility which resulted for those consulting the work.[44]

The compiler of the *Florilegium angelicum*, assembled in the second half of the twelfth century, gives interesting information in the preface to the anthology. There, he admits to having borrowed part of his work from existing florilegia *(defloravi flosculos)* so as to present a spray *(manipulos)* that is easy to use.[45]

This recovery of already exisiting material will continue later, and a large number of philosophical florilegia, composed from the thirteenth century, will contain earlier extracts which a compiler will complete with the aid of extracts either from newly translated texts or from contemporary commentaries. These anthologies, aimed at introducing those who so wished to Aristotelianism, would be reviewed and added to regularly to keep them up to date. Since it was a question of tools which were very frequently consulted, readers and users also added supplementary extracts in the margins as well as explicative glosses which progressively entered the content and became an integral part of the work as it continued to be copied. It is, therefore, very difficult to give a precise date to anthologies which circulated in this manner.

One may conceive of a florilegium in several ways. Either one limits oneself to a single author from whose works one culls representative selections, which obviously implies a certain subjectivity on the part of the compiler, and what might be important for one individual will not be for another, or, on the contrary, one organizes information from one or several authors on the same subject, or, again, one chooses a series of concepts accompanied by extracts from diverse works. In this last instance, the compiler generally classifies the concepts in alphabetical order so that users can find rapidly and without a problem all the passages relevant to the study of a particular term. One ends up then with three types of florilegia: the florilegium devoted to a single or multiple authors which follows the order of the original text; systematic florilegia classified by subject; and, finally, florilegia classified by an alphabetical listing of citations.

One can already find this type of classification in certain anthologies from the early Middle Ages, and it will continue to the scholastic era. Most of these anthologies were used in scholarly and then university settings, providing the basics from works of authors on the reading list. Next came tools meant for preachers, assembling *distinctiones* or *exempla* or *auctoritates* which could be used in sermons.[46] From the thirteenth century, one notices that the same florilegium could be composed for university students as well as for preachers.[47] This double intent explains in part the general ethos of most of the chosen extracts. Exercises which students were forced to undertake in the course of their studies accustomed them to memorizing a great deal of the subject matter. It is not surprising, then, that a large number of citations transmitted by florilegia passed literally into the obligatory scholarly exercises or the drafting of commentaries or the explanations of texts. The same is true also for the extracts used in sermons.

In this period, florilegia in general were the repositories of *auctoritates*. But, as one has just seen, the citations were intended to serve in diverse contexts. Compilers also felt free to modify the text or even sometimes the sense to bring the extracts into conformity with theological doctrines and to give them a universal meaning. The citations no longer faithfully reproduced the original texts.

In the scholastic period, recourse to *auctoritates* was part and parcel of the explanation of texts and had become indispensable for giving added weight to the original philosophical doctrines expounded by intellectuals, and this explains the unparalleled success of Aristotle and the large number of research tools based on his works. If, in the early Middle Ages, one also made reference to *auctoritates,* it was because classical authors were the only witnesses available. But with the introduction of Aristotelianism, the study of philosophy develops in university settings and changes considerably the way in which one approaches the study of nature and speculative questions. Christian doctrine no longer was sufficient to answer speculations about the creation of the world and physical and metaphysical problems. Theology, which had nourished intellectuals, did not answer all the questions they asked themselves, and it was appropriate to have recourse to new doctrines to shore up the elaboration of diverse philosophical theories.

Thus, in order to provide information which was to the point and aimed at all audiences, often in the religious orders several members worked together to gather the information necessary for scientific work and study, as Albert the Great and Vincent of Beauvais bear witness. The mendicant orders played an important role in the composition and diffusion of florilegia from the thirteenth century. Since many theologians feared that the new perspectives elaborated by the doctrines of Aristotle might be in contradiction with the teachings of the Church, representatives of these orders censored numerous texts to give them a more universal viewpoint. Compilers, therefore, began to expurgate numerous texts and to include in the florilegia they composed only extracts that could be placed in everyone's hands, but that no longer took into account the substance of Aristotelian philosophy. From the thirteenth century, theologians exercised censorship, fearful that new theories would corrupt minds and be erroneously interpreted by students who did not have a sufficient background to question or interpret them. It was absolutely essential, therefore, to make a choice in the assembled extracts and to eliminate ambiguous passages to escape Church condemnation. For this reason one finds many passages of a general meaning and which have a universal scope adaptable to numerous contexts.

For all these reasons, most of the philosophical florilegia of this period are only a pale reflection of the original doctrines of Aristotle. However, they had the advantage of being able to be used by all, whether students or preachers. Thanks to their practical and synthetic character, they could be copied easily by impoverished scholars who did not have the means to acquire complete manuscripts of authors, and this factor explains their success.

As in earlier periods, some compilers employed already existing material to compose their florilegia. The *Parvi flores,* an anthology dedicated to Aristotelian philosophy dating from the end of the thirteenth century, included a prologue which could not have been composed by the compiler since it is attested independently in earlier manuscripts. To this example may be added an older florilegium containing extracts from works of logic, as well as another containing extracts of ethical import from classical authors (Seneca, Boethius, and Apuleius), already in circulation earlier and recovered in this new philosophical research tool. Since the compiler strove to give extracts from all the works of Aristotle translated into Latin and known during the period, he added to this borrowed material extracts from works which had not yet been anthologized. In carrying out his work, he often makes choices that are not the most judicious. Most of the citations are not literal. A single phrase sometimes suffices to summarize an entire chapter. The passages chosen are very short and can be readily memorized. They generally follow the order of the text for each work, but the content absolutely does not reflect the subtleties of many of Aristotle's doctrines. In assembling the information, the compiler has visibly censored many passages so as to place his work in a universal context. This fact is not surprising from a Franciscan professor teaching in his convent at Montpellier.[48] Since he is working at a period when Thomistic philosophy was condemned by the Church authorities, he borrows numerous extracts from Thomas Aquinas without ever giving his name, but citing them under the name of *Commentator,* which, as one knows, designated Averroes at that time.

LOCATING SOURCES, THE IDENTIFICATION OF CITATIONS, AND THE EDITING OF ANTHOLOGIES

As is clearly seen from what has preceded, we are dealing with the fluid transmission of material, which poses many problems for modern editors. The compilers themselves modified the text of certain citations, sometimes abbreviating outrageously entire passages and not hesitating to censor certain doctrines. Sometimes they placed extracts from certain authors under the name of authors recognized as authorities, either due to ignorance or to thwart the attention of the censors. Moreover, not all compilers were aware of the contribution of the latest translations or discoveries concerning the attribution of certain works. Thus, one finds citations from *De formula vitae honestae,* the work of Martin of Braga, also entitled *De quattuor virtutibus cardinalibus,* under the name of Seneca, as well as citations from the *Liber de causis* attributed to Aristotle at that period, whereas Thomas Aquinas had shown that this treatise was not by him as early as the second half of the thirteenth century. Obviously the compiler was unaware of this fact and had not followed the progress made on this level.

It could also happen that a compiler would make a first collection of material and then augment or correct it before giving it its definitive form. As well, users, who recopied the anthologies either for references or pedagogical reasons, enriched progressively their content by adding citations or supplementary extracts, as well as marginal glosses which during later transmission were often integrated into the text. As many exemplars disappeared with the passage of time, how to reconstruct a stemma of the manuscripts and the original of the compilation? How is it possible to find the totality of sources and identify every citation contained in a florilegium? This involves long and fastidious work, especially if a critical edition of the original text does not exist. The extant manuscripts often present significant variants, and it is not easy to rediscover the affiliations among them, especially when one is dealing with a florilegium which had a wide readership and a broad diffusion. Besides the usual textual variants, some witnesses have preserved supplementary citations missing in other witnesses. For some extracts, the text is so corrupt that one may only find the exact source for the phrase by chance. Finally, in certain places the copyists or users rewrote the passage.

A concrete example will demonstrate the difficulties involved in this work. One finds the following phrase in the *Parvi flores*: "Genus multorum semper est scibile."[49] According to the compiler, this extract comes from citations taken from the *De generatione animalium* of Aristotle. Reading the text where Aristotle treats of sterility in the Latin translation made by William of Moerbeck gives the following: "Sed hoc genus totum sterile est quod multorum." How to find the origin of the textual corruption? The error stems from an error in transmission. Since this florilegium has been preserved in more than 300 manuscirpts, one may take soundings to figure out what happened. One finds in one of the witnesses the following citation: "Genus multorum semper est sterile," whose content is incomprehensible. In a later manuscript, one can read "scibile" in place of "sterile," which allows one to understand the meaning of the phrase. In order to make it understandable, either the coypist had misinterpreted the abbreviation in his model or he corrected the text to make sense, remembering the passage from the *Categories* "Multa sunt scibilia de quibus non est scientia."[50] The phrase is now comprehensible, but it still does not come from the citations taken from the *De generatione animalium*. Its place is to be found among the citations from the *Categoriae*, citations from which are found at the end of the anthology. In this case, one was able to find the source of the problem, but many other passages cannot be identified, unless one has access to the orginal compilation. How to find then an identification in other cases where the intermediary exemplars have disappeared and for which conjectures are sometimes hazardous?

One understands, therefore, why many florilegia have not been edited. The multiple difficulties encountered in identifying the texts also illustrate the problems posed by the transmission of these anthologies, especially if they circulated in many manuscripts. Moreover, the manuscripts in which they are preserved, especially those which date from the scholastic period, are often difficult to transcribe. Recopied and used by students and scholars for their own purposes, they are written very carelessly, and the Cursive script of many of the manuscripts, full of abbreviations that are difficult to read and resolve, makes their consultation difficult, even for the best palaeographers. These manuscripts were for personal use and were not intended for circulation. Chapter titles and paragraph divisions are often missing. There is no attempt to organize the page; the only thing that matters is the quantity of citations written on a page. The more the script is abbreviated, the more one can get on a page. That most of these manuscripts were for private study explains these changes, the additions and remarks made to the content. This was a distinctive feature of these tools recopied with little care and serving as indispensible information consulted as much in education as in preaching.

In addition, since one is dealing with a sort of "secondhand" literature, modern researchers resist undertaking the work necessary to establish a critical text. Such an attitude, though understandable, does not further the identification of the numerous citations made by medieval authors in their works. Fortunately, we have today text databases which greatly help in identifying sources. However, the variants attached to the phrase in the course of transmission are often impediments to precise identifica-tion. To arrive at a satisfactory result, teams should be put in place which could be given the responsibility of finding the citations of an author in the literature of a period and could perhaps construct for some of them lists of identified citations.

The following question arises concerning the editing of florilegia: Given the com-plexity of the manuscript tradition and the fluid transmission of the text, is it worth a researcher spending several years trying to reconstruct the original of an anthology? One cannot give an answer which can be applied to every kind of florilegium. Each case is unique: What is the manuscript tradition and has the information been copied literally over the course of transmission? Does the identification of extracts cause problems because of their rewriting? Great scholars, such as Father L.-J. Bataillon, answered this question by advising one to give the text of the oldest preserved manuscript and to identify the extracts as far as possible so as to aid researchers in finding the sources of texts used in the medieval period.

In certain cases one might envisage another solution: in the case where a florilegium was widely copied and continued to be used into the Renaissance and even in certain instances right up to the end of the seventeenth century, one finds a printed tradition of the text. With the appearance of printing, one or sometimes two versions of an original anthology continued in circulation. This text is not reworked and is transmitted such as it is. One can, therefore, base the editing on the printed tradition of the anthology. This is obviously not an ideal solution, but it does make accessible for all a text which circulated at a given time. The example of the "Auctoritates Aristotelis," a version printed in hundreds of incunables and ancient editions, made it possible for the *Parvi flores* to circulate in a certain form, and to identify the citations contained within it and render service to numerous researchers confronted with identifying the sources from Aristotle in the philosophical texts of the scholastic period. For this precise case, the solution proved useful. This was the only way to circulate a version of the text.

The complexity of these anthologies is evident. There are numerous problems one encounters in studying them, and since florilegia cover very different spheres of sources, each category should be studied by a specialist in the subject. Since certain points in common emerge from studies conducted previously, this chapter has tried to take them into account by placing them within chronological limits. There is also an evolution between the early and High Middle Ages which one must take account of. More could be written on these anthologies, which had an enormous success. In numerous cases, they constituted privileged witnesses to earlier texts, the basis of culture or teaching.

Their content clearly reflects the cultural level of an environment and illustrates the working method of intellectuals at a certain period. In them, one may trace the interests of the users of each period and thus see established a sort of repertory of the most widely read texts and those most appreciated by medieval writers. Their use in scholarly, monastic, and university circles reveals their universal character, in spite of their content essentially having been put together at second hand.

While recognizing their usefulness, one must confess that these anthologies are often disappointing because of the poverty they bring to the richness of their originals. Certain medieval authors, aware of their limits, did not hesitate to judge the antholgies and to underline their inherent faults. As early as the twelfth century, Robert of Melun had already signaled the dangers in having too frequent recourse to anthologies of glosses, since they often obscured the original meaning of the text, when the reader restricted himself to reading or studying only a collection of more or less interesting explications instead of trying to grasp the deep meaning of a passage.[51] Similarly, Engelbert of Admont, O.S.B. (1250–1331), who had studied with the Dominicans of Padua, a center which had a great reputation at the time, underlines the limits of compilations after his return to the monastery, where he had access henceforth to the entire text of several works. He illustrated their deficiencies and their faults and criticized certain professors for obscuring the originality of an author's thought by basing their lectures on anthologies of extracts rather than complete works. Regrettably, teaching suffered greatly because the professors oversimplified the difficulties of understanding and suppressed nuances. He was overjoyed, therefore, to return to his monastery, where he had access to *originalia* of the authors explicated in the courses and to find again in these works the original expressions and the difficult questions which his professor did not take up in his teaching.[52]

It is, therefore, very surprising to see that in spite of their doctrinal poverty, their always incomplete nature, and often the inexact references given or the corruption of the text in certain passages, some florilegia continued to be used in the Renaissance and even later. Though humanists criticized florilegia, certain anthologies still appeared, enriched and diffused. The invention of printing gave them new life. Early printers set up shop often close to universities and chose bestsellers to make new editions. Research tools were part of this and always found buyers among students who were looking for practical and useful aids.

But thanks also to printing, complete editions of authors began to circulate and became accessible to all. The reading practice of intellectuals henceforward was based on reading complete works. Florilegia no longer served for the acquisition of an indispensable culture. They remained in circulation only because they were practical and were considered as repositories of citations that were easier to handle and transport. Many intellectuals would seek out the original text of the sources, and the philological sense of the printers would develop to the detriment of this "secondhand" literature. One notices also a change of mentality during the same period. Recourse to *auctoritates*, so much an integral part of the scholastic method, gradually disappears and is replaced with the quest for *ratio*. Experimentation will develop in every domain and will replace recourse to arguments of the past. After having known a long and happy existence, this literary genre will be replaced by a different manner of thought, and the critical spirit will finally carry it off, strongly limiting the scope of medieval citations. New translations of texts made from original, newly discovered Greek manuscripts will give a new impetus to study, and by the end of the seventeenth century medieval anthologies will become completely obsolete.

NOTES

1. Darbo-Peschanski (2004).
2. Cf. Tuomarla (1999).
3. Rauner (1989) gives an interesting overview of the complexity of these anthologies and the problems one confronts when one wishes to study them.
4. As Talbot (1956, 6) wrote:

   The *Florilegium* differs, on the one hand, from the collection of thoughts drawn by an author as the distillation of his own personal creative activity and, on the other, from a collection of proverbs which reflect the wisdom of human experience handed down by oral tradition and which is for the most part anonymous; it is a kind of nosegay, a selection of the thoughts of other writers gathered together to suit the purposes of the compiler. It necessarily bears the personal imprint of the compiler and reflects his aims, his interests and his prejudices.

5. The best overview for the entire period is Spallone (1990). Her very complete and well-researched study takes into account classical florilegia of the early Middle Ages. Moreover, B. Munk Olsen has produced several publications on the Latin classics (1979, 1980), a very useful catalogue of manuscripts (1985–9) in three volumes, the second of which has a chapter dedicated to florilegia (pp. 837–77), and a collection of articles (1995). But this scholar's work does not go beyond the twelftth century. For the thirteenth century, one may complement the work assembled by Munk Olsen with the article by Falmagne (1997).

6. For patristic florilegia, see Rouse and Rouse (1982); Dekkers (1990).
7. Rouse and Rouse (1982).
8. See Hamesse (1990).
9. Our first attestation, given the present state of our knowledge, is found in Mirabellius et al.(1621), the *Florilegium magnum, seu polyanthea floribus novissimis sparsa* (cited in Pérennès 1859, col. 256).
10. Ovidius, *Met.* 15.366.
11. See Melville (1970).
12. See Imbs (1971–94, T.VIII, 992).
13. See Rouse (1991).
14. Rigg (1982, 317) seeks to clearly differentiate "anthology" from "florilegia":

    The words "anthology," "florilegium" and "excerpt" are all closely connected and derive from the image of plucking flowers...In modern critical terminology, however, anthology is usually distinguished from florilegium : the former is a collection of complete texts, the latter consists of extracts or excerpts from longer works. One might describe the *Golden Treasury of English Verse* as an anthology but the *Oxford Book of Quotations* as a florilegium.

15. See Hathaway (1989, 19).
16. In regards to technical vocabulary, one should mention Clasen (1960); see also the series of publications by Weijers (1988–2000) under the auspices of the Comité International des Institutions et de la Communication Intellectuelles au Moyen Âge (CIVICIMA) and especially Teeuwen (2003), which comprises a list of all technical terms studied in the nine previous volumes, and particularly Hamesse (1990).
17. See Hamesse (1974).
18. See Falmagne (2001, 328).
19. See Compagnon (1979).
20. For example, the *Dicta Catonis*, the work of a pupil of Alcuin, is composed of extracts from the commentary of Calcidius on the *Timaeus*, of the *De trinitate* and the *De civitate Dei* of St. Augustine, of the commentary of Boethius on the *Categories* of Aristotle, of the glosses of Prudentius, and of citations taken from the *Libri quaestionum naturalium* of Seneca. One finds there citations of ancient philosophical texts, but the title given to the anthology in some manuscripts, namely, *De imagine Dei,* well illustrates the theological interests of the compiler. See Zimmerann (1929); Marenbon (1981, 33–4); Contreni (1989, 100–1).
21. See Munk Olsen (1995, 21–3).
22. One may find in the same anthology citations of pagan authors in contrast to those of the saints and Christian authors, either citations of pagan authors who dealt with morality in relation to the *auctores*, literary authors, or again citations of prose authors in relation to poets. Likewise, poets are called *auctores*, while prose authors are called *philosophi*. See Paré, Brunet, and Tremblay (1933, 153–4).
23. For proverbs and sentences in antiquity, see Roos (1984).
24. See Woelfflin (1869); Giancotti (1963); Reeve (1986).
25. See Boas (1914); Boas and Botschuyver (1952).
26. See Hamesse (2008).
27. See Sanford (1924).
28. This florilegium was published by Schwenke (1889).
29. See Vat. Reg. Lat. 1762, fol.4: "Incipit de divina natura **colletio** quaedam secundum Tullium Ciceronem ceterosque philosophos ab ipso commemoratos."

30. See Delhaye (1964).
31. Thus, manuscript Douai, Bibliothèque municipale, 749-II, has the following incipit on fol. 23r: "Incipit proverbia ex diversorum auctorum libris in unum collecta moribus instruendis viciisque destruendis proferenda."
32. Gibson (1969, 124).
33. See Rouse (1976); Falmagne (1997).
34. See Fernandez de la Cuesta Gonzalez (2008, 39), who explains that the three manuscripts which conserve the *Florilegium Duacense* have a prologue which mentions explicitly the economic and cultural circumstances which account for the anthology.
35. The best overall study of this literature remains that of Grabmann (1939). The publication goes far beyond the framework of Aristotelian florilegia to encompass all kinds of tools made in the Middle Ages to facilitate the study of Aristotelianism.
36. Cf. Rouse and Rouse (1974), (1979).
37. See Holtz (1994).
38. See Fransen (1984).
39. See Fransen (1988).
40. Vatican City, BAV, Reg. lat. 1762 fol. 4r.
41. See Munk Olsen (1979, 53, n.2, and 100).
42. We have the proof from the pen of the compiler of the *Florilegium Sancticrucianum*: "et ut [sententie memoria digne] edificatione proficerent, saniori sensui cooptavi." Cited in Munk Olsen (1970, 53, n.2).
43. See Glauche (1971, 305, n.25): "ex maiori parte scolasticos libellos meos postpositurus... in quo quaedam inveniuntur quae ethice, quaedam phisice, quaedam vero quae theorice supponuntur."
44. See Quain (1945); Spallone (1990, 392–412).
45. Munk Olsen (1973, 195) has edited the complete preface.
46. These florilegia answer a wish made by Humbert de Romans in the first book of his *De eruditione praedicatorum*: "Circa materias sermonum sive collationum nota, quod interdum multis difficiulius est invenire materias utiles, et laudabiles, de quibus fiat sermo, quam inventa materia, de ipsa sermonem contexere. Et ideo expedit quod praedicator semper habeat in promptu materias ad praedicandum vel conferendum de Deo." Cited by Heintke (1993, 110).
47. See von Nolcken (1981).
48. See Hamesse (1995).
49. Aristoteles, *De generatione animalium*, B7, 746 b 19–20.
50. Aristoteles, *Categoriae*, 7, 7 b 30–5.
51. See *De modis colligendi summas et docendi*. Such is the title given in the preface in certain manuscripts of the *Sententiae*. See Martin (1947, XIV–XV).
52. See Wichner (1889, 509):

    Deinde post quinquennium audivi Theologiam Paduae in domo Praedicatorum sub magistris lectoribus. Tunc ibidem in eodem studio quatuor annos mansi. Et deinde ad claustrum meum rediens in Admundam, totum studium meum posui **ad originalia inquirenda et perlegenda**: quorum Deo dante pervidi et perlegi numerum competentem, et inveni in qubusdam eorum multa breviter et succincte posita et dicta. Quae aliqui magni doctores **in terminacionibus aliquarum difficilium quaestionum**, non expressis nominatim, nec in dictis eorum auctoritatibus posuerunt quod **forsitan factum est gracia brevitatis**.

Bibliography

Boas, M. 1914. "De librorum Catonianorum historia atque compositione." *Mnemosyne* 42: 17–46.

Boas, M. and H. J. Botschuyver. 1952. *Disticha Catonis recensuit et apparatu critico instruxit M. Boas. Opus post Marci Boas mortem edendum curavit H. J. Botschuyver.* Amsterdam: North-Holland.

Clasen, S. 1960. "Collectanea zum Studien- und Buchwesen des Mittelalters." *Archiv für Geschichte der Philosophie* 42: 159–206, 247–71.

Compagnon, A. 1979. *La Seconde Main ou le travail de la citation.* Paris: Éditions du Seuil.

Contreni, J. J. 1989. "The Carolingian School: Letters from the Classroom." In *Giovanni Scoto nel suo tempo. L'organizzazione del sapere in età carolingia* (Atti dei Convegni dell'Accademia Tudertina e del Centro di studi sulla spiritualità medievale. Nuova Serie, 1). Spoleto: Centro italiano di studi sull'alto Medioevo.

Darbo-Peschanski, C., ed. 2004. *La Citation dans l'Antiquité* (Actes du Colloque du PARSA, Lyon ENS, 6–8 novembre 2002). Grenoble: Éditions Jérôme Millon.

Dekkers, E. 1990. "Quelques notes sur des florilèges augustiniens anciens et médiévaux." In *Collectanea Augustiniana. Mélanges T. J. Van Bavel,* 27–44. Louvain: Institut historique augustinien.

Delhaye, P. 1964. "Florilèges médiévaux d'éthique." In *Dictionnaire de spiritualité: ascétique et mystique, doctrine et histoire,* ed. Marcel Villier, vol. 5, col. 460. Paris : Beauchesne.

Falmagne, T. 1997. "Les Cisterciens et les nouvelles formes d'organisation des florilèges aux 12ᵉ et 13ᵉ siècles." *Archivum latinitatis medii aevi* 55: 73–176.

Falmagne, T. 2001. Un Texte en contexte. *Les "Flores Paradisi" et le milieu culturel de Villers-en-Brabant dans la première moitié du 13e siècle.* Turnhout: Brepols.

Fernandez de la Cuesta Gonzalez, B. 2008. *En la senda del "florilegium Gallicum": Edicion y estudio del florilegio del manuscrito Cordoba, Archivo Capitular 150* (Textes et études du moyen âge 45), Louvain-la-Neuve: Fédération internationale des instituts d'études médiévales.

Fransen, P.-I. 1984. "Description de la collection hiéronymienne de Florus de Lyon sur l'Apôtre." *Revue bénédictine* 94: 195–228.

Fransen, P.-I. 1988. "Description de la collection de Florus de Lyon sur l'Apôtre." *Revue bénédictine* 98: 278–317.

Giancotti, F. 1963. *Ricerche sulla tradizione manoscritta delle Sentenze di Publilio Siro* (Biblioteca di cultura contemporanea LXXIX). Messina and Florence: G. d'Anna.

Gibson, M. 1969. "The *Artes* in the Eleventh Century." In *Arts libéraux et philosophie au moyen âge. Actes du 4e Congrès international de philosophie médiévale,* 121–6. Montreal and Paris: Institut d'études médiévales–J. Vrin.

Glauche, G. 1971. "Einige Bemerkungen zum Florileg von Heiligenkreuz." In *Festschrift Bernhard Bischoff zu seinem 65. Geburtstag,* ed. J. Autenrieth and F. Brunhölzl, 295–306. Stuttgart: A. Hiersemann.

Grabmann, M. 1939. *Methoden und Hilfsmittel des Aristotelesstudiums im Mittelalter* (Sitzungsberichte der Bayerischen Akademie der Wissenschaften. Philosophisch-historische Abteilung. Jahrgang 1939, Heft 5). Munich: Verlag der Bayerischen Akademie der Wissenschaften.

Hamesse, J. 1974. *Les "Auctoritates Aristotelis". Un florilège médiéval. Étude historique et édition critique* (Philosophes médiévaux XVII). Louvain and Paris: Publications universitaires.

Hamesse, J. 1990. *Le Vocabulaire des florilèges médiévaux*. In *Méthodes et instruments du travail intellectuel au moyen âge. Études sur le vocabulaire* (CIVICIMA – Études sur le vocabulaire intellectuel du moyen âge III), ed. O. Weijers, 209–30. Turnhout: Brepols.

Hamesse, J. 1995. "Johannes de Fonte, compilateur des 'Parvi flores.' Le témoignage de plusieurs manuscrits conservés à la Bibliothèque Vaticane." *Archivum Franciscanum Historicum* 88: 515–31.

Hamesse, J. 2008. "La Survie de quelques auteurs classiques dans les collections de textes philosophiques du moyen âge." In *Classica et beneventana. Essays presented to Virginia Brown on the Occasion of her 65th Birthday*, ed. F. T. Coulson and A. A. Grotans (Textes et études du moyen âge 36), 73–86. Turnhout: Brepols.

Hathaway, N. 1989. "Compilatio: from Plagiarism to Compiling." *Viator* 20: 19–44.

Heintke, F. 1993. *Humbert von Romans der fünfte Ordenmeister der Dominikaner* (Historisches Studien, Heft 222). Berlin: Ebering.

Holtz, L. 1994. "La Minuscule marginale et interlinéaire de Florus de Lyon." In *Gli autografi medievali. Problemi paleografici e filologici*, ed. P. Chiesa and L. Piselli (Quaderni di cultura mediolatina 5), 149–66. Spoleto: Centro italiano di studi sull'alto medioevo.

Imbs, P., ed. 1971–94. *Trésor de la langue française. Dictionnaire de la langue du XIXe et du XXe siècle (1789–1960)*. Paris: Éditions du Centre national de la recherche scientifique.

Marenbon, J. 1981. *From the Circle of Alcuin to the School of Auxerre: Logic, Theology and Philosophy in the early Middle Ages* (Cambridge Studies in Medieval Life and Thought. Third Series, 15). Cambridge: Cambridge University Press.

Martin, R. M. 1947. *Œuvres de Robert de Melun*. T. III: *Sententie*, vol. I. Texte inédit (Spicilegium Sacrum Lovaniense 21). Louvain: Bureaux.

Melville, G. 1970. "Zur 'Flores-Metaphorik' in der Mittelalterlichen Geschichtsschreibung. Ausdruck eines Formungsprinzips." *Historisches Jahrbuch* 90: 65–80.

Mirabellius, N. *et al.* 1621. *Florilegii Magni seu Polyantheae floribus novissimis sparsai libri xx*. Frankfurt: Heirs of Lazarus Zetzner.

Munk Olsen, B. 1973. "Note sur quelques préfaces de florilèges latins du XIIe siècle." *Revue romane* 8: 185–91.

Munk Olsen, B. 1979. "Les Classiques latins dans les florilèges médiévaux antérieurs au XIIIe siècle." *Revue d'histoire des textes* 9: 47–121.

Munk Olsen, B. 1980. "Les Classiques latins dans les florilèges médiévaux antérieurs au XIIIe siècle (*suite*)." *Revue d'histoire des textes* 10: 115–64.

Munk Olsen, B. 1985–9. *L'Étude des auteurs classiques latins aux XIe et XIIe siècles*. Paris: Éditions du CNRS.

Munk Olsen, B. 1995. *La Réception de la littérature classique au moyen âge (IXe–XIIe siècle): choix d'articles publié par des collègues à l'occasion de son soixantième anniversaire*. Copenhagen: Museum Tusculanum Press.

Paré, G., A. Brunet, and P. Tremblay. 1933. *La Renaissance du XIIe siècle. Les écoles et l'enseignement* (Publications de l'Institut d'Études médiévales d'Ottawa III). Paris and Ottawa: J. Vrin.

Pérennès, F. 1859. *Dictionnaire de bibliographie catholique*. Paris: J.-P. Migne.

Quain, E. A. 1945. "The Mediaeval 'Accessus ad Auctores'." *Traditio* 3: 215–64.

Rauner, E. 1989. "Florilegien." In *Lexikon des Mittelalters*, ed. R.-H. Bautier *et al.*, IV, 566–9. Munich and Zurich: Artemis.

Reeve, M. D. 1986. "Publilius." In *Texts and Transmission. A Survey of the Latin Classics*, ed. L. D. Reynolds, 327–9. Oxford: Clarendon Press.

Rigg, A. G. 1982. "Anthologies and Florilegia." In *Dictionary of the Middle Ages*, ed. Joseph R. Strayer, 1, 317. New York : Scribner.

Roos, P. 1984. *Sentenza e Proverbio nell'Antichità e i "Distici di Catone." Il testo latino e volgarizzamenti italiani. Con una scelta e traduzione delle massime e delle frasi proverbiali latine classiche più importanti o ancora vive oggi nel mondo moderno.* Brescia: Editrice Morcelliana.

Rouse, M. A. and R. H. Rouse. 1982. "Florilegia of Patristic Texts." In *Les Genres littéraires dans les sources théologiques et philosophiques médiévales. Définition, critique, exploitation* (Publications de l'Institut d'Études Médiévales. Textes, Études, Congrès 5), 165–80. Louvain-la-Neuve: Université catholique de Louvain.

Rouse, R. H. 1976. "Cistercian Aids to Study in the Thirteenth Century." *Studies in Cistercian History* 2: 123–34.

Rouse, R. H. 1991. "The 'Florilegium Angelicum': Its Origin, Content and Influence." In *Authentic Witnesses: Approaches to Medieval Texts and Manuscripts*, 101–52. Notre Dame, IN: University of Notre Dame Press.

Rouse, R. H. and M. A. Rouse. 1974. "Biblical Distinctions in the Thirteenth Century." *Archives d'histoire doctrinale et littéraire du Moyen Âge* 41: 27–37.

Rouse, R. H. and M. A. Rouse. 1979. *Preachers, Florilegia and Sermons: Studies on the "Manipulus florum" of Thomas of Ireland* (Studies and Texts 47). Toronto: Pontifical Institute of Medieval Studies.

Sanford, E. M. 1924. "The Use of Classical Latin Authors in the Libri Manuales." *Transactions and Proceedings of the American Philological Association* 55: 190–248.

Schwenke, P. 1889. "Des Presbyter Hadoardus Cicero-Excerpte nach E. Narducci's Abschrift des Cod. Vat. Reg. 1762." *Philologus, Zeitschrift für das klassische Alterthum*, Supplementband 5: 397–588.

Spallone, M. 1990. "I percorsi del testo: 'accessus,' commentari, florilegi." In *Lo spazio letterario di Roma antica* III: *La ricezione del testo*, ed. G. Cavallo, P. Fedeli, and A. Giardina, 387–471. Rome: Salerno Editrice.

Talbot, C. H. 1956. *Florilegium Morale Oxoniense. Secunda Pars: Flores Auctorum* (Analecta Mediaevalia Namurcensia, 6). Louvain and Lille: Nauwelaerts.

Teeuwen, M. 2003. *The Vocabulary of Intellectual Life in the Middle Ages* (CIVICIMA, Études sur le vocabulaire intellectuel du moyen âge 10). Turnhout: Brepols.

Tuomarla, U. 1999. *La Citation mode d'emploi. Sur le fonctionnement discursif du discours rapporté direct.* Helsinki, Academia Scientiarum Fennica.

von Nolcken, C. 1981. "Some Alphabetical Compendia and How Preachers Used them in Fourteenth-Century England." *Viator* 12: 271–88.

Weijers. O. 1988-2000. *Études sur le vocabulaire intellectuel du Moyen Âge.* (CIVICIMA 1–9). Turnhout: Brepols.

Wichner, P. T. 1889. "Zwei Bücherverzeichnisse des 14. Jahrh. in der Admonter Stiftsbibliothek." *Zentralblatt für Bibliothekswesen* 1(4): 461–531.

Woelfflin, E., ed. 1869. *Publilii Syri Sententiae ad fidem codicum optimorum primum recensuit E. Woelfflin.* Leipzig: B. G. Teubner.

Zimmerann, F. 1929. "*Candidus*, Ein Beitrag zur Geschichte der Frühscholastik." *Divus Thomas, Jahrbuch für Philosophie und speculative Theologie* 7: 30–60.

CHAPTER 59

THEOLOGICAL TEXTS

LESLEY SMITH

THE manuscripts which preserve for us the varied materials of medieval Latin theology are of especial interest because they show such obvious adaptations to the contexts in which they were used. During the period from the late eleventh century to the late thirteenth, the cutting edge of biblical study moved from monasteries to "secular" schools (those attached to cathedrals or run by individual masters), where it became the academic discipline of theology. The group of those who taught and those who learned was broadened to include, as well as monks, secular scholars and mendicant friars. These were men in a hurry, and the slow, contemplative study of the Bible practiced in the monasteries was transformed into an examinable subject with its own time-limited curriculum and newly created textbooks. Unlike the monks, who had a lifetime of meditative reading ahead of them, and whose goal was the shaping of their spiritual lives, both schoolmen and friars had a more immediate purpose. The students in the schools were intent on qualifications, and the friars were eager to take their learning into the naughty world.

Monastic reading began at the beginning and read slowly through to the end, needing only a bookmark to show the reader where he had left off. But the schools required that books be searchable; rather than aiding contemplation, books provided swiftly retrievable information. This differing purpose led to the composition of new sorts of text, and to familiar texts being produced in novel ways. Moreover, the schools participated in the shift from a largely oral to a more written culture that took place over the twelfth and thirteenth centuries. Although medieval teaching was always founded on the oral exposition of authoritative texts, the twelfth-century reluctance to commit that exposition to writing was slowly replaced by a scholasticism used to reading the latest works, and by readers such as the friars who wanted to be able to take their texts with them wherever they went.

Paris became the center of the study of theology, and it is at Paris that we can trace the development of a commercial book trade. The size and wealth of the city, the royal court and administration, and the masters and scholars of the thriving schools combined to provide a living for dozens of *libraires* and their allied tradesmen. Theological books were no longer made only in monasteries by monks or those employed by them, but by businessmen supplying a market; schoolmen and friars experimented with innovation, and the theological texts which were produced balanced ease of production against the increasingly demanding requirements of their users. It is not possible in this short chapter to cover all types of theological texts and the issues surrounding them. Instead, we can look at manuscripts of the Bible, of biblical commentary, and finally, of *summae*, as particularly good examples of how theological books were responsive to didactic and institutional changes.

Although there were exceptions, when books were made for wealthy patrons or to mark special occasions, most books made by monks followed an archetypal form. Monastic Bibles were typical of monastic book production—large and relatively plain books, with the text framed by generous margins and empty space, made to be read at a reading desk (Plate 59.1). They were bound in thick wooden boards, covered in leather. These Bibles generally took up numerous volumes, epitomizing the medieval notion of the Bible as a *bibliotheca*—a library—rather than a single book. Not all biblical books were equally popular and equally copied; the Psalms, Gospels, and Pauline Epistles were the most frequently read sections, and they each circulated in separate copies with an independent life. Decoration tended to be focused on the initials beginning each book, and often encapsulated a scene or more from the narrative, acting as a reminder to the reader of what was to come.

The biblical text was commonly Jerome's Vulgate translation, but by the twelfth century it had become corrupted by miscopying, poor emendation, and all the other errors that manuscript transmission can accumulate. Chapter and verse division was not yet fixed, and in many copies is not signaled. These are texts whose page layout is best suited for a reader starting at the beginning and simply reading to the end; finding a particular passage can be time-consuming and difficult. Partly for this reason, plain text Bibles were much less in use in the schools than in monasteries. Students in the schools appear to have needed other aids to help them through the text, and the later-twelfth century produced a series of works that made the Bible more accessible to beginners. Chief amongst these was the extraordinarily popular *Historia scholastica* of Peter Comestor (d. 1179), a sort of paraphrase and exposition of the text to the end of the Gospels, setting out the narrative straightforwardly but keeping flavorful sections of dialogue. A similar paraphrastic introduction to the text was Peter of Riga's (d. 1209) poem *Aurora*, sometimes known simply as *Biblia versificata*—the verse form was designed to make it easier to remember. These two text-based works were joined by a pictorial exposition attributed to yet a third Peter, Peter of Poitiers (d. 1216?). His *Compendium historiae* traced the genealogy of Christ through the patriarchs of the Old Testament. In one form, it was made as a long, colorful roll, the medieval equivalent of a wall chart for classroom use (Plate 59.2).

By the second quarter of the thirteenth century, the friars were beginning to make their mark on scholarship, and the results of their study are evident in books. Most of the innovation can be credited to the Dominicans, whose house of study on the rue St. Jacques in Paris was an important center for research. They seem to have worked in

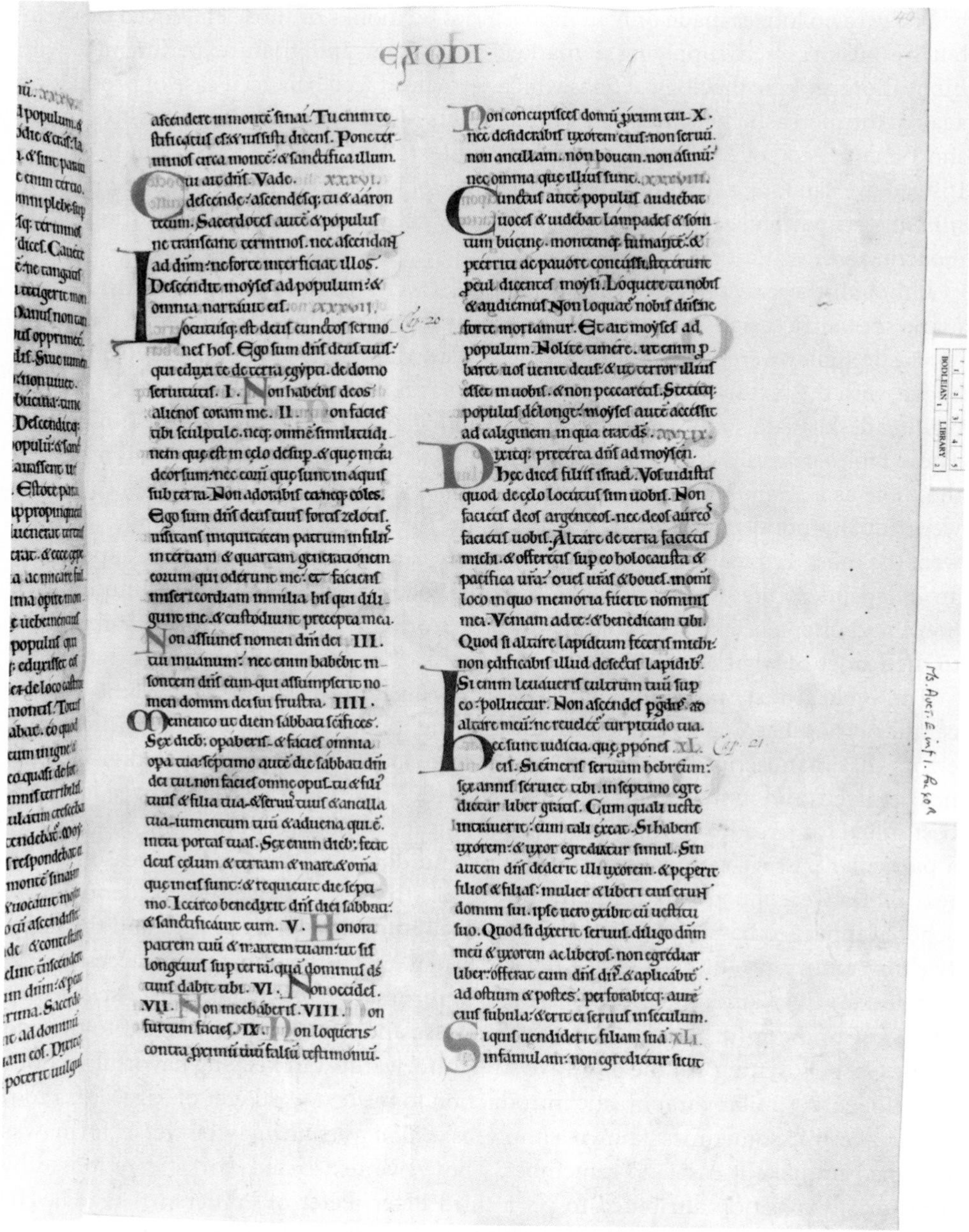

PLATE 59.1 Monastic Bible. Oxford, Bodleian Library, MS Auct. E. inf. 1, fol. 40r; twelfth century; Winchester.

PLATE 59.2 Peter of Poitiers, *Compendium historiae genealogiae Christi*. Oxford, Bodleian Library, MS Lat. th. b. 1 (R); mid-thirteenth century; England.

teams, initially under the direction of master Hugh of St. Cher (d. 1263), a method which suited the kind of work they were interested in. One of the order's key strengths was its mobility: unlike the orders who lived by the Rule of St. Benedict, the mendicants were not tied to a particular place. Their pastoral ministry was centered on the Bible, but the existing large-format monastic copies were no use to them in their wandering life. Instead, they developed books in smaller and smaller formats, right down to tiny (10 × 15 cm), one-volume (pandect) Bibles, written on onion-skin parchment in tiny script and able to be carried in pockets or hanging from a belt (Plate 59.3). Running titles and chapter numbers were among the other additions which made finding one's way easier. Despite their small size, these books could be finely made; and they included not only Jerome's Vulgate text but also his general introduction to the Bible, his specific prologues to each book or group of books, and his works translating and interpreting the Hebrew proper names in the text. Dominicans used these smaller formats for other pastoral texts they developed, such as confessors' manuals, books of model sermons or sermon exempla, and expositions of vices and virtues; it meant that friars on the move were not deprived of materials for their ministry. Although small, they were still protected in bindings made from wooden boards and leather covering, although some were made in limp parchment bindings—the medieval equivalent of paperbacks. One corollary of these small format personal copies is evident in the library inventories of mendicant houses, which are surprisingly thin. Ironically, given their vow of personal poverty, individual friars seem to have retained the ownership of their books, which were not credited as the possessions of a particular house.

The Bible was the grist to the Dominican mill, and sometime before 1247, the scholars at St. Jacques created the first of three biblical concordances that are associated with them. This first pioneering publication paved the way for the others to follow (Plate 59.4). Similarly, the *Correctorium* was a list of improvements to the biblical text drawn from early Bible manuscripts and patristic quotation, which attempted to render it more literally accurate. Although the Dominicans are not thought to have pioneered such lists, they did produce at least two more versions, beginning in the mid-thirteenth century. To aid them in their research into the text, and in their ministry overseas, they also embarked upon a serious study of languages, which resulted in (for instance) bilingual copies of the Psalms and translation of Hebrew and Arabic texts. Comparison of texts of the Psalms, in particular, was not new: a feature of Herbert of Bosham's twelfth-century copy of Peter Lombard's commentary on the Psalms, made for Thomas Becket, is its parallel text, with two of Jerome's translations, the Gallican and the Hebraicum, written out side by side.

Common though the Bible was as a theological text in the Middle Ages, in the twelfth century it was overtaken by manuscripts of biblical commentaries, and in particular by the multivolume compendium of patristic and later exegesis known as the Gloss, thousands of copies of which still survive. Indeed, so useful was the Gloss that when in the thirteenth century the University of Paris came to designate a Bible as the official version for study, they chose just such a glossed Bible, rather than the bare text. Up to this point, biblical exegesis was usually a single author expounding a

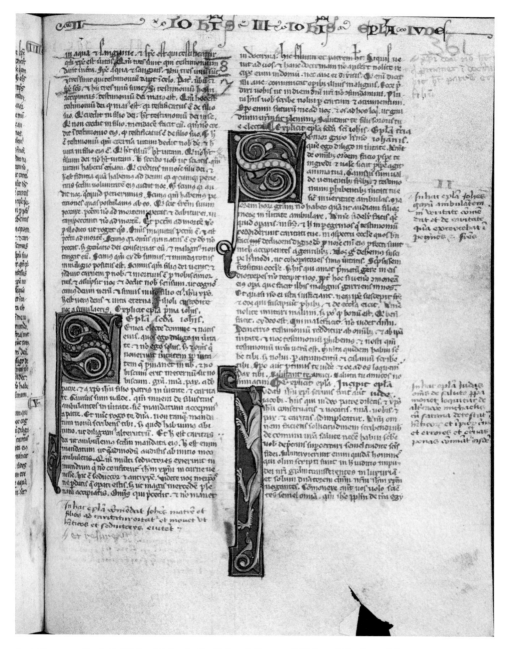

PLATE 59.3 Pocket Bible. Oxford, Bodleian Library, MS Lat. bib. f. 3, fol. 361r; AD 1254; ? France.

PLATE 59.4 Biblical concordance. Oxford, Bodleian Library, MS Canon. Pat. Lat. 7, fols. 3v–4r; thirteenth century, second half; probably Paris.

single book, such as Gregory the Great on Job, or Augustine on Genesis. The common layout for such commentary was the lemmatized text (Plate 59.5). The scribe wrote the page as a single or double column; each portion of commentary was preceded by a short quotation or lemma from the Bible, generally underlined or otherwise set apart. Not all of the biblical text need be present in this layout, since, if there is no commentary, the text will not appear. A related version of this form is the *catena* commentary. Again, the page is divided at most into two columns, but the commentary text is headed by a longer quotation from the Bible, at least a verse or two in length, often in a larger or different script. In this form, the whole biblical text is usually included, though broken up into pieces.

From its beginnings at the school of Laon at the outset of the twelfth century, the Gloss employed an entirely different layout, one borrowed from copies of arts faculty textbooks, such as Priscian and Boethius. Each page (Plate 59.6) is laid out in three columns—the outer and central columns of roughly the same width, the inner column about half as wide. Initially, only the central column is ruled, and the scribe copies the text of a complete biblical book, which forms a continuous and distinct whole. This is then surrounded, in the inner and outer columns, and between the lines of the text itself, by a series of glosses—short comments on and explanations of the text, drawn from the works of authoritative interpreters; in this case, the Church Fathers such as Augustine, Ambrose, Jerome, Gregory, and on up to Bede, Isidore, and Rabanus Maurus. The inner and outer columns are ruled only as and when needed to add a gloss; and because the ruling is not related to that of the central column, the ratio of lines of text script and glossing script is not fixed, and can go from around two lines of gloss to one of text to almost four to one. These glosses are not informal jottings but still written in relatively formal hands. Color is used sparingly, and is almost invariably confined to the biblical text; the paragraphs of gloss are distinguished not by colored initials but by a paragraph sign in ink. It is very rare for there to be any extra reader aids such as running headers or chapter numbers. More interestingly, however, there are very seldom lemmata—or any other form of tie mark—to show which gloss relates to which part of the text. Beyond the outer column there is often a broad empty margin for readers' notes, as well as a particularly deep lower margin.

Anyone who has ever taught a set text will recognize the strength of this form of layout as a classroom teaching tool. The keystone of medieval teaching was the oral exposition by a master of an authoritative text—most often a book of the Bible. The rules of exposition required that the master not simply give his own interpretation of the text, but provide a summary and discussion of previous commentary on it. The Gloss form allowed a master to have the whole text in front of him, along with the short glosses as a sort of starting point for his exposition of the authorities. The Gloss was most useful in the hands of a knowledgeable teacher who could take its often lapidary glosses and expound them in a way his student audience could understand; on its own, it can be hard to penetrate. Nevertheless, having the whole biblical text rather than just selected lemmata meant that the teacher could deviate from his prepared lecture, if he

PLATE 59.5 Lemmatized biblical commentary (Isaiah). Oxford, Bodleian Library, MS e Mus. 3, fol. 29r; c.1200; England.

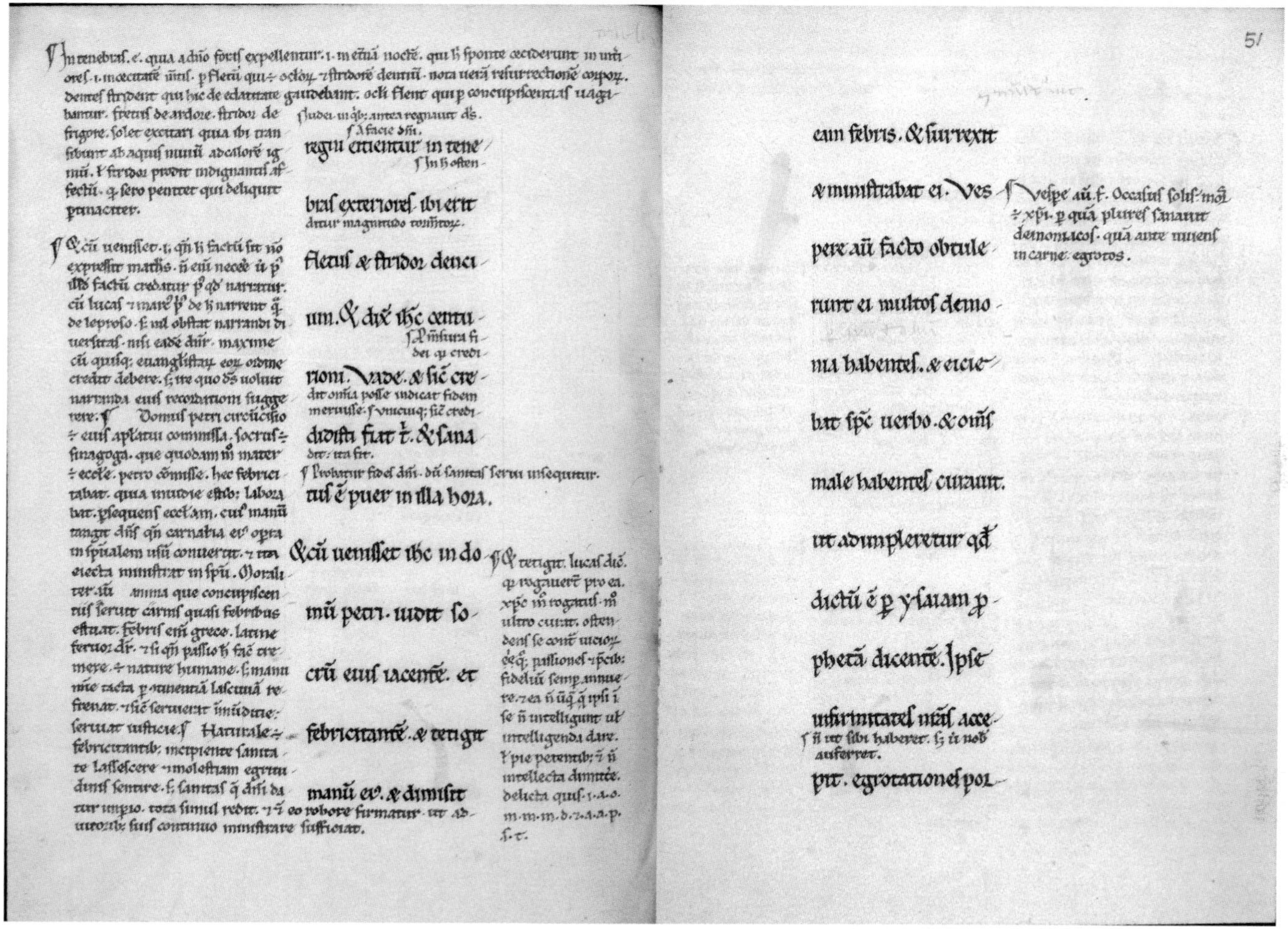

PLATE 59.6 *Glossa ordinaria*: simple format. Oxford, Bodleian Library, MS E. D. Clarke 35, fols. 50v–51r; twelfth century; Troisfontaines, France.

wished. The immediate visual difference between the appearance of the biblical text and the glosses meant that the master could switch quickly between the two.

Glossed books in this layout are relatively easy for a scribe to make, since the text can be written out first in the invariant central column, and the glosses put in afterward. Ruling the glossing columns only as they were needed also saved work and meant that size of script could be varied, depending on how much gloss there was to include. But the unchanging width of the central column had its limitations. At the beginning of almost any biblical book there was usually much to be said, and the glosses often continue into the top and bottom margins, as well as being crammed between the lines. But long before the end of the text, almost everything that needed to be said had already been said. The majority of the precious parchment page is empty. So it was partly in order to save space that around the middle of the twelfth century scribes begin to experiment with variations on this simple Gloss layout and developed a more complex form sometime in the 1160s. In these copies, each page is designed individually, to maximize the use of space. More than three columns may inhabit the page, and the height and width (even within a column) of every column can vary depending on the ratio of text to gloss (Plate 59.7). To make the scribe's job easier, the whole page (not just the text column) was ruled at the same time, at the height of the gloss script, so that the number of lines of gloss to lines of text becomes fixed at a ratio of two to one. These copies also use color to delineate sections of text (though not usually gloss), and for running headers and marginal chapter numbers. The variable number of columns on each page prompts the use of tie marks to link continuing glosses across page breaks. All is designed to help readers find their way through a text which does indeed look *textus*—woven—onto the page.

The move to the complex layout meant that the Gloss could be copied using fewer pages than before; but more importantly, it signals that the Gloss was no longer being used directly in the classroom as a tool for oral teaching, but for silent reading, whether by masters in preparation for a lecture or to provide follow-up material for students to consolidate what had been heard. Although the biblical text and the glosses were still distinct, the whole effect of the complex layout and the motility of its columns on the page was too dense for immediate use in oral teaching. The Gloss was still full of useful material, but it was material for the reader, not the speaker.

The Gloss was not the only commentary from this period to be laid out in an uncommon way. Gilbert de la Porrée (d. 1154), one of Anselm's students, used a distinctive format for his own commentaries, whether on the Psalms and Pauline Epistles or on school texts such as Boethius (Plate 59.8), which comprised a layout of two unequal columns, with the text in the narrower, inner column and the commentary in the other. This layout has the unusual feature that the commentary (with biblical lemmata underlined) had to be written out before the text, to make sure it could all be fitted in; the text is added subsequently in the inner column, spaced out so that text and commentary do not get too far out of step. As well as the two-column layout, Gilbert seems to have introduced a number of features (not all his own creation) into his works, to give the reader information, such as numbering the psalms. Gilbert

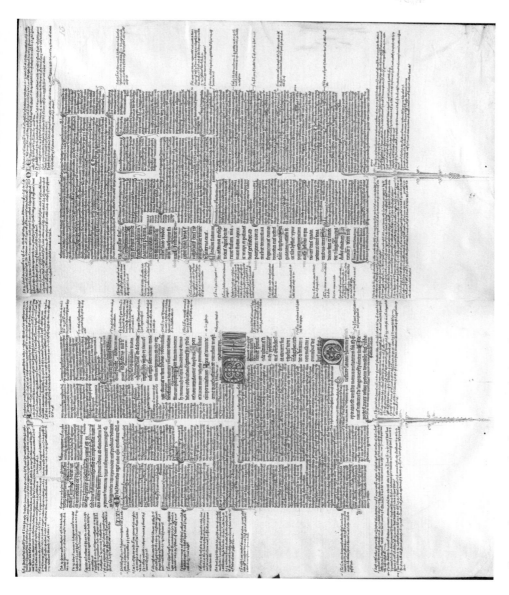

PLATE 59.7 *Glossa ordinaria*: complex format. Oxford, Bodleian Library, MS Laud Lat. 9, fols. 14v–15r; mid-thirteenth century; France.

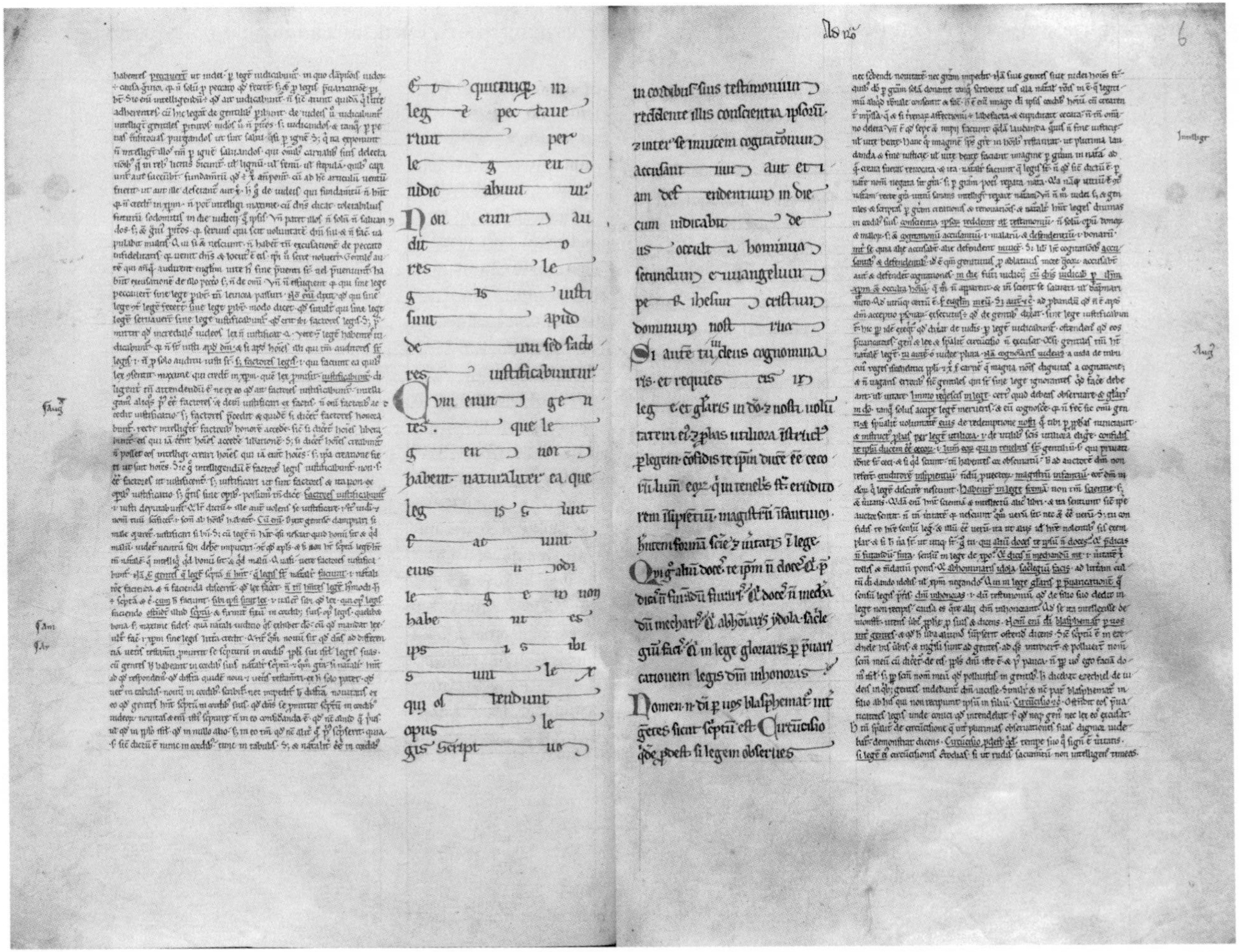

PLATE 59.8 Gilbert of Poitiers (de la Porrée): commentary format (Pauline Epistles). Oxford, Bodleian Library, MS Lat. th. c. 21, fols. 5v–6r; twelfth century; France.

also divided the Psalms into twelve categories according to their subject (Resurrection, Penitence, Love), each with a symbol to designate the relevant psalms. Even more unusually, Gilbert is very particular about giving citations to the authorities he quotes, giving their names in the outer margin, in space left specifically for the purpose—a variation on modern footnotes. This was not a new invention: like the two-column page layout, which can be found in manuscripts of Bruno of Würzburg's commentary on the Psalms, references like these were not unknown; they can be found, for instance, in manuscripts of some of the works of Bede or Rabanus Maurus.

Peter Lombard (d. 1160) was a slightly younger contemporary of Gilbert, also working in Paris on biblical commentary, and he too seems to have specified that his works be laid out with particular characteristics. Peter's intercut ("*intercisum*") layout was even easier for a scribe to produce in a way that would keep text and commentary together (Plate 59.9); it must have developed from the *catena* format, where a section of text is followed by a section of commentary. Once again, the page has a two-column format, fully ruled at the height of the glossing script. But now a chunk of text (exactly how much depends on the amount of gloss it attracts) is written out in a block at the left-hand side of the column, but across only part of its width, and the block is surrounded on three sides with the relevant section of commentary. The text is written at double height on alternate lines, making it distinct from the surrounding gloss. The scribe can keep text and commentary together because he does not have to write out the next part of the text before the previous commentary is complete. Peter retained and enhanced Gilbert's referencing system. As well as naming his authors, he marks the extent of the quotation in the margin with a vertical line; in the commentary, the beginning of the quotation is noted by a symbol allotted to the particular author, with the end signaled by two dots. If a reader knows the symbol allotted to each quoted author, he can instantly know who is being cited, without even having to check the name in the margin.

Why are these different layouts important? The Psalms and Pauline Epistles were the most read and taught parts of the Bible in the schools. All three of these commentaries—the Gloss, Gilbert de la Porrée, and Peter Lombard—circulated widely, at the same time. They had much material in common. However, the characteristic look of each one means that a reader can tell at a glance which of the three he is dealing with. Yet by no means all manuscripts of Gilbert's and Peter's commentaries are made in this way, or manage to retain all of the characteristics. The reference system, in particular, proved too much of a challenge to scribes, and often falls away; by the thirteenth century, their commentaries mostly appear in a familiar two-column lemmatized or catenated layout. Nevertheless, their appearance in the mid-twelfth century shows that at least some scholars and book producers were experimenting with the way that layout and "reader aids" could enhance the reading experience. Few other scholars seem to have taken up the referencing or indexing systems, although one significant exception is Robert Grosseteste (d. 1253), who developed his own set of indexing symbols. But Grosseteste made these symbols for his own use, so that he could

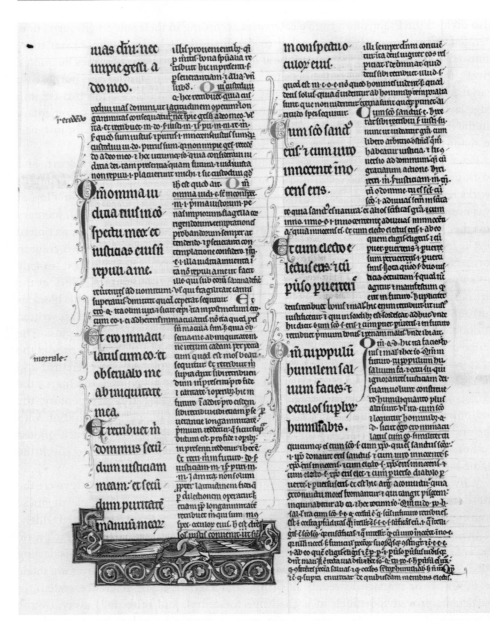

PLATE 59.9 Peter Lombard: commentary format (Psalms). Oxford, Bodleian Library, MS Auct. D. 1. 19, fol. 28r; mid- thirteenth century; England.

find what he needed in his books, and he did not mean them to be used by other readers.

In contrast to the experiments of the twelfth century, by the thirteenth, apart from copies of the Gloss, theological books tended to be produced in a standard format of two equal columns. Even the great monuments of thirteenth- and fourteenth-century biblical commentary, the *Postillae* of Hugh of St. Cher and Nicholas of Lyra (d. 1349), were not produced, as they might have been, in Gloss format, but as plain lemmatized text. Not until they were printed were they given a Gloss-type format. On the whole, thirteenth-century books were smaller, so they did not have to be read on stands, and book producers used means other than textual layout to help the reader through the text. The majority of theological books were produced in Paris, as a consequence of the schools there, and even those which were not were influenced by the look of Paris copies. The characteristic theological text of the thirteenth century and later was the *summa*, which developed from earlier collections of *sententiae* on important themes: Peter Lombard's renowned *Four Books of Sentences* became a set text in the schools. *Summae* proceeded by posing questions, which they answered by arraigning a series of arguments pro and con, until they came to a conclusion and answered the objections. Instead of distinctive textual layout, these volumes used color (especially blue and red) and a hierarchy of size of script and of decoration to lead the reader through the text (Plate 59.10). Each item of the argument, for or against the proposition, began with a colored initial, alternating red and blue so that the eye could skip with minimum effort through the points. The amount and complexity of decoration or flourishing for each initial indicates the level of division of the text: the more important the division, the bigger the initial. Running headers (again, alternating red and blue), numbering (of points, sections, or chapters, for instance), titles, subject headings, and summaries (often diagrammatic) in the margins, chapter lists and alphabetical indices all became standard parts of a text. These additions meant that a reader could quickly find any portion of a text or part of an argument without having to read from the beginning.

Although the Paris book trade grew up alongside the schools, not all students could afford to buy books from professional producers; and the Paris *libraires* introduced (probably from Bologna) the pecia system of book copying. Students could hire from the official university booksellers copies of their textbooks section (*pecia*) by section, and copy them out for themselves. As theological texts got longer (a thirteenth-century characteristic), the script used in these texts grew smaller and more abbreviated.

In what state have theological texts reached us? This is a difficult question to answer for medieval manuscripts in general. Some luxury, bespoke books are bewildering to modern scholars because of their unfinished state. It is not clear why a volume made with lavish resources should not have been completed, and yet incompleteness seems not to have disturbed medieval readers (or owners) in the way that it does us. We can be reasonably sure that the productions of thirteenth-century professional manuscript workshops show us theological texts in a state which was approved by their authors, but other texts may be drafts or classroom notes. Texts from the twelfth century, with its more oral culture, are even more difficult to place. Some monastic authors, such as

MS. Add. C. 265

PLATE 59.10 Thomas Aquinas, *Summa theologiae*. Oxford, Bodleian Library, Ms Add. C. 265, fol. 1r; fourteenth century; Bologna.

Anselm of Bec or Bernard of Clairvaux, worked outside a classroom situation and have left behind a number of texts; but it is clear from the lack of material evidence of some of the greatest twelfth-century teachers, such as Anselm of Laon or William of Champeaux, that "publishing" written texts was much less important to them than the oral teaching they did in their schools. Partly, this may be because pupils brought in fees in the way that written texts, in a pre-copyright age, could not; partly, there was danger in committing ideas to writing which was not present in simply oral discussion. In some sense, the work of these masters was always work in progress. According to his pupil, Herbert of Bosham, Peter Lombard did not intend to publish his Psalms and Pauline Epistles commentaries, but kept them for private use, presumably updating them as he taught them year by year. Yet, immediately on his death, Herbert seems to have taken over the texts and produced (very successful) editions, thus both preserving Peter's reputation and fixing the texts in aspic, in a way that the Lombard may not himself have intended. A few volumes seem to preserve *reportationes*—classroom notes taken by designated students and subsequently approved by the master. Other texts, such as the *sententiae* collections associated with Anselm's Laon school, which have some (but not all) of their material in common, appear more likely to be individual students' records of their classes. For some theological texts, a number of similar but not identical copies exist. Are they editions or redactions made by the master, or are they classroom (or post-classroom) notes made by his pupils, perhaps to begin lecturing from themselves? The aim of the schools was to produce people trained to do similar things with the same texts, not to be original or strike out on their own. This makes establishing the manuscript record and textual tradition in theology particularly difficult.

Theological texts are not generally illustrated, and where they are, they illustrate biblical scenes rather than any form of commentary. Of those which are, decorated and illustrated Psalters are the most prolific, and illustrated Apocalypses enjoyed something of a vogue in England in the thirteenth century. From the fourteenth century onward, the *Biblia pauperum* presented the text almost in comic-book illustrated form, with captions; it was particularly popular in monasteries. The exception to this illustration rule is the thirteenth-century *Bible moralisée*, luxury volumes made for a very select audience, which illustrate both the text and a spiritualized interpretation of it.

In their variety, interest and adaptation to changing circumstances, theological texts present a group of manuscripts which demonstrates the entrepreneurship of the book trade, the virtuosity of scribes, and the changing circumstances of scholarship in the central Middle Ages.

CHAPTER 60

··

TEXT AND GLOSS

··

GRETI DINKOVA-BRUUN

DESPITE their variety, ingenuity, and versatile use, glosses generally remain subordinate to the text they comment upon. The text is the inspiration; the gloss is the explanation. The text provides the idea; the gloss documents the idea's intellectual afterlife. The text weaves together meaning; the gloss teases it apart. When written as interlinear and marginal notes, the glosses show their dependency on the text both through what they say and by where they are located, and even the more independent variety of glossing, the continuous or chain commentary, is still inspired by an original composition which provides a precise point of departure and an inherent principle of organization. Often the glosses are more than a simple reflection on the grammatical, literary, or doctrinal reality of the text they explicate; they frequently bring more detail to the original composition, reinforce its message, and broaden its appeal. Even when they argue against the text, the glosses nevertheless enrich the understanding of the work's readership. The most extreme case and a complete reversal of roles is seen on rare occasions where the text makes little, if any sense at all without the accompanying notes. Here, the glosses have become an integral part of the process of creation, not just a scholarly afterthought.

The basic relationship between text and gloss was well understood during the Middle Ages, as is seen in Huguccio's popular etymological dictionary *Derivationes*, written sometime in the later twelfth century.[1] Huguccio says that one needs to distinguish between comment, gloss, translation, and text. A comment does not consider the joining of words but their sense (*verborum iuncturam non considerans, sed sensum*), whereas a gloss provides a clarification of the meaning of individual phrases and even words (*non solum sententiam sed etiam verba attendit*). The text, in contrast, is the book of the author without any further explanatory notes (*textus est liber . . . sine littere vel sententie expositione*).[2]

Thus, it is clear that clarifying grammar, explaining the meaning of words, and unlocking the deeper significance of the text are the main concerns of glossing, at least until the gloss transforms itself to become a textual construct in its own right and thus inspires its own glossing. The continuous *catena* commentaries organized by lemmata as textual cues are the best examples of this gloss metamorphosis. The different levels of gloss sophistication can be and often are brought into play simultaneously, even though frequently the process of glossing seems to be shaped by the intellectual needs of a particular readership. Especially when texts were used for teaching, the complexity of their annotations would reflect the educational stage at which these texts were incorporated into the curriculum. In some medieval textbooks we might even find multiple layers of glosses introduced independently of each other by various users of the book over an extended period of time. In such cases the glosses are seen to be in dialogue not only with the text proper but also with the other layers of annotation. Even when they result from private reading and study, the individual glosses vary in difficulty and purpose, reflecting the scholarly proclivities of the person who wrote them.

This chapter explores the complex intellectual interplay between text and gloss, using examples from the vast but lesser known field of Latin biblical versification from the later Middle Ages.[3] The poems of Peter Riga (d. 1209), Leonius of Paris (d. c.1201), Alexander of Ashby (d. 1208 or 1214), and William de Montibus (d. 1213),[4] as well as some anonymous compositions, such as the *Liber Generationis Iesu Christi* (late eleventh century), the *Liber Prefigurationum Christi et Ecclesiae* (late eleventh century–early twelfth century), and the *Capitula euangeliorum* (late thirteenth–early fourteenth century)[5] will be mined for representative and instructive occurrences of text and gloss interaction which will demonstrate the various approaches the glossators employed in their work. And finally, it has to be remembered that apart from interacting with the text itself, the glosses are also an intermediary between text and reader. Sometimes they may even require a very active involvement from the reader, especially when the position of the glosses is ambiguous and their textual anchors (or lemmata) difficult to establish. In any case, the centrality of the glosses to the understanding of the text's message is undeniable not only for medieval students, masters, and scholars but also for their modern counterparts.

Interlinear Glosses: Clarifying the Meaning of the Word

On this first level the role of the glosses was to provide help with the basic understanding of how the text was constructed. Avoiding confusion and explaining uncertainties must have been the guiding principles of the glossator at this stage. It was of primary importance to make sure that the reader, who probably was a beginner Latin student, grasped the literal meaning of the text, from where he could then move to uncovering its deeper significance. Thus, it is evident that this first level of glossing is closely related to teaching and is generally meant for younger or less advanced students.

The interlinear glosses can be non-verbal, i.e., construe signs, accentual marks, numerals (Roman and later also Arabic), small letters, and other symbols, as well as verbal, explaining various introductory but essential aspects of the text. In the field of prosody the glosses usually deal with issues of accents, meter, and poetic techniques. The problems of grammar, both morphological and syntactical, are exemplified by supplying omitted prepositions, explaining cases, clarifying subjects and objects, especially when they are expressed by pronouns, and providing help with word order and clause subordination. In the matters of vocabulary the glossators normally offer synonyms (rarely antonyms), give Latin equivalents for Greek words or vernacular translations for Latin ones, and supply names that both aid and enrich the reader's understanding. Because of their highly localized nature, these types of glosses are commonly placed between the lines and in close proximity to their lemmata but because of special limitations they can be displaced, sometimes even as far as the margins. In such cases, the critical judgment of the reader is required in order to connect them to their intended place in the text. Despite these occasional difficulties, interlinear glosses are generally short, clear, and unambiguous. Their illuminating quality and educational value are unmistakable.

The examples of medieval interlinear glosses are innumerable and ubiquitous. They are found in manuscripts throughout the Middle Ages and in a variety of languages, even though Latin is best represented. Here only an illustrative selection will be included. For instance, in the *Liber Generationis Iesu Christi* we see the following concise treatment in the story of Ruth coming to Boaz's bed in the middle of the night in order to convince him to marry her (see Ruth 3:7–13):[6]

.i. nox, ut iret dormitum   Booz   somno
Venerat hora thori,   uir se dedit ille sopori,

          alloquitur eum   et tangit
Ruth uenit et   tangit uerbis   et tactibus angit

per legem   derelictum esse   suscitare   cognati
Lege sibi   linqui semen   recreare   propinqui

  .i. in prima uice renuit   secunda uice
Vir prius   excusat minimeque   secundo recusat.

The glosses to these four Leonine hexameters are all useful for a number of reasons. First, they help with simply grasping the meaning of the poem by identifying the protagonist of the story Boaz ("uir" = "Booz"), by providing the morphological gloss "per legem" for the less obvious ablative of manner "lege" ("by law"), and by explaining the adverbs "prius" and "secundo" with the more easily understood, especially for "secundo," "in prima uice" and "secunda uice" ("at first...but then...."). In addition, the glosses simplify the poetic language of the verse by annotating poetic expressions such as "uenerat hora thori" ("the hour for going to bed had come"), "tangit uerbis" ("she touched him with her words") and "tactibus angit" ("and ensnared him with her caresses") with the more prosaic "i.e. nox ut iret dormitum" ("that is, the night, so that he might go to sleep"), "alloquitur eum" ("she spoke to him") and "et tangit" ("and she touched him"). The rest of the glosses provide useful synonyms, i.e., "sopori" = "somno," "recreare" = "suscitare," "propinqui" = "cognati," and "excusat" = "renuit." All in all, in this passage the explanations of the glossator are manifestly aimed at helping the reader's understanding of the Latin and at elucidating the basic meaning of the poetic text.

Another type of interlinear gloss is seen when non-verbal marks (i.e., dots in various configurations, superscript letters, or Roman numerals) are placed above or more rarely below the words in order to help the reader construe the correct meaning of the sentence. Such annotating is necessary because of the well-known fact that the demands of metrical versification often lead to a transformation of the customary ways of expression found in prose texts. An example of this glossing technique is seen in the early twelfth-century poem the *Liber Prefigurationum Christi et Ecclesiae*, vv. 233–4, where the mystery of the Eucharist is explained as follows:[7]

b	c	f	e	d	a
Esse	tuum	panem	benedictum	corpus	aisti,
Quodque	tuus	uinum	sanguis	fiat	benedictum.

Verse 233, containing four potentially confusing accusatives, must have been considered especially difficult. Thus, superscript *lettrine* were added telling the reader how to rearrange the words following the alphabetical order of the letters. As a result, the sentence has to be construed as follows: "Aisti esse tuum corpus benedictum panem" ("You said that your body was the holy bread"). By providing this help the glossator is making sure that "corpus" is linked with "tuum" and "panem" with "benedictum," and not vice versa. The point of this annotation contains doctrinal significance as well as grammatical import.

One extreme case, in which the text of the poem makes little sense without its glosses, is found in the mnemonic composition *Capitula Euangeliorum*, which dedicates one verse to each chapter of the four Gospels. Because of this excessive brevity, the text of this work makes no grammatical sense whatsoever; rather, each line of the poem represents a string of unconnected words that are lifted directly out of their biblical context without any attempt to connect them into a coherent sentence. Thus, the glosses added to the poem are extremely useful. They not only help the readers understand better the cryptic text in front of them, but also provide clues to identifying the precise biblical verse to which the poet refers. A short example from the beginning of the Gospel of Matthew will suffice here:[8]

Liber	generationis	cum esset			regit
	Abraham,	sponsata,	nollet traducere,		donec.
	transit				uocabitur
	Bethleem,	Egiptum,	Rachel,	Arthelaus,	Nazareus.

	de pilis		ad radicem	modo	descendentem
	Camelorum,	uipera,	securis,	sine,	columbam.
temptatus	in deserto	terra	uocat	apostolos	multorum
	Desertum,	Zabulon,	piscatores,	sanitates.	

At a first glance it is not easy to grasp the meaning of these verses. However, it quickly becomes apparent that each of the words that constitute this mnemonic composition represents a verse or rarely a section from the first four chapters of the Gospel of Matthew. For example, the biblical references for the last poetic line are: desertum] Mt 4:1; Zabulon] Mt 4:15; piscatores] Mt 4:18; sanitates] Mt 4:24. The glosses are really helpful here since they explain that "desertum" refers to Christ being tempted in the desert (*temptatus in deserto*), while "piscatores" ("fishermen") brings to mind the encounter between Jesus and the future Apostles Simon (Peter) and his brother Andrew (*uocat apostolos*). Also, "Zabulon" is glossed with "terra" ("the land of Zebulun"), which tells the reader both that "Zabulon" has to be understood as a genitive and that the poet is indeed taking this particular mnemonic cue from Matthew 4:15, where we see the expression "terra Zabulon," and not from Matthew 4:13, where the biblical text reads "in finibus Zabulon." Finally, the gloss "multorum" above "sanitates" is a general reminder of the multiple healing miracles performed by Jesus during his ministry in Galilee. All in all, the interlinear glosses to the anonymous *Capitula Euangeliorum* are indispensable facilitators in the understanding of a very fragmented and often cryptic text.

MARGINAL GLOSSES: EXPLAINING THE ORGANIZATION AND THE MEANING OF THE TEXT

The simplest marginal glosses are short notes that assist the retrieval of information, provide a reference, or simply draw the reader's attention to important elements in the narrative. A passage from the Book of Daniel included in Alexander of Ashby's biblical versification *Breuissima comprehensio historiarum*, vv. 565–80, illustrates this annotating approach. The marginal glosses are indeed numerous and very useful for finding a specific biblical episode in the poetic account (i.e., "The first vision of Daniel," "About the three boys in the furnace," "About Susanna," and so on), as well as for identifying the protagonists of the narrative (i.e., "Daniel," "Ananias, Azarias, Misael," "Susanna") and even for indicating when the action is taking place (i.e., "At the time of Darius, king of the Medes"):[9]

In sompnis regi quid uisa notaret ymago,   Prima uisio Danielis
    Hic uidet et recitat et subit inde decus.

Qui socii fuerant in penis et prece secum,	Ananias, Azarias, Misael
Consociat Daniel tres in honore sibi.	
Cum regis statue capud inclinare recusant,	Secunda uisio Danielis
Vis in fornacem regia trudit eos.	De tribus pueris in fornacio
Ignis parcit eis, hostes perimit, stupet inde	
Rex et laudandum predicat inde Deum.	
In sompnis arbor regi quid uisa minetur,	Tercia uisio Danielis
Dicit ei Daniel, res ea dicta probat.	
Quid manus in muro scripsit, scriptura quid illa	Mane, Techel, Phares
Signaret regi, nouerat atque notat.	Sexta uisio Danielis
Illi parcit, obest, tutum facit esse, leonum	Tempore Darii Medorum
Rictus, consortum fraus, pietasque Dei.	
Urget Susannam seniorum perfida lingua,	De Susanna
Dampnat plebs, Daniel liberat arte noua.	

In addition to these types of notes, the outer margins can contain information on the sources used by the author. An interesting example is seen in the biblical poem *Historie ueteris testamenti* by Leonius of Paris, who includes himself, i.e. *Autor*, among the authorities he draws on in his work, i.e., Moses (i.e., the Bible) and Flavius Josephus for the material added to the biblical narrative. In both instances the marginal source glosses provide only general indications rather than useful text references. The passage below represents Leonius's versification of Genesis 22:14–19:[10]

Quodque piis oculis Deus hic uidisset utrumque,	Moses
Inde loco nomen "Dominus uidet" indidit illi.	
Tunc uelut in uitam certa de morte remissum	Iosephus
Natum amplexitur, nato pater oscula figit.	
Gaudia nec celant lacrime, uix pectore toto	Autor
Leticiam capit ipse suam pietasque paterna	
Plena redit. Mouet inde gradum puerosque reuisit	Moses
Tantarum ignaros rerum campoque relictos.	

Often, when every single word in the verse is commented upon, we find letters or variously shaped signs placed above the words in the body of the poetic text. These non-verbal cues, also called *signes-de-renvoi*, are then repeated in the margins, followed by the intended comment. In this case the superscript signs are not glosses per se; rather, they designate links to the real comments, which are written somewhere else on the page. The reader is supposed to look for the corresponding twin marks in the margins or sometimes between the lines and uncover for himself the point of the annotation. This technique is attested in William de Montibus's *Versarius*, a rich collection of short epigrams on numerous topics organized alphabetically.[11] The following piece, entitled *Dedicatio ecclesie* is from the section on the letter "D." The text and glosses are transcribed here from London, BL, MS Add. 16164, fol. 26r. The title of the epigram is written in red ink in the left margin of the manuscript. The glosses appear both to the left and to the right of the text of the verses:

Octo concurrunt ad templum^d sanctificandum:

Sal, scriptura, cinis, aqua, uinum, crismaque, lux, thus.
(e   f   g   h   i   k   l   ..)

Circuit, aspergit mentes, inscribit, inungit
(m   ∴)

Iustorum Christus illuminat et benedicit.
(n)

Right Margin		Left Margin	
d	.i. ecclesiam dedicandam.	l	Operis boni.
e	Hec est sapientia.	..	Oracio.
f	Doctrina.	m	Custos.
g	Memoria mortis.	∴	Sanguine.
h	Contricio penitencialis.	n	Gratia.
i	Leticia spiritualis.		
k	Vbi oleum misericordie.		

In the cases discussed above, the marginal glosses are still very short and relatively straightforward (i.e. *sal* means *sapientia*, *scriptura* stands for *doctrina*, and *uinum* denotes *leticia spiritualis*). With the exception of their location, many of these marginal notes are not very different from the interlinear glosses. In what follows, the tenor of the marginal glosses changes. They become complex comments on sense and doctrine either recording the thoughts of the medieval scholars studying the text or providing help to students at a higher level of education. Such marginal commentaries are found in countless medieval manuscripts. They are not restricted to subjects and disciplines but demonstrate universal applicability. Here the phenomenon will be illustrated by a short excerpt from the anonymous poem *Liber Generationis Iesu Christi* that outlines the allegorical meaning of 2 Kings 11 (Plate 60.1):[12]

Bersabeae   aliud misticum ostenditur in ea
Coniunx Vriae   plus affert allegoriae,

     litteram   nobis   spirituale   intellectum
Legis scripturam signando siue figuram,

spirituali intellectu   lex in se   misterii
     Pneumate fecundum quae continet omne profundum

scil. prepucium   seruari
     Pellem   tollendo uel sabbata precipiendo.

In addition to the interlinear glosses explaining that yet another mystical interpretation is to be uncovered in the figure of Uriah's wife Bathsheba (*aliud misticum ostenditur*

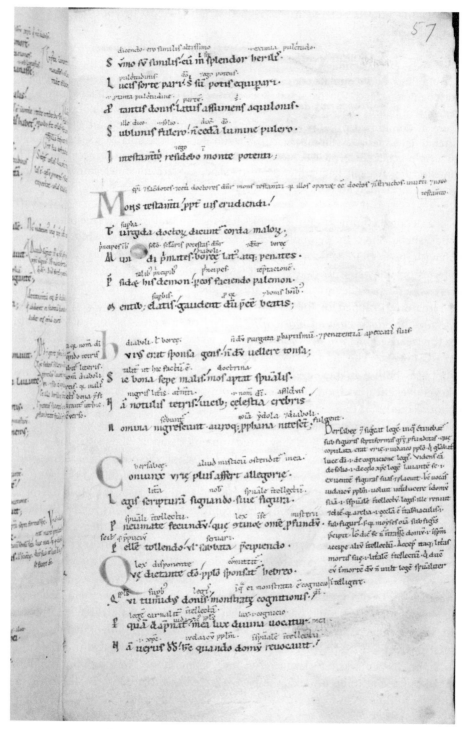

in ea), a long note is entered in the right margin close to the opening verse of the excerpt. It reads:

> Bersabeae etiam significat legem, in qua continebatur sub figuris septiformis gratiae profunditas, quae copulata erat Vriae, .i. Iudaico populo, qui gloriabatur luce Dei, .i. de cognicione legis. Videns eam de solio, .i. de caelo Christus, legem lauantem se, .i. exuentem figuras suas, et placuit. Tunc uocans Iudaicum populum uoluit introducere in domum suam, .i. in spiritualem intellectum legis; ille renuit et dicit, quia archa, .i. aecclesia, est in tabernaculis, .i. sub figuris, scil. quia Moyses omnia sub figuris precipit. Ideo dicit se non intrare domum, .i. in spiritum accipere alium intellectum. Accepit itaque literas mortis suae, .i. literalem intellectum, qui ducit eum in mortem, dum non uult legem spiritualiter intelligere.

This is a detailed comment on the typological meaning of the marriage between Uriah and Bathsheba. She is the symbol of the sevenfold grace of the law, while he represents the Jewish people, to which the law binds itself. The rest of the marginal gloss elaborates on the well-known exegetical trope of the inability of the Jewish people to perceive the deeper allegorical significance of the Bible *(spiritualem intellectum legis)*, thus remaining trapped in the deadly realm of the literal understanding *(literalem intellectum qui ducit eum ad mortem)*. The text of this gloss is copied in its entirety from the treatise *Enarrationes in Matthaeum*, which has been attributed to Anselm of Laon (d. 1117).[13] The complexity of the argument presented in this marginal note presupposes both a higher level of Latinity and at least a basic familiarity with the medieval exegetical method. The gloss not only explains the meaning of the poetical text but also takes it to a new level of sophistication.

Occasionally, the marginal glosses become so extensive that they completely surround and even dwarf the text they are commenting upon. This situation is seen in manuscripts containing glossed Bibles and other scholastic books, where the primary compositions are copied in a confined writing block in the middle of the page, while the surrounding gloss fills the rest of the page.[14] In these cases the gloss has become the main exposition, whereas the original composition which inspired it is included as a point of reference. The two textual entities are connected either through *signes-de-renvoi*, as we saw above, or through lemmata, that is, words and phrases from the main composition that are repeated in the commentary in order to make the reader aware which sections of the text have been subjected to scrutiny.

The margins of the manuscript page had been used for so long as useful space where notes on the main text could be written that the practice continued even after books began to be printed. Various early humanists, known and unknown, would collate in the margins of their freshly printed tomes variant readings of the text in front of them in addition to remarks of clarification and explanation. The medium might have changed but the attitude towards the page attested in these books is still the same as during the Middle Ages.[15]

Catena Commentaries:
Becoming the Text

Whether short or long, simple or intricate, the interlinear and marginal glosses are still physically joined with the texts, which they explicate. This localized unity is broken in the so-called *catena* commentaries, which represent continuous chains of notes copied independently of the text they annotate, but linked to it through lemmata cues like the ones that were mentioned already in relationship to the marginal glosses. In this the *catena* commentaries break away from the immediacy of the text/gloss page continuum and claim the status of independent expositions, which in turn might inspire their own glossing activity. The examples of *catena* commentaries are numerous. The format was used for annotating both classical and scholastic texts.[16] In the field of medieval biblical studies a famous *catena* commentary is the so-called *Catena Aurea* to the four Gospels compiled from various sources by Thomas Aquinas in the 1260s.[17]

The example presented here is from an anonymous *catena* commentary to Peter Riga's poem the *Aurora* found in Salzburg, Stiftsbibliothek Sankt Peter, MS a.VII.6. Only a short section of this *catena* has ever been printed, and the excerpt below is taken from this partial edition.[18] For the reader's convenience I also give the full text of the *Aurora*, which is then followed by the anonymous Salzburg *Glose*.

> Peter Riga's *Aurora, Liber Genesis*, vv. 21–36.[19]
>
> Principium Iesus est; **celum creat** auctor in isto,
>   Per quem celestes efficit esse uiros.
> **Terra** prius **uacua** notat ecclesiam sine fructu,
>   Donec Christus adest et sibi iungit eam.
> 25 Eius in aduentu datur ecclesie **noua proles**,
>   Nam breuis aut nullus ad bona fructus erat.
> Scripture **tenebras** caligo figurat abyssi:
>   Mystica scripta quidem clausa fuere **diu**,
> Sed ueniente Iesu reserauit scripta beatum
> 30 Pneuma, **superferri quod memoratur aquis**.
> Hinc merito sequitur quod facta luce recedunt
>   Et fugiunt tenebre, lucida terra patet:
> Nempe sacri flatus reseratur claue magistra
>   Quidquid scripture **ianua clausa tenet**.
> 35 **Lux notat** a tenebris diuisa quod a tenebrosis
>   Distinguat uitiis lucida facta bonus.

This passage from the *Aurora* offers the reader an allegorical interpretation of the narrative of the first day of Creation: the beginning of everything is Christ; the empty and barren earth (*terra uacua sine fructu*) symbolizes the Church before the arrival of the Saviour who makes her fertile with his good deeds; the shadows of the abyss (*caligo abyssi*) denote the hidden meaning of Holy Scripture; light separated from darkness (*lux a tenebris diuisa*) symbolizes the division between the bright virtues and the dark vices. The anonymous commentary on this text reads as follows (the lemmata selected by the glossator and underlined in his commentary are printed in bold typescript in Riga's text presented above) (Plate 60.2):

> celum creat, hoc est, in filio qui est sapientia patris; potentia diuinitatis persona patris, sapientia persona filii, uoluntas persona spiritus sancti. Nota quod procedit allegorice quod sumitur multis modis, ut habes superius. terra uacua, quia erat infructuosa ecclesia usque ad aduentum Christi. noua proles, hec est fides et exibitio bonorum operum. diu, donec Christus uenit qui regnauit omnia. et tenebre. Super faciem abissi erant tenebre, hoc est, super terram uel super materiam quatuor elementorum. superferri quod memoratur aquis spiritus Domini, idest prouidentia diuina siue uoluntas, nam spiritus suus uoluntas sua est; prudenter excogitabat more artificis qualiter de terra diuersas eliceret creaturas; uel *spiritus Domini ferebatur super aquas*,[20] idest super terram, quia terra adhuc flexibilis erat ad recipiendam omnem formam. ianua clausa tenet. Vnde Dauid: *Tenebrosa aqua in nubibus aeris*,[21] hoc est, sententia in prophetis, idest nostra doctrina latebat sub figuris ueteris legis. lux notat. Diuisit angelos malos ab angelis bonis.

It is clear from this example that, even though the *catena* commentary clarifies, explains, and supplements Riga's poem, it is still very much dependent on its structure and literary expression. The gloss might look like an independent composition because of its continuously flowing text, but in reality it is not. The *catena* commentaries are separated from the texts they explicate physically rather than conceptually. One advantage of this format for the commentating tradition is that it removes the constraints which the limited dimensions of the page impose on the glossator and allows him to include extensive and complex comments alongside the short and simple ones. A second advantage might be related to aesthetic concerns; for whatever reasons, a glossator might prefer to leave the manuscript of the original work he is commenting upon unmarred by interlinear and marginal notes: in that case, the creation of a separate chain commentary would be the preferred working method. Finally, it should be noted that in addition to the annotations, the actual lemmata found in the chain commentaries are also worthy of study because they can exhibit textual variations that have been lost or obscured in the text's modern critical edition. All in all, the *catena* commentaries contain a wealth of information about the intellectual and often didactic concerns of their creators.

OBSERVATIONS ON LAYOUT

The discussion presented above intimates that the different glossing systems occupy clearly defined registers on the page, i.e., the interlinear glosses are found within the

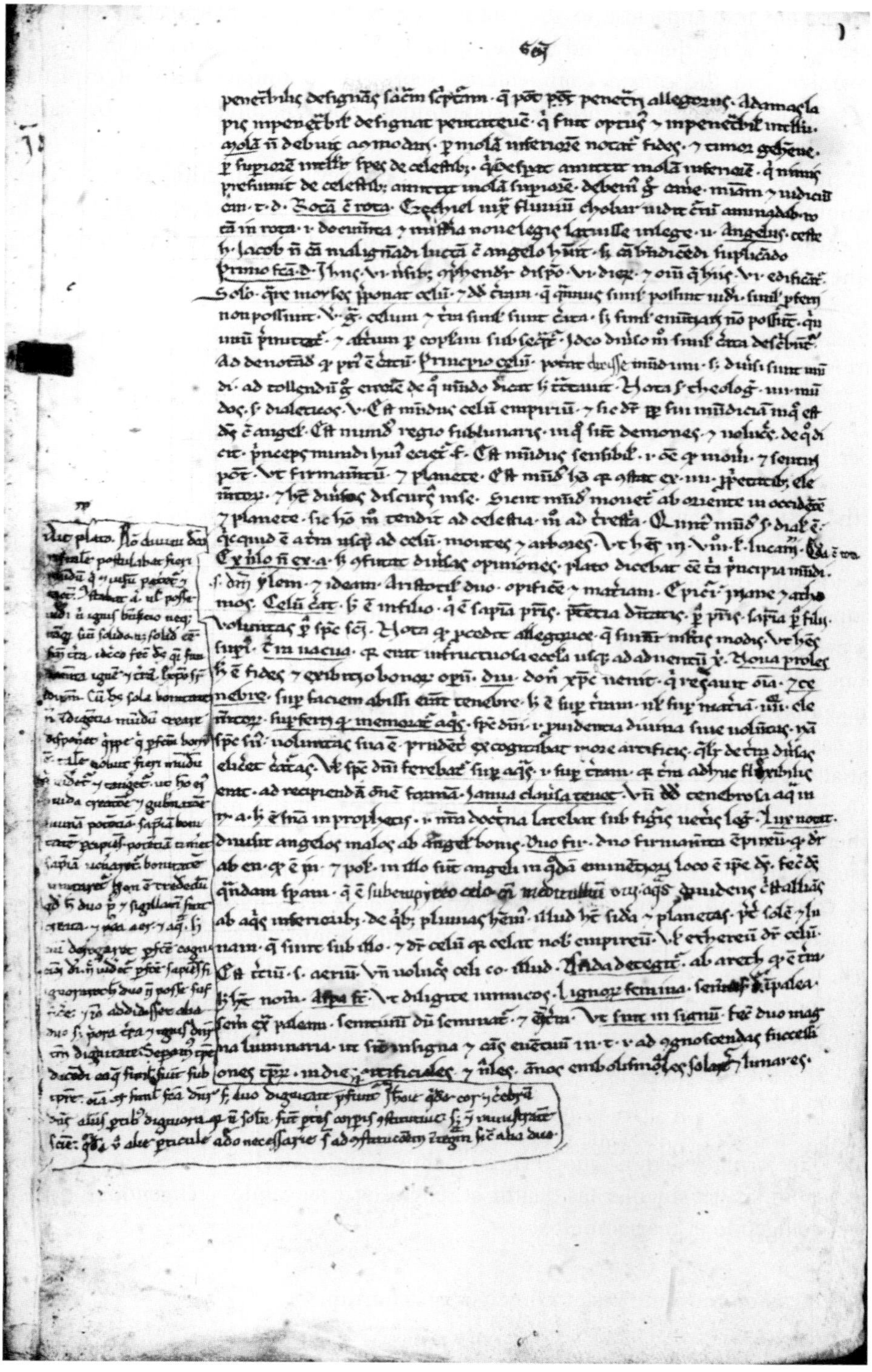

PLATE 60.2 © Salzburg, Stiftsbibliothek St. Peter, MS A.VII.6, fol. 49v.

body of the text and close to the words they explicate; the marginal glosses fill the space surrounding the text and are keyed to it either by *signes-de-renvoi* or by general proximity; and the *catena* commentaries represent continuous texts of explanatory notes removed from the primary composition but still linked to it by carefully chosen lemmata.

While this is generally true, the situation in medieval manuscripts is not always so uncompromising, especially in the case of the interlinear and marginal glosses, which can easily run into each other's spatial registers. A good example of this fluidity is seen in the *Liber Generationis Iesu Christi*, vv. 224–7 (Plate 60.3):[22]

illa sapientia patris, .i. filius, dedit   quia sine omni peccato originali et actuali erat caro Christi
Carnis naturam dedit in se uiuere puram,

Christus dico   quia nullus umquam natus fuit qui esset sine peccato nec infans unius hore nisi Christus
                 qui est absque omni macula peccati in conceptione et in natiuitate.
Liber   precunctis humano corpore functis.

In the first verse the gloss explaining that the body of Christ was pure because it was free of all original and actual sin is so long that it starts as an interlinear gloss but extends into the right margin. The same is also true for the even longer note on the second verse, which continues the same argument: Christ does not have a human body like everybody else "because nobody was ever born without sin, not even an infant that is one hour old, except for Christ, who remains without any stain of sin both in his conception and in his birth." The placement of these glosses shows that sometimes it is not easy to label a particular comment as either interlinear or marginal because spatially it represents a merging of the two.

Occasionally, glosses that normally would appear in the margins of the page are gathered together into something like short *catena* commentaries and copied above the verse which they expound. This practice has the advantage of eliminating the confusion that could result when glosses were displaced or cue marks omitted. However, the inclusion of such extensive fields of commentary into the actual body of the poetic work interferes with the continuous reading of the text and thus suggests that this annotating format could have been meant for teaching purposes. An example is seen in William de Montibus's *Versarius*, where the epigram *Monachus* is glossed as follows in Cambridge, CCC, MS 186, fol. 16r (the cue letters are written in red ink; Plate 60.4):[23]

m .i. in formationem n Quod est monachus .i. unicus uel singularis; monos enim
grece unitas uel singularitas dicitur et religiosus a religando .i. eligendo
uel colligendo et mariambulus

          m   n
Ad formam morum prestat nomen monachorum

Dicta quadriga di · quid tractat materiei

Inpathmos uilla · septem monstrata sigilla

Que soluit magnus · septem cu cornibus agnus

Nomine mutato · septe benefacta uocato

Que sunt natalis de uirgine non genialis

Postea baptismus · sordis nre catarismus

Mors maledicta crucis · nre raparacio lucis

Queq; die trina · fuit intumulo lubumia

Gloria surgendi · spes nobis id faciendi

Spe unde datus · carnis supastra meatus

Iudicii flagru · iosaphat quod spectat adagru

Dogma septenum · typico carismate plenum

Sacris summistis · septem contexit istis;

Vt typicis uinclis · iungantur singula singlis

Yox ysaie · preponit pneuma sophie

Qua sit natalis · mirandus non genialis

Nam carne matris · mundana sapientia patris

Per generis massam · peccati pondere quassam

Carnis naturam dedit · inse uiuere puram

Liber precunctis · humano corpore functis; pecca inceptoie 7 inatturitate

Bis duo natales · sed tres non sunt geniales;

Lex non mutatur · cu pcoitum generatur · p m modus.

Hanc eneruauit ds · ada quando creauit · Secds modus.

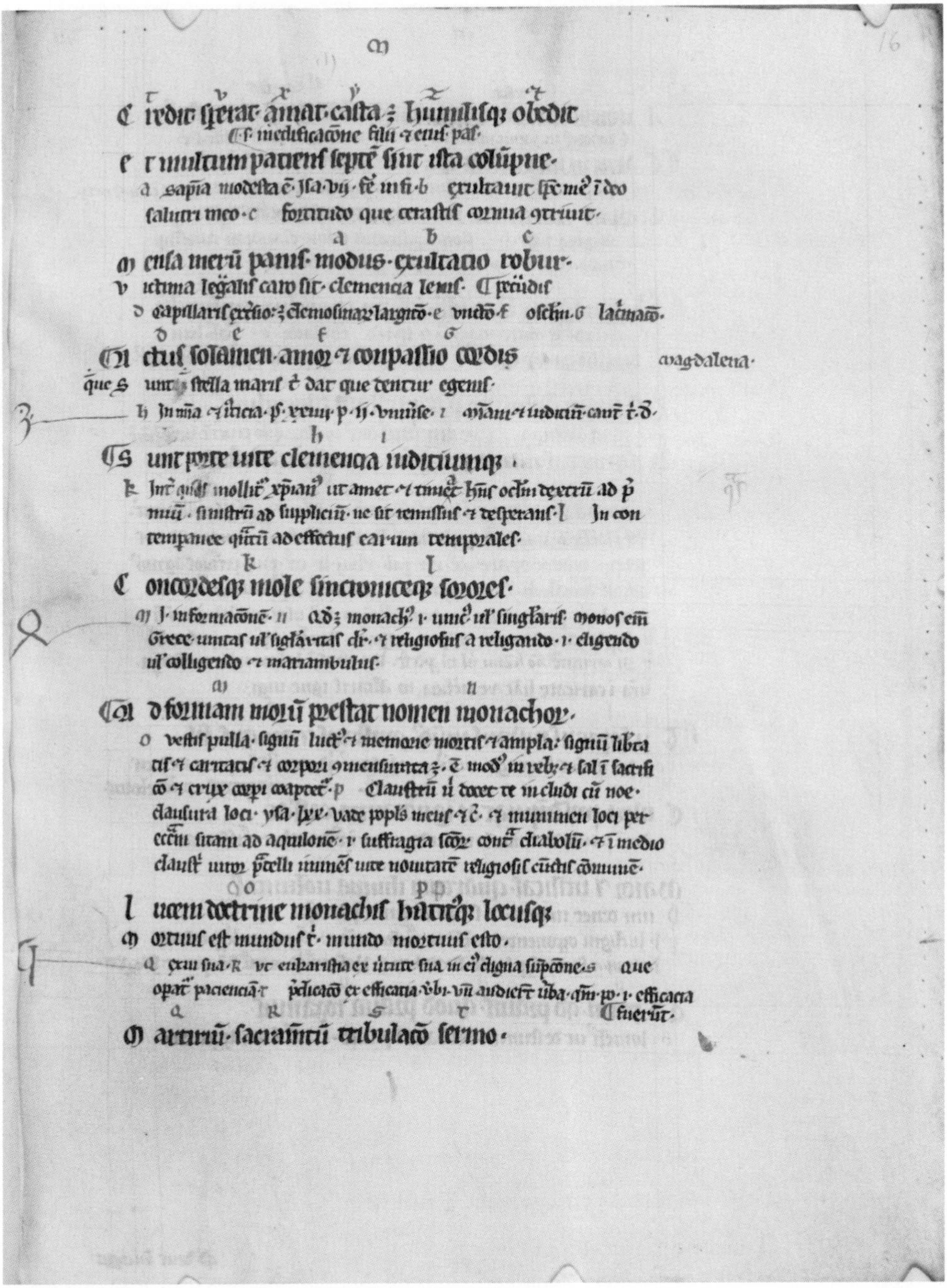

PLATE 60.4 © Cambridge, Corpus Christi College, MS 186, fol. 16r.

o uestis pulla signum luctus et memorie mortis. et ampla signum liberta-
tis et caritatis et corpori commensurata est; est modus in rebus et sal in sacrifi-
cio et crux corpori coaptetur. p Claustrum ubi docet te includi cum Noe
clausura loci; ysa. lxx: *Vade populus meus* etc.[24] et munimen loci per
ecclesiam sitam ad aquilonem .i. suffragia sanctorum contra diabolum et in medio
claustri uiror pratelli iminens uite nouitatem religiosis cunctis communem

o   p

Lucem doctrine monachis habitusque, locusque.

The various glosses and layout formats presented in this chapter demonstrate the
fruitful relationship between medieval texts and their commentaries. The purpose of
the glosses is first and foremost practical, but it is clear from the arrangements we see
on the manuscript page that aesthetic considerations also played a role in organizing
the material at hand. As a result, the primary composition and the secondary commentary are mutually shaped into a new textual reality which is both richer in meaning
and more complex in form. It is simplistic to claim that glosses and commentaries were
written only to provide the elucidation of obscure and difficult texts. The medieval
glossing enterprise is much more than that. It represents a mode of thinking, a way of
expression, and an intricate method of intellectual engagement with the inherited
literary and scholarly tradition.

Notes

1. Huguccio died in 1210. For a brief but useful introduction to medieval lexicography, see
   Weijers (1989).
2. For the full text of Huguccio, see Cecchini *et al.* (2004, II, 536–7: GLOSSA). The purpose,
   use, and function of medieval glosses are analyzed in Teeuwen (2011).
3. The medieval glosses and commentaries on both the classical and late-antique poets have
   been the object of numerous important studies but there is very little comparable work
   done in regard to the poetic production of the later Middle Ages in general and biblical
   versification in particular. Among the landmark works that deal with classical and late-
   antique authors are Marti (1958); Wieland (1983); Coulson (1991); O'Sullivan (2004) and
   (2016); Rieker (2005); and Petruccione (2013).
4. For some studies and editions concerning the glossing traditions of these texts, see
   Dinkova-Bruun (2004), (2005b), and (2006).
5. For critical editions of these poems, see Dinkova-Bruun (2005a), (2007), and (2009b).
6. These are verses 237–40 of the abbreviated edition of Dinkova-Bruun (2005a, 50–1) or
   verses 800–3 in the complete edition of Rödel (1999, 110).
7. See Dinkova-Bruun (2007, 13). The poem was written during the reign of Philip Augustus
   (1060–1108), and more precisely between 1093–1108 (see Dinkova-Bruun 2007, ix). For
   more examples, see Wieland (1983, 98–107).
8. See Dinkova-Bruun (2009b, 262–4). The poem was written in the late thirteenth or early
   fourteenth century, probably in Central Europe.

9. See Dinkova-Bruun (2004, 49–50). The marginal notes presented here are found in the apparatus criticus to the edition. They are preserved only in one of the manuscripts containing the poem, i.e. Durham, University Library, MS Add. 767 (saec. XIVin).

10. See Dinkova-Bruun (2005b, 300). For another study and a partial edition of Leonius (*Liber Ruth*), see Dinkova-Bruun (2009a). For a translation of this text, see Dinkova-Bruun (2015).

11. The *Versarius* is preserved in two manuscripts and is still unedited. The life and works of William are discussed in Goering (1992). For another glossing enterprise originating in William's classroom, see Dunning (2016).

12. These are verses 634–7 of the abbreviated edition of Dinkova-Bruun (2005a, 94–5), or verses 1325–8 in the complete edition of Rödel (1999, 138). The actual layout of the text is seen in Heidelberg, Universitätsbibliothek, MS Salem IX 15, fol. 57r. I thank Sigrun Schall-Thiery for providing the images from the University Library in Heidelberg, as well as granting me permission to use them in this essay.

13. The text is printed in *PL* 162, col. 1244BC. For the different commentaries on the Gospel of Matthew that are linked with Anselm, see Giraud (2010, 92–5).

14. Excellent reproductions are found in de Hammel (1986, especially Chapter IV: "Books for Students," pp. 108–41). For images from manuscripts relating exclusively to medieval law, see L'Engle and Gibbs (2001). Teeuwen (2017) offers an engaging discussion on how to measure and evaluate the annotating activity in Carolingian manuscripts.

15. For a superb discussion of this phenomenon, see Sciarra (2011).

16. For *catena* commentaries on classical texts, see Coulson (2010); Gura (2010); and Stover (2010).

17. For an edition of this monumental compilation, see Guarienti (1953).

18. See Dinkova-Bruun (2006, 252).

19. See Beichner (1965, I, 22–3).

20. Gen. 1:2.

21. Ps. 17:12.

22. The text and glosses are edited in Rödel (1999, 78–9). The actual layout of the text is seen in Heidelberg, Universitätsbibliothek, MS Salem IX 15, fol. 32v. Similar observations are made in O'Sullivan (2017).

23. I thank Gill Cannell from the Parker Library in Cambridge for providing the image and the permission to use it in this essay.

24. Is. 26:20. It is necessary to observe here that the medieval numbering of the biblical verses differs from our own.

BIBLIOGRAPHY

Beichner, P., ed. 1965. *Aurora Petri Rigae Biblia Versificata* (Publications in Mediaeval Studies, vol. 19.1–2). Notre Dame, IN: University of Notre Dame Press.

Cecchini, E. *et al.*, eds. 2004. *Uguccione da Pisa Derivationes*. Florence: Edizioni del Galluzzo.

Coulson, F. T. 1991. *The "Vulgate" Commentary on Ovid's Metamorphoses: The Creation Myth and the Story of Orpheus* (Toronto Medieval Latin Texts 20). Toronto: PIMS.

Coulson, F. T. 2010. "The *Catena* Commentary and its Renaissance Progeny." *Manuscripta* 54/2: 153–70.

de Hammel, C. 1986. *A History of Illuminated Manuscripts*. New York: Phaidon Press [last repr. 2004].

Dinkova-Bruun, G. 2004. *Alexandri Essebiensis Opera Poetica, Corpus Christianorum Continuatio Mediaevalis* 188A. Turnhout: Brepols.

Dinkova-Bruun, G. 2005a. *The Ancestry of Jesus. Excerpts from "Liber Generationis Iesu Christi Filii Dauid Filii Abraham"* (Matthew 1:1–17) (Toronto Medieval Latin Texts 28). Toronto: PIMS.

Dinkova-Bruun, G. 2005b. "Leonius of Paris and his *Liber Ruth.*" In *Schrift, Schreiber, Schenker. Studien zur Abtei Sankt Viktor in Paris und den Viktorinern* (Corpus Victorinum. Instrumenta 1), ed. Rainer Berndt, 293–316. Berlin: Akademie Verlag.

Dinkova-Bruun, G. 2006. Peter Riga's *Aurora* and its Gloss from Salzburg, Stiftsbibliothek Sankt Peter, Ms. a.VII.6." In *Insignis Sophiae Arcator. Medieval Latin Studies in Honour of Michael W. Herren on his 65th Birthday* (Publications of the Journal of Medieval Latin 6), ed. Gernot R. Wieland, Carin Ruff, and Ross G. Arthur, 237–60. Turnhout: Brepols.

Dinkova-Bruun, G. 2007. *Liber Prefigurationum Christi et Ecclesiae and Liber de Gratia Noui Testamenti, Corpus Christianorum Continuatio Mediaevalis* 195. Turnhout: Brepols, 2007. With a *Supplementum*. Turnhout: Brepols, 2014.

Dinkova-Bruun, G. 2009a. "*Autor*, Authorship and the Literal Sense of the Bible: The Case of Leonius of Paris." In *Bibel und Exegese in der Abtei Sankt Viktor zu Paris. Form und Funktion eines Grundtextes im europäischen Raum* (Corpus Victorinum. Instrumenta 3), ed. Rainer Berndt, 259–77. Münster: Aschendorf.

Dinkova-Bruun, G. 2009b. "Remembering the Gospels in the Later Middle Ages: The Anonymous *Capitula Euangeliorum Versifice Scripta.*" *Sacris Eruditi* 48: 235–73.

Dinkova-Bruun, G. 2015. "Leonius of Paris. *Histories of the Old Testament: The Book of Ruth.* Introduction and Translation." In *Interpretation of Scripture: Practice* (Victorine Texts in Translation 6), ed. Frans van Liere and Franklin T. Harkins, 475–96. Turnhout: Brepols.

Dunning, A. 2016. *Samuel Presbiter. Notes from the School of William de Montibus. Edited from Oxford, Bodleian Library, MS Bodley 860* (Toronto Medieval Latin Texts 33). Toronto: PIMS.

Giraud, C. 2010. *Per verba magistri: Anselme de Laon et son école au XIIe siècle*. Turnhout: Brepols.

Goering, J. 1992. *William de Montibus (c. 1140–1213). The Schools and the Literature of Pastoral Care*. Toronto: PIMS.

Guarienti, A., ed. 1953. *S. Thomae Aquinatis Catena aurea in quatuor evangelia*, 2 vols. Turin and Rome: Marietti.

Gura, D. T. 2010. "From the *Orléanais* to Pistoia: The Survival of the *Catena* Commentary." *Manuscripta* 54.2: 171–88.

L'Engle, S. and R. Gibbs. 2001. *Illuminating the Law: Legal Manuscripts on Cambridge Collections*. London and Turnhout: Harvey Miller-Brepols.

Marti, B. M. 1958. *Arnulfi Aurelianensis Glosule super Lucanum*. Rome: American Academy.

O'Sullivan, S. 2004. *Early Medieval Glosses on Prudentius' Psychomachia: The Weitz Tradition*. Leiden: Brill.

O'Sullivan, S. 2016. "Servius in the Carolingian Age: A Case Study of London, British Library, Harley 2782." *The Journal of Medieval Latin* 26: 77–123.

O'Sullivan, S. 2017. "Reading and the Lemma in Early Medieval Textual Culture," in *The Annotated Book in the Early Middle Ages. Practices of Reading and Writing*, ed. Mariken Teeuwen and Irene van Renswoude, 371–96. Turnhout: Brepols.

Petruccione, J. 2013. "The Glosses of Prudentius's *Peristephanon* in Leiden, Universiteitsbibliotheek, Burmann Quarto 3 (Bur. Q.3) and their Relationship to a Lost Commentary." *The Journal of Medieval Latin* 23: 295–333.

Sciarra, E. 2011. "I copisti e la stampa. Interazioni tra testo e margine nelle cinquecentine delle raccolte romane." *Segno e testo* 9: 247–68 and 6 plates.

Stover, J. 2010. "An Encyclopedia in the Margins: *Catena* Commentaries, Marginal Glosses, and the Decline of Platonic Studies." *Manuscripta* 54.2: 189–206.

Rieker, J. R. 2005. *Arnulfi Aurelianensis Glosule Ovidii fastorum*. Florence: SISMEL.

Rödel, M. 1999. *"De generatione Christi": Ein typologisches Lehrgedicht des hohen Mittelalters (Inc. Prima luce deum)* (Europäische Hochschulschriften, Reihe 15: Klassische Sprachen und Literaturen 79). Frankfurt: Peter Lang.

Teeuwen, M. 2011. "Marginal Scholarship: Rethinking the Function of Latin Glosses in Early Medieval Manuscripts," in *Rethinking and Recontextualizing Glosses* (Textes et Études du Moyen Âge 54), ed. Patrizia Lendinara, Loredana Lazzari, and Claudia di Sciacca, 19–37. Turnhout: Brepols.

Teeuwen, M. 2017. "Voices from the Edge: Annotating Books in the Carolingian Period," in *The Annotated Book in the Early Middle Ages. Practices of Reading and Writing*, ed. Mariken Teeuwen and Irene van Renswoude, 13–36. Turnhout: Brepols.

Weijers, O. 1989. "Lexicography in the Middle Ages." *Viator* 20: 139–54.

Wieland, G. 1983. *The Latin Glosses on Arator and Prudentius in Cambridge University Library, MS GG.5.35*. Toronto: PIMS.

CHAPTER 61

ANGLO-SAXON GLOSSES AND GRAMMARS

PATRIZIA LENDINARA

GLOSSES

GLOSSES are explanations of words written between the lines of the text or in the margins of a manuscript. The English word *gloss* "gloss" is a loan-word from Latin *glōs(s)a*, which, in turn, was borrowed from Greek γλῶσσα "tongue (of men or animals), language, provincialism, obsolete or dialectal word." Latin *glōs(s)a* meant "obscure term requiring an interpretation," and was used to signify both a "rare or difficult word for which an explanation is needed" and the explanation itself. The Latin word eventually came to signify "interpretation of a word" as well as "explanation added to a word and hereafter excerpted from its context along with the word it referred to." By gloss is now generally intended the couple formed by the lemma (that is the Latin word of a set text or the first part of a glossary entry) and its interpretation (or *interpretamentum*).

Glossing is a scribal practice in use since antiquity, but by the early Middle Ages glosses attained a different status, acquiring a new meaning. The Germanic West, including the British Isles, saw a large output of glosses and glossaries that stretches for many centuries and includes different typologies of glossing. Glosses in the English vernacular began to appear beside Latin glosses quite early, at the end of the seventh century, and Anglo-Saxon manuscripts preserve a large corpus of glosses and several glossaries, also of a large size.

As far as the distribution in the folio of a codex is concerned, glosses might be either occasional or continuous, and might vary in number from a few items or even a single word to a fairly dense apparatus of interpretations. The frequency of the glosses which may accompany a text is unpredictable, as is the choice of the words which were furnished by an interpretation. Unpredictability is one of the features of glossarial activity in the Middle Ages: glosses often accompany Latin words which are not particularly hard, and often occur in texts which are not that difficult. However, at a time when and in a land where the vocabulary of Latin had to be mastered through memory, the difference between commonplace and hard is a fine one.

The hierarchical relationship between Latin and the vernacular is generally evident in the layout of interlinear versions. There are manuscripts which were ruled from the outset to contain interlinear glosses. In other instances one or more layers of glosses, either in Latin or in the vernacular, were added between the lines of the text or in the margins of the manuscript. The arrangement of the folio yields invaluable evidence for the study of glosses and allows establishing, for example, whether a gloss was occasional or copied along with the main text. Glosses might be written in the hand of the main text, or added at a subsequent time by the same or a different hand.

Throughout the Anglo-Saxon period different genres of works were provided with continuous glosses in Old English. Of the many manuscripts of Latin Psalters, for example, 13 have continuous glossing in the vernacular and others are partially provided with interlinear glosses.

There was a well-established tradition of Psalter scholarship and interpretation, and both Roman and Gallican versions of the Psalter were glossed in Old English. A network of relationships has been established between the glossed Psalters, with two groups emerging: A (Psalters A, B, C, with B and C independently derived from A) and D, which is the prototype of most Psalters of a later date (Psalters D, F, G, H, J, K, L). The apparatus of glosses in some of these Psalters is very complex, with more layers of glossing. The Lambeth Psalter (I) (London, Lambeth Palace Library, 427), for example, provides evidence of a process of correction and revision of the interlinear glosses.

Besides the original ten Biblical canticles, the five non-Biblical canticles which formed part of the Roman Office in use in England were supplied with a continuous Old English gloss. Hymnals too were glossed in the vernacular, and two Anglo-Saxon hymnaries (London, BL, Cotton Julius A.vi and Vespasian D.xii) also contain an "Expositio hymnorum," in which the hymns sung in the Divine Office are set out in plain prose and furnished with glosses. This is also the case with the so-called Monastic canticles.

A late seventh-century and a late eighth or early ninth century manuscript of the Gospels (London, BL, Cotton Nero D.iv and Oxford, Bodleian Library, Auct. D. 2.19) were provided with continuous interlinear glosses in the second half of the tenth century: these are the so-called Lindisfarne and Rushworth glosses, the former of which still await a new edition after the nineteenth-century one by Skeat.

A number of manuscripts contain Latin prayers accompanied by glosses; the small private prayer book in London, BL, Royal 2.A.xx features a peculiar sort of glossing. In this instance the glossator seems to have confected a kind of interlinear gloss which approaches a proper Old English translation of the prayers. This sort of gloss was probably intended to help laypeople or less erudite clerics to understand the Latin prayers.

Continuous interlinear glosses in Old English accompany Latin texts pertinent to monastic life, such as rules and monastic customs (the *Regula Sancti Benedicti* and the *Regularis Concordia*).

Latin works used as school texts rarely have a complete gloss in Old English, with the few exceptions of rather recent works coming from the Continent such as Book 3 of the *Bella Parisiacae urbis* by Abbo of Saint-Germain-des-Prés. Manuscripts of the works of Boethius, Caelius Sedulius, Prosper of Aquitaine, and Prudentius contain glosses in Old English; these works and those of Arator and Juvencus and the *Disticha Catonis* were also accompanied by glosses in Latin, in large part still unprinted. As the program of study was largely inherited by the Carolingian one, the same intellectual indebtedness has been surmised for the Latin apparatuses of glosses and commentaries. The fact that a gloss appears in several manuscripts seems to indicate that it was not the spontaneous reaction of a teacher or student. In many instances Latin glosses to late antique and medieval authors seem to have travelled from the Continent to tenth-century England along with the works they were meant to explicate. There are several examples of manuscripts where the glossator stopped glossing a text after the first page, and this procedure still awaits a proper justification. Only when all the corpora of glosses to a set author are published will we be in a position to evaluate the insular debt to masters such as Remigius of Auxerre.

Anglo-Saxon manuscripts feature both commentaries and glosses drawn from his commentaries, which were copied along with the works of authors such as Boethius, Sedulius, and Martianus Capella. As regards the commentaries attributed to Remigius, manuscripts show the circulation in England of those to the *De consolatione Philosophiae* of Boethius, the *Disticha Catonis*, the *Ars minor* of Donatus, the *De nuptiis Philologiae et Mercurii* of Martianus Capella, the *Institutio de nomine et pronomine et verbo* of Priscian, and the *Carmen paschale* and the Hymns of Sedulius. There are also three manuscripts of the commentary on Martianus Capella's work attributed to Dunchad.

The arrangement of the commentaries, the glosses excerpted from the commentaries, and the text of reference varies from manuscript to manuscript. For example, a complicated system of reference marks links the glosses to the text in Cambridge, Trinity College, O.3.7, containing the *De consolatione Philosophiae* of Boethius, with Latin glosses stemming from Remigius's commentary.

In the tenth century, the English curriculum became quite distinct from any Continental curriculum. The study of "hermeneutic" texts was unique to England, and glosses and glossaries were indispensable tools for the practitioners of the hermeneutic style, which is one of the hallmarks of tenth-century Anglo-Saxon literature.

When Latin learning was reinstituted in the tenth century, Aldhelm's writings became immensely popular. Aldhelm's prose *De virginitate* is the most heavily glossed work from Anglo-Saxon England. Already influential in his lifetime, Aldhelm continued to be popular in England until the Viking attacks of the mid-ninth century. Later on, in the 920s, interest in Aldhelm's work was revived and, within a generation, he became a major curriculum author who was studied, in some centres, even beyond the turn of the twelfth century. The prose *De virginitate* and the *Epistola ad Acircium* received layers of Latin and Old English glosses which form a corpus with approximately 60,000 glosses preserved in 14 manuscripts (the oldest from c.800, the latest from *c.*1350), ranging from single letters or symbols to entire paragraphs—a density which is amazing, the more so when contrasted with the length of the text (which is about 20,000 words long). The most heavily glossed manuscripts are London, BL, Royal 7.D.xxiv, Brussels, BR 1650, Oxford, Bodleian Library, Digby 146, and London, BL, Royal 6.B.vii. In Brussels, BR 1650 five different scribes—hands A, B, C (two layers), CD, and R—were at work: these five scribes added 5,500 Old English glosses and 8,500 Latin ones.

Glosses might range in format from single letters to encyclopedic commentaries. These single- or multi-letter glosses—called merographs—(e.g. "spiritalis: *<gastli>cere*" or "electionis: *geco<rennysse>*": Aldhelm's prose *De virginitate*, ed. Ehwald, p. 240, 5 and p. 247, 21 respectively) are quite hard to unravel. Since it was the ending that was generally omitted, merographs were meant to emphasize the meaning of a word rather than its grammatical function.

These shortened forms were often incised in the vellum with a stylus and therefore are called scratched or dry-point glosses. The majority of the dry-point glosses in Anglo-Saxon and Continental manuscripts are in the vernacular and seem to reflect the ad hoc responses of individual readers to textual difficulties. These glosses were sometimes scratched twice and in some cases repeated a gloss already given in ink.

Quite frequent are "construe marks," used to indicate word order. This glossing (which belongs to the category of syntactical glosses) involved a complex system of diacritics (letters, dots, commas, and virgules) which were to aid the analysis and understanding of the Latin text. London, BL, Cotton Tiberius A.iii, for example, contains a copy of the *Regula Sancti Benedicti* with a continuous interlinear gloss in Old English accompanied by a complex system of letters from *a* to *z*. Unfortunately the above-mentioned kinds of glosses, which lack an immediate lexicographical interest, have often been neglected by editors.

As regards the taxonomy, the five main types are glosses on prosody, lexical glosses, grammatical glosses, syntactical glosses, and commentary glosses (some categories have two or more subtypes). Glosses on prosody include acute accents which indicate that a monosyllabic word should be emphasized; accentual marks also give the correct stress of polysyllabic words and help to elucidate possible ambiguities such as *aérius* or *díí*. Lexical glosses were concerned with meaning, but also with the morphological structure of the lemma. Morphological glosses elucidate or expand the grammatical properties or functions of a word, for example, the addition of the Old English preposition *mid* clarifies instrumentality, whereas *o* or *s.o.* indicates the vocative in the lemma. Syntactical glosses clarify the Latin word order. Commentary glosses reveal or explain a figure, conceit, or allusion.

There is a close relationship between interlinear glosses and the glossaries. One part of the entries which went to form Anglo-Saxon glossaries originated in a process of selection from glossed manuscripts. These entries combined with sequences of words of different origin are the core of the glossaries preserved by Anglo-Saxon manuscripts. Glosses originally written above or alongside a word of a Latin text could be excerpted along with the respective *interpretamenta* to form a "batch," that is, a sequence of glosses, the items of which maintain their original order. The lemma and the Latin or

Old English interpretation were often separated off by a simple point or by the abbreviation. *i.* (for *id est*).

As far as Medieval Latin *glos(s)are* "to gloss" is concerned, the earliest occurrence of the verb dates from the middle of the twelfth century, whereas the first occurrences of *glos(s)arium*, "glossary, collection of glosses" date back to the ninth century. This word is used to mean a collection of lexical items, each followed by an interpretation, listed—though not necessarily and not exclusively—in alphabetical order.

Three types of glossary are witnessed by Anglo-Saxon manuscripts: those consisting of one or more sections of *glossae collectae*, the class glossaries, and the alphabetical glossaries. In all types a Latin lemma was followed by one or more *interpretamenta* in Latin or Old English. With the exception of subject glossaries, where all the entries have a vernacular interpretation, the Anglo-Saxon glossaries are characterized by a random distribution of Latin and Old English interpretations.

At the stage of gloss collecting known as *glossae collectae*, one or more sets of words would be gathered in the order in which they occurred in the original text (the compiler now and then going twice over the same ground), without any alphabetical arrangement. Such words, now the lemmata of the glossary, generally kept their original inflexions, sometimes accompanied by a preposition. The different sequences of glosses might subsequently be reshuffled in alphabetical order. For example, in the Leiden Glossary the entries in chs. I and II are arranged alphabetically (in *A*-order). This kind of glossary was divided into chapters or sections, each one preceded by a rubric and including entries drawn from the books of the Bible or the Benedictine Rule or, for example, the *Historiae adversus paganos* by Orosius.

The oldest glossary of English origin was made up of *glossae collectae*. This compilation is said to date from the time of Archbishop Theodore of Tarsus (602–90) and Abbot Hadrian (*c.*630–709) and likely stems from their school at Canterbury, possibly deriving from notes taken down by students attending Theodore's lectures. The English archetype is lost (though abundantly witnessed by the entries in English glossaries such as the Second Corpus Glossary), and the oldest witness of *glossae collectae* of this stock dates from at least a century after Theodore's death. The large family of derivative glossaries, mainly preserved in Continental manuscripts, is known as the "Leiden Family" of glossaries, owing this name to the glossary in Leiden, Bibliotheek der Rijksuniversiteit, Voss. Lat. Q. 69, written at St Gall *c.*800, but featuring many *interpretamenta* in Old English.

A number of the glosses in the Épinal (Épinal, Bibliothèque municipale, 72) and First Erfurt glossaries (Erfurt/Gotha, Universitäts- und Forschungsbibliothek, Dep. Erf., CA 2° 42) were likely drawn from a source akin to the Leiden Glossary and go back to the common archetype compiled between *c.*675 and the end of the seventh century. Cognate entries are also found in the Second Corpus Glossary, but since this glossary is quite large and its entries listed in a different order, the so-called É-E glosses are no longer grouped together. From the Second Corpus Glossary entries akin to É-E and Leiden passed into the First Cleopatra Glossary. In later glossarial collections the old material was combined with new.

Whilst the oldest *glossae collectae* eventually merged in larger glossaries, new sets of *glossae collectae* were being produced all through the Anglo-Saxon period, testifying to the vitality of this selection technique. A working model is represented by the glossary (with all-Latin entries) in London, BL, Cotton Domitian i, which is drawn, for the most part, from Book 3 of the *Bella Parisiacae urbis* by Abbo of Saint-Germain-des-Prés.

Class (or subject or encyclopedic) glossaries were made up of separate lists of words belonging to particular semantic fields such as the parts of the body, the members of family and society, names of animals, common objects, and parts of the house; the entries occurred in "dictionary form." This kind of glossary goes back to the subject glossaries included in *Hermeneumata pseudodositheana*, which furnished ready-made lists of words to be memorized and used for more or less practical aims.

The *Hermeneumata* glossaries themselves provided entries to several Anglo-Saxon glossaries. Their *capitula* of classified vocabulary were drawn upon by ch. XLVII of the Leiden Glossary. Small batches of *Hermeneumata* glosses and single items drawn from the same source occur in the Épinal, Erfurt, and Corpus glossaries (where they passed independently from Leiden). The entries drawn from the glossaries of the *Hermeneumata* were modified by eliminating the Greek lemma and adding an Old English interpretation; a few glosses such as "Philocain (= Gk φιλοκάλιον) grece scopon" (Leiden Glossary XLVII, 95) preserve an echo of the original entries.

One large class glossary is to be found among the glossary material copied in the margins of Antwerp, Plantin-Moretus Museum 16.2 + London, BL, Add. 32246: this includes about 3,000 entries, arranged in nine topical sections. Smaller glossaries of this kind occur in Oxford, Bodleian Library, Bodley 730 and London, BL, Harley 107. Akin to the class glossaries, but of different origin and with a likely different use, are the plant names compilations, such as the Durham and the Laud Herbal glossaries.

A good example of class glossary is represented by Ælfric's *Glossary*. The three works written by Ælfric of Eynsham to meet the needs of monastic schools, that is, the *Grammar*, the *Glossary*, and the *Colloquy*, clearly belong together and feature a number of interconnections. For example, the lists of words of a semantic field could easily be memorized and, to aid memorization, the same vocabulary could be employed in a scholastic colloquy devised to provide students practice in speaking Latin.

Ælfric's *Glossary*, which is made up of eight sections, enjoyed a large circulation and was also excerpted (cf. Oxford, Bodleian Library, Barlow 35). Unlike the other glossaries produced in England, it is witnessed by several manuscripts. Moreover, in these codices the glossary is evidently part of larger plan and occurs alongside the *Grammar* by the same author and anonymous grammatical works, as well as glossaries and Latin texts accompanied by Old English glosses (see below).

Alphabetical glossaries were to become the most common type of glossary in England: entries could either occur in the nominative form, as in class glossaries, or could retain the same grammatical case which they had in the original text, as in the case of *glossae collectae*, which were one of their sources.

The alphabetical glossaries compiled in England were indebted to monolingual (that is, all-Latin) glossaries circulating in Italy, France, and Spain. These glossaries were characterized by an elementary alphabetic order of the entries and small-scale *interpretamenta*, and had many sources in common. Among the sources were works such as Festus's *De verborum significatu* in the epitome of Paulus Diaconus, Nonius Marcellus's *De compendiosa doctrina*, Fulgentius's *Expositio sermonum antiquorum*, and Isidore's *Etymologiae*. These compilations also contain lists of synonyms and scholia to classical authors such as Terence and Vergil, either drawn from the original texts or culled from the writings of grammarians. These medieval glossaries are now known by their first entry, for example *Abolita, Abstrusa*, or *Affatim*. Another Continental glossary whose lemmata found somehow found a way to Anglo-Saxon England is the so-called *Placidus Glossary*.

The most famous of the medieval glossaries is the *Liber glossarum*, a vast encyclo-paedic compilation originating in seventh-century Visigothic Spain. It is an immense, though unfinished achievement, with all-Latin entries (including transcriptions from Greek and Hebrew), besides passages taken from the *Etymologiae* of Isidore and other classical, late antique and patristic works (many of the glossary's items come from the *Abolita, Abstrusa*, and *Placidus* glossaries). On the Continent there were also in circulation Latin-Greek and Greek-Latin glossaries, e.g. *Pseudo-Philoxenus* and *Pseudo-Cyril*—this last to be distinguished from the all-Greek *Pseudo-Cyrillus*—where entries from Greek authors and the *Hermeneumata pseudodositheana* had found a place.

Anglo-Saxon alphabetical glossaries drew their basic material from the above-mentioned (all-Latin) glossaries, combining it with batches of *glossae collectae* from the Bible, Orosius, etc., and interlinear glosses drawn from manuscripts of insular authors such as Aldhelm. The entries were reorganized under each letter of the alphabet, and in many cases the Latin *interpretamentum* was replaced by an Old English one. At first the entries were alphabetized in *A*-order, that is, they were arranged according to the first letter of the lemma, as in the Épinal and First Erfurt glossaries (but note that entries were rearranged according to the first two initial letters (*AB*-order) in the last part of almost all the alphabetical sections of the two glossaries). In a more advanced stage of alphabetization, lemmata were arranged in *AB*-order, as in the Second Corpus Glossary (Cambridge, Corpus Christi College, 144). Alphabetical glossaries underwent progressive refinement, finally reaching an *ABC*-stage with the Harley Glossary (London, BL, Harley 3376). In this glossary there are even traces of attempts to arrive at an *ABCD*-order, e.g. "Blandus . lenis . placidus . iocundus . suavis . *liþe*" (B 456),..., "Blasphemia . vituperatio . *tæl*" (B 466), "Blatis . *bitelum*" (B 467),..., "Blavum . color est vestis . *bleo*" (B 474).

The Second Corpus Glossary, which bears the title of "Incipit glosa secundum ordinem elimentorum alphabeti," is the largest alphabetical glossary from Anglo-Saxon England, having more than 8,700 entries, over 2,000 of them with an Old English *interpretamentum*.

The alphabetical glossaries of the late period (which still preserve much material of the earliest period) were probably even bigger and were progressively approaching the format of a modern dictionary. The Harley Glossary (London, BL, Harley 3376), written around the turn of the tenth and eleventh centuries, should have contained about 12,000 to 14,000 entries. At present it features 5,563 entries, more than 1,500 with an *interpretamentum* in Old English, which cover the letters A–F (the remainder is lost, with the exception of two leaves: Oxford, Bodleian Library, Lat. Misc. a. 3, f. 49 and Lawrence, University of Kansas, Kenneth Spencer Research Library, Pryce P2 A : 1).

Whereas subject glossaries were designed for teaching and self-instruction, alphabetical glossaries were undeniably meant for reference purposes.

Glossary entries could be either set in columns or written as a continuous text (e.g., in the Harley Glossary), with the end of each *interpretamentum* signalled by a point. The entries of the Leiden Glossary, for example, are arranged in columns, each page being divided into two columns. Old English *interpretamenta* could be written in the same line as the respective lemmata or above the line. In the First Cleopatra Glossary, the Old English interpretations are usually written above the Latin lemmata, in a script which is smaller than that of the Latin headwords. The two glossaries in Cambridge, CCC 144 were compiled and transmitted together as parts of a single whole which occupies the entire manuscript. Each section of both glossaries is given graphical prominence by appropriate spacing and the use of a hierarchy of decorated initials.

On the other hand, English manuscripts feature several instances where lists of glosses were added, at a later time, on full pages that were left blank, or in the blank spaces of manuscripts, and this layout is responsible for the general disrespect given in the past to such glossarial compilations.

Larger compilations have fared better, although, in some instances, editions were limited to the publication of the Latin-Old English glosses. The linguistic approach prevailing in the past put a premium on glosses in the vernacular. As a result, where a glossary alternated, as is frequently the case, monolingual with bilingual *interpretamenta*, only the glosses in Old English and their respective lemmata were published, while monolingual glosses were omitted. This practice prevents a full appreciation of the structure of a glossary and obscures the relationships and ratios existing between the sequences of entries, hampering the identification of their sources.

A manuscript might be entirely made up by glossaries. This is the case with London, BL, Cotton Cleopatra A.iii, which contains three glossaries. The first (fols. 5r–75v) is an alphabetical glossary (mainly in *A*-order) of about 5,000 glosses, breaking off with the letter P. On fols. 76r–88r there is a subject glossary which includes a few alphabetical sections (known as the Second Cleopatra Glossary), followed by lemmata from the Gospels (fols. 88r–91v) and, on fols. 92r–117r, by a series of words taken from Aldhelm's prose and verse *De virginitate* (these two known as the Third Cleopatra Glossary). The same applies to Cambridge, CCC 144 with its two glossaries. These codices were repositories of learning and reference tools for the communities hosting the volumes in their library.

A not much studied codex, Brussels, BR 1828–30 features a large sylloge of glossaries of different typology, including excerpts from a version of the *Hermeneumata* and a few sections of a class glossary with Old English *interpretamenta*. This manuscript represents a *unicum* with its combination of monolingual and bilingual glossaries (alongside patristic excerpts, grammatical notes, and a commentary).

Anglo-Saxon glossators were well aware of the importance of their role. Aldred, the author of the Old English gloss to the Lindisfarne Gospels, wrote in the colophon at the end of the Gospel of John "7 Aldred presbyter indignus . . . hit ofergloesade on englisc" ("and Aldred, unworthy priest, glossed it in English between the lines"). Contemporary readers as well understood the relevance of glossaries as a specific genre of text: a list of books and ecclesiastical vestments, added on blank folios at the end of Oxford, Bodleian Library, Tanner 3 names a "Glosarius" (no. 5), another "Glosarius" (no. 17) and a "Glosarius per alfabetum" (no. 44).

We do not know much about what went on in Anglo-Saxon scriptoria and class-rooms— the two likely places whence glosses could derive. The presence of glosses, marginal notes, and commentaries in Carolingian manuscripts has generally been connected to the activity of teachers. It was in the Carolingian period that codices began to feature many more glosses, notes, and scholia and all sort of additions than the antique ones.

The process of interpreting texts by means of glosses—sparse rather than continuous—is a constant practice in England, but it is particularly valued in the tenth and eleventh centuries. The reason behind these glosses is still far from being completely clear. It remains uncertain whether these glosses were written by a single scholar trying to master a Latin work in the silence of his room, and, afterward, copied over and over again along with the main text. By another view, glosses were a crib either for the teacher, who used them when lecturing, or for the student who had to master a difficult text. However, it is unlikely that glossaries were used in the classroom itself for teaching purposes; they are rather a sort of reference work, to be consulted by the master at points of difficulty.

In the last period of Anglo-Saxon England, beginning with the Benedictine reform, Latin literacy was aided by translations and vernacular glossing. Ælfric's *Grammar*, which presented Latin grammar through the medium of Old English, was not an innovation in teaching, but an innovation in written composition.

Old English glosses to Latin texts were a common learning tool. Interlinear versions were undoubtedly instrumental in vocabulary learning because, by their nature and physical layout, they encouraged a regular coupling of lemma and *interpretamentum*. As noted above, lexical glossing was not confined to the explanation of unfamiliar words, but also provided a share of synonyms for familiar words, expanding the repertoire of basic vocabulary.

The concern of modern scholars with the semantic aspect of glosses has tended to overlook the wider cultural (and educational) purposes for which they were designed. Glosses, as well as the other vernacular activities of tenth- and eleventh-century grammar, witness a deep scholarly preoccupation with the English language. It has been remarked that the breadth and quality of the products of this activity are unparalleled elsewhere in Europe.

GRAMMAR

In Anglo-Saxon England any person striving for a good degree of literacy needed grammatical knowledge to read and master Latin. Education was mostly dedicated to attaining and improving the Latin literacy that was necessary for interpreting literary texts, above all the Bible.

As well as in other countries, in the Middle Ages, grammar occupied a central position and was a most necessary discipline concerned not only with literacy (*ratio recte scribendi et loquendi*), but also with all the aspects of a literary text (*scientia interpretandi*). In both England and Ireland, which were non-Romance speaking areas, proficiency in Latin could have been acquired not just by means of one of the grammars devised for Latin-speaking countries, but by combining the study of grammatical tracts and lists of exempla (such as the *Declinationes nominum* and the *Coniugationes verborum*, which often circulated separately) with the reading of set texts, likely accompanied by glosses. This new and wider sense given to grammar was responsible for the creation of a specific type of manuscript where *artes* and *auctores* formed a cluster. It also influenced the layout of manuscripts in which the latter were usually accompanied by interpretational frames in the form of glosses.

What was understood by the term "grammar" dominated the Anglo-Saxon curriculum, to the virtual exclusion of other disciplines. Rhetoric and dialectic were less essential than grammar, though it should be mentioned that Bede was sympathetic to the techniques of classical rhetoric and added an appendix to his *De arte metrica*, entitled *De schematibus et tropis*, where the descriptions of figures are, in large part, borrowed word for word from Donatus.

In the very early period, Anglo-Saxon schools would have used late Latin grammars inherited from the Continent, and the surviving manuscripts bear witness to the circulation of a number of Latin grammarians. The textbooks introduced from the Continent were intended for Latin speakers and took for granted knowledge of the declension of nouns and conjugation of verbs. Hence the need of new textbooks and collections of paradigms, each one accompanied by a list ranging from tens to hundreds of words that inflected similarly. A number of graphical devices were used to make Latin grammars more accessible, such as word separation, and also the word order of the texts was sometimes modified.

The composition of indigenous grammatical textbooks is dated to the end of the seventh century. Among the earliest works were also works on metre. Knowledge of Latin verse was considered essential: Bede wrote on metrics, composing a *De arte metrica*, and Aldhelm was the author of the *De metris* and the *De pedum regulis* (both of which are parts of his *Epistola ad Acircum*). The *De metris*, mostly about the dactylic hexameter, was accompanied by a hundred riddles (*enigmata*) in that metre. Boniface too will be responsible for a short treatise on metre, the *Caesurae versuum*.

Tatwine and Boniface wrote two grammars based on the *Ars maior* of Donatus. Another reworking of Donatus, the *Ars Asporii*, that probably originated in late sixth- or early seventh-century Gaul (and was a foreign-learner-oriented textbook as well) is among the sources of both Tatwine and Boniface. The two insular textbooks provide essential information on Latin grammar, improving the content and structure of the *Ars maior* and allowing more space to the description of accidence. That of Tatwine in particular contains a number of carefully arranged paradigms and lists of examples. The main core of such examples will be used over and over in insular elementary grammars. The two textbooks were exported to the Continent, whereas their impact in England seems to have been short-lived, and they were probably among the many texts to disappear in the ninth century.

A fragmentary copy of Boniface's *Ars grammatica* survives in Marburg, Hessisches Staatsarchiv Hr 2,18, a manuscript dating to the middle of the eighth century and a fragment of Tatwine's is preserved in Karlsruhe, Badische Landesbibliothek, fragm. Aug. 119, written at the end of the eighth century in an Anglo-Saxon scriptorium, probably on the Continent.

The two grammars are preserved by a number of Continental manuscripts; particularly interesting is the case of a group of four codices of the *Ars grammatica* of Tatwine which features a few Latin and Old English glosses with an evident overlap with the common core of entries of the Épinal, Erfurt, and Leiden glossaries, which might have been added either at Canterbury (where Tatwine was appointed archbishop in 731) or at a Continental centre where both his grammar and the Canterbury glossary material was available.

The standard works until the beginning of the ninth century are reference grammars dealing with each part of speech in turn, which did not include drills or practice material, apart lists of examples. For this reason it is necessary to surmise a joint use of this sort of grammars and elementary texts such as the Psalter or the *Disticha Catonis*. Studying grammar had a pragmatic bent, and teaching was meant to enable pupils to read intelligently Latin works, particularly the Bible, but also patristic writings and to allow them an active participation in the Mass and Office.

Alcuin's output includes a number of *opera didascalica*: the *Ars grammatica*, the *De dialectica*, the *De orthographia*, and the *Dialogus Franconis et Saxonis de octo partibus orationis*. All these works are made up of a series of questions and answers. A number of grammatical topics were also addressed in his *Disputatio Pippini regalis et nobilissimi iuvenis cum Albino scholastico*, which included questions such as "Quid est littera?" and "Quid est verbum?" ("What is a letter?" and "What is a word?").

The *Ars grammatica* draws on the classical sources available at Tours, where Alcuin was abbot from 796 to 804. Still keeping the framework of Donatus, this grammar takes advantage of Priscian's *Institutiones grammaticae* (note that the first manuscript of Priscian's *Partitiones XII versuum Aeneidos principalium* also comes from Tours). Alcuin's *De orthographia* was largely based on Bede's handbook of the same title and bears witness to a keen interest in synonyms and *differentiae verborum*, also evident in the glossators' practice. The two works were intended for use in formal instruction, but also as reference tools.

As far as the circulation of Alcuin's works in Anglo-Saxon England is concerned, there are two manuscripts of *De dialectica* and two of *De orthographia*. Moreover an "Alchuinum" is number eight in the list of books owned by an unknown grammarian named Æthelstan included in London, BL, Cotton Domitian i.

A new kind of grammar, devised by Carolingians grammarians would become popular in England, replacing the insular elementary grammars. Although the technique of parsing had been in use in teaching for a long time, the "parsing grammar" represents a new genre of textbook whose compilation was likely influenced by the rediscovery of Priscian's *Partitiones*. One of the first parsing grammars is the *Ars* of Peter of Pisa, which included questions such as "Pater quae pars" ("What part of speech is *father*?"). These manuals had a different and peculiar structure: one particular example, such as *pater* "father" or *anima* "soul," was taken as starting point and used to convey basic grammatical information (cf. the parsing grammar "Anima quae pars" in Worcester, Cathedral Library, Q.5). Note that there is a limited number of manuscripts containing grammatical works dating from the ninth century.

Later grammars were based on a modification of Priscian, in which the formal criterion for nouns was the type of declension, rather than gender, as in Donatus. This system resulted in a further development in insular grammars reducing the number of paradigms and formulating rules by applying analogy. By the end of tenth century, a renovated range of grammatical works was available in England, alongside a continued circulation of standard works such as Priscian's.

Almost all of Priscian's grammatical writings were known in Anglo-Saxon England: there is an early copy of the *Institutio* in Karlsruhe, Badische Landesbibliothek, Fragm. Aug. 122 (s. viii ex). The tract also occurs in Columbia, University of Missouri, Ellis Library, Fragm. manuscripta F.M.2 (s. ix) from Wales, St. Petersburg, RNL, O.v.XVI.1, ff. 1–16, and Worcester, Cathedral Library, Q.5. The *Institutiones* are found in Cambridge, Jesus College, 28 (s. xi ex), from France, where they are followed by the *De accentibus* attributed to Priscian, as well as in English manuscripts such as Cambridge, Trinity College, O.2.51, part ii, Cambridge, UL, Add. 4406, Cambridge, Magdalene College, Pepys 2981 (7), and Canterbury, Cathedral Library and Archives, Add. 127/19. There is one manuscript of the *Partitiones*: Rheims, Bibliothèque municipale 1097.

An abridgment of the *Institutiones*, the *Excerptiones de Prisciano* is preserved in two Anglo-Saxon manuscripts, Paris, BnF, nouv. acq. lat. 586, ff. 16–131 and Antwerp, Plantin-Moretus Museum 16.2 + London, BL, Add. 32246.

There is no copy of Donatus's *Ars minor* and only one complete copy of the *Ars maior* among surviving manuscripts: London, BL, Cotton Cleopatra A.vi. Eutyches's *Ars de verbo* occurs in Oxford, Bodleian Library, Auct. F.4.32 and Phocas's *Ars de nomine et verbo* in Oxford, Bodleian Library, Auct. F.2.14.

A foreign master, Abbo of Fleury, called to teach at Ramsey from 955 to 957, after he had returned to France, composed a treatise entitled *Quaestiones grammaticales*, which he dedicated and sent to his former students in England.

It was Ælfric's *Grammar*, however, that superseded all the other handbooks on grammar. Around 998 Ælfric composed a *Grammar* which owes much to an abbreviated version of Priscian's *Institutiones* known as the *Excerptiones de Prisciano*. Ælfric's *Grammar*, like most other grammars written in England, provides a description of Latin at a rather elementary level, laying much stress on accidence. The *Grammar* differs from its predecessors in only one respect, the use of Old English as a medium. It was the most successful of Ælfric's didactic works and is preserved by thirteen manuscripts; in six of these it is followed by his *Glossary*.

As was underscored above, typical Anglo-Saxon educational manuscripts were to contain a grammar and the text of one or more *auctores*, accompanied by related commentaries. In Geneva, Bibliotheca Bodmeriana 175, for example, excerpts from Book I of Donatus's *Ars maior* occur alongside the *De consolatione Philosophiae*, and the commentaries to Boethius's work by Remigius of Auxerre and Lupus of Ferrières. Oxford, St. John's College 154 features Ælfric's *Grammar* and *Glossary*, followed by a series of scholastic colloquies in Latin (provided with occasional interlinear glosses in both Latin and Old English) and a part of Book 3 of the *Bella Parisiacae urbis*, also accompanied by a continuous gloss in Old English.

The *Grammar* of Ælfric is found in combination with other kinds of primers (anonymous grammatical treatises, possibly composed in England) and school texts. London, BL, Cotton Julius A.ii, fols. 10–135 combines Ælfric's *Grammar* and *Glossary* with a treatise on Latin verbs. London, BL, Harley 3271, an eleventh-century codex likely written at Winchester, contains a copy of Ælfric's *Grammar* and three other elementary works: the grammatical treatise "Beatus quid est," an acephalous list of nouns and verbs classified by declension and conjugation (starting with the third declension), and notes on the first two nominal declensions. In addition, the manuscript features a variety of works which may well have served the needs of a master, such as Book 3 of the *Bella Parisiacae urbis* and a word-for-word Old English rendering of a prose version of the same poem.

"Beatus quid est" is a parsing grammar most likely composed in England in the early years of the eleventh century. It survives only in this copy and represents a written reflection of the pedagogical techniques which had served the Anglo-Saxons for centuries. As well as Ælfric's *Grammar*, "Beatus quid est" represents the result of centuries of attempts to adjust grammatical teaching to the need of those with no native knowledge of Latin.

London, BL, Harley 3826 contains *De orthographia* by Alcuin, followed by Bede's work of the same title and texts such as Abbo's and Martianus Capella's. A long series of glosses—with a few exceptions, hitherto unpublished—takes up the majority of the manuscript and includes a copy of the "Grammarian's Glossary" (*incipit*: "Poeta id est vates...."), an interesting collection of entries on grammar and metrics which is also found in several Continental manuscripts.

There are also all-grammatical codices, such as London, BL, Cotton Cleopatra A.vi, ff. 2–53, where Donatus's *Ars maior* is combined with the parsing grammar "Iustus quae pars," and Worcester, Cathedral Library, Q.5, which contains a rich collection of grammatical texts (Bede's *De arte metrica* and *De schematibus et tropis*, Priscian's *Institutio* and Israel the Grammarian's *De arte metrica*), alongside other instructional works.

As was remarked above, the question-and-answer format was particularly suitable for grammatical teaching. A small prose dialogue on declensions, "Prima declinatio quot litteras terminales habet?" ("How many final letters has the first declension?") (still unprinted) is found in Durham, Cathedral Library, B.III.32, London, BL, Cotton Faustina A.x, ff. 3–101, and Harley 107. The first manuscript also contains Ælfric's *Grammar* and the other two both the *Grammar* and the *Glossary*.

Only with the Benedictine reform movement was the educational background for Latin scholarship firmly established: it was the second generation of men involved in the English reform that brought to full growth the efforts of scholars such as Æthelwold. Both glossaries and grammars were powerful tools in the hands of these masters.

BIBLIOGRAPHY

Gneuss, H. 1990. "'The Study of Language in Anglo-Saxon England.' The Toller Memorial Lecture 1989." Bulletin of the John Rylands University Library of Manchester 72: 3–32 [repr. in Language and History in Early England (Variorum Collected Studies Series, CS559), Aldershot: Ashgate, 1996].

Gneuss, H. and M. Lapidge. 2014. *Anglo-Saxon Manuscripts. A Bibliographical Handlist of Manuscripts and Manuscript Fragments Written or Owned in England up to 1100* (Toronto Anglo-Saxon Series, 15). Toronto, Buffalo,, NY, and London: University of Toronto Press.

Ker, N. R. 1957. *Catalogue of Manuscripts Containing Anglo-Saxon*. Oxford: Clarendon Press [reissued with suppl., 1990].

Lapidge, M. 1982. "The Study of Latin Texts in Late Anglo-Saxon England: The Evidence of Latin Glosses." In Latin and the Vernacular Languages in Early Medieval Britain, ed. Nicholas Brooks, Leicester: Leicester University Press, 99–140 [repr. in *Anglo-Latin Literature 600-899*, London and Rio Grande, OH: Hambledon Press, 1996, 455–98].

Lapidge, M. 2006. *The Anglo-Saxon Library*. Oxford: Oxford University Press [including a reprint of his "Surviving Booklists from Anglo-Saxon England," 133–47].

Law, V. 1982. *The Insular Latin Grammarians* (Studies in Celtic History, 39). Woodbridge: Boydell.

Law, V. 1997. *Grammar and Grammarians in the Early Middle Ages*. London and New York: Longman.

Lendinara, P. 1999. *Anglo-Saxon Glosses and Glossaries* (Variorum Collected Studies Series, CS622). Aldershot: Ashgate.

CHAPTER 62

THE HISTORY OF MANUSCRIPTS SINCE 1500

GREGORY HAYS

INTRODUCTION

INDIVIDUAL manuscripts can change hands in various ways: through sale, gift, inheritance or theft. Since the sixteenth century, however, such transfers have been augmented by the forcible dissolution of monastery libraries, a process that took place in two distinct stages. In England and much of Northern Europe it was a result of the Protestant reformation of the sixteenth century. In Catholic countries it came only in the late eighteenth and early nineteenth centuries, through state action in Germany and Austria, the revolution and its aftermath in France, and the Napoleonic conquests and rise of the new national state in Italy. These dissolutions and dispersions were balanced by the formation of new collections, especially those of religious and secular rulers, many of which in time developed into the large national or public libraries of Europe. Individual collectors played a significant role throughout the process (see Fig. 62.1).[1]

FROM MEDIEVAL INSTITUTION TO PRIVATE COLLECTORS

In England the dispersal began with Henry VIII's dissolution of the monasteries between 1536 and 1539.[2] The fates of their libraries varied widely.[3] Cathedral libraries often had a better chance at preservation, and substantial collections remain at Salisbury, Durham, Lincoln, and Hereford.[4] Books from Canterbury passed into the

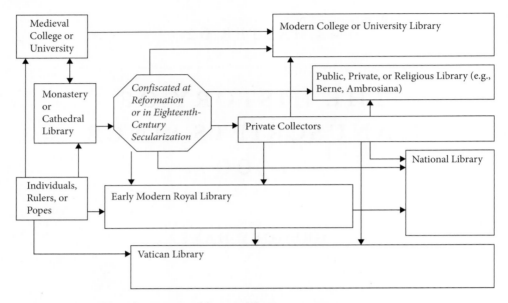

FIG. 62.1 Movement of manuscripts, late Middle Ages to present.

possession of Archbishop Cranmer. Some monastic books were saved by former monks, by antiquarians, or by Protestants interested in grounding the new English church in a historical context.[5] John Leland (1506–52), commissioned by the government to survey monastery property, was instrumental in arranging for the transfer of some to the royal library.[6] Still other manuscripts were preserved in, or found their way to, the universities.

Much of the salvage is due to private collectors.[7] Matthew Parker (1504–75), archbishop of Canterbury from 1559, left over 400 codices to Corpus Christi College, Cambridge.[8] Another major library (subsequently dispersed) was formed by the astrologer and courtier Dr. John Dee (1527–1608 or 1609).[9] Many books from northern monasteries found their way into the library of Henry Saville of Banke (1568–1617).[10] Many of Dee's and Saville's books were in turn absorbed into the library of Sir Robert Cotton (1571–1631).[11] Substantial collections were also assembled by Sir Simonds d'Ewes (1602–50),[12] Thomas Howard, fourteenth earl of Arundel (1585–1646),[13] and James Ussher (1581–1656), archbishop of Armagh.[14]

In Germany private collectors had been active before 1500; the Book Collector appears among the passengers of Sebastian Brant's *Narrenschiff* (1494). One such was Amplonius Ratinck von Berka (*c.*1365–1435), who bequeathed his large library to the university at Erfurt. German students who had studied in Italy brought manuscripts back with them: a notable example is the scholar-physician Hartmann Schedel (1440–1514), the compiler of the Nuremberg Chronicle.[15] With the advent of the Reformation, monasteries in Protestant-controlled areas were dissolved and their libraries appropriated or dispersed. The rich holdings of Lorsch, for example, were incorporated into the library of the Elector Palatine in Heidelberg. Among private individuals, noteworthy manuscript collections were assembled by various members of the Fugger family of Augsburg.[16] Later collectors include the brothers Heinrich (1570–1642) and Friedrich Lindenbruch (1573–1648), who acquired manuscripts for the princes of Holstein-Gottorp. Many of these subsequently passed to the diplomat and antiquarian Marquard Gude (1635–89).[17]

France offers a complex picture.[18] Some monastery libraries remained intact until the revolution, but others were plundered during the Wars of Religion, or diminished gradually by neglect, theft, and sale to collectors. Exemplary is the case of St. Benoît at Fleury, whose surviving manuscripts are dispersed among five libraries in four different countries (see Fig. 62.2).[19] A large number fell into the hands of the Orléans advocate and philologist Pierre Daniel (1530–1603 or 1604).[20] Part of Daniel's collection went to Jacques Bongars, whose heir, Jakob Gravisset, donated it to the town of Berne in 1632. The other half of Daniel's library went to Paul Petau, whose collection was sold by his son Alexandre in 1650 to Queen Christina of Sweden (1626–89).[21] In 1654 Christina converted to Catholicism and abdicated, taking with her an already extensive manuscript collection (in part the spoils of the Thirty Years War). This she enlarged still further by buying other libraries, including that of Jean Bourdelot (d. 1638), briefly her court physician, and his nephew Pierre Michon-Bourdelot (1610–85).[22] She spent the remainder of her life in Rome, where her collection passed to the Vatican as the Codices Reginenses.[23]

Fleury manuscripts and fragments were also acquired by a Parisian circle of scholar-administrators that included Pierre Pithou (1539–96) and his brother François,[24] Jacques-Auguste de Thou (1553–1617),[25] and Claude Dupuy (1545–94).[26] Most of these

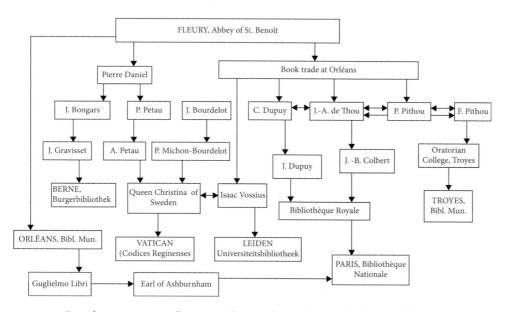

FIG. 62.2 French manuscript collectors with special attention to the library of Fleury.

manuscripts eventually found their way into the royal library. Dupuy's books were given directly by his son Jacques. Pierre Pithou's manuscripts were split between his brother François and his friend and fellow collector de Thou. De Thou's library (including manuscripts left him by Pierre Pithou) was in turn bought by Jean-Baptiste Colbert (1619–83), Louis XIV's minister of finance, and passed to the royal library from him.[27]

In Italy, early modern collectors could draw on the rich remains of fifteenth-century private libraries, and on manuscripts sold or discarded with the coming of print. The Paduan antiquarian Gian Vicenzo Pinelli (1535–1601) accumulated a sizable library of both Greek and Latin manuscripts.[28] In Rome Angelo Colocci (1467–1549)[29] and Fulvio Orsini (1529–1600)[30] built up significant collections, now in the Vatican. Orsini also served as librarian to Alessandro Farnese (Pope Paul III, d. 1569), whose own manuscripts would later end up in Naples. Other ecclesiastical collectors included Cardinal Marcello Cervini (1501–55), whose manuscripts (including some from the Cambridge Friars) were later acquired by Cardinal Sirleto.[31] A late figure in this tradition was the Florentine Antonio Magliabecchi (1633–1714), who left his collection to his native city.[32]

THE RISE OF PRINCELY LIBRARIES

Private libraries, unless left to an institution, were typically dispersed within a generation of the owner's death. The case was potentially different with royal libraries, but even of these, only two can trace substantial continuity back beyond 1500.

One of these is the Vatican.[33] Medieval popes, like other rulers, had libraries, but these were more personal than institutional. The conception of an institutional library is credited to Nicholas V (reigned 1447–55), though its development in fact owes more to Sixtus IV (reigned 1471–84).[34] In the sixteenth century the original collection, the Vaticani latini, absorbed the libraries of scholars and antiquarians like Colocci and Orsini. The seventeenth saw the accession of three important collections: the mostly German Palatini (plundered from Heidelberg), the mainly French Reginenses (purchased from Queen Christina's heirs), and the Italian Urbinates (once owned by the duke of Urbino, Federico da Montefeltro).[35] New accessions continued to arrive, notably the codices Ottoboniani (including manuscripts of Marcello Cervini) in 1748.[36]

The other princely library that can claim a foundation date before 1500 is the French Bibliothèque Royale.[37] In the late fifteenth century it had been enriched by the Aragonese royal library at Naples, large portions of which were seized by Charles VIII in 1494,[38] and by the Visconti-Sforza family library at Milan, captured by Louis XII in 1499.[39] Kept first at Fontainebleau, then at Blois, it was eventually moved to Paris in 1666.

In Germany, political fragmentation is mirrored in a plethora of princely libraries, of which three stand out. In Munich Albrecht V of Bavaria founded an extensive court library in 1558, incorporating books of Hartmann Schedel, the humanist Johann Albrecht Widmanstetter, and Johann Jakob Fugger.[40] The collection of the Electors

Palatine at Heidelberg reached its acme under the Dutch humanist Jan Gruter (1560–1627). It included not one but two libraries successively built up by Ulrich Fugger (1526–84). Captured during the Thirty Years War, it was sent to the Vatican by the Catholic Maximilian of Bavaria.[41] Finally, in 1572 Duke Julius of Brunswick established a court library at Wolfenbüttel, subsequently refounded as the Bibliotheca Augusta by Julius's descendant, Duke August (1579–1666).[42] Important accessions of manuscripts soon followed: from the monastery of Weissenburg in 1690 and the library of Marquard Gude in 1710.

The Hapsburgs were not left behind. In Vienna, the Hofbibliothek acquired the collection of Georg Fugger (1517–69) from his heirs in 1655. Fugger's manuscripts joined many codices purchased from the Hungarian humanist Joannes Sambucus (1531–84).[43] In Spain, Philip II built up two collections intended to aid in the defense of Catholicism: those of the Biblioteca Nacional in Madrid and the monastery-palace of the Escorial. The latter incorporated the library of the humanist archbishop and legal scholar Antonio Agustín (1516–86).[44] But Philip was also ruler of the Low Countries, and as such the ultimate founder of the Bibliothèque Royale in Brussels, established in 1559.[45] The core of its rich manuscript collection descends from the library of the dukes of Burgundy (notably Philip the Good), which Philip merged with the books bequeathed him by his aunt, Mary of Austria.

ITALIAN LIBRARIES IN THE COUNTER-REFORMATION

Italy is unique for the number and variety of libraries with significant manuscript holdings.[46] Some of these descend from private or family libraries of the late Renaissance. The earliest of these was the Florentine Biblioteca Medicea-Laurenziana, opened in 1571 by Grand Duke Cosimo I, and essentially an outgrowth of the Medici family library, incorporating the libraries of Coluccio Salutati and Niccolò Niccoli. Other examples include the Biblioteca Riccardiana, Florence (assembled in the late 1600s; publicly available from 1715), and the library of the Este at Modena (opened to the public in 1764). Individuals sometimes left their collections to the public. Francesco Marucelli's (1625–1703) collection became the Biblioteca Marucelliana (opened 1752). Antonio Magliabechi (1633–1714) left his library to the city of Florence, though it was not opened to the public until 1747. Its collections subsequently formed the basis of the Biblioteca Nazionale Centrale in Florence.[47]

Still other institutions were founded by churchmen, such as Cardinal Bessarion, who in 1467 left his collection of manuscripts (predominantly Greek but also Latin) to the Republic of Venice, as the foundation collection of the Biblioteca Marciana.[48] Sadly, the gift sat in crates for decades and was not made publicly available until after 1550.[49] By that time, other libraries were coming on the scene. In Rome,

Filippo Neri, the creator of the Oratorian Order, founded the Biblioteca Vallicelliana (1581), which incorporated the library of the Portuguese humanist Achilles Statius.[50] Other Roman foundations include the Biblioteca Angelica, founded by the Augustinian Angelo Rocca (1546–1622) and, a century later, the Biblioteca Casanatense, left to the Dominicans as a public resource by Cardinal Girolamo Casanate (d. 1700).

By far the greatest, however, is the Biblioteca Ambrosiana, founded in Milan by Cardinal Federico Borromeo (1564–1631).[51] Important early accessions came from Bobbio (including a number of manuscripts later revealed as palimpsests) and from the library of the fifteenth-century humanist Francesco Pizolpasso.[52] Milanese religious establishments contributed to the collection. So did private libraries; when Gian Vicenzo Pinelli's manuscripts were auctioned at Naples in 1608, it was Borromeo's representatives who emerged victorious.[53]

The newer (or newly important) monarchies of eighteenth-century Italy created royal libraries to match. That of the House of Savoy eventually became the Biblioteca Nazionale Universitaria at Turin.[54] The former Farnese library was inherited by the Bourbon Charles III of Spain (son of Elizabeth Farnese), who moved it to Naples in 1734. It was combined with other collections in the late eighteenth century to form the royal library, ancestor of the present Biblioteca Nazionale.

Italian university libraries are less significant for manuscript holdings. A partial exception is Bologna's Biblioteca Universitaria (originally part of the eighteenth-century Istituto delle Scienze), which housed the manuscripts of Pinelli's friend Ulisse Aldrovandi (1522–1605) in 1742, and a major bequest from Pope Benedict XIV (d. 1758).

Collectors and Libraries in Holland and England

Protestant countries were not without their resources. In Holland the Leiden Universiteitsbibliotheek, active from 1587, embarked on an aggressive program of acquisition.[55] Important early accessions included manuscripts from Leiden professors like Bonaventura Vulcanius and J. J. Scaliger, as well as the printer Hieronymus Commelinus and the Flemish philologist Franciscus Nansius.[56] A small but significant acquisition was the manuscripts of Justus Lipsius in 1722.[57] The university libraries of Oxford and Cambridge date back to the fifteenth century, but were revitalized in the early seventeenth. In Cambridge the University Library's holdings remained inferior to some college libraries', notably those of Trinity and Corpus Christi.[58] The case was otherwise in Oxford, where Thomas Bodley (1545–1613) gave money and books to re-establish the university library in 1602.[59] One early benefactor was Kenelm Digby (1603–65), who left the library manuscripts originally collected by Bodley's friend Thomas Allen. But the Bodleian missed its chance at the over 700 manuscripts of Isaac Vossius (1618–89), previously employed by Christina of Sweden. They went instead to Leiden.[60]

Private collectors remained important.[61] Book auctions (introduced to London in 1676) fed the appetites of collectors like Samuel Pepys, who left his library to Magdalene College, Cambridge.[62] The Cotton library was soon to be rivaled, and then surpassed, by the collection of over 7,000 manuscripts assembled by Robert Harley, earl of Oxford (1661–1724) and his son Edward (1689–1741), with the aid and guidance of their librarian Humfrey Wanley.[63] But the Harleys were merely the peak of a range that also included men like Richard Rawlinson (1690–1755), who left his manuscripts to the Bodleian,[64] Thomas Coke, earl of Leicester (1698–1759), whose library at Holkham Hall included manuscripts commissioned for Raphael de Marcatellis,[65] and the physician William Hunter (1718–83), who left his manuscripts to his old university, Glasgow.[66] These collectors preserved English manuscripts: among the elder Harley's first large purchases was the library of Sir Simonds D'Ewes. But their collections were European in scope. Collectors like Rawlinson and Coke brought Continental (especially Italian) manuscripts back from the Grand Tour. The Harleys had agents on the continent and bought up manuscripts formerly owned by the Dutch philologist J. G. Graevius, the French Chancellor Pierre Séguier, and the humanist cardinal Nicholas of Kues.[67] Hunter bought through agents in Paris, bidding against French collectors like the duc de la Vallière (1708–80) and the marquis de Paulmy (1722–87), whose collection would form the basis of the Bibliothèque de l'Arsenal.[68]

Sir Robert Cotton's library had always been open to other antiquarians, and was left to the state on his grandson's death. But the key step in the development of a national library was a somewhat later legacy, that of the physician and antiquarian Hans Sloane (1660–1753), whose collections became the core of the British Museum.[69] Sloane's more than 4,000 manuscripts formed one of the museum's three "foundation" collections, together with the Cotton library and the Harleian manuscripts, the latter purchased by the state from Edward Harley's widow and daughter. The museum was further enriched by the royal library donated by George II in 1757 (now the Royal manuscripts). His successor, George III, set about building a new collection; this would be transferred to the museum in 1823 by George IV as the King's manuscripts.

SECULARIZATION AND REVOLUTION

The British Museum's growth owed something to rivalry with the Bibliothèque du Roi in Paris, by this period a national library de facto. A major stimulus to the rise of other such institutions was the wave of secularizations in the second half of the eighteenth century that dissolved most remaining European monasteries.[70] The movement began with suppression of the Jesuits in the 1760s. In France the confiscations included manuscripts from the College of Anchin, now in the Bibliothèque municipale at Douai, and the Collège de Clermont, purchased en bloc by the Dutch collector Gerard Meerman (1722–71).[71]

This proved merely the prologue to a vaster confiscation.[72] Between 1782 and 1787 the Hapsburg Emperor Joseph II closed a third of Austrian monasteries.[73] Bavarian monasteries suffered a similar fate under the Elector Maximilian III Joseph (d. 1777) and his successors, culminating in the full-scale secularizations of 1802–3 under Maximilian Joseph IV, overseen by the energetic Johann Christoph von Aretin (1772–1824).[74] The libraries of major foundations such as Benediktbeuern, St. Emmeram (Regensburg), Ranshofen, Tegernsee, and the cathedral library at Freising were absorbed into the Bayerische Staatsbibliothek, whose manuscript collection swelled almost overnight from some 2,000 codices to over 20,000.[75] The public and university libraries in Würzburg, Bamberg, and Augsburg were enriched on a somewhat lesser scale. Manuscripts from Reichenau went to Karlsruhe, those from Fulda to Kassel and elsewhere.

In France, meanwhile, the revolution completed the process of secularization begun a generation before with the Jesuits.[76] In Paris the former royal library was transformed into the Bibliothèque Nationale and doubled in size by accessions from religious and other confiscated libraries, including those of Saint-Germain-des-Prés and the abbey of St. Victor, as well as the Sorbonne.[77] Books from provincial monasteries were handed over to the municipalities. In many cases a Bibliothèque municipale still preserves the core of a neighboring monastery's collection, as at Valenciennes (St. Amand), Dijon (Cîteaux), and Troyes (Clairvaux).

The revolution and Napoleon's subsequent campaigns unleashed a wider phase of plunder and confiscation.[78] At least 1,600 Italian manuscripts were transported to Paris, as were many from Belgian, Austrian, and German libraries. Most, though not all, were returned after Waterloo. A more lasting consequence of Napoleon's campaigns was the suppression of Italian monasteries. What remained of the Bobbio library after earlier accessions to the Biblioteca Ambrosiana made its way to Turin, probably in 1820. The process was extended to the new unified state by Cavour and Victor Emmanuel in 1866. Religious libraries like the Angelica were nationalized. Manuscripts confiscated from Roman libraries formed the basis of the Biblioteca Nazionale Centrale in that city, and "Conventi soppressi" shelf marks are found at the Biblioteca Medicea-Laurenziana and the Biblioteca Nazionale Centrale in Florence. In smaller centers a religious library was commonly transformed into a Biblioteca Comunale.

The nineteenth century was the age of the national library.[79] The Bibliothèque Royale at Brussels was enlarged by the spoils of confiscated Jesuit libraries (including the collections of the Bollandists) and monasteries such as Gembloux. In Vienna, the Hofbibliothek became the Österreichisches Nationalbibliothek with the final collapse of the Hapsburg regime in World War I. Germany, not formally united until 1871, has no official national library, but the role is split de facto between the Bayerische Staatsbibliothek in Munich and the Deutsche Staatsbibliothek—Preussischer Kulturbesitz in Berlin.[80] The latter traces its foundation to Elector Frederick William of Brandenburg in 1659; its initially unimpressive manuscript holdings were augmented by purchase in the late nineteenth century.[81] The picture is still more complex in Italy, where many libraries can claim "national" status.[82]

COLLECTORS IN THE NINETEENTH
AND EARLY TWENTIETH CENTURIES

Secularization also put manuscripts on the market to private collectors. In Paris, the Russian diplomat Peter Dubrovsky acquired manuscripts from Corbie and Saint-Germain, which are now in St. Petersburg.[83] The Venetian ex-Jesuit Luigi Matteo Canonici (1727–1807) formed a large collection, purchased after his death by the Bodleian.[84] The spoils of Continental monasteries fed the London book market of the early and mid-nineteenth century. They contributed, for example, to the enormous collection formed by Sir Thomas Phillipps (1792–1872),[85] which took a century to disperse, and to the smaller one bequeathed to the Bodleian by Francis Douce (1757–1834).[86]

Manuscript collecting had its own fashions.[87] The dilettante William Beckford (1760–1844) leaned toward illuminated Italian manuscripts and Books of Hours, and affected disdain for the early medieval manuscripts ("putrid yellow parchments of Psalms and Gospels") collected by his son-in-law, the duke of Hamilton.[88] But the rise of the "Gothic" aesthetic and the Pre-Raphaelite movement brought new interest in all things medieval.[89] Significant manuscript collections were assembled by John Ruskin[90] and William Morris.[91] Meanwhile, the Oxford Movement was prompting a new interest in liturgiology. Keble College, founded in 1870 and named for one of the movement's leaders, has few classical manuscripts, but one of the finest collections of Books of Hours in Britain.[92]

Many private collections eventually found their way to institutions. Examples are the two manuscript collections formed by the colonial governor Sir George Grey (1812–98), one now in the National Library of South Africa in Cape Town, the other in Auckland, New Zealand.[93] The Fitzwilliam Museum, Cambridge, inherited about 200 manuscripts from the astronomer Frank McClean (1837–1904). The Berlin Staatsbibliothek bought the collection of some 600 manuscripts formed by the duke of Hamilton (1767–1852), incorporating about 80 previously owned by his father-in-law Beckford.[94] Some of the Phillipps library, including the former Meerman manuscripts, also went to Berlin, while another large bloc was sold to the Bibliothèque Royale in Brussels.

The half-century from 1880–1930 saw a new generation of wealthy collectors.[95] By far the greatest of these was J. P. Morgan, whose collection remains in the Morgan Library in New York.[96] Others included Henry Yates Thompson, the Worcestershire sauce heir Dyson Perrins, and the Irish-American mining engineer Chester Beatty.[97] The Baltimore railroad magnate Henry Walters (1848–1931) bought illuminated manuscripts as an adjunct to his art collections.[98] But men of lesser means competed too. The London solicitor James Lyell left a hundred manuscripts (somewhat less than half his collection) to the Bodleian.[99] Interest in fifteenth-century Italian manuscripts was stimulated by Sir Sydney Cockerell (1867–1962), longtime director of the Fitzwilliam Museum in Cambridge.[100] Another collector with strong holdings in this period was Major J. R. Abbey, whose collection was sold off between 1965 and 1989.[101] Their American counterparts included the publisher George Plimpton (1855–1936), who left manuscripts to Wellesley and Columbia,[102] and Thomas E. Marston, whose collection was bought by Yale in 1962.

By this time, the supply of manuscripts was beginning to dry up. One new source was the large library of the Carthusian house at Buxheim in Germany, which passed into private hands at secularization and was released onto the market in the 1880s.[103] What remained of the Phillipps library in 1945 was bought en bloc by the London firm of William H. Robinson, Ltd. and sold off gradually in the following decades. On the positive side, the diminishing supply of "new" manuscripts has stimulated research in other areas. Increasingly, new discoveries come from the investigation of manuscript fragments used as pastedowns and binding materials in other manuscripts or printed books.[104]

OLD HAZARDS AND
NEW TECHNOLOGIES

Manuscripts are vulnerable to many hazards. A third of Pinelli's library was lost shortly after his death when the ship carrying it from Venice to Naples was attacked by Turkish pirates. In 1687 a fire at the monastery of San Antonio di Castello in Venice claimed the library of the Venetian Cardinal Grimani (1461–1523), which included the massive collection of Pico della Mirandola.[105] Other conflagrations destroyed the library of Westminster Abbey (1694) and much of the royal library in Stockholm (1697). Most famous is the fire that destroyed or damaged part of the Cotton library (then stored at Ashburnham House), in 1731.

Private collectors preserved manuscripts that might otherwise have perished. But they did not leave them untouched.[106] Like earlier readers, they wrote in their books.[107] Often they had them rebound, destroying evidence of provenance and trimming away marginal notes. Acephalous texts at the opening of a volume might be discarded, or missing text supplied from other sources. Integral manuscripts were sometimes split up and shorter, unrelated manuscripts bound together.[108] Victorian amateurs snipped out miniatures and illuminated initials; dealers broke up manuscripts to sell the pages individually.[109] The foremost twentieth-century dismemberer may have been the Cleveland academic and book-dealer Otto Ege (1888–1951), who assembled portfolios of single leaves for sale to American libraries.[110]

Custodianship of manuscripts by university and national libraries provided a measure of stability. Yet dangers still lurked. Early attempts to recover the lower script of palimpsests through the use of chemical reagents left some virtually unreadable. A major fire in 1904 destroyed large numbers of manuscripts at Turin.[111] Others fell victim to the flooding of the Arno in 1966. Theft was another risk. The most colorful case is that of Count Guglielmo Libri (1803–69), appointed in 1836 to a position involving the inspection of French regional libraries.[112] He was thus enabled to acquire surreptitiously a considerable collection of manuscripts (including many from Tours, Orléans, and Lyons), which he sold in 1847 to Bertram, fourth earl of Ashburnham.[113] The bulk of the French thefts were restored through negotiations with Ashburnham's heirs.[114] As it turned out, Libri had also filched a number of Italian manuscripts; these were repurchased by Italy in 1884 and now form the Ashburnham collection at the Biblioteca Medicea-Laurenziana in Florence.

The increasingly indiscriminate nature of modern warfare has not left manuscripts unscathed. Strasbourg's Bibliothèque municipale was destroyed during the Franco-Prussian War in August, 1870, while the University Library at Louvain perished in World War I. World War II took a still greater toll. Many collections were moved to storage, but three French bibliothèques municipales (Tours, Chartres, and Metz) suffered heavily.[115] Completely destroyed were the National Library in Warsaw (including some manuscripts returned from St. Petersburg after 1918), the University Library at Louvain (again), and the Hessische Landesbibliothek in Darmstadt. A number of Berlin manuscripts vanished during (or shortly after) the war, but ultimately turned up in Krakow.[116] The aftermath of the war produced its own difficulties. Like Berlin itself, the Deutsche Staatsbibliothek was split in two, with considerable confusion to shelf marks and catalogues. (The two halves were reunited in 1989.) Cold War rivalry slowed the cataloguing of German collections and impeded access to collections in the Eastern bloc countries.

Some insurance against these dangers was provided by the advent of photography.[117] A major advance was the development in 1907 of the photostat (a primitive form of photocopier) and its successor technologies, microfilm and microfiche, whose potential was recognized by the mid-1930s. The advent of digital photography has opened up the field still further. At the time of writing, for example, substantial collections of St. Gall and Cologne manuscripts are available on the Web, as is an increasing proportion of the huge Munich and Vatican collections.[118] Digital reproduction is allowing the virtual reconstruction of dismembered manuscripts and dispersed libraries. Progress can also be expected on more conventional fronts: new and improved cataloguing of extant collections, research on thousands of surviving booklists (many still unpublished), studies of institutions and individual owners, and of broader intellectual trends over the last four centuries.[119] Despite considerable advances, much of the modern history of medieval manuscripts still remains to be written.[120]

NOTES

1. Synoptic treatments of this topic are rare. Brief but still worth reading is James (1919). Also valuable are the manuscript catalogues of individual collections (which are cited only exceptionally below); for these, see Kristeller and Krämer (1993); Krämer (2006.) For an updated online edition, see Kristeller and Krämer (2016).

2. Ker (1942–3); Wright (1958a); De Hamel (1997); Carley (2002); Ramsay (2004); Carley (2006).
3. Ker (1964) with the supplement Watson (1987).
4. Ker (1964, xiv–xv).
5. Fritze (1983).
6. Birrell (1987). On Henry's own collecting, see Carley (2004).
7. Watson (2004); Roberts (2006).
8. James (1899); Pearce (1925); Dickins (1972); Page (1993); Graham (2006).
9. Roberts and Watson (1990); Sherman (1995).
10. Watson (1969).
11. Wright (1958b); Sharpe (1979, esp. 48–83); Carley and Tite (1982); Tite (1994); Parry (1995, 70–94); Wright (1997); Brown (1998).
12. Watson (1966).
13. Howarth (1985) touches on manuscripts only incidentally.
14. O'Sullivan (1956).
15. Stauber (1908).
16. Lehmann (1956–60). See the review-summary by Vernet (1961).
17. Horváth (1987).
18. Fundamental for this period is Vernet and Jolly (1988–92, vol. 2). Cf. also Dupruigrenet Desroussilles (2005).
19. See Mostert (1989, 29–33).
20. Hagen (1873).
21. Meyier (1947).
22. Omont (1891); Pellegrin (1986). For other sources, see Pellegrin (1973).
23. Montfaucon (1964); Bignami Odier (1962).
24. Bibolet (1998).
25. Vernet and Jolly (1988–92, vol. 2, 101–26).
26. Solente (1927); Delatour (1998).
27. Delisle (1868–81, vol 1, 439–86); Balayé (1988a, 71–99); Vernet and Jolly (1988–92, vol. 2, 157–80).
28. Grendler (1980), not just on the Greek MSS, and (1981); Nuovo (2005), (2007). The Latin manuscripts are surveyed by Rivolta (1933).
29. Lattès (1931); Fanelli (1972).
30. Nolhac (1887).
31. Ker (1978); Fossier (1979).
32. Totaro (1993).
33. Vian and D'Aiuto (2011). On the foundational period, see Müntz and Fabre (1887); Grafton (1993).
34. Bignami Odier (1973); Manfredi (1994).
35. Moranti and Moranti (1981).
36. Bignami Odier (1966).
37. Delisle (1868–81); Balayé (1988a); Vernet and Jolly (1988–92, vol. 2, 77–84, 209–34).
38. De Marinis (1947–52); Toscano (1993).
39. Pellegrin (1955).
40. Hartig (1917).
41. Mittler (2000).
42. Haase (1973); Schmidt-Glintzer (1998).

43. Gerstinger (1926).
44. Mayer (1997).
45. Wittek (1969), with a focus on illuminated MSS.
46. Bottasso (1984), (1990); Rozzo (2005).
47. Totaro (1993).
48. Bianca (1980); Zorzi (1987).
49. Lowry (1974).
50. Rosa Corsini (1995).
51. Paredi (1981); Paredi and Rodella (1992).
52. Paredi (1961).
53. Hobson (1971).
54. Cf. Vitale-Brovarone (2004).
55. Hulshoff Pol (1975).
56. Hulshoff Pol (1976).
57. Lieftinck (1962).
58. Oates (1958).
59. Philip (1983).
60. Blok (1974), (2000).
61. De Ricci (1930, 33–70).
62. Ramsay (2001); Beadle (2004).
63. Wright (1960), (1962); Wright and Wright (1966, xi–lxxxiii).
64. Enright (1990).
65. Hassall (1959).
66. Ker (1983); Hindman *et al.* (2001, 35–6).
67. Clark (1891); Wright (1972); Hallauer (1986).
68. Muzerelle (1983); Vernet and Jolly (1988–92, vol. 2, 303–17); Hindman *et al.* (2001, 33f).
69. Miller (1973); Harris (1998).
70. Beales (2003).
71. After the death of his son Johan, the manuscripts were sold at auction in 1824; many bought then and subsequently by Sir Thomas Phillipps were acquired en bloc after his death by the Staatsbibliothek in Berlin. See van Heel (2007).
72. Garrett (1992).
73. Buchmayr (2004).
74. Ruf (1962), all published; Hauke (1991). For Aretin, see Ruf (1962, 7–48).
75. Hartig (1932).
76. Vernet and Jolly (1988–92, vol. 3, 9–97); Varry (2000), (2004).
77. Balayé (1988a, 323–440), (1988b).
78. Hobson (1989); Laffitte (1989); Zorzi (2000).
79. Humphreys (1988, 1–32).
80. Olson (1996).
81. Schmidt (1978).
82. See Lazzari (1990).
83. Voronova (1978); Thompson (1984).
84. Madan (1897, 313–14); Hobson (2000).
85. De Ricci (1930, 119–30); Munby (1954), (1956), (1960). See also Munby (1967), an abridgement of his earlier volumes.
86. Gillam (1984); Hindman *et al.* (2001, 37–8).

87. Fundamental is Munby (1972).
88. Hobson (1976).
89. Hindman *et al.* (2001, 177–213).
90. Dearden (1966).
91. Needham (1976).
92. Parkes (1979).
93. Kerr (2006).
94. Boese (1966, ix–xxii); Hobson (2000).
95. De Ricci (1930, 169–93).
96. Taylor (1957); Hindman *et al.* (2001, 218–23).
97. On Yates Thompson, see De Hamel (1991a); on Perrins, see Cleaver (2020); on Beatty, see De Hamel (1991b); Cleaver (2017).
98. Hindman *et al.* (2001, 223–7). Johnston (1999) has little to say about the manuscripts.
99. Hunt (1950).
100. De Hamel (1987), (2006a), (2006b), (2006c); Panayotova (2008).
101. Hobson and Munby (1961); Alexander and de la Mare (1969).
102. Plimpton (1993, 51–67).
103. Hogg (1984); Honemann (1995), mainly on the printed books.
104. The importance of pastedowns was already recognized by Humfrey Wanley; cf. Hindman *et al.* (2001, 18).
105. Kibre (1936, 18–21); Lowry (1974).
106. For examples, see Page (1993).
107. Work in this area has so far focused mostly on printed books: see Baron (2001); Sherman (2007).
108. To take an example at random, Paris, BnF, lat. 8048, once owned by Claude Dupuy, consists of ten unrelated fragments of various sizes dating from the eleventh to the fourteenth century. No medieval reader ever owned or used this "manuscript."
109. De Hamel (1996); Wieck (1996); Hindman *et al.* (2001, 47–101).
110. Hindman *et al.* (2001, 255–9); Shailor (2003); Porcheddu (2007); Gwara (2013).
111. Vitale-Brovarone (1983); Giaccaria (1984); Giaccaria (1986).
112. De Ricci (1930, 131–8); Munby (1977a); Maccioni Ruju and Mostert (1995); Hobson (2004); Norman (2013).
113. In addition to his purchases from Libri, Ashburnham had also acquired manuscripts from Joseph Barrois of Lille, many of which proved to have been stolen from the Bibliothèque Nationale.
114. Munby (1977b).
115. For the losses, see Masson (1962).
116. Milde (1986).
117. On imaging technologies, see Hindman *et al.* (2001, 103–75).
118. *e-codices—Virtual Manuscript Library of Switzerland*, https://www.e-codices.unifr.ch/en, accessed March 30, 2020; *CEEC. Codices Electronici Ecclesiae Coloniensis*, http://www.ceec.uni-koeln.de/, accessed March 30, 2020. For Munich, see the website of the Bayerische Staatsbibliothek.
119. A particularly valuable resource for provenance research is the Schoenberg Database of Manuscripts, https://sdbm.library.upenn.edu/, accessed March 31, 2020.
120. This chapter was submitted to the editors in October, 2009. I have added references to a few items published after that date but have not been able to update it systematically.

BIBLIOGRAPHY

Alexander, J. J. G. and A. C. de la Mare. 1969. *The Italian Manuscripts in the Library of Major J. R. Abbey*. London: Faber.

Balayé, S. 1988a. *La Bibliothèque Nationale des origines à 1800*. Geneva: Droz.

Balayé, S. 1988b. "De la Bibliothèque du roi à la Bibliothèque nationale." In *La Carmagnole des muses: l'homme de lettres et l'artiste dans la révolution*, ed. J.-C. Bonnet, 37–48. Paris: A. Colin.

Baron, S. A., ed. 2001. *The Reader Revealed*. Washington, DC: Folger Shakespeare Library.

Beadle, R. 2004. "Medieval English Manuscripts at Auction, 1676–c.1700." *The Book Collector* 53: 46–63.

Beales, D. 2003. *Prosperity and Plunder: European Catholic Monasteries in the Age of Revolution, 1650–1815*. Cambridge: Cambridge University Press.

Bianca, C. 1980. "La formazione della biblioteca latina del Bessarione." In *Scrittura, biblioteche e stampa a Roma nel Quattrocento. Aspetti e problemi*, ed. C. Bianca, P. Farenga, G. Lombardi, A. G. Luciani, and M. Miglio, 103–65. Vatican City: Scuola Vaticana di paleografia, diplomatica e archivistica.

Bibolet, F. 1998. "Bibliotheca Pithoeana." In *Du copiste au collectionneur*, ed. D. Nebbiai-Dalla Guarda and J.-F. Genest, 497–521. Turnhout: Brepols.

Bignami Odier, J. 1962. "Le Fonds de la reine à la Bibliothèque vaticane." In *Collectanea Vaticana in honorem Anselmi M. card. Albareda*, vol. 1, 159–89. Vatican City: Biblioteca Apostolica Vaticana.

Bignami Odier, J. 1966. *Premières recherches sur le fonds Ottoboni*. Vatican City: Biblioteca Apostolica Vaticana.

Bignami Odier, J. 1973. *La Bibliothèque vaticane de Sixte IV à Pie XI*. Vatican City: Biblioteca Apostolica Vaticana.

Birrell, T. 1987. *English Monarchs and their Books: From Henry VII to Charles II*. London: British Library.

Blok, F. F. 1974. *Contributions to the History of Isaac Vossius's Library*. Amsterdam: North-Holland.

Blok, F. F. 2000. *Isaac Vossius and his Circle: His Life until his Farewell to Queen Christina of Sweden*. Groningen: E. Forsten.

Boese, H. 1966. *Die lateinischen Handschriften der Sammlung Hamilton zu Berlin*. Wiesbaden: Harrassowitz.

Bottasso, E. 1984. *Storia della biblioteca in Italia*. Milan: Bibliografica.

Bottasso, E. 1990. "The Network of Libraries in the Old Italian States." *Libraries and Culture* 25: 334–44.

Brown, M. P. 1998. "Sir Robert Cotton, Collector and Connoisseur?" In *Illuminating the Book: Makers and Interpreters: Essays in Honour of Janet Backhouse*, ed. M. P. Brown and S. McKendrick, 281–98. London: British Library.

Buchmayr, F. 2004. "Secularization and Monastic Libraries in Austria." In *Lost Libraries: The Destruction of Great Book Collections since Antiquity*, ed. J. Raven, 145–62. London: Palgrave Macmillan.

Carley, J. 2002. "Monastic Collections and their Dispersal." In *The Cambridge History of the Book in Britain*, ed. J. Barnard and D. F. McKenzie, vol. 4, 339–47. Cambridge: Cambridge University Press.

Carley, J. 2004. *The Books of King Henry VIII and his Wives*. London: British Library.

Carley, J. 2006. "The Dispersal of the Monastic Libraries and the Salvaging of the Spoils." In *The Cambridge History of Libraries in Britain and Ireland*, vol. 1, ed. E. Leedham-Green and T. Webber, 265–91. Cambridge: Cambridge University Press.

Carley, J. and C. G. C. Tite. 1982. "Sir Robert Cotton as Collector of Manuscripts." *The Library* (ser. 6) 14: 94–9.

Clark, A. C. 1891. "The Library of J. G. Graevius." *Classical Review* 5: 365–72.

Cleaver, L. 2017. "The Western Manuscript Collection of Alfred Chester Beatty (ca. 1915–1930)," *Manuscript Studies* 2: 445–482.

Cleaver, L. 2020. "Charles William Dyson Perrins as a Collector of Medieval and Renaissance Manuscripts *c.*1900–1920." *Perspectives médiévales* 41, http://journals.openedition.org/peme/19776, accessed March 30, 2020.

Dearden, J. S. 1966. "John Ruskin, the Collector." *The Library* (ser. 5) 21: 124–54.

De Hamel, C. 1987. "Medieval and Renaissance Manuscripts from the Library of Sir Sydney Cockerell (1867–1962)." *British Library Journal* 13: 186–210.

De Hamel, C. 1991a. "Was Henry Yates Thompson a Gentleman? " In *Property of a Gentleman: The Formation, Organisation and Dispersal of the Private Library 1620–1920*, ed. R. Myers and M. Harris, 77–89. Winchester: St. Paul's Bibliographies.

De Hamel, C. 1991b. " Chester Beatty and the Phillipps Manuscripts." *The Book Collector* 40: 358–70.

De Hamel, C. 1996. *Cutting up Manuscripts for Pleasure and Profit*. Charlottesville, VA: Book Arts Press.

De Hamel, C. 1997. "The Dispersal of the Library of Christ Church, Canterbury, from the Fourteenth to the Sixteenth Centuries." In *Books and Collectors 1200–1700: Essays Presented to Andrew Watson*, ed. J. P. Carley and C. G. C. Tite, 263–79. London: British Library.

De Hamel, C. 2006a. "Cockerell as Entrepreneur." *The Book Collector* 55: 49–72.

De Hamel, C. 2006b. "Cockerell as Museum Director." *The Book Collector* 55: 201–23.

De Hamel, C. 2006c. "Cockerell as Collector." *The Book Collector* 55: 339–66.

Delatour, J. 1998. *Les Livres de Claude Dupuy. Une bibliothèque humaniste au temps des guerres de religion*. Paris: École des Chartes.

Delisle, L. 1868–81. *Le Cabinet des manuscrits de la Bibliothèque impériale* [*Bibliothèque nationale* for vols. 2–3], 3 vols. in 4. Paris: Imprimerie impériale.

De Marinis, T. 1947–52. *La biblioteca napoletana dei re d'Aragona*, 4 vols. Milan: Hoepli [1969. 2 vol. supplement. Verona: Stamperia Valdonega].

De Ricci, S. 1930. *English Collectors of Books and Manuscripts (1530–1930)*. Cambridge: Cambridge University Press.

Dickins, B. 1972. "The Making of the Parker Library." *Transactions of the Cambridge Bibliographical Society* 6: 19–34.

Gillam, S. G., ed. 1984. *The Douce Legacy : An Exhibition to Commemorate the 150th Anniversary of the Bequest of Francis Douce (1757–1834)*. Oxford: Bodleian Library.

Gwara, S. 2013. *Otto Ege's Manuscripts*. Cayce, SC: De Brailes Publishing.

Dupruigrenet Desroussilles, F. 2005. "Biblioteche umanistiche in area francese (XVI–XVII secolo)." In *Federico Borromeo. Fondatore della Biblioteca Ambrosiana*, ed. F. Buzzi and R. Ferro, 105–17. Milan: Biblioteca Ambrosiana.

Enright, B. J. 1990. "'I Collect and I Preserve': Richard Rawlinson 1690–1755 and Eighteenth-Century Book Collecting." *The Book Collector* 39: 27–54.

Fanelli, V., ed. 1972. *Atti del convegno di studi su Angelo Colocci (Jesi, 13–14 settembre 1969)*. Jesi: Amministrazione Comunale di Jesi.

Fossier, F. 1979. "Premières recherches sur les manuscrits latins du Cardinal Marcello Cervini (1501–1555)." *Mélanges de l'École française de Rome* 91: 381–456.

Fritze, R. H. 1983. "'Truth Hath Lacked Witnesse, Tyme Wanted Light.'" *Journal of Library History* 18: 274–91.

Garrett, J. 1992. "Aufhebung im doppelten Wortsinn: The Fate of Monastic Libraries in Central Europe, 1780–1810." *Verbum. Analecta Neolatina* 2: 15–27.

Gerstinger, H. 1926. "Johannes Sambucus als Handschriftensammler." In *Festschrift der Nationalbibliothek in Wien*, 251–400. Vienna: Staatsdruckerei.

Giaccaria, A. 1984. "I fondi medievali della Biblioteca Nazionale Universitaria di Torino. Guida al fondo manoscritto." *Pluteus* 2: 175–94.

Giaccaria, A. ed. 1986. *Biblioteca Nazionale Universitaria di Torino. Manoscritti danneggiati nell'incendio del 1904*. Turin: Biblioteca Nazionale Universitaria.

Grafton, A., ed. 1993. *Rome Reborn: The Vatican Library and Renaissance Culture*. Washington, DC: Library of Congress.

Graham, T. 2006. "Matthew Parker's Manuscripts: An Elizabethan Library and its Use." In *The Cambridge History of Libraries in Britain and Ireland*, vol. 1, ed. E. Leedham-Green and T. Webber, 322–41. Cambridge: Cambridge University Press.

Grendler, M. 1980. "A Greek Collection in Padua: The Library of Gian Vincenzo Pinelli (1535–1601)." *Renaissance Quarterly* 33: 386–416.

Grendler, M. 1981. "Book Collecting in Counter-Reformation Italy: The Library of Gian Vincenzo Pinelli (1535–1601)." *Journal of Library History* 16: 143–51.

Haase, Y. A. 1973. "Die Geschichte der Herzog August Bibliothek." *Wolfenbütteler Beiträge* 2: 17–42.

Hagen, H. 1873. *Der Jurist und Philolog Peter Daniel aus Orléans*. Berne [repr. 1879. In *Zur Geschichte der Philologie und zur römischen Litteratur*, 1–30. Berlin: S. Calvary].

Hallauer, H. J. 1986. "*Habent sua fata libelli.* Von der Mosel zur Themse: Handschriften des St. Nikolaus-Hospitals in der Bibliotheca Harleiana." *Mitteilungen und Forschungsbeiträge der Cusanus-Gesellschaft* 17: 21–56.

Harris, P. R. 1998. *A History of the British Museum Library, 1753–1973*. London: British Library.

Hartig, O. 1917. *Die Gründung der Münchener Hofbibliothek*. Munich: Verlag der Königlich-Bayerischen Akademie der Wissenschaften.

Hartig, O. 1932. "Die Erschließung der Münchener Handschriftensammlung." *Bayerland* 43: 393–402.

Hassall, W. O. 1959. "Portrait of a Bibliophile II: Thomas Coke, Earl of Leicester, 1697–1759." *The Book Collector* 8: 249–61.

Hauke, H. 1991. "Die Bedeutung der Säkularisation für die bayerischen Bibliotheken." In *Glanz und Ende der alten Klöster: Säkularisation im bayerischen Oberland 1803*, ed. J. Kirmeier and M. Treml, 89–97. Munich: Süddeutscher Verlag.

Hindman, S. *et al.* 2001. *Manuscript Illumination in the Modern Age*. Evanston, IL: Mary and Leigh Block Museum of Art.

Hobson, A. 1971. "A Sale by Candle in 1608." *The Library* (ser. 5) 26: 215–33.

Hobson, A. 1976. "William Beckford's Library." *The Connoisseur* 191: 298–305.

Hobson, A. 1989. "Appropriations from Foreign Libraries during the French Revolution and Empire." *Bulletin du bibliophile* 2: 255–72.

Hobson, A. 2000. "L'abate e il marchese." *La bibliofilia* 102: 103–8.

Hobson, A. 2004. "Guglielmo Libri." In *Against the law: Crime, Sharp Practice, and the Control of Print*, ed. R. Myers, 133–50. New Castle, DE, and London: Oak Knoll Press and British Library.

Hobson, A. R. A. and A. N. L. Munby, "Contemporary Collectors XXVI: John Roland Abbey." *The Book Collector* 10: 40–8.

Hogg, J. 1984. "Buxheim Manuscripts in American Libraries." In *Die Kartäuser und die Reformation: Internationaler Kongress vom 24. bis 27. August 1983*, ed. J. Hogg, 222–36. Salzburg: Institut für Anglistik und Amerikanistik.

Honemann, V. 1995. "The Buxheim Collection and its Dispersal." *Renaissance Studies* 9: 166–88.

Horváth, E. 1987. "Marquard Gudes Gottorper Handschriften." *Wolfenbütteler Beiträge* 7: 125–47.

Howarth, D. 1985. *Lord Arundel and his Circle*. New Haven, CT: Yale University Press.

Hulshoff Pol, E. 1975. "The Library." In *Leiden University in the Seventeenth Century*, ed. T. H. Lunsingh Scheurler and G. H. M. Posthumus Meyjes, 394–459. Leiden: Brill.

Hulshoff Pol, E. 1976. "Franciscus Nansius und seine Handschriften." In *Essays Presented to G. I. Lieftinck. 4. Miniatures, Scripts and Collections*, ed. J. P. Gumbert and M. J. M. de Haan, 79–102. Amsterdam: Van Gendt.

Humphreys, K. 1988. *A National Library in Theory and in Practice*. London: British Library.

Hunt, R.W. 1950. "The Lyell Bequest." *Bodleian Library Record* 3: 68–82.

James, M. R. 1899. *The Sources of Archbishop Parker's Collection of MSS at Corpus Christi College, Cambridge*. Cambridge: Cambridge Antiquarian Society.

James, M. R. 1919. *The Wanderings and Homes of Manuscripts*. London: Society for Promoting Christian knowledge.

Johnston, W. R. 1999. *William and Henry Walters: The Reticent Collectors*. Baltimore, MD: Johns Hopkins University Press.

Ker, N. R. 1942–3. "The Migration of Manuscripts from the English Medieval Libraries." *The Library* (ser. 4) 23: 1–11 [repr. 1985, in *Books, Collectors and Libraries*, ed. A. G. Watson, 459–70. London: Hambledon Press].

Ker, N. R. 1964. *Medieval Libraries of Great Britain: A List of Surviving Books*, 2nd ed. London: Royal Historical Society.

Ker, N. R. 1978. "Cardinal Cervini's Manuscripts from the Cambridge Friars." In *Xenia Medii Aevi Historiam Illustrantia Oblata Thomae Kaeppeli O.P.*, ed. R. Creytens and P. Künzle, 51–71. Rome: Edizioni di storia e letteratura [repr. 1985, in *Books, Collectors and Libraries*, ed. A. G. Watson, 437–58. London: Hambledon Press].

Ker, N. R. 1983. "William Hunter as a Collector of Medieval Manuscripts" (The First Edwards Lecture on Palaeography Delivered in the University of Glasgow). Glasgow: University of Glasgow Press.

Kerr, D. J. 2006. *Amassing Treasures for All Times: Sir George Grey, Colonial Bookman and Collector*. New Castle, DE, and Dunedin, New Zealand: Oak Knoll Press and Otago University Press.

Kibre, P. 1936. *The Library of Pico della Mirandola*. New York: Columbia University Press.

Krämer, S. 2006. *Latin Manuscript Books before 1600. Ergänzungsband 2006*. Hanover: Hahnsche Buchhandlung.

Kristeller, P. O. and S. Krämer. 1993. *Latin Manuscript Books before 1600*. Munich: Monumenta Germaniae Historica.

Kristeller, P.O. and S. Krämer. 2016. *Latin Manuscript Books before 1600*, revised digital ed., http://www.mgh-bibliothek.de/kristeller/index.html, accessed March 31, 2020.

Laffitte, M. P. 1989. "La Bibliothèque nationale et les 'conquêtes artistiques' de la Révolution et de l'Empire." *Bulletin du Bibliophile* 2: 273–323.

Lattès, S. 1931. "Recherches sur la bibliothèque d'Angelo Colocci." *Mélanges d'archéologie et d'histoire* 48: 308–44.

Lazzari, G. 1990. "The Heritage of the pre-1861 States in the Italian Library System." *Libraries and Culture* 25: 345–57.

Lehmann, P. 1956–60. *Eine Geschichte der alten Fuggerbibliotheken*, 2 vols. Tübingen: Mohr.

Lieftinck, G. I. 1962. "Les Manuscrits de Juste Lipse conservés à la Bibliothèque Universitaire de Leyde." *Scriptorium* 16: 380–5.

Lowry, M. C. J. 1974. "Two Great Venetian Libraries in the Age of Aldus Manutius." *Bulletin of the John Rylands University Library of Manchester* 57: 128–66.

Maccioni Ruju, P. A. and M. Mostert. 1995. *The Life and Times of Guglielmo Libri (1802–1869), Scientist, Patriot, Scholar, Journalist and Thief.* Hilversum: Verloren Publishers.

Madan, F. 1897. *A Summary Catalogue of Western Manuscripts in the Bodleian Library at Oxford.* vol. 4. Oxford: Clarendon Press.

Manfredi, A. 1994. *I codici latini di Niccolò V.* Vatican City: Biblioteca Apostolica Vaticana.

Masson, A. 1962. *Catalogue général des manuscrits des bibliothèques publiques de France. Vol. 53: Bibliothèques sinistrées de 1940 à 1944.* Paris: Bibliothèque nationale de France.

Mayer, M. 1997. "Towards a History of the Library of Antonio Agustín." *Journal of the Warburg and Courtauld Institutes* 60: 261–72.

Meyier, K.A. de. 1947. *Paul en Alexandre Petau en de geschiedenis van hun handschriften.* Leiden: Brill.

Milde, W. 1986. "Lateinische Handschriften der ehemaligen Preußischen Staatsbibliothek Berlin in der Biblioteka Jagiellonska Krakau." *Codices Manuscripti* 12 : 85–9.

Miller, E. 1973. *That Noble Cabinet: A History of the British Museum.* London: Deutsch.

Mittler, E. 2000. "Une Collection éclatée: la Bibliotheque Palatine." In *Le Livre voyageur. Constitution et dissémination des collections livresques dans l'Europe moderne 1450–1830*, ed. D. Bougé-Grandon, 179–94. Paris: Klincksieck.

Montfaucon, B. 1964. *Les Manuscrits de la reine de Suède au Vatican. Réédition du catalogue de Montfaucon et cotes actuelles.* Vatican City: Biblioteca Apostolica Vaticana.

Moranti, M. and L. Moranti. 1981. *Il trasferimento dei Codices Urbinates alla Biblioteca Vaticana.* Urbino: Accademia Raffaello.

Mostert, M. 1989. *The Library of Fleury.* Hilversum: Verloren Publishers.

Munby, A. N. L. 1954. *The Formation of the Phillipps Library up to 1840* (Phillipps Studies 3). Cambridge: Cambridge University Press.

Munby, A. N. L. 1956. *The Formation of the Phillipps Library from 1841 to 1872* (Phillipps Studies 4). Cambridge: Cambridge University Press.

Munby, A. N. L. 1960. *The Dispersal of the Phillipps Library* (Phillipps Studies 5). Cambridge: Cambridge University Press.

Munby, A. N. L. 1967. *Portrait of an Obsession: The Life of Sir Thomas Phillipps.* London: Constable.

Munby, A. N. L. 1972. *Connoisseurs and Medieval Miniatures 1750–1850.* Oxford: Clarendon Press.

Munby, A. N. L. 1977a. "The Earl and the Thief." In *Essays and Papers*, ed. N. Barker, 175–91. London: Scolar Press.

Munby, A. N. L. 1977b. "The Triumph of Delisle." In *Essays and Papers*, ed. N. Barker, 193–205. London: Scolar Press.

Müntz, E. and P. Fabre. 1887. *La Bibliothèque du vaticane au XVe siècle d'après des documents inédits*. Paris: Libraire des Écoles Françaises d'Athènes et de Rome.

Muzerelle, D. 1983. "Les Fonds médiévaux de la Bibliothèque de l'Arsenal (Paris)." *Pluteus* 1: 177–89.

Needham, P. 1976. "William Morris: Book Collector." In *William Morris and the Art of the Book*. New York: Pierpont Morgan Library.

Nolhac, P. de. 1887. *La Bibliothèque de Fulvio Orsini*. Paris: H. Champion.

Norman, J. 2013. *Scientist, Scholar and Scoundrel: A Bibliographical Investigation of the Life and Exploits of Count Guglielmo Libri*. New York: Grolier Club.

Nuovo, A. 2005. "Dispersione di una biblioteca privata: La biblioteca di Gian Vicenzo Pinelli dall'agosto 1601 all'ottobre 1604." In *Biblioteche private in età moderna e contemporanea*, ed. A. Nuovo, 43–54. Milan: Bonnard.

Nuovo, A. 2007. "The Creation and Dispersal of the Library of Gian Vincenzo Pinelli." In *Books on the Move: Tracking Copies through Collections and the Book Trade*, ed. R. Myers et al., 39–67. New Castle, DE, and London: Oak Knoll Press and British Library.

Oates, J. C. T. 1958. "The Libraries of Cambridge, 1570–1700." In *The English Library before 1700*, ed. F. Wormald and C.E. Wright, 213–35. London: Athlone Press.

Olson, M. P. 1996. *The Odyssey of a German National Library: A Short History of the Bayerische Staatsbibliothek, the Staatsbibliothek zu Berlin, the Deutsche Bücherei, and the Deutsche Bibliothek*. Wiesbaden: Harrassowitz.

Omont, H. 1891. "Catalogue des manuscrits de Jean et Pierre Bourdelot, médecins parisiens." *Revue des Bibliothèques* 1: 81–103.

O'Sullivan, W. 1956. "Ussher as a Collector of Manuscripts." *Hermathena* 88: 34–58.

Page, R. I. 1993. *Matthew Parker and his Books*. Kalamazoo, MI: Medieval Institute Publications.

Panayotova, S. 2008. *I Turned it into a Palace. Sydney Cockerell and the Fitzwilliam Museum*. Cambridge: Fitzwilliam Museum.

Paredi, A. 1961. *La biblioteca del Pizolpasso*. Milan: Hoepli.

Paredi, A. 1981. *Storia dell'Ambrosiana*. Milan: N. Pozza [trans. 1983. *A History of the Ambrosiana*. Notre Dame, IN: University of Notre Dame Press].

Paredi, A. and M. Rodella. 1992. "Le raccolte manoscritte e i primi fondi librari." In *Storia dell'Ambrosiana 1. Il Seicento*, ed. M. Lanza, 45–88. Milan: Cassa di Risparmio dell provincie lombarde.

Parkes, M. B. 1979. *The Medieval Manuscripts of Keble College, Oxford*. London: Scolar Press.

Parry, G. 1995. *The Trophies of Time: English Antiquarians of the Seventeenth Century*. Oxford: Oxford University Press.

Pearce, E. C. 1925. "Matthew Parker." *The Library* (ser. 4) 6: 209–28.

Pellegrin, E. 1955. *La Bibliothèque des Visconti et des Sforza*, 2 vols. Paris: Publications de l'Institut de recherche et d'histoire des textes; 1969. Supplement. Florence: Olschki.

Pellegrin, E. 1973. "Possesseurs français et italiens de manucrits latins du fonds de la reine à la Bibliothèque Vaticane." *Revue d'histoire des textes* 3: 271–97 [repr. 1988. *Bibliothèques retrouvées*, 457–83. Paris: Éditions du Centre national de la recherche scientifique].

Pellegrin, E. 1986. "Catalogue des manuscrits de Jean et Pierre Bourdelot. Concordance." *Scriptorium* 40: 202–32.

Philip, I. G. 1983. *The Bodleian Library in the Seventeenth and Eighteenth Centuries*. Oxford: Clarendon Press.

Plimpton, G. A. 1993. *A Collector's Recollections*. New York: Columbia University Libraries.

Porcheddu, F. 2007. "Otto Ege: Teacher, Collector, and Biblioclast." *Art Documentation* 26: 4–14.

Ramsay, N. 2001. "English Book Collectors and the Salerooms in the Eighteenth Century." In *Under the Hammer: Book Auctions Since the Seventeenth Century*, ed. R. Myers *et al.*, 89–110. New Castle, DE, and London: Oak Knoll Press and British Library.

Ramsay, N. 2004. "'The Manuscripts Flew about like Butterflies': The Break-Up of English Libraries in the Sixteenth Century." In *Lost Libraries. The Destruction of Great Book Collections since Antiquity*, ed. J. Raven, 125–44. London: Palgrave Macmillan.

Rivolta, A. 1933. *Catalogo dei Codici Pinelliani dell'Ambrosiana*. Milan: Tipografia Pontificia Arcivescovile S. Giuseppe.

Roberts, J. 2006. "Extending the Frontiers: Scholar Collectors." In *The Cambridge History of Libraries in Britain and Ireland*, vol. 1, ed. E. Leedham-Green and T. Webber, 292–321. Cambridge: Cambridge University Press.

Roberts, J. and A. G. Watson. 1990. *John Dee's Library Catalogue*. London: Oxford University Press.

Rosa Corsini, M. T. 1995. *I libri di Achille Stazio. Alle origini della Biblioteca Vallicelliana*. Rome: Edizioni de Luca.

Rozzo, U. 2005. "Le biblioteche umanistiche nell'Italia medievale e moderna." In *Federico Borromeo. Fondatore della Biblioteca Ambrosiana*, ed. F. Buzzi and R. Ferro, 71–104. Milan: Biblioteca Ambrosiana.

Ruf, P. 1962. *Säkularisation und Bayerische Staatsbibliothek. Vol. I: Die Bibliotheken der Mendikanten und Theatiner (1799–1802)*. Wiesbaden: Harrassowitz.

Schmidt, W. 1978. "Von der Kurfürstlichen Bibliothek zur Preußischen Staatsbibliothek: Geschichtlicher Überblick von 1661–1945." In *Staatsbibliothek Preussischer Kulturbesitz. Festgabe zur Eröffnung des Neubaus in Berlin*, ed. E. Vesper, 1–95. Wiesbaden: Reichert.

Schmidt-Glintzer, H., ed. 1998. *A Treasure House of Books: The Library of Duke August of Brunswick-Wolfenbüttel*. Wiesbaden: Herzog August Bibliothek.

Shailor, B. 2003. "Otto Ege: His Manuscript Fragment Collection and the Opportunities Presented by Electronic Technology." *Journal of the Rutgers University Libraries* 60: 1–22.

Sharpe, K. 1979. *Sir Robert Cotton 1586–1631: History and Politics in Early Modern England*. Oxford: Oxford University Press.

Sherman, W. H. 1995. *John Dee. The Politics of Reading and Writing in the English Renaissance*. Amherst, MA: University of Massachusetts Press.

Sherman, W. H. 2007. *Used Books. Marking Readers in Renaissance England*. Philadelphia, PA: University of Pennsylvania Press.

Solente, S. 1927. "Les Manuscrits des Dupuy à la Bibliothèque nationale." *Bibliothèque de l'École des chartes* 88: 177–250.

Stauber, R. 1908. *Die Schedelsche Bibliothek*. Freiburg im Breisgau: Herdersche Verlagshandlung.

Taylor, F. H. 1957. *Pierpont Morgan as Collector and Patron, 1837–1913*. New York: Pierpont Morgan Library.

Thompson, P. Z. 1984. "Biography of a Library: The Western European Manuscript Collection of Peter P. Dubrovsky in Leningrad." *Journal of Library History* 19: 477–503.

Tite, C. G. C. 1994. *The Manuscript Library of Sir Robert Cotton*. London: British Library.

Toscano, G. 1993. "La Librairie des rois d'Aragon à Naples." *Bulletin du bibliophile* 2: 265–83.

Totaro, G. 1993. "Antonio Magliabecchi e i libri." In *Bibliothecae selectae. Da Cusano a Leopardi*, ed. E. Canone, 549–58. Florence: Olschki.

van Heel, J. 2007. "From Venice and Naples to Paris, The Hague, London, Oxford, Berlin… The Odyssey of the Manuscript Collection of Gerard and Johan Meerman." In *Books on the Move: Tracking Copies through Collections and the Book Trade*, ed. R. Myers *et al.*, 87–111. New Castle, DE, and London: Oak Knoll Press and British Library.

Varry, D. 2000. "Le Livre, otage de la Révolution. Conséquences bibliographiques des saisies politiques." In *Le Livre voyageur. Constitution et dissémination des collections livresques dans l'Europe moderne 1450–1830*, ed. D. Bougé-Grandon, 207–26. Paris: Klincksieck.

Varry, D. 2004. "Revolutionary Seizures and their Consequences for French Library History." In *Lost Libraries. The Destruction of Great Book Collections since Antiquity*, ed. J. Raven, 181–96. London: Palgrave Macmillan.

Vernet, A. 1961. "L'Histoire de la Bibliothèque des Fugger." *Scriptorium* 15: 302–7.

Vernet, A. and C. Jolly. 1988–92. *Histoire des bibliothèques françaises*, 4 vols. Paris: Promodis-Éditions du Cercle du librairie.

Vian, P. and F. D'Aiuto. 2011. *Guida ai fondi manoscritti, numismatici, a stampa della Biblioteca Vaticana. I. Dipartimento Manoscritti*. Vatican City: Biblioteca Apostoloca Vaticana.

Vitale-Brovarone, A. 1983. "Verso una ricostituzione del fondo manoscritto della Bibloteca Nazionale di Torino." *Accademie e Bibblioteche d'Italia* 51: 458–69.

Vitale-Brovarone, A. 2004. "Momenti di storia del fondo manoscritto della Biblioteca Nazionale Universitaria." In *Il palazzo dell'università di Torino e le sue collezioni*, ed. A. Quazza and G. Romano, 343–52. Turin: Cassa di risparmio di Torino.

Voronova, T. P. 1978. "P. P. Dubrovskii, 1754–1816, and the Saint-Germain Manucripts." *The Book Collector* 27: 469–78.

Watson, A. G. 1966. *The Library of Sir Simonds D'Ewes*. London: British Museum.

Watson, A. G. 1969. *The Manuscripts of Henry Savile of Banke*. London: Bibliographical Society.

Watson, A. G. ed. 1987. *Medieval Libraries of Great Britain, a List of Surviving Books: Supplement to the Second Edition*. London: Royal Historical Society.

Watson, A. G. 2004. *Medieval Manuscripts in Post-Medieval England*. Aldershot: Ashgate.

Wieck, R. 1996. "Folia Fugitiva: The Pursuit of the Illuminated Manuscript Leaf." *Journal of the Walters Art Gallery* 54: 233–54.

Wittek, M. 1969. "Le Cabinet des manuscrits." In *Bibliothèque Royale. Mémorial 1559–1969*, 159–201. Brussels: La Bibliothèque.

Wright, C. E. 1958a. "The Dispersal of the Libraries in the Sixteenth Century." In *The English Library before 1700*, ed. F. Wormald and C. E. Wright, 148–75. London: Athlone Press.

Wright, C. E. 1958b. "The Elizabethan Society of Antiquaries and the Formation of the Cottonian Library." In *The English Library before 1700*, ed. F. Wormald and C. E. Wright, 176–212. London: Athlone Press.

Wright, C. E. 1960. "Humfrey Wanley: Saxonist and Library-Keeper." *Proceedings of the British Academy* 46: 99–129.

Wright, C. E. 1962. "Portrait of a Bibliophile VIII: Edward Harley, 2nd Earl of Oxford, 1689–1741." *The Book Collector* 11: 158–74.

Wright, C. E. 1972. *Fontes Harleiani: A Study of the Sources of the Harleian Collection of Manuscripts Preserved in the Department of Manuscripts in the British Museum.* London: British Museum.

Wright, C. E. and R. C. Wright, eds. 1966. *The Diary of Humfrey Wanley.* London: Bibliographical Society.

Wright, C. J., ed. 1997. *Sir Robert Cotton as Collector.* London: British Library.

Zorzi, M. 1987. *La libreria di San Marco.* Milan: Mondadori.

Zorzi, M. 2000. "Les Saisies napoléoniennes en Italie." In *Le Livre voyageur. Constitution et dissémination des collections livresques dans l'Europe moderne 1450–1830,* ed. D. Bougé-Grandon, 251–70. Paris: Klincksieck.

CHAPTER 63

....

CATALOGUING
MEDIEVAL MANUSCRIPTS

....

CONSUELO W. DUTSCHKE

INTRODUCTION

....

THIS chapter offers an abstract template for cataloguing western European medieval and Renaissance manuscripts in codex format. Given the book that hosts the chapter, most of the delimiting terms in this first sentence are expected: nothing in Arabic, Armenian, Ethiopian, not even Greek; no notice of the manuscript book after *c.*1520; nothing of archival, documentary, or notarial nature. The one word that the attentive reader will have seized upon is "abstract." What follows is a series of proposals with commentary. Which areas (for such is the name I shall use for the large groupings of categories of information) and which fields (this being the name for the individual categories) will carry weight for the individual cataloguer or for the individual user of catalogues will depend upon his goal. But first, who is the cataloguer? He may be the scholar who collects evidence for a study of an author, or of a text, or of a certain kind of text; he may be an art historian or a musicologist, or work in another academic specialization; for this scholar cataloguer, the choice of fields and the depth to which he pushes any one field or area are essentially independent of outside constraint. He may be a member of a collaborative group in the planning stages for a long-term shared project such as an exhibition catalogue or online academic resource; the group's decisions will determine the data to be recorded. A third possibility is that the cataloguer may work in an established commercial firm, such as Christie's or Sotheby's. The cataloguer may work in an institutional library, and that institution may have subscribed to the cataloguing rules of a larger group; in this case, the cataloguer's choices will be limited (although, given quotas applied in some libraries, imperative restrictions affecting the time available for each manuscript description may prove of greater constraint than those regarding categories of information).

This chapter also assumes that the cataloguer has the languages, the palaeography, and the knowledge of texts and of history to be capable of his tasks. One of the early statements that I am aware of, dating from 1791, addresses the competencies necessary in the field in a straightforward manner: "Il est cependant essentiel que ceux qui seront chargés de ce travail [i.e., cataloguing, inter alia, medieval manuscripts] aient quelque teinture des lettres, & qu'ils sachent au moins la langue latine" ("It is essential that those who take up this work have a sprinkling of culture and that they at least know Latin"). The same pamphlet later adds: "Il seroit sans doute à desirer qu'il se trouvât sur les lieux des personnes en état de déterminer le siècle où chaque manuscrit auroit été écrit; mais comme il est rare d'en rencontrer qui aient cette connoissance, il suffira d'indiquer si l'écriture du manuscrit est ancienne ou moderne"[1] ("It is to be desired that one should have at hand people who can determine the century when each manuscript was written, but as it is rare to find someone with this knowledge, it will suffice to indicate if the writing of the manuscript is ancient or modern"). Latin and some palaeography are expectations; but if it was deemed rare to find people with expertise in palaeography in the eighteenth century, we note that it is hardly common today either.

Who the cataloguer is today is, in fact, a very real question, if not a problem. Even if the person exists who has the qualifications and interests, he will be deterred by the two communities that host and need his services. Within the library, when administrators focus on content, cataloguing of medieval manuscripts tends to be judged a "niche" specialization (as addressing a comparatively small body of material, and thus as disproportionately expensive); when the focus is on process, administrators may judge the cataloguing of medieval manuscripts in the same vein as the cataloguing of any manuscript, and place it in the hands of staff ill-equipped for the task.[2] Within the non-medievalist academic world, cataloguing of medieval manuscripts is often viewed as an exercise of small value, perhaps because of a perceived parallel with the cataloguing of modern printed books ("any librarian can do it"; "it is just raw data"). This last accusation has some foundation in reality: is a catalogue of medieval manuscripts ever the final goal in a process or is it always a step towards a larger goal? It may be that certain statistical studies are served by the resources of the catalogue alone; some comparative textual studies and quantitative codicology could use large databases of catalogued medieval manuscripts to answer certain questions (e.g., "What is the survival rate of manuscripts of Thomas Aquinas versus those of Cicero?"; "Proportionately, do more fifteenth-century manuscripts survive on paper from Germany or from Italy?").[3]

Thus, the cataloguer, with years of learning behind him and aware of the demands that impinge more or less greatly on his task, sits down at his desk, on whichever side of the library door that desk resides. Before he picks up his pencil, he must reflect upon the goal of his catalogue and what questions will be asked of it: his own questions now; his own questions toward the end of his scholarly career; his colleagues' questions, and those of a larger public. The goal of the catalogue has implications on the choices of categories of information, and ultimately on the arrangement of those categories; the goal of the catalogue will determine depth and emphasis of cataloguing. At the two extremes, and if I may be allowed to invoke stereotypes, the scholar's goal may result in intensive, highly detailed cataloguing on a related and rather small set of manuscripts that form a "virtual" collection united to address a particular question; the librarian's catalogue may be less detailed, cover a wide range of heterogeneous subjects, and include a large number of codices that exist together in an actual collection. The librarian's verbalized goal may consist of "bibliographic control" (a corral to keep those wild manuscripts from running amuck), and it implies an undifferentiated welcome to study the manuscripts directly (itself an ultimately arguable position, since medieval manuscripts are hardly a renewable resource). Whichever end of the spectrum instigates the catalogue, it may remain the only means of access to the manuscripts for years to come; this is a plea, therefore, for a balance in both deep and broad thinking, for drilling horizontally and for reaching vertically at the same time, so that the work invested retains value.

Time available for cataloguing will also have an effect on choice and depth of fields. If the graduate student researching materials for his dissertation has travel funding for six months, or if the library has received an outside grant for three years, both will have performed a simple operation of division on the number of manuscripts and the number of days available. If time limitations have not been formally imposed, the cataloguer should nevertheless estimate and track his rate of progress for his own information or as part of a reporting process. The wise cataloguer, however, should expect deviation from a schedule: our reasons for working with medieval manuscripts are the surprises and the new knowledge that they bring; if we could predict in advance all that manuscripts have to tell us, there would be small value to cataloguing and studying them.

The next set of decisions may seem mundane, and until very recently they would not have been posed as questions, the answers being obvious. What computer-based application(s) will host the catalogue during its gestation? In what manner will the catalogue be delivered in its final form? Whether the final presentation is planned as a printed book or as online delivery, a computer will have aided the cataloguer in some aspect of his work. In either case, it behooves us to consider how the catalogue's information might be structured in order to move it readily from its original container to another one, because the need for that migration will almost certainly arise, from print to electronic, or from one form of electronic to another, or from one purpose to another. Specifically, the more database-like the information is, the simpler any sort of movement will be: this means that categories of information should be as granular as possible (it is easier to amalgamate pieces of data later on than to tease joined statements apart), as intellectually distinct as possible (a country is one category of information; a city is another), and as consistent in location as possible (e.g., always or never discuss flyleaves from a separate manuscript in the Binding field). Incompatibility among data containers is inevitable, but the more clearly the cataloguer has understood the categories as separate building blocks, the more easily in the future those blocks could be reconstructed to form a different edifice. It is not only technological obsolescence that may prompt a move: to shift to a different container is also to repurpose the content while minimizing the labor. Ease of crosswalking from one electronic system to another will also decide how well data from one country aggregates with data from other countries; international collaboration is an active desideratum, with a proof of concept already in place (see note 12).

It is not within the scope of this chapter to address advantages and disadvantages of various computer applications beyond general reminders. The first general comment focuses on gestation programs, with the division between proprietary (e.g., the Microsoft suite) and non-proprietary software, with applications that function as a word processor or as a relational database (in increasing level of initial complexity in setting up the program). These would serve to collect the information in a systematic manner with increasing levels of computer-enforced obligation and thus resulting in increasingly "cleaner" data (e.g., with a word processor you might forget to note the Secundo Folio; in a database, you could have set the program to reject a record in which you had not put data into the Secundo Folio field). Depending upon your catalogue's goal, either of these levels might be sufficient (e.g., if you intended to publish the catalogue as a PDF), or might constitute an intermediate step towards a final container in XML (i.e., eXtensible Markup Language), which is machine-readable.

XML, while theoretically neutral, will be employed according to an establishable XML DTD or schema (i.e., a set of declarations that make explicit what elements will be used and in what circumstances). In its simplest form a document encoded in XML is roughly analogous to structured word-processed document, but you can build obligations into the XML schema so that the document will not validate (i.e., be accepted by the program) unless it meets those obligations. An XML schema is more complicated to set up initially than word-processing protocols, but because an XML document's data is born in that format, it is assured as long a life as any of us can predict, with readability extended almost indefinitely (not the case with proprietary software issued in new versions at frequent intervals; in all probability XML is also longer lived than non-proprietary word-processing software).[4] If the data is to be aggregated with data from another source, if it is to be programmatically analyzed, indexed, searched, retrieved, and displayed for presentation on the Web, it would benefit greatly by existence in XML, whether it originated in XML or was reformatted to XML at some point along the line.

In terms of final delivery of the information, the scholar cataloguer may not intend that his catalogue ever be publicly viewable, it having served to systematically collect evidence for an interpretive study. Requirements for printed catalogues will have been negotiated in advance with the publisher (but all will want text in e-format, as surely will the author to reduce errors in rekeying). Online catalogues allow for correction and updating; whether or not there will be people to accomplish continued attention to the catalogue is another matter. Medieval manuscripts held by American libraries are frequently included in the institution's own OPAC, which means that, behind the scenes, the manuscripts were catalogued in MARC format, often following the subset of AACR2 rules known as AMREMM.[5] While MARC is intended for modern printed books (and is, therefore, not well suited to the cataloguing of rare books of any ilk, since it concentrates attention on text to the detriment of physical and historical matters), it has the advantage of its ubiquitousness: it mainstreams medieval manuscripts in accommodating them to the same rules as followed by modern printed books and thus protects their records from isolation and technical obsolescence. Nor is MARC the final statement, as even the library world begins to look for better solutions such as those to be offered by RDA.[6]

The one truly different aspect in cataloguing today compared to even a fairly recent past is that cataloguing can now hardly take place without images, not only of figurative decoration (miniatures, bas-de-page scenes, historiated initials, etc.) but of all aspects of the book: layout, ruling, script, music, quire markings, plain and flourished initials, reader notes, ownership notes, dealer codes and markings, binding; every aspect of the book is served well by images. Images also provide excellent service in recognition of texts: imaged opening and closing pages allow for transcription of crucial rubrics, incipits, and explicits. Images build future into a catalogue because they will permit the present cataloguer to revise his own work in 20 years' time when he will have acquired 20 years of experience; they allow the specialist right now to correct or to add greater specificity;[7] they may even answer a question that today's world has not learned to ask. Images as a systematic part of a catalogue break down the age-long division between the scholar and the librarian, by sharing the burden of the cataloguing: the librarian, responsible for a wide variety of material, entrusts some of the cataloguing information to the image, while the scholar, an expert in a particular set of manuscripts, can extrapolate from the image information that is not verbally present in the catalogue and return it to the librarian for eventual updating of the catalogue, especially in an online delivery system.[8] When, in cataloguing, librarians embrace, and scholars accept that "lo mejor es enemigo de lo bueno,"[9] imperfect cataloguing will become a mutually fruitful venture, encouraging cataloguers to put forth into public view a record with uncertainties and defects, and enabling scholars to accept responsibility for reporting corrections and discoveries back to the holding institution.

Thus, online catalogues, images, the recognition of the positive value of imperfection, and collaboration can combine to increase the rate of production and the quality in the cataloguing of medieval manuscripts. More online catalogues bring hope to the century-long question: "How do I find the manuscripts relevant to my research?" There is also a broader question that will be answered only with more extensive cataloguing: "How can we advance our knowledge of the Middle Ages?" It is only when we plumb the riches of *all* medieval manuscripts that we can be confident of our research.

Template for a Description of a Codex

63.2.1 Heading
    63.2.1.1 Date(s) of Work with the Manuscript
    63.2.1.2 Shelf Mark
    63.2.1.3 Tombstone Title
    63.2.1.4 Place of Origin
    63.2.1.5 Date of Origin
    63.2.1.6 Notes
63.2.2 Intellectual Content
    63.2.2.1 Span of Folios
    63.2.2.2 Rubric
    63.2.2.3 Incipit
    63.2.2.4 Explicit
    63.2.2.5 Colophon
    63.2.2.6 Author
    63.2.2.7 Title
    63.2.2.8 Overview
    63.2.2.9 Bibliography Relevant to Text
    63.2.2.10 Acknowledgments
63.2.3 Physical Description
    63.2.3.1 Support
    63.2.3.2 Number of Leaves in Codex
    63.2.3.3 Measurements in Millimeters
        63.2.3.3.1 Book Block
        63.2.3.3.2 Text Block
    63.2.3.4 Collation
        63.2.3.4.1 Quire Signatures
        63.2.3.4.2 Leaf Signatures
        63.2.3.4.3 Catchwords
    63.2.3.5 Layout
    63.2.3.6 Script
        63.2.3.6.1 Alphabet
    63.2.3.7 Scribe(s)
    63.2.3.8 Musical Notation
    63.2.3.9 Decoration
        63.2.3.9.1 Artist(s) or Style(s)
        63.2.3.9.2 Miniatures
        63.2.3.9.3 Borders
        63.2.3.9.4 Historiated Initials
        63.2.3.9.5 Painted Initials
        63.2.3.9.6 Pen-flourished Initials

63.2.3.10 Evidence of Reader(s)

63.2.3.11 Accompanying Material

63.2.3.12 Binding

63.2.3.13 Acknowledgments

63.2.3.14 Condition

63.2.4 History of the codex

63.2.4.1 Origin

63.2.4.2 Provenance

63.2.4.3 Former Shelf Marks

63.2.4.4 Secundo Folio

63.2.5 Other

63.2.5.1 Bibliography Relevant to Manuscript

63.2.5.2 Acknowledgments

63.2.5.3 Available Reproductions

63.2.5.4 Images

63.2.5.5 Administrative Information

The template works from a number of assumptions:[10]

(1) that the cataloguer recognize this template for what it is: a series of suggestions open to modification in order and in content. The cataloguer, or the institution directing the cataloguer, may prefer to describe first the physical aspect of the book, and then its texts. There may be a decision to add fields not listed here (e.g., punctuation; standardized ruling patterns via a coded system; colors via assigned reference numbers from a color chart).

(2) that the cataloguer comprehend the goal of his catalogue in order to place consistently greater or lesser emphasis on fields of greater or lesser relevance to that goal.

(3) that the cataloguer have adequate time at his disposal; if not, it would be good at the start to decide which fields will be abandoned (e.g., collation can be very time-consuming; determining the number of scribes can require much slow and precise work; compiling a full bibliography may not be an option).

(4) that the unit of work is the codex; if the description addresses an incomplete item, even down to the single leaf or cutting, it will be sufficient to eliminate the fields that pertain only to a full book (e.g., collation and its subsets). If the description considers a number of codices that share certain characteristics, it may be time-saving to write the collection-level information once (e.g., provenance; binding) and then refer back to it (or link to it, if online).

(5) that the value of a template, once it is determined, lies in its consistent application, so that a reader of the description (who may be the cataloguer himself many years later) will have confidence in the presence or absence of a field in the description, and so that the reader will be able to reliably and quickly locate certain segments of information at certain points in the description.

The template divides its information into five areas: Heading; Intellectual Content; Physical Description; History; Other.

63.2.1 Heading

This information is presented in database-like, telegraph-style brevity, allowing the reader to quickly decide if the description contains material of interest. If time available for the description is very tight, and the intent is to compile little more than an inventory, the description might consist of no more than the Heading's five fields and one other field for notes. Or, since work on a catalogue of manuscripts often proceeds in an iterative manner, the Heading with its fields may be compiled as the first tracking phase of what will eventually become a fully descriptive catalogue.

63.2.1.1 Date(s) of work with the manuscript
63.2.1.2 Shelf Mark
63.2.1.3 Tombstone Title
63.2.1.4 Place of origin
63.2.1.5 Date of origin
63.2.1.6 Notes

63.2.1.1 *Date(s) of the cataloguer's work with the manuscript*

Although it may seem obvious to the point of superfluity to record the date(s) when the cataloguer has the manuscript on a desk in front of him, within a few years' time, one will not remember, and the date may become important for tracking, for example, if it was before or after the cataloguer attended a crucial lecture, or if it was during a period of initial or more advanced study; the date might be important if the manuscript is later refoliated, worked on by conservation, damaged, or stolen.

63.2.1.2 *Shelf Mark (Class Mark; Call Number)*

It becomes ever more crucial with increasing electronic access to medieval manuscripts to record the precise format of the shelf mark used by the holding institution. Arbitrary rules to always/never include MS or Ms. or Cod. (in whatever position) imposed by an editor or a set of cataloguing rules cannot be accepted, since a search engine may reject an imperfect match. The cataloguer should follow in-house capitalization, spacing. and punctuation marks for the same reason. The cataloguer is forewarned, however, that institutions with online catalogues may prefix the shelf mark with added zeros to the left of the item number to assure correct stacking in a computer-generated list; presumably one omits them in reporting such a call number.

Some libraries, and perhaps only American libraries, impose class marks on medieval manuscripts, i.e., an identifying system that ties the intellectual content of the manuscript to a modern classification system (e.g., Dewey Decimal; Library of

Congress). If the cataloguer has a choice in the matter, it will be better to avoid such square-peg, round-hole solutions since they are often inappropriate in equating modern subject divisions to premodern materials; they do not simplify the cataloguer's task; and they do not aid the browsing reader in open shelves. Classification systems are also more cumbersome and more difficult to recopy accurately than a sequential numbering that usually represents order of acquisition (MS 1, MS 2, etc.). Sequential numbering may also be tied to a language (e.g., Paris, Bibliothèque nationale de France, nouv[elles] acq[uisitions] fr[ançaises] 934), or to provenance (e.g., Vatican City, Biblioteca Apostolica Vaticana, Ottob[oniani] lat[ini] 1641). The term "call number" seems to be of American, rather than British usage, and while it implies class marks (since it is used for modern printed books), it appears to have acquired a generic meaning as the identifier by which one calls for a book, whether manuscript or printed.

While on the subject of shelf marks, it is pertinent to note that a catalogue of medieval manuscripts will include throughout its text citations of other manuscripts beyond those of the actual or fictive collection in question. When citing other manuscripts, the formal citation should be given in full at each occurrence to save later verification: city (programmatically either always in the language of the country or always in the language of the catalogue), institution (always in the language of the country), repository (always in the language of the country), then the shelf mark/class mark/call number.

It may, of course, not be a simple matter to discover the modern location of a cited manuscript that is referred to in older bibliography as in a private collection or in a sale/auction catalogue. It is surprising how successful a simple online keyword search can be and will increasingly be, but only when the desired manuscript is describable with almost unique words. Tools specific to the movement of medieval manuscripts continue to be developed.[11] There are also increasing numbers of online tools that aggregate multiple collections.[12]

See also Section 63.2.4.3.

63.2.1.3 *Tombstone Title*

As its name implies, this field contains the barest essentials to indicate the intellectual content of a manuscript. It might consist of a short author/title statement, such as "Augustinus, Sermones" (in Latin) or "Cicero, Letters" (in English); it might be yet broader, such as "Rolle, Writings" (author last name, and a generic title); it might list several authors and no titles, such as "Bruni; Filelfo; Petrarch; Porcari," or it might sum up the contents in a short, comprehensive title assigned by the cataloguer, such as "Humanistic miscellany"; it might contain a mention of a vernacular language, such as "Devotional prayers in German."

63.2.1.4 *Place of Origin*

The place of origin of a manuscript[13] should precede a statement of its date of origin, because the former information helps the cataloguer to determine the latter: not all shifts in scribal features, not all changes in style of decoration take place across Europe at the same time. Nevertheless, one's level of precision about the place of origin may vary: "Italy, Abbey of Morimondo," or "France," or "England?" or "Southern France or northern Spain." Because we are presently discussing the area of the Heading, any of the above would be appropriate, and the discussion as to a France/Spain uncertainty or the pinpointed precision of "Morimondo" can wait until the area for the History of the manuscript for nuanced presentation. What one will want to include consistently is the name of the country, which usually is cited according to modern political divisions (although it may be debatable to give a manuscript to France when it was produced in a very German style and signed as Strasbourg).

When a medieval manuscript is localized by an explicit statement from its scribe, he designates his space by a city name (as, therefore, did early printers, and as, therefore, our printed books continue to do today). Nevertheless, it will behoove the cataloguer to step backward from the city to the larger unit that is the country in order to maintain consistency in the cataloguing fields. A manuscript signed by its scribe as copied "in civitate senarum in domo domini Francisci Lutii equitis insignis" is not usefully catalogued in the Heading as "Siena, Sir Francesco Luti's house" but rather "Italy, Siena."[14] As mentioned above, with the ubiquitous presence of computers in our work, we need to catalogue with formal consistency: to mix a city name and a country name in the same field is to find oneself at the end with "dirty" data. Let the field begin consistently with the same category of information; depending upon the container for the catalogue, it might be reasonable to devise a number of fields to represent subsets of the concept of Place of Origin (e.g., Country; Cardinal Position; Region/Province/ Département; City; Monastery or Locale).

63.2.1.5 *Date of Origin*

Just as with the place of origin, the date of origin of a manuscript is often very difficult to determine.[15] Consequently, just as with the field for Place of Origin, one may need to express in the Heading area one's knowledge of this crucial information in a simple, even simplistic manner, and reserve fuller justification to the cataloguing area for History. There is one very useful difference, however, in the expression of date: convention distinguishes when the date has been assigned by the cataloguer, as opposed to an assertion of date by the scribe. When assigned in modern times, the date is shown either as Roman numerals with superscript letter/numbers (the way it is handled in the academic world by manuscript scholars) or it is written in Arabic numerals enclosed within square brackets (the system used by the library world). If the scribe's own signed date is in the manuscript, it is presented in the catalogue in straightforward Arabic numerals.

For example: "s. XVex," "late fifteenth century," "circa 1490–1500" and "[1490–1500]" all tell the reader—albeit with variation in meaning—that the date has been determined in modern times (i.e., the manuscript is not dated); but a date given as "1496" is understood to represent the scribe's own assertion (i.e., the manuscript is dated). The convention of writing palaeographically assigned dates with Roman numerals for the centuries and superscript letters/numbers for the segments of centuries was laid out for the English-speaking world in 1969 by Ker (1969–2002, I, vii); ten years later, Parkes (1979, xix) gave a more detailed explanation of the system.

Between the extremes of not-dated and dated, lies the category of datable, when a combination of factors internal and external to the manuscript combines to limit the possible span of time during which the manuscript could have been copied. For example, one might say that a manuscript was "datable to between 1493 and 1496" if its text was composed in 1493 and if the original owner's signature is in the book, and the owner is known to have died in 1496. The explanation for a datable range of time is best handled in the field for Origin, internal to the area for History (see Section 63.2.4.1).

As with the cataloguing for Place of Origin, the prescient cataloguer will take computers into consideration on the manner of expressing dates. Computers of any sort, at least as matters stand at the time of writing, are not prepared to sort successfully on Roman numerals or on dates that include non-numeric characters such as square brackets. Therefore, the cataloguer, even producing descriptions for his own benefit, will include fields for BeginDate and EndDate. The palaeographically assigned date, for example, of "s. XIII^{med}" will be accompanied by two further statements with conventional values: "BeginDate: 1240" and "EndDate: 1260."

Note that there is no convention for indicating that a manuscript has been localized in modern times versus the manuscript's own statement of place of origin in a scribal colophon. When the location is by country alone, one assumes that it was assigned by the cataloguer; when a city is present, one might wonder whether the more tightly defined localization was due to the scribe's statement.

The above discussion works from the most common situation: that one codex has one place of origin and one date of origin. Not always true, of course. Composite manuscripts exist whereby booklets or fascicules with separate text(s) and of separate origins are bound together; composite manuscripts also exist whereby a single text may have been composed in segments of differing place and date of origin (for example, if the book had lost its final quires in some mishap, a scribe of later times and a different nationality might have undertaken completion of the text). The Heading area could include such information or not, depending upon the cataloguer's judgment: is the different material significant enough to warrant a separate statement in the Heading? Or is the different material slight enough to simply include a mention of the separate section in the Intellectual Content and/or in the History areas?

63.2.1.6 *Notes*

Medieval manuscripts as hand-produced items in a pre-standardization era do not fall into neat categories, such as the present template seems to suggest. By including a field for Notes even in the area for Heading, the cataloguer is encouraged to be aware of (and pleased with) some aspect of the manuscript that he deems worthy of comment, even though it may not match an official category. Note that some cataloguing traditions may also include a statement in the heading about the language of the text, about the kind of support, about the number of leaves, etc.

63.2.2 Intellectual Content

The area of Intellectual Content has been the traditional focus of cataloguing in the past; significantly, Title is the only required field in today's cataloguing for institutional libraries that use the omnipresent MARC system.[16] This hints at the centuries of effort to sort out the definition of title, and to distinguish its many permutations. The present article will not attempt that; a cataloguer who requires a deeper knowledge is encouraged to look to printed-book cataloguing rules for systematic classes.[17] Specifically in the fraught and complex issues of authors and titles in medieval manuscripts, the cataloguer should read (and reread) Sharpe (2003).[18]

Although a cataloguer could decide to place the modern title of a text in the first position in his catalogue, this discussion begins with the evidence for the text's identification in the manuscript itself. The list of fields outlined here will be repeated for each successive text in the manuscript.

63.2.2.1. Span of Folios
63.2.2.2. Rubric
63.2.2.3. Incipit
63.2.2.4. Explicit
63.2.2.5. Colophon
63.2.2.6. Author
63.2.2.7. Title
63.2.2.8. Overview
63.2.2.9. Bibliography Relevant to Text
63.2.2.10. Acknowledgments

63.2.2.1 *Span of Folios*

Most medieval manuscripts received foliation in early modern or modern times, rather than pagination; unless there is strong reason to the contrary, it is better to stay with whichever system is present, and it is preferable to not refoliate even if the present counting has an occasional mistake. One sometimes encounters modern foliation that skips numbers intentionally in order to represent what are imagined to be missing leaves (mimicking the situation of a printed book, where missing pages have taken their page numbers away with them). Such an unfortunate action leads the readers of the catalogue to assume that leaves were removed recently, and it misleads unwary readers into thinking that the manuscript is more extensive that it actually is. Decisions to skip imagined missing leaves in foliation often forget that a singleton leaf might be an addition to the manuscript, rather than the remaining orphan from a subtraction; a skipped number in the foliation simply proves the cataloguer's ignorance. If the cataloguer must refoliate (or repaginate), he could with his pencil put a line through the to-be-superseded numbering (but not erase it, since there could be reference to it in print), and add the new number below; he should then record publicly the date of the new foliation.

In reporting pagination, "p." and "pp." are standard abbreviations. With foliation, the noun may be abbreviated as "f." or "fol." for the singular, and "ff." or "fols." for the plural; the recto of the leaf may be abbreviated as "r" and the verso as "v" (without a period, as a matter of common usage). The designation of recto is sometimes implied, so that "f. 1" is understood to refer to the recto of the leaf. The habit may have originated in the days of taking notes by hand, when a lowercase handwritten "r" and a lowercase handwritten "v" looked very much like one another; to always omit the "r" meant that one's notes could later be transcribed with accuracy. Another pitfall with regard to designation of location in a manuscript is to handle the recto and the verso of one leaf as if it were a matter of several leaves, giving, for example, the erroneous "ff. 1r–v." Occasionally in older catalogues one might find the letters "a" and "b" to designate the recto and the verso of a leaf; when the letters occur today, they are more likely to indicate columns.

63.2.2.2 *Rubric*

The opening and closing rubrics (for the latter, see Section 63.2.2.5) contain author- and/or title-like information in the manuscript,[19] often set off from the main body of the text by a colored ink, (usually red), underlining, lining-through, display script, or spacing; the cataloguer might choose to represent this paratextual information also in a typographic manner, for example, in italics or by underlining, or he might choose to signal it verbally. Since the rubrics contain what the manuscript's scribe or owner thought was the text's author and/or title, even if we no longer accept the attribution, it is important to transcribe the rubrics precisely, and to indicate if later owners rejected or corrected the attribution. The wording of the "titulus" in the rubrics may also point to the particular redaction of a text, which is an important part of a text's circulation.[20]

This is the primary-source information that will eventually help us to pinpoint the identity of an author or a text (it is not a given that today's attributions are more correct than the medieval statement of author or title), or help us to understand medieval library catalogues, or to study reception of a text (with rubric differing when a text circulates under one author or another).

The opening rubric of a text often contains the words "incipit" or "here begins" or the like, and thus risks being mistaken for the actual incipit; the closing rubric often contains the words "explicit" or "here ends" or the like, and thus risks being mistaken for the explicit (for Incipit and Explicit, see Sections 63.2.2.3 and 63.2.2.4, respectively). The physical display mechanisms in the manuscript (red ink, etc.) are not in and of themselves sufficient to meet the definition of "rubric," which must contain some sort of non-textual title-page-like information.

Because Rubric is the first field discussed here that requires transcription, it becomes necessary to touch upon that vast and complicated topic. To begin, we note that there are no immutable rules for all transcriptions from all medieval manuscripts. Differing vernacular languages, differing national traditions for Latin, differing habits according to type of text (e.g., literary vs. archival) all play into the matter. The goal of the particular catalogue will have an effect on transcription decisions. One of the most important actions of the cataloguer will be to determine his rules for transcription, to declare those rules, and to adhere to those rules. He should not apply differing transcription conventions, for example, to the Middle English manuscripts in his catalogue, and to the Latin texts that may well be in the same manuscripts. If the goal of his catalogue is to accompany an edition of the text, he may need to signal openly the expansion of an abbreviation (usually with italics; printed-book cataloguing rules such as AACR2 require square brackets). If the goal of his catalogue is to aid others in finding a text, abbreviations are best expanded silently. Other areas of uncertainty include the supplying of an omitted initial letter (in the space reserved by the scribe for a *littera notabilior*), the supplying of illegible text, the transcription of numbers as words (both cardinal and ordinal), as well as approaches to differing forms of medieval spelling, including the post-medieval distinctions of *i/j* and *u/v*; even capitalization and punctuation are matters of concern in transcription. It is, however, never appropriate to correct the scribe silently; at most one takes such a step with open declaration at every occurrence. The scribe's "mistake" may derive from his exemplar, and a silent correction by the cataloguer would mask the earlier manuscript; the scribe's "mistake" may be due to spelling common at the place or time, whereby the "correction" would falsify localization or dating of the manuscript. An option, when there is an undoubted scribal error, is to comment on it via the usual methods, either [!] or [*sic*]; but these should be used sparingly, when the cataloguer himself, at a later proofreading, runs the risk of considering something in the transcription his own mistake.

Transcription represents the specific instance of a concrete reality; normalization belongs to the abstraction of a modern title. At the same time, transcription is a balance between fidelity to the original and modern readability, which by now perforce includes readability by a computer. Remember that a computer can find all the occurrences of "Hic incipit liber psalmorum" but without special programming it cannot find "[H]ic i[n]cipit lib[er] psalmo[rum]" or "Hic incit [*sic*] liber psalmorum" (unless, of course, it occurs to the user of the catalogue to phrase his search with those particular sets of square brackets).

63.2.2.3 *Incipit*

The incipit, or opening words of a text or of a division of a text, functioned in the Middle Ages as a more certain form of textual identifier than the title, the latter often being a modern editor's construct; incipits are understood to serve the function of text identifier still today, justifying the omnipresence of incipit lists in catalogues of medieval manuscripts and the existence of the online tool, In Principio.[21] When a text begins with a biblical citation (as is the case with sermons), or a legal lemma, or a prologue, or a translator's dedicatory letter, ideally all its incipits should be transcribed into the catalogue. Especially in the case of an unidentified text, or of a generically identified text (e.g., "Sermons"; "Theological treatise"; "Medical tract") or one of uncertain authorship, the incipit becomes all the more necessary in its function as text identifier. However, transcription of the incipit may be less imperative in the case of complete bibles, liturgical books, and statute books because these begin in the same way (essentially) in all copies of the same text, and the signifying words, if any, are often buried quite deeply.

The length of the incipit is at the cataloguer's discretion: medieval reportings of incipits are often quite short; in modern usage, it is recommended to transcribe far enough into the text to include a finite verb, and in any case never to break within a syntactical unit. At times the incipits to several different texts correspond through a sustained number of phrases; the cataloguer will not be aware of potential ambiguity until he begins bibliographic work on the text. Poetry has its own requirements, and at least the first two verses (with the break signaled by a diagonal slash? but see below) may constitute a reasonable amount.

Fragments of manuscripts pose quandaries with regard to incipits. The first is that today medieval manuscripts all too frequently lack their first leaf, when the decoration proved too tempting. A second situation arises when the incipit is incomplete (i.e., left so by its scribe and/or decorator), as opposed to having become defective through defacing and cutting away. The third quandary is represented by single-leaf fragments. Does the cataloguer supply the missing material, employing some sort of typographical signal, e.g., brackets? Or does he transcribe the incipit as it actually stands in the manuscript today, prefacing the truncated transcription with another typographical signal, e.g., a double slash? Whatever the decision, it will be well to be able to programmatically separate the "real" incipits from those produced by the chance of survival (and which are necessarily internal to their no longer extant complete texts). As has been noted before, computers cannot happily read strings of text that incorporate non-alphanumeric characters, so the use of brackets and double slashes will be seen and correctly interpreted by the human, but not by the machine unless provision is made, for example, via XML markup.

The transcription issues noted in Section 63.2.2.2 for Rubric are also pertinent for Incipit.

63.2.2.4 *Explicit*

Explicit (or Desinit, or Finit, as it is less commonly called) is the field for the closing words of a text, or of a division of a text. When a cataloguer includes the explicit in his description, it becomes immediately possible for the reader to verify at some level the completeness of a text, as well as to obtain information that may point to the particular recension of the text. Whether the explicit is incomplete (i.e., left so by its scribe and/or decorator), or has become defective through defacing and cutting away, its problematic nature can be signaled by double slashes (which will have the same problems of computer legibility, as noted in Section 63.2.2.3).

Depth of transcription depends upon the cataloguer's wise decisions (see Section 63.2.2.3 regarding the length of transcription of incipits); in particular, he will remember that medieval copies of texts not infrequently end with some form of doxology and his transcription will, therefore, push backward beyond these pious words of thanks.

Again, as with Incipit, the cataloguer will not be led into confusion: the closing rubric is the phrase beginning with the word "Explicit" that frequently stands at the very end of a medieval text, in red ink, such as "Explicit Liber Psalmorum" or "Here ends the Book of Psalms," or in the plural, "Expliciunt libri Titi Livii qui supersunt" or "Here end the books of Livy that survive." The explicit, however, contains the words that close the text itself, which, in the case of the Psalter, are "Omne quod spirat laudet Dominum" or "Let every thing that hath breath praise the Lord."

The transcription issues noted in Section 63.2.2.3 for Rubric are also pertinent for Explicit.

63.2.2.5 *Colophon*

The colophon may contain various kinds of information: a ditty on the joys of finishing, the scribe's name, the name of the person for whom the manuscript was copied, the place of production, the date of production, the reasons for copying the text, the weather, and so on. The validity of a "dated manuscript" as a touchstone for undated and codices not localized depends upon the accuracy of the cataloguer's transcription of the colophon and the correct interpretation of it[22] (see Sections 63.2.1.5 and 63.2.4.1).

In summary, at the end of a text, the cataloguer faces the possibility of three intellectually separate categories: the explicit, the closing rubric, and the colophon, as shown in this example from Vatican City, BAV, Ottob. lat. 1875, fol. 73v:

- *Explicit*: . . . girfalchi et herodii seu falcones peregrini in copia magna qui inde postmodum ad diversas regiones et provincias deferuntur.
- *Closing rubric*: Explicit liber tercius et ultimus de conditionibus et consuetudinibus orientalium regionum translatus de vulgari Italico in latinum per fratrem Franciscum Pipini Bononiensem ordinis fratrum predicatorum. Deo gratias. Amen.
- *Colophon*: Iohannes Magnus Gothus Lincopensis Anno domini 1520 per mensem Augusti scripsit Rome in domo Sancte brigide.

In the manuscript, division between the last two may not jump to the eye, since they both might be in red ink and written straight on, but the rubric contains information about the text and the colophon contains information about the copy. In the representation of these categories of information in a printed catalogue the user will read and understand the difference without difficulty; in a computer-friendly catalogue, however, the fields should be distinguished.

The transcription issues noted in Section 63.2.2.2 for Rubric are also pertinent for Colophon.

63.2.2.6 *Author*

The Author field contains the name of the person with primary intellectual responsibility for a bibliographic unit. The author of a particular text may be anonymous or pseudonymous; there may be multiple "authors," each with a defined relationship to the text (e.g., translator, composer of prologue, or glossator); one may define a collective authorship, if the work emanated from a council or other such body. The author may have titles of nobility or sainthood; the language in which his name is to be cited may be uncertain; spelling is always an issue. Even the order of the name, if it includes a patronymic, might be uncertain (Dante Alighieri or Alighieri, Dante?) as well as punctuation in the name (Leonardo da Vinci or Leonardo, da Vinci?).

The problems of medieval nomenclature make consistency in the form of names difficult to achieve, and the normalized form of the name determined by the cataloguer in all likelihood will not match the medieval designation of the author as contained in the rubric. The form of the name is, however, of singular importance in the indexing or searching for authors, and thus should be assigned with care, and with attention to other catalogues or authority sources. Just what other catalogues or authority sources a cataloguer consults will depend in large part upon the goal of his catalogue. If his catalogue contains his own documentation for a more theoretical study, his choice of authority can be personal preference; if his work is internal to a national cataloguing system, or if his work is part of a collaborative or international project, the system or project may have dictated the choice.

It should be noted that there is no single overarching international authority; various national systems have devised their own lists, sometimes privileging their own language in the form of a medieval name, sometime according ascendency to a Latin form, and sometimes choosing the language of the author's major writings. There is, however, progress in sharing the content of the multiple authority lists via a concordance (VIAF) hosted online by the American national bibliographic utility, OCLC, which has a simple interface and provides the series of approved national forms, each identified by the flag of the country (and a mouseover expands the flag to the country name).[23] In a print-based world, choice of a format of a name matters; in a computer-based world, it may come to matter less when (if?) name equivalences are put in place, so that a search on any form of a name retrieves all forms of the name.

VIAF may help a cataloguer decide whether to call a certain author Richard of Middleton or Ricardus de Mediavilla (by letting him know which national authorities accept which form), but it will not serve to tie a particular author and a particular text together. The limited scope of this chapter will not attempt to address that complex problem.[24] The present few words can only recognize that identification of the text is one of the most crucial and most time-consuming of the cataloguer's tasks.

63.2.2.7 *Title*

The field for Title contains the word or words that identify a given work by a name that may be specific to that work (i.e., the form accepted as normative by an authority; e.g., *Roman de la rose*), or conventional (again, even though generic, in a form accepted as normative, and perhaps more correctly indicating a category of books, but taken here as an instance of that group; e.g., missal). As with Author, the Title is determined by the cataloguer and may or may not match the content of the medieval designation of title as contained in the rubric. It is, however, of singular importance in the indexing or searching for titles, and thus should be assigned with care, and with attention to other catalogues or authority sources.

The regularized form should omit the opening definite or indefinite articles, so that the title will alphabetize on its first indexable word, not on its initial stopwords (e.g., not *Le Roman de la rose*), although this is not a grammatical option for what is now taken as if a Latin title, i.e., those statements of subject that begin with the preposition "de." Also for the sake of alphabetization, and when possible, the signifying term should come first (e.g., Book of Hours, Sarum Use rather than Sarum use, Book of Hours). The field may be used to characterize in a general way a number of texts when there is not time to list each one individually (e.g., Letters) but, if possible, the cataloguer should plan to expand the field to its individual components; otherwise the texts remain in limbo not only for the single manuscript, but bibliographically for other manuscripts that may or may not match the present series with precision.

The language of the title is usually that of the catalogue in the case of generic or collective titles (e.g., Missal; Sermons; Medical Recipes); it is usually in the language of the text for a specific title (e.g., *De vulgari eloquentia* in Latin but *Vita nuova* in Italian). Sometimes, when the situation of the many titles under which a work circulates is too nebulous, the cataloguer might resort to a modern construct, but he should be aware of the conventionality of this shortcut; his consciousness plays out in multiple cross-referenced entries in an index of a printed book, or in appropriate markup or separate fields in a computer-based situation.

In any case, because a title is a normalized abstraction, its orthography no longer needs to reflect the specific manuscript copy. Classical Latin's "ti" and "mn" probably trump the manuscript's medieval spelling with "ci" and "mpn"; there seems some uncertainty, however, with regard to "ae" vs. "e" (*Lumen anim*ae or *Lumen anim*e?).

63.2.2.8 *Overview*

The field, Overview, introduces a section of the description of the Intellectual Content by announcing in an abbreviated way what will follow in detail; it could also serve in place of any further detail. In practice, this has been used in descriptions of the contents of bibles: the Overview in a few lines summarizes the full description (which will be quite long with folio numbers, incipits of prologues, rubrics, Stegmüller repertory numbers[25] of a Bible, with a thumbnail comparison to N. R. Ker's touchstone description of London, Lambeth Palace, MS 1364.[26]

63.2.2.9 *Bibliography Relevant to Text*

The amount of bibliography for a text in a catalogue will depend upon the nature of the catalogue (auction catalogues, lists of library holdings, editions of a text, and exhibition catalogues have different demands), and on the possibility of updates, which in turn depends ultimately on the catalogue's method of delivery (if in print, updates are difficult; if online, updates are feasible). It seems reasonable to cite a printed edition, if one exists; if a study of the transmission has been written, with a list of manuscripts, it will be helpful to include it in the bibliography. If there is a standard repertory for the text or others of similar nature, that repertory and the text's number should be cited; one could use an abbreviated author/title for it (but making sure that the abbreviated form is offered in full form somewhere in the catalogue). See also Section 63.2.5.1.

63.2.2.10 *Acknowledgments*

The field for Acknowledgments is proposed here (see also Section 63.2.5.2) as a reminder that it is always correct to recognize another person's contribution to one's work. Medievalists seem to be particularly cognizant of the need for the assistance of specialists, and a person who catalogues medieval manuscripts will almost certainly find himself asking others for help.

63.2.3 Physical Description

It is in the area of the physical description that today's catalogue of medieval manuscripts most fully differentiates itself from its progenitors. One could go so far as to assert that to some of today's readers of medieval manuscripts the text may be irrelevant: for certain kinds of art historical study, the scholar may be equally interested in a codex whether it contains a breviary or a chronicle. With the advent of codicology after World War II as an area of study,[27] and with the more recent approach termed quantitative codicology,[28] interest in the physical book as a historical artifact has intensified. Note that the importance of the physical description poses barriers to the successful use of MARC for medieval manuscripts (perhaps more of an issue to American libraries than European ones), since many of the scholarly points of interest can only be accommodated in MARC's undifferentiated Notes fields, and are, therefore, unsearchable and less portable to other data containers.[29]

It was mentioned above in Sections 63.2.1.4 (Place of Origin) and 63.2.1.5 (Date of Origin) that composite manuscripts will require duplication of those two fields. The definition of "composite manuscript" is tied to the concept of a campaign of production; multiple campaigns, whether separated in time or across space or both, may call for treatment of the physical evidence in repetitions of the fields of the area of Physical Description. The cataloguer will decide if the diversified physical evidence is such that he will invoke multiple instances of Physical Description or if the matter can (should?) be handled simply as a note. The decision will result in greater or lesser searchability on the varying Places and Dates of Origin, and possibly other fields.

Arrangement of the area for Physical Description follows an imagined plan for producing a manuscript, beginning with the choice of support and ending with the binding.

63.2.3.1 Support
63.2.3.2 Number of Leaves in Codex
63.2.3.3 Measurements in Millimeters
   63.2.3.3.1 Book Block
   63.2.3.3.2 Text Block

63.2.3.1 *Support*

The field Support contains a description of the physical material on which the manuscript's writing, musical notation, decoration and/or other signifiers are placed, or are intended to be placed. In the case of medieval manuscripts, there are three common choices: parchment (or vellum), paper, or the combination of parchment and paper together.

The term "palimpsest" describes reused writing support for a manuscript from which the previous text or set of signs was made more or less to disappear (whether by erasing it or washing it or scraping it) so that a new text could be placed on the same support; in practice this is almost always parchment. If the support is palimpsest, the cataloguer will be sure to notice that (and treat the underlying text as a part of a composite manuscript).

If the support is paper, the cataloguer will attempt to identify the watermark; a watermark is the imprint, usually figurative, left on paper during its manufacture by the slim wire sewn or soldered onto the paper-making frame.[30]

The main pitfall while talking about Support lies in the words "folio," "quarto," and "octavo." These words are explained to represent "format," which entails two different but related situations: (1) the number of times the writing support has been folded (mainly in reference to paper); and (2) the general designation of the size of the codex when its measurements are not expressed by measured dimensions (whether parchment or paper). The same set of words has been used by cataloguers to express both situations, although the literal meaning is the first; the cataloguer should be wary of such labels and determine the actual foldings of the paper himself. Note that some institutions have incorporated format indications into the call numbers of their manuscripts, and they must be retained in citing the shelf mark.[31]

63.2.3.2 *Number of Leaves in Codex*

This number might be expressed as a unit (e.g., ff. 198) or as a span (ff. 1–198v) according to the project cataloguing rules; the first seems the more common. It is conventional to describe the flyleaves with small roman numerals (e.g., ff. ii + 198 + i). See Section 63.2.2.1 (Span of Folios) for further discussion.

63.2.3.3 *Measurements In Millimeters*

63.2.3.3.1 BOOK BLOCK

63.2.3.3.2 TEXT BLOCK

Of these two fields, the first might be more pertinent to the librarian's interest ("How much space does the book occupy on the shelf?" "Should I order a case for it?"), and the second to the scholar's interest ("Can I use these numbers as an indicator of type of book, or place, or date of origin?"). The reason for the double set of measurements is that, in rebinding, a book is usually guillotined, and thus its present overall size may no longer give reliable information on its original size; on the other hand, the measurements of the text block have presumably not changed.

Some people measure the text block according to its ruled space, while others measure it according to its written space, i.e., from the top of the first line's ascenders to the bottom of the last line's descenders. To work from the ruled space is less subject to interpretation. If very accurate measurements are necessary, the cataloguer could measure several pages and report a range; or he could measure one page and state which page it was. On the other hand, if the support is parchment, shifts of temperature and humidity may change the size of the page over a period of days. Since the books in question date from before the precision of machines, variation of a millimeter or so does not seem significant.

If the manuscript consists of cropped or mutilated fragments, the cataloguer could give the measurement of the largest fragment, i.e., of the one which comes closest to what the original non-damaged shape would have been.

The standard unit of measurement is millimeters, and the order of the measurements is usually Height × Width (× Depth, if desired).

63.2.3.4 *Collation*

63.2.3.4.1 QUIRE SIGNATURES

63.2.3.4.2 LEAF SIGNATURES

63.2.3.4.3 CATCHWORDS

The field for Collation contains the description of the gathering-by-gathering composition of a codex, or segment of a codex, expressed sometimes in prose, and perhaps more usually in a formula. In the latter there will be two sets of numbers, one representing the gatherings (or quires) and one representing the leaves; the two sets might be distinguished with Roman vs. Arabic numerals, or with one set of numbers in superscript, or with the second set of numbers set off from the first via a colon. However the structure is represented, it is assumed to consist of bifolia nested one inside another. There will most often be an even number to express the number of leaves of a given quire; the final computation may result in an odd number when single leaves have been added to or cut from the basic structure. If the quire structure is expressed according to the number of its bifolia, the quire designation might be even or odd, as in the formulae used in Germany. An example of two possible types of collation formula for the same situation would be:

$$1^{\wedge}6^{\wedge}\ 2\text{--}5^{\wedge}10^{\wedge}\ 6^{\wedge}10^{\wedge}(-7, \text{after f. } 52)$$
$$\mathrm{III}^{\wedge}6^{\wedge} + 4\ \mathrm{V}^{\wedge}46^{\wedge} + (\mathrm{V} - 1)^{\wedge}55^{\wedge}$$

Both types of formula show an initial gathering of a ternion (i.e., of six leaves), followed by four quinions (i.e., gatherings of ten leaves each), ending with a quinion that is lacking a leaf. The first example offers a running count of the gatherings, while the second keeps track of the number of folios; the first notes the position within the final gathering of the missing leaf, while the second, representing the number of missing leaves, does not.

Because the collation gives the first hint as to whether the text may be incomplete or manipulated (i.e., when a gathering contains subtracted or added leaves), collation is an effort worth making, albeit potentially a time-consuming one. With tight bindings, and with no written indicators of the structure of the gatherings (such as quire/leaf signatures or catchwords), collation may be impracticable, and that should be stated, so that a user of the catalogue understands the reason why no collation is supplied. In a tight binding, if quire signatures, leaf signatures, or catchwords are present, even sporadically, it may be possible to determine what a normal structure might be, so that in lieu of a collation expressed as a formula, one may assert "apparently in gatherings of four bifolia" or the like.

After the collation has been finished, the cataloguer would do well to add up its numbers, and to compare that total against the number of leaves said to be in the codex; if the numbers do not match, either the collation or the foliation counting the leaves is wrong, so both will require checking until the error is discovered and corrected.

Be aware that textual scholars employ the term "collation" to designate the comparison of one version of a text against another in order to establish a better text.

The fields for Quire and Leaf Signatures contain information about progressive marking of fascicules and/or of leaves (usually only through the first half of the gathering), so that they may be assembled in correct order by the binder. The marking usually consists of a letter to indicate the gathering (a, b, c, etc.) and a number to indicate the leaf (Roman numerals may be preferred, although Arabic numerals are certainly not unknown); but ad hoc sequences for leaf signatures can also occur, such as Ave-maria-gratia-plena on the first four leaves of each quire; or increasing numbers of circles, or horizontal slashes, etc. On occasion, one also encounters a mark (in the form of an X?) at the center of the gathering, usually in the gutter of the centermost bifolium.

In pre-twelfth-century manuscripts, only the quires are numbered (not the leaves); this numbering is placed in the center lower margin of the first leaf recto or the last leaf verso.

The field for Catchwords provides space for a description of the system of word(s), written in the lower margin of the last leaf verso of a gathering, as a preview of the first word(s) of the first leaf recto of the successive gathering, to ensure correct ordering of the quires by the binder. During the fifteenth century Italian humanists began to position the catchword vertically along the inner bounding line—a practice carefully assessed by Albert Derolez.[32] During the sixteenth century, one begins to see preview words at the foot of each page, referring to the first words of the next page, as an aid to the reader.

All these variations should be noticed by the cataloguer, because they may point to an individual scribe, an organized group of scribes, or a place or date of production, as Derolez has so definitively demonstrated.

The cataloguer should be aware that for the printed book community the term "signature" denotes the set of nested leaves that the manuscript world calls "gathering" or "quire."

63.2.3.5 *Layout*

The field Layout (or *mise-en-page* as it often called, even in an English context) contains the description of the way in which text is arranged on the page, specifying, for example, the disposition and shape of the prick marks, the number and medium of the ruled or written lines, and the number of columns. It can also accommodate descriptions of how the gloss is handled, and the way in which illustration and musical notation are integrated with the text.

63.2.3.6 *Script*

63.2.3.6.1 ALPHABET

63.2.3.7 *Scribe(s)*

63.2.3.8 *Musical Notation*

This grouping of fields pertains to the physical manner in which the message of the text is produced. While there are a few codices that contain only illustration, without text or musical notation, they are so extraordinary that they force us as readers to mentally supply the text; in that manner the text is in some fashion still present.[33]

Alphabet should have been placed hierarchically above script, but the context of the present chapter is so geared to Western European manuscripts that it may be an unnecessary field. Nevertheless, it is worth remarking upon the difference between Alphabet, Script, Hand, and Scribe, since some confusion reigns. Alphabet refers to the primary writing system, which in the present context is usually the Latin (or Roman) alphabet. It is the use of "Latin" qua alphabet that is attested in the fundamental series known generally as the CMD (for "Catalogues de manuscrits datés") of which several national sets carry titles of this sort, *Catalogue des manuscrits en écriture latine portant des indications de date, de lieu ou de copiste* (sponsored since 1953 by the Comité international de paléographie latine; see Section 63.2.2.5). It is also the meaning of the title of P. O. Kristeller's (1993) invaluable aid (updated by Sigrid Krämer), *Latin Manuscript Books before 1600*.[34] In these cases, and when used to designate Alphabet in a catalogue, the adjective does not refer to language, but to the writing system. It happens with some frequency that manuscripts in the Greek alphabet (and language) are included in the same catalogue as manuscripts copied using the Latin alphabet; there may even be a few in the Hebrew or Cyrillic alphabets, so it is well that the cataloguer keep the difference between alphabet and language clear in his mind.

Script in the context of the present chapter is a term that designates a particular configuration of the Latin alphabet. While for the early centuries of the Latin alphabet and for certain geographic areas, as attested in manuscripts, there is some common acceptance of script terminology (e.g., Capitals, Uncials, Half-uncials, Beneventan, Visigothic), for the later Middle Ages, national traditions and vast variety resist suggested classifications; no single set of terms is entirely accepted. The cataloguer, therefore, is at liberty to choose the system (or non-system) that he prefers, bearing in mind that script names have two functions in a catalogue: they tell the reader which script is used in a given manuscript (but if the manuscript is illustrated with an image, an elaborate naming system may be superfluous); they aid the reader in finding manuscripts written in a certain script (and therefore the more generic the script term used, the more likely that the term will be discovered in a printed index or via an online search engine).[35] Today's cataloguing tends to reject adjectives of aesthetic nature (e.g., elegant, controlled, crabbed, idiosyncratic, uncertain). If the final catalogue is in print, the cataloguer might explain his choice of script nomenclature in his introduction.

The concept of Hand refers to the particular configurations of a script. While Script represents an ideal type, Hand is the present instance of that ideal. Hand not only brings to our mind the curved back, the stretched arm and the fingers of the scribe seated at his desk, but even the same man at differing moments, writing in differing scripts. To distinguish the divisions among hands in a manuscript is a slow and often difficult task: is this section copied by a different person, i.e., hand? Or is it the same person who is cramping up the script into a smaller tighter module to make the text's end correspond to the quire's end? Were the rubrics, written in a hierarchically more important script, inserted by the same hand as the one that copied the body of the text?

Scribe is the Hand for whom we have a name or an assigned pseudonym, such as "Richardus Franciscus" or "Scribe D of the Trinity College Gower." The source of the name could be a colophon in the present manuscript, or a payment record, or a scholar's recognition privately communicated, or a printed article or another catalogue. The cataloguer should be explicit about the source, and if the attribution to a scribe derives from private communication, the cataloguer should thank the person in the Acknowledgments.

Musical Notation is to music as letters are to words; it is the set of symbols used to make a written record of musical sounds. Musicologists have not been well served by traditional catalogues of medieval manuscripts; the cataloguer will wish to consult a specialist for the manuscripts that contain music; if images are an option, he should try to include music in a systematic way, so that the specialized reader can form his own judgment.

63.2.3.9 *Decoration*

63.2.3.9.1 ARTIST(S) OR STYLE(S)

63.2.3.9.2 MINIATURES

63.2.3.9.3 BORDERS

63.2.3.9.4 HISTORIATED INITIALS

63.2.3.9.5 PAINTED INITIALS

63.2.3.9.6 PENFLOURISHED INITIALS

Although it was said at the beginning of Section 63.2.3, the discussion of Physical Description, that the order of presentation would follow the imagined production of a medieval manuscript, that order is turned upside down for Decoration. Miniatures, which were normally added to the manuscript after the other decoration had been completed, are instead presented here before other decoration. Art historians (and cataloguers) are more interested in the figurative aspects of a manuscript; why adhere to a self-imposed rule when it has no function? Similarly, if one has a named artist or wishes to attribute an aspect of the decoration to a personage or style, it makes some sense to open the discussion of decoration with that name or style.

The artist's name or the artistic style may be an assigned or associative term; the source of an actual name could be an inscription in the present manuscript, or a payment record, or a scholar's recognition privately communicated, or a printed article or other catalogue. If the attribution derives from private communication, the cataloguer should thank the person in the Acknowledgments; as always, he should be explicit about the source. If the attribution derives from legacy data (e.g., an exhibition label from an exhibition of 30 years ago), and if the cataloguer has not consulted a specialist, cautionary wording is prudent.

As a rule of thumb, give the number of occurrences of each type of decoration (when feasible, i.e., it is not expected that a cataloguer count out the some 128 painted initials in a Bible), size/shape, and technique if other than standard tempera; include notice of major decoration now missing; mention also the decoration added to the manuscript at later dates. If gold is used in the decoration, a mention of that metal immediately gives the reader a sense of the expense level of the manuscript. Under the heading of decoration, one may also include mention of charts, diagrams, and tables.

Set iconography of scenes depicted in miniatures, historiated initials, marginal scenes, and so on can both help and hinder the cataloguer. Commonly accepted terminology can provide shortcuts (e.g., "Annunciation" vs. "Scared girl in blue dress talking to boy with wings"), but the cataloguer may not always recognize a scene; if in doubt, read the text, look for other catalogues containing manuscripts with the same text, or consult a specialist.

It is almost impossible to describe pen-flourishing in such a manner that someone else can recognize other instances of the same pen-flourishing in another book, and yet scholars have demonstrated the value of pen-flourishing in localization[36] and in dating,[37] and in determining matters of production.[38] The only solution is to supply images; depending upon the type of catalogue, this may or may not be an option.

63.2.3.10 *Evidence of Reader(s)*

The field, Evidence of Reader(s), serves to record any written or drawn additions to the original state of the manuscript, such as marginalia, scribblings, or doodles. These matters can be very important: think of the recognizable manicules that Petrarch drew in the margins of his books.[39] If the catalogue can accommodate images, this sort of material is better handled with a picture than with a description, although words are what a computer searches on.

63.2.3.11 *Accompanying Material*

This field recognizes that physically separate items sometimes are associated with a medieval manuscript; they usually pertain to earlier owners (an armorial *ex libris* removed from a pastedown in a rebinding and retained with the manuscript; exchange of correspondence between an owner and the bookseller from whom the manuscript was purchased), or they may reflect a long-dead scholar's unpublished work, donated to the library by his heirs (a collation of the manuscript's text against a printed edition).

63.2.3.12 *Binding*

The field for Binding contains the description of the binding and its date (or at least an approximation: original; early; early modern; modern); if the name of the binder and his dates are known, they should be given. In addition, whatever knowledge or estimations that the cataloguer can make with regard to previous bindings should certainly be included (e.g., green stains on flyleaves from a previous binding in green vellum might point to the Archinto collection). Description of the structure of the binding, however, as opposed to its appearance, usually lies within the purview of specialists; if the library has a conservation department, the conservation staff may be consulted with much profit.

Because the cover, or the wrappers, or the flyleaves may be waste from another manuscript, they should be described as a separate Part of a composite manuscript, with all the Intellectual Content, the Physical Description, and the History fields that are appropriate.

63.2.3.13 *Acknowledgments*

The field for Acknowledgments is proposed here as a further reminder: always ask for help; always recognize it publicly (see also Sections 63.2.2.10, and 63.2.5.2).

63.2.3.14 *Condition*

The field for Condition summarizes the physical state of a manuscript. It will probably be of most use to describe various unpleasant conditions (catalogue descriptions seldom comment on the excellent health of a codex). In any case, it should not be used to describe technical conservation repairs to a manuscript; these are more appropriately described in in-house files (presumably open to readers upon request).

63.2.4 History of the Codex

This area contains information about the history of a manuscript from the moment of its production to the present day, but rather than the telegraph-style or bullet-point data that was recommended for the area for Heading, here the cataloguer gives his reasoning and pulls together seemingly disparate notices in the description to make an argument (for example, if the description of the intellectual content mentions the presence of saints Romanus and Audoenus in the litany, and if the description of the physical book notes that the four Evangelists share a single miniature at the beginning of the Gospel pericopes, the cataloguer might recall these details in the present section of his description and conclude that the book was produced in Rouen).

> 63.2.4.1 Origin
> 63.2.4.2 Provenance
> 63.2.4.3 Former Shelf Marks
> 63.2.4.4 Secundo Folio

63.2.4.1 *Origin*

The present chapter breaks down the history of a book's life into two parts: Origin and Provenance. The first contains information concerning the place, date, and other circumstances of the production of a manuscript. The cataloguer is assumed to have the competency to make these judgments himself, whether on palaeographic or on art historical grounds; in this case he usually expresses the matter as a simple statement, e.g., "Written in England during the first half of the fourteenth century." If more evidence is available, the statement on place and date is phrased more fully, e.g., "Written by Ranulph Higden at Werburg, Chester, between 1299 and his death in 1363–4."[40] If the evidence is not clear-cut, the statement will of necessity suggest nuanced reasons, e.g., "Written in Bavaria on the basis of the dialect and the origin of the woodcuts, in the middle of the fifteenth century; the dates 1433 and 1435 on ff. 53 and 70 are thought to be the dates of translation of the texts rather than the dates of transcription."[41] Bibliography will then include documentation, e.g., on the recognition of Ranulph Higden's hand and on Bavarian woodcuts. If the documentation has not been printed, but has been a private communication to the cataloguer, the scholar who provided the evidence for the Origin should be acknowledged, e.g., "Written in Venice and decorated by the Master of the Putti, who flourished between 1469 and 1473" with acknowledgment to Prof. Lilian Armstrong.[42] If the cataloguer is uncertain about a manuscript's origin, and if he finds himself without specialist assistance, he may decide to repeat (one hopes as an interim measure) a place or date derived from nineteenth-century cataloguing, from an exhibition label, or from an unknown bookseller's slip. In these circumstances, he should remind himself and his readers that these crucial pieces of information derive from legacy data by stating the source as precisely as possible. Because the places and dates of origin of manuscripts are assessed by the scholarly community in varying levels according to the solidity of the catalogue's evidence, the nature of the evidence should be clear.

The field Origin also allows the cataloguer to explain the "datable" nature of a manuscript, should it fall into this group. The concept means that we have knowledge about the production of the manuscript derived from some aspect of the book itself: a chronicle that breaks abruptly in a certain year, and then picks up in another scribe's hand; a text composed in a certain year with a slightly later acquisition note on a flyleaf; an Easter table with a cross next to one year's column, and so forth. If it is a question of a range of years, they usually fall within parameters that are ever tighter the closer one moves to the modern world: a manuscript datable to a 25-year range in the ninth century should be so designated with a clear explanation; a fifteenth-century Italian manuscript datable to the same range of time is not of as strong an interest on this account. The decision to highlight (or not) a manuscript as "datable" is placed in the capable hands of the cataloguer. (See Section 63.2.1.5 for a discussion of dating composite manuscripts and of the formats for expressing dates.)

It should be said that in the majority of cases the date is applied to the manuscript by the cataloguer, according to his own experience and expertise. This is not proposed as the least desirable form of dating (and localizing); indeed, assertions that a manuscript is dated or datable rest on shaky grounds if they are not supported by visible palaeographic evidence (a scribal colophon may have been copied word for word from the exemplar; the cross on an Easter table's date may have been scratched in the manuscript by a later owner).

It is also worth keeping in mind that when we, as cataloguers, designate a place or a date of origin, we are in reality stating that X manuscript shares the characteristics of other manuscripts of X place or X date of origin; strictly speaking, we do not actually *know* where or when that manuscript was produced. In most cases, assertion of the production data and recognition of shared characteristics are the same thing, at least to the extent that one cannot concretely distinguish one situation from the other. There are occasions, however, when we need to remember the existence of that gap, and be prepared to think more flexibly. Consider, for example, a certain manuscript written by two scribes: the first seemingly French, the second seemingly Italian. The first reserved triangular spaces for the rubrics; the second left rectangular ones. All the rubrics were then supplied in a rectangular manner (leaving empty the pointed part of the bottom of the triangular space). Was the unfinished manuscript taken from France to Italy, and completed in the local manner? Or was the manuscript produced in France by two people, the second of whom was Italian temporarily away from home? Or was it produced in Italy, and the first part of the work was done by a visiting Frenchman? We cannot neatly separate the two styles of production and assign two countries as places of production as if this were a composite manuscript, because the two styles overlap, suggesting that the two were happening at essentially the same time. Our problem here is that we are faced with two sets of localizing characteristics, but one location (presumably, at any rate); to keep the gap between style and origin in mind helps us to recognize the situation, even when it is unresolvable.[43]

The existence of a gap is all the more comprehensible when considering the date of production of a manuscript. One hears tell of the "30-Year Rule" as a reminder that an old man, writing in the script he learned when young, may be entirely contemporary to the very young scribe who lives next door, and who is copying according to latest and newest of fashions. Visually, the old scribe's work will appear to date from 30 years earlier, while the young man's script is not only that of the moment, but may itself remain unchanged for the coming 30 years. Again, when dating a manuscript, we are in reality stating that its characteristics are normal to a certain date; we are not affirming (in any objective way) that it was actually produced at that time.[44]

63.2.4.2 *Provenance*

The second field of the area for History is called Provenance; it is concerned with aspects of the history of the manuscript from the time of its production until the present day; the cataloguer's knowledge of libraries, of collectors, of booksellers— indeed of history itself—[45] comes into play to interpret the marks that have remained in the book, and those that are no longer documented but that may be conjectured through knowledge of the book's siblings. Some cataloguers prefer to construct a third category in the area of History, which has been termed Acquisition, intending that it contain the passage of a manuscript into its present home (the field's name, however, is ambiguous since the codex was "acquired" by its new owner at each passage in its history). When the acquisition was by purchase, and in particular if it was via an auction house, the amount paid is a matter of public record and is knowable; there are arguments for and against including the amounts in a catalogue.

If the manuscript includes coats of arms, whether painted within the border of the first leaf or engraved on an owner's bookplate or stamped on a binding, the arms should be not only identified with the names of the families, but also described, and if possible imaged, so that a reader discovering the same arms in another codex will be able to recognize them. Mottoes fall into the same category as heraldry: it is not enough to identify them: they also need to be documented.

63.2.4.3 *Former Shelf Marks*

Changed or supplementary numbering is a matter of concern; the cataloguer should include in his catalogue any other call numbers that the manuscript in question has carried in the past and while in the present location, specifying the nature of the additional shelf mark or number, e.g., "Phillipps n. 10603" (for San Marino, CA, Huntington Library, HM 00505); or "Previous call numbers MAR 39, and 2MS B665 D2" (for Berkeley, University of California, Berkeley, Bancroft Library BANC MS UCB 002). (See also Section 63.2.1.2.)

63.2.4.4 *Secundo Folio*

Medieval librarians not infrequently included in their inventories the several words that occurred in certain predetermined positions in the books in their collections, the most usual location being the opening words of the second leaf. Since all copies of a text begin the same way (the principle that validates the use of incipits as textual identifiers), but since (presumably) each scribe copies at a different pace, he will have arrived at a different point in the text when he begins the second leaf. The Secundo Folio thus is intended to provide a unique and unchangeable identification of the one codex, since it pinpoints the intersection between text and physical book. The system is not infallible: texts in verse and manuscripts copied according to set layouts result in identical Secundo Folio words. Modern cataloguers sometimes include this information in the description of a manuscript as an aid to matching a present codex with one listed in a medieval catalogue.

Medieval library catalogues, rather like modern ones, run the gamut from inventory lists to more complex bibliographic tools; and like modern library catalogues of medieval manuscripts, it is often difficult to know whether they exist for a certain collection, and if so, how to find the catalogue. Efforts to remedy the problem usually depend upon national studies: England, France, and Germany, for example, have publications that will aid today's scholar and cataloguer to locate a medieval library catalogue.[46]

63.2.5 Other

This amorphous area is included by way of encouraging the cataloguer to consider what other categories of information will be useful to his goal. No claims are made that the categories listed in this chapter are the only fields that might be necessary, nor is it prescribed that this is the only position in a catalogue for "other" information. In some cases it may be preferable to collect the information in a separate container, so that part or all of this information is more readily updatable (e.g., the main catalogue may be printed, and the updates maintained online), more readily added to (e.g., an institution may maintain a separate website of images available for purchase), or more easily annotated (e.g., in-house but cross-departmental notes on correspondence about loan exhibitions).

63.2.5.1 Bibliography Relevant to Manuscript
63.2.5.2 Acknowledgments
63.2.5.3 Available Reproductions
63.2.5.4 Images
63.2.5.5 Administrative Information

63.2.5.1 *Bibliography Relevant to Manuscript*

Bibliography risks engulfing a cataloguing effort, so the cataloguer should consider what his time will allow and pose some limits; the different goals of the cataloguer and the scholar will undoubtedly come into play. If, however, the catalogue will be maintained by staff at a large library, a retrospective and complete bibliography might be a possibility;[47] continuous updating may be possible.[48] See Section 63.2.2.9. for additional commentary on Bibliography Relevant to Text; the distinction between the two fields may not always be self-evident in practice.

63.2.5.2 *Acknowledgments*

The field for Acknowledgments has been repeated several times, in reference to texts, to scribal and artistic identification, and to establishing place and date of origin. The field placed here at the end of a description reminds the cataloguer to take a larger look at the help he has received; it might be that this field contains the recognition to be placed at the beginning of a catalogue for funding received from the National Endowment for the Humanities (United States), or the Joint Steering Committee (Great Britain), or another funding agency; it could contain recognition of help from individuals at many levels (including the technical staff of an institution). There will certainly be gratitude expressed to other cataloguers and scholars. Bottom line: a catalogue produced by a cataloguer who has never talked with anyone will not be satisfactory.

63.2.5.3 *Available Reproductions*

Interest in this field may wane in years to come, or the field may become all the more necessary. It is the space for a scholar to note the reproductions of the manuscript that were available to him when he prepared his catalogue entry (slides; photographs; digital images; microfilm, etc.) and the extent of these surrogates (folio numbers; details); he may wish to register the place where he consulted the surrogate.[49] If the catalogue is produced by the holding library, this slot might serve to alert readers as to what surrogates are available; it might contain a link to the partially or fully digitized manuscript available online.

63.2.5.4 *Images*

This field is intended to hold the file names of the digital images associated with the manuscript; the difference between this field and the preceding one is readability: the preceding field assumes a human reader; the present field is for the sake of the computer's data and may live well in a separate container: the columns of a spreadsheet can easily coordinate image file name, shelf mark, folio number, caption (if desired), date of capture, capture equipment, etc.

It is important to remember that image file names are not a repeat of the cataloguing information; the single goal of an image file name is to be unique (since otherwise the second image with the same name will overwrite the first), so the simpler the system, the lower the chance of duplication and of typographical error. If the cataloguer wants to guarantee no duplication, he will need to take the step beyond spreadsheet to database, where he can constrain behavior of a field (to refuse duplication if he is hand-entering the image file name, or, if the naming depends upon the computer, to autogenerate the image file name as sequential numbers, padded with zeros to the left to as many digits as desired). This chapter is not the place to offer technical information; it is merely a reminder to the cataloguer of the issues he should consult on very early in the process. The scholar in particular needs to consider this matter very carefully; it is not because his images are for his private use that he should form his image names casually; quite the contrary, since he will not have the expertise of the in-house technology staff to aid him in the way that the institutional cataloguer will. In addition, the private scholar might profitably meditate on matters of scale: while at present he may imagine his collection at only several hundred images, by the end of his academic career, he will have thousands of images; the image file name patterns should allow for close to unlimited growth.[50]

63.2.5.5 *Administrative Information*

This field is another that might not remain part of the same entry or record as the main body of the cataloguing. If the catalogue is that of an institution, one may wish to separate physically or via encoding certain kinds of information irrelevant to the public (e.g., price paid for the codex; priorities for conservation work; ongoing negotiations for loan). If the catalogue is that of a scholar aiming for eventual publication, he may wish to record the names and contact points of librarians who were helpful (or those who were not) in case he has last-minute questions. Again, the mention of such a field in this chapter serves as a memento of the sorts of considerations that might be useful.

In conclusion, I can do no better than to repeat the words of Humfrey Wanley, from his letter of 1701 (see n. 44): "But then, whether all this can be always done, done easily and without Errors, is the doubt."[51]

Notes

1. See Massieu (1791, 3, 14): "It is nevertheless essential that those who are entrusted with this task should have some appearance of learning, and that they should at least know Latin" and later, "It's certainly desirable that there should be someone available on the premises capable of determining the century when each manuscript was copied, but because it's unusual to come across people with this knowledge, it will be enough to indicate whether the handwriting of the manuscript is ancient or modern."

2. I was once asked to catalogue the "oriental" manuscripts at my library; the reaction to my protests that I could not read them, much less catalogue them, was surprise that I found this problematic: the items were "hand-produced" and "old" just like the Western medieval manuscripts that I dealt with.

3. For a formal statement on the goals of quantitative codicology, see Bozzolo and Ornato (1982).

4. For an excellent discussion, see Lee and O'Donnell (2009). More broadly, and with chapters dedicated to a range of topics, is the print and online publication Schreibman, Siemens, and Unsworth (2004).

5. Acronyms are endemic to the library word: OPAC = Online Public Access Catalogue; MARC = MAchine Readable Cataloguing; AACR2 = Anglo-American Cataloguing Rules, 2nd ed. (for MARC and AACR2, see below at nn. 16, 17); AMREMM = Pass (2003).

6. Resource Description and Access; see n. 17.

7. An example in point is the catalogue of the medieval manuscripts of the Chapter Library of Verona that was prepared for print during the early years of the 1900s; at the end of that century, some 80 years after the cataloguer's death, his material was published with updating of the bibliography, and, crucially, one image for each manuscript. Although neither the original nor the later editor commented on the fact, one of the manuscripts is certainly of English origin: CCXXXIV (221); courtesy of the image supplied in the printed catalogue, the reader of the catalogue can supply the manuscript's origin for himself. See Marchi (1996, 273–4 and color plate after p. 256).

8. It is telling that auction catalogues have long since provided images as the mechanism to bridge the space between an auction house and its public; the intention is to convey accurately things that cannot be expressed in words, such as style and quality, both of which relate to financial value.

9. The proverb exists in many languages, but I always heard it in Spanish and in discussions of cataloguing from my friend and the co-founder of Digital Scriptorium, Charles Faulhaber.

10. Much of the present discussion originates in two similar documents, of which the first is the data dictionary that I compiled in 1997 to ensure parallel cataloguing for a specific project, the Digital Scriptorium, then in its infancy at the University of California, Berkeley and at Columbia University in the City of New York (revised 2011, with additions by J. Nelson, University of California, Berkeley for AACR2-related matters). The second document, intended for a broader and less proscriptive purpose, was the fruit of collaboration of the team of people who formed the TEI Working Group for Manuscript Description, TEI–MSS, during the years 1998–2003; in alphabetical order, they were: Consuelo Dutschke, Peter Kidd, Eva Nylander, Ambrogio Piazzoni, and Merrilee Proffitt. It was a privilege to work with such an experienced, intelligent, and good-willed group of people, from whom I learned much in details and in concepts; I hope that the present chapter, while taking advantage of the group's contributions, does not at this distance in time, distort their thinking. The documents are available online at: http://www.columbia.edu/cu/libraries/inside/projects/tei-ms, accessed February 16, 2020; the Working Group's materials were revised by the TEI and are available on their website at: http://www.tei-c.org/release/doc/tei-p5-doc/en/html/MS.html, accessed February 16, 2020. In particular, I would like to thank Peter Kidd for his comments on several versions of this chapter.

11. As a growing index to vast numbers of sale and auction catalogues, see the *Schoenberg Database of Manuscripts*: http://dla.library.upenn.edu/dla/medren/index.html, accessed February 16, 2020. For the movement of manuscripts in North America since the publication of de Ricci and Wilson (1935–7) and its supplement by Faye and Bond (1962), see Conway and Davis (2015).

12. For example, see for Europe, the Consortium of European Research Libraries: http://www.cerl.org/web/en/resources/cerl_portal, accessed February 16, 2020; for Europe and Middle East, the Hill Museum and Monastic Library: http://www.hmml.org/, accessed February 16, 2020; for France: Initiale, through the Institut de Recherche et d'Histoire des Textes: http://initiale.irht.cnrs.fr/, accessed March 23, 2020; for Germany, Manuscripta Medievalia: http://www.manuscripta-mediaevalia.de/, accessed February 16, 2020; for the Netherlands, Medieval Manuscripts in Dutch Collections: http://www.mmdc.nl/static/site/, accessed February 16, 2020; for Switzerland, e-codices: http://www.e-codices.unifr.ch/, accessed February 16, 2020; and for the United States, Digital Scriptorium: http://www.digital-scriptorium.org, accessed February 16, 2020.

13. A. Petrucci, in his otherwise incomparable book affirms (Petrucci 2001, 65) that localizing a manuscript is not necessary, "Se datare un codice è indispensabile, localizzarlo non lo è." This extraordinary assertion may be due to national cataloguing traditions, in that most Italian and Vatican catalogues do not provide a place of origin, although blaming habit only pushes the question about the origin of Petrucci's statement backward one step, and the problem remains. Petrucci comments that localization of a manuscript is very difficult to accomplish, and indeed it is, but not more so than the dating of a manuscript, and he does not attempt to sidestep that difficulty.

14. New York, Columbia University, Rare Book & Manuscript Library, Plimpton MS 120, f. 193.

15. Muzerelle (2008).

16. A basic overview is Furrie (2009).

17. The *Anglo-American Cataloguing Rules*, edited by Michael Gorman, were first published in 1967, and have been reviewed and re-edited several times (see Gorman and Winkler 1978); this set of rules is available in print and online for a fee via the Cataloguer's Desktop: http://www.loc.gov/cds/desktop/, accessed February 16, 2020. June 2010 saw the first release of a new standard, the Resource Description and Access (referred to as RDA) which is intended to offer more flexibility for cataloguing in a digital environment; see http://www.rda-jsc.org/rda.html, accessed February 16, 2020.

18. Sharpe (2003) argues convincingly the fundamental obligation of cataloguers to provide evidence from the manuscripts in full reporting of tituli (or rubrics, as they are called in the present chapter), incipits, and explicits, and to assign author and title designations from other evidence-based studies, with extreme caution in the use of repertories; on pp. 251–301, "A Shelf of Reference Books," he gives an annotated bibliography on the key tools in the field.

19. Sharpe (2003), uses the term "titulus" or inscription, which focuses on the intellectual content rather than its physical manifestation in the way "rubric" does.

20. For example, these three rubrics all represent what a uniform title in English would identify as "Travels of Marco Polo. Latin," but to cite the identification of the text without the rubric hides our first awareness of the version that the particular manuscript carries: "De conditionibus et consuetudinibus orientalium regionum" in, for example, London, BL, Add. 19952 (Latin translation by Francesco Pipino; classified in the stemma as P); "De mirabilibus mundi" in Milan, Biblioteca Ambrosiana, X.12.sup. (Latin version deriving from the main Venetian version; classified as LB); "De morum et gentium

varietatibus" in, for example, Vatican City, BAV, Barb. lat. 2687 (highly abbreviated Latin text, related, but at a distance, to the main Venetian version; classified as LA).

21. Available for a fee as part of a suite of Brepols databases.

22. For the Comité International de Paléographie Latine, and a link from its website to the ongoing production of Catalogues de Manuscrits Datés, see http://www.palaeographia. org/cipl/cipl.htm, accessed February 16, 2020. The group of scholars currently producing volumes in Italy have published the protocols of their working method: see De Robertis *et al.* (2007).

23. For the concordance, Virtual International Authority File, see http://viaf.org/, accessed February 16, 2020. One of the very significant components of the VIAF is the *Personennamen des Mittelalters*, produced by the German National libraries; its most recent version in print is Fabien (2000), containing the names, with variant forms, of more than 13,000 persons who died after AD 500 and before AD 1501; the German online contribution to VIAF is yet larger than that of the 2000 print publication.

24. One could consult Berlioz *et al.* (1994) as well as the section entitled "A Shelf of Reference Books" in Sharpe (2003, 251–301).

25. Stegmüller (1940–76).

26. Ker (1969–2002, vol. 1, 96–7).

27. As dates of departure, one could point to the founding of the journal, *Scriptorium* in 1946, and to 1956 for an early study according to the principles of codicology, Delaissé (1956).

28. Published in 1982, the manifesto of this approach is Bozzolo and Ornato (1982).

29. See Section 63.1 on delivery methods and Section 63.2.2.7 (Title).

30. The basic tools for medieval paper are Briquet (1923), and Piccard (1961–97). All the print material in Piccard, plus large amounts of added material, is available online at http://www.piccard-online.de/start.php, accessed February 16, 2020; the description of the online Piccard project is at http://www.landesarchiv-bw.de/web/44577, accessed February 16, 2020.

31. German libraries in particular adhere to this tradition: Berlin uses "fol.," qu.," and "oct."; Erfurt uses "F.," Q.," and "O."; Wolfenbüttel uses "2°," "4°," and "8°."

32. Derolez (1984).

33. For example, London, BL, Add. 24189 consists of 14 leaves, with 28 full-page miniatures in grisaille and no text; in 1889 Sir George Warner associated the images with the *Travels of Sir John Mandeville*.

34. Kristeller (1993) and (2007), the latter an additional volume of updates by Sigrid Krämer and Birgit Christine Arensmann.

35. To use script names, especially complex ones that propose relationships, requires necessarily abstract thinking about concretely shared or rejected characteristics of letterforms; this kind of trained observation and thinking has led to profitable results in the field of palaeography. It may be less productive, however, for cataloguing, which has different goals.

36. Korteweg (1992).

37. Stirnemann (1990).

38. Armstrong (1999).

39. Fiorilla (2005, images 2, 9–11, 13–14, 16, and 50).

40. San Marino (CA), Huntington Library, HM 00132.

41. San Marino (CA), Huntington Library, HM 00195.

42. San Marino (CA), Huntington Library, HM 01031.

43. New York, Columbia University, Rare Book & Manuscript Library, Plimpton MS 060.

44. In 1701 Humfrey Wanley commented on the gap between the style of a script and the actual date, although he widened the space to 50–60-year span:

> And what may make a Man yet more liable to mistakes (besides the want of Dates in the most Antient Greek, Latin and other MSS) was the Practice of many Writers, still to Use the very same Hand when in Years, as they learnt when they were Young; like as many Antient People, who do yet continue to write the Roman and Secretary Hands, which were more fashionable 50 or 60 years ago, than now.
>
>   (Heyworth 1989, 172, in Letter 79, to Narcissus March, July 11, 1701;
>   the entire letter is on pp. 166–79).

45. James (1919).

46. For France, see Genevois *et al.* (1987). For Germany, see Krämer (1989–90). For Great Britain, see the modern editions of the medieval inventories in the series of the Corpus of British Medieval Library Catalogues, published by the British Library in association with the British Academy.

47. For example, the retrospective bibliographies of the Vatican Library: Buonocore (1994), covering the years up to 1968; Buonocore (1986); then picked up by Ceresa (1991), and by the same author, for the years 1986–90 (1998), and for the years 1991–2000 (2005).

48. For example, the Morgan Library & Museum in New York, whose OPAC, named Corsair, contains links from records for individual manuscripts to PDFs with citation of bibliography on the particular manuscript.

49. As well as or instead of the holding library itself, he may have availed himself of an aggregated online union location such as the IRHT, HMML, DS, cited in Section 63.2.1.2.

50. While there is much advice on the Web on the formation of image file names, not all of it is valid for the purposes of a catalogue and should be evaluated carefully.

51. Heyworth (1989, 178).

BIBLIOGRAPHY

Armstrong, L. 1999. "Nicolaus Jenson's *Breviarium Romanum*, Venice, 1478: Decoration and Distribution." In *Incunabula: Studies in the Fifteenth-Century Printed Book Presented to Lotte Hellinga*, ed. Martin Davies, 421–67. London: British Library Publications [repr. 2003, in *Studies of Renaissance Miniaturists in Venice*, vol. 2, 534–87 and color Plate VIII. London: Pindar Press].

Berlioz, J. *et al.* 1994. *Identifier sources et citations* (L'Atelier du Médiéviste vol. 1). Turnhout: Brepols.

Bozzolo, C. and E. Ornato. 1982. "Pour une codicologie 'expérimentale'." *Scrittura e civiltà* 6: 263–302 [repr. 1997. in *La Face cachée du livre médiéval. L'histoire du livre vue par Ezio Ornato, ses amis et ses collègues*, 3–31. Rome: Viella].

Briquet, C. M. 1923. *Les Filigranes: dictionnaire historique des marques du papier*. Leipzig: Hiersemann [facsimile repr. 1984. Hildesheim and New York: Georg Olms].

Buonocore, M. 1986. *Bibliografia dei fondi manoscritti della Biblioteca vaticana, 1968–1980*. Vatican City: Biblioteca apostolica vaticana.

Buonocore, M. 1994. *Bibliografia retrospettiva dei fondi manoscritti della Biblioteca vaticana*. Vatican City: Biblioteca apostolica vaticana.

Ceresa, M. 1991. *Bibliografia dei fondi manoscritti della Biblioteca vaticana, 1981–1985*. Vatican City: Biblioteca apostolica vaticana.

Conway, M. and L. F. Davis. 2015. "Directory of Collections in the United States and Canada with Pre-1600 Manuscript Holdings." *Papers of the Bibliographical Society of America* 109:3: 273–420, https://www.journals.uchicago.edu/doi/full/10.1086/682342?mobileUi= 0&, accessed March 23, 2020.

Delaissé, L. M. J. 1956. *Le Manuscrit autographe de Thomas à Kempis et l'imitation de Jésus-Christ. Examen archéologique et édition diplomatique du Bruxellensis 5855–61*. Paris: Éditions Érasme.

de Ricci, S. and W. J. Wilson. 1935–7. *Census of Medieval and Renaissance Manuscripts in the United States and Canada*. New York: American Council of Learned Societies.

De Robertis, T. *et al.*, eds. 2007. *Norme per i collaboratori dei manoscritti datati d'Italia*, 2nd ed. Padua: CLEUP.

Derolez, A. 1984. *Codicologie des manuscrits en écriture humanistique sur parchemin*. Turnhout: Brepols.

Fabien, C. 2000. *Personennamen des Mittelalters*. Munich: K. G. Saur.

Faye, C. U. and W. H. Bond. 1962. *Supplement to the Census of Medieval and Renaissance Manuscripts in the United States and Canada*. New York: Bibliographical Society of America.

Fiorilla, M. 2005. *Marginalia figurati nei codici di Petrarca*. Florence: Olschki.

Furrie, B. 2009. *Understanding MARC Bibliographic: Machine-Readable Cataloging*, 8th ed. Washington, DC: Network Development and MARC Standards Office, Library of Congress: http://www.loc.gov/marc/umb/, accessed February 16, 2020.

Genevois, A.-M. *et al.*, eds. 1987. *Bibliothèques de manuscrits médiévaux en France: relevé des inventaires du VIIIe au XVIIIe siècle*. Paris: Éditions du Centre national de la recherche scientifique: Diffusion Presses du CNRS.

Heyworth, P. L., ed. 1989. *Letters of Humfrey Wanley, Palaeographer, Anglo-Saxonist, Librarian, 1672–1726*. Oxford: Clarendon Press.

James, M. R. 1919. *The Wanderings and Homes of Manuscripts*. London and New York: Society for Promoting Christian knowledge–Macmillan.

Ker, N. R. 1969–2002. *Medieval Manuscripts in British Libraries*. Oxford: Clarendon Press.

Korteweg, A. S. 1992. *Kriezels, aubergines en takkenbossen: randversiering in Noordnederlandse handschriften uit de vijftiende eeuw*. Zutphen: Walburg Pers.

Krämer, S. 1989–90. *Handschriftenerbe des deutschen Mittelalters*. Munich: Beck.

Kristeller, P. O. 1993. *Latin Manuscript Books before 1600: A List of the Printed Catalogues and Unpublished Inventories of Extant Collections*, 4th rev. and enl. ed., ed. Sigrid Krämer. Munich: Monumenta Germaniae Historica.

Kristeller, P. O. 2007. *Latin Manuscript Books before 1600: A List of the Printed Catalogues and Unpublished Inventories of Extant Collections. Ergänzungsband 2006*, ed. Sigrid Krämer with Birgit Christine Arensmann. Hanover: Hahnsche Buchhandlung.

Lee, S. D. and D. P. O'Donnell. 2009. "From Manuscript to Computer." In *Working with Anglo-saxon Manuscripts*, ed. G. R. Owen-Crocker, 252–84 and 288 [bibliography]. Exeter: University of Exeter Press.

Marchi, S., ed. 1996. *I manoscritti della Biblioteca Capitolare di Verona: catalogo descrittivo redatto da Antonio Spagnolo*. Verona: Casa Editrice Mazziana.

Massieu, J.-B. 1791. *Instruction pour procéder à la confection du Catalogue de chacune des Bibliothèques sur lesquelles les Directoires on dû ou doivent incessamment apposer les scellés*. Paris: Imprimerie Nationale, http://gallica.bnf.fr/ark:/12148/bpt6k64658219/f1.image, accessed February 16, 2020,

Muzerelle, D. 2008. "Dating Manuscripts: What is at Stake in the Steps Usually (but Infrequently) Taken." *Journal of the Early Book Society* 11: 167–80.

Parkes, M. B. 1979. *The Medieval Manuscripts of Keble College, Oxford.* London: Scolar Pres.

Pass, G. A., ed. 2003. *Descriptive Cataloguing of Ancient, Medieval, Renaissance and Early Modern Manuscripts*, 2nd ed. Chicago: Association of College and Research Libraries.

Petrucci, A. 2001. *La descrizione del manoscritto: storia, problemi, modelli*, 2nd ed. Rome: Carocci.

Piccard, G. 1961–97. *Die Wasserzeichenkartei Piccard im Hauptstaatsarchiv Stuttgart: Findbuch.* Stuttgart: Kohlhammer, http://www.piccard-online.de/start.php, accessed February 16, 2020.

Schreibman, S., R. Siemens, and J. Unsworth, eds. 2004. *A Companion to Digital Humanities.* Oxford: Blackwell, http://www.digitalhumanities.org/companion/, accessed February 16, 2020.

Sharpe, R. 1997. *A Handlist of the Latin Writers of Great Britain and Ireland before 1540.* Turnhout: Brepols [repr. with addenda 2002. Turnhout: Brepols].

Sharpe, R. 2003. *Titulus: Identifying Medieval Latin Texts, an Evidence-Based Approach.* Turnhout: Brepols.

Gorman, Michael and Paul W. Winkler. 1978. *Anglo-American Cataloging Rules*, 2nd ed. Chicago: American Library Association [1st ed. by C. Sumner Spalding, 1967].

Stegmüller, F. 1940[i.e., 1950]–76. *Repertorium Biblicum Medii Aevi.* Madrid: Consejo Superior de Investigaciones Científicas, Instituto Francisco Suárez.

Stirnemann, P. 1990. "Fils de la Vierge: l'initiale à filigranes parisienne, 1140–1314." *Revue de l'art* 90: 58–73, https://www.persee.fr/, accessed March 23, 2020.

LIST OF PERMISSIONS

We are grateful to the following libraries and institutions for permission to reproduce images from material in their collections. They retain all rights to these images, which may not be reproduced without their express written permission.

Amiens, Bibliothèque municipale
Amsterdam, Bibliotheek der Universiteit
Auxerre, Bibliothèque municipale
Bamberg, Staatsbibliothek
Barcelona, Biblioteca de Catalunya
Bari, Archivio del Capitolo Metropolitano
Berlin, Staatsbibliothek zu Berlin-Preußischer Kulturbesitz
Bratislava, Archiv mesta Bratislavy
Bratislava, Slovenský národný Archiv
Brussels, Bibliothèque Royale Albert I
Brussels, Société des Bollandistes
Budapest, Országos Széchényi Könyvtär
Cambridge, Corpus Christi College
Cambridge, Sidney Sussex College
Cambridge, University Library
Carpentras, Bibliothèque Inguimbertine
Cesena, Biblioteca Malatestiana
Cologne, Dombibliothek
Digital Scriptorium
Douai, Bibliothèque municipale
Dublin, Trinity College Library
Durham, University Library
Florence, Biblioteca Nazionale Centrale
Florence, Biblioteca Medicea Laurenziana
Florence, Biblioteca Riccardiana
Ghent, Universiteitsbibliotheek
Güssing, Klosterbibliothek
Heidelberg, Universitätsbibliothek
Huesca, Archivio de la Catedral
Ivrea, Biblioteca Capitolare
Kew, National Archives
La Seu d'Urgell, Arxiu de la Catedral d'Urgell
Laon, Bibliothèque municipale

Leiden, Universiteitsbibliotheek
London, British Library
Lucca, Biblioteca Capitolare
Madrid, Real Academia de la Historia
Milan, Archivio Capitolare della Basilica di S. Ambrogio
Milan, Biblioteca Ambrosiana
Milan, Istituto Toniolo-Università Cattolica del S. Cuore
Modena, Biblioteca Estense Universitaria
Monreale, Biblioteca Comunale
Monte Cassino, Archivio della Badia
Montpellier, Bibliothèque Interuniversitaire, Faculté de Médecine
Monza, Biblioteca Capitolare
Munich, Bayerische Staatsbibliothek
Nantes, Musée Dobrée
New Haven, Yale University, Beinecke Rare Book and Manuscript Library
Oxford, Bodleian Library
Oxford, Corpus Christi College
Oxford, New College
Paris, Bibliothèque de l'Arsenal
Paris, Bibliothèque nationale de France
Périgueux, Archives départementales de la Dordogne
Pistoia, Archivio Capitolare
Reims, Bibliothèque municipale
Roermond, Stedelijk Museum
Salzburg, Stiftsbibliothek Sankt Peter
Utrecht, Universiteitsbibliotheek
Vatican City, Archivio Capitolare di San Pietro
Vatican City, Biblioteca Apostolica Vaticana
Vercelli, Archivio e Biblioteca Capitolare
Verona, Biblioteca Capitolare
Vic, Arxiu i Biblioteca Episcopal
Vienna, Österreichische Nationalbibliothek
Wolfenbüttel, Herzog August Bibliothek
Würzburg, Universitätsbibliothek

Index of Manuscripts

I. Manuscripts (Shelfmark)

Aberdeen, University Library
  49 c (Papyrus 21) 87–8
  106 799
Alba Iulia, Batthyaneum
  R II 134 475
  R III 78 477–8
Albi, Bibliothèque municipale
  17 839, 845
Albi, Médiathèque Pierre-Amalric
  4 539
Alençon, Bibliothèque municipale
  84 256
Amiens, Bibliothèque municipale
  6 199
  7 199, 238
  8 199
  9 199
  11 199
  220 195
  223 256
Amsterdam, Bibliotheek der Universiteit
  53 449
Angers, Bibliothèque municipale
  24 256, 719
  148 295
Antwerp, Museum Plantin-Moretus
  312 244
  16.2 948, 954
Arezzo, Biblioteca della Città de Arezzo
  405 131, 799–800

Austin, University of Texas, Harry Ransom
  Humanities Research Center
  HRC 35 541
Autun, Bibliothèque municipale
  3 102
  19 244
  20 199
  27 146, 147, 148
Auxerre, Bibliothèque municipale
  212 745
Avezzano, Curia Vescovile, Archivio Diocesano
  Exultet s.n. 795
Avignon, Bibliothèque municipale
  1086 30

Baltimore, Walters Art Gallery
  W 1 256
Bamberg, Staatsbibliothek
  Can. 5 272
  Class. 5 244, 246
  Hist. 162 253
  Iur. 1 289
  Lit. 131 239, 242
  Msc. Bibl. 40 247
  Msc. Bibl. 100 395–6
Barcelona, Biblioteca de Catalunya
  2541/1 161
Bari, Archivio del Capitolo Metropolitano
  Benedizionale 136
Basel, Universitätsbibliothek
  AN.IV.18 253
  N.1.4 193
Bergamo, Biblioteca Capitolare
  1046 271
Bergamo, Curia Vescovile, Archivio Vescovile
  s.n. 270
Berkeley, University of California, Berkeley,
  Bancroft Library

IV. References to *Chartae latini antiquiores*

General Index